The
DOUBLEDAY COOKBOOK
Volume 2

The DOUBLEDAY COOKBOOK

Volume 2

Complete Contemporary COOKING

*Jean Anderson
and Elaine Hanna*

ILLUSTRATIONS BY MEL KLAPHOLZ
PHOTOGRAPHS BY WILL ROUSSEAU

Doubleday & Company, Inc.
GARDEN CITY, NEW YORK

Copyright © 1975 by Doubleday & Company, Inc.
All Rights Reserved
Printed in the United States of America

ACKNOWLEDGMENTS

We are greatly indebted to the following companies for providing equipment to use in the testing and development of recipes:

General Electric Company, Housewares Division, Bridgeport, Connecticut (for portable appliances); *KitchenAid, The Hobart Manufacturing Company,* Troy, Ohio (dishwashers and heavy-duty electric mixers); *Ronson Corporation,* Woodbridge, New Jersey (electric cook-and-stir blenders); *The West Bend Company,* West Bend, Wisconsin (small electric appliances, cookware, and bakeware); and *Whirlpool Corporation,* Benton Harbor, Michigan (gas and electric ranges).

We also wish to thank the following for their gracious co-operation and for supplying quantities of valuable information:

Agricultural Extension Service, University of Wyoming; Aluminum Association; American Dietetics Association; American Home Economics Association; American Institute of Baking; American Lamb Council; American Meat Institute; American Museum of Natural History; American Mushroom Institute; American Spice Trade Association; Bourbon Institute; Brooklyn Botanic Garden; California Foods Research Institute; Cling Peach Advisory Board; Council on Foods and Nutrition, American Medical Association; Dried Fruit Association of California; Fishery Council; Florida Board of Conservation; Florida Citrus Commission; Food and Nutrition Board, National Academy of Sciences, National Research Council; French National Federation of Regional Committees for Promotion and Development of Agricultural Products; French National Wines Committee; Gas Appliance Manufacturers' Association; Glass Container Institute; Idaho Potato and Onion Commission; Madeira Wine Association; Maine Department of Sea and Shore Fisheries; Metal Cookware Manufacturers Association; Maryland Department of Economic Development; Massachusetts Department of Fisheries and Game; National Apple Institute; National Broiler Council; National Canners Association; National Coffee Association; National Dairy

Council; National Electrical Manufacturers Association; National Fisheries Institute; National Live Stock and Meat Board; National Macaroni Institute; National Turkey Federation; New York Botanical Garden; New York State College of Agriculture, Cornell University; New York State College of Human Ecology, Cornell University; New York State Cooperative Extension Service; North Carolina Agricultural Extension Service; Nutrition Foundation; Pan-American Coffee Bureau; Porto Wine Institute; Potato Growers Association of California; Poultry and Egg National Board; Rice Council; Roquefort Association; Tea Council of the U.S.A.; Shrimp Association of the Americas; United Fresh Fruit and Vegetable Association; U. S. Department of Agriculture; U. S. Department of Health, Education and Welfare; U. S. Department of the Interior, Fish and Wildlife Service; Washington State Apple Commission; Wine Advisory Board; Wine Institute; Wisconsin Conservation Department

We wish to thank Hammacher Schlemmer, 147 East 57th Street, New York, New York 10022, for providing the accessories for the photographs.

CONTENTS
Volume 2

Acknowledgments	v
List of Color Illustrations	xi
How to Use This Book	xiii

12 EGGS AND CHEESE   1

Buying Tips – Special Cooking Techniques – Serving Tips – Chart of Popular Cheeses

13 CEREALS, RICE, AND PASTA   34

Varieties – Ways to Cook – Ways to Dress Up Cooked Cereals – What to Do with Leftovers

14 SAUCES, GRAVIES, AND BUTTERS   72

Special Terms and Techniques – White Sauces – Brown Sauces and Gravies – Egg-Thickened Sauces – Mayonnaise-Based Sauces – Oil and Vinegar Sauces – Sour Cream Sauces – Butter Sauces – Tomato and Pasta Sauces – Barbecue Sauces and Marinades

15 STUFFINGS AND FORCEMEATS   113

Cooking Tips – Stuffing Quantity Chart – Easy Ways to Spice Up Package Stuffings

16 VEGETABLES   125

How to Recognize Quality – Shopping Tips – Food Values – Basic Ways of Cooking – Vegetable Seasoning Charts – Ways to

Dress Up Canned Vegetables – Ways to Glamorize Frozen Vegetables

17 SALADS AND SALAD DRESSINGS — 285

Green Salads – Vegetable Salads – Meat Salads – Seafood Salads – Egg Salads – Pasta Salads – Fruit Salads – Gelatin Salads – Frozen Salads – Salad Oils and Vinegars – Salad Dressings – Salad Herbs

18 BREADS — 334

Quick Breads – Yeast Breads – Steamed Breads – Fried Breads – Pancakes and Waffles – Crackers – Methods of Mixing – Ways to Shape and Decorate – Flavored Toasts – Bread Cubes, Crumbs, Croutons

19 SANDWICHES — 391

About Breads and Spreads – Plain and Fancy Party Sandwiches – Open-Face and Closed Sandwiches – Danish Sandwiches – Sandwiches in Quantity – Sandwiches to Go – Garnishes

20 DESSERTS AND DESSERT SAUCES — 408

Fruit Desserts – Custards, Creams, and Puddings – Steamed Puddings – Gelatin Desserts – Ice Cream, Sherbets, Ices, Bombes, and Mousses – Some Specialty Desserts – Sauces and Toppings – Garnishes

21 PIES AND PASTRIES — 481

Conventional Pastry – Torte Pastry – Puff Paste – Choux Paste – Crumb Crusts – Meringue Pies – Fruit Pies, Tarts, and Turnovers – Custard and Cream Pies – Chiffon Pies – Chess Pies – Cheese Cakes – Fancy Pastries – Methods of Mixing – Special Terms and Techniques – Pastry Decorations

22 CAKES, FILLINGS, AND FROSTINGS — 529

Butter Cakes – Sponge and Angel Cakes – Chiffon Cakes – Fruit Cakes – Wedding Cakes – Cupcakes – Methods of Mixing – Special

CONTENTS

Terms and Techniques – Cooked and Uncooked Frostings and Fillings – Bake-On Glazes – Ways of Decorating Cakes

23 COOKIES 575

Drop Cookies – Rolled Cookies – Molded and Pressed Cookies – Refrigerator Cookies – Bar Cookies – No-Bake Cookies – Methods of Mixing – How to Decorate Cookies – How to Pack and Ship – How to Dress Up Commercial Slice-and-Bake Cookies – Cookie Chart (Which Recipes to Halve or Double, Let Children Make, Pack and Ship)

24 CANDIES AND NUTS 628

Candy-Making Temperatures and Tests – Terms and Techniques – How to Decorate and Dip Candies – Cooked Candies (Fondant, Fudge, Divinity, Penuche, Pralines, Pulled Mints, Taffy, Brittle) – Uncooked Candies (Fudge, Fondant, Marzipan, Fruit Candies) – The Kinds of Nuts – Buying Tips – How to Roast, Sugar, Glaze

25 PICKLES, PRESERVES, JAMS, AND JELLIES 650

Basic Methods – Special Equipment – Special Ingredients – Storage Tips

26 CANNING AND FREEZING 683

Special Equipment – Basic Canning and Freezing Methods – Special Terms and Techniques – Canning Guide for Fruits and Vegetables – Freezing Guide for Fruits and Vegetables – How to Freeze Meats, Game, Poultry, Seafood – How to Freeze Herbs – How to Freeze Eggs and Dairy Products – Guide to Freezing Precooked Foods

APPENDIX 717

EAT WELL, KEEP WELL
Good Nutrition, What It Is, What It Does – The 4 Basic Food Groups – About Individual Nutrients – About Calories – Height-Weight Charts for Women and Men

CONTENTS

Recommended Daily Dietary Allowances	722
ADDRESS BOOK	725
Where to Order Special Cooking Equipment, Foreign Foods	
INDEX	727
HOW TO USE THIS BOOK	776
ABOUT INGREDIENTS	777
WHAT IT MEANS TO COOK WITH METRIC MEASURES	778

LIST OF COLOR ILLUSTRATIONS

Volume 2

following page 154

V. HOMESPUN AMERICAN FAVORITES:

Indoor Clambake
Baked Country Cured Ham with Baking Powder Biscuits
Caesar Salad
The home pantry

following page 298

VI. NEW FLAVOR COMBINATIONS:

Raw Zucchini Salad
Fillets of Sole
Poulet Basquais

following page 466

VII. ENTERTAINING:

Planked Steak with Vegetables
Rice à l'Impératrice and Crown Roast of Pork
From the home candy kitchen

following page 610

VIII. EATING ALFRESCO:

Charcoal Broiled Shish Kebabs and Spit-Roasted Leg of Lamb
"All-American" picnic
Spiced Blue Crabs
French Chocolate Ice Cream

Acknowledgment

We wish to thank Hammacher Schlemmer, 147 East 57th Street, New York, New York 10022, for providing the accessories for the photographs.

HOW TO USE THIS BOOK

All recipes in this book call for specific products by their generic (general descriptive) names, not the brand names; "quick-cooking rice," for example, is the fully precooked minute variety, "liquid hot red pepper seasoning" is the fiery bottled sauce made with tabasco peppers.

Whenever the name of a recipe is capitalized (Medium White Sauce, for example, or Flaky Pastry I), the recipe is included elsewhere in the book; consult Index for page numbers.

Whenever a method or technique is marked with an asterisk,* ("build a moderately hot charcoal fire,*" for example), how-to information is described in full detail elsewhere in the book; see Index for page numbers.

Three symbols are used throughout the book to key recipes:

⚖=Low-Calorie
¢=Budget
🗷=Quick and Easy

Specific sizes of pan, casserole, or mold are given whenever those sizes are essential to the success of a recipe.

Unless a recipe specifies alternate ingredients, do not make substitutions—margarine for butter, for example; oil for shortening; syrup for sugar. *And never substitute soft margarine for regular margarine or no-sift flour for sifted all-purpose flour.*

Suggestions for garnishes, seasonings, and leftovers are included within each chapter wherever appropriate.

Preheat oven or broiler a full 15 minutes before using. *Tip:* Have oven checked frequently for accuracy (many utility companies provide this service free of charge).

Use middle oven rack for general baking and roasting; whenever a higher or lower rack position is essential, recipe will so direct.

CHAPTER 12

EGGS AND CHEESE

"They know, in France, 685 different ways of dressing eggs, without counting those which our savants invent every day." *De la Reynière*

Add to those 685 the dozens of ways other countries know to prepare eggs and the total staggers. No food is more versatile. Eggs can be cooked in the shell or out, simply or lavishly, solo or with something sweet or savory. They leaven angel-food cakes and soufflés, color and thicken sauces, bind croquettes, emulsify mayonnaise, clarify aspics, give batter-fried food crisp fragile crusts, glaze baked goods, smooth ice creams and candies, and enrich the flavor and food value of everything. Eggs have been called nature's "nutritional bombshells" because of their near-perfect protein and high vitamin and mineral content. Yet they are low in calories, about 80 per large egg.

About Buying Eggs

Quality: There are three federal grades for eggs, marked on the carton or tape sealing it: USDA AA (the very top quality), USDA A (second best) and USDA B. All are widely available. Choose top grades when appearance counts (as in poached or hard-cooked eggs); these eggs have excellent shape, firm whites, and high-standing yolks. Grade B eggs have thinner whites, flatter yolks, cost less, and are good "cooking eggs" to use in making cakes and cookies, pies and puddings.

Size: Size has nothing to do with grade; weight determines. The four most common sizes, usually included in the grade stamp (see opposite):

Egg Size	Weight per Dozen
Extra Large	27 ounces
Large	24 ounces
Medium	21 ounces
Small	18 ounces

Note: Recipes in this book are based on large eggs.

Color: The breed of hen determines shell color and personal preference which you buy; white and brown eggs are equally flavorful and nutritious. Yolk color is affected by the hen's diet. Cloudy whites mean extra-fresh eggs.

Freshness: The fresher the better—except if eggs are to be hard-cooked. Shells cling to fresh eggs, making them difficult to peel, so use eggs several days or a week old. To determine if an egg is fresh, cover with cold water; if it floats, it's old. Beware of cracked eggs—they spoil rapidly. If you should accidentally crack an egg, use as soon as possible.

Blood Specks: Bloody eggs are removed during grading, but occasionally flecks of blood show in the yolk. They're harmless, do not mean an egg is fertile or bad. Remove with a piece of shell or paper toweling.

Fertile Eggs: These contain no magical properties, as some health faddists insist, and are no more nutritious than infertile eggs. They are overpriced and quick to spoil.

Other Kinds of Eggs

Because "eggs" so automatically mean hen eggs, we tend to overlook those of other fowl. Duck eggs are delicious (especially if ducks have swum in unbrackish ponds) and can be used interchangeably with large hen eggs (try them in custard). Eggs of geese and other domestic fowl may also be used. Simply multiply the number of hen's eggs in a recipe by 2 ounces, then substitute an equivalent weight of other fowl eggs.

Other Forms of Eggs

Commercially frozen egg products (whole mixed eggs, egg whites, and yolks), are available, but almost altogether on the wholesale level. Dried egg solids (whole eggs, whites, and yolks) are sometimes available in 5- or 8-ounce cartons. They are prey to bacteria, however, and should be used only for baking or in other thoroughly cooked dishes. To simplify measuring and using:

1 ounce dried whole egg=2 large eggs
1 ounce dried egg yolk =3½ fresh yolks
1 ounce dried egg white=6¼ fresh whites

About Storing and Freezing Eggs
See separate chapters on Freezing and Storage.

Some Special Terms and Techniques of Egg Cookery

To Break an Egg: Rap center of egg sharply against the edge of a counter or bowl, pull halves apart, letting egg fall into bowl. If using many eggs, break each separately into a small dish so that 1 bad egg won't destroy the lot. Here's a quick table of equivalents:

4–6 whole raw eggs=1 cup
10–12 raw whites =1 cup
13–14 raw yolks =1 cup

To Separate an Egg: Break egg, catch yolk in half shell, and let white fall into a small bowl; transfer yolk to empty shell, again letting white drain into bowl. Place yolk in a separate bowl.

To Remove a Speck of Yolk from White: The merest dot of yolk will keep whites from whipping. To remove, scoop up with a piece of shell or paper toweling.

To Remove Shell Fragments: Scoop out with a piece of shell.

To Beat Whole Eggs: The point is to blend whites and yolks so that eggs will mix more quickly with other ingredients or to make the eggs fluffy and of uniform color.

To Beat Whites: For best results, bring whites to room temperature and beat just before using; beaten egg whites quickly break down on standing. French chefs use unlined copper bowls and balloon whisks for greatest volume. Next best, a whisk and conventional bowl. Rotary beaters work well, electric mixers less so because they tend to break down the beaten whites. The greatest danger in beating whites is *overbeat-*

EGGS AND CHEESE

ing. For most recipes, whites are beaten either to *soft* peaks (as shown below), or to *stiff* peaks (also described as *stiff but not dry*). Peaks can be very soft; firm but too soft to "peak"; or stiff enough to stand straight up when beater is withdrawn. But the beaten whites should never look dry. If so, they've been overbeaten and their volume is lost forever. Volume is the point of beating egg whites, because the air incorporated into them is what leavens a soufflé or omelet or angel-food cake (overbeating causes more flops than underbeating). (*Note:* Whites beaten with a pinch of salt, sugar, or cream of tartar or a drop of lemon juice or vinegar will have greater volume and stability than those beaten without.)

To Beat Yolks: These need not be at room temperature. When used to thicken sauces or custards, yolks should be beaten *lightly*, just to blend; further beating weakens their thickening power. Cake recipes often call for beating yolks until *thick and lemon-colored* (not the best description because yolks are more nearly the color of mayonnaise) or if beaten with sugar, until mixture *makes a ribbon* (drops from beater in a thin flat ribbon that doubles back on itself in bowl).

About Folding in Beaten Egg Whites: Easy does it! Once whites are beaten, they must be combined with a base mixture so that very little volume is lost. The gentle, over-and-over folding motion shown

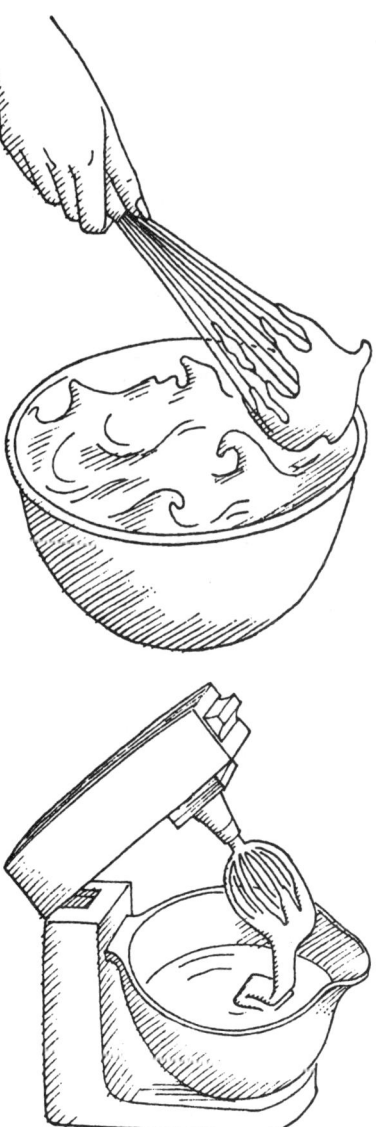

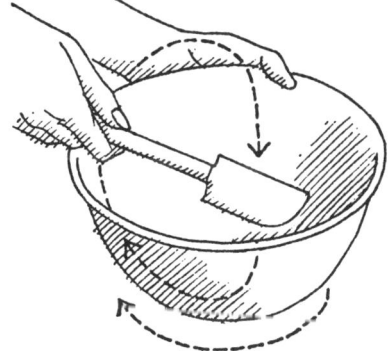

is the technique and a rubber spatula or flat whisk the best implement. If base mixture is thick, *stir in ¼–½ cup* of whites to lighten it, then *fold in* the rest.

About Adding Eggs to Hot Mixtures: Eggs or yolks are often blended into soups, sauces, or cream dishes shortly before serving—to thicken them, add flavor and color. Not a difficult technique, except that eggs curdle easily.

To Prevent Curdling: Beat eggs lightly, quickly blend in a little hot mixture (about ½ cup), then return to pan, stirring briskly. Burner should be at lowest point or, better still, topped with an asbestos "flame tamer." Cook, stirring constantly, about 2 minutes, *just* until mixture coats a metal spoon (leaves a thin, even, custard-like film).

About Cooking Egg-Thickened Mixtures: The old theory was that all egg mixtures had to be cooked in the top of a double boiler over simmering, not boiling, water. And there are times when they still should be—if the cooking is prolonged, for example, as with Stirred Custard or Zabaglione, if the cook is a beginner. But most cooks can deal with simple egg-thickened mixtures over direct low heat if they stir constantly, watch closely, and take the mixture from the heat the instant it thickens. *An important point to remember: Egg mixtures continue cooking off heat and, unless taken from it at the critical moment, may curdle on the counter top.*

To Rescue Curdled Egg Mixtures: Strain through a fine sieve or double thickness of cheesecloth. If mixture is thin, rethicken with additional egg, taking every precaution.

What to Do with Leftover Yolks and Whites

Yolks:
– Make custard or any creamy pudding or pie filling, using 2 yolks for each egg.
– Make Mayonnaise, Hollandaise, Zabaglione, or other egg yolk sauce.
– Add yolks to creamed soups, seafood, meats, or vegetables (about 1 yolk per cup).
– Add an extra yolk or 2 to scrambled eggs.
– Hard-cook yolks,* sieve, and use in making cocktail spreads or as a garnish.

Whites:
– Make a soufflé, adding 3–4 extra whites.
– Make an angel-food cake.
– Make meringues or a meringue-topped pie.
– Make divinity or seafoam candy.
– Make Prune or Apricot Whip.
– Make a chiffon pie.
– Add an extra egg white or 2 to scrambled eggs or omelets.

How to Cook Eggs

Like other high-protein foods, eggs toughen and shrivel if cooked too long, too fast or furiously. With a couple of exceptions: French omelets, which go from pan to plate in about a minute, and French-fried eggs, which bubble in deep fat. Both remain moist and tender. For egg cookery in general, however, the basic rule stands: low to moderate heat and gentle handling. *Dishwashing tip:* Soak "eggy" dishes in cold water before washing; hot water will cook egg on the dishes, making them twice as hard to wash.

To Cook in the Shell: To keep shells from cracking (especially important in Boiling Water Method), bring eggs to room temperature

EGGS AND CHEESE

Degree of Doneness	Description	Approximate Cooking Time (in Minutes)	
		Cold Water Method	Boiling Water Method
Very soft-cooked	Jelly-like white, runny yolk	1	3
Soft-cooked	Just-set white, runny yolk	2	4
Medium-soft	Firm-tender white, soft yolk	3	5
Oeufs Mollets (a French favorite)	Firm-tender white, yolk beginning to set around the edges	—	6
Hard-cooked	Firm-tender white *and* yolk	15	10–12

before cooking or warm quickly under hot tap. Use 3–4-day-old eggs for hard-cooking so eggs will peel easily. (*Note:* Eggshells badly discolor aluminum, so use pans made of other materials.)

Cold Water Method: Place eggs in pan, add enough cold water to come 1″ above eggs, bring to a boil, turn off heat, cover, and cook to desired doneness, using above table as a guide. Begin timing *after* heat is turned off. Drain eggs and plunge in cold water to stop cooking, prevent formation of dark green around yolk, and facilitate peeling.

Boiling Water Method (Coddling): Gently lower eggs into about 6 cups boiling water (it should come 1″ above eggs). Adjust heat so water is *just below* simmering and cook according to table. Drain and chill eggs as in Cold Water Method.

To Peel: Soft-cooked eggs are usually sliced in half and scooped into small dishes or served large end up in egg cups; to eat, slice off top, sprinkle in seasonings, and eat from shell. *Oeufs mollets* and hard-cooked eggs are peeled: Crack gently on a flat surface, roll egg over surface or between hands to craze and loosen shell. Starting at the large end where there is an air space, peel off shell and membrane, dipping as needed in cold water to make the going easier. Take care not to tear white.

To Keep Peeled Eggs Warm: Immerse in hot water, *not* on the stove.

To Hard-Cook Egg Yolks: Place yolks in individual ramekins, set in 1–1½″ simmering water, cover, and cook 5–7 minutes until firm. Use in salads or spreads or as a garnish.

To Tell if an Egg Is Hard-Cooked or Raw: Spin egg on counter. If it wobbles, it's cooked; if it spins neatly, it's raw.

To Poach: Pour about 2″ water into a shallow saucepan or skillet (not iron) and bring to a boil; adjust heat so water simmers, break eggs, 1 at a time, into a small dish. Stir water into a whirlpool, slip egg in, stirring in the same direction. Repeat with other eggs and cook 3–5 minutes to desired firmness. Lift out with a slotted spoon and serve. (*Note:* It's not necessary, as once thought, to add salt or vinegar to the water.)

VARIATION: Poach as directed, but use milk or broth instead of water.

To Steam-Poach: Break eggs into buttered cups of an egg poacher, set over simmering water, cover, and steam 3–4 minutes.

To Fry:

Method I: Heat 1–2 tablespoons butter, margarine, or bacon drippings for each egg in a large, heavy skillet over moderate heat about 1 minute, break eggs into skillet, spacing so they don't run together, reduce heat slightly, and cook, basting with fat or turning, to desired firmness. Soft-fried eggs "sunny side up" will take 2–3 minutes; "over easy" eggs about 2 minutes on the first side and 1–2 minutes on the second.

Method II: Lightly grease a large, heavy skillet (not iron) and heat over moderate heat just until a drop of water will dance. Break eggs into skillet, turn heat to low, and cook just until edges turn milky, about 1 minute. Add ½ teaspoon water for each egg, cover, and steam to desired firmness.

To French-Fry: Pour about 3″ cooking oil into a small deep saucepan and heat over moderately high heat until almost smoking. Break egg into a small dish, slide into fat, roll over with 2 wooden spoons until nearly round. Fry until puffed and golden, 2–2½ minutes; drain on paper toweling and serve. (*Note:* These eggs should be cooked 1 at a time.)

To Scramble (*Note:* Never try to scramble just 1 egg; allow 2 per person or, if scrambling many eggs, 1½ per person):

Method I: Beat eggs just enough to blend whites and yolks, season lightly with salt and pepper. Pour into a heavy skillet (not iron) lightly coated with melted butter, margarine, or bacon drippings and cook and stir over low heat 2–3 minutes until creamy-firm.

Method II: Break eggs into a bowl, for each egg add 1 tablespoon cream, milk, or water; season lightly with salt and pepper. Beat until frothy, pour into a heavy skillet (not iron) lightly coated with melted butter, margarine, or bacon drippings, and cook and stir over low heat 2–3 minutes until creamy-firm.

Method III: Prepare eggs as for Method II. Melt 2–3 tablespoons butter in the top of a double boiler, pour in eggs, and cook and stir over simmering water 3–4 minutes to desired firmness. These eggs are super-creamy.

Some Variations on Scrambled Eggs: Prepare 6–8 eggs by any of the above methods and, about 1 minute before they're done, mix in any of the following:
– ⅓ cup minced sautéed chicken livers or pâté
– ⅓ cup minced cooked sausages or frankfurters
– ⅓ cup minced cooked ham, tongue, luncheon meat, or salami
– ⅓ cup minced cooked fish, shellfish, chicken, or turkey
– ⅓ cup minced sautéed mushrooms, yellow onions, sweet red or green peppers
– ⅓ cup coarsely grated sharp Cheddar, Swiss, or Gruyère cheese
– ⅓ cup cooked asparagus tips, minced cooked cauliflower or broccoli
– ⅓ cup crisp, crumbled bacon
– ⅓ cup minced cooked artichoke hearts
– ⅓ cup sour cream and 2 tablespoons minced chives
– ⅓ cup sour cream and 2 tablespoons red or black caviar
– ⅓ cup peeled, seeded, minced tomato
– 1 tablespoon fresh minced herb (parsley, chives, dill, tarragon, chervil, marjoram)

EGGS AND CHEESE

To Bake or Shirr (Oeufs en Cocottes):

These two techniques are similar, the only difference being that shirred eggs are started on the top of the stove and finished in the oven and baked eggs are cooked altogether in the oven. Break eggs into buttered ramekins or custard cups and top each, if you like, with 1 tablespoon light cream. Set cups in a shallow baking pan, pour in enough warm water to come halfway up cups.
To Shirr: Cook over low heat just until whites begin to set, then transfer to a 325° F. oven and bake, uncovered, about 5 minutes until whites are milky and yolks soft but not runny. *To Bake:* Place eggs in ramekins, set in water bath, and bake uncovered 15–20 minutes at 325° F. (*Note:* Do not sprinkle eggs with salt and pepper until after they are done, otherwise, the yolks will be spotted.)

VARIATIONS:
– Place about 2 tablespoons minced cooked ham, chicken, chicken livers, fish, or shellfish into the bottom of each ramekin before adding eggs.
– Place 1 cooked artichoke bottom into each ramekin before adding eggs or, if you prefer, 2–3 tablespoons minced sautéed mushrooms, onions, or sweet peppers.
– Before baking eggs, top with a little crumbled bacon or grated cheese.
– Before baking eggs, sprinkle with a little minced parsley, fresh dill, tarragon, chervil, or chives.
– Before baking eggs, top with 2–3 tablespoons tomato, mushroom, or cheese sauce.

A Note About Serving Eggs: Have plates or platter warm, *not hot,* or eggs may cook beyond the point of desired doneness—especially important for omelets, scrambled eggs, and other simple egg dishes that quickly overcook.

Some Garnishes for Eggs

Almost anything savory and colorful is appropriate: crisp bacon strips, frizzled ham or Canadian bacon slices, glistening sausage links or patties, kippered herring, anchovy strips or rolls, sautéed chicken livers, tomato wedges or cherry tomatoes, clusters of green or black olives. And, of course, the old standbys— parsley, paprika, and watercress.

SKILLET EGG AND POTATO BREAKFAST

Makes 4 servings

8 *slices bacon*
2 *cups diced cooked potatoes*
¼ *cup minced yellow onion*
½ *teaspoon salt*
¼ *teaspoon pepper*
4 *eggs*
¾ *cup coarsely grated sharp Cheddar cheese*

Fry bacon until crisp in a large, heavy skillet; drain on paper toweling and crumble. Pour off all but 2 tablespoons drippings and brown potatoes and onions 10–12 minutes over moderate heat. Sprinkle with half the salt and pepper. Break eggs over potatoes, spacing evenly. Turn heat to low, cover, and cook 3–4 minutes or until eggs are done to your liking. Sprinkle with remaining salt and pepper, cheese, and crumbled bacon and serve. About 285 calories per serving.

SCOTCH WOODCOCK

There are two ways to make Scotch Woodcock; the easiest is simply to spread hot buttered toast with anchovy paste and top with softly

scrambled eggs. This is a more elaborate version.
Makes 6 entree servings, 2 dozen appetizers

6 slices hot buttered toast, trimmed of crusts
2 (2-ounce) cans anchovy fillets, drained and mashed
Freshly ground pepper
1 tablespoon minced parsley

Sauce:
1 cup heavy or light cream
4 egg yolks, lightly beaten
2 tablespoons butter (no substitute)

Make sauce first: Heat cream in the top of a double boiler over simmering water, mix a little into yolks, return to pan, and heat, stirring constantly, 7–10 minutes until smooth and thickened. (*Note:* Do not let water underneath boil or mixture will be scrambled eggs, not sauce.) Drop in butter and beat well; remove top of double boiler from bottom. Spread toast with anchovies, and halve diagonally, or, if to be served as appetizers, cut in "fingers." Arrange on hot plates, spoon or spread sauce over each piece, and top with a hearty grinding of pepper and sprinkling of parsley. About 285 or 340 calories per entree serving, depending upon whether made with light or heavy cream; 70 or 85 calories per appetizer.

⚖️ **EGG IN A NEST**

Makes 1 serving

1 slice firm-textured white bread
1 tablespoon butter or margarine
1 egg
⅛ teaspoon salt
Pinch pepper

Spread both sides of bread with butter, then, using a 2½" round cutter, cut out center of slice. Place both slice and cut-out circle in a small skillet and brown lightly on both sides over moderate heat, 2–3 minutes. Remove bread circle and keep warm. Break egg into hole in slice, cover, and cook about 4 minutes until white is firm. Transfer to a heated plate, taking care not to break the yolk. Season with salt and pepper. Top with bread circle and serve. About 245 calories per serving.

VARIATION:

⚖️ Spread sautéed circle with ketchup, deviled ham, or cheese spread and place, spread side down, on egg. About 250 calories per serving made with ketchup, 260 if made with deviled ham or cheese spread.

EGGS BENEDICT

Makes 4 servings

4 thin slices boiled ham or Canadian bacon
1 tablespoon butter or margarine
2 hot, split, toasted, and buttered English muffins
4 poached eggs
1 cup hot Hollandaise Sauce

Lightly brown ham in butter over moderate heat; arrange on muffins, trimming to fit. Top with eggs, cover with sauce, and serve. About 300 calories per serving.

VARIATION:

🔲 ⚖️ **Benedict-Style Eggs:** Prepare as directed but instead of Hollandaise use 1 (10½-ounce) can cream of celery, mushroom, tomato, or cheese soup, heated and thinned with ⅓ cup milk. Calories per serving: About 240 if made with tomato soup, about 270 if made with celery or mushroom soup, and about 285 if made with cheese soup.

EGGS AND CHEESE

⚖ EGGS FLORENTINE

Makes 6 servings

2 (10½-ounce) packages frozen chopped spinach, cooked by package directions and drained
6 poached eggs
1½ cups hot Mornay Sauce
¼ cup finely grated Parmesan cheese

Preheat oven to 350° F. Spoon spinach into a buttered 1 quart *au gratin* dish or shallow casserole or into 6 buttered custard cups set on a baking sheet. Make 6 depressions in spinach and slip a poached egg into each. Spoon sauce evenly over eggs, covering completely, and sprinkle with cheese. Bake uncovered, 15 minutes, then broil 5″ from heat until speckled with brown. About 160 calories per serving.

▨ EGGS AMERICANO

Poached eggs on toast topped with a mild curry sauce.
Makes 4 servings

2 tablespoons minced yellow onion
2 tablespoons cooking oil
1 (10½-ounce) can condensed cream of celery soup blended with ¼ cup milk
Dash liquid hot red pepper seasoning
¼ teaspoon curry powder
¼ teaspoon rosemary
¼ teaspoon oregano
4 slices hot lightly buttered toast
¼ cup finely grated Parmesan cheese
8 poached eggs

Sauté onion in oil in a saucepan over moderate heat 5–8 minutes until pale golden. Stir in soup mixture and all seasonings, reduce heat to moderately low, cover, and simmer about 5 minutes, stirring occasionally. Arrange toast on 4 individual heated plates, sprinkle 1 tablespoon cheese over each slice and top with a poached egg. Spoon sauce over eggs and serve. About 380 calories per serving.

HUEVOS RANCHEROS

Fried eggs on tortillas smothered with a chili-flavored tomato sauce. A Mexican classic.
Makes 2–4 servings

4 tortillas (homemade or packaged)
3 tablespoons lard or cooking oil
4 eggs
1 small yellow onion, peeled and minced
¼ cup minced sweet green pepper or 2 tablespoons minced hot green chili pepper
½ clove garlic, peeled and crushed
¾ cup canned tomato sauce
1½ teaspoons chili powder
¼ teaspoon salt
⅛ teaspoon sage
Pinch crushed dried hot red chili peppers (optional)

Preheat oven to 200° F. Fry tortillas on 1 side in 2 tablespoons lard in a large, heavy skillet over moderately low heat about 1 minute until pliable; drain on paper toweling, arrange on heatproof plates and set in oven. Fry eggs in drippings *just* until whites are set, then arrange on tortillas and keep warm in oven. Stir-fry onion and pepper in remaining lard 3–4 minutes, add remaining ingredients, and heat and stir until bubbling; turn heat to low and simmer, uncovered, 1–2 minutes. Spoon sauce over eggs and serve. About 370 calories for each of 2 servings, about 190 for each of 4.

EGGS FOO YOUNG

Eggs Foo Young are a good way to use leftovers, which explains the many variations served in Chinese restaurants.
Makes 4 servings

6 eggs, lightly beaten
1 cup well-drained bean sprouts
¼ cup minced scallions (include some tops)
¼ cup minced bamboo shoots, celery, or shredded Chinese cabbage
4 water chestnuts, minced
⅓–½ cup slivered cooked ham, chicken, or lean roast pork or minced cooked shrimp
1 teaspoon soy sauce
2–3 tablespoons peanut or other cooking oil

Sauce:
1 cup chicken broth
1 teaspoon soy sauce
½ teaspoon sugar
2 teaspoons cornstarch blended with 1 tablespoon cold water

Prepare sauce first: Heat and stir all ingredients in a small saucepan over moderate heat until slightly thickened; keep warm until needed. Mix eggs with all vegetables, meat, and soy sauce. Heat 2 teaspoons oil in a heavy 4″–6″ skillet over moderate heat ½ minute, add ⅓ cup egg mixture and fry as you would a pancake until lightly browned on bottom; turn and brown flip side. Keep warm (but do not stack) while you fry remaining "pancakes," adding more oil as needed and stirring egg mixture before each new "pancake." Serve hot topped with sauce. About 300 calories per serving if made with chicken or shrimp; about 330 per serving if made with pork or ham.

About Omelets

Omelets aren't as temperamental as they're rumored to be. Still, people approach them with trembling. By heeding the tips below, you should be able to make an acceptable omelet (the perfect one will take practice).

There are two kinds of omelets: *the plain or French*, made on top of the stove, and *the soufflé or puffed*, begun on the stove top but finished in the oven. For plain omelets, yolks and whites are beaten together just to mix; for soufflé omelets, the whites are whipped separately and folded in at the last.

Tips for Making Better Omelets

– Assemble all ingredients and implements beforehand. If omelet is to be filled, have filling ready.
– Use the freshest eggs possible and have them at room temperature (you'll get better volume). For an extra-tender omelet, add 1 teaspoon cold water per egg—*not* milk or cream, which will toughen it.
– Do not overbeat eggs. For a plain omelet, 20–30 seconds with a fork or whisk will do it. For a soufflé omelet, yolks should be briskly beaten with a fork and the whites beaten with a whisk until soft but firm peaks form.
– Use unsalted butter for cooking omelets.
– *Use a proper omelet pan* (without it, even an expert would have trouble). If the pan is too heavy, it cannot be manipulated easily as the omelet cooks; if too light, eggs may scorch. It should be round bottomed with sides that flare at the top, no more than 6″–8″ in diameter, of medium weight and made of cast aluminum, tin-lined copper, thick stainless steel, enameled cast iron, or teflon-lined aluminum. It should be well seasoned and used exclusively for making omelets. *To season an omelet pan:* Half fill with cooking oil, set over lowest heat, and warm uncovered 1 hour. Turn off heat and let oil cool in pan to room tempera-

ture; pour out (save for cooking, if you like) and wipe pan with paper toweling. *To care for an omelet pan:* Wipe after each use with paper toweling but do not wash. If something burns on the bottom, scour with salt and fine steel wool (not soap-filled). Rinse, dry, and reseason if necessary.

– Make only 1 small omelet at a time; large ones are difficult to handle and cook unevenly.

– Once eggs are in the pan, raise burner heat to moderately high—or as high as your proficiency allows without scorching eggs. Omelets are an exception to the low-heat rule of egg cookery. If they are to be lightly browned on the bottom, creamy inside and moist on top, the heat must be high and the handling deft.

– Serve an omelet the second it comes from the pan on a *warm*—not hot—plate.

About Filled Omelets

Plain omelets are easier to fill than the puffy, which are too bulky to fold well; these should be filled either by mixing filling with uncooked eggs or, better still, by ladling it over finished omelets before they are turned out. Plain omelets can be filled with almost any meat, fish, poultry, cheese, vegetable, fruit, preserve, or nut. Meat and vegetable fillings are usually warmed in butter in the omelet pan, then topped with the eggs (by the time the omelet is cooked, the filling will be in the center). Cheese, fruit, nuts, and other delicate fillings can be scattered over the omelet just before it's folded. Most fillings (cheese and nuts excepted) should be warm so that they do not cool the omelet.

Some Fillings for Savory Omelets

Cheese: Hard cheeses (Parmesan, romano, sapsago) can be mixed with the uncooked eggs; grate fine and allow 2–3 tablespoons cheese per 3-egg omelet. Softer cheeses (Cheddars, Gruyère, Roquefort, mozzarella, cottage or cream cheese) should be added in small dabs just before omelet is folded; again allow 2–3 tablespoons cheese per 3-egg omelet.

Meat: Any cooked, minced meat can be used. Allow ¼–⅓ cup per 3-egg omelet and warm in butter in omelet pan before adding eggs.

Seafood: Any drained canned, thawed frozen, or cooked fish or shellfish can be used. Bone and flake, allow ¼–⅓ cup per 3-egg omelet, and warm in butter in omelet pan before adding eggs.

Vegetable: Raw and cooked vegetables both make good fillings. In either case, they should be minced or diced; allow ¼–⅓ cup per 3-egg omelet. *Best vegetables to use raw:* tomato, avocado, finocchio, spinach, sweet red or green pepper. *Best cooked vegetables:* asparagus, broccoli, cauliflower, zucchini, yellow squash, carrots, green peas, potatoes, mushrooms, spinach, onions, artichokes.

Combination Fillings: Leftover meats, seafoods, and vegetables can be minced, mixed, and used to fill omelets. Allow ¼–⅓ cup per 3-egg omelet and warm in butter in omelet pan before adding eggs. *Some good combinations:* ham and asparagus or spinach; corned beef and potatoes; franks and baked beans; beef and potatoes or onion; pork and apples or sweet potatoes; chicken and rice; rice and minced ripe or green olives; chicken liver and crumbled bacon; sautéed sausages and onions, potatoes or apples.

Dessert Omelet Fillings

Fruit: Well-drained canned, thawed frozen, or fresh fruits are suitable. Small berries can be added whole, but larger fruits should be sliced thin, minced, or puréed. Allow about ⅓–½ cup fruit per 3-egg omelet and add just before folding. If fruits are cold, warm slightly before adding.

Jelly, Jam, or Preserves: Use ⅓ cup warmed jelly, jam, or preserves per 3-egg omelet; pour over omelet just before folding.

Nut: Use ⅓ cup minced, ground, or thinly sliced nuts per 3-egg omelet (thinly sliced *marrons glacés* are especially good). Scatter over omelet just before folding.

Liquor or Liqueur: Drizzle 1–2 tablespoons warmed liquor or liqueur (rum, cognac, kirsch, calvados, etc.) over omelet just before folding. Fold, drizzle with 2–3 tablespoons more liquor or liqueur. Blaze with a match, if you like, and serve flaming.

PLAIN OR FRENCH OMELET

Omelets should be made to order, one at a time.
Makes 1 serving

1 tablespoon unsalted butter or margarine
3 eggs, at room temperature
1 tablespoon cold water
½ teaspoon salt
⅛ teaspoon white pepper

Warm butter in a 6″–8″ omelet pan over low heat while you mix eggs. Beat eggs, water, salt, and pepper vigorously with a fork or whisk 20–30 seconds until blended and frothy. When butter is bubbly but not brown, tip to coat sides of pan and pour in eggs. Turn heat to moderately high and, using a fork, draw edges of eggs as they cook in toward center, at the same time tilting and gently shaking pan so uncooked portions flow underneath. Continue until omelet is just set and top creamy and moist. Take pan from heat at once, loosen omelet edges with fork, shaking gently. If omelet should stick, slide a dab of butter underneath and tilt pan so it runs over bottom. Fold omelet in ½ or, if you prefer, let fold over as shown as you turn onto a warmed plate. Serve as is or topped with Tomato, Mornay, Mushroom, or other savory sauce. About 345 calories per serving.

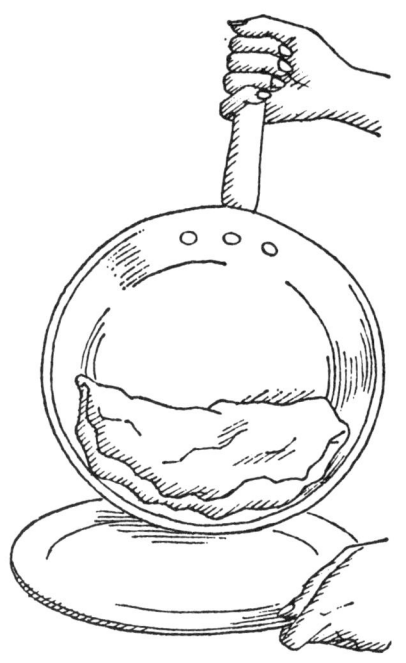

To Glaze: Fold omelet in pan, brush with melted butter, and brown quickly under broiler.

To Fill: There are 2 techniques (for filling ideas, see Some Fillings for Omelets):
– Lightly sauté filling in pan, add eggs, and cook as directed; when omelet is done, filling will be in center.
– Sprinkle filling over omelet just before folding.

VARIATIONS:

Fines Herbes Omelet: Gently warm 1 teaspoon minced chives, ½ teaspoon minced fresh chervil, and ¼ teaspoon minced fresh tarragon (or ½ teaspoon dried *fines herbes*) in melting butter. Add eggs and cook as directed. About 345 calories per serving.

Lorraine Omelet: Prepare omelet as directed and, just before folding, top with 2 tablespoons coarsely grated Gruyère cheese, 1 tablespoon minced parsley, and 2 crisp brown slices of bacon. Fold and serve. About 490 calories per serving.

Lyonnaise Omelet: Prepare omelet as directed and, just before folding, top with 1 thinly sliced, sautéed yellow onion. Fold and serve. For extra zip, top with a drizzling of vinegar and browned butter. About 415 calories per serving.

Caviar Omelet: Prepare omelet as directed and, just before folding, top with ¼ cup caviar (red or black) and 2 tablespoons each sour cream and minced Spanish or Bermuda onion. Fold and serve. About 555 calories per serving.

Spanish Omelet: Stir-fry 1 slivered pimiento, 1 small peeled, cored, seeded, and coarsely chopped tomato, 1 crushed clove garlic, and 1 tablespoon minced parsley in 1 tablespoon butter 5–7 minutes over moderate heat. Cook omelet as directed, top with tomato mixture, fold, and serve. About 390 calories per serving.

Ham, Mushroom, and Tomato Omelet: Sauté ½ cup thinly sliced mushrooms in 1 tablespoon butter over moderate heat 3–5 minutes until golden; add ¼ cup julienne strips cooked ham, and 1 small peeled, cored, seeded, and coarsely chopped tomato; cook and stir 5–7 minutes. Cook omelet as directed, top with ham mixture, fold, and serve. About 420 calories per serving.

Dessert Omelet: Beat eggs with water called for and 2 tablespoons sugar instead of salt and pepper. Cook as directed, sprinkle with sugar, and serve. If you like, fill with a sweet filling or top with a favorite dessert sauce. About 435 calories per serving without filling or topping.

Note: You can put almost anything you want into an omelet—pâté and truffles if you're rich, minced luncheon meat if you're not. Once you get the feel of omelet making, improvise with the fillings. One New York City restaurant prepares 553 different omelets, so the sky is really the limit.

⚜ PUFFED OR SOUFFLÉ OMELET

Makes 2 servings

4 eggs, separated (at room temperature)
¼ cup cold water
½ teaspoon salt
⅛ teaspoon white pepper
1 tablespoon butter or margarine

Preheat oven to 350° F. Beat yolks briskly with a fork. In a separate bowl beat whites until frothy; add water, salt, and pepper and beat until soft peaks form; fold gently into yolks. Heat butter in an 8″ omelet pan with a heatproof handle over moderate heat until bubbly but not brown; tip pan so butter coats bottom and sides. Pour in eggs and cook, uncovered, without stirring 5 minutes until underside is pale golden. Transfer to oven and bake, uncovered, 12–15 minutes until puffy and delicately browned. Loosen omelet with a spatula, divide in half, using 2 forks, invert on a heated platter, and turn out. Or crease center with a spatula and fold omelet in half as you tip out of pan. About 215 calories per serving.

VARIATIONS:

Filled Soufflé Omelet: When omelet comes from oven, sprinkle filling over ½ nearest pan handle and fold as above. Or, fold filling into eggs *just before* cooking. (See Some Fillings for Omelets.)

Sweet Soufflé Omelet: Prepare as directed but omit salt and pepper, and beat ¼ cup sugar into egg whites. Cook as directed, sprinkle with sugar, and top with a favorite dessert sauce. About 310 calories per serving without sauce.

GREEK SHEPHERD'S OMELET

Makes 1 serving

1 tablespoon olive oil
1 clove garlic, peeled and halved lengthwise
2 bay leaves
3 eggs, at room temperature
1 tablespoon cold water
3 tablespoons crumbled feta cheese

Warm oil, garlic, and bay leaves in an 8″ omelet pan over lowest heat 3–4 minutes. Meanwhile, beat eggs and water briskly with a fork to blend. Remove garlic and bay leaves from pan, raise burner heat to moderately high, and heat 1–2 minutes, tilting pan so that oil coats bottom and sides. When oil is hot but not smoking, pour in eggs and, using a fork, draw curling edges in toward center. Keep tilting and gently shaking pan so uncooked eggs flow underneath. After 1–1½ minutes (eggs should still be creamy), sprinkle feta over half the omelet, fold as directed for plain omelet. Gently slide omelet onto a heated plate and serve. About 405 calories per serving.

⊠ ONION FRITTATA

An Italian omelet that is browned on both sides.
Makes 2–4 servings

1 medium-size Bermuda onion, peeled and sliced paper thin
3 tablespoons olive or other cooking oil
1 clove garlic, peeled and crushed
4 eggs, lightly beaten
¾ teaspoon salt
⅛ teaspoon pepper
1 teaspoon basil
2 tablespoons grated Parmesan cheese

Sauté onion in half the oil over moderately low heat 5–8 minutes until limp, not brown; add garlic and stir-fry 1 minute. Mix onion and garlic with eggs, seasonings, and cheese. Heat remaining oil in a heavy 9″ or 10″ skillet over moderate heat ½ minute, add egg mixture, and cook without stirring 3–4 minutes until browned underneath and just set on top. Cut in quarters, turn, and brown flip side 2–3 minutes. About 390 calories for each of 2 servings, 195 for each of 4.

VARIATIONS:

Ham and Tomato Frittata: Omit onion; sauté ½ cup slivered prosciutto or cooked ham and 1 coarsely chopped, peeled, and seeded tomato in oil 5 minutes, then proceed as directed. About 425 calories for each of 2 servings, 215 for each of 4.

Artichoke Frittata: Omit onion; sauté ½ cup thinly sliced parboiled or drained canned artichoke hearts in oil 3–4 minutes, add garlic, and proceed as directed. About 390 calories for each of 2 servings, 195 for each of 4.

PIPERADE

This Basque "omelet" is closer to scrambled eggs, cooked until soft and creamy and topped with onions, tomatoes, sweet peppers, and ham.

Makes 4–6 servings

3 medium-size yellow onions, peeled and sliced thin
2 sweet green peppers, cored, seeded, and cut in strips ¼" wide
1 sweet red pepper, cored, seeded, and cut in strips ¼" wide
2 tablespoons lard, olive or other cooking oil
3 tablespoons butter or margarine
1 clove garlic, peeled and crushed
4 medium-size ripe tomatoes, peeled, cored, seeded, and coarsely chopped
1½ teaspoons salt
⅛ teaspoon pepper
½ cup cooked ham strips cut ¼" wide and 2" long
8 eggs, lightly beaten

Stir-fry onions and pepper in lard and 1 tablespoon butter in a large, heavy skillet over moderately low heat about 10 minutes until limp, not brown. Add garlic and tomatoes and stir-fry 5–8 minutes until almost all liquid has evaporated. Add seasonings and ham and keep warm. Melt remaining butter in a heavy 10" skillet over moderately low heat, add eggs, and scramble *just* until set. Remove from heat, spread with ham mixture, and stir lightly into

surface of eggs. Cut in wedges and serve. Good with crusty French bread and a crisp green salad. About 420 calories for each of 4 servings, 280 for each of 6.

VARIATION:

Prepare as directed but just before spreading with ham mixture sprinkle with ¼–⅓ cup coarsely grated Gruyère cheese. About 450 calories for each of 4 servings, 300 for each of 6.

⚖ ☒ BAKED EGGS IN TOMATOES

Nutritious diet fare.

Makes 4 servings

2 large firm ripe tomatoes, halved crosswise
4 eggs
¼ cup soft white bread crumbs
¼ cup coarsely grated sharp Cheddar
1 tablespoon minced parsley
¼ teaspoon salt
⅛ teaspoon pepper
2 tablespoons melted butter or margarine

Preheat oven to 425° F. Scoop pulp from tomatoes, then stand cut sides up in a greased 9" piepan and bake, uncovered, 5–7 minutes. Break eggs, 1 at a time, into a custard cup and slide into a tomato. Mix crumbs, cheese, parsley, salt, and pepper, sprinkle over eggs, and drizzle with butter. Bake, uncovered, about 15 minutes until eggs are just set and topping golden. About 205 calories per serving.

VARIATIONS:

⚖ **Low-Calorie Baked Eggs in Tomatoes:** Prepare as directed but omit drizzling of butter. About 160 calories per serving.

⚖ **Baked Eggs in Toast Cups:** Prepare 4 toast cups.* Slide an egg into each cup, sprinkle with topping, drizzle with butter, and bake 15–20 minutes at 350° F. until eggs are set. Good with hot Cheese or Mushroom Sauce. About 220 calories per serving.

STUFFED EGGS BAKED IN CHEESE SAUCE

Makes 4 servings

1 recipe Basic Stuffed Eggs or Deviled Eggs
2 tablespoons butter or margarine
2 tablespoons flour
1 cup milk
½ teaspoon salt
⅛ teaspoon pepper
1 teaspoon Worcestershire sauce
½ teaspoon prepared mild yellow mustard
1 cup coarsely grated sharp Cheddar cheese

Preheat oven to 350° F. Arrange eggs 1 layer deep in a buttered 9" piepan or *au gratin* dish. Melt butter over moderate heat in a small saucepan; blend in flour, slowly add milk and seasonings, and heat and stir until thickened; add cheese, stirring until melted. Pour over eggs and bake, uncovered, 20–30 minutes until bubbly; if you like, brown lightly under broiler. About 455 calories per serving.

VARIATIONS:

Stuffed Eggs in Mushroom Sauce: Prepare as directed but substitute 1½ cups Mushroom Sauce for the cheese sauce; if you like, sprinkle with ¼ cup grated Cheddar just before baking. About 400 calories per serving (with cheese).

Baked Stuffed Eggs the French Way: Prepare as directed, but substitute 1½ cups Béchamel, Velouté, Suprême, or Mornay Sauce for the cheese sauce. About 455 calories per serving for Suprême or Mornay Sauce, 340 if made with Béchamel or Velouté.

Rosy Baked Stuffed Eggs: Prepare as directed but substitute 1½ cups Tomato Sauce for cheese sauce. About 375 calories per serving.

EGGS AND BROCCOLI AU GRATIN

Makes 4 servings

1 (2-pound) bunch broccoli, parboiled
4 hard-cooked eggs, peeled and quartered
3 tablespoons butter or margarine
3 tablespoons flour
¼ teaspoon powdered mustard
¼ teaspoon salt
⅛ teaspoon white pepper
1½ cups milk
1½ teaspoons Worcestershire sauce
2 cups coarsely grated sharp Cheddar cheese

Preheat oven to 350° F. Drain broccoli well and arrange in an ungreased shallow 2-quart casserole; distribute eggs evenly over broccoli. Melt butter in a saucepan over moderately low heat, blend in flour, mustard, salt, and pepper; slowly stir in milk and cook and stir until thickened and smooth. Mix in Worcestershire sauce and 1½ cups cheese. Pour sauce evenly over broccoli and eggs, top with remaining cheese, and bake uncovered 20–30 minutes until lightly browned and bubbly. Serve hot as a main dish. About 490 calories per serving.

BACON AND EGG PIE

Makes 6–8 servings

1 recipe Flaky Pastry II
1 egg, lightly beaten (glaze)

Filling:
12 slices crisply cooked bacon
6 eggs
¼ teaspoon salt
⅛ teaspoon pepper

Preheat oven to 425° F. Prepare pastry as directed, roll out into 2 (12") circles and fit 1 in a 9" pie-pan. Lay 6 slices bacon over bottom crust. Break eggs, 1 at a time, into a cup and gently slide on top of bacon, spacing evenly. Top with remaining bacon. Dampen rim of bottom crust; cut steam slits in top crust and fit over filling. Press edges of pastry together, trim, and crimp to seal. Brush with glaze, being careful not to cover steam slits, and bake 25–30 minutes until golden. Serve hot or cold. About 475 calories for each of 6 servings, 355 for each of 8.

RANCH-STYLE EGG AND POTATO "PIE"

Makes 4 servings

4 medium-size potatoes, peeled
¼ cup cooking oil
1 teaspoon salt
⅛ teaspoon pepper
2 tablespoons minced chives
1 cup coarsely grated Cheddar cheese
8 eggs

Slice potatoes paper thin into a bowl of cold water; drain and pat dry on paper toweling. Heat oil 1–2 minutes over moderately low heat in a large, heavy skillet or flameproof casserole, spread potato slices over bottom and press down with a pancake turner. Sauté about 30 minutes, without stirring, until a crisp brown crust forms on bottom and potatoes are tender. Meanwhile, preheat oven to 350° F. Sprinkle salt, pepper, chives, and cheese over potatoes. Break eggs, 1 at a time, into a cup and gently slide on top of cheese, spacing evenly. Bake, uncovered, 5–8 minutes until eggs are cooked to your liking. Cut into portions, including an egg with each, and serve. About 480 calories per serving.

▨ BASIC CREAMED EGGS

Makes 4 servings

2 cups hot Medium White Sauce
1 teaspoon Worcestershire sauce (optional)
1 tablespoon minced parsley
6 hard-cooked eggs, peeled and quartered or sliced thin
Salt to taste

Mix all ingredients and serve over hot buttered toast or English muffins, boiled rice or frizzled ham, cooked asparagus or broccoli, or in puff pastry shells. About 325 calories per serving (without toast, etc.).

VARIATIONS:

Eggs in Cheese Sauce: Mix 1 cup coarsely grated sharp Cheddar cheese and 1 teaspoon prepared mild yellow mustard into sauce along with above seasonings, heat and stir until cheese melts, fold in eggs, and serve. About 440 calories per serving.

Scalloped Eggs: Prepare as directed, then layer into a buttered 1½-quart casserole with 1½ cups soft buttered bread crumbs, beginning and ending with eggs. Top with ⅓ cup fine buttered crumbs and bake, uncovered, ½ hour at 350° F. until browned and bubbly. About 450 calories per serving.

Eggs Goldenrod: Mix sauce with seasonings and coarsely chopped egg whites. Spoon over toast and top with sieved egg yolks. About 390 calories per serving.

Curried Eggs: Prepare as directed

but omit parsley; add 2 teaspoons curry powder warmed 3–5 minutes in 2 tablespoons butter over low heat, and, if you like, ¼ cup toasted slivered almonds. Serve over rice. About 470 calories per serving without rice.

Deviled Creamed Eggs: Prepare as directed but substitute 6 deviled eggs (12 halves) for the hard-cooked. Arrange in an ungreased shallow *au gratin* dish, cover with sauce (made without parsley), and bake uncovered 15 minutes at 350° F. About 545 calories per serving.

Eggs à la King: Prepare as directed, then fold in 1 cup sautéed sliced mushrooms, ½ cup cooked green peas, and 2 tablespoons minced pimiento. About 360 calories per serving.

Creamed Eggs, Bacon, and Onion: Prepare as directed but omit parsley and add ½ cup each minced sautéed onion and crisp crumbled bacon. About 400 calories per serving.

Some Additional Ways to Vary Basic Creamed Eggs: Prepare recipe as directed, then just before serving mix in any of the following:
– ¾–1 cup diced cooked ham, tongue, luncheon meat, or sliced cooked sausages
– ¾–1 cup chipped beef
– 6–8 coarsely chopped sautéed chicken livers or 3–4 sautéed lamb kidneys
– ¾–1 cup tiny whole shelled and deveined boiled shrimp, or minced cooked crab meat or lobster
– ¾–1 cup flaked tuna or salmon
– 1 peeled and diced ripe avocado
– ¾–1 cup leftover cooked vegetables (peas, diced carrots, corn, lima beans, asparagus tips, cauliflower or broccoli flowerets)
– 1–1½ cups diced boiled potatoes

⚖ DEVILED EGGS

Makes 4 servings

6 hard-cooked eggs, peeled and halved lengthwise
¼ cup mayonnaise
2 teaspoons lemon juice
¼ teaspoon powdered mustard or 1 teaspoon prepared spicy brown mustard
1 teaspoon grated yellow onion (optional)
1 teaspoon Worcestershire sauce
¼ teaspoon salt
Pinch white pepper
Some Suggested Garnishes:
Parsley, watercress, tarragon, dill, or chervil sprigs
Minced chives, dill, or parsley
Pimiento strips
Sliced pitted ripe or green olives
Capers
Rolled anchovy fillets
Paprika

Mash yolks well, mix in remaining ingredients, mound into whites, and chill ½ hour. Garnish as desired and serve. About 225 calories per serving without garnish.

VARIATIONS:

Deviled Eggs with Cheese: Prepare yolk mixture as directed, then beat in ⅓ cup finely grated sharp Cheddar, Parmesan, or Gruyère cheese or crumbled blue cheese. About 310 calories per serving.

⚖ **Anchovy Eggs:** Prepare yolk mixture as directed but omit mustard; mix in instead 2 tablespoons anchovy paste. About 230 calories per serving.

⚖ **Mexican Deviled Eggs:** When preparing yolk mixture, omit mustard, reduce mayonnaise to 2 tablespoons, and add 2 tablespoons chili sauce and 1 teaspoon chili powder. About 185 calories per serving.

⚱ **Curried Deviled Eggs:** Prepare yolk mixture as directed but increase grated onion to 2 teaspoons and add 2 teaspoons curry powder. About 230 calories per serving.

☒ ⚱ **JIFFY DEVILED EGGS**

Makes 4–6 servings

8 hard-cooked eggs
½ cup relish-type sandwich spread
1 tablespoon milk
1 teaspoon prepared spicy brown mustard
¼ teaspoon salt
Pinch pepper

Chill eggs, then peel and halve lengthwise. Mash yolks with a fork and blend in remaining ingredients; stuff into whites, mounding mixture up, and serve. (*Note:* Flavor will be better if eggs are chilled about 1 hour before serving.) About 280 calories for each of 4 servings, 185 for each of 6.

⚱ **BASIC STUFFED EGGS**

Makes 4 servings

6 hard-cooked eggs, peeled and halved lengthwise
¼–⅓ cup milk, heavy, light, or sour cream
¼ teaspoon salt
Pinch white pepper

Mash yolks well, blend in remaining ingredients, and mound into whites, using a pastry bag fitted with a large decorative tip if you like. Chill ½ hour, garnish as desired (see Some Suggested Garnishes for Deviled Eggs), and serve. Calories per serving: about 130 if made with milk, 160 if made with light or sour cream, 190 if made with heavy cream.

Some Quick Stuffing Variations:
Blend any of the following into yolk mixture, adjusting liquid as needed to make a creamy consistency:
– 1 (2¼–2½-ounce) can deviled ham, meat, or chicken spread or pâté
– ¼ cup ground cooked ham, tongue, luncheon meat, chicken, or chicken livers
– ¼ cup crisp crumbled bacon
– ¼ cup minced cooked fish or shellfish
– ¼ cup red caviar and 2 teaspoons lemon juice
– 2 tablespoons anchovy paste and 1 tablespoon minced capers
– ¼ cup minced pitted ripe or green olives
– 2 tablespoons each minced scallions and celery and 1 tablespoon finely grated onion
– ¼ cup grated sharp cheese (any kind) and 2 tablespoons minced chutney or nuts
– ¼ cup cottage or cream cheese, 1 tablespoon each minced chives and pimiento and 2–3 dashes liquid hot red pepper seasoning
– ¼ cup puréed cooked spinach, asparagus, beets, peas, or carrots

⚱ **ROSEMARY EGGS**

Makes 4 servings

6 hard-cooked eggs
2 tablespoons mayonnaise
1 tablespoon light cream
1 teaspoon white wine vinegar
1 tablespoon minced shallots or yellow onion
¼ teaspoon minced fresh rosemary or ⅛ teaspoon dried rosemary
⅛ teaspoon powdered mustard
½ teaspoon salt
Pinch white pepper

Chill eggs well, then peel and halve lengthwise. Scoop yolks into a small mixing bowl and mash with a fork. Add remaining ingredients to yolks and beat with a fork until creamy. Stuff whites with yolk mixture, mounding it up well. Chill at least 1 hour before serving. About 180 calories per serving.

EGG CROQUETTES

Makes 4 servings

4 *hard-cooked eggs, peeled and minced*
⅔ *cup cold Thick White Sauce*
½ *cup soft white bread crumbs*
½ *teaspoon salt*
⅛ *teaspoon pepper*
1 *egg, lightly beaten*
½ *cup toasted fine bread crumbs*
Shortening or cooking oil for deep fat frying

Mix hard-cooked eggs, sauce, soft crumbs, salt, and pepper. Using about ¼ cup for each, shape into 6 logs about 3" long and 1" across. Dip in beaten egg, then crumbs to coat well. Cover and chill ½ hour. Meanwhile, heat fat in a deep fat fryer with basket and deep fat thermometer over moderate heat to 375° F. Fry rolls, a few at a time, about 1½ minutes until golden. Drain on paper toweling and serve. Good with Tomato Sauce. About 325 calories per serving.

VARIATION:

Cheese Croquettes: Omit hard-cooked eggs; while sauce is still hot, stir in 1 cup coarsely grated sharp Cheddar cheese. Cool, add crumbs and seasonings, and proceed as directed. About 355 calories per serving.

⚜ **EGGS IN ASPIC**

Makes 4 servings

2 *cups aspic* made with beef or chicken broth*
2–3 *tablespoons Madeira or cognac*
Truffle or pimiento cutouts
4 *firm poached eggs, chilled*

Mix aspic and Madeira, chill until syrupy, then spoon 2–3 tablespoons into each of 4 ungreased custard cups or ramekins, swirling round to coat sides and bottom; chill until firm. Keep remaining aspic syrupy. Decorate chilled aspic with cutouts, trim poached eggs to fit cups and arrange on aspic, attractive side down. Fill cups with aspic and chill until firm. Unmold and sprig with watercress. Serve with mayonnaise as a light main course or salad. About 120 calories per serving (without mayonnaise).

VARIATIONS:

⚜ **Stuffed or Deviled Eggs in Aspic:** Prepare as directed but substitute 2 stuffed or deviled eggs (4 halves) for the poached, arranging stuffed sides down on aspic. About 150 calories per serving.

⚜ **Eggs in Madrilène Aspic:** Prepare as directed but substitute madrilène for aspic; heat and stir madrilène with 1 envelope unflavored gelatin until gelatin dissolves, cool, and mix in 3 tablespoons dry sherry or port. Chill until syrupy and proceed as directed. About 140 calories per serving.

⚜ **Tarragon Eggs in Aspic:** Begin as directed, chilling a layer of aspic in ramekins; decorate with fresh tarragon leaves and truffle diamonds, add 2 paper thin slices boiled ham cut to fit, top with a little aspic, and chill until tacky. Add a poached or hard-cooked egg (with end sliced off so yolk shows), fill with aspic, and chill until firm. About 130 calories per serving.

⚜ **Hard-Cooked Eggs in Aspic:** Prepare as directed, substituting medium-size hard-cooked eggs for the poached. Cut off about ⅓ of ends and place cut sides down in

EGGS AND CHEESE

cups so yolks show when eggs are unmolded. About 125 calories per serving.

⚜ ¢ **PICKLED EGGS**

Good picnic fare.
Makes 4–6 servings

1½ cups white vinegar
1 teaspoon mixed pickling spices
1 clove garlic, peeled and bruised
1 bay leaf
6 hard-cooked eggs, peeled

Simmer vinegar and spices, uncovered, 10 minutes; cool slightly, add garlic and bay leaf. Pack eggs into a screw-top jar, add vinegar mixture, cover, and cool to room temperature. Refrigerate 7–10 days before serving—longer for stronger flavor. Serve as an appetizer or with cold cuts and salad. About 135 calories for each of 4 servings, 90 for each of 6.

VARIATION:

⚜ **Pickled Eggs and Beets:** Prepare as directed but add 6–8 small whole boiled and peeled beets to eggs before adding vinegar. Marinate 2–3 days before serving. About 150 calories for each of 4 servings, 100 for each of 6.

CHEESE

No one knows who first made cheese, though legend credits an early wayfarer whose milk ration, carried in a skin pouch, turned to curds and whey. That ancient cheese would have been much like our cottage cheese. Pungent ripened cheeses arrived later, again by accident. A shepherd boy, the story goes, found that a cheese he'd left in a cave was covered with mold. He tried it, liked it, and blue cheese came into being.

Cheese is made from the milk or cream of many animals; some is unripened (cottage and cream cheese), some is mold-ripened (the whole family of blues), some bacteria-ripened (Limburger, Liederkranz). Cheeses range from hard to soft, bland to overpowering, white to dark brown. All are excellent meat substitutes because of their high quality protein, vitamin, and mineral content. Depending upon whether cheese is made from skim or whole milk or cream, it can be low in calories or loaded.

The kinds of cheese available today are bewildering. France alone produces hundreds, including most of the great classics. Italy, Holland, England, Switzerland, Scandinavia, America, and Canada are also major producers. America's appetite for cheese has become so insatiable that cheese shops are proliferating and supermarket dairy counters are offering obscure imported varieties as well as the familiar domestics.

Confronted with dozens of cheeses, the buyer wonders which to try. Which to use in cooking, which to serve with cocktails, which to offer as dessert. The best way to bring order to the confusion is to group cheeses by type and use. But first, some oft-used terms defined:

Pasteurized Cheese: America's cheese, like its other dairy products, is pasteurized. This means, of course, that the cheese is wholesome; but it also means that the organisms responsible for the cheese's character have been destroyed and that the color, texture, and flavor won't change much as the cheese ages.

Process Cheese: Watered-down cheese; preservatives, emulsifiers, artificial coloring, and flavoring are often added.

Process Cheese Food: Further watered-down and adulterated cheese, which in some instances isn't cheese at all.

Some Popular Cheeses Grouped by Type and Use

Soft, Unripened Cheeses (highly perishable): Serve slightly chilled; curd cheeses can be served anytime or used in cooking. The cream cheeses, teamed with fresh berries or tart preserves, make elegant desserts, especially if accompanied by chilled champagne or moderately sweet white wine.

Cheese	*Country of Origin*	*Description*
Cottage, pot, and farmer's cheese	U.S.A.	Bland but sour curd cheeses; cottage cheese is moistest (especially cream style, which has fresh cream added), pot cheese is next, and farmer's cheese driest; it is often shaped.
Cream cheese	U.S.A.	Rich, bland, and buttery
Gervais	France	Sour, doubly rich cream cheese
Petit-Suisse	France	Mild, doubly rich cream cheese
Neufchâtel	France, U.S.A.	Soft cream cheese, pungent if ripe
Ricotta	Italy	Fine-cured cousin of cottage cheese

Soft, Ripened Cheeses: Serve at room temperature. Excellent with fruit, wine, and French bread between the main course and dessert; also good before dinner with cocktails. (*Note:* Cheese crusts are not cut away but eaten.)

Compatible Fruits: Apples, pears, peaches, grapes. *Compatible Wines:* Dry reds, *except* for Liederkranz and Limburger, which are better with beer.

Cheese	*Country of Origin*	*Description*
Brie	France	The cheese that sends gourmets into ecstasy; perfectly ripened, it is golden and creamy throughout, neither too bland nor pungent.
Camembert	France	France's favorite and a rival of Brie. It should be ivory-hued, butter-soft but not runny. Mild to strong.
Crema Dania	Denmark	Rich, creamy, and zippy when ripe
Liederkranz	U.S.A.	Strong and creamy
Limburger	Belgium	Creamy-firm and strong enough "to blow a safe"; not for the meek

EGGS AND CHEESE

Semisoft Cheeses: Serve at room temperature. Excellent between the main course and dessert, accompanied by fruit and wine. Also good as anytime snacks and as cocktail party fare. (*Note:* Cut away any rind before eating; cheeses are usually served in the rind, unless it's unsightly.) Fontina, mozzarella, and Monterey Jack are excellent cooking cheeses because they melt smoothly; feta is delicious crumbled into salads or omelets. *Compatible Fruits:* Tart apples, crisp pears, grapes; feta is especially good with dried figs or apricots and pistachio nuts. *Compatible Wines:* Dry, full-bodied reds except for feta, which is better with a white retsina.

Cheese	Country of Origin	Description
Bel Paese	Italy	Smooth, mellow, and nutty
Feta	Greece	Snowy, salty, crumbly sheep's milk cheese preserved in brine
Fontina	Italy	Pale, mild, and nutty
Monterey Jack	U.S.A.	Pale, mild to sharp Cheddar type
Mozzarella	Italy	The pizza cheese—white and delicate
Muenster	France (Alsace), U.S.A.	American Muenster is pale and bland; the European is sharper and darker. Sometimes has caraway seeds.
Oka	Canada	Smooth, mellow, and mild
Pont l'Évêque	France	France's fourth most important cheese (after Brie, Camembert, and Roquefort). Soft, pale yellow, and piquant; shot through with tiny "eyes."
Port du Salut	France	Pale, butter smooth, but robust
Reblochon	France	Ivory-colored under its russet skin; soft but authoritative
Tilsit	Germany	The color of cream, full of small "eyes," fairly sharp
Wensleydale	England	Pale yellow, sharp, butter-flavored; there is also a blue Wensleydale.

Firm Cheeses: Serve at room temperature. Good anytime as snacks, also between the main course and dessert with fruit and wine. These are cooking favorites because of their robust flavor and smooth-melting quality. *Compatible Fruits:* Apples, pears, grapes, plums. *Compatible Wines:* Full-bodied dry reds except for the Cheddar types, which are better with beer, ale, or stout.

Cheese	Country of Origin	Description
Caerphilly	Wales	Smooth, white, and salty
Cheddar	England, U.S.A., Canada	Huge family ranging from sharp to mild, white to orange. Good U.S. Cheddars: Colby, Coon, Herkimer, Pineapple, Vermont, Wisconsin
Cheshire	England	Rich, zesty red or white Cheddar type; popular for Welsh Rabbit
Edam	Netherlands	Mild, golden "cannonball" cheese, coated with red wax
Gjetost	Norway	Curious, sweet-salty, fudge-textured brown cheese made of caramelized goat's milk. Norwegians like it for breakfast, sliced paper thin, on buttered rye bread; also for dessert.
Gloucester	England	There are two—single and double, or mild and sharp; both are velvety.
Gouda	Netherlands	Mild, creamy cheese much like Edam; well aged, it is crumbly and piquant.
Gruyère	Switzerland	Rich, nutty-sweet, cream colored, shot with small "eyes"; superb for cooking
Kashkaval	Bulgaria	Salty, crumbly, white sheep cheese
Lancashire	England	White with lots of bite; when young, cheese is mellow and butter-smooth.
Leicester	England	Bright orange-rose, crumbly, sharp, and lemony
Provolone	Italy	Smoky-mellow pale yellow giant trussed with rope and swung from rafters
Swiss or Emmentaler	Switzerland	Pale cream to tan cheese with big holes; nutty-sharp with a sweet aftertaste

The "Blues": Serve at room temperature. Good with cocktails before dinner; delicious with fruit, rough bread, and wine between the entree and dessert; excellent crumbled into salads, salad dressings, casseroles, and omelets. *Compatible Fruits:* Apples and pears. *Compatible Wines:* Robust dry reds except for Stilton, which is committed to vintage port.

EGGS AND CHEESE

Cheese	Country of Origin	Description
Danish blue	Denmark	Creamy-white with blue-green marbling; salty with lots of bite
Gorgonzola	Italy	Pale green-veined, soft cheese; pungent
Roquefort	France	Made of sheep's milk and "Queen of the Blues"; crumbly, creamy-white with deep blue-green mottling; extra strong
Stilton	England	Oyster white, blue-green-veined cheese, mellower than other blues because of a vaguely Cheddarish flavor

Hard ("Grating") Cheeses: Except for Parmesan, good eaten out of hand, these are used almost altogether as toppings (soup and pasta) or to heighten the flavor of sauces, salads, and casseroles. Use sparingly.

Cheese	Country of Origin	Description
Parmesan	Italy	Sharp, grainy, and golden; the foundation of Italian cuisine
Romano	Italy	Sheep's milk cheese, similar to but more pungent than Parmesan
Sapsago	Switzerland	Hard, conical green cheese, sour and pungent with dried Alpine clover

Some Tips on Cooking with Cheese

– Use low to moderate heat. Cheese becomes rubbery, tough, and indigestible when cooked too long or at too high a heat.
– Use well-aged cheeses for cooking —especially for sauces and fondues, where smoothness counts. Badly aged cheeses will clump and separate and nothing can be done to bring them back together. Should this happen, it's best to discard the rubbery clumps and thicken the sauce with a flour paste.
– When cheeses are to be melted into a sauce, coarsely grate or dice.
– Use strong cheeses sparingly so their flavors don't dominate.
– If a particular cheese called for in a recipe is unavailable, substitute a similar one from the same group (see Some Popular Cheeses Grouped by Type and Use).

Some Tips on Serving Cheese

In General:
– Serve soft, unripened cheeses cold, *but all others at room temperature.* Bringing cheese to room temperature can take from ½–3 hours, depending on the cheese and the weather. Soft cheeses warm faster than hard, small cheeses faster than large. All, of course, come to room temperature faster in hot weather than in cold.
– Serve cheeses in their rinds or crusts unless unsightly. Crusts are usually edible; rinds are not.
– Present cheese on a simple board,

wooden tray, or marble slab, not on crystal, china, or silver, which are incompatible with its earthiness.
– Put out only what cheese you expect to be eaten.
– Allow plenty of space between cheeses on a board and don't group the strongs with the milds. Provide a separate knife for each cheese.
– Don't clutter a cheese board with garnishes, which will only wilt and get smeared with cheese. The best garnish is no garnish.
– Choose simple rough breads (French or Italian) and unseasoned, unsalted crackers for cheese. Highly seasoned ones overpower the cheese.
– Serve breads and crackers separately, not on the cheese board.

Before Dinner:
– Serve 1 or, at most, 2 cheeses— rich or sharp ones (blue or Brie, perhaps) that guests aren't apt to overeat. It's easy to nibble away at bland cheeses until the appetite's gone.

At Cocktail Parties:
– Vary the cheeses, striking a balance between hard and soft, sharp and bland. A good practice is to choose one from each of the following categories: Soft, Ripened; Semisoft; Firm; Blue.
– Avoid the superstrong Limburger and Liederkranz. In a hot crowded room, they'll soon smell to high heaven.
– Put out plenty of cheese (¼–½ pound per guest is a good estimate) and in whole wheels or 2–3-pound slabs so there will be enough to go around.

At the End of a Meal:
– Suit the cheese to the meal. If dinner has been rich, cheese is out of order. It is also inappropriate following an Oriental or Indian meal. But after a French, Italian, Viennese, or Scandinavian meal, it is perfect. Elegant menus deserve queenly cheeses, rougher fare, coarser cheeses. As a general rule, French cheeses are best with French wines, Italian cheeses with Italian wines, and English or Nordic cheeses with beer or ale.
– Set out a single tray of cheese and bowl of fruit from which everyone can help themselves.

About Keeping and Storing Cheese
See the chapter on storage.

WELSH RABBIT

Makes 4 servings

1 tablespoon butter or margarine
½ cup milk, ale, or beer
½ teaspoon powdered mustard
Pinch cayenne pepper
1 tablespoon Worcestershire sauce
¾ pound sharp Cheddar cheese, coarsely grated

Heat butter, milk, mustard, cayenne, and Worcestershire sauce in the top of a double boiler or chafing dish over *just* simmering water 7–10 minutes. Add cheese, a little at a time, stirring constantly until smooth and quite thick. Remove from heat immediately and serve over hot buttered toast. About 365 calories per serving if made with milk, 355 if made with ale or beer, not including toast. Add about 120 calories for each slice buttered toast.

⚔ TOMATO-CHEESE RABBIT

Makes 6 servings

2 tablespoons butter or margarine
¼ cup unsifted flour
¼ teaspoon oregano
¼ teaspoon basil
½ teaspoon salt
¼ teaspoon cayenne pepper
1 cup light cream

1 tablespoon onion juice
½ cup coarsely grated sharp
   Cheddar cheese
1 cup tomato juice
⅛ teaspoon baking soda

Melt butter in a small saucepan over moderate heat and blend in flour, herbs, salt, and pepper. Mix in cream and heat, stirring, until thickened and smooth. Turn heat to low, add onion juice and Cheddar, and heat, stirring, until cheese is melted. Meanwhile, in a separate small saucepan, bring tomato juice to a boil over high heat; off heat, stir in soda. Add tomato juice slowly to cheese sauce, stirring constantly. Serve over hot buttered toast. About 185 calories per serving not including toast. Add about 120 calories for each slice buttered toast.

CHEESE FONDUE

Sometimes, despite all precautions, a fondue will "lump." The cheese, not the cook, is usually to blame. If the cheese is poorly aged or not *Swiss* Gruyère or Emmentaler, it may never melt smoothly. The Swiss like to drink kirsch with fondue (usually a pony halfway through the proceedings) and to follow with broiled sausage and crisp apples or pears.
Makes 4 servings

⅔ pound well-aged imported
   Gruyère cheese, cut in ¼" cubes
⅓ pound well-aged imported
   Emmentaler cheese, cut in ¼"
   cubes
3 tablespoons flour
½ teaspoon paprika
¼ teaspoon nutmeg or mace
⅛ teaspoon white pepper
1 clove garlic, peeled and halved
1¾ cups Neuchâtel, Chablis, or
   Riesling wine
1 tablespoon lemon juice

2 tablespoons kirsch
¼ teaspoon baking soda (optional)
1½ loaves day-old French bread,
   cut in 1½" cubes (each should
   have crust on 1 side)

Toss cheeses in a bowl with flour, paprika, nutmeg, and pepper. Rub a 2-quart fondue *caquelon* or heavy round flameproof earthenware pot well with garlic. Add wine and heat, uncovered, over low heat until bubbles dot bottom of pot. Begin adding dredged cheeses (and any loose bits of flour and spices) by the handful, stirring with a wooden spoon in a figure 8 motion. Raise heat to moderate, continue stirring and adding cheese, flour, and spices a little at a time until all are in. Mix in lemon juice. At first, cheese will clump, but keep stirring. After 15–20 minutes, fondue should begin to "cream up." When fondue is smooth and bubbling gently, stir in kirsch and, for a lighter fondue, the soda. Set caquelon over its warmer and adjust flame so fondue bubbles *gently*—too much heat will make it rubbery. Serve with bread cubes and long-handled fondue forks. (*Note:* If fondue should separate and lump, return to moderately low stove heat and beat gently with a whisk; blend ½ teaspoon cornstarch with ¼ cup wine (same kind as in recipe) and blend into fondue. If fondue becomes too thick, thin with a little warmed wine.) About 990 calories per serving.

CHEDDAR-BEER FONDUE

Much easier and almost as good as Swiss fondue. Somewhat lower in calories, too.
Makes 4 appetizer servings; 2 entree servings

1 clove garlic, peeled and halved
1 tablespoon butter or margarine

2 cups coarsely grated sharp Cheddar cheese or ½ pound American cheese, finely diced
1 tablespoon flour
⅓ cup beer
1–2 tablespoons aquavit (*optional*)
1 small loaf day-old French or Italian bread, cut in 1" cubes (*each should have crust on 1 side*)

Rub inside of the top of a double boiler with garlic. Add butter and melt over simmering water. Toss cheese and flour together, add to butter along with beer and, if you like, aquavit. Heat, stirring rapidly, until smooth. Transfer to a chafing dish, set over simmering water, and serve with crusts of bread, long-handled fondue forks, and plenty of napkins. About 855 calories for each of 2 servings, 425 for each of 4.

⚕ HOMEMADE COTTAGE CHEESE

Rennet tablets, necessary for making cottage cheese, have disappeared from grocery shelves but are still available at drugstores.
Makes about 1 quart

1 gallon skim milk
½ cup sour cream
¼ penny-size rennet tablet, crushed in 2 tablespoons cold water
1–1½ teaspoons salt
⅓ cup heavy cream (*optional*)

Warm milk over lowest heat in a large stainless-steel or enamel kettle to 70° F. (a household thermometer can be used to test temperature) or let stand covered at room temperature 2–3 hours. Blend ½ cup of this milk with sour cream, return to kettle, and mix well. Stir in rennet, cover with a dry towel, and let stand undisturbed at room temperature (about 70° F.) 12–18 hours until a firm curd forms (mixture will look set with whey visible around edges). With a long stainless-steel knife, cut curd in kettle into ½" cubes; set kettle on a large, heavy rack *over* simmering water in a larger kettle and heat, uncovered, to 110–15° F. (use a candy thermometer), stirring every 2–3 minutes. Maintain 110–15° F. temperature for ½ hour, stirring every 5 minutes. Ladle into a colander lined with a double thickness of cheesecloth and let whey drain 2–3 minutes, lifting corners of cheesecloth occasionally, to move curd. Lift cheesecloth and curd, twisting top to form a bag, and plunge into cold water; move cloth gently to rinse curd. Drain and plunge into ice water; let stand 1–2 minutes. Lay bag of curd in a colander and drain well. Remove curd from cloth, season to taste with salt, and, if you like, mix in cream. Cover and chill before serving. Use within 2–3 days. About 95 calories per ½ cup serving (without heavy cream).

⚕ ▨ CURDS AND SOUR CREAM

A Slavic specialty eaten on pumpernickel.
Makes 4 servings

1 pound cottage or pot cheese
1 cup sour cream
½ cup minced scallions (*include some tops*)
½ cup minced cucumber
½ cup minced radishes
1 teaspoon salt
Freshly ground pepper

Mix all but last ingredient and chill well. Sprinkle with pepper and serve on lettuce or, as the Slavs do, with buttered pumpernickel. Also good spooned over buckwheat kasha or hot boiled new potatoes. About 230 calories per serving (on lettuce).

VARIATION:

⚖ **Calorie Counter's Curds:** Prepare as directed but substitute yogurt for sour cream. Serve on lettuce. About 140 calories per serving.

¢ **SWISS CHEESE PUFF**

Makes 4 servings

8 slices firm-textured white bread, trimmed of crusts
3 cups coarsely grated Swiss cheese
3 eggs, lightly beaten
2 cups milk
1 teaspoon salt
⅛ teaspoon white pepper
2 tablespoons minced scallions
⅛ teaspoon paprika

Preheat oven to 300° F. Alternate layers of bread and cheese in a buttered shallow 1½-quart casserole, beginning with bread and ending with cheese. Mix all remaining ingredients except paprika and pour into casserole. Sprinkle with paprika and bake, uncovered, 35–40 minutes until puffed, golden, and *just* set (a silver knife inserted midway between center and rim should come out clean). Serve immediately. About 575 calories per serving.

VARIATION:

Cheddar Bake: Prepare as directed but substitute sharp or mild Cheddar for the Swiss cheese and omit scallions. About 600 calories per serving.

About Soufflés

Like omelets, soufflés have a reputation for being difficult. They aren't, once the basic technique is learned. Soufflés are nothing more than sauces into which beaten egg whites are folded. It is the air, whipped into the whites, that leavens soufflés, so the point is to achieve the greatest possible volume of whites and to maintain it. This is done by using a balloon whip or wire whisk (and, if you have one, an unlined copper bowl), also by lightening the base sauce a bit by *stirring in* ¼–½ cup beaten whites before *folding in* the balance (see To Beat Egg Whites and About Folding in Beaten Egg Whites at the beginning of this chapter).

To Grease or Not to Grease the Soufflé Dish: Opinions are sharply divided. Some insist that soufflés climb to greater heights in greased and crumbed dishes; others say not, that it's like making a monkey climb a greased pole. Recipes in this book call for ungreased dishes and have produced cloud-high soufflés. But by all means, try both methods.

To Make a Top Hat Soufflé: Just before baking soufflé, insert a table knife into soufflé mixture about 1″–1½″ from rim of dish and draw a circle concentric with dish. When baked, soufflé center will puff way up, forming the top hat.

Note: Other soufflé recipes are included in the meat, poultry, seafood, vegetable and dessert chapters.

⚖ **BASIC CHEESE SOUFFLÉ**

Makes 4 servings

3 tablespoons butter or margarine
3 tablespoons flour
1 cup milk
1¼ cups coarsely grated Cheddar cheese or ¾ cup coarsely grated Swiss or Gruyère cheese
3 eggs, separated
1 teaspoon salt
⅛ teaspoon pepper

Melt butter in a saucepan over moderate heat, blend in flour, slowly stir in milk, and heat, stirring, until thickened. Add cheese and stir until melted. Beat yolks lightly, blend in a little hot sauce and return to pan; heat and stir 1–2 minutes over lowest heat. Off heat, mix in salt and pepper; lay a piece of wax paper flat on surface of sauce and cool to room temperature. Meanwhile, preheat oven to 350° F. Beat egg whites until stiff but not dry, stir about ¼ cup into sauce, then fold in remaining whites. Spoon into an ungreased 5-cup soufflé dish and bake, uncovered, 35–40 minutes until puffy and browned. Serve at once, accompanied, if you like, with Mushroom Sauce or Tomato Sauce. About 335 calories per serving if made with Cheddar, 285 if made with Swiss cheese.

⚔ **To Make with Process Cheese:** Prepare as directed but use only ⅓ cup process cheese; it is gummy and will make soufflé heavy. About 260 calories per serving.

VARIATIONS:

⚔ **Herbed Cheese Soufflé:** Prepare as directed, but add any of the following to cheese sauce: 1 tablespoon minced fresh dill or parsley; 1 teaspoon oregano, basil, sage, thyme, tarragon, or marjoram. Same calorie counts as for Basic Cheese Soufflé.

Deviled Cheese Soufflé: Prepare as directed but to cheese sauce add: 1 teaspoon each Worcestershire sauce and prepared spicy brown mustard, 1 tablespoon ketchup, ¼ teaspoon garlic powder, and ⅛ teaspoon cayenne pepper. About 345 calories per serving if made with Cheddar, 295 if made with Swiss cheese.

⚔ **Wine and Cheese Soufflé:** Prepare as directed but substitute ½ cup dry white wine for ½ cup of the milk. Serve, if you like, with hot Mornay Sauce (lightly laced with white wine). Same calorie counts as Basic Cheese Soufflé, not including sauce.

Cheese and Onion Soufflé: Prepare sauce as directed but before cooling mix in ½ cup thinly sliced Bermuda onion rings sautéed until limp, not brown. Cool sauce, fold in whites, and bake as directed. About 340 calories if made with Cheddar, 290 if made with Swiss cheese.

Some Additional Ways to Vary Cheese Soufflé: Prepare basic recipe as directed but before cooling cheese sauce mix in any of the following:
– ¼–⅓ cup minced cooked ham, crisp crumbled bacon, or minced sautéed chicken livers
– ¼ cup deviled ham or pâté
– ¼ cup minced sautéed mushrooms and 2 tablespoons minced pimiento
– ⅓ cup minced cooked vegetable (asparagus, spinach, broccoli, cauliflower, cabbage, or Brussels sprouts)
– ¼ cup each sautéed minced yellow onion and sweet green or red peppers
– ¼ cup minced ripe or green olives
– ¼ cup minced cooked fish or shellfish

❑ **TOP-OF-THE-STOVE SOUFFLÉED CHEESE**

Makes 4 servings

4 eggs, lightly beaten
1 cup cottage cheese
¼ cup milk
¾ teaspoon salt
⅛ teaspoon white pepper
1½ cups hot Tomato Sauce or Mushroom Sauce

EGGS AND CHEESE

Mix all ingredients except sauce in the top of a double boiler set over simmering water. Beat with a whisk or rotary beater until mixture thickens, 2–3 minutes. Cover, pull pan from heat, but leave over hot water, undisturbed, 5–10 minutes. Spoon onto warm plates and top with sauce. About 320 calories per serving.

VARIATION:

⚜ **Low-Calorie Souffléed Cheese:** Prepare as directed but serve topped with minced chives instead of sauce. About 140 calories per serving.

QUICHE LORRAINE

Makes 10 appetizer servings; 6 entree servings

Pastry:
1 recipe Flaky Pastry I

Filling:
½ pound crisply cooked bacon, crumbled
½ pound Gruyère or Swiss cheese, coarsely grated
4 eggs, lightly beaten
1 teaspoon salt
⅛ teaspoon white pepper
Pinch cayenne pepper
⅛ teaspoon nutmeg (optional)
1¾ cups light cream
1 tablespoon melted butter

Preheat oven to 425° F. Prepare pastry, roll into a 12" circle, and fit into a 9" piepan, making a high, fluted edge. Prick bottom and sides of pastry well with a fork; cover with wax paper and fill with uncooked rice or dried beans. Bake 5–7 minutes until firm but not brown, then cool slightly on a wire rack. Remove paper and rice. Sprinkle bacon and cheese evenly over pie shell. Mix together remaining ingredients and strain through a fine sieve. Place pie shell on partly pulled-out oven rack, then pour in egg mixture. Bake, uncovered, 15 minutes at 425° F., reduce heat to 350° F., and bake 10–15 minutes longer or until a knife inserted halfway between center and rim comes out clean. Cool on a wire rack 8–10 minutes before cutting into wedges. Serve as an appetizer or luncheon entree. About 620 calories for each of 6 servings, 375 calories for each of 10.

VARIATIONS:

Roquefort Quiche: Prepare as directed, using ¼ pound each Roquefort and Gruyère. Approximately the same calories per serving as *Quiche Lorraine.*

Quiche Bourbonnaise: Prepare as directed but substitute ½ pound slivered cooked ham for the bacon and reduce cheese to ¼ pound. About 550 calories for each of 6 servings, 335 for each of 10.

Onion Quiche: Prepare as directed but substitute 1 thinly sliced, lightly sautéed Bermuda onion for the bacon; separate into rings and arrange over crust. Reduce cream to 1½ cups. About 475 calories for each of 6 servings, 285 for each of 10.

Quiche Niçoise: Prepare as directed but omit bacon; arrange thinly sliced tomatoes over crust, overlapping slices slightly; scatter with ⅓ cup thinly sliced ripe olives and sprinkle with ¼ teaspoon garlic powder. Reduce amount of cheese to ¼ pound and cream to 1½ cups. About 465 calories for each of 6 servings, 280 for each of 10.

Clam Quiche: Prepare as directed but substitute 1 cup well-drained minced clams for the bacon. Make egg mixture using 1 cup heavy cream and ½ cup clam liquid instead of 1¾ cups cream. About 545 calories for each of 6 servings, 330 for each of 10.

CHEDDAR ONION TART

Makes 6 servings

1 recipe Flaky Pastry I
1 medium-size Bermuda onion, peeled, sliced paper thin, and separated into rings
1½ cups milk
1½ cups coarsely grated sharp Cheddar cheese
3 eggs, lightly beaten
¾ teaspoon salt
⅛ teaspoon pepper
⅛ teaspoon paprika

Preheat oven to 425° F. Prepare pastry, roll into a 12" circle, and fit into a 9" piepan, making a high, fluted edge; prick bottom and sides well with a fork. Cover with wax paper and fill with uncooked rice or dried beans. Bake 5–7 minutes until firm, not brown; cool briefly on a wire rack. Remove paper and rice and scatter onion evenly into pie shell. Scald milk, add cheese, and stir until melted. Off heat, stir a little hot mixture into eggs, return to pan, and mix well. Add salt and pepper and pour over onion. Sprinkle with paprika and bake, uncovered, 15 minutes, lower heat to 350° F., and bake 15 minutes longer until knife inserted midway between center and rim comes out clean. Cool 10 minutes on a wire rack before cutting. About 390 calories per serving.

CROQUE-MONSIEUR

An egg-dipped, fried cheese and ham "sandwich" to be eaten with knife and fork.
Makes 2 servings

4 thin slices firm-textured white bread, trimmed of crusts and buttered on 1 side
3 (1-ounce) packages Gruyère or Swiss cheese, coarsely grated
2 thin slices boiled ham, cut to fit bread
2 eggs lightly beaten with 2 tablespoons cold water
2–3 tablespoons butter or margarine
½ cup hot Medium White Sauce blended with 2 tablespoons finely grated Parmesan cheese

Sandwich cheese and ham between slices of bread pressing lightly, dip in egg, making sure edges are well coated, and brown on both sides in butter over moderate heat. Lift to warm plates and top with sauce. About 695 calories per serving.

VARIATION:

Croque-Madame: Prepare as directed but substitute very thinly sliced white meat of chicken or turkey for the ham. About 690 calories per serving.

⚖ CROSTINI ALLA MOZZARELLA (BREADED, FRIED MOZZARELLA CHEESE)

Don't cut cheese cubes any larger than ¾" or they won't cook properly.
Makes 6 entree servings or 36 appetizers

Shortening or cooking oil for deep fat frying
½ pound mozzarella cheese (low moisture type is best), cut in ¾" cubes
¼ cup unsifted flour
2 eggs, lightly beaten
3 cups soft white bread crumbs

Begin heating shortening over moderate heat; insert deep fat thermometer. Dredge cheese in flour, dip in eggs, then in crumbs, then in eggs and crumbs again; press crumbs lightly so they stick. When fat

EGGS AND CHEESE

reaches 375° F., fry cheese, a few cubes at a time, 30–40 seconds until well browned. (*Note:* Timing and temperature are important; cheese should be slightly runny just underneath the crumbs but firm in the center.) Lift out with slotted spoon, drain on paper toweling, and keep warm while you fry the rest. Serve as soon as possible, as entree, if you like, with hot Tomato Sauce, or with toothpicks as an appetizer. About 225 calories for each of 6 servings, about 40 calories per appetizer.

CHEESE BLINTZES

Makes 1 dozen

½ cup sifted flour
¼ teaspoon salt
2 eggs, lightly beaten
¾ cup milk or a ½ and ½ mixture of milk and cold water
1 tablespoon melted butter or margarine
1–2 tablespoons butter or margarine

Filling:
1 pound cottage or pot cheese
2 egg yolks, lightly beaten
3–4 tablespoons sugar
⅛ teaspoon salt
⅛ teaspoon cinnamon
1–2 tablespoons milk (*optional*)

Topping:
1 cup sour cream

Sift flour and salt into a bowl; mix eggs, milk, and melted butter, slowly add to flour, and beat until smooth. Butter bottom and sides of a heavy 6″ skillet and heat over moderately high heat until a drop of water will dance. Using about 2 tablespoons batter for each blintze, add to skillet and tip back and forth until bottom is evenly coated. Brown lightly on 1 side, about ½ minute, turn out, browned side up, on a kitchen towel or paper toweling. Cook remaining blintzes the same way. Mix filling ingredients, adding milk to moisten if needed. Place about 1½ tablespoons filling in center of each blintze, fold bottom up and sides in over filling, then roll up. Brown in remaining butter over moderate heat and serve with sour cream. About 175 calories per blintze if made with cottage cheese, 165 if made with pot cheese.

VARIATION:

Season filling to taste with finely grated lemon or orange rind and top with stewed fruit instead of sour cream.

UKRAINIAN CHEESE TURNOVERS

Makes about 10

1 recipe Sour Cream Pastry or Flaky Pastry I
1 egg, lightly beaten with 1 tablespoon cold water (*glaze*)

Filling:
1 cup minced scallions (include some tops)
¼ cup butter or margarine
¼ cup minced parsley
2 cups coarsely grated Swiss cheese

Prepare pastry, wrap in wax paper, and chill while you make the filling. Preheat oven to 450° F. Stir-fry scallions in butter over moderately low heat 5–7 minutes until limp; off heat, mix in parsley and cheese. Roll pastry, ½ at a time, and cut in rounds using a 4″ saucer as a guide. Brush edges with glaze, spoon a little filling onto lower halves of rounds, fold over, and crimp edges with a fork. Brush with glaze and bake, uncovered, on ungreased baking sheets 15 minutes; lower heat to 350° F. and bake 15 minutes longer until golden. Serve hot. About 340 calories per turnover if made with sour cream pastry, 250 per turnover if made with flaky pastry.

CHAPTER 13

CEREALS, RICE, AND PASTA

When man discovered that seeds of certain grasses were edible, that they could be planted to provide food for himself and his family, he emerged from savagery. It was no longer necessary to kill in order to survive. Such life-giving foods, inevitably, were held sacred and became the basis of much mythology. Our word *cereal*, in fact, derives from Ceres, Roman goddess of grain and harvest.

The family of cereals is vast. All, to greater or lesser degrees, are high energy foods with B vitamins in abundance. The more refined or polished the cereal, the less nutritious because most of the nutrients are contained in the husk. Enrichment programs, however, are replacing vitamins and minerals lost in the milling. A cereal marked *"restored"* has had the nutritive content restored to the level of whole grain. *"Enriched cereal"* has been given the added boost of nutrients not present in the whole grain (usually vitamins A or D).

The Kinds and Forms of Cereals

The vast array of cereals available today can be divided into three basic categories: the *regular cooking*, the *quick cooking*, and the *ready to eat*. Briefly, here are the kinds of grains and forms in which they're sold:

Barley: One of man's first foods but not commonly used today except for making beer. The polished grain, or *pearl*, comes in three sizes—coarse, medium, and fine—and is a good extender of soups and stews. *Scotch barley*, sold primarily in health food stores, is husked and coarsely ground. It must be soaked overnight before using.

Bran: Not a single grain but the husk of any grain separated out in the milling.

Buckwheat: No relation to wheat but another species altogether; it is Siberian and the foundation of many Russian dishes, notably *kasha*, a pilaf-like dish of braised buckwheat groats. Kasha has become something of a generic term today, meaning any braised or baked cracked cereal and, in fact, some bulgur wheat is marketed as kasha. True kasha, however, is a particular recipe made of buckwheat.

Bulgur: (see Wheat).

Corn: America's gift to the world and the grain upon which much of Latin America lives yet. Both yellow and white meal are available, enriched and the old-fashioned unbolted (unsifted) stone or water ground (ground on millstones), which Southerners prefer to all others. *Hominy* is white flint corn, the kernels of which have been skinned either mechanically or in a lye bath. It is available dry (cracked or whole) or canned (whole). *Hominy grits* are simply dried hominy ground to meal; they can be prepared like corn meal.

Couscous: The Arabic word for semolina (see Wheat).

Farina: Broadly speaking, any ground grain. Today, however, farina usually means ground wheat, either the whole grain (*dark farina*) or the refined (*light farina* or *cream of wheat*).

Grits: Finely ground grain, now almost always meaning *hominy grits* (see Corn).

Groats: Coarsely ground grain, usually buckwheat.

Kasha: (see Buckwheat).

Masa Harina: A special corn flour popular throughout Mexico and Latin America; it is what gives tortillas their characteristic nutty-sweet flavor.

Millet: An Asian grain little used in this country except as forage. Health food stores sell millet flour, also millet seeds, which can be cooked like other whole grains.

Oats: One of the most nutritious and important grains. Most are rolled into oatmeal, ground into flour or puffed into breakfast cereal.

Rice: The "bread" of the Orient and a grain once so revered only emperors were permitted to plant it. There are dozens of varieties of rice, but, to simplify, there are the *long grain* and the *short grain*. Long grain rice is best for serving solo or using in casseroles because the grains remain separate; short grain rice cooks down into a softness more suitable for puddings. *Brown rice* is simply unpolished rice (only the husks have been removed). It is more nutritious than polished rice, cheaper, and, some people think, of better flavor. *Wild rice* is not rice (see description that follows). Polished rice is available in three popular forms: *regular, converted* (also known as processed or parboiled), and *quick cooking* (fully cooked, dehydrated rice that needs only stand in boiling water a few minutes). (*Note:* Recipes in this book, unless otherwise noted, were tested using converted rice). This rice has been steam-treated so that its grains become tender without gumming up or losing their identity.

Rye: The bulk of rye grown goes either into whiskey or flour. Rye groats are sometimes available, however, and should be cooked like buckwheat or other groats.

Semolina: (see Wheat).

Wheat: The staff of life for much of the world, source of flours, myriad breakfast cereals, also such ethnic exotics as *cracked wheat;* that Middle Eastern favorite called *bulgur* (parched, cracked wheat from which some of the bran has been removed); and *semolina* (the hard heart of durum wheat, ground either into the flour from which pasta is made or into granules, cooked much like farina and known to Arabs as *couscous*). Other wheat products include *wheat germ,* the tender, perishable embryo; it can be scattered over cereals, mixed into meat loaves and croquettes, slipped into casseroles and salads, or used as a topping.

Wild Rice: A luxurious, nut-flavored, long grain marsh grass of the northern Lake States, so expensive still that Indians of the area (by law the only persons allowed to harvest it) carry small pouches of it in place of money. The longer the grain, the greater the price.

How to Cook Cereals

Except for rice and wild rice, which will be discussed separately, all cereals are cooked more or less the same way. The only variable is the proportion of liquid to cereal, determined by size of grain (whether whole, cracked, or ground) rather than by species. It's always best to cook cereal by package directions because each manufacturer knows his product best. As a general rule, however, the following methods work for all cereals (except for the quick-cooking, which should be prepared strictly as the label directs).

Direct Heat Method: Bring water and salt to a full rolling boil in a heavy saucepan. Gradually sprinkle in cereal, stirring all the while. Turn heat to low and cook uncovered, stirring often, 15–20 minutes until tender and no raw taste of starch remains. Toward end of cooking, use an asbestos flame-tamer, if possible, to keep cereal from scorching.

Double Boiler Method (slower but surer): Place water and salt in top part of a double boiler and bring quickly to a boil over direct heat. Sprinkle cereal in gradually, stirring constantly. When cereal begins to thicken, set over simmering water and cook uncovered, stirring occasionally, 20–30 minutes until done.

Some Ways to Dress Up Cooked Cereals

— Cook in milk or a ½ and ½ mixture of cream and water instead of in water.
— To the cooking water, add 1 tablespoon sugar mixed with 1 teaspoon cinnamon and, if you like, a pinch nutmeg, allspice, or cloves.

PROPORTIONS FOR 4 SERVINGS

Cereal	Quantity	Water	Salt
Rolled oats or wheat	1 cup	2 cups	½ teaspoon
Buckwheat or other groats, bulgur and cracked wheat, other cracked or coarsely ground cereals	1 cup	2 cups	1 teaspoon
Farina, corn meal, grits, and other granular cereals	1 cup	5 cups	1 teaspoon

– About 5 minutes before cereal is done, stir in ½–1 cup seedless raisins, dried currants, diced dates, dried apricots, figs, or prunes.
– About 5 minutes before cereal is done, stir in ¾ cup coarsely chopped pecans, walnuts, roasted almonds, or peanuts.
– When serving, mound into a Baked Apple or on top of baked or fried bananas.
– When serving, make a well in the center of each portion and fill with Melba Sauce or any fruit jam, jelly, or preserves.
– When serving, top with any of the following:
  – Maple or brown sugar and, if you like, a pinch of cinnamon or nutmeg
  – Maple syrup, honey, or molasses and heavy cream
  – A ½ and ½ mixture of brown sugar and wheat germ
  – Brown sugar, minced fresh mint, and yogurt or sour cream
  – Heavy or sour cream and thawed frozen berries or peaches

Note: Chicken or beef broth can be used for cooking rice instead of water, but salt should be reduced accordingly.

Basic Method (for fluffy, tender rice): Bring water and salt to a rapid boil over high heat in a heavy saucepan, add rice, cover, reduce heat so rice bubbles gently, and cook until rice is tender and all water absorbed. Regular and converted rice will take 20–25 minutes, brown rice 40–45. If you like, uncover and let dry out 3–5 minutes before serving. Fluff with a fork.

Open Pan Method (for firm, tender white rice; especially good to use if rice is to be added to casseroles or stuffings): Bring water and salt to a rapid boil over high heat in an extra-heavy saucepan, stir in rice, reduce heat slightly, and cook, uncovered, *without stirring* until water is barely visible, about 10 minutes. Turn heat to low and continue cooking, uncovered, until all moisture is absorbed, about 8–10 minutes. Fluff with a fork.

Oven Method (for mellow, nutty flavor): Preheat oven to 400° F. In a heavy flameproof casserole, melt 2 tablespoons butter or margarine over direct moderate heat. Add rice and stir-fry about ½ minute. Add water and salt, cover tightly, and bake until rice is tender and all liquid absorbed. White rice will take about 20 minutes, brown about 45. Fluff with a fork and serve.

VARIATION:

Stir-fry 2 tablespoons minced yellow onion in butter 2–3 minutes, then add rice and proceed as directed. For added zip, add a parsley sprig or celery top and 2–3 dashes liquid hot red pepper seasoning. Remove parsley or celery before serving.

HOW TO COOK RICE

Kind of Rice	Quantity of Uncooked Rice	Water	Salt	Yield of Cooked Rice	Number of Servings
White (regular)	1 cup	2 cups	1 teaspoon	3 cups	4
White (converted)	1 cup	2–2½ cups	1 teaspoon	4 cups	4–6
White (quick-cooking)	1 cup	(cook by package directions)		2 cups	2–3
Brown	1 cup	2½ cups	1 teaspoon	4 cups	4–6

Tips for Making Better Rice

- Be sure to use a large enough pan; rice will quadruple or triple in bulk during cooking. Also make sure pan is heavy so there is little danger of scorching.
- Once rice comes to a boil, stir as little as possible, and use a fork if you must stir—less chance of mashing or breaking the rice.
- To help keep rice grains beautifully distinct, add 1 or 2 drops cooking oil or a dab of butter or margarine to the cooking water. Also gives rice a lovely glisten.
- If rice must be held before serving, transfer to a colander and set over simmering water; keep covered. Rice will keep hot without overcooking. *Or* transfer rice to a heavy casserole and set in oven turned to lowest heat. Keep tightly covered.

What to Do with Leftover Rice

To Reheat: Place rice in a large, fine sieve and with moistened hands break up any clumps. Set sieve over simmering water, cover, and steam about 10 minutes. Rice will be almost as good as it was the first time around. *Or* place rice in a buttered casserole and break up clumps with moistened hands. Dot well with butter, cover, and bake ½ hour at 325° F.

To Use Up Small Amounts:
- Mix into meat loaves, croquettes, or stuffings.
- Combine with leftover meat and vegetables in a casserole or soup.
- Add to any creamed meat or vegetable mixture.
- Marinate in Garlic or Herb Dressing and serve in hollowed-out tomatoes.
- Toss with mixed greens in a salad.
- Add to pancake batter.
- Scramble with eggs.
- Team with custard sauce and/or fresh fruit as a dessert.

Some Quick Ways to Dress Up Rice

During Cooking (amounts based on 1 cup uncooked rice and basic method of cooking):

Saffron Rice: Add ⅛ teaspoon powdered saffron to cooking liquid or soak ¼ teaspoon saffron in ¼ cup cooking liquid about 10 minutes, then cook as directed. Season to taste with salt and pepper.

Arroz Amarillo (Yellow Mexican Rice): Stir-fry rice in 3 tablespoons olive oil with 1 small minced yellow onion and 1 crushed clove garlic about 5 minutes over moderate heat until pale golden; mix in ⅔ cup canned tomato sauce and 2 cups chicken broth and cook by basic method. Season to taste with salt and freshly ground pepper.

Pineapple Rice: Cook rice in a ½ and ½ mixture of pineapple juice and chicken broth. Just before serving, mix in 1 (8-ounce) drained can pineapple tidbits and, if you like, 1 cup coarsely chopped cashew nuts. Omit salt and pepper.

Orange Rice: Cook rice in a ½ and ½ mixture of orange juice and chicken broth with 2 teaspoons grated orange rind and ⅛ teaspoon nutmeg. Just before serving, mix in ½ cup diced, seeded orange sections. Add a pinch of salt but omit pepper.

Raisin, Currant, Date, Apricot, or Fig Rice: Cook as directed but add ¼ cup seedless raisins or dried currants, diced dates, dried apricots, or figs to the pot. Season to taste with salt and pepper. Especially good with curry.

Onion Rice: Stir-fry 1 minced Bermuda onion and the rice in 3 tablespoons butter about 5 minutes over moderate heat until pale golden; then cook as directed and season to taste.

Garlic Rice: Stir-fry 1 minced clove garlic in 2 tablespoons butter 2 minutes over moderate heat; add rice and stir-fry 3 minutes longer, then cook as directed. Season to taste.

Savory Rice: Stir-fry ¼ cup each minced yellow onion and celery and 1 crushed clove garlic in 2 tablespoons butter over moderate heat 8–10 minutes until golden. Add rice and cook as directed, using beef broth. Season to taste with salt and pepper and, if you like, Worcestershire sauce.

Green Rice: Stir-fry ½ cup minced scallions (include tops) in 2 tablespoons butter 3–4 minutes over moderate heat until limp; add rice and cook as directed, using chicken broth. Season to taste and mix in 1 cup minced parsley.

Confetti Rice: Stir-fry ⅓ cup each minced yellow onion, sweet red and green pepper in 3 tablespoons butter or olive oil; add rice and cook as directed, using chicken broth. Season to taste with salt and liquid hot red pepper seasoning.

Curried Rice: Warm 2 teaspoons curry powder in 1 tablespoon butter 1–2 minutes over moderate heat; add rice and cook as directed, using chicken broth. Season to taste.

Chili Rice: Warm 2 teaspoons curry powder and ½ teaspoon each garlic and onion powder in 2 tablespoons olive oil 2 minutes over moderate heat; add rice and cook as directed, using beef or chicken broth. Season to taste with salt and crushed dried hot red chili peppers. Just before serving, mix in ⅓ cup crisp crumbled bacon.

Herbed Rice: Warm 2 tablespoons minced fresh dill, basil, chives, or parsley or 1 tablespoon minced fresh sage or thyme in 2 tablespoons butter 2 minutes over moderate heat; add rice and cook as directed, using chicken broth. Season to taste. (*Note:* 1 teaspoon of the dried herb may be substituted for the fresh, but the flavor will not be as good.)

Mushroom Rice: Stir-fry ½ pound thinly sliced or coarsely chopped mushrooms in 3 tablespoons butter over moderately high heat 2–3 minutes until golden; add rice and cook as directed, using beef or chicken broth. Season to taste.

Just Before Serving: Cook 1 cup rice by basic method, season with salt and pepper, then mix in any of the following:

Poppy or Caraway Seed Rice: 2 tablespoons each poppy or caraway seeds and melted butter.

Rice Amandine: ⅓ cup butter-browned slivered blanched almonds.

Nut Rice: 2 tablespoons melted butter and ⅓ cup coarsely chopped pecans, walnuts, macadamia, piñon, or pistachio nuts or toasted peanuts or cashews.

Olive Rice: ½ cup minced pitted ripe or pimiento-stuffed green olives and 1–2 tablespoons olive oil.

Avocado-Tomato Rice: 1 coarsely chopped small firm-ripe avocado and ½ cup coarsely chopped, peeled, seeded tomato.

Minted Rice (delicious with lamb): ¼ cup minced fresh mint warmed 2–3 minutes in 2 tablespoons butter.

Soy Rice: ¼ cup minced scallions sautéed in 2 tablespoons peanut oil 2–3 minutes over moderate heat, 2 tablespoons each soy sauce and minced pimiento and ½ teaspoon sugar; reduce salt as needed. Cover and let stand off heat 2–3 minutes; toss and serve.

Sour Cream Rice: ¾–1 cup warmed sour cream; cover rice and let stand off heat 5 minutes. Sprinkle with 1–2 tablespoons minced chives, toss lightly and serve.

Cheesy Rice: ⅓–½ cup grated sharp Cheddar, Parmesan, Swiss, or mozzarella cheese; cover rice and let stand off heat 4–5 minutes to melt cheese; toss lightly and serve.

TOASTED RICE

If you like the nutty flavor of toasted rice, toast a pound, store airtight, and use as needed.
Makes 4 servings

1 cup uncooked rice

Preheat oven to 350° F. Spread rice out in a shallow baking pan and toast, stirring now and then, 8–10 minutes until golden. Cook as you would regular rice. About 180 calories per serving.

VARIATION:

Toasted Rice and Vegetable Casserole: In a greased 2-quart casserole, mix 1 cup toasted rice, 1 (10-ounce) package frozen mixed vegetables thawed just enough to separate, 1 (4-ounce) can drained sliced mushrooms, 2 cups chicken or beef broth, and ½ teaspoon salt. Cover and bake about 20 minutes at 350° F. until rice is tender. About 245 calories per serving.

RICE RING

White, brown, and wild rice can all be molded by the following method. So can cracked or bulgur wheat, buckwheat groats, and all of the flavored rices (Curried, Herbed, etc.) except for very soft ones containing sauce. For variety, mold in individual ramekins or 1½-quart fluted or decorative molds instead of a ring mold.
Makes 8 servings

6 cups hot seasoned cooked rice
¼ cup melted butter or margarine

Mix rice and butter with a fork and pack lightly into a *well-buttered* or oiled 1½-quart ring mold. Let stand 1 minute, then invert on a hot platter. Fill center with any creamed mixture, stew, or curry. (*Note:* If dinner must be held, don't mold rice until the very last minute; it will keep hot in the pan far better than in the mold.) About 190 calories per serving.

RICE PILAF

Makes 4 servings

¼ cup butter or margarine
1 cup uncooked rice
2 cups hot chicken or beef broth
½ teaspoon salt (about)
⅛ teaspoon pepper

Melt butter in a heavy saucepan over moderately low heat, add rice, and stir-fry about 5 minutes until straw-colored. Add broth, salt, and pepper, cover, and cook over lowest heat without stirring 18–20 minutes until all liquid is absorbed. Uncover and cook 3–5 minutes longer to dry out. Fluff with a fork, taste for salt and adjust as needed. About 305 calories per serving.

VARIATIONS:

Baked Pilaf (a good way to make pilaf in quantity): Stir-fry rice as directed in a flameproof casserole or

Dutch oven-type kettle, add broth and seasonings, cover, and bake about ½ hour at 350° F. until all liquid is absorbed. For drier rice, uncover and bake 5 minutes longer. About 305 calories per serving.

Middle East Pilaf: Stir-fry 1 small minced yellow onion in butter along with rice, add broth and seasonings, also ¼ cup seedless raisins or dried currants, ¼ teaspoon each cinnamon and allspice, ⅛ teaspoon each turmeric and cardamom. Cover and cook as directed. About 330 calories per serving.

Indian Pilaf: Stir-fry 1 medium-size minced yellow onion in butter along with rice, add 2 teaspoons curry powder, and stir-fry ½ minute. Add broth and seasonings, also ¼ cup sultana or seedless raisins. Cover and cook as directed. Add ¼ cup coarsely chopped toasted blanched almonds, then fluff with a fork. About 390 calories per serving.

Bulgur Pilaf: Prepare any of the preceding pilafs as directed, but substitute 1 cup uncooked bulgur or cracked wheat for rice. Calorie counts approximately the same as for any of the pilafs made with rice.

Main Dish Pilaf: Prepare rice or bulgur pilaf as directed; just before serving, add 1½ cups diced cooked meat, chicken, fish, or shellfish and toss lightly to mix. Recipe too flexible for a meaningful calorie count.

BROWN RICE PILAF

Makes 4–6 servings

¼ cup butter or margarine
1 cup uncooked brown rice
1 (10½-ounce) can condensed beef broth
1 cup water
⅛ teaspoon pepper

Preheat oven to 325° F. Melt butter in a flameproof 2-quart casserole over moderately low heat, add rice, and cook, stirring constantly, 3–4 minutes; do not brown. Off heat, stir in remaining ingredients. Cover and bake 1–1¼ hours until rice is tender. Fluff with a fork and serve. About 310 calories for each of 4 servings, 205 calories for each of 6 servings.

VARIATION:

Just before serving, toss in any of the following: ½ cup chopped, cooked chicken livers, shrimp, ham, sweetbreads, poultry, game, or leftover meat. (*Note:* By adding as much as 2 cups of any of these, you can serve pilaf as a main dish.) Recipe too flexible for a meaningful calorie count.

ARMENIAN RICE

Delicious with roast lamb or shish kebabs.
Makes 6 servings

6 tablespoons butter or margarine
⅔ cup fine egg noodles
1½ cups uncooked rice
3 cups boiling water
1 tablespoon salt

Melt butter in a large, heavy kettle over moderately high heat, toss in noodles and stir-fry 3–5 minutes until pale brown. Add rice and stir-fry 5 minutes until tweedy and golden. Add water and salt, stir well, cover, and boil gently over moderate heat about 20 minutes until rice is tender and all water absorbed. About 300 calories per serving.

RISOTTO ALLA MILANESE

There are dozens of *risotti* (soft rice mixtures that are to the north of Italy what pasta is to the south).

This one is a classic. Delicious with veal or chicken.

Makes 4 servings

2 tablespoons each butter and beef marrow or ¼ cup butter or margarine
1 small yellow onion, peeled and minced
1 cup uncooked rice
2 cups hot chicken or beef broth
Pinch powdered saffron or ⅛ teaspoon saffron, soaked in ¼ cup of the hot broth (strain and reserve broth)
½ teaspoon salt (about)
⅛ teaspoon pepper
¼ cup grated Parmesan cheese

Melt butter and marrow in a heavy saucepan over moderately low heat, add onion and rice, and stir-fry about 5 minutes until rice is straw-colored. Add broth, saffron, salt, and pepper, cover, and cook over lowest heat 18–20 minutes until all liquid is absorbed. Uncover and dry out 3–5 minutes. Add Parmesan and fluff with a fork; taste for salt and adjust as needed. About 330 calories per serving.

VARIATIONS:

Mushroom Risotto: Stir-fry ½ pound minced mushrooms along with onion and rice; proceed as directed and toss in ¼ cup piñon nuts along with the Parmesan. About 405 calories per serving.

Savoy Risotto: Omit onion, but stir-fry rice as directed, adding 1 crushed clove garlic during last 2 minutes. Add 1 cup each dry white wine and chicken broth, the seasonings, and proceed as directed. Substitute ⅓ cup grated Emmentaler or Gruyère cheese for the Parmesan, fork into rice, cover, and let stand off heat 5 minutes to melt cheese. About 375 calories per serving.

Risi e Bisi (Makes 6 servings): Prepare as directed, omitting saffron if you like. When rice has cooked in liquid 10 minutes, add 1 (10-ounce) package frozen green peas (break up in package before adding). Cover and proceed as directed. About 380 calories per serving.

CHICKEN LIVER RISOTTO

Makes 4 servings

1 pound chicken livers
6 tablespoons butter or margarine
1 large yellow onion, peeled and minced
½ cup thinly sliced mushrooms
1 cup uncooked rice
2½ cups hot chicken broth
½ teaspoon salt
⅛ teaspoon pepper
2 tablespoons minced parsley
¼ cup grated Parmesan cheese

Halve livers at the natural separation and pat dry on paper toweling. Melt ¼ cup butter in a large skillet or flameproof casserole that has a tight fitting lid over moderately high heat. Add livers and sauté 3–4 minutes, stirring, until lightly browned; remove with a slotted spoon to a heated plate, cover, and keep warm. Melt remaining butter in the same skillet, add onion, and stir-fry 4–5 minutes. Add mushrooms and stir-fry 5 minutes longer until onion and mushrooms are brown. Add rice, broth, salt, and pepper, mix well, and heat uncovered until just boiling. Turn heat to low, cover, and simmer 15–20 minutes until rice is tender. Add livers, parsley, and Parmesan, toss lightly with 2 forks, and serve. About 555 calories per serving.

VARIATION:

Calf's Liver Risotto: Prepare as directed, substituting 1 pound calf's liver, cut in bite-size pieces, for the chicken livers. About 565 calories per serving.

¢ ⚖ SPANISH RICE
Makes 4 servings

1 large yellow onion, peeled and minced
2 tablespoons cooking oil
1 small sweet green pepper, cored, seeded, and minced
½ cup uncooked rice
¼ teaspoon chili powder
1 (1-pound) can tomatoes (do not drain)
½ cup water
1 bay leaf, crumbled
¾ teaspoon salt
⅛ teaspoon pepper
¼ teaspoon sugar

Sauté onion in oil in a heavy saucepan over moderate heat 5–8 minutes until limp. Add green pepper and stir-fry 5 minutes. Stir in rice and chili powder and brown rice lightly. Add remaining ingredients, chopping up tomatoes, cover, and simmer 20 minutes. Uncover and cook 5 minutes longer. About 195 calories per serving.

VARIATIONS:

¢ ⚖ **Baked Spanish Rice with Cheese:** Brown vegetables and rice in a flameproof casserole, add remaining ingredients and ½ cup grated sharp Cheddar cheese. Mix lightly, cover, and bake ½ hour at 350° F.; uncover and bake 5 minutes longer. Serve as a main dish. About 250 calories per serving.

⚖ **Spanish Rice with Olives and Saffron:** Soak ¼ teaspoon saffron in the ½ cup water called for, 10 minutes, then strain, reserving liquid. Prepare recipe as directed, using saffron water and adding ½ cup thinly sliced pimiento-stuffed green or ripe olives along with tomatoes. About 210 calories per serving.

¢ JAMBALAYA

Jambalaya is a Creole rice classic. Originally made with ham (its name comes from *jamón*, the Spanish word for ham), it is as likely to be made today with sausage, shrimp, or chicken. But the method remains the same, which means making a *roux*, browned flour and fat mixture. A roux is such an integral part of Creole cooking that many recipes begin simply, "First, you make a roux." It's assumed everyone knows how. Old-time Creole cooks will "work a roux" 4 or 5 times as long as the recipe below calls for to obtain a rich caramel flavor. But it really isn't necessary.
Makes 6 servings

1¼ pounds pork sausage meat or diced cooked ham
¼ cup bacon drippings (optional)
3 tablespoons flour
2 medium-size yellow onions, peeled and coarsely chopped
12 scallions, sliced ½" thick (include tops)
2 cloves garlic, peeled and crushed
¼ cup minced parsley
2 teaspoons salt (slightly less if ham is used)
1 teaspoon cayenne pepper
2 cups uncooked rice
2⅔ cups chicken broth or water

Stir-fry sausage in a large, heavy kettle over moderately high heat 5 minutes, remove to a bowl with a slotted spoon. (*Note:* If using ham, stir-fry in bacon drippings. Measure drippings and add additional bacon drippings as needed to make ¼ cup.) Blend in flour and heat and stir 1–2 minutes to make a rich brown roux. Add onions, scallions, and garlic and stir-fry 10–12 minutes over moderate heat until golden brown and well worked into roux. Return sausage to kettle, add all remaining ingredients except broth and stir-fry 1–2 minutes. Add broth, bring to a boil, then turn heat to lowest point, cover, and simmer 45 minutes. Uncover, stir well, and heat 10 minutes, stirring occasionally, until rice dries out a bit. Serve hot as a budget main dish or potato substitute. About 770 calories per serving if made with sausage, 625 calories per serving if made with diced cooked ham.

¢ **CAJUN "DIRTY RICE"**

Makes 4 servings

½ cup minced red onion
3 tablespoons bacon drippings
2 chicken livers, minced
2 scallions, minced (include tops)
1 clove garlic, peeled and crushed
2 tablespoons minced parsley
½ cup water
½ teaspoon salt (about)
⅛–¼ teaspoon crushed dried hot red chili peppers
4 cups hot boiled rice

Stir-fry onion in drippings in a large, heavy skillet over moderate heat 10–12 minutes until lightly browned. Add livers and brown. Add scallions, garlic, and parsley and stir-fry about 5 minutes until limp. Add water, salt, and peppers to taste and cook and stir 5–10 minutes over low heat to blend flavors. Pour over rice, toss lightly to mix, and serve. About 310 calories per serving.

VARIATION:

¢ **Baked Cajun Rice:** Prepare as directed, spoon into a greased 1½-quart casserole, dot liberally with butter, and bake uncovered about 20 minutes at 350° F. to brown lightly. About 350 calories per serving.

¢ **LOUISIANA RED BEANS AND RICE**

Makes 4 servings

1 cup dried red kidney beans, washed and sorted
1 quart cold water
1 (⅛-pound) chunk salt pork
1 medium-size yellow onion, peeled and coarsely chopped
1 clove garlic, peeled and crushed
1 stalk celery, coarsely chopped
1 bay leaf, crumbled
¼ teaspoon cumin
⅛ teaspoon pepper
1 tablespoon light brown sugar
½ teaspoon salt (about)
4 cups hot boiled rice
2 tablespoons minced parsley

Soak beans overnight in 2 cups water or use the quick method.* Drain, measure soaking water, and add enough cold water to make 2 cups. Place beans, water, and salt pork in a large, heavy saucepan, cover, and simmer ¾ hour. Add all but last 3 ingredients, cover, and simmer ½–¾ hour longer until tender. Discard salt pork; season to taste with salt. Ladle over rice, sprinkle with parsley, and serve. About 480 calories per serving.

¢ **JAMAICAN-STYLE RICE**

A spicy mixture of rice, onions, and kidney beans
Makes 6 servings

3 cups water
1 teaspoon butter or margarine
1⅓ cups uncooked rice
2 medium-size yellow onions, peeled and minced
3 tablespoons olive oil
1 (1-pound 4-ounce) can red kidney beans, drained
1 teaspoon salt
⅛ teaspoon pepper
⅛ teaspoon allspice

CEREALS, RICE, AND PASTA

Place water in a large saucepan and bring to a boil; stir in butter and rice and boil rapidly, uncovered, 10–15 minutes, without stirring, until most of the water is absorbed. Turn heat to low and cook, uncovered, 5 minutes longer until all water is absorbed. While rice cooks, stir-fry onions in oil in a large, heavy skillet 8–10 minutes over moderate heat until golden; stir in beans, salt, pepper, and allspice, turn heat to low, and sauté, stirring occasionally, 10–15 minutes. When rice is done, add to bean mixture and toss lightly to mix. Serve hot. About 320 calories per serving.

❒ CHINESE FRIED RICE

Makes 4 servings

- *3 cups cold cooked rice*
- *3 tablespoons peanut or other cooking oil*
- *½ cup julienne strips of lean cooked roast pork or ham*
- *4 scallions, minced (white part only)*
- *¼ cup chicken broth*
- *1 tablespoon soy sauce*
- *¼ teaspoon sugar*
- *⅛ teaspoon pepper*

Stir-fry rice in oil in a large, heavy skillet over moderate heat, pressing out any lumps, until pale golden. Add pork and scallions and stir-fry 1 minute. Add remaining ingredients, cover, and heat 1 minute. Serve very hot. About 295 calories per serving.

VARIATION:

Chinese Fried Eggs and Rice: Stir-fry rice, pork, and scallions as directed, then push to side of skillet; omit broth but add 1 or 2 lightly beaten eggs; scramble lightly, then mix into rice along with soy sauce, sugar, and pepper. About 330 calories per serving.

JAPANESE GINGER RICE WITH TOASTED SEAWEED

The Japanese like short grain rice because it cooks down to pudding softness. They're also fond of dried seaweed (available in pressed sheets at gourmet shops and Oriental groceries; separate sheets before measuring). The two are delicious together.

Makes 4 servings

- *1 cup uncooked short grain rice*
- *2 cups boiling chicken broth or weak tea*
- *1 (1″) piece fresh gingerroot, peeled and minced*
- *¼ teaspoon salt*
- *2 teaspoons soy sauce*
- *1 cup crumbled dried seaweed*

Preheat oven to 350° F. Mix rice, broth, ginger, salt, and soy sauce in a heavy saucepan, cover, and bring to a boil over high heat; turn heat to low, stir once, then cover and cook 15 minutes. Meanwhile spread seaweed on an ungreased baking sheet and toast, uncovered, 12–15 minutes until slightly crisp. When rice has cooked 15 minutes, uncover and cook 3–5 minutes longer. Fluff with a fork and serve sprinkled with seaweed. About 225 calories per serving.

¢ KHICHIRI (EAST INDIAN RICE AND LENTILS)

Good topped with yogurt or chutney and especially good with curry.

Makes 4–6 servings

- *½ cup dried lentils, washed and sorted*
- *1 medium-size yellow onion, peeled and minced*
- *2½ cups chicken broth or water*
- *½ cup uncooked rice*
- *¾ teaspoon salt (about)*

*Pinch crushed dried hot red chili
  peppers*
2 tablespoons margarine
2 teaspoons cumin seeds

Simmer lentils and onion in broth in a covered heavy saucepan 25 minutes, stirring occasionally. Add rice, salt, and chili peppers, cover, and simmer 20 minutes until rice is tender and all liquid absorbed. Uncover and cook 2–3 minutes to dry out. Meanwhile, melt margarine in a small skillet over moderately low heat, add cumin seeds, and stir-fry ½ minute until they begin to pop. Pour over rice and toss with a fork. Taste for salt and adjust as needed. Calories per serving: about 230 for each of 4 servings if made with water and 260 if made with chicken broth; about 155 for each of 6 servings if made with water and 170 if made with chicken broth.

¢ BAKED RICE IRANIAN STYLE (CHELOU)

It takes long cooking and a heavy casserole to make this Middle Eastern favorite. The aim is to get a crusty bottom layer of rice (use a flameproof glass dish so you can tell at a glance) that can be broken up and sprinkled over the softer rice on top.
Makes 4 servings

*4 tablespoons melted butter or
  margarine*
4 cups hot cooked rice
1 egg yolk, lightly beaten

Preheat oven to 400° F. Pour 2 tablespoons butter into a heavy 1½-quart casserole and swirl to coat bottom and sides. Mix ½ cup rice with the egg yolk and spread evenly over bottom of casserole, packing lightly. Spoon remaining rice on top, mounding it up. With a spoon handle, make a hole down through center of rice, then cover and bake 15 minutes. Uncover, sprinkle with remaining butter, re-cover, and bake 40–50 minutes until crusty and brown on the bottom. Remove from oven and cool on a wire rack 10 minutes. Fluff rice with a fork, turn onto a hot platter, then scrape out crusty layer and scatter evenly over all. About 300 calories per serving.

RICE CROQUETTES

Makes 6–8 servings

2 tablespoons butter or margarine
2 tablespoons flour
½ cup milk
1 egg, lightly beaten
3 cups cooked rice (leftover is fine)
¼ teaspoon salt (about)
⅛ teaspoon pepper
*Shortening or cooking oil for deep fat
  frying*
¼ cup unsifted flour
*1 egg, lightly beaten with 1
  tablespoon cold water*
½ cup toasted fine bread crumbs

Melt butter in a small saucepan over moderate heat, blend in flour, slowly stir in milk, and heat, stirring until thickened. Off heat, beat in egg; mix in rice, salt, and pepper, taste for seasoning and adjust. Cool to room temperature; shape into logs about 3″ long and 1″ wide and chill 1 hour. Begin heating shortening in a deep fat fryer with basket and deep fat thermometer over moderately high heat. Dredge logs in flour, dip in egg mixture, and roll in crumbs to coat well. When fat reaches 375° F., fry croquettes, a few at a time, 2–3 minutes until golden. Drain on paper toweling and keep warm while frying the rest. Serve hot as a potato substitute. About 270 calories for

CEREALS, RICE, AND PASTA

each of 6 servings, 200 for each of 8 servings.

VARIATIONS:

Savory Rice Croquettes: Prepare as directed but substitute Curried, Herbed, Mushroom or Amandine Rice for the plain. About 270 calories for each of 6 servings if made with Curried or Herbed Rice, 330 if made with Mushroom Rice, and 365 if made with Amandine Rice. About 200 calories for each of 8 servings if made with Curried or Herbed Rice, 250 if made with Mushroom Rice, and 275 if made with Amandine Rice.

Main Dish Rice Croquettes: Prepare as directed but use 2 cups rice and 1 cup any minced leftover meat, poultry, or seafood. Good topped with Mushroom or Tomato Sauce. Recipe too flexible for a meaningful calorie count.

Bulgur or Kasha Croquettes: Prepare as directed but substitute cooked bulgur wheat or buckwheat groats for rice. Approximately the same number of calories per serving as for croquettes made with rice.

EASY RICE AND CHEESE CROQUETTES

Makes 4 servings

Shortening or cooking oil for deep fat frying
2 cups cold cooked rice
2 egg yolks, lightly beaten
⅓ cup grated Parmesan, Gruyère, or mozzarella cheese
1 tablespoon minced parsley
1 teaspoon prepared spicy brown mustard
¼ cup unsifted flour
2 egg whites, lightly beaten
½ cup toasted fine bread crumbs

Begin heating fat in a deep fat fryer with basket and deep fat thermometer over moderately high heat. Mix rice, egg yolks, cheese, parsley, and mustard and shape into logs 3″ long and 1″ wide. Dredge in flour, dip in egg whites, and roll in crumbs to coat. When fat reaches 375° F., fry croquettes, a few at a time, 2–3 minutes until golden. Drain on paper toweling and keep warm while frying the rest. Serve hot as a potato substitute. About 300 calories per serving if made with Parmesan or Gruyère cheese, about 290 per serving if made with mozzarella cheese.

¢ ⚖ **RICE PANCAKES**

Good for breakfast with ham or bacon. And a good way to use up leftover rice.

Makes 4 servings

1 cup cooked rice
1 tablespoon finely grated yellow onion
⅓ cup plus 2 tablespoons milk
1 egg, lightly beaten

Simmer rice, onion, and ⅓ cup milk in a covered saucepan over lowest possible heat (a flame-tamer is good) 15–20 minutes until all milk is absorbed and rice very soft. Off heat, mix in remaining milk and the egg. Heat an oiled griddle over moderate heat until a drop of water will dance (or to 350° F. if using an electric griddle). Drop mixture by rounded tablespoonfuls, spread to about 3″ in diameter, and brown lightly on both sides. Keep warm while browning the rest. Pass syrup or warm honey. About 95 calories per serving (without syrup).

¢ ⚖ **Dessert Rice Pancakes:** Prepare as directed but omit onion and add 2 tablespoons each sugar and seedless raisins. About 135 calories per serving.

¢ **Savory Rice Pancakes:** Prepare as directed but use Curried, Herbed, Mushroom, or other flavored rice instead of plain. Recipe too flexible for a meaningful calorie count.

BASIC BOILED WILD RICE

Wild rice is expensive, but it's richer than regular rice and goes further —1 cup uncooked rice equals 3⅓ cups cooked rice, enough for 4–6 servings. To extend, mix ½-and-½ with cooked brown rice or bulgur wheat.

Makes 4–6 servings

1 cup wild rice
3 cups water
1 teaspoon salt
2–3 tablespoons melted butter or margarine

Wash rice well in a strainer under cold running water. Place in a heavy saucepan with water and salt, cover, and bring to a boil over moderate heat. Uncover and boil gently, without stirring, about 35 minutes until *just* tender. Drain, set uncovered over lowest possible heat (an asbestos flame-tamer is handy), and dry 5 minutes, shaking pan occasionally. Mix in butter with a fork and serve. (*Note:* To keep hot, transfer to the top of a double boiler, cover, and set over simmering water. Don't try to keep warm more than 20 minutes or lovely crisp texture will be lost.) About 220 calories for each of 4 servings, 150 calories for each of 6 servings.

VARIATIONS:

Wild Rice for Game and Poultry: Sauté 1 minced yellow onion in 2 tablespoons butter 5–8 minutes until limp, add rice, 3 cups giblet stock or chicken broth, the salt, and ¼ teaspoon each sage, thyme, and marjoram. Cook as directed but do not add butter at the end. About 240 calories for each of 4 servings, 160 calories for each of 6 servings.

Wild Rice with Ham: Stir-fry ¼ pound finely diced cooked ham in 2 tablespoons bacon drippings over moderate heat 3–5 minutes until golden, add rice, water, and salt and proceed as directed but omit butter at the end. About 270 calories for each of 4 servings, 180 calories for each of 6 servings.

Wild Rice with Mushrooms and Bacon: Brown 6 slices bacon until crisp, remove to paper toweling, and crumble. In drippings, sauté ½ pound coarsely chopped mushrooms 3–5 minutes until golden. Add rice, 3 cups chicken broth, and ½ teaspoon salt and cook as directed. Add crumbled bacon (but not butter) and toss lightly to mix. About 275 calories for each of 4 servings, 185 calories for each of 6 servings.

Herbed Wild Rice: Cook rice in 3 cups chicken broth with 2 tablespoons minced chives or scallions, 1 tablespoon minced parsley, 1 teaspoon basil or savory, and ½ teaspoon salt. Mix in butter and serve. About 255 calories for each of 4 servings, 170 calories for each of 6 servings.

Wild Rice with Sour Cream and Chives: Cook rice as directed but omit butter. Transfer to the top of a double boiler, set over simmering water, and fork in ¾ cup sour cream, 3 tablespoons minced chives, and, if you like, ¼ cup cooked crumbled bacon. Cover and heat 10 minutes, fluff with a fork, and serve. About 290 calories for each of 4 servings, 195 calories for each of 6 servings.

WILD RICE AMANDINE

Makes 6 servings

6 scallions, minced (include some tops)
¼ cup unsalted butter
1 clove garlic, peeled and crushed
1 cup wild rice, washed in cold water
2 cups chicken broth
½ cup dry white wine
½ teaspoon salt (about)
⅛ teaspoon pepper
⅓ cup slivered toasted blanched almonds

Preheat oven to 325° F. Stir-fry scallions in butter in a 1-quart flameproof casserole over moderately low heat 3–5 minutes until limp. Add garlic and rice and stir-fry 1–2 minutes, add remaining ingredients except almonds, and boil gently, uncovered, without stirring 20 minutes. With a fork, mix in almonds and bake, uncovered, 15–20 minutes until all liquid is absorbed. About 240 calories per serving.

VARIATION:

Brandied Wild Rice: Cook as directed but use 2¼ cups chicken or beef broth instead of broth and wine and mix in 4–6 tablespoons brandy along with almonds. Bake as directed. About 265 calories per serving.

▨ WILD RICE CAKES

Makes 6 servings

1 recipe Basic Boiled Wild Rice (do not drain)
3 tablespoons white corn meal
¼ cup bacon drippings or cooking oil

While rice is still hot, mix in corn meal, 1 tablespoon at a time, and cool to room temperature. Shape into 3″ patties, brown in drippings in a heavy skillet over moderate heat, drain on paper toweling, and serve. Good with ham, Canadian bacon, or sausages. About 240 calories per serving.

CASSEROLE OF WILD RICE, CHICKEN LIVERS, AND SAUSAGE

A festive accompaniment for poultry or game birds.

Makes 12 servings

1 pound pork sausage meat
¾ pound chicken livers, halved at the natural separation
2 large yellow onions, peeled and minced
1 pound mushrooms, wiped clean and sliced thin
2 cups wild rice, washed in cold water
1 quart chicken broth
1½ teaspoons salt
¼ teaspoon pepper
1 teaspoon poultry seasoning
1 cup light cream

Break up sausage meat in a large, heavy kettle and brown lightly over moderate heat, stirring now and then. Lift out with slotted spoon and reserve; drain off all but ¼ cup drippings and reserve. Sauté chicken livers in drippings over moderately high heat 3–4 minutes until lightly browned, remove, coarsely chop, and add to sausage. Add 2 tablespoons reserved drippings to kettle and sauté onions over moderate heat 5–8 minutes until pale golden; add mushrooms and sauté 2–3 minutes longer. Stir in rice, broth, and all seasonings and boil gently, uncovered, 20 minutes. Meanwhile, preheat oven to 325° F. With a fork mix in sausage, chicken livers, and cream. Spoon into a greased 3-quart casserole and bake, uncovered, 20–30 minutes until all liquid is absorbed. Fluff with a fork before serving. About 350 calories per serving.

BASIC BUCKWHEAT KASHA

To be strictly accurate, *kasha* is braised buckwheat groats. But the word has become a generic meaning for any braised, cracked cereal. Serve in place of potatoes.
Makes 4–6 servings

1 cup buckwheat groats
1 egg, lightly beaten
¼ cup butter or margarine
2 cups chicken or beef broth or water
1 teaspoon salt (about)
¼ teaspoon pepper

Mix groats and egg in a large, heavy skillet or saucepan set over moderate heat and cook and stir until dry, not brown. Add remaining ingredients, cover, and simmer 15 minutes until liquid is absorbed and groats are tender. Fluff with a fork, taste for salt and adjust if needed. About 355 calories for each of 4 servings, 240 calories for each of 6 servings.

VARIATIONS:

Old World Buckwheat Kasha: Sauté 1 large minced yellow onion in the butter 8–10 minutes until golden, add groats mixed with egg and ⅓ cup minced celery, and stir-fry 1–2 minutes. Add chicken broth, salt, pepper, 1 teaspoon poultry seasoning, and ⅛ teaspoon curry powder. Cover and cook as directed. About 375 calories for each of 4 servings, 250 calories for each of 6 servings.

Buckwheat-Mushroom Kasha: Sauté 1 cup coarsely chopped mushrooms in the butter 3–4 minutes until golden, add groats mixed with egg, and stir-fry 1–2 minutes. Cook as directed. Just before serving, mix in ⅓ cup minced toasted almonds, pecans, walnuts, or piñon nuts. About 445 calories for each of 4 servings, 295 calories for each of 6 servings.

Kasha Varnishkas (Makes 6 servings): Cook the groats as directed and while they cook boil ½ pound broad noodles by package directions; also stir-fry 1 large peeled and minced yellow onion in the ¼ cup butter 8–10 minutes until golden. Mix groats with drained noodles, onion, and 1 tablespoon poppy seeds. Place in a buttered 2½-quart casserole and bake, uncovered, 15 minutes at 350° F. About 405 calories per serving.

BULGUR WHEAT KASHA

Makes 4–6 servings

1 large yellow onion, peeled and minced
¼ cup butter or margarine
1 cup bulgur wheat
2 cups chicken or beef broth
1 teaspoon salt
¼ teaspoon pepper

Preheat oven to 350° F. Sauté onion in butter in a flameproof casserole over moderate heat 5–8 minutes until pale golden. Add bulgur wheat and stir-fry 2–3 minutes until golden. Add remaining ingredients, cover, and bake ½ hour until liquid is absorbed and bulgur tender. Fluff with a fork and serve as a potato substitute. About 335 calories for each of 4 servings, 225 calories for each of 6 servings.

VARIATIONS:

Apple-Almond Kasha: Prepare as directed but stir-fry 1½ cups peeled, minced tart apples along with bulgur wheat. Also add ¼ teaspoon each thyme, sage, and celery seeds and 1 tablespoon minced parsley. Cover and bake as directed; just before serving top with ½ cup slivered blanched almonds sautéed in ¼ cup butter. About 560 calories for each of 4 servings, 375 calories for each of 6 servings.

Bulgur-Mushroom Kasha: Prepare as directed but stir-fry 1 cup thinly sliced mushrooms along with bulgur wheat; add 1 teaspoon poultry seasoning along with salt, and just before serving mix in ⅓ cup warmed heavy cream or sour cream. About 410 calories for each of 4 servings if made with heavy cream, 385 if made with sour cream; about 275 calories for each of 6 servings if made with heavy cream, 255 if made with sour cream.

BAKED KASHA WITH WALNUTS

Especially good with roast lamb. Makes 4 servings

1 medium-size yellow onion, peeled and minced
3 tablespoons bacon drippings, butter, or margarine
2 cups cooked buckwheat groats, bulgur, or cracked wheat
½ teaspoon salt
⅛ teaspoon pepper
½ cup coarsely chopped walnuts

Preheat oven to 350° F. Brown onion in 2 tablespoons drippings in a small skillet over moderate heat 10–12 minutes; mix into *kasha* along with salt, pepper, and walnuts and toss well. Spoon into a greased 1½-quart casserole, sprinkle with remaining drippings, cover, and bake ½ hour. Serve in place of potatoes. About 320 calories per serving.

⚖ ¢ STEWED BARLEY AND VEGETABLES

Makes 4–6 servings

1 cup medium pearl barley
1 large yellow onion, peeled and minced
3 carrots, peeled and cut in small dice
2 stalks celery, cut in small dice
1 cup diced rutabaga
2 tablespoons minced parsley
2 teaspoons salt (about)
¼ teaspoon pepper
1 quart beef broth

Mix all ingredients in a large, heavy saucepan, cover, and simmer 1–1¼ hours until barley is tender. Taste for salt and adjust. Serve as a vegetable. About 225 calories for each of 4 servings, 150 for each of 6 servings.

BAKED BARLEY AND MUSHROOM CASSEROLE

Makes 4–6 servings

1 cup medium pearl barley
4 tablespoons butter or margarine
1 large yellow onion, peeled and minced
1 cup coarsely chopped mushrooms
3 cups chicken or beef broth
2 teaspoons salt
¼ teaspoon pepper

Preheat oven to 350° F. Stir-fry barley in 2 tablespoons butter in a skillet over moderate heat about 2 minutes until lightly browned; transfer to an ungreased 1½-quart casserole. Sauté onion in remaining butter 5–8 minutes until pale golden, add mushrooms, if you like, and sauté 3–5 minutes longer; add to casserole. Mix in all remaining ingredients, cover, and bake about 1¼ hours until barley is tender, stirring now and then. Fluff with a fork and serve as a potato substitute. About 330 calories for each of 4 servings, 220 for each of 6 servings.

CHEESE GNOCCHI

Serve hot as a luncheon entree or as a potato substitute with veal or chicken.
Makes 4 servings

Gnocchi:
½ pound ricotta cheese
½ cup sifted flour
6 tablespoons grated Parmesan cheese
2 tablespoons melted butter or margarine
½ teaspoon salt
Pinch nutmeg
2 eggs, lightly beaten

Topping:
⅓ cup melted butter or margarine
⅓ cup grated Parmesan cheese

Preheat oven to 350° F. Mix gnocchi ingredients and spoon about half into a pastry bag fitted with a large plain tube (opening should be about ½" across). Heat about 5 quarts salted water to boiling in a large kettle; adjust heat so water bubbles *very gently*. Squeeze out gnocchi over water, cutting with a knife at 1" intervals and letting drop into water. Simmer, uncovered, 2–3 minutes until gnocchi float, then remove with a slotted spoon and drain in a colander. Arrange gnocchi 1 layer deep in a buttered 1½-quart *au gratin* dish or shallow casserole, drizzle with melted butter, and sprinkle with cheese. Bake, uncovered, 10 minutes, then broil about 2 minutes to brown lightly. About 400 calories per serving.

POTATO GNOCCHI

Serve as an accompaniment to veal or chicken.
Makes 4 servings

Gnocchi:
2 cups hot mashed potatoes (*without milk or seasoning*)
1 cup sifted flour
2 eggs, lightly beaten
1½ teaspoons salt
⅛ teaspoon white pepper
Pinch nutmeg

Topping:
1½ cups hot Italian Tomato Sauce
¼ cup grated Parmesan cheese

Mix all *gnocchi* ingredients and spoon about half into a pastry bag fitted with a large, plain tube (opening should be about ½" in diameter). Bring about 5 quarts salted water to a boil in a large kettle, then adjust heat so water bubbles *very gently*. Squeeze out gnocchi over water, cutting with a knife at 1" intervals and letting drop into water. Simmer, uncovered, until gnocchi float, then simmer 1 minute longer. Lift out with slotted spoon, drain in a colander, and keep hot in a shallow serving dish. When all gnocchi are done, cover with sauce and sprinkle with cheese. If you like, pass extra Parmesan. About 310 calories per serving.

VARIATION:

Cool uncooked gnocchi mixture to room temperature, then roll on a lightly floured board into a rope about ½" thick. Cut in 1" lengths and imprint lightly with the back of a fork. Cook and serve as directed. About 310 calories per serving.

CEREALS, RICE, AND PASTA

FARINA GNOCCHI PARMIGIANA

Makes 6 servings

3 cups milk
2 teaspoons salt
Pinch nutmeg
1 cup quick-cooking farina
2 tablespoons melted butter or margarine
3 egg yolks, lightly beaten
½ cup butter
½ cup finely grated Parmesan cheese

Heat milk, salt, and nutmeg, covered, in the top of a double boiler over just boiling water until steaming. Add farina slowly, stirring with a wooden spoon; cook and stir until smooth and very thick, about 10 minutes. Set double boiler top on a damp cloth, mix in melted butter and yolks. Brush a large, shallow pan or casserole with cold water.

Add farina mixture, spreading to a thickness of ½", cover, and chill 1–2 hours. Cut into strips ¾" wide, turn out on a board, and roll under your palms into ropes; cut in 1" lengths. (*Note:* Dip knife in cold water to prevent sticking.) Preheat oven to 400° F.

Arrange half of *gnocchi*, slightly overlapping, over bottom of a buttered 1½-quart *au gratin* dish or shallow casserole. Dot with ¼ cup butter and ¼ cup Parmesan; repeat to make a second layer. Bake, uncovered, 10–15 minutes, then broil 4"–5" from heat 2–3 minutes until lightly browned. Serve hot as a potato substitute with veal scaloppine, veal chops, or chicken, or as a luncheon entree with soup and salad. About 380 calories per serving.

BOILED COUSCOUS (SEMOLINA)

Couscous is the Arabic word for finely ground semolina. It is also the name of the North African lamb stew served over it (see the chapter on lamb). Boiled couscous can be served in place of rice or potatoes. Makes 6 servings

1 quart beef or chicken broth or water
2 cups uncooked couscous (available in gourmet shops and Middle Eastern groceries)
¼ cup butter or margarine
1 teaspoon salt (*about*)

Bring broth to a rapid boil in a large, heavy saucepan, gradually add *couscous*, stirring briskly to prevent lumping. Cook and stir 2–3 minutes, add butter and salt, and mix lightly. Remove from heat, cover, and let stand 10–15 minutes until all moisture is absorbed and no raw taste remains.

Fluff with a fork and serve smothered with gravy. (*Note:* If using to make the lamb stew called Couscous, place cooked couscous in a large colander lined with a triple thickness of dampened cheesecloth, set over kettle of stew, cover, and let steam while stew cooks.

Prepared this way, the couscous will be light and moist and delicately lamb-flavored.) About 295 calories per serving.

♨ POLENTA

Polenta, or corn meal mush Italian style, often takes the place of bread in Northern Italy. The mush is cooked until very thick, turned out, cut in chunks, and eaten with chicken, rabbit, or fish stew. Sometimes polenta is topped with the stew, sometimes with Italian sausages and Tomato Sauce. Leftovers are good fried or baked with cheese and sauce. If you have the time and patience, cook polenta the Italian way in a very heavy kettle, *stirring constantly.* Otherwise, use the more foolproof double boiler. Makes 6 servings

1 cup yellow corn meal
1 cup cold water
1½ pints boiling water
1 teaspoon salt

Mix meal and cold water in the top of a double boiler set over simmering water or in a heavy 4-quart kettle over moderately low heat (if you have one, use the unlined copper polenta pot). Stir in boiling water and salt and cook about 45 minutes until very thick; stir every 5 minutes if using double boiler, constantly if using the kettle to avoid lumping. Mixture is ready to serve when a crust forms on sides of pan. Scrape polenta onto a hot buttered platter, cool 2–3 minutes, then slice as you would bread or cut in squares and serve. (*Note:* To cut more cleanly, use string and a sawing motion.) About 85 calories per serving.

VARIATIONS:

⚔️ **Fried Polenta:** Cut cold leftover polenta in 2″ squares ½″–¾″ thick, brown lightly, 2–3 minutes on each side, in 2 tablespoons olive oil or bacon drippings over moderately low heat. About 130 calories per serving.

⚔️ **Polenta Parmigiana:** Prepare polenta as directed and, while hot, spoon into a buttered 8″ or 9″ square pan; smooth top and cool. Cut in 2″ or 3″ squares, arrange in a single layer in a buttered *au gratin* dish or shallow casserole. Drizzle with ⅓ cup each melted butter and grated Parmesan cheese. Bake, uncovered, ½ hour at 400° F., then brown lightly under broiler. Serve as potato substitute. About 190 calories per serving.

Baked Polenta with Italian Sausages: Arrange 2″ squares cold cooked polenta in a single layer in a buttered 2-quart *au gratin* dish or shallow casserole. Top with 6 cooked sweet Italian sausages, split lengthwise, and 2 cups Tomato Sauce; sprinkle with ¼ cup grated Parmesan cheese. Bake, uncovered, ½ hour at 400° F. Serve as an entree. About 390 calories per serving.

⚔️ ¢ **BAKED HOMINY CASSEROLE**

Makes 6 servings

1 (1-pound 12-ounce) can hominy
Liquid drained from hominy plus
 enough milk to measure 1⅓ cups
3 eggs, lightly beaten
1 cup soft white bread crumbs
1½ teaspoons salt
⅛ teaspoon white pepper
2 tablespoons minced parsley

Preheat oven to 350° F. Mix all ingredients and spoon into a buttered 2-quart casserole. Set casserole in a larger pan half full of hot water and bake, uncovered, about 1 hour until just firm. Serve hot as a potato substitute. About 150 calories per serving.

VARIATIONS:

Baked Hominy and Cheese Casserole: Prepare as directed but reduce eggs to 2 and add ½ pound grated sharp Cheddar cheese. Serve as a luncheon entree. About 265 calories per serving.

Baked Hominy Casserole with Sausages or Franks: Prepare casserole as directed and bake ½ hour; ar-

CEREALS, RICE, AND PASTA

range 6 browned link sausages or frankfurters spoke fashion on top and bake ½ hour longer. About 270 calories per serving if made with sausages, 290 calories per serving if made with frankfurters.

⚱ ⊠ HOMINY, BACON, AND EGG SCRAMBLE

A simple dish that is suitable for breakfast, lunch, or supper.

Makes 4 servings

8 slices bacon
1 (1-pound) can hominy, drained
2 eggs, lightly beaten with ¼ cup milk
2 tablespoons grated Parmesan cheese
⅛ teaspoon pepper

Brown bacon in a large, heavy skillet, lift to paper toweling, crumble, and reserve. Drain off all but ¼ cup drippings, add hominy, and stir-fry over moderate heat 2–3 minutes. Add eggs and scramble until soft; mix in cheese and pepper. Spoon onto warm plates and top with bacon. About 220 calories per serving.

¢ ⊠ HOMINY, BEANS, AND SALT PORK

Makes 4–6 servings

½ pound salt pork, trimmed of rind and cut in small dice
1 (1-pound) can hominy, drained
2 cups boiled dried or drained canned white or lima beans
½ teaspoon salt (about)
¼ teaspoon pepper

Stir-fry salt pork 8–10 minutes in a heavy kettle over moderate heat until lightly browned. Pour off all but ¼ cup drippings, mix in remaining ingredients, cover, and heat until piping hot, stirring now and then. Taste for salt and adjust as needed. Serve for breakfast (with eggs) or as a potato substitute. About 505 calories for each of 4 servings, 340 calories for each of 6 servings.

GRITS AND GRUYÈRE FRITTERS

Makes 6 servings

Shortening or cooking oil for deep fat frying
2 cups cooked hominy grits, chilled
¾ cup coarsely grated Gruyère cheese
¼ teaspoon pepper
⅛ teaspoon nutmeg
1 egg, lightly beaten with 1 tablespoon cold water
¾ cup fine dry bread crumbs

Begin heating shortening in a deep fat fryer with a deep fat thermometer. Mash grits with a fork, mix in cheese, pepper, and nutmeg. Shape into logs about 2½" long and 1" across. Dip in egg, then in bread crumbs. When fat reaches 375° F., fry, a few at a time, 2–3 minutes until golden brown. Drain on paper toweling and serve hot as a potato substitute. About 230 calories per serving.

VARIATION:

Grits and Gruyère Appetizers (Makes about 2½ dozen): Prepare as directed but shape into small balls (about 1") instead of logs. Deep-fry, spear with toothpicks, and serve hot. About 45 calories each.

GRITS AND SMITHFIELD HAM PATTIES

Makes 6 servings

2 cups cooked hominy grits, chilled
1 cup minced Smithfield ham
¼ teaspoon black pepper
⅛ teaspoon cayenne pepper

1 egg, lightly beaten with 1
  tablespoon cold water
¾ cup fine dry bread crumbs
⅓ cup peanut or other cooking oil
2 cups hot Mushroom or Cheese
  Sauce

Mash grits with a fork, mix in ham and peppers. Shape into patties about the size of small hamburgers. Dip in egg, then in crumbs to coat evenly. Heat oil in a large, heavy skillet over moderately high heat until very hot but not smoking. Add patties and brown about 2 minutes on a side. Drain on paper toweling and serve topped with sauce. About 335 calories per serving.

PASTA

There are dozens of stories about how pasta came to Italy from China, probably none of them true. It's now thought noodles may have originated in both places, quite independently of the other. The Chinese noodles would have been first, and they would have been made in those ancient days as they are today, of rice or soy flour. First mention of spaghetti in Italy occurred early in the Middle Ages, well before Marco Polo is said to have brought it back from the Orient. But this was pasta made of wheat flour, particularly semolina, ground from the hard golden heart of durum flour. Pasta rapidly became an Italian staple. It was cheap, satisfying, quick to prepare, and so versatile it combined equally well with harvests of land and sea. Why so many shapes and sizes? No one knows, though perhaps it was a way of adding variety to what might have become a boring routine.

Basically, there are two types of Italian pasta: *macaroni and spaghetti,* made of semolina and water and just enough egg to bind them, and *egg pasta or noodles,* containing a high proportion of egg. Green noodles have simply had spinach added. There is other European pasta, notably the German *Spätzle* and Middle European *Nockerln,* both soft noodle-like dumplings used to extend the main dish and catch the gravy or sauce.

Some Popular Kinds of Pasta

Spaghettis (String Shapes):
Fedeline
Capellini
Spaghettini
Vermicelli
Spaghetti
Fusilli

Flat and Ribbon Shapes:
Linguine (egg pasta)
Taglierini (egg pasta)
Fettuccine (egg pasta)
Lasagne
Mafalde

Noodles:
Tagliatelle
Fine Noodles
Medium Noodles
Wide or Broad Noodles

Stuffed Pasta:
Ravioli
Cappelletti Tortellini

Macaronis (Tubular or Hollow Shapes):
Bucatini
Tubetti
Tufoli
Rigatoni
Ziti
Ditalini
Ditali
Cannelloni
Manicotti
Elbow Macaroni

CEREALS, RICE, AND PASTA

Fancy Shapes:
Farfalline (little bows)
Farfalle (bows)
Conchiglie (seashell macaroni)

Soup Pasta:
Stellette (little stars)
Semini (little seeds)
Alphabet
Peperini (pepper seeds)
Anelli Campanelline (small rings)
Quadruccini (little squares)
Conchigliette (little seashells)

Oriental Noodles:
Chow Mein Noodles (crisp-fried and ready to use)
Cellophane Noodles (also called bean thread and Chinese vermicelli)
Harusame (Japanese noodles made of soy flour)
Soba (Japanese buckwheat noodle)
Rice Stick (fine rice flour noodles)

How to Use Pasta

Generally speaking, long, thin pasta and small tubes are boiled and sauced. Broad flat pasta, also the larger fancy shapes, are boiled, then baked *en casserole* with cheese, meat, seafood, or vegetable and sauce. Large tubes are boiled, stuffed, sauced, and baked. Soup pasta is added to soups or thin stews minutes before serving so that the rawness cooks out but not the firm-tenderness.

Italians intensely dislike soft or mushy pasta and eat it *al dente* (to the tooth, meaning there's still a bit of resilience). They are also likely to eat it before the main course or as an accompaniment to meat, which is why Italian cookbooks often state that a pound of pasta will serve 8 to 10. It won't the way we eat it.

How Much Pasta per Person: Figure 4 servings per pound if the pasta is to be eaten as the main dish, 6–8 if it is an accompaniment.

How to Cook Pasta

Spaghetti and Macaroni: For each 1 pound pasta, bring 6–7 quarts water and 2 tablespoons salt to a full rolling boil in a large, heavy kettle over high heat. To keep pasta from clumping, add about a teaspoon olive or other cooking oil. Do not break strands of pasta, even if very long, but ease into the kettle, pushing farther in as ends soften, until completely submerged. Water should be boiling rapidly all the while, so if necessary add pasta a little at a time. As soon as all pasta is in the pot, begin timing it; do not cover but *do* move pasta occasionally with a long-handled fork. Depending on size and shape, pasta will take 5–10 minutes to become *al dente;* very large pasta may take 15–20 minutes. Begin testing after 4 minutes, and test regularly thereafter, pulling out a strand and biting it. There should be no raw starch taste but pasta should be firm-tender. The second it's done, pull off the fire. If you've cooked a small amount, fork out or lift with tongs to serving platter, letting excess moisture run back into kettle. This method won't work, however, for more than a pound of pasta, because you can only lift out a bit at a time and that left in the pot goes mushy. So drain in a colander —fast—and return to kettle. *Do not rinse.* Set kettle over low heat and shake about ½ minute, then serve pasta immediately. Mound on a hot platter or individual serving plates (wide-rimmed soup plates are best), top, if you like, with a hearty lump of softened butter, then with sauce. If sauce is mixed into pasta before serving, do so with a lifting and turning motion, as though tossing salad; never stir.

If Pasta Must Wait: As soon as

pasta is drained, return to kettle and dot well with butter. Cover and set in oven turned to lowest heat. Pasta will hold about ½ hour this way. If dinner is delayed longer than that, cook a new batch (the old can be used in stuffings, meat loaves, or casseroles).

To Reheat Leftover Pasta: Sauced pasta is no problem; simply heat slowly in a covered saucepan to serving temperature. Unsauced pasta should be covered with boiling water and allowed to stand about 2 minutes, then drained well.

Noodles and Egg Pasta: These are softer than spaghetti and cook faster. They're also slightly saltier. Follow procedure for spaghetti but use half the amount of salt. Add noodles by handfuls to rapidly boiling water and cook uncovered. Fine noodles will be done in about 3 minutes, larger ones in 5–7. (*Note:* Homemade noodles will cook faster than the commercial, so watch carefully and taste often.) When noodles taste done, they are done. Drain quickly in a colander, again do not rinse, mound in serving dish, mix in a few dabs of butter, then sauce. Noodles do not wait well, so serve as soon as they're done.

Oriental Noodles: All of these hair-fine, translucent noodles are prepared more or less the same way. Soak in warm water about 10 minutes to soften, then drain well and use as recipes direct. They may also be deep-fat-fried without being soaked. Heat oil (preferably peanut oil) to 380° F., crumble noodles into fat a little at a time, and fry, stirring gently with a slotted spoon, ½–1 minute until frizzled and pale golden. Drain on paper toweling and use as a crunchy topping for Chinese dishes.

How to Eat Pasta

It's the long slithery strands that intimidate. With practice, however, eating spaghetti is as easy as eating scrambled eggs. Simply catch a few strands on the ends of your fork, then twirl round and round against your plate (the Italian way) or against the bowl of a large spoon (the American way) until the pasta is wound into a neat mouthful. That's all there is to it.

About Sauces for Pasta

In addition to the recipes that follow, there are a number of sauces suitable for pasta in the chapter on sauces and gravies.

¢ HOMEMADE PASTA DOUGH

Makes about 1½ pounds

4 cups sifted flour
1½ teaspoons salt
4 eggs, lightly beaten
¼ cup lukewarm water
2 teaspoons olive or other cooking oil

Sift flour with salt; make a well in center and pour in eggs, water, and oil. Gradually draw dry ingredients from edges of bowl into liquid to form a fairly stiff dough (you may need to use hands at the end). Or mix with a dough hook on an electric mixer (hold a dry towel over bowl so flour doesn't fly). Knead dough on lightly floured board about 10 minutes until smooth and elastic. Cover with dry cloth and let rest ½ hour. Quarter dough and roll paper thin, one piece at a time, into a 13″–14″ square on a lightly floured board, using as little additional flour as possible and keeping edges straight.

For Noodles (including lasagne noodles): Roll dough up loosely, jelly-roll fashion, cut crosswise in strips of desired width, and unroll. Cover with dry cloth and let dry at room temperature 1 hour. Cook by basic recipe but remember that homemade noodles will cook faster than the commercial. (*Note:* Noodles may be dried overnight [turn now and then] and stored airtight; use within 1 week.)

For Cannelloni, Manicotti, or Ravioli: Cut rolled dough into squares of desired size.

To Use a Pasta Machine: Prepare as directed up to point of rolling. Flatten each piece of dough into a rectangle and feed into machine following manufacturer's instructions. For the first rolling, set dial at widest opening (No. 10), then decrease for each successive rolling until desired thickness is reached. No. 3 or 4 is good for noodles, No. 2 for cannelloni, manicotti, and ravioli. If strips become unwieldy in the rolling, halve crosswise. (*Note:* Keep remaining dough covered while rolling each piece.) About 360 calories per ¼-pound serving.

VARIATION:

Pasta Verde (Green Pasta): Sift the flour with 1 teaspoon salt; add 2 lightly beaten eggs, 2 tablespoons lukewarm water, 2 teaspoons olive oil, and 1 cup well-drained, puréed, cooked spinach; proceed as directed. About 370 calories per ¼-pound serving.

¢ NOODLE RING

A festive way to serve plain buttered noodles.
Makes 4 servings

½ *pound noodles, cooked and drained by package directions*
¼ *cup melted butter*
1 teaspoon salt
⅛ *teaspoon white pepper*

Preheat oven to 375° F. Toss noodles with butter, salt, and pepper then *pack* into a *well-buttered* 1½-quart ring mold. Place mold in a larger pan half filled with water and bake, uncovered, 20–30 minutes. Lift mold from water bath, loosen edges, and invert on a hot platter. Ring is now ready to fill with any creamed meat, fish, or vegetable. About 320 calories per serving (without filling of any sort).

VARIATIONS:

Egg-Noodle Ring: Prepare noodle mixture as directed but add 2 lightly beaten eggs and ½ cup heavy cream. Bake as directed, allowing 35–40 minutes until ring is firm. Unmold and fill with something delicate—Creamed Sweetbreads, perhaps, or asparagus tips. About 465 calories per serving (without filling).

Cheese-Noodle Ring: Prepare noodle mixture as directed but add 2 lightly beaten eggs, ½ cup milk, and 1 cup coarsely grated sharp Cheddar cheese. Butter ring mold and coat with fine dry bread crumbs; pack in noodle mixture and bake as directed about 40 minutes. Fill with creamed spinach, broccoli, cauliflower, chicken, or turkey. About 535 calories per serving (without filling).

Some Quick Ways to Dress Up Noodles

The following amounts are for 1 pound noodles, cooked and drained by package directions. Depending upon richness of sauce, each will serve 6–8 if noodles are used as a potato substitute, 4–6 if a main course.

Savory Noodles: Dress noodles with ⅓–½ cup seasoned butter: Browned, Garlic, Dill, Herb, or Parsley-Lemon.

Noodles Noisette: Toss noodles with ⅓ cup minced, blanched, toasted almonds or peanuts, pecans, cashews, walnuts, piñon, or pistachio nuts and ⅓–½ cup melted butter.

Noodles Amandine: Sauté ½ cup slivered, blanched almonds in ½ cup butter until golden; off heat mix in 2 teaspoons lemon juice, pour over noodles, and toss to mix.

Fried Noodles: Slowly brown cooked noodles in ½ cup melted butter (you'll probably have to do 2 batches), stirring occasionally, about 15 minutes.

Herbed Noodles: Toss noodles with ½ cup melted butter and ¼ cup minced chives or parsley, or 1–2 tablespoons minced fresh or 1 teaspoon dried basil, oregano, savory, marjoram, dill, or chervil.

Poppy Seed Noodles: Toss noodles with ½ cup melted butter and 2 tablespoons poppy seeds. (*Note:* Toasted sesame seeds and caraway seeds are equally good.)

Garlic Noodles: Toss noodles with 1 cup coarse dry bread crumbs browned in ½ cup Garlic Butter.

Creamed Noodles: Toss noodles with 1–1½ cups hot Thin White Sauce and, if you like, ⅓ cup sautéed sliced mushrooms, ⅓ cup minced pimiento or scallions, or ½ cup mixed cooked vegetables (diced carrots, green beans, and peas).

Sauced Noodles: Toss noodles with ½ cup hot milk and 1 cup hot Parsley, Mushroom-Cheese, Velouté, Curry, Mornay, or Egg Sauce. Or toss with 1½ cups hot Tomato Sauce, Sauce Verte, or any gravy.

Noodles Florentine: Toss noodles with 1 cup minced, well-drained, cooked spinach and ⅓ cup melted butter.

Noodles Smetana: Toss noodles with ½ cup melted butter, 1 pint sour cream, 1½ teaspoons garlic salt, ¼ cup minced chives, and ⅛ teaspoon pepper.

Noodles Hungarian: Return drained noodles to pan, add 1 pound cottage cheese, ½ cup melted butter or bacon drippings, and pepper to taste. Toss gently over lowest heat to warm cheese. Serve topped with crisp, crumbled bacon or crisply browned, diced salt pork.

Cheese Noodles: Return drained noodles to pan, add ⅔ cup hot milk, 1 cup grated sharp Cheddar or Swiss cheese or ½ cup grated Parmesan or crumbled blue cheese. Toss lightly over lowest heat until cheese melts.

Creamed Noodles and Onions: Return drained noodles to pan, add 1 cup coarsely chopped, boiled white onions and a little cooking liquid, ⅔ cup heavy cream, and 2 tablespoons butter. Toss over lowest heat just until heated through.

Noodles Lyonnaise: Stir-fry 1 thinly sliced large Bermuda onion in ½ cup butter over moderate heat until pale golden, 5–8 minutes. Serve on top of buttered noodles.

Noodles Polonaise: Lightly brown 1 cup coarse white bread crumbs in ⅓ cup butter. Off heat, mix in the sieved yolks of 4 hard-cooked eggs and 2 tablespoons minced parsley. Serve on top of buttered noodles.

¢ **SPÄTZLE**

These tiny teardrop-shaped German noodles are served as a potato substitute (though in Germany often *in addition* to potatoes). They're good with all kinds of meats, also as a soup garnish.

Makes 4 servings

1 cup sifted flour
½ teaspoon salt
Pinch nutmeg (*optional*)
Pinch paprika (*optional*)
1 egg, lightly beaten
⅓ cup cold water
2 tablespoons melted butter or margarine

Sift flour with salt and, if you like, spices. Mix egg and water and add slowly to dry mixture; beat hard until smooth (batter will be quite thick). Bring about 2 quarts well-salted water (or chicken or beef broth) to a slow boil in a large, heavy saucepan. Balance a colander on rim of saucepan so that it is well *above* water. Spoon about ⅓ of batter into colander, then carefully press through holes, letting *spätzle* fall into water. Cook 3–4 minutes, lift out with a slotted spoon and keep warm while cooking remaining spätzle. Toss spätzle with melted butter and serve hot. About 170 calories per serving.

¢ NOCKERLN

These delicate little Middle European dumplings are made to be smothered with the sauces and gravies of goulash and *paprikash*. Makes 6 servings

¼ cup butter or margarine
1 egg, lightly beaten
6 tablespoons milk
½ teaspoon salt
1 cup sifted flour

Cream butter until light; mix egg with milk and salt. Add flour alternately to butter with egg mixture, beginning and ending with flour, then beat until smooth. Bring 4 quarts well-salted water to a slow boil. Drop in *nockerln* from a ½ teaspoon and cook, uncovered, a few at a time, 4–5 minutes. (*Note:* Cook no more than 1 layer of nockerln at a time and wet each spoon each time you dip it in the batter.) Lift cooked dumplings from kettle with a slotted spoon and keep warm while you cook the rest. About 160 calories per serving.

VARIATION:

Swirl cooked nockerln in ¼ cup melted butter in a large, heavy kettle over moderately low heat, just to coat, then serve. About 230 calories per serving.

¢ DELUXE MACARONI AND CHEESE

Makes 6 servings

¼ cup butter or margarine
¼ cup unsifted flour
1 teaspoon powdered mustard
2½ cups milk
3 cups coarsely grated sharp Cheddar cheese
¼ teaspoon salt (*about*)
⅛ teaspoon white pepper
1 tablespoon Worcestershire sauce
1 tablespoon finely grated yellow onion (*optional*)
½ pound elbow macaroni, cooked and drained by package directions

Preheat oven to 350° F. Melt butter in a saucepan over moderate heat, blend in flour and mustard, slowly stir in milk, and cook, stirring until thickened. Mix in 2 cups grated cheese and all remaining ingredients except macaroni. Taste for salt and add a little more if needed. Cook and stir until cheese melts. Off heat, mix in macaroni; turn into a buttered 2 quart casserole, sprinkle with remaining cheese, and bake uncovered about ½ hour until bubbly and lightly browned. About 515 calories per serving.

¢ ITALIAN MACARONI, PIMIENTO, AND CHEESE LOAF

Makes 6–8 servings

½ pound elbow macaroni, cooked and drained by package directions
2 cups milk, scalded
3 eggs, lightly beaten
2 cups soft white bread crumbs
1 cup coarsely grated mozzarella cheese
1 cup finely grated Parmesan cheese
1 cup coarsely grated provolone cheese
¼ cup minced scallions (include some tops)
2 tablespoons minced parsley
¼ cup minced pimiento
1 teaspoon salt (about)
¼ teaspoon white pepper
2–3 cups hot Tomato or Mushroom Sauce (optional)

Preheat oven to 350° F. Mix all ingredients but sauce, taste for salt and adjust. Spoon into a well-buttered 9″×5″×3″ loaf pan and bake, uncovered, about 1 hour until firm in the center. Let stand upright 5 minutes; loosen and invert on a hot platter. If you like, spoon some sauce over each serving and pass the rest. Slice, not too thin, as you would a meat loaf. About 475 calories for each of 6 servings (without sauce), about 355 calories for each of 8 servings.

VARIATION:

Macaroni and Cheddar Loaf: Prepare as directed but substitute ¾ pound coarsely grated sharp Cheddar for the 3 Italian cheeses. About 500 calories for each of 6 servings (without sauce), about 370 calories for each of 8 servings.

¢ FISHERMAN'S BAKED SHELLS

You can vary this next recipe by varying the fish. Use mussels, for example, instead of clams (but don't mince—they're nicer left whole). Or use tiny squid instead of shrimp, salmon instead of tuna.

Makes 6 servings

1 medium-size yellow onion, peeled and minced
1 clove garlic, peeled and crushed
1 medium-size carrot, peeled and cut in fine dice
1 stalk celery, cut in fine dice
2 tablespoons butter or margarine
2 tablespoons flour
1 (7½-ounce) can minced clams, drained (reserve liquid)
Liquid drained from clams plus enough bottled clam juice to make 2 cups
1 cup dry white wine or water
¼ teaspoon basil
¼ teaspoon savory
¾ pound raw shrimp, shelled and deveined
2 tablespoons cooking oil
1 (7-ounce) can tuna, drained and flaked
½ pound seashell macaroni, cooked and drained by package directions
2 tablespoons minced parsley

Stir-fry onion, garlic, carrot, and celery in butter in a 2-quart saucepan over moderate heat 3–5 minutes until limp. Mix in flour, add clam juice, wine, and herbs, cover, and simmer 30 minutes, stirring now and then. Meanwhile, stir-fry shrimp in oil over moderate heat 3–5 minutes until pink; remove and reserve. Preheat oven to 350° F. When sauce is ready, mix in clams, shrimp, and tuna. Layer macaroni and sauce in a buttered 3-quart casserole, cover, and bake 30 minutes. Sprinkle with parsley and serve. About 385 calories per serving.

CEREALS, RICE, AND PASTA

¢ SPAGHETTI AND MEAT BALLS IN TOMATO SAUCE

Makes 4 servings

Sauce:
- 1 (1-pound) can tomatoes (do not drain)
- 1 (6-ounce) can tomato paste
- 1 cup water
- 1 teaspoon salt
- ¼ teaspoon pepper
- 2 teaspoons sugar
- 2 teaspoons basil
- 1 tablespoon minced onion
- ½ teaspoon garlic juice

Meat Balls:
- 1 pound ground beef
- 1 cup soft white bread crumbs
- ¼ cup water
- ¼ cup milk
- 1 small yellow onion, peeled and minced
- 1 tablespoon Worcestershire sauce
- 1 teaspoon salt
- ¼ teaspoon pepper
- 2 tablespoons cooking oil (for browning)

Pasta:
- 1 pound spaghetti

Place all sauce ingredients in a large saucepan, cover, and simmer 1 hour, stirring occasionally and breaking up tomatoes. Meanwhile, mix meat ball ingredients except oil and shape into 1" balls. Brown 4-5 minutes in the oil in a large, heavy skillet over moderate heat, doing only ⅓ of balls at a time and draining on paper toweling. Pour all but 2 tablespoons drippings from skillet, mix in a little sauce, scraping up browned bits, and return to saucepan. Add meat balls, cover, and simmer 15 minutes. Cook spaghetti by package directions, drain, and arrange on a large, deep platter. Place meat balls on top, spoon a little sauce over all, and pass the rest. About 860 calories per serving.

SPAGHETTI AL PESTO (GENOESE-STYLE SPAGHETTI WITH FRESH BASIL SAUCE)

In Italy, women laboriously pound garlic, piñon nuts, basil, and spinach into *pesto* sauce using a mortar and pestle. The electric blender does a faster, better job.

Makes 4 servings

Sauce:
- 2 cloves garlic, peeled and crushed
- ⅓ cup piñon nuts
- 1¾ cups fresh basil leaves, minced
- 1 cup fresh spinach leaves, washed well and minced
- 1 cup olive oil
- ½ cup finely grated Parmesan cheese

Pasta:
- 1 pound thin spaghetti
- ¼ cup olive oil

Purée garlic, nuts, basil, and spinach with ½ cup oil in an electric blender at low speed. (*Note:* Because mixture is thick, you'll have to stop blender often and stir.) Pour purée into a small bowl and add remaining oil, a little at a time, beating well with a fork after each addition; mix in cheese and let sauce "mellow" at room temperature at least 1 hour. Cook spaghetti by package directions, adding 1 tablespoon olive oil to the cooking water; meanwhile, warm remaining oil over low heat. When spaghetti is *al dente* (just tender), drain quickly and return to kettle; add hot oil and toss well. To serve, divide spaghetti among 4 plates and top each portion with a generous ladling of pesto sauce. Set out more freshly grated Parmesan. About 1165 calories per serving (without additional Parmesan).

¢ SPAGHETTI WITH WHITE CLAM SAUCE

Makes 2–4 servings

Sauce:
2 cloves garlic, peeled and minced
¼ cup olive or other cooking oil
2 tablespoons flour
2 cups clam juice (use liquid drained from clams, rounding out measure as needed with bottled clam juice)
1½ cups finely chopped fresh clams or 2 (10½-ounce) cans minced clams, drained (save liquid)
1 tablespoon minced parsley
⅛ teaspoon pepper

Pasta:
½ pound thin spaghetti, cooked by package directions and drained
¼ cup coarsely chopped parsley (garnish)

Stir-fry garlic in oil in a saucepan about 1 minute over low heat; do not brown. Blend in flour, add clam juice, and heat, stirring constantly, until mixture thickens slightly; cover and simmer 10–15 minutes. Add clams, minced parsley, and pepper, cover, and simmer 3–5 minutes. Pour sauce over hot spaghetti and toss with 2 forks to mix well. Sprinkle with coarsely chopped parsley and serve. About 885 calories for each of 2 servings, 445 calories for each of 4 servings.

¢ SPAGHETTI ALL'AMATRICIANA

Spaghetti topped with a peppy salt-pork and tomato sauce.
Makes 4 servings

Sauce:
½ pound salt pork, trimmed of rind and cut in small dice
Salt pork drippings plus enough bacon drippings to total ¼ cup
1 small yellow onion, peeled and minced
1 clove garlic peeled and stuck on a toothpick
1 (1-pound 12-ounce) can Italian plum tomatoes (do not drain)
1 small chili pepper, cored, seeded, and minced (optional)

Pasta:
1 pound thin spaghetti, cooked and drained by package directions

Topping:
⅓ cup grated Romano cheese mixed with ⅓ cup grated Parmesan cheese
Freshly ground pepper

Brown salt pork 8–10 minutes in a large, heavy skillet over moderate heat; drain on paper toweling and reserve. In ¼ cup drippings, sauté onion 8–10 minutes until golden. Add remaining ingredients, breaking up tomatoes, and reserved salt pork and simmer, uncovered, ½ hour, stirring now and then. Discard garlic. Heap pasta in 4 large bowls, top with sauce, a generous sprinkling of cheese, and a grinding of pepper. Pass remaining cheese. About 1075 calories per serving.

✎ SPAGHETTI WITH BUTTER, CREAM, AND PARMESAN

A refreshing change from potatoes. Also makes a nice light entree.
Makes 8 servings

½ cup butter (no substitute)
½ cup heavy cream
1 pound thin spaghetti, cooked and drained by package directions
½ cup grated Parmesan cheese
Salt and pepper to taste

Heat butter and cream in a small saucepan but do not boil. Mound pasta in a buttered warm large bowl, pour in cream, sprinkle with cheese, and toss thoroughly but lightly. Season to taste and serve. About 390 calories per serving.

VARIATIONS:

Spaghetti with Butter, Cream, Parmesan, and Piñon Nuts: Toss in ⅓ cup minced piñon nuts (or minced, blanched almonds) along with cream and cheese. About 425 calories per serving.

Spaghetti with Butter, Cream, Parmesan, and Truffles: Toss in 2–3 minced truffles along with cream and cheese. About 430 calories per serving.

Spaghetti with Butter, Cream, Parmesan, and Mushrooms: Toss in ½ cup minced, sautéed mushrooms along with cream and cheese. About 420 calories per serving.

Spaghetti with Herbs: Heat ½ teaspoon each basil and oregano along with butter and cream. Pour sauce over pasta; omit cheese but add 2 tablespoons each minced chives and parsley, and toss to mix. About 365 calories per serving.

SPAGHETTI CARBONARA

Spaghetti dressed with cream, cheese, bacon, and eggs.

Makes 4 servings

1 pound thin spaghetti
¼ cup bacon drippings
6 eggs, lightly beaten
½ teaspoon salt
⅛ teaspoon white pepper
¾ cup light cream
½ pound crisply cooked bacon, crumbled
½ cup finely grated Parmesan cheese

Cook spaghetti by package directions, timing carefully so it is done just as you begin cooking the eggs. The spaghetti must be *very hot* when the eggs are poured over it so they will cling and continue to cook a bit. Heat drippings in a large, heavy skillet over moderate heat 1–2 minutes. Mix eggs, salt, pepper, and cream, pour into drippings, cook and stir 2–3 minutes until eggs just *begin* to thicken—they should be creamy but *not set;* remove from heat. Quickly drain spaghetti and arrange on a heated platter, pour eggs on top and toss to mix. Sprinkle with bacon and Parmesan and toss again. Serve at once.

VARIATION:

Prepare as directed, substituting linguine, macaroni, or fusilli for the spaghetti.

Both versions: About 875 calories per serving.

☒ NOODLES ALFREDO

If you prepare this recipe with homemade noodles, so much the better.

Makes 4 servings

1 pound hot thin or medium-wide noodles, cooked by package directions
1 pound unsalted butter, sliced ¼" thick and softened to room temperature
1 pound Parmesan cheese, grated fine

Quickly drain noodles and return to kettle. Add butter and cheese and toss lightly but rapidly until noodles are evenly coated. Serve on heated plates. About 1700 calories per serving.

VARIATION:

Creamed Noodles Alfredo (not as authentic but almost as good, and certainly less caloric): Toss hot drained noodles with 1 cup melted butter, 2 cups finely grated Parmesan cheese, and 1 cup warm heavy cream. About 1255 calories per serving.

¢ ⊠ LINGUINE ALLA ROMANA

Makes 4 servings

½ *pound ricotta cheese*
½ *cup unsalted butter (no substitute)*
1 pound linguine or spaghetti, cooked and drained by package directions
½ *cup grated Parmesan cheese*
½ *teaspoon salt (about)*
Freshly ground pepper

Mix ricotta and butter in a heavy saucepan and simmer, uncovered, over lowest heat 5–7 minutes, stirring now and then. Place linguine in 4 large bowls, top with sauce, sprinkle with cheese and salt and, finally, a grinding of pepper. Toss to mix and serve. About 755 calories per serving.

¢ FETTUCCINE AND FISH

Makes 4 servings

Sauce:
1 medium-size yellow onion, peeled, sliced thin, and separated into rings
1 medium-size sweet green or red pepper, cored, seeded, and minced
2 tablespoons olive or other cooking oil
1 (1-pound) can Italian plum tomatoes (do not drain)
2 tablespoons tomato paste
½ *cup water*
¾–1 *pound haddock or any lean fish fillets, cut in 1″ cubes*
1 (2-ounce) can anchovy fillets, drained and minced (optional)

Pasta:
1 pound fettuccine, cooked and drained by package directions

Topping:
1 tablespoon minced fresh basil or parsley

Stir-fry onion and pepper in oil in a large skillet over moderate heat 3–5 minutes until limp. Add tomatoes, chopping as you add, tomato paste, and water; simmer, uncovered, 15 minutes. Scatter fish on top, cover, and simmer 10 minutes. Place pasta in a hot deep serving dish, top with sauce, and toss lightly. Sprinkle with basil and serve with grated Parmesan. (*Note:* If not using anchovies, taste for salt and adjust.) About 670 calories per serving.

VARIATION:

¢ **Fettuccine and Dried Salt Cod (Fettuccine con Baccalà):** Use ¾ pound filleted salt cod instead of haddock; soak in cold water to cover for 4 hours, drain, pat dry, and cube. Make sauce as directed, omitting anchovies. If you like, add ¼ cup each piñon nuts and sultana raisins just before pouring over pasta. About 645 calories per serving (without piñon nuts and raisins).

¢ BEEF AND SAUSAGE STUFFED RIGATONI OR TUFOLI

Makes 6 servings

½ *pound rigatoni or tufoli, cooked by package directions until barely al dente, then drained and rinsed in cool water*

Filling:
½ *pound ground beef chuck*
½ *pound sweet or hot Italian sausages, removed from casings and minced*
¼ *pound mushrooms, wiped clean and minced*
¾ *cup hot Italian Tomato Sauce*
⅓ *cup diced mozzarella cheese*

Topping:
2½ *cups hot Italian Tomato Sauce*
¼ *cup grated Parmesan cheese*

Preheat oven to 350° F. While rigatoni cool, prepare filling: Stir-fry beef and sausages in a large, heavy skillet over moderate heat 4–5 minutes until no longer pink; add mushrooms and stir-fry 2–3 minutes. Mix in sauce and simmer, uncovered, 5 minutes; cool slightly and stir in cheese. Using a small teaspoon, stuff into rigatoni; layer in an oiled 2½-quart casserole or *au gratin* dish, topping with some of the 2½ cups sauce as you go. Add remaining sauce, sprinkle with cheese, and bake uncovered 30 minutes until bubbly. About 520 calories per serving.

VARIATIONS:

Prepare as directed but substitute one of the following fillings for that above: Chicken and Prosciutto, Spinach and Ricotta, or Cheese Stuffing for Ravioli. About 320 calories per serving if made with Spinach and Ricotta Filling, 430 calories per serving if made with Chicken and Prosciutto Filling, and 525 calories per serving if made with Cheese Stuffing.

¢ **MEAT-FILLED RAVIOLI**

Ravioli, plump little pasta pillows stuffed with meat, eggs, vegetables, or cheese, can be made ahead, then baked in sauce just before serving. If you like, make a quantity and freeze *uncooked* (simply place 1 layer deep on foil-lined trays, roll up inside foil, and freeze until needed). Makes 6 servings

½ recipe *Homemade Pasta Dough*

Filling:
1 pound beef chuck, ground twice
1 small yellow onion, peeled and minced
1 clove garlic, peeled and crushed
1 tablespoon olive or other cooking oil
2 tablespoons flour
¾ cup beef broth
¼ cup tomato paste
1 teaspoon salt
⅛ teaspoon pepper

Topping:
1 cup grated Parmesan cheese
3 cups hot Italian Tomato or Marinara Sauce

Prepare dough as directed and let rest while making filling. Stir-fry beef, onion, and garlic in oil in a saucepan over moderate heat 4–5 minutes until no longer pink; put through finest blade of meat grinder. Return to pan, set over moderate heat, sprinkle in flour, and slowly mix in remaining filling ingredients. Cook and stir until thickened, reduce heat, and simmer uncovered 5 minutes; cool to room temperature. Meanwhile, roll half of the dough on a lightly floured board into a paper thin 14" square. Drop rounded teaspoonfuls of filling over dough, spacing 2" apart in neat rows. Roll remaining dough into a square of the same size and lay over the first. Press lightly around mounds of filling, then cut in 2" squares with a ravioli cutter or pastry wheel forming "pillows." (*Note:* If you have ravioli pans [trays with 12 depressions and sharp raised edges], lay 1 sheet of rolled dough on pan, drop filling into depressions, cover with second dough sheet, and roll with a rolling pin to separate squares. Make sure edges are sealed so filling won't ooze out.) Place ravioli 1 layer deep on a lightly floured tray, dust with flour, and let stand uncovered ½ hour; turn and let stand ½ hour longer. Bring about 5 quarts salted water to a boil in a large kettle (to keep ravioli from sticking, add 1 teaspoon cooking oil). Drop in about a dozen ravioli and cook 7–10 minutes, moving them around so they don't stick. Lift to a hot, buttered large platter with a slotted spoon, top with 2 tablespoons cheese and 3–4 tablespoons sauce, and keep warm. Continue cooking ravioli, adding to dish and topping with cheese and sauce. Serve very hot with remaining cheese and sauce. About 570 calories per serving.

VARIATIONS:

¢ **Mushroom, Eggplant, or Cheese Ravioli:** Prepare as directed but use Italian Mushroom-Eggplant or Italian Cheese Sauce instead of tomato sauce. About 585 calories per serving if made with Mushroom-Eggplant Sauce, 600 if made with Italian Cheese Sauce.

¢ **Sausage Stuffed Ravioli:** Prepare as directed but substitute ¾ pound sweet Italian sausages and ¼ pound salami, removed from casings and minced, for the beef. About 665 calories per serving.

Chicken and Prosciutto Stuffed Ravioli: Prepare as directed but use the following filling: 1 cup each ground cooked chicken and prosciutto ham mixed with 2 lightly beaten egg yolks, ⅛ teaspoon each nutmeg and pepper, and 2 tablespoons each melted butter and grated Parmesan cheese. About 545 calories per serving.

¢ **Spinach and Ricotta Stuffed Ravioli:** Prepare as directed but for the meat filling substitute: 1 cup each ricotta cheese and well-drained, puréed, cooked spinach mixed with 1 lightly beaten egg yolk and a pinch nutmeg. About 435 calories per serving.

¢ **Cheese Stuffed Ravioli:** Prepare as directed but fill with the following mixture: 1 pound ricotta cheese mixed with ½ cup grated Parmesan or mozzarella cheese, 1 lightly beaten egg, 1 teaspoon each minced parsley and basil, and ¾ teaspoon salt. Omit sauce and sprinkle layers with 2–3 tablespoons each melted butter and grated Parmesan. About 640 calories per serving.

¢ **LASAGNE**

Makes 8–10 servings

1 pound sweet Italian sausages
2 quarts (about) hot Savory Beef and Tomato Sauce for Pasta, or Marinara Sauce
1 pound lasagne, cooked and drained by package directions
1 pound ricotta cheese
⅔ cup finely grated Parmesan cheese
¾ pound mozzarella cheese, coarsely grated

Preheat oven to 350° F. Sauté sausages 15–20 minutes over moderate heat or until cooked through, drain on paper toweling, and slice ½″ thick. Spoon a thin layer of sauce into an ungreased 13″×9″×2″ baking pan and arrange a single layer of lasagne (about ¼ of the total) on top, slightly overlapping. Add another thin layer of sauce, top with ⅓ of the sausage and ricotta, and sprinkle with ¼ of the Parmesan and mozzarella. Continue building up layers until all ingredients are in the pan, ending with Parmesan and mozzarella. (*Note:* Recipe can be prepared to this point early in the day or days ahead. Cool, cover, and refrigerate or freeze until needed. Bring to room temperature before proceeding.) Bake, uncovered, 35–45 minutes until lightly browned and bubbling. Cut into squares and serve. If made with Savory Beef and Tomato Sauce, about 1115 calories for each of 8 servings, 890 for each of 10 servings. If made with Marinara Sauce, about 870 calories for each of 8 servings, 695 for each of 10.

CEREALS, RICE, AND PASTA

VARIATION:

Meat Ball Lasagne: Prepare 1 recipe Savory Meat Balls as directed but omit the gravy. Simmer the meat balls 10–15 minutes in 2 quarts Marinara Sauce, then prepare the lasagne as above, substituting the meat balls, sliced ¼" thick, for the Italian sausages. About 865 calories for each of 8 servings, 690 calories for each of 10 servings.

¢ CANNELLONI OR MANICOTTI SQUARES

Cannelloni and manicotti are large pasta squares (or, if bought, tubes). In this country the larger tube or square (usually 5") is manicotti, the smaller (4") one, cannelloni. Tufoli may be substituted for either.

Makes 1½ dozen 4" squares

½ recipe Homemade Pasta Dough
5 quarts water
2 tablespoons salt
1 teaspoon cooking oil

Prepare and roll dough as directed; cut in 4" squares, cover with cloth, and let dry 1 hour at room temperature. Bring water, salt, and oil to a boil in a large kettle and cook, uncovered, about 6 squares at a time, in rapidly boiling water 7–10 minutes until tender. Lift with a slotted spoon to a dampened dish towel. Squares are now ready to fill. About 60 calories per manicotti or cannelloni square.

¢ CANNELLONI WITH MEAT FILLING

Makes 6 servings

1 recipe Cannelloni Squares

Filling:
1 teaspoon cooking oil
1 pound ground beef chuck
2 tablespoons minced yellow onion
2 teaspoons salt
¼ teaspoon pepper
1 teaspoon savory
2 tablespoons flour
¾ cup beef consommé
Few drops liquid gravy browner

Sauce:
3 cups Italian Tomato Sauce or Marinara Sauce or canned meatless spaghetti sauce

Topping:
½ pound mozzarella cheese, coarsely grated

Prepare and cook cannelloni squares as recipe directs, then reserve. Preheat oven to 375° F. Brush a large skillet with oil and heat 1–2 minutes over moderately high heat. Add beef and brown well 4–5 minutes, stirring constantly. Add onion, salt, pepper, and savory. Sprinkle flour over beef, then slowly stir in consommé. Cook and stir until thickened; mix in gravy browner, reduce heat to low, cover, and simmer 15–20 minutes, stirring now and then. Remove from heat and cool 10 minutes. Drop 1½ tablespoons filling in center of each cannelloni square, fold bottom edge up over filling, then roll up jelly-roll style and arrange seam side down in a single layer in a buttered shallow 3-quart casserole. Cover with sauce, sprinkle with mozzarella, and bake uncovered 25–30 minutes until bubbling and lightly browned. (*Note:* If not brown enough, broil 4" from heat 1–2 minutes.) About 585 calories per serving if made with Italian Tomato Sauce, 590 calories per serving if made with Marinara Sauce, and 520 calories per serving if made with canned meatless spaghetti sauce.

CANNELLONI ALLA NERONE

A classic chicken liver, chicken and ham stuffing rolled up in homemade cannelloni, but good, too, in Manicotti Pancakes or boiled tufoli.
Makes 6 servings

1 recipe Cannelloni Squares

Filling:
4 chicken livers, halved at the natural separation
1 tablespoon butter or margarine
2 small cooked chicken breasts, boned and skinned
4 slices prosciutto ham
½ cup grated Parmesan cheese
1½ pints hot Béchamel Sauce

Prepare and cook cannelloni squares as directed. Preheat oven to 375° F. For the filling: Sauté chicken livers in butter 2–3 minutes over moderate heat, just until firm, then put through finest blade of meat grinder along with chicken and ham. Mix in ¼ cup cheese and ⅓ cup sauce, taste for salt and adjust. Place about 1½ tablespoons filling on each cannelloni square, roll up tightly, and arrange seam side down in a single layer in a buttered 3-quart shallow casserole. Sprinkle with remaining cheese and pour sauce over all. (*Note:* Recipe can be prepared to this point early in the day, covered, and chilled until ready to bake.) Bake, uncovered, about ½ hour until bubbling; if you like, brown lightly under broiler. About 625 calories per serving.

¢ CANNELLONI GARIBALDI

Cannelloni filled with sweet Italian sausages, chopped spinach, and grated Parmesan cheese.
Makes 6 servings

1 recipe Cannelloni Squares

Filling:
1 pound sweet Italian sausages
1 (10-ounce) package frozen chopped spinach, cooked by package directions but not seasoned
¼ cup finely grated Parmesan cheese
1 egg, lightly beaten

Sauce:
3 cups Mushroom Marinara Sauce

Topping:
¼ cup finely grated Parmesan cheese

Prepare and cook cannelloni squares as recipe directs, then reserve. Preheat oven to 375° F. Remove sausage meat from casings and brown in a large, heavy skillet over moderately low heat 10–15 minutes, stirring occasionally and breaking up large clumps with a spoon; transfer with a slotted spoon to a bowl. Drain spinach in a sieve, pressing out as much water as possible with a spoon. Add spinach, cheese, and egg to sausage and toss well to mix. Divide filling evenly among cannelloni squares, roll up, and arrange seam side down in a single layer in a buttered shallow 3-quart casserole. Spoon sauce evenly over all and top with cheese. Bake, uncovered, about 30 minutes until bubbling. About 625 calories per serving.

¢ BAKED MEATLESS "MANICOTTI"

A cheese-rich meat substitute.
Makes 6 servings

Manicotti Pancakes:
2 eggs, lightly beaten
¾ cup milk
½ teaspoon salt
1 cup sifted flour

Filling:
1 pound ricotta cheese
3 tablespoons grated Parmesan cheese

2 tablespoons minced parsley
1 teaspoon salt
1 egg, lightly beaten

Topping:
1½ pints hot Marinara or Italian Tomato Sauce

Preheat oven to 350° F. For the pancakes, mix eggs, milk, and salt; slowly add flour and beat until smooth. Using 1 tablespoon batter for each pancake, drop onto a greased griddle set over moderate heat and spread into 4" circles. Brown lightly, turn, and brown flip side. Lay most attractive side *down* on paper toweling while you cook the rest. Mix filling ingredients, spoon about 1½ tablespoons on center of each pancake, then fold top and bottom toward center, envelope fashion. Arrange seam side down in a buttered 13"×9½"×2" baking pan and top with sauce. Bake, uncovered, ½ hour until bubbling. Serve hot with extra grated Parmesan. About 355 calories per serving if made with Italian Tomato Sauce (without extra Parmesan), 365 if made with Marinara Sauce.

VARIATION:

⚔ **Meatless Cannelloni:** Substitute 1 recipe Cannelloni Squares or ¾ pound packaged cannelloni or tufoli for Manicotti Pancakes. Cook, drain, and fill; top with sauce and bake as directed. About 285 calories per serving if made with Italian Tomato Sauce and Manicotti Pancakes, about 255 calories per serving if made with Italian Tomato Sauce and packaged cannelloni or tufoli. About 295 calories per serving if made with Marinara Sauce and Manicotti Pancakes, 265 calories per serving if made with Marinara Sauce and packaged cannelloni or tufoli.

CHICKEN AND MUSHROOM STUFFED MANICOTTI

1 recipe Manicotti Pancakes or Manicotti Squares

Filling:
½ pound mushrooms, wiped clean and minced (include stems)
2 tablespoons butter or margarine
2 cups cooked minced chicken (preferably white meat)
1 teaspoon grated lemon rind
½ teaspoon salt
⅛ teaspoon pepper

Sauce:
2 cups Thick White Sauce
1 cup heavy cream
⅓ cup grated Parmesan cheese

Prepare manicotti as directed. Preheat oven to 375° F. For the filling: Sauté mushrooms in butter over moderate heat 3–4 minutes until golden; off heat, mix in remaining ingredients. Mix sauce and cream and blend ⅓ cup into chicken mixture. Spoon about 1½ tablespoons filling on each manicotti, roll up, and arrange seam side down in a buttered 3-quart casserole. Sprinkle with cheese and top with remaining sauce. Bake, uncovered, ½ hour, then brown lightly under broiler. About 645 calories per serving.

CHAPTER 14

SAUCES, GRAVIES, AND BUTTERS

Sauce cookery is neither mysterious nor complicated if you consider that there are five, perhaps six, "mother" sauces from which most of the others descend: *White Sauce* (and its richer cousin Béchamel), *Velouté* (similar to White Sauce except that the liquid is light stock instead of milk), *Espagnole* (rich brown stock-based sauce), *Hollandaise* (cooked, egg-thickened sauce), *Mayonnaise* (an uncooked oil and egg emulsion), and *Vinaigrette* (oil and vinegar—it and mayonnaise are included in the salad chapter). No sauce is difficult to make (though some are tedious) and none requires more than learning a few basic techniques. The time required to prepare certain sauces may seem overlong. In some cases, slow simmering is needed to boil down liquids and concentrate flavors. In others, it is needed to give the sauce a particular finish or finesse.

In addition to the classic sauce families, there are a few orphan sauces that defy categorization: flavored butters, purées, barbecue sauces, sweet-sour sauces, not to mention the myriad sauce mixes crowding supermarket shelves and the jiffy sauces that can be made from canned soups. All sauces, however, the thick and the thin, the hot, the cold, the quick, and the classic, serve the same purpose: to enhance the food they accompany. They should never dominate, never inundate the food with which they are served.

Some Terms and Techniques of Sauce Making

Beurre Manié: Butter-flour mixture, pinched off, a bit at a time, or rolled into small balls and beaten into hot sauces to thicken them. A wire whisk is the best tool to use when adding *beurre manié*.

Beurre Noir: Literally "black butter"; but actually, butter heated to an even nut brown.

SAUCES, GRAVIES, AND BUTTERS

Beurres Composés: The French term for flavored butters.

Brunoise: Finely shredded or diced vegetables, poached in stock and used in making sauces. The most often used are leeks, onions, and carrots.

Caramel: Liquid melted sugar, used to color and flavor sauces. See soup chapter for recipe for Caramelized Sugar.

Clarified Butter: Melted butter, skimmed of milk solids; it is clear and golden and much less likely to burn than unclarified butter. *To Make:* Melt butter over low heat, watching that it does not brown. Remove from heat and let stand 2–3 minutes until solids settle. Skim off clear liquid butter and discard sediment. (*Note:* ½ cup butter=about ⅓ cup clarified butter.)

Cream: To mix a white or light sauce with coarsely chopped or diced meat, fish, fowl, or vegetables. A good ratio: 1 cup sauce to 2 cups solids.

Deglaze: To scrape up browned bits in a pan in which meat, fowl, or fish has browned, usually by adding a small amount of liquid and bringing to a boil. These pan scrapings enrich the color and flavor of brown sauces and gravies.

Degrease: To remove grease. The easiest—but slowest—way is to chill a mixture until fat rises to the top and hardens so that it can be lifted off. Liquid fat may be skimmed off hot sauces, or, if quantity is small, blotted up with paper toweling.

Drawn Butter: The same as clarified butter.

Fond: The French word for stock used as a base for soups and sauces. *Fond blanc* is white stock, *fond brun*, brown stock.

Fumet: A concentrated stock used to give body to sauces.

Ghee: The East Indian version of clarified butter.

Glace de Viande: A meat glaze made by greatly reducing brown beef stock. It is used to color and flavor sauces and gravies. Commercial beef extract makes a good substitute.

Liaison: The French term for "thickener." The ways of thickening sauces are many, each requiring a different technique:

Starch Thickeners: Starches such as flour, cornstarch, or arrowroot, when heated in liquid, swell and coagulate, thickening the liquid. Whether the liquid thickens smoothly depends upon whether the starch particles were kept separate during cooking. And that depends on the cook. Raw flour, cornstarch, or other powdery thickener tossed into a bubbling liquid will lump, but if blended first with fat or a small amount of cold liquid, then blended into the hot liquid and stirred until after thickening, each will produce a silky-smooth sauce. (*Note:* The easiest way to blend starch and cold liquid is with the fingers or, if there is slightly more liquid than starch, in a shaker jar. Not all starches have the same thickening power, not all produce the same results, i.e., some will make a sauce opaque, some translucent, and others sparklingly clear. Here's a quick table (on following page).

A Note about Flours: The new nonlumping "sauce" flours ensure satiny sauces, even for the haphazard cook who forgets to stir; but they are more expensive than conventional all-purpose flours.

Eggs as Thickeners: Egg yolks are more commonly used than whole eggs; they not only thicken a sauce but enrich its color and flavor as well. Generally speaking, it will take 2 egg yolks to make 1 cup liquid about the consistency of Medium White Sauce. The egg yolks should be beaten briskly with a fork, just until uniformly liquid, then blended with a little cold liquid or beaten hard with a small amount of a hot sauce before being added to that sauce. Otherwise, the eggs will curdle. For best results, cook and stir egg-thickened sauces over lowest heat (insulated by an asbestos flame-tamer) or in the top of a double boiler over *simmering,* not boiling, water. Cook and stir only until sauce is thickened (about the consistency of stirred custard) and no raw taste of egg remains. If, despite all care,

Thickener	Thickening Power	Use to Thicken	Special Techniques	Sauce Appearance
Flour	1 T. will slightly thicken 1 cup liquid (see White Sauce chart)	Gravies, sweet and savory sauces	Blend with an equal quantity fat or cold liquid before adding. Cook several minutes *after thickening* to remove raw taste.	Opaque
Brown Flour	½ that of flour	Gravies, brown sauces	Same as flour	Opaque
(*Note: To Make Brown Flour:* Heat and stir flour in a dry heavy skillet over low heat until a pale amber color.)				
Cornstarch	Twice that of flour	Sweet-sour or sweet sauces	Same as flour. Do not cook more than 3 minutes or sauce may thin.	Almost transparent
Rice Flour (available in Oriental groceries)	1–1½ times that of flour	Sweet-sour or sweet sauces; also gravies	Same as flour	Translucent
Potato Flour or Starch (available in specialty shops)	2–2½ times that of flour	Gravies, savory sauces	Same as flour but do not boil or cook after thickening—the sauce will thin out.	Translucent
Arrowroot (available in specialty shops)	2–2½ times that of flour	Sweet sauces and glazes	Mix with equal amount of sugar or about twice as much cold liquid; do not boil or reheat —sauce will thin.	Sparkling, clear

a sauce should curdle, strain through a fine sieve or double thickness of cheesecloth. If mixture is thin, rethicken with egg, taking every precaution. If sauce is Hollandaise or one of its descendants, you can salvage by following directions in the Hollandaise recipe.

Blood as a Thickener: Game sauces and gravies are sometimes thickened with blood. It should be absolutely fresh (mixing with a little vinegar helps keep it liquid), strained, then added to the sauce shortly before serving. Swirl it in slowly, as you would an egg yolk mixture, and cook and stir over low heat just until sauce thickens. Never boil a blood-thickened sauce or it will curdle.

Marinade: A spicy or piquant mixture in which food is soaked so that it absorbs some of the flavors.

Marinate: To soak in a marinade.

Mirepoix: A mixture of diced, sautéed vegetables (usually carrots, onions, shallots, celery) used as a base for sauces.

Paste: A blend of starch and cold liquid, usually 1 part starch to 2 parts liquid, used to thicken sauces.

Reduce: To boil a liquid uncovered so that it reduces in volume. The purpose is to thicken a sauce and concentrate the flavors.

Roux: A smooth blend of melted butter and flour used in thickening sauces. When the butter and flour are not browned, the roux is a *roux blanc* (white roux); when the roux is worked over low heat until pale tan it is a *roux blond,* and when it is browned still further, it becomes a *roux brun.*

Salpicon: Diced ingredients (vegetables, meats, fish, or a mixture) served in a sauce.

Skim: To scoop fat from the top of a sauce with a skimmer or large, flat spoon.

Thickener: See Liaison.

Some Tips for Making Better Sauces

– Use heavy, flat-bottom pans of enamel, tin-lined copper, stainless steel, porcelain, or flameproof glass. Aluminum is apt to turn white sauces gray and discolor those made with egg or vinegar.
– Use a comfortable wooden spoon for stirring or, if you prefer, a wire whisk.
– When making a thick or moderately thick sauce, keep burner heat low and stir often to prevent sauce from scorching (especially important if starch is the thickener).
– If doubling or tripling a sauce recipe, allow more cooking time so that sauce can thicken and mellow properly.
– To enrich color of gravies and brown sauces, add Caramelized Sugar or liquid gravy browner.
– To enrich flavor of gravies and brown sauces, add bouillon cubes, Glace de Viande, or beef extract.
– Taste sauces often as they cook, adjusting seasonings as needed. Remember that cold sauces can take more seasoning than hot ones—cold numbs the palate.
– To prevent a skin from forming on a sauce as it cools, place a circle of wax paper *flat on sauce.*
– To smooth out a lumpy sauce, strain. Whirling in an electric blender can turn a starch-thickened sauce gluey.

About Keeping and Holding Sauces

Egg- or starch-thickened sauces, as a rule, keep poorly. About 4–5 days in the refrigerator is a maximum. Place wax paper flat on surface of sauce, then add a cover so that sauce will not absorb refrigerator odors. *Health Tip:* Never try to hold these sauces at room (or more than room) temperature for more than 20–30 minutes. You invite food poisoning. And when making creamed dishes, do not mix the sauce and the minced foods until shortly before serving unless each is cooled separately, refrigerated, and reheated. At buffets, creamed foods should be kept bubbly-hot in chafing dishes, again to reduce the risk of food poisoning.

Acid sauces are less perishable, especially tomato or other puréed vegetable sauces. Properly refrigerated, they should keep well about 2 weeks.

About Freezing Sauces

Egg- and starch-thickened sauces do not freeze successfully. Many of the pasta sauces do, however. For details, see chapter on freezing.

WHITE SAUCES

⊠ BASIC WHITE SAUCE
Makes 1 cup

Melt fat in a small saucepan (not aluminum) over low heat and blend in flour to form a smooth paste. Gradually stir in milk and heat, stirring constantly, until thickened and smooth. (*Note:* Don't be alarmed if sauce seems to "curdle" as milk is added—it's merely the fat hardening on contact with the cold milk; sauce will soon smooth out.) Add seasonings, then let mellow about 5 minutes, stirring occasionally over lowest heat. (*Note:* If sauce must be held a short while— up to 20–25 minutes—transfer to the top of a double boiler, set over simmering water, and cover. To hold longer, remove from heat, place a circle of wax paper flat on sauce [to prevent a skin from forming], and cool to room temperature; refrigerate until needed. Reheat in the

Type	Fat (Butter, Margarine, or Drippings)	Flour	Milk	Seasonings	Use
Very thin	1 tablespoon	½ tablespoon	1 cup	¼ teaspoon salt, pinch pepper	For thickening thin cream soups
Thin	1 tablespoon	1 tablespoon	1 cup	¼ teaspoon salt, pinch pepper	For thickening standard cream soups
Medium	2 tablespoons	2 tablespoons	1 cup	¼ teaspoon salt, pinch pepper	As a base for sauces and creamed dishes
Thick	3 tablespoons	3 tablespoons	1 cup	¼ teaspoon salt, pinch pepper	For binding casserole ingredients
Very thick	¼ cup	¼ cup	1 cup	¼ teaspoon salt, pinch pepper	For binding croquettes

SAUCES, GRAVIES, AND BUTTERS

top of a double boiler. Calories for each 1 cup: About 275 for Very Thin White Sauce, 285 for Thin White Sauce, 410 for Medium White Sauce, 535 for Thick White Sauce, and 660 for Very Thick White Sauce.

VARIATIONS:

Parsley Sauce: To each cup Medium White Sauce, add 2 tablespoons minced parsley and let mellow, stirring, about 5 minutes. Good with fish, carrots, or beets. About 25 calories per tablespoon.

Mint Sauce: To each cup Medium White Sauce, add 1 tablespoon minced mint and let mellow, stirring, about 5 minutes. Good with boiled onions. About 25 calories per tablespoon.

Cheese Sauce: To each cup Medium White Sauce, add ¾–1 cup coarsely grated Cheddar, American, or Gruyère cheese, 1 teaspoon Worcestershire sauce, and a pinch each powdered mustard and cayenne. For a peppier sauce, increase mustard and cayenne slightly and add 1 teaspoon grated onion and ¼ minced clove garlic. Heat and stir sauce until cheese is melted and flavors blended. Thin, if needed, with a little milk. About 35 calories per tablespoon.

Quick Mushroom Sauce: To each cup Thick White Sauce, add 1 undrained (3-ounce) can sliced or chopped mushrooms; heat and stir 3–5 minutes to blend flavors. About 40 calories per tablespoon.

Mushroom Sauce: Begin 1 recipe Medium White Sauce as directed, but before blending in flour stir-fry 1 cup minced mushrooms in the butter 3–5 minutes. Blend in flour and proceed as directed. If you like, spike sauce with a little dry sherry or vermouth. About 30 calories per tablespoon.

Mushroom and Cheese Sauce: Begin 1 recipe Medium White Sauce as directed, but before blending in flour stir-fry 2 tablespoons minced yellow onion 3–5 minutes until limp; add ½ pound button mushrooms, cover, and simmer 7–8 minutes, stirring once or twice. Blend in flour, add 1 cup light cream or milk, ¾ cup coarsely grated sharp Cheddar cheese, and the seasonings called for. Heat and stir until thickened and smooth, then let mellow about 5 minutes longer over lowest heat, stirring occasionally. Good over boiled potatoes or summer squash. About 35 calories per tablespoon if made with milk, 50 calories per tablespoon if made with cream.

Mustard Sauce: Into each cup Medium White Sauce blend ¼ cup prepared mild yellow or spicy brown mustard and 1–2 teaspoons cider vinegar; let mellow over lowest heat 3–5 minutes before serving. Good with ham. About 30 calories per tablespoon.

Hot Mustard Sauce: Begin 1 recipe Medium White Sauce as directed but blend ½ teaspoon powdered mustard into butter along with flour. Proceed as for Mustard Sauce (above), adding 1 teaspoon Worcestershire sauce and 2 or 3 drops liquid hot red pepper seasoning. Good with ham. About 30 calories per tablespoon.

Chiffon Sauce: Prepare 1 recipe Medium White Sauce in the top of a double boiler, omitting pepper and reducing salt to ⅛ teaspoon; blend a little hot sauce into 1 lightly beaten egg yolk, return to pan, set over simmering water, and cook and stir 2–3 minutes. Place a circle of wax paper flat on sauce and cool 20–30 minutes. Beat 2 tablespoons tarragon vinegar into sauce in a slow steady stream. Whip 1 egg white to soft peaks and fold into sauce; cover and chill 1–2 hours. Good with cold shellfish. About 30 calories per tablespoon.

❋ BEURRE MANIÉ

Makes about 3 tablespoons, enough to thicken slightly 1½ cups liquid

3 tablespoons butter, softened slightly
2 tablespoons flour

Blend butter and flour until smooth. Pinch off small pieces and add, 1 at a time, stirring constantly, to hot liquids, gravies, and sauces to thicken. About 120 calories per tablespoon.

BÉCHAMEL SAUCE

A French white sauce from which many other sauces descend. Depending upon the food to be sauced, make with part milk, part broth (chicken broth for meat or poultry, fish stock for seafood, vegetable cooking water for eggs, cheese, or vegetables).
Makes 1⅔ cups

4 tablespoons butter (no substitute)
¼ cup unsifted flour
2 cups milk or 1 cup each milk and chicken broth, Easy Fish Stock, or vegetable cooking water
½ teaspoon salt (about)
⅛ teaspoon white pepper
2 tablespoons minced yellow onion
2 ounces ground veal (use only if sauce is for meat or poultry)
1 small sprig fresh thyme or a pinch dried thyme
¼ bay leaf
Pinch nutmeg

Melt 3 tablespoons butter in a double boiler top over direct moderate heat; blend in flour, slowly add milk, and heat, stirring, until thickened. Mix in salt and pepper. Set over simmering water. Stir-fry onion in remaining butter 3–5 minutes over moderate heat until limp, add veal if sauce is for meat or poultry, and stir-fry until no longer pink; add to sauce along with remaining ingredients, cover and cook 1 hour over simmering water, beating now and then with a whisk and scraping bottom and sides of pan with a rubber spatula. (*Note:* Be careful when removing lid not to let water condensed there drop in sauce.) Strain sauce, taste for salt and adjust. Serve hot or use as a base for other sauces. From about 20 to 35 calories per tablespoon depending upon whether made with milk, a combination of milk and broth, and whether made with or without meat.

VARIATIONS:

Anchovy Sauce (Makes 1⅔ cups): Prepare Béchamel using milk and fish stock and omitting salt; before setting to simmer, blend in 4 teaspoons anchovy paste and a pinch cayenne. Proceed as above. Good with fish. About 30 calories per tablespoon.

Caper Sauce (Makes 2 cups): Prepare Béchamel using milk and fish stock and omitting salt; just before serving, mix in ⅓ cup coarsely chopped capers and 1 tablespoon lemon juice. Serve with fish. About 20 calories per tablespoon.

Caper and Horseradish Sauce (Makes 2 cups): Prepare Caper Sauce and mix in 2 tablespoons prepared horseradish. Good with boiled beef brisket. About 22 calories per tablespoon.

Hot Horseradish Sauce (Makes 2 cups): Prepare Béchamel, mix in ¼–⅓ cup drained prepared horse-

SAUCES, GRAVIES, AND BUTTERS

radish, ⅛ teaspoon powdered mustard blended with 2 tablespoons light cream, and heat 2–3 minutes. Good with corned or boiled beef. About 35 calories per tablespoon.

Mornay Sauce (Makes 2½ cups): (*Note:* This delicate cheese sauce can be used with seafood, poultry, eggs, or vegetables; let recipe decide which stock you use in making it.) Prepare Béchamel, add ½ cup of the same stock used in the Béchamel, and heat uncovered in the top of a double boiler until sauce reduces to 2 cups. Add ¼ cup each grated Parmesan and Gruyère and heat and stir until melted. Off heat, beat in 2 tablespoons butter, 1 teaspoon at a time. (*Note:* If Mornay is to be used for a gratiné, use half as much cheese and butter.) About 35 calories per tablespoon.

Nantua Sauce (Makes about 3 cups): Prepare Béchamel using milk and fish stock, mix in ⅓ cup heavy cream, and keep warm. Boil ¼–⅓ pound crayfish or shrimp in 1½ cups water with ½ teaspoon salt 3–5 minutes; shell, devein, and mince. Boil cooking liquid, uncovered, until reduced to ¼ cup; mix into sauce along with crayfish; add a pinch cayenne and, if you like, 1 tablespoon brandy. Off heat, beat in 2 tablespoons Shrimp Butter, 1 teaspoon at a time. Good with seafood or eggs. About 26 calories per tablespoon.

Soubise Sauce (Makes about 1 quart): Prepare Béchamel and keep warm. Meanwhile, simmer 4 coarsely chopped yellow onions, covered, with 1½ cups water (or a ½-and-½ mixture of water and chicken or beef broth) and 3 tablespoons butter about ¾ hour until mushy. Uncover and boil until liquid reduces to 1 cup. Purée onions and liquid at low speed in an electric blender or put through a food mill. Mix into sauce, season to taste with salt, pepper, and nutmeg. Good with poultry, fish, brains, and sweetbreads. About 20 calories per tablespoon.

VELOUTÉ SAUCE

If a velouté is used to sauce poultry, egg, or vegetable dishes, make with chicken broth; if to sauce meat, use veal stock; if seafood, fish stock. Makes about 1⅔ cups

6 tablespoons butter (no substitute)
6 tablespoons flour
2 cups chicken broth, Veal (White) Stock or Easy Fish Stock
¼ teaspoon salt (about)
Pinch white pepper
2–3 tablespoons coarsely chopped mushrooms (optional)

Melt butter in a heavy saucepan over moderate heat. Blend in flour, gradually stir in broth, and heat, stirring constantly, until thickened and smooth. Add seasonings, mushrooms, if you like, reduce heat, and simmer uncovered ½ hour, stirring often and skimming light scum from sides of pan as it collects. Turn heat to lowest point, cover, and simmer ½ hour, stirring now and then. (*Note:* When uncovering sauce, don't let moisture on lid drop into sauce.) Strain sauce through a fine sieve and serve hot. About 30 calories per tablespoon (with or without mushrooms).

VARIATIONS:

⚜ **Allemande Sauce** (Makes 1 quart): Prepare Velouté with chicken broth and keep warm. Heat 2 cups chicken broth in the top of a double boiler and blend ½ cup into 4 lightly beaten egg yolks; return to pan, set over simmering water, and cook and stir 3–4 minutes until thickened and no raw egg taste remains. Blend in Velouté and, if you like, 3–4 teaspoons lemon juice. Strain and serve with chicken, fish, brains, or sweetbreads. About 18 calories per tablespoon.

⚔ **Poulette Sauce** (Makes 1 quart): Prepare Allemande Sauce, using lemon juice, and keep warm in double boiler. Meanwhile, boil 1½ cups chicken broth and ¼ pound minced mushrooms, uncovered, 20 minutes, stirring occasionally, until liquid is reduced to ½ cup. Strain liquid into Allemande Sauce and heat and stir 2–3 minutes. Mix in 2–3 tablespoons minced parsley and serve with vegetables, sweetbreads, or brains. About 15 calories per tablespoon.

Aurore Sauce (Makes 2 cups): Make Velouté with chicken broth or fish stock, blend in ½ cup tomato purée, cover, and simmer 5–7 minutes. Beat in 2 tablespoons butter, 1 teaspoon at a time. Taste and, if tart, add ¼ teaspoon sugar. Good over eggs, poultry, or sweetbreads. About 35 calories per tablespoon.

Bercy Sauce (Makes 2 cups): Make Velouté with fish stock and keep warm. Stir-fry 2 tablespoons minced shallots or scallions (white part) in 2 tablespoons butter over moderate heat 3–4 minutes until limp. Add ½ cup each dry white wine and fish stock and boil slowly, uncovered, until liquid reduces to ½ cup; mix into sauce along with 1 tablespoon minced parsley. Good with fish. About 35 calories per tablespoon.

Marinière Sauce (Makes 2½ cups): Begin Bercy Sauce as directed, using strained liquid from Steamed Mussels in the Velouté and in the wine-shallot mixture instead of fish stock. When wine-shallot mixture is reduced, blend into 2 lightly beaten egg yolks, mix into sauce, set over simmering water, and cook and stir 3–4 minutes until no raw egg taste remains. Beat in 2 tablespoons butter, 1 teaspoon at a time; add salt and pepper to taste, strain, mix in the parsley, and serve with seafood. About 28 calories per tablespoon.

Bontemps Sauce (Makes 3 cups): Prepare Velouté with chicken broth or veal stock and keep warm. Stir-fry 1 small minced yellow onion in 2 tablespoons butter 3–5 minutes until limp, add 2 cups apple cider, ¾ teaspoon salt, and ⅛ teaspoon paprika, and boil slowly uncovered until reduced to 1 cup. Mix into Velouté, add 2 teaspoons Dijon mustard, and simmer uncovered 10 minutes. Beat in 2–3 tablespoons butter, 1 teaspoon at a time. Serve with broiled meat. About 29 calories per tablespoon.

Chivry Sauce (Makes 2 cups): Prepare Velouté with chicken broth or fish stock and keep warm. Boil 1 cup dry white wine, uncovered, with 1 tablespoon each minced fresh (or 1 teaspoon each dried) tarragon and chervil until reduced to ½ cup; strain liquid into sauce. Beat in 2 tablespoons Green Butter and 1 tablespoon Tarragon Butter, 1 teaspoon at a time. Serve with eggs or seafood. About 35 calories per tablespoon.

Egg Sauce (Makes 2 cups): Prepare Velouté with fish stock, mix in 2 minced hard-cooked eggs and, if you like, 1 teaspoon minced parsley. Serve with white fish. About 30 calories per tablespoon.

Indienne (Indian) Sauce (Makes 2 cups): Before beginning Velouté, stir-fry 1 minced large yellow onion, 1 minced stalk celery, and 2 tablespoons minced celery root in butter called for 5–8 minutes over moderate heat until limp. Blend in 2 teaspoons curry powder, the flour called for, and proceed with Velouté as directed, adding ¼ teaspoon thyme, ⅛ teaspoon mace and ½ bay leaf along with other seasonings. Strain sauce, mix in ½ cup heavy cream and 1 tablespoon lemon juice. Good with cold roast lamb. About 40 calories per tablespoon.

Lobster Sauce (Makes 2 cups): Prepare Velouté with fish stock, add 1 cup dry white wine, and simmer uncovered until sauce reduces to 2 cups; beat in, 1 teaspoon at a time, ¼ cup Lobster Butter or 1 tablespoon anchovy paste and 2 tablespoons butter. Mix in ⅓ cup minced cooked lobster and a pinch cayenne. Serve with seafood. About 43 calories per tablespoon.

Normande (Normandy) Sauce (Makes 2 cups): Prepare Velouté with fish stock and keep warm. Boil 1½ cups chicken broth, uncovered, with ¼ pound minced mushrooms until reduced to ½ cup, stirring occasionally; strain liquid into sauce, add ½ cup fish stock, and simmer uncovered about ½ hour until reduced to 2 cups. Lightly beat 2 egg yolks with ¼ cup heavy cream, blend in ⅓ cup hot sauce, return to pan, and cook and stir about 3 minutes over lowest heat until no raw egg taste remains; do not boil. Mix in a pinch cayenne. Good with fish, especially sole. About 39 calories per tablespoon.

Diplomate Sauce (Makes 2½ cups): Prepare Normande Sauce and pour into a double boiler top set over simmering water. Beat in ¼ cup Lobster Butter, 1 tablespoon at a time. Mix in ¼ cup minced cooked lobster, 2 tablespoons brandy, and, if you like, 2 tablespoons minced truffles. Good over white fish. About 43 calories per tablespoon.

Joinville Sauce (Makes 2½ cups): Prepare Normande Sauce and pour into a double boiler top set over simmering water. Beat in ¼ cup each Lobster Butter and Shrimp Butter, 1 tablespoon at a time. Good with fish. About 43 calories per tablespoon.

Oyster Sauce (Makes about 3 cups): Prepare Normande Sauce and keep warm in a double boiler top set over simmering water. Poach ½ pint small shucked oysters in their liquor over moderately low heat 3–4 minutes until edges ruffle; remove and reserve oysters; boil liquor, uncovered, until reduced to ¼ cup, strain through a cheesecloth-lined sieve, mix into sauce, and heat 2–3 minutes. Mix in oysters and serve with white fish fillets. About 30 calories per tablespoon.

Ravigote Sauce (Makes 2 cups): Prepare Velouté (use mushrooms) and keep warm. Boil ¼ cup each dry white wine and white wine vinegar, uncovered, with 1 teaspoon each minced fresh (or ¼ teaspoon each dried) tarragon and chervil, 1 tablespoon each minced chives and shallots or scallions, and 1 parsley sprig until reduced to ⅓ cup; strain liquid into sauce. Blend in ¼ cup heavy cream and a pinch cayenne pepper. Good with seafood. About 39 calories per tablespoon.

Suprême Sauce (Makes 3 cups): Prepare Velouté, using chicken broth, and keep warm. Boil 1½ cups chicken broth and ¼ pound minced mushrooms, uncovered, about 20 minutes until liquid reduces to ½ cup; strain liquid into sauce and simmer, uncovered, ½ hour, skimming scum from pan's sides as it collects. Slowly blend in 1 cup heavy cream, then serve with poultry, sweetbreads, or brains. About 37 calories per tablespoon.

Albuféra Sauce (Makes 3 cups): Prepare Suprême Sauce (above) using no salt in the Velouté, mix in ⅓ cup Glace de Viande or 2 teaspoons beef extract, then beat in 3 tablespoons Pimiento Butter, 1 tablespoon at a time. Good with sweetbreads or brains. About 44 calories per tablespoon.

Talleyrand Sauce (Makes about 3½ cups): Prepare Velouté with chicken broth, mix in 2 cups chicken broth, and simmer uncovered until sauce reduces to 2 cups. Turn heat to low, mix in ½ cup each heavy cream and dry Madeira; beat in 2 tablespoons butter, one at a time, then strain sauce. Mix in 2 tablespoons each minced truffles, pickled tongue, and 1 tablespoon each butter-sautéed minced onion, celery, and carrot seasoned with a pinch of thyme. About 32 calories per tablespoon.

⊠ ITALIAN CHEESE SAUCE

In Italy, cheese sauce is made with any available cheese and sometimes with a mixture of them. Try ½ cup Parmesan mixed with ¼ cup finely grated, aged provolone or Romano. Serve over pasta, accompanied, if you like, by separate bowls of grated Parmesan and minced Italian parsley. Makes about 2½ cups, enough for 4 servings

¼ cup butter or margarine
2 tablespoons flour
1 cup milk
1 cup light cream
1 clove garlic, peeled, bruised, and stuck on a toothpick
¾ cup finely grated Parmesan cheese
Freshly ground black pepper

Melt butter in a saucepan over moderate heat, blend in flour, slowly stir in milk and cream, add garlic, and heat, stirring constantly, until thickened. Turn heat to low, add cheese, a little at a time, and heat, stirring, until melted. Partially cover and simmer 2–3 minutes. Remove garlic, add a grating of pepper, and serve hot over pasta. (*Note:* If well-aged cheese is used, no salt is needed in this sauce.) About 35 calories per tablespoon. About 355 calories for each of 4 servings.

LIGHT CURRY SAUCE

Makes 2 cups

2 medium-size yellow onions, peeled and minced
1 stalk celery, minced
1 clove garlic, peeled and crushed (optional)
¼ cup butter or margarine
1 tablespoon curry powder
¼ cup unsifted flour
2 cups chicken broth, Veal (White) Stock, or water
1 teaspoon salt
⅛ teaspoon black pepper
Pinch cayenne pepper

Stir-fry onions, celery, and, if you like, garlic in butter in a saucepan over moderate heat 5–8 minutes until limp, not brown. Add curry powder and stir-fry 1 minute. Blend in flour, slowly add broth, salt, pepper, and cayenne pepper, and heat, stirring, until thickened. Cover and simmer ½ hour, stirring now and then.

VARIATION:

Brown Curry Sauce: Prepare as directed but brown flour in the fat.

Substitute beef broth for chicken broth, also stir in 1 tablespoon each tomato paste and lemon juice and ⅛ teaspoon crushed dried hot red chili peppers.

Both versions: About 21 calories per tablespoon.

⚔ LEMON SAUCE

Serve with veal loaf or fish.
Makes 2 cups

- 2 cups Veal (White) Stock, chicken broth, or Easy Fish Stock (depending upon dish to be sauced)
- 2 tablespoons cornstarch mixed with 2 tablespoons cold water
- ¼ cup butter
- 1 egg yolk, lightly beaten with 1 tablespoon cold water
- 3 tablespoons lemon juice
- Salt
- White pepper
- 1 teaspoon minced parsley (optional)

Heat stock, mix in cornstarch, and cook, stirring constantly, until thickened. Add butter and beat to blend. Reduce heat, cover, and simmer 2–3 minutes. Blend a little hot sauce into egg yolk, return to pan, and heat and stir 1–2 minutes; do not boil. Off heat, mix in remaining ingredients, adding salt and pepper to taste. About 18 calories per tablespoon.

✕ SHRIMP SAUCE

Makes about 2 cups

- 2 tablespoons butter or margarine
- 2 tablespoons flour
- 1 cup milk or light cream
- 2 teaspoons tomato paste
- ½ teaspoon salt
- ⅛ teaspoon paprika
- 1 cup coarsely chopped cooked shrimp
- 2 tablespoons dry sherry (optional)

Melt butter in a saucepan over low heat, blend in flour, gradually stir in milk and heat, stirring constantly, until thickened and smooth. Mix in remaining ingredients and cook and stir about 5 minutes to blend flavors. Serve hot as a sauce for poached, baked, or broiled white fish, for seafood soufflés or mousses. About 18 calories per tablespoon if made with milk, 29 calories per tablespoon if made with cream.

CHAUD-FROID SAUCE

Chaud-froid sauce is used to glaze cooked foods that are served cold, usually whole chickens, small game birds, or chicken breasts.
Makes about 2 cups

- 3 tablespoons butter or margarine
- 3 tablespoons flour
- 2 cups clear chicken broth
- 1 envelope unflavored gelatin
- 1 egg yolk, lightly beaten with ¼ cup heavy cream
- Salt
- White pepper

Melt butter over moderate heat, blend in flour, gradually stir in 1½ cups chicken broth, and heat, stirring constantly, until thickened. Mix gelatin and remaining broth, add to sauce, and stir until dissolved. Reduce heat, cover, and simmer 3–4 minutes. Blend a little hot sauce into egg yolk, return to pan, and cook and stir 1–2 minutes; do not boil. Season to taste with salt and pepper, bearing in mind that cold sauces need slightly more seasoning. Place a circle of wax paper flat on sauce and cool to room temperature. Uncover, stir well, and chill until sauce coats the back of a metal spoon thickly but is still of pouring consistency. Use as recipes direct. (*Note:* If sauce becomes too thick, set over a bowl of hot water and stir until sauce thins.) About 23 calories per tablespoon.

VARIATION:

Omit butter, flour, and broth; use instead 1 recipe hot Velouté Sauce and proceed as directed, adding gelatin, egg yolk mixture, and salt and pepper to season. About 33 calories per tablespoon.

BROWN SAUCES AND GRAVIES

⚖ ☒ **PAN GRAVY**

While a roast "rests," make gravy of your choice.
Makes about 2 cups

¼ cup roasting pan drippings (*round out amount as needed with bacon drippings or butter*)
2 cups hot water, vegetable cooking water, or beef broth or any combination of the 3
¼ cup unsifted flour
Liquid gravy browner (*optional*)
Salt
Pepper

Drain drippings from roasting pan and reserve ¼ cup. Pour water into roasting pan and stir, scraping up browned bits (heat, if necessary, to loosen bits). Pour drippings into a large skillet, blend in flour, and cook and stir over moderate heat until light brown. Add water mixture and heat, stirring, until thickened; reduce heat and simmer 3–5 minutes. Add gravy browner to color, if you like, salt and pepper to taste. For a silken gravy, strain through a fine sieve. About 16 calories per tablespoon.

For Thin Gravy: Reduce flour to 2 tablespoons. About 14 calories per tablespoon.

For Thick Gravy: Increase flour to 5–6 tablespoons. About 18 calories per tablespoon.

For Stronger Flavor: Dissolve 1 or 2 beef bouillon cubes in the hot water.

For Extra-Large Roasts: Double the recipe. About 16 calories per tablespoon.

VARIATIONS:

☒ ⚖ **Au Jus Gravy:** Drain all but 1 tablespoon clear drippings from roasting pan, add water, and heat and stir, scraping up browned bits, 2–3 minutes until slightly reduced. If you like, add a touch of gravy browner and/or dry red wine. Season to taste and ladle over each portion. About 3 calories per tablespoon.

⚖ ☒ **Chicken (or Turkey) Gravy:** Prepare as directed using Chicken or Turkey Broth. (*Note:* If turkey is a big one, double the recipe.) About 17 calories per tablespoon.

☒ **Chicken (or Turkey) Cream Gravy:** Prepare as directed using 1½ cups Chicken or Turkey Broth and ½ cup light cream. About 25 calories per tablespoon.

⚖ ☒ **Giblet Gravy:** Prepare as directed using Giblet Stock. Mix in minced cooked giblets and neck meat just before serving. About 17 calories per tablespoon.

⚖ ☒ **Herb Gravy:** Prepare as directed, warming any of the following herbs in drippings before blending in flour: ½ teaspoon savory, thyme, or marjoram (good with beef), 1

SAUCES, GRAVIES, AND BUTTERS

teaspoon tarragon or mint, or ¼ teaspoon rosemary (lamb or veal), ½ teaspoon sage and/or thyme (pork or poultry). About 16 calories per tablespoon.

⚔ **Jus Lié:** Drain all drippings from roasting pan; pour 2 cups hot Veal (White) Stock or chicken broth into pan and heat, stirring, to scrape up browned bits. Stir in 2 tablespoons cornstarch blended with 2 tablespoons cold water and heat and stir until thickened and clear. Season to taste. Good with veal and chicken. About 4 calories per tablespoon.

☒ **Milk Gravy:** Prepare Pan Gravy as directed but use 1 cup each milk and broth. Add no gravy browner. Especially good with poultry. About 21 calories per tablespoon.

Mushroom Gravy: Prepare Pan Gravy and mix in ½ pound thinly sliced mushrooms and 1 minced yellow onion that have been sautéed 3–5 minutes in 2 tablespoons butter. Cover and simmer 4–5 minutes; taste for seasoning and adjust as needed. About 25 calories per tablespoon.

⚔ **Onion Gravy:** Stir-fry 2 thinly sliced medium-size yellow onions in pan drippings 8–10 minutes over moderate heat until golden, blend in flour, and proceed as Pan Gravy recipe directs. About 18 calories per tablespoon.

⚔ ☒ **Quick Mushroom Gravy:** Drain all drippings from roasting pan; pour 1 cup beef broth and 1 (10½-ounce) can condensed cream of mushroom soup into pan and heat and stir about 5 minutes, scraping up browned bits. Mix in 1 (4-ounce) can drained mushroom stems and pieces and 1 teaspoon Worcestershire sauce. About 13 calories per tablespoon.

☒ **Sour Cream Gravy** (Makes 2½ cups): Prepare Pan Gravy as directed, smooth in 1 cup sour cream, and adjust seasonings as needed. Heat briefly but do not allow to boil. About 25 calories per tablespoon.

⚔ ☒ **Wine Gravy:** Make Pan Gravy using 1 cup each dry red wine and beef broth (for beef), 1 cup each rosé and water (for lamb or veal), or 1 cup each dry white wine and chicken broth (for poultry). About 18 calories per tablespoon.

⚔ ☒ **MADEIRA-MUSHROOM SAUCE**

Makes about 1¾ cups

2 tablespoons butter or margarine
½ pound button mushrooms, wiped clean and halved
4 teaspoons flour
1 cup condensed beef broth
1 teaspoon Worcestershire sauce
1 tablespoon minced chives
3 tablespoons sweet Madeira wine

Melt butter in a heavy skillet over moderately high heat, add mushrooms, and sauté 3–4 minutes until golden. Push to side of pan, blend in flour, slowly stir in broth and cook, and stir until thickened. Add remaining ingredients and cook and stir 3–5 minutes. Serve with steaks, London Broil, or sautéed kidneys. About 15 calories per tablespoon.

ESPAGNOLE SAUCE

Serve with broiled meats, poultry, or fish or use as a base for the variations that follow. Makes about 2⅔ cups

4 slices bacon, minced
1 medium-size yellow onion, peeled and minced
1 medium-size carrot, peeled and minced
1 stalk celery, minced

6 tablespoons butter (*no substitute*)
6 tablespoons flour
5 cups beef broth or Easy Fish Stock (depending upon whether sauce is for meat or seafood)
Pinch minced fresh or dried thyme
½ bay leaf
¼ cup tomato purée

Stir-fry bacon over moderate heat 3-4 minutes until crisp; drain on paper toweling. Sauté onion, carrot, and celery in drippings 8-10 minutes until golden; drain on paper toweling. Melt butter in a saucepan over moderate heat, blend in flour, then cook and stir 1-2 minutes until lightly browned. Gradually mix in broth and cook, stirring constantly, until slightly thickened. Add bacon, sautéed vegetables, and herbs. Reduce heat and boil, uncovered, very slowly ½ hour, skimming light scum from pan sides as it collects. Strain sauce through a fine sieve into a clean saucepan, pressing vegetables lightly to extract juices. Mix in tomato purée, set lid on askew, and simmer 20-30 minutes until sauce coats a metal spoon. Skim or blot off any fat, then serve hot. About 28 calories per tablespoon.

VARIATIONS:

Bigarade (Orange) Sauce (Makes about 1 quart): Prepare Espagnole with beef broth and keep warm. Add 1 cup dry white wine to pan drippings from roast duck or goose, heat, and stir, scraping up brown bits, then boil uncovered until reduced to ½ cup. Strain, skim off fat, and mix into sauce along with 1 cup orange juice and 1 tablespoon lemon juice. Boil ½ cup sugar and ½ cup water 15 minutes until amber colored and blend into sauce. Also boil finely slivered rind (orange part only) of 4 oranges in 1 cup water 3-4 minutes; drain rind, then add rind to sauce. If you like, add 2 tablespoons curaçao. Serve with roast duck or goose. About 29 calories per tablespoon.

Diable Sauce (Makes about 3½ cups): Prepare Espagnole with beef broth and keep warm. Boil 1 cup red or white wine vinegar, uncovered, with 2 tablespoons minced shallots or scallions until reduced to ½ cup. Mix into sauce along with 2 tablespoons each Worcestershire and tomato purée and ¼ teaspoon cayenne. Good with broiled poultry, also sweetbreads, brains, and tongue. About 23 calories per tablespoon.

Piquante Sauce: (Makes about 1 quart): Prepare Diable and mix in ¼ cup minced gherkins and 2 tablespoons minced parsley. Good with liver, tongue, and tripe. About 20 calories per tablespoon.

Poivrade (Pepper) Sauce (Makes about 3½ cups): Prepare Espagnole with beef broth and keep warm. Boil ¾ cup dry white wine with ¾ cup white wine vinegar until reduced by half; mix into sauce along with 6-8 crushed peppercorns, ½ bay leaf, and a pinch fresh or dried thyme. Cover and simmer 5 minutes, strain through a cheesecloth-lined sieve, and serve with broiled steaks or chops. About 21 calories per tablespoon.

Chevreuil (Roebuck) Sauce (Makes about 1 quart): Prepare Poivrade, add ½ cup dry red wine and a good pinch cayenne; simmer, uncovered, 10 minutes. Good with meat and game. About 19 calories per tablespoon.

Grand Veneur Sauce (Makes about 1 quart): Prepare Poivrade, stir in ¾ cup gooseberry jelly or strained gooseberry jam, and simmer uncovered 10 minutes. If you like, mix in ⅓ cup heavy cream. Serve with venison. About 36 calories per tablespoon without heavy cream, 41 calories per tablespoon with heavy cream.

Réforme (Reform) Sauce (Makes about 1 quart): Prepare Poivrade and keep warm. Sauté ¼ pound minced mushrooms in 2 tablespoons butter 3–4 minutes, then add to sauce along with ¼ cup diced cooked smoked tongue, 2 tablespoons minced gherkins, and 2 minced truffles. Simmer, uncovered, 5 minutes, mix in 2 minced hard-cooked egg whites, and serve with lamb or mutton chops. About 25 calories per tablespoon.

Rich Brown Sauce (Demi-Glace): See separate recipe that follows.

Victoria Sauce (Makes about 1 quart): Prepare Espagnole with beef broth, add 1½ cups tawny port wine, ⅓ cup red currant jelly, 3 cloves, ¼ teaspoon pepper, and 2 tablespoons finely grated orange rind. Boil slowly, uncovered, stirring now and then, until reduced to about 3½ cups. Remove cloves, mix in ⅓ cup orange juice and ⅛ teaspoon cayenne. Serve with roast poultry, game, or game birds. About 27 calories per tablespoon.

Yorkshire Sauce (Makes about 3 cups): Prepare ½ recipe Espagnole and keep warm. Simmer 2 cups tawny port wine, uncovered, with 2 tablespoons finely slivered orange rind 10 minutes; mix into sauce along with 2 tablespoons red currant jelly, ¼ cup orange juice, and a good pinch cinnamon and cayenne pepper. Simmer, uncovered, 5 minutes. Good with ham or roast duck. About 26 calories per tablespoon.

RICH BROWN SAUCE (DEMI-GLACE, OR HALF GLAZE)

Makes 3¼ cups

1 recipe Espagnole Sauce
1 cup beef broth or Easy Fish Stock *(depending upon whether sauce is to be used with meat or fish)*
¼ cup dry Madeira or sherry

Mix Espagnole and broth and boil slowly, uncovered, until reduced to 3 cups (sauce should coat a metal spoon). Mix in wine and serve or use as a base for other sauces. About 25 calories per tablespoon.

VARIATIONS:

Bordelaise Sauce (Makes about 1 quart): Prepare Rich Brown Sauce and keep warm. Boil 2 cups dry red wine, uncovered, with 2 tablespoons minced shallots or scallions, a small sprig fresh thyme (or ¼ teaspoon dried thyme), and 1 small bay leaf until reduced to 1⅓ cups. Strain wine into sauce and simmer, uncovered, until reduced to 1 quart. Mix in ½ cup minced marrow from Marrowbones and 1 tablespoon minced parsley. Adjust salt, if needed, and serve with broiled or roasted meat, poultry, or game. About 25 calories per tablespoon.

Rouennaise Sauce (Makes 1 cup): Mince 1 raw duck liver (or 2 chicken livers) and mix with 1 cup Bordelaise. Add a pinch allspice and simmer, uncovered, ½ hour. Strain and serve with duck. About 31 calories per tablespoon.

Bourguignonne (Burgundy) Sauce (Makes about 1 quart): Prepare Rich Brown Sauce and keep warm. Stir-fry ¼ cup minced yellow onion in 2 tablespoons butter 3–5 minutes over moderate heat until limp, add 3 cups red Burgundy and 1 *bouquet garni** tied in cheesecloth and boil, uncovered, until reduced by half. Stir into sauce, reduce to about 1 quart, strain, season to taste with salt and pepper, and serve with roasts, steaks, chops, or fish. (*Note:* For extra flavor, reduce wine in pan meat was cooked in.) About 30 calories per tablespoon.

Brown Sauce Fines Herbes (Makes 1 cup): Mix 1 cup Rich Brown Sauce with ¼ teaspoon lemon juice and 1 tablespoon each minced fresh (or 1 teaspoon each dried) parsley, tarragon, and chervil; let stand about a minute to blend flavors. Serve with broiled meats or poultry, baked or poached fish. About 25 calories per tablespoon.

Charcutière Sauce (Makes about 1 quart): Prepare Rich Brown Sauce with beef broth and keep warm. Stir-fry ⅓ cup minced yellow onion in 2 tablespoons butter 5–8 minutes over moderate heat until pale golden; mix into sauce along with ⅓ cup minced gherkins and serve with pork. About 24 calories per tablespoon.

Chasseur Sauce (Makes about 3 cups): Prepare ½ recipe Rich Brown Sauce with beef broth and keep warm. Sauté ½ pound minced mushrooms in 2 tablespoons each olive oil and butter over moderate heat 2–3 minutes until pale golden; add 2 tablespoons minced shallots and sauté 2 minutes. Add 1 cup dry white wine and boil until reduced by half. Mix into sauce along with 1 cup hot Tomato Sauce and 1 tablespoon each minced fresh (or 1 teaspoon each dried) parsley, tarragon, and chervil. Adjust salt as needed and serve with roasts, steaks or chops, poultry or game. About 26 calories per tablespoon.

Chateaubriand Sauce (Makes about 1 quart): Prepare Rich Brown Sauce with beef broth and keep warm. Boil 2 cups dry white wine with 2 tablespoons minced shallots or scallions, a small sprig fresh thyme (or ¼ teaspoon dried thyme), and ½ bay leaf until reduced to 1⅓ cups; strain into sauce and boil until reduced to 1 quart. Stir in 2 tablespoons minced fresh (or 1½ teaspoons dried) tarragon, 1 tablespoon lemon juice, ¼ teaspoon salt, and ⅛ teaspoon cayenne. Serve with chateaubriand or other broiled steak. About 19 calories per tablespoon.

Duxelles Sauce (Makes about 5 cups): Prepare Rich Brown Sauce and keep warm. Sauté ½ pound minced mushrooms, 1 minced small yellow onion, and 2 minced shallots or scallions in 3 tablespoons butter 5 minutes over moderate heat until limp; add 1 cup dry white wine, ½ teaspoon salt, and ⅛ teaspoon each pepper and nutmeg and boil, uncovered, until liquid is reduced to ½ cup. Stir into sauce along with 1 cup tomato purée and 2 tablespoons minced parsley and simmer 5 minutes. Good with meat or game fish. About 22 calories per tablespoon.

Italienne (Italian) Sauce (Makes about 5 cups): Prepare Duxelles, mix in ⅓ cup minced lean cooked ham and 2 tablespoons each minced fresh (or 2 teaspoons each dried) tarragon and chervil. Serve with brains, sweetbreads, or liver. About 24 calories per tablespoon.

Lyonnaise Sauce (Makes about 3½ cups): Prepare Rich Brown Sauce with beef broth and keep warm. Stir-fry 2 minced large yellow onions in 2 tablespoons butter 8–10 minutes over moderate heat until golden. Stir into sauce along with ⅓ cup dry white wine, 3 tablespoons white or red wine vinegar, and, if you like, 2 tablespoons tomato paste. Simmer, uncovered, ½ hour. Serve with steaks and chops. About 28 calories per tablespoon.

Madeira Sauce (Makes 1¼ cups): Simmer 1 cup Rich Brown Sauce with ¼ cup dry Madeira wine 2–3 minutes. Good with broiled poultry or steaks, ham, sweetbreads, brains, heart, or kidneys. About 28 calories per tablespoon.

Financière Sauce (Makes 1¼ cups): Prepare Madeira Sauce and mix in 2 tablespoons minced truffles. Serve with sweetbreads or brains. About 28 calories per tablespoon.

Port Wine Sauce (Makes 1¼ cups): Prepare like Madeira Sauce but use tawny port wine instead of Madeira. Good with ham. About 28 calories per tablespoon.

Raisin Sauce (Makes 1½ cups): Prepare Madeira or Port Wine Sauce as directed and mix in ¼–⅓ cup seedless raisins; simmer slowly about 10 minutes to plump raisins. Good with ham and tongue. About 35 calories per tablespoon.

Marchands de Vin Sauce (Makes about 1 quart): Prepare Rich Brown Sauce with beef broth and keep warm. Stir-fry 2 minced bunches scallions (white part) and ½ pound minced mushrooms in ⅓ cup butter 3–4 minutes over moderate heat; add 1½ cups dry red wine and boil, uncovered, until reduced by half. Stir into sauce along with 1 tablespoon lemon juice. Good with steaks. About 31 calories per tablespoon.

Périgueux Sauce (Makes 1 cup): Mix 2 tablespoons minced truffles into 1 cup Rich Brown Sauce. Good with steak, game, and game birds. About 25 calories per tablespoon.

Périgourdine Sauce (Makes 1 cup): Mix 2 thinly sliced truffles into 1 cup Rich Brown Sauce. Good with steak, game, and game birds. About 25 calories per tablespoon.

Régence (Regency) Sauce (Makes about 1 quart): Prepare Rich Brown Sauce with beef broth and keep warm. Stir-fry 1 cup minced lean cooked ham and 2 peeled and quartered yellow onions in 2 tablespoons butter 5 minutes over moderate heat until onions are pale golden. Add 1 cup chicken broth and ½ cup dry white wine, cover, and simmer until onions are mushy, about ¾ hour. Uncover and boil until liquid reduces to about 1 cup, then purée at low speed in an electric blender or put through a food mill. Mix into sauce and simmer 5 minutes. Good with brains and sweetbreads. About 29 calories per tablespoon.

Robert Sauce (Makes about 1 quart): Prepare Rich Brown Sauce with beef broth and keep warm. Sauté 1 minced large yellow onion in 2 tablespoons butter 5–8 minutes over moderate heat until pale golden, add 1 cup dry white wine and boil, uncovered, until reduced to ½ cup. Stir into sauce along with ¼ teaspoon sugar and 1½ teaspoons powdered mustard blended with 1 teaspoon cold water. Simmer, uncovered, 20 minutes and serve with pork or ham, veal chops, sweetbreads, or brains. About 24 calories per tablespoon.

Romaine Sauce (Makes about 1 quart): Prepare Rich Brown Sauce with beef broth and keep warm. Boil ¼ cup sugar with ¼ cup water, uncovered, 8–10 minutes until amber colored. Off heat, stir in 2 tablespoons white wine vinegar and ½ cup chicken broth; boil until reduced to ½ cup, add ¼ cup toasted piñon nuts and 2 tablespoons each dried currants and seedless raisins, cover, and simmer 10 minutes. Stir into sauce and serve with game, lamb chops, or steaks. About 28 calories per tablespoon.

Tarragon Sauce (Makes about 3½ cups): Prepare Rich Brown Sauce with beef broth and keep warm. Boil 1 cup dry white wine, uncovered, with 3 tablespoons minced fresh (or 2 teaspoons dried) tarragon until reduced to ¼ cup. Mix into sauce, simmer uncovered 5 minutes, then strain and mix in 1–2 tablespoons minced fresh tarragon. Good with roast veal. About 25 calories per tablespoon.

Tortue Sauce (Makes about 1 quart): Prepare Rich Brown Sauce with beef broth and keep warm. Simmer 1 cup dry white wine, uncovered, with 2 sprigs fresh thyme (or ¼ teaspoon dried thyme), ½ bay leaf, 1 sprig each parsley, fresh sage, and rosemary (or ¼ teaspoon of the dried), 3 fresh basil leaves (or ¼ teaspoon dried basil) 15–20 minutes; strain liquid into sauce, add ¼ cup minced mushrooms, ½ cup tomato purée, ½ cup Veal (White) Stock, and simmer uncovered until reduced to 1 quart. Mix in ¼ cup dry Madeira and ⅛ teaspoon each allspice and cayenne. Serve with kidneys or tongue. About 22 calories per tablespoon.

Zingara Sauce (Makes about 1 quart): Prepare Rich Brown Sauce with beef broth, mix in ½ cup tomato purée, 2 tablespoons each julienne strips cooked ham and boiled tongue, minced mushrooms and truffles, and 1 teaspoon paprika. Good with roast veal. About 23 calories per tablespoon.

⚖ ▒ **GLACE DE VIANDE**

Never salt a sauce until after *glace de viande* is added; then taste and salt as needed. Use sparingly to add flavor to sauces, soups, and gravies. Makes ⅓ cup

1 cup Brown Beef Stock or canned condensed beef broth

Boil stock, uncovered, over high heat until reduced to ⅓ cup. (*Note:* A similar flavor can be obtained by dissolving 1 tablespoon beef extract in ¼ cup cold water.) About 6 calories per tablespoon.

COLBERT SAUCE

Makes about 1 cup

¼ cup Glace de Viande or 1 tablespoon beef extract
1 tablespoon hot water
½ cup butter, softened to room temperature (no substitute)
2 tablespoons lemon juice
1 tablespoon minced parsley
Pinch nutmeg
Pinch cayenne pepper
2 tablespoons dry Madeira wine

Heat *glace de viande* with hot water in a small saucepan. Slowly beat in butter, 1 tablespoon at a time, then mix in remaining ingredients. Drizzle sparingly over broiled meat or fish. About 55 calories per tablespoon.

⚖ ▒ **SHALLOT SAUCE**

Makes about ¾ cup

3 tablespoons minced shallots
2 tablespoons butter or drippings from broiled or panfried steak
½ cup beef broth
2 tablespoons dry red wine or red wine vinegar
1 teaspoon minced parsley (optional)

Sauté shallots in butter (preferably in pan steak was cooked in) over moderate heat 3–5 minutes until limp. Add remaining ingredients,

SAUCES, GRAVIES, AND BUTTERS

heat, stirring, to boiling, then pour over steaks. About 15 calories per tablespoon.

⚜ GARLIC SAUCE

Makes about 2 cups

1 cup beef broth
1 cup water
1 clove garlic, peeled and bruised
1 medium-size yellow onion, peeled and minced
1 bay leaf
2 tablespoons minced celery leaves
¼ teaspoon salt (about)
⅛ teaspoon pepper
¼ cup heavy cream
3 thin slices lemon

Simmer all but last 2 ingredients, covered, 20 minutes, then strain into a clean saucepan. Add cream and heat over lowest heat 3–5 minutes; taste for salt and pepper and adjust. Serve hot with lemon slices floating on top. Good with roast lamb or veal. About 10 calories per tablespoon.

HERB SAUCE

Delicious with steaks and chops.
Makes 2 cups

2 cups beef broth
4 scallions, peeled and minced
1 tablespoon minced chives
¼ teaspoon each marjoram, thyme, savory, sage, and basil
⅛ teaspoon nutmeg
⅛ teaspoon pepper
¼ cup butter or margarine
¼ cup unsifted flour
¼ teaspoon salt (about)
1 tablespoon lemon juice
1 teaspoon minced fresh tarragon or ¼ teaspoon dried tarragon
1 teaspoon minced fresh chervil or ¼ teaspoon dried chervil

Simmer broth, scallions, chives, herbs, nutmeg, and pepper covered 15 minutes; strain broth through a cheesecloth-lined sieve and reserve. Melt butter in a saucepan over moderate heat, blend in flour, and cook and stir 1–2 minutes until light brown. Slowly mix in reserved broth and heat, stirring, until thickened. Lower heat and simmer 5 minutes. Mix in salt, lemon juice, tarragon, and chervil and serve. About 20 calories per tablespoon.

HOLLANDAISE AND OTHER EGG-THICKENED SAUCES

HOLLANDAISE SAUCE

If you remember one basic rule—that too much heat will curdle an egg-thickened sauce—you should have little difficulty making Hollandaise. Cook over *simmering*, not boiling, water, take from the heat the minute sauce thickens, and remember that all is not lost if the sauce does curdle. It can be rescued. Hollandaise should be served warm, not hot, not cold.

Makes about 1⅓ cups

4 egg yolks
1 tablespoon cold water
½ cup butter, softened to room temperature (no substitute)
¼ teaspoon salt
Pinch white pepper
1–2 tablespoons lemon juice

Beat yolks until thick and lemon colored, mix in water and transfer to the top of a double boiler set over barely simmering water. Heat and stir 2–3 minutes until warm, not hot.

Add butter, 2 tablespoons at a time, stirring continuously and not adding more butter until previous addition is well blended in. When all butter is in, cook and stir 2–3 minutes until sauce thickens enough to coat the back of a metal spoon. Set double boiler top on counter, mix in salt, pepper, and lemon juice and stir 1–2 minutes. Serve with vegetables or seafood. About 50 calories per tablespoon.

To Salvage Curdled Hollandaise: Add 2 tablespoons boiling water and beat vigorously until smooth. Or set pan in an ice bath, beat hard until smooth, then warm very gently over just simmering water, stirring constantly.

To Make Hollandaise Ahead of Time: Prepare as directed, then transfer to a small bowl; place a circle of wax paper flat on sauce to prevent a skin from forming. About 15 minutes before serving, set bowl of sauce in very hot—not boiling—water and stir now and then as sauce warms; replenish hot water as needed. If sauce seems thick, beat in 1–2 tablespoons hot water.

VARIATIONS:

Béarnaise Sauce (Makes about 1⅓ cups): Before beginning sauce, boil ¼ cup dry white wine, uncovered, with ¼ cup white wine vinegar, 1 tablespoon each minced fresh (or 1 teaspoon each dried) tarragon and chervil, 1 tablespoon minced shallots or scallions (white part), ⅛ teaspoon salt, and a pinch white pepper until liquid reduces to 2 tablespoons; strain liquid and cool to room temperature. Prepare Hollandaise as directed, substituting reduced liquid for lemon juice. Just before serving, mix in ½ teaspoon each minced fresh tarragon and chervil and a pinch cayenne. Good with broiled meats. About 50 calories per tablespoon.

Choron Sauce (Makes about 1⅓ cups): Prepare Béarnaise and blend in 2 tablespoons tomato paste. Good with steak. About 51 calories per tablespoon.

Paloise Sauce (Makes about 1⅓ cups): Prepare Béarnaise as directed but substitute 2 tablespoons minced fresh mint for the tarragon and chervil in the vinegar mixture; also mix in 1 teaspoon minced mint instead of tarragon and chervil at the end. Good with roast veal or lamb. About 50 calories per tablespoon.

Mousseline (Chantilly) Sauce (Makes 2 cups): Prepare Hollandaise, then fold in ½ cup heavy cream beaten to soft peaks. Add extra salt and pepper if needed. Good with seafood and vegetables. About 69 calories per tablespoon.

Figaro Sauce (Makes 1⅔ cups): Prepare Hollandaise, blend in ⅓ cup tomato purée and 1 tablespoon minced parsley, and heat and stir over barely simmering water 2–3 minutes. Good with seafood. About 51 calories per tablespoon.

Maltaise (Maltese) Sauce (Makes 1⅔ cups): Prepare Hollandaise, then blend in the juice of 1 orange, heated to lukewarm, and ¼ teaspoon finely grated orange rind. Good with boiled vegetables, especially asparagus, green beans, and broccoli. About 51 calories per tablespoon.

Mustard Hollandaise (Makes about 1⅓ cups): Prepare Hollandaise as directed but blend ½ teaspoon powdered mustard with lemon juice before adding to sauce. Good with boiled vegetables and fish. About 50 calories per tablespoon.

SAUCES, GRAVIES, AND BUTTERS

BLENDER HOLLANDAISE

Quicker and easier than old-fashioned Hollandaise.
Makes about 1⅓ cups

4 egg yolks
2 tablespoons lemon juice
¼ teaspoon salt
Pinch white pepper
½ cup hot melted butter

Blend yolks, lemon juice, salt, and pepper in an electric blender at high speed ½ minute; uncover and continue blending at high speed, at the same time adding butter drop by drop. As mixture thickens, add butter in a thin slow stream. When about half the butter is in, you can pour a little faster. Continue blending until thick and satiny, then serve. About 50 calories per tablespoon.

VARIATIONS:

Blender Béarnaise: Prepare reduced vinegar-herb mixture as for regular Béarnaise, then prepare recipe above, substituting vinegar mixture for lemon juice. Just before serving, mix in ½ teaspoon each minced fresh tarragon and chervil. About 50 calories per tablespoon.

Note: Any of the variations on standard Hollandaise can be made with the blender variety.

AVGOLEMONO SAUCE

A favorite Greek sauce, thickened with egg and lightly flavored with lemon. Serve with asparagus, broccoli, or globe artichokes. Also good with roast veal.
Makes 1½ cups

1¼ cups chicken broth
Pinch nutmeg
3 egg yolks, lightly beaten
3–4 tablespoons lemon juice
Salt
Pepper

Heat broth and nutmeg in the top of a double boiler over simmering water. Blend about ½ cup broth into egg yolks, return to pan, and cook, stirring constantly, until thickened. Off heat, mix in lemon juice, 1 tablespoon at a time; season to taste with salt and pepper. About 10 calories per tablespoon.

BATARDE SAUCE

An imitation Hollandaise, less caloric than the real thing.
Makes about 1⅔ cups

2 tablespoons butter (no substitute)
2 tablespoons flour
1¼ cups water, vegetable cooking water or Easy Fish Stock (depending upon dish to be sauced)
1 egg yolk, lightly beaten with 1 tablespoon cold water
⅓ cup butter, softened to room temperature
½ teaspoon salt
⅛ teaspoon white pepper
1–2 tablespoons lemon juice

Melt butter over moderate heat, blend in flour, gradually mix in water, and cook, stirring, until thickened. Blend ¼ cup hot sauce into egg yolk, return to pan, and cook and stir over lowest heat 2 minutes until no raw taste of egg remains; do not boil. Off heat, beat in softened butter, 1 tablespoon at a time. Season with salt, pepper, and lemon juice. Serve warm—not hot—with fish or vegetables. About 32 calories per tablespoon.

MAYONNAISE SAUCES

Note: Other mayonnaise sauces can be found in the chapter on salads and salad dressings.

⊠ SOME EASY MAYONNAISE SAUCES

To make any of the following sauces of pouring consistency, use ½ cup milk or cream and ½ cup mayonnaise instead of 1 cup mayonnaise. The cold mayonnaises will be more flavorful if allowed to stand 15–20 minutes at room temperature before serving.

Aioli Sauce (Makes 1 cup): Blend 1 cup mayonnaise with 4 crushed garlic cloves and a pinch each sugar and cayenne. Serve slightly chilled or at room temperature with hot or cold seafood or meat, cold poultry or vegetables. Also good floated on Gazpacho. About 110 calories per tablespoon.

Anchovy Mayonnaise (Makes 1 cup): Blend 1 cup mayonnaise with 7–8 minced anchovies (or 2 tablespoons anchovy paste) and ½ crushed clove garlic. Let mellow 1 hour before serving. (*Note:* If preparing homemade mayonnaise, omit salt.) Serve with cold seafood. About 115 calories per tablespoon.

Andalouse Mayonnaise (Makes 1½ cups): Blend 1 cup mayonnaise with ⅓ cup tomato purée, 2 diced pimientos, and ½ crushed clove garlic. Good with cold meat or fish. About 75 calories per tablespoon.

Applesauce Mayonnaise (Makes 2 cups): Blend 1 cup each mayonnaise and applesauce, season with ⅛ teaspoon each cinnamon and nutmeg, and serve with cold pork, ham, or tongue. About 60 calories per tablespoon.

Avocado Mayonnaise (Makes 1½ cups): Blend 1 cup mayonnaise with 1 puréed ripe avocado, 1 minced pimiento, 1 tablespoon lemon juice, and salt to taste. Good with cold shellfish. About 90 calories per tablespoon.

Buttermilk Mayonnaise (Makes 1½ cups): Blend 1 cup mayonnaise, ½ cup buttermilk, 2 tablespoons minced chives, and a few drops liquid hot red pepper seasoning. Serve over cold vegetables. About 75 calories per tablespoon.

Caviar Mayonnaise (Makes 1 cup): Mix ¼ cup red or black caviar into 1 cup mayonnaise. (*Note:* Reduce salt if preparing homemade mayonnaise.) Serve with seafood. About 120 calories per tablespoon.

Chutney Mayonnaise (Makes 1¼ cups): Mix 1 cup mayonnaise with ¼ cup minced chutney. Serve with cold meat or poultry. About 100 calories per tablespoon.

Cranberry Mayonnaise (Makes 1½ cups): Mix 1 cup mayonnaise with ½ cup whole or jellied cranberry sauce and 1 teaspoon finely grated orange rind. Serve with cold pork, ham, or poultry. About 75 calories per tablespoon.

Dill Mayonnaise (Makes 1 cup): Blend 1 cup mayonnaise with 1–2 tablespoons minced fresh dill. Serve with seafood. About 110 calories per tablespoon.

French Mayonnaise (Makes 1⅓ cups): Blend 1 cup mayonnaise with ⅓ cup French dressing, 1 teaspoon finely grated onion, and ½ crushed clove garlic. Heat and stir over lowest heat 2–3 minutes; do not boil. Serve over broccoli, asparagus, or green beans. About 100 calories per tablespoon.

Grenache Mayonnaise (Makes 1¾ cups): Blend 1 cup mayonnaise with ½ cup warm red currant jelly and 2 tablespoons each prepared horseradish and Madeira wine. Chill and serve with cold meat, poultry, or

SAUCES, GRAVIES, AND BUTTERS

game. About 85 calories per tablespoon.

Herb Mayonnaise (Makes 1 cup): Blend 1 cup mayonnaise with 1 teaspoon each minced fresh tarragon, chervil, chives, and parsley. Serve with seafood or cold meat or poultry. About 110 calories per tablespoon.

Mint Mayonnaise (Makes 1 cup): Blend 1 cup mayonnaise with 2–3 teaspoons minced fresh mint or ¼ cup mint jelly. Serve with cold lamb or veal. About 110 calories per tablespoon made with fresh mint, 115 calories made with mint jelly.

Perfection Mayonnaise (Makes 1¾ cups): Blend 1 cup mayonnaise with ½ cup sour cream and 2 tablespoons each ketchup, steak sauce, tarragon vinegar, and minced parsley. Serve with seafood. About 75 calories per tablespoon.

Pimiento and Olive Mayonnaise (Makes 1½ cups): Mix 1 cup mayonnaise with ½ cup minced pimiento-stuffed green olives or ¼ cup each minced pimiento and pitted ripe olives. Serve with cold meat or seafood. About 75 calories per tablespoon.

Quick Lemon-Caper Sauce (Makes 1½ cups): Mix 1 cup mayonnaise with 3 tablespoons lemon juice and 2 tablespoons each minced capers and parsley. Serve with seafood. About 75 calories per tablespoon.

Mustard Mayonnaise Sauce (Makes 1¼ cups): Blend 1 cup mayonnaise with ¼ cup milk, 3 tablespoons prepared spicy brown mustard, and 1 tablespoon cider vinegar. Warm 2–3 minutes, stirring, over lowest heat; do not boil. Serve with ham, pork, tongue, boiled beef, or poached chicken. Also good with hot green vegetables. About 90 calories per tablespoon.

Shellfish Cocktail Mayonnaise (Makes 1¼ cups): Mix 1 cup mayonnaise with ¼ cup each chili sauce and minced mustard pickles and 1 tablespoon each cider vinegar and Worcestershire sauce. Serve with shellfish. About 100 calories per tablespoon.

Tuna Mayonnaise (See Vitello Tonnato).

Vincent Sauce (Makes 1½ cups): Mix 1 cup mayonnaise with 2 tablespoons each minced chives, parsley, and watercress, 1 minced hard-cooked egg, and 1 teaspoon Worcestershire sauce. Serve with cold meat or seafood. About 80 calories per tablespoon.

Watercress Mayonnaise (Makes 1¼ cups): Mix 1 cup mayonnaise with ¼ cup minced watercress leaves and 2 tablespoons minced scallions. Serve with cold poultry or seafood. About 80 calories per tablespoon.

☒ MOCK HOLLANDAISE SAUCE

A good quick substitute for real Hollandaise.
Makes about 1½ cups

¼ *cup butter or margarine*
Juice of ½ *lemon*
1¼ cups mayonnaise

Melt butter in a small saucepan over low heat. Beat in lemon juice and mayonnaise, then heat and beat about 2 minutes. Serve as a sauce for broccoli, cauliflower, asparagus, or globe artichokes. About 110 calories per tablespoon.

TARTAR SAUCE I

Nice and tart.
Makes about 1¼ cups

1 cup mayonnaise
3 shallots, peeled and minced, or 3 scallions, minced

1 tablespoon minced parsley
1 tablespoon minced fresh tarragon
¼ cup minced gherkins or dill pickle
2 tablespoons capers
1 teaspoon prepared Dijon-style mustard
½ teaspoon sugar
2 tablespoons red wine vinegar

Mix all ingredients, cover, and chill 2–3 hours. Serve with any seafood. (*Note:* If sauce seems thick, thin with red wine vinegar.) About 90 calories per tablespoon.

TARTAR SAUCE II

Olives give this version special character.
Makes about 1 cup

1 cup mayonnaise
1 tablespoon drained sweet pickle relish
1 tablespoon minced green olives
1 tablespoon minced parsley
1 tablespoon minced scallion
2 teaspoons drained, minced capers
1 teaspoon prepared Dijon-style mustard

Mix all ingredients and let stand at room temperature 10–15 minutes. Serve with any seafood. About 113 calories per tablespoon.

HORSERADISH CREAM SAUCE

Makes about 1 cup

½ cup heavy cream
½ cup mayonnaise or mayonnaise-type salad dressing
2 tablespoons prepared horseradish
1–2 tablespoons lemon juice
1 tablespoon finely grated lemon rind
Pinch cayenne pepper

Gradually beat cream into mayonnaise and, when smooth, stir in remaining ingredients. Chill ½ hour and serve with cold roast beef, ham, tongue, or poultry. About 80 calories per tablespoon.

VARIATION:

Whipped Horseradish Sauce: Beat cream to soft peaks, omit mayonnaise, and fold in remaining ingredients; season to taste with salt and pepper. About 30 calories per tablespoon.

TAPENADE

Makes about 1½ cups

1 cup mayonnaise
1 (2-ounce) can anchovy fillets, drained and minced
⅓ cup capers, minced
1 clove garlic, peeled and crushed
1 teaspoon finely grated lemon rind
1 tablespoon minced parsley

Mix all ingredients, cover, and chill 1–2 hours. Serve as a dunk for chilled raw vegetables. About 75 calories per tablespoon.

OIL AND VINEGAR SAUCES

Note: Other oil and vinegar sauces can be found in the chapter on salads and salad dressings.

DIJONNAISE SAUCE

Makes ¾ cup

2 hard-cooked eggs, shelled
½ cup olive or other cooking oil
2 tablespoons white or red wine vinegar
1–2 tablespoons Dijon mustard
¼ teaspoon salt
⅛ teaspoon white pepper

Press egg yolks through a fine sieve (save whites for sandwiches or salads). Beat in ¼ cup oil, drop by drop; beat in 1 tablespoon vinegar. Add remaining oil in a fine steady stream, beating vigorously all the while. (*Note:* If mixture curdles, beat in 1–2 tablespoons boiling water.) Mix in mustard, salt, and pepper. Serve with steak or ham. About 100 calories per tablespoon.

GRIBICHE SAUCE

A rich tartar-like sauce that is superb with cold fish or shellfish.

Makes 1 cup

2 *hard-cooked eggs, shelled*
½ *cup olive or other cooking oil*
2 *tablespoons white vinegar*
2 *tablespoons minced gherkins*
2 *tablespoons minced capers*
1 *tablespoon minced parsley*
1 *teaspoon minced fresh chervil or*
 ¼ *teaspoon dried chervil*
1 *teaspoon minced fresh tarragon or*
 ¼ *teaspoon dried tarragon*
¼ *teaspoon salt*

Press egg yolks through a fine sieve and beat in ¼ cup oil, drop by drop. Beat in 1 tablespoon vinegar, then add remaining oil in a fine, steady stream, beating vigorously all the while. (*Note:* If mixture curdles, beat in 1–2 tablespoons boiling water.) Add remaining vinegar along with other ingredients and the finely chopped egg whites. Chill slightly before serving. About 75 calories per tablespoon.

COLD RAVIGOTE SAUCE

Makes about 1⅓ cups

¾ *cup olive or other cooking oil*
¼ *cup white or red wine vinegar*
¼ *teaspoon salt*
⅛ *teaspoon pepper*
2 *tablespoons minced capers*
2 *tablespoons minced yellow onion*
2 *tablespoons minced chives*
1 *tablespoon minced parsley*
1 *teaspoon minced fresh tarragon or*
 ¼ *teaspoon dried tarragon*
1 *teaspoon minced fresh chervil or*
 ¼ *teaspoon dried chervil*

Beat oil, vinegar, salt, and pepper until slightly thickened. Mix in remaining ingredients and let stand at room temperature ½ hour. Beat lightly with a fork and use to dress seafood or chicken salad. About 70 calories per tablespoon.

GREEN SAUCE (SALSA VERDE)

Makes about 1 cup

¼ *cup red or white wine vinegar*
¼ *teaspoon salt*
⅛ *teaspoon white pepper*
¼ *teaspoon powdered mustard*
1 *tablespoon minced parsley*
1 *tablespoon minced chives*
1 *tablespoon minced watercress or spinach*
2 *shallots, peeled and minced, or 2 scallions, minced (include tops)*
¾ *cup olive oil*

Mix vinegar, salt, pepper, and mustard in a bowl with a fork. Mix in parsley, chives, watercress, and shallots. Add oil and beat vigorously until blended and slightly thickened. Chill slightly and beat again before serving. Good with Bollito Misto, boiled beef, or boiled tongue. About 88 calories per tablespoon.

⊠ SOME EASY SOUR CREAM SAUCES

All but the first sauce can be served hot or cold. For best results, bring sour cream to room temperature before mixing sauce. Heat gently, preferably in the top of a double boiler so sour cream doesn't curdle. As a general rule, serve hot with hot food, cold with cold food.

Sour Cream-Almond Sauce (Makes 1¼ cups): Mix ¼ cup minced toasted almonds (or piñon, pistachio, or peanuts) with 1 cup sour cream; salt to taste. Good with baked potatoes and broiled fish. About 35 calories per tablespoon.

Sour Cream-Anchovy Sauce (Makes 1¼ cups): Blend 1 cup sour cream with 3 tablespoons each milk and anchovy paste and 1 tablespoon lemon juice. Serve with fish. About 30 calories per tablespoon.

Sour Cream-Bacon Sauce (Makes 1¼ cups): Mix 1 cup sour cream with ¼ cup crisp crumbled bacon and 2 tablespoons melted bacon drippings. Good with baked potatoes, seafood, and green vegetables. About 40 calories per tablespoon.

Sour Cream-Blue Cheese Sauce (Makes 2 cups): Blend 1 cup sour cream with 1 (3-ounce) package softened cream cheese, ⅓ cup crumbled blue cheese, and 3 tablespoons evaporated milk. Good with green vegetables. About 35 calories per tablespoon.

Sour Cream-Caper Sauce (Makes 1⅓ cups): Mix 1 cup sour cream with 3 tablespoons each lemon juice (or white vinegar) and minced capers and 2 tablespoons minced chives. Serve with seafood. About 30 calories per tablespoon.

Sour Cream-Cheese Sauce (Makes 1¾ cups): Melt 1 cup finely grated sharp Cheddar cheese with ¼ cup milk and 1 teaspoon steak sauce in the top of a double boiler over simmering water. Blend in 1 cup sour cream. Good with fish, baked potatoes, and green vegetables. About 35 calories per tablespoon.

Sour Cream-Chive Sauce (Makes 1¼ cups): Mix 1 cup sour cream with 3-4 tablespoons minced chives and salt and pepper to taste. If you like, add ½ crushed clove garlic or ¼ teaspoon garlic powder. Good with baked potatoes, carrots, and seafood. About 25 calories per tablespoon.

Sour Cream-Chutney Sauce (Makes 1¼ cups): Mix 1 cup sour cream with ¼ cup minced chutney and 2 tablespoons Worcestershire sauce. Good with cold meat or poultry. About 35 calories per tablespoon.

⚖ **Sour Cream-Cucumber Sauce** (Makes 2 cups): Mix 1 cup each sour cream and peeled, diced, seeded cucumber with 2 tablespoons white wine vinegar, 1 tablespoon minced fresh dill, and salt and pepper to taste. Good with fish or ham. About 17 calories per tablespoon.

Sour Cream-Curry Sauce (Makes 1 cup): Blend 1 cup sour cream with 1 teaspoon curry powder warmed 2-3 minutes with 1 tablespoon each butter and finely grated onion; add salt and pepper to taste. Good with meat or fish. About 35 calories per tablespoon.

Sour Cream-Dill Sauce (Makes 1¼ cups): Mix 2 tablespoons each minced fresh dill and mayonnaise with 1 cup sour cream; add salt and pepper to taste. Good with seafood. About 35 calories per tablespoon.

Sour Cream-Herb Sauce (Makes 1 cup): Mix 1 tablespoon each minced fresh tarragon, chervil, and parsley with 1 cup sour cream; add salt and pepper to taste. Good with meat, seafood, or vegetables. About 25 calories per tablespoon.

Sour Cream Hollandaise (Makes 1½ cups): Heat and stir 1 cup sour cream, 6 lightly beaten egg yolks, ¾ teaspoon salt, and ⅛ teaspoon white pepper in the top of a double boiler over simmering water 2-3

SAUCES, GRAVIES, AND BUTTERS

minutes until no raw taste of egg remains. Off heat, mix in 4–5 teaspoons lemon juice. Good with green vegetables, seafood, or poultry. About 35 calories per tablespoon.

Sour Cream-Horseradish Sauce (Makes 1¼ cups): Blend 2 tablespoons each cider vinegar and prepared horseradish with 1 cup sour cream. Good with beef, ham, or pork. About 30 calories per tablespoon.

Sour Cream-Mustard Sauce (Makes 1 cup): Blend 2–3 tablespoons any prepared mustard and 1 tablespoon cider vinegar with 1 cup sour cream. Good with beef, ham, or pork. About 30 calories per tablespoon.

Sour Cream-Red Currant Sauce (Makes 1½ cups): Blend 1 cup sour cream with ½ cup warmed red currant jelly (or apple, guava, or cranberry jelly) and a pinch allspice. Good with game and game birds. About 45 calories per tablespoon.

Sour Cream Sauce (Makes 1¼ cups): Blend 1 cup sour cream with ¼ cup mayonnaise and salt and pepper to taste. Good with boiled red or green cabbage. About 45 calories per tablespoon.

Sour Cream-Sesame Sauce (Makes 1 cup): Mix 2 tablespoons toasted sesame seeds (or poppy or caraway seeds) with 1 cup sour cream. Good with green vegetables. About 30 calories per tablespoon.

Sour Cream-Sherry Sauce (Makes 1¼ cups): Blend 3–4 tablespoons dry sherry and a pinch nutmeg with 1 cup sour cream. Good with poultry or shrimp. About 30 calories per tablespoon.

Sour Cream-Soup Sauce (Makes 2 cups): Heat and stir 1 (10-ounce) can condensed cream of chicken, mushroom, or celery soup with 1 cup sour cream over low heat until smooth. Add 1 tablespoon each minced parsley and chives and serve hot over meat, poultry, or vegetables. About 25 calories per tablespoon.

Sour Cream-Tomato Sauce (Makes 1¼ cups): Mix ¼ cup tomato paste, chili sauce, or ketchup and 1 tablespoon lemon juice with 1 cup sour cream. If you like, add 1 tablespoon minced parsley or dill. Good with seafood. About 30 calories per tablespoon.

⚖ LOW-CALORIE VARIATIONS

The following "sour cream" sauces will be low-calorie if made with yogurt instead of sour cream:

Sour Cream-Caper: 8 calories per tablespoon

Sour Cream-Chive: 8 calories per tablespoon

Sour Cream-Chutney: 15 calories per tablespoon

Sour Cream-Cucumber: 6 calories per tablespoon

Sour Cream-Curry: 15 calories per tablespoon

Sour Cream-Dill: 8 calories per tablespoon

Sour Cream-Herb: 8 calories per tablespoon

Sour Cream-Horseradish: 8 calories per tablespoon

Sour Cream-Mustard: 10 calories per tablespoon

SMITANE SAUCE

Serve with steaks and chops. Also good as a topping for baked potatoes and green vegetables.

Makes about 1 cup

1 large yellow onion, peeled and minced
2 tablespoons butter or margarine
½ cup dry white wine
1 cup sour cream
¼ teaspoon salt
Paprika

Stir-fry onion in butter over moderate heat 3–5 minutes until limp, not brown. Add wine and simmer, uncovered, until liquid reduces to about 2 tablespoons. Turn heat to low, gradually stir in sour cream and salt, and heat gently; do not boil. Dust with paprika and serve warm. About 50 calories per tablespoon.

⊠ DRAWN BUTTER SAUCE

Makes 1 cup

¼ cup clarified butter* or melted margarine
2 tablespoons flour
1 cup any warm fish or vegetable stock or water
½ teaspoon salt
⅛ teaspoon paprika
½–1 teaspoon lemon juice

Warm butter in a small saucepan over low heat and blend in flour. Add stock and heat, stirring constantly, until thickened and smooth. Mix in salt, paprika, and lemon juice to taste. Good with broiled fish or steamed green vegetables. (*Note:* Traditionalists strain this sauce before serving, but doing so is unnecessary if the sauce is correctly made and satin-smooth.) About 30 calories per tablespoon.

⊠ SOME FLAVORED BUTTERS

Each makes enough to dress 6 servings of meat, fish, or vegetables

Anchovy Butter: Cream ½ cup butter until light; mix in 4 teaspoons anchovy paste (or 4–5 minced anchovy fillets), ½ teaspoon lemon juice, and 2–3 drops liquid hot red pepper seasoning. Let stand 15 minutes before using. Spread on fish before or after broiling, on broiled steaks, or use as a sandwich spread with seafood fillings. About 140 calories per serving.

Bercy Butter: Boil ½ cup dry white wine with 1 tablespoon minced shallots until reduced to 3 tablespoons; cool. Mix in ½ cup melted butter, ¼ cup diced poached marrow from Marrowbones (optional), 1 tablespoon lemon juice, 2 teaspoons minced parsley, ¼ teaspoon salt, and a pinch pepper. Serve warm with broiled meat or fish. About 135 calories per serving (without marrow).

Beurre Noir ("Black" Butter): Melt ½ cup butter over moderate heat and cook until nut brown. Off heat, mix in 1 tablespoon each minced parsley, capers, and cider vinegar. Serve with fish, vegetables, sweetbreads, or brains. About 135 calories per serving.

Browned Butter: Mix ½ cup lightly browned butter and 4 teaspoons Worcestershire sauce; use to dress steaks, chops, fish, or vegetables (especially good with cauliflower). About 140 calories per serving.

Caper Butter: Mix ½ cup melted butter, ¼ cup small capers, 1 tablespoon lemon juice, and a pinch cayenne pepper; serve with fish, brains, sweetbreads, or vegetables. About 140 calories per serving.

SAUCES, GRAVIES, AND BUTTERS

Chili Butter: Mix ½ cup melted butter and 1 teaspoon chili powder; warm gently 5 minutes and use to baste broiled tomatoes, meat, fish, or poultry. About 135 calories per serving.

Chive Butter: Mix ½ cup melted butter, 2 tablespoons minced chives, ¼ teaspoon salt, and a pinch pepper. *Or,* cream butter until light, blend in remaining ingredients, spoon into a small crock, and chill until firm. Serve poured or dotted over steak, chops, fish, or vegetables. About 135 calories per serving.

Curry Butter: Warm ½ cup melted butter and 1 teaspoon curry powder gently 5 minutes; serve with broiled meat, poultry, fish, or tomatoes. Also good with boiled broccoli or cauliflower. About 135 calories per serving.

Dill Butter: Let ½ cup melted butter, 3–4 tablespoons minced fresh dill, and ⅛ teaspoon nutmeg stand in warm place 1 hour; use to dress fish or vegetables. About 135 calories per serving.

Garlic Butter: Mix ½ cup melted butter, 1 or 2 crushed cloves garlic, ¼ teaspoon salt, and a pinch pepper; warm 5 minutes and strain if you like. *Or,* cream butter until light and blend in remaining ingredients. Serve on broiled meat or fish, with steamed lobster, or use to make Garlic Bread. About 135 calories per serving.

Green Butter: Simmer ¼ cup minced fresh spinach leaves with 2 tablespoons each minced parsley, chives, and water 2–3 minutes; press through a fine sieve, drain, and mix into ½ cup creamed butter along with a pinch each of salt and pepper. Chill and serve with fish or vegetables. About 135 calories per serving.

Herb Butter: Mix ½ cup creamed unsalted butter with ½ teaspoon each minced fresh sweet marjoram and thyme (or substitute ½ teaspoon minced fresh rosemary). Cover and chill until firm. Serve with fish or vegetables. (*Note:* With rosemary it's delicious with lamb chops and green peas.) About 135 calories per serving.

Horseradish Butter: Mix ½ cup creamed butter and 1 tablespoon prepared horseradish; cover and chill 1 hour. Serve with steaks and chops. About 140 calories per serving.

Lemon Butter: Warm ½ cup melted butter, 2 tablespoons lemon juice, and a pinch pepper 2–3 minutes. Serve with fish or vegetables. *Parsley-Lemon Butter:* Add 2–3 tablespoons minced parsley to Lemon Butter. Each version: about 135 calories per serving.

Lobster Butter: Finely grind 1 cup mixed cooked lobster meat, coral, and some shell. Mix with ½ cup melted butter and blend at high speed in an electric blender. Heat until butter melts, then blend again at high speed. Rub through a fine sieve, cool, beat with a fork, season to taste with salt and pepper, and chill until firm. Serve with fish. About 160 calories per serving.

Maître d'Hôtel Butter (Parsley Butter): Mix ½ cup creamed butter with 2 tablespoons each minced parsley and lemon juice, ¼ teaspoon salt, and ⅛ teaspoon white pepper. On foil shape into a roll about 1¼″ in diameter, wrap, and chill until firm. Or roll into balls about ½″ in diameter, place in a piepan, cover, and chill until firm. Use to season broiled steaks, chops, chicken, or fish by topping each serving with 2 or 3 balls or ¼″ thick pats. About 135 calories per serving.

Marchands de Vin Butter: Boil ½ cup dry red wine with 2 tablespoons minced shallots until reduced to ¼ cup. Beat in ½ cup soft butter, 2 tablespoons at a time, add 1 tablespoon Glace de Viande or 1 teaspoon beef extract, 1 tablespoon each minced parsley and lemon juice, and a pinch pepper. Serve on steaks and chops. About 135 calories per serving.

Mushroom Butter: Sauté ¼ pound minced mushrooms in 2 tablespoons butter 3–5 minutes until browned and tender; press through a fine sieve and cool slightly. Mix in 6 tablespoons creamed butter, 1 tablespoon sherry, ¼ teaspoon salt, and a pinch pepper. Cover and chill; spread on steaks and chops. About 145 calories per serving.

Mustard Butter: Cream ½ cup softened butter with ½ teaspoon powdered mustard and 1–2 tablespoons any prepared mustard. Use to dress broiled meats and fish or boiled vegetables (especially good with broccoli and asparagus). About 135 calories per serving.

Noisette Butter: Lightly brown ½ cup butter over moderate heat; stir in 3 tablespoons lemon juice and pour sizzling hot over vegetables or fish. About 135 calories per serving.

Orange Butter: Let ½ cup melted butter and 1 tablespoon finely slivered orange rind (orange part only) steep in a warm place ½ hour. Warm gently and serve with boiled beets, carrots, parsnips, peas, winter squash, turnips, or rutabagas. About 135 calories per serving.

Paprika Butter: Blend ½ cup creamed butter with 1–2 teaspoons paprika (Hungarian rose, preferably), cover, and chill. Use to dress fish and vegetables. About 135 calories per serving.

Pimiento Butter: Pound 2 seeded canned pimientos to a smooth paste in a mortar and pestle. Blend into ½ cup creamed butter along with ¼ teaspoon salt. Cover, chill, and serve with meat, fish, or vegetables. About 140 calories per serving.

Seasoned Butter: Mix ½ cup melted butter, 1 teaspoon salt, and ¼ teaspoon freshly ground black pepper. Use to dress seafood or vegetables. About 135 calories per serving.

Shallot Butter: Crush 6–8 peeled shallots in a garlic press, mix into ½ cup creamed butter along with ¼ teaspoon salt and a pinch pepper. Cover and chill 1 hour; serve with steaks, chops, and seafood. About 135 calories per serving.

Shrimp Butter: Mince ¼ pound cooked, shelled, and deveined shrimp, add 1 tablespoon lemon juice, then pound to a paste in a mortar and pestle. Blend into ½ cup creamed butter, add a pinch each salt and paprika, cover, and chill 2 hours. *Or,* mix 1–2 tablespoons shrimp paste into ½ cup melted butter, season, and let stand in a warm place 1 hour. Serve with seafood. About 155 calories per serving.

Tarragon Butter: Let ½ cup melted butter steep with 1 tablespoon each minced fresh tarragon and tarragon vinegar 1 hour in a warm place. *Or,* mix tarragon and vinegar into creamed butter and chill. Serve with meat, fish, poultry, and vegetables. About 135 calories per serving.

Tomato Butter: Blend ½ cup creamed butter with ¼ cup tomato paste, ¼ teaspoon salt and a pinch pepper; cover and chill until firm.

Serve with fish. About 145 calories per serving.

Tuna Butter: Pound ¼ cup drained canned tuna with 1 tablespoon lemon juice to a paste in a mortar and pestle. Blend in ½ cup creamed butter and ⅛ teaspoon pepper. Cover and chill until firm. Serve with seafood. About 155 calories per serving.

Watercress Butter: Mix ¼ cup minced watercress leaves and ¼ cup soft butter to a paste in a mortar and pestle. Blend in ¼ cup creamed butter and add ¼ teaspoon salt and a pinch pepper. Serve with meat, seafood, poultry, or vegetables. Good as a sandwich spread, especially with egg salad or cheese. About 135 calories per serving.

TOMATO AND PASTA SAUCES

Note: Other pasta sauces can be found in the chapter on cereals, rice, and pasta.

⚜ **TOMATO SAUCE**

Makes about 1 quart

2 tablespoons diced salt pork or bacon
1 tablespoon butter or cooking oil
2 medium-size yellow onions, peeled and minced
1 medium-size carrot, peeled and minced
1 tablespoon flour
1 (1-pound 13-ounce) can tomato purée
1 cup Veal (White) Stock or water
1 bouquet garni,* tied in cheesecloth
1 clove garlic, peeled and stuck on a toothpick
1½ teaspoons salt (about)
¼ teaspoon pepper
1 teaspoon sugar

Stir-fry pork in a large, heavy saucepan over moderate heat 3–4 minutes until pale golden. Add butter, onions, and carrot and sauté 5–8 minutes until limp, not brown. Blend in flour, mix in purée and stock, then add remaining ingredients. Cover and simmer, stirring occasionally, 1 hour; remove *bouquet garni* and garlic. Purée, a little at a time, at low speed in an electric blender or put through a food mill. Reheat, taste for salt and adjust as needed. About 10 calories per tablespoon.

VARIATIONS:

⚜ **Creole Sauce:** Prepare as directed, using oil instead of butter; also sauté 2 minced and seeded sweet green peppers and 2 stalks minced celery along with onions and carrot; use 2 cloves garlic and add 1 teaspoon paprika and ⅛ teaspoon cayenne pepper along with other seasonings. Simmer, purée, then stir in 1 teaspoon filé powder, reheat briefly, and serve. Good with seafood. About 15 calories per tablespoon.

⚜ **Portugaise (Portuguese) Sauce** (Makes 1½ quarts): Prepare as directed but omit salt pork and use 3 tablespoons olive oil for sautéing vegetables. Simmer and purée as directed; mix in 2 cups Rich Brown Sauce (or rich brown gravy), cover, and simmer 10 minutes. Stir in 3 tablespoons minced parsley and serve. Good with poultry and seafood. About 15 calories per tablespoon.

Provençal Sauce: Prepare as directed, using ¾ cup each dry white wine and veal stock instead of 1 cup stock. Just before serving, stir in 1 tablespoon minced parsley.

Good with seafood. About 20 calories per serving.

ITALIAN TOMATO SAUCE

Good with any pasta. This sauce freezes well. Makes about 1 quart, enough for 4 servings

2 cloves garlic, peeled and crushed
¼ cup olive or other cooking oil
1 (1-pound 12-ounce) can tomato purée
½ cup water
1½ teaspoons salt
1 teaspoon sugar
1 teaspoon basil
1 bay leaf, crumbled
⅛ teaspoon crushed dried hot red chili peppers

Sauté garlic in oil in a saucepan over moderate heat 1–2 minutes until golden. Add remaining ingredients, cover, and simmer 30–40 minutes, stirring now and then. (*Note:* If doubling recipe, use 3 cloves garlic; if tripling, 4 cloves.) About 215 calories for each of 4 servings.

VARIATIONS:

Bolognese Tomato Sauce (Makes 5 cups): Stir-fry ½ pound ground beef chuck with garlic, breaking beef up with a spoon, 8–10 minutes until browned. Proceed as directed, adding 1 teaspoon oregano along with other herbs. About 335 calories per serving.

Italian Mushroom-Eggplant Sauce (Makes 5 cups): Stir-fry ½ pound thinly sliced mushrooms and 1 peeled and diced medium-size eggplant with garlic 4–5 minutes until lightly browned. Proceed as directed but simmer sauce 1 hour. About 260 calories per serving.

Red Clam Sauce (Makes 6 cups): Prepare as directed but substitute liquid drained from 2 (7½-ounce) cans minced clams for the water. About 5 minutes before serving, mix in clams. About 295 calories per serving.

MARINARA SAUCE

Makes about 1½ quarts

1 cup minced yellow onion
2 cloves garlic, peeled and crushed
¼ cup olive or other cooking oil
1 (2-pound 3-ounce) can Italian plum tomatoes (*do not drain*)
1 (6-ounce) can tomato paste
½ cup dry red wine
½ cup water
2 teaspoons salt
1½ teaspoons sugar
¼ teaspoon pepper
1 tablespoon minced fresh oregano or 1 teaspoon dried oregano
¼ cup finely grated Romano cheese (*optional*)

Sauté onion and garlic in oil in a large, heavy saucepan over moderate heat 8–10 minutes until golden. Add remaining ingredients except cheese, cover, and simmer 1 hour, stirring occasionally. Press sauce through a sieve or purée, a little at a time, in an electric blender at low speed. Reheat to simmering, add cheese if you wish, and serve hot with any pasta. About 225 calories per 1-cup serving (without cheese).

VARIATIONS:

Mushroom-Marinara Sauce: Prepare as directed but mix in ¾–1 pound sautéed sliced mushrooms just before serving. About 275 calories per 1-cup serving.

Anchovy-Marinara Sauce: Prepare as directed but omit salt; just before serving, mix in 2 (2-ounce) cans

SAUCES, GRAVIES, AND BUTTERS

anchovy fillets, drained and minced. About 285 calories per 1-cup serving.

MOLE SAUCE

Makes about 2 cups

3 ripe tomatoes, peeled, cored, seeded, and coarsely chopped
½ cup ground blanched almonds or unsalted peanuts
1 (4-ounce) can peeled green chilies, drained, or 1 tablespoon chili powder
2 cloves garlic, peeled and crushed
2 tablespoons grated yellow onion
1 tablespoon sesame seeds
¼ teaspoon coriander
¼ teaspoon salt
⅛ teaspoon cinnamon
1 cup chicken broth
1 (1-ounce) square unsweetened chocolate, coarsely grated

Purée all ingredients in an electric blender at high speed 1 minute. Transfer to a saucepan and simmer, uncovered, stirring now and then, ½ hour. Sauce is now ready to add to braised chicken or turkey. About 370 calories per 1-cup serving, 25 calories per tablespoon.

⚜ SALSA FRÍA

Mexican green tomatoes (*tomatillos*), available canned in Latin-American groceries, make a good addition to *salsa fría*. Chop 2 or 3 fine and add along with the other tomatoes.

Makes about 2 cups

4 ripe tomatoes, peeled, cored, seeded, and coarsely chopped
1 large red onion, peeled and minced
1 medium-size sweet green pepper, cored, seeded, and minced
½ small hot red chili pepper, cored and seeded, or 1 (4-ounce) can peeled green chilies, drained and minced very fine

1 clove garlic, peeled and crushed
1 tablespoon red wine vinegar
1 tablespoon olive oil
1 teaspoon salt (*about*)
¼ teaspoon coriander or 1 teaspoon minced fresh coriander leaves
Pinch cloves

Mix all ingredients and chill well; taste for salt and adjust as needed. Serve cold with steaks or fish either on the side of the plate or in individual bowls. About 10 calories per tablespoon.

VARIATION:

⚜ Prepare as directed but substitute 1 (1-pound) can tomatoes, drained and coarsely chopped, for fresh tomatoes, and ⅛–¼ teaspoon crushed dried hot red chili peppers for the fresh or canned. About 10 calories per serving.

BEEF, SAUSAGE, AND MUSHROOM SAUCE FOR PASTA

Here's a versatile sauce that freezes beautifully and can be used for making lasagne or ladled over steaming spaghetti, linguine, or macaroni.
Makes about 1 gallon, enough for 16–18 servings

1 pound sweet Italian sausages
1½ pounds ground beef chuck
3 large yellow onions, peeled and minced
4 cloves garlic, peeled and crushed
4 teaspoons salt
2 tablespoons oregano
1 tablespoon basil
1 teaspoon chili powder
⅛ teaspoon crushed dried hot red chili peppers
1 (8-ounce) can mushrooms (do not drain)
1 (1-quart 14-ounce) can tomato juice
4 (6-ounce) cans tomato paste
1 cup water

Slit sausage casings and remove meat; sauté over moderate heat in a large, heavy skillet, breaking meat up with a fork, about 10 minutes until golden brown. Transfer to a large kettle with a slotted spoon. Drain all but 3 tablespoons drippings from skillet, add beef and brown over moderate heat; transfer to kettle, using a slotted spoon. Again drain all but 3 tablespoons drippings from skillet; add onions and garlic and sauté, stirring occasionally, 8–10 minutes until golden. Transfer to kettle. Mix remaining ingredients into kettle, cover, and simmer 2 hours over moderate heat, stirring occasionally. Serve hot over pasta, or cool to room temperature and freeze for use later. About 195 calories for each of 16 servings, 175 calories for each of 18 servings.

SAVORY BEEF AND TOMATO SAUCE FOR PASTA

Makes about 1 quart, enough for 4 servings

2 medium-size yellow onions, peeled and coarsely chopped
1 clove garlic, peeled and crushed
2 tablespoons olive oil
1 pound ground beef chuck
1 large bay leaf, crumbled
½ teaspoon oregano
¼ teaspoon summer savory
¼ teaspoon nutmeg
1½ teaspoons salt
⅛ teaspoon pepper
2 tablespoons bourbon (optional)
1 tablespoon light brown sugar
1 (1-pound 12-ounce) can tomatoes (do not drain)
1 (6-ounce) can tomato paste
⅔ cup water

Sauté onions and garlic in oil in a large, heavy skillet over moderate heat, stirring occasionally, 10 minutes, until golden. Add beef, breaking it up with a spoon, and sauté 8–10 minutes until just pink. Stir in bay leaf, oregano, savory, nutmeg, salt, pepper, bourbon, if you like, and brown sugar and heat, stirring, 5 minutes. Reduce heat to low, stir in remaining ingredients, and simmer uncovered, stirring occasionally, 1½ hours. Serve hot over pasta. About 470 calories for each of 4 servings.

✠ WHITE CLAM SAUCE FOR SPAGHETTI

Makes about 3 cups, enough for 4 servings

2 cloves garlic, peeled and crushed
1 medium-size yellow onion, peeled and minced
2 tablespoons olive or other cooking oil
2 (10½-ounce) cans minced clams, drained (reserve liquid)
¼ teaspoon basil
¼ teaspoon oregano
1 tablespoon minced parsley
⅛ teaspoon white pepper
¼ teaspoon salt

Stir-fry onion and garlic in oil in a heavy saucepan over moderate heat 8–10 minutes until golden. Add clam liquid (but not clams) and all remaining ingredients; cover and simmer 15 minutes. Add clams, cover, and simmer 5–7 minutes. Serve over hot spaghetti or linguine. About 140 calories for each of 4 servings.

✠ TUNA SAUCE FOR PASTA

Makes about 1 cup, enough for 2 servings

1 clove garlic, peeled and crushed
2 tablespoons olive oil
2 tablespoons butter or margarine
1 (7½-ounce) can tuna in olive oil (do not drain)
2 anchovy fillets, minced

1 teaspoon minced parsley
⅛ teaspoon freshly ground black pepper

Sauté garlic in oil and butter in a saucepan 1–2 minutes over moderate heat until golden. Mix in tuna and anchovies, turn heat to low, and warm, breaking up tuna chunks. Cover and simmer 5 minutes. Ladle into a sauceboat, sprinkle with parsley and pepper, and serve with spaghetti or linguine. About 360 calories for each of 2 servings.

VARIATION:

✗ **Anchovy-Olive Sauce for Pasta:** Sauté garlic in ¼ cup each olive oil and butter. Add 2 (2-ounce) cans anchovy fillets, drained and minced, instead of tuna and anchovies called for and cook and stir until anchovies disintegrate. Mix in ¼ cup coarsely chopped pitted ripe olives, the parsley and pepper and serve. About 630 calories for each of 2 servings.

BARBECUE SAUCES AND MARINADES

Note: Other barbecue sauces and marinades can be found in the individual meat, poultry, and seafood sections.

¢ **ALL-PURPOSE BARBECUE SAUCE**

Makes about 1¼ cups

¼ cup cider vinegar
½ cup water
2 tablespoons sugar
1 tablespoon prepared mild yellow mustard
½ teaspoon pepper
1½ teaspoons salt
¼ teaspoon paprika
1 thick slice lemon
½ medium-size yellow onion, peeled and sliced thin
¼ cup butter or margarine
½ cup ketchup
2 tablespoons Worcestershire sauce

Simmer all but last 2 ingredients, uncovered, 20 minutes, stirring occasionally; off heat, mix in ketchup and Worcestershire sauce. Use in making any barbecued dish. About 585 calories per cup, 37 calories per tablespoon.

✗ **BARBECUE SAUCE FOR BEEF**

Makes 2 cups

½ cup cooking oil
½ cup dry red wine or red wine vinegar
2 tablespoons Worcestershire sauce
1 clove garlic, peeled and crushed
¼ teaspoon seasoned pepper
1 cup tomato juice

Shake all ingredients in a shaker jar to blend; use as a marinade for beef or as a brush-on basting. About 575 calories per cup, 36 calories per tablespoon.

⚔ ✗ **BARBECUE GRAVY FOR BEEF**

Makes about 2½ cups

½ cup Barbecue Sauce for Beef
1 cup tomato juice
1 cup condensed beef broth
2 tablespoons cornstarch blended with 2 tablespoons cold water

Heat and stir all ingredients over moderate heat until thickened and clear. Reduce heat and let mellow 3–5 minutes. Serve with any barbecued beef. About 11 calories per tablespoon.

SOUTH AMERICAN HOT BARBECUE SAUCE

Hot and spicy. Especially good for basting charcoal-broiled meats.
Makes about 3 cups

½ cup minced yellow onion
½ cup minced sweet green pepper
2 cloves garlic, peeled and crushed
¼ cup olive oil
2 teaspoons chili powder
2 cups tomato purée
½ cup red wine vinegar
⅓ cup firmly packed dark brown sugar
¼ teaspoon crushed dried hot red chili peppers
1½ teaspoons salt

Stir-fry onion, green pepper, and garlic in oil in a saucepan over moderate heat 5–8 minutes until onion is pale golden. Add chili powder and stir-fry 1–2 minutes. Add remaining ingredients, cover, and simmer ½ hour. Use as a basting sauce for spareribs, beef, or poultry. About 320 calories per cup, 20 calories per tablespoon.

⊠ CALIFORNIA ORANGE-GINGER BARBECUE SAUCE

Makes about 3 cups

1 cup orange juice
1 cup ginger ale
½ cup ketchup
¼ cup cooking oil
¼ cup honey or light corn syrup
¼ cup sweet sherry
2 tablespoons frozen orange juice concentrate
1 teaspoon ginger
1 teaspoon salt
Pinch cayenne pepper

Mix all ingredients and use to baste poultry, lamb, or pork. About 427 calories per cup, 27 calories per tablespoon.

⊠ CHINESE BARBECUE SAUCE

Makes about ½ cup

⅔ cup firmly packed dark brown sugar
2 tablespoons cider vinegar
2 tablespoons soy sauce
⅛ teaspoon curry powder
¼ teaspoon garlic powder

Mix together all ingredients until sugar dissolves. Use for brushing barbecued spareribs, loin of pork, leg of lamb, or lamb shanks. About 70 calories per tablespoon.

⊠ ⚔ TERIYAKI SAUCE

A strong sauce best added with a light hand.
Makes about ¾ cup

½ cup soy sauce
¼ cup mirin (sweet rice wine), sake, or medium-dry sherry
1 tablespoon sugar (if sake or sherry is used)
2 teaspoons finely grated fresh gingerroot or 1 tablespoon minced preserved ginger
¼ clove garlic, peeled and crushed (optional)

Mix all ingredients and use as a marinade or basting sauce for broiled beef or chicken or roast pork. About 11 calories per tablespoon if made with *mirin*, 15 calories per tablespoon if made with *sake* and sugar or with sherry and sugar.

⊠ POULTRY MARINADE

Suit the wine or vinegar in the marinade to the bird—white for chicken, Cornish game hens, or turkey; red for duckling, goose, or game birds.
Makes 2 cups

1 cup medium-dry white or red wine, sweet or dry Vermouth, or ½ cup each wine vinegar and water

1 cup olive or other cooking oil
1 clove garlic, peeled and crushed (optional)
Few crushed sprigs fresh rosemary, tarragon, or thyme
¼ teaspoon crushed juniper berries

Place all ingredients in a large jar, cover, and shake vigorously. Use to marinate and/or baste poultry. If made with wine: About 1100 calories per cup, 69 calories per tablespoon. If made with water and vinegar: About 1012 calories per cup, 63 calories per tablespoon.

⚔ ⊠ BUTTERMILK MARINADE
Makes 1 quart

1 quart buttermilk
2 tablespoons white vinegar
1 large yellow onion, peeled and sliced thin
2 teaspoons prepared horseradish
½ teaspoon sage
1 teaspoon salt
⅛ teaspoon pepper

Mix all ingredients and use to marinate poultry, game, or lamb. About 105 calories per cup, 6 calories per tablespoon.

⊠ BEER MARINADE
Makes 2 cups

1 (12-ounce) can beer
½ cup French dressing
1 clove garlic, peeled and crushed
1 teaspoon powdered mustard
½ teaspoon salt
¼ teaspoon pepper

Mix all ingredients and use to marinate poultry, beef, game, or shrimp. About 315 calories per cup, 20 calories per tablespoon.

OTHER SAUCES

⚔ ⊠ QUICK AND EASY CHILI SAUCE
Makes about 5½ cups

1 (1-pound) can tomatoes (do not drain)
1 (1-pound 12-ounce) can tomato purée
1 large yellow onion, peeled and grated fine
2 cloves garlic, peeled and crushed
¼ cup cider vinegar
1 tablespoon chili powder
1½ teaspoons salt
1 teaspoon sugar
⅛ teaspoon crushed dried hot red chili peppers
⅛ teaspoon allspice
2 tablespoons cornstarch mixed with 2 tablespoons cider vinegar

Purée tomatoes in an electric blender or put through a food mill. Mix with all but last ingredient and heat in a large saucepan until bubbling. Stir in cornstarch paste and heat, stirring constantly, 2–3 minutes. Reduce heat and simmer, uncovered, 10 minutes. Cool, ladle into sterilized jars, and seal. Sauce will keep in a cool place without refrigeration 2–3 weeks, longer in refrigerator. About 5 calories per tablespoon.

⊠ COCKTAIL SAUCE
Makes 1 cup

1 cup ketchup or chili sauce
1–2 tablespoons prepared horseradish
1 tablespoon lemon juice
2–3 dashes liquid hot red pepper seasoning

Mix all ingredients and let stand ½ hour for flavors to blend. Serve with seafood. About 20 calories per tablespoon.

VARIATION:

☒ **Fin and Claw Cocktail Sauce:** Prepare as directed but use ½ cup mayonnaise and ½ cup chili sauce instead of all ketchup. About 75 calories per tablespoon.

BREAD SAUCE

Traditional with game birds but good, too, with any poultry.
Makes 2 cups

1 large yellow onion, peeled and stuck with 6 cloves
2 cups milk
2 tablespoons butter
1 teaspoon salt (about)
¼ teaspoon white pepper
Pinch mace (optional)
Pinch cayenne pepper
1 cup fine dry bread crumbs
2 tablespoons light or heavy cream

Simmer onion, covered, in milk with butter and seasonings ¾ hour until mushy; remove onion, pick out cloves and discard. If you like mince onion and return to milk. Mix in crumbs and heat, stirring constantly, over low heat until the consistency of oatmeal. Taste for salt and adjust, blend in cream, and serve. About 20 calories per tablespoon.

CUMBERLAND SAUCE

Serve with venison.
Makes about 2 cups

2 tablespoons finely slivered orange rind (orange part only)
1 tablespoon finely slivered lemon rind (yellow part only)
1 shallot, peeled and minced, or 1 scallion, minced (white part only)
⅓ cup water
1 cup red currant jelly
1 cup tawny port wine
½ teaspoon powdered mustard mixed with 1 teaspoon water
¼ cup orange juice
2 tablespoons lemon juice
½ teaspoon salt
⅛ teaspoon ginger
Pinch cayenne pepper

Boil orange and lemon rind and shallot in water 3–4 minutes; drain off water. Simmer remaining ingredients, covered, stirring now and then, 10 minutes. Add rinds and shallots, cover, and simmer 5 minutes. About 45 calories per tablespoon.

☒ ⚖ SWEET-SOUR SAUCE

Makes 1⅔ cups

1 cup water or pineapple juice or a ½ and ½ mixture of water and beef or chicken broth
¼ cup cider vinegar
¼ cup soy sauce
⅓ cup firmly packed light brown sugar
1 teaspoon finely grated fresh gingerroot or ⅛ teaspoon powdered ginger
½ clove garlic, peeled and crushed
2 tablespoons cornstarch blended with 2 tablespoons cold water

Heat together all but last ingredient; when steaming, mix in cornstarch paste and cook and stir until thickened and clear. Lower heat, cover, and simmer 5 minutes. Serve with roast pork, spareribs, broiled shrimp, or Chinese-style vegetables. About 15 calories per tablespoon.

VARIATIONS:

Pineapple-Pepper Sweet-Sour Sauce: Drain liquid from 1 (8¾-ounce) can pineapple tidbits and add enough pineapple juice to total 1 cup. Prepare sauce as directed, using the pineapple juice and adding ½ cup minced sweet green pepper before simmering. Just before serving, stir in pineapple tidbits. About 20 calories per tablespoon.

Chinese-Style Sweet-Sour Sauce: Stir-fry 1 medium-size sweet green pepper, cored, seeded, and cut in ½" squares, with 1 carrot, peeled and cut in julienne strips, in 2 tablespoons peanut or other cooking oil 2–3 minutes over moderate heat; do not brown. Mix in liquid and proceed as recipe directs, reducing soy sauce to 2 tablespoons. Before serving, mix in 1 tablespoon dry sherry and, if you like, ½ cup pineapple tidbits. About 25 calories per tablespoon (without pineapple tidbits).

☒ JAPANESE STEAK SAUCE

Makes about 1 cup

¼ cup minced yellow onion
2 tablespoons butter or margarine
½ cup Japanese soy or teriyaki sauce
1 tablespoon chili sauce or ketchup
2 tablespoons dry sherry or sake
2 teaspoons powdered mustard
½ teaspoon pepper

Stir-fry onion in butter in a small saucepan over moderate heat 8–10 minutes until golden. Mix in remaining ingredients and simmer, uncovered, 5 minutes. Serve hot over any broiled steak. Good, too, with lamb and pork chops. About 20 calories per tablespoon.

⚖ ☒ TEMPURA SAUCE

Makes about 1½ cups

¼ cup Japanese soy sauce
1 cup hot beef broth
1 teaspoon light brown sugar
2 tablespoons dry sherry or sake
1 medium-size radish, grated fine

¼ teaspoon monosodium glutamate
¼ teaspoon finely grated fresh gingerroot

Mix all ingredients and let stand at room temperature 10 minutes. Mix well again and serve with Japanese Butterfly Shrimp or tempura. About 5 calories per tablespoon.

⚖ ¢ ☒ HOT CHINESE MUSTARD SAUCE

Very hot. Use sparingly.
Makes ¼ cup

2 tablespoons powdered mustard
1 tablespoon cold water
1 tablespoon white vinegar
¼ teaspoon salt
¼ teaspoon sugar
2 or 3 drops liquid hot red pepper seasoning
Pinch turmeric
Pinch ginger

Blend mustard with water and vinegar until smooth, mix in remaining ingredients, and let stand 10 minutes to develop and blend flavors. Serve as a dip for spareribs or Chinese egg rolls. About 5 calories per tablespoon.

☒ FRESH MINT SAUCE

Makes about 1 quart

1½ cups cider or white vinegar
1½ cups sugar
1 cup minced fresh mint leaves
  (measure loosely packed)

Wash and sterilize enough preserving jars and closures to hold 1 quart (baby food jars are ideal). Stir vinegar and sugar together in a large bowl until sugar dissolves. Add mint and mix well; ladle into jars, distributing mint evenly. Screw lids on and store in a dark, cool place (sauce will keep 2–3 months). Serve with hot or cold roast lamb, lamb

⊠ EASY RAISIN SAUCE

Makes about 2½ cups

3 tablespoons cornstarch
2 cups apple cider
1 tablespoon orange juice
1 teaspoon finely grated orange rind
2 tablespoons butter or margarine
1 cup seedless raisins

In a closed shaker jar, blend cornstarch with ½ cup apple cider until smooth. Pour into a small saucepan, add all remaining ingredients, and heat, stirring constantly over moderate heat, until thickened and clear and no raw starch taste remains. Turn heat to low and let sauce mellow 2–3 minutes, stirring occasionally. Serve warm with ham or tongue. About 25 calories per tablespoon.

PLUM SAUCE

Makes about 1½ cups

½ cup mango chutney
1 cup red plum jelly
2 teaspoons light brown sugar
2 teaspoons red wine vinegar

Drain and reserve liquid from chutney; chop solids fine. Mix chutney liquid and chopped chutney with remaining ingredients, cover, and let stand at room temperature 1 hour. Serve with Barbecued or Chinese-Style Spareribs. About 30 calories per tablespoon.

⊠ WHOLE CRANBERRY SAUCE

Makes about 1 quart

2 cups water
2 cups sugar
1 pound fresh or frozen cranberries, washed and stemmed

Bring water and sugar to a boil in a large, heavy saucepan over moderate heat, stirring constantly; boil, uncovered, 5 minutes without stirring. Add cranberries, cover, and simmer 5–7 minutes until skins pop open. Serve warm or chilled with poultry or pork. About 30 calories per tablespoon.

VARIATIONS:

⊠ **Spicy Whole Cranberry Sauce:** Prepare as directed but add 1 stick cinnamon and 18 whole cloves tied in cheesecloth along with cranberries, remove before serving. About 30 calories per tablespoon.

⊠ **Orange-Cranberry Sauce:** Prepare as directed but substitute light brown sugar for the granulated and the juice of 3 oranges and ¼ cup water for the 2 cups water. If you like, add a cinnamon stick. About 30 calories per tablespoon.

CHAPTER 15

STUFFINGS AND FORCEMEATS

Many a routine dish has been transformed into something unique by the addition of a stuffing or forcemeat (*farce*, the French call these savory mixtures of finely minced meat and vegetables). Most are easy to make (if not quick), most are economical and a good way to stretch the number of servings. The varieties of stuffings are as broad as the imagination. They can be made wholly or partly from scratch or they can be stirred up in minutes, using any of the package mixes available. Stuffings and forcemeats, by the way, are an excellent way to use up odds and ends of meats, vegetables, and breads.

Some Tips on Making and Using Stuffings and Forcemeats

– Mix stuffings and forcemeats just before using—there is danger of food poisoning if they are made far ahead of time.
– To save last minute frenzy, have all ingredients chopped or minced beforehand, but do not mix. Keep ingredients in separate containers in the refrigerator and put together just before using.
– Never put stuffing into a bird, roast, or fish until just before cooking.
– Never stuff anything that is to be frozen, either before or after cooking. It is true that prestuffed frozen turkeys are available, but commercial packers have access to preservatives the housewife doesn't.
– Always remove stuffing from leftover bird, roast or fish, wrap and refrigerate separately—again to reduce risk of food poisoning.
– Team rich stuffings with not so rich poultry, meat, or fish, light stuffings with heavier poultry, meat, or fish. (*Note:* Best stuffings for specific seafoods and poultry are named in the charts of Sauces, Gravies, and Seasonings in each of those sections.)
– Never use raw pork or pork sausage in a stuffing or forcemeat; always sauté first in a skillet until no pink color remains.
– To mellow flavor of minced onions, garlic, celery, and mushrooms, sauté lightly before mixing into stuffing.
– When using soft white commercial bread in stuffings, reduce amount of

moisture in recipe slightly. These breads are already oversoft and if mixed with additional liquid may produce a soggy stuffing. (*Note:* At holiday time, many supermarkets sell special "stuffing" breads.)
– Always mix stuffings with a light hand. Never pack them into a bird, fish, or roast—just drop or spoon in lightly. Stuffings expand on heating and, if too tightly packed, may become leaden. Moreover, they may rupture the bird, fish, or roast.
– Mix forcemeats with a deft hand from start to finish. Properly made, they should be moist, velvety, and airy.

How Much Stuffing Is Enough?

For stuffing lovers, there is never enough. For practical purposes, however, figure ½–¾ cup stuffing per pound of food to be stuffed. It is unlikely that you will be able to get the full amount into the bird, fish, or roast—don't try. Wrap any extra stuffing in heavy foil, then add to roasting pan about 1 hour before bird, fish, or roast is done. Or, if there is as much as 4 cups, spoon into a lightly greased casserole and bake, uncovered, during the last ¾–1 hour of cooking, just until touched with brown. Use the following chart as a guide in determining quantity of stuffing needed.

Quantity of Stuffing	Size Bird It Will Stuff	Number of Servings
1 pint	3–4 pounds	2–3
1½ pints	5–6 pounds	4–5
1 quart	6–8 pounds	6
1½ quarts	8–10 pounds	8
2 quarts	10–12 pounds	10
3 quarts	12–15 pounds	12–14
4 quarts (1 gallon)	15–20 pounds	18–20

What to Do with Stuffing Leftovers

– Slice and serve cold with roast poultry or meat.
– Fluff with a fork, place on a heavy piece of foil, dot with softened butter, wrap, and heat 15–20 minutes at 350° F.
– Fluff with a fork, place in a well-greased small casserole or shallow baking pan, drizzle with melted butter or smother with sliced sautéed mushrooms, and bake about 20 minutes at 375° F. until heated through.
– Fluff with a fork and spoon into hollowed-out tomatoes or parboiled onions or parboiled, scooped-out halves of summer squash. Dot well with butter and bake 20–30 minutes at 375° F. until vegetables are tender and stuffing lightly browned.

¢ ▨ **BASIC BREAD STUFFING**

Makes about 2 quarts, enough to stuff a 10–12-pound turkey

1 cup minced yellow onion
¾ cup minced celery (include some leaves)
½ cup butter or margarine or bacon drippings
2 quarts (½″) stale bread cubes or 2 quarts soft white bread crumbs
2 teaspoons poultry seasoning or ¾ teaspoon each sage, thyme, and marjoram
1½ teaspoons salt
½ teaspoon pepper

¼ cup minced parsley
1–2 eggs, lightly beaten (optional)

Sauté onion and celery in butter in a skillet over moderate heat 5 minutes until pale golden. Mix with remaining ingredients, tossing with 2 forks. (*Note:* For moister stuffing, mix in ⅓ cup chicken broth.) Use to stuff poultry or pork. Or, if you prefer, bake uncovered in a well-greased 2½-quart casserole at 325° F. about 1 hour until lightly browned. About 235 calories per cup if made without eggs, 255 calories per cup if made with 2 eggs.

VARIATIONS:

Stuffing Balls (Makes 1 dozen): Prepare as directed using 2 lightly beaten eggs or 1 egg and ⅓ cup chicken broth. Shape into 1 dozen balls and arrange 1" apart on a well-greased baking sheet. Bake, uncovered, 35–40 minutes at 325° F. until golden brown. About 165 calories per stuffing ball if made without eggs, 170 per stuffing ball if made with 2 eggs.

Chestnut Stuffing: Prepare as directed but reduce bread cubes to 1½ quarts and poultry seasoning to 1½ teaspoons. Mix in 1 pound coarsely chopped Boiled, Sautéed, or peeled Roasted Chestnuts. About 300 calories per cup if made without eggs, 320 calories per cup if made with 2 eggs.

Pecan Stuffing: Prepare as directed but reduce bread cubes to 1½ quarts and add 1½ cups coarsely chopped pecans (or walnuts, filberts, almonds, or Brazil nuts); toast nuts first if you like. About 330 calories per cup if made without eggs, 350 per cup if made with 2 eggs.

Water Chestnut Stuffing (nice for Cornish game hens or fish): Reduce bread cubes to 1½ quarts, omit poultry seasoning but add 1 teaspoon thyme; also mix in 2 cups coarsely chopped or thinly sliced water chestnuts and 2 minced pimientos. About 230 calories per cup if made without eggs, 250 calories per cup if made with 2 eggs.

Sage and Mushroom Stuffing: Sauté 1½ pounds thinly sliced mushrooms (include stems) along with onion and celery in ⅔ cup butter. Add 1½ quarts bread cubes, 1 teaspoon sage, ½ teaspoon marjoram, and the salt and pepper called for; omit poultry seasoning and parsley. Excellent with veal. About 215 calories per cup if made without eggs, 235 per cup if made with 2 eggs.

Oyster Stuffing: Prepare recipe using 3 cups bread cubes and 3 cups coarsely crushed crackers; reduce poultry seasoning to 1½ teaspoons and add 1 pint oysters, drained and minced. About 290 calories per cup if made without eggs, 310 per cup if made with 2 eggs.

Ham and Pepper Stuffing: Sauté 1 large cored, seeded, and minced sweet green or red pepper along with onion and celery. Reduce bread cubes to 7 cups and add 1½ cups diced cooked ham. About 270 calories per cup if made without eggs, 290 per cup if made with 2 eggs.

Apple-Raisin Stuffing: Reduce minced onion to ½ cup, bread cubes to 1½ quarts, and poultry seasoning to 1 teaspoon. Add 3 cups coarsely chopped, peeled, tart apple and ¾ cup seedless raisins. Good with pork. About 255 calories per cup if made without eggs, 275 per cup if made with 2 eggs.

Corn Bread Stuffing: Prepare as directed but sauté vegetables in bacon drippings and use 3 cups bread cubes and 5 cups corn bread crumbs (preferably from corn bread made without sugar). About 285 calories per cup if made without eggs, 305 per cup if made with 2 eggs.

Amish Potato Stuffing: Prepare as directed, using 1 quart bread cubes and 3 cups unseasoned mashed potatoes (or sweet potatoes); reduce poultry seasoning to 1½ teaspoons and add ¼ teaspoon nutmeg. About 235 calories per cup if made without eggs, 255 per cup if made with 2 eggs.

Savory Sausage Stuffing: Sauté 1 pound sausage meat slowly in a heavy skillet, breaking up with a fork, until lightly browned and cooked through, about 20 minutes; transfer to a bowl with slotted spoon. Proceed as directed, using ½ cup drippings for sautéing vegetables and reducing bread cubes to 7 cups. About 370 calories per cup if made without eggs, 390 per cup if made with 2 eggs.

Bread and Apricot Stuffing: Cover 1½ cups dried apricots with boiling water and soak 10 minutes; drain and coarsely chop. Reduce onion to ½ cup, bread cubes to 1½ quarts, and poultry seasoning to ½ teaspoon. Prepare as directed, adding apricots along with bread and mixing in ½ teaspoon cinnamon and ¼ teaspoon nutmeg. About 315 calories per cup if made without eggs, 335 per cup if made with 2 eggs.

Black Olive and Onion Stuffing: Reduce onion to ½ cup and sauté with 2 minced, seeded pimientos and the celery. Reduce bread cubes to 1½ quarts and poultry seasoning to 1 teaspoon; add 2 cups coarsely chopped pitted ripe olives. About 260 calories per cup if made without eggs, 280 per cup if made with 2 eggs.

BASIC RICE STUFFING

Makes about 1 quart, enough to stuff a 6–8-pound bird

1 medium-size yellow onion, peeled and minced
¼ cup minced celery
¼ cup butter or margarine
1 cup uncooked rice
2 cups chicken broth
¾ teaspoon salt (about)
¼ teaspoon pepper
¼ teaspoon each sage, thyme, and marjoram

Sauté onion and celery in butter in a heavy saucepan over moderate heat 5 minutes until pale golden. Add rice and stir-fry 1–2 minutes; add remaining ingredients, cover, reduce heat so rice bubbles gently, and cook 20–25 minutes until all liquid is absorbed. Uncover and fluff with a fork. Taste for salt and adjust as needed. Cool and use as a stuffing. About 265 calories per cup.

VARIATIONS:

Rice and Kidney Stuffing (Makes 5 cups): Sauté ¾ pound lamb kidneys in the butter called for 3–5 minutes over moderately high heat; remove and mince. Stir-fry vegetables in drippings and proceed as directed, adding kidneys along with seasonings. About 290 calories per cup.

Rice and Chicken Liver Stuffing (Makes 5 cups): Prepare like Rice and Kidney Stuffing, but substitute ½ pound chicken livers for kidneys. About 270 calories per cup.

Sherried Rice with Raisins and Almonds (Makes 5 cups): Prepare Basic Rice Stuffing as directed but omit celery and herbs, use 1½ cups beef broth and ½ cup dry sherry instead of chicken broth, and add ½ cup each seedless raisins and toasted slivered almonds and ¼ teaspoon each nutmeg and allspice along with broth. About 360 calories per cup.

Rice and Mushroom Stuffing (Makes 5 cups): Sauté ½ pound minced mushrooms (include stems) along with onion and celery in ⅓ cup butter; proceed as directed for Basic Rice Stuffing. About 245 calories per cup.

Avocado-Rice Stuffing (Makes 5 cups): Prepare basic recipe as directed but omit herbs; cool and mix in 2 firm-ripe, coarsely chopped, pitted, and peeled avocados tossed with 2 tablespoons lemon juice. About 360 calories per cup.

BASIC WILD RICE STUFFING

Expensive as wild rice is, putting it in a stuffing is not a waste of money, because only it can provide a certain crunch and nuttiness. Use for elegant birds—game birds or a plump young turkey. If 1 cup wild rice seems an extravagance, use ½ cup wild rice and ½ cup rice, brown rice, or bulgur wheat.
Makes about 1 quart, enough to stuff a 6–8-pound bird

1 *medium-size yellow onion, peeled and minced*
⅓ *cup celery*
¼ *cup bacon drippings*
¼ *cup minced cooked ham*
1 *cup wild rice, washed well*
½ *teaspoon rosemary*
3 *cups chicken broth or water*
1 *teaspoon salt (about)*
⅛ *teaspoon pepper*

Sauté onion and celery in drippings in a large, heavy saucepan over moderate heat 5–8 minutes until pale golden; add ham and stir-fry 1 minute; add rice and rosemary and stir-fry ½ minute. Add broth, salt, and pepper, cover, and bring to a boil; uncover and boil gently, without stirring, about 30 minutes until barely tender. Drain and set, uncovered, over lowest heat to dry 2–3 minutes, shaking pan now and then. Taste for salt and adjust as needed. About 250 calories per cup.

VARIATIONS:
Wild Rice and Grape Stuffing: Prepare stuffing as directed, then mix in 1–1½ cups halved, seedless green grapes. About 275 calories per cup.

Wild Rice and Cranberry Stuffing: Let 1 (8-ounce) can whole cranberry sauce drain in a fine sieve while preparing stuffing as directed; then mix in cranberries and 1 teaspoon finely grated lemon rind. About 270 calories per cup.

Wild Rice and Mushroom Stuffing: Sauté ½ pound minced mushrooms along with onion and celery, then proceed as directed. About 265 calories per cup.

Wild Rice and Liver Pâté Stuffing: Prepare stuffing as directed. Blend ¼ pound liver pâté, liverwurst, or *pâté de foie gras* with ¼ cup brandy, then mix into stuffing. About 400 calories per cup.

BRANDIED WILD RICE, CORN BREAD, AND CHESTNUT STUFFING

Makes 1 gallon or enough to stuff a 15–20-pound turkey or suckling pig

1 *(½-pound) piece lean bacon, cut in ¼" cubes*
4 *medium-size yellow onions, peeled and coarsely chopped*
3 *cloves garlic, peeled and crushed*
1½ *cups finely diced celery*
1½ *pounds mushrooms, wiped clean and sliced thin*
½ *cup minced parsley*
¼ *cup minced fresh sage or 1½ tablespoons dried sage*

1 (8-ounce) box wild rice, cooked by package directions
8 cups crumbled corn bread or 2 (8-ounce) packages corn bread stuffing mix
1½ pounds chestnuts, shelled, peeled, and quartered
1¼ cups melted butter or margarine
1 cup chicken broth or water
½ cup brandy
¼ teaspoon pepper

Brown bacon in a large, heavy skillet over moderately high heat and drain on paper toweling. Stir-fry onions, garlic, and celery in drippings 8–10 minutes until golden. Add mushrooms, parsley, and sage and sauté, stirring occasionally, 8–10 minutes. Mix with all remaining ingredients (you'll have to use a very large kettle for this job) and use for stuffing a large turkey or suckling pig. Wrap any leftover stuffing in heavy foil and chill until about 1 hour before serving; place foil package in roasting pan alongside turkey or pig and let heat as turkey or pig finishes roasting. About 470 calories per cup.

CORN BREAD AND SAUSAGE STUFFING

Makes about 2 quarts, enough to stuff a 10–12-pound turkey

1½ pounds sausage meat
1 cup minced yellow onions
1 cup minced celery
2 (8-ounce) packages corn bread stuffing mix
½ teaspoon sage
½ teaspoon thyme
1 teaspoon poultry seasoning
2½ teaspoons salt
½ teaspoon pepper
1 cup melted butter or margarine

Sauté sausage slowly in a heavy skillet, breaking up with a fork, until lightly browned and thoroughly cooked, about 20 minutes; transfer to a large bowl with a slotted spoon. Drain all but ¼ cup drippings from skillet; add onions and celery and stir-fry over moderate heat 8–10 minutes until golden. Add to sausage along with remaining ingredients and toss lightly to blend. Use to stuff turkey, any poultry or game bird. About 690 calories per cup.

VARIATIONS:

Corn Bread and Oyster Stuffing: Omit sausage and sauté onion and celery in ¼ cup bacon drippings as directed. Toss with stuffing mix, seasonings, and butter, then mix in 1 pint minced, well-drained oysters. About 465 calories per cup.

Corn Bread, Ham, and Olive Stuffing: Omit sage and sauté onion and celery in ¼ cup bacon drippings as directed; add ½ pound finely diced cooked ham and stir-fry 2 minutes. Toss with stuffing mix, seasonings, and butter, then mix in ½ cup minced ripe or green olives. About 500 calories per cup.

Corn Bread and Cranberry Stuffing: Omit sage and sauté onion and celery in ¼ cup butter in a large saucepan as directed; add 1 pint washed and stemmed cranberries and ½ cup water, cover, and simmer until berries pop. Cool slightly and toss with stuffing mix, seasonings, and ¼ cup melted butter. About 440 calories per cup.

¢ SAGE AND ONION DRESSING

Makes about 2 quarts, enough to stuff a 10–12-pound bird

4 medium-size yellow onions, peeled and minced
1 cup water

STUFFINGS AND FORCEMEATS

6 cups soft white bread cubes
2 teaspoons sage
½ cup melted butter or margarine
2 teaspoons salt
¼ teaspoon pepper

Simmer onions and water, covered, 20 minutes. Off heat, mix in remaining ingredients. Use to stuff poultry or spoon lightly into a well-greased 2½-quart casserole. Bake, uncovered, 1 hour at 325° F. and serve with roast pork, ham, chicken, turkey, duckling, or goose. About 215 calories per cup.

PECAN-BULGUR WHEAT STUFFING

Makes about 1 quart, enough to stuff a crown roast or 6–8-pound bird

1 medium-size yellow onion, peeled and minced
½ cup minced celery
½ pound mushrooms, wiped clean and minced
½ cup butter or margarine
1 cup bulgur wheat
1¾ cups chicken broth
1 teaspoon salt (about)
1 teaspoon sage
1 teaspoon thyme
¼ teaspoon pepper
½ cup minced pecans

Sauté onion, celery, and mushrooms in butter in a saucepan over moderate heat 5–8 minutes until pale golden. Add bulgur wheat and stir-fry 2–3 minutes. Add remaining ingredients except pecans, cover, and simmer ½ hour until liquid is absorbed and bulgur wheat tender. Mix in pecans, taste for salt and adjust as needed. (*Note:* If you wish to bake stuffing separately, spoon into a well-greased casserole and bake 20 minutes at 350° F.) About 310 calories per cup.

CHESTNUT MUSHROOM STUFFING

Makes 3 quarts or enough to stuff a 12–15-pound turkey or suckling pig

4 medium-size yellow onions, peeled and coarsely chopped
2 cloves garlic, peeled and crushed
4 large stalks celery, coarsely chopped (*do not include tops*)
¼ cup butter or margarine
1 pound fresh mushrooms, wiped clean and sliced thin
¼ cup minced parsley
½ teaspoon sage
½ teaspoon thyme
1 tablespoon salt
¼ teaspoon pepper
¾ cup melted butter or margarine
8 cups soft bread crumbs or 2 (8-ounce) packages poultry stuffing mix
1 pound chestnuts, shelled, peeled, and quartered
¼ cup dry sherry

Stir-fry onions, garlic, and celery in butter in a large, heavy skillet over moderate heat 8–10 minutes until golden; add mushrooms, parsley, sage, thyme, salt, and pepper and heat, stirring occasionally, 8–10 minutes. Mix with all remaining ingredients (use a 6-quart kettle) and use to stuff turkey or suckling pig. Wrap any leftover stuffing in heavy foil and chill until about an hour before serving; place foil package in roasting pan and let heat while turkey or pig finishes roasting. About 465 calories per cup.

ORANGE-SWEET POTATO STUFFING

Makes about 1½ quarts, enough to stuff an 8–10-pound bird

½ cup minced yellow onion
1 medium-size carrot, peeled and cut in small dice

¼ cup butter or margarine
2 cups hot mashed sweet potatoes
2 eggs, lightly beaten
2 cups stale bread crumbs
¼ cup minced celery leaves
3 oranges, peeled, seeded, sectioned, and coarsely cut up
1 teaspoon finely grated orange rind
½ teaspoon salt (about)
¼ teaspoon rosemary
¼ teaspoon pepper

Sauté onion and carrot in butter in a skillet over moderate heat 5 minutes until onion is pale golden, reduce heat, and stir-fry 2–3 minutes longer until carrot is crisp tender. Beat sweet potatoes and eggs together until light and fluffy, mix in onion and carrot and all remaining ingredients. Taste for salt and adjust as needed. About 250 calories per cup.

❊ TANGERINE CRACKER STUFFING

Makes about 3 cups, enough to stuff a 5-pound bird

4 slices bacon
⅓ cup minced scallions (include tops)
⅓ cup minced celery
2 cups coarsely crushed soda crackers
1 (8-ounce) can tangerine (mandarin orange) sections, drained and coarsely cut up
⅓ cup coarsely chopped toasted almonds
1 teaspoon finely grated orange rind

Fry bacon in a skillet over moderate heat until crisp, drain on paper toweling, and crumble. Sauté scallions and celery in drippings 3–5 minutes until limp, not brown. Toss with remaining ingredients including bacon. Taste for salt and pepper and adjust as needed. About 370 calories per cup.

SAUERKRAUT STUFFING

Makes about 1½ quarts, enough to stuff a 10-pound goose

1 large Spanish onion, peeled and minced
1 clove garlic, peeled and minced
⅓ cup butter, margarine, or bacon drippings
2 tart cooking apples, peeled, cored, and coarsely chopped
¼ cup firmly packed light brown sugar
2 (1-pound 4-ounce) cans sauerkraut drained and chopped moderately fine
½ teaspoon thyme or celery seed

Sauté onion and garlic in butter in a large skillet over moderately low heat about 5 minutes until onion is limp not brown. Add apples and sugar and stir until sugar is dissolved, then mix in sauerkraut and thyme. About 175 calories per cup.

SOME EASY WAYS TO SPICE UP STUFFINGS MADE FROM PACKAGE MIXES

Each variation makes about 1½ quarts, enough to stuff an 8–10-pound bird

Prepare 1 (8-ounce) package poultry stuffing mix by package directions, then vary any of the following ways. To bake separately, spoon into a well-greased 1½-quart casserole and bake, uncovered, about 35 minutes at 325° F. until lightly browned.

Apple and Pecan Stuffing: Mix in ¾ cup moderately finely chopped pecans and 2 peeled, cored, and coarsely chopped tart cooking apples. About 255 calories per cup.

Herbed Bread Stuffing: Mix in ½ cup minced yellow onion sautéed in ¼ cup butter over moderate heat 5

minutes until pale golden; also mix in ½ teaspoon each sage, thyme, chervil, and savory and 2 tablespoons minced parsley. About 215 calories per cup.

Sausage and Mushroom Stuffing: Prepare Herbed Bread Stuffing as directed. Also sauté ½ pound sausage meat or thinly sliced link sausages in a skillet over moderately low heat about 15 minutes until cooked through. Remove with a slotted spoon to paper toweling, pour off all but ⅓ cup drippings, then stir-fry ½ cup minced yellow onion and ½ pound thinly sliced mushrooms (include stems) 5 minutes until pale golden. Toss into stuffing along with sausage and 1 tablespoon Worcestershire sauce. About 270 calories per cup.

Herbed Fruit Stuffing: Prepare Herbed Bread Stuffing as directed, then mix in ½ cup each seedless raisins and halved seedless green or seeded red grapes, 2 peeled, seeded, and sectioned oranges, ¼ cup minced celery, and, if you like, ¼ cup minced walnuts. About 315 calories per cup if made with walnuts, about 280 calories per cup if made without walnuts.

Giblet Stuffing: To the prepared stuffing mix, add the cooked and minced giblets from the bird to be stuffed; if you like, use giblet stock in stuffing instead of liquid called for and add an extra 2-3 sautéed minced chicken livers. About 200 calories per cup.

Oyster and Almond Stuffing: Add ½ cup minced yellow onion sautéed in ¼ cup butter until pale golden, also 1 cup minced, drained oysters, ¼ cup oyster liquor, and 1 cup coarsely chopped toasted almonds. About 380 calories per cup.

Chicken Liver and Mushroom Stuffing: Dredge ½ pound chicken livers in flour and sauté in ¼ cup butter or bacon drippings over moderately high heat about 5 minutes until browned. Remove with slotted spoon and mince. Sauté ¼ pound sliced mushrooms in drippings 2-3 minutes until golden. Mix livers, mushrooms, and 1 tablespoon minced parsley into stuffing. About 270 calories per cup.

Corn and Pepper Stuffing: Sauté ½ cup minced yellow onion and 6 minced yellow-green sweet Italian peppers in ¼ cup cooking oil over moderate heat 5 minutes until pale golden; reduce heat and simmer 2-3 minutes until peppers are tender. Mix into stuffing along with 1 cup drained canned whole kernel corn. (*Note:* This recipe is also good made with corn bread stuffing mix.) About 270 calories per cup.

Mincemeat Stuffing: Add ½ cup each minced yellow onion and celery sautéed in ¼ cup butter until pale golden. Also mix in 1 cup well-drained prepared mincemeat. About 330 calories per cup.

Prune, Apple, and Cranberry Stuffing: Prepare fruit before stuffing. Simmer 1 cup fresh cranberries with ¼ cup sugar and ½ cup water until berries pop. Off heat, mix in 1 cup diced, pitted prunes and let stand 10 minutes. Drain off liquid and use as part of liquid called for in stuffing. Prepare mix, toss in prepared fruit, 1 diced, peeled, and cored tart cooking apple, and ¼ teaspoon allspice. About 290 calories per cup.

VEAL AND PORK FORCEMEAT

Pounding is necessary for a smooth forcemeat, though vigorous beating with a wooden spoon or electric mixer works fairly well. Any meat can be used for forcemeat, but this combination is unusually good. Use for Galantine or Ballottine or to stuff chicken or game birds. For a 10-pound turkey, double recipe. Forcemeat balls can be used to garnish soup, a poultry or pork platter, leftovers can be cooked like hamburgers. Small panfried patties or balls make excellent hors d'oeuvre.

Makes about 1½ pints, enough to stuff a 5-pound bird

½ cup finely minced yellow onion
2 tablespoons butter or margarine
⅓ cup scalded milk
1 cup dry bread crumbs
½ pound veal, ground twice
½ pound lean pork, ground twice
¼ pound ground pork fat
1 turkey liver, 2–3 chicken livers, or livers from bird to be stuffed, ground fine (optional)
1 egg, lightly beaten
¼ cup brandy
1 teaspoon finely grated lemon rind
¾ teaspoon salt
½ teaspoon thyme
Pinch mace
⅛ teaspoon white pepper

Sauté onion in butter in a skillet 5 minutes over moderate heat until pale golden; set aside. Pour milk over crumbs, mix until smooth, and cool. Pound onion, all meats and fat, a little at a time, in a mortar and pestle until very smooth. Mix in remaining ingredients, including crumb paste, and knead until well blended. Use as a stuffing. About 795 calories per cup if made without turkey or chicken livers, about 815 calories per cup if made with livers.

VARIATIONS:

Veal and Ham Forcemeat: Prepare as directed but substitute ½ pound twice-ground lean cooked ham for the pork. (*Note:* Forcemeat may also be made with veal.) About 745 calories per cup if made without turkey or chicken livers, about 775 calories per cup if made with livers.

Veal and Pork Forcemeat Balls (Makes about 4 dozen): Prepare as directed but omit onion and liver, also substitute ¼ cup light cream for the brandy. Shape into marble-size balls. *To Use as a Soup Garnish:* Poach balls, a few at a time, in salted simmering water, chicken or beef broth 4–5 minutes until just cooked through. Remove with a slotted spoon and add to hot soup just before serving. (*Note:* Recipe can be halved for small amounts of soup; use all veal and serve in a delicately flavored soup.) About 50 calories per ball.

To Use as a Garnish: Brown balls, a few at a time, in about ½" hot lard or vegetable shortening over moderate heat 3–4 minutes, turning often. Drain on paper toweling and mound at one end of a poultry platter or use to fill center of a pork crown roast. About 65 calories per ball.

¢ **BASIC BREAD STUFFING FOR FISH**

Makes about 2 cups, enough to stuff a 3–4-pound fish

1 medium-size yellow onion, peeled and minced
½ cup minced celery
¼ cup butter or margarine
2 cups soft white bread crumbs or 2 cups (½") stale bread cubes
½ teaspoon salt
⅛ teaspoon pepper
1 tablespoon minced parsley

STUFFINGS AND FORCEMEATS

¼ teaspoon each thyme and sage or
½ teaspoon poultry seasoning
1 egg, lightly beaten

Sauté onion and celery in butter in a large, heavy skillet over moderate heat 5 minutes until pale golden. Add all remaining ingredients and toss well to mix. About 410 calories per cup.

LEMON BREAD STUFFING FOR FISH

Makes about 1½ cups, enough to stuff a 3-pound fish

¼ cup minced yellow onion
¼ cup minced celery
2 tablespoons butter or margarine
1¼ cups toasted ½" bread cubes
1½ teaspoons finely grated lemon rind
1 tablespoon lemon juice
1 tablespoon minced parsley
¼ teaspoon salt
¼ teaspoon sage
⅛ teaspoon pepper
2 tablespoons milk

Stir-fry onion and celery in butter in a large, heavy skillet over moderate heat 5–8 minutes until golden. Pour over bread crumbs, add remaining ingredients, and toss lightly to mix. About 175 calories per cup.

VEGETABLE STUFFING FOR FISH

Makes about 2 cups, enough to stuff a 3–4-pound fish

⅓ cup minced scallions
½ cup minced celery
1 small sweet green pepper, cored, seeded, and minced
1 medium-size carrot, peeled and cut in small dice
½ pound mushrooms, wiped clean and minced (include stems)
½ clove garlic, peeled and crushed (optional)
2 tablespoons olive or other cooking oil
2 tomatoes, peeled, seeded, and coarsely chopped
1 pimiento, seeded and minced
¼ cup minced ripe olives
¾ teaspoon salt
⅛ teaspoon pepper

Stir-fry scallions, celery, green pepper, carrot, mushrooms, and, if you like, the garlic in oil in a large, heavy skillet over moderate heat 5–8 minutes until pepper and carrot are crisp tender. Off heat, mix in remaining ingredients. About 230 calories per cup.

TOMATO AND GREEN PEPPER STUFFING FOR FISH

Makes about 2 cups, enough to stuff a 3–4-pound fish

1 small yellow onion, peeled and minced
1 medium-size sweet green pepper, cored, seeded, and minced
¼ cup butter or margarine
1½ cups dry bread crumbs or coarse cracker crumbs
½ cup coarsely peeled, seeded, and chopped tomato
1 hard-cooked egg, peeled and minced
1 teaspoon minced parsley
½ clove garlic, peeled and minced
½ teaspoon salt
⅛ teaspoon pepper

Sauté onion and green pepper in butter in a skillet over moderate heat 5 minutes until onion is pale golden. Off heat, mix in remaining ingredients. About 430 calories per cup.

✠ QUICK MUSHROOM STUFFING FOR FISH

Especially good for stuffed, baked shad. Makes about 2 cups, enough to stuff a 3–4-pound fish

1½ cups soft white bread crumbs
2 tablespoons minced chives
2 tablespoons minced parsley
½ teaspoon dried tarragon or marjoram
1 (4-ounce) can mushroom stems and pieces, drained and minced
½ teaspoon salt
⅛ teaspoon white pepper
3 tablespoons melted butter or margarine
1 egg, lightly beaten

Place all ingredients in a bowl and toss lightly to mix. About 315 calories per cup.

✠ FRUIT STUFFING FOR FISH

Makes about 2 cups, enough to stuff a 3–4-pound fish

1 cup cold cooked rice
1 cup well-drained crushed pineapple
1 orange, peeled, sectioned, seeded, and coarsely cut up
¼ cup sultana raisins
2 tablespoons melted butter
1 teaspoon finely grated lemon rind

Place all ingredients in a bowl and toss lightly to mix. About 360 calories per cup.

CRAB OR SHRIMP STUFFING FOR FISH

Makes about 3 cups, enough to stuff a 5–6-pound fish

¼ cup minced scallions (include some tops)
¼ cup minced celery
⅓ cup butter or margarine
2 cups (½") soft bread cubes
1 cup flaked cooked or canned crab meat or minced cooked, shelled, and deveined shrimp
1 tablespoon lemon juice
Pinch nutmeg
Pinch cayenne pepper

Stir-fry scallions and celery in butter in a skillet over moderate heat 2–3 minutes. Add bread cubes and stir-fry until lightly browned. Off heat, add remaining ingredients and toss lightly to mix. About 305 calories per cup.

VARIATION:

Clam Stuffing for Fish: Prepare as directed but substitute 1 (7½-ounce) can drained minced clams for crab meat. About 315 calories per cup.

✠ EASY ALMOND STUFFING FOR FISH

Especially good for trout.
Makes about 2 cups, enough to stuff a 3–4-pound fish

1 cup poultry stuffing mix
3 tablespoons melted butter
¼ cup minced celery
2 tablespoons minced parsley
¾ cup finely chopped, toasted, blanched almonds

Toss all ingredients together to mix. About 565 calories per cup.

CHAPTER 16

VEGETABLES

Of all the world's foods, none has greater color or variety than vegetables. None can lift a meal more quickly from the humdrum to the dramatic. And few offer cooks greater challenge.

It takes experience to whip potatoes into snowy drifts without cooling them down, to lift asparagus from the pot the second it's turning from crisp to tender, to build a soufflé out of spinach. Few people understand the art of vegetable cookery better than the Chinese and Japanese, to whom every leaf, stalk, and root is a living thing to be cooked as quickly and kindly as possible. They use practically no water, preferring to cut vegetables into delicate shapes and stir-fry them in a smidgen of oil (there are few better ways, incidentally, of preserving vitamins).

The French, too, have a talent with vegetables, particularly green vegetables, which they blanch in boiling salted water, then "refresh" in ice water. This sets the color, crunch, and flavor, meaning that a vegetable can be held several hours if necessary. It then needs only a warming in butter, broth, or sauce. Americans, strangely, have been cool toward vegetables until recently. Something—travel, perhaps, or the proliferation of ethnic restaurants—has glamorized vegetables, given them an importance long overdue.

How to Bring Out the Best in Vegetables

– The quicker vegetables go from plot to pot, the better. If you grow your own, you're lucky. If not, shop on days fresh shipments arrive.
– Buy only what perishable vegetables you can use within a day or two.
– Wash vegetables before cooking, *not* before refrigerating.
– Slice or dice vegetables as you're ready to cook them; never soak in water (except for potatoes and artichokes, which will darken if not soaked).
– Boil vegetables whole and unpeeled whenever possible. The smaller the pieces, the greater the nutrient loss.
– Boil vegetables quickly in a minimum of water (potatoes and artichokes excepted) and use any "pot

likker" in soups and sauces. The French method may seem to contradict this rule but doesn't because the final heating is the cooking.

– Cook only as much of a vegetable as you need (leftovers fade fast). The best way to reheat vegetables is in the top of a double boiler with enough broth, water, milk, or sauce to moisten and revitalize them.

Basic Ways of Cooking Vegetables

Boiling: Cooking *in* boiling or simmering liquid. Start vegetables in boiling liquid, then time after liquid returns to a boil. Adjust heat so liquid boils gently throughout cooking. Cover pot or not as individual recipes recommend.

Parboiling: Partial cooking; often called for when vegetables are to be added to stews, casseroles, or other recipes.

Poaching: A variation of boiling in which asparagus or broccoli is simmered flat in a skillet in an inch or so of water.

Steaming: Cooking in a covered pot on a rack over boiling water. Though standing in some water, artichokes and stalked vegetables are technically steamed; only those parts *in* water are boiled.

Frying (Sautéing): Cooking, uncovered, in a small amount of fat until tender and/or brown. Use a skillet or French sauté pan and moderately high heat.

Stir-Frying: The Oriental technique of tossing finely cut foods as they fry.

French or Deep Fat Frying: Cooking immersed in hot fat, 360–400° F. You'll need 3 pounds shortening or 2 quarts oil to do a proper job, also a deep fat fryer and thermometer. Vegetables to be deep fat fried should be cut in small pieces if they're to cook through by the time they brown.

Braising (Panning): A combination of sautéing and boiling. A popular method is to brown a vegetable lightly in butter, then add broth or wine and simmer, covered, until tender—either on top of the stove or in a 325–350° F. oven.

Pressure Cooking: High speed steaming in a pressure cooker.

Baking: Cooking uncovered without liquid or fat in the oven (this refers to baking potatoes and other vegetables solo, not *en casserole*).

Roasting: Oven cooking, usually uncovered in some fat, often in tandem with a roast.

Broiling: Quick cooking under or over intense heat. Only a few vegetables—tomatoes, eggplant—broil well; they must be sliced thick and brushed with oil or marinade.

Charcoal Broiling: Cooking over hot coals; again tomatoes and eggplant are best.

About Storing, Canning, and Freezing Vegetables

(See chapters on the larder, canning, and freezing)

How to Dress Up Canned Vegetables

Because canned vegetables are already cooked, they should only be heated through. Two ways to do it:
– Drain can liquid into saucepan and

ABOUT PRESSURE COOKING VEGETABLES

Handy as pressure cookers are, they shouldn't be used for all vegetables. Delicate ones will overcook and become mushy or slimy, dried ones may break apart, clog the safety valve, and threaten to blow the lid off the cooker.

Vegetables That Pressure Cook Poorly:

Jerusalem artichokes	Corn (on the cob or off)	Eggplant	Mushrooms
Asparagus	Cucumbers	Endive	Okra
Celery	Dried beans, peas,	Ferns	Peppers
Chestnuts	or lentils	Fennel	Tomatoes
Chinese cabbage		Leeks	Zucchini

Vegetables That Pressure Cook Well: Most other vegetables pressure cook nicely in jig time, particularly such slow boilers as potatoes, parsnips, rutabagas, and turnips. Always add water to a pressure cooker as its manufacturer directs, and use his instructions for sealing, building up, and reducing pressures. Use the chart below as a guide for vegetable preparation, seasoning, and approximate cooking times (count time *after* 15 pounds pressure is reached).

Vegetable	Preparation	For Better Flavor Cook With	Time at 15 Pounds Pressure
Globe artichokes	Wash and trim as for steaming; leave whole.	1/4 teaspoon salt	6-10 minutes depending on size
Beans (green or wax)	Prepare as for boiling; leave whole, snap or French.	—	1-2 minutes for Frenched beans 2-3 minutes for whole or snapped
Beans (lima)	Shell.	—	2 minutes for baby limas 3-5 minutes for Fordhooks
Beets	Prepare as for boiling leave whole.	—	10-20 minutes depending on size and age
Beet greens	Prepare as for steaming.	—	2-3 minutes
Broccoli	Prepare as for steaming.	1/4 teaspoon salt	1½-2 minutes
Brussels sprouts	Prepare as for boiling.	1/4 teaspoon salt	2 minutes
Cabbage (green)	Cut into thin wedges or shred medium fine.	1/4 teaspoon salt	5-6 minutes for wedges 3 minutes for shredded cabbage
Cabbage (red)	Shred medium fine.	1-2 tablespoons lemon juice or vinegar	3-4 minutes

ABOUT PRESSURE COOKING VEGETABLES (continued)

Vegetable	Preparation	For Better Flavor Cook With	Time at 15 Pounds Pressure
Cardoons	Prepare as for boiling.	1/4 teaspoon salt	15 minutes
Carrots	Prepare as for boiling; leave whole, slice, or sliver.	1/2 teaspoon sugar	2-3 minutes for sliced or slivered carrots 4-6 minutes for whole carrots
Cauliflower	Wash and divide into large flowerets of equal size.	—	3-4 minutes
Celeriac	Trim, wash, peel, and slice or dice.	1/2 teaspoon salt	5 minutes
Chard, collards, kale, mustard	Prepare as for boiling.	—	3-5 minutes
Dandelion greens	Prepare as for cooking.	—	4 minutes
Kohlrabi	Prepare as for boiling.	1/4 teaspoon salt	4-5 minutes
Onions (white)	Peel but leave whole.	—	5-6 minutes
Onions (yellow)	Peel but leave whole.	—	6-8 minutes
Parsnips	Prepare as for boiling. If young, leave whole; otherwise slice or dice.	1 teaspoon light brown sugar	2 minutes for sliced or diced parsnips 6-8 minutes for whole young parsnips
Green peas	Shell.	A few pea pods	1 minute
Irish potatoes (use boiling varieties only)	Scrub but do not peel.	—	10-15 minutes for new potatoes 15-20 minutes for mature boiling potatoes
Sweet potatoes	Scrub but do not peel.	—	8-10 minutes

Vegetable	Preparation	For Better Flavor Cook With	Time at 15 Pounds Pressure
Pumpkin	Cut in chunks 4" long and 2" wide but do not peel.	—	15 minutes
Rutabaga	Peel and cut in 1" cubes.	—	10-12 minutes
Salsify	Prepare as for boiling; cut in 2" chunks, slice, or sliver.	1/4 teaspoon salt	4-8 minutes for slices or slivers 10-12 minutes for chunks
Spinach	Prepare as for steaming.	1/2 teaspoon salt	1 minute
Summer squash (yellow and pattypan only)	Prepare as for boiling or steaming and cut in slices 1/4" thick.	1/4 teaspoon salt	2 minutes
Winter squash Acorn	Halve, remove seeds and stringy portions.	—	8-10 minutes
Butternut	Peel and cut in 2"-3" chunks.	—	5-9 minutes
Hubbard and other thick-fleshed varieties	Peel and cut in 2"-3" chunks.	—	12-15 minutes
Turnip greens	Prepare as for boiling.	—	3-5 minutes
Turnips	Peel and cut in 1/2" cubes.	—	3-5 minutes

VEGETABLE SEASONING CHART

If vegetables are really fresh, they need only the simplest seasoning. But when they've stood too long in the bin, are canned or must be reheated, they profit by a bit of dressing up. Picking combinations from the chart below, add to each cup of cooked vegetables: 2-3 tablespoons sauce, butter, or topping; or 1/2 teaspoon minced fresh herbs (1/4 teaspoon of the dried); and/or a pinch of spice. If vegetables are to be warmed in the sauce, use 1/3-1/2 cup for each cup of vegetables.

Vegetable	For Hot Vegetables			For Hot or Cold Vegetables	For Cold Vegetables
	Sauces	Butters	Toppings	Herbs and Spices	Sauces and Dressings
Globe Artichokes *Asparagus*	Béchamel Hollandaise Mock Hollandaise Mornay Mousseline Poulette Velouté	Browned Lemon Seasoned	Chopped, hard-cooked egg Crisp bacon bits Crushed cheese crackers Grated Cheddar or Parmesan Minced pimiento	Basil Chervil Chives Curry Dill Oregano Parsley	Toasted sesame seeds *Artichokes only:* Bay leaves Coriander Garlic	Aioli Chiffon French Oil and Vinegar Rémoulade Russian
Beans: *Green* *Wax* *Lima*	Béchamel Cheese Hollandaise Mock Hollandaise Mornay Mustard Poulette Velouté	Browned Garlic Herb Lemon	Chopped toasted almonds or pecans Crumbled French-fried onions Crumbled Roquefort Grated Cheddar, Swiss, or Parmesan cheese Minced scallions	Basil Bay leaves Celery seeds Chervil Dill Garlic Marjoram Mustard	Oregano Parsley Savory Tarragon Thyme	Blue Cheese French Garlic Green Goddess Mayonnaise Spanish Vinaigrette

	Sauces	Seasonings	Herbs and spices	

Beets
Carrots
Parsnips
	Béchamel
	Medium White
	Mousseline
	Parsley
	Poulette
	Velouté
		Herb
		Lemon
		Maître
		  d'Hôtel
		Orange
		Seasoned
			Buttered, browned bread
			  crumbs
			Currant jelly or orange
			  marmalade
			Light brown sugar
			Maple sugar or syrup
			Carrots only: seedless
			  green grapes
				Caraway seeds
				Cardamom
				Celery seeds
				Chervil
				Chives
				Cinnamon
				Coriander
				Cumin
				Dill
				Fennel
				Ginger
					Horseradish
					Mace
					Marjoram
					Mint
					Nutmeg
					Oregano
					Parsley
					Rosemary
					Savory
					Tarragon
					Thyme
						Beets and Carrots only:
						Oil and Vinegar
						Ravigote
						Sour Cream Horseradish

Broccoli
Brussels sprouts
Cauliflower
Collards
Green cabbage
Kale
	Béchamel
	Cheese
	Hollandaise
	Mock Hollandaise
	Mousseline
	Poulette
		Browned
		Lemon
		Maître
		  d'Hôtel
			Buttered bread crumbs
			Capers
			Crisp bacon bits
			Fried parsley
			Grated Cheddar or Parmesan
			  cheese
			Toasted, chopped almonds,
			  pecans, or peanuts
				Basil
				Caraway seeds
				Cardamom
				Celery seeds
				Chervil
				Chives
				Cumin seeds
				Curry powder
				Dill
				Ginger
					Mustard
					Paprika
					Saffron
					Savory
					Tarragon
					Thyme
					Turmeric
					Cabbage only:
					Horseradish
					Juniper berries
						Broccoli and cauliflower
						only:
						Aioli
						Chiffon
						Ravigote
						Spanish Vinaigrette

Red cabbage	Medium White Parsley Velouté	Lemon Maître d'Hôtel	Apple cider Red wine vinegar Sour cream	Anise seeds Caraway seeds Celery seeds Chervil Coriander Cumin seeds Dill	Fennel Horseradish Juniper berries Mace Nutmeg Savory Tarragon	

VEGETABLE SEASONING CHART (continued)

Vegetable	For Hot Vegetables			For Hot or Cold Vegetables		For Cold Vegetables
	Sauces	Butters	Toppings	Herbs and Spices		Sauces and Dressings
Celeriac Celery Cucumbers Endive Fennel	Béchamel Cheese Medium White Mornay Parsley Poulette Velouté	Browned Herb Lemon Seasoned	Buttered bread crumbs Chopped, toasted almonds, pecans, or piñon nuts; Brazil nut slivers Grated Cheddar, Parmesan or Swiss cheese Minced pimiento	Basil Bay leaves Chervil Chives Cumin seeds Dill Fennel Mace	Marjoram Mint Oregano Paprika Parsley Savory Tarragon Thyme	Aioli French Mayonnaise Rémoulade Russian Thousand Island
Corn	*Whole kernel only:* Cheese Medium White Parsley	Browned Chili Curry Herb Maitre d'Hôtel Seasoned	*Whole kernel only:* Crisp bacon bits Crumbled French-fried onions Minced green pepper or pimiento Minced ripe or green olives Minced scallions or red onion	Chervil Chives Dill Parsley Savory Thyme	*Whole kernel only:* Celery seeds	
Greens: Beet Chard Mustard Spinach Turnip	Béchamel Cheese Hollandaise Italian dressing Mock Hollandaise Mornay Mustard	Browned Lemon	Chopped, toasted almonds, pecans or peanuts Crisp bacon bits Crumbled corn bread Crushed cheese crackers Minced hard-cooked egg Minced onion	Basil Bay leaves Curry powder Mustard	Oregano Parsley Tarragon Thyme	Oil and Vinegar

Mushrooms	Cheese Mousseline Parsley	Browned Garlic Maitre d'Hôtel	Crisp bacon bits Cognac (try flaming) Medium sweet sherry Medium sweet Madeira Sour cream	Basil Bay leaves Chervil Chives Curry powder Dill	Fennel Marjoram Oregano Savory Tarragon Thyme	Herb Oil and Vinegar
Okra	Cheese Mushroom Tomato Velouté	Browned Lemon	Crisp bacon bits Grated Parmesan Sour cream	Basil Bay leaves Chervil Chives	Dill Fennel Savory Thyme	
Onions Leeks Scallions	Béchamel Cheese Medium White Mornay Parsley Velouté	Browned Herb Orange	Buttered bread crumbs Chopped, toasted pecans or peanuts Crisp bacon bits Medium dry sherry Medium dry Madeira	Basil Bay leaves Chervil Chili powder Curry powder Dill Fennel Mace	Mustard Nutmeg Paprika Parsley Sage Savory Tarragon Thyme	French Herb Oil and Vinegar

Green peas	Béchamel
	Cheese
	Mint
	Mustard
	Mushroom and
	   Cheese
		Herb
		Maitre
		   d'Hôtel
		Orange
		Seasoned
			Buttered bread crumbs or
			   poultry stuffing mix
			Chopped, toasted almonds,
			   pecans, or peanuts
			Crumbled French-fried onions
			Sliced scallions
			Sliced water chestnuts
				Basil
				Chervil
				Fennel
				Ginger
				Mint
				Mace
					Parsley
					Rosemary
					Savory
					Tarragon
					Thyme
					Turmeric	

VEGETABLE SEASONING CHART (continued)

	For Hot Vegetables			For Hot or Cold Vegetables		For Cold Vegetables
Vegetable	Sauces	Butters	Toppings	Herbs and Spices		Sauces and Dressings
Irish potatoes	Cheese Medium White Mushroom and Cheese Parsley	Browned Herb Lemon Maître d'Hôtel	Crumbled French-fried onions Grated Cheddar or Gruyère cheese Minced dill pickle Sour cream	Basil Bay leaves Caraway seeds Celery seeds Chervil Chives Cumin Curry powder Dill	Marjoram Mint Oregano Parsley Rosemary Sage Savory Tarragon Thyme	Herb Mayonnaise Oil and Vinegar Spanish Vinaigrette
Summer squash Eggplant	Béchamel Cheese Mornay Mushroom and Cheese Parsley	Herb Maître d'Hôtel Seasoned	Buttered bread crumbs or poultry stuffing mix Chopped, toasted almonds or pecans Crumbled French-fried onions Grated Parmesan or Cheddar cheese Minced sautéed green or red pepper	Basil Bay leaves Chervil Chives Cinnamon Cumin seeds Curry powder Dill Mace Mayonnaise	Mint Nutmeg Oregano Parsley Rosemary Sage Savory Tarragon Thyme	French Herb Italian Oil and Vinegar Spanish Vinaigrette
Winter squash Pumpkin Sweet potatoes Yams	Medium White Parsley	Herb Lemon Orange	Dark or light brown sugar Maple sugar or syrup Molasses Sweet sherry Sweet Madeira	Allspice Cinnamon Cloves Ginger Mace	Nutmeg Parsley Savory Thyme	

Tomatoes	*For baked, broiled, or fried slices only:*		Basil	French
	Béarnaise	Buttered bread crumbs or poultry stuffing mix	Bay leaves	Herb
	Béchamel	Chili		Chervil	Italian
	Cheese	Curry	Deviled or minced ham	Chili powder	Oil and Vinegar
	Hollandaise	Garlic	Duxelles or sautéed, minced mushrooms	Chives	Russian
	Mock Hollandaise	Herb		Cumin seeds	Spanish Vinaigrette
	Mustard	Maître d'Hôtel	Crumbled French-fried onions	Curry powder	Thousand Island
	Mushroom and Cheese	Seasoned	Grated Cheddar, Parmesan, or Swiss cheese	Dill	
	Parsley		Puréed peas or spinach	Horseradish	
			Mustard (especially Dijon)		
			Any seafood salad		
Turnips Rutabaga	Béchamel	Browned	Crisp bacon bits	Cardamom	
	Cheese	Herb	Crumbled French-fried onions	Chervil	
	Medium White	Lemon	Grated Cheddar or Parmesan cheese	Cinnamon	
	Parsley	Orange		Cumin	
				Dill	
				Fennel	

Marjoram, Mint, Mustard, Oregano, Paprika, Parsley, Sage, Tarragon, Thyme

Ginger, Mace, Nutmeg, Paprika, Savory, Tarragon

Use fresh, frozen, canned, or leftover vegetables in soufflés, but drain them *very well* before puréeing or chopping and measuring so that they will not thin the sauce too much. The chart below indicates which liquid ingredients and seasonings are most compatible with which vegetable, and notes any modifications that should be made in the *Basic Vegetable Soufflé* recipe. Choose the type of soufflé you want to make from the chart, then prepare according to the *Basic Vegetable Soufflé* recipe that precedes. *NOTE:* T = tablespoon, t = teaspoon.

BASIC VEGETABLE SOUFFLÉ CHART

Vegetable	Liquid	Seasonings	Special Instructions
Artichoke (globe) About 240 calories per serving if made with milk, 280 per serving if made with cream.	1/2 cup milk or light cream + 1/2 cup chicken broth	1 t. grated onion, 1/4 cup minced mushrooms, and 1 T. grated Parmesan	Use artichoke hearts or bottoms. Stir-fry onion and mushrooms in butter called for, then blend in flour. Mix in cheese along with egg yolks.
Asparagus About 235 calories per serving if made with milk, 275 if made with cream.	1/2 cup milk or light cream + 1/2 cup chicken broth	1 T. grated Parmesan and 2 T. minced pimiento	—
Broccoli About 230 calories per serving.	1/2 cup milk + 1/2 cup chicken broth	1 t. finely grated lemon rind or 2 T. minced capers	Purée stems and flowerets together or use flowerets only.
Carrot About 230 calories per serving if made with milk, 275 per serving if made with cream.	1/2 cup milk or light cream + 1/2 cup chicken broth	1 T. grated onion, 1 T. minced parsley, and a pinch of thyme OR 1 t. each finely grated orange rind and mint flakes and a pinch nutmeg or mace	Purée carrots for a full-flavored soufflé.
Cauliflower About 230 calories per serving if made with milk, 275 if made with cream.	1/2 cup milk or light cream + 1/2 cup cooking water or chicken broth	1 T. grated Parmesan, 1/4 t. minced chives, chervil, or dill, and 1/8 t. nutmeg	Purée stems and flowerets together or use flowerets only.
Celery About 250 calories per serving if made with milk, 290 if made with cream.	1/2 cup milk or light cream + 1/2 cup cooking water or chicken broth	1 minced small yellow onion, 3 T. grated Parmesan, and a pinch of thyme	Cook onion with celery. Add cheese and thyme to hot sauce.

136

Vegetable	Liquid	Seasonings	Instructions
Corn (whole-kernel) About 315 calories per serving if made with milk, 360 if made with cream.	1/2 cup milk or light cream + 1/2 cup cooking water or chicken broth	2 T. minced onion and 2 T. each minced green pepper and pimiento	Stir-fry onion in butter called for, mix remaining seasonings into hot sauce.
Green pea About 315 calories per serving.	1/2 cup light cream + 1/2 cup cooking water or chicken broth	1 T. grated onion, 1 t. finely grated orange rind, 1 T. mint flakes, and a pinch each of rosemary and nutmeg	Stir-fry onion and orange rind in butter called for, then blend in flour. Mix remaining seasonings into hot sauce.
Mushroom About 255 calories per serving.	1/2 cup light cream + 1/2 cup beef broth	2 T. minced onion and a pinch each of thyme and mace	Stir-fry 1½ cups minced raw mushrooms with onion, thyme, and mace in butter called for, then blend in flour.
Onion About 295 calories per serving.	1/2 cup light cream + 1/2 cup beef broth	1/2 small minced clove of garlic, 1/2 t. thyme, pinch of nutmeg, and 3 T. grated Parmesan	Use 2 cups chopped raw onion instead of 1⅓ cups cooked vegetable called for in basic vegetable soufflé. Stir-fry in butter with garlic, thyme, and nutmeg. Blend in flour; add cheese to hot sauce.
Potato About 290 calories per serving if made with milk, 330 if made with cream.	1/2 cup milk or light cream + 1/2 cup beef or chicken broth	1/4 cup minced onion, 2 T. minced parsley, 1/4 t. each sage and thyme, and a pinch of mace	Use hot, unseasoned mashed potatoes. Stir-fry all seasonings in butter called for; blend in flour.
Pumpkin, yam, sweet potato, winter squash About 255 calories per serving for pumpkin or winter squash soufflé, 300 per serving for yam or sweet potato soufflé.	1/2 cup milk + 1/2 cup chicken broth	2 T. minced onion, 1 T. light brown sugar, 1 t. each apple-pie spice and finely grated orange rind	Use hot, unseasoned mashed pumpkin, yams, sweet potatoes, or winter squash. Stir-fry all seasonings in butter called for, then blend in flour.
Spinach About 275 calories per serving.	1/2 cup light cream + 1/2 cup beef broth	1 minced small yellow onion and 1/4 t. nutmeg	Brown butter called for, add onion and stir-fry until limp; blend in flour and nutmeg.
Summer squash About 230 calories per serving if made with milk, 275 per serving if made with cream.	1/2 cup milk or light cream – 1/2 cup chicken broth	1 minced small yellow onion and 1/4 t. each rosemary and nutmeg	Stir-fry all seasonings in butter called for, then blend in flour.

boil, uncovered, until reduced by half. Add vegetable, a fat chunk of butter, and heat and stir 2–3 minutes. For seasoning ideas, see the Vegetable Seasoning Chart.
– Pick a sauce compatible with the vegetable (see Vegetable Seasoning Chart), then prepare, using can liquid. Add ⅓–½ cup sauce to each cup of vegetable, warm and stir until heated through, about 5 minutes.

Some Ways to Glamorize Frozen Vegetables

With so many specialty frozen vegetables available, we tend to neglect the plain-frozen standbys. Almost any of them improve when cooked in chicken or beef broth instead of water, also with the simplest additions to the pot. For example (amounts for a 9- or 10-ounce package unless otherwise indicated):

Artichoke hearts and asparagus:
 – To the pot add a sprig fresh tarragon or dill or a pinch of the dried.
 – Cook in ¼ cup each butter and water with a strip of lemon rind.
 – Cook artichokes in a ½-and-½ mixture of tarragon vinegar and water.

Beans (green, wax, or Italian):
 – To the pot add 1 peeled clove garlic, 1 bay leaf, and 2 tablespoons olive oil.
 – Cook in Italian or herb dressing instead of water; omit seasonings called for.
 – Cook with 1 (4-ounce) can undrained sliced mushrooms; add no water.
 – Cook 2 packages beans with 1 (1-pound) can undrained white onions; add no water.
 – Cook in ¼ cup each dry white wine and water with a little mint or fennel.
 – Cook in ¼ cup each wine vinegar, and water with 2 tablespoons sugar.
 – Cook with 1 cup minced celery, using water called for.

Beans (Lima):
 – To the pot add ⅓ cup minced scallions.
 – To the pot add a *bouquet garni** or rosemary sprig.
 – Cook in milk (or evaporated milk) instead of water (simmer, don't boil).

Broccoli, Brussels sprouts and cauliflower:
 – Place frozen vegetable in a shallow casserole, top with 1 (10½-ounce) can condensed cream of mushroom, chicken, or celery soup mixed with ½ cup milk. Cover and bake 40–50 minutes at 350° F. (The cheese soup works well too.)
 – Cook broccoli in a skillet with 2 tablespoons each cooking oil, vinegar, and water with a peeled clove of garlic.

Carrots:
 – To the pot add 1 thick orange or lemon slice or 2 tablespoons orange marmalade.
 – To the pot add a *bouquet garni** or rosemary sprig.
 – Cook with 1 bunch small scallions (white part only), using water called for.
 – Cook with 2 tablespoons butter and a small piece peeled fresh gingerroot, using water called for.

Corn:
 – Cook frozen ears in ginger ale or a ½-and-½ mixture of milk and water.
 – Cook cut corn in milk or light cream instead of water; add 1 teaspoon sugar.
 – Cook cut corn in light cream instead of water with 1 tablespoon minced chives.
 – Cook cut corn with ¼ cup frozen chopped sweet green pepper and 2 tablespoons butter; add no water.

VEGETABLES 139

Green peas—Use *no water;* cook instead in any of the following:
- 2 tablespoons butter with a mint sprig or small peeled white onion.
- 2 tablespoons butter with 1 teaspoon each grated orange rind and chopped mint.
- 2 tablespoons each butter and small cocktail onions.
- ¼ cup heavy cream and 2 shredded lettuce leaves.

Squash (butternut):
- Sprinkle with a little nutmeg, cinnamon, and cloves, bake as directed, and stir before serving.
- Drizzle with a little maple syrup or honey before baking; stir before serving.
- Dot with Herb Butter before baking; stir before serving.

Squash (zucchini and summer)—Use *no water;* cook instead with:
- 1 large peeled and chopped tomato and 1 tablespoon each olive oil and minced fresh basil.
- 1 large, peeled and sliced onion that has been sautéed in 2 tablespoons butter or olive oil. Simply add squash to skillet after sautéeing onion, and cook covered, until tender. Season with a little summer savory or oregano.

Spinach—Use *no water;* instead, cover and cook with:
- 2 tablespoons olive oil and 1 peeled clove garlic.
- 2 tablespoons butter and ¼ cup minced scallions.
- 3 tablespoons heavy cream, a pinch nutmeg or mace.
- 2 tablespoons butter and ¼ cup chopped mushrooms.

BASIC VEGETABLE SOUFFLÉ

Because the basic proportions and methods of preparing any vegetable soufflé are very much the same, you can, by using the master recipe below, make a variety of different vegetable soufflés. If, for example, you choose to make a Mushroom Soufflé, turn first to the Basic Vegetable Soufflé Chart that precedes to determine what liquid ingredient you should use, what seasonings, what special instructions you should note, then prepare the Mushroom Soufflé following the recipe below. Makes 4 servings

3 tablespoons butter or margarine
3 tablespoons flour
1 cup liquid (see Basic Vegetable Soufflé Chart)
4 eggs, separated
1 teaspoon salt
Pinch white pepper
Seasonings (see Basic Vegetable Soufflé Chart)
1⅓ cups puréed, mashed, or finely chopped cooked vegetable (see Basic Vegetable Soufflé Chart)
Pinch cream of tartar

Melt butter in a saucepan over moderate heat, blend in flour, slowly stir in liquid, and heat, stirring, until thickened and no raw taste of flour remains. Beat egg yolks lightly, blend in a little hot sauce, then stir back into pan; heat and stir 1–2 minutes over lowest heat. Off heat, mix in salt, pepper, seasonings, and vegetable. Lay a piece of wax paper flat on sauce and cool to room temperature. (*Note:* You can make recipe up to this point ahead of time, then cover and chill until about 2 hours before serving. Let mixture come to room temperature before proceeding.) Preheat oven to 350° F. Beat egg whites until frothy, add cream of tartar, and continue beating until stiff but not dry. Fold whites into vegetable mixture, spoon into an ungreased 5-cup soufflé dish. Bake, uncovered, on center rack of oven 35–45 minutes until puffy and browned. Serve at once, accompanied, if you like, with an appropriate sauce (see Some Sauces, Butters, and Toppings for Vegetables).

VEGETABLE FRITTERS

A variety of vegetables lend themselves to batter frying. Some should be parboiled first; others need not be. But all should be cut in small—about bite-size—pieces and all should be thoroughly dry before being dipped in batter and deep fried.
Makes 4 servings

Suitable Vegetables:
Artichoke Hearts (2 9-ounce packages frozen artichoke hearts, parboiled, drained, and patted dry on paper toweling)
Carrots (1 pound carrots, peeled, sliced ½" thick, parboiled, drained, and patted dry on paper toweling)
Cauliflowerets (flowerets from 1 large head, parboiled, drained, and patted dry on paper toweling)
Parsley Fluffs (3 cups, washed and patted dry on paper toweling)
Parsnips (1 pound parsnips, peeled, sliced ½" thick, parboiled, drained, and patted dry on paper toweling)
Sweet Potatoes (4 medium-size potatoes, parboiled, peeled, sliced ¼" thick, and patted dry on paper toweling)
Turnips or Rutabaga (2 cups 1" cubes, parboiled, drained, and patted dry on paper toweling)
Zucchini or Yellow Squash (4 medium-size squash, scrubbed and sliced ½" thick)

Shortening or cooking oil for deep fat frying
1 recipe Basic Batter for Fried Foods

Prepare vegetable as directed and set aside. Heat shortening or oil in a deep fat fryer over moderately high heat to 380° F. on a deep fat thermometer. Dip vegetable, a few pieces at a time, into batter, allowing excess to drain off. Drop into fat and fry 2–5 minutes until golden brown (time will vary according to vegetable). Drain on paper toweling, then keep warm in a 250° F. oven while you fry the rest (don't cover or fritters will become soggy). Serve piping hot with lemon wedges or, if you prefer, with soy sauce. Recipe too flexible for a meaningful calorie count.

VEGETABLES À LA GRECQUE

Certain vegetables—summer squash, mushrooms, leeks, to name three—are delicious served cold in a fragrant lemon and oil dressing. Here's how to prepare them.
Makes 4 servings

Suitable Vegetables:
Artichoke Hearts (2 9-ounce packages frozen artichoke hearts boiled 10 minutes and drained)
Asparagus (2 pounds asparagus, washed, trimmed, parboiled, and drained)
Celery Hearts (6 medium-size celery hearts, parboiled and drained)
Cucumbers (8 small cucumbers, peeled, quartered, seeded, parboiled, and drained)
Endives (6 medium-size endives, parboiled, drained, and halved)
Fennel (4 bulbs of fennel, parboiled and drained)
Green or Wax Beans (1 pound green or wax beans, tipped, parboiled, and drained)
Hearts of Palm (one 14-ounce can hearts of palm, drained and sliced ½" thick)
Leeks (2 bunches leeks, trimmed, parboiled, and drained)

Mushrooms (1 pound medium-size mushrooms, stemmed and peeled)
Zucchini or Yellow Squash (2 pounds zucchini or yellow squash, scrubbed, sliced ½" thick, parboiled, and drained)

1 recipe À la Grecque Marinade

Prepare vegetable as directed above, cover with marinade, and chill 2–3 hours, turning occasionally. Serve cold as a vegetable, salad, or first course, spooning a little marinade over each portion.

VARIATION:

Vegetables à la Dijonnaise: Prepare vegetable as directed. Blend 1 tablespoon Dijon mustard into À la Grecque Marinade, pour over vegetable, and marinate as directed. Recipes too flexible for meaningful calorie counts.

GLOBE ARTICHOKES

(Also known as French or Italian Artichokes)
These large, green flowerlike buds are possibly the most beautiful of the world's vegetables; certainly they are one of the most delicate and elegant. Native to Mediterranean Europe, artichokes were brought first to America by the French who settled in Louisiana in the eighteenth century. But it was the Spaniards, settling in California, who first grew them with success. The mild California climate proved ideal for artichokes, and the fertile Salinas Valley below San Francisco particularly favorable (the Salinas Valley is today the "artichoke capital of the world"). With millions of artichokes now being harvested each year, we can all enjoy a luxury once reserved for the rich and the royal.

Season	For Top Quality	Amount to Buy	Nutritive Value	Calories (unseasoned)
October–June; peak months: April, May	Pick tight, plump green buds heavy for their size.	1 (⅓–¾ pound) artichoke per person.	Poor	Low: 30–50 per steamed artichoke; 80 per cup of hearts

To Prepare Artichokes for Cooking:
Snap off stems, pulling any tough fibers from bottom of artichokes. Cut off ragged stem edges, remove blemished outer petals, then snip off prickly petal tips. Wash under cold running water and rub cut edges with lemon to prevent darkening.

To Remove Choke (this can be done before or after cooking), spread petals and reach down into the center, pulling out thistly pieces. With a teaspoon, scoop out any remaining prickly bits. (*Note:* De-

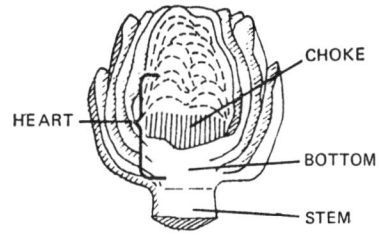

choked artichokes will cook twice as fast as those with chokes in.) If artichokes are not to be cooked immediately, keep covered with cold acidulated water (1 tablespoon lemon juice or white vinegar to 1 quart water).

To Prepare Artichoke Hearts: Break off stems and trim away ragged edges. Remove all but inner cone of petals, lay each heart on its side and slice off prickly tips. Rub cut edges with lemon and drop into acidulated water. To keep creamy-white, don't dechoke until after cooking.

To Prepare Artichoke Bottoms: These can be made before or after cooking. In either case, begin with the hearts, remove all petals and chokes. If raw, rub with lemon and soak in acidulated water; boil as you would artichoke hearts.

To Slice an Artichoke: Cut off stem and top ⅓ of artichoke and discard; remove choke. Lay artichoke on its side and cut horizontally straight across the bud in ¼" slices, letting them fall in acidulated water. Pat dry before sautéing or frying.

Cooking Tip: Cook artichokes in an enamel, stainless-steel, or teflon-lined pan so they won't discolor or taste of metal.

Serving Tip: Don't serve artichokes with wine or tea—for some reason, the flavors cancel one another out.

How to Eat an Artichoke: Eating an artichoke is like playing "he-loves-me, he-loves-me-not" with a daisy. Pluck off one petal at a time, dip base in accompanying sauce, then nibble off flesh. If the choke hasn't been removed, lift out or loosen with knife and fork. Cut bottom into bite-sized chunks and eat with a fork, first dunking each into sauce.

BASIC STEAMED GLOBE ARTICHOKES

Steaming is the preferred method for cooking artichokes because there is less chance of their overcooking. Steamed artichokes, moreover, are easier to drain than boiled artichokes because they have not been submerged in cooking water.
Makes 4 servings

4 large globe artichokes, prepared for cooking
Boiling water (about 3 cups)
¼ cup cider vinegar
1 teaspoon salt
1 clove garlic, peeled and quartered (optional)

Stand artichokes stem down in a deep enamel, stainless-steel, or teflon-lined kettle just big enough to hold them snugly. (You can stand them on a trivet, if you like, but it's not necessary.) Pour in boiling water to a depth of 1", add remaining ingredients, cover, and steam 45 minutes over moderate heat or until you can pull a leaf off easily (remember that dechoked artichokes will cook twice as fast). Lift artichokes from kettle with tongs and drain upside down in a colander. Serve hot as a first course or vegetable with melted butter or hot sauce (see Vegetable Seasoning Chart for ideas). Or chill and serve as a first course or salad. About 140 calories per serving topped with 1 tablespoon melted butter.

To Boil Artichokes: Follow above recipe but add enough boiling water to cover.

To Boil Artichoke Hearts: For 4 servings you will need 8 artichokes. Prepare hearts* as directed. Bring 1 quart water, 2 tablespoons lemon juice, and 1½ teaspoons salt to a boil in a large, deep saucepan, add hearts, cover, and simmer 30–40 minutes until tender (liquid should cover hearts at all times, so add additional water if necessary). Drain upside down in a colander, remove chokes,* season with melted butter or margarine, and serve. About 140 calories per serving topped with 1 tablespoon melted butter.

To Parboil Artichokes or Artichoke Hearts for Use in Other Recipes: Boil as directed above, but reduce cooking time to 25 minutes. Omit butter. (*Note:* Dechoked artichokes will parboil in 15 minutes.)

VARIATIONS:

To Serve Cold: Cool artichokes or artichoke hearts in cooking liquid, then cover and chill until ready to use. Drain, pat dry on paper toweling, and remove chokes. Serve cold as a first course or salad with Italian or French Dressing. About 110 calories per serving with 1 tablespoon Italian dressing, 135 with 1 tablespoon French dressing.

⚖ **Low-Calorie Artichokes or Artichoke Hearts:** Instead of serving with butter or sauce, sprinkle artichokes with seasoned salt or drizzle with low-calorie herb or Italian dressing. About 48 calories per serving.

Artichoke Hearts DuBarry: Boil and drain artichoke hearts as directed. Return to pan, add 2 tablespoons butter, 8 small sautéed button mushrooms, 8 boiled baby carrots, and/or 8 braised small white onions. About 100 calories per serving.

ARTICHOKE BOTTOMS STUFFED WITH VEGETABLES

Makes 4 servings

8 *globe artichoke hearts, boiled and drained*
¼ *cup butter or margarine*
1½ *cups hot seasoned vegetables* (*asparagus tips or cauliflowerets; chopped spinach; peas and diced carrots; or sautéed chopped mushrooms*)
2 *tablespoons minced parsley*

Strip all leaves from the hearts and remove chokes.* Melt butter in a large skillet over moderately low heat and sauté bottoms 3–4 minutes, basting all the while. Fill with vegetables and sprinkle with parsley. For extra glamour, top with Lemon Butter. About 160 calories per serving if stuffed with asparagus, cauliflower, or spinach, 180 per serving if stuffed with peas and carrots, 200 per serving if stuffed with sautéed chopped mushrooms.

VARIATIONS:

To Serve Cold: Instead of sautéing bottoms in butter, marinate 2–3 hours in the refrigerator in French dressing. Fill with cold, seasoned, cooked vegetables.

Florentine Style: Fill with chopped buttered spinach, top with Mornay Sauce and grated Parmesan, and brown quickly under the broiler.

Lyonnaise Style: Fill with a mixture of sautéed sausage and minced onion.

Piedmontese Style: Fill with Risotto, top with grated Parmesan, and broil quickly to brown.

Argenteuil Style: Fill with puréed, cooked, seasoned white asparagus.

Brittany Style: Fill with puréed, cooked, seasoned white haricot beans.

Artichoke Bottoms Soubise: Fill with puréed, creamed onions.

Artichoke Bottoms Princesse: Fill with puréed, cooked, seasoned green peas. All variation recipes too flexible for meaningful calorie counts.

STUFFED ARTICHOKE BOTTOMS À LA PARISIENNE

Here's an excellent dish for a ladies' lunch.
Makes 4 servings

8 globe artichoke hearts, boiled and drained
1½ cups creamed chicken, ham, or shellfish
¼ cup soft white bread crumbs
¼ cup grated Parmesan cheese

Preheat oven to 375° F. Strip all leaves from hearts and remove chokes.* Arrange in a buttered shallow casserole and fill with one of the creamed mixtures. Mix crumbs with Parmesan and sprinkle over filling. Bake, uncovered, in top half of the oven 20–25 minutes until browned and bubbly. Serve as a light entree. About 150 calories per serving if stuffed with creamed chicken or shellfish, 175 calories per serving if stuffed with ham.

ROMAN ARTICHOKES STUFFED WITH ANCHOVIES

Stuffed artichokes are eaten like the steamed: pluck off petals, one at a time, then finish by eating the heart and stuffing with knife and fork.
Makes 4 servings

4 large globe artichokes, prepared for cooking
½ cup soft white bread crumbs
4 anchovy fillets, chopped fine
2 tablespoons minced parsley
¼ teaspoon pepper
½ cup olive oil
2 cups boiling water

Remove chokes from artichokes.* Mix crumbs, anchovies, parsley, pepper, and 2 tablespoons olive oil and spoon into centers of artichokes. Place remaining oil and the water in a large kettle and stand artichokes in the liquid stem end down. (The liquid should only half cover artichokes, so ladle from—or add to—the pot as needed.) Cover and simmer 35–45 minutes until a leaf will pull off easily. Serve hot as a first course or vegetable with Drawn Butter Sauce or Lemon Butter. About 150 calories per serving (without Drawn Butter Sauce or Lemon Butter). Add about 30 calories per serving for each tablespoon of Drawn Butter Sauce added, 135 calories for each tablespoon of Lemon Butter added.

BRAISED ARTICHOKES PROVENÇAL

Makes 6 servings

6 large globe artichokes, parboiled and drained
1 medium-size yellow onion, peeled and sliced thin
1 carrot, peeled and sliced thin
1 clove garlic, peeled and crushed
2 tablespoons butter or margarine
2 tablespoons olive oil
½ teaspoon salt
⅛ teaspoon white pepper
1 sprig parsley
½ bay leaf
1 cup dry white wine
1 cup chicken broth
2 tablespoons lemon juice
1 tablespoon minced parsley (garnish)

Preheat oven to 325° F. Cut off top ⅓ of each artichoke and discard, then quarter remaining ⅔ lengthwise and remove chokes.* In a large flameproof casserole over moderately low heat, stir-fry onion, carrot, and garlic in butter and oil 5 minutes (don't allow to brown). Lay artichokes over onion mixture and sprinkle with salt and pepper. Add all remaining ingredients except garnish and cover. When casserole begins to boil, set in oven and bake, covered, 1¼–1½ hours until most of the liquid has bubbled away and artichokes are tender. To serve, strain cooking liquid, spoon over artichokes, and sprinkle with minced parsley. Provide a fork and spoon for scraping flesh from artichoke petals—they are too messy to eat with your fingers. About 125 calories per serving.

Season	For Top Quality	Amount to Buy	Nutritive Value	Calories (unseasoned)
October–March	Pick firm, unscarred tubers with tender beige-to-brown skins.	3–4 artichokes (about ¼ pound) per person.	Poor	Fairly low—about 60 per average serving

⚜ ITALIAN-STYLE MARINATED ARTICHOKE HEARTS

Makes 4–6 servings

½ cup low-calorie Italian dressing
1 clove garlic, peeled and crushed
Juice of ½ lemon
Pinch pepper
2 (9-ounce) packages frozen artichoke hearts, boiled and drained

Mix dressing, garlic, lemon juice, and pepper and pour over artichoke hearts. Cover and marinate in the refrigerator 2–3 hours, turning hearts occasionally. Toss well and serve cold as a vegetable or salad. About 75 calories for each of 4 servings, 50 calories for each of 6.

JERUSALEM ARTICHOKES

There's no reason why Jerusalem artichokes should be called Jerusalem artichokes. They aren't from Jerusalem and they aren't artichokes. Nut-brown and potato-flavored, they're actually tubers of a sunflower that grows wild in the Eastern United States. Eat them out of hand like a radish, or, better still, boil, bake, mash, hash, or picklo.

To Prepare for Cooking: Scrub well in cool water with a vegetable brush, cut away eyes, small knobs, or blemishes but do not peel unless the skins seem tough and inedible (because of their knobbiness, Jerusalem artichokes are the very dickens to peel).

BOILED JERUSALEM ARTICHOKES

Makes 4 servings

1 pound Jerusalem artichokes, prepared for cooking
2 cups boiling water
½ teaspoon salt
Butter or margarine
Salt
Pepper

Place artichokes in a large saucepan, add water and the ½ teaspoon salt, and simmer, covered, 8–10 minutes until just tender (artichokes will seem quite crisp and raw throughout most of the cooking, then quite suddenly become soft). Drain well and serve with plenty of butter, salt, and pepper. About 160 calories per serving with 1 tablespoon of butter or margarine.

VARIATIONS:

⚖ **Low-Calorie Jerusalem Artichokes:** Instead of serving with butter, sprinkle with seasoned salt or drizzle with a little low-calorie Italian salad dressing. About 70 calories per serving.

Jerusalem Artichoke Purée: Follow above recipe, increasing cooking time to 10–12 minutes so artichokes are very soft. Press flesh from skins and mash or whip until creamy with an electric mixer. Beat in 2 tablespoons each butter and heavy cream (just enough to give artichokes a good consistency), then season to taste with salt, pepper and nutmeg. Warm 1–2 minutes, stirring over lowest heat, and serve. About 135 calories per serving.

BAKED JERUSALEM ARTICHOKES

Makes 4 servings

1 pound uniformly large Jerusalem artichokes (they should be about 2" long and 1½" across), prepared for cooking
Butter or margarine
Salt
Pepper

Preheat oven to 400° F. Place artichokes in a shallow roasting pan and bake, uncovered, 15–20 minutes until tender. (As with boiled artichokes, they'll seem quite crisp until 1–2 minutes before they're done, so watch carefully.) Serve oven-hot with lots of butter, salt and freshly ground pepper. About 160 calories per serving with 1 tablespoon of butter.

HASHED BROWN JERUSALEM ARTICHOKES

Makes 4 servings

1 pound Jerusalem artichokes, prepared for cooking
2 tablespoons butter or margarine
¼ teaspoon salt
Pepper

Peel artichokes and slice thin. Melt butter in a large skillet over moderate heat, add artichokes, and fry 5–7 minutes, stirring now and then, until tender and lightly tinged with brown. Season with salt and pepper and serve. About 110 calories per serving.

CREAMED JERUSALEM ARTICHOKES

It's best to make the cream sauce while the artichokes cook so the two are done at the same time.

Makes 4–6 servings

1½ pounds Jerusalem artichokes, prepared for cooking
2 cups boiling water
1 tablespoon lemon juice
2 tablespoons butter or margarine
2 tablespoons flour
½ teaspoon salt
Pinch white pepper
Pinch mace
1 cup light cream
1 egg yolk
1 tablespoon minced parsley or chives

Peel artichokes and cut in ½" cubes. Place in a large saucepan, add water and lemon juice, cover, and simmer 5–7 minutes until just tender; drain. Meanwhile, melt butter over moderate heat in a small saucepan and blend in flour, salt, pepper and mace. Add cream, then cook, stirring constantly, until thickened. Beat egg yolk with a fork, mix in a little

V. HOMESPUN AMERICAN FAVORITES

Indoor Clambake – Baked Country Cured Ham – Caesar Salad – The home pantry

Indoor Clambake (vol. 1, p. 679)

Baked Country Cured Ham (vol. 1, pp. 437–39); and Baking Powder Biscuits (vol. 2, pp. 338–39)

Caesar Salad (vol. 2, p. 292)

The Home Pantry (vol. 2, pp. 650–70 and 683–99)

VEGETABLES

of the hot sauce, then stir back into sauce in pan. Mix parsley or chives into sauce, pour over artichokes, toss lightly, and serve. About 295 calories for each of 4 servings, 195 calories for each of 6 servings.

ASPARAGUS

Spring's first asparagus begins coming to market about the end of February with slim young stalks the color of budding leaves and snug, pointed tips faintly tinged with lavender. This is the asparagus Americans know best, but Europeans prefer the chunky, buttersmooth white varieties, particularly the French Argenteuil asparagus and the German *Stangenspargel*. Both of these are sometimes available in big-city American markets. Try them, if you should find them in your market, and prepare them as you would green asparagus—their flavor is slightly more delicate, their texture somewhat softer. Both the green and the white asparagus are fragile vegetables, best when cooked gently and *quickly* (the greatest crime perpetrated against asparagus is overcooking—when properly cooked, the stalks will be bright green, tender but *crisp*, never soft, never mushy).

To Prepare for Cooking: Snap off tough stem ends, wash asparagus well in tepid water, remove scales (they harbor grit), and, if skins seem coarse, peel with a vegetable peeler.

Season	For Top Quality	Amount to Buy	Nutritive Value	Calories (*unseasoned*)
Late February–July; peak months: April, May	Choose straight, bright green (or pale ivory) stalks of uniform size with tight tips and moist bases.	Allow 8–10 stalks (about ½ pound) per person; bundles average 2–2½ pounds, contain 3–4 dozen stalks.	Green has some Vitamin C and A, the white far less.	Low–35–40 per average serving

Serving Tip: Serve steamed asparagus, drizzled with melted butter or sauced with Hollandaise, as a separate course before or after the entree.

How to Eat: Use a fork whenever stalks are tender, limp or drippy. It's proper, however, to eat crisp spears with your fingers (except at formal dinners).

STEAMED ASPARAGUS

Makes 4 servings

2 pounds asparagus, prepared for cooking
½ cup boiling water
¼ cup melted butter or margarine
1 teaspoon salt
⅛ teaspoon pepper

Tie stalks in serving-size bunches, keeping strings loose so asparagus does not bruise. Stand stems down in a deep saucepan or double boiler bottom (by inverting top over bottom, you can improvise a steamer). Add water, cover, and simmer 15–20 minutes until stems are tender. Drain, remove strings, and season with butter, salt, and pepper. *Or* omit butter and top with Hollandaise or other appropriate sauce (see Vegetable Seasoning Chart). About 85 calories per serving (with butter).

To Poach: Lay individual asparagus stalks flat in a large, heavy skillet, preferably in 1 layer but never more than 2. Add 1 teaspoon salt, enough boiling water to cover (about 2 cups), then cover skillet and simmer 15–20 minutes until crisp-tender. Drain well and season with butter and pepper.

To Parboil for Use in Other Recipes: Prepare as directed but reduce cooking time to 12 minutes; omit seasonings.

VARIATIONS:

To Serve Cold: Lay steamed asparagus flat in a large bowl and cover with ice water. When cold, drain well, cover, and chill until ready to use. (See Vegetable Seasoning Chart for sauce suggestions.)

Low-Calorie Asparagus: Omit butter; dress with 2 tablespoons lemon juice or ¼ cup low-calorie Italian or Roquefort dressing. About 40 calories per serving.

Asparagus with Dill: Add 1 tablespoon minced fresh dill to the melted butter. About 85 calories per serving.

Asparagus with Capers: Reduce salt to ½ teaspoon and mix 1 tablespoon minced capers with the melted butter. About 90 calories per serving.

Buttered Asparagus Tips: Use the top 2" of each stalk only, prepare as for Steamed Asparagus, but cook just 5–8 minutes. Season as directed. About 80 calories per serving.

Creamed Asparagus Tips: Prepare Buttered Asparagus Tips but omit *all* seasonings. To each cup asparagus, add ½ cup hot Medium White Sauce, mix lightly, heat through, and serve. (*Note:* The Cheese, Mushroom, and Mustard variations of Basic White Sauce are equally good with asparagus tips.) About 85 calories per serving.

ASPARAGUS POLONAISE

Makes 4 servings

2 pounds hot steamed asparagus or 2 (10-ounce) packages boiled frozen asparagus
3 hard-cooked egg yolks
1 tablespoon minced parsley
⅓ cup soft white bread crumbs
3 tablespoons Browned Butter

Preheat broiler. Drain asparagus well and arrange in rows in a shallow buttered casserole. Press egg yolks through a fine sieve, mix with parsley, and sprinkle over asparagus. Toss crumbs in butter and sprinkle on top. Broil 4"–5" from the heat 2–3 minutes until lightly browned. About 170 calories per serving.

CHEESE AND ASPARAGUS CASSEROLE

Makes 4 servings

2 (15-ounce) cans asparagus or 2 (10-ounce) packages boiled frozen asparagus (do not drain either one)
1 pint light cream (about)
6 tablespoons butter or margarine
6 tablespoons flour
¾ teaspoon salt
⅛ teaspoon white pepper
2 cups coarsely grated sharp Cheddar cheese
1 cup poultry stuffing mix

Preheat oven to 400° F. Drain canned asparagus liquid or asparagus cooking water into a quart measure and add enough light

cream to measure 3 cups. Melt 4
tablespoons butter over moderate
heat and blend in flour. Add the 3
cups liquid and heat, stirring constantly,
until thickened. Add salt,
pepper, and 1 cup cheese; cook and
stir until cheese is melted. Arrange
asparagus in a buttered shallow 2-
quart casserole and top with cheese
sauce. Toss remaining cheese with
stuffing mix, sprinkle over sauce and
dot with remaining butter. Bake, uncovered,
10–12 minutes until bubbly
and touched with brown. About
645 calories per serving.

ASPARAGUS DIVAN

Makes 6 servings

2 *pounds cooked Buttered Asparagus
Tips*
6 *slices hot buttered white toast*
2 *tablespoons sweet Madeira or
sherry*
2 *cups hot Cheese Sauce*
¼ *cup grated Parmesan cheese*

Preheat broiler. Arrange hot asparagus
tips on toast in an ungreased
shallow roasting pan. Stir wine into
sauce, pour evenly over asparagus,
and sprinkle with Parmesan. Broil
4″ from the heat 3–4 minutes until
sauce is speckled with brown and
bubbly. About 375 calories per
serving.

VARIATIONS:

Asparagus Divan on Ham: Substitute
a thick slice of cooked ham for
each piece of toast. Serve as an
entree. About 390 calories per
serving.

Asparagus and Egg Divan: Top asparagus
with 6 very soft poached
eggs before adding sauce and Parmesan.
Serve as an entree. About 455
calories per serving.

CHINESE ASPARAGUS

Makes 4–6 servings

2 *pounds asparagus, prepared for
cooking*
1 *tablespoon cornstarch*
2 *tablespoons cold water*
1 *cup chicken broth*
2 *teaspoons soy sauce*
1 *tablespoon dry sherry*
¼ *teaspoon sugar*
¼ *teaspoon MSG (monosodium
glutamate)*
3 *tablespoons peanut or other
vegetable oil*
¼ *cup thinly sliced water chestnuts
or bamboo shoots*

Cut each asparagus stalk diagonally
into slices ¼″ thick. Blend cornstarch
with water in a small saucepan,
add broth, soy sauce, sherry,
sugar, and MSG, and heat, stirring,
over moderate heat until slightly
thickened. Remove from burner but
keep warm. Heat oil in a large,
heavy skillet or *wok* over moderate
heat 1 minute. Add asparagus and
stir-fry 3 minutes until crisp-tender.
Slowly stir in sauce and heat 2
minutes longer, stirring constantly.
Add water chestnuts or bamboo
shoots and serve. About 155 calories
for each of 4 servings, 105 calories
for each of 6 servings.

SPANISH-STYLE ASPARAGUS BAKE

Makes 4 servings

2 *pounds asparagus, steamed or
poached, or 1 (1-pound) can cut
asparagus*
2 *hard-cooked eggs, peeled and
halved*
2 *pimientos, cut in small dice*
2 *tablespoons lemon juice*
2 *tablespoons cooking oil*
2 *tablespoons light cream*
1 *tablespoon minced chives*

¼ teaspoon salt
⅛ teaspoon white pepper

Preheat oven to 350° F. Drain asparagus well; if using the fresh, halve crosswise. Arrange in an ungreased shallow 1-quart casserole. Scoop egg yolks from whites and set aside. Mince egg whites, mix with pimientos, and scatter over asparagus. Press yolks through a fine sieve, then beat in the lemon juice, oil, and cream, one at a time. Mix in remaining ingredients, pour over asparagus, and bake uncovered ½ hour. Serve at once. About 165 calories per serving.

BEANS

Of all vegetable families, none is quite so big or bountiful as the bean family. There are big beans and little beans, delicate and hearty beans, black beans and white (and every color in between). There are foreign exotics and American favorites: limas, green beans, and kidney beans. These three, nutritionists maintain, are America's most valuable contribution to the world table, more so than potatoes or tomatoes because, as a protein-rich food, beans, down the ages, have nourished people unable to afford meat. The easiest way to learn the many kinds of beans is to subdivide them by type: the *fresh* and the *dried*.

The Varieties of Beans Cooked Fresh

Green Beans (also known as *snap, string,* and *haricot beans*): A kidney bean tender enough to eat pod and all.

Wax Beans: Yellow "green" beans.

Italian Green Beans: Broader, flatter than green beans, brighter, too. Most often available frozen.

Lima Beans (the *"butter beans"* of the South): There are large limas (Fordhooks) and baby limas, better all-round beans because they are less starchy and do not cook down to mush.

Cranberry Beans (also called *shellouts* and *shell beans*): These pods look like outsize, splotchy red wax beans. The pods are tough but the inner cream-colored beans are nutty and tender.

Black-Eyed Peas: A Deep South favorite, small, pale green beans with black eyes. Pods are misshapen, russeted green, inedible.

To Prepare for Cooking:

Green, Wax, or Italian Green Beans: There are few "strings" today because science has bred them out. Wash in cool water and snap off ends. If beans are tender, leave whole; if not, snap in 2″ lengths.

Season	For Top Quality	Amount to Buy	Nutritive Value	Calories (unseasoned)
Summer for Italian green beans, black-eyed peas. Year round for all others.	Choose firm, well-filled pods with lots of snap; wax and green beans should also be of uniform size and fairly straight.	1 pound green or wax beans will serve 4; 1 pound unshelled limas, cranberry beans, or black-eyed peas 1–2 persons.	All but wax beans are fairly high in vitamin A and contain some C.	Low for green and wax beans, 30–40 per serving; high for shelled types: limas 180 per serving.

Green and wax beans may be Frenched for variety (slivered the long way); most vegetable peelers have Frenchers at one end. Frenched beans will cook faster than the snapped.

Limas, Cranberry Beans, Black-Eyed Peas: Shell. To hasten the job, peel a strip from outer curved edge with a vegetable peeler or snip seam open with scissors.

Cooking Tip: Never add soda to the cooking water to brighten green beans—makes them soapy and destroys vitamin C.

An Alphabet of Dried Beans

Black Beans (also called *turtle beans*): Black skinned, creamy fleshed; the staple of South American soups and stews.

Black-Eyed and *Yellow-Eyed Peas:* Southern favorites called "peas" because their flavor resembles that of field peas. They differ only in the color of their "eyes." Black-eyed peas are available fresh in summer. Yellow-eyed peas are also known as yellow-eyed beans in some parts of the country.

Cannellini: White Italian kidney beans, available dry in Italian groceries, canned in supermarkets. Good *en casserole* with tomatoes and sausages.

Chick-Peas (also called *garbanzo beans* and *cece*): Chick-peas resemble withered filberts and are, in fact, the most nutlike of beans. They work equally well in soups, salads, and casseroles.

Cowpeas: A sort of baby black-eyed pea used in much the same way.

Cranberry Beans: (See Fresh Beans.)

Fava Beans (also called *horse beans* and *English broad beans*): Wrinkled, beige-skinned, strong-flavored giants as big as your thumb.

Flageolets: In France green beans are grown just for the tender, pale green inner beans known as *flageolets*. Though they're available fresh abroad, we must be content with the dried or canned.

Kidney Beans: Old friends, these, the red-brown beans of chili and the basis of many a Mexican recipe. They are also a popular "baking" bean in New England.

Lima Beans: Baby limas are more often dried than Fordhooks because they hold their shape better.

Pink Beans: A kissing cousin of the kidney bean, this is the bean of refried beans and other Southwestern favorites.

Pinto Beans: Another kidney bean, this one pink with brown freckles.

Red Beans: Yet another kidney bean, a smaller, redder variety that's Mexico's favorite.

White Beans: This isn't a single bean but a family of four: the big *marrowfat*, the medium sized *Great Northern*, and the smaller *navy* (or *Yankee*) and *pea beans*.

To Prepare for Cooking: Place beans in a colander or large sieve and rinse well in cool water. Sort carefully, removing withered or broken beans and any bits of stone. Soak, using one of the following methods:

Basic Method: Allowing 1 quart cold water for 1 pound dried beans, soak overnight or for 6–8 hours (discard any beans that float). If your kitchen is very warm, soak

For Top Quality	Amount to Buy	Nutritive Value	Calories (unseasoned)
Most dried beans are boxed, so buy brands you know and trust; if buying from a bin, choose clean, unwithered, unbuggy beans.	1 pound dried beans will serve 4–6 persons.	All dried beans are high in iron, most B vitamins and protein (*incomplete* protein, but valuable in rounding out meals).	High—from 230 per cup (white beans, black-eyed peas, red or pinto beans) to 260 (limas)

beans, covered, in the refrigerator so they don't sour.

Quick Method: Allow 1 quart cold water for 1 pound of beans. Place beans and water in a large kettle, cover, and bring to a boil over high heat. Reduce heat to moderate and let beans boil gently 2 minutes. Remove from heat and let stand 1 hour with the lid on.

Cooking Tips:

(1) Always use some soaking water for cooking beans (it contains vitamins).
(2) Don't salt beans (or add tomatoes or other acid foods) until toward the end of cooking because they toughen the beans.
(3) To keep the pot from boiling over, add 1 tablespoon margarine, drippings, or cooking oil. A chunk of bacon or salt pork will do the trick too. So will a ham bone.

Some Special Beans and Bean Products

Mung Beans: We don't often see these dark, bb-sized Oriental beans, though we're thoroughly familiar with their sprouts. Many Americans today, in fact, are growing their own bean sprouts.

Soybeans: "Superbeans" might have been a better name because these beans provide oil for our margarines, a high protein flour, soy sauce, bean pastes and curds, and a yellow sprout prized by the Chinese.

Bean Powders: These are relatively new, flours, really, that can be used for thickening gravies and sauces, dredging foods to be fried, enriching breads, croquettes, and meat loaves.

BOILED FRESH GREEN OR WAX BEANS

Because beans can so easily cook dry and burn it's best to cook them covered.
Makes 4 servings

1 pound green or wax beans, prepared for cooking
1 teaspoon salt
1 cup boiling water
2 tablespoons butter or margarine
⅛ teaspoon pepper

Place beans in a large saucepan, add salt and water, cover, and simmer until crisp-tender, about 15 minutes for Frenched beans, 20–25 for the snapped or whole. Drain, season with butter and pepper, and serve. About 80 calories per serving of green beans, 90 per serving of wax beans.

To Parboil for Use in Other Recipes: Follow method above, reducing cooking time to 10 minutes. Omit seasonings.

VARIATIONS:

To Serve Cold: Omit seasonings. Chill beans in ice water, drain, pat dry on paper toweling, wrap in Saran, and refrigerate until ready to use. Dress with a tart oil and vinegar dressing and serve as a salad.

Low-Calorie Beans: Dress with ¼ cup low-calorie Italian dressing instead of butter. About 35 calories per serving of green beans, 45 for the wax.

Green Beans Amandine: Increase butter to ⅓ cup, melt in a small skillet, add ⅓ cup slivered blanched almonds, and stir-fry 3–5 minutes until golden. Toss with beans and serve. About 175 calories per serving.

Green Beans with Mushrooms: Stir ½ cup sautéed sliced mushrooms or 1 (3-ounce) can drained sliced mushrooms into beans along with butter. About 85 calories per serving.

Beans with Bacon and Dill: Just before serving, stir in ⅓ cup crisp cooked bacon and 1 tablespoon minced fresh dill. About 120 calories per serving of green beans, 130 per serving of wax beans.

Beans with Oil and Vinegar: Omit butter and dress beans with 3 tablespoons olive oil and 2 tablespoons tarragon-flavored white wine vinegar. About 125 calories per serving of green beans, 135 calories per serving of wax beans.

Sweet-Sour Beans: Omit butter and toss beans with ¼ cup cider vinegar and 1–1½ tablespoons sugar. Serve hot or chill and serve cold. About 45 calories per serving of green beans, 55 calories per serving of wax beans.

GREEN BEANS IN MUSTARD SAUCE

Makes 4 servings

1 pound green beans, boiled and drained (reserve cooking water)
1 tablespoon butter or margarine
1 tablespoon flour
Green bean cooking water plus enough milk to total ¾ cup
3 tablespoons prepared mild yellow mustard
1 tablespoon Worcestershire sauce
½ teaspoon salt
¼ teaspoon cayenne pepper

Keep beans warm. Melt butter over moderate heat and blend in flour. Add the ¾ cup liquid and heat, stirring constantly, until thickened. Mix in remaining ingredients and heat, stirring, 2–3 minutes to blend flavors. Pour sauce over beans, toss lightly to mix, and serve. About 75 calories per serving.

GREEN BEANS AND ONIONS IN SOUR CREAM

Makes 6–8 servings

2 pounds green beans, prepared for cooking
1 (1⅜-ounce) package dry onion soup mix
1½ cups boiling water
2 tablespoons butter or margarine
½ cup sour cream
⅛ teaspoon pepper

Place beans in a large saucepan with onion soup mix and water, cover, and boil gently 20–25 minutes until tender and most of the cooking liquid has evaporated. Mix in butter, sour cream, and pepper and serve. About 130 calories for each of 6 servings, 100 calories for each of 8 servings.

GREEN OR WAX BEANS AU GRATIN

Makes 4 servings

1 pound green or wax beans or 2 (10-ounce) packages frozen green, wax, or Italian beans, boiled and drained
1½ cups hot Cheese Sauce or Mornay Sauce
⅓ cup coarsely grated sharp Cheddar cheese
1 tablespoon melted butter or margarine

Preheat broiler. Arrange beans in an ungreased 2-quart *au gratin* dish or shallow casserole, cover with sauce, sprinkle with cheese, and dot with butter. Broil 5″ from heat 3–4 minutes until cheese melts and is nicely browned. Green beans: about 280 calories per serving made with Mornay Sauce, 320 made with Cheese Sauce. Wax beans: about 290 calories per serving with Mornay Sauce, 330 with Cheese Sauce.

VARIATION:

Lima Beans au Gratin: Substitute boiled baby lima beans (you'll need 3 pounds in the pod) or 2 (10-ounce) packages frozen limas for the green beans. About 430 calories per serving made with Mornay Sauce, 470 calories per serving made with Cheese Sauce.

¢ BEANS LYONNAISE

Makes 4 servings

1 pound green or wax beans, Frenched and parboiled
3 tablespoons butter or margarine
1 large yellow onion, peeled and sliced thin
1 teaspoon salt
⅛ teaspoon white pepper
1 teaspoon minced parsley
1 teaspoon white wine vinegar

Drain beans well and pat dry between paper toweling. Melt butter in a large, heavy skillet over moderate heat 1 minute. Add onion and sauté 5–8 minutes until pale golden. Add beans and stir-fry 3–4 minutes until *just* tender. Add remaining ingredients, toss lightly to mix, and serve. About 115 calories per serving if made with green beans, 125 calories per serving if made with wax beans.

¢ GREEN BEANS PROVENÇAL

Don't try to stir-fry more than this amount of beans in one skillet; if you double the recipe, use two.

Makes 4 servings

1 pound green beans, parboiled
2 tablespoons olive oil
1 small clove garlic, peeled and crushed
2 teaspoons minced parsley
¾ teaspoon salt
⅛ teaspoon pepper

Drain beans well and pat dry between paper toweling. Heat oil in a large, heavy skillet over moderate heat 1 minute. Add beans and stir-fry 3–4 minutes, until crisp-tender and *very lightly* browned. Add garlic and stir-fry 1 minute. Off heat, mix in parsley, salt, and pepper and serve. About 90 calories per serving.

BEANS FROM POMPEII

Makes 4 servings

1 pound young green or wax beans, prepared for cooking
1½ cups canned Italian-style plum tomatoes (include some liquid)
½ cup beef bouillon
1 teaspoon salt
⅛ teaspoon pepper
1 teaspoon minced parsley

Place beans in a large, heavy skillet, add tomatoes, breaking them up, then add all remaining ingredients except parsley. Cover and boil slowly 25–30 minutes until beans are tender. Add parsley and serve with plenty of "sauce." For extra savor, sprinkle each serving with a little grated Parmesan. About 110 calories per serving if made with green beans (without Parmesan), 120 calories per serving if made with wax beans.

SOFRITO WAX BEANS

Makes 6 servings

Sofrito Sauce:
- *3 slices bacon, diced*
- *2 tablespoons lard*
- *1 medium-size yellow onion, peeled and chopped fine*
- *1 clove garlic, peeled and crushed*
- *1 small sweet green pepper, cored, seeded, and chopped fine*
- *1 sweet red pepper, cored, seeded, and chopped fine*
- *1 large ripe tomato, peeled, seeded, and coarsely chopped*
- *Pinch coriander or 2 leaves fresh coriander*
- *4 pitted green olives, chopped fine*
- *¼ teaspoon capers, chopped fine (optional)*
- *1 teaspoon oregano*
- *⅓ cup water*
- *½ teaspoon salt*

1½ pounds hot wax beans, boiled and drained

Fry bacon 2–3 minutes over moderate heat in a large, heavy skillet, add lard, onion, garlic, green and red peppers, and sauté 7–8 minutes until onion is pale golden. Add remaining sauce ingredients, cover, and simmer slowly 7–10 minutes, stirring once or twice. Pour sauce over beans, toss lightly to mix, and serve. About 225 calories per serving.

ORIENTAL-STYLE BEANS WITH WATER CHESTNUTS

Makes 4 servings

- *1 pound green beans*
- *3 tablespoons peanut or other cooking oil*
- *12 small scallions, trimmed of green tops*
- *¼ cup chicken broth*
- *1 teaspoon salt*
- *⅛ teaspoon pepper*
- *1 (5-ounce) can water chestnuts, drained and sliced paper thin*

Cut beans diagonally, into ¼" slices or sliver lengthwise into matchstick strips. Heat oil in a large, heavy skillet or *wok* over moderate heat, add beans and scallions, and stir-fry 5–7 minutes. Add chicken broth, cover tightly, reduce heat to low, and simmer 4–5 minutes until beans are tender. Off heat, mix in salt, pepper, and water chestnuts and serve. About 145 calories per serving.

BOILED FRESH BABY LIMA BEANS

The basic way to cook lima beans and a handy beginning for a number of flavor variations.
Makes 4 servings

- *3 pounds baby lima beans, shelled*
- *1 teaspoon salt*
- *2 cups boiling water*
- *2 tablespoons butter or margarine*
- *⅛ teaspoon pepper*

Place limas in a large saucepan, add salt and water, cover, and simmer 20–30 minutes until tender. Drain, season with butter and pepper, and serve. About 230 calories per serving.

To Parboil for Use in Other Recipes: Use above method but reduce cooking time to 10–15 minutes; omit seasonings.

VARIATIONS:

To Serve Cold: Omit seasonings; chill beans in ice water, drain, pat dry between paper toweling, wrap in Saran, and refrigerate until ready to use. (See Vegetable Seasoning Chart for Sauce Suggestions.)

Lima Beans with Cheese: Reduce butter to 1 tablespoon, add ¼ cup Cheddar or blue cheese spread or 1 (3-ounce) package cream cheese with chives to beans and warm over lowest heat, stirring, until cheese melts. About 230 calories per serving with Cheddar or blue cheese, 280 per serving with cream cheese.

Lima Beans with Bacon and Sour Cream: Reduce butter to 1 tablespoon and stir in ½ cup sour cream and ¼ cup crisp, crumbled bacon just before serving. About 290 calories per serving.

Lima Beans with Parsley and Paprika: Toss in 2 tablespoons minced parsley and 1 teaspoon paprika just before serving. About 230 calories per serving.

Lima Beans with Dill: Reduce butter to 1 tablespoon and stir in ½ cup sour cream and 1 tablespoon minced fresh dill just before serving. About 265 calories per serving.

▨ BABY LIMAS WITH PECANS

Makes 2–4 servings

1 (10-ounce) package frozen baby lima beans (do not thaw)
¼ cup boiling water
2 tablespoons butter or margarine
¼ cup sour cream
1 cup pecan halves
½ teaspoon salt
Pinch pepper

Place beans, water, and butter in a small saucepan, cover, and boil gently 15–20 minutes until tender. Uncover and cook 2–3 minutes longer or until most of the liquid has evaporated. Watch the beans closely at this point, as they're apt to scorch. Mix in remaining ingredients, reduce heat to low, warm 3–5 minutes to blend flavors, and serve. About 680 calories for each of 2 servings, 340 calories for each of 4 servings.

LIMA BEANS WITH CARROTS AND BACON

Makes 4–6 servings

1 (¼-pound) piece bacon, diced
2 medium-size carrots, peeled and sliced thin
1 medium-size yellow onion, peeled and sliced thin
3 pounds baby lima beans, shelled
¾ cup boiling water
1 teaspoon salt
1 teaspoon paprika
Pinch pepper
¼ cup dry white wine
¾ cup sour cream
3 tablespoons minced fresh dill

Brown the bacon in a large, heavy skillet over moderately high heat, then drain on paper toweling. Sauté carrots and onion in the drippings over moderate heat about 8 minutes until onion is golden. Add beans to skillet along with water, salt, paprika, and pepper. Cover, reduce heat to moderately low, and simmer 20–25 minutes until beans are tender. Mix in bacon, wine, sour cream, and dill, heat, stirring, 1–2 minutes longer, and serve. About 370 calories for each of 4 servings, 250 calories for each of 6 servings.

▨ QUICK SUCCOTASH

Makes 4 servings

1 (10-ounce) package frozen baby lima beans (do not thaw)
½ cup boiling water

VEGETABLES

1 teaspoon salt
2 tablespoons butter or margarine
1 tablespoon onion flakes
1 (10-ounce) package frozen whole kernel corn (do not thaw)
½ teaspoon paprika
⅛ teaspoon pepper
½ cup heavy cream

Place limas, water, salt, butter, and onion flakes in a saucepan, cover, and simmer 8–10 minutes. Add corn, re-cover, and simmer 10 minutes longer, stirring occasionally, until vegetables are tender. Mix in remaining ingredients and heat, uncovered, 1–2 minutes more. Ladle into soup bowls and serve. About 285 calories per serving.

VARIATION:

New England Succotash: Substitute raw shelled cranberry beans (1½ pounds in the pod should be enough) for the frozen limas and fresh corn cut from the cob for the frozen (about 2 ears will be sufficient). Also substitute 1 minced onion for the onion flakes and increase amount of boiling water to 1 cup. Proceed as directed, increasing cooking time slightly so that both beans and corn are crisp-tender. About 285 calories per serving.

¢ **BOILED FRESH CRANBERRY BEANS**

These beans can be used in place of limas in recipes.
Makes 4 servings

3 pounds cranberry beans in the pod
1 teaspoon salt
2 cups boiling water
2 tablespoons butter or margarine
⅛ teaspoon pepper

Shell beans just before you're ready to use them and place in a saucepan. Add salt and water, cover, and boil slowly 10–12 minutes until tender.

Drain, season with butter and pepper, and serve. About 230 calories per serving.

¢ **BOILED FRESH BLACK-EYED PEAS**

Makes 4 servings

3 pounds black-eyed peas in the pod
1 teaspoon salt
1½ quarts boiling water
1 (¼-pound) piece lean bacon, cut in large chunks
⅛ teaspoon pepper

Shell peas, place in a saucepan, add salt, water, and bacon, cover, and boil slowly 1–1½ hours or until of desired tenderness. Check pot occasionally and add more water if necessary. Season with pepper, taste for salt and adjust as needed. Serve peas and "pot likker" in small bowls. About 415 calories per serving.

VARIATION:

¢ **Carolina-Style Black-Eyed Peas:** Prepare as directed but increase water to 2 quarts, omit salt, and substitute 1 (¼-pound) chunk salt pork or fat back for the bacon. Simmer slowly 2½–3 hours until soft-tender, adding water as needed to keep mixture soupy. Taste for salt and adjust as needed. Season with pepper. Serve peas in cooking liquid with freshly baked corn bread to accompany. About 430 calories per serving.

¢ **BOILED DRIED BEANS**

This method works for the whole family of dried beans—only the cooking time varies.
Makes 6 servings

1 pound dried beans, washed and sorted
2 quarts cold water (about)
1 tablespoon margarine, roast drippings, or cooking oil

Soak beans in 1 quart water overnight or use the quick method.* Drain, measure soaking water, and add enough cold water to make 1 quart. Simmer beans, covered, in the water with margarine, drippings, or oil, stirring now and then, as follows:

30–40 minutes	for black-eyed peas, cowpeas
50 minutes–1 hour	for lima beans
1–1½ hours	for chick-peas (garbanzos), flageolets, cannellini, pink or red kidney beans
1½–2 hours	for pea, navy, Great Northern, marrowfat, black or pinto beans

Use the beans in other recipes or add salt and pepper to taste and serve. To dress them up, season with a fat chunk of Herb Butter or top with Parsley Sauce or Cheese Sauce. From 250 to 280 calories per serving depending on kind of beans. (Limas are the most caloric).

VARIATIONS:

¢ **To Serve Cold** (for all but black beans): Cool beans in their cooking water, drain, then rinse under cold running water. Cover and chill until ready to use. Serve cold as a vegetable, dressed with oil, vinegar, and garlic, or toss into salads.

¢ **Savory Beans** (for white or light beans): Simmer a ham bone or pig's knuckle with the beans, a chunk of bacon or salt pork, leftover beef bones, even bouillon cubes. Other good additions to the pot: parsley sprigs, young carrots, a clove of garlic, a yellow onion stuck with a clove or two, almost any leftover vegetable. Recipe too flexible for a meaningful calorie count.

Black Beans and Sour Cream: Simmer beans with a ham bone, a medium-size onion, chopped fine, and a crushed clove of garlic. Top each serving with a dollop of sour cream. About 300 calories per serving with 1 tablespoon of sour cream.

CREAMED PURÉE OF DRIED BEANS

Makes 4 servings

½ *pound dried white or lima beans, boiled and drained*
¼ *cup milk*
¼ *cup light cream*
2–4 *tablespoons melted butter or margarine*
½ *clove garlic, peeled and crushed*
Pinch *white pepper*
2 *tablespoons grated Parmesan cheese (optional)*

Preheat oven to 350° F. Mash beans with a potato masher. (If you want to remove bean skins, do not drain; press beans *and* their liquid through a coarse sieve.) Beat in remaining ingredients, spoon into a buttered shallow 1½-quart casserole, roughen surface with a fork and bake, uncovered, 25–30 minutes. To brown, broil 5″ from the heat about 4 minutes. About 220 calories per serving made with white beans, 235 per serving made with limas.

VARIATIONS:

Purée of Beans au Gratin: Omit Parmesan. Just before broiling, sprinkle purée with ⅓ cup grated sharp Cheddar cheese and 2 tablespoons melted butter. About 360 calories per serving with white beans, 375 per serving with limas.

Purée of Vegetables au Gratin: Combine equal quantities of puréed beans and carrots or rutabaga, then proceed as for Purée of Beans au Gratin. Recipe too flexible for a meaningful calorie count.

VEGETABLES

¢ BOSTON BAKED BEANS

A good meat substitute, although in New England, Boston Baked Beans are traditionally accompanied by ham, hot dogs, sausages, or meat loaf.

Makes 4–6 servings

2 cups dried pea beans, washed and sorted
2 quarts cold water (about)
2 teaspoons salt
½ teaspoon powdered mustard
3 tablespoons dark brown sugar
3 tablespoons molasses
1 medium-size yellow onion, peeled and coarsely chopped (optional)
1 (¼-pound) piece salt pork

Soak beans overnight in 1 quart water or use the quick method.* Drain, measure soaking water, and add cold water to make 1 quart. Place beans in a large kettle, add the water, cover, and simmer, stirring occasionally, 1 hour. Drain, reserving 2 cups cooking water. Meanwhile, preheat oven to 400° F. Place beans in an ungreased 2-quart bean pot. Mix reserved cooking water with salt, mustard, sugar, and molasses and stir into beans; add onion if you like. Score rind of salt pork at ½" intervals, then push into beans so only the rind shows. Cover and bake 1 hour; reduce temperature to 250° F. and bake 4 hours; uncover pot and bake 1 hour longer. Stir about every hour. Serve bubbling hot from the pot. About 530 calories for each of 4 servings, 355 calories for each of 6 servings.

RUMMY BAKED BEANS

Makes 6 servings

1 pound dried pea beans, washed and sorted
2½ quarts cold water
1 (¼-pound) piece bacon, diced
2 medium-size yellow onions, peeled and cut in thin wedges
⅓ cup molasses
¼ cup firmly packed light brown sugar
1 teaspoon powdered mustard
¼ teaspoon baking soda
2½ teaspoons salt
⅛ teaspoon pepper
¼ cup rum

Soak beans overnight in 1 quart water or use the quick method.* Drain and rinse in cold water. Place beans in a large kettle, add bacon and remaining water, cover, and simmer very slowly 40 minutes. Drain, reserving 1 cup cooking water. Meanwhile, preheat oven to 275° F. Place beans and bacon in an ungreased 2½-quart bean pot. Add onion wedges, pushing them well down into beans. Mix reserved water with remaining ingredients and stir into beans. Cover and bake 6½ hours until beans are richly amber brown. Serve hot as a meat substitute. About 430 calories per serving.

▨ EASY BRANDIED BEANS

Makes 8 servings

4 (1-pound 2-ounce) jars "oven"-baked beans (do not drain)
¼ cup molasses
⅓ cup brandy
2 tablespoons light brown sugar
1½ teaspoons powdered mustard
2 tablespoons onion flakes
2 tablespoons ketchup
½ teaspoon ginger

Preheat oven to 350° F. Place beans in an ungreased shallow 3-quart casserole and stir in all remaining ingredients. Bake, uncovered, about 1 hour, stirring now and then, until bubbly. About 485 calories per serving.

⊠ ¢ THREE BEAN CASSEROLE

Makes 8–10 servings

1 (*1-pound*) *can pork and beans* (do not drain)
1 (*1-pound*) *can small lima beans, drained*
1 (*1-pound*) *can red kidney beans* (do not drain)
1 (*10½-ounce*) *can condensed onion soup* (do not dilute)
¼ *cup chili sauce*
1 *tablespoon prepared hot spicy mustard*
¼ *cup molasses*

Preheat oven to 350° F. Empty beans into an ungreased 2-quart casserole. Mix all remaining ingredients together, then stir into beans. Bake, uncovered, 45 minutes to 1 hour, stirring once or twice. Serve as a vegetable or meat substitute. About 245 calories for each of 8 servings, 195 calories for each of 10 servings.

¢ ESTOUFFAT (WHITE BEAN STEW)

In France, *estouffade* means "stew," and this hearty white bean dish *is* a stew. Its name probably comes from the way people in the southern province of Languedoc pronounce *estouffade* (like Southern Americans, they've *quite* an accent).

Makes 6 servings

1 *pound dried white beans, flageolets, or limas, boiled just 1 hour but not drained*
½ *pound salt pork, cut into slices* ¼″ *thick*
1 *large yellow onion, peeled and chopped fine*
3 *large ripe tomatoes, peeled, seeded, and coarsely chopped*
2 *cloves garlic, peeled and crushed*
1 *bouquet garni,** *tied in cheesecloth*
Salt to taste

Keep beans warm in their cooking water. Brown salt pork in a large, heavy skillet over moderate heat and drain on paper toweling. Sauté onion in the drippings 6–8 minutes until pale golden; add tomatoes and garlic and sauté 1–2 minutes longer. Add sautéed mixture to beans, also salt pork and *bouquet garni*. Cover and simmer 1 hour, stirring occasionally. Add salt to taste and serve. About 575 calories per serving.

¢ BEAN AND CABBAGE HOT POT (OUILLADE)

Here's a traditional dish from the French Pyrenees, where the vegetables grow big and beautiful on the terraced hillsides.

Makes 6–8 servings

½ *pound dried white beans, flageolets, or limas, boiled but not drained*
2 *cups boiling water*
2 *teaspoons salt*
6 *small potatoes, peeled*
1 *large yellow onion, peeled and sliced thin*
1 *pound small young carrots, peeled*
1 *small rutabaga, peeled and cut in* ½″ *cubes*
1 *small cabbage, cored and cut in 8 wedges*
¼ *teaspoon pepper*

Keep beans warm in their cooking liquid. Place all remaining ingredients in a second kettle, cover, and boil gently 25–30 minutes or until potatoes and rutabaga are tender. Drain beans and add to other vegetables. Stir *gently*, then simmer, covered, about 10 minutes. Serve hot with pot roast, boiled tongue, or corned beef. Or serve in place of meat. If made with white beans, about 265 calories for each of 6 servings and 200 calories for each of 8 servings. If made with limas, about 280 calories for each of 6 servings and 210 calories for each of 8 servings.

¢ BEANS IN ONION SAUCE

A husky French country dish that is both easy and economical to make. Makes 4 servings

4 *large yellow onions, peeled and quartered*
¾ *cup water*
3 *tablespoons butter or margarine*
¾ *cup hot Medium White Sauce*
½ *teaspoon salt (about)*
⅛ *teaspoon white pepper*
3 *cups hot boiled dried white or lima beans*

Place onions, water, and butter in a saucepan, cover, and simmer 45 minutes or until onions are mushy. Uncover, boil slowly until liquid reduces to about ½ cup, then purée in an electric blender at slow speed or put through a food mill. Mix in white sauce, salt, and pepper. Taste for salt and add a little more if needed. Pour onion sauce over hot, drained beans, mix gently, and serve. About 365 calories per serving.

TURKISH "FRIED" WHITE BEANS AND CARROTS

Makes 6–8 servings

1 *pound dried white beans, boiled just 1 hour but not drained*
3 *large yellow onions, peeled and chopped fine*
2 *cloves garlic, peeled and minced*
1 *cup olive oil*
4 *medium-size carrots, peeled and cut into rounds ¼" thick*
1 *tablespoon salt (about)*
¼ *teaspoon pepper*

Keep beans warm in their cooking liquid. Meanwhile, sauté onions and garlic in the oil in a large skillet over moderately low heat 5–8 minutes until pale golden; stir into beans (include all olive oil). Add carrots, salt, and pepper, cover, and simmer 45 minutes, stirring occasionally, until vegetables are tender. About 600 calories for each of 6 servings, 450 calories for each of 8 servings.

NEAPOLITAN BEANS WITH PARMESAN

Makes 6 servings

1 *pound dried cannellini beans, boiled but not drained*
2 *tablespoons bacon drippings*
¼ *teaspoon sage*
½ *cup tomato paste*
4 *Italian plum tomatoes, peeled, seeded, and coarsely chopped, or 4 canned tomatoes, drained and coarsely chopped*
2½ *teaspoons salt*
¼ *teaspoon pepper*
½ *cup grated Parmesan cheese*
1 *tablespoon minced parsley*
Grated Parmesan cheese (topping)

To the beans add all remaining ingredients except parsley and cheese topping, cover, and simmer 1 hour, stirring now and then. Mix in parsley and serve with a sprinkling of Parmesan. About 340 calories per serving.

¢ SAVORY LIMA BEANS WITH WINE

If the pork hock is meaty enough, this can double as a main dish. Makes 6–8 servings

1 *pound dried large lima beans, washed and soaked*
Soaking water plus enough cold water to measure 3 cups
1 *pork hock or pig's foot*
1 *medium-size yellow onion, peeled and stuck with 6 cloves*
1 *bay leaf, crumbled*

1 tablespoon salt
⅛ teaspoon pepper
1 cup dry white wine

Place beans, water, pork hock, onion, and bay leaf in a large kettle, cover, and simmer 1 hour. Add remaining ingredients, cover, and simmer 45 minutes longer. Remove onion and pork hock. Cut meat from bones, add to beans, and serve. About 335 calories for each of 6 servings, 275 calories for each of 8 servings.

¢ MEXICAN FRIED BEANS (FRIJOLES FRITOS)

Makes 4 servings

¼ cup lard
1 recipe Mexican Beans (opposite)

Melt lard in a large, heavy skillet over moderate heat. Ladle in a few of the beans and mash, adding a tablespoon or so of the bean liquid. Continue to add beans, mashing with bean liquid, until all are used up (you'll need about ½ cup liquid to give the beans the right consistency). (Note: You can mash all the beans, or leave about half of them whole.) Heat, stirring, until piping hot. To be really Mexican, serve with ham and Huevos Rancheros. About 320 calories per serving.

VARIATIONS:

¢ **Fried Beans with Cheese:** Just before serving add ½ cup coarsely grated Monterey Jack or sharp Cheddar cheese to beans and heat, stirring, about ½ minute until cheese melts. About 375 calories per serving.

¢ **Fried Beans with Tomato:** After mashing beans, mix in ½ cup tomato paste, ¼–½ teaspoon chili powder, and, if you like, a touch of garlic. Heat and serve. About 355 calories per serving.

¢ **Refried Beans (Frijoles Refritos):** As the title suggests, simply refry leftover fried beans in more lard until heated through and crisp here and there. Recipe too flexible for a meaningful calorie count.

¢ MEXICAN BEANS (FRIJOLES MEXICANOS)

Makes 4 servings

1 cup dried pinto or red kidney beans, washed and soaked
Soaking water plus enough cold water to measure 3 cups
1 tablespoon lard
1 large yellow onion, peeled and coarsely chopped (optional)
4 slices bacon, diced (optional)
1½ teaspoons salt

Place all ingredients except salt in a large saucepan, cover, and simmer until tender: 1–1½ hours for red kidney beans, 1½–2 hours for pinto beans. Mix in salt and serve. The cooking liquid should be quite thick; if not, simmer uncovered until the consistency of gravy (don't boil, however, or beans may break up). About 195 calories per serving (without onion and bacon), 255 calories per serving (with onion and bacon).

¢ BARBECUED BEANS

This casserole improves on standing, so bake the day before and refrigerate until needed. About ½ hour before serving, pop, covered, into a 350° F. oven.

Makes 6–8 servings

1 pound dried red kidney beans, washed and soaked
2 large yellow onions, peeled and chopped fine
2 cloves garlic, peeled and crushed
2 tablespoons bacon drippings
½ cup ketchup

VEGETABLES

½ cup chili sauce
½ cup cider vinegar
½ cup firmly packed dark brown sugar
½ teaspoon powdered mustard
½ teaspoon chili powder
2 teaspoons salt (about)
½ teaspoon pepper
5 cups water (about)

Preheat oven to 350° F. Drain beans, place in an ungreased 3-quart bean pot or casserole, and mix in all remaining ingredients. Cover tightly (use a double thickness of foil if casserole has no lid) and bake 5–6 hours, stirring occasionally, until beans are tender and sauce thick. If mixture gets too dry before beans are done, stir in a little warm water. About 400 calories for each of 6 servings, 300 calories for each of 8 servings.

¢ SOUTH-OF-THE-BORDER BEAN POT

A robust Mexican main dish filled with kidney beans, green pepper, and tomatoes. It's peppery, so if you are unaccustomed to hot dishes, reduce the amount of chili peppers to suit you.
Makes 4–6 servings

1 pound dried red kidney beans, washed and soaked
1 medium-size yellow onion, peeled and coarsely chopped
1 clove garlic, peeled and crushed
½ cup minced sweet green pepper
1 (1-pound 12-ounce) can tomatoes (do not drain)
3 tablespoons olive oil
½ teaspoon oregano
1 teaspoon crushed coriander
1¼ teaspoons salt
⅛ teaspoon black pepper
2 teaspoons minced parsley
1 tablespoon honey or light corn syrup
2 teaspoons red wine vinegar
¼ teaspoon crushed hot red chili peppers (optional)

Preheat oven to 275° F. Drain beans, rinse under cold running water, and place in an ungreased 2½-quart bean pot. Mix in all remaining ingredients. Bake, uncovered, 2½ hours, stirring well every hour. Cover and bake 2–2½ hours longer or until beans are tender yet still firm, again stirring every hour. If beans seem to be drying out before they're tender, mix in a little hot water. Serve bubbling hot from the pot. About 510 calories for each of 4 servings, 340 calories for each of 6 servings.

¢ SWEDISH BAKED BEANS

Somewhat like Boston Baked Beans, but more spicily flavored. These beans are popular at smorgasbords.
Makes 6–8 servings

1 pound dried red kidney, cranberry, or pinto beans, boiled but not drained
1 medium-size yellow onion, peeled and chopped fine
1 clove garlic, peeled and crushed
½ cup ketchup or tomato sauce
1 tablespoon Worcestershire sauce
⅔ cup firmly packed light brown sugar
2 tablespoons molasses
¼ cup cider vinegar
¼ teaspoon powdered mustard
1½ teaspoons cornstarch
2 tablespoons cold water
6 slices bacon

Preheat oven to 325° F. Transfer beans and their cooking liquid to an ungreased 3-quart casserole and mix in onion and garlic. Blend ketchup, Worcestershire sauce, sugar, molasses, vinegar, and mustard and stir into beans. Blend cornstarch and water until smooth and mix in well.

Lay bacon on top of beans, cover, and bake 1½ hours. Raise oven temperature to 400° F., uncover, and bake 10 minutes to crisp bacon. About 485 calories for each of 6 servings, 360 calories for each of 8 servings.

¢ SPANISH BEAN POT

Richly glazed, rum-and-coffee-flavored baked beans.

Makes 6 servings

1 pound dried pinto beans, boiled but not drained
1 clove garlic, peeled and crushed
¼ teaspoon thyme
⅛ teaspoon crushed hot red chili peppers
1 large Spanish onion, peeled and sliced thin
2 tablespoons olive oil or other cooking oil
2 tablespoons cider vinegar
2 tablespoons prepared mild yellow mustard
2 tablespoons sugar
½ cup hot strong coffee
1 jigger dark Jamaica rum (optional)

Preheat oven to 350° F. Transfer beans and their cooking liquid to an ungreased 3-quart casserole and mix in all remaining ingredients except coffee and rum. Cover and bake 1 hour. Mix in coffee and, if you like, the rum, re-cover, and bake 15 minutes longer. Taste for salt and adjust if needed. About 300 calories per serving.

¢ SOUTHERN-STYLE BLACK-EYED PEAS

Makes 4–6 servings

1 pound dried black-eyed peas, washed
1 (¼-pound) piece bacon or salt pork, cut in 1" cubes
1½ quarts water
1 tablespoon salt
¼ teaspoon cayenne pepper

Place peas, bacon, and water in a large, heavy kettle, cover, and simmer *very slowly* 2–2½ hours until tender. Season with salt and pepper and serve. About 545 calories for each of 4 servings, 365 calories for each of 6 servings.

¢ HOPPING JOHN

Makes 6 servings

2 (10-ounce) packages frozen black-eyed peas (do not thaw)
3 cups boiling water
1 (¼-pound) piece lean bacon
1 yellow onion, peeled and coarsely chopped
3 cups hot fluffy cooked rice
2 tablespoons bacon drippings, butter, or margarine
2 teaspoons salt
⅛–¼ teaspoon crushed hot red chili peppers
⅛ teaspoon black pepper

Place peas, water, bacon, and onion in a large saucepan, cover, and simmer 30–35 minutes until peas are tender. Remove bacon, lightly mix in remaining ingredients, and serve in place of potatoes. About 360 calories per serving.

¢ BAKED CHICK-PEA PILAF

Makes 6 servings

½ medium-size Spanish onion, peeled and chopped fine
3 tablespoons olive or other cooking oil
1 (1-pound 4-ounce) can chick-peas (do not drain)
½ cup uncooked rice
1 beef or chicken bouillon cube
¼ cup boiling water

1 pimiento, seeded and coarsely chopped
1 teaspoon salt

Preheat oven to 325° F. Sauté onion in oil over moderate heat 5–8 minutes until pale golden. Place chickpeas and rice in an ungreased 1½-quart casserole and mix lightly. Dissolve bouillon cube in boiling water, add to casserole along with onion and remaining ingredients, and stir to mix. Cover and bake 1–1¼ hours, stirring occasionally, until rice is tender. About 215 calories per serving.

CHICK-PEAS AND KASHA

To be really authentic, each serving of this Syrian dish should be topped with a dollop of yogurt.
Makes 4–6 servings

2 cups canned or boiled dried chickpeas
2 cups cooked buckwheat groats
½ cup beef bouillon
2 tablespoons butter or margarine

Preheat oven to 350° F. Drain peas, then remove skins by rubbing each pea between your thumb and forefinger. Coarsely chop peas, add buckwheat, and toss to mix. Spoon into a buttered 1½-quart casserole, pour bouillon over all, and dot with butter. Cover and bake 30 minutes. About 275 calories for each of 4 servings, 180 calories for each of 6 servings.

¢ GREEK-STYLE CHICK-PEAS AND TOMATOES

This dish has the consistency of a good, rich "spoon soup" and is easiest to eat out of soup bowls. It can also be served over spaghetti as a pasta sauce.
Makes 6 servings

¼ cup olive or other cooking oil
1 medium-size Spanish onion, peeled and sliced thin
2 cloves garlic, peeled and crushed
2 (1-pound 4-ounce) cans chick-peas, drained, or 1 pound dried chick-peas, boiled and drained
2 cups tomato or marinara sauce
1 tablespoon minced parsley
¼ teaspoon finely chopped mint

Heat oil in a large saucepan over moderate heat 1 minute. Add onion and garlic and stir-fry 5 minutes, then mix in chick-peas and tomato sauce. Reduce heat to low, cover, and simmer 30 minutes. Mix in parsley and mint and serve. About 310 calories per serving.

¢ FLORIDA BLACK BEANS AND PEPPERS

If you like black bean soup, you will also like black beans prepared this way with minced green and red peppers.
Makes 6 servings

1 pound dried black beans, boiled but not drained
½ cup olive or other cooking oil
1 large Spanish onion, peeled and sliced thin
2 large sweet green peppers, cored, seeded, and chopped fine
1 large sweet red pepper, cored, seeded, and chopped fine
1 clove garlic, peeled and crushed
1 teaspoon salt (about)
⅛ teaspoon pepper
½ cup cider vinegar
2 tablespoons sugar

Keep beans warm in their cooking liquid. Heat oil in a large skillet over moderate heat 1 minute. Add onion, peppers, and garlic, sauté 5–8 minutes until onion is pale golden, then stir into beans. Add salt and pepper, cover, and simmer 45 minutes. Mix in vinegar and sugar, re-cover, and simmer 5–10 minutes longer. About 435 calories per serving.

▣ BRAZILIAN BLACK BEANS

Makes 4 servings

6 slices bacon, cut crosswise in julienne strips
1 medium-size yellow onion, peeled and coarsely chopped
1 clove garlic, peeled and crushed
2 bay leaves
2 (1-pound) cans black beans (drain 1 can)
1 tablespoon white corn meal
1 tablespoon cider vinegar
⅛ teaspoon crushed hot red chili peppers

Brown bacon in a large, heavy skillet over moderate heat and drain on paper toweling. Pour off all but 2 tablespoons drippings, add onion and garlic to skillet, and stir-fry 8 minutes until golden. Add remaining ingredients, turn heat to low, and simmer uncovered, stirring occasionally, about 15 minutes. Serve, topping each portion with bacon. About 375 calories per serving.

BEETS

To the ancient Greeks, the beet was a food fit for the gods (it was, in fact, the one vegetable considered worthy enough to offer the god Apollo). The first beet recipes come to us from Apicius, the first-century Roman epicure whose cookbook is still sold today. These ancients, however, ate the greens and threw away the beet (it remained for the Russians and Germans to discover how delicious the roots were). Today we have learned to enjoy both the sweet crimson beet root and the crinkly-tart green tops.

To Prepare for Cooking:
Beets: Cut off all but 1″ of the tops and leave root ends on so beets won't fade. Scrub in cold water, taking care not to break skins. Do not peel.

Greens: Sort, discarding coarse stems and blemished leaves, then wash by plunging up and down in cool water. To perk up limp leaves, soak briefly in ice water.

¢ BOILED BEETS

Makes 4 servings

2 pounds beets, prepared for cooking
1½ teaspoons salt
1 quart boiling water
2 tablespoons butter or margarine
Pinch pepper

Place beets, salt, and boiling water in a large saucepan, cover, and boil 35–45 minutes until tender. Drain, plunge in cold water 1–2 minutes, then peel and remove any stem or root ends. If beets are small, leave whole; if not, slice thin. Return to pan, add butter and pepper, and

Season	For Top Quality	Amount To Buy	Nutritive Value	Calories (unseasoned)
Year round; peak months for greens and beets: June–October	Pick crisp-tender greens; firm, unscarred beets of equal size, 1½–2″ in diameter.	½ pound beets or greens per person.	Greens are rich in vitamins A and C, beets are considerably less nutritious.	Low for greens about 25 per serving; Moderate for beets—about 50 a serving

VEGETABLES

warm uncovered, shaking pan gently, until butter melts and gilds beets. About 125 calories per serving.

To Parboil for Use in Other Recipes: Boil as directed but reduce cooking time to 20–25 minutes.

VARIATIONS:

¢ **To Serve Cold:** Cook, drain, and plunge in cold water as directed. When cool, peel, remove root and stem ends, and, if you like, slice. Toss with about 1 cup good tart dressing (see Vegetable Seasoning Chart) and chill 2–3 hours.

¢ **Orange-Glazed Beets:** Boil, drain, and peel as directed; stir ¼ cup orange marmalade into beets with butter and warm, uncovered, shaking pan gently, about 5 minutes until beets are glazed. About 185 calories per serving.

¢ **Beets with Sour Cream and Dill:** Boil, drain, and peel; reduce butter to 1 tablespoon and stir in ⅓ cup sour cream and 1 tablespoon minced dill. Warm 2–3 minutes (but do not boil) and serve. About 140 calories per serving.

¢ **Beets with Horseradish:** Cook, drain, and peel; mix 2 tablespoons each prepared horseradish and white wine vinegar into beets along with butter. Warm and serve. About 125 calories per serving.

¢ **BAKED BEETS**

Baked beets are mellower, sweeter, nuttier than the boiled.
Makes 4 servings

2 pounds beets, prepared for cooking
1 teaspoon salt
Pinch pepper
2 tablespoons butter or margarine

Preheat oven to 350° F. Place beets in a roasting pan, cover with foil, and bake 2–2½ hours until tender. Cool until easy to handle (if you're in a hurry, plunge in ice water), then peel. If the beets are small, leave whole; otherwise slice, dice, or cut in julienne strips. Place in a saucepan with salt, pepper, and butter and warm, uncovered, over low heat, shaking pan gently, 2–3 minutes. About 125 calories per serving.

¢ **HARVARD BEETS**

Makes 4–6 servings

½ cup sugar
2 tablespoons cornstarch
1 teaspoon salt
¼ teaspoon pepper
1 cup cider vinegar
¼ cup water
¼ cup butter or margarine
2 pounds boiled fresh beets, peeled and diced or cut in julienne strips, or 2 (1-pound) cans julienne beets, drained

Mix sugar, cornstarch, salt, and pepper in a large saucepan and slowly stir in vinegar. Add water and butter and cook, stirring, over moderate heat until thickened and clear. Reduce heat to low, add beets, cover, and simmer 15 minutes. About 295 calories for each of 4 servings, 200 calories for each of 6 servings.

HOT SPICY SHREDDED BEETS

Particularly good with pork, poultry, or ham.
Makes 4 servings

2 pounds beets, trimmed, peeled, and coarsely grated
½ cup coarsely grated onion
3 tablespoons butter or margarine
½ cup water
¼ cup dry red wine
Juice of ½ lemon
¼ teaspoon cinnamon
¼ teaspoon nutmeg
½ teaspoon salt
⅛ teaspoon pepper

Simmer all ingredients, covered, 25–30 minutes until beets are tender and flavors well blended. Stir once or twice during cooking. About 175 calories per serving.

BEETS IN ORANGE-LEMON SAUCE

Makes 4–6 servings

1 tablespoon cornstarch
2 tablespoons sugar
1 cup orange juice
2 tablespoons lemon juice
2 pounds boiled fresh beets, peeled, or 2 (1-pound) cans small whole beets, drained
2 tablespoons butter or margarine
1–2 teaspoons grated orange rind

Mix cornstarch and sugar, slowly add fruit juices, then cook and stir over moderate heat until thickened and clear. Add beets and butter, turn heat to low, cover, and simmer 10–15 minutes to blend flavors. Add rind to taste and serve. About 180 calories for each of 4 servings, 120 calories for each of 6 servings.

BEETS BAKED WITH SOUR CREAM AND CARAWAY SEEDS

Makes 4–6 servings

2 pounds fresh beets, boiled, peeled, and diced, or 2 (1-pound) cans julienne beets, drained
1½ cups sour cream
1 teaspoon caraway seeds
Pinch nutmeg or mace

Preheat oven to 350° F. Mix beets with remaining ingredients and spoon into an ungreased small casserole. Bake, uncovered, 20–25 minutes to heat through. About 255 calories for each of 4 servings, 170 calories for each of 6 servings.

✖ BEETS TOKAY

Beets and grapes in a smooth white sauce. Delicious!
Makes 4–6 servings

2 pounds fresh beets, boiled, peeled, and sliced, or 2 (1-pound) cans sliced beets, drained
1½ cups hot Medium White Sauce
½ cup diced celery
1 cup halved, seeded Tokay grapes

Preheat oven to 350° F. Mix all ingredients, place in a buttered 1½-quart casserole, cover, and bake 25 minutes. Stir and serve. About 255 calories for each of 4 servings, 170 calories for each of 6 servings.

✖ BEETS IN BURGUNDY

Spicy, finely cut beets in dry red wine.
Makes 3 servings

1 (1-pound) can julienne beets (do not drain)
1 tablespoon cornstarch
⅓ cup sugar
⅛ teaspoon cloves
Pinch salt
¼ cup red wine vinegar
½ cup red burgundy wine
2 tablespoons butter or margarine

Drain beets, saving ¼ cup liquid. Mix cornstarch, sugar, cloves, and salt in a saucepan, slowly add beet liquid, vinegar, and wine, and cook, stirring, over moderate heat until thickened and clear. Add beets and butter, turn heat to low, cover, and simmer 15 minutes to blend flavors. About 250 calories per serving.

STEAMED BEET GREENS

(See recipe for Steamed Spinach.)

BREADFRUIT

In Florida, California, and large metropolitan areas, these big pebbly green-brown fruits are not unfamiliar. Their flesh is the color and texture of bread, tastes something like globe artichokes, and is best when boiled, mashed, creamed, or baked and stuffed.

To Prepare for Cooking: Scrub well, halve, and peel deep enough that no green shows. Cut around hard, stringy core and pull out. Leave as halves or cut in 1–1½" chunks.

To Boil: Cover with lightly salted boiling water and boil, covered, until tender: about 2–2½ hours for halves, 1½–1¾ hours for chunks. Drain, season with butter, salt, and pepper, and serve.

To Parboil for Use in Other Recipes: Boil as directed, reducing cooking time to 1¼ hours for halves, 1 hour for chunks.

To Mash: Boil chunks as directed, increasing time to 2 hours so they are very soft. Drain, mash with a potato masher, and mix with a little cream, butter, salt, and pepper.

To Cream: Boil chunks as directed, drain, and mix with 1½ cups hot Medium White Sauce.

To Bake and Stuff: Parboil halves and drain; fill with any mixture you would use for stuffing yellow squash, wrap halves in foil, and bake 30–40 minutes at 350° F. Unwrap and serve, allowing a half for each person.

Season	For Top Quality	Amount To Buy	Nutritive Value	Calories (unseasoned)
July–August	Choose plump, firm but not too hard breadfruit with fairly clean skins.	1 breadfruit serves 2–4	Some vitamin C	Moderate —about 85 per average serving

BROCCOLI

First cousin to cauliflower, second cousin to cabbage, broccoli was almost unknown in this country until the late 1920's, when an enterprising Italian farmer in California began advertising his broccoli crop over the radio.

To Prepare for Cooking: Discard coarse stem ends and leaves. Wash broccoli in cold water; separate into stalks of about the same size and make deep X-cuts in the base of each so they'll cook as quickly as the tender heads.

STEAMED BROCCOLI
Makes 4 servings

1 (2-pound) head broccoli, prepared for cooking
1¼ cups boiling water
½ teaspoon salt
⅛ teaspoon pepper
3 tablespoons butter or margarine

Stand stalks stem end down in a deep saucepan (the top of a double boiler is perfect). Add water and salt, cover (or invert double boiler bottom over top), and simmer 15–20 minutes until crisp-tender. Drain, return to pan, season with pepper and butter, and warm over low heat just until butter is melted. Taste for salt and add more if needed. About 125 calories per serving.

To Parboil for Use in Other Recipes: Steam as directed, reducing cooking time to 10 minutes. Omit seasonings.

Season	For Top Quality	Amount To Buy	Nutritive Value	Calories (unseasoned)
Year round with supplies at their best in spring and again in fall	Look for crisp, moist stalks and dark green or purplish heads. Reject any that are yellowed or flowering.	½ pound per person	High in vitamins A and C, fairly high in calcium	Low—about 40 per average serving

VARIATIONS:

To Serve Cold: Steam as directed, then chill in ice water. Drain, pat dry on paper toweling, cover, and refrigerate until ready to use (see Vegetable Seasoning Chart for sauce and dressing ideas). Serve as an appetizer, vegetable, or salad.

△ **Low-Calorie Steamed Broccoli:** Dress with seasoned salt or low-calorie Italian dressing instead of butter. About 50 calories per serving.

Broccoli Amandine: Increase butter to ⅓ cup, melt over moderate heat, and in it sauté ⅓ cup slivered blanched almonds, stirring, 3–5 minutes until golden brown. Add 1 tablespoon lemon juice, the pepper and pour over drained broccoli. About 280 calories per serving.

BROCCOLI PARMIGIANA

Makes 4 servings

1 (2-pound) head broccoli, steamed, or 2 (10-ounce) packages frozen broccoli spears, boiled and drained

Sauce:
3 tablespoons butter or margarine
3 tablespoons flour
1½ cups milk
1 egg yolk, lightly beaten
¾ teaspoon salt
⅛ teaspoon white pepper
¾ cup grated Parmesan cheese

Topping:
¾ cup soft white bread crumbs

mixed with 2 tablespoons grated Parmesan cheese

Prepare sauce while broccoli cooks: melt butter over moderate heat and blend in flour. Add milk and heat, stirring, until thickened. Mix a little sauce into yolk, stir back into sauce in pan, and mix in remaining sauce ingredients. Cook and stir 1 minute but do not boil. Preheat broiler. Spoon a little sauce into an unbuttered shallow 1½-quart casserole, add broccoli, pour in remaining sauce and sprinkle with topping. Broil 4″ from the heat 2–3 minutes until flecked with brown. About 335 calories per serving.

VARIATION:

Eggs and Broccoli Parmigiana: For a light entree, arrange 4 soft poached eggs on broccoli before adding sauce and topping. About 415 calories per serving.

BROCCOLI WITH ANCHOVIES ROMAN STYLE

Makes 6 servings

2 (2-pound) heads broccoli, prepared for cooking
¼ cup olive oil
2 cloves garlic, peeled
¼ cup boiling water
1 tablespoon anchovy paste
½ cup dry white wine
⅛ teaspoon pepper

Divide broccoli into flowerets of equal size (save stalks for soup).

Heat oil in a large, heavy skillet over moderate heat 1 minute, add garlic, sauté 1–2 minutes, and discard. Reduce heat to moderately low and stir-fry broccoli in the oil 4–5 minutes. Add water, cover, and simmer 5–7 minutes until crisp-tender. Lift broccoli to a heated vegetable dish and keep warm. Mix anchovy paste, wine, and pepper into cooking liquid and heat, stirring, 1–2 minutes. Pour over broccoli and serve. About 180 calories per serving.

BROCCOLI IN WHITE WINE SAUCE

Makes 4 servings

2 tablespoons butter or margarine
¼ cup dry white wine
1 (2-pound) head broccoli, parboiled and drained
¼ teaspoon salt
⅛ teaspoon pepper
Pinch nutmeg

Add butter and wine to broccoli, cover, and simmer 5 minutes over low heat. Uncover and simmer 5–10 minutes longer, basting with pan liquid, until tender. Season with salt, pepper, and nutmeg and serve. About 115 calories per serving.

CASTILIAN SAUTÉED BROCCOLI WITH RIPE OLIVES

Makes 4 servings

1 (2-pound) head broccoli, parboiled and drained
1 small clove garlic, peeled and crushed
2 tablespoons olive oil
1 tablespoon butter or margarine
¾ cup thinly sliced, pitted ripe olives
¼ teaspoon salt (about)

Cut broccoli in 2″ lengths. Sauté garlic in oil and butter in a large skillet over moderate heat 1 minute, add broccoli, and stir-fry 5–7 minutes. Add olives, stir gently, cover, and let steam 3–4 minutes. Add salt to taste and serve. About 150 calories per serving.

VARIATION:
Sautéed Broccoli with Parmesan: Cook broccoli by the recipe above, leaving out olives. Just before serving, squeeze a lemon wedge over broccoli and sprinkle with about ⅓ cup grated Parmesan cheese. About 125 calories per serving.

⊠ BROCCOLI WITH PEANUT BUTTER SAUCE

Peanut butter may sound an odd seasoning for broccoli, but when smoothed into a golden brown sauce, it brings out the best in the broccoli.

Makes 4 servings

1 (2-pound) head broccoli, steamed, or 2 (10-ounce) packages frozen broccoli spears, boiled
⅓ cup butter or margarine
2 tablespoons chopped, toasted, blanched peanuts
2 tablespoons cream-style peanut butter

Drain broccoli, place in a heated serving dish, and keep warm. Melt butter over moderately low heat, add peanuts, and sauté 2–3 minutes. Blend in peanut butter, reduce heat to low, and heat, stirring, about 2 minutes. Pour over broccoli and serve. About 295 calories per serving.

⊠ OSAKA SKILLET BROCCOLI

Chilled, this makes an unusually good hors d'oeuvre.

Makes 2–4 servings

1 (2-pound) head broccoli, prepared for cooking

¼ cup peanut oil
1 clove garlic, peeled and crushed
2 (½″) cubes fresh gingerroot, peeled and crushed
¼ cup water
2 tablespoons Japanese soy or teriyaki sauce

Divide broccoli into small flowerets (save stalks for soup). Heat oil in a large heavy skillet over moderate heat 1 minute, add garlic and ginger, and stir-fry 1 minute. Add broccoli and remaining ingredients, cover, and simmer 8–10 minutes until crisp-tender. Serve, topping each portion with a little pan liquid. About 355 calories for each of 2 servings, 180 calories for each of 4 servings.

BROCCOLI BAKED IN MUSTARD SAUCE

Makes 8 servings

2 (2-pound) heads broccoli, parboiled and drained (reserve cooking liquid)
Sauce:
¼ cup butter or margarine
¼ cup unsifted flour
Broccoli cooking liquid plus enough milk to measure 2¼ cups
¼ cup dry vermouth
1 cup coarsely grated Gruyère cheese
2 tablespoons prepared mild yellow mustard
2 tablespoons prepared spicy brown mustard
¼ teaspoon salt
⅛ teaspoon cayenne pepper
Topping:
¼ cup fine dry bread crumbs mixed with 1 tablespoon melted butter or margarine

Preheat oven to 375° F. Cut broccoli in 2″ lengths and place in a buttered shallow 2½-quart casserole. Melt butter over moderate heat and blend in flour. Add broccoli cooking liquid-milk mixture and heat, stirring, until thickened. Mix in remaining sauce ingredients and pour over broccoli. Sprinkle with topping and bake, uncovered, 35–40 minutes until browned and bubbling. About 170 calories per serving.

BROCCOLI, EGG, AND SOUR CREAM CASSEROLE

Makes 4 servings

1 (2-pound) head broccoli, steamed, drained, and coarsely chopped, or 2 (10-ounce) packages frozen chopped broccoli, boiled and drained
2 hard-cooked eggs, peeled and sliced
1 cup sour cream
½ cup mayonnaise
2 tablespoons tarragon vinegar
⅛ teaspoon paprika

Preheat oven to 350° F. Arrange broccoli in an ungreased shallow 1½-quart casserole, top with egg slices, and set aside. Over lowest heat warm sour cream with mayonnaise and vinegar, stirring, 4–5 minutes (do not boil); pour over broccoli. Bake, uncovered, 10 minutes, sprinkle with paprika, and serve. About 430 calories per serving.

BROCCOLI CREPES AU GRATIN

For a small luncheon an elegant entree that's not difficult to make.
Makes 4 servings

1 (10-ounce) package frozen chopped broccoli, boiled and drained
8 (6″) thin pancakes made from any pancake mix
1 teaspoon salt
⅛ teaspoon pepper
1 hard-cooked egg, sliced thin

VEGETABLES

1 (10½-ounce) can condensed cream of asparagus or celery soup (do not dilute)
¼ cup light cream
½ cup coarsely grated sharp Cheddar cheese

Preheat oven to 350° F. Spoon a little broccoli in the center of each pancake, sprinkle with salt and pepper, and top with a slice of egg. Roll pancakes up and place, seam side down, in a buttered 1½-quart *au gratin* dish or shallow casserole. Blend soup with cream, spoon over crepes, and sprinkle with cheese. Bake, uncovered, 20–25 minutes until bubbly, then broil 3″ from the heat 2–3 minutes to brown. About 325 calories per serving.

VARIATION:

Asparagus Crepes au Gratin (4 servings): Prepare as directed, substituting 2 (10-ounce) packages frozen asparagus spears for broccoli. Lay 2 or 3 stalks across center of each crepe, then season, roll, and proceed as directed. About 335 calories per serving.

BRUSSELS SPROUTS

Little more than a curiosity in this country until frozen foods made them widely available, these baby cabbages have long been popular abroad. French royalty used to reject any larger than a pea, Belgians insist yet that they be the size of a grape.

To Prepare for Cooking: Since most sprouts are washed and trimmed before they're packed, about all that's needed is a quick sorting to remove withered leaves. Trim off stems (but not too close or sprouts will fall apart). To ensure even cooking, make an X-cut in the base of each sprout with the point of a knife. Rinse sprouts in cold, lightly salted water, then drain well.

BOILED BRUSSELS SPROUTS

Makes 4–6 servings

1 quart Brussels sprouts, prepared for cooking
1½ cups boiling water
1 teaspoon salt
¼ teaspoon pepper
2 tablespoons butter or margarine

Place sprouts in a saucepan with water and salt, cover, and boil gently 15–20 minutes until crisp-tender. Drain, season with pepper and butter and serve. About 95 calories for each of 4 servings, 65 calories for each of 6 servings.

To Parboil for Use in Other Recipes: Follow recipe above but cut cooking time in half. Omit seasonings.

VARIATIONS:

⚖ **Low-Calorie Brussels Sprouts:** Season with 1–2 tablespoons lemon juice or tarragon vinegar and a pinch of nutmeg instead of butter. About 45 calories for each of 4 servings, 30 calories for each of 6.

Season	For Top Quality	Amount To Buy	Nutritive Value	Calories (unseasoned)
September–March; peak months: October and November	Choose firm, clean compact heads of a crisp green color.	A 1-pint carton will serve 2–3 persons.	Very high in vitamin C, fairly high in vitamin A	Low—about 45 per average serving

Brussels Sprouts Véronique: Boil and season sprouts as directed, then toss in ¾ cup seedless green grapes and a pinch of nutmeg or mace. About 115 calories for each of 4 servings. 75 calories for each of 6 servings.

Brussels Sprouts Parmigiana: Boil and drain as directed but do not season. Place sprouts in a buttered 2-quart casserole, top with ½ cup melted butter and ⅓ cup grated Parmesan. Bake, uncovered, 15 minutes at 350° F. About 115 calories for each of 4 servings, 75 calories for each of 6 servings.

Dilled Sprouts in Sour Cream: Boil and drain as directed but do not season. Quarter each sprout or, if small, halve. Return to pan and stir in 1½ cups sour cream, 4 minced scallions, 2 teaspoons minced fresh dill (or ½ teaspoon of the dried), ½ teaspoon salt, and a pinch each garlic salt and white pepper. Set over lowest heat, cover, and warm 5-7 minutes, taking care cream doesn't boil. About 275 calories for each of 4 servings, 185 calories for each of 6 servings.

BRUSSELS SPROUTS AU GRATIN

Makes 6 servings

1 quart fresh Brussels sprouts or 2 (10-ounce) packages frozen sprouts, boiled and drained
1½ cups hot Cheese Sauce or Mornay Sauce
⅓ cup coarsely grated sharp Cheddar cheese
1 tablespoon melted butter or margarine

Preheat broiler. Arrange sprouts in an ungreased 1½-quart *au gratin* dish or shallow casserole. Cover with sauce, sprinkle with cheese, and drizzle with butter. Broil 4″–5″ from the heat 3–4 minutes until lightly browned. About 195 calories per serving if made with Mornay Sauce, 220 per serving if made with Cheese Sauce.

BRUSSELS SPROUTS WITH CHESTNUTS

Makes 6 servings

1 quart fresh Brussels sprouts or 2 (10-ounce) packages frozen sprouts, boiled and drained
2 tablespoons butter or margarine
1 tablespoon flour
½ cup chicken broth
Pinch salt
Pinch pepper
1 teaspoon lemon juice
1 cup coarsely chopped cooked or canned chestnuts

Return sprouts to pan and keep warm. Melt butter over moderate heat and blend in flour. Add chicken broth slowly and cook, stirring until slightly thickened. Mix in remaining ingredients, pour over sprouts, toss lightly, and serve. About 140 calories per serving.

BRUSSELS SPROUTS IN ONION SAUCE (SOUBISE)

Makes 6 servings

3 large yellow onions, peeled and quartered
½ cup boiling water
2 tablespoons butter or margarine
½ cup hot Béchamel Sauce or Medium White Sauce
¼ teaspoon salt (about)
Pinch white pepper
1 quart Brussels sprouts, boiled and drained

Simmer onions, covered, in water and butter 45 minutes until mushy. Uncover, boil slowly to reduce liquid to ¼ cup, then purée all in an electric blender at low speed or put through a food mill. Mix butter or margarine, Béchamel or White Sauce, salt, and pepper into onion purée; taste for salt and add more if needed. Place sprouts in an ungreased shallow 1½-quart casserole, top with onion purée mixture, cover, and bake 15–20 minutes, stirring once or twice. About 125 calories per serving.

VARIATION:

Just before serving, sprinkle casserole with ½ cup finely grated sharp Cheddar cheese and broil 4″–5″ from the heat 2–3 minutes to brown. About 170 calories per serving.

CREAMED BRUSSELS SPROUTS AND CELERY

Makes 4–6 servings

2 *(10-ounce) packages frozen Brussels sprouts (do not thaw)*
1 *cup diced celery*
1 *cup boiling water*
¼ *teaspoon salt*
½ *cup light cream*
Pinch white pepper
2 *tablespoons butter or margarine*
2 *tablespoons flour blended with 2 tablespoons cold water*

Place sprouts, celery, water, and salt in a saucepan, cover, and boil 10 minutes until sprouts are *barely* tender. Mix in cream, pepper, and butter and turn heat to low. Blend in flour-water paste and heat, stirring, until thickened and smooth. Cover, simmer 10 minutes longer to blend flavors, and serve. About 175 calories for each of 4 servings, 115 calories for each of 6 servings.

CABBAGE

Few vegetables are surrounded by more legends than cabbage. According to Greek myth, the first cabbage sprang from the tears of a prince whom Dionysus, god of wine, punished for trampling grapes. From this legend arose another—that cabbage could prevent drunkenness. Aristotle, it's said, dined well upon cabbage before setting out for a night on the town. And the Romans preceded their orgies by consuming quantities of cabbage. The cabbages of myth, however, were sprawling varieties, not the firm round heads we know today. These were brought to America by English colonists and thrived so well in the New World they soon rivaled potatoes as "the most popular vegetable." Available to us today are not only the smooth green cabbage but also the crinkly green Savoy, the red and the long slim Chinese, or celery, cabbage.

Season	For Top Quality	Amount To Buy	Nutritive Value	Calories (unseasoned)
Year round for all cabbages	Buy firm, heavy heads with crisp, unblemished leaves. Green cabbages fade in storage, so a white head may be old	A medium size head (3–3½ pounds) will serve 4–6.	All raw cabbage is fairly high in vitamin C, the cooked somewhat less so.	Low—from 30–60 per cup, Savoy being lowest, red cabbage highest

To Prepare for Cooking: Strip away coarse or soiled outer leaves, halve head, and core. Slice, shred, or cut in thin wedges as individual recipes specify.

Serving Tip: Instead of discarding cabbage cores, trim off woody bits, parboil 10–15 minutes in lightly salted water, cool, and slice into salads.

¢ STEAMED GREEN OR RED CABBAGE

Though many recipes recommend steaming cabbage 7 to 11 minutes, we've found it's really quite raw unless cooked for 25. If you like yours crisp and pungent, by all means use the shorter time. To make red cabbage really red, add a little lemon juice, vinegar (any flavor), or dry red wine to the cooking water.
Makes 4–6 servings

1 medium-size cabbage, cored and cut in thin wedges or 1" slices
1 cup boiling water
3 tablespoons butter or margarine
1 teaspoon salt
Pinch pepper

Place cabbage in a large pot, add water, cover, and steam over moderate heat 20–25 minutes, stirring occasionally. Drain, add butter, salt, and pepper, return to heat, and warm, uncovered, tossing cabbage occasionally, 2–3 minutes. Green cabbage: About 110 calories for each of 4 servings, 75 calories for each of 6. Red cabbage: about 135 calories for each of 4 servings, 90 calories for each of 6.

To Parboil for Use in Other Recipes: Use method above but steam only 15 minutes; omit seasonings.

VARIATIONS:

¢ ⚖ **Low-Calorie Cabbage:** *For the green,* reduce butter to 1 tablespoon. About 45 calories for each of 6 servings, 60 for each of 4. *For the red,* omit butter and dress with 2 tablespoons vinegar. About 50 calories for each of 6 servings, 70 for each of 4.

Austrian Cabbage: Steam and season green cabbage as directed above, then chop coarsely and mix in 1 cup sour cream and 2 teaspoons poppy seeds. Spoon into a buttered 3-quart casserole, cover, and bake 15–20 minutes at 350° F. About 230 calories for each of 4 servings, 155 calories for each of 6 servings.

Creamy Cabbage: Steam green cabbage by recipe above, adding butter to cooking water. Do not drain. Stir in salt, pepper, 1 (6-ounce) can evaporated milk, and ¼ teaspoon nutmeg. Heat, stirring, 5 minutes (do not boil). Serve in soup bowls with lots of the cooking liquid. About 175 calories for each of 4 servings, 115 calories for each of 6 servings.

CREOLE CABBAGE

Makes 4 servings

1 large yellow onion, peeled and minced
1 small sweet green pepper, cored, seeded, and minced
1 small sweet red pepper, cored, seeded, and minced
1 stalk celery, minced (do not include top)
1 clove garlic, peeled and crushed
2 tablespoons cooking oil
3–4 ripe tomatoes, peeled, seeded, and coarsely chopped
1 small cabbage, shredded medium fine

1½ teaspoons salt
⅛ teaspoon pepper

Stir-fry onion, sweet peppers, celery, and garlic in the oil in a large kettle 5–8 minutes until onion is pale golden. Add tomatoes and stir-fry 2 minutes; add cabbage, salt, and pepper, cover, turn heat to low, and simmer 15–20 minutes until cabbage is tender. About 135 calories per serving.

SAFFRON CABBAGE

Makes 4–6 servings

3 slices bacon
1 medium-size yellow onion, peeled and sliced thin
1 medium-size cabbage, shredded medium fine
½ teaspoon salt
⅛ teaspoon powdered saffron
½ cup beef bouillon
Pinch pepper

Brown bacon in a large kettle over moderate heat; drain on paper toweling, crumble, and reserve. Sauté onion in the drippings 5–8 minutes until pale golden; add cabbage, sprinkle with salt and saffron, and mix in bouillon. Cover and boil slowly 10–15 minutes until cabbage is tender. Drain and season with pepper. Serve topped with bacon. About 125 calories for each of 4 servings, 85 calories for each of 6 servings.

¢ PENNSYLVANIA DUTCH CABBAGE KNABRUS

Makes 4 servings

¼ cup bacon drippings, butter, or margarine
1 small cabbage, shredded medium fine
3 medium-size yellow onions, peeled and sliced thin
1–2 teaspoons salt
¼ teaspoon pepper

Melt fat in a large kettle over moderate heat, layer cabbage and onions into kettle, sprinkling each with salt (use 1 teaspoon in all). Cover and simmer 15–20 minutes, stirring once or twice, until cabbage is tender. Season with pepper, taste for salt and add more if needed. About 160 calories per serving.

¢ COLCANNON

Originally, Colcannon was a leftover dish, the mashed potatoes and cabbage or kale being stirred up and set in the oven to warm while the supper cooked.
Makes 4 servings

1 small cabbage, steamed and chopped fine
2 cups hot seasoned mashed potatoes
2 tablespoons bacon drippings, butter, or margarine
¼ teaspoon salt
Pinch white pepper

Preheat oven to 400° F. Mix cabbage with remaining ingredients, spoon into a well-buttered 1½-quart casserole, and roughen surface with a fork. Bake, uncovered, 35–45 minutes until lightly browned. About 140 calories per serving.

VARIATIONS:

– Follow recipe above, substituting 1½ pounds kale, steamed and finely chopped, for the cabbage. About 140 calories per serving.
– Follow recipe above, stirring 1–2 tablespoons minced parsley into colcannon before baking. About 140 calories per serving.
– Follow recipe above, adding 1–2 finely chopped, steamed leeks (they can be steamed in the same pot with

the cabbage). About 145 calories per serving.

¢ BAKED CABBAGE

Makes 6 servings

1 medium-size cabbage, cut in 8 wedges and parboiled
1 medium-size yellow onion, peeled and coarsely chopped
¼ cup butter or margarine
1 cup coarse dry bread crumbs
2 tablespoons minced parsley
1 tablespoon minced fresh dill or ½ teaspoon dried dill
½ cup canned condensed beef consommé
1 teaspoon salt
⅛ teaspoon pepper

Preheat oven to 350° F. Drain cabbage and arrange in a buttered 2½-quart casserole. Sauté onion in butter over moderate heat 10–12 minutes, stirring until browned; mix in crumbs, parsley, and dill. Pour consommé over cabbage, sprinkle with salt and pepper, and top with sautéed mixture. Cover and bake 45–50 minutes until cabbage is tender. Uncover and bake 15–20 minutes longer to brown. About 125 calories per serving.

¢ SCALLOPED CABBAGE

The perfect companion for roast pork or ham.
Makes 6 servings

1 medium-size cabbage, cut in ½" slices, parboiled, and drained (save cooking water)

Sauce:
¼ cup butter or margarine
¼ cup unsifted flour
1 teaspoon salt
⅛ teaspoon mace

Pinch cayenne pepper
Pinch black pepper
Cabbage cooking water plus enough milk to total 2 cups

Topping:
1 cup toasted fine bread crumbs mixed with 3 tablespoons melted butter or margarine

Preheat oven to 350° F. Place cabbage in an ungreased 2-quart au gratin dish or shallow casserole and set aside. Melt butter and blend in flour, salt, mace, and peppers. Add the 2 cups liquid and heat, stirring, over moderate heat until thickened. Pour over cabbage, sprinkle with topping, and bake uncovered 30 minutes until bubbly. About 275 calories per serving.

SPICY EAST INDIAN BAKED CABBAGE

Here's an unusual vegetable to serve with curry.
Makes 4 servings

4 cups finely chopped cabbage
1 medium-size yellow onion, peeled and minced
1 teaspoon salt
¼ cup flaked coconut
½ teaspoon chili powder
¼ teaspoon turmeric
Very small pinch crushed hot red chili peppers
2 eggs, lightly beaten
¼ cup cold water

Preheat oven to 350° F. Mix all ingredients and spoon into a buttered 1½-quart casserole. Cover and bake about 50 minutes until cabbage is tender; uncover and bake 10 minutes longer to crispen surface slightly. About 105 calories per serving.

VEGETABLES

¢ SWEET AND SOUR RED CABBAGE

Makes 4–6 servings

1 medium-size red cabbage, sliced very thin
⅔ cup boiling water
3 tablespoons butter or margarine
¼ cup red wine vinegar
½ teaspoon caraway seeds
⅛ teaspoon salt
⅛ teaspoon pepper
2 teaspoons light brown sugar
⅛ teaspoon nutmeg

Place all ingredients in a large pot, toss to mix, cover, and simmer, stirring once or twice, 15–20 minutes until cabbage is crisp-tender. Serve hot in soup bowls with plenty of the cooking liquid. About 145 calories for each of 4 servings, 100 calories for each of 6 servings.

SHREDDED RUBY CABBAGE

Makes 4–6 servings

1 cup water
3 tablespoons sugar
1 teaspoon salt
¼ cup red currant jelly
1 medium-size red cabbage, coarsely grated
1½ cups finely chopped yellow onion
2 tablespoons cider vinegar

Heat water, sugar, salt, and jelly in a very large saucepan over moderate heat 2–3 minutes, stirring until sugar dissolves. Stir in cabbage and onion, cover, and simmer 20 minutes until cabbage is crisp-tender. Uncover and boil, stirring constantly, 4–5 minutes until liquid evaporates. Add vinegar, toss to mix, and serve. About 195 calories for each of 4 servings, 130 calories for each of 6 servings.

RED CABBAGE AND CHESTNUTS

This combination of cabbage and chestnuts goes particularly well with game.

Makes 6 servings

1 medium-size red cabbage, shredded medium fine
¾ cup beef bouillon
2 teaspoons cider vinegar
½ teaspoon salt
¼ teaspoon pepper
18–20 chestnuts, boiled, peeled, and coarsely chopped
2 tablespoons bacon drippings

Place cabbage, bouillon, vinegar, salt, and pepper in a large pot, cover, and simmer 20–25 minutes until cabbage is barely tender. Mix in chestnuts and drippings and boil, uncovered, 5–7 minutes until most of the liquid has evaporated. About 150 calories per serving.

VARIATION:

Savoy Cabbage and Chestnuts: Follow recipe above, substituting Savoy cabbage for the red and reducing simmering time to 15 minutes. About 145 calories per serving.

FLEMISH RED CABBAGE AND APPLES

If you make this recipe a day or so ahead, then reheat slowly in a covered kettle, it will taste even better.

Makes 4–6 servings

1 small red cabbage, shredded medium fine
½ large Spanish onion, peeled and sliced thin
4 apples (Baldwin, McIntosh, or Jonathan), peeled, cored, and sliced thin

¼ cup firmly packed dark brown sugar
1½–2 teaspoons salt
½ cup dry red wine or red wine vinegar
2 tablespoons butter or margarine
Pinch pepper

Place cabbage, onion, apples, sugar, 1½ teaspoons salt, and wine in a large, heavy kettle, toss to mix, cover, and boil slowly, stirring once or twice, 20–25 minutes until cabbage is just tender. Mix in butter and pepper; taste for salt and add more if needed. About 255 calories for each of 4 servings, 170 calories for each of 6 servings.

STEAMED CHINESE CABBAGE

Makes 4 servings

2–3 heads Chinese cabbage, cut crosswise into fine shreds
½ cup boiling water
¾ teaspoon salt
Pinch pepper
2 tablespoons butter or margarine

Place cabbage, water, and salt in a large saucepan, cover, and boil slowly 7–9 minutes until crisp-tender. Drain, add pepper and butter, and shake pan uncovered over low heat 1–2 minutes until butter melts and gilds cabbage. About 85 calories per serving.

To Parboil for Use in Other Recipes: Steam as directed above, reducing cooking time to 5 minutes; omit seasonings.

VARIATION:

⚖️ **Low-Calorie Chinese Cabbage:** Omit salt and butter and dress with a sprinkling of seasoned salt or drizzling of low-calorie Italian or herb dressing. About 32 calories per serving.

SAUTÉED CHINESE CABBAGE WITH SESAME SEEDS

Makes 4 servings

3 tablespoons peanut or other cooking oil
2–3 heads Chinese cabbage, shredded fine
1 teaspoon sesame seeds
2 teaspoons Japanese soy sauce

Heat oil in a large, heavy skillet or wok over moderately low heat 1 minute, add cabbage, and stir-fry 4 minutes. Add sesame seeds and stir-fry 1 minute. Mix in soy sauce. Cabbage should be crisp-tender; if not, stir-fry 1–2 minutes longer. About 115 calories per serving.

VARIATION:

Follow recipe above, stir-frying 6–8 minced scallions (include green tops) along with the cabbage. About 120 calories per serving.

SAUERKRAUT

Sauerkraut isn't, as most of us think, a German invention. The Chinese stumbled upon the recipe centuries ago while the Great Wall was being built. Among the coolies' rations was a mixture of shredded cabbage and rice wine which, over the weeks, softened and soured into the world's first kraut. If you want to try making your own sauerkraut, you'll find the recipe in the chapter Pickles, Preserves, Jams, and Jellies.

To Prepare for Cooking: Always taste sauerkraut before cooking or heating. If it seems too salty (the fresh often is), soak 15 minutes in cold water, rinse, and drain.

To Cook Fresh Sauerkraut: Drain kraut, place in large saucepan, add just enough water, beef or chicken broth, or dry white wine to cover, and simmer, covered, 30–40 minutes until tender. Drain and serve (sauerkraut needs no additional seasoning).

To Heat Precooked Sauerkraut: Heat sauerkraut, covered, in its own liquid or, if salty, in ¾–1 cup water or dry white wine 5–10 minutes. Drain and serve

⚜ ¢ CARAWAY SAUERKRAUT

Makes 6–8 servings

1 large yellow onion, peeled and chopped fine
2 tablespoons butter or margarine
2 (1-pound) cans sauerkraut (do not drain)
2–3 tablespoons caraway seeds

Sauté onion in butter in a large, heavy kettle over moderate heat 5–8 minutes until pale golden. Add sauerkraut, cover, and simmer slowly 20 minutes. Drain, mix in caraway seeds, cover, and let stand over lowest heat 5–7 minutes to blend flavors. About 70 calories for each of 6 servings, 50 calories for each of 8 servings.

BRAISED SAUERKRAUT WITH JUNIPER BERRIES

Makes 4 servings

1 (1-pound 4-ounce) can sauerkraut, drained
¼ pound salt pork, cut in small dice
3 small white onions, each peeled and stuck with 2 cloves
1 carrot, peeled and quartered
1 bouquet garni* and 1 tablespoon juniper berries tied in cheesecloth
½ cup beef broth
½ cup water

Preheat oven to 350° F. Squeeze sauerkraut as dry as possible. Brown salt pork in a heavy kettle over moderate heat; add sauerkraut and all remaining ingredients, cover, and bring to a boil. Transfer kettle to oven and bake, covered, 45–50 minutes, until onions are very tender. (*Note:* Check kettle occasionally and add a little hot water, if necessary, to keep it from boiling dry.) Discard carrot, cheesecloth bag, and cloves. Chop onions coarsely into sauerkraut and serve. About 245 calories per serving.

For Top Quality	Amount To Buy	Nutritive Value	Calories (unseasoned)
Buy brands you know and like. Precooked kraut is sold in cans and, more recently, in refrigerated plastic bags. Fresh kraut is sold by delicatessens, specialty groceries.	¼–⅓ pound per person	Fairly high in vitamin C	Low–about 45 per cup

CARDOONS

Few of us know these giant prickly green stalks, although in France and Italy they're as common as cauliflower. Cardoons are related to artichokes and, according to some botanists, they're the *original* artichoke. They are available, occasionally, in big-city specialty food shops and are a delicacy worth trying.

To Prepare for Cooking: Discard tough stalks and all leaves. Wash each stalk well, cut in 3″ lengths, remove stringy parts, and rub cut edges with lemon. Like celery stalks, cardoons have a heart; trim and quarter it.

To Cook Cardoons: Whether they're to be served in a salad or as a vegetable, cardoons must be cooked. Cover with lightly salted boiling water or chicken broth and simmer, covered, about 2 hours until tender. Drain. Chill and slice into salads, marinate in Vinaigrette or Italian Dressing, or use hot to prepare:

Herbed Cardoons: Toss cardoons with a little melted butter, minced chives, tarragon, or chervil, and salt and pepper to taste.

Sautéed Cardoons: Pat cardoons dry on paper toweling, then sauté 8–10 minutes in butter or olive oil until golden. Season with salt, pepper, and mace.

Breaded Cardoons: Dry cardoons on paper toweling, dip in beaten egg, roll in fine dry crumbs, and fry in deep fat (380° F.) 3–4 minutes until golden.

Sauced Cardoons: Warm cardoons in hot Béchamel or Mornay Sauce (1 cup sauce to 2 cups cardoons) 3–5 minutes, stirring.

Season	For Top Quality	Amount To Buy	Nutritive Value	Calories (unseasoned)
Winter	Look for crisp, unblemished stalks	1 pound cardoons serves 2–4.	Not determined	Not determined

CARROTS

When carrots first appeared in England some 350 years ago, ladies were so enchanted by the lacy tops they wore garlands of them in their hair. It was the English who brought carrots to America, the Indians who carried them cross country. Southwestern tribes grow much of today's crop, and to visit these areas at harvest time is to see miles of flatlands herringboned with the orange and green of freshly pulled carrots.

To Prepare for Cooking: Mature carrots should be peeled and trimmed of stem and root ends; young tender carrots need only be trimmed and scrubbed. Always try to cook carrots whole; if they seem too large, halve or quarter; if tough, slice, dice, or cut into julienne strips.

Season	For Top Quality	Amount To Buy	Nutritive Value	Calories (unseasoned)
Year round	Look for firm, bright orange carrots of equal size without cracks or splits. If buying by the bunch, make sure tops are not wilted.	1 pound carrots serves 3–4. There are 6–8 medium-size carrots per pound, 12–14 slim ones, 2–3 dozen babies.	High in vitamin A	Low—about 25 per raw, medium-size carrot

¢ BOILED CARROTS

Makes 3–4 servings

6–8 medium-size carrots, prepared for cooking
1½ cups boiling water, ginger ale, beef or chicken broth
½ teaspoon salt
Pinch pepper
2 tablespoons butter or margarine

Boil carrots, covered, in lightly salted boiling water (or one of the alternate cooking liquids) as follows: 35–45 minutes for whole carrots; 20–25 for the halved or quartered; 10–15 for the thickly sliced; 5–10 for the thinly sliced, diced, or julienne. Drain, add seasonings, and warm uncovered over low heat 1–2 minutes until butter melts. (*Note:* When boiling cut carrots, reduce cooking liquid to 1 cup.) About 120 calories for each of 3 servings, 90 calories for each of 4 servings.

Boiled Baby Carrots: Follow method above and boil 10–15 minutes.

To Parboil for Use in Other Recipes: Use recipe above but boil whole carrots only 20–25 minutes; the halved or quartered 10; thickly sliced or whole baby carrots 7; thinly sliced, diced, or julienne carrots 3–4. Omit seasonings.

VARIATIONS:

¢ **To Serve Cold:** Boil and drain as directed, then chill in ice water. Drain, cover, and refrigerate. See Vegetable Seasoning Chart for appropriate cold dressings.

⚖ ¢ **Low-Calorie Carrots:** Omit butter; dress with lemon or orange juice and/or 1 tablespoon minced chives. About 50 calories for each of 3 servings, 40 for each of 4.

¢ **Lemon-Glazed Carrots:** Boil and drain carrots by above recipe and keep warm. Melt butter, mix in pepper, ¼ cup light brown sugar, and ½ teaspoon grated lemon rind, and warm, stirring, 3–5 minutes until sugar dissolves. Pour over carrots and serve. About 190 calories for each of 3 servings, 140 calories for each of 4 servings.

¢ **Carrots Rosemary:** Boil and drain carrots as directed above. Return to heat, add pepper and butter, ½ teaspoon each minced fresh rosemary and summer savory (or ¼ teaspoon of the dried), 1 tablespoon each lemon juice and light brown sugar. Warm over lowest heat, turning carrots now and then, about 5 minutes to glaze. About 140 calories for each of 3 servings, 105 calories for each of 4 servings.

MASHED CARROTS

Makes 4 servings

6–8 medium-size hot boiled carrots
¼ teaspoon salt
2 tablespoons butter or margarine, softened to room temperature
2 tablespoons heavy cream
Pinch nutmeg or mace (*optional*)

Mash carrots with a potato masher, beat with an electric mixer or purée in an electric blender at high speed. Add all remaining ingredients and beat well with a fork. About 115 calories per serving.

VARIATIONS:

Mashed Carrots and Potatoes: Add 1½ cups hot mashed potatoes to mashed carrots, mix in all seasonings, and beat until light. About 160 calories per serving.

Mashed Carrots and Yams: Add 1½ cups hot mashed yams or sweet potatoes, 2 tablespoons honey or maple syrup, and a pinch cinnamon to mashed carrots. Mix in the salt, butter, cream, and nutmeg and beat until light. About 205 calories per serving.

Mashed Carrots and Rutabagas: Mix 1½ cups hot mashed rutabagas into carrots, add all seasonings, and beat until light. About 145 calories per serving.

Mashed Carrots and Turnips: Mix 1½ cups hot mashed turnips into carrots, add seasonings, and beat until fluffy. About 130 calories per serving.

Mashed Carrots and Parsnips: Mix 1½ cups hot mashed parsnips into carrots, add seasonings, and beat until light. About 185 calories per serving.

CARROTS VICHY

If you have a bottle of Vichy water, try cooking young carrots in it for particularly rich flavor. If not, use the following recipe, which substitutes tap water and a pinch of soda but tastes like the real thing.
Makes 4 servings

12–14 small young carrots, peeled
2 tablespoons sugar
½ teaspoon salt
½ cup boiling water
2 tablespoons butter or margarine
Pinch baking soda
Pinch white pepper
1 tablespoon minced parsley

Place carrots, sugar, salt, water, butter, and soda in a saucepan. Cover and boil gently 10–15 minutes until carrots are fork tender. Uncover and boil until almost all liquid is gone, shaking pan frequently so carrots become lightly glazed. Sprinkle with pepper and parsley and serve. About 110 calories per serving.

HOT MACÉDOINE OF VEGETABLES

A macédoine of vegetables is a mixture of cooked vegetables of similar size and shape. Usually they're diced, sometimes cut in diamonds or small balls. Almost any mixture can be used if the colors and flavors go well together (avoid using beets because their color runs).
Makes 4–6 servings

1 cup diced cooked carrots
1 cup diced cooked turnips
1 cup diced cooked celery
1 cup cooked green peas
1 cup baby limas
1 cup cooked green or wax beans, cut in ½" lengths
3–4 tablespoons butter or margarine
Salt
Pepper

Drain all vegetables well and place in a saucepan with butter and salt and pepper to taste. Warm over low heat 2–3 minutes, shaking pan, until butter melts and serve. About 180 calories for each of 4 servings, 120 calories for each of 6 servings.

VARIATION:

Cold Macédoine of Vegetables: Chill cooked vegetables in ice water, drain, pat dry on paper toweling, and refrigerate until ready to use. Instead of seasoning with butter, salt, and pepper, dress with Spanish Vinaigrette Dressing or thin mayonnaise. Serve as a salad, cold vegetable, or hors d'oeuvre. About 180 calories for each of 4 servings, 120 calories for each of 6 servings (with 4 tablespoons dressing).

VENETIAN CARROTS IN CREAM

Carrots prepared this way go well with roast fresh ham or spring lamb.
Makes 4 servings

12–14 small young carrots, peeled
½ cup chicken broth
¼ teaspoon salt
Pinch white pepper
Pinch nutmeg
⅓ cup heavy cream

Place carrots and broth in a saucepan, cover, and simmer 10–15 minutes until tender. (*Note:* There should be very little liquid left, so uncover and boil rapidly to reduce, if necessary.) Add remaining ingredients and simmer, uncovered, 2–3 minutes longer, basting carrots occasionally. Do not allow to boil. About 115 calories per serving.

FLEMISH-STYLE CARROTS

Belgians have a particular talent with vegetables. Flemish-style carrots are sautéed in butter until faintly caramel, then seasoned with lemon so that they aren't too sweet.
Makes 4 servings

¼ cup butter or margarine
6–8 medium-size carrots, peeled and cut in matchstick strips
⅓ cup boiling water
1 tablespoon light brown sugar
1 teaspoon salt
⅛ teaspoon mace
2 egg yolks
½ cup light cream
1 tablespoon lemon juice

Melt butter in a large, heavy skillet over moderate heat, add carrots, and sauté, stirring, 12–15 minutes until lightly glazed. Add water, brown sugar, salt, and mace, cover, and simmer 8–10 minutes until carrots are crisp-tender. Uncover and cook 2 minutes longer. Beat egg yolks with cream, mix into carrots, season with lemon juice, and serve. About 245 calories per serving.

CARROTS PROVENCAL

An unusual combination of carrots, onion, garlic, and tomatoes.
Makes 4 servings

2 tablespoons olive or other cooking oil
1 medium-size yellow onion, peeled and chopped fine
1 clove garlic, peeled and crushed
2 ripe tomatoes, peeled, seeded, and coarsely chopped
6–8 medium-size carrots, cut in julienne strips and parboiled
½ teaspoon salt
⅛ teaspoon pepper

Heat oil in a large, heavy skillet over moderate heat 1 minute. Add onion and garlic and sauté 5–8 minutes until onion is pale golden. Add tomatoes, sauté 1–2 minutes, then add drained carrots, cover, reduce heat to low, and simmer 5 minutes until carrots are tender. Uncover and simmer 2–3 minutes longer, stirring. Season with salt and pepper and serve. About 130 calories per serving.

CANTONESE CARROTS WITH GREEN PEPPER AND CELERY

Makes 4 servings

12–14 small young carrots, peeled
3 stalks celery
½ medium-size sweet green pepper, cored and seeded
2 tablespoons peanut or other cooking oil
1 scallion, chopped fine (include tops)
Pinch MSG (monosodium glutamate)
¾ teaspoon salt

Cut carrots on the bias into diagonal slices about ¼" thick. Cut celery the same way, making slices ⅛" thick. Cut green pepper into matchstick strips. Heat oil in a large, heavy skillet over moderately low heat 1 minute. Add carrots and celery and stir-fry 4 minutes. Add green pepper and scallion and stir-fry 5 minutes or until carrots are crisp-tender. Sprinkle vegetables with MSG and salt, toss, and serve. About 105 calories per serving.

CARROT AND ONION "PIE"

Makes 4 servings

6–8 medium-size carrots, peeled and halved or quartered
1 large yellow onion, peeled and coarsely chopped
1½ cups boiling water
2 tablespoons melted butter or margarine
1 teaspoon salt (about)
⅛ teaspoon pepper
2 tablespoons butter or margarine
1 teaspoon minced parsley
1 teaspoon minced chervil (optional)

Preheat oven to 350° F. Boil carrots and onion in the water, covered, about 20 minutes until tender. Drain and put through a food mill or purée in an electric blender at high speed. Beat melted butter, salt, and pepper into carrot purée, taste for salt and add more if needed. Spoon into a well-buttered 9" or 10" piepan and dot with remaining butter. Bake, uncovered, 15–20 minutes. Sprinkle with parsley and, if you like, the chervil and serve. About 150 calories per serving.

BAKED CARROTS AND RICE

A mellow, crunchy combination of shredded carrots and rice that makes an unusual potato substitute.
Makes 6 servings

¼ cup butter or margarine
3 cups coarsely grated raw carrots
½ cup minced onion
1 teaspoon minced parsley
1½ teaspoons salt
¼ teaspoon summer savory
¼ teaspoon mace
Pinch rosemary
Pinch pepper
3 tablespoons dry sherry
3 cups cooked rice
1 cup milk
2 eggs, lightly beaten

Preheat oven to 325° F. Melt butter in a large, heavy skillet over moderate heat, add carrots and onion, and sauté, stirring occasionally, about 15 minutes until carrots are crisp-tender. Mix in parsley, salt, savory, mace, rosemary, pepper and sherry and heat, stirring, 1–2 minutes. Off heat, mix in rice. Beat milk with eggs, add to carrots, and stir until well blended. Spoon into a buttered 9"×9"×2" baking dish, cover with foil, and set in a shallow pan; pour ½" water into pan. Bake 45 minutes, remove foil, and bake 30 minutes longer. About 245 calories per serving.

CAULIFLOWER

Snowy . . . succulent . . . a little bit sweet, a little bit nutty . . . that's cauliflower. "Cabbage with a college education," Mark Twain called it. Certainly it's the most elegant cabbage, a vegetable grown only for emperors and kings until twentieth-century farming made it available to all.

To Prepare for Cooking: Remove green leaves, cut off heavy stem close to base, and wash head well in cool water, holding it upside down. Leave head whole, making a deep X-cut in the base of the heavy stem to hasten cooking; or divide into bite-size flowerets, trimming each stem to a length of 1".

Serving Tip: Try serving raw cauliflowerets with seasoned salt or Curry Dip as a cocktail hors d'oeuvre.

VEGETABLES

Season	For Top Quality	Amount To Buy	Nutritive Value	Calories (unseasoned)
Year round; peak months: September–December	Choose snowy, compact heads with crisp green leaves and few or no dark spots. Reject any open, spongy heads.	1 large (3–3½-pound) cauliflower will serve 4.	High in vitamin C	Low–25–30 per average serving

BOILED CAULIFLOWER

Some say cauliflower should be cooked uncovered, some say it should be uncovered the first 5 minutes only, some say it should be covered at all times. We've tried all three ways and prefer the third because it minimizes the "cabbage-y" cooking odor. The same technique works for all members of the cabbage family.
Makes 4 servings

1 large cauliflower, prepared for cooking
1½ cups boiling water
1 slice lemon (to keep cauliflower snowy)
½ teaspoon salt
⅛ teaspoon white pepper

Place cauliflower stem down in a large saucepan, add all but last ingredient, cover, and boil until crisp-tender: 20–30 minutes for a head, 5–7 for flowerets. Drain well. To keep head intact while transferring to serving dish, tilt pan and ease it out. Sprinkle with pepper, dress with Browned Butter or one of the sauces listed in the Vegetable Seasoning Chart. About 30 calories per serving without Browned Butter or sauce.

To Steam Cauliflower: Place cauliflower on a rack in a steamer, pour in boiling water to a depth of 1", cover, and steam head 30–40 minutes, flowerets 10–15.

To Parboil for Use in Other Recipes: Use either method above, reducing cooking times thus: boil heads 10 minutes, flowerets 3–5; steam heads 20 minutes, flowerets 7–10. Omit seasonings.

VARIATIONS:
To Serve Cold: Chill boiled or steamed cauliflower in ice water, drain, and pat dry on paper toweling; refrigerate until ready to use. Serve as a salad or cold vegetable dressed with one of the sauces listed in the Vegetable Seasoning Chart.

⚖ **Low-Calorie Cauliflower:** Boil or steam as directed, drain and dress with low-calorie herb or Italian dressing instead of butter or sauce. If you like, add a sprinkling of minced chives, parsley, or dill. About 35 calories per serving.

CAULIFLOWER POLONAISE

Makes 4–6 servings

1 large cauliflower, steamed and drained
2 tablespoons butter or margarine
1 cup soft white bread crumbs
2 hard-cooked eggs, peeled and chopped fine
1 tablespoon minced parsley

Transfer cauliflower to a vegetable dish and keep warm. Melt butter in a small skillet over moderate heat, add crumbs, and stir-fry 4–5 minutes until lightly browned. (*Note:* Crumbs brown slowly at first, quickly toward the end, so watch carefully.) Off heat, mix in eggs and parsley. Sprinkle crumb mixture over cauliflower and serve. About 155 calories for each of 4 servings, 105 calories for each of 6 servings.

CAULIFLOWER IN CIDER AND CREAM

Makes 4–6 servings

2 tablespoons butter or margarine
2 tablespoons flour
1 cup heavy cream
½ cup apple cider
½ teaspoon salt
Pinch white pepper
1 large cauliflower, divided into flowerets, parboiled, and drained

Melt butter in the top of a double boiler over simmering water and blend in flour; slowly mix in cream and cider. Heat, stirring, until thickened. Season with salt and pepper, add cauliflowerets, and toss gently to mix. Cover and warm, still over simmering water, 10–15 minutes to blend flavors. About 315 calories for each of 4 servings, 210 calories for each of 6 servings.

DEVILED CAULIFLOWER

To give this dish special zip, add a beef bouillon cube to the cooking water.
Makes 4 servings

1 large cauliflower, divided into flowerets, boiled and drained (save cooking water)
¼ cup butter or margarine
3 tablespoons flour
1 teaspoon powdered mustard
Cauliflower cooking water plus enough milk to total 1⅔ cups
1 tablespoon Worcestershire sauce
1 tablespoon prepared spicy brown mustard
½ teaspoon salt
1 teaspoon ketchup
⅛ teaspoon pepper

Keep cauliflower warm. Melt butter over moderate heat and blend in flour and powdered mustard. Mix in the 1⅔ cups liquid and heat, stirring, until thickened. Mix in remaining ingredients and heat, stirring, 2–3 minutes. Pour sauce over cauliflower, toss lightly to mix, and serve. About 180 calories per serving.

CAULIFLOWER CARUSO

A piquant dish that goes well with veal cutlets, scaloppine, or broiled chicken.
Makes 4–6 servings

1 large cauliflower, divided into flowerets, boiled and drained
1 small yellow onion, peeled and chopped fine
2 tablespoons olive or other cooking oil
1 tablespoon minced anchovies
¼ cup dry white wine or chicken broth
1 tablespoon lemon juice
1 teaspoon minced parsley
1 teaspoon minced fresh chervil or ½ teaspoon dried chervil
½ teaspoon minced fresh basil or ¼ teaspoon dried basil
Pinch pepper

Keep cauliflower warm. Sauté onion in oil in a large skillet over moderate heat 5–8 minutes until pale golden. Add anchovies and sauté 1 minute. Stir in wine or broth and lemon juice, reduce heat to low, cover, and simmer 10 minutes. Add cauliflower, mix gently, sprinkle with parsley, herbs, and pepper. Cover and simmer 5–7 minutes until heated through, basting cauliflower once or twice with sauce. About 120 calories for each of 4 servings, 80 calories for each of 6 servings.

PURÉED CAULIFLOWER À LA DU BARRY

Makes 4 servings

1 large cauliflower, boiled until very tender and drained
1 cup hot, seasoned mashed potatoes
¼ cup heavy cream
2 tablespoons melted butter or margarine
1 teaspoon salt
⅛ teaspoon white pepper
Pinch mace
2 tablespoons butter or margarine

Preheat oven to 350° F. Purée cauliflower in an electric blender at high speed or put through a food mill. With a wooden spoon or wire whisk, beat purée with potatoes and cream until fluffy. Mix in melted butter, salt, pepper, and mace. Spoon into a buttered shallow 1½-quart casserole and dot with butter. Bake, uncovered, 1 hour until golden brown. About 215 calories per serving.

VARIATION:

Mix in any of the following just before baking: ¼ cup minced scallions (include some tops); ½ cup coarsely chopped toasted almonds; ¼ cup finely chopped pecans. About 215 calories per serving if made with scallions, 320 calories per serving if made with almonds, and 245 calories per serving if made with pecans.

CAULIFLOWER SOUFFLÉ

Topped with Cheese Sauce or Mornay Sauce, this makes a luscious luncheon entree.
Makes 4 servings

¼ cup butter or margarine
¼ cup sifted flour
½ cup cauliflower cooking water
½ cup light cream
4 eggs, separated
¾ teaspoon salt
Pinch white pepper
2 cups puréed, cooked cauliflower
Pinch cream of tartar

Preheat oven to 350° F. Melt butter over moderate heat and blend in flour. Mix in cauliflower cooking water and cream and heat, stirring, until thickened and smooth. Beat egg yolks lightly, mix in a little hot sauce, then stir back into sauce in pan. Cook, stirring, 1–2 minutes, but do not boil. Mix sauce, salt, and pepper into cauliflower purée. (*Note:* You can make recipe up to this point well ahead of time, then cool, cover, and chill until about 2 hours before serving. Let sauce come to room temperature before proceeding.) Beat egg whites until frothy, add cream of tartar, and continue beating until fairly stiff peaks form. Fold whites into sauce, then spoon into an ungreased 5-cup soufflé dish. Bake, uncovered, on center rack about 45 minutes or until puffed and golden. Rush to the table and serve. About 280 calories per serving (without sauce).

CAULIFLOWER PUDDING

A rich cauliflower custard aromatic of savory and mace.
Makes 4–6 servings

2 medium-size cauliflowers, divided into flowerets and parboiled
1 (13-ounce) can evaporated milk
2 tablespoons melted butter or margarine
2 eggs
2 teaspoons salt
¼ teaspoon pepper
¼ teaspoon summer savory
⅛ teaspoon mace

Preheat oven to 300° F. Drain cauliflower thoroughly and chop coarsely. Place all remaining ingredients in a large bowl and beat with an electric mixer or rotary beater until frothy. Mix in cauliflower. Transfer to a lightly buttered 2-quart casserole or soufflé dish and bake, uncovered, 1–1½ hours until no longer liquid. Stir mixture 1 or 2 times from the bottom as it cooks. About 280 calories for each of 4 servings, 185 calories for each of 6 servings.

CAULIFLOWER AU GRATIN

Such an easy, elegant recipe.
Makes 4–6 servings

1 large cauliflower, divided into flowerets, boiled, and drained
½ teaspoon salt
⅛ teaspoon white pepper
1½ cups hot Cheese Sauce or Mornay Sauce
⅓ cup coarsely grated sharp Cheddar cheese
1 tablespoon melted butter or margarine

Preheat broiler. Arrange flowerets in an ungreased *au gratin* dish or shallow casserole. Season with salt and pepper and cover evenly with sauce. Sprinkle with cheese and drizzle with butter. Broil 5″ from heat 3–4 minutes until cheese melts and is dappled with brown. About 280 calories for each of 4 servings and 185 calories for each of 6 if made with Mornay Sauce. About 320 calories for each of 4 servings and 210 for each of 6 if made with Cheese Sauce.

VARIATION:

After browning, top with ½ cup toasted, slivered almonds. About 385 calories for each of 4 servings and 255 calories for each of 6 if made with Mornay Sauce. About 425 calories for each of 4 servings and 280 for each of 6 if made with Cheese Sauce.

CAULIFLOWER BAKED IN WINE AND CREAM SAUCE

Makes 4–6 servings

1½ cups chicken broth
1 large cauliflower, divided into flowerets
⅔ cup heavy cream (about)
¼ cup butter or margarine
¼ cup unsifted flour
Pinch mace
2 tablespoons dry white wine
½ cup finely grated Parmesan cheese
⅛ teaspoon salt
Pinch pepper

Topping:
⅔ cup cracker meal
3 tablespoons melted butter or margarine
1 tablespoon finely grated Parmesan cheese

Bring broth to a boil in a large saucepan, add cauliflower, cover, and simmer 20–25 minutes until crisp-tender. Drain, reserving broth. Measure broth and add cream to make 2 cups. Melt butter over moderate heat and blend in flour and mace. Add broth mixture and heat, stirring, until thickened. Off heat, mix in wine, Parmesan, salt, and pepper. Arrange flowerets in an ungreased 2-quart *au gratin* dish and top with sauce. Mix topping and sprinkle over surface. Preheat broiler, then broil 5″ from heat 3–4 minutes until browned and bubbly. About 520 calories for each of 4 servings, 345 calories for each of 6 servings.

VEGETABLES

CELERIAC

(Also called Knob Celery, Turnip Celery, and German Celery)

Long treasured in Europe, this plump root celery has never become popular in this country. It tastes like strong celery, has the texture of a turnip, and is best when creamed, puréed, or prepared *au gratin*.

To Prepare for Cooking: Cut off all stalks and root ends and discard; scrub knob well in cool water, then peel (the skin is very tough and stringy). Slice, cube, or cut into julienne strips.

Cooking Tip: Substitute celeriac for celery in soups and stews.

Serving Tip: Marinate raw julienne strips of celeriac 2–3 hours in the refrigerator in a good tart dressing and serve in—or as—a salad.

BOILED CELERIAC

If you've never tasted celeriac, try it one of these easy ways. You may discover that you like it very much.
Makes 4 servings

3 knobs celeriac, prepared for cooking
1½ cups boiling water or chicken broth
1 teaspoon salt (about)
⅛ teaspoon white pepper
2 tablespoons melted butter or margarine

Place celeriac, water or broth, and salt (reduce to taste if you use broth) in a saucepan, cover, and boil until crisp-tender: 15 minutes for julienne strips, 20–30 for cubes and slices. Drain, add pepper and butter, and toss to mix. About 95 calories per serving.

To Parboil for Use in Other Recipes: Use method above but reduce cooking time to 10 minutes for julienne strips, to 15 for cubes and slices. Omit seasonings.

VARIATIONS:

To Serve Cold: Cook and drain as recipe directs; chill in ice water. Drain, pat dry on paper toweling, and refrigerate until needed. Serve as a cold vegetable or salad, with one of the dressings recommended in the Vegetable Seasoning Chart.

⚖ **Low-Calorie Celeriac:** Season with lemon juice instead of butter, use seasoned salt for ordinary salt, and sprinkle with 2 tablespoons minced chives. About 45 calories per serving.

Creamed Celeriac: Omit butter and mix boiled, drained celeriac with 1½ cups hot Medium White Sauce. About 195 calories per serving.

Puréed Celeriac: Cook 1 small peeled cubed Irish potato with celeriac. Purée vegetables with ¼ cup cooking liquid in an electric blender at low speed or put through

Season	For Top Quality	Amount To Buy	Nutritive Value	Calories (unseasoned)
August–May	Look for firm, crisp knobs 2–4" in diameter with few scars or blemishes.	A 2–4" knob serves 1–2.	Low	Low—about 45 per average serving

a food mill. Mix in ⅛ teaspoon white pepper, 2 tablespoons heavy cream, a pinch of nutmeg, and, for a rich purée, 2 tablespoons melted butter. If mixture has cooled, warm over low heat, stirring. About 145 calories per serving (without additional butter), 195 calories per serving (with additional butter).

CELERIAC AU GRATIN

An especially good casserole. Easy, too.

Makes 4 servings

3 knobs celeriac, cut in julienne strips, boiled and drained
1½ cups hot Cheese Sauce
½ cup soft white bread crumbs
¼ cup finely grated Parmesan cheese
1 tablespoon minced parsley
2 tablespoons melted butter or margarine

Preheat oven to 400° F. Arrange celeriac in an ungreased 1½-quart *au gratin* dish or shallow casserole and top with sauce. Toss remaining ingredients together and sprinkle over sauce. Bake, uncovered, 20 minutes until crumbs are lightly browned. About 370 calories per serving.

CELERY

Celery is a Mediterranean vegetable, which ancients looked upon as medicine rather than food (it was said to purify the blood). When the French began to cultivate wild celery, it was the seed they prized (and used as an herb), not the stalk. No one knows who first thought to eat the crisp, succulent stalks—odd considering how much we rely on them today to give crunch to salads and stuffings, delicate savor to soups and stews.

To Prepare for Cooking: Cut root end and green leafy tops from celery (save for stock pot); separate head into individual stalks. Wash well in cool water, slice or chop as individual recipes specify.

To Prepare Celery Hearts: Peel away all but inner 4 or 5 stalks (save for salads, soups, or stews), halve lengthwise, then trim off root ends and leafy tops so each heart is about 5" long. Soak hearts ½ hour in ice water; rinse.

Serving Tip: To make raw stalks supercrisp, pull threads from outer side of each; soak stalks 20–30 minutes in 1 gallon ice water mixed with ¼ cup sugar.

¢ ⚖ **BOILED CELERY**

Cooked celery makes a delicious, low-calorie vegetable.

Makes 4 servings

Season	For Top Quality	Amount To Buy	Nutritive Value	Calories (unseasoned)
Year round	Whether buying white or green (Pascal) celery, choose crunchy stalks, neither cracked nor bruised, with crisp green leaves.	1 large head (1½ pounds), cooked, will serve 4.	Some minerals; rather low in vitamins	Very Low— about 5 per stalk

1 large bunch celery, prepared for
    cooking
1½ cups boiling water
½ teaspoon salt
Pinch pepper
2 tablespoons melted butter or
    margarine

Cut stalks in 1½" lengths or dice. Boil, covered, in lightly salted water 20–30 minutes if cut in lengths, 10–15 if diced. Drain, add pepper and butter, and serve. About 65 calories per serving.

To Parboil for Use in Other Recipes: Use recipe above but reduce cooking time to 10 minutes for celery cut in lengths, to 5 minutes for the diced. Omit seasonings.

VARIATIONS:

¢ **To Serve Cold:** Boil and drain as directed; chill in ice water, drain, pat dry on paper toweling, and refrigerate until needed. Serve as a salad or cold vegetable with one of the dressings recommended in the Vegetable Seasoning Chart.

⚖ ¢ **Low-Calorie Celery:** Instead of seasoning with butter, dress with 2 tablespoons low-calorie herb or Italian dressing, 2 tablespoons minced chives, and a dash of Worcestershire sauce. About 15 calories per serving.

Celery Amandine: Boil and drain celery as directed and sprinkle with pepper. Omit butter and top instead with 1–1½ cups hot Medium White Sauce. Mix lightly, sprinkle with 2–3 tablespoons toasted slivered almonds, and serve. About 145 calories per serving.

Celery au Gratin: Cut celery in 1½" lengths, boil and drain as directed. Sprinkle with pepper but omit butter. Mix with 1½ cups hot Mornay Sauce, spoon into an ungreased 1-quart *au gratin* dish, sprinkle with ⅓ cup grated sharp Cheddar cheese, and broil 5" from the heat 3–4 minutes until lightly browned. About 240 calories per serving.

BRAISED CELERY HEARTS

Makes 4 servings

4 celery hearts, parboiled and drained
2 tablespoons butter or margarine
1 cup water, chicken or beef broth or
    ¾ cup water or broth and ¼ cup
    dry vermouth
⅛ teaspoon pepper
½ teaspoon salt (optional)

Pat celery dry between several layers of paper toweling. Heat butter until bubbly in a heavy skillet over moderately low heat, add celery and cook gently, turning frequently until pale golden. Add water, sprinkle with pepper and salt (omit salt if using broth), cover, and simmer about ½ hour until fork tender. When serving, top each portion with a little cooking liquid. About 65 calories per serving if cooked in water, 75 calories per serving if cooked in broth or in broth and vermouth.

CELERY AND CARROT CURRY

Good with ham, pork, lamb, or chicken.

Makes 4–6 servings

6–8 medium-size carrots, peeled and
    cut in matchstick strips
¾ cup boiling water
2 beef bouillon cubes
4 large stalks celery, cut in matchstick
    strips
1¼ cups milk (about)
2 tablespoons butter or margarine
1 small yellow onion, peeled and
    minced

2 tablespoons flour
1 tablespoon curry powder
¼ teaspoon ginger
Pinch nutmeg

Place carrots in a large saucepan, add water and bouillon cubes, cover, and simmer 8–10 minutes. Add celery, re-cover, and simmer 10 minutes longer until vegetables are crisp-tender. Drain cooking liquid into a measuring cup and add enough milk to total 1½ cups. In a separate saucepan, melt butter over moderate heat and sauté onion, stirring, 5–8 minutes until pale golden. Blend in flour and spices, add milk mixture, and heat, stirring, until thickened. Pour sauce over vegetables, toss to mix, and let "season," uncovered, over lowest heat 5–10 minutes, stirring occasionally. About 170 calories for each of 4 servings, 110 for each of 6 servings.

SCALLOPED CELERY WITH ALMONDS

Makes 4–6 servings

1 large bunch celery, prepared for cooking
1½ cups boiling water
1–1¼ teaspoons salt
3 tablespoons butter or margarine
3 tablespoons flour
½ cup light cream
⅛ teaspoon white pepper
½ cup finely chopped blanched almonds
½ cup fine dry bread crumbs

Preheat oven to 350° F. Cut celery stalks in 3″ lengths; arrange in an ungreased shallow 2-quart flameproof casserole, add water and 1 teaspoon salt. Cover and simmer 20–25 minutes over moderate heat until crisp-tender. Drain off cooking water, reserving 1 cup. Melt butter over moderate heat and blend in flour. Mix in cooking water and cream and cook and stir about 5 minutes until thickened. Season with pepper, taste for salt and add remaining ¼ teaspoon if needed. Pour sauce over celery. Mix almonds with crumbs and sprinkle on top. Bake, uncovered, 30 minutes until browned and bubbly. About 295 calories for each of 4 servings, 200 calories for each of 6 servings.

BLUE CHEESE-CELERY CASSEROLE

Makes 4 servings

4 cups coarsely chopped celery (you'll need about 1 bunch)
1 cup chicken broth
1 cup hot seasoned mashed potatoes
½ teaspoon salt
⅛ teaspoon pepper
¼ cup crumbled blue cheese

Topping:
1 cup soft white bread crumbs mixed with 2 tablespoons melted butter or margarine

Simmer celery, covered, in broth 1 hour until mushy (when celery is about ⅔ done, begin preheating oven to 400° F.). Purée celery with cooking liquid in an electric blender at low speed or put through a food mill. Mix in remaining ingredients except topping and spoon into a buttered 1-quart casserole. Sprinkle with topping and bake, uncovered, 35–45 minutes until lightly browned. About 190 calories per serving.

⊠ ¢ CHINESE STIR-FRIED CELERY

Makes 4 servings

1 large bunch celery, prepared for cooking
¼ cup peanut or other cooking oil

Cut each stalk diagonally into slices

⅛" thick, discarding any strings. Heat oil in a *wok* or large, heavy skillet over moderate heat, add celery, and stir-fry 5–7 minutes until crisp-tender but not brown. About 140 calories per serving.

VARIATIONS:

◨ ¢ **Chinese Celery with Soy and Sesame Seeds:** Stir-fry as directed; just before serving toss in 1 tablespoon each soy sauce and sesame seeds. About 145 calories per serving.

¢ **Stir-Fried Celery, Pepper, and Scallions:** Stir-fry ½ thinly slivered sweet red pepper and 3–4 minced scallions along with the celery. About 145 calories per serving.

Stir-Fried Celery and Mushrooms: Stir-fry ⅔ cup thinly sliced mushrooms along with the celery. About 145 calories per serving.

CHARD
(Also called Swiss Chard)

Chard is a bonus vegetable: the crinkly green leaves can be steamed much like spinach, the silvery stalks can be simmered like asparagus, or the two can be chopped and cooked together.

To Prepare for Cooking: Discard root ends and separate stalks from leaves. Wash leaves 2 or 3 times in cool water to remove all grit; trim stalks of tough or woody ribs and wash well in cool water. Keep stalks and leaves separate.

BOILED CHARD
Makes 4 servings

2 pounds chard, prepared for cooking
½ cup boiling water
½ teaspoon salt
Pinch pepper
2 tablespoons melted butter or margarine

Coarsely chop stalks and leaves but keep the two separate. Place stalks in a large pot, add water and salt, cover, and boil 5 minutes. Add leaves, cover, and boil 5–10 minutes longer until tender. Drain, toss with pepper and butter, and serve. About 90 calories per serving.

To Boil Stalks Alone: Prepare stalks for cooking, leave whole or cut in 2–3" lengths. Place in a pot with 1 cup boiling water and ½ teaspoon salt and boil, covered, 10–15 minutes until tender. Drain, season with pepper and butter, and serve.

Steamed Chard Leaves: Prepare leaves for cooking, place in a large pot with ½ cup boiling water and ½ teaspoon salt, cover, and steam 5–10 minutes until tender. Drain and season with butter and pepper or oil and vinegar. About 90 calories per serving.

To Parboil for Use in Other Recipes: Boil stalks by method above but reduce cooking time to 5–7 minutes; omit seasonings. The leaves don't need parboiling.

Season	For Top Quality	Amount To Buy	Nutritive Value	Calories (unseasoned)
June–November	Look for crisp leaves and fleshy stalks free of insect injury.	A 1-pound bunch serves 2 amply.	Very high in vitamin A	Low—less than 40 per ½-pound serving

VARIATIONS:

To Serve Cold: Boil or steam as directed and drain; chill stalks and/or leaves in ice water. Drain, toss with a good tart dressing, and refrigerate several hours.

⚜️ **Low-Calorie Chard:** Season with red or white wine vinegar instead of butter. About 40 calories per serving.

Puréed Chard: Boil and drain as directed; purée in an electric blender at high speed or put through a food mill. Mix in 2 tablespoons each butter and heavy cream, a pinch pepper and warm 1–2 minutes, stirring, over low heat. About 115 calories per serving.

CHAYOTES

(Also called Christophene, Cho-Cho, Mango Squash, Mirliton, and Vegetable Pear)

These Caribbean squashes, fairly common in the Gulf States, are beginning to appear elsewhere. The size and shape of an avocado, they have deeply furrowed, waxy, pale yellow skins. They taste like summer squash and can be substituted for it in recipes.

To Prepare for Cooking: Scrub well in cool water, then peel unless chayotes are to be stuffed and baked (you'll notice a sticky substance on your hands—it's harmless and washes right off). Halve chayotes and with a table knife pry out long, slender seed. Leave as halves, cut each in two lengthwise, or slice crosswise ¾" thick.

To Boil: Cover with lightly salted boiling water and simmer, covered, until firm but tender: about 45 minutes for halves, 30 for quarters, 20 for slices. Drain, season with butter, salt, and pepper or top with Mornay, Basic Cheese, or Medium White Sauce.

To Parboil for Use in Other Recipes: Use method above but reduce cooking time to 30 minutes for halves, 20 for quarters, and 10–15 for slices.

To Bake and Stuff: Fill parboiled, *unpeeled,* scooped-out halves with any mixture you would use for stuffing summer squash. Bake, uncovered, at 350° F. about 30–40 minutes.

To Serve as Salad: Cool and chill boiled chayote halves or slices. Fill halves with any meat or fish salad; marinate slices in a tart dressing and toss into green salad.

CHESTNUTS

(Also called Marrons)

To us chestnuts are a luxury, something to savor before the fire with a glass of fine sherry, something to save for that special Thanksgiving stuffing. To Europeans, however,

Season	For Top Quality	Amount To Buy	Nutritive Value	Calories (unseasoned)
Year round	Choose plump, firm, clean chayotes with few nicks, blemishes.	1 chayote serves 2.	Not determined	Thought to be low

they're commonplace, a popular potato substitute. Try them their way in place of potatoes.

To Shell and Peel Chestnuts: This is a tedious job, so have patience. Make an X-cut into shell on flat side of each nut. Cover nuts with cold water, bring to a boil, cover, and boil 1–2 minutes. Remove from heat but do not drain. Using a slotted spoon, scoop 2–3 nuts from the pan at a time and peel off both the hard outer shell and the inner brown skin (use a small knife to loosen skins if necessary). Keep chestnuts in hot water until you're ready to peel them. If any seem unduly stubborn, simply reheat briefly in boiling water and try again to peel.

BOILED CHESTNUTS

Serve in place of potatoes with poultry, pork, game, or game birds.
Makes 4 servings

1 pound shelled, peeled chestnuts
2 cups boiling water or chicken broth
3 tablespoons butter or margarine
Salt
Pepper

Simmer chestnuts, covered, in water or broth 15–20 minutes until tender but not mushy. Drain, add butter, salt, and pepper to taste, and warm uncovered over low heat, shaking pan gently, until butter melts and gilds nuts. About 295 calories per serving (if cooked in water), 310 per serving (if cooked in broth).

To Boil Dried Chestnuts: Wash and sort, carefully removing any that are withered, discolored, or buggy. Cover with cold water, remove any that float, then soak overnight. Drain, rinse several times, and scrape off bits of brown skin remaining. Cover with fresh cold water and simmer, covered, 1–1½ hours until plump and tender. Drain and use cup-for-cup in place of fresh boiled chestnuts.

VARIATIONS:

Sautéed Chestnuts: Boil and drain chestnuts by recipe above, add salt and pepper but omit butter. Sauté instead in ¼ cup butter 4–5 minutes until lightly browned. About 320 calories per serving (if cooked in water), 335 per serving (cooked in broth).

Creamed Chestnuts: Boil and drain chestnuts as recipe directs, then halve. Add butter, salt, and pepper called for, also ½ cup heavy cream. Warm, uncovered, over lowest heat until just simmering. Stir occasionally. About 400 calories per serving (if cooked in water), 415 per serving (if cooked in broth).

Riced Chestnut Pyramid: Boil and drain chestnuts as directed, season with salt and pepper but omit butter. Put chestnuts through a potato

Season	For Top Quality	Amount To Buy	Nutritive Value	Calories (unseasoned)
Fall and winter	Choose plump, unshriveled nuts with unscarred, uncracked shells.	1½ pounds unshelled nuts will yield 1 pound shelled nuts and serve about 4.	Some incomplete protein, iron and B vitamins	Very high—about 20 per fresh nut, 40 per dried nut

ricer, letting them mound into a pyramid on a heated plate. Serve with melted butter. About 220 calories per serving (if cooked in water), 235 per serving (if cooked in broth)—without butter.

Puréed Chestnuts: Boil as directed in chicken broth; drain and purée in an electric blender at high speed or put through a food mill. Beat in 2 tablespoons each butter and light cream; add salt and pepper to taste. About 310 calories per serving.

ROASTED CHESTNUTS

Makes 4 servings

1½ pounds chestnuts in the shell
¼ cup cooking oil

Preheat oven to 400° F. With a sharp knife, make an X-shaped cut on the flat side of each shell. Arrange nuts in a roasting pan, sprinkle with oil, and toss lightly. Roast, uncovered, 10–15 minutes. Cool just until easy to handle, then shell and remove inner brown skins. The chestnuts are now ready to use in recipes or to eat out of hand. About 245 calories per serving.

VARIATION:

Hearth-Roasted Chestnuts: Do not make X-cuts on chestnuts, do not use oil. Lay chestnuts at edge of fire near glowing coals (you don't need a pan) and roast about 10 minutes, turning frequently, until nuts "pop." Shell and eat. About 220 calories per serving.

BRAISED CHESTNUTS

These chestnuts can be served as a vegetable, alone, or mixed with creamed onions, boiled cabbage, Brussels sprouts, or broccoli. They can also be used to garnish roast chicken, turkey, or game platters. Makes 4 servings

¼ cup melted butter or margarine
1 small yellow onion, peeled and minced
1 stalk celery, minced (include green tops)
1 pound shelled, peeled chestnuts, whole or halved
⅛ teaspoon white pepper
1½ cups chicken broth or ¾ cup each beef consommé and water
1 star anise (optional)

Preheat oven to 350° F. Pour butter into a 1½-quart casserole, add onion and celery, and top with chestnuts. Sprinkle with pepper, pour in broth, and, if you like, add anise. Cover and bake 35–45 minutes until chestnuts are very tender. When serving, top each portion with some of the pan juices. About 340 calories per serving.

COLLARDS

Nearly every Southern farm has its collard patch, every kitchen its "mess o' greens" simmering on the back of the stove with a chunk of streaky bacon or salt pork. There's always lots of "pot likker" and oven-fresh corn bread for sopping it up.

To Prepare for Cooking: Wash well in cool water to remove grit and sand. Discard tough stems and leaf midribs; cut large leaves into bite-size pieces.

Cooking Tip: Try stir-frying finely shredded young collard leaves in bacon drippings 8–10 minutes over moderately high heat until crisp-tender.

VEGETABLES

¢ BOILED COLLARDS, TURNIP GREENS, OR MUSTARD GREENS

Makes 4 servings

2 pounds collards, turnip greens, or mustard greens, prepared for cooking
½ cup boiling water
¾ teaspoon salt
Pinch pepper
2 tablespoons bacon drippings, melted butter or margarine

Break leaves into bite-size pieces or chop fine. Place in a large pot, add water and salt, cover, and simmer until tender: 10–15 minutes for turnip or mustard greens, 15–20 for collards. (*Note:* Very young leaves may cook in 5–7 minutes.) Drain, add pepper and drippings, and toss to mix. About 105 calories per serving.

VARIATION:

⚖ ¢ **Low-Calorie Boiled Greens:** Omit drippings and dress with a sprinkling of white wine vinegar and a pinch nutmeg. About 55–60 calories per serving.

Season	For Top Quality	Amount To Buy	Nutritive Value	Calories (unseasoned)
Year round; supply short only in April, May.	Choose crisp, clean frosty blue-green leaves free of insect injury.	1 pound serves 2.	Very high in vitamins A and C, also calcium	Moderately low—55 per cup of cooked collards

CORN

(Also called Maize)

One of the joys of summer is feasting upon sugary ears of sweet corn, dripping with butter and so hot you can hardly hold them. A gift from the American Indian, corn provides not only kernels to nibble off the cob but also corn meal, cornstarch, corn syrup, hominy, hominy grits, and bourbon. There are hundreds of varieties of corn, but those we like best are sweet—truly sweet, unfortunately, only when rushed from stalk to pot. If you live in a corn-growing area, try to befriend a farmer who will let you pick your own.

To Prepare for Cooking: Just be-

Season	For Top Quality	Amount To Buy	Nutritive Value	Calories (unseasoned)
May–October; in big cities corn is available year round, but best only in summer.	Buy ears in the husk preferably from iced bins; husks should be bright green and snug-fitting; kernels bright, plump, and milky.	2 ears per person	Fair source of vitamin A and certain of the B complex	High—70 for quite a small ear; 170 per cup of whole kernel corn

fore cooking—*no earlier*—peel away husks, remove tassels and silks. Break off tip and stem end. Do not wash.

To Cut Corn off the Cob: For *cream-style,* cut down the center of each row of kernels, then, using

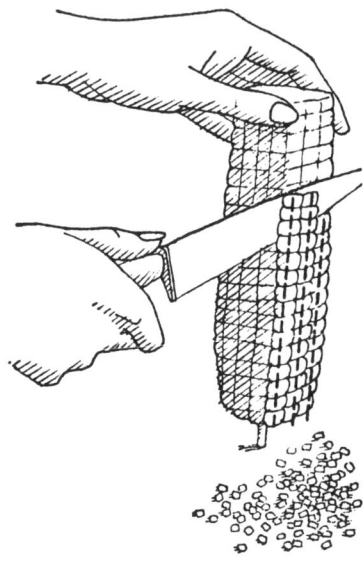

the back of the knife, scrape corn into a bowl. For *whole kernel corn,* simply cut kernels from cob, doing 3 or 4 rows at a time.

Cooking Tip: To give not so fresh corn a just-picked flavor, add 1–2 tablespoons sugar to the cooking water. Never cook corn in salted water.

☒ BOILED FRESH CORN ON THE COB

For truly sweet and tender corn, don't salt the cooking water. Add a teaspoon of sugar, if you like, but *no* salt.

Allow 2 ears per person

Fresh ears sweet corn, prepared for cooking
4–5 quarts boiling water
Salt
Pepper
Butter or margarine

Place water in a 1½-gallon kettle over high heat and, when boiling vigorously, drop in corn. Cover and boil 5–8 minutes, depending on the size of the ears. Lift ears from water with tongs and serve with salt, pepper, and plenty of butter. About 70 calories per ear of corn (without butter).

VARIATION:

Substitute 1 quart milk for 1 quart water and boil as directed. About 70 calories per ear of corn (without butter).

CHARCOAL-ROASTED FRESH EARS OF CORN

Allow 2 ears per person

Prepare a moderately hot charcoal fire.* Pull back husks to expose kernels but do not tear off. Remove silks, then smooth husks back over ears and tie at tips. Lay ears on a grill 3–4″ from coals and roast 12–15 minutes, turning frequently. Husk while piping hot (wear gloves) and serve at once with salt, pepper, and butter. About 70 calories per ear of corn (without butter).

VARIATIONS:

– After removing silks and tying husks at the tips as directed above, soak ears 10–15 minutes in ice water. Drain, shake off excess water, and roast as directed. If you want to roast directly in coals, soak 30 minutes. Bury in coals and roast 10 minutes. About 70 calories per ear of corn (without butter).
– Husk ears, wrap in buttered squares of aluminum foil, and roast

VEGETABLES

3" from coals 20–30 minutes, turning frequently. About 75 calories per ear of corn (without additional butter).

OVEN ROASTING EARS

An unusually good way to prepare frozen corn on the cob is to roast in the oven—it's firm yet tender and has a delightful nutty flavor.

Makes 2–4 servings

2 (2-ear) packages frozen corn on the cob (do not thaw)
Butter or margarine
Salt
Pepper

Preheat oven to 400° F. Wrap each solidly frozen ear in several thicknesses heavy foil, twisting ends to seal. Place on lowest oven rack and roast 1 hour. Unwrap and serve with butter, salt, and pepper. About 70 calories per ear of corn (without butter).

VARIATION:

Charcoal-Roasted Frozen Ears: Prepare a moderate charcoal fire.* Wrap frozen ears as directed above and roast 3–4" from coals 1 hour, giving them a quarter turn every 15 minutes. Unwrap and serve with butter, salt, and pepper. About 70 calories per ear of corn (without butter).

BOILED FRESH WHOLE KERNEL CORN

Makes 4–6 servings

6–8 ears sweet corn, prepared for cooking
1 cup boiling water or skim milk
½ teaspoon sugar
½ teaspoon salt
Pinch white pepper
2 tablespoons butter or margarine

Cut corn from cob.* Place in a saucepan with water or milk and sugar, cover, and simmer 5–8 minutes until tender. Drain and season with salt, pepper, and butter. About 155 calories for each of 4 servings, 105 calories for each of 6 servings.

VARIATIONS:

Boiled Corn and Vegetables: Just before serving corn, mix in 1½ cups boiled green peas, asparagus tips, or diced carrots; or ½ cup sautéed minced red or green pepper or Spanish onion. Recipe too flexible for a meaningful calorie count.

Creamy Corn: Simmer corn with sugar as directed above but use ½ cup cream (heavy, light, or half-and-half) instead of water or milk. Do not drain. Add all seasonings called for and serve in soup bowls. If made with heavy cream, about 260 calories for each of 4 servings, 175 calories for each of 6 servings. If made with light cream, about 210 calories for each of 4 servings, 140 calories for each of 6 servings. If made with half-and-half, about 195 calories for each of 4 servings, 130 calories for each of 6 servings.

⊠ HERBED CORN IN CREAM

Makes 4–6 servings

4 cups fresh whole kernel sweet corn or 2 (1-pound) cans whole kernel corn, drained
¾ cup heavy cream
2 tablespoons butter or margarine
2 tablespoons minced chives (fresh, frozen, or freeze-dried)
¼ teaspoon minced fresh basil or ⅛ teaspoon dried basil
¼ teaspoon minced fresh chervil or ⅛ teaspoon dried chervil
Salt
Pepper
Pinch paprika

Place all but last 3 ingredients in

the top of a double boiler over simmering water, cover, and cook 10 minutes until corn is tender. Add salt and pepper to taste, ladle into soup bowls, and sprinkle with paprika. About 380 calories for each of 4 servings, 255 calories for each of 6 servings.

OLD-FASHIONED SUCCOTASH

Makes 4–6 servings

2 cups fresh whole kernel sweet corn
2 cups fresh baby lima or cranberry beans, parboiled
1 cup light cream
2 tablespoons butter, margarine, or bacon drippings
2 teaspoons sugar
Pinch white pepper
1 teaspoon salt

Place all ingredients but salt in a saucepan and simmer, uncovered, stirring occasionally, 10–12 minutes until beans are tender. Mix in salt; ladle into soup bowls. About 360 calories for each of 4 servings, 240 calories for each of 6 servings.

VARIATIONS:

Green Bean Succotash: Substitute ½ pound parboiled cut green beans for the lima beans and prepare as recipe directs. About 290 calories for each of 4 servings, 195 calories for each of 6 servings.

Hominy-Green Bean Succotash: Instead of using recipe above, place 2 cups each of boiled, drained hominy and boiled, drained cut green beans in a large saucepan, add ½ cup heavy cream, 3 tablespoons bacon drippings, and salt and pepper to taste. Warm, stirring, 3–4 minutes just to blend flavors. Serve in soup bowls, topped, if you like, with crisp bacon bits. About 245 calories for each of 4 servings, 165 calories for each of 6 servings.

☒ CONFETTI CORN

Makes 4 servings

1 large sweet green pepper, cored, seeded, and chopped fine
1 (3½-ounce) can pimiento, drained and chopped fine
1 small yellow onion, peeled and chopped fine
¼ cup butter or margarine
1 (1-pound 1-ounce) can whole kernel corn, drained
¼ teaspoon salt
Pinch pepper

Stir-fry green pepper, pimiento, and onion in butter 8–10 minutes until onion is golden. Add corn, salt, and pepper, cover, and simmer 3–4 minutes, just long enough to heat through. About 210 calories per serving.

SCALLOPED CORN

A marvelously mellow corn casserole.

Makes 4 servings

2 tablespoons butter or margarine
2 tablespoons flour
1¼ cups milk
1 teaspoon salt
⅛ teaspoon pepper
1 egg, lightly beaten
¼ teaspoon prepared mild yellow mustard
2 cups whole kernel corn (fresh; drained frozen cooked or canned)
1 cup coarse soda cracker crumbs
2 tablespoons melted butter or margarine

Preheat oven to 350° F. Melt butter over moderate heat, blend in flour, then add milk and heat, stirring, until thickened and smooth. Off heat mix in salt, pepper, egg, mustard, and corn. Pour into a lightly buttered 1½-quart casserole, sprinkle with crumbs, and drizzle with melted butter. Bake, uncovered,

VEGETABLES

30 minutes until lightly browned. About 350 calories per serving.

CORN GUMBO

Makes 4–6 servings

1 medium-size yellow onion, peeled and minced
½ medium-size sweet green pepper, cored, seeded, and chopped fine
1 stalk celery, chopped fine
2 tablespoons bacon drippings
1½ cups coarsely chopped, seeded, peeled tomatoes
2 cups fresh, thawed frozen, or canned whole kernel corn (drain the frozen or canned)
4–6 baby okra pods, sliced ½" thick
1 teaspoon salt
¼ teaspoon gumbo filé
⅛ teaspoon pepper

Sauté onion, green pepper, and celery in drippings in a large saucepan 8–10 minutes over moderate heat until onion is golden. Add all remaining ingredients except salt, gumbo filé, and pepper, cover, and simmer slowly 10–15 minutes, stirring occasionally. Mix in salt, gumbo filé, and pepper. Ladle into soup bowls and serve. About 175 calories for each of 4 servings, 115 calories for each of 6 servings.

CORN PUDDING

Everyone's favorite.
Makes 6 servings

3 tablespoons butter or margarine
2 (10-ounce) packages frozen whole kernel corn (do not thaw)
¼ teaspoon nutmeg
4 eggs
¼ cup unsifted flour
½ teaspoon baking powder
1 tablespoon sugar
1 teaspoon salt
⅛ teaspoon white pepper
1 (13-ounce) can evaporated milk
⅓ cup light cream

Preheat oven to 325° F. Melt butter in a large saucepan over moderate heat, add corn, and simmer, uncovered, stirring occasionally, 8–10 minutes until heated through. Do not drain; stir in nutmeg. Beat eggs until foamy in a large mixing bowl. Mix flour with baking powder, sugar, salt, and pepper, add to eggs, and beat until smooth. Mix in corn, then milk and cream. Pour into a buttered, shallow 1½-quart casserole, set in a shallow roasting pan, and pour in enough cold water to come about halfway up casserole. Bake, uncovered, about 1 hour and 20 minutes or until a knife inserted in center of pudding comes out clean. About 355 calories per serving.

CORN PIE

Makes 6 servings

Pastry:
1 recipe Flaky Pastry I

Filling:
4 eggs, lightly beaten
1¼ cups milk or light cream
1¼ teaspoons salt
Pinch white pepper
1 tablespoon grated yellow onion
1½ cups whole kernel corn (fresh or drained canned)

Preheat oven to 425° F. Prepare pastry and fit into a 9" piepan, making a high, fluted edge. Prick bottom and sides of pastry with a fork, cover with wax paper, and fill with uncooked rice or dried beans. Bake 5–7 minutes until firm but not brown, remove rice or beans. Stir together all filling ingredients and pour into pie shell. Bake 10 minutes at 425° F., reduce heat to 350° F., and bake 30 minutes longer or until center is almost firm. Cool about 10 minutes before cutting. About 310 calories per serving (if made with milk), 380 per serving (if made with cream).

VARIATIONS:

Bacon and Corn Pie: Add ½–¾ cup crumbled cooked bacon to filling and bake as directed. About 360 calories per serving (if made with milk), 430 calories per serving (if made with cream).

Corn Quiche: Add ¾ cup coarsely grated Gruyère or Swiss cheese to filling and bake as directed. About 380 calories per serving (if made with milk), 450 calories per serving (if made with cream).

CORN OYSTERS

These corn cakes are delicious for breakfast, lunch, or supper. Top, if you like, with maple syrup.

Makes 6 servings

½ cup sifted flour
¾ teaspoon salt
½ teaspoon baking powder
¼ cup milk
1 egg, lightly beaten
2 cups whole kernel corn (fresh or drained canned)
⅓ cup cooking oil

Sift flour with salt and baking powder into a bowl. Slowly add milk and beat until smooth. Beat in egg and mix in corn. Heat oil in a large, heavy skillet over moderate heat 1 minute. Drop batter by tablespoonfuls into skillet and fry, a few "oysters" at a time, 3–4 minutes until browned on both sides. Drain on paper toweling and set, uncovered, in a 250° F. oven to keep warm while you fry the rest. About 160 calories per serving (without syrup).

CORN FRITTERS

Makes 6 servings

Lard, shortening, or cooking oil for deep fat frying

Fritters:
1½ cups sifted flour
1½ teaspoons salt
2 teaspoons baking powder
2 eggs, lightly beaten
½ cup milk
2 cups cooked whole kernel corn, drained well

Begin heating fat in a deep fat fryer over moderately high heat; insert deep fat thermometer. Meanwhile, sift flour, salt, and baking powder together into a bowl. Add eggs, a little of the milk and beat until smooth. Add remaining milk and beat again. Stir in corn. When fat reaches 375° F., drop in batter from a measuring tablespoon. Do only 5 or 6 fritters at a time, frying each until crisply golden and turning as needed to brown evenly. Drain on paper toweling and set, uncovered, in a 250° F. oven to keep warm while you fry the rest. About 250 calories per serving.

VARIATION:

Corn-Cheese Fritters: Add 1 cup coarsely grated sharp Cheddar cheese to batter. (If mixture seems thick, stir in 1–2 tablespoons cold water.) Fry as directed. About 325 calories per serving.

CUCUMBERS

It was cucumbers the Israelites craved in the Wilderness, cucumbers the Emperor Tiberius ate daily, and cucumbers Charlemagne ordered grown lest he run out of pickles. Delicious raw, cucumbers are equally so baked in butter, stir-fried in peanut oil, or smothered in cream

VEGETABLES

Season	For Top Quality	Amount To Buy	Nutritive Value	Calories (unseasoned)
Year round	Choose uniformly firm green cucumbers with no dark, soft spots.	1 medium-size cucumber will serve 1–2.	Poor	Low—about 30 per medium-size cucumber

sauce. The French and Chinese are the masters of cucumber cooking, and we include some of their favorite recipes here.

To Prepare for Cooking: Most cucumbers today are dipped in wax to keep them crisp and fresh, so it's a good idea to peel before using. Cut up and seed as individual recipes specify. The easiest way to seed cucumbers is simply to scoop them out with a teaspoon.

BOILED CUCUMBERS

Makes 4 servings

3 medium-size cucumbers, peeled, halved, and seeded
½ cup boiling water
¼ teaspoon salt
Pinch white pepper
2 tablespoons butter or margarine

Leave cucumbers as halves or cut in 1" cubes. Place in a saucepan with water and salt, cover, and simmer until crisp-tender: 8–10 minutes for cubes, 10–12 for halves. Drain, add pepper and butter, set over low heat, and warm uncovered until butter melts. About 70 calories per serving.

To Steam Cucumbers: Place halves or cubes in a steamer over rapidly boiling water, cover, and steam 8–10 minutes for cubes, 10–12 for halves. Season as above and serve. About 70 calories per serving.

To Parboil for Use in Other Recipes: Boil or steam as directed above, reducing cooking times as follows: to 5 minutes for cubes, to 8 for halves. Omit seasonings.

VARIATIONS:

⚔ **Low-Calorie Cucumbers:** Omit butter and dress with 1–2 tablespoons lemon juice and/or a sprinkling minced chives, parsley, or dill. For additional savor, substitute seasoned salt for salt. About 25 calories per serving.

Cucumbers au Gratin: Boil by recipe above, drain, season with pepper, and place in a buttered 1½-quart *au gratin* dish. Top with ½ cup grated Parmesan mixed with ½ cup soft white bread crumbs and drizzle with 2 tablespoons melted butter. Broil 5" from heat 2 minutes until browned (watch closely so cucumbers don't burn). About 190 calories per serving.

SAUTÉED CUCUMBERS

Makes 4 servings

3 medium-size cucumbers, peeled, seeded, and cut in 1½" cubes, parboiled and drained
2 tablespoons butter or margarine
1 tablespoon cooking oil
1 egg, lightly beaten
½ cup toasted seasoned bread crumbs

Pat cucumbers dry on paper toweling. Melt butter in a heavy skillet over moderate heat, add oil and heat ½ minute. Dip cucumber in egg, then in crumbs to coat evenly. Sauté, a few cubes at a time, 4–5 minutes, until golden brown and crisp. Drain on paper toweling, set, uncovered, in a 250° F. oven to keep warm while you sauté the rest. Good with lemon wedges or Tartar Sauce. About 120 calories per serving.

⚜ CHINESE-STYLE CUCUMBERS IN SOY SAUCE

Makes 4 servings

3 medium-size cucumbers, peeled, quartered lengthwise, and seeded
2 tablespoons peanut oil
1 tablespoon Japanese soy sauce
1 tablespoon minced chives (fresh, frozen, or freeze-dried)

Cut each cucumber quarter into slices ¼" thick and pat dry on paper toweling. Heat oil in a large, heavy skillet or *wok* over moderate heat 1 minute. Add cucumbers and stir-fry 3–4 minutes, until crisp-tender. Add soy sauce and toss to mix; sprinkle with chives and serve. About 60 calories per serving.

CUCUMBERS BRAISED IN WHITE WINE AND CHICKEN BROTH

Makes 4 servings

3 medium-size cucumbers, peeled, halved, and seeded
¼ cup melted butter or margarine
½ cup medium-dry white wine
½ cup chicken broth

Preheat oven to 350° F. Place cucumbers in an ungreased shallow 1½-quart casserole and pour butter evenly over all. Bake, uncovered, 10 minutes. Pour wine and broth into casserole, cover, and bake 30 minutes longer until fork tender. About 150 calories per serving.

VARIATION:

Braised Vegetable-Stuffed Cucumbers: Prepare and bake as directed, then fill hollow of each cucumber with cooked, seasoned peas, cauliflowerets, diced carrots, or creamed spinach. Recipe too flexible for a meaningful calorie count.

CUCUMBERS PROVENÇAL

Makes 4 servings

3 medium-size cucumbers, peeled, seeded, cut in 1" cubes, parboiled, and drained
2 tablespoons butter or margarine
2 tablespoons olive or other cooking oil
1 clove garlic, peeled and crushed
2 medium-size ripe tomatoes, peeled, seeded, and coarsely chopped
1 tablespoon minced parsley
½ teaspoon salt
⅛ teaspoon pepper

Pat cucumbers dry on paper toweling. Melt butter in a large, heavy skillet over moderate heat, add oil and heat ½ minute. Sauté garlic ½ minute until pale golden, add cucumbers and tomatoes, and sauté 4–5 minutes until tender, stirring constantly. Off heat, add remaining ingredients, toss lightly to mix, and serve. About 150 calories per serving.

BAKED STUFFED CUCUMBERS

Makes 4 servings

2 medium-size cucumbers, peeled and halved
5–6 tablespoons melted butter or margarine
2 cups soft white bread crumbs
¼ teaspoon salt

⅛ teaspoon pepper
1 teaspoon dried chervil
½ cup coarsely chopped, peeled, seeded tomatoes
3 tablespoons sliced blanched almonds

Preheat oven to 350° F. Scoop seeds and center pulp from cucumbers so they are boat-shaped. Coarsely chop pulp and reserve ¼ cup. Parboil cucumbers 5 minutes, then drain and arrange in a well-buttered shallow baking pan. (*Note:* Use a pancake turner for handling cucumbers because they're delicate and break easily.) Brush cucumbers lightly all over with a little melted butter. Toss crumbs with reserved cucumber pulp, ¼ cup melted butter, and all remaining ingredients except almonds and stuff cucumbers. Top with almonds and drizzle with melted butter. Bake, uncovered, 35 minutes until cucumbers are fork tender and almonds lightly browned. About 260 calories per serving.

DANDELIONS

Ever wonder how dandelions got their name? It's a corruption of *dent de lion* ("tooth of the lion"), which is the way the French described the dandelion's jagged leaves. It is these leaves that are good to eat, particularly if cooked gently like spinach in a small amount of water, then tossed with butter or dressed with oil and lemon. These are the same dandelions that blight our lawns, though those sold in groceries have been especially grown for the table.

To Prepare for Cooking: Trim away roots and sort, removing yellowed or wilted leaves. Wash well in cool water and tear into bite-size pieces.

Serving Tip: Add crisped dandelion greens to tossed salads for special bite and zest.

Season	For Top Quality	Amount To Buy	Nutritive Value	Calories (*unseasoned*)
Spring	Choose clean, tender leaves with stems and roots attached.	1 pound serves 2.	High in vitamin A and iron	Low—about 50 per average serving

WILTED DANDELIONS OR NETTLES

Makes 4 servings

4 slices bacon
2 pounds (3–4 quarts) dandelion or nettle leaves, prepared for cooking
¼ cup red wine vinegar
1–2 tablespoons sugar
½ teaspoon salt
Pinch pepper

Brown bacon in a large, heavy kettle over moderate heat and drain on paper toweling. Add leaves to kettle along with all remaining ingredients, cover, and simmer 10–15 minutes until tender. Remove leaves from kettle and chop fine. Serve topped with any cooking liquid and crumbled bacon. About 160 calories per serving.

DASHEENS

(Also known as Taro)

Cooked, mashed, and fermented, dasheens are the *poi* of Hawaii; boiled or baked, they are the "potatoes" of Jamaica. Like potatoes, dasheens are mealy and nutty; unlike them, they are gray-lavender inside. Some are no bigger than pullet eggs, but coconut-size dasheens are more common.

To Prepare for Cooking: Scrub in cool water with a vegetable brush. Peel and cut in 1½" chunks if dasheens are to be boiled; leave whole and do not peel if they are to be baked.

To Boil: Cover dasheens with lightly salted boiling water, cover, and simmer about 1 hour until tender. Drain and mash as you would potatoes, seasoning with butter, salt, and pepper; or instead of mashing, mix cubes with hot Medium White Sauce (about 1 cup sauce to 2 cups dasheens).

To Bake: Parboil whole, unpeeled dasheens 30 minutes. Drain and bake, uncovered, in a shallow roasting pan 1–1½ hours at 375° F. until a fork pierces them easily. Halve or quarter dasheens, also peel, if you like, and season as you would baked potatoes.

Season	For Top Quality	Amount To Buy	Nutritive Value	Calories (unseasoned)
Year round	Choose clean, unscarred tubers of uniform size.	1 average dasheen serves 2–4.	Some minerals but generally poor	Moderate–high–110 per serving

EGGPLANT

(Sometimes called by the French name *aubergine*)

For centuries eggplant stood high on Europe's list of "dangerous and immoral foods," the rumor being it drove men mad. Fortunately, Arabs and Orientals knew better; they ate eggplant with relish and created many of the recipes we consider classics. Today we appreciate eggplant for what it is—one of the most versatile of vegetables.

To Prepare for Cooking: Wash well in tepid water; peel or not as individual recipes specify (the skin is often left on to give dishes color, flavor, and texture).

Serving Tip: Salt thin strips of raw peeled eggplant, pat dry on paper toweling, toss with Vinaigrette Dressing and minced tarragon or chervil, and serve as a salad.

FRIED EGGPLANT

Eggplant cooks so quickly that, when fried, it need only be browned on both sides. Use, if possible, the slim, drier "frying" variety that doesn't have to be salted and blotted on paper toweling.

Makes 4–6 servings

1 medium-size eggplant or 6 slim "frying" eggplants cut in ½" rounds (do not peel)
2 teaspoons salt (about)
1 egg, lightly beaten
⅛ teaspoon mace
⅛ teaspoon pepper
⅓ cup olive or other cooking oil
½ cup cracker meal

If using the large eggplant, sprinkle about 1 teaspoon salt over rounds and weight down between paper toweling 1 hour. Mix egg with 1 teaspoon salt, the mace, and pepper.

VEGETABLES

Season	For Top Quality	Amount To Buy	Nutritive Value	Calories (unseasoned)
Year round	Choose firm, evenly purple eggplants, without cuts or scars, that weigh heavy for their size.	1 medium-size eggplant will serve 4; allow 1–2 "frying" eggplants per person.	Poor	Low—about 40 per average serving

Heat 3–4 tablespoons oil 1–2 minutes in a large, heavy skillet over moderately high heat. Dip rounds in egg, a few at a time, then in crumbs and brown on both sides, adding more oil to skillet as needed. Drain browned rounds on paper toweling and set, uncovered, in a 250° F. oven to keep warm while you fry the rest. About 280 calories for each of 4 servings, 190 calories for each of 6 servings.

⊠ BROILED EGGPLANT

Makes 4 servings

1 medium-size eggplant, cut in rounds ½" thick (do not peel)
⅓ cup olive or other cooking oil (about)
1 teaspoon salt
⅛ teaspoon pepper

Preheat broiler. Brush eggplant rounds generously with oil and broil 4–5" from heat about 5 minutes until speckled with brown. Turn, brush again with oil, and broil 5 minutes longer. Sprinkle with salt and pepper and serve. For extra dash, top with chopped parsley, grated Parmesan cheese, or Tomato Sauce. About 190 calories per serving (without grated Parmesan or Tomato Sauce).

VARIATION:

⚖ **Low-Calorie Broiled Eggplant:** Brush rounds with lemon juice or low-calorie Italian dressing instead of oil and broil as directed. About 40–45 calories per serving.

BASQUE-STYLE EGGPLANT, PEPPERS, AND TOMATOES

Makes 6–8 servings

1 medium-size eggplant, peeled and cut in ¾" cubes
2 tablespoons flour
¼ cup olive or other cooking oil
3 large sweet green peppers, cored, seeded, and cut in ½" squares
3 cups coarsely chopped, seeded, peeled ripe tomatoes
1 teaspoon salt
1 tablespoon minced parsley

Dredge eggplant in flour and stir-fry in oil in a large, heavy skillet over moderately high heat 7–8 minutes until browned. Add peppers and sauté 3–4 minutes, then add tomatoes and cook 2–3 minutes longer, stirring. Cover, reduce heat to low, and simmer 15 minutes. Mix in salt and parsley and, if mixture seems too liquid, turn up heat and boil, uncovered, stirring, until the consistency of stew. Serve with garlic bread. About 160 calories for each of 6 servings, 120 calories for each of 8 servings.

IZMIR EGGPLANT

Want an unusual—unusually good—vegetable to go with roast lamb?

Then try this Turkish way of preparing eggplant.

Makes 4–6 servings

1 medium-size eggplant, cut in ½" cubes (do not peel)
2 medium-size yellow onions, peeled and coarsely chopped
2 cloves garlic, peeled and crushed
2 bay leaves
⅓ cup olive oil
1 (8-ounce) can tomato sauce
Juice of ½ lemon
¼ teaspoon oregano
¼ teaspoon salt
⅛ teaspoon pepper

Stir-fry eggplant, onions, garlic, and bay leaves in the oil in a large, heavy skillet over moderate heat 12–15 minutes until eggplant is tender. Mix in remaining ingredients, reduce heat to low, and simmer uncovered, stirring now and then, 10 minutes longer. About 250 calories for each of 4 servings, 165 calories for each of 6 servings.

RATATOUILLE (EGGPLANT, ZUCCHINI, AND TOMATO STEW À LA PROVENÇALE)

Ratatouille takes some doing, but once the pot's on, perfuming the air, the effort seems worthwhile. This dish keeps well, is even better the second time around.
Makes 4–6 servings

1 medium-size eggplant, peeled and sliced in ¼" rounds
3 medium-size zucchini, cut in ¼" rounds
1 tablespoon salt (about)
¾ cup olive oil (about)
2 medium-size yellow onions, peeled and sliced thin
2 medium-size sweet green peppers, cored, seeded, and sliced thin
2 cloves garlic, peeled and crushed
4 medium-size tomatoes, peeled, juiced, seeded, and coarsely chopped
⅛ teaspoon pepper
3 tablespoons minced parsley

Sprinkle eggplant and zucchini with 1 teaspoon salt and weight down between paper toweling 1 hour. Cut eggplant in ¼" strips and stir-fry, about ¼ at a time, 3–5 minutes in 2–3 tablespoons oil over moderately high heat. Drain on paper toweling. (Eggplant soaks up oil, but don't use more than 2–3 tablespoons for each batch or the ratatouille will be greasy). Brown all zucchini in 2 tablespoons oil and drain. Stir-fry onions with peppers and garlic in remaining oil 10 minutes over moderate heat until golden, lay tomatoes on top, add 1½ teaspoons salt and the pepper, cover, and simmer 8–10 minutes. Uncover and simmer 10 minutes longer. In an ungreased shallow 2½-quart flameproof casserole, build up alternate layers as follows: onion mixture (sprinkle with parsley), eggplant-zucchini (sprinkle with salt), onions (parsley), eggplant-zucchini (salt), onions (parsley). (*Note:* At this point ratatouille can be cooled, covered, and held in the refrigerator 1–2 days. Bring to room temperature before proceeding.) Simmer, covered, over low heat 35–40 minutes until vegetables are tender—don't stir. Uncover and simmer 40 minutes longer, also without stirring, until almost all juices are gone. Serve hot or cold as a vegetable or use for filling Crepes. About 500 calories for each of 4 servings, 335 calories for each of 6 servings.

VEGETABLES

¢ PISTO (SPANISH VEGETABLE STEW)

Pisto, Spanish cousin to *ratatouille*, can be eaten hot or cold, as an appetizer, vegetable, or main dish, depending on how much meat goes into it.

Makes enough appetizers for 50, vegetable servings for 16

1 cup diced lean cooked ham
½ cup olive oil
4 large yellow onions, peeled and sliced thin
2 medium-size sweet red peppers, cored, seeded, and coarsely chopped
1 (7½-ounce) can pimientos, drained and cut in ¼" strips
4 cloves garlic, peeled and crushed
1 medium-size eggplant, washed and cut in ½" cubes (do not peel)
½ pound mushrooms, wiped clean and sliced thin
2–3 teaspoons salt
2 (9-ounce) packages frozen artichoke hearts (do not thaw)
2 (1-pound) cans tomatoes (do not drain)

Brown ham in the oil in a large kettle over moderate heat. Add onions, peppers, pimientos, garlic, eggplant, and mushrooms, cover, and simmer slowly, stirring occasionally, 15 minutes until onions are golden. Add remaining ingredients and simmer, covered, 30–40 minutes until artichokes are tender. Cool, cover, and chill 4–5 hours. Serve cold or reheat and serve hot. About 45 calories for each of 50 appetizer servings, 135 calories for each of 16 vegetable servings.

VARIATIONS:

Main Dish Ham Pisto: Make as directed, increasing ham to 4 cups. Serve hot with fluffy cooked rice. Makes 12–14 servings. About 250 calories for each of 12 servings, 215 calories for each of 14 servings (without rice).

Main Dish Beef Pisto: Substitute 2 pounds ground beef chuck for the ham, brown lightly in the oil, then proceed as recipe directs and serve hot with rice. Makes 12–14 servings. About 320 calories for each of 12 servings, 275 calories for each of 14 servings (without rice).

SULTAN'S EGGPLANT

Makes 4 servings

1 large eggplant
½ teaspoon lemon juice
¼ cup light cream
¼ cup soft white bread crumbs
½ teaspoon salt (about)
2 teaspoons grated Parmesan cheese
⅛ teaspoon white pepper
2 tablespoons butter or margarine
1 tablespoon minced parsley

Preheat oven to 400° F. Prick eggplant all over with a sharp fork and bake, uncovered, about 1 hour until soft. Cool until easy to handle and slip off skin. Beat eggplant briskly with a fork or rotary beater, mix in lemon juice, and heat slowly, stirring, just until warm. Add all remaining ingredients except parsley and heat, stirring, 3–5 minutes. Sprinkle with parsley and serve. About 140 calories per serving.

VARIATION:

Roasting the eggplant over charcoal will give the dish a woodsy flavor. Simply place well-pricked eggplant on a grill over a moderate charcoal fire and roast 5" from the coals, turning frequently, about 45 minutes. Peel, mix with remaining ingredients, heat, and serve as directed. About 140 calories per serving.

EGGPLANT PARMIGIANA

When making a *parmigiana*, do as the Italians do—use a light hand with the garlic and a heavy one with Parmesan.
Makes 6–8 servings

2 small eggplants, cut in ¼" rounds (*do not peel*)
2 eggs, lightly beaten
1½ cups dry bread crumbs mixed with ½ teaspoon salt and ⅛ teaspoon pepper
1 clove garlic, peeled and halved
¾ cup olive oil (*about*)
1 (*1-pound 4-ounce*) can Italian plum tomatoes (*do not drain*)
⅓ cup tomato paste
2 tablespoons minced fresh basil or 2 teaspoons dried basil
1 teaspoon salt
⅛ teaspoon pepper
1 cup grated Parmesan cheese
½ pound mozzarella cheese, sliced very thin

Dip eggplant rounds in eggs, then in seasoned crumbs. Cover loosely and chill 20 minutes. Sauté garlic in 2 tablespoons olive oil 1–2 minutes in a large saucepan over moderate heat, then remove. Add tomatoes, tomato paste, basil, salt, and pepper, cover, and simmer, stirring occasionally, 30 minutes. Preheat oven to 350° F. Pour oil in a large, heavy skillet to a depth of ¼" and brown eggplant over moderately high heat, doing a few rounds at a time and adding more oil as needed. Drain on paper toweling. Spoon a thin layer of tomato sauce into an ungreased, shallow 2½-quart casserole, then build up alternate layers of eggplant, tomato sauce, Parmesan, and mozzarella, dividing ingredients equally and ending with mozzarella. Bake, uncovered, 30 minutes until bubbly. Serve as a vegetable or, for an Italian dinner, as a main dish following a hearty soup or pasta. About 590 calories for each of 6 servings, 440 calories for each of 8 servings.

EGGPLANT STUFFED WITH PILAF AND RAISINS

Makes 4 servings

1 medium-size eggplant
1–1½ teaspoons salt
1 medium-size yellow onion, peeled and chopped fine
2 tablespoons olive oil
2 tablespoons water
1¼ cups Rice Pilaf
¼ cup seedless raisins
⅛ teaspoon pepper
1 teaspoon minced fresh dill or ½ teaspoon dried dill
1 teaspoon minced parsley

Slice 1" off stem end of eggplant to make a lid, then, using a sharp knife, hollow out eggplant, leaving a shell ½" thick; sprinkle inside lightly with salt. Chop flesh medium fine. Sauté onion in the oil 8–10 minutes over moderately high heat until golden, add chopped eggplant, and stir-fry 2–3 minutes. Add water, cover, and simmer over lowest heat 10–15 minutes until eggplant is tender. Mix with pilaf and remaining ingredients, fill eggplant shell, and cover with stem lid. Stand eggplant upright in a deep kettle, pour in water to a depth of 3", cover, and simmer about 45 minutes until fork tender. Check pot occasionally to see that eggplant isn't slipping from its upright position. Lift eggplant from water, cut into wedges, and serve. About 185 calories per serving.

VEGETABLES

BAKED EGGPLANT STUFFED WITH MUSHROOMS AND CHICK-PEAS

Makes 4 servings

1 medium-size eggplant, halved lengthwise (do not peel)
2 teaspoons salt
1 large yellow onion, peeled and chopped fine
1 clove garlic, peeled and crushed
3 tablespoons cooking oil
1 cup finely chopped mushrooms
1 cup cooked chick-peas, chopped fine
⅛ teaspoon pepper
1½ cups tomato sauce
½ cup water

Score eggplant halves in a crisscross pattern and sprinkle each with ½ teaspoon salt. Let stand 1 hour, then press out as much liquid as possible. Rinse in cold water and pat dry on paper toweling. Scoop out centers, leaving shells ½" thick; chop centers fine. Preheat oven to 375° F. Sauté onion and garlic in 2 tablespoons oil in a large skillet over moderate heat 6–8 minutes until pale golden. Add remaining oil, mushrooms, and chopped eggplant and sauté 4–5 minutes until mushrooms brown. Off heat, stir in chick-peas, remaining salt, and the pepper. Brush rims of eggplant shells with oil and fill with sautéed mixture. Place halves in an ungreased shallow casserole and spread ¼ cup tomato sauce over each. Mix remaining tomato sauce with water and pour into casserole. Bake, uncovered, 1 hour until shells are fork tender. Serve, topped with some of the sauce. About 235 calories per serving.

TURKISH STUFFED EGGPLANT (IMAM BAYILDI)

A Turkish imam's wife once served her husband an eggplant dish so delicious he swooned. Here's the recipe, appropriately named Imam Bayildi, meaning "the parson fainted." Serve it hot as a vegetable, cold as an appetizer.

Makes 4 servings

1 medium-size eggplant, halved lengthwise (do not peel)
2 teaspoons salt
1 large yellow onion, peeled and minced
2 cloves garlic, peeled and crushed
½ cup olive oil
3 medium-size tomatoes, peeled, seeded, and coarsely chopped
⅛ teaspoon pepper

Score cut surfaces of eggplant halves in a crisscross pattern, sprinkle each with ½ teaspoon salt, and let stand 1 hour. Press out as much liquid as possible, rinse in cold water and pat dry on paper toweling. Scoop out centers, leaving shells ½" thick, and brush rims with oil. Cut centers in ½" cubes. Preheat oven to 350° F. Sauté onion and garlic in ¼ cup oil over moderate heat 8–10 minutes until golden; drain on paper toweling and reserve. Sauté tomatoes in 2 tablespoons oil 5 minutes and mix with onion; brown eggplant cubes in remaining oil, add to onion, and season with pepper and remaining salt. Taste and, if too tart, mix in a little sugar. Place eggplant shells in a lightly greased shallow casserole, cutting a slice off the bottoms, if necessary, to make them stand. Fill and bake, uncovered, 45–50 minutes until tender. About 330 calories per serving.

BELGIAN ENDIVE

(Also known as French Endive, Witloof, and Chicory)

Endive was one of the "bitter herbs" God commanded the Israelites to eat with lamb at the Feast of Passover. Earlier, it was a favorite of the Egyptians, who tossed the leaves into salads and brewed the roots into a bitter drink. The recipes we prize today, however, come from the Belgians and French.

To Prepare for Cooking: Pull off any wilted or discolored outer leaves and cut a thin slice from the root end of each stalk; wash well in cool water.

Serving Tip: Crispen individual endive leaves in ice water and serve with seasoned salt as a low-calorie cocktail snack.

Season	For Top Quality	Amount To Buy	Nutritive Value	Calories (unseasoned)
October–May	Choose crisp, clean stalks with tightly clinging leaves.	1 stalk per person.	Poor	Very low— about 20 per stalk

BOILED BELGIAN ENDIVES

Makes 4 servings

4 medium-size Belgian endives, prepared for cooking
1 cup boiling water or chicken broth
1 tablespoon lemon juice
¼ teaspoon salt
Pinch white pepper
2 tablespoons melted butter or margarine

Leave endives whole, halve lengthwise, or cut in rounds ⅛" thick. Boil, covered, in water or broth with lemon juice and salt until tender: 5 minutes for rounds, 14 for halves, 20 for stalks. Drain, add pepper and butter, and toss gently to mix. About 70 calories per serving (if made with water), 80 per serving (if made with broth).

To Parboil for Use in Other Recipes: Use method above but reduce cooking time to 2–3 minutes for rounds, 5–8 for halves, and 10 for whole stalks. Omit seasonings.

VARIATIONS:

To Serve Cold: Boil and drain as directed but do not season. Chill stalks in ice water, drain, and marinate in the refrigerator several hours in a good tart dressing (see Vegetable Seasoning Chart). Serve as a salad or cold vegetable.

Low-Calorie Endives: Boil and drain as directed; omit butter and dress with low-calorie herb, Italian, or French dressing. About 25 calories per serving.

Belgian Endives au Gratin: Boil, drain, and season endives by recipe above; place in an ungreased 1-quart *au gratin* dish, top with 1½ cups hot Cheese Sauce and ¼ cup grated Cheddar cheese. Broil 5" from heat 3–4 minutes to brown. About 270 calories per serving.

Endives and Ham au Gratin: For additional elegance, roll each endive in 2 thin slices boiled ham before arranging in *au gratin* dish. Cover with sauce and cheese and broil as directed. About 340 calories per serving.

Swiss-Style Endives: Boil, drain, and season endives by recipe above; place in a buttered 1-quart *au gratin* dish, sprinkle with about 1 teaspoon sugar and ⅓ cup grated Gruyère or Swiss cheese; broil 5" from heat

2–3 minutes until browned. About 120 calories per serving.

BRAISED BELGIAN ENDIVES

This recipe brings out the delicate flavor of endives.
Makes 4 servings

4 medium-size Belgian endives, prepared for cooking
2 tablespoons butter
¼ cup chicken broth
¼ teaspoon salt
1 teaspoon lemon juice
Minced parsley or chives (optional garnish)

Sauté endives in butter in a heavy skillet over moderately low heat 7–12 minutes, turning frequently so they become an even nut-brown. Add all remaining ingredients except garnish, cover, and simmer 10–12 minutes until tender. Serve topped with cooking liquid and, if you like, a little minced parsley or chives. About 75 calories per serving.

FENNEL

(Also called Finochio)

This aromatic Mediterranean vegetable deserves more recognition. It looks like bulbous celery, tastes faintly of licorice, and is delicious raw in salads or cooked in a variety of ways.

To Prepare for Cooking: Discard coarse or blemished outer stalks, trim off feathery tops (save to use as a seasoning) and tough base. Wash well in cool water, using a vegetable brush if necessary to remove stubborn grit. Leave whole or cut up as individual recipes specify.

To Prepare Fennel Hearts: Peel away all heavy outer stalks (save for soups). Quarter bulbs lengthwise and wash in cool water.

Cooking Tip: Mince feathery fennel tops and use as an herb to season salads, boiled carrots, beets, parsnips, or cabbage. Fennel also adds delicate fragrance to broiled chicken and white fish.

Season	For Top Quality	Amount To Buy	Nutritive Value	Calories (unseasoned)
Summer	Choose crisp, plump, unscarred bulbs with fresh, feathery tops.	1 bulb will serve 1–2.	Some vitamin A and C	Low—about 35 per average serving

BOILED FENNEL

Makes 4 servings

4 bulbs fennel, prepared for cooking
1½ cups boiling water or chicken broth
1 teaspoon salt (about)
Pinch white pepper
2 tablespoons butter or margarine

Prepare hearts* or cut stalks in 1" slices. Bring water or broth to a boil, add salt (reducing amount if broth is salty) and fennel, cover, and boil until crisp-tender: 7–10 minutes for slices, 12–15 for hearts. Drain, add pepper and butter, and toss. About 85 calories per serving (if made with water), 95 per serving (made with broth).

To Parboil for Use in Other Reci-

pes: Use recipe above but reduce cooking time to 5 minutes for slices, 10 for hearts. Omit seasonings.

VARIATIONS:

To Serve Cold: Boil and drain hearts as directed but do not season. Chill in ice water, drain, top with dressing (see Vegetable Seasoning Chart), and chill several hours. Serve as an appetizer, a salad, or cold vegetable.

⚖ **Low-Calorie Fennel:** Boil and drain as directed. Omit butter and dress with low-calorie French or Italian dressing. About 35 calories per serving.

Butter-Braised Fennel: Parboil and drain hearts but do not season. Sauté in 3 tablespoons butter 3–4 minutes, turning constantly. Add 2 tablespoons water, cover, and simmer 5–7 minutes until hearts are glazed and golden brown. Add pepper and serve. About 110 calories per serving (cooked in water), 120 per serving (cooked in broth).

Fennel Parmigiana: Parboil hearts, drain and place in an ungreased 1-quart *au gratin* dish. Drizzle with ¼ cup melted butter, sprinkle with ¼ cup grated Parmesan, and broil 4″ from heat 3–4 minutes until lightly browned. About 170 calories per serving (if fennel is cooked in water), 180 per serving (if cooked in broth).

FERNS

(Also called Fiddleheads)

The tender shoots of ferns that grow along mossy creek banks are one of spring's rare treats. Most highly prized is the cinnamon fern, which tastes of both asparagus and artichoke. Bracken and ostrich ferns are good too, though tougher and saltier. Canned ferns are available in specialty shops, but the best are those you pick fresh yourself.

To Prepare for Cooking: Sort, discarding any ferns that are discolored. Cut off stems—you want only the tightly curled "heads." Wash carefully in cool water to remove all traces of sand.

BUTTERED FERNS

Makes 4 servings

2 cups ferns, prepared for cooking
½ teaspoon salt
⅛ teaspoon white pepper
½ cup boiling water
¼ cup melted butter or margarine

Place ferns in a saucepan along with salt, pepper, and boiling water. Cover and simmer 20–30 minutes until tender. Drain well, add butter,

Season	For Top Quality	Amount Needed	Nutritive Value	Calories (unseasoned)
May	Pick young, silvery green shoots no more than 2″ above the ground and tightly curled like the scroll at the top of a fiddle.	Allow ½ cup per person.	Not determined	Not determined but probably low

VEGETABLES

Season	For Top Quality	Amount To Buy	Nutritive Value	Calories (unseasoned)
Spring	Choose firm, moist, fairly clean hearts with few cuts, scars or blemishes.	1 heart, trimmed, will weigh 1½–2½ pounds and serve 2–3. Canned hearts are smaller and will serve 1.	Not determined	Not determined

and toss lightly to mix. Calorie counts for ferns unavailable.

HEARTS OF PALM

(Also called Swamp Cabbage, Cabbage Palm, and Palmetto Cabbage)

These smooth ivory palmetto shoots are rarely seen fresh, though once in a great while they appear in gourmet markets. Canned hearts of palm, cooked and ready to eat, are widely available.

To Prepare for Cooking: Fresh hearts are bitter and must be soaked and sometimes blanched before cooking. Peel away coarse outer layers, cut off fibrous tops, then wash well in tepid water. Leave whole or slice into rounds ½" thick; soak 1 hour in cool water. Drain and taste for bitterness. If still bitter, boil 5 minutes in acidulated water to cover (1 tablespoon lemon juice to 1 quart water) and drain.

To Boil: Place prepared hearts in a saucepan, add lightly salted boiling water to cover, and simmer, covered, until tender: about 45 minutes for slices, 1½–2 hours for whole hearts (when cooking whole hearts, change water at least 3 times to extract as much bitterness as possible). Drain well, drizzle with melted butter, or serve as you would asparagus with Hollandaise Sauce. Or chill in ice water, drain, and use in salads.

HEARTS OF PALM BRAISED IN WHITE WINE

Makes 3–4 servings

1 (14-ounce) can hearts of palm, drained
2 tablespoons butter or margarine
¼ cup sauterne
1 tablespoon finely chopped pimiento (garnish)
1 hard-cooked egg yolk, sieved (garnish)

Slice hearts crosswise into ½" rounds and sauté in butter 5 minutes over low heat, stirring once or twice. Add wine, cover, and simmer 10 minutes, basting now and then. Transfer hearts to a heated vegetable dish and keep warm; reduce cooking liquid to about 2 tablespoons by boiling rapidly, uncovered. Spoon over hearts, sprinkle with pimiento and egg, and serve. Calorie counts for hearts of palm unavailable.

HEARTS OF PALM IN CREAM CHEESE SAUCE

Makes 4 servings

1 (14-ounce) can hearts of palm, drained (reserve liquid)

Sauce:
1 tablespoon butter or margarine
1 tablespoon flour
¾ cup milk

1 (3-ounce) package cream cheese, softened to room temperature
¼ teaspoon salt
Pinch white pepper

Slice hearts crosswise into rounds ½" thick; simmer, covered, in reserved liquid 10 minutes. Meanwhile prepare sauce: melt butter over moderate heat and blend in flour. Slowly add ½ cup milk and reserved can liquid and heat, stirring, until thickened. Reduce heat to low and simmer, uncovered, 2–3 minutes. Blend remaining milk with cheese, mix into sauce, and simmer, stirring, 2–3 minutes. Drain hearts, top with sauce, and serve. Calorie counts for hearts of palm unavailable.

SAUTÉED HEARTS OF PALM MEDALLIONS

Makes 4 servings

1 (14-ounce) can hearts of palm, drained
1 egg, lightly beaten with 1 tablespoon cold water
⅔ cup toasted seasoned bread crumbs
3 tablespoons butter or margarine

Slice hearts crosswise into rounds ½" thick and pat very dry on paper toweling. Dip rounds in egg, then in crumbs to coat evenly; place on a wire rack and let dry 15 minutes. Melt butter in a large skillet over moderate heat, add rounds, a few at a time, and brown lightly about 1 minute on a side. Drain on paper toweling and set, uncovered, in a 250° F. oven to keep warm while you brown the rest. Calorie counts for hearts of palm unavailable.

KALE

(Also known as Borecole and Colewort)

This sprawling, crinkly cousin of cabbage is so ancient no one knows where it originated. It is from "keal," the Scottish word for the vegetable, that we get "kale." It was also from the Scots that we obtained our first kale plants.

To Prepare for Cooking: Discard woody stems and coarse leaf midribs, then wash thoroughly in cool water. Tear large leaves into bite-size pieces.

Serving Tip: Toss tender young kale leaves into green salads for refreshing crunch.

BOILED KALE

To minimize the strong cooking odor of kale, keep the pot tightly covered.

Makes 4 servings

Season	For Top Quality	Amount To Buy	Nutritive Value	Calories (unseasoned)
Fall, winter	Choose clean, crisp green leaves whether kale is sold loose or prewashed, pretrimmed, and bagged in plastic.	1 pound serves 2.	Very high in vitamin A; high in vitamin C and calcium	Low—about 30 per average serving

2 pounds kale, prepared for cooking
3 cups boiling water
1 teaspoon salt
⅛ teaspoon pepper
2 tablespoons butter, margarine, or bacon drippings

Coarsely chop kale and place in a large saucepan along with water and salt. Cover and boil slowly 15–20 minutes until tender (to keep kale as green as possible, lift lid once or twice during cooking). Drain well and, if you like, chop kale more finely. Season with pepper and butter or drippings and serve. About 80 calories per serving.

VARIATIONS:

⚖ **Low-Calorie Kale:** Boil and drain as directed; omit salt and butter or drippings, and dress with seasoned salt and lemon juice. About 30 calories per serving.

Kale 'n' Cabbage: Combine equal amounts boiled kale and hot Steamed Green Cabbage, dress with Lemon Butter, and toss to mix. About 80 calories per serving.

KOHLRABI

(Also known as Cabbage Turnip)

Kohlrabi is the most unusual member of the cabbage family. It looks more like a large pale green turnip than a cabbage and has a delicate, nutlike flavor all its own. It is delicious simply boiled and buttered, mashed, creamed, or baked in a casserole with a grated cheese topping.

To Prepare for Cooking: Remove leaves and stems and discard (if they're very young and tender, they can be cooked with other greens or tossed into salads). Wash bulbs, peel, and cut up as individual recipes specify.

Serving Tip: If you should find really young delicate kohlrabi, peel and slice raw into a green salad.

BOILED KOHLRABI

Makes 4–6 servings

8 bulbs kohlrabi, prepared for cooking
1½ cups boiling water
1 teaspoon salt
⅛ teaspoon pepper
2 tablespoons butter or margarine

Cut kohlrabi in ½" cubes, place in a saucepan with water and salt, cover, and boil gently 20–25 minutes until fork tender. Drain, add pepper and butter, and shake pan, uncovered, over low heat until butter melts. About 85 calories for each of 4 servings, 60 calories for each of 6 servings.

To Parboil for Use in Other Recipes: Use recipe above but reduce cooking time to 15 minutes; omit seasonings.

Season	For Top Quality	Amount To Buy	Nutritive Value	Calories (unseasoned)
May–December; peak months: June, July	Choose firm, crisp bulbs about 3" in diameter with fresh green leaves.	Allow 1–2 bulbs per person.	High in vitamin C	Low—about 35 per average serving

VARIATIONS:

⚖ **Low-Calorie Kohlrabi:** Boil and drain as directed; omit butter and sprinkle with minced chives and lemon juice. About 35 calories per serving.

Mashed Kohlrabi: Boil and drain as directed, then mash with a potato masher before seasoning. Sprinkle with pepper, add 2 tablespoons butter and 1 tablespoon heavy cream, and mix well. About 100 calories for each of 4 servings, 70 calories for each of 6 servings.

Kohlrabi au Gratin: Boil, drain, and season kohlrabi by recipe above. Place in an unbuttered 1½-quart *au gratin* dish, top with 1½ cups hot Cheese Sauce and ¼ cup grated Cheddar cheese, and broil 5" from heat 3–4 minutes to brown. About 290 calories for each of 4 servings, 190 calories for each of 6 servings.

Creamed Kohlrabi: Boil and drain as directed but do not season; mix with 1½ cups hot Medium White Sauce or Béchamel Sauce, add a pinch of mace, and serve. If made with White Sauce: about 190 calories for each of 4 servings, 125 for each of 6. If made with Béchamel Sauce: about 220 calories for each of 4 servings, 145 for each of 6.

LEEKS

Leeks, of course, are onions, but they are so special and so elegant they deserve a section to themselves. Strangely, though peasant food abroad, they've never been widely grown in this country and have thus remained a luxury.

To Prepare for Cooking: Cut off roots and tough green tops, peel away coarse outer layers of stalk, and wash thoroughly in tepid water to remove all sand and grit.

BOILED LEEKS

Makes 4 servings

2 bunches leeks, prepared for cooking
1 cup boiling water, chicken or beef broth
2 tablespoons butter or margarine
½ teaspoon salt (about)
Pinch pepper

Lay leeks in a large skillet, add water or broth, cover, and simmer 12–15 minutes until crisp-tender. Drain, add butter, salt, and pepper to taste, and warm uncovered, shaking skillet gently, 1–2 minutes until butter is melted. About 85 calories per serving (if cooked in water), 95 per serving (if cooked in broth).

To Parboil for Use in Other Recipes: Use method above but reduce cooking time to 8–10 minutes; omit seasonings.

VARIATIONS:

To Serve Cold: Boil and drain as directed; chill in ice water, and drain. Cover with a fragrant dress-

Season	For Top Quality	Amount To Buy	Nutritive Value	Calories (unseasoned)
Year round; two peak seasons: September–December and April–July	Look for fresh green tops and crisp, white clean stalks.	A bunch weighs about 1 pound and serves 2.	Some minerals and vitamin C, otherwise poor	Low–about 35 per leek

⚖️ **Low-Calorie Leeks:** Boil and drain leeks; omit butter and dress with 2 tablespoons lemon juice or tarragon vinegar or 3 tablespoons low-calorie Italian or garlic dressing. About 60 calories per serving.

Leeks au Gratin: Parboil and drain leeks; place in an ungreased 1½-quart *au gratin* dish and add 1 cup beef bouillon. Cover and bake 20 minutes at 350° F.; uncover and bake 10 minutes longer. Mix 1½ cups soft white bread crumbs with ¼ cup each grated Parmesan and melted butter. Sprinkle over leeks and broil 4″ from heat 2–3 minutes until lightly browned. About 275 calories per serving.

LEEK PIE

Delicious as a first course or as a luncheon or light supper entree. Makes 6–8 servings

1 recipe Torte Pastry
6 medium-size leeks, washed, trimmed, and sliced thin
1 cup boiling water
1½ teaspoons salt
1 (13-ounce) can evaporated milk
⅓ cup milk
2 (3-ounce) packages cream cheese, softened to room temperature
2 eggs, lightly beaten
⅛ teaspoon white pepper
Pinch mace

Preheat oven to 325° F. Make pastry according to the recipe and fit into a 9″ piepan, making a high, fluted edge; do not bake. Place leeks, boiling water, and ½ teaspoon salt in a small saucepan, cover, and simmer 10–12 minutes; drain leeks well and reserve. In a separate saucepan, heat evaporated milk, milk, cream cheese, and remaining salt over moderate heat about 10 minutes, beating with a whisk until cheese is melted and mixture smooth. Mix a little hot sauce into yolks, then return to pan; stir in leeks, pepper, and mace. Pour into crust and bake, uncovered, 45–50 minutes until filling is set and crust lightly browned. Cool 15–20 minutes on a wire rack, then cut into wedges and serve warm. About 540 calories for each of 6 servings, 405 calories for each of 8 servings.

LENTILS

The pottage Esau sold his birthright for was made of lentils, probably the red lentils of Egypt. Those we know better are the khaki-colored French lentils, although the smaller Egyptian red lentils are sometimes available in big city Armenian or Turkish groceries. Both the red lentils and the green are only available dried.

To Prepare for Cooking: Place lentils in a colander and rinse under cool water, sorting to remove any bits of gravel or shriveled lentils.

For Top Quality	*Amount To Buy*	*Nutritive Value*	*Calories (unseasoned)*
Buy brands you know or, if buying in bulk, choose lentils that are clean, firm, and unshriveled.	1 pound dried lentils will serve 4 persons.	High protein food rich in vitamin A, most of the B complex, and minerals	Very high— about 350 per cup of cooked lentils

¢ BOILED LENTILS

A good topping for lentils is crisply browned croutons or salt pork cubes.
Makes 4 servings

1 pound dried lentils, washed and sorted
3 cups cold water, chicken or beef broth
½ teaspoon salt (about)
⅛ teaspoon pepper

Place all ingredients except pepper in a heavy saucepan, cover, and bring to a boil over high heat. Reduce heat to low and simmer about 45 minutes, stirring occasionally, until lentils are tender but not mushy. (*Note:* Most of the water will be absorbed during cooking, so keep a close eye on the pot to make sure lentils don't stick.) Mix in pepper, taste for salt and add more if needed. About 350 calories per serving (if cooked in water), 370 per serving (if cooked in broth).

VARIATIONS:

Lentils and Ham: Add a ham bone or pork hock and boil as directed in water. Cut meat from bone and mix into lentils before serving. About 420 calories per serving.

Savory Lentils: Cook lentils in chicken or beef broth with 1 peeled and chopped large yellow onion, 1 bay leaf, ¼ teaspoon dried thyme or rosemary, or a *bouquet garni.** About 380 calories per serving.

DHAL

Dhal is the Indian word for lentils, the "meat" of vegetarian sects. This dhal *can* double as meat, although you may prefer it as a potato substitute, a side dish for curry, or even a spaghetti sauce.
Makes 4–6 servings

1 cup dried lentils, washed and sorted
1 quart cold water
¾ teaspoon salt
½ teaspoon chili powder
¼ teaspoon turmeric
2 large yellow onions, peeled and chopped fine
2 tablespoons Clarified Butter
3 medium-size ripe tomatoes, peeled, cored, seeded, and coarsely chopped

Place lentils, water, salt, chili powder, and turmeric in a heavy saucepan, cover, and bring to a boil over high heat. Reduce heat to low and simmer 45 minutes, stirring occasionally, until lentils are tender, not mushy. Meanwhile, sauté onions in butter over moderate heat 8–10 minutes until golden. Add tomatoes and stir-fry 4–5 minutes. Set aside. When lentils are tender, stir in onions and tomatoes, cover, and simmer 5 minutes. If you plan to serve the dhal over rice or pasta, thin with about 1 cup boiling water until the consistency of a spaghetti sauce. About 445 calories for each of 4 servings, 300 calories for each of 6 servings.

RED LENTILS AND RICE

Red lentils and rice are popular throughout the Middle East. Sometimes they're curried, sometimes reinforced with bits of meat, fish, hard-cooked eggs, or cheese (a good way to stretch the meat budget). Lebanese women top lentils and rice with salad greens—it's unusual but good.
Makes 6 servings

1 cup red lentils, washed and sorted
1 quart cold water, beef or chicken broth (about)
2 teaspoons salt (about)
2 medium-size yellow onions, peeled and sliced thin
¼ cup olive or other cooking oil

¼ teaspoon pepper
½ cup uncooked rice
1 teaspoon curry powder (optional)
1 tablespoon minced parsley

Place lentils, water, and salt (reduce amount to taste if using broth) in a large, heavy saucepan, cover, and bring to a boil; adjust heat so mixture simmers gently and cook 20 minutes. Meanwhile, sauté onions in oil 5–8 minutes until pale golden. Set aside. When lentils have cooked 20 minutes, stir in onions and all remaining ingredients except parsley. Simmer, covered, 20–25 minutes until rice is tender. (*Note:* Watch pot carefully so mixture doesn't stick; add a little water if necessary to give it the consistency of thick applesauce.) Sprinkle with parsley and serve. About 370 calories per serving (if made with water), 400 per serving (if made with broth).

LETTUCES

(See chapter on salads for descriptions of the different varieties.)

Romaine . . . iceberg lettuce . . . watercress . . . escarole . . . all can be cooked and served as vegetables, either by themselves or in tandem with other vegetables. Because of their delicacy, lettuces should be cooked a few minutes only so that they lose none of their fresh green color.

PANNED LETTUCE, ONIONS AND CAPERS

Makes 4 servings

2 tablespoons butter or margarine
4 small white onions, peeled and chopped fine
2 heads iceberg lettuce, romaine, or escarole or 4 heads Boston lettuce, washed and shredded medium fine
¼ cup water

¾ teaspoon salt
2–3 tablespoons capers
Pinch white pepper

Melt butter in a large, heavy saucepan over moderate heat, add onions and sauté 5–8 minutes until pale golden. Add lettuce, water, and salt, cover, turn heat to low, and steam 4–5 minutes. Add capers and pepper, toss to mix, and serve. About 95 calories per serving.

BUTTER-BRAISED HEARTS OF LETTUCE

Makes 4 servings

2 heads romaine or 4 heads Boston lettuce, trimmed of stems and coarse leaves and washed
2 tablespoons butter or margarine
¼ cup chicken or beef broth
¾ teaspoon salt (about)
Pinch pepper

If using romaine, slice off tops so hearts are 8" or 9" long. Place butter and broth in a large skillet, cover, and bring to a simmer. Add lettuce, cover, and simmer 10 minutes until just tender. Halve hearts lengthwise, transfer to serving dish, and salt to taste. Boil remaining cooking liquid, uncovered, until reduced to about 2 tablespoons. Mix in pepper, pour over lettuce, and serve. About 80 calories per serving.

VARIATIONS:

Braised Lettuce with Sour Cream: Braise as directed; mix ¾ cup sour cream into reduced cooking liquid along with pepper. Warm (but do not boil) 1–2 minutes, pour over lettuce, and serve. About 170 calories per serving.

Butter-Braised Iceberg Lettuce: Core and quarter a large (about 2 pounds) trimmed head iceberg lettuce and braise by method above.

Serve with Hollandaise Sauce, Herb or Lemon Butter. About 80 calories per serving (without sauce).

BUTTERED WATERCRESS

Being naturally salty, watercress needs no salt.
Makes 4 servings

3 bunches watercress
⅔ cup boiling water
Pinch pepper
3 tablespoons butter or margarine

Trim stalks of watercress so they're 1" long, then wash cress in cold water, discarding any yellowed or wilted leaves. Place cress in a saucepan with water, cover, and simmer 8–10 minutes until just tender. Drain, add pepper and butter, and shake pan uncovered over low heat until butter melts. If you like, chop watercress before serving. About 105 calories per serving.

MUSHROOMS

To ancient Egyptians, mushrooms were "sons of gods" sent to earth on thunderbolts; to the medieval Irish they were leprechaun umbrellas, and to the English they were food, edible only if gathered under a full moon. During Louis XIV's reign, the French began growing mushrooms in caves near Paris. They're grown that way yet. Because gathering wild mushrooms is risky, we concentrate here on the commercially grown and edible wild species sometimes available in groceries: the beige *morel*, the yellow *chanterelle*, and the creamy *shaggy mane*. You can buy the strong French *crêpes* canned and the Oriental black mushrooms and wood ears dried.

To Prepare for Cooking: Discard woody stem ends and wipe mushrooms clean with a damp cloth; never wash or soak—you'll send the delicate flavor down the drain.

To Peel: With a paring knife, catch a bit of loose skin on underside of cap and pull up toward top of cap. Repeat until all skin is removed. It isn't necessary to peel mushrooms unless they're to be served raw (try them in salads or stuffed with a salty spread as an hors d'oeuvre).

To Prepare Dried Mushrooms for Cooking: Black mushrooms and wood ears should be soaked in boiling water to cover 15 minutes. Drain and squeeze as dry as possible before cooking.

✠ SAUTÉED MUSHROOMS

So simple and yet so elegant.
Makes 2 servings

½ pound small- to medium-size mushrooms, wiped clean
3 tablespoons butter or margarine
¼ teaspoon salt
⅛ teaspoon pepper

If mushrooms are small and tender, trim stems to within ½" of the caps. Otherwise, pull stems out of caps and save for soups, stuffings, or meat loaves. Sauté mushrooms rapidly in butter over moderately high heat, stirring or shaking skillet, until lightly browned, about 3 minutes. Drain on paper toweling, season with salt and pepper, and serve. About 180 calories per serving.

VARIATIONS:

Sautéed Sliced Mushrooms: Thinly slice mushrooms and sauté by method above but reduce cooking time to 2 minutes. About 180 calories per serving.

VEGETABLES

BROILED MUSHROOMS

Makes 4 servings

1 pound medium-size mushrooms, wiped clean and stemmed
¾ cup melted butter or margarine or cooking oil
1 teaspoon salt
⅛ teaspoon pepper

Using your hands, toss mushrooms in butter or oil until well coated. Cover loosely and let stand at room temperature 30 minutes, tossing once or twice. Preheat broiler. Arrange caps, cup side down, on a broiler rack and brush lightly with butter or oil. Broil 5" from heat 5 minutes until lightly browned; turn caps, brush again with butter or oil, and broil 3 minutes longer until fork tender. Sprinkle with salt and pepper. About 335 calories per serving.

SKILLET MUSHROOMS

Makes 4 servings

1 teaspoon salt
1 pound mushrooms, wiped clean and sliced ¼" thick (include stems)
2 tablespoons water
Pinch pepper
4 pats Maître d'Hôtel Butter (optional)

Heat a large, heavy skillet over high heat 1 minute. Sprinkle in salt, add mushrooms and stir-fry 2–3 minutes, until golden. Keep mushrooms moving constantly to avoid burning. Add water and pepper, turn heat to low, and cook 1 minute. Serve topped, if you like, with pats of Maître d'Hôtel Butter. About 30 calories per serving (without butter), 135 calories per serving (with butter).

VARIATION:

⚜ **Low-Calorie Skillet Mushrooms:** Omit butter pats and dress with a few drops onion, garlic, or lemon juice. About 30 calories per serving.

CREAMED MUSHROOMS

Ladled over hot buttered toast or used to fill puff pastry shells, Carolines, or hollowed-out rolls, these mushrooms can be served as a luncheon entree.

Makes 4 servings

1 pound medium-size mushrooms, wiped clean and sliced ¼" thick (include stems)
¼ cup butter or margarine
2 tablespoons flour
1¼ cups milk or ½ light cream and ½ chicken broth
¾ teaspoon salt
Pinch white pepper
½ teaspoon Worcestershire sauce

Season	For Top Quality	Amount To Buy	Nutritive Value	Calories (unseasoned)
Year round though supplies may be short in summer.	Choose clean, snowy, plump mushrooms of equal size; the veil that joins cap to stem should be intact, hiding brown gills.	1 pound will serve 2–4.	Poor except for being fairly high in niacin	Low—about 40 per cup

Stir-fry mushrooms in butter in a large skillet over moderately high heat 2–3 minutes until golden. Blend flour with milk (or cream and broth) until smooth, then slowly stir into mushrooms. Reduce heat to low and cook and stir until thickened. Mix in salt, pepper, and Worcestershire sauce and serve. About 190 calories per serving (if made with milk), 240 calories per serving (if made with cream and broth).

VARIATION:

Mushrooms in Madeira Sauce: Prepare recipe above and just before serving stir in 2 tablespoons sweet Madeira wine. About 200 calories per serving (if made with milk), 250 calories per serving (if made with cream and broth).

MUSHROOMS, ONIONS AND GREEN PEPPERS

Delicious over broiled steak.
Makes 6 servings

1 medium-size Spanish onion, peeled and chopped fine
3 tablespoons cooking oil
1 pound mushrooms, wiped clean and sliced thin (include stems)
1 large sweet green pepper, cored, seeded, and thinly slivered
1 teaspoon salt
⅛ teaspoon pepper
Pinch mace

Sauté onion in oil in a large, heavy skillet over moderately high heat 8 minutes until golden. Add mushrooms and green pepper and sauté 4–5 minutes until lightly browned. Reduce heat to low and stir-fry 2–3 minutes until pepper is tender. Season with salt, pepper, and mace and serve. About 95 calories per serving.

BAKED MUSHROOM CAPS STUFFED WITH HAZELNUTS

A luscious garnish for a roast platter.
Makes 4–6 servings

24 perfect small- to medium-size mushrooms, wiped clean
½ cup unsalted butter, softened to room temperature
⅔ cup finely chopped unblanched hazelnuts or pecans
2 tablespoons minced chives
2 tablespoons minced parsley
1 teaspoon salt
⅛ teaspoon pepper
2 tablespoons cognac
¼ cup cracker meal
1½ cups milk (about)

Preheat oven to 300° F. Carefully remove mushroom stems from caps; set caps aside and chop stems fine. Mix chopped stems with all remaining ingredients except milk and stuff each mushroom cap, mounding mixture in the center. Place stuffed caps in an ungreased 9"×9"×2" baking pan and pour in milk to a depth of ¾". Bake, uncovered, basting every 15 minutes with milk, 1 hour or until tender. Lift mushrooms from milk and use to garnish a roast or steak platter or serve hot as a vegetable with a little of the milk spooned over each serving. About 505 calories for each of 4 servings, 335 calories for each of 6 servings.

MUSTARD GREENS

(Also called Chinese Mustard and Mustard Spinach)

It's said that Aesclepius, god of medicine, gave mustard to man. He intended that the plant be used medicinally, but man soon learned how delicious the greens were if gathered young and cooked like spinach. They still are.

VEGETABLES

Season	For Top Quality	Amount To Buy	Nutritive Value	Calories (unseasoned)
Year round; peak season: June–October	Choose crisp, tender leaves without holes or blemishes.	1 pound greens will serve 2.	High in vitamins A and C, also in calcium	Low—about 40 per average serving

To Prepare for Cooking: Pick over greens carefully, removing any roots, woody stems or blemished leaves. Wash 2–3 times in cool water to remove all grit and sand.

To Boil: See recipe for Boiled Collards, Turnip Greens or Mustard Greens under *Collards.*

OKRA

(Also sometimes called Gumbo)

People are generally of two minds about okra—they either adore it or abhor it. It's not the flavor they dislike (that is delicate, rather like eggplant) but the texture (too often slimy). The best preventive: don't overcook.

To Prepare for Cooking: Cut off stems (but not stem ends of pods); scrub okra well in cool water. Leave whole or slice as individual recipes specify.

Cooking Tip: Never cook okra in iron or tin pans because it will turn black (it's edible, just unattractive).

⊠ BOILED OKRA

Makes 4 servings

1 pound okra, prepared for cooking
¾ cup boiling water
1 teaspoon salt
⅛ teaspoon pepper
2 tablespoons butter or margarine

Leave pods whole if small; if large, slice 1" thick. Place okra in a saucepan with water and salt, cover, and boil gently until just tender: 6–10 minutes for whole pods, 3–4 minutes for slices. Drain, add pepper and butter, and set uncovered over low heat, shaking pan gently, until butter melts. About 85 calories per serving.

To Steam Okra: Place okra in a steamer over boiling water, cover, and steam until tender: 3–5 minutes for slices, 8–10 minutes for whole pods. About 85 calories per serving.

To Parboil for Use in Other Recipes: Boil or steam as directed but reduce cooking time to 2 minutes for slices, 5 minutes for pods.

VARIATIONS:

⚖ **Low-Calorie Boiled Okra:** Omit butter and dress with low-calorie herb dressing. About 35 calories per serving.

⚖ **Combo:** Mix drained, parboiled okra with 1 cup coarsely chopped canned tomatoes (do not drain), ⅛ teaspoon garlic powder, 2 tablespoons chili sauce, and 1 tablespoon minced parsley. Cover and simmer 3–5 minutes until okra is tender. Serve over (or with) hot Garlic Bread. About 60 calories per serving (without bread).

SOUTHERN FRIED OKRA

One of the very best ways to cook okra because little of the original crispness is lost.
Makes 4 servings

Season	For Top Quality	Amount To Buy	Nutritive Value	Calories (unseasoned)
Year round; peak months: July–October	Choose young, tender clean pods 2–4″ long; reject any with bruises or punctures.	1 pound will serve 2–4.	Some vitamin C and A	Low—about 35 per average serving

1 pound small okra pods, prepared for cooking
¼ cup unsifted flour
1 egg, lightly beaten with 1 tablespoon cold water
1 cup white or yellow corn meal, fine dry bread crumbs, or cracker meal
3 tablespoons butter or margarine, lard, or bacon drippings
¾ teaspoon salt
Pinch pepper

Cut off okra stem ends and tips and slice pods crosswise into rounds ¼″ thick. Pat dry on paper toweling. Dip rounds in flour, then in egg, then roll in meal or crumbs to coat evenly. Set on paper toweling. Heat butter, lard, or drippings in a large, heavy skillet 1 minute over moderate heat. Add okra and sauté about 2 minutes on a side until golden brown. Drain on paper toweling, sprinkle with salt and pepper. About 215 calories per serving.

BATTER-FRIED OKRA

Makes 4 servings

1 pound small okra pods, parboiled and drained
Lard, shortening, or cooking oil for deep fat frying

Batter:
1 cup sifted flour
1 teaspoon salt
1 cup milk
1 egg, lightly beaten

Pat okra dry on paper toweling. Begin heating fat in a deep fat fryer over moderately high heat; insert deep fat thermometer. Sift flour and salt together into a bowl, slowly add milk and beat until smooth. Beat in egg. When fat reaches 375° F., dip okra, a few pieces at a time, into batter, allowing excess to drain off, then drop into fat. Fry 1–2 minutes until golden brown. Using a slotted spoon, remove to paper toweling to drain. Set uncovered in a 250° F. oven to keep warm while you fry the rest. About 150 calories per serving.

VEGETABLE GUMBO

A Creole vegetable stew.
Makes 4 servings

3 slices bacon, diced
¼ cup finely chopped yellow onion
¼ cup finely chopped celery
1 (1-pound) can tomatoes (do not drain)
1 (10-ounce) package frozen whole baby okra (thaw only to separate pods, then slice in 1″ rounds)
1 (10-ounce) package frozen whole kernel corn (do not thaw)
1 teaspoon salt
⅛ teaspoon pepper
Pinch powdered saffron
Pinch filé powder
2 cups hot cooked rice

Fry bacon in a large skillet over moderate heat 2–3 minutes; add

VEGETABLES

onion and celery and sauté 8–10 minutes until golden. Add tomatoes and okra, cover, and boil gently 3–4 minutes. Add corn, salt, pepper, and saffron, re-cover, and boil 3–4 minutes longer until okra is tender. Stir in filé powder, ladle over rice, and serve. About 270 calories per serving.

ONIONS

During the Civil War, General Grant notified the War Department, "I will not move my army without onions." He got them; moreover, no one thought the request odd, because armies had always traveled with onions. Originally, they were said to make men valiant, later they were used to enliven dull army food. There are many kinds of onions, each a specialist. The best way to distinguish them is to categorize as follows: *dry onions, green or fresh onions, specialty onions.*

Dry Onions

These are dry-skinned, not very perishable onions that keep well unrefrigerated.

Bermuda Onions: These large flat onions can be white, tan, even red skinned; all are mild and sweet, perfect for slicing into salads or onto hamburgers. About 2–3 per pound.

Spanish Onions: Often mistakenly called Bermudas, these fawn-colored jumbos average ½ pound apiece. They're mild, sweet, and juicy, good raw, French-fried, or stuffed and baked.

White Onions: Mild, shimmery little silverskins about the size of a walnut (there are 18–24 per pound) that are best creamed or simmered in stews. Those less than 1″ in diameter are *pickling onions;* those smaller still, *cocktail onions.*

Yellow Onions: The strongest of the dry onions, these are the round, golden skinned "cooking" onions we chop or slice and stir into everything from chili to chop suey. About 3–5 per pound.

Red or Italian Onions: Strong, purple-red onions that are best eaten raw in antipasti or salads. About 3–4 per pound.

To Prepare for Cooking: Peel. A quick and tearless way to do small white onions is to let stand 1 minute in boiling water until skins begin to shrivel, then to drain and plunge in ice water. The skins will slip off neatly as peach skins.

Green or Fresh Onions

These are perishable, freshly pulled onions that should be kept in the refrigerator.

Season	For Top Quality	Amount To Buy	Nutritive Value	Calories (unseasoned)
Year round for red, white, and yellow onions; March–June for Bermudas; and August–May for Spanish onions	Choose firm, well-shaped onions with dry, clean, bright skins. Reject any that are sprouting.	1 pound will serve 2–4.	Poor	Low—about 30 per ¼ pound of cooked onions; 40 per ¼ pound raw onions

Spring or Green Onions: Long, strong, slim onions with green tops and slightly bulbous stems.

Scallions: A sister to the spring onion but slimmer and sweeter.

Leeks: (see the special section on leeks).

Chives: These fragrant wispy green "tops" are the most delicate of all onions. Buy by the pot if possible, set on a sunny window sill, and use as an herb.

To Prepare for Cooking: Scallions and spring onions must be trimmed of roots, wilted tops, and any coarse outer stem coverings. Leave whole or cut up as individual recipes specify. Chives should be washed in cool water, patted dry on paper toweling gathered into a bunch, and minced or snipped with scissors.

Specialty Onions

There are only two, both available year round, both used sparingly as seasonings.

Garlic: An average bulb, composed of cloves that fit together rather like sections of a tangerine, is about the size of a tangerine. Individual cloves can be small as a lima bean or big as a walnut. When a recipe calls for a clove of garlic, use one about the size of the end of your little finger (or the equivalent). Buy only one bulb of garlic at a time (they quickly dry out) and choose one that is plump and firm. Always peel garlic before using; leave whole, mince, or crush as individual recipes specify, but bear in mind that crushed garlic has about 3 times the impact of the minced.

Shallots: Copper skinned and about the size of hazelnuts, shallots are milder than garlic but stronger than most onions. Buy about ¼ pound at a time (shallots quickly dry up) and select ones that are plump and firm. Peel before using and cut as individual recipes specify.

In addition to the onions described above, there is an ever-widening array of *convenience onions*—powders, juices, flakes, salts, and dry soup mixes that save much in time and tears but cannot compare with fresh onions for flavor.

Season	For Top Quality	Amount To Buy	Nutritive Value	Calories (*unseasoned*)
Year round for all fresh onions	Choose spring onions and scallions with succulent white stems 2–3″ long and crisp green tops. If potted chives are unavailable, choose those with a "just-cut" look.	1 bunch scallions or spring onions contains 5–6 stalks and will serve 1–2.	Poor	Very low— about 4 per spring onion or scallion

BOILED ONIONS

Makes 4 servings

1½ pounds small white onions, peeled
1½ cups boiling water, chicken or beef broth
1½ teaspoons salt (about)
3 tablespoons butter or margarine
¼ teaspoon paprika
Pinch mace
Pinch pepper

Place onions in a saucepan with water or broth and 1 teaspoon salt, cover, and boil 20 minutes until tender. Drain, add remaining salt if onions were boiled in water, the butter, paprika, mace, and pepper and warm, shaking pan gently, 1–2 minutes until butter melts. About 115 calories per serving (cooked in water), 125 per serving (cooked in broth).

To Parboil for Use in Other Recipes: Use recipe above but reduce cooking time to 15 minutes; omit all seasonings.

VARIATIONS:

Low-Calorie Boiled Onions: Cook onions as directed in water. Omit butter and spices and dress with low-calorie Italian or herb dressing. About 40 calories per serving.

Creamed Onions: Boil and drain onions as directed but do not season; combine with 1½ cups hot Medium White Sauce, 1 tablespoon light brown sugar, and a pinch nutmeg and cayenne pepper. Warm, stirring, 2–3 minutes to blend flavors. About 200 calories per serving (cooked in water), 210 calories per serving (cooked in broth).

Glazed Onions: Boil and drain onions as directed (reserve 1 tablespoon cooking liquid). Do not season. Melt ¼ cup butter in a large skillet, add reserved cooking liquid, ⅓ cup light brown sugar, a pinch each mace and pepper, and simmer, stirring, 3–4 minutes until syrupy. Add onions and heat 5–8 minutes, turning frequently, until evenly glazed. Serve hot as a vegetable or use to garnish a roast platter. About 210 calories per serving (cooked in water), 220 calories per serving (cooked in broth).

PAN-BRAISED ONIONS

Makes 4–6 servings

2 pounds small white onions, peeled
¼ cup unsalted butter
½ cup dry vermouth
¼ teaspoon salt
Pinch pepper

Sauté onions in butter in a large, heavy skillet over moderately high heat, turning frequently, 10 minutes until golden. Add vermouth, reduce heat to moderately low, cover, and simmer 15 minutes until crisp-tender. Sprinkle with salt and pepper and turn onions in pan juices to glaze evenly. Serve hot as a vegetable or use in making such stews as Boeuf à la Bourguignonne. About 185 calories for each of 4 servings, 125 calories for each of 6 servings.

SAUTÉED ONIONS

Makes 4 servings

6 medium-size yellow onions, peeled
2–3 tablespoons flour (optional)
¼ cup butter, margarine, or cooking oil
Salt
Pepper

Thinly slice onions and separate into rings or chop medium fine. Dredge, if you like, in flour (onions will be a bit browner). Heat butter or oil in a large, heavy skillet over moderate heat 1 minute (or use an electric skillet with temperature control set at 350° F.). Sauté onions, turning frequently, 8–10 minutes for golden, 10–12 minutes for well browned. If you like them slightly crisp, raise heat to moderately high at the end of cooking and stir-fry 1 minute. Drain quickly on paper toweling, sprinkle with salt and pepper, and serve. About 160 calories per serving (made without flour).

FRENCH-FRIED ONION RINGS

Crisp and sweet.
Makes 4 servings

1 large Spanish onion, peeled and sliced ¼" thick
Lard, shortening, or cooking oil for deep fat frying

Batter:
⅔ cup sifted flour
¾ teaspoon salt
¼ teaspoon baking powder
⅔ cup milk

Begin heating fat in a deep fat fryer over moderately high heat; insert deep fat thermometer. Separate onion slices into rings. Sift flour, salt, and baking powder together into a bowl. Slowly add milk and beat until bubbles appear on surface of batter. When fat reaches 375° F., dip onion rings, 4 or 5 at a time, into batter, allowing excess to drain off, then drop into fat. Fry 1 minute until golden brown; turn rings to brown evenly if they don't flip on their own. Remove to a paper-towel-lined baking sheet and set uncovered in a 250° F. oven while you fry the rest. (*Note:* Skim bits of batter from fat between fryings before they burn.) About 160 calories per serving.

VARIATION:

Shallow Fried Onion Rings: Pour 1½" cooking oil into an electric skillet (temperature control set at 375° F.) or large, heavy skillet set over moderately high heat. When hot, not smoking, dip onion rings into batter and fry as recipe directs. About 160 calories per serving.

BAKED ONIONS

Baked onions are mellower and sweeter than boiled onions. They are delicious with roast meats or fowl.
Makes 4 servings

4 medium-size Spanish onions (do not peel)
⅓ cup water
1 teaspoon salt
⅛ teaspoon pepper
¼ cup melted butter or margarine

Preheat oven to 400° F. Trim root end from onions and arrange in a buttered shallow casserole. Pour in water. Bake, uncovered, 1½ hours until fork tender. Using a small piece of paper toweling as a pot holder, grasp skin of onion at the top and pull off. Sprinkle onions with salt and pepper, drizzle with butter, and serve. About 160 calories per serving.

ROASTED ONIONS

Oven-roasted onions glazed with drippings.
Makes 4 servings

8 medium-size yellow or Bermuda onions or 4 medium-size Spanish onions, peeled
½ cup bacon drippings, shortening, or lard
Salt
Pepper

Preheat oven to 400° F. Place onions in a roasting pan or casserole, add drippings, shortening, or lard. Roast, uncovered, until fork tender: 45–50 minutes for yellow or Bermuda onions; 1¼–1½ hours for Spanish onions. Turn onions halfway through cooking so they'll brown evenly. Drain on paper toweling, sprinkle with salt and pepper, and serve. About 180 calories per serving.

CREAMED SCALLIONS

Scallions are a good substitute for the more expensive, less available leeks, especially when creamed. Makes 4 servings

4 bunches scallions, washed and trimmed of roots and tops
1 cup boiling water
1 teaspoon salt
½ cup heavy cream
2 tablespoons butter or margarine
2 tablespoons flour blended with 2 tablespoons cold water
⅛ teaspoon white pepper

Place scallions, water and salt in a saucepan, cover, and boil gently 5–7 minutes until just tender. Lift scallions from liquid and keep warm. Add cream and butter to scallion liquid, then stir in flour-water paste. Heat, stirring, until thickened and smooth. Add pepper, taste for salt and add more if needed. Pour sauce over scallions, mix lightly, and serve. About 190 calories per serving.

ONIONS IN CHEDDAR SAUCE

Makes 4 servings

1½ pounds small white onions, boiled and drained (reserve cooking water)
2 tablespoons butter or margarine
2 tablespoons flour
⅛ teaspoon cinnamon
⅛ teaspoon mace
Onion cooking water plus enough evaporated milk to total 1½ cups
1¼ cups coarsely grated sharp Cheddar cheese
1 teaspoon prepared spicy brown mustard
1 teaspoon ketchup
½ teaspoon Worcestershire sauce
¼ teaspoon cayenne pepper
1 tablespoon cream sherry

Keep onions warm. In a separate saucepan melt butter over moderate heat and blend in flour, cinnamon, and mace. Add the 1½ cups liquid and heat, stirring constantly, until thickened. Mix in cheese and all remaining ingredients and heat, stirring, 1–2 minutes until smooth. Pour sauce over onions, heat 1–2 minutes longer, and serve. About 280 calories per serving.

¢ ONION STEW

Makes 4 servings

4–5 medium-size yellow onions, peeled
1 quart water
1 teaspoon salt (about)
Pinch white pepper
¼ cup butter or margarine
Croutons (optional garnish)

Place onions, water, and salt in a saucepan, cover, and boil gently 30 minutes until very soft. Remove from heat and let stand, covered, 1 hour. Quarter each onion and return to liquid. Stir in pepper, cover, and heat slowly until piping hot. Taste for salt and adjust as needed. Ladle into heated soup bowls, add 1 tablespoon butter to each, and serve. Pass croutons to be sprinkled on top if you like. About 140 calories per serving (without croutons).

CHAMP

Champ is a traditional dish from Northern Ireland made with scallions and mashed potatoes.
Makes 4 servings

3 bunches scallions, prepared for cooking and coarsely chopped (include tops)
½ cup boiling water
½ teaspoon salt
3 cups hot seasoned mashed potatoes
2 tablespoons butter or margarine

Place scallions, water, and salt in a small saucepan, cover, and boil 4–5 minutes until scallions are very tender. Drain well and briskly beat scallions into potatoes with a fork. Spoon into a heated vegetable dish, dot with butter, and serve. About 160 calories per serving.

VARIATION:

Baked Champ: Spoon mixture into a buttered 1½-quart casserole, roughen surface with a fork, and drizzle with melted butter. Bake, uncovered, 20 minutes at 400° F., then broil 4" from the heat 1–2 minutes to brown. About 160 calories per serving.

STUFFED ONIONS

Boiled Spanish or yellow onions, hollowed out, can be filled with many vegetables: buttered peas and mushrooms; creamed diced carrots and peas; puréed spinach; mashed sweet potatoes; Harvard Beets; Mexican-Style Corn and Peppers.
Makes 4 servings

4 medium-size Spanish onions, peeled
2⅓ cups water
1 teaspoon salt
1 tablespoon cooking oil

Stuffing:
2 tablespoons butter or margarine
¾ cup soft white bread crumbs
1 teaspoon salt
⅛ teaspoon pepper
¼ cup finely grated sharp Cheddar cheese
Minced parsley (garnish)

Preheat oven to 400° F. Cut a ½" slice from the top of each onion (save for other recipes). Place onions, 2 cups water, and salt in a large saucepan, cover, and simmer 20–25 minutes. Drain well. With a spoon, scoop out center of each onion, leaving a shell ½" thick; place shells in a buttered shallow 1-quart casserole, and brush with oil. Pour remaining water into casserole. Chop onion centers fine and sauté 5 minutes in butter over moderate heat. Mix in all remaining stuffing ingredients except parsley, spoon into onion shells, and bake uncovered 30–40 minutes until lightly browned. Sprinkle with parsley and serve. About 200 calories per serving.

Some Additional Stuffings for Onions

To the chopped sautéed onion centers, add any of the following:
– ¾ cup hot cooked rice, ¼ cup chopped peeled tomatoes, and a pinch each garlic salt and powdered saffron.
– ½ cup each hot cooked rice and slivered boiled ham and 2 tablespoons grated Parmesan cheese.
– ¾ cup minced ripe olives, ¼ cup finely chopped toasted almonds, and 1 tablespoon heavy cream.
– 1 cup poultry stuffing mix and 2 tablespoons melted butter.
– 1 cup seasoned mashed potatoes and 2 tablespoons melted butter. Fill onion shells and bake as directed in basic recipe above.

VEGETABLES

FINNISH ONION FRY IN SOUR CREAM

Makes 4 servings

¼ cup butter or margarine
1 pound Spanish onions, peeled and chopped fine
½ pound mushrooms, wiped clean and sliced thin
2 pimientos, seeded and slivered
1 cup sour cream
½ teaspoon salt
⅛ teaspoon paprika

Melt butter in a very large, heavy skillet over moderately low heat, add onions, and cook, stirring occasionally, 10–12 minutes until tender but not browned; lift from skillet and reserve. Raise heat to moderately high and sauté mushrooms 2–3 minutes until golden. Return onions to skillet, add pimientos, and mix well. Reduce heat to low, mix in sour cream and salt, and heat, stirring, 1–2 minutes (do not boil). Sprinkle with paprika and serve. About 280 calories per serving.

PISSALADIÈRE (ONION TART À LA NICOISE)

Nearly every French town has an onion tart, but only in Nice, where the cooking is as much Italian as French, does it resemble pizza (it's called *pissaladière*).

Makes 6 servings

1 recipe Pizza Dough (see Pizza in the bread chapter)
6 medium-size yellow onions, peeled and sliced thin
1 clove garlic, peeled and crushed
1 bay leaf
¼ cup olive oil
1 teaspoon salt
⅛ teaspoon pepper
1 (2-ounce) can anchovy fillets, drained
1 cup brined, pitted ripe Italian olives

Make pastry according to recipe and fit into a 12″ pizza pan. Preheat oven to 450° F. Sauté onions, garlic, and bay leaf in oil in a large, heavy skillet over moderate heat 8–10 minutes until onions are golden. Stir in salt; remove bay leaf. Spread onions evenly over pastry and sprinkle with pepper. Arrange anchovies, spoke fashion, over onions and dot olives here and there. Bake, uncovered, 15 minutes until pastry is browned. Cut into wedges and serve as a light entree or cut into smaller wedges and serve as an appetizer. About 480 calories per serving.

PARSNIPS

The Roman Emperor Tiberius was so fond of parsnips he sent to the Rhine country each year for his supply because in that climate they grew to plump and sugary perfection. His cooks were ordered to treat the parsnips with reverence, to boil them gently and sauce them with honey wine. Parsnips later fell from favor and they have never regained their popularity. In Tudor England they were used primarily for making bread, in Ireland for brewing beer. Even today, few people relish parsnips, possibly because they have been eclipsed by their cousin, the carrot, whose sweeter, nuttier flavor most of us prefer. Parsnips are worth trying, however, because they are economical and make a welcome change of pace.

To Prepare for Cooking: Remove root ends and tops; scrub well in cool water and peel. If parsnips seem large, halve and remove woody central cores. Otherwise leave whole or cut as individual recipes specify.

Cooking Tip: To improve the flavor of parsnips, add a little brown sugar to the cooking water and, if you like, a peeled 1" cube gingerroot or blade of mace.

¢ **BOILED PARSNIPS**

Makes 2–4 servings

1 pound parsnips, prepared for cooking
1½ cups boiling water
2 tablespoons butter or margarine
1 teaspoon salt
⅛ teaspoon pepper

Place parsnips in a large saucepan, add water, cover, and boil 30–35 minutes until tender; drain. Cut into thin slices or small cubes and return to pan. Add remaining ingredients and warm, uncovered, over low heat, shaking pan gently, 2–3 minutes until butter is melted and parsnips lightly glazed. About 250 calories for each of 2 servings, 125 calories for each of 4 servings.

To Parboil for Use in Other Recipes: Boil as directed above but reduce cooking time to 10 minutes; omit seasonings.

VARIATIONS:

¢ **Mashed Parsnips:** Quarter and core parsnips, boil as directed, but reduce cooking time to 15–20 minutes. Drain and mash with a potato masher. Beat in butter, salt, and pepper called for, also, if you like, 1–2 tablespoons heavy cream. About 250 calories for each of 2 servings (without heavy cream), 125 calories for each of 4.

¢ **Currant-Glazed Parsnips:** Add 2 tablespoons currant jelly to parsnips along with butter, salt, and pepper and warm as directed to glaze. About 320 calories for each of 2 servings, 160 calories for each of 4 servings.

¢ **Orange-Glazed Parsnips:** Add 2 tablespoons orange marmalade to parsnips along with butter and seasonings and warm as directed to glaze. About 320 calories for each of 2 servings, 160 calories for each of 4 servings.

¢ **Caramel-Glazed Parsnips:** To drained parsnips add ¼ cup each butter and light brown sugar, 1 tablespoon lemon juice, ⅛ teaspoon nutmeg, and the salt and pepper called for. Warm, uncovered, over lowest heat 10 minutes, stirring occasionally, until evenly glazed. About 450 calories for each of 2 servings, 225 calories for each of 4.

¢ **Gingery Parsnips:** Add 2 tablespoons minced preserved ginger and ⅛ teaspoon mace to parsnips along with butter, salt, and pepper and warm as directed to glaze. About 300 calories for each of 2 servings, 150 calories for each of 4.

Season	For Top Quality	Amount To Buy	Nutritive Value	Calories (unseasoned)
Year round; peak seasons: fall, winter, and spring	Look for clean, firm, well-shaped roots of medium size (large parsnips may be woody).	A 1-pound bunch will serve 2–4.	Poor	Moderate— about 74 per ¼ pound serving

¢ ROASTED PARSNIPS

Makes 4 servings

½ cup melted bacon or beef
   drippings or shortening
1½ pounds medium-size parsnips,
   prepared for cooking and halved
½ teaspoon salt

Preheat oven to 400° F. Pour drippings or shortening into a 10" flameproof glass piepan, add parsnips, turning in drippings to coat. Roast, uncovered, 40–45 minutes until lightly browned and fork tender, turning once or twice so they brown evenly. Drain on paper toweling, sprinkle with salt, and serve. About 210 calories per serving.

¢ PARSNIP CAKES

Makes 4–6 servings

1 egg, lightly beaten
Pinch nutmeg
Salt
Pepper
2 pounds parsnips, boiled and
   mashed
1 egg lightly beaten with 1 tablespoon cold water
¾ cup toasted seasoned bread
   crumbs
¼ cup butter or margarine

Mix egg, nutmeg, salt, and pepper to taste into parsnips. Cool to room temperature, cover, and chill 1 hour. Using ⅓ cup as a measure, shape mixture into 8 cakes and flatten; dip in egg, then in crumbs to coat evenly, cover, and chill ½ hour. Melt butter in a large skillet over moderate heat, add half the cakes, and brown well on both sides, about 3–4 minutes. Drain on paper toweling and set, uncovered, in a 250° F. oven to keep warm while you brown the rest. About 365 calories for each of 4 servings, 245 calories for each of 6 servings.

FRENCH-FRIED PARSNIPS

Makes 4 servings

1½ pounds parsnips, parboiled and
   cut in ⅜" strips as for French fries
Lard, shortening, or cooking oil for
   deep fat frying
Salt

Pat parsnip strips dry on paper toweling. Meanwhile, begin heating fat in a deep fat fryer over moderately high heat; insert wire basket and deep fat thermometer. When fat reaches 375° F., drop in about half the parsnips and fry 1–2 minutes until golden brown and crisp. Transfer to a paper-towel-lined baking sheet and set, uncovered, in a 250° F. oven to keep warm while you fry the rest. Sprinkle with salt and serve. About 160 calories per serving.

VARIATION:

Batter-Fried Parsnips: Parboil parsnips and cut into strips as directed above; also heat fat for deep frying. Prepare a batter: sift together 1 cup flour and 1 teaspoon salt, slowly add 1 cup milk, then beat well. Add 1 lightly beaten egg and beat again. Dip parsnip strips, a few at a time, into batter, allowing excess to drain off, then fry as recipe directs. About 210 calories per serving.

PEAS

"This subject of peas continues to absorb all others," wrote Madame de Maintenon of the new fad at Louis XIV's court. "Some ladies, after having supped at the Royal Table and well supped, too, returning to their own homes, at the risk of suffering from indigestion, will again eat peas before going to bed. It is both a fashion and a madness." These were *petits pois*, a tiny variety of today's green peas and a far cry from the mealy, unsweet field peas

Season	For Top Quality	Amount To Buy	Nutritive Value	Calories (unseasoned)
Year round for all peas; peak season: April–August	Choose bright green, tender, slightly velvety pods. Green pea pods should be well filled, snow pea pods slender and crisp. Cook as soon after buying as possible.	1 pound green peas in the pod serves 1–2; 1 pound snow peas 4–6; 1 pound dried peas 4–6.	Green and snow peas have fair amounts of vitamins A, C, and niacin; dried peas are high in protein and iron.	High—about 115 per cup of green peas; 290 per cup of dried peas. Not known for snow peas.

of old (these are now almost unavailable except as dried whole or split yellow peas). The newest member of the pea family (at least the newest to Americans) is the tender snow or sugar pea of Chinese cooking.

To Prepare for Cooking:
Green Peas: Shell *just* before cooking, no sooner.

Snow or Sugar Peas: Trim off stem ends; wash pods (but don't soak) in cool water.

Dried Whole Peas: Wash, sort, and soak overnight in 1 quart cold water. Or use the quick method* recommended for soaking dried beans.

Dried Split Peas: Wash and sort.

Cooking Tip: Add a pea pod to the pot when cooking green peas—gives them a just-picked flavor.

BOILED FRESH GREEN PEAS

Makes 4 servings

3 pounds green peas in the pod
½ cup boiling water
1 teaspoon sugar
1 teaspoon salt
Pinch pepper
2 tablespoons butter or margarine

Shell peas, place in a saucepan with water and sugar, cover, and boil 8–10 minutes until tender. Drain, add salt, pepper, and butter, and toss lightly to mix. About 110 calories per serving.

To Parboil for Use in Other Recipes: Boil as directed but reduce cooking time to 5 minutes; omit seasonings.

VARIATIONS:

To Serve Cold: Boil and drain as directed, then chill in ice water. Drain and refrigerate until needed. Use in salads or other recipes calling for cold peas.

Minted Green Peas: Boil as directed, adding a mint sprig to the pot. About 110 calories per serving.

Green Peas with Rosemary: Tuck a sprig fresh rosemary into the pot, letting it perfume the peas as they boil, or add a pinch dried rosemary to peas before serving. About 110 calories per serving.

Green Peas in Cream: Boil and drain peas by method above, stir in ¼ cup heavy cream and a pinch mace or nutmeg along with seasonings called for; serve in soup bowls. About 160 calories per serving.

VEGETABLES

Puréed Green Peas: Purée boiled, drained peas in an electric blender at high speed or put through a food mill. Mix in 2 tablespoons heavy cream along with seasonings called for and beat until light. (*Note:* Makes 2–3 servings.) About 275 calories for each of 2 servings, 185 calories for each of 3 servings.

Some Vegetables to Team with Green Peas: Diced, cooked carrots or celery; boiled tiny new potatoes; sautéed, sliced mushrooms; cooked or canned whole kernel or cream-style corn; boiled cauliflowerets; canned pearl onions or sautéed, sliced scallions.

GREEN PEAS WITH MINT AND ORANGE

Makes 4 servings

3 pounds green peas, shelled and boiled, or 2 (10-ounce) packages frozen peas, cooked by package directions
¼ cup butter or margarine
2 tablespoons finely slivered orange rind (use only the orange part)
2 tablespoons minced fresh mint or 1 teaspoon mint flakes
½ teaspoon salt
Pinch pepper

While peas are cooking, melt butter in a small saucepan over low heat. Add orange rind and heat, uncovered, 2–3 minutes, stirring occasionally. Drain peas well. Add butter and rind, also mint, salt, and pepper. Toss lightly to mix and serve. About 160 calories per serving.

GREEN PEAS AND DUMPLINGS

Makes 4 servings

3 pounds green peas, shelled
1¼ cups boiling water
1 cup light cream
2 tablespoons butter or margarine
1 tablespoon sugar
1 mint sprig
1 teaspoon salt
Pinch pepper

Dumplings:
1 cup sifted flour
1 tablespoon sugar
1½ teaspoons baking powder
½ teaspoon salt
1 tablespoon butter or margarine
½ cup milk

Place peas, boiling water, cream, butter, sugar, mint, salt, and pepper in a large saucepan, cover, set over moderate heat, and let come to a full boil. Meanwhile, quickly sift flour with sugar, baking powder, and salt into a small bowl and cut in butter with a pastry blender until mixture is the texture of coarse meal. Pour in milk and stir briskly with a fork *just* to mix, no longer. Drop dumplings from a tablespoon on top of *boiling* pea liquid, covering surface. Cover and simmer exactly 15 minutes (don't peek or dumplings won't be light). Remove mint and serve in soup bowls, spooning lots of cooking liquid over each portion. About 400 calories per serving.

⊠ SOY GREEN PEAS

The Chinese usually prepare snow peas this way, but the recipe works equally well with green peas.
Makes 4 servings

2 (10-ounce) packages frozen green peas (do not thaw)
2 tablespoons peanut oil
1½ teaspoons sugar
3 tablespoons soy sauce
½ teaspoon ginger

Hit packages of frozen peas against the edge of a counter to break up the solid mass. Heat peanut oil in a large, heavy skillet over moderately high heat about 1 minute. Add peas and stir-fry 5–7 minutes until heated through. Add remaining ingredients, stir-fry 1 minute longer, and serve. About 130 calories per serving.

PEAS À LA FRANÇAISE

Makes 4 servings

3 pounds green peas, shelled
1 cup finely shredded romaine or iceberg lettuce
12 scallions, trimmed and cut in rounds ¼" thick
1 bouquet garni
¼ teaspoon sugar
¼ cup boiling water
¼ cup butter or margarine
1 teaspoon salt
Pinch pepper

Place all ingredients except butter, salt, and pepper in a saucepan, cover, and boil 8–10 minutes, stirring once or twice, until peas are tender. Drain and remove *bouquet garni*. Add butter, salt, and pepper, cover, and shake pan gently over low heat until butter melts. Toss lightly and serve. About 175 calories per serving.

VARIATION:

Substitute 2 (10-ounce) packages frozen green peas for the fresh, reducing amount of boiling water to 2 tablespoons. Add butter to saucepan before cooking, then boil peas, covered, 5–7 minutes, breaking up any large chunks after 2 minutes of cooking. Season and serve. About 175 calories per serving.

PEAS À LA BONNE FEMME

Peas and onions cooked in chicken broth.
Makes 6 servings

2 tablespoons butter or margarine
12 very small white onions, peeled
2 slices bacon, diced
4 teaspoons flour
1 cup chicken broth
3 pounds green peas, shelled, or 2 (10-ounce) packages frozen peas (do not thaw)
Salt
Pepper

Melt butter in a large skillet over moderately high heat. Brown onions slowly all over, 6–8 minutes, then push to one side of skillet. Add bacon and sauté 2–3 minutes until crisp and golden. Stir in flour, slowly add chicken broth, and mix until smooth. Cook, stirring constantly, until thickened. Reduce heat to moderately low, cover, and simmer 10 minutes until onions are crisp-tender. Add peas, cover, and simmer 8–10 minutes for the fresh, 5–7 for the frozen (break these up after 2 minutes of cooking). Season to taste with salt and pepper. About 140 calories per serving.

FARM-STYLE GREEN PEAS

Carrots, onion, lettuce, and green peas cooked in apple cider and lightly flavored with bacon.
Makes 6 servings

2 tablespoons bacon drippings, butter, or margarine
2 medium-size carrots, peeled and diced
1 medium-size yellow onion, peeled and sliced thin
2 leaves romaine or iceberg lettuce
3 pounds green peas, shelled, or 2 (10-ounce) packages frozen peas (do not thaw)
¼ teaspoon sugar
1 teaspoon salt
⅛ teaspoon pepper
1 teaspoon minced parsley
¾ cup apple cider or juice
1 teaspoon minced fresh chervil or ½ teaspoon dried chervil

Melt drippings or butter in a saucepan over moderate heat, add carrots and onion, and stir-fry 2–3 minutes. Lay lettuce leaves on top of carrots and onion and add all remaining ingredients except chervil. Cover and simmer 10 minutes for fresh peas, 5–7 for the frozen (break these up after 2 minutes of cooking). Drain, reserving cooking liquid; discard lettuce. Sprinkle chervil over vegetables and toss gently to mix. Spoon into a heated vegetable dish and keep warm. Boil cooking liquid, uncovered, until reduced to ¼ cup, pour over vegetables, and serve. About 100 calories per serving.

✻ BOILED FRESH SNOW PEA PODS

Makes 4–6 servings

1 pound small snow pea pods, prepared for cooking
2 cups boiling water
½ teaspoon salt
Pinch pepper
2–4 tablespoons melted butter or margarine

Place pea pods in a large saucepan, pour in boiling water, and set over high heat. The instant water returns to a full rolling boil, time peas and boil, uncovered, exactly 2 minutes. Drain in a colander, transfer to a heated vegetable dish, sprinkle with salt and pepper, and drizzle with butter. Toss very gently and serve. About 70 calories for each of 4 servings (with 2 tablespoons butter), 80 for each of 6 (with 4 tablespoons butter).

VARIATIONS:

Snow Peas and Water Chestnuts: Add 3–4 thinly sliced water chestnuts to peas just before serving. About 75 calories for each of 4 servings, 85 calories for each of 6.

Snow Peas and Scallions: Add 8 finely chopped scallions (white part only) to peas just before serving. About 75 calories for each of 4 servings, 85 calories for each of 6.

✻ CHINESE-STYLE SNOW PEAS

Makes 4–6 servings

1 pound small snow pea pods, prepared for cooking
3 tablespoons peanut or sesame oil
¾ teaspoon salt
Pinch pepper
Pinch MSG (monosodium glutamate)

Pat pods dry on paper toweling. Heat oil in a large, heavy skillet or *wok* over moderately high heat 1 minute. Add pea pods, reduce heat to moderate, and stir-fry 2 minutes. Cover skillet and cook 1–2 minutes longer, shaking pan frequently, until peas are crisp-tender. Toss in remaining ingredients and serve. About 115 calories for each of 4 servings, 75 calories for each of 6 servings.

VARIATION:

Substitute 2 (7-ounce) packages frozen snow peas for the fresh. Plunge solidly frozen pods into boiling water for 1 minute or just long enough to separate them. Drain, pat dry on paper toweling, then proceed as recipe directs. About 115 calories for each of 4 servings, 75 calories for each of 6.

¢ BOILED DRIED WHOLE PEAS

For special piquancy, drizzle a little vinegar over these peas before serving. Makes 4–6 servings

1 pound dried whole green or yellow peas, washed and sorted

2½ quarts cold water (about)
2 tablespoons butter, margarine, bacon or roast drippings
2–3 teaspoons salt
⅛ teaspoon pepper

Soak peas in 1 quart water overnight or use the quick method.* Drain, measure soaking water, and add enough cold water to total 1½ quarts. Simmer peas, covered, in the water 1¾–2 hours, stirring occasionally, until tender and almost all water has evaporated. If mixture seems soupy, simmer uncovered a few minutes. Stir in butter or drippings, salt to taste, and pepper and serve. About 340 calories for each of 4 servings, 230 calories for each of 6 servings.

¢ **SPLIT PEA PURÉE**

Makes 4 servings

1 cup dried split green or yellow peas, washed and sorted
2 cups cold water
¾ teaspoon salt
1 small yellow onion, peeled and chopped fine
2 tablespoons butter or margarine

Place all ingredients in a heavy saucepan, cover, and bring to a boil over high heat. Reduce heat to moderately low and simmer 35–40 minutes, stirring occasionally, until peas are mushy. (*Note:* If lid does not fit tightly, you may have to add an extra ¼ cup boiling water toward the end of cooking so peas don't stick.) Remove from heat and beat peas with a wooden spoon or, if you prefer, purée in an electric blender at high speed or press through a fine sieve. Reheat, if necessary, and serve hot. About 235 calories per serving.

VARIATION:

Savory Split Pea Purée: Use 2 cups chicken or beef broth for cooking peas instead of water. Add all seasonings called for above, also 1 minced carrot, 2 stalks celery, chopped fine, 1 crushed clove garlic, and 1 bay leaf. Cover and simmer as recipe directs. Remove bay leaf and purée in an electric blender at high speed. Top, if you wish, with crisp crumbled bacon or Croutons. About 255 calories per serving (without bacon or croutons).

PEPPERS

When Columbus discovered the West Indies, he found island natives eating scarlet and emerald pods that contained all the fire of costly East Indian black pepper. He called these pods "peppers" and "peppers" they have remained, although botanically they are not peppers but members of a large family that also includes tomatoes and potatoes. Old World cooks applauded the New World peppers, found them "more pungent than the peppers of the Caucasus," and devised delightful new ways of using them. The peppers we know today can be lumped into two large categories—the sweet and the hot. Either may be green or red because peppers, like tomatoes, turn red (or in some instances, sunny yellow) as they ripen.

To Prepare for Cooking: Wash in cool water; cut up as individual recipes specify. Always wash your hands well after cutting or working with hot peppers.

To Prepare for Stuffing: Using a small sharp knife, cut a wide circle around stem of pepper and lift off (save if stem-lids are to be used to cover stuffing during baking). Scoop out core and seeds and discard.

VEGETABLES

Season	For Top Quality	Amount To Buy	Nutritive Value	Calories (unseasoned)
Year round for all; Peak season: June–October	Choose bright, firm fleshy pods. Pimientos are available only canned.	1 sweet pepper per person; 2–3 Italian peppers	The red are high in vitamins A and C, the green in vitamin C.	Very low—15–20 per pepper, the red being the higher

To Parboil Before Stuffing: Because peppers will not always cook as fast as their stuffing, they must sometimes be parboiled. To do so, prepare for stuffing by method above, then lay peppers on their sides in a large kettle and add lightly salted boiling water to cover. If tops are to be used, add to kettle. Cover and boil 6–8 minutes until crisp-tender (remove tops after 4 minutes). Pour off water and drain peppers upside-down on paper toweling.

PEPPERS STUFFED WITH SPANISH RICE

Makes 4 servings

4 large sweet green or red peppers, washed
4 cups Spanish Rice
¼ cup coarsely grated Monterey Jack or sharp Cheddar cheese
1 cup water (about)

Preheat oven to 375° F. Prepare peppers for stuffing and parboil.* Stand close together in an ungreased shallow 1-quart casserole, fill with Spanish Rice, and sprinkle with cheese. Pour water around peppers. Bake, uncovered, 45 minutes until peppers are tender, checking occasionally to make sure water hasn't boiled away—there should be a little in the bottom of the casserole at all times. Using 2 large spoons, lift peppers to a heated dish and serve. About 290 calories per serving.

VARIATIONS:

Peppers Stuffed with Spanish Rice and Meat: Reduce amount of Spanish Rice to 2½ cups and mix with 1½ cups chopped, cooked meat, poultry, or seafood (this is a splendid way to use up leftover cold cuts, ham, or hot dogs). Stuff and bake peppers as directed. Serve hot, topped if you like, with Tomato Sauce. About 305 calories per serving (without Tomato Sauce).

Peppers Stuffed with Macaroni Marinara: Instead of stuffing peppers with Spanish Rice, stuff with 3 cups boiled macaroni shells mixed with 2 cups Marinara Sauce. Sprinkle peppers with cheese. Pour 1½ cups Marinara Sauce into kettle with peppers and bake as directed above. Serve from casserole, spooning some of the sauce over each portion. About 215 calories per serving.

Some Other Stuffings for Peppers (allow 1 cup per pepper and bake as directed above): Macaroni and cheese, chili con carne, corned beef hash, franks or pork and beans, Izmir Eggplant, Rice Pilaf, Saffron Rice, Ratatouille, Pisto, Jambalaya, any *risotto*.

SAUTÉED SWEET GREEN OR RED PEPPERS

Serve these peppers as a vegetable or use to garnish meat or egg platters. They're also good mixed with sautéed sliced mushrooms, hashed brown potatoes, boiled whole kernel corn, or buttered baby limas. Makes 2–4 servings

2 tablespoons cooking oil
2 large sweet green or red peppers, washed, cored, seeded, and cut in long, thin strips
¼ teaspoon salt
Pepper

Heat oil in a heavy skillet over moderate heat 1 minute. Add peppers and sauté, stirring frequently, 4–6 minutes until lightly browned. Turn heat to low, cover, and simmer 2–3 minutes until crisp-tender. Using a slotted spoon, transfer to a heated vegetable dish, sprinkle with salt, a grinding or two of the pepper mill, and serve. About 125 calories for each of 2 servings, 65 calories for each of 4 servings.

ITALIAN PEPPERS AND ONIONS

Makes 4 servings

3 tablespoons olive oil
3 large sweet red or green peppers or 8 Italian sweet green peppers, washed, cored, seeded, and cut in long, thin strips
1 medium-size Spanish onion, peeled and sliced thin
1 clove garlic, peeled and crushed
½ teaspoon salt
Pinch pepper

Heat oil in a large, heavy skillet over moderate heat. Add peppers, onion, and garlic and stir-fry 8 minutes until onion is golden. Cover, turn heat to low, and simmer 5 minutes, shaking pan occasionally. Uncover, cook, stirring, 1–2 minutes to drive off excess moisture; add salt and pepper and serve. Especially good with veal or chicken or in a hero sandwich with hot Italian sausages. About 125 calories per serving.

⚔️ MARINATED ROASTED PEPPERS

An elegant cold appetizer or salad. Makes 2–4 servings

4 medium-size sweet green peppers, washed
1 tablespoon olive oil
1 tablespoon red wine vinegar
1 clove garlic, peeled and quartered
4 bay leaves
¼ teaspoon salt
Pinch pepper

Preheat broiler. Lay peppers on their sides on broiler pan and broil 2″ from the heat, turning frequently, 15–20 minutes until skins are blackened all over. Cool under running cold water and slake off blackened skin. Core peppers, seed, and cut into 1″×2″ strips. Place in a small bowl, add remaining ingredients and toss gently to mix. Cover and marinate at room temperature several hours, turning occasionally. Remove garlic and bay leaves and serve. About 90 calories for each of 2 servings, 45 calories for each of 4 servings.

PEPPERS IN SWISS CHEESE SAUCE

Makes 4 servings

5 large sweet green peppers, washed
Sauce:
2 tablespoons butter or margarine
2 tablespoons flour
1¼ cups milk
¼ pound Swiss cheese, coarsely grated
½ teaspoon salt
Pinch white pepper

Preheat broiler. Lay peppers on their sides on broiler pan and broil

2" from heat, turning frequently, 15–20 minutes until black all over. Turn oven control from broil to 375° F. Cool peppers under cold running water and rub off blackened skins; core, seed, and cut into 2" squares. Place peppers in an ungreased 1-quart casserole and set aside while you make the sauce. Melt butter in a saucepan over moderate heat, blend in flour, then slowly stir in milk. Heat, stirring constantly, until thickened. Add cheese, salt, and pepper, cook, and stir 1–2 minutes longer until cheese melts and sauce is smooth. Pour over peppers and mix lightly. Cover and bake 20–25 minutes until peppers are very tender. About 160 calories per serving.

PLANTAIN

Wherever explorers sailed in warm waters, they found plantains, starchy banana-shaped fruits for which natives knew as many ways to cook as we do potatoes. Plantains taste rather like yams and, like them, are best when baked, sautéed, or candied.

To Prepare for Cooking: Peel (just as you would a banana) unless plantains are to be baked in their skins.

To Bake: Choose ripe plantains; do not peel but slit skins lengthwise down one side. Place on a baking sheet and bake, uncovered, 20 minutes at 350° F. Turn and bake 25–30 minutes longer until tender. Serve hot with lots of butter, salt and pepper.

To Sauté: Use ripe plantains; peel and quarter lengthwise. Sauté in ¼ cup butter over moderate heat, turning often, 15–20 minutes until tender. Roll in sugar and serve.

To Deep-Fry: Peel hard green plantains and slice very thin on the bias so slices are oval. Soak 1 hour in lightly salted water, drain, and pat dry on paper toweling. Fry, a few chips at a time, in 2" cooking oil over high heat 2–3 minutes until golden. Drain on paper toweling, sprinkle with salt, and serve at room temperature.

To Candy: Peel ripe plantains, quarter lengthwise, and soak ½ hour in lightly salted water. Drain, place in a buttered 9"×9"×2" baking dish, dot well with butter, and sprinkle heavily with light brown sugar. Bake, uncovered, 20–25 minutes at 350° F., turn, dot again with butter, and sprinkle with sugar. Bake 25–30 minutes longer until tender.

IRISH POTATOES

The Irish potato isn't Irish. It's South American, one of the New World foods brought to Europe by the conquistadors. Europe wasn't impressed and potatoes might never have been accepted if they hadn't

Season	For Top Quality	Amount To Buy	Nutritive Value	Calories (unseasoned)
Year round	Choose ripe black-skinned plantains unless they are to be deep-fat-fried.	1 plantain will serve 1–3 depending on size.	Some vitamin A, also some of the B group	Very high— about 125 per ¼ pound serving

had boosters like Sir Francis Drake, Sir Walter Raleigh, Frederick the Great, even Marie Antoinette, who wore potato flowers in her hair.

The real credit for establishing potatoes, however, belongs to the poor of Ireland and Germany, who proved that they were *enjoyable* as well as edible. There are so many kinds of potatoes even experts can't keep them straight. Grocers usually classify them simply as *all-purpose, baking* or *boiling potatoes*. New potatoes, often billed separately, are boiling potatoes (*new* refers both to immature potatoes and to those that haven't been in storage; they are in best supply between mid-May and mid-September). Here are *America's Top Potatoes and How to Use Them:*

For Top Quality: Regardless of type, choose firm, well shaped, clean, blemish-free potatoes. Reject any with large green "sunburn spots" and those that are sprouting.

Calories: MODERATE—90–100 per medium-size potato. *Nutritive Value:* Some vitamin C.

To Prepare for Cooking: Scrub and remove eyes. To preserve nutrients, do not peel.

¢ **BOILED POTATOES**

Makes 4–6 servings

6 medium-size potatoes, scrubbed
2 cups boiling water, chicken or beef broth
1 teaspoon salt

Peel potatoes only if they're to be boiled in broth or a stew, at the same time cutting out eyes and green "sunburned" spots; drop in cold

Potato	Best Uses	Season	Amount To Buy
Round Whites, also marketed as Maine, Eastern, or All-purpose potatoes.	Boiling, frying, and, if a mealy type, baking	Year round but supplies may be short in late summer and early fall.	1 potato per person; there are 3–4 per pound.
Round Reds, which include the luscious little New Potatoes.	Boiling	Year round but best in the spring	2–4 potatoes per person, depending on size; there are 4–8 per pound, depending on size
California Long Whites or White Rose; also sometimes marketed as California News	Boiling	Mid-May to Mid-September; Mid-December to Mid-March	1 potato per person; there are 3–5 per pound.
Russet Burbank, more often sold as Idaho Potatoes or Bakers	Baking, frying; if closely watched, can be boiled.	Year round but supplies may be short in summer.	1 potato per person; there are 2–3 per pound

VEGETABLES

water to prevent darkening. Place potatoes, water or broth, and salt (reduce amount if broth is salty) in a large saucepan, cover, and boil slowly about 30 minutes until tender. Drain and peel (if not already done). Return to pan, set uncovered over lowest heat, and shake briskly 1–2 minutes to drive off steam. Serve piping hot with butter, salt, and pepper. About 150 calories for each of 4 servings (without butter), 100 calories for each of 6 servings.

To Parboil for Use in Other Recipes: Peel potatoes and leave whole or halve. Boil halves 10 minutes in lightly salted water, whole potatoes 15–20 minutes. Do not season.

VARIATIONS:

¢ **Parsleyed Potatoes:** Roll boiled, peeled potatoes in ¼ cup each melted butter and minced parsley (or for special fragrance, ½-and-½ minced parsley and mint or basil). About 250 calories for each of 4 servings, 170 calories for each of 6 servings.

¢ **Potato Balls:** With a melon baller, cut raw, peeled potatoes into 1″ balls. (*Note:* Because of waste, you'll need 9–12 potatoes for 4–6 servings; scraps can be cooked separately and used for mashed potatoes.) Boil potato balls 15–20 minutes until just tender; drain and serve with salt, pepper, and butter or, if you like, sprinkled with minced parsley. Recipe too flexible for a meaningful calorie count.

¢ **Riced Potatoes:** Force boiled, peeled potatoes through a ricer or fine sieve, letting them mound in a serving dish. Drizzle with ¼ cup melted butter and sprinkle with 1 tablespoon minced parsley, basil, or chives. About 250 calories for each of 4 servings, 170 calories for each of 6 servings.

¢ **Mashed Potatoes:** Boil potatoes in skins as directed, drain, and dry out over low heat but do not season. Mash or beat with an electric mixer. Add ⅓ cup softened butter, salt and pepper to taste, and, depending on how creamy you like your potatoes, ¼–⅓ cup hot milk, evaporated milk, or cream. Beat briskly with whisk or mixer *just* until light. If potatoes grow cold, or if dinner is delayed, spoon into a buttered casserole, cover, and warm 8–10 minutes in a 250° F. oven. About 295 calories for each of 4 servings, 200 calories for each of 6 servings (if made with cream).

¢ **BAKED POTATOES**

Allow 1 large Idaho or other mealy type potato per person (*always choose those of uniform size with few eyes and no green spots*).

Preheat oven to 425° F. (Potatoes *can* be baked at any temperature between 300° F. and 450° F., but they'll be flakiest done at 425° F. They can also be baked along with other foods, but again, won't be so nice and dry.) Scrub potatoes well, then pierce almost to the center with a sharp fork so steam can escape. Bake directly on oven racks about 1 hour until tender (those baked at lower temperatures will take longer, of course, sometimes as much as ½ hour). Make an X-shaped cut in the top of each potato, press sides gently to open, then push a fat chunk of butter down inside each and sprinkle with salt and pepper.

To Oil (or Not to Oil) the Skins: If you like a soft-skinned potato, oil.

To Wrap (or Not to Wrap) in Foil: Again it's a matter of choice. Foil-wrapped potatoes will be soft skinned and moist inside. They'll also bake about 15 minutes faster.

To Speed Baking: Insert aluminum potato nails and potatoes will cook twice as fast.

To Charcoal Bake: Wrap each potato in foil and bake at edge of a moderate charcoal fire ¾–1 hour, turning 2 or 3 times. If you like crisp, charred skins, bake without wrapping (test for doneness after ½ hour).

About 100 calories per baked potato (without butter or other topping).

To Give Baked Potatoes Special Flair, top with any of the following:
– Sour cream (or, for fewer calories, cottage cheese) and minced chives
– Melted butter and minced chives, dill, basil, parsley, or marjoram
– Melted butter, minced dill pickle, and crisp bacon bits
– Melted butter and minced onion or scallions

¢ FRANCONIA POTATOES (OVEN-ROASTED POTATOES)

Makes 4 servings

½ *cup melted beef or bacon drippings or cooking oil*
6 *medium-size potatoes, peeled, halved, parboiled, and drained*
Salt

Preheat oven to 400° F. Pour drippings in a shallow roasting pan, add potatoes, turning in fat to coat. Roast uncovered, turning occasionally, about 40 minutes until tender and nut brown. Drain on paper toweling, sprinkle with salt, and serve. About 200 calories per serving.

VARIATIONS:

¢ **Potatoes Roasted with Meat:** When roast has about 1 hour longer to cook, add peeled, halved, parboiled potatoes to pan and roast uncovered, turning occasionally, until meat is done. If there are few pan drippings, add 2–3 tablespoons cooking oil. About 200 calories per serving.

¢ **Château Potatoes:** Peel 6 *raw* potatoes, quarter, and then trim each quarter until it is the size and shape of a jumbo olive. Roast as directed above, reducing cooking time to 30 minutes. Drain, season, and, if you like, sprinkle with minced parsley. About 175 calories per serving.

¢ **Parisienne Potatoes:** With a melon baller, cut raw, peeled potatoes into 1″ balls. Roast and season as for Château Potatoes. About 150 calories per serving.

¢ **Sautéed Château or Parisienne Potatoes:** Cut potatoes as directed but, instead of roasting, sauté in ¼ cup clarified butter* 15–20 minutes over moderately low heat, turning frequently. About 175 calories per serving for Château Potatoes, 150 per serving for Parisienne Potatoes.

SOME WAYS TO USE LEFTOVER POTATOES

About 2–4 servings

MASHED:

Potato Casserole: Mix 2 cups mashed potatoes with ¼ cup heavy cream and 1 teaspoon onion flakes. Spoon into a buttered 1-quart casserole, top with ¼ cup grated sharp Cheddar or Swiss cheese, and bake uncovered 30 minutes at 350° F. About 345 calories for each of 2 servings, 170 calories for each of 4 servings.

Potato Cups: Beat 1 egg into 2 cups mashed potatoes and spoon into 4 buttered custard cups. Press a

VEGETABLES

½″ cube Camembert, Port du Salut, or Brie cheese into the center of each, top with cracker meal, and bake 10–15 minutes at 425° F. About 300 calories for each of 2 servings, 150 calories for each of 4 servings.

Potato Patties or Croquettes: Shape into patties, roll in flour, dip in lightly beaten egg, then in toasted bread crumbs. Brown 1–2 minutes on a side in 2 tablespoons butter. *For additional flavor,* mix in any of the following before shaping (1 tablespoon to 1 cup mashed potatoes): grated or fried chopped onion; minced parsley, dill, or chives; cooked crumbled bacon; finely chopped toasted peanuts, almonds, pecans, or piñon nuts. Recipe too flexible for a meaningful calorie count.

Substitute for freshly mashed potatoes when making Farmhouse Potato Topping, Cottage Potato Casserole, or Easy Potato Soufflé-Pudding.

BOILED OR BAKED (peel before using):

Creamed Potatoes: Slice or dice potatoes. Measure, place in a saucepan, add ¼ cup heavy cream for each 1 cup potatoes, and simmer uncovered over low heat, stirring now and then, until cream has reduced by ½. Season with salt and white pepper to taste, sprinkle with minced chives, parsley, or dill, and serve. Recipe too flexible for a meaningful calorie count.

Potatoes au Gratin: Mix 2 cups sliced, diced, or coarsely grated potatoes with 1 cup Medium White Sauce or Parsley Sauce. Spoon into a buttered 1-quart *au gratin* dish, top with cracker meal or grated Cheddar cheese, and bake uncovered 20 minutes at 350° F. Brown under the broiler and serve. *Variation:* If you like, mix in any leftover peas, beans, corn, chopped asparagus, broccoli, or cauliflower and bake as directed. Recipe too flexible for a meaningful calorie count.

Potato-Onion Pie: Mix 2 cups thinly sliced potatoes with 1 thinly sliced sautéed yellow onion. Place in a buttered 9″ piepan, spread with ½ cup sour cream, and bake uncovered 20 minutes at 350° F. Sprinkle with paprika and serve. About 400 calories for each of 2 servings, 200 calories for each of 4 servings.

Substitute for freshly cooked potatoes when making any potato salad (if potatoes are firm), Hashed Brown Potatoes, O'Brien Potatoes, or Lyonnaise Potatoes.

SOME WAYS TO GLAMORIZE INSTANT MASHED POTATOES

For 4 servings

– Prepare by package directions but substitute milk, beef or chicken broth for the water and heat with 2 tablespoons each butter and Cheddar cheese spread. When potatoes are fluffy, beat in a pinch each savory and mace.
– Prepare by package directions, adding 2 tablespoons onion, celery, parsley, or mint flakes to the cooking liquid.
– Prepare by package directions, reducing amount of liquid by 2–3 tablespoons. Stir in ¼ cup sour cream and ½ teaspoon paprika before serving.
– Prepare by package directions, reducing amount of liquid by 2–3 tablespoons. Omit salt. Beat in ½ (2-ounce) tube anchovy paste, ¼

cup sour cream, and 2 tablespoons each grated yellow onion, minced fresh parsley, and tarragon.
– Prepare by package directions but omit butter and salt. Mix in ¼ cup minced stuffed green olives and 2 tablespoons each olive oil and grated yellow onion.
– Prepare by package directions and, just before serving, stir in 2 tablespoons of any of the following: prepared horseradish or spicy brown mustard; minced fresh basil, chives, dill, parsley, or scallions.
– Prepare by package directions and, just before serving, mix in ¼ cup of any of the following: any cheese spread; chopped toasted almonds, pecans, or peanuts; chopped French-fried onion rings.

STUFFED BAKED POTATOES

Makes 4 servings

4 large, hot baked potatoes
½ cup hot milk
¼ cup butter or margarine, softened to room temperature
1 teaspoon salt
⅛ teaspoon white pepper
Melted butter or margarine

Preheat broiler. Cut a ¼" lengthwise slice from top of each potato, then scoop flesh into a bowl, taking care not to break skins. Mash potatoes and beat in milk, butter, salt, and pepper. Spoon into skins, roughen surface with a fork, and brush with melted butter. Place on a lightly greased baking sheet and broil 3"–4" from heat 2–3 minutes until lightly browned. About 245 calories per serving.

VARIATION:

Add any of the following to the mashed potato mixture: 1 cup grated sharp Cheddar cheese; ½ cup crumbled blue cheese; ¼ cup minced onion, scallions, or chives;

1 (7-ounce) can drained, flaked tuna or salmon; 1 cup cooked sausage meat. Recipe too flexible for a meaningful calorie count.

¢ HASHED BROWN POTATOES

Makes 4 servings

6 large potatoes, boiled, peeled, and cut in ½" cubes
1 medium-size yellow onion, peeled and minced
3 tablespoons bacon drippings, butter, margarine, or cooking oil
1 teaspoon salt
⅛ teaspoon pepper

Brown potatoes and onion 5–7 minutes in fat in a heavy skillet over moderate heat, pressing into a pancake. Shake pan often so mixture doesn't stick. Sprinkle with salt and pepper, cut in 4 wedges, turn, brown other sides, and serve. About 235 calories per serving.

VARIATIONS:

¢ **O'Brien Potatoes:** Follow recipe above, frying ½ minced sweet green pepper and 2 tablespoons coarsely chopped pimiento with onion and potatoes. Fry 10–15 minutes, turning often, until potatoes are lightly crisp. Add salt and pepper. About 240 calories per serving.

¢ **Lyonnaise Potatoes:** Slice potatoes ¼" thick instead of cubing; omit onion. Fry potatoes in fat 10–12 minutes until golden. In a separate skillet, sauté 2 thinly sliced, peeled yellow onions in 2 tablespoons butter 8–10 minutes until golden; add to potatoes, fry 1–2 minutes longer, sprinkle with salt, pepper, and minced parsley. About 295 calories per serving.

¢ **Country Fried Potatoes:** Cut raw, peeled potatoes in ½" slices; omit onion. Place potatoes in a skillet with drippings called for, cover, and cook 10 minutes. Uncover and fry 10–12 minutes, stirring, until browned. Add salt and pepper and serve. About 225 calories per serving.

¢ **Oven-Fried Potatoes for a Crowd:** Peel 9 pounds potatoes and cut in ½" cubes. Place in 2 large roasting pans and drizzle each with ½ cup melted drippings or oil. Cover with foil and bake 15 minutes at 400° F.; uncover, stir, and bake 30 minutes. Raise heat to 500° F., stir, and bake 10–15 minutes until brown. Sprinkle well with salt and pepper and serve, using a slotted spoon. Makes about 20 servings. About 200 calories per serving.

FRENCH-FRIED POTATOES

Makes 4–6 servings

3 pounds Idaho or all-purpose potatoes
Shortening or oil for deep fat frying
Salt
Pepper

Peel potatoes, 1 at a time, cut into strips the length of the potato and ⅜" wide, letting each fall into cold water. When all strips are cut, soak 10 minutes in cold water. Drain and pat dry on paper toweling. Meanwhile, heat shortening or oil in a deep fat fryer over high heat (use a deep fat thermometer). When fat reaches 375° F., place ⅓ of the potatoes in frying basket and fry 8–10 minutes until golden brown. Drain on paper toweling and keep warm in a 250° F. oven while you fry the rest. Sprinkle with salt and pepper and serve very hot. About 230 calories for each of 4 servings, 155 calories for each of 6 servings.

VARIATIONS:

Twice-Fried French Fries: Prepare potatoes as directed. Heat shortening or oil to 330° F., add potatoes, about 1 cup at a time, and fry 2 minutes until lightly golden and all sputtering stops. Drain on paper toweling. Potatoes can now be held until just before serving. For the second frying, heat fat to 375° F. and fry, ⅓ of the potatoes at a time, 5 minutes until crisply golden. About 230 calories for each of 4 servings, 155 calories for each of 6 servings.

Shoestring Potatoes: Cut potatoes into matchstick strips about 2" long and ⅛" thick. Soak in cold water as for French fries, drain, and pat dry. Fry about ⅓ of the potatoes at a time in deep fat (375° F.) 3–5 minutes until crisp and golden. Drain on paper toweling and serve. About 230 calories for each of 4 servings, 155 calories for each of 6 servings.

SOUFFLÉ POTATOES

For this tricky recipe, you *must* have mature storage potatoes with plenty of starch. If you can't find them, don't even try to make Soufflé Potatoes. Even when the potatoes are perfect, a few slices may refuse to "puff."

Makes 4 servings

6 large mature Idaho potatoes
Cooking oil, shortening, or lard for deep fat frying
Salt

Peel potatoes, trimming so they're uniformly oval. Cut *lengthwise* into slices ⅛" thick (they must be of uniform thickness) and soak 20 minutes in ice water. Meanwhile, heat fat in a deep fat fryer over moderately high heat; insert wire basket and deep fat thermometer. Drain potatoes and pat dry on paper toweling. When fat reaches 300° F., lift pan from heat and drop in enough slices to form a single layer. As they rise to surface, agitate basket to keep them covered with fat. When fat temperature drops to 200° F. (after about 4 minutes), remove slices to paper toweling to drain. Repeat with remaining slices. (*Note:* You can prepare recipe to this point early in the day; cool potatoes and cover until shortly before serving. No need to refrigerate.) Reheat fat to 400° F. Drop in slices 1 at a time. They should bob to the surface at once and puff. Cook 1–2 minutes, turning as needed to brown puffs evenly. Drain on paper toweling, sprinkle with salt, and serve. Puffs will deflate on standing but may be repuffed by dropping in 400° F. fat. (*Note:* If you have 2 deep fat fryers, use one for the partial cooking, the other for the puffing.) About 150 calories per serving.

SCALLOPED POTATOES

Makes 4–6 servings

1 quart very thinly sliced, peeled potatoes (you'll need 4–5 medium-size potatoes)
2 small yellow onions, peeled and sliced paper thin
¼ cup butter or margarine
2 tablespoons flour
1 tablespoon minced fresh dill or ¼ teaspoon dried dill
¼ teaspoon summer savory (optional)
1 teaspoon salt
⅛ teaspoon pepper
1½ cups milk

Preheat oven to 325° F. In a buttered 2-quart casserole build up alternate layers of potatoes and onions, beginning and ending with potatoes. Dot each onion layer with butter and sprinkle with flour, herbs, salt and pepper. Pour in milk, cover, and bake 45 minutes. Uncover and bake 30–40 minutes until potatoes are tender and almost all liquid is absorbed. Broil, if you like, to brown and serve. About 290 calories for each of 4 servings, 195 calories for each of 6 servings.

VARIATIONS:

Cream-Scalloped Potatoes: Follow recipe above, substituting light or heavy cream for milk and omitting flour. Bake as directed. If made with light cream: about 420 calories for each of 4 servings, 285 for each of 6. If made with heavy cream: 545 calories for each of 4 servings, 365 calories for each of 6 servings.

¢ **Budget-Scalloped Potatoes:** Follow recipe above, substituting bacon drippings for butter and water for milk. Bake as directed. About 315 calories for each of 4 servings, 210 calories for each of 6 servings.

Scalloped Potatoes with Ham: Use a 2½-quart casserole. Layer 2 cups diced cooked ham in with other ingredients but omit flour. Mix 1 (10½-ounce) can condensed cream of celery or mushroom soup with ¾ cup milk and pour into casserole in place of milk. Bake as directed. About 695 calories for each of 4 servings, 465 calories for each of 6 servings.

Scalloped Potatoes with Cheese: Use a 2½-quart casserole. Layer 1½ cups grated Gruyère or sharp Cheddar cheese in with other ingredients, omitting flour. Pour 2 cups milk over all and bake as directed. About 465 calories for each of 4 servings, 310 calories for each of 6 servings.

STE. MICHELE SCALLOPED POTATOES

Potatoes scalloped the French way, with scallions, Gruyère cheese,

VEGETABLES

plenty of butter and cream. Makes 4 servings

3–4 large potatoes
½ cup thinly sliced scallions (include tops)
1 (6-ounce) package Gruyère cheese, grated
1 teaspoon salt
¼ teaspoon white pepper
½ teaspoon minced garlic
¼ cup butter or margarine
⅓ cup light cream

Preheat oven to 400° F. Peel potatoes and slice ⅛" thick, letting them drop into cold water. Drain and pat dry on paper toweling. Layer ⅓ of the potatoes in a buttered 1½-quart *au gratin* dish or shallow casserole. Add half the scallions and cheese and sprinkle with ⅓ of the salt, pepper, and minced garlic. Dot with ⅓ of the butter. Add a second layer of potatoes, scallions, and cheese and season as before. Top with remaining potatoes, seasonings, and butter. Pour cream over all and bake, uncovered, ½ hour. Reduce oven to 350° F. and bake 20–25 minutes longer until potatoes are crusty golden and fork tender. About 375 calories per serving.

EASY POTATO SOUFFLÉ-PUDDING

Makes 4 servings

2 cups hot seasoned mashed potatoes
½ cup milk
3 eggs, separated
¼ teaspoon dill
½ teaspoon salt
⅛ teaspoon white pepper

Preheat oven to 375° F. Mix potatoes and milk. Beat egg yolks lightly, then stir into potatoes along with dill, salt, and pepper. Cover loosely and cool to room temperature. Beat egg whites until soft peaks form and fold into potato mixture. Spoon into an ungreased 5-cup soufflé dish and bake, uncovered, on center rack about 35 minutes until puffed and golden. About 145 calories per serving.

FARMHOUSE POTATO TOPPING

Makes 4 servings

3 cups hot unseasoned mashed potatoes
1 egg, lightly beaten
2 tablespoons softened butter or margarine
¾ cup sour cream
⅛ teaspoon white pepper
1 teaspoon salt
¼ teaspoon nutmeg

Mix together all ingredients and use as a topping for oven-baked stews. Or spoon into a buttered shallow 1-quart casserole and broil 4" from heat 3–4 minutes. About 255 calories per serving.

COTTAGE POTATO CASSEROLE

Makes 6 servings

3 cups cream-style cottage cheese
4 cups hot unseasoned mashed potatoes
¾ cup sour cream
2 tablespoons finely chopped scallions (include tops)
2 teaspoons salt
⅛ teaspoon white pepper
1–2 tablespoons melted butter or margarine

Preheat oven to 350° F. Sieve cottage cheese or purée in an electric blender at medium speed. Mix with potatoes and all remaining ingredients except butter. Spoon into a buttered 2-quart casserole, roughen surface with a fork, and brush with melted butter. Bake, uncovered, 30 minutes until lightly browned. About 360 calories per serving.

DUCHESS POTATOES

Makes 6 servings

6 medium-size potatoes, boiled and drained
¼ cup butter or margarine
Pinch nutmeg
⅛ teaspoon white pepper
1 teaspoon salt
2 tablespoons milk
1 egg, lightly beaten
1 egg yolk, lightly beaten
1 egg beaten with 1 tablespoon cold water (glaze)

Peel potatoes, mash, and measure 4 cups. Beat butter, nutmeg, pepper, salt, milk, egg and egg yolk into potatoes. Meanwhile, preheat broiler. Fill a pastry bag fitted with a large rosette tip with potatoes and press out onto a lightly greased baking sheet, forming 12 spiral cones about 2½" in diameter. Or simply spoon potatoes into 12 mounds. Brush lightly with egg glaze. Broil 5" from heat 3–5 minutes until lightly browned and serve. About 210 calories per serving.

VARIATIONS:

– Bake 10 minutes at 450° F. instead of broiling.

– Beat any one of the following into the potatoes: ¼ teaspoon minced garlic, 1 tablespoon minced parsley or chives, 1 teaspoon minced basil, dill, or chervil. Broil or bake as directed. About 210 calories per serving.

Planked Potatoes: These usually accompany planked steak, chops, or fish. When meat has browned on one side, turn and transfer to oiled plank. Pipe a ruffled border of potatoes around edge of plank, brush with egg glaze, and broil until meat is done. If potatoes brown too fast, cover loosely with foil. About 210 calories per serving.

DAUPHINE POTATOES

These deep-fried potatoes, admittedly, are somewhat tedious to make. But they're puffy and light and so very worth the trouble. Makes 4–6 servings

2 cups hot unseasoned mashed potatoes (add no milk or cream)
¼ the recipe for Choux Pastry (do not cook)
1 teaspoon salt
Pinch pepper
Pinch nutmeg or mace
Cooking oil, shortening, or lard for deep fat frying
Flour

Mix potatoes, pastry mixture, salt, pepper and nutmeg until smooth and chill 1 hour. Begin heating fat in a deep fat fryer over moderately high heat; insert deep fat thermometer. Using a rounded teaspoon as a measure, shape potato mixture into small balls, logs, or cork shapes, then roll in flour. When fat reaches 375° F., fry potatoes, a few at a time, 2–3 minutes until golden. Drain on paper toweling and keep warm while you fry the rest by setting, uncovered, in a 250° F. oven. Serve piping hot. About 260 calories for each of 4 servings, 175 calories for each of 6 servings.

VARIATIONS:

Breaded Dauphine Potatoes: Mix and shape potatoes by recipe above. Roll in flour as directed, then dip in 1 egg beaten with 1 tablespoon cold water and roll in fine dry bread crumbs. Let dry on a rack 10 minutes, then fry as above. About 320 calories for each of 4 servings, 215 calories for each of 6 servings.

Lorette Potatoes: Add ¼ cup grated Gruyère cheese to potato mixture, shape into small crescents, roll gently in flour, dip in egg mixture, then roll in crumbs as for Breaded Dauphine Potatoes (above). Fry as directed. About 370 calories for each of 4 servings, 245 calories for each of 6 servings.

¢ POTATO PANCAKES

Makes 4 servings

2 large Idaho potatoes, peeled
1 egg, lightly beaten
2 tablespoons flour
1 small yellow onion, peeled and finely grated
¼ teaspoon baking powder
1 teaspoon salt
2 tablespoons cooking oil

Coarsely grate potatoes into a bowl of cold water and let stand 15–20 minutes. Meanwhile mix egg and flour until smooth and stir in all remaining ingredients except oil. Drain potatoes, squeeze as dry as possible, and stir into batter. Heat oil in a large, heavy skillet over high heat 1–2 minutes. Drop potato mixture by spoonfuls into oil, shaping into 4 or 5 large cakes and flattening slightly with a spatula. Brown 1–2 minutes on each side, turn heat down low, and cook pancakes 20–25 minutes, turning frequently, so they're cooked through. Drain on paper toweling and serve piping hot. Good with sour cream or applesauce. About 150 calories per serving (without sour cream or applesauce).

RÖSTI

In German Switzerland this pie-sized potato pancake is served almost every day.
Makes 4 servings

3 large Idaho potatoes
¼ cup lard, butter, or margarine
1½ teaspoons salt
⅛ teaspoon pepper

Peel potatoes, 1 at a time, and grate moderately coarsely, letting shreds fall into cold water. When all are grated, drain well and pat dry on paper toweling. Heat fat in a heavy 9" skillet over moderate heat 1 minute, add potatoes, salt, and pepper, toss lightly in the fat, then press down gently with a pancake turner to level the surface. Turn heat to moderately low and fry slowly about 15 minutes, without stirring, until a golden-brown crust forms on the bottom. Loosen "pancake" with a spatula and turn by easing out onto a plate. Invert onto a second plate, then slide back into skillet and brown the other side. To serve, slide onto platter and cut in wedges. About 160 calories per serving.

VARIATION:

Mix a little finely grated yellow onion into potatoes before frying. About 165 calories per serving.

POTATOES ANNA

One of the great classic potato recipes, this one is said to have been created by a lovesick French chef in honor of a beautiful lady named Anna.
Makes 6 servings

⅓ cup clarified butter*
5 large potatoes (the baking varieties won't work)
1½ teaspoons salt mixed with ¼ teaspoon pepper

Preheat oven to 450° F. Brush a 9" ovenproof glass pie dish or shallow 1½-quart casserole with butter. (Glass is better because you can check on the final browning.) Peel potatoes and slice very thin, letting slices drop into cold water. Drain and measure potatoes (you should have 6 cups); pat dry on paper toweling. Arrange the most perfect slices in slightly overlapping concentric circles over the bottom of the pie dish, then add a row around the sides. Brush generously with butter and sprinkle with salt and pepper. Layer remaining slices the same way, brushing with butter and sprinkling with salt and pepper. You needn't be so artistic about the middle layers, but do make sure potatoes are well packed. Cover dish with foil, weight down with a heavy lid, and bake on center rack 50–55 minutes until potatoes are *just* tender. Uncover, reduce heat to 425° F., move dish to lowest rack, and bake 15–20 minutes until bottom slices turn amber-brown. Take from oven, let stand 4–5 minutes, then loosen sides and bottom with a spatula, trying not to disturb the design. Invert on a heated platter and ease out potatoes. (If any should stick to the dish, simply lift out and replace in design.) Cut in wedges and serve. About 180 calories per serving.

VARIATIONS:

– Sprinkle a little finely grated Parmesan cheese between potato layers. About 195 calories per serving.

– Sprinkle a little minced fresh basil or chives between potato layers. About 180 calories per serving.

– Spread sautéed chopped onions between potatoes, using ½ cup in all. About 190 calories per serving.

¢ BOILED NEW POTATOES

Really fresh new potatoes, those dug in the spring or early summer, will cook faster than those that have been in storage. The not so new sometimes take as long as an hour to become tender.

Makes 4 servings

12 medium-size new potatoes, scrubbed
3 cups boiling water
1 or 2 sprigs mint (optional)

Place all ingredients in a large saucepan, cover, and boil gently 30–45 minutes until fork tender. Drain, discarding mint, if used, and serve potatoes in or out of their skins with butter, salt, and freshly ground pepper. About 90 calories per serving (without butter).

VARIATIONS:

¢ **Parsleyed New Potatoes:** Just before serving, peel potatoes, roll in ¼ cup melted butter, then in ¼ cup minced parsley. About 190 calories per serving.

¢ **Herbed New Potatoes:** Certain fresh herbs—chives, dill, basil, marjoram—go beautifully with new potatoes. Simply roll the boiled, peeled potatoes in ¼ cup melted butter, then in 2 tablespoons minced herbs. About 190 calories per serving.

¢ **Lemon-Glazed New Potatoes:** When potatoes are tender, peel, then warm 10–12 minutes in a heavy skillet over low heat with ¼ cup firmly packed light brown sugar and 2 tablespoons each butter, water, and lemon juice, basting constantly to glaze. About 190 calories per serving.

NEW POTATOES IN DILL SAUCE

Makes 4 servings

16 small new potatoes, boiled in their skins

VEGETABLES

Sauce:

3 tablespoons unsalted butter
2 tablespoons minced fresh dill
2 tablespoons flour
1 cup light cream
¾ teaspoon salt
⅛ teaspoon white pepper

Drain potatoes, peel, return to pan, and keep warm. Melt butter in a small saucepan over moderate heat, add dill, and heat, stirring, 1–2 minutes. Blend in flour, then add cream, salt, and pepper and heat, stirring constantly, about 5 minutes until thickened and smooth. Pour sauce over potatoes, set over lowest heat, and warm uncovered, stirring occasionally, 10–12 minutes. About 305 calories per serving.

DANISH-STYLE NEW POTATOES

Delectable! Young new potatoes in a buttery, brown sugar glaze.

Makes 6–8 servings

18 medium-size new potatoes, boiled in their skins

Glaze:
½ cup firmly packed light brown sugar
¼ cup water
2 tablespoons butter or margarine
1 teaspoon salt
2 tablespoons minced fresh dill

Drain potatoes and let cool 10 minutes. Meanwhile, heat all glaze ingredients except dill in a large, heavy skillet over moderate heat, stirring, 5–8 minutes until slightly thickened and bubbly. Reduce heat to low and stir in dill. Peel potatoes, add to skillet, and warm 10–15 minutes, rolling in glaze, until they glisten and are the color of topaz. About 255 calories for each of 6 servings, 190 calories for each of 8 servings.

SWEET POTATOES

It was Columbus who introduced America's sunny, honey sweet yams to Europe. Europeans apparently liked them from the start, because they were well established by the time Irish potatoes became acceptable.

To Prepare for Cooking: Scrub well; to preserve vitamins, cook in the skins.

¢ BOILED SWEET POTATOES OR YAMS

Makes 4 servings

4 medium-size sweet potatoes or yams
2 cups boiling water
1 teaspoon salt

Scrub potatoes well in cold water, cut off root end, and remove any bruised spots. Place in a large saucepan with water and salt, cover and boil 35–40 minutes until *just* tender (sweet potatoes tend to be mushy, so watch closely during the last 5–10 minutes). Drain and serve in or out of the skins with plenty of butter, salt, and pepper. About 150 calories per serving (without butter).

To Parboil for Use in Other Recipes: Boil as directed but reduce cooking time to 20 minutes.

VARIATIONS:

¢ **Mashed Sweet Potatoes:** Boil and drain by method above and peel. Mash with a potato masher or whip in an electric mixer. Beat in ¼ cup softened butter, 3 tablespoons honey, ¼ teaspoon each salt and mace, and a pinch pepper. About 270 calories per serving.

¢ **Orange-Flavored Mashed Sweet Potatoes:** Prepare mashed potatoes as directed above and beat in 2

Season	For Top Quality	Amount To Buy	Nutritive Value	Calories (unseasoned)
Year round	Choose firm, clean scar-free potatoes of uniform size.	1 potato per person; there are 2-3 per pound	Very high in vitamin A, some vitamin C	Very high— 150-70 per medium-size potato

tablespoons orange juice and 1 teaspoon grated orange rind along with other seasonings. About 270 calories per serving.

¢ **Maple-Flavored Mashed Sweet Potatoes:** Prepare and season mashed potatoes by basic method above, substituting maple syrup for honey and adding ¼ teaspoon vanilla. About 265 calories per serving.

¢ BAKED SWEET POTATOES OR YAMS

Makes 4 servings

4 medium-size sweet potatoes or yams

Preheat oven to 400° F. Scrub potatoes well in cold water but do not peel. Bake directly on oven rack or in a shallow baking pan 45 minutes to 1 hour or until tender. Serve piping hot with lots of butter, salt, and pepper. About 150 calories per serving (without butter).

VARIATION:

To Charcoal Bake: Wrap in foil and bake as directed for Irish potatoes.* About 150 calories per serving (without butter).

ORANGE-CANDIED SWEET POTATOES OR YAMS

Makes 4 servings

2 tablespoons butter or margarine
½ cup firmly packed dark brown sugar
¼ cup orange juice
1 teaspoon finely grated orange rind
4 medium-size sweet potatoes or yams, parboiled, peeled, and halved
1 navel orange, peeled and sectioned (garnish)

Heat butter, sugar, orange juice and rind, uncovered, in a very large, heavy skillet over moderately low heat, stirring occasionally, until sugar dissolves. Add potatoes and simmer, uncovered, 10-15 minutes, basting and turning to glaze evenly. Transfer to serving dish and keep warm. Warm orange sections in skillet 2-3 minutes, garnish potatoes, and serve. About 330 calories per serving.

VARIATION:

Substitute 1 (1-pound 8-ounce) can sweet potatoes or yams, drained, for the fresh and simmer 8-10 minutes to glaze. About 330 calories per serving.

SWEET POTATO CAKES

Nice and spicy. Delicious with baked ham.
Makes 6 servings

3 medium-size sweet potatoes, boiled and peeled
¼ cup milk
¼ cup melted butter or margarine
3 eggs
1 teaspoon baking powder
½ teaspoon ginger
¼ teaspoon cinnamon
⅛ teaspoon mace

½ teaspoon salt
Pinch pepper
¼ cup cooking oil

Mash potatoes, mix in all remaining ingredients except oil, and beat until fluffy. Heat 2 tablespoons oil in a large, heavy skillet 1–2 minutes over moderately high heat, then drop in potato mixture by the tablespoon and brown 2–3 minutes (don't try to do more than 4 or 5 cakes at a time). Using a pancake turner, turn cakes gently, flatten slightly, and brown the flip side 2–3 minutes. Keep warm in a 250° F. oven while you do the rest. Fry remaining cakes in the same way, adding more oil to the skillet as needed. Serve piping hot. About 225 calories per serving.

SWEET POTATO PUFF

Makes 6–8 servings

4 medium-size sweet potatoes, boiled and peeled
½ cup melted butter or margarine
⅓ cup milk
3 tablespoons honey or maple syrup
4 eggs
Juice and grated rind of 1 orange
1 teaspoon baking powder
½ teaspoon cinnamon
½ teaspoon cardamom
¼ teaspoon mace
¼ teaspoon salt

Preheat oven to 350° F. Mash potatoes well, mix in all remaining ingredients, and beat until fluffy. Spoon into a lightly buttered 2-quart casserole and bake, uncovered, about 45 minutes until puffy and lightly browned. About 330 calories for each of 6 servings, 250 calories for each of 8 servings.

VARIATION:

Marshmallow-Frosted Sweet Potato Puff: Stud casserole with marshmallows, then bake as directed, reducing cooking time to about 30 minutes so marshmallows are just nicely tinged with brown. About 350 calories for each of 6 servings, 265 calories for each of 8 servings.

YAM, APPLE, AND RAISIN CASSEROLE

Makes 4–6 servings

4 medium-size yams, peeled and sliced ½" thick
2 apples (McIntosh, Baldwin, or Jonathan), peeled, cored, and cut in ¼" rings
½ cup seedless raisins
½ teaspoon salt
½ cup firmly packed light or dark brown sugar
¼ cup butter or margarine
1 cup soft white bread crumbs
2 tablespoons melted butter or margarine

Preheat oven to 375° F. Layer yams, apples, and raisins into a buttered 2-quart casserole, sprinkling with salt as you go. Top with sugar and dot with butter. Cover and bake 50 minutes until yams are tender, basting once or twice. Mix crumbs and melted butter and scatter over yams. Bake, uncovered, 10 minutes to brown lightly. About 530 calories for each of 4 servings, 355 calories for each of 6 servings.

YAM-PECAN SOUFFLÉ

Makes 6 servings

2 teaspoons cornstarch
⅔ cup pineapple or orange juice
¼ cup firmly packed light brown sugar
4 eggs, separated
1 (1-pound 8-ounce) can yams, drained and mashed
1 teaspoon salt
⅛ teaspoon pepper
¼ cup finely chopped pecans

Preheat oven to 375° F. Blend cornstarch with ⅓ cup fruit juice in a small saucepan, add remaining juice and the brown sugar. Cook and stir 2–3 minutes over moderate heat until mixture boils and thickens. Beat egg yolks lightly, mix in a little of the hot fruit sauce, then return all to pan. Heat, stirring, 1–2 minutes but do not allow to boil. Mix sauce into yams, then add salt, pepper, and pecans. Beat egg whites until firm peaks form and fold into yams. Spoon into an ungreased 1½-quart soufflé dish and bake, uncovered, on center oven rack 40–45 minutes until puffed and golden. Rush to the table and serve. About 235 calories per serving.

VARIATION:

Dessert Yam-Pecan Soufflé: Double the amount of light brown sugar, omit salt and pepper, then proceed as recipe directs. Top with sweetened whipped cream flavored with a little grated orange rind or slivered crystallized ginger. About 320 calories per serving (including 2 tablespoons sweetened whipped cream to top).

PUMPKIN

When baked or boiled and served with butter or smoky-flavored bacon drippings, pumpkin fills that need for a different vegetable.

To Prepare for Cooking: How you plan to cook the pumpkin determines what should be done with it. Small pumpkins, for example, can be baked whole, in which case you need only cut a circle around the stem, making a "lid," and scoop out seeds and pulp. Pumpkins to be boiled should be cut into 2–3" chunks or strips and peeled.

BOILED PUMPKIN

Makes 4 servings

1 (3–4-pound) ripe pumpkin, cut in 2–3" chunks or strips and peeled
1 quart boiling water
1½ teaspoons salt
Pinch pepper
2–3 tablespoons butter or margarine

Place pumpkin, water, and salt in a saucepan, cover, and boil gently 25–30 minutes until fork tender. Drain, add pepper and butter, and serve. About 110 calories per serving.

To Parboil for Use in Other Recipes: Boil as directed but reduce cooking time to 15 minutes; omit seasonings.

To Steam: Place pumpkin chunks or strips in a steamer over rapidly boiling water, cover, and steam 30–35 minutes until fork tender. Season and serve. About 110 calories per serving.

VARIATIONS:

Mashed Pumpkin: Boil and drain as directed, then mash. Heat, un-

Season	For Top Quality	Amount To Buy	Nutritive Value	Calories (unseasoned)
Autumn	Choose small, firm, bright orange pumpkins, 6–7" in diameter, that seem heavy for their size.	1 pound raw pumpkin yields 1 cup cooked pumpkin or 1 serving.	High in vitamin A	Moderate —about 75 per cup

covered, over low heat, shaking pan now and then, 3–5 minutes to drive off excess moisture. Add pepper and butter and, if you like, 2–3 tablespoons heavy cream; mix well or beat until fluffy with an electric mixer. Also good with a little brown sugar or honey added. About 135 calories per serving (without cream, brown sugar or honey).

Pumpkin au Gratin: Prepare Mashed Pumpkin as directed, spoon into a buttered 1½-quart casserole, and top with ½ cup grated Parmesan cheese mixed with ½ cup dry white bread crumbs; drizzle with 2–3 tablespoons melted butter. Bake, uncovered, 25–30 minutes at 400° F. until golden. About 255 calories per serving.

Pumpkin and Potatoes: Mix equal parts seasoned mashed pumpkin and seasoned mashed potatoes, spoon into a buttered casserole, roughen top with a fork, and broil 5″ from heat 2 minutes until browned. Recipe too flexible for a meaningful calorie count.

BAKED WHOLE PUMPKIN

Makes 4–6 servings

1 (4-pound) ripe pumpkin
1 teaspoon salt
⅛ teaspoon pepper
3 tablespoons melted butter or margarine

Preheat oven to 375° F. Cut a 3″ circle around stem, remove and save to use as a "lid." Scoop out seeds and strings and sprinkle inside of pumpkin evenly with salt and pepper. Place pumpkin on an ungreased baking sheet and set lid on tray skin side down. Bake, uncovered, 1–1½ hours until fork tender; test lid for doneness after ¾ hour, remove if tender and set aside, otherwise continue cooking. When pumpkin is tender, remove liquid inside with a bulb baster. Using a pancake turner, lift to a large platter, pour in butter, and cover with lid. Carry to table and carve in wedges, serving skin and all. About 160 calories for each of 4 servings, 105 calories for each of 6 servings.

VARIATIONS:

Foil-Baked Pumpkin: Cut pumpkin into pieces about 4″ square; remove strings and seeds but do not peel. Sprinkle each piece with salt and pepper, dot with butter, and wrap in foil. Place on a baking sheet and bake 1–1½ hours at 375° F. until fork tender. Partially unwrap and serve each portion as you would a baked potato with extra butter, salt, and pepper. Recipe too flexible for a meaningful calorie count.

New England Baked Pumpkin: Prepare Foil-Baked Pumpkin as directed, substituting bacon drippings for butter and sprinkling each piece with 1–2 teaspoons maple or dark brown sugar and, if you like, a little cinnamon, nutmeg, and/or orange juice. Serve topped with crisply cooked crumbled bacon or diced salt pork. Recipe too flexible for a meaningful calorie count.

PUMPKIN PURÉE

Use in Pumpkin Pie or any recipe calling for pumpkin purée.
Makes about 1 quart

1 (6–7-pound) ripe pumpkin
¼ teaspoon salt

Preheat oven to 375° F. Halve pumpkin crosswise and scoop out seeds and strings. Place halves in a large baking pan, hollow side down, and bake uncovered 1½–2 hours until fork tender. Remove from oven and cool. Scrape pulp from shells and purée in an electric blender, a little at a time, or put through a food mill. Mix in salt. About 75 calories per cup.

PUMPKIN AND ONION CASSEROLE

Makes 4–6 servings

3 medium-size yellow onions, peeled, sliced thin, and separated into rings
3 tablespoons bacon drippings
1 (3–4-pound) ripe pumpkin, cut in 1" cubes, peeled, parboiled, and drained
½ teaspoon salt
⅛ teaspoon pepper
2 teaspoons minced parsley

Preheat oven to 375° F. Stir-fry onions in drippings over moderate heat 3–5 minutes until limp, not brown. Layer pumpkin and onions (include drippings) in an ungreased 1½-quart casserole, seasoning with salt and pepper as you go. Cover and bake 1 hour. Uncover, sprinkle with parsley, and serve. About 195 calories for each of 4 servings, 130 calories for each of 6 servings.

RUTABAGA

Rutabagas aren't just big yellow turnips but a distinct species altogether. Botanists believe they're a hybrid of turnips and cabbage and that they originated in Russia only about 250 years ago.

To Prepare for Cooking: Peel (rutabagas are dipped in melted paraffin before shipping so they'll stay fresh longer), then cut in 1" cubes or strips for easier handling. Rutabagas are often extremely hard, so use your sharpest knife and cut carefully.

¢ BOILED RUTABAGA

Makes 4 servings

1 medium-size rutabaga, prepared for cooking
1½ cups boiling water
1½ teaspoons salt
⅛ teaspoon pepper
3–4 tablespoons butter or margarine

Place rutabaga in a large saucepan with water and salt, cover, and boil 20–30 minutes until tender. Drain well, add pepper and butter, set over low heat and warm, shaking pan, until butter melts. Toss to mix and serve. About 150 calories per serving.

To Parboil for Use in Other Recipes: Boil by method above but reduce cooking time to 12–15 minutes; omit seasonings.

VARIATIONS:

⚖ ¢ **Low-Calorie Rutabaga:** Boil and drain as directed but substitute seasoned salt for salt. Omit butter and sprinkle with mace. About 75 calories per serving.

¢ **Mashed Rutabaga:** Boil, drain, and season as directed, then mash

Season	For Top Quality	Amount To Buy	Nutritive Value	Calories (unseasoned)
Year round; peak months: October and November	Choose firm, fairly smooth, 2- or 3-pound rutabagas with few leaf scars around the crown.	Figure ½ pound rutabaga per serving.	High in vitamin C, fairly high in vitamin A and iron	Moderate— about 75 per ½ pound serving

with a potato masher. Heat, stirring, 2–3 minutes to dry off excess moisture and serve. About 150 calories per serving.

¢ **Cottage-Style Rutabaga:** Boil 1 peeled, cubed potato and 1 peeled, sliced carrot with rutabaga. Drain, season as directed, and mash. About 180 calories per serving.

Rutabaga au Gratin: Boil and drain but do not season. Mix with 1½ cups hot Cheese Sauce and spoon into an ungreased 2-quart *au gratin* dish. Top with ⅓ cup grated sharp Cheddar cheese and broil 5" from heat 3–4 minutes until bubbly. About 335 calories per serving.

Rutabaga with Bacon and Sour Cream: Boil, drain, and season as directed. Stir in ½ cup sour cream and 4 slices cooked, crumbled bacon and serve. About 260 calories per serving.

¢ **HASHED BROWN RUTABAGA**

Makes 6–8 servings

3 tablespoons butter or margarine
1 medium-size rutabaga, boiled and mashed
2 cups hot seasoned mashed potatoes
2 tablespoons grated yellow onion

Melt butter in a large, heavy skillet over moderate heat. Mix rutabaga, potatoes, and onion, spoon into skillet, and pat down with a pancake turner. Brown bottom slowly about 5–7 minutes. Stir to distribute brown bits throughout, pat down again, and brown as before. Using a pancake turner, scoop into a heated vegetable dish, turning so that browned parts are on top. About 160 calories for each of 6 servings, 120 calories for each of 8 servings.

SCALLOPED RUTABAGA AND APPLES

Makes 6 servings

1 medium-size rutabaga, quartered and peeled
3 apples (Baldwin, McIntosh, or Jonathan), peeled, cored, and sliced thin
¼ cup butter or margarine
1½ teaspoons salt
⅛ teaspoon pepper
¼ cup firmly packed light brown sugar
1½ cups water

Preheat oven to 400° F. Halve rutabaga quarters lengthwise, then cut crosswise into slices ⅛" thick. Arrange ½ the slices in a buttered 2-quart flameproof casserole and top with apples. Dot with ½ the butter and sprinkle with ½ the salt, pepper, and sugar. Top with remaining rutabaga, butter, salt, pepper, and sugar. Pour water over all, cover, set over high heat until mixture boils, then transfer to oven and bake 1 hour. Stir gently and bake, uncovered, 20–30 minutes longer until almost all liquid is gone. About 185 calories per serving.

SALSIFY

(Also called Oyster Plant)

Once fairly popular, salsify now falls into the category of "forgotten vegetables." Too bad, because it has a pleasing, delicate flavor. Some people think it tastes like oysters (hence its nickname), others insist it's more like artichokes. Actually, there are two kinds of salsify, the common, or white skinned, and the rarer, more delicate black salsify. Both are prepared exactly the same way.

To Prepare for Cooking: Remove tops and upper part of roots that

Season	For Top Quality	Amount To Buy	Nutritive Value	Calories (*unseasoned*)
Summer, fall, and winter	Choose firm roots the size and shape of small carrots.	Allow 3 roots (⅓–½ pound) per person.	Some minerals	Moderate —85–90 per average serving

look to have been wound with cord. Scrub roots with a vegetable brush in cold water. Peel roots, 1 at a time, and cut into 2″ chunks, letting them fall into acidulated water (1 quart cold water mixed with the juice of 1 lemon) to keep them from turning brown. When all roots are prepared, soak 10 minutes longer in acidulated water.

BOILED SALSIFY

Makes 4 servings

2 bunches salsify, prepared for cooking
1½ cups boiling water
2 tablespoons butter or margarine
½ teaspoon salt
Pinch pepper

Place salsify in a saucepan with water, cover, and boil 20–25 minutes until tender. Drain, add butter, salt, and pepper, set over low heat, and warm uncovered, shaking pan gently, 2–3 minutes until butter melts. About 140 calories per serving.

To Parboil for Use in Other Recipes: Boil as directed but reduce cooking time to 15 minutes; omit seasonings.

VARIATIONS:

Herbed Salsify: Prepare as directed, adding 1 tablespoon each minced parsley and chives along with butter, salt, and pepper. About 140 calories per serving.

Salsify with Dill and Sour Cream: Prepare as directed, adding ¼ cup sour cream and 2 tablespoons minced dill along with butter, salt, and pepper. About 195 calories per serving.

Creamed Salsify: Boil and drain as directed but do not season; mix with 1½ cups hot Medium White Sauce, season to taste with salt and white pepper, and warm uncovered over low heat, stirring occasionally, 5 minutes to blend flavors. About 245 calories per serving.

SORREL

(Also called Sour Dock and Patience)

Most of us find these crisp leaves too bitter to eat alone (except when puréed into sorrel soup), so we toss the youngest leaves into salads to add refreshing bite and steam the older with spinach—just a handful—to add character.

To Prepare: Wash by plunging up and down in a sinkful of tepid water; drain.

To Steam: Place sorrel in an enamel, stainless-steel, or teflon-lined pot, add no water, cover, and steam over moderate heat 10–15 minutes until tender. Toss with melted butter or bacon drippings, season to taste with salt and pepper.

To Steam with Spinach: Use 1 part sorrel to 3 parts spinach and steam following the recipe for Steamed Spinach.

VEGETABLES

Season	For Top Quality	Amount To Buy	Nutritive Value	Calories (unseasoned)
Year round	Choose young, tender, crisp leaves about 2–3" long.	¼–½ pound per person, depending on whether sorrel is to be served alone or mixed with other greens.	High in vitamins A and C	Low—about 40 per cup

SPINACH

"Many English people that have learned it of the Dutch," wrote a seventeenth-century British herbalist, "doe stew the herbe in a pot without any other moisture than its owne and after the moisture is a little pressed from it, they put butter and a little spice unto it, and make therewith a dish that many delight to eate of." The "herbe" was spinach and we haven't found a better way to cook it today, whether it's crinkly or plain leafed or that supermarket newcomer, New Zealand spinach. It, by the way, isn't spinach at all; we include it here because it's best when cooked like spinach.

To Prepare for Cooking:

Bulk Spinach: Sort, removing any blemished leaves; trim off roots and coarse stems. Wash leaves by plunging up and down in a sinkful of tepid water (this helps float out sand) and rinse several times in cool water. Lift from rinse water, shake lightly, and place directly in cooking pot.

Bagged Spinach: Remove coarse stems and deteriorating leaves; rinse well.

Cooking Tip: Always cook spinach in an enamel, stainless-steel, or teflon-lined pot so it will not darken or taste of metal.

Season	For Top Quality	Amount To Buy	Nutritive Value	Calories (unseasoned)
Year round for spinach; peak months: March–July; spring and early summer for New Zealand spinach	Buy loose or bulk spinach if possible and choose crisp, dark green moist leaves with roots attached. If buying prewashed, bagged spinach, make sure it's not wilted, slimy, or dry.	½ pound bulk spinach per person; 1 (10-ounce) bag serves 2.	Very high in vitamin A; high in iron and vitamin C	Low—about 40 per cup

STEAMED SPINACH

Makes 4 servings

2 pounds bulk spinach or 2 (10-ounce) bags prewashed spinach, prepared for cooking
3 tablespoons melted butter or margarine
1 teaspoon salt
⅛ teaspoon pepper

Place spinach in a large pot, add no water, cover, and steam 3–5 minutes over moderate heat until slightly wilted but still bright green. Drain, add seasonings, and toss to mix. About 115 calories per serving.

VARIATIONS:

To Serve Cold: Steam as directed but do not drain or season; cool, then cover and chill (see Vegetable Seasoning Chart for dressing ideas). Drain before dressing.

Low-Calorie Spinach: Steam and drain as directed but omit butter. Dress with 3 tablespoons lemon juice or low-calorie Italian dressing. About 40 calories per serving.

Chopped Spinach: Chop steamed, drained spinach and toss with butter, salt, and pepper. About 115 calories per serving.

Puréed Spinach: Purée steamed, *undrained* spinach in an electric blender at high speed or put through a food mill. Return to pan, add seasonings, cover, and warm, stirring occasionally, 3–4 minutes. About 115 calories per serving.

Italian-Style Spinach: Steam and drain as directed; omit butter and dress with 3 tablespoons olive oil; if you like, toss in ¼ crushed clove garlic. About 135 calories per serving.

Spinach with Bacon: Steam and drain as directed; omit butter and toss with 2 tablespoons bacon drippings and ¼ cup crisp crumbled bacon. About 115 calories per serving.

Creamed Spinach: Steam as directed; drain in a fine sieve, pressing as dry as possible, chop fine, and return to pan. Add 1 cup hot Medium White Sauce and warm, uncovered, over low heat, stirring occasionally, 3–5 minutes. About 140 calories per serving.

Spinach au Gratin: Steam as directed; drain in a fine sieve, pressing as dry as possible, chop fine, and return to pan. Mix with 1 cup hot Cheese Sauce, place in an ungreased 1-quart casserole, top with ½ cup grated Cheddar cheese mixed with ½ cup coarse dry bread crumbs, and broil 4–5″ from heat 2–3 minutes to brown. About 280 calories per serving.

SPINACH RING

A showy way to shape spinach for a special dinner.

Makes 6 servings

7 (10-ounce) packages frozen chopped spinach, cooked by package directions
3 tablespoons butter or margarine
1 teaspoon salt
⅛ teaspoon pepper
⅛ teaspoon nutmeg

Drain spinach in a strainer, pressing as dry as possible. Mix with remaining ingredients. Pack *tightly* in a lightly buttered 1-quart ring mold, then invert at once on a hot platter. If you like, fill center with hot Creamed Mushrooms or a small bowl of sauce (see Vegetable Seasoning Chart). About 110 calories per serving (unfilled).

VARIATION:

Baked Spinach Ring: Drain spinach as directed, mix in 2 lightly beaten eggs and all seasonings called for. Pack into mold and bake, uncovered, in a water bath at 350° F. 30–40 minutes until firm. Loosen edges, invert, and serve. About 140 calories per serving.

⊠ CURRIED SPINACH

Exotic and easy.

Makes 4 servings

2 (10-ounce) packages frozen chopped spinach, cooked by package directions and drained well
1 tablespoon butter or margarine
2 tablespoons sour cream
2 teaspoons curry powder
⅛ teaspoon nutmeg
½ teaspoon salt
Pinch pepper

Keep spinach warm. In a separate small saucepan, melt butter over low heat. Blend in remaining ingredients, pour over spinach, toss well to mix, and serve. About 80 calories per serving.

⊠ SPINACH DRESSED WITH OIL AND VINEGAR

The Italian way to season spinach. And very good, too.

Makes 4 servings

¼ cup olive oil
2 (10-ounce) packages frozen leaf spinach (do not thaw)
1 clove garlic, peeled and crushed
3 tablespoons cider vinegar
½ teaspoon salt
Pinch pepper

Place olive oil, spinach, and garlic in a saucepan and simmer, uncovered, about 15 minutes until spinach is heated through. Stir from time to time, breaking up any frozen chunks. Remove from heat, add remaining ingredients, and toss well to mix. Serve hot or at room temperature. About 165 calories per serving.

SPINACH BAKED WITH MUSHROOMS

Makes 4–6 servings

2 pounds fresh spinach, steamed, or 2 (10-ounce) packages frozen chopped spinach, cooked by package directions
⅔ cup light cream
½ teaspoon salt
Pinch pepper
3 tablespoons butter or margarine
½ pound mushrooms, wiped clean and sliced thin

Topping:
2 tablespoons butter or margarine
1 cup coarse dry white bread crumbs
¼ cup coarsely chopped toasted, blanched almonds

Preheat oven to 375° F. Drain spinach in a sieve, pressing as dry as possible. If using fresh spinach, chop fine. Mix spinach with cream, salt, and pepper. Melt butter in a skillet over moderately high heat, add mushrooms, and sauté 2–3 minutes until golden. Mix mushrooms and spinach, then spoon into a buttered 1-quart casserole. For the topping, melt butter in a small saucepan over moderate heat, stir in crumbs, and brown lightly 1–2 minutes. Add almonds, toss to mix, and sprinkle over spinach. Bake, uncovered, 20–30 minutes until lightly browned. About 355 calories for each of 4 servings, 235 calories for each of 6 servings.

SPINACH-ONION-SOUR CREAM BAKE

Makes 4 servings

2 tablespoons butter or margarine
1 medium-size yellow onion, peeled and minced

2 (*10-ounce*) *packages frozen chopped spinach* (do not thaw)
¼ *teaspoon mace*
1 *teaspoon salt*
⅛ *teaspoon pepper*
1 *cup sour cream*

Preheat oven to 325° F. Melt butter in a large saucepan over moderate heat, add onion, and stir-fry 5–8 minutes until pale golden. Add spinach, mace, salt, and pepper, cover, and simmer 15 minutes. Uncover, break up any frozen chunks, and simmer uncovered 10 minutes longer until all moisture has evaporated. Mix in sour cream. Spoon into an unbuttered 9″ piepan, bake uncovered ½ hour, and serve. About 220 calories per serving.

SPINACH CUSTARDS

These custards are especially good with cold baked ham.

Makes 2 servings

1 (*10-ounce*) *package frozen chopped spinach, cooked by package directions*
¼ *teaspoon cornstarch*
½ *cup milk*
½ *teaspoon salt*
2 *eggs, lightly beaten*
1 *tablespoon finely grated yellow onion*
1 *tablespoon finely chopped pimiento* (*optional*)

Preheat oven to 375° F. Drain spinach in a fine sieve, pressing as dry as possible. Chop very fine, then return to saucepan and set over low heat to dry, 1–2 minutes. Remove from heat and set aside. Blend cornstarch with 1 tablespoon milk and mix into spinach along with all remaining ingredients including remaining milk. Ladle into 2 well-buttered custard cups, set in a shallow baking pan, and pour hot water into pan to a depth of about 1″. Bake, uncovered, on center oven rack 30–35 minutes until a knife inserted near the center of a custard comes out clean. Remove cups from water bath and cool 3–5 minutes. Serve in cups or, if you prefer, loosen edges with a spatula and invert to unmold. About 165 calories per serving.

SQUASH

No American Indian food seems to have impressed Europeans more than squash, perhaps because there are so many varieties of it. Fortunately they can be classified as either *summer* or *winter squash*. Our word "squash," incidentally, comes from the Indian *"askutasquash,"* meaning "green thing eaten green."

The Three Kinds of Summer Squash

These tender skinned, delicately flavored squash take equally well to saucepan, skillet, or oven. Most can be used interchangeably for one another.

Season	For Top Quality	Amount To Buy	Nutritive Value	Calories (unseasoned)
Year round for all three types	Choose firm, tender skinned, blemish-free squash that are heavy for their size.	½ pound per person	Some vitamins A and C	Very low—about 30 per cup

VEGETABLES

Yellow Squash: There are two types, the *crookneck* and the slightly plumper *straightneck*. Both are sunny yellow outside, pale and succulent inside. About 2–4 per pound.

Pattypan (also called *cymling*): Flat, round, pale green squash with scalloped edges. They can be small as a biscuit or big as a pie. The large may weigh 1–2 pounds; the small a fraction of that.

Zucchini (also called *courgette*): This isn't one squash but three, all green skinned and white fleshed. The one called *zucchini* is cucumber-sized with dark lacy stripes. The other two are the slimmer yellow and green striped *cocozelle*, and the more rounded *caserta* with two-tone green stripes. About 2–4 per pound.

To Prepare for Cooking:

Yellow Squash and Zucchini: Cut off ends and scrub well; peel only if skins are old. If young and tender leave whole; otherwise cut in ½" slices, or halve and seed.

Pattypan: Wash in cool water, peel, seed, and cut in ½" cubes.

Four Favorite Winter Squash

These hard-skinned varieties are best when boiled and mashed or baked in the skins.

Acorn Squash: Not much bigger than a large avocado, these are small enough to handle easily. Usually green, but sometimes orange, they're moist and tender. About 1–2 pounds each.

Butternut: A large pear-shaped squash with thin, fawn-colored skin and fine, bright orange flesh. About 2–3 pounds each.

Buttercup: Smallish, turban-shaped, green- and gray-striped squash with faintly sweet orange flesh. About 2 pounds each.

Hubbard: A rough, tough, green or orange skinned giant often sold by the chunk. It is drier and stringier than smaller squash.

To Prepare for Boiling: Halve, scoop out seeds and pulp; peel and cut in 1–2" chunks. Work slowly and carefully because squash are hard and their skins slippery. *To Prepare for Baking:* If very small, leave whole; otherwise halve lengthwise and remove seeds and pulp. If extra large, quarter or cut in sixths or eighths. Do not peel. When squash are baked whole, halve and seed before serving.

Some Lesser Lights: In addition to the winter squash above, there are others, most of them used as decoration because they're not very moist or tender. Still, if cooked like Hubbard squash, they can be palatable. These varieties are: Warren Turban, Delicious, Marblehead, Boston Marrow, Cushaw

Season	For Top Quality	Amount To Buy	Nutritive Value	Calories (unseasoned)
Year round for acorn squash; fall and winter for the others	Choose heavy squash with hard, clean unblemished skins.	½ pound per person	Very high in vitamin A, some vitamin C and iron	Very high—about 130 per cup

BOILED SUMMER SQUASH

Makes 4 servings

2 pounds summer squash (yellow, pattypan, or zucchini), prepared for cooking
1 teaspoon salt
½ cup boiling water
⅛ teaspoon pepper
3 tablespoons butter or margarine

Place squash in a large saucepan, add salt and water, cover, and boil until crisp-tender—10–15 minutes for slices or cubes, 20–25 for halves, 30–40 for whole squash. Drain well, return to pan, and warm uncovered, shaking pan occasionally, 2–3 minutes to drive off moisture. Season with pepper and butter and serve. About 105 calories per serving.

To Steam: Place prepared squash in a steamer over boiling water, cover, and steam, using times above as a guide. Remove from steamer and season with salt, pepper, and butter. About 105 calories per serving.

To Parboil for Use in Other Recipes: Boil or steam as directed, reducing cooking time to 5 minutes for slices or cubes, 10–15 for halves, 15–20 for whole squash. Omit seasonings.

VARIATIONS:

To Serve Cold: Slice or cube; boil and drain as directed. Chill in ice water, drain, mix with dressing (see Vegetable Seasoning Chart for ideas), and chill until ready to serve.

⚖ **Low-Calorie Squash:** Boil and drain as directed but omit butter. Dress with low-calorie herb, garlic, or Italian dressing. About 35 calories per serving.

Squash and Carrots: Combine equal amounts sliced boiled carrots and squash, season as directed, then stir in 1 teaspoon minced fresh mint or basil. About 120 calories per serving.

Squash and Scallions: Cook 4–6 minced scallions with squash and season as directed. About 110 calories per serving.

Italian-Style Zucchini: Cook 1 clove peeled, halved garlic with zucchini and dress with 2 tablespoons olive oil and 1 tablespoon red wine vinegar instead of butter. About 95 calories per serving.

SKILLET SQUASH AND ONIONS

Makes 4 servings

3 tablespoons butter, margarine, or olive oil
2 pounds yellow squash or zucchini, scrubbed and sliced ½" thick
3 medium-size yellow onions, peeled and sliced ¼" thick
1 teaspoon salt
¼ teaspoon summer savory
¼ teaspoon oregano
⅛ teaspoon nutmeg
⅛ teaspoon pepper

Heat butter or oil over low heat in a large skillet 1–2 minutes. Add remaining ingredients and stir gently to mix. Cover and cook over low heat, stirring occasionally, 30–35 minutes until squash is fork tender. About 135 calories per serving.

SCALLOPED SUMMER SQUASH

Makes 4 servings

2 pounds summer squash, boiled
3 tablespoons butter or margarine
3 tablespoons grated yellow onion
¾ teaspoon salt
⅛ teaspoon pepper

Topping:
½ cup fine cracker crumbs mixed with 1 tablespoon melted butter or margarine

Preheat oven to 350° F. Drain squash well and mash with a potato masher. Mix in all remaining ingredients except topping. Spoon into a buttered shallow 1½-quart casserole and top with buttered crumbs. Bake, uncovered, 25–30 minutes until lightly browned. About 170 calories per serving.

PARMESAN STUFFED SQUASH

Good for a party because the squash can be prepared well ahead of time.

Makes 4–6 servings

6 *medium-size zucchini or yellow squash, halved and parboiled*
1½ *teaspoons salt*
¼ *teaspoon pepper*
¼ *cup butter or margarine*
½ *cup finely chopped yellow onion*
3 *cups soft bread crumbs*
⅛ *teaspoon paprika*
½ *cup grated Parmesan cheese*
1 *tablespoon minced parsley*

Scoop out squash halves, leaving shells ¼" thick; discard seedy centers. Sprinkle with 1 teaspoon salt and the pepper; arrange in a lightly buttered 13"×9"×2" pan. Preheat oven to 425° F. Melt butter in a skillet over moderate heat, add onion, and sauté 8 minutes until golden. Remove from heat and mix in all remaining ingredients including remaining ½ teaspoon salt. Stuff shells with crumb mixture. (*Note:* You may prepare recipe to this point early in the day; cool, cover, and chill. Bring to room temperature before proceeding.) Bake, uncovered, 20–30 minutes until crumbs are lightly browned and squash tender. About 300 calories for each of 4 servings, 200 calories for each of 6 servings.

BAKED YELLOW SQUASH PUDDING

Makes 6–8 servings

4 *pounds yellow squash, scrubbed and sliced ¼" thick*
3 *medium-size yellow onions, peeled and cut in thin wedges*
¼ *cup boiling water*
¼ *cup butter or margarine*
¼ *teaspoon thyme*
⅛ *teaspoon rosemary*
⅛ *teaspoon nutmeg*
1 *teaspoon salt*
⅛ *teaspoon pepper*
1 *tablespoon light brown sugar*
¼ *cup minced parsley*

Preheat oven to 350° F. Place squash, onions, water, and butter in a large kettle, cover, and simmer 25–30 minutes until squash is mushy. Uncover and simmer 10 minutes longer, mashing large pieces with a fork. Stir in all remaining ingredients. Transfer to a buttered 3-quart *au gratin* dish and bake, uncovered, 2½ hours until light caramel in color. About 135 calories for each of 6 servings, 100 calories for each of 8 servings.

YELLOW SQUASH AND CHIVE CHEESE AU GRATIN

Makes 6–8 servings

4 *pounds yellow squash, scrubbed and sliced 1" thick*
1 *(10½-ounce) can condensed beef consommé*
2 *tablespoons minced onion*
¼ *cup butter or margarine*
6 *(3-ounce) packages cream cheese with chives, softened to room temperature*
2 *tablespoons minced parsley*
2 *tablespoons minced fresh dill or*
½ *teaspoon dried dill*

Topping:
½ cup cracker meal mixed with
2 tablespoons melted butter or
margarine

Preheat oven to 375° F. Place squash, consommé, and minced onion in a large saucepan, cover, and simmer 15 minutes until squash is crisp-tender. Meanwhile, in a separate saucepan, heat butter and cheese over lowest heat, stirring, until melted and smooth. Stir in parsley and dill. When squash is done, drain consommé into cheese sauce and beat until smooth. Place squash in a buttered shallow 3-quart casserole and pour cheese sauce over all. Sprinkle topping over squash and bake, uncovered, 40 minutes until browned. About 450 calories for each of 6 servings, 335 calories for each of 8 servings.

BAKED ZUCCHINI WITH ROSEMARY

Makes 4–6 servings

2 pounds zucchini, scrubbed
2 cups boiling water
1 medium-size yellow onion, peeled and chopped fine
1 clove garlic, peeled and crushed
¼ cup olive oil
Juice of ½ lemon
3 tablespoons flour mixed with ¼ cup cold water
⅛ teaspoon rosemary
⅛ teaspoon summer savory
⅛ teaspoon nutmeg
1 teaspoon salt
⅛ teaspoon pepper
¼ cup grated Parmesan cheese
¼ cup minced parsley

Topping:
1½ cups soft white bread crumbs
2 tablespoons grated Parmesan cheese
⅓ cup melted butter or margarine

Preheat oven to 325° F. Quarter each zucchini by cutting in half lengthwise, then in half crosswise. Place in a large saucepan with boiling water, cover, and boil 15–20 minutes until crisp-tender. Drain, reserving 1 cup cooking water. Sauté onion and garlic in oil in a heavy skillet over moderate heat 8 minutes until onion is golden. Stir in cooking water and all remaining ingredients except cheese, parsley, and topping. Heat, stirring constantly, until thickened and smooth. Off heat, mix in cheese and parsley. Arrange half the zucchini in a buttered 8″×8″×2″ baking dish. Cover with half the sauce. Add remaining zucchini and sauce. Mix topping and sprinkle over surface. Bake, uncovered, about 1 hour until browned and bubbly. About 455 calories for each of 4 servings, 305 calories for each of 6 servings.

ZUCCHINI AND LEEK PUDDING-SOUFFLÉ

Half soufflé, half pudding, and one of the best ways we know to prepare zucchini.
Makes 4 servings

4 medium-size zucchini, scrubbed and coarsely grated
2 leeks or scallions, trimmed and sliced
3 shallots, peeled and minced
1 tablespoon olive oil
1½ teaspoons salt
¼ teaspoon marjoram
Pinch nutmeg
⅛ teaspoon freshly ground black pepper
2 tablespoons margarine
3 tablespoons flour
1 cup condensed beef consommé
2 tablespoons grated Parmesan cheese
2 egg yolks, lightly beaten

6 egg whites
⅛ teaspoon cream of tartar

Stir-fry zucchini, leeks, and shallots in olive oil with 1 teaspoon of the salt, the marjoram, nutmeg, and pepper in a large, heavy skillet over moderately high heat about 5 minutes until lightly golden. Reduce heat to lowest point and keep warm. Meanwhile, melt margarine in a small saucepan over moderate heat and blend in flour. Off heat, whisk in consommé, return to heat, and cook, stirring, 3–5 minutes until thickened and no raw flour taste remains. Remove from heat and mix in 1 tablespoon of the Parmesan, ¼ teaspoon of salt, and zucchini mixture. Whisk in egg yolks, place plastic wrap flat on top, and cool to room temperature. (*Note:* You may prepare recipe up to this point ahead of time and chill until about 2 hours before serving. Let sauce come to room temperature before proceeding.) Preheat oven to 375°. Butter a 1-quart soufflé dish, add remaining tablespoon of Parmesan, and tilt dish round and round to coat. Tap out excess cheese. Beat egg whites until frothy, add cream of tartar and remaining ¼ teaspoon salt, and beat until fairly stiff peaks form. Whisk about ¼ of the beaten whites into the zucchini mixture, then fold in remaining whites with a rubber spatula. Pour into prepared soufflé dish and bake, uncovered, on center oven rack 40–45 minutes until puffed and touched with brown. Serve at once. About 215 calories per serving.

ARMENIAN ZUCCHINI CUSTARD

Makes 4–6 servings

2 *pounds zucchini, scrubbed and coarsely grated*
1 *medium-size yellow onion, peeled and minced*
1 *clove garlic, peeled and crushed*
3 *tablespoons olive oil*
⅓ *cup minced parsley*
⅛ *teaspoon thyme*
⅛ *teaspoon rosemary*
1 *teaspoon salt*
⅛ *teaspoon pepper*
5 *eggs*
½ *cup sifted flour*
¾ *cup grated Parmesan cheese*

Preheat oven to 300° F. Stir-fry zucchini, onion, and garlic in oil in a large, heavy skillet over moderate heat 10–12 minutes until zucchini is tender. Mix in parsley, thyme, rosemary, salt, and pepper. Beat eggs until frothy, then mix in flour and Parmesan. Stir zucchini mixture into eggs, spoon into a buttered 1½-quart casserole, and bake uncovered 1–1¼ hours until a silver knife inserted in the center comes out clean. About 360 calories for each of 4 servings, 240 calories for each of 6 servings.

BOILED WINTER SQUASH

Makes 4 servings

2 *pounds winter squash (butternut, acorn, buttercup, or Hubbard), prepared for boiling*
1½ *cups boiling water*
1 *teaspoon salt*
Pinch pepper
2 *tablespoons butter or margarine*

Place squash, water, and salt in a saucepan, cover, and boil gently 15–20 minutes until fork tender. Drain, add pepper and butter, and serve. About 180 calories per serving.

To Parboil for Use in Other Recipes: Boil as directed, reducing cooking time to 10 minutes; omit seasonings.

VARIATIONS:

Mashed Winter Squash: Boil and

drain as directed and mash with a potato masher. Add pepper and butter and, if you like, 2 tablespoons cream. Mix or beat with an electric mixer until fluffy. About 180 calories per serving (without cream).

Spicy Mashed Squash in Orange Cups: Fill 4–6 large orange cups* with hot mashed squash, sprinkle each with cinnamon sugar, and top with a marshmallow. Broil 4–5″ from heat 2 minutes until marshmallow is lightly browned. About 220 calories per serving (with 1 teaspoon cinnamon sugar to top each orange cup).

BAKED BUTTERNUT OR ACORN SQUASH

Makes 4 servings

1 (2-pound) butternut or acorn squash, halved lengthwise and seeded
1 teaspoon salt
¼ teaspoon pepper
2 tablespoons butter or margarine

Preheat oven to 375° F. Place each piece of squash hollow side up on a square of foil large enough to wrap it; sprinkle with salt and pepper and dot with butter. Wrap tightly. Place squash on a baking sheet and bake 45 minutes until fork tender. Unwrap and serve with extra butter if you like. About 180 calories per serving.

To Charcoal Bake: Season and wrap each piece of squash as directed. Bake on a grill set 3–4″ above a moderately hot charcoal fire ¾–1 hour, turning 2 or 3 times. About 180 calories per serving.

VARIATION:
Before wrapping add a little honey or maple syrup, brown, maple, or cinnamon sugar, or orange marmalade to squash along with butter, salt, and pepper (about 2 tablespoons in all will be enough). Wrap and bake as directed. About 210 calories per serving.

BAKED HUBBARD SQUASH

Because this is such a giant squash, it requires special baking instructions.

Makes 8 servings

4–5 pounds Hubbard squash (try to get a whole small squash rather than a chunk of a giant one), prepared for baking*
1½ teaspoons salt
¼ teaspoon pepper
¼ cup butter or margarine

Preheat oven to 400° F. Place each piece of squash hollow side up on a piece of foil large enough to wrap it, sprinkle evenly with salt and pepper, and dot with butter; wrap tightly and place in a roasting pan. Bake about 1 hour until fork tender. Unwrap and serve with extra butter if you like. About 180 calories per serving.

VARIATIONS:

Mashed Hubbard Squash: Bake as directed, then scoop flesh from skin and mash with a potato masher; taste for salt and pepper and adjust. Add 2 tablespoons melted butter and beat until fluffy. About 205 calories per serving.

"Candied" Hubbard Squash: Just before wrapping squash pieces, sprinkle with ¼ cup light brown sugar, or drizzle with ¼ cup maple syrup or honey. Wrap and bake as directed. About 205 calories per serving.

FRUIT-GLAZED BUTTERNUT OR ACORN SQUASH

Makes 4 servings

1 (2-pound) butternut or acorn squash, halved, seeded, peeled, and sliced ½" thick
1½ cups pineapple or orange juice
¼ cup firmly packed light brown sugar
½ teaspoon salt
3 tablespoons melted butter or margarine

Preheat oven to 350° F. Arrange squash in an ungreased 1½-quart casserole. Mix remaining ingredients and pour over squash. Cover and bake about 45 minutes, basting 2 or 3 times, until fork tender. Uncover, baste, and bake 10 minutes longer to glaze lightly. About 310 calories per serving.

VARIATION:

Substitute Hubbard squash for the butternut or acorn and increase baking time to about 1 hour. About 310 calories per serving.

BUTTERNUT SQUASH PARMIGIANA

An unusual way to prepare butternut squash, but the butter, cheese, and bread crumbs enhance its mellow flavor.

Makes 4 servings

1 (2-pound) butternut or acorn squash, halved, seeded, peeled, cut in 1" chunks, and parboiled
1 teaspoon salt
Pinch pepper
2 tablespoons butter or margarine
¼ cup toasted fine bread crumbs
¼ cup grated Parmesan cheese

Preheat oven to 350° F. Arrange squash in an ungreased shallow 1½-quart casserole, sprinkle evenly with salt and pepper, and dot with butter. Mix crumbs and cheese and sprinkle on top. Cover and bake 25–30 minutes until fork tender. Raise oven temperature to 400° F., uncover, and bake 10 minutes longer to brown. About 230 calories per serving.

VARIATION:

Substitute Hubbard squash for the butternut or acorn and prepare as directed. About 230 calories per serving.

TOMATOES

The astonishing truth about tomatoes is that for centuries people considered them poisonous. They weren't eaten in this country until about 150 years ago, when a New Jersey farmer stood on the Salem County Courthouse lawn and ate one publicly to prove he would neither sicken nor die. He made his point and soon the most doubting Thomases were eating tomatoes. Today, of course, it's difficult to imagine life without them. Here are the most popular types and how to use them:

Red Globe Tomatoes: These are the juicy, everyday tomatoes, good either raw or cooked. There are 3–4 per pound.

Beefsteak Tomatoes: These large, firm tomatoes are perfect for broiling or slicing into sandwiches. About 1–2 per pound.

Cherry Tomatoes: Juicy, bite-size tomatoes ideal for picnics or cocktail snacks. About 30 in a 1-pint carton.

Plum Tomatoes: Sometimes red, sometimes golden, these plump, mellow Italian tomatoes cook superbly. About 5–6 per pound.

Cranberry Tomatoes: These are the tiny, tart "wild" tomatoes occa-

Season	For Top Quality	Amount To Buy	Nutritive Value	Calories (unseasoned)
Year round but the best are summer tomatoes	Choose firm, well-formed tomatoes of good strong color (whether red, green, or yellow) with smooth, unblemished skins.	1 medium-size tomato per person; 1 pound will serve 4.	Fairly high in vitamins A and C	Very low—about 35 per medium-size tomato

sionally carried by gourmet groceries. Toss into salads or serve as a cocktail snack to be eaten like nuts. About 100 per pint.

Green Tomatoes: There are two types: the small *immature green* that are used in pickles and relishes and the larger *mature green* that are excellent for frying or broiling. From 3–8 per pound.

To Ripen: Do not (repeat DO NOT) stand green tomatoes on a sunny window sill, because they'll ripen unevenly and become pithy. Instead, place in a perforated bag or box with a ripe apple and set in a cool (65–75° F.) spot.

To Peel: Do not core. Spear stem end with a long-handled fork and twirl slowly over an open flame just until skin splits. Or, if you prefer, twirl slowly in boiling water about ½ minute. Plunge into ice water, core, and slip off skin.

To Seed and Juice: Halve tomatoes crosswise and squeeze gently in your hand—seeds and juices will spurt out. To save juice, squeeze over a strainer set in a bowl. The strainer catches the seeds, which can be tossed out.

Serving Tip: If tomatoes are to go into a sandwich, slice from top to bottom instead of crosswise. There'll be much less juice to make the bread soggy.

⊠ FRIED TOMATOES

Makes 4 servings

3 tablespoons butter, margarine, bacon drippings, or cooking oil
4 large, firm, ripe beefsteak tomatoes, washed and sliced ¾" thick (do not peel)
½ teaspoon salt
⅛ teaspoon pepper

Heat butter 1 minute in a large, heavy skillet over moderate heat. Add tomatoes and fry 3–4 minutes on a side until golden brown. Sprinkle with salt and pepper and serve. About 110 calories per serving.

VARIATIONS:

⊠ **Fried Tomatoes with Sour Cream:** Transfer fried tomatoes to platter and keep warm. Blend 2 teaspoons flour into skillet drippings, mix in ½ cup milk, and heat, stirring 1–2 minutes until thickened. Off heat, mix in ½ cup sour cream, ⅛ teaspoon paprika, and ¼ teaspoon salt. Pour over tomatoes and serve. About 185 calories per serving.

⊠ **Fried Green Tomatoes:** Use green tomatoes instead of ripe, fry as directed, but sprinkle slices with sugar halfway through cooking. About 150 calories per serving.

VEGETABLES

▣ **Fried Tomatoes Lyonnaise:** Spread ½ cup sautéed minced onions on serving plate, arrange fried tomatoes on top, then add ½ cup more sautéed onions. About 185 calories per serving.

▣ **Fried Tomatoes Provençal:** Fry tomatoes in 3 tablespoons olive oil with 1 crushed clove garlic. Season with salt and pepper and serve. About 130 calories per serving.

▣ PENNSYLVANIA DUTCH FRIED TOMATOES

These tomatoes, unlike plain fried tomatoes, are lightly sugared and topped with heavy cream.
Makes 4 servings

4 large firm, ripe tomatoes or 4 large green tomatoes, washed and sliced ¾" thick (do not peel)
¼ cup unsifted flour
3 tablespoons bacon drippings
¼ cup firmly packed light brown sugar
½ teaspoon salt
1 cup heavy cream

Dip tomato slices in flour to dredge lightly. Heat drippings, in a large, heavy skillet over moderate heat 1 minute, add tomatoes, and fry 3–4 minutes on a side until lightly browned; sprinkle with brown sugar and salt. Pour cream into skillet and heat 1–2 minutes, basting tomatoes once. Transfer tomatoes to a heated platter, pour cream over all, and serve. About 395 calories per serving.

▣ BROILED TOMATOES

For an Italian touch, brush the tomatoes lightly with olive oil before sprinkling in the seasonings. And omit the butter.
Makes 4 servings

4 large firm, ripe tomatoes, washed and halved crosswise (do not peel)
½ teaspoon salt
⅛ teaspoon pepper
1 tablespoon minced fresh chervil or 1 teaspoon dried chervil (optional)
1 tablespoon minced fresh basil or 1 teaspoon dried basil (optional)
¼ cup butter or margarine

Preheat broiler. Arrange tomatoes cut side up in a lightly greased shallow pan. Mix salt, pepper, and, if you like, the herbs and sprinkle over tomatoes; dot with butter. Broil 5–6" from heat 10–12 minutes until lightly browned. About 135 calories per serving.

VARIATIONS:

Deviled Tomatoes: Mix ¼ cup cracker meal, 2 tablespoons melted butter, 1 tablespoon each grated Parmesan and minced chives, 1 teaspoon prepared mild yellow mustard, and a pinch pepper. Pat on tomato halves instead of seasonings called for above and broil 5" from heat about 3 minutes until browned. About 130 calories per serving.

Broiled Tomatoes with Anchovies and Cheese: Place each tomato half cut side up on a 3–4" circle of buttered toast spread with anchovy paste. Sprinkle lightly with minced fresh basil and grated Cheddar cheese and broil 5–6" from heat 3–4 minutes until bubbly and browned. About 205 calories per serving.

▣ BAKED TOMATOES

Serve at breakfast or brunch accompanied by ham, bacon or sausage, and eggs.
Makes 4 servings

4 large firm, ripe beefsteak tomatoes, washed and halved crosswise (do not peel)

1 teaspoon salt
⅛ teaspoon pepper
¼ cup butter or margarine

Preheat oven to 375° F. Place tomatoes cut side up in a buttered roasting pan or shallow casserole. Sprinkle with salt and pepper and dot with butter. Bake, uncovered, 15–20 minutes until fork tender. (*Note:* Winter tomatoes, being drier, will take longer to bake than summer tomatoes.) About 135 calories per serving.

STUFFED TOMATOES

A good basic recipe to vary as you wish. Experiment with some of the stuffing variations given below or concoct one of your own.
Makes 4 servings

4 large firm, ripe tomatoes, washed
½ teaspoon salt
⅛ teaspoon pepper

Stuffing:
1 tablespoon butter or margarine
¼ cup finely chopped yellow onion
2 cups soft white bread crumbs
¾ teaspoon salt
⅛ teaspoon pepper
1 cup chopped tomato pulp (saved from tomato centers)
¼ cup grated Parmesan cheese

Preheat oven to 375° F. Cut a thin slice from top of each tomato and reserve. Using a teaspoon, scoop out pulp and seeds. Coarsely chop pulp and reserve 1 cup (use the rest in soups or stews). Sprinkle inside of tomatoes with salt and pepper. Melt butter in a small skillet over moderate heat, add onion, and sauté 8–10 minutes until golden. Mix onion with all remaining stuffing ingredients except Parmesan. Stuff tomatoes, sprinkle with Parmesan, and, if you like, replace reserved tops. Stand tomatoes in a buttered shallow casserole and bake, uncovered, ½ hour until tender. About 160 calories per serving.

Some Other Ideas for Stuffing Tomatoes:

– Substitute any of the following combinations for the recipe given above, allowing ½ cup stuffing per tomato and using chopped tomato pulp to moisten as needed:
• 1¾ cups poultry stuffing mix or cooked rice mixed with ¼ cup each sautéed chopped onion and celery. About 185 calories per tomato stuffed with stuffing mix, 110 per tomato stuffed with rice.
• 1 cup browned sausage meat mixed with 1 cup cooked rice and 1 tablespoon minced parsley. About 200 calories per serving.
• 1 cup coarsely chopped sautéed mushrooms mixed with 1 cup Savoy Risotto. About 195 calories per serving.
• ½ cup finely chopped hard-cooked eggs mixed with ¼ cup crisp crumbled bacon, ¼ cup minced pitted green olives, and 1 cup soft white bread crumbs. About 145 calories per serving.

– Instead of making stuffing, mix 1 cup reserved tomato pulp with 1 cup cooked vegetables: small cauliflowerets, whole kernel or cream-style corn, green peas, baby limas, cut green beans, or sautéed diced eggplant. Recipe too flexible for a meaningful calorie count.
– Drain hollowed-out tomatoes upside-down on paper toweling and fill with any of the following: macaroni and cheese; creamed spinach, mushrooms or celery; creamed chicken, ham, brains, sweetbreads, shrimp, crab, or lobster. Top with buttered crumbs before baking. (*Note:* If filling is very delicate

VEGETABLES

[like sweetbreads or brains], bake empty tomato shells right side up 20 minutes at 375° F., fill, and bake 10 minutes longer. Otherwise, fill and bake ½ hour as directed in basic recipe.) Recipe too flexible for a meaningful calorie count.

⚱ ⊠ ¢ STEWED TOMATOES

Another basic recipe that invites improvisation.
Makes 4 servings

4 large ripe tomatoes, peeled, cored, and quartered, or 1½ pounds Italian plum tomatoes, peeled
1 tablespoon water (optional)
¾ teaspoon salt
¼ teaspoon sugar
Pinch pepper

Place tomatoes in a heavy saucepan, add water (if they seem dry) and remaining ingredients. Cover and simmer 5–7 minutes until *just* soft; uncover and simmer ½ minute longer. Serve in small bowls as a vegetable. About 35 calories per serving.

VARIATIONS:

⚱ ⊠ ¢ **Savory Stewed Tomatoes:** Cook any of the following with the tomatoes: 2 tablespoons minced yellow onion or scallions and ½ crushed clove garlic; ¼ cup minced celery or sweet green pepper; 1 bay leaf; 1 teaspoon minced fresh basil, oregano, or marjoram, or ½ teaspoon of the dried. About 40 calories per serving.

⊠ ¢ **Dressed-Up Stewed Tomatoes:** Just before serving add any one of the following: 2 tablespoons butter or grated Parmesan; 1–2 tablespoons maple syrup; 1 tablespoon minced parsley; ⅓ cup soft white bread crumbs or croutons. Recipe too flexible for a meaningful calorie count.

⊠ ¢ **Stewed Vegetables:** Just before serving, stir in any of the following: 1 cup hot cooked whole kernel corn or cream-style corn; 1 cup sautéed sliced mushrooms; 1½ cups hot cooked green beans; 2 cups hot cooked baby okra pods. Recipe too flexible for a meaningful calorie count.

⊠ EASY SCALLOPED TOMATOES

Makes 3–4 servings

1 (1-pound) can whole tomatoes (do not drain)
1 cup poultry stuffing mix
¼ cup finely chopped scallions (include green tops)
¼ teaspoon tarragon or chervil
⅛ teaspoon crushed fennel seeds (optional)
2 tablespoons butter or margarine

Preheat oven to 375° F. Empty tomatoes into a buttered 9" piepan and cut them into quarters. Toss together all remaining ingredients except butter and scatter evenly over tomatoes. Dot with butter and bake, uncovered, 20 minutes. About 205 calories for each of 3 servings, 155 calories for each of 4 servings.

TOMATO-CHEESE-CORN PIE

A vegetable dish hearty enough to serve as an entree.
Makes 6 servings

Pastry:
1 recipe Flaky Pastry I

Filling:
2 tablespoons butter or margarine
1 large yellow onion, peeled and sliced thin
2 cups coarsely grated sharp Cheddar cheese

2 medium-size, firm ripe tomatoes, peeled and sliced ½" thick
½ teaspoon salt
⅛ teaspoon pepper
1 (1-pound) can cream-style corn

Preheat oven to 425° F. Make pastry and roll to a diameter of 9½". Cut 3 V-shaped slits or decorative holes near the center. Cover with cloth while you make the filling. Melt butter in a small skillet over moderate heat, add onion, and stir-fry 5–8 minutes until pale golden; set aside. Sprinkle ½ cup cheese over bottom of an ungreased 9" piepan and top with tomato slices. Sprinkle with salt, pepper, and onion. Spread corn evenly over tomatoes and top with remaining cheese. Brush rim of pan lightly with cold water. Cover pie with pastry, roll overhang under even with rim, and crimp. Bake 25 minutes until lightly browned. (*Note:* Put a piece of foil on the rack below pie to catch any drips.) About 440 calories per serving.

TRUFFLES

Truffles grow only at the roots of certain trees and only in a few areas of the world; they're dug once a year by especially trained pigs or dogs and bring about $60 a pound. Oddly, though gourmets rave about truffles, they cannot agree on the flavor. Some say that truffles taste like oysters, others like mild garlic, still others like well-ripened Brie. It is flavor for which truffles are cherished, not nutritive value or beauty. Truffles are wrinkled, warty, black, brown or beige fungi usually about the size of chestnuts or golf balls. The choicest are the black Périgord truffles of Southern France; second best are the white (actually beige) truffles from Northern Italy. Though fresh truffles make rare appearances in New York specialty markets, most of us must be content with the canned. And even these are a great luxury.

How to Heighten the Flavor of Canned Truffles: Open can but do not drain; add 1–2 tablespoons Madeira and let truffles stand 30–45 minutes before using.

How to Use Canned Truffles (1 truffle is usually enough for any recipe):
– Mince and stir into meat stuffing, an omelet, or potato salad (use a light hand with herbs or omit them altogether so you don't overpower the truffle).
– Slice tissue thin, cut into fancy shapes with truffle cutters, and use to decorate pâté, ham or fowl in aspic, or canapés.
– Save can liquid and use to season sauces and meat stuffings.

How to Save Leftover Canned Truffles: Wrap in foil and freeze. Or leave in the can, cover with melted bacon drippings, and refrigerate (they'll keep several weeks).

TURNIPS AND TURNIP GREENS

(The greens are often called Turnip Salad)

Most vegetables as ancient as turnips (more than 4,000 years old) have been in and out of favor half a dozen times. Not so turnips. They've never been particularly popular and only today are we beginning to appreciate their gingery piquancy.

To Prepare for Cooking:

Turnips: Trim off any stems and root ends and discard. Very tiny

VEGETABLES

Season	For Top Quality	Amount To Buy	Nutritive Value	Calories (unseasoned)
Year round for turnips; peak season: fall. January–April for greens	Choose firm, smooth turnips 2–3" across with few leaf scars or roots; clean, tender, crisp greens.	¼ pound turnips per person; ½ pound greens	Greens are very high in vitamins A and C; turnips contain some vitamin C.	Very low— about 30 per cup of greens; 35 per cup of turnips

tender turnips can be scrubbed and cooked whole in their skins; larger turnips should be peeled and quartered or cut in ½" cubes.

Turnip Greens: Discard coarse stems and leaf midribs; sort greens, rejecting any that are wilted, blemished, or yellow. Wash by plunging up and down in tepid water, rinse several times, then lift from water, shake lightly, and place directly in pot.

To Boil Turnip Greens: See recipe for Boiled Collards, Turnip Greens, or Mustard Greens.

Cooking Tips:
– Always cook turnip greens in enamel, stainless-steel, or teflon-lined pots so they don't darken or taste of metal.
– Toss young greens or thin strips of raw turnip into salads for refreshing zing.

Serving Tip: Don't serve turnips with seafood because they overpower it. They're best with pork, ham, or pot roasts.

¢ **BOILED TURNIPS**

To give turnips richer flavor, boil in beef or chicken broth instead of water.
Makes 4 servings

1¼ *pounds turnips, prepared for cooking*

1½ *cups boiling water, beef or chicken broth*
1 *teaspoon salt (about)*
2 *tablespoons butter or margarine*
⅛ *teaspoon pepper*

Place turnips, water or broth, and salt (reduce amount if broth is salty) in a saucepan, cover, and boil until tender: 35–40 minutes for whole small turnips, 25–30 for quarters, and 15–20 for cubes. Drain, then shake pan, uncovered, over low heat to drive off steam. Add butter and continue to shake over low heat until butter melts. Add pepper and serve. About 85 calories per serving (if cooked in water), 95 per serving (cooked in broth).

To Parboil for Use in Other Recipes: Boil as directed, reducing cooking time to 25 minutes for small whole turnips, 15–20 for quarters, and 10 for cubes. Omit seasonings.

VARIATIONS:

⚖ ¢ **Low-Calorie Turnips:** Boil in water and drain as directed; omit butter and sprinkle with 2 tablespoons minced chives, dill, or fennel. About 35 calories per serving.

¢ **Parsleyed Turnips:** Boil in broth and season as directed; just before serving stir in 1 tablespoon lemon juice and 1 tablespoon minced parsley. About 95 calories per serving.

¢ **Mashed Turnips:** Boil and drain

as directed; mash with a potato masher or, if stringy, press through a fine sieve. Beat in butter and pepper and warm 2–3 minutes over low heat, stirring. Sprinkle with minced parsley and serve. About 85 calories per serving (if cooked in water), 95 calories per serving (if cooked in broth).

¢ **Glazed Turnips:** Parboil quartered turnips in beef broth as directed; drain, reserving broth, but do not season. Brown turnips in a heavy skillet 3–5 minutes in 3 tablespoons oil over moderately high heat. Add broth, 2 tablespoons each sugar and butter, cover, and simmer 15–20 minutes until tender. If cooking liquid hasn't become syrupy, boil uncovered to reduce, turning turnips until well glazed. Sprinkle with pepper and minced parsley and serve. About 260 calories per serving.

TURNIPS AU GRATIN

Those who don't like turnips will probably like them prepared this way.
Makes 4 servings

1¼ pounds turnips, peeled, cubed, boiled, and drained
2 tablespoons butter or margarine
2 tablespoons flour
1 cup milk
½ teaspoon salt
⅛ teaspoon pepper
Pinch powdered mustard
¾ cup coarsely grated sharp Cheddar cheese

Preheat oven to 400° F. Arrange turnips in an ungreased 1½-quart *au gratin* dish or shallow casserole. Melt butter over moderate heat, blend in flour, and slowly stir in milk. Heat, stirring constantly, until thickened; mix in salt, pepper, mustard, and ½ cup cheese. Pour sauce over turnips and mix lightly; sprinkle remaining cheese on top. Bake, uncovered, 20 minutes until bubbly. About 220 calories per serving.

¢ ROASTED TURNIPS

Sweeter than boiled turnips, less watery, too.
Makes 4 servings

1¼ pounds medium-size turnips, peeled
½ cup lard, bacon drippings, or cooking oil
1 teaspoon salt

Preheat oven to 375° F. Place turnips in an ungreased shallow casserole and add lard, drippings, or oil. Bake, uncovered, 50 minutes, turning turnips after ½ hour. Raise oven temperature to 400° F. and bake 10–15 minutes longer until lightly browned and tender. Drain on paper toweling, sprinkle with salt, and serve. About 135 calories per serving.

¢ SKILLET TURNIPS AND RED ONIONS

Makes 4 servings

1¼ pounds medium-size turnips, peeled and cubed
1 large red onion, peeled and sliced thin
⅓ cup water
3 tablespoons butter or margarine
¾ teaspoon salt

Place all ingredients in a large, heavy skillet, cover, and simmer 15–20 minutes, shaking skillet frequently. Uncover toward end of cooking and stir gently so turnips become nicely glazed. If mixture seems dry, add 1 tablespoon water. About 125 calories per serving.

TURNIPS STUFFED WITH MUSHROOM RISOTTO

Makes 4 servings

8 medium-size turnips, parboiled and drained
1½ cups Mushroom Risotto
¼ cup grated Parmesan cheese
1½ cups chicken broth

Preheat oven to 350° F. Hollow out turnips to form "cups" (save centers for soup or stew). Stuff with risotto, sprinkle with cheese, and arrange in an ungreased shallow casserole. Pour broth around turnips, cover, and bake 20 minutes. Uncover, bake 15 minutes longer, basting 2 or 3 times. About 215 calories per serving.

WILD GREENS

Milkweed . . . nettles . . . pokeweed . . . purslane. They're yours for the picking, and very good they are. Like other greens, they're low in calories and high in vitamins A and C. All should be cooked in enamel, stainless-steel, or teflon-lined pots so that they don't darken or taste of metal.

Milkweed

Milkweed grows throughout the Eastern United States and almost every part of it is edible—the fragile young shoots and leaves, the flower buds and small, tender seed pods. All are naturally bitter and need special treatment to remove the astringency. Allow about ½ pound per person.

To Prepare: Whether cooking shoots, leaves, buds, or pods, wash well in cool water. Place in a large pot, cover with boiling water, and boil 1 minute. Drain and cover with fresh boiling water. Repeat boiling and draining process 3 or 4 times until all bitterness is gone, then boil 5–10 minutes longer until crisp-tender. Drain, season with butter, salt, and pepper, and serve.

Nettles

"Baby" nettle leaves are delicious. Look for them in early spring (wear thick gloves). Allow about 1½ pints per person.

To Prepare: Wash as you would spinach by plunging up and down in tepid water. Rinse, lift from water, shake lightly, and place in a pot. Add no water, cover, and steam over moderate heat until tender: about 10 minutes for youngest leaves, 20–30 for the not so young. Drain and purée in an electric blender at high speed or put through a food mill. Season with butter, salt, and pepper and serve on hot buttered toast or in pastry shells. *Or,* follow the recipe for Wilted Dandelions or Nettles.

Pokeweed

Although the mature stems, roots, and berries are mildly poisonous, the first shoots of spring are good to eat. Look in open fields for the tall, silvery stalks of last year's crop; at their base you'll find plump new shoots. Choose those no more than 6" to 8" high and allow 3 to 4 per person.

To Prepare: Wash well in tepid water, peeling off any coarse outer layers of stalk. Place shoots in a large pan, cover with boiling water, and boil covered 10 minutes. Drain, cover with fresh boiling water, and boil covered 8–10 minutes longer until tender. Drain, dress with butter or heavy cream, salt, and pepper. *Or,* chill and serve cold with oil and vinegar.

Purslane

(Also called Portulaca)

If gardeners knew how savory purslane is, they wouldn't work so hard to weed it out of their flower beds. The stems, leaves, and flower buds are all good to eat, but the young shoots are the most succulent of all. Allow about 1 cup per person.

To Prepare: Wash in tepid water and discard any tough or blemished portions. Place in a saucepan, add lightly salted water to cover, and boil covered about 10 minutes until tender. Drain, season with butter, salt, and pepper, and serve. *Or,* sauté young shoots in 2–3 tablespoons bacon drippings over moderate heat 2–3 minutes, then cover and steam 6–8 minutes until tender. Drizzle with white wine vinegar, season with salt and pepper, and serve. *Or,* use in gumbos and other Creole dishes in place of okra.

CHAPTER 17

SALADS AND SALAD DRESSINGS

The Romans, who liked most things twice-gilded, took their salads straight—lettuce sprinkled with salt. It is, in fact, from their word for salt (*sal*) that our word salad derives. Our salads are a good deal more complex than the Roman and may appear at almost any point in a meal. Californians begin dinner with crisp green salads, simply dressed, and Southerners often end it with frozen fruit salads. The French prefer salad either before or after the main course (so that the dressing doesn't overpower the wine) and Swedes construct whole smorgasbords out of cold marinated fish and vegetables.

Salads can be nothing more than greens tossed with oil and vinegar, or they can be elaborate concoctions of meat, seafood, poultry, vegetables, pasta, or fruit. They may be bland or tart, savory or sweet, light or lavish, and they may be served hot or cold, jellied or frozen.

The Salad Greens

Most salads are built around—or upon—greens. Time was when green salad was a wedge of iceberg lettuce drenched with French or Thousand Island dressing. No more, thanks to the variety of greens now available year round. Nutritionally, salad greens are low in calories and relatively high in vitamins C and A (the darker the green, the greater the vitamin content), iron, and calcium. Here, then, are the varieties of greens available:

Lettuces:

Crisphead or Iceberg: The old standby, tightly packed, crunchy, pale green heads. Sweet, succulent, and bland.

Leaf or Simpson: Loose-leafed, medium to bronzy green, depending on variety (Salad Bowl, Garden, Bronze, Ivy, and Oak are popular leaf lettuces). Coarser textured and stronger flavored than iceberg.

Boston or Butterhead: Smallish, loose, medium green heads with buttery, easily bruised leaves. Exceptionally good flavor.

Bibb or Limestone: Loveliest of lettuces. Tulip-shaped, tiny, crinkly-crisp heads of medium to pale yellow-green. Not widely available but worth hunting up. These need extra-careful washing to float out hidden caches of soil. Delicate, mellow flavor.

Romaine or Cos: Supercrisp, green, elongated heads from the Aegean island of Cos. Essential to tossed green salads for crunch and a certain amount of tang.

Other Salad Greens:

Chicory or Curly Endive: Frilly, sprawling heads, bright green around the edges, pale in the center. Bitter, somewhat coarse, and best when teamed with more delicate greens.

Escarole: A coarse cousin of chicory with fairly broad, bitter, flat green leaves.

Field Salad (also known as *Corn Salad, Lamb's Lettuce,* and *Lamb's Quarter*): Small, dark, spoon-shaped leaves, loosely clustered into rosettes. A rarity in most markets and available only in fall and winter. Flavor is biting, radish-like.

Garden Cress or Peppergrass: Small, spicy-hot plants of the mustard family gathered when barely out of the ground. Not often marketed in this country but worth growing from seed. A handful of leaves will revitalize a listless salad.

Nasturtium: Leaves of this sunny flower have lots of dash and bite. They're good alone or tossed with other greens. The blossoms are edible, too, and contribute color and pungency.

Rugula (Arugula) or Rocket: Rugula is the Italian name and the one most often used, since these dark, bitter-sharp greens are an Italian favorite. Use sparingly in green salads.

Sorrel or Dock: Crisp, sour, tongue-shaped leaves with a fresh, spring green color. Add with a light hand.

Watercress: Deep green, succulent, tart, and burning. The leaves and tender young stems provide welcome crunch and piquancy.

Belgian Endive, Cabbage, Chinese Cabbage, Dandelions, and *Spinach,* all popular additions to the salad bowl, are described in detail in the vegetable chapter. So are *Beet, Mustard,* and *Turnip Greens,* which, if young, fresh, and tender, team well with other greens.

About Buying Salad Greens

Choose crisp greens free of blemishes, bruises or soft spots, nicks or cuts. Also avoid those with "rust spots" (these may go clear through the head), wilted or yellow leaves. If you are buying a head of lettuce, be sure the head is firm and compact. Whenever possible, buy unpackaged greens that you can inspect closely.

How to Wash and Crisp Salad Greens

There are two schools of thought. One insists that greens will keep longer if they are not washed until shortly before using. The second (to which we belong) maintains just the opposite, that greens should be attended to as soon as they come home from garden or grocery. Peel off and discard any wilted or damaged outer leaves, then *wash* carefully (never allow to soak).

Headed Lettuces: With point of paring knife, cut out stem end, then hold head under a stream of cold water; it will force leaves apart and cleanse them. Drain well and wrap head in paper or cloth toweling, then pop into a plastic bag and place in hydrator compartment of refrigerator. If salad is to be made fairly soon, separate leaves, blot on toweling, and roll up; refrigerate until needed. *To Make Lettuce Cups:* Carefully pull off outer leaves (they will be nicely cup-shaped) and place on a towel-lined tray. Top with another towel and crisp in refrigerator until needed.

Loose-Leafed Lettuces: Cut out stem end, pull off leaves, and slosh up and down several times in a sinkful of cool water. Repeat, changing water as needed, to float out grit and soil. Blot leaves dry on paper toweling, roll loosely in cloth or paper toweling, then store in hydrator until needed. If greens are not to be used within a day or so, slip into a plastic bag, towel and all.

Watercress, Field Salad, and Other Stemmed Greens: Open bunch and discard roots and coarse stems. Swish leaves and tender young stems up and down in several changes of cool water until free of dirt. Rinse in cold water, blot on several thicknesses of paper toweling, then roll up in dry cloth and store in hydrator. (*Note:* If watercress is not to be used right away, open bunch but do not trim; stand in a glass of cold water, cover with a plastic bag, and store in refrigerator.)

A Word About Wire Salad Baskets: Many cooks wash greens in wire baskets, then whirl them dry by swinging the baskets through the air. An all-right method for sturdy greens, but not for fragile ones because the wire mesh will bruise them.

About Making Tossed Green Salads

The Bowl: Wooden salad bowls have become absurdly sacrosanct, hallowed things never to be rinsed, let alone washed. So they go on and on, gathering oils, essence of garlic, and rancidity. "Wash" does not mean "soak"—which would indeed ruin a wooden bowl—but a quick sudsing, rinsing, and drying after each use is good practice. Better still, choose a non-porous, washable ceramic, glass, or metal bowl, a *big* one (it's impossible to toss salad in a small bowl).

Choosing the Greens: The best green salads provide contrasts—of color (greens range from near-white to near-black), texture, shape, and flavor. But the contrasts must be subtle lest one flavor or texture overshadow the others. Salad artists devote years to their art, experimenting with combinations of greens, dressings, and herbs until they achieve a delectable balance. Consider the whole meal when constructing the salad, and select greens that will complement it—strong entrees demand delicate salads, light ones something substantial.

Good Salad Herbs: Because a handful of herbs have become known as "salad herbs," we tend to slight a number of others that work very well with tossed greens. The best herbs to use are fresh herbs (if you have a sunny window and a halfway green thumb, try growing your own; it isn't difficult). Don't load a salad with herbs, but settle upon one or two (and no more than three) that are compatible with one another and your choice of greens (tasting is the best way to tell). As a rule, two tablespoons of minced fresh herbs are sufficient for one quart prepared greens. Sprinkle the herbs into the greens, or mix into the oil. If you use dried herbs, crush between your fingers, add to the oil, and let stand twenty to thirty minutes at room temperature so they will gain fragrance. Dried herbs are stronger than the fresh, so use only one-third to one-fourth as much.

Favorite Salad Herbs:
Basil Tarragon
Chervil Fines Herbes (a mix
Chives of chervil, chives,
Dill parsley, and
Parsley tarragon)

Others to Try:
Borage ⎫ Both are cool, cucumber-
Burnet ⎭ flavored
Coriander Leaves (flavor is a cross between carrots and parsley)
Fennel
Marjoram
Mint
Oregano
Rosemary
Summer Savory
Thyme

Good Vegetable Additions to Green Salads: Raw cucumbers, carrots, and radishes are naturals for tossed salads, but so are a lot of other raw vegetables. As for cooked vegetables, nearly any vegetable that can be served cold can be tossed into a green salad. Here are some suggestions (all vegetables should be cut in bite-size or at least easy-to-eat pieces):

Raw Vegetables: Carrots, cauliflowerets, celeriac, celery, cucumbers (these are often coated with wax to retard spoilage; if so, peel before using), fennel, kale, and kohlrabi (if young and tender), mushrooms, onions (the whole huge family), radishes, sweet peppers, turnips, and zucchini. (*Note:* Tomatoes are not particularly suitable because of their juiciness. To keep them from watering down the salad: Slice tomatoes vertically instead of horizontally; marinate tomato wedges in dressing and add at the very last minute as a garnish, or best of all, use whole cherry tomatoes.)

Cooked Vegetables: Artichoke hearts and bottoms, asparagus, beans (the whole family of fresh and dried), beets, broccoli, carrots, celeriac, celery, cucumbers, eggplant, hearts of palm, leeks, lentils, green peas and snow pea pods, sweet green or red peppers (especially Marinated Roasted Peppers), and Irish potatoes.

Good Fruit Additions to Green Salads: Grapefruit, orange, mandarin orange, and tangerine sections (make sure all seeds and white pith are removed); diced or sliced avocados or apples (dip in lemon juice to prevent darkening); peeled seeded grapes.

Other Flavorful Additions to Green Salads:
— Cheese: Cubes of Cheddar, Swiss, or Gruyère cheese, crumbles of Roquefort or blue cheese
— Croutons (plain or seasoned)
— Capers, sweet or sour pickles, ripe or green olives, slivered pimiento
— Bacon crumbles, slivered prosciutto or boiled ham
— Truffles—especially good with delicate greens and French dressing
— Nuts: toasted slivered almonds, piñon nuts, peanuts, water chestnuts
— Seeds: celery, caraway, and toasted sesame seeds
— Flower petals: chrysanthemums, marigolds, roses, nasturtiums, violets, pumpkin or squash blossoms

SALADS AND SALAD DRESSINGS

About Adding Garlic: Someone once said there was no such thing as "a touch of garlic." Perhaps not, but that doesn't mean you have to add enough to blow a safe. For fairly subtle garlic flavor, use one of the following techniques:
- Rub salad bowl with a cut clove of garlic before adding greens; or for slightly stronger flavor, sprinkle a little salt in bowl, then rub with garlic.
- Toss a *chapon* with salad, then remove before serving. A *chapon* is a stale chunk of French bread rubbed well with a cut or crushed clove of garlic.
- Slice garlic into salad oil, then warm briefly over lowest heat. Cool oil to room temperature and remove garlic before dressing salad. (*Note:* Never let garlic stand long in oil; it will become bitter.)

Choosing the Dressing: Salad greens team happily with a huge variety of dressings—any oil and vinegar type (except very sweet ones), any tart creamy dressing, any savory cheese dressing. Consider the make-up of the salad—and the entire meal—then pick a dressing compatible with both. If there are dieters, also consider the calories (there is a good selection of low-calorie dressings in the recipe section that follows).

Putting Tossed Green Salads Together

Prepare the Dressing—at least a half hour ahead of time so that flavors will mellow. If you are going to make an oil and vinegar dressing, combine herbs and other seasonings with oil and let stand a half hour at room temperature. (*Note:* It's best to make dressings in small quantities; few keep well. If adding cooked or raw vegetables to salad, let marinate in a little of the dressing for about a half hour at room temperature.)

Prepare the Greens—just before making the salad. Use only those that have been well washed and crisped in the refrigerator. If greens still show drops of water, blot gently on paper toweling. Break, tear, or cut greens into bite-size or easy-to-eat pieces and drop into salad bowl. (*Note:* Until recently, people thought cutting greens bruised them, destroyed the food value. But that theory is being questioned. The best way today seems to be whichever is easiest, most efficient. Endive, for example, is simpler to cut than tear; iceberg lettuce just the opposite.) *How many greens for a salad?* Allow one to two cups prepared greens per person (depending on appetites).

Dress and Toss the Salad: Place all salad ingredients in a large bowl and drizzle with a small amount of dressing; toss lightly, lifting greens from the bottom to the top, until leaves glisten. Taste, add more dressing if needed, also salt and pepper. (*Note:* If you are dressing salad with oil and vinegar, drizzle oil in first and toss until leaves are lightly coated. Then sprinkle vinegar on top and toss again, tasting as you go and adding extra vinegar as needed.) Vinegar and salt should always be added to tossed greens at the very last minute because they will quickly wilt a salad. The best way to avoid overdressing a salad is to underdress, then to add more dressing if necessary. As a rule, three to four tablespoons dressing per quart of prepared greens is sufficient.

Other Kinds of Salads

There are dozens of different salads in addition to the tossed, which may be grouped roughly as follows: *Vegetable* (both cooked and raw), *Fruit* (both raw and cooked), *Main Dish* (meat, poultry, seafood, egg, and pasta salads), *Molded*, and *Frozen*. Main dish, molded, and frozen salads are treated fully in the accompanying recipe section (and there are additional recipes in the meat, poultry, seafood, and egg chapters). Vegetable and fruit salads, however, are less a matter of specific recipes than of improvisation. Here is the place to let your imagination run wild, mixing and matching flavors, combining tints and textures, tasting as you go. These salads can be presented as *platter salads*—fruits and/or vegetables grouped on a platter rather than tossed.

Some Good Vegetable Salad Combinations: (*Note:* To shave calories, substitute a low-calorie dressing for that recommended below.)

– Diced cooked potatoes, carrots, green peas, baby limas, and minced red onion; add enough mayonnaise to bind.
– Diced cooked beets, hard-cooked eggs, elbow macaroni, minced sweet green pepper, and yellow onion; add enough mayonnaise to bind.
– Cooked asparagus tips and halved cherry tomatoes marinated in French Dressing.
– Cooked artichoke bottoms filled with Russian Salad.
– Drained sauerkraut mixed with minced raw celery, yellow onion, and sweet green or red pepper. Dress with French, Shallot, or Wine Dressing.

Some Good Fruit Salad Combinations: *Note:* Apples, peaches, bananas, and avocados must be dipped in lemon or other citrus juice to prevent darkening. They should be added to the salad just before serving. Slice, dice, or cube fruits, keeping each in proportion to the other. Dress with any dressing suitable for fruit salads.

– Oranges or tangerines, apples, grapes, and pecans or toasted almonds
– Bananas, oranges or tangerines, and dates
– Bananas, oranges, pineapple, and mango or papaya
– Pineapple and strawberries and/or grapes
– Melon balls, grapes, and pineapple
– Melon balls and lemon-dipped avocado cubes
– Cooked plums, peaches, and figs

About Garnishing Salads

Tossed Salads should look casual, so the simpler the garnish the better—strategically placed radish roses or carrot curls, clusters of ripe or green olives, crumbles of bacon or French-fried onions, shreds of fresh horseradish, Cheddar cubes, or paprika-dusted cream cheese balls.

Vegetable and Main Dish Salads: These are best dressed up by serving in hollowed-out tomatoes, vegetable cases, or avocado halves (these must be well brushed with lemon juice to keep them from darkening).

Savory Aspics, Molded Vegetable, Meat, or Fish Salads: Trim with ruffs of greenery (parsley, watercress, chicory), clusters of ripe or green olives, plain or fancily cut radishes, carrot or celery curls, pickle fans, clusters of tiny cooked shrimp, cherry tomatoes.

Fruit and Molded Fruit Salads: Decorate with clusters of green and red grapes, preserved kumquats, melon balls, lemon-dipped unpeeled red apple cubes, and avocado cubes or crescents, mandarin oranges, orange or grapefruit sections, any fresh berries or any compatible combinations of these. For greenery: mint or fennel sprigs, rose geranium or lemon verbena leaves. A touch of color is all that's needed.

About Salads to Go

Most salads are poor travelers. Best choices—*if* they can be kept well chilled in transit—are cooked vegetable, meat, or seafood salads. Salad greens are apt to wilt or crush, but if wrapped in several thicknesses of *damp* paper toweling, then tied in a plastic bag and kept cool, they should arrive on location crisp and fresh. The dressing should travel separately and be added at the very last minute.

Some Ways to Serve Tomatoes

French-Style: Arrange ripe tomato slices on a large plate, alternating, if you like, with cucumber slices and overlapping slightly. Sprinkle with salt and freshly ground pepper, drizzle with olive oil and red wine vinegar, and let stand at room temperature about a half hour before serving.

Belgian-Style: Alternate slices of tomato and Bermuda onion rings on a large plate, overlapping slightly. Sprinkle with salt, sugar, freshly minced chives and chervil. Sprinkle lightly with celery seeds, drizzle with French Dressing, cover, and marinate one to two hours in refrigerator.

Italian-Style: Arrange ripe tomato slices, slightly overlapping, on a large plate, alternating, if you like, with thin slices of mozzarella cheese. Sprinkle with salt and freshly ground pepper, drizzle with olive oil and red wine vinegar or lemon juice, and scatter lavishly with minced fresh basil. Let stand at room temperature about one hour before serving.

Mediterranean-Style: Arrange ripe tomato slices on a large plate but do not overlap. Sprinkle with salt and freshly ground pepper, olive oil and lemon juice. Mound with Caponata, garnish with ripe olives and watercress, and serve.

Tomatoes Finlandia: Mix equal parts minced cooked shrimp or pickled herring and hard-cooked eggs, add mayonnaise to bind, salt, pepper, and minced fresh dill to taste. Mound on tomato slices and serve.

"Frosted" Tomatoes: Spread tomato slices with thick layers of cottage cheese, sprinkle with minced chives and dill, and serve.

Marinated Tomatoes and Artichokes: Marinate equal parts tomato wedges and cooked artichoke hearts in French or other tart dressing two to three hours in the refrigerator. Toss and serve.

Roquefort Tomatoes and Avocados: Marinate equal parts slim tomato wedges and lemon-dipped avocado slices in any Roquefort or blue cheese dressing about 1 hour in refrigerator.

Provençal Tomato Hash: Mix equal

quantities diced, peeled, seeded tomatoes, diced cucumber, and pitted ripe or green olives. Dress with olive oil and red wine vinegar, season with minced fresh parsley and dill or fennel, and let stand at room temperature about 1 hour. Sprinkle with freshly ground pepper and serve in lettuce cups.

CAESAR SALAD

Makes 6 servings

1 clove garlic, peeled
⅔ cup olive oil (about)
2 cups ½" bread cubes made from stale French or Italian bread
1 large head romaine, washed and crisped
½ teaspoon salt
¼ teaspoon pepper
1 egg (either raw or boiled in the shell 1 minute)
3–4 tablespoons lemon juice
6 anchovy fillets, drained and minced
⅓ cup grated Parmesan cheese

Crush garlic into oil, cover, and let stand overnight at room temperature. Next day, drain oil from garlic; discard garlic. Heat ⅓ cup of the oil in a heavy skillet over moderately high heat 1–2 minutes. When hot but not smoking, add bread cubes and brown on all sides, tossing constantly. Drain on paper toweling and reserve. (*Note:* You can do these well ahead of time to avoid a last minute rush.) Break romaine in bite-size pieces into a salad bowl. Sprinkle with remaining oil, the salt and pepper and toss; add a few extra drops oil if needed to coat all leaves lightly. Break egg into a cup and slide onto salad, pour lemon juice directly on egg, and toss lightly. Add anchovies, Parmesan, and bread cubes, toss again, and serve. About 295 calories per serving.

VARIATION:

⊠ **Jiffy Caesar Salad:** Rub a large salad bowl with a cut clove garlic; break romaine into bowl, top with the egg and anchovy fillets. Toss, add 1–1½ cups packaged plain or seasoned croutons, ⅓ cup grated Parmesan, and ⅓ cup French dressing, and toss again. About 205 calories per serving.

⚖ WINTER HEALTH SALAD

A brilliant combination of vegetables.

Makes 4–6 servings

2 cups finely shredded cabbage
1 sweet green pepper, cored, seeded, and cut in julienne strips
1 pimiento, seeded and cut in julienne strips
1 medium-size carrot, coarsely grated (scrub but do not peel)
1 small red onion, peeled and minced, or ¼ cup minced scallions (include tops)
½ cup minced celery (include tops)
½ cup minced cucumber (do not peel unless cucumbers are waxed)
½ small white turnip, peeled and finely grated
⅓ cup tiny cauliflowerets or broccoli flowerets (optional)
4 radishes, thinly sliced
¼–⅓ cup French dressing

Chill all vegetables well; add just enough dressing to coat all lightly, toss, and serve. For lunch, top with a scoop of cottage cheese or cubed sharp Cheddar. About 65 calories for each of 4 servings, 45 calories for each of 6 (without cheese).

VARIATION:

⚖ **Extra-Low-Calorie Winter Health Salad:** Prepare as directed but dress with Tangy Low-Calorie Salad Dressing. About 45 calories for each of 4 servings, 30 calories for each of 6 (without cheese).

SALADS AND SALAD DRESSINGS

NASTURTIUM SALAD

Nasturtium leaves make a sharp and pungent salad.
Makes 4–6 servings

1 pint young nasturtium leaves, washed and patted dry on paper toweling
1 quart prepared mixed salad greens

Dressing:
⅓ cup olive oil
½ clove garlic, peeled and crushed
1 tablespoon minced parsley
½ teaspoon minced fresh marjoram or ¼ teaspoon dried marjoram
¼ teaspoon salt
⅛ teaspoon pepper
¼ cup sour cream
2 tablespoons tarragon vinegar

Place nasturtium leaves and greens in a salad bowl. Beat dressing ingredients until creamy, pour over greens, toss lightly to mix, and serve. About 220 calories for each of 4 servings, 150 calories for each of 6 servings.

WILTED SPINACH SALAD WITH HOT BACON DRESSING

Makes 4–6 servings

1 (10-ounce) bag fresh spinach

Dressing:
6 slices bacon, cut crosswise in julienne strips
2 scallions, washed and sliced thin (include some tops)
½ cup red wine vinegar
2 tablespoons ketchup
½ teaspoon salt
⅛ teaspoon pepper

Sort spinach carefully, removing blemished leaves and coarse stems; wash in a colander under cold running water. Pat dry on paper toweling, then place in a large salad bowl. Brown bacon in a skillet and drain on paper toweling. Stir-fry scallions in drippings 5–8 minutes until tender, mix in remaining dressing ingredients, and heat, stirring, about 5 minutes. Pour hot dressing over spinach and toss well. Sprinkle in bacon crumbles, toss again, and serve. About 180 calories for each of 4 servings, 120 calories for each of 6 servings.

WILTED LETTUCE

An old Southern salad, slightly sweet-sour.
Makes 4 servings

4 slices bacon
2 tablespoons cider vinegar
1 teaspoon sugar
¼ teaspoon salt
⅛ teaspoon pepper
1 quart prepared mixed salad greens
¼ cup minced scallions (optional)

Fry bacon until crisp, drain on paper toweling, crumble, and reserve. Drain all but 3 tablespoons drippings from skillet; mix in vinegar, sugar, salt, and pepper and heat and stir just until simmering. Pour over greens and, if you like, scallions, add bacon, toss, and serve. About 165 calories per serving.

VARIATION:

Carolina-Style Wilted Lettuce: Heat ¼ cup bacon or ham drippings in a small skillet; mix in ½ cup boiling water, the vinegar, sugar, salt, and pepper and bring to a boil. Pour over 1 quart prepared iceberg lettuce, toss, and garnish with sliced hard-cooked eggs and scallions. Delicious with fried country ham. About 185 calories per serving.

STUFFED LETTUCE

Makes 6 servings

1 medium-size head iceberg lettuce

Stuffing:
1 (8-ounce) package cream cheese, softened to room temperature
1 tablespoon mayonnaise
1 teaspoon finely grated yellow onion
¼ cup finely grated carrot
¼ cup minced sweet red or green pepper
¼ cup peeled, minced, well-drained tomato
Few drops liquid hot red pepper seasoning
¼ teaspoon salt

Core lettuce and make a small hollow (save scraps for another salad). Mix stuffing ingredients and pack firmly into hollow. Wrap lettuce in foil or Saran and chill well. Slice crosswise about ¾" thick and serve with French or Thousand Island Dressing. About 155 calories per serving.

VARIATION:

Fruit-Stuffed Lettuce: Core and hollow out lettuce as directed. Instead of the stuffing above, mix 1 (8-ounce) package softened cream cheese with 1 tablespoon each mayonnaise and lemon juice, ½ cup well-drained crushed pineapple, fruit salad, or chopped raw apple, and ¼ cup minced toasted almonds, pecans, or walnuts. Stuff and chill as directed. About 220 calories per serving.

JAPANESE VEGETABLE SALAD WITH TOASTED SESAME SEED DRESSING

Toasted sesame seeds provide a rich nutty flavor.
Makes 4 servings

2 cups prepared mixed salad greens
1 cup finely shredded or sliced red cabbage
1 cup fine julienne strips of peeled, seeded cucumber
½ cup finely shredded radishes
½ cup finely shredded carrot or raw broccoli stalks
½ cup minced cooked shrimp, scallops, or delicate white fish (optional)

Dressing:
3 tablespoons peanut or other salad oil
2 tablespoons sesame seeds
¼ cup rice vinegar or 2 tablespoons cider vinegar
2 tablespoons mirin or cream sherry
1 tablespoon lemon juice
1 tablespoon soy sauce

Place greens, vegetables, and, if you like, shrimp in a large salad bowl. Heat and stir oil and sesame seeds in a small, heavy skillet over moderately high heat about 1 minute until pale caramel colored; remove from heat and stir 1 minute longer. (*Note:* Be careful not to overbrown seeds—they'll be bitter.) Mix in remaining dressing ingredients, pour over salad mixture, toss lightly, and serve. About 165 calories per serving (with shrimp).

CREAMY SWEET-SOUR COLESLAW

This coleslaw is even better the second day.
Makes 6–8 servings

2 quarts moderately finely grated cabbage
¼ cup finely grated Bermuda or Spanish onion
2 medium-size carrots, peeled and grated moderately fine
2 tablespoons minced sweet green pepper
½ cup relish-type sandwich spread
½ cup sour cream
2 tablespoons tarragon vinegar
1 teaspoon salt
⅛ teaspoon pepper

SALADS AND SALAD DRESSINGS

Place all ingredients in a large bowl and toss thoroughly to mix. Cover and chill 2–3 hours. Stir well and serve. About 165 calories for each of 6 servings, 125 calories for each of 8 servings.

CARAWAY COLESLAW WITH CREAMY OIL AND VINEGAR DRESSING

A fragrant sweet-sour slaw. Olive oil makes the difference.
Makes 6–8 servings

2 *quarts moderately finely grated cabbage*
1 *medium-size yellow onion, peeled and grated fine*

Dressing:
⅓ *cup olive oil*
⅓ *cup tarragon vinegar*
2 *tablespoons superfine sugar*
1 *tablespoon caraway seeds*
1 *teaspoon salt*
⅛ *teaspoon pepper*
1 *cup sour cream*

Place cabbage and onion in a large bowl. Mix all dressing ingredients except sour cream and stir until sugar dissolves; blend in sour cream. Pour dressing over cabbage and toss well to mix. Cover and chill several hours before serving. About 250 calories for each of 6 servings, 185 calories for each of 8 servings.

VARIATION:

Red and Green Slaw: Prepare as directed, using a ½ and ½ mixture of moderately finely grated red and green cabbage. About 260 calories for each of 6 servings, 195 calories for each of 8 servings.

OLD-FASHIONED CAROLINA COLESLAW WITH CELERY SEED DRESSING

The mustardy dressing has plenty of bite.
Makes 6 servings

1 *medium-size cabbage, trimmed, cored, and quartered*

Dressing:
2 *eggs*
1½ *teaspoons powdered mustard*
3 *tablespoons sugar*
½ *teaspoon salt*
¾ *cup heavy cream*
⅓ *cup boiling cider vinegar*
1 *tablespoon butter or margarine*
1½ *teaspoons celery seeds*

Slice cabbage quarters paper thin and place in a large mixing bowl. Lightly beat eggs in the top of a double boiler and mix in mustard, sugar, and salt. Beat in cream, then add vinegar in a slow stream, stirring constantly. Heat and stir over simmering water 3–5 minutes until the consistency of stirred custard. Off heat, mix in butter and celery seeds; pour dressing over cabbage and toss well to mix. Cover and chill 2–3 hours. Just before serving, toss well again. About 230 calories per serving.

MARINATED HEARTS OF PALM

Makes 3–4 servings

1 *(14-ounce) can hearts of palm, drained*
3 *tablespoons olive oil*
1–2 *tablespoons red wine vinegar or lemon juice*
Freshly ground black pepper
1 *tablespoon minced fresh tarragon, chervil, dill, chives, or parsley*
1 *pimiento, slivered*

Halve hearts of palm lengthwise and

arrange in a large flat-bottomed bowl. Drizzle evenly with olive oil and vinegar, add a couple of grindings of pepper, sprinkle with tarragon, cover, and marinate in refrigerator 2–3 hours, turning occasionally. Garnish with pimiento and serve as is or on a bed of dark crisp greens. Calorie counts unavailable for hearts of palm.

VARIATION:

Prepare as directed but substitute ¼–⅓ cup French or Garlic Dressing (or any favorite tart dressing) for the oil and vinegar. Calorie counts unavailable for hearts of palm.

RAW ZUCCHINI SALAD

Use only the tenderest young zucchini for making this salad. Otherwise it may be too bitter.
Makes 4–6 servings

2 cups thinly sliced unpeeled baby zucchini, chilled
2 medium-size firm-ripe tomatoes, cored and thinly sliced
1 medium-size red onion, peeled, sliced paper thin, and separated into rings
¾ cup thinly sliced raw, peeled mushrooms (optional)
⅓ cup French dressing
2 cups prepared mixed salad greens

Mix all ingredients except greens, cover, and chill 1 hour, turning now and then. Line a salad bowl with the greens, mound zucchini mixture on top, and toss at the table (there should be enough dressing for the greens, too; if not add a little more). About 185 calories for each of 4 servings, 125 calories for each of 6 servings.

VARIATION:

Okra Salad: Prepare as directed but substitute baby okra for zucchini. About 205 calories for each of 4 servings, 140 calories for each of 6 servings.

¢ RADISH SALAD

Makes 4 servings

¾ cup very thinly sliced red radishes
¾ cup very thinly sliced white radishes
1 small sweet green pepper, cored, seeded, and cut in julienne strips
¼ cup minced celery root
¼ cup French dressing
1 teaspoon sugar

Toss all ingredients together, chill ½ hour, and serve on crisp greens. About 110 calories per serving.

RAW MUSHROOM SALAD

A perfectly elegant salad aromatic of tarragon. Plan it for a special dinner. Delicious with poultry or seafood.
Makes 4 servings

1 pound medium-size mushrooms, rinsed in cold water, patted dry, and sliced thin
2 tablespoons minced fresh tarragon or 1 teaspoon dried tarragon
1 tablespoon minced chives
⅔ cup olive oil
2 tablespoons tarragon vinegar
Juice of ½ lemon
¼ teaspoon salt
⅛ teaspoon pepper

Place all ingredients in a mixing bowl and toss well to mix. Cover and marinate 1–3 hours at room temperature. Drain and serve as is or on crisp lettuce leaves. About 185 calories per serving.

RAW CAULIFLOWER SALAD WITH SOUR CREAM-PARMESAN DRESSING

Makes 4–6 servings

1 medium-size cauliflower, trimmed, divided into flowerets, and sliced paper thin
1 cup thinly sliced radishes
½ cup minced watercress leaves
2 tablespoons minced scallions

Dressing:
1 cup sour cream
½ clove garlic, peeled and crushed
Juice of ½ lemon
2 tablespoons olive or other salad oil
1 tablespoon finely grated Parmesan cheese
½ teaspoon salt
⅛ teaspoon black pepper
Pinch cayenne pepper

Toss cauliflower with radishes, watercress, and scallions and chill about ½ hour. Meanwhile, blend together dressing ingredients. Pour dressing over salad mixture, toss well, and serve. About 215 calories for each of 4 servings, 145 calories for each of 6 servings.

¢ ⚖ WILTED CUCUMBERS

Makes 4 servings

2 medium-size cucumbers, peeled or not (as you like) and sliced paper thin
1½ teaspoons salt
2 tablespoons boiling water
2 tablespoons sugar
⅓ cup white, tarragon, or cider vinegar
Grinding of pepper

Layer cucumbers in a bowl, salting as you go, weight down, cover, and let stand at room temperature 1–2 hours. Drain, wash in a colander under cold running water, then drain and press out as much liquid as possible; pat dry on paper toweling. Mix water and sugar until sugar dissolves, add vinegar, pour over cucumbers, and toss well. Cover and chill 1–2 hours, mixing now and then. Top with a grinding of pepper and serve as is or in lettuce cups. About 40 calories per serving.

CUCUMBERS IN SOUR CREAM

Good with fish, shellfish, or ham.
Makes 4 servings

¾ cup sour cream
1 tablespoon tarragon vinegar
1 tablespoon lemon juice
1 tablespoon minced fresh dill
¼ teaspoon salt
⅛ teaspoon pepper
2 medium-size cucumbers, peeled and sliced ¼" thick

Blend all ingredients but cucumbers, add cucumbers, and toss to mix. Cover and chill 1–2 hours. Toss again and serve. About 110 calories per serving.

TURKISH CUCUMBER SALAD (CACIK)

A cooling salad dressed with yogurt and seasoned with fresh mint and dill.
Makes 6–8 servings

4 medium-size cucumbers, peeled and quartered lengthwise

Dressing:
1 pint yogurt
1 clove garlic, peeled and crushed
2 tablespoons olive oil
Juice of ½ lemon
1 tablespoon minced fresh mint
2 tablespoons minced fresh dill
½ teaspoon salt
⅛ teaspoon white pepper

Slice cucumber quarters ⅛" thick and drain on paper toweling. Beat dressing ingredients until creamy, add cucumbers, and toss well to mix. Cover and chill several hours. Toss again, serve in small bowls or, if you prefer, crisp lettuce cups. About 105 calories for each of 6 servings, 80 calories for each of 8 servings.

⚔ ¢ ORIENTAL CUCUMBER SALAD

Sliced cucumbers in an unusual soy-red wine vinegar dressing.
Makes 6 servings

3 large cucumbers, scrubbed well and sliced thin
3 tablespoons soy sauce
3 tablespoons red wine vinegar
3 tablespoons peanut oil
⅛ teaspoon pepper

Place cucumber slices in a large, shallow bowl. Mix remaining ingredients and pour over cucumbers. Toss well, cover, and chill several hours, tossing occasionally so all cucumber slices are marinated. Serve cold. About 85 calories per serving.

SALADE NIÇOISE

When served as a luncheon entree, this classic salad usually contains tuna (see seafood chapter for recipe).
Makes 4 servings

1 clove garlic, peeled and halved
1 head Boston lettuce, trimmed, broken in bite-size pieces, and chilled
½ cup French dressing
2 cups cold diced cooked potatoes
2 cups cold cooked cut green beans
½ cup ripe olives
2 tomatoes, cored and cut in wedges
1 (2-ounce) can rolled anchovies, drained
1 tablespoon capers
1 teaspoon minced fresh chervil
1 teaspoon minced fresh tarragon

Rub a salad bowl with garlic, add lettuce, 2–3 tablespoons dressing, and toss. Mix ¼ cup dressing with potatoes and beans, then pile on lettuce. Garnish with olives, tomatoes, and anchovies, sprinkle with capers, herbs, and remaining salad dressing. Do not toss. About 340 calories per serving.

RUSSIAN SALAD

Makes 6 servings

1 cup cold diced cooked potatoes
1 cup cold cooked cut green beans
1 cup cold diced cooked carrots
1 cup cold cooked green peas
⅓ cup French dressing
⅓ cup mayonnaise
1 cup cold diced cooked beets
1 head Boston or romaine lettuce, trimmed, and chilled
1 tablespoon capers

Mix all vegetables except beets with French dressing, cover, and chill 2–3 hours. Drain and save dressing; mix 1 tablespoon with mayonnaise, add to vegetables along with beets, and toss well. Mound on lettuce and top with capers. About 245 calories per serving.

MOLDED COTTAGE CHEESE AND SPINACH SALAD

Makes 6–8 servings

1 quart lightly packed prepared fresh spinach leaves, minced
3 hard-cooked eggs, peeled and diced
1½ cups cottage cheese
1 medium-size sweet green pepper, cored, seeded, and minced
½ cup minced celery
½ cup mayonnaise
1¼ teaspoons salt
⅛ teaspoon pepper

Mix all ingredients and pack into a lightly oiled 5-cup ring mold. Cover and chill 3–4 hours. Unmold and garnish, if you like, with tomato wedges and parsley or watercress sprigs. About 300 calories for each of 6 servings, 225 calories for each of 8 servings.

OLD-FASHIONED POTATO SALAD

Nothing fancy but unusually good.
Makes 6 servings

6 medium-size boiled potatoes, chilled, peeled, and cubed
4 hard-cooked eggs, chilled, peeled, and diced
½ medium-size sweet green pepper, cored, seeded, and minced
1 medium-size yellow onion, peeled and minced
2 stalks celery, diced
1 cup mayonnaise
¼ cup sweet pickle relish
1½ teaspoons salt
⅛ teaspoon pepper

Stir all ingredients together to mix, cover, and chill several hours before serving. Serve as is or in crisp lettuce cups. About 480 calories per serving.

HERBED POTATO SALAD

Dill and marjoram make this salad especially fragrant.
Makes 6–8 servings

6 medium-size boiled potatoes, chilled, peeled, and cubed
6 hard-cooked eggs, chilled, peeled, and diced
1 medium-size yellow onion, peeled and minced
4 stalks celery, diced
½ cup minced sweet green pepper (optional)
½ cup minced dill pickle
1 cup mayonnaise
½ cup light cream
2 tablespoons white wine vinegar
2 tablespoons minced fresh dill or ¼ teaspoon dried dill
½ teaspoon minced fresh marjoram or ¼ teaspoon dried marjoram
1½ teaspoons salt
⅛ teaspoon pepper

Mix all ingredients in a very large bowl, cover, and chill several hours before serving. About 545 calories for each of 6 servings, 410 calories for each of 8 servings.

GERMAN POTATO SALAD

Nice and tart.
Makes 6 servings

1 tablespoon flour
¾ cup cold water
¼ cup cider vinegar
2 tablespoons sugar
¼ teaspoon white pepper
2–3 teaspoons salt
6 medium-size warm boiled potatoes, peeled and cubed
½ cup minced yellow onion
½ cup minced sweet green pepper
1 cup coarsely chopped celery
3–4 slices crisp cooked bacon, crumbled
6 hard-cooked eggs, peeled and diced

Blend flour and 2 tablespoons water in a small saucepan, add remaining water, vinegar, sugar, pepper, and 2 teaspoons salt, and cook, stirring, until mixture boils. Place potatoes, onion, green pepper and celery in a large bowl and toss lightly. Pour in hot dressing and mix well. Cool to room temperature, add bacon and eggs, and toss again. Taste for salt and add more if needed. Serve at room temperature. About 250 calories per serving.

VARIATION:

Hot German Potato Salad: Cut 4 strips bacon crosswise in julienne strips, brown in a large skillet, and drain on paper toweling. In drippings stir-fry ⅔ cup minced onion until golden, 5–8 minutes. Blend in 1 tablespoon flour, add ¾ cup water or beef broth and the vinegar, sugar, salt, and pepper called for above. Heat and stir until mixture boils; keep warm. While potatoes are still hot, slice thin into a large bowl; scatter with bacon, omit green pepper, celery, and eggs. Pour hot dressing over potatoes, toss gently to mix, sprinkle with 1 tablespoon minced parsley, and serve. About 195 calories per serving.

SPANISH POTATO SALAD

What makes it Spanish are the green olives and olive oil dressing.
Makes 6 servings

6 *medium-size boiled potatoes, chilled, peeled, and sliced thin*
¾ *cup minced pimiento-stuffed green olives*
2 *tablespoons finely grated Spanish or Bermuda onion*
⅓ *cup olive oil*
2 *teaspoons white wine vinegar*
⅛ *teaspoon pepper*

Mix all ingredients in a large bowl, cover, and chill several hours before serving. About 240 calories per serving.

CELERY VICTOR

This cool American classic was created by Victor Hirtzler, for years chef at San Francisco's stately old St. Francis Hotel.
Makes 4 servings

1 *large bunch celery, prepared for cooking*
1½ *cups boiling beef bouillon*
1 *cup French dressing*
1 *small bunch watercress or 1½ cups finely shredded iceberg lettuce*
¼ *teaspoon salt*
⅛ *teaspoon pepper*

1 *tablespoon minced parsley*
8 *anchovy fillets*
1 *large ripe tomato, cut in 8 wedges*
8–12 *ripe olives*

Cut celery in 3″ lengths and simmer, covered, in bouillon 30 minutes until tender. Drain celery, toss with dressing, cover, and marinate in the refrigerator 4–6 hours or overnight. To serve, arrange watercress or lettuce on individual salad plates. Lift celery from dressing and arrange on top. Sprinkle each portion with salt, pepper, and parsley and decorate with anchovies, tomato wedges, and olives. Serve as an appetizer or salad. About 175 calories per serving.

ASPARAGUS VINAIGRETTE

Makes 4 servings

2 *pounds asparagus, steamed or poached, or 2 (10-ounce) packages frozen asparagus spears, cooked by package directions*
⅔ *cup French Dressing or Spanish Vinaigrette*

Drain asparagus well. Arrange in a large, shallow bowl, pour in dressing, cover, and marinate in refrigerator several hours, turning now and then. Serve on a bed of lettuce as a salad or first course. About 135 calories per serving (if made with French Dressing), 140 per serving (if made with Spanish Vinaigrette).

VARIATION:

Other Vegetables to Serve Vinaigrette:
Artichoke hearts and bottoms, beans (green, wax, and lima), broccoli, carrots, cauliflower, celeriac, celery (especially the hearts), cucumbers, endive, fennel, hearts of palm, leeks, green peas, zucchini. Simply cook by basic method, drain well, add enough French Dressing to coat

SALADS AND SALAD DRESSINGS

lightly, and marinate several hours in the refrigerator. Recipe too flexible for a meaningful calorie count.

CURRIED ASPARAGUS SALAD

Makes 3–4 servings

1 pound hot steamed asparagus or 1 (1-pound) can asparagus, drained
½ cup French Dressing
6–8 lettuce leaves, washed and crisped
1 pimiento, drained and cut in ¼" strips

Curry Dressing:
½ cup mayonnaise
1 tablespoon sour cream
½ teaspoon curry powder
½ teaspoon lemon juice

Marinate asparagus in French Dressing 3–4 hours in refrigerator, turning occasionally. Shortly before serving, mix Curry Dressing. Drain asparagus (reserve French Dressing for other salads later) and arrange on lettuce. Top with Curry Dressing, garnish with pimiento, and serve. About 375 calories for each of 3 servings, 280 calories for each of 4 servings.

GREEN BEAN SALAD

Cooked green beans in a spicy red dressing. Especially good with pork, ham, or lamb.
Makes 6 servings

1½ pounds green beans, boiled and drained, or 2 (9-ounce) packages frozen cut green beans, cooked and drained by package directions
1 medium-size red onion, peeled and sliced thin

Dressing:
2 tablespoons minced fresh tarragon or ½ teaspoon dried tarragon
1 clove garlic, peeled and crushed
2 teaspoons prepared spicy brown mustard
1 tablespoon ketchup
½ teaspoon salt
Pinch pepper
½ cup olive oil
3 tablespoons red or white wine vinegar

Place beans and onion in a large bowl. Blend together dressing ingredients, pour over beans and onion, and toss to mix. Cover and let stand at room temperature about 1 hour. Toss again and serve. About 200 calories per serving.

THREE BEAN SALAD

Green, wax, and kidney beans marinated in a sweet-sour dressing.
Makes 6 servings

1 (1-pound) can cut green beans, drained
1 (1-pound) can wax beans, drained
1 (1-pound) can red kidney beans, drained
1 cup minced celery
1 cup minced sweet green pepper
1 cup minced yellow onion
½ cup minced sweet or dill pickle (optional)
½ cup olive oil
6 tablespoons cider vinegar
3 tablespoons sugar
1 teaspoon salt
⅛ teaspoon pepper

Mix all ingredients, cover, and chill several hours before serving. About 355 calories per serving.

HOT SWEET-SOUR BEAN SPROUT SALAD

Delicious with roast pork, ham, chicken, or turkey.
Makes 4 servings

1 pound fresh bean sprouts (readily available in Oriental groceries and occasionally in supermarkets)

Dressing:
6 slices bacon, cut crosswise in julienne strips
1 small yellow onion, peeled and coarsely chopped
½ small sweet green pepper, cored, seeded, and coarsely chopped
1 tablespoon ketchup
¼ cup tarragon vinegar
¼ teaspoon salt
Pinch pepper

Wash sprouts several times in cool water, discard any that are dark or blemished, and drain the rest in a colander. Brown bacon in a small skillet and drain on paper toweling. Stir-fry onion and green pepper in drippings over moderate heat 8–10 minutes until onion is golden. Mix in remaining dressing ingredients and simmer, uncovered, 5 minutes. Just before serving, set colander of sprouts in sink and turn on hot water full blast. Move colander about so all sprouts are heated—this will take 3–4 minutes. Quickly drain sprouts and place in a salad bowl. Pour in hot dressing, add bacon, toss to mix, and serve. About 210 calories per serving.

DRIED BEAN SALAD

Makes 4 servings

2 cups any cold boiled dried beans
⅓ cup minced celery
⅓ cup minced sweet green pepper
⅓ cup minced yellow onion
3 tablespoons olive or other salad oil
2 tablespoons cider vinegar
1–2 tablespoons sugar
½ teaspoon salt (about)
⅛ teaspoon pepper
2 tablespoons minced parsley

Mix all ingredients, cover, and chill several hours or overnight, tossing now and then. Taste for salt and adjust. About 235 calories per serving.

VARIATIONS:

Creamy Dried Bean Salad: Prepare as directed but omit oil and add ⅓ cup mayonnaise and 2–3 tablespoons chili sauce. About 300 calories per serving.

Parmesan Bean Salad: Prepare and chill salad as directed. Just before serving toss in ¼ cup finely grated Parmesan cheese. About 260 calories per serving.

Bean and Beet Salad (Makes 6 servings): Prepare as directed but add 1 (1-pound) can pickled beets, drained and diced, and 2 extra tablespoons olive oil. About 325 calories per serving.

CHICK-PEA AND TOMATO SALAD

Keeps well in the refrigerator and is actually better after 1 or 2 days. Makes 6–8 servings

2 medium-size ripe tomatoes, peeled, cored, seeded, and cubed
½ cup minced sweet green pepper
½ cup minced Bermuda or Spanish onion
1 clove garlic, peeled and crushed
3 (1-pound 4-ounce) cans chick-peas, drained well
¼ cup minced parsley
1 tablespoon minced chives
1 teaspoon minced fresh marjoram or ½ teaspoon dried marjoram or oregano
½ teaspoon salt
⅛ teaspoon pepper
¼ cup olive oil
3 tablespoons red wine vinegar

Place all ingredients in a large bowl and toss well to mix. Cover and marinate at room temperature at least 1 hour. Toss well again and serve. About 200 calories for each of 6 servings, 150 calories for each of 8 servings.

RICE AND BLACK-EYED PEA SALAD

Makes 6 servings

1 quart hot boiled rice
1 (10-ounce) package frozen black-eyed peas, cooked and drained by package directions
1 medium-size yellow onion, peeled and minced
1 clove garlic, peeled and crushed
1 large carrot, peeled and coarsely grated
¼ cup minced parsley
1½ teaspoons salt
⅛ teaspoon black or cayenne pepper
3–4 tablespoons olive oil

Mix all ingredients together, adding just enough oil to coat all lightly. Serve warm or at room temperature as a main dish salad. Good mounded in hollowed-out tomatoes. About 240 calories per serving.

BASIC MACARONI SALAD

Makes 6 servings

½ pound elbow macaroni, cooked and drained by package directions and chilled
1 cup diced celery
½ cup minced scallions or 1 small yellow onion, peeled and minced
⅓ cup minced sweet green and/or red pepper
1 cup mayonnaise or mayonnaise-type salad dressing
2 tablespoons white vinegar or lemon juice
2 teaspoons prepared mild yellow mustard
1½ teaspoons salt (about)
⅛ teaspoon pepper

Mix all ingredients, cover, and chill several hours; taste for salt and adjust. Serve garnished with tomato wedges and quartered hard-cooked egg. About 465 calories per serving.

VARIATIONS:

Cheese-Macaroni Salad: Prepare as directed but add 1 cup diced sharp Cheddar, Swiss, or Gruyère cheese and use ½ cup each mayonnaise and Roquefort or blue cheese dressing. About 540 calories per serving.

Macaroni and Meat, Chicken or Shellfish Salad: Prepare as directed but add 3 cups cubed cooked ham, tongue, chicken, turkey or shellfish and an extra ⅓ cup mayonnaise or ¼ cup French dressing. Serve as an entree. About 705 calories per serving (made with ham or tongue), 655 per serving (made with chicken or turkey), 630 (made with shellfish).

German Macaroni Salad: Omit mayonnaise and vinegar; dress instead with ½ cup olive oil and ¼ cup white wine vinegar; also add 1 large minced dill pickle. About 345 calories per serving.

"Deli" Salad: Mix 2 cups Basic Macaroni Salad with 2–2½ cups mixed cubed salami, bologna, corned beef, ham, tongue, luncheon meat, or chicken roll—whatever combination pleases you; chill well and serve as an entree. About 575 calories per serving (if made with any of the meats), 545 calories per serving (made with chicken).

RICE-STUFFED TOMATOES AL PESTO

Makes 8 servings

8 large ripe beefsteak tomatoes

Stuffing:
2 cups water
¼ cup olive oil
1 cup uncooked rice
1 medium-size yellow onion, peeled and minced

1 clove garlic, peeled and crushed
2 tablespoons minced parsley
2 tablespoons minced fresh basil
½ cup piñon nuts
2 tablespoons finely grated Parmesan cheese
¾ teaspoon salt
Pinch pepper

Core tomatoes, scoop out seeds and pulp, leaving only firm outer walls; drain upside down on several thicknesses paper toweling. Bring water and 1 tablespoon olive oil to a boil in a small saucepan, stir in rice, and boil rapidly uncovered, stirring occasionally, 10–12 minutes until almost all water is absorbed; turn heat to low and let rice dry out. Meanwhile, stir-fry onion and garlic in remaining oil in a large, heavy skillet over moderate heat 8–10 minutes until golden. Mix in rice and remaining stuffing ingredients, turn heat to low, and heat, stirring occasionally, 5 minutes; cool to room temperature. Stuff tomatoes with mixture and serve as an entree. About 245 calories per serving.

TABBOULEH

A Middle Eastern salad that can also be served as a first course.
Makes 4–6 servings

1 cup uncooked bulgur wheat
2 cups boiling chicken broth or water
1 cup minced parsley
¼ cup minced fresh mint or 2 tablespoons dried mint
1 medium-size yellow onion, peeled and minced
2 ripe tomatoes, peeled, cored, and coarsely chopped
¼ cup olive oil
¼ cup lemon juice
½ teaspoon salt (*about*)
⅛ teaspoon pepper
½ head romaine lettuce, trimmed and chilled

Mix bulgur wheat and broth, cover, and let stand at room temperature 2 hours. Fluff with a fork, add parsley, mint, onion, and tomatoes, and toss to mix. Beat oil, lemon juice, salt, and pepper until well blended, add to salad, and toss again. Cover and chill well. Taste for salt and adjust if needed. Arrange romaine leaves spoke fashion on a platter or in a shallow bowl and mound salad in center. Diners can serve themselves by scooping up salad with romaine leaves, or individual portions can be served on leaves. About 310 calories for each of 4 servings, 210 calories for each of 6 servings.

CHEF'S SALAD

Makes 4 servings

3 cups prepared mixed salad greens (*include watercress if possible*)
½ medium-size cucumber, peeled and cut in ¼″ cubes
½ medium-size Spanish onion, peeled and sliced thin
1 cup julienne strips boiled ham, chilled
½ cup julienne strips cooked smoked tongue, chilled
1 cup julienne strips cooked white meat of chicken or turkey, chilled
½ cup julienne strips Swiss cheese, chilled
4 radishes, washed and sliced thin
½–¾ cup French dressing

Toss greens lightly with cucumber and onion in a large salad bowl. Group ham, tongue, chicken, and cheese on greens in a spoke fashion; fill center with radishes. Cover and chill until serving time. Dress at the table by adding about ½ cup dressing and tossing gently. About 410 calories per serving.

VARIATIONS:
— Use any combination of meat and cheese instead of those listed—luncheon meat, salami, headcheese, Cheddar cheese, etc.
— Substitute boneless sardines, flaked tuna, or cooked, smoked, flaked haddock for the ham and/or tongue.
— Use washed, crisped spinach leaves as part of the greens.
— Use any favorite salad dressing instead of French—Russian, Thousand Island, Italian, Green Goddess, etc.

Recipe variations all too flexible for meaningful calorie counts.

CHICKEN OR TURKEY SALAD

A good basic salad to vary according to whim.

Makes 6 servings

3 cups diced cold cooked chicken or turkey meat
1 cup diced celery
¼ cup minced yellow onion or scallions
¼ cup minced sweet green pepper (optional)
2 tablespoons minced pimiento
¾ cup mayonnaise
2 tablespoons French dressing, lemon juice, or milk
¼ teaspoon salt (about)
⅛ teaspoon pepper
1 tablespoon minced parsley (garnish)

Mix all ingredients except parsley, cover, and chill 2–3 hours. Taste for salt and adjust. Sprinkle with parsley and serve. For a party, mound in avocado halves or hollowed-out tomatoes. About 425 calories per serving (if made with French dressing), 395 calories per serving (if made with lemon juice or milk).

To Use for Sandwiches: Mince chicken instead of dicing, then proceed as directed.

VARIATIONS:

Chicken, Egg, and Caper Salad: Prepare as directed using French dressing, but mix in 3 diced, peeled, hard-cooked eggs and 2 tablespoons each capers and minced sweet or dill pickle. About 470 calories per serving.

Chicken and Vegetable Salad: Reduce celery to ½ cup and mix in 1–1½ cups any of the following combinations: mixed cooked peas and diced carrots; diced avocado and cucumber; diced cooked potatoes and cooked cut green beans; cooked asparagus tips and diced radishes; diced unpeeled raw baby zucchini and diced, peeled, cored, and seeded tomatoes; drained canned bean sprouts, shredded Chinese cabbage, and slivered water chestnuts. Recipe too flexible for a meaningful calorie count.

Chicken, Olive, and Walnut Salad: Reduce celery to ½ cup and add ½ cup each sliced pitted ripe or green olives and ⅓ cup coarsely chopped walnuts. About 500 calories per serving (if made with French dressing), 470 per serving (if made with milk or lemon juice).

Chicken and Ham Salad: Prepare as directed, using 1½ cups each diced, cooked ham (or tongue, luncheon meat, corned beef, cooked veal or lamb) and chicken. Recipe too flexible for a meaningful calorie count.

Chicken and Seafood Salad: Prepare as directed, using 1½ cups each diced, cooked fish or shellfish and chicken. About 425 calories per serving (if made with French dressing), 395 calories per serving (if made with lemon juice or milk).

Some Quick Ways to Vary the Flavor: Mix any of the following into mayonnaise before adding to salad:
- 2 teaspoons curry or chili powder
- ¼ cup minced hot chutney, hot mustard pickle, or hot pepper relish
- 1 tablespoon prepared spicy brown mustard or prepared horseradish
- 2 tablespoons soy sauce and 1 tablespoon Worcestershire sauce (omit salt)
- ¼ cup chili sauce or any thick bottled salad dressing (Roquefort, Russian, Thousand Island, etc.)
- 2 tablespoons minced fresh dill, basil, or chives (or 1 teaspoon dried).

Flavor variations too flexible for meaningful calorie counts.

CHICKEN WALDORF SALAD

Makes 4 servings

3 cups ½" *cubes of cold cooked chicken meat*
2 *medium-size tart apples, peeled, cored, and diced*
⅔ *cup minced celery*
¼ *cup coarsely chopped pecans*
2 *tablespoons toasted, blanched, slivered almonds*
1½ *cups mayonnaise*
1 *teaspoon salt*
⅛ *teaspoon white pepper*

Mix all ingredients well, cover, and chill 2–3 hours. Stir, taste for salt and add more if needed. Serve in lettuce cups, avocado halves, or hollowed-out tomatoes. About 875 calories per serving (in lettuce cups).

CHOW CHOW CHICKEN OR TURKEY SALAD

Makes 4 servings

1½–1¾ *cups cold diced, cooked chicken or turkey meat (preferably white meat)*
1 *cup finely chopped celery*
⅓ *cup coarsely chopped mustard pickles*
1 *pimiento, drained and minced*
¼ *cup coarsely chopped, blanched almonds*
1 *teaspoon finely grated yellow onion*
½–1 *teaspoon salt*
⅛ *teaspoon white pepper*
¼ *cup French dressing*
⅓ *cup mayonnaise*

Mix together all ingredients, cover, and chill 2–3 hours to blend flavors. Serve as is or in lettuce cups, hollowed-out tomatoes, or avocado halves. For a touch of the exotic, serve in mango or small papaya halves. About 380 calories per serving.

EGG SALAD

Makes about 3 cups, enough for 4 salads, 6–8 sandwiches

12 *hard-cooked eggs, chilled, peeled, and coarsely chopped*
1 *tablespoon minced yellow onion*
¼ *cup minced celery (optional)*
1 *tablespoon minced parsley (optional)*
1 *teaspoon salt*
⅛ *teaspoon pepper*
¼–⅓ *cup mayonnaise or mayonnaise-type salad dressing*
3–4 *tablespoons milk*

Mix all ingredients together, adding just enough mayonnaise and milk to give salad a good consistency. Cover and chill several hours. Stir well and use as a main course salad—in lettuce cups or hollowed-out tomatoes—or as a sandwich spread. About 480 calories per cup, 30 calories per tablespoon.

VARIATIONS:

Pickle-Egg Salad: Prepare as directed but add 2 tablespoons minced dill or sweet pickle and substitute 1–2

VI. NEW FLAVOR COMBINATIONS
Raw Zucchini Salad – Fillets of Sole – Poulet Basquais

Raw Zucchini Salad (vol. 2, p. 296)

Fillets of Sole à la Marinière (vol. 1, p. 637); Fillets of

Sole à la Niçoise; (vol. 1, p. 638); and Fillets of Sole à la Florentine (vol. 1, p. 637)

Poulet Basquais (vol. 1, p. 568); and Buttered Noodles (vol. 2, p. 58)

SALADS AND SALAD DRESSINGS

tablespoons pickle juice for 1–2 tablespoons milk. About 490 calories per cup, 31 calories per tablespoon.

Dilly Egg Salad: Prepare as directed, adding 1 tablespoon each minced fresh dill and capers. About 490 calories per cup, 31 calories per tablespoon.

Herbed Egg Salad: Prepare as directed, adding 1 tablespoon each minced parsley and chives and 1 teaspoon minced fresh or ¼ teaspoon dried tarragon, chervil, marjoram, or rosemary. About 480 calories per cup, 30 calories per tablespoon.

Anchovy-Egg Salad: Prepare as directed, adding 2 tablespoons anchovy paste and omitting salt. About 510 calories per cup, 32 calories per tablespoon.

Curried Egg Salad: Prepare as directed, adding 2–3 teaspoons curry powder and 1–2 tablespoons minced chutney. About 500 calories per cup, 31 calories per tablespoon.

Olive-Egg Salad: Prepare as directed, but omit salt and add ⅓ cup minced green or ripe olives. About 510 calories per cup, 32 calories per tablespoon.

Caviar-Egg Salad: Prepare as directed but mix in 1 (1-ounce) jar black caviar and omit salt. About 525 calories per cup, 33 calories per tablespoon.

Mustard-Egg Salad: Prepare as directed, but add 1 tablespoon prepared spicy brown mustard and 3–4 dashes liquid hot red pepper seasoning. Use 2 tablespoons tarragon vinegar for 2 tablespoons milk. About 480 calories per cup, 30 calories per tablespoon.

Deviled Egg Salad: Prepare as Mustard-Egg Salad directs, but substitute relish-type sandwich spread for the mayonnaise. About 480 calories per cup, 30 calories per tablespoon.

BASIC HAM OR TONGUE SALAD

Makes 4–6 servings

2 cups cubed, cooked ham or tongue or 1 cup of each
3 hard-cooked eggs, peeled and coarsely chopped
½ medium-size sweet green pepper, cored, seeded, and cut in julienne strips
2 tablespoons minced yellow onion (optional)
1 large dill pickle, minced
½ cup mayonnaise or mayonnaise-type salad dressing
1 tablespoon lemon juice
1 tablespoon light cream
1 teaspoon Worcestershire sauce
½ teaspoon prepared mild yellow mustard

Mix all ingredients, cover, and chill 2–3 hours. Serve mounded in lettuce cups or in the center hollow of a tomato aspic or jellied vegetable salad ring. About 435 calories for each of 4 servings (served in lettuce), 290 calories for each of 6.

VARIATION:

Ham and Cheese Salad: Prepare as directed, using 1½ cups cubed ham and 1 cup cubed sharp Cheddar, Swiss, or Gruyère cheese. About 510 calories for each of 4 servings, 340 calories for each of 6 servings.

EASY TUNA SALAD

Makes about 3 cups, enough for 4 salads or 6–8 sandwiches

2 (7-ounce) cans tuna, drained and flaked

½ cup minced Bermuda onion
Juice of ½ lemon
¾–1 cup mayonnaise (depending on how creamy a mixture you want)
2 tablespoons minced parsley
Pinch salt
⅛ teaspoon pepper

Mix all ingredients and chill several hours before serving. Serve as a salad in hollowed-out tomatoes or on crisp lettuce leaves or as a sandwich spread. About 600 calories per cup, 38 calories per tablespoon.

VARIATIONS:

Tart Tuna Salad: Prepare as directed but add 2 tablespoons minced capers and 1 tablespoon minced fresh dill or ½ teaspoon dried dill. About 600 calories per cup, 38 calories per tablespoon.

Herbed Tuna Salad: Prepare as directed but increase parsley to 3 tablespoons and add 1 tablespoon minced fresh marjoram or ½ teaspoon dried marjoram. About 600 calories per cup, 38 calories per tablespoon.

Tuna-Cheese Salad: Prepare as directed but reduce mayonnaise to ½ cup and add ¼ cup sour cream; also add ¾ cup coarsely grated Cheddar cheese and 1 tablespoon capers. About 600 calories per cup, 38 calories per tablespoon.

Tuna-Cucumber Salad: Prepare as directed but add ⅓ cup minced cucumber or, if you prefer, diced celery. About 600 calories per cup, 38 calories per tablespoon.

Tuna-Anchovy Salad: Prepare as directed but omit salt and add 3–4 minced, drained anchovy fillets. About 605 calories per cup, 38 calories per tablespoon.

Tuna-Olive Salad: Prepare as directed but omit salt and lemon juice and add ½ cup minced green or ripe olives. About 610 calories per cup, 38 calories per tablespoon.

SCANDINAVIAN HERRING SALAD (SILDESALAT)

Serve as an appetizer or entree. Makes 4 entree servings, enough appetizers for 6–8

3 herring in brine
2 cups cold diced, boiled potatoes
2 cups cold diced, boiled beets
1 small yellow onion, peeled and minced
½ teaspoon powdered mustard blended with 1 tablespoon cider vinegar
1 teaspoon sugar
¾ cup heavy cream, whipped to soft peaks
⅛ teaspoon pepper

Soak herring in cold water 24 hours, changing water several times. Remove heads, fillet and skin* herring, and cut in 1″ cubes. Mix herring with vegetables; add remaining ingredients and mix again. Chill well before serving. About 390 calories for each of 4 entree servings, 260 calories for each of 6 appetizer servings, and 195 calories for each of 8 appetizer servings.

BASIC SHELLFISH SALAD

The flavor will be best if shellfish is freshly cooked and still slightly warm when mixed into salad.
Makes 4 servings

1 pound cooked, shelled, and deveined shrimp, diced, cooked lobster, crab meat, or scallops
½ cup mayonnaise
2 tablespoons lemon juice or French dressing
Pinch cayenne pepper

½ teaspoon anchovy paste
   (optional)
1 tablespoon minced chives
½ cup diced celery, chilled
½ cup diced cucumber, chilled

Mix all but last 2 ingredients, cover, and chill 2–3 hours. Add celery and cucumber, mix well, and taste for salt if anchovy paste is not used. Serve mounded in lettuce cups, hollowed-out tomatoes, halved avocados, or in the center of a tomato aspic or jellied vegetable salad ring. About 350 calories per serving (made with lemon juice), 395 (made with French dressing).

VARIATIONS:

Shellfish, Egg, and Avocado Salad: Prepare as directed but add 3 coarsely chopped hard-cooked eggs and 1 diced, peeled avocado along with celery and cucumber; toss very gently. About 500 calories per serving (made with lemon juice), 545 calories per serving (made with French dressing).

Shellfish Salad Louisiana: Prepare as directed, using 2 cups mixed, cooked shrimp, lobster, and crab meat and adding ¼ cup chili sauce and ¼ teaspoon prepared horseradish. About 405 calories per serving (made with lemon juice), 450 (made with French dressing).

Spanish Shellfish Salad: Prepare as directed but blend ⅛ teaspoon powdered saffron into lemon juice before mixing into salad; omit celery and cucumber and add 1 cup cubed, cooked potatoes, ½ cup cooked green peas, ⅓ cup coarsely chopped, pitted ripe olives, and 1 cup shredded Boston lettuce or romaine. Add a little extra mayonnaise if needed. About 470 calories per serving (without extra mayonnaise).

Shellfish and Saffron Rice Salad: Prepare as directed, adding 1½ cups cold Saffron Rice, ¼ cup minced sweet green pepper, and 1 tablespoon each olive oil and cider vinegar along with celery and cucumber. About 450 calories per serving (if made with lemon juice), 495 calories per serving (if made with French dressing).

☒ QUICK CURRIED SHRIMP SALAD

Makes 4 servings

⅓ cup mayonnaise
3 tablespoons sour cream
1 teaspoon curry powder
1 teaspoon lemon juice
1 teaspoon minced chives
⅛ teaspoon pepper
1 pound cooked, shelled, and
   deveined shrimp, chilled
Crisp lettuce cups

Mix all ingredients except shrimp and lettuce; add shrimp and toss to mix well. Cover and chill 30 minutes or longer. Serve in lettuce cups. Or divide in 6 smaller portions and serve as an appetizer. About 300 calories per entree serving, 200 calories for each of 6 appetizers.

VARIATION:

Quick Curried Chicken or Turkey: Prepare as directed, substituting 3 cups ½″ cubes cooked chicken or turkey meat for shrimp and adding, if you like, ½ cup diced celery and/or apple. About 310 calories per entree serving (made with ½ cup each diced celery and apple).

CRAB RAVIGOTE

Makes 6 servings

1½ pounds fresh lump or backfin
   crab meat, well picked over, or 4
   (6-ounce) packages frozen Alaska
   king crab meat, thawed and drained

¼ cup tarragon vinegar
¾ cup mayonnaise
½ medium-size yellow onion, peeled and minced
2 tablespoons capers, minced
1 tablespoon minced chives
1 teaspoon minced parsley
1 teaspoon minced fresh chervil
1 teaspoon minced fresh tarragon
1 tablespoon slivered pimiento

Mix crab meat and vinegar, cover, and marinate in refrigerator 2 hours, turning now and then. Drain off vinegar and mix it with all but last ingredient, pour over crab, toss well, and arrange on lettuce or in avocado halves. Garnish with pimiento and serve. About 210 calories per serving (in lettuce).

GRAPEFRUIT AND AVOCADO SALAD

Makes 6 servings

2 grapefruit, peeled and sectioned
2 medium-size ripe avocados
Juice of 1 lemon
½ cup French, Roquefort French, or Sweet French Dressing

Make sure all white pith is removed from grapefruit sections. Halve, pit, and peel avocados; slice into thin crescents and dip in lemon juice to prevent darkening. Place in a large bowl with grapefruit, add dressing, and toss to mix. Serve as is or on a bed of crisp mixed greens. About 290 calories per serving (with French Dressing), 305 (with Roquefort French Dressing), and 325 (with Sweet French Dressing).

VARIATIONS:

Orange and Avocado Salad: Prepare as directed but substitute 4 navel oranges for the grapefruit. Calorie counts the same as for Grapefruit and Avocado Salad.

Papaya and Avocado Salad: Prepare as directed but substitute 1 large, ripe papaya, pitted, peeled, and thinly sliced, for the grapefruit. Use Sweet French Dressing. About 300 calories per serving.

Tomato and Avocado Salad: Prepare as directed but use 3 large, ripe beefsteak tomatoes, peeled, cored, and cut in slim wedges, instead of grapefruit. Use French or Roquefort French Dressing. About 280 calories per serving (with French Dressing), 295 (with Roquefort French Dressing).

Avocado and Endive Salad: Prepare as directed but substitute 4–6 Belgian endives, cut in 1″ chunks and separated into individual leaves, for the grapefruit. Use French or Roquefort French Dressing. About 275 calories per serving (with French Dressing), 290 (with Roquefort French Dressing).

WALDORF SALAD

Makes 4 servings

4 medium-size tart red apples, cored and diced (do not peel)
¾ cup finely chopped celery
⅓ cup coarsely chopped walnuts
⅔–1 cup mayonnaise

Stir all ingredients together, adding just enough mayonnaise for good consistency. Cover and chill 2–3 hours. Stir well and serve on lettuce leaves. About 425 calories per serving.

VARIATIONS:

Date-Marshmallow Waldorf Salad: Prepare as directed but reduce celery to ⅓ cup and add ½ cup diced, pitted dates and 16 miniature marshmallows. About 545 calories per serving.

SALADS AND SALAD DRESSINGS

Red Grape Waldorf Salad: Prepare as directed but add 1 cup halved, seeded red grapes. About 440 calories per serving.

Pear Waldorf Salad: Prepare as directed but substitute 4 ripe pears for apples. About 455 calories per serving.

Banana Waldorf Salad: Prepare as directed but add 2 peeled, thinly sliced bananas. About 465 calories per serving.

Sour Cream Waldorf Salad: Prepare as directed, but add 1 tablespoon honey and substitute ½ cup sour cream for ½ cup mayonnaise. About 305 calories per serving.

AMBROSIA SALAD

A Southern favorite served both as salad and dessert.
Makes 4–6 servings

1 cup well-drained mandarin oranges
1 cup miniature marshmallows
1 cup well-drained pineapple chunks
1 cup flaked coconut
1 cup coarsely chopped pecans (optional)
1 cup sour cream

Mix all ingredients, cover, and chill about 1 hour. Serve as is, on pineapple rings, or in lettuce cups. About 535 calories for each of 4 servings, 355 calories for each of 6 servings.

FIVE FRUIT SALAD

A more elaborate ambrosia.
Makes 6 servings

1½ cups well-drained pineapple chunks or diced apricot halves
2 bananas, peeled and diced
2 oranges or tangerines, peeled, sectioned, seeded, diced, and drained
2 apples or pears, peeled, cored, and diced
1 cup diced, pitted dates
1 cup miniature marshmallows (optional)
1¼ cups mayonnaise or Fruit Mayonnaise

Mix all ingredients, cover, and chill several hours. Stir well and serve as is or mounded in lettuce cups. About 560 calories per serving (without marshmallows).

About Gelatins and Molded Salads

Cool, shimmering, jewel-bright, these are the glamour salads. They're good party choices because they're showy, also because they can be made hours, even days, ahead of time. The vital ingredient, of course, is gelatin, either unflavored or fruit-flavored. Unflavored gelatin is 85 per cent protein and low in calories. Flavored gelatins are sweetened either with sugar or one of the noncaloric artificial sweeteners. Depending upon the calorie value of the foods being molded, gelatin salads are excellent choices for dieters.

How Much Gelatin? The perfect molded salad is tender yet strong enough to stand on its own. Too much gelatin makes the salad rubbery, too little makes it collapse. Here is the standard ratio:

To Mold 2 cups of Liquid, Use: 1 envelope (1 tablespoon) unflavored gelatin *or* 1 (3-ounce) package fruit-flavored gelatin.

Note: Very sweet mixtures will "set up" softer than tart or savory ones. *Do not attempt to mold fresh or frozen pineapple or pineapple juice; they contain an enzyme that breaks* down the gelatin and keeps it from setting. Canned pineapple, however, can be used.

To Dissolve Gelatin:

Unflavored Gelatin: There are 4 techniques; which you use is determined by the individual recipe.

Over Direct Heat: Sprinkle gelatin over cold liquid, then heat and stir constantly over low heat until dissolved. (*Note:* If cream or milk is used, gelatin will take about twice as long to dissolve.)

By Adding Hot Liquid: Soften gelatin in a small amount of cold liquid, then pour in simmering-hot liquid and stir until dissolved.

By Mixing with Sugar: Mix sugar with dry gelatin, add cold liquid, and heat and stir over low heat until dissolved, or pour boiling liquid over sugar-gelatin mixture and stir until dissolved.

Over Boiling Water: Soften gelatin in a small amount of cold liquid, set over boiling water (or place in a ramekin and stand in a small amount of boiling water), and heat and stir until dissolved. Combine with remaining liquid.

Flavored Gelatins: One simple method: Pour boiling or simmering-hot liquid over gelatin and stir until dissolved.

About Combining Solid Foods with Gelatin: If minced fruits, meats, or vegetables are added to gelatin while it is still liquid, they will sink or float, depending upon whether they're lighter or heavier than the gelatin. Celery, apples, pears, bananas, avocados, and peaches are all floaters. Grapes, most citrus and canned fruits, most cooked meats and vegetables are sinkers. To distribute foods evenly throughout gelatin, chill gelatin mixture until thick and syrupy (it should be about the consistency of raw egg white), then fold in foods and chill until firm.

(*Note:* Always drain all foods well before adding so that they do not water down gelatin. For 2 cups of gelatin mixture, allow 1–2 cups solids, either minced, cubed, or cut in small pieces.)

Gelatin Setting Times: These will vary somewhat even in standard gelatin mixtures, depending upon sweetness or tartness of mixture, shape and size of mold (large molds take proportionately longer to set up than small ones), temperature and humidity of refrigerator. The following times, however, are average *minimums:*

Clear Gelatin (with no foods mixed in): about 2 hours

Gelatins with Foods Mixed in: about 4 hours

Layered Gelatins: about 12 hours (*Note:* A detailed discussion of layered gelatins and ribbon loaves follows.)

To Hasten Jelling: Dissolve 1 package gelatin in 1 cup boiling liquid, then add 7–10 ice cubes and stir until mixture is syrupy; remove any unmelted ice cubes. Or, prepare gelatin mixture as recipe directs, then set in an ice water bath or in a large bowl of crushed ice and stir until syrupy. (*Note:* It's generally bad practice to quick-jell a mixture in the freezer—except for mousses and chiffon-type molds—because the gelatin may freeze and break down.)

About Molds: Clear gelatins can be molded in deeply sculptured molds (and come out as sparkling and

SALADS AND SALAD DRESSINGS

faceted as jewels), but mixtures containing solids should be molded in something simpler; if not, they will be difficult to unmold and the intricacy of the design will be lost. Recipes occasionally call for oiled or greased molds (to facilitate unmolding), but oil leaves an unpleasant film on the gelatin. A better method is simply to rinse mold quickly in cold water, then to add gelatin mixture to the wet mold.

How to Unmold Gelatin Salads: Keep mold refrigerated and do not unmold until ready to serve.
– Dip mold in *warm* (not hot) water to depth of gelatin mixture.
– Remove from water, loosen edges with tip of a paring knife.
– Place a serving plate, quickly rinsed in cold water but not dried, flat on top of mold, then invert so plate is on the bottom and shake gently. Gelatin should ease right out. By having serving plate moist, you can easily center mold.
– Wipe up any drops of liquid, garnish as desired, and serve.

TOMATO ASPIC

Plenty of variations here to try, some simple, some sophisticated.
Makes 4–6 servings

1 quart tomato juice
2 sprigs parsley
1 stalk celery, coarsely chopped (include tops)
2 tablespoons minced onion
1 bay leaf, crushed
1½ teaspoons salt
1½ teaspoons sugar
¼ teaspoon basil
1–2 drops liquid hot red pepper seasoning
2 envelopes unflavored gelatin
2 tablespoons lemon juice
1 pint prepared mixed salad greens

Simmer 2 cups tomato juice, covered, 20 minutes with parsley, celery, onion, bay leaf, salt, sugar, basil, and pepper seasoning, stirring occasionally; strain tomato juice, discarding the solids, mix in gelatin, and stir to dissolve. Mix in remaining tomato juice and lemon juice. Pour into an ungreased 1-quart ring mold and chill until firm, at least 4 hours. To serve, unmold on a flat round platter, fill center, and decorate base with greens. Pass French dressing or mayonnaise. About 75 calories for each of 4 servings (without dressing), 50 for each of 6 servings.

VARIATIONS:

Tomato, Cream Cheese, and Olive Aspic: Begin aspic as directed and smooth 2 (3-ounce) packages softened cream cheese into hot tomato juice-gelatin mixture. Stir in remaining tomato juice and lemon juice and chill until syrupy. Mix in ¼ cup thinly sliced pimiento-stuffed green olives, pour into a 5-cup mold, and chill until firm. About 245 calories for each of 4 servings, 165 calories for each of 6 servings.

Egg-Tomato Aspic: Prepare aspic, chill until syrupy, and divide in 3 equal parts; pour ⅓ into a 1-quart mold and arrange 1 sliced hard-cooked egg on top (it will sink about halfway), chill until tacky; keep remaining aspic syrupy. Arrange another sliced hard-cooked egg on tacky layer, pour in another ⅓ of aspic and chill until tacky. Top with a third sliced hard-cooked egg and remaining aspic. Chill until firm. About 135 calories for each of 4 servings, 90 calories for each of 6 servings.

Vegetable Aspic (Makes 6 servings): Prepare aspic as directed and chill until syrupy; fold in 1½–2 cups mixed, diced raw or cooked vegetables (any combination you fancy). Spoon into a 1½-quart mold and chill until firm. Recipe too flexible for a meaningful calorie count.

Tomato-Cheese Aspic (Makes 6 servings): Prepare aspic and chill until syrupy; fold in 1 cup cottage cheese and ¼ cup each minced sweet green pepper and celery. Mold as directed in a 1½-quart mold. *For a 2-Layer Aspic:* Pour half of syrupy aspic into mold and chill until tacky. Mix remaining aspic with the cheese and vegetables, spoon on top, and chill until firm. About 120 calories per serving.

⚜️ **Seafood Aspic** (Makes 6 servings): Prepare aspic and chill until syrupy; fold in 1 teaspoon anchovy paste and 1½ cups coarsely chopped cooked fish or shellfish; mold as directed in a 1½-quart mold. About 95 calories per serving.

Ham or Tongue Aspic (Makes 6 servings): Prepare aspic and chill until syrupy; fold in 1½ cups diced, cooked ham or tongue and ¼ cup minced mustard pickle; mold as directed in a 1½-quart mold. About 185 calories per serving.

Chicken or Turkey Aspic (Makes 6 servings): Prepare aspic and chill until syrupy; fold in 1½ cups diced cooked chicken or turkey and ¼ cup applesauce. Mold as directed in a 1½-quart mold. About 145 calories per serving.

⚜️ **CUCUMBER ASPIC**

Makes 6–8 servings

4 small cucumbers, peeled
2 cups water
1 teaspoon salt
2 envelopes unflavored gelatin
1 tablespoon finely grated yellow onion
4 teaspoons lemon juice
½ teaspoon Worcestershire sauce
Pinch cayenne pepper
2 or 3 drops green food coloring

Coarsely chop 2 cucumbers and simmer, covered, with water and salt about 20 minutes until mushy; drain liquid into gelatin, set over low heat, and heat and stir until dissolved. Press cooked cucumbers through a fine sieve, then mix into gelatin along with onion, lemon juice, Worcestershire, cayenne, and coloring. Cover and chill until syrupy. Meanwhile, halve and seed remaining cucumbers and coarsely grate. Mix into gelatin, spoon into an ungreased 5-cup mold, and chill until firm. Unmold and serve on crisp greens. Pass mayonnaise, if you like, or Old-Fashioned Cooked Dressing. About 25 calories for each of 6 servings (without mayonnaise), 20 for each of 8.

LEMON-AVOCADO ASPIC

Makes 4–6 servings

1 (3-ounce) package lemon-flavored gelatin
1 teaspoon salt
1¾ cups boiling water
1 teaspoon lemon juice
Few drops liquid hot red pepper seasoning
1 teaspoon finely grated yellow onion
1½ cups thinly sliced avocado
¼ cup finely shredded red cabbage

Mix gelatin and salt with boiling water, stirring until dissolved; mix in lemon juice, pepper seasoning, and onion and chill until syrupy. Fold in avocado and cabbage, spoon into an ungreased 1-quart mold, and chill until firm. Unmold and serve with mayonnaise. About 180 calories for each of 4 servings (without mayonnaise), 120 calories for each of 6 servings.

VARIATIONS:

Creamy Lemon and Avocado Mold: Mix gelatin and salt with 1 cup boiling water, blend in ¾ cup sour cream, and proceed as directed. About 260 for each of 4 servings, 175 calories for each of 6 servings.

Lime-Avocado Mousse: Mix 1 (3-ounce) package lime-flavored gelatin with the salt and 1 cup boiling water, stirring until dissolved. Cool but do not chill. Mix in ¾ cup mayonnaise or sour cream, the seasonings called for above, and 1½ cups puréed avocado; omit cabbage. Mold as directed. Good topped with cold marinated shellfish. If made with mayonnaise: About 325 calories for each of 4 servings, 215 for each of 6. If made with sour cream: About 260 calories for each of 4 servings, 175 for each of 6 servings.

MOLDED COTTAGE AND CREAM CHEESE SALAD

Makes 14–16 servings

1 envelope unflavored gelatin
1 cup cold water
1 (3-ounce) package lemon-flavored gelatin
2 cups boiling water
¼ cup cider vinegar
¼ cup canned pineapple juice
1 teaspoon finely grated yellow onion
½ teaspoon prepared horseradish
1 teaspoon salt
1 cup cottage cheese
1 (3-ounce) package cream cheese, softened to room temperature
⅔ cup evaporated milk or light cream
½ cup coarsely chopped pimiento-stuffed green olives
1 cup minced celery
¼ cup minced sweet green pepper
2 canned pineapple rings, coarsely chopped
⅓ cup toasted, slivered almonds

Sprinkle unflavored gelatin over cold water, then heat and stir until dissolved; pour over lemon gelatin along with boiling water and stir until dissolved. Stir in vinegar, canned pineapple juice, onion, horseradish, and salt, then cover and chill until syrupy; beat with a rotary beater or electric mixer until frothy. Blend cheeses and milk and fold into gelatin along with remaining ingredients. Spoon into an ungreased 2-quart mold and chill several hours or overnight until firm. Unmold and serve with mayonnaise or Old-Fashioned Cooked Dressing. About 135 calories for each of 14 servings (without mayonnaise or dressing), 120 calories for each of 16 servings.

AVOCADO MOUSSE

If an avocado seems green, you can "ripen" by letting stand ¾–1 hour in an oven turned to lowest possible temperature (150–200° F.). Cool and chill before using.

Makes 6 servings

1 envelope unflavored gelatin
1 cup cold water
1 tablespoon minced yellow onion
½ teaspoon salt
Pinch cayenne pepper
1 cup puréed ripe avocado (about 2 small ones)
¼ cup mayonnaise or sour cream

Sprinkle gelatin over water, then heat and stir until dissolved. Mix in remaining ingredients, spoon into an ungreased 3-cup mold, cover tightly, and chill until firm. Unmold (especially pretty on a bed of watercress) and serve at once (the mousse discolors rapidly on standing); wrap any leftovers airtight. About 195 calories per serving (if made with mayonnaise), 145 calories per serving (if made with sour cream).

JELLIED GARDEN VEGETABLE SALAD

Makes 8 servings

3 envelopes unflavored gelatin
½ cup sugar
3½ cups water
½ cup white vinegar
1 teaspoon salt
1 tablespoon minced parsley
1 tablespoon minced chives
½ cup cooked green peas
½ cup diced, cooked carrots or finely grated raw carrots
1 cup finely shredded cabbage
¼ cup thinly sliced radishes
½ cup diced celery
½ cup diced cucumber
¼ cup minced sweet green or red pepper
1 small red onion, peeled and minced
2 medium-size firm-ripe tomatoes, peeled, cored, seeded, and coarsely chopped

Heat and stir gelatin, sugar and 1 cup water until dissolved. Add remaining water, vinegar, salt, parsley, and chives and chill until syrupy. Mix in remaining ingredients and spoon into an ungreased 2-quart ring mold or 9"×5"×3" loaf pan; cover and chill until firm. Unmold and top, if you like, with a thin mayonnaise-type dressing. About 90 calories per serving (without mayonnaise).

To Use Other Vegetables: Substitute any compatible combination of cooked and raw vegetables for those listed above. You'll need 1 quart minced vegetables, total.

VARIATION:

Vegetable Ribbon Salad: Prepare gelatin mixture as directed and divide into 4 equal parts. Chill 1 part until syrupy, mix in peas and carrots, spoon into an ungreased decorative 2-quart mold, cover and chill until tacky. Meanwhile, chill second part of gelatin until syrupy, mix in cabbage and radishes, spoon into mold, cover, and chill until tacky. Chill third part of gelatin until syrupy, mix in celery, cucumber, and green pepper, add to mold, cover, and chill until tacky. Chill remaining gelatin until syrupy *but do not add onion and tomatoes;* pour into mold, cover, and chill until firm. Unmold and serve as directed. About 90 calories per serving.

⚜ PERFECTION SALAD

Makes 6 servings

1 envelope unflavored gelatin
¼ cup sugar
1¼ cups water
2 tablespoons lemon juice
1 tablespoon cider vinegar
¾ teaspoon salt
1½ cups finely shredded green, red, or Chinese cabbage or ½ cup of each
½ cup diced celery
¼ cup coarsely chopped pimiento-stuffed green olives
¼ cup minced sweet red or green pepper
2 tablespoons finely grated carrot

Sprinkle gelatin and sugar over water and heat, stirring, over moderately low heat until dissolved. Off heat, stir in lemon juice, vinegar, and salt; chill until syrupy. Fold in remaining ingredients, spoon into an ungreased 1-quart mold, and chill until firm. Unmold on lettuce leaves and serve with mayonnaise. About 55 calories per serving (without mayonnaise).

SALADS AND SALAD DRESSINGS

VARIATION:

⚜ **Perfection Salad for a Crowd:** (Makes 12 servings.) Double recipe and spoon into an ungreased 13"×9"×2" baking pan. Chill until firm and cut in large squares. About 55 calories per serving.

SOUFFLÉ SALAD

No need for salad dressing—it's built in.
Makes 4–6 servings

1 cup boiling water
1 (3-ounce) package lemon, lime, or apple-flavored gelatin
½ cup cold ginger ale
½ cup mayonnaise or mayonnaise-type salad dressing
½ teaspoon salt (about)
Few drops liquid hot red pepper seasoning
1 tablespoon minced yellow onion
1½ cups mixed diced cooked vegetables or finely shredded cabbage or thinly sliced avocado

Pour boiling water over gelatin and stir until dissolved. Add all but last ingredient and mix well, using a rotary beater or wire whisk. Pour into a shallow pan and chill in freezer about 15–20 minutes until there's a 1" frozen border all round (mixture should still be liquid in center). Scrape into a bowl and whip until fluffy. Fold in vegetables, spoon into an ungreased 1-quart mold, and chill until firm. Unmold and serve on a bed of greens. If made with diced cooked vegetables: about 335 calories for each of 4 servings, 225 calories for each of 6 servings. If made with shredded cabbage: about 310 calories for each of 4 servings, 205 calories for each of 6. If made with sliced avocado: about 395 calories for each of 4 servings, 265 calories for each of 6.

JELLIED CHICKEN OR TURKEY SALAD

For small families, this recipe may be halved and molded in a 1-quart mold or 4 custard cups.
Makes 8 servings

2 envelopes unflavored gelatin
½ cup cold water
3 cups chicken broth
2 tablespoons lemon juice
½ teaspoon salt
3 cups minced cold cooked chicken or turkey meat (preferably white meat)
¼ cup minced celery
¼ cup minced sweet green pepper
¼ cup minced scallions
2 tablespoons minced pimiento

Heat and stir gelatin with water and broth until dissolved; mix in lemon juice and salt. Chill until thick and syrupy, mix in remaining ingredients, spoon into an ungreased 9"×5"×3" loaf pan, cover, and chill until firm. Loosen edges and unmold. If you like, pass a thin mayonnaise-type dressing. About 110 calories per serving (without mayonnaise).

VARIATIONS:

Jellied Meat Salad: Prepare as directed, substituting 1½ cups each water and beef broth for chicken broth and 3 cups minced cooked lean beef, lamb, or veal for chicken. If you like, reduce lemon juice to 1 tablespoon and add 1 teaspoon Worcestershire sauce. About 180 calories per serving.

Jellied Ham or Tongue Salad: Prepare as directed, using 1½ cups each beef and chicken broth and 3 cups minced, cooked ham or tongue instead of chicken. About 160 calories per serving.

Jellied Shellfish Salad: Prepare as directed, using 1½ cups each chicken broth and water or tomato juice and 3 cups minced, cooked shellfish instead of chicken. About 90 calories per serving.

Jellied Meat, Poultry, or Shellfish and Vegetable Salad: Prepare any of the above salads as directed but omit celery and green pepper and add ¾–1 cup any leftover mixed cooked vegetables. Recipe too flexible for a meaningful calorie count.

Creamy Jellied Meat, Poultry, or Shellfish Salad: Heat and stir gelatin in ½ cup cold water until dissolved; blend in 1 pint mayonnaise and 1 cup water, tomato juice, chicken or beef broth; add lemon juice called for above and salt to taste. Chill until syrupy, mix in 3 cups minced, cooked meat, poultry, or shellfish, ¼ cup minced scallions, and 1 cup any leftover mixed cooked vegetables. Mold as directed. Recipe too flexible for a meaningful calorie count, but because of the mayonnaise used, approximately 5 times the calorie count of Jellied Chicken or Turkey Salad.

MOLDED GRAPEFRUIT AND PINEAPPLE SALAD

Makes 4–6 servings

1 (3-ounce) package lime or lemon-flavored gelatin
1 cup boiling water
1 cup fresh or canned grapefruit sections, cut up (include juice)
1 (13½-ounce) can pineapple chunks, drained
¼ cup quartered maraschino or candied cherries
¼ cup coarsely chopped pecans

Mix gelatin with boiling water, stirring until dissolved; cool, then chill until syrupy and stir in remaining ingredients. Spoon into an ungreased 3-cup mold or 4–6 individual molds. Chill until firm, unmold, and serve with mayonnaise or Cream Cheese and Fruit Dressing. About 240 calories for each of 4 servings, 160 calories for each of 6 servings (without mayonnaise or dressing).

APRICOT-PINEAPPLE SALAD

Good as dessert or salad.
Makes 6–8 servings

½ cup boiling water
1 (3-ounce) package orange-flavored gelatin
1 (8¾-ounce) can pitted apricots (drain and save liquid)
1 (8½-ounce) can crushed pineapple (drain and save liquid)
Canned fruit liquid plus enough cold water to total 1 cup
1 tablespoon lemon juice
½ cup heavy cream, whipped to soft peaks

Pour boiling water over gelatin and stir until dissolved; add fruit liquid and lemon juice, pour into a shallow pan, and chill in freezer 15–20 minutes until there is a 1″ frozen border all round. Meanwhile, dice apricots. Scrape gelatin mixture into a bowl and whip until fluffy. Fold in remaining ingredients, spoon into an ungreased 5-cup mold, and chill until firm. Unmold and serve as is or on greens. No dressing needed. About 195 calories for each of 6 servings, 145 calories for each of 8 servings.

MOLDED CHERRY-PECAN SALAD

Makes 8 servings

1 (1-pound) can pitted sour red cherries (do not drain)
1 cup sugar
½ cup water
1 (3-ounce) package cherry-flavored gelatin

SALADS AND SALAD DRESSINGS

1 envelope unflavored gelatin
Grated rind of 1 orange
2 oranges, peeled, seeded, and diced
1 (8½-ounce) can crushed pineapple (do not drain)
½ cup coarsely chopped pecans

Heat cherries, sugar, and water to boiling, stirring occasionally. Off heat, mix in gelatins and stir until dissolved. Cool, then chill until syrupy; mix in remaining ingredients, spoon into an ungreased 5-cup mold or 8 individual molds. Chill until firm. Unmold and, if you wish, serve with a thin mayonnaise-type dressing. About 285 calories per serving (without mayonnaise).

MOLDED SPICY CRANBERRY SALAD

Makes 8 servings

1 pound fresh or frozen cranberries, washed
2 cups water
2 cinnamon sticks and 24 cloves, tied in cheesecloth
1 cup sugar
½ teaspoon salt
2 envelopes unflavored gelatin
⅔ cup minced celery
1 cup canned crushed pineapple, drained
1 cup minced walnuts

Simmer cranberries, water, and spices covered until cranberry skins pop, 5–7 minutes; discard spice bag. Purée cranberries and cooking liquid, a little at a time, in an electric blender at low speed or put through a food mill. Return to pan, stir in sugar, salt, and gelatin, and simmer, stirring, until gelatin dissolves. Cool, then chill, stirring occasionally, until thick and syrupy. Mix in remaining ingredients, ladle into an ungreased 5-cup mold or 8 individual molds, and chill until firm. To serve, unmold and garnish with chicory or other crisp greens. About 255 calories per serving.

MOLDED CRANBERRY-PECAN SALAD

Makes 10–12 servings

1 (3-ounce) package cherry-flavored gelatin
2 (3-ounce) packages black raspberry-flavored gelatin
1 teaspoon unflavored gelatin
1 cup sugar
1 quart boiling water
1 pound fresh or frozen cranberries, put through fine blade of food grinder
2 small tart red apples, cored and ground fine (do not peel)
1 large seedless orange, ground fine (do not peel or seed)
1¾ cups coarsely chopped pecans
1¼ cups finely diced celery

Dissolve gelatins and sugar in boiling water; cool to room temperature, cover, and chill just until syrupy. Mix in remaining ingredients, pour into an ungreased 2½-quart decorative mold, and chill 6–8 hours until firm. To serve, unmold and cut into slim wedges. No dressing is needed. About 315 calories for each of 10 servings, 260 calories for each of 12 servings.

About Making Gelatin Ribbon Loaves

Any compatible gelatin mixtures can be layered—jellied meat and vegetables, jellied poultry and tart fruit or vegetables, aspic with almost anything savory. Bear in mind *combined yield* of gelatin mixtures and use a mold large enough to accommodate both. For best results:

— Keep thickness of layers in proportion to each other.
— Do not try to mold more than 3 or 4 layers in a 1- or 2-quart mold or 9″×5″×3″ loaf pan (it holds 2 quarts).
— Always chill 1 layer until *tacky-firm* before adding another. If gelatin is too firm, layers will not stick together; if too liquid, they will run together.
— Have gelatin mixtures at room temperature or, better still, chilled *just* until syrupy before adding to mold.
— Add heaviest layers last (those containing minced foods) so that when loaf is unmolded, they will be on the bottom; otherwise they may topple or slide off.
— Give a ribbon loaf plenty of time to set up before unmolding—at least 12 hours.

TOMATO AND CHEESE RIBBON LOAF

Makes 8–10 servings

1 recipe Tomato Aspic
2 envelopes unflavored gelatin
¾ cup water
3 cups sieved cottage cheese
⅔ cup sour cream
2 tablespoons minced parsley
2 tablespoons minced scallions (include some tops)
1 teaspoon salt
⅛ teaspoon white pepper

Prepare aspic as directed and pour half into an ungreased 9″×5″×3″ loaf pan; chill until tacky-firm; keep remaining aspic syrupy over tepid water. Meanwhile, sprinkle gelatin over water and heat and stir over moderately low heat until dissolved. Mix with remaining ingredients and chill quickly until syrupy either by setting in freezer or in a bowl of cracked ice. Pour half of cheese gelatin on molded tomato aspic and chill until tacky; keep remaining cheese mixture syrupy over tepid water. Add remaining tomato aspic to mold, chill until tacky, then top with remaining cheese gelatin. Chill overnight until firm. Slice about ½″ thick and serve on crisp greens. Good with a thin mayonnaise-type dressing. About 355 calories for each of 8 servings (without mayonnaise), 285 calories for each of 10 servings.

VARIATIONS:

Tomato-Avocado Ribbon Aspic: Prepare 1 recipe each Tomato Aspic and Lemon-Avocado Aspic; beginning with Tomato Aspic, layer into a loaf pan following technique above. About 250 calories for each of 8 servings, 200 calories for each of 10.

Tomato-Chicken Ribbon Loaf: Prepare 1 recipe Tomato Aspic and ½ recipe Jellied Chicken Salad. Starting with Tomato Aspic, layer into loaf pan. About 270 calories for each of 8 servings, 215 calories for each of 10 servings.

FROZEN FRUIT SALAD

More dessert than salad. It's rich but not too sweet.
Makes 6–8 servings

1 tablespoon water mixed with 1 tablespoon lemon juice
1 teaspoon unflavored gelatin
1 tablespoon confectioners' sugar
1 (3-ounce) package cream cheese, softened to room temperature
⅓ cup mayonnaise
½ cup heavy cream
1 (1-pound) can fruit cocktail, drained, or 1½ cups mixed diced fresh fruit

Place water mixture in a custard cup, sprinkle in gelatin and sugar, and set in a small pan of simmering water;

heat and stir until gelatin dissolves. Beat cream cheese and mayonnaise until blended and stir in gelatin mixture; whip cream to soft peaks and fold in along with fruit. Spoon into a 9" square pan and freeze just until firm. Cut in squares and serve on lettuce. About 275 calories for each of 6 servings, 205 calories for each of 8 servings.

VARIATION:

Frozen Fruit and Nut Salad: Prepare as directed but omit cream cheese and increase mayonnaise to ½ cup. Add ¼ cup minced nuts (pistachios are especially good) and 6 minced maraschino cherries along with fruit. (*Note:* To keep cherries from coloring mixture, rinse briefly in cold water and pat dry.) About 325 calories for each of 6 servings, 245 calories for each of 8 servings.

✠ FROZEN CRANBERRY RIBBON SALAD

Makes 6–8 servings

1 (1-pound) can whole or jellied cranberry sauce
¼ cup lemon juice
½ cup mayonnaise
⅓ cup sugar
1 cup heavy cream
¼ cup minced pecans, walnuts, or toasted almonds (optional)

If using jellied cranberry sauce, soften by standing unopened can in very hot water; mix lemon juice into sauce, spoon into a refrigerator tray, and freeze until firm. Mix mayonnaise and sugar; beat cream to soft peaks and fold in. Spread on top of cranberry layer, sprinkle, if you like, with nuts, and freeze until firm. Cut in squares and serve on lettuce. About 500 calories for each of 6 servings and 375 calories for each of 8 servings (if made with nuts); about 470 calories for each of 6 servings and 350 calories for each of 8 servings (if made without nuts).

✠ FROZEN MARSHMALLOW AND PINEAPPLE SALAD

Really a dessert.
Makes 6–8 servings

2 (3-ounce) packages cream cheese, softened to room temperature
1 cup drained crushed pineapple
2 cups miniature marshmallows
¼ cup coarsely chopped maraschino cherries
1 teaspoon lemon juice
½ cup coarsely chopped pecans or walnuts

Blend cheese and pineapple; mix in remaining ingredients and spoon into a refrigerator tray. Freeze until firm, cut in squares, and serve. About 285 calories for each of 6 servings, 215 calories for each of 8 servings.

SALAD DRESSINGS

The parade of bottled dressings along supermarket shelves is so long it may seem foolish to make a dressing from scratch. It isn't. Good as some commercial dressings are, they can never match the delicacy and bouquet of those made at home from first quality oils, vinegars, and seasonings.

The Salad Oils: Keep a selection of oils on hand—on a cool, dark shelf, never in the refrigerator (cold turns oils cloudy). Unless you use oils frequently, buy in small amounts so that you can use up a bottle before it becomes rancid. Oils give salads a special mellowness and are the medium in which all flavors mingle. They are also, alas, what add calories to salads (1 tablespoon salad oil averages about 115). So if you are dieting, use one of the low-calorie types. A more detailed discussion of oils is included in the chapter The Larder.

The Vinegars: Nearly every supermarket stocks a good variety of plain and flavored vinegars. Keep an assortment on hand on a cool, dark shelf. It's best to buy in fairly small bottles because vinegars do mold and produce sediment. The sediment can be strained out, but a moldy vinegar should be discarded.

Cider Vinegar: The all-purpose, golden brown vinegar made from apples. It is good for cooked or highly seasoned dressings but too rough and coarse to use solo with oil.

Distilled Vinegar: White vinegar, acid and sour and better for pickles than salads.

Malt Vinegar: An English favorite, tart but mellow; use interchangeably with cider vinegar.

Wine Vinegars: These are simply wines that have gone a step too far, which explains why there are white, red, and rosé wine vinegars. (*Note:* Save any tag ends of the wine bottle; when the wine sours into vinegar, use to dress salads.)

Flavored Vinegars: These, usually made from cider or white wine vinegar, include all the herb vinegars, also garlic, onion, and shallot vinegars. You can buy them at any grocery or, if you have an herb garden, make your own (recipes follow).

Rice Vinegar: A delicate white Japanese vinegar, about half as acid as cider vinegar. To achieve a proper salad tartness, you'll have to use about twice as much.

Pear Vinegar: A fairly new item with a fresh flowery bouquet.

Tips on Making Salad Dressings

– Most dressings do not keep well, so make in small quantities.
– For best flavor, dressings should be made at least a half hour ahead of time, sometimes even longer. Oil and vinegar types should stand at room temperature so flavors marry, but cream or mayonnaise dressings should be kept refrigerated.
– Do not use garlic or onion powders and salts; they rapidly become stale and can ruin an otherwise excellent salad. It's far better to mince fresh garlic and onion; more effort, true. But worth it.
– Use fresh herbs in preference to the dry. And when using the dry, make sure they haven't been sitting on the shelf for months. An old herb adds about as much character to salad as dried grass.
– Use the finest quality oils, vinegars, and seasonings.
– Use coarse salt or kosher salt if possible and, of course, freshly ground black pepper.
– When dressing salads with oil and vinegar, use a heavy hand with the oil and a light one with the vinegar. *The classic proportion is 3 or 4 parts oil to 1 part vinegar.* For variety, try substituting lemon or lime juice (or part lemon or lime juice) for the vinegar.

⚔ GARLIC VINEGAR

Makes 1 pint

1 pint boiling cider vinegar
6 cloves garlic, peeled and halved

Pour vinegar into a jar, drop in garlic, cover, and let stand 24 hours at room temperature. Discard garlic, strain vinegar through a double thickness of cheesecloth into a fresh pint jar. Use for making salad dressings and sauces. About 3 calories per tablespoon.

⚜ HERB VINEGAR

Herbs will be at their peak of flavor if picked just before they bloom.

Makes 1 pint

2 cups tender fresh herb leaves or sprigs (tarragon, chervil, dill, basil, or thyme) washed gently in cool water and patted dry on paper toweling
1 pint boiling vinegar (cider or white wine)

Place herbs in a wide-mouthed heatproof jar and crush lightly with the handle of a wooden spoon. Pour in vinegar and cool to room temperature. Screw on lid and let stand in a cool spot (not refrigerator) 10 days to 2 weeks; once every day, turn jar upside down, then right side up again. Taste vinegar after 10 days and, if strong enough, strain through several thicknesses of cheesecloth into a fresh pint jar. If too weak, let stand the full 2 weeks. If still too weak, strain off vinegar and bring to a boil; fill a fresh jar with freshly picked herbs, cover with boiling vinegar, and let stand a week to 10 days, turning once a day. Strain vinegar and use for making salad dressings and sauces. About 3 calories per tablespoon.

À LA GRECQUE MARINADE

Leeks, zucchini, and certain other cooked vegetables are delicious when marinated in this delicate lemon and oil dressing. They may be served as a first course, a salad, or a vegetable.

Makes about 3 cups

⅓ cup lemon juice
½ cup olive oil
1 pint hot water
½ teaspoon salt
⅛ teaspoon each fennel and coriander seeds tied in cheesecloth
1 bay leaf
1 (4") sprig fresh thyme or ⅛ teaspoon dried thyme
Pinch white pepper

Mix all ingredients together and use in preparing vegetables that are to be served *à la grecque*. About 20 calories per tablespoon.

☒ FRENCH DRESSING (VINAIGRETTE)

Called *vinaigrette* in France, French dressing is simply 3–4 parts olive oil to 1 part vinegar, seasoned with salt and pepper.

Makes 1 cup

¼ cup red or white wine vinegar
¼ teaspoon salt
⅛ teaspoon white pepper
¾ cup olive oil

In a bowl mix vinegar, salt, and pepper with a fork. Add oil and mix vigorously until well blended and slightly thickened. (*Note:* For a creamier dressing, beat over ice 1–2 minutes.) Use to dress green or vegetable salads. (*Note:* If you prefer, substitute any good salad oil for the olive oil and cider or malt vinegar for the wine vinegar.) About 95 calories per tablespoon.

VARIATIONS:

Garlic French Dressing: Drop 1 peeled, bruised clove garlic into dressing and let stand 2–3 days at room temperature; remove garlic before using dressing. About 95 calories per tablespoon.

Tarragon French Dressing: Make dressing with tarragon vinegar and add 1 tablespoon minced fresh or ½ teaspoon dried tarragon. About 95 calories per tablespoon.

Roquefort French Dressing: Prepare dressing as directed and crumble in 3 tablespoons Roquefort cheese. Cover and let stand several hours at room temperature before using. About 105 calories per tablespoon.

Spanish Vinaigrette: Prepare dressing as directed and place in a shaker jar with 1 tablespoon minced green olives and 1 teaspoon each minced chives, capers, parsley, and gherkin, and 1 sieved hard-cooked egg yolk. Shake, let stand at room temperature ½ hour; shake again before using. About 100 calories per tablespoon.

Lorenzo Dressing: Prepare dressing as directed and blend in 2 tablespoons chili sauce or ketchup. About 100 calories per tablespoon.

Chiffonade Dressing: Prepare dressing as directed, then mix in 2 tablespoons each minced ripe olives, chives, and sweet green pepper and 1 minced hard-cooked egg. About 105 calories per tablespoon.

Sweet French Dressing: Prepare dressing as directed, then mix in ¼ cup each orange juice and honey or superfine sugar. Use to dress fruit salads. About 110 calories per tablespoon if made with sugar, 115 calories per tablespoon if made with honey.

FRESH HERB DRESSING

Makes ¾ cup

½ cup olive oil
1 tablespoon minced fresh dill, tarragon, chervil, or fennel
1 tablespoon minced chives
¼ teaspoon minced fresh marjoram (optional)
½ teaspoon salt
⅛ teaspoon pepper
¼ cup tarragon vinegar

Place oil, herbs, salt, and pepper in a shaker bottle or large glass measuring cup and let stand at room temperature 3–4 hours. Add vinegar and shake or stir well to blend. Use to dress any crisp green salad, using only enough to coat each leaf lightly. Save leftover dressing to use for other salads later (dressing will keep about 1 week). About 85 calories per tablespoon.

FRESH BASIL-MINT DRESSING

Makes about ½ cup

⅓ cup olive oil
1 tablespoon minced fresh basil
1 teaspoon minced fresh mint
1 teaspoon minced chives
3 tablespoons red wine vinegar
¼ teaspoon salt
Pinch pepper

Place oil in a small bowl, add herbs, and let stand at room temperature at least 1 hour. Mix in remaining ingredients and use to dress sliced tomatoes or crisp salad greens. About 85 calories per tablespoon.

GARLIC-HERB DRESSING

Makes about ⅓ cup

1 clove garlic, peeled and crushed
½ teaspoon tarragon
½ teaspoon marjoram
½ teaspoon powdered mustard
¼ teaspoon salt
⅛ teaspoon pepper
¼ cup olive oil
2 tablespoons red wine vinegar

Shake all ingredients in a small jar with a tight-fitting lid and let stand at room temperature at least 1 hour.

SALADS AND SALAD DRESSINGS

Shake again and use to dress any crisp green salad. About 95 calories per tablespoon.

SHALLOT DRESSING

Makes about ½ cup

1 tablespoon minced shallots
½ teaspoon paprika
½ teaspoon powdered mustard
¼ teaspoon tarragon or chervil
½ teaspoon salt
Pinch pepper
⅓ cup olive oil
3 tablespoons tarragon vinegar

Place all ingredients except vinegar in a small bowl, stir well to mix, cover, and let stand at room temperature about 1 hour. Stir again, mix in vinegar, and use to dress crisp green salads. About 85 calories per tablespoon.

SWEET-SOUR DRESSING

Makes about 1¾ cups

1 cup salad oil
⅓ cup red wine vinegar
¼ cup mayonnaise or mayonnaise-type salad dressing
¼ cup chili sauce
¼ teaspoon salt
2 tablespoons sugar
Pinch cayenne pepper
1 clove garlic, peeled and crushed

Shake all ingredients in a large, wide-mouthed jar with a tight-fitting lid. Cover and chill several hours. Before using, shake well. Use to dress crisp green salads. About 95 calories per tablespoon.

⚖ ☒ BUTTERMILK DRESSING

Dieters, note just *how* low the calories are.

Makes about 1½ cups

½ cup cider vinegar
1 tablespoon salad oil
1 teaspoon salt
⅛ teaspoon white pepper
1 cup buttermilk

Shake all ingredients in a jar with a tight-fitting lid and use to dress cabbage or crisp green salads. (*Note:* Dressing will keep about a week in the refrigerator.) About 10 calories per tablespoon.

☒ LEMON-LIME DRESSING

Makes about 1 cup

Juice of 1 lemon
Juice of ½ lime
2 tablespoons honey
⅔ cup olive oil
1 tablespoon minced chives
1 tablespoon minced fresh basil or dill
Pinch salt
Pinch pepper

Shake all ingredients in a jar and use to dress sliced tomatoes or crisp green salads. About 95 calories per tablespoon.

WINE DRESSING

A good way to use up any tag ends of wine.

Makes 1¼ cups

⅓ cup dry red or white wine
¼ cup red or white wine vinegar
1 clove garlic, peeled, bruised, and stuck on a toothpick
¼ teaspoon salt
¼ teaspoon powdered mustard
⅛ teaspoon white pepper
⅔ cup olive or other salad oil

Mix wine, vinegar, and garlic, cover, and let stand at room temperature 2 hours; remove garlic. Beat in salt, mustard, and pepper, then drizzle in oil, beating constantly. Shake well and use to dress green salads. About 70 calories per tablespoon.

▣ SOUR CREAM DRESSING

Makes 1¼ cups

1 cup sour cream
3 tablespoons white or cider vinegar
2 tablespoons sugar
½ teaspoon salt
Pinch cayenne pepper

Mix all ingredients, cover, and chill well. Use to dress fruit or green salads. For a thinner dressing, blend in a little milk or French dressing. About 30 calories per tablespoon.

VARIATIONS:

⚕ **Low-Calorie Yogurt Dressing:** Prepare as directed but substitute yogurt for sour cream, reduce vinegar to 2 tablespoons and sugar to ½ teaspoon; also add ¼ cup skim milk and 2 tablespoons minced chives or 1 tablespoon finely grated yellow onion. About 10 calories per tablespoon.

California Sour Cream Dressing: Prepare as directed but use 2 tablespoons lemon juice instead of the vinegar; add 2 sieved hard-cooked egg yolks and, if you like, 1 tablespoon minced fresh dill. About 35 calories per tablespoon.

Fruity Sour Cream Dressing: Prepare as directed but use 2 tablespoons lemon juice instead of the vinegar; increase sugar to 3 tablespoons and add 2 tablespoons orange juice and 1 teaspoon finely grated orange rind. Thin, if needed, with a little extra orange juice. About 35 calories per tablespoon.

Sour Cream-Roquefort Dressing: Prepare as directed, then mix in 2 tablespoons finely crumbled Roquefort cheese. About 35 calories per tablespoon.

CREAMY ROQUEFORT DRESSING

Makes about 2½ cups

1 (8-ounce) jar mayonnaise-type salad dressing
1 tablespoon sugar
1 teaspoon prepared mild yellow mustard
½ teaspoon prepared horseradish
½ teaspoon Worcestershire sauce
½ teaspoon minced garlic
1 tablespoon grated onion
½ pound Roquefort cheese
3–4 tablespoons cider vinegar

Blend salad dressing with sugar, mustard, horseradish, Worcestershire sauce, garlic and onion. Crumble in Roquefort and stir well. Mix in 3–4 tablespoons vinegar, depending upon how thick a dressing you want, and use to dress green salads. (*Note:* Dressing keeps well in refrigerator several days.) About 65 calories per tablespoon.

▣ BLENDER GARLIC-ROQUEFORT DRESSING

Makes about 1½ cups

¾ cup olive oil
⅓ cup tarragon or red wine vinegar
2 tablespoons honey
½ (3-ounce) package Roquefort cheese, softened to room temperature
1 clove garlic, peeled and crushed
½ teaspoon powdered mustard
1 teaspoon paprika
⅛ teaspoon salt
⅛ teaspoon pepper

Buzz all ingredients in an electric blender at high speed 1–2 minutes until creamy. Pour into a jar, cover, and chill until ready to use. Shake well, then use to dress crisp green salads. (*Note:* Dressing keeps well about 2 weeks in refrigerator, so

make a double batch if you like.)
About 80 calories per tablespoon.

CAMEMBERT CREAM DRESSING

Makes about 1 pint

4 ounces Camembert cheese, trimmed of rind and softened to room temperature
1 (8-ounce) package cream cheese, softened to room temperature
⅓ cup buttermilk
⅓ cup tarragon vinegar
½ teaspoon sugar
⅛ teaspoon pepper

Cream cheeses together, add remaining ingredients, and beat well; cover and chill 1–2 hours. Beat well just before serving. Use to dress any crisp green salad. (*Note:* Dressing keeps well about a week in refrigerator.) About 40 calories per tablespoon.

AVOCADO DRESSING

It's best to make this dressing just before using, because it darkens on standing. If it must be made in advance, spread with a thin film of mayonnaise, then cover and refrigerate until needed (this will minimize discoloration). Stir mayonnaise in before serving.

Makes about 1 cup

2 fully ripe medium-size avocados, halved and pitted
3 tablespoons lemon juice
1 tablespoon finely grated yellow onion
½ teaspoon salt
¼ teaspoon sugar
Few drops liquid hot red pepper seasoning

Scoop flesh from avocados and press through a fine sieve; beat in remaining ingredients. Serve over wedges of lettuce, halved endive spears, or in hollowed-out tomatoes. Or use to dress any seafood salad instead of mayonnaise. About 50 calories per tablespoon.

⊠ CREAM CHEESE AND FRUIT DRESSING

Makes 1 cup

1 (3-ounce) package cream cheese, softened to room temperature
½ cup orange or pineapple juice
2 tablespoons lemon juice
2 tablespoons sugar
Pinch cayenne pepper

Whip cheese until fluffy, then beat in remaining ingredients; cover and chill. Serve over fruit salads, avocado halves, or lettuce wedges. About 30 calories per tablespoon.

VARIATIONS:

Cream Cheese and Nut Dressing: Prepare as directed, then mix in ¼ cup minced pecans or toasted almonds. About 40 calories per tablespoon.

Cream Cheese and Chutney Dressing: Prepare as directed but use ⅓ cup milk in place of orange juice and add ¼ cup minced chutney (include some liquid). About 40 calories per tablespoon.

⚖ LOW-CALORIE FRUIT DRESSING

Makes 1⅓ cups

1 clove garlic, peeled, bruised, and stuck on a toothpick
5 tablespoons lemon juice
1 cup pineapple, orange, or tangerine juice
1 tablespoon light corn syrup or honey
½ teaspoon salt
¼ teaspoon paprika

Let garlic stand in lemon juice at room temperature 2 hours, then remove. Beat in remaining ingredients, cover, and chill. Shake well and use to dress fruit salads. About 20 calories per tablespoon.

About Making Mayonnaise

Mayonnaise isn't tricky to make—*if* you follow these basic rules:
- Have all ingredients at room temperature before beginning.
- Measure oil accurately into a widemouthed container so you can dip it out by spoonfuls during early stages of mixing.
- If mixing by hand, place a damp cloth under bowl to keep it from sliding around as you mix. Use a fork or wire whisk for beating.
- Add oil in the beginning *by the drop* so that it will emulsify with the egg yolks.
- If you substitute vinegar for lemon juice, use the very finest quality so mayonnaise will have a delicate flavor.

—If mayonnaise separates, use 1 of the following remedies:
- Beat in 1–2 teaspoons hot water.
- Beat 1 egg yolk with 2 or 3 drops oil until very thick, then beat in curdled mayonnaise *drop by drop.*
- Buzz in an electric blender at high speed.

HOMEMADE MAYONNAISE

Makes 1½ cups

2 egg yolks
¾ teaspoon salt
½ teaspoon powdered mustard
⅛ teaspoon sugar
Pinch cayenne pepper
4–5 teaspoons lemon juice or white vinegar
1½ cups olive or other salad oil
4 teaspoons hot water

Beat yolks, salt, mustard, sugar, pepper, and 1 teaspoon lemon juice in a small bowl until very thick and pale yellow. (*Note:* If using electric mixer, beat at medium speed.) Add about ¼ cup oil, *drop by drop,* beating vigorously all the while. Beat in 1 teaspoon each lemon juice and hot water. Add another ¼ cup oil, a few drops at a time, beating vigorously all the while. Beat in another teaspoon each lemon juice and water. Add ½ cup oil in a very fine steady stream, beating constantly, then mix in remaining lemon juice and water; slowly beat in remaining oil. If you like, thin mayonnaise with a little additional hot water. Cover and refrigerate until needed. (*Note:* Store in warmest part of refrigerator—less chance of the mayonnaise separating—and do not keep longer than one week.) About 130 calories per tablespoon.

VARIATIONS:

Blender Mayonnaise: Place yolks, salt, mustard, sugar, pepper, and 3 teaspoons lemon juice in blender cup and buzz at low speed 15 seconds. Increase speed to moderately high and slowly drizzle in ¼ cup oil. As mixture begins to thicken, continue adding oil in a fine steady stream, alternating with hot water and remaining lemon juice. Stop blender and scrape mixture down from sides as needed. About 130 calories per tablespoon.

Sauce Verte: Prepare mayonnaise as directed and set aside. Place ¼ cup each minced fresh spinach, watercress leaves, and parsley in a small pan, add 2 tablespoons each minced chives and water and 1 teaspoon minced fresh or ½ teaspoon dried tarragon, cover, and simmer 2 minutes. Press mixture through a fine sieve, drain briefly and blend into mayonnaise. Serve with cold cooked seafood or use to dress green salads. About 130 calories per tablespoon.

Rémoulade Dressing: Prepare mayonnaise as directed, then mix in 1 tablespoon each minced capers and gherkins, 2 teaspoons each anchovy paste and Dijon mustard, and 1 teaspoon each minced parsley and fresh chervil. Serve with seafood or use to dress cold vegetable salads or sliced tomatoes. About 130 calories per tablespoon.

Sauce Niçoise: Prepare mayonnaise as directed and set aside. Mix 2 tablespoons tomato purée with 2 minced pimientos and ½ crushed clove garlic; press through a fine sieve and blend into mayonnaise. About 135 calories per tablespoon.

Russian Mayonnaise: Prepare mayonnaise, then mix in ¼ cup black or red caviar, ½ cup sour cream, and 1 tablespoon minced fresh dill. About 145 calories per tablespoon.

Mustard Mayonnaise: Prepare mayonnaise, then mix in 4 teaspoons Dijon mustard. About 130 calories per tablespoon.

Curry Mayonnaise: Prepare mayonnaise, then blend in 1–2 teaspoons curry powder. About 130 calories per tablespoon.

Chantilly Mayonnaise: Prepare mayonnaise, then fold in ½ cup heavy cream, beaten to soft peaks. About 150 calories per tablespoon.

Fruit Mayonnaise: Prepare mayonnaise, then beat in 3 tablespoons each orange juice and superfine sugar, 1 teaspoon finely grated orange rind, and a pinch nutmeg. For added zip, mix in 1 tablespoon Grand Marnier or other fruit liqueur. Serve with fruit salads. About 140 calories per tablespoon.

Thin Mayonnaise: Prepare mayonnaise, then thin to desired consistency by beating in hot water, a tablespoon at a time. About 130 calories per tablespoon.

COOKED SALAD DRESSING

Note to cholesterol counters: this dressing contains only a third as many egg yolks as old-fashioned cooked dressing.
Makes about 1¼ cups

2 tablespoons flour
2 tablespoons sugar
1 teaspoon powdered mustard
¾ teaspoon salt
Pinch cayenne pepper
¾ cup cold water, or ½ cup milk and ¼ cup water
2 egg yolks, lightly beaten
¼ cup lemon juice or white wine vinegar
2 tablespoons salad oil

Mix flour, sugar, mustard, salt, cayenne, and water in the top of a double boiler over simmering water; beat egg yolks and lemon juice just to blend, then mix in. Heat, stirring constantly, until thickened. Beat in oil, 1 tablespoon at a time. Place a piece of wax paper flat on dressing and cool to room temperature; chill before serving. If you like, thin with a little water or milk. About 25 calories per tablespoon if made with water, 30 calories per tablespoon if made with milk and water.

VARIATIONS:

Cooked Salad Dressing à la Crème: Prepare dressing as directed, then fold in ½ cup heavy cream, beaten to soft peaks. About 45 calories per tablespoon if made with water, 50 calories per tablespoon if made with milk and water.

Piquant Cooked Dressing: Prepare dressing, cool, and mix in ½ cup sour cream, 1 teaspoon each prepared horseradish, grated yellow onion, and Worcestershire sauce. Bruise a peeled clove garlic, stick on a toothpick, and chill in dressing; remove before serving. About 35 calories per tablespoon if made with water, about 40 calories per tablespoon if made with milk and water.

Cooked Fruit Salad Dressing: Prepare dressing as directed but substitute 1 tablespoon cornstarch for the flour and use ½ cup orange juice and ¼ cup pineapple juice for the water; reduce lemon juice to 2 tablespoons. If you like, fold in ¼ teaspoon bruised celery, dill, or caraway seeds, also ½ cup heavy cream, whipped to soft peaks. About 30 calories per tablespoon (without whipped cream), 50 calories per tablespoon (with whipped cream).

OLD-FASHIONED COOKED DRESSING

This is such a versatile dressing. Make without seeds and serve over cold poached salmon. Or use in any of the ways that you would use mayonnaise.
Makes 1 pint

6 egg yolks, lightly beaten
½ teaspoon powdered mustard
½ cup sugar
½ cup heavy cream
1 teaspoon salt
½ cup melted butter or margarine
1 cup warm cider vinegar
1½ teaspoons celery or poppy seeds (optional)

Mix yolks, mustard, sugar, cream, salt, and butter in the top of a double boiler; slowly beat in vinegar, set over simmering water, and heat and stir until the consistency of custard sauce. Remove from heat and stir 1 minute; mix in seeds if you like. Place a piece of wax paper flat on dressing and cool to room temperature. Cover and chill well. Stir before using. About 60 calories per tablespoon.

⚖ **TANGY LOW-CALORIE SALAD DRESSING**

Good with any green salad.
Makes 1½ cups

1 tablespoon cornstarch
1 cup cold water
3 tablespoons salad oil
¼ cup cider vinegar
1 teaspoon salt
1 teaspoon sugar
2 tablespoons ketchup
1 teaspoon prepared mild yellow mustard
½ teaspoon paprika
½ teaspoon prepared horseradish
½ teaspoon Worcestershire sauce
½ teaspoon oregano

Blend cornstarch and water and heat and stir over moderate heat until thickened and clear. Off heat, beat in remaining ingredients with a rotary beater or electric mixer. Cover and chill well. Shake before using. About 20 calories per tablespoon.

⚖ **MUSTARD SALAD DRESSING**

Makes about 1½ cups

2 tablespoons butter or margarine
2 tablespoons flour
1 cup milk
1 teaspoon salt
1½ teaspoons sugar
2 teaspoons powdered mustard blended with 2 tablespoons cold water
⅓ cup cider vinegar

Melt butter in a small saucepan over moderately low heat, blend in flour, add milk slowly, and cook and stir until thickened and smooth. Mix in salt, sugar, and mustard paste. Add vinegar, 1 tablespoon at a time, beating well after each addition. Cool dressing, then cover and chill 2–3 hours. Beat well before using. Use to dress any cooked vegetable or seafood salad. (*Note:* Dressing keeps well about a week in refrigerator.) About 20 calories per tablespoon.

VARIATION:

⚖ **Extra-Low-Calorie Mustard Dressing:** Prepare as directed but use skim milk instead of regular. About 15 calories per tablespoon.

THOUSAND ISLAND DRESSING

Makes about 1½ cups

1 cup mayonnaise
1 hard-cooked egg, peeled and chopped fine
1 tablespoon minced onion, scallion or chives
¼ cup chili sauce
¼ cup minced pimiento-stuffed green olives
1 tablespoon minced sweet green pepper
2–3 drops liquid hot red pepper seasoning

Mix all ingredients well, cover, and chill about 2 hours. Use to dress crisp wedges of lettuce. (*Note:* This dressing keeps well in the refrigerator for several days.) About 80 calories per tablespoon.

VARIATIONS:

⚖ **Low-Calorie Thousand Island Dressing** (Makes about 1 cup): Substitute yogurt for mayonnaise and 2 tablespoons minced parsley for the olives; use minced egg white only and reduce chili sauce to 1 tablespoon. About 10 calories per tablespoon.

Extra-Creamy Thousand Island Dressing (Makes about 2½ cups): Prepare as directed but substitute minced parsley for the green pepper; mix in ¼ cup minced dill pickle, 1 tablespoon Worcestershire sauce, and ¼ teaspoon paprika; finally, fold in ½ cup heavy cream beaten until glossy but not stiff. About 100 calories per tablespoon.

⊠ RUSSIAN DRESSING (AMERICAN STYLE)

Makes about 1¾ cups

1 cup mayonnaise or mayonnaise-type salad dressing
¼ cup French Dressing
¼ cup chili sauce
2 tablespoons minced sweet green pepper
2 tablespoons minced pimiento
1 tablespoon minced yellow onion
1 teaspoon prepared horseradish

Blend all ingredients together and use to dress green salads. About 80 calories per tablespoon.

VARIATION:

Russian Dressing (Russian Style): Prepare dressing as directed and mix in 2–3 tablespoons black caviar. About 85 calories per tablespoon.

GREEN GODDESS DRESSING I

Years ago when George Arliss was opening in San Francisco in *The Green Goddess,* the Palace Hotel chef created a salad dressing in his honor. Of the two versions below, the first is the most like the original, the second a popular, easy variation. Makes about 1 quart

1 clove garlic, peeled and halved
⅓ cup minced parsley
⅓ cup minced chives
1 tablespoon minced scallions
¼ cup minced fresh tarragon

8 anchovy fillets, rinsed, drained, and minced
3 cups mayonnaise
⅓ cup tarragon vinegar

Rub a small bowl well with cut sides of garlic; discard garlic. Add remaining ingredients and mix well; cover and chill 1–2 hours. Use to dress crisp green salads. (*Note:* Dressing keeps well in refrigerator about 1 week.) About 85 calories per tablespoon.

VARIATION:

Green Goddess Dressing II: Prepare as directed but substitute ½ (2-ounce) tube anchovy paste for the minced anchovies and 1 cup sour cream for 1 cup of the mayonnaise. About 70 calories per tablespoon.

GREEN MAYONNAISE I

Green Mayonnaise I is nippier than Green Mayonnaise II, which substitutes spinach for watercress.

Makes about 1½ cups

½ cup minced parsley
⅓ cup minced watercress
2 tablespoons minced chives
1 tablespoon minced fresh dill
1¼ cups mayonnaise
1 teaspoon lemon juice
¼ teaspoon salt
2–3 drops liquid hot red pepper seasoning

Mix all ingredients well, cover, and chill several hours. Serve with cold boiled shellfish (especially lobster) or use to dress fish or vegetable salads. About 50 calories per tablespoon.

VARIATION:

Green Mayonnaise II: Prepare as directed, substituting minced raw spinach for the watercress and minced fresh tarragon or chervil for the dill. Omit chives if you like. About 50 calories per tablespoon.

WATERCRESS DRESSING

Makes 1½ cups

½ bunch watercress, washed
½ teaspoon celery salt
1 cup mayonnaise
1 tablespoon lemon juice

Pick leaves from watercress and mince; mix with remaining ingredients, cover, and chill 30 minutes. Good over wedges of lettuce, Belgian endives, halved lengthwise, or a mixture of avocado, orange, and grapefruit sections. About 75 calories per tablespoon.

CAVIAR DRESSING

Makes about 1 pint

1 hard-cooked egg, peeled and halved
1 cup mayonnaise
1 cup sour cream
Juice of ½ lemon
1 tablespoon prepared spicy brown mustard
1 scallion, minced (do not include tops)
1 (1-ounce) jar black caviar

Rub egg yolk through a fine sieve and mince the white; mix with remaining ingredients, cover, and chill about 1 hour. Stir well and use to dress tossed green salads or tomato aspic. Good, too, with cold boiled shrimp or lobster. (*Note:* Dressing keeps well several days in refrigerator.) About 75 calories per tablespoon.

CREAMY BUTTERMILK-CHIVE DRESSING

Makes 1½ cups

½ cup buttermilk
1 cup mayonnaise or mayonnaise-type salad dressing
2 tablespoons minced chives

¼ teaspoon salt
Pinch white pepper

Blend all ingredients together, cover, and chill 2 hours. Mix well again and use to dress green salads. (*Note:* Dressing keeps well about 1 week in refrigerator.) About 75 calories per tablespoon.

CHAPTER 18

BREADS

Making bread is one of cooking's true joys, yet many of us have lost that joy, if indeed we ever knew it. Every woman should make bread once, at least, if only to feel the warm dough responding to her touch, if only to fill her house with the promise of fresh loaves and the memories of her children with happiness.

Basically, there are two kinds of bread: *quick breads* (biscuits, muffins, pancakes, etc.), which can be cooked as soon as they're mixed, and *yeast breads,* which require more time and attention.

The Ways of Mixing Breads

Different breads require different techniques in handling; all are basic, most are easy:

Muffin Method (for muffins, popovers, waffles, pancakes, most corn breads): Dry ingredients are sifted together into a mixing bowl, liquid ingredients are combined, added all at once, and mixed in *just* enough to dampen the dry ingredients. There is great temptation to overbeat these batters, but if the bread—especially the muffin—is to be light and meltingly tender, the batter must be lumpy. If flecks of flour show, no harm done. Too much mixing makes the muffin tough.

Biscuit or Pastry Method (for biscuits and dumplings): Dry ingredients are sifted together into a bowl, the fat is cut in with a pastry blender or 2 knives until the texture of coarse meal, then the liquid is sprinkled over the mixture and stirred briskly. Kneading follows, usually about 20 seconds on a lightly floured board. It is the distribution of small fat particles throughout the dough that produces a flaky biscuit.

Cake Method (for most quick fruit and/or nut loaves): The shortening is creamed with the sugar and eggs, then the sifted dry ingredients added alternately with the liquid; nuts and fruit are folded in at the end.

Yeast Bread: Not one method but several; see Yeast Breads.

Tips for Making Better Breads

About Pans and Preparing Pans:

– Always use pan sizes recipes specify.
– Use baking sheets for biscuits and individually shaped rolls; if you

have none, use a turned-upside-down large baking pan.
- For richly browned loaves (especially yeast loaves), use heatproof glass or dull finish, dark metal pans.
- For greasing pans, use cooking oil, shortening, or clarified* unsalted butter. Brush over bottom and sides of pans, applying in a thin, even film with a crumple of paper toweling or a pastry brush.
- If bread contains sticky fruit or filling, grease *and* flour pans (sprinkle a little flour into greased pans, tilt from one side to the other to coat with a thin film, then tap out excess flour).
- When using muffin tins, grease only those cups that will be used; if you've greased more cups than you need, wipe grease from those not to be used.

About Mixing Breads:

- Read recipe carefully before beginning.
- Assemble all utensils and measure ingredients before beginning.
- Use as light a hand as possible in mixing breads. Muffins, especially, need a delicate touch.
- Unless recipes indicate otherwise, mix breads by hand, using a comfortable long-handled wooden spoon.
- To avoid last minute confusion, measure all ingredients for quick breads well ahead of time, then mix shortly before time to serve.

About Rolling Doughs:

- Use a lightly floured surface and rolling pin (experienced cooks prefer a pastry cloth and stockinette-covered pin), adding only what flour is needed to keep dough from sticking to board. Too much flour will toughen the dough.
- Roll doughs with quick, firm strokes from the center outward, keeping in mind the ultimate shape you want—circle, rectangle, square—and adjusting position of dough as needed to achieve that shape with a minimum of handling.
- Use floured cutters when cutting dough, floured scissors or knives for snipping or slicing it.

About Placing Breads and Rolls in Pans:

- Never fill muffin pan cups more than two-thirds full when making muffins or popovers; to make popover batter go farther, half fill cups.
- For soft-sided biscuits or rolls, place close together; for crusty sides, space about 1" apart.
- Always brush any loose topping or wipe any spilled glaze from baking sheets before baking breads.

About Baking Breads (also see About Baking Yeast Breads for special techniques applying to yeast breads only):

- Let oven preheat a full 15 minutes before baking.
- Bake breads as near center of oven as possible unless recipes direct otherwise.
- When baking several pans of bread at once, stagger carefully so heat will circulate as evenly as possible; never let pans touch each other or oven walls.
- Check bread after minimum cooking time, then bake full time if needed.

To Tell if Breads Are Done:

Biscuits, Muffins, Rolls, and other Small Breads: They should be dappled with brown, firm and springy to the touch, and, if baked in muffin tins, slightly pulled from sides of cups.

Quick Loaves: They should have

pulled slightly from sides of pans, be golden brown and springy to the touch.

Yeast Loaves: They should have pulled slightly from sides of pans, be richly browned and sound hollow when tapped.

About Cooling Breads:

– Unless recipes direct to the contrary, always remove breads from pans as soon as they come from the oven.
– Cool breads on wire racks and allow plenty of space around loaves for air to circulate. This keeps moisture from condensing on breads and spoiling them.

About Serving Breads:

– Serve muffins, biscuits, corn breads, popovers, and yeast rolls oven hot; cool yeast breads and fruit or nut loaves to room temperature before serving.
– Nestle hot breads in napkin-lined baskets so they will stay hot.
– If muffins or rolls should be done before the rest of the meal, tip each slightly in its muffin cup, turn off heat, and let stand in oven until ready to serve.
– To slice fresh loaves more easily, use a hot serrated bread knife (run quickly under hot water, then dry). Or use a fine strong thread in a sawing motion.

About Reheating Breads:

Biscuits: Wrap in foil, not individually but en masse, and heat 15–20 minutes at 375° F. *Or* set unwrapped on a trivet in a large skillet, add 2–3 tablespoons water, cover and let steam over moderate heat 5–8 minutes.

Rolls, Muffins, Corn Breads: Bundle in foil and heat 8–10 minutes at 350° F. *Or* use the steaming method described for biscuits.

About Keeping Breads: Breads do not keep well; in damp weather they mold, in fair weather they harden and dry. Wrap tightly in foil, plastic bags, or wax paper and store in a breadbox in a cool, dry place. Or, if weather is unusually damp or muggy, in the refrigerator. The refrigerator, contrary to what many people believe, is not a good place to store bread because it *hastens* staling.

About Freezing Breads: See chapter on freezing.

QUICK BREADS AND BATTERS

Note: Unless recipes specify otherwise, use all-purpose flour in the recipes that follow and double-acting baking powder.

¢ ⊠ **BASIC MUFFINS**

Makes about 1¼ dozen

2 cups plus 2 tablespoons sifted flour
1 tablespoon baking powder
2 tablespoons sugar
1 teaspoon salt
1 egg, beaten until frothy
1 cup milk
3 tablespoons cooking oil, melted butter or margarine

Preheat oven to 425° F. Sift all dry ingredients together into a mixing bowl. Mix egg, milk, and oil. Make a well in center of dry ingredients and pour in egg mixture all at once; stir lightly and quickly just to mix; *batter should be lumpy*. Spoon into muffin pans—bottoms of cups should be greased but *not* sides—filling each cup two-thirds. Bake about 20 minutes until lightly browned. Serve oven hot with plenty of butter. About 105 calories per muffin (without butter).

VARIATIONS:

Bacon Muffins: Sift dry ingredients as directed but reduce salt to ½ teaspoon; add ¼ cup minced crisp bacon and toss to dredge. Lightly beat egg and milk with 2 tablespoons each cooking oil and melted bacon drippings; mix into dry ingredients by basic method and bake as directed. About 115 calories per muffin (without butter).

Date, Raisin, or Currant Muffins: Sift 2¼ cups flour, 3 tablespoons sugar, 1 tablespoon baking powder, and ½ teaspoon salt into mixing bowl; add 1 teaspoon finely grated lemon rind and 1 cup diced, pitted dates, seedless raisins, or dried currants; toss to dredge. Lightly beat egg and milk with ¼ cup cooking oil, mix into dry ingredients by basic method, and bake as directed. About 130 calories per muffin (without butter).

Nut Muffins: Sift 2¼ cups flour, ¼ cup light brown sugar, 1 tablespoon baking powder, and ½ teaspoon salt into bowl; add ¾ cup minced nuts (any kind) and toss to dredge. Lightly beat egg and milk with ¼ cup oil or melted butter; mix into dry ingredients by basic method and bake as directed. About 140 calories per muffin (without butter).

Blueberry Muffins: Sift 2¼ cups flour, ¼ cup sugar, 1 tablespoon baking powder, and ¼ teaspoon salt into mixing bowl. Add 1 cup washed and dried blueberries and toss to mix. Beat egg and milk with ¼ cup melted butter; mix into dry ingredients by basic method and bake as directed. About 130 calories per muffin (without butter).

Orange Muffins: Sift 2¼ cups flour, ¼ cup sugar, 2½ teaspoons baking powder, ½ teaspoon baking soda, and ¼ teaspoon salt into mixing bowl. Add finely grated rind of 1 orange and toss to dredge. Lightly beat egg with ½ cup each milk and orange juice and ¼ cup melted butter (no substitute). Mix egg mixture into dry ingredients by basic method and bake as directed. About 120 calories per muffin (without butter).

¢ **WHOLE WHEAT MUFFINS**

Makes 1 dozen

¾ cup unsifted whole wheat flour
1 cup sifted all-purpose flour
3 tablespoons sugar
1 tablespoon baking powder
1 teaspoon salt
1 egg
1 cup milk
¼ cup cooking oil
1 tablespoon molasses

Preheat oven to 425° F. Place whole wheat flour in a large mixing bowl, then sift all-purpose flour with sugar, baking powder, and salt directly into bowl; toss well to mix. Beat egg with milk, oil, and molasses until foamy. Make a well in the center of the dry ingredients, pour in liquid all at once and stir lightly and quickly just to mix; batter should be quite lumpy. Spoon into greased muffin pans, three-fourths filling each cup. (*Note:* For best results, only bottoms of cups should be greased, not sides.) Bake 20–22 minutes until lightly browned. Serve hot with plenty of butter. About 135 calories per muffin (without butter).

¢ BRAN MUFFINS

Makes 1 dozen

1¼ cups ready-to-eat bran cereal
1 cup milk
1¼ cups sifted flour
1 tablespoon baking powder
½ teaspoon salt
¼ cup sugar
1 egg
¼ cup cooking oil, melted butter or margarine

Preheat oven to 425° F. Soak bran in milk 2–3 minutes. Sift dry ingredients together into a mixing bowl. Beat egg and oil until blended, then stir into bran and milk. Make a well in center of dry ingredients and pour in bran mixture all at once. Stir lightly and quickly just to mix (batter should be lumpy). Spoon into muffin pans—bottoms of cups should be greased but not sides—filling each cup two-thirds. Bake about 25 minutes until lightly browned and springy to the touch. Serve hot with lots of butter. About 140 calories per muffin (without butter).

VARIATIONS:

Raisin-Bran Muffins: Prepare as directed, adding ¾ cup seedless raisins to the sifted dry ingredients; toss well to dredge before combining with liquid ingredients. About 170 calories per muffin (without butter).

Nut-Bran Muffins: Prepare as directed, adding ¾ cup minced pecans or walnuts to the sifted dry ingredients; toss well to dredge before mixing with liquid ingredients. About 185 calories per muffin (without butter).

¢ RYE MUFFINS

Not unlike pumpernickel.
Makes 1 dozen

1 tablespoon caraway seeds
2 tablespoons boiling water
¾ cup unsifted rye flour
3 tablespoons light brown sugar
1 cup sifted all-purpose flour
1 tablespoon baking powder
1 teaspoon salt
1 egg
1 tablespoon dark molasses
¾ cup milk
¼ cup cooking oil

Preheat oven to 425° F. Soak caraway seeds in boiling water 15–20 minutes. Place rye flour and sugar in a bowl and rub well between your fingers, breaking up any lumps of sugar. Sift all-purpose flour, baking powder, and salt directly into another bowl and toss well to mix. Beat egg with molasses, milk, and oil until foamy, then stir in caraway seeds and water. Make a well in center of dry ingredients and pour in milk mixture all at once. Stir quickly and lightly just enough to mix; batter should be lumpy. Spoon into muffin pans—bottoms of cups should be greased but not sides—filling each cup two-thirds. Bake about 20 minutes until lightly browned. Serve hot with lots of butter. About 135 calories per muffin (without butter).

¢ BAKING POWDER BISCUITS

These will be light and feathery if you follow the directions exactly.
Makes 1½ dozen

2 cups sifted flour
1 teaspoon salt
1 tablespoon baking powder
⅓ cup chilled shortening
¾ cup milk
Milk, melted butter or margarine (optional glaze)

Preheat oven to 450° F. Sift flour with salt and baking powder into a bowl and cut in shortening with a pastry blender until the texture of very coarse meal; make a well in center, pour in milk, and stir briskly with a fork just until dough holds together. Knead gently on a lightly floured board 7 or 8 times. Roll ½" thick and cut in rounds with a floured biscuit cutter; reroll and cut scraps. Place on ungreased baking sheets—1" apart for crusty-sided biscuits, almost touching for soft. For glistening brown tops, brush with glaze. Bake 12–15 minutes until lightly browned. Serve oven hot with lots of butter. (*Note:* For hot-hot-hot biscuits, bake in piepans that can come to the table. To reheat leftover biscuits, wrap together in a large foil package and warm 15–20 minutes at 350° F.) About 85 calories per biscuit (without butter).

VARIATIONS:

¢ **Drop Biscuits:** Prepare basic recipe but increase milk to 1 cup. Do not knead or roll but drop by tablespoonfuls 1" apart on greased baking sheets. Bake as directed. About 85 calories per biscuit (without butter).

¢ **Biscuit Topping for Casseroles:** Prepare 1 recipe Drop Biscuits (above) and drop by rounded tablespoonfuls, almost touching, on top of hot casserole mixture. (*Note:* Bake any leftover dough as basic recipe directs.) Bake casserole, uncovered, as recipe directs or 15–20 minutes at 425° F. until lightly browned. To serve: Cut through biscuit topping as you would piecrust. About 250 calories for each of 6 pie-shaped wedges, 190 calories for each of 8 wedges.

¢ **Quick Biscuit Topping for Casseroles:** For Drop Biscuits (above), substitute packaged biscuit mix prepared by label directions or canned refrigerated biscuits; drop onto casserole and bake as directed. About 80 calories per biscuit.

¢ **Stir-and-Roll Biscuits:** Sift dry ingredients into bowl as directed. Pour ⅓ cup cooking oil into a measuring cup, and add ⅔ cup milk; *do not stir* but pour all at once into well in dry ingredients. Mix briskly with a fork until dough holds together. Knead in bowl 10 times without adding more flour. Turn onto an *unfloured* board, top with a sheet of wax paper and roll ½" thick. Cut and bake on ungreased baking sheets 12–14 minutes at 475° F. About 85 calories per biscuit (without butter).

▫ **Extra-Quick Biscuits:** Prepare basic dough as directed, pat into a rectangle ½" thick and cut in 1½" squares or 2" triangles. Bake as directed. About 85 calories per biscuit (without butter).

Extra-Rich Biscuits: Prepare basic dough as directed but add 2 tablespoons sugar to dry ingredients and increase shortening to ½ cup. About 90 calories per biscuit (without butter).

¢ **Buttermilk Biscuits:** Prepare basic or stir-and-roll dough as directed but reduce baking powder to 2 teaspoons, add ¼ teaspoon baking soda, and substitute cold buttermilk for milk. About 85 calories per biscuit (without butter).

Sweet Pinwheel Biscuits: Prepare basic dough and roll into a rectangle about 12" long, 6"–7" wide, and ¼" thick. Spread with softened butter, sprinkle with ¼ cup light brown sugar, 1 teaspoon cinnamon, ⅛ teaspoon nutmeg, and ¼–⅓ cup seedless raisins, dried currants, or coarsely chopped pecans or walnuts.

Or, if you prefer, top butter with marmalade, jam, or a drizzling of honey. Roll the short way, jelly roll style, pinch seam to seal, then slice 1″ thick. Lay pinwheels flat in greased muffin pans, brush lightly with milk, and bake 12–15 minutes at 425° F. Recipe too flexible for a meaningful calorie count.

Savory Pinwheel Biscuits: Prepare like Sweet Pinwheel Biscuits (above) but spread with deviled ham or any cheese or meat spread instead of sugar and spices. About 105–115 calories per serving depending on filling (cheese would tend to run higher than meat).

Party Biscuits: Prepare and roll basic dough as directed; cut with a 1½″ cutter and bake 10–12 minutes at 450° F. Split biscuits, fill with slices of Smithfield ham, roast chicken, or turkey, and serve as buffet food. About 95 calories per biscuit.

¢ **Herb Biscuits:** Prepare basic recipe as directed, but before adding milk lightly toss in any of the following: ½ teaspoon each sage and thyme (nice with pork), ½ teaspoon each basil and oregano (good with veal), ¼ cup minced chives or parsley (delicious with chicken), 2 teaspoons dill or 1½ teaspoons caraway seeds. About 85 calories per biscuit (without butter).

¢ **Onion Biscuits:** Prepare basic recipe as directed, but before adding milk toss in 1–2 tablespoons instant minced onion or ¼ cup crumbled French-fried onion rings. About 85 calories per biscuit (without butter).

Bacon Biscuits: Prepare basic recipe as directed, but before adding milk toss in ⅓–½ cup finely crumbled, crisp bacon. About 100 calories per biscuit (without butter).

¢ **Cheese Biscuits:** Prepare basic recipe as directed, but before adding milk toss in ½ cup coarsely grated sharp Cheddar cheese. About 100 calories per biscuit (without butter).

¢ **Orange or Lemon Biscuits:** Prepare extra rich dough as directed, but before adding milk toss in the finely grated rind of 1 orange or ½ lemon. About 90 calories per biscuit (without butter).

Berry Biscuits: Mix drop biscuits as directed, then stir in 1 cup washed, well-dried blueberries, raspberries, or very small strawberries. Sprinkle biscuits with sugar before baking. About 90 calories per biscuit (without butter).

¢ **Make-Ahead Biscuits:** Prepare any biscuit recipe as directed, then bake 7–8 minutes at 450° F. until risen but not browned. Cool, wrap, and freeze. To serve, arrange solidly frozen biscuits on ungreased baking sheets and bake in top ⅓ of a 450° F. oven 8–10 minutes until browned.

Some Quick Toppings to Jazz Up Biscuits: Before baking, brush tops of biscuits with a little milk, melted butter or margarine, then sprinkle with any of the following:
– Cinnamon sugar
– Poppy, caraway, or sesame seeds
– Finely ground pecans, walnuts, almonds, or peanuts
– Grated Parmesan cheese
– Corn meal
– Seasoned salt

¢ **CHEESE-CORN MEAL BISCUITS**

Makes about 1½ dozen

½ *cup corn meal*
¾ *cup milk, scalded*

1 cup sifted flour
1 tablespoon baking powder
¾ teaspoon salt
3 tablespoons butter, margarine, or lard
¾ cup coarsely grated mild Cheddar cheese
1 egg yolk, lightly beaten (glaze)

Preheat oven to 450° F. Briskly mix corn meal into hot milk, cover, and set aside. Sift flour with baking powder and salt into a bowl. Using a pastry blender, cut in butter until mixture resembles coarse meal. Add corn meal mixture and cheese and stir lightly to blend. Turn onto a lightly floured board, knead gently about ½ minute. Roll ½" thick and cut into rounds with a biscuit cutter. Arrange 1½" apart on an ungreased baking sheet and brush tops with glaze. Bake 12–15 minutes or until well risen and golden. About 85 calories per biscuit.

¢ ☒ BANNOCKS

A husky Scottish griddlecake made with oatmeal.
Makes 2 dozen

4¼ cups uncooked oatmeal (not quick-cooking)
2 teaspoons salt
1 teaspoon baking soda
¼ cup melted bacon drippings or lard
1 cup very hot water

Preheat griddle over moderately high heat while you mix bannocks, or, if using an electric griddle, preheat to 400° F. Place 4 cups oatmeal in a mixing bowl; buzz the rest in an electric blender at high speed until moderately fine, then reserve to use in rolling out dough. Add remaining ingredients to bowl and mix well. Knead on a board lightly dusted with the fine oatmeal 1 minute, roll ¼" thick, and cut into rounds with a 3" cutter. Cook on an *ungreased* griddle 5–6 minutes per side until lightly browned and cooked through. Serve hot with plenty of butter. About 110 calories per bannock (without butter).

¢ IRISH SODA BREAD

In Ireland this bread is made as often with whole wheat flour as with white, and usually without shortening. It's a close-textured loaf. When serving, cut straight across the loaf into thin slices instead of dividing into wedges.
Makes a 6" round loaf

1 cup sifted all-purpose flour
2 teaspoons baking soda
1½ teaspoons salt
¼ cup shortening or margarine
3 cups unsifted whole wheat flour
1⅔ cups buttermilk or sour milk

Preheat oven to 400° F. Sift all-purpose flour, soda, and salt together into a large bowl. With a pastry blender cut in shortening until the texture of coarse meal. Mix in whole wheat flour. Pour in buttermilk all at once and mix well to blend (you may have to use your hands). Turn out on a lightly floured board and knead until fairly smooth, about 5 minutes. Shape into a round loaf about 6" across, with a sharp knife cut a cross ¼" deep in top and sprinkle with a very little flour. Place cross side up in a well-greased round 2-quart casserole about 2½" deep. Bake, uncovered, about 40 minutes until crusty brown and hollow sounding when tapped. Turn loaf out on wire rack and cool before cutting. About 110 calories for each of 20 slices.

VARIATION:

¢ **White Irish Soda Bread:** Sift 4

cups all-purpose flour with soda and salt and cut in shortening; omit whole wheat flour and reduce buttermilk to 1½ cups; otherwise proceed as directed. About 110 calories for each of 20 slices.

¢ HILDA'S YORKSHIRE SCONES

Makes about 10

1½ cups sifted flour
¼ cup sugar
¼ teaspoon salt
1½ teaspoons baking powder
¼ cup margarine
⅓ cup seedless raisins
1 egg, lightly beaten
2 tablespoons milk

Preheat oven to 425° F. Sift flour, sugar, salt, and baking powder into a bowl. Using a pastry blender or 2 knives, cut in margarine until the texture of coarse meal. Add raisins and toss to mix. Add egg and milk and mix with a fork until mixture forms a soft dough. Roll on a floured board or pat into a circle about ½" thick, adding only enough flour to keep dough from sticking. Cut into rounds with a floured 2" cutter; reroll and cut scraps. Bake 2" apart on a greased baking sheet 12–15 minutes until golden. Let cool 1–2 minutes on a wire rack. Scones are best eaten warm, not hot—split in half and slathered with butter. About 145 calories per scone (without butter).

¢ POPOVERS

Makes about 6 popovers

1 cup sifted flour
½ teaspoon salt
¾ cup milk
¼ cup cold water
2 eggs

Preheat oven to 450° F. Beat all ingredients in a small bowl with a rotary beater until just smooth. Scrape bottom of bowl with rubber spatula once or twice during beating. Spoon into a well-greased muffin tin, filling each cup two-thirds. Bake 40 minutes until well browned, puffed, and firm. (*Note:* For dry, crisp popovers, bake 35 minutes, quickly cut a small slit in the side of each popover so steam can escape, and bake 5–10 minutes longer.) Serve immediately with plenty of butter. About 115 calories per popover (without butter).

¢ YORKSHIRE PUDDING

A 100-year-old Yorkshire recipe adapted for today's silken flours. Like a soufflé, Yorkshire pudding will not wait, so serve straight from the oven.

Makes 6 servings

½ cup sifted flour
½ teaspoon salt
½ cup milk
¼ cup cold water
2 eggs, lightly beaten
1 tablespoon melted roast beef drippings

Mix flour and salt in a small bowl, add milk, a little at a time, beating with a rotary beater or electric mixer until smooth. Add water and eggs and beat until bubbly. Cover loosely and let stand in a cool place (not refrigerator) about ½ hour. Meanwhile, preheat oven to 500° F. (*Note:* If you've been doing a roast, shove temperature up after roast comes from oven.) Beat batter 1–2 minutes until bubbles appear on surface. Pour ½ teaspoon drippings into each of 6 muffin pan cups and heat in the oven 1–2 minutes until almost smoking hot. Spoon 3 tablespoons batter into each cup and bake 8 minutes *without opening oven door*. Reduce temperature to 400° F. and bake 8–10 minutes longer until well browned, risen, and crisp. (*Note:* Do not pierce with a fork or puddings will collapse.) Arrange puddings around roast and serve at once, allowing 1 pudding with each portion of meat and topping with plenty of hot gravy. About 80 calories per serving (without gravy).

VARIATION:

¢ **Old-Fashioned Yorkshire Pudding:** Prepare batter and preheat oven to 500° F. Pour 3 tablespoons melted roast beef drippings into a 13"×9"×2" baking pan (or similar-size pan in which beef was roasted) and heat in oven 2 minutes. Meanwhile beat batter until bubbles appear. Pour batter into pan and bake 10 minutes, reduce temperature to 450° F., and bake 12–15 minutes longer until well browned and crisp. Cut in large squares and serve. About 80 calories per serving (without gravy).

CHEESE CRACKERS

Makes about 6 dozen

1½ cups sifted flour
1 teaspoon salt
⅛ teaspoon paprika
⅛ teaspoon cayenne pepper
½ cup chilled margarine (no substitute)
½ pound sharp Cheddar cheese, coarsely grated
2½–3 tablespoons ice water

Mix flour, salt, paprika and cayenne in a shallow bowl and cut in margarine with a pastry blender until mixture resembles coarse meal. Add cheese and toss to mix. Sprinkle ice water evenly over surface, 1 tablespoon at a time, mixing lightly with a fork; dough should just hold together. Divide dough into 2 parts, turn out on a lightly floured board, and shape each into a roll about 9" long and 1½" in diameter; wrap in foil and chill well. About 10 minutes before crackers are to be baked, preheat oven to 375° F. Slice rolls ¼" thick and space crackers 1" apart on ungreased baking sheets. Bake 10 minutes until golden, then transfer at once to wire racks to cool. Store airtight. Serve at room temperature or, if you prefer, reheat about 5 minutes at 350° F. About 30 calories per cracker.

¢ **BASIC CORN BREAD**

Makes an 8"×8"×2" loaf

1 cup sifted flour
1 cup sifted corn meal
1 tablespoon baking powder
¾ teaspoon salt
1 tablespoon sugar (optional)
1 egg
1 cup milk
¼ cup cooking oil, melted shortening, or bacon drippings

Preheat oven to 400° F. Sift flour, corn meal, baking powder, salt, and, if you like, sugar into a bowl; beat egg with milk and oil just to blend. Make a well in dry ingredients, pour in egg mixture, and stir until well blended. Pour into a well-greased 8"×8"×2" baking pan and bake 20–25 minutes until bread pulls slightly from edges of pan, is lightly browned and springy to the touch. Cut in large squares and serve oven hot with lots of butter. About 110 calories for each of 16 squares (without butter), 145 calories for each of 12 squares.

VARIATIONS:

¢ **Corn Sticks** (Makes 14): Preheat oven to 425° F. Grease corn stick pans, set in oven, and let heat while oven preheats. Mix batter as directed, spoon into hot pans, and bake 15–20 minutes until nicely browned and springy to the touch. Serve at once. About 125 calories per corn stick.

¢ **Corn Muffins** (Makes 1 dozen): Preheat oven to 425° F. Mix batter as directed, spoon into greased muffin pans, filling each cup two-thirds. Bake 15–20 minutes until lightly browned and springy to the touch. Serve hot. About 145 calories per muffin.

¢ CRACKLING BREAD

Cracklings are the crunchy brown bits left over after rendering pork fat into lard. In the old days there were plenty of cracklings at hog butchering time. Today, unless you raise hogs, you'll have to buy fresh pork fat from your butcher (some will give it to you) and make your own cracklings. Here's how.

Makes 8 small patties

Cracklings:
2 cups diced fresh pork fat

Bread:
¾ cup sifted flour
1½ cups corn meal
½ teaspoon baking soda
¾ teaspoon salt
1 cup diced cracklings
2 tablespoons drippings from cracklings
1 cup plus 2 tablespoons buttermilk

Render pork fat in a large iron skillet over moderately low heat, stirring now and then, until all fat is melted and cracklings are crisp and golden brown; this will take about 45 minutes. Watch carefully and reduce heat if fat threatens to smoke and burn. Drain cracklings on paper toweling and cut up any big pieces; save drippings to use in cooking. Preheat oven to 400° F. Mix flour with corn meal, soda, and salt; add cracklings and toss to mix. Combine drippings and buttermilk, pour into meal mixture, and stir to mix. Shape into hamburger-size patties or oblong cakes and bake on a greased baking sheet about 25 minutes until lightly browned and firm. Serve hot—no butter needed. About 200 calories per piece.

¢ BAKED JOHNNYCAKE

Makes an 8″×8″×2″ loaf

1 cup sifted flour
1 cup corn meal, preferably white
1 teaspoon salt
1 tablespoon baking powder
1 egg, lightly beaten
¼ cup melted butter or margarine
2 tablespoons dark molasses
1⅓ cups milk

Preheat oven to 375° F. Sift flour, meal, salt, and baking powder together into a bowl. Add remaining ingredients and beat just until blended. Spoon into a greased 8″×8″×2″ pan and bake 25–30 minutes until pale golden and springy to the touch. Turn out on a wire rack and cool 1–2 minutes; turn upright, cut in 2″ squares, and serve hot with plenty of butter. About 110 calories for each of 16 squares (without butter).

⌧ ¢ RHODE ISLAND JONNYCAKES

There are Rhode Island jonnycakes and Rhode Island jonnycakes (*not* spelled johnnycake, by the way). If you come from "South County," Rhode Island, you like your jonnycakes thick—the batter should be about the consistency of a soft drop-cookie dough so that it mounds on a spoon and stands up on the griddle.

And the cakes themselves will be thick, ½–¾ inch, and cooked at least 10 minutes on each side until crispy-brown. "You can't hurry jonnycakes," they say in "South County." But if, on the other hand, you're from Northern Rhode Island, you like your jonnycakes thin—almost as thin as a crepe. The recipe below is a basic one, and you can experiment with batter thickness until you determine just the consistency you like. It's best to cook jonnycakes on an old-fashioned iron griddle, but you can use an electric skillet or griddle set at a low temperature.
Makes 4 servings

1 cup fine water-ground white corn meal
½ teaspoon salt
1 tablespoon sugar
1 cup boiling water (about)
Milk (to thin batter)
3–4 tablespoons bacon drippings or shortening

Mix together corn meal, salt, and sugar. Pour in boiling water and toss with a fork just to mix. There should be enough water just to dampen the ingredients so that no dry particles show. Next, add enough milk to thin batter to the consistency you like. Heat 2 tablespoons bacon drippings or shortening on a heavy griddle over moderate heat until a drop of water will dance about. Then drop batter by rounded tablespoonfuls onto griddle, reduce heat, and brown slowly, a few at a time, 5–10 minutes on a side, depending on thickness, until crispy and brown. Jonnycakes should be about 2½" in diameter. Lift to paper toweling and keep warm while frying the remainder (add more bacon drippings or shortening as needed). Serve hot with butter or, if you prefer, with butter and maple syrup. If the cakes are thick, try splitting and tucking in a slice of sharp Cheddar cheese—delicious! About 225 calories per serving (without butter, syrup, or cheese).

OLD-FASHIONED DEEP SOUTH SPOON BREAD

This custard-like corn meal pudding makes a good potato substitute.
Makes 4–6 servings

1 pint light cream
⅓ cup milk
¼ cup unsalted butter
2 tablespoons sugar
1 teaspoon salt
1 cup sifted stone- or water-ground white corn meal
4 eggs, separated
1 teaspoon baking powder

Preheat oven to 375° F. Heat cream, milk, butter, sugar, and salt uncovered, stirring occasionally, until scalding; off heat, mix in corn meal, beating until smooth and thick. Lightly beat yolks and stir in baking powder. Stir a little of the hot mixture into yolks, then return to pan and blend well. Beat whites until soft peaks form and fold in. Bake, uncovered, in a lightly buttered 2-quart casserole or soufflé dish 30–35 minutes until puffy and lightly browned. Serve oven hot with lots of butter, salt, and freshly ground black pepper. About 625 calories for each of 4 servings (without butter), 420 calories for each of 6 servings.

¢ CORN MEAL MUSH

A Southern breakfast favorite.
Makes 4 servings

½ cup corn meal, preferably enriched yellow meal
2½ cups boiling water
¾ teaspoon salt

Sprinkle meal into rapidly boiling water, add salt, and heat, stirring, over very low heat about ½ hour until quite thick. Ladle into bowls, top with pats of butter, and serve hot for breakfast. About 60 calories per serving (without butter).

VARIATION:

Fried Mush: Prepare mush as directed and pour into heatproof water glasses or small tin cans (the soup size is perfect) that have been rinsed out in cold water. Cool until firm. Unmold, slice mush ½"–¾" thick and brown in hot bacon drippings, butter, or margarine. Serve with hot syrup in place of pancakes or waffles. About 135 calories per serving (without syrup).

HUSHPUPPIES

For this recipe you *must* use old-fashioned, stone- or water-ground white corn meal—enriched yellow meal flies to pieces in the hot fat. Hushpuppies, it's said, were originally tag ends of corn bread dough, deep fat fried and tossed to dogs at mealtime to "hush them up." Serve hushpuppies with seafood, especially breaded or batter-fried fish.
Makes about 2 dozen

Shortening or cooking oil for deep fat frying
2 cups sifted fine stone- or water-ground white corn meal
1 tablespoon sugar
¾ teaspoon baking soda
2 teaspoons salt
1 tablespoon minced yellow onion
1 egg
1 cup buttermilk
4–5 tablespoons cold water

Begin heating fat in a deep fat fryer; use a deep fat thermometer. Stir corn meal, sugar, soda, and salt together to mix. Place onion in a small bowl, add egg and buttermilk, and beat until frothy; pour all at once into meal and stir lightly to mix. Add just enough water to make dough a good dropping consistency—it should be about the same as drop biscuit dough. When fat reaches 375° F., scoop up rounded ½ tablespoons of dough, shape lightly on end of spoon to smooth out rough edges, drop into fat, and fry about 2 minutes until evenly browned. Drain quickly on paper toweling and serve—hushpuppies should be sizzling hot. About 70 calories each.

¢ **TORTILLAS**

Masa harina is a special corn flour used to make tortillas and other Mexican breads. It's available in gourmet food shops, Latin American and Spanish groceries.
Makes 15

2 cups masa harina
1 teaspoon salt
1¼ cups very hot water

Mix masa and salt, stir in water, and blend well. Pinch off a piece of dough and roll into a ball about 1½" in diameter; flatten in a tortilla press or, if you have none, between 2 dampened 6" double thickness squares of cheesecloth, pressing as hard as possible with a cutting board. Remove board and roll with a rolling pin until about 5" across. Lift off top cheesecloth, very gently invert tortilla on palm of hand, and peel off bottom cheesecloth. Cook in an ungreased, heavy skillet over moderately high heat or on an electric griddle set at 400° F. ½–1 minute on each side, just until tortilla begins to color. It should not brown. Keep warm in a napkin or linen towel while you shape and cook remaining tortillas. Serve hot. About 70 calories each.

VARIATION:

Chili Tostados: Prepare and cook tortillas as directed, then fry, a few at a time, in ½" cooking oil over moderate heat until lightly browned. Drain on paper toweling, spread with hot chili con carne, top with shredded lettuce, a drizzling of French dressing, and a sprinkling of grated Parmesan or Cheddar cheese. Fold tortilla over filling and serve. About 200 calories each.

EASY DATE-NUT BREAD

Start this recipe the day before you bake it.
Makes 2 9"×5"×3" loaves

- *cups coarsely cut-up pitted dates*
- *2 cups boiling water*
- *2 teaspoons baking soda*
- *1 cup sugar*
- *1 tablespoon melted butter or margarine*
- *1 egg, lightly beaten*
- *2¾ cups sifted flour*
- *1 cup coarsely chopped pecans or walnuts*
- *1 teaspoon vanilla*

Mix dates, water, and soda; cool, cover, and let stand at room temperature overnight. Next day preheat oven to 325° F. Add sugar, butter, and egg to date mixture and stir until sugar dissolves. Add flour, a few spoonfuls at a time, mixing after each addition until smooth. Stir in nuts and vanilla. Spoon into 2 greased and floured 9"×5"×3" loaf pans and bake about 1 hour, until loaves shrink slightly from sides of pan and are springy to the touch. Cool upright in pans on wire rack 10 minutes, turn out, and cool completely. Wrap airtight and store overnight before cutting. (*Note:* These loaves freeze well.) About 90 calories for each of 20 slices.

PRUNE AND WALNUT BREAD

This loaf tastes better and cuts more easily if wrapped airtight and "seasoned" about a day.
Makes a 9"×5"×3" loaf

- *2 cups sifted flour*
- *1 teaspoon baking powder*
- *½ teaspoon salt*
- *1 cup boiling water*
- *1 teaspoon baking soda*
- *1 cup coarsely chopped pitted prunes*
- *⅔ cup sugar*
- *1 egg*
- *2 tablespoons melted butter or margarine*
- *½ teaspoon vanilla*
- *⅔ cup coarsely chopped walnuts*

Preheat oven to 300° F. Sift flour with baking powder and salt and set aside. Mix boiling water, soda, and prunes and cool to lukewarm; drain off liquid and reserve. Beat sugar, egg, butter, and vanilla until well blended. Add flour mixture, about ⅓ at a time, alternately with reserved prune liquid, beginning and ending with flour; beat just until smooth. Mix in prunes and walnuts. Spoon into a greased 9"×5"× 3" loaf pan and bake 1 hour until loaf shrinks slightly from sides of pan and is springy to the touch. Cool upright in pan on a wire rack 20 minutes before turning out. Cool thoroughly, slice, and serve. About 135 calories for each of 20 slices.

VARIATIONS:

Apricot-Pecan Bread: Prepare as directed, substituting dried apricots for the prunes and pecans or blanched almonds for the walnuts. About 130 calories for each of 20 slices.

Raisin or Currant and Nut Bread: Prepare as directed, substituting seedless raisins or dried currants for the prunes. For the nuts use walnuts, pecans, filberts, or blanched almonds. About 135 calories for each of 20 slices.

ORANGE NUT BREAD

Delicious spread with cream cheese. Makes a 9"×5"×3" loaf

2¾ cups sifted flour
2½ teaspoons baking powder
½ teaspoon baking soda
½ teaspoon salt
2 tablespoons butter or margarine, softened to room temperature
1 cup strained honey
1 egg, lightly beaten
1½ teaspoons finely grated orange rind
¾ cup orange juice
¾ cup coarsely chopped pecans, walnuts, or blanched almonds

Preheat oven to 325° F. Sift flour with baking powder, soda, and salt and set aside. Blend butter with honey until creamy; add egg and orange rind and mix well. Add sifted ingredients alternately with orange juice, beginning and ending with the sifted. Fold in nuts. Spoon into a greased 9"×5"×3" loaf pan and bake 1–1¼ hours until loaf pulls slightly from sides of pan and is springy to the touch. Let cool upright in pan 10 minutes, then turn out and cool on a wire rack. About 155 calories for each of 20 slices.

CRANBERRY NUT BREAD

Makes a 9"×5"×3" loaf

1 cup cranberries (fresh or frozen)
1 cup sugar
3 cups sifted flour
4 teaspoons baking powder
½ teaspoon salt
½ cup coarsely chopped walnuts or pecans

Grated rind of 1 orange
1 egg, lightly beaten
1 cup milk
2 teaspoons melted butter or margarine

Preheat oven to 350° F. Put cranberries through coarse blade of meat grinder and mix with ¼ cup sugar. Sift remaining sugar with flour, baking powder, and salt; mix in nuts and orange rind. Lightly beat egg with milk and melted butter and stir into flour mixture. Fold in cranberries. Spoon into a buttered 9"×5"×3" loaf pan and bake about 1 hour until loaf pulls slightly from sides of pan and is springy to the touch. Cool upright in pan 10 minutes, then turn out on a wire rack and cool before slicing. About 140 calories for each of 20 slices.

BANANA TEA BREAD

Makes a 9"×5"×3" loaf

1¾ cups sifted flour
2 teaspoons baking powder
¼ teaspoon baking soda
½ teaspoon salt
⅓ cup shortening
⅔ cup sugar
2 eggs, well beaten
1 cup mashed ripe bananas

Preheat oven to 350° F. Sift flour with baking powder, soda, and salt and set aside. Cream shortening until light, add sugar gradually, continuing to cream until fluffy. Beat in eggs. Add flour mixture alternately with bananas, beginning and ending with flour. Spoon into a well-greased 9"×5"×3" loaf pan and bake about 1 hour and 10 minutes until loaf pulls slightly from sides of pan and is springy to the touch. Cool upright in pan 10 minutes, then turn out on a wire rack and cool before slicing. About 110 calories for each of 20 slices.

CINNAMON COFFEE CAKE

Makes 2 9" × 5" × 3" loaves

2½ cups sifted flour
2½ teaspoons baking powder
1 cup butter or margarine
1 cup sugar
3 eggs
1 teaspoon vanilla
1 cup sour cream
½ cup coarsely chopped pitted dates
½ cup finely chopped pecans or walnuts
½ cup firmly packed light brown sugar mixed with 2 teaspoons cinnamon

Preheat oven to 350° F. Sift flour with baking powder and set aside. Cream butter and sugar until light, then beat in eggs, 1 at a time; mix in vanilla. Add flour, a few spoonfuls at a time, alternately with sour cream, beginning and ending with flour. Stir in dates and nuts. Spoon about half the batter into 2 greased and floured 9" × 5" × 3" loaf pans and sprinkle with half the brown sugar mixture. Add remaining batter and sprinkle with remaining sugar mixture. Bake about 1 hour until loaves pull slightly from sides of pan and are springy to the touch. Cool upright in pans on a wire rack 10 minutes, then turn out and cool completely. Slice and serve with butter. (*Note:* These loaves freeze well.) About 130 calories for each of 20 slices.

¢ BOSTON BROWN BREAD

A rich, dark steamed bread, which New Englanders eat with baked beans.
Makes 3 small round loaves

1 cup sifted all-purpose flour
1 teaspoon salt
1 teaspoon baking powder
1 teaspoon baking soda
1½ cups unsifted whole wheat flour
½ cup corn meal
¾ cup dark molasses
2 cups sour milk or buttermilk
1 cup seedless raisins

Grease 3 clean small shortening tins (the 14-ounce size) and line bottoms with greased circles of wax paper. Sift all-purpose flour with salt, baking powder, and soda into a large bowl, stir in whole wheat flour and corn meal, then mix in molasses and sour milk. Stir in raisins. Spoon into cans, filling no more than two-thirds, cover with a *greased* double thickness of foil and tie or tape securely. Place on a rack in a large kettle, pour in enough boiling water to come halfway up cans, cover, and steam about 1 hour until well risen and a metal skewer inserted in center of bread comes out clean. Lift cans from water, cool upright 1–2 minutes on a wire rack, then invert and ease loaves out. Cool slightly on racks before cutting or cool to room temperature. Slice ¼" thick. (*Note:* The best way to cut this bread is with fine strong thread, using a sawing motion.) The bread can be steamed in any well-greased molds instead of shortening tins. Just make sure to fill no more than two-thirds and to cover with greased foil. 1–1½-pint molds will take 1–1½ hours, 1-quart molds 2–2½ hours, and 1½-quart molds about 3 hours. About 85 calories per slice.

SPICY BAKING POWDER DOUGHNUTS

Children love these.
Makes 2 dozen

3½ cups sifted flour
½ teaspoon salt
2 teaspoons baking powder
1 teaspoon baking soda
½ teaspoon cinnamon

½ teaspoon nutmeg
2 eggs
1 cup sugar
2 tablespoons cooking oil or shortening
¾ cup buttermilk or sour milk
Shortening or cooking oil for deep fat frying

Topping:
½ cup superfine sugar mixed with 1 teaspoon cinnamon

Sift flour with salt, baking powder, soda, and spices and set aside. In a large mixer bowl, beat eggs, sugar, and oil at medium speed; add buttermilk. Add dry ingredients all at once and beat just until smooth. Cover and chill 1 hour. Meanwhile, begin heating fat in a deep fat fryer; insert deep fat thermometer. Roll dough ½" thick on a lightly floured surface and cut with a doughnut cutter; reroll and cut scraps. When fat reaches 375° F., slide 4 doughnuts into fat. (*Note:* To transfer doughnuts without pushing them out of shape, use a slotted pancake turner dipped in the hot fat.) Fry doughnuts 2–3 minutes until brown all over, using tongs to turn. Drain on paper toweling; roll in topping while still warm or dip in Easy White Icing. About 150 calories each.

VARIATIONS:

Chocolate Doughnuts: Prepare as directed but omit spices; increase sugar to 1⅓ cups and add along with it 2 squares melted unsweetened chocolate. After frying, dust doughnuts with sifted confectioners' sugar. About 190 calories each.

Orange or Lemon Doughnuts: Prepare as directed, mixing 4 teaspoons finely grated orange or lemon rind and ¼ teaspoon orange or lemon extract into egg mixture. About 150 calories each.

Sugar Puffs (Makes about 3½ dozen): Prepare as directed but reduce flour to 2 cups, eggs to 1, and sugar to ⅓ cup. Do not chill. Fry scant tablespoonfuls in deep fat as directed and roll in superfine sugar while warm. About 40 calories each.

ROSETTES (SWEDISH PATTY SHELLS) FOR SAVORY FILLINGS

Rosette irons with patty shell attachments can be bought in housewares departments of many large stores. Read accompanying instructions before beginning this recipe.
Makes about 4 dozen

Shortening or cooking oil for deep fat frying
2 eggs
1 cup milk
1 teaspoon sugar
½ teaspoon salt
1 cup sifted flour

Begin heating fat in a deep fat fryer; use a deep fat thermometer. Beat eggs, milk, sugar, and salt just to blend, sprinkle in flour, a little at a time, and beat until smooth. When fat reaches 355–65° F., heat iron by submerging in hot fat 10 seconds. Lift out, shake off excess fat, and dip iron carefully into batter so top is *exactly level* with surface of batter—any deeper and patty shell will not come off the iron. Plunge coated iron into fat and, as soon as batter begins to puff, gradually ease iron out—patty shell should slip back into fat. When lightly browned, lift out with a slotted spoon and drain on paper toweling. (*Note:* You'll have to work fast, the whole procedure takes only a few seconds.) Heat iron and repeat with remaining batter, never frying more than 2 patty shells at a time and keeping fat as near 365° F.

as possible. Cool patty shells in a single layer on paper toweling. When ready to use, warm, uncovered, 7–10 minutes in a 325° F. oven, then fill with hot creamed chicken, seafood, or vegetables. Stored airtight, patty shells will keep well about 1 week. About 20 calories each (unfilled).

¢ ▨ BASIC PANCAKES

Electric griddles or skillets are ideal for cooking pancakes because they maintain a constant heat. Follow manufacturer's directions for greasing and preheating. Batters containing fat or oil can usually be cooked in an ungreased skillet.

Makes 1 dozen

1 cup sifted flour
½ teaspoon salt
2 tablespoons sugar
2 teaspoons baking powder
1 egg, lightly beaten
¾ cup milk
2 tablespoons cooking oil, melted butter or margarine

Preheat griddle over moderate heat while you mix batter or, if using an electric griddle, preheat as manufacturer directs. Sift flour, salt, sugar, and baking powder into a bowl or wide-mouthed pitcher. Combine egg, milk, and oil, slowly stir into dry ingredients, and mix only until dampened—batter should be lumpy. When a drop of cold water will dance on the griddle, begin cooking pancakes, using about 3 tablespoons batter for each, allowing plenty of space between them and spreading each until about 4″ across. Cook until bubbles form over surface, turn gently, and brown flip side. (*Note:* For extra-light and tender pancakes, turn *before* bubbles break and turn 1 time only.) Stack 3–4 deep on heated plates and keep warm while cooking the rest. Serve as soon as possible with butter, maple syrup, or other topping (see Some Toppings for Waffles and Pancakes). About 80 calories per pancake (without butter, syrup, or topping).

For Thinner Pancakes: Add 2–3 extra tablespoons milk.

If Batter Has Stood a While: Mix in about ¼ teaspoon additional baking powder before cooking.

VARIATIONS:

Nut Pancakes: Prepare batter as directed and just before cooking fold in ½ cup coarsely chopped pecans, walnuts, almonds, or roasted peanuts. About 115 calories per pancake (without butter or syrup).

Berry Pancakes: Prepare batter as directed and just before cooking fold in ½ cup fresh, slightly thawed frozen or drained canned berries (any kind as long as they're small). About 85 calories per pancake (without butter or syrup).

¢ **Apple Pancakes:** Prepare as directed, sifting ¼ teaspoon each cinnamon and nutmeg along with dry ingredients; just before cooking, fold in ½–¾ cup minced, peeled tart apple. About 90 calories per pancake (without butter or syrup).

¢ **Rice Pancakes:** Prepare as directed but increase eggs to 2 and milk to 1 cup; just before cooking, fold in ½ cup cooked rice or wild rice. About 90 calories per pancake (without butter or syrup).

¢ **Buttermilk Pancakes:** Prepare as directed but reduce baking powder to 1 teaspoon, add ¾ teaspoon baking soda, and use 1 cup buttermilk or sour milk instead of sweet milk. About 75 calories per pancake (without butter or syrup).

¢ **Whole Wheat Pancakes:** Prepare as directed, using ½ cup each unsifted whole wheat flour and sifted all-purpose flour; increase milk to 1 cup. About 85 calories per pancake (without butter or syrup).

¢ **Buckwheat Pancakes:** Prepare as directed, using ½ cup each unsifted buckwheat flour and sifted all-purpose flour, increase milk to 1 cup. About 85 calories per pancake (without butter or syrup).

Sausage Pancakes: Prepare as directed but reduce sugar to 1 teaspoon. Cook pancakes until bubbles break, dot with thin slices of cooked sausages or frankfurters, turn, and brown. Serve for lunch or supper. About 115 calories per pancake.

Cheese Pancakes: Prepare as directed but reduce sugar to 1 teaspoon. Just before cooking, mix in ½ cup grated sharp Cheddar or processed cheese. Cook as directed and serve for lunch or supper, topped with any creamed meat or vegetable. About 100 calories per pancake (without topping).

Onion Pancakes: Prepare as directed but reduce sugar to 1 teaspoon. Just before cooking, mix in ½ cup sautéed minced onion and a pinch each sage and thyme. Cook as directed and serve for lunch or supper, topped with Welsh Rabbit or any creamed or curried meat or vegetable. About 80 calories per pancake (without topping).

Corn and Pepper Pancakes: Prepare as directed but reduce sugar to 1 teaspoon. Just before cooking, mix in ½ cup well-drained canned whole kernel corn and ¼ cup minced sweet red or green pepper. Cook as directed and serve as is in place of potatoes or topped with chili as a main course. About 90 calories per pancake (without topping).

SOUFFLÉ PANCAKES

Don't stack these rich, puffy pancakes. They will flatten out.
Makes 8

¼ *cup packaged biscuit mix*
1 tablespoon sugar
¼ *cup sour cream*
4 eggs, separated

Preheat griddle over moderate heat while you mix the batter or, if using an electric griddle, preheat to 375° F. Stir biscuit mix, sugar, sour cream, and egg yolks, together until well blended. Beat egg whites until soft peaks form, stir half of whites into batter, and fold in the rest. When a drop of cold water will dance across the griddle, grease lightly and add pancakes, using about 3 tablespoons batter for each and spacing far apart. Spread pancakes so they are about 4" across and cook about 1 minute until 1 or 2 bubbles appear on surface and undersides are brown; turn and brown flip sides. Lift to hot plates and serve with maple syrup (no butter needed because these pancakes are rich). About 90 calories per serving (without syrup).

¢ **YEAST-RAISED PANCAKES**

Makes 1½ dozen

1¾ cups scalded milk
2 tablespoons sugar
½ teaspoon salt
¼ cup warm water (105–15° F.)
1 package active dry yeast
1 egg, lightly beaten
2 tablespoons cooking oil, melted butter or margarine
2 cups sifted flour

Mix milk, sugar, and salt and cool to lukewarm. Pour water into a warm mixing bowl, sprinkle in yeast and stir to dissolve; mix in cooled mixture, also egg and oil. Slowly add flour and beat until smooth. Cover and let rise in a warm draft-free place until doubled in bulk, about 35 minutes. Toward end of rising, preheat griddle over moderate heat, or, if using an electric one, by manufacturer's instructions. When batter is fully risen, stir down and pour about ¼ cup onto griddle for each pancake; allow plenty of space between pancakes, then spread each until about 4" across. Cook until bubbles form on surface and underside is brown, turn, and brown flipside. Keep warm while cooking the rest. Serve hot with butter and syrup or other suitable topping (see Some Toppings for Waffles and Pancakes). About 85 calories per pancake (without butter, syrup, or topping).

VARIATIONS:

Blini: Prepare and cook pancakes as directed; fill each with 1 tablespoon red or black caviar, fold in half, and serve with sour cream. About 85 calories per pancake (without sour cream).

¢ **English Crumpets** (Makes 14): Prepare batter as directed but reduce flour to 1⅓ cups. Cook as directed, but until bubbles on pancakes *break;* brown flip side very lightly only. Cool pancakes. When ready to serve, toast, smother "holey" sides with butter, quarter crumpets, and serve hot as a teatime snack. About 75 calories per crumpet (without butter).

¢ **Yeast-Raised Waffles** (Makes 8): Prepare as directed but reduce flour to 1½ cups. Bake in a preheated waffle iron. About 160 calories per waffle (without butter or syrup).

About Using Waffle Irons

Automatic waffle irons take the frustrations out of waffle baking. But old irons, properly used, produce exquisitely crisp, nut-brown waffles. Here are a few tips for using them:
– Heat iron until a drop of water will dance over the grids.
– Pour batter in center of iron until ½–⅔ full, then close and bake until all steaming stops. Open iron gently. If top sticks, waffle probably needs to bake longer. The first waffle often sticks to an old iron, so bake it a little browner than you like and discard. Doing so will temper the iron nicely for the waffles to follow.
– Never wash or grease an iron once it has been seasoned.

¢ **BASIC WAFFLES**

More than a half-dozen variations here to try.
Makes 8

2 cups sifted flour
2 tablespoons sugar
1 tablespoon baking powder
1 teaspoon salt
2 eggs, separated
1¾ cups milk
6 tablespoons cooking oil, melted butter, margarine, or bacon drippings

Preheat waffle iron according to manufacturer's directions. Sift flour, sugar, baking powder, and salt into a bowl. Combine egg yolks, milk, and oil, pour into flour mixture, and beat with a rotary beater or electric mixer just until smooth. Beat egg whites until soft peaks form and fold into batter. Pour batter into waffle iron as manufacturer directs and bake at medium heat until steaming stops and waffle is golden. Serve with plenty of butter and warm syrup or other topping. About 260 calories per waffle (without butter or syrup).

VARIATIONS:

Extra-Rich Waffles: Prepare as directed but reduce flour to 1¾ cups and milk to 1½ cups; increase eggs to 3 and oil to ½ cup. About 285 calories per waffle (without butter or syrup).

¢ **Buttermilk Waffles:** Prepare as directed, substituting buttermilk or sour milk for sweet; reduce baking powder to 2 teaspoons and add 1 teaspoon baking soda. About 245 calories per waffle (without butter or syrup).

Ham Waffles: Prepare as directed but omit sugar; add 1 cup finely diced lean boiled ham to batter before folding in egg whites. About 310 calories per waffle (without butter).

Cheese Waffles: Prepare as directed but omit sugar; add ½ cup finely grated sharp Cheddar or Parmesan cheese to batter before folding in egg whites. About 275 calories per waffle (without butter).

Nut Waffles: Prepare as directed and add ⅓–½ cup coarsely chopped walnuts, pecans, almonds, hazelnuts, peanuts, or piñon nuts to batter before folding in egg whites. About 295 calories per waffle (without butter or syrup).

Blueberry Waffles: Prepare as directed; scatter a few (about 2 tablespoons) washed and dried blueberries over batter in iron before baking. About 260 calories per waffle (without butter or syrup).

Savory Waffles: Prepare as directed but omit sugar; serve topped with creamed chicken or turkey, tuna or chipped beef, Welsh Rabbit or Shrimp Newburg. About 385 calories per serving (with topping).

Dessert Waffles: Prepare extra-rich waffles and top with ice cream or sweetened sliced peaches or berries and whipped cream. About 340 calories per serving (topped with a scoop of ice cream).

¢ **CREPES FOR SAVORY FILLINGS**

Makes 10 crepes

½ cup sifted flour
¼ teaspoon salt
2 eggs, lightly beaten
½ cup milk
1 tablespoon cold water
1 tablespoon melted butter or margarine

Sift flour and salt together into a bowl; mix all remaining ingredients and add slowly to dry ingredients, beating until smooth. Let stand at room temperature 15 minutes. Brush bottom and sides of a heavy 6" skillet with cooking oil and set over moderate heat ½ minute. Stir batter, then add 2 tablespoonfuls to skillet, tipping it back and forth so batter *just* coats bottom (crepe should be *very thin*). Brown lightly on 1 side, about 30 seconds, turn and brown other side. Place on a paper-towel-lined baking sheet, most attractive side down so that when crepe is rolled it will be on the outside. Cook remaining crepes the same way; they are now ready to be filled. About 55 calories per crepe (unfilled).

VARIATION:

¢ **Simple Dessert Crepes:** Add 1 tablespoon sugar to dry ingredients, then mix and cook crepes as directed; keep warm in a 250° F. oven until all are done. To serve, spread with jam, honey, or marmalade, fill with crushed berries, or simply drizzle with melted butter and sprinkle with sugar. Roll and top with dollops of sour cream. About 105 calories for each crepe (filled with ¼ cup unsweetened crushed berries and topped with 1 tablespoon sour cream).

Some Toppings for Waffles and Pancakes

For Breakfast:
Butter and
– Any syrup or honey
– A sprinkling of sugar–granulated, brown, maple, or raw
– Any tart jam, preserves, or marmalade
Whipped cream cheese and
– Any tart jam, preserves, jelly, or marmalade
– Any syrup or honey
– Applesauce
– Any sliced fresh fruit
– Stewed prunes, apricots, or figs

For Lunch or Supper (make basic pancakes or waffles as directed but reduce sugar to 1 teaspoon):
– Any creamed meat, seafood, or vegetable
– Any curried meat, eggs, or seafood
– Welsh Rabbit
– Chop Suey
– Chili con Carne and sprinklings of minced onion, grated sharp Cheddar, and shredded lettuce

For Dessert:
– Sour cream and any fruit preserves
– Sour cream and a thick sprinkling of brown or maple sugar (a dusting of cinnamon or nutmeg adds zip)
– Vanilla ice cream or sweetened whipped cream and fresh sliced or thawed frozen berries or peaches
– Vanilla ice cream and any dessert sauce
– Chocolate ice cream and Fudge or Butterscotch Sauce

– Fruit cocktail or crushed pineapple and sweetened whipped cream

¢ **DUMPLINGS (BASIC RECIPE)**

The new way to cook dumplings is uncovered for 10 minutes, then tightly covered for another 10 so that the steam will fluff up the dumplings.
Makes 7–8 dumplings

1 cup sifted flour
1½ teaspoons baking powder
½ teaspoon salt
2 tablespoons chilled shortening
½ cup milk

Sift flour, baking powder, and salt together into a bowl; cut in shortening with a pastry blender until mixture resembles coarse meal. Add milk all at once and mix lightly *just* until dough holds together. Drop by rounded tablespoonfuls on top of gently bubbling soup or stew. Adjust burner so liquid just simmers, then simmer *uncovered* 10 minutes; cover and simmer 10 minutes longer. (*Note:* If soup or stew needs thickening, do so *after* removing dumplings.) About 100 calories for each of 7 dumplings, 90 calories for each of 8 dumplings.

VARIATIONS:

¢ **Parsley or Chive Dumplings:** Prepare as directed, mixing 2 tablespoons minced parsley or chives into dry ingredients. About 100 calories for each of 7 dumplings, 90 calories for each of 8.

¢ **Sage, Thyme, and Onion Dumplings:** Prepare as directed, mixing ¼ teaspoon each sage and thyme and 1 teaspoon instant minced onion into dry ingredients. About 100 calories for each of 7 dumplings, 90 calories for each of 8.

¢ **Caraway Dumplings** (especially good with goulash): Prepare as directed, mixing 1½ teaspoons caraway seeds into dry ingredients. About 100 calories for each of 7 dumplings, 90 calories for each of 8.

Saffron Dumplings: Prepare as directed, mixing ⅛ teaspoon each powdered saffron and sage or thyme into dry ingredients. About 100 calories for each of 7 dumplings, 90 calories for each of 8.

¢ **Cheese Dumplings:** Prepare as directed, mixing 2–3 tablespoons coarsely grated sharp Cheddar cheese to dry ingredients. About 115 calories for each of 7 dumplings, 100 calories for each of 8.

▧ QUICK DUMPLINGS

Makes about 1 dozen

2 cups packaged biscuit mix
½ teaspoon salt
1 egg, lightly beaten
½ cup milk

Mix biscuit mix and salt. Combine egg and milk, add to dry ingredients all at once, and stir lightly and quickly with a fork to form a soft dough. Drop by rounded tablespoonfuls on top of just boiling stew or soup. Simmer, uncovered, over low heat 10 minutes, then cover and simmer 10 minutes longer. About 60 calories per dumpling.

VARIATION:

▧ **Biscuit Dumplings:** Separate biscuits from a can of refrigerated biscuits and arrange on top of bubbling stew or soup. Cover and simmer 15–20 minutes. Sprinkle with minced parsley just before serving. About 60 calories per dumpling.

¢ BREAD DUMPLINGS

A delicious way to use up stale bread. These dumplings are good in soups or stews.

Makes 14–16

3 cups ½" cubes stale bread, trimmed of crusts
¼ cup unsifted flour
1 teaspoon salt
⅛ teaspoon pepper
¼ teaspoon baking powder
⅛ teaspoon nutmeg (optional)
1 tablespoon minced parsley
2 tablespoons minced yellow onion
¼ cup milk
1 egg, lightly beaten
1 tablespoon melted butter or margarine

Mix all ingredients together, let stand 5 minutes, and mix again. Drop by rounded teaspoonfuls into a little flour, then roll into balls. Drop into *just* boiling soup or stew, simmer uncovered 5 minutes, cover, and simmer 2–3 minutes longer. Do not cook more than 1 layer deep at a time. Serve in soup or stew, allowing 3–4 per serving. (*Note:* For stew, the dumplings can be made twice as large; simmer uncovered 7–10 minutes, cover, and simmer 5–7 minutes longer.) About 65 calories for each of 14 dumplings, 55 calories for each of 16 dumplings.

BASIC BATTER FOR FRIED FOODS

An all-purpose batter that can be used for almost any foods to be fried: chicken, fish fillets, shellfish, vegetables, fruit.

Makes about 1½ cups

1 cup sifted flour
1 teaspoon baking powder
½ teaspoon salt
1 egg, lightly beaten
1 cup milk
2 tablespoons cooking oil

Sift flour with baking powder and

salt. Mix egg, milk, and oil, slowly add to dry ingredients, and beat until smooth. Pat food to be fried very dry and, if you like, dredge lightly in flour. Dip pieces, 1 at a time, in batter, then fry in deep fat as individual recipes direct. About 890 calories for the 1½ cups, about 37 calories per tablespoon (about what it would take to coat a shrimp or small piece of fruit or vegetable).

TEMPURA BATTER

Beer is what gives this batter its exceptional lightness.
Makes about 1 pint

3 eggs
1⅔ cups rice flour
1½ teaspoons salt
1 teaspoon baking powder
1 (12-ounce) can beer

Beat eggs until frothy. Sift rice flour with salt and baking powder and add to eggs alternately with beer. Use for Japanese Butterfly Shrimp or for coating bite-size chunks of cucumber, carrot, cauliflower, and zucchini or parsley fluffs to be fried in deep fat. About 1060 calories for the 1 pint, about 32 calories per tablespoon.

To Halve Recipe: Use 1 extra-large egg, ¾ cup plus 2 tablespoons rice flour, ¾ teaspoon salt, ½ teaspoon baking powder, and ¾ cup beer. About 500 calories for 1 cup, about 31 calories per tablespoon.

VEGETABLE FRITTER BATTER

Makes about 1½ cups

¾ cup sifted flour
1 teaspoon baking powder
1 teaspoon salt
¾ cup milk
1 egg, lightly beaten

Sift flour, baking powder, and salt together into a bowl. Slowly add milk and beat until smooth. Add egg and beat well. Use for dipping vegetables that are to be deep-fat-fried. About 605 calories for the 1½ cups, about 25 calories per tablespoon.

▧ GARLIC FRENCH BREAD

Everyone's favorite. And so easy to prepare.
Makes 6 servings

¼ pound butter or margarine, softened to room temperature
1 clove garlic, peeled and crushed
1 loaf French bread about 18" long

Blend garlic with butter and let stand at room temperature about 1 hour. About ½ hour before serving, preheat oven to 375° F. Meanwhile, slice bread 1" thick, cutting *to* but not *through* the bottom and holding knife at a slight angle. Spread both sides of each slice with garlic butter and wrap loaf snugly in heavy foil. Place on a baking sheet and warm 20–25 minutes. Unwrap and serve in a long napkin-lined bread basket or break into chunks and serve in a round napkin-lined basket. About 250 calories per serving, 83 calories per slice.

VARIATIONS:

Herbed Garlic Bread: Mix 1 teaspoon minced parsley and ¼ teaspoon each thyme and oregano or marjoram into garlic butter; proceed as directed. About 250 calories per serving, 83 calories per slice.

Cheese-Garlic Bread: Mix 1 tablespoon grated Parmesan, ¼ teaspoon salt, ⅛ teaspoon pepper, and ¼ teaspoon each savory and oregano or thyme into garlic butter; proceed as directed. About 255 calories per serving, 85 calories per slice.

Curry or Chili-Garlic Bread: Mix

1–2 teaspoons curry or chili powder into garlic butter and proceed as directed. About 250 calories per serving, 83 calories per slice.

☒ SOME FLAVORED TOASTS

Enough for 4 slices

Cinnamon Toast: Mix 4 teaspoons sugar with 1 teaspoon cinnamon, sprinkle on well-buttered toast, and heat 3–5 minutes at 350° F. About 125 calories per slice.

Honey Toast: Toast bread on 1 side. Butter untoasted sides, then drizzle with honey (about 2 teaspoons in all) and sprinkle lightly with nutmeg or mace. Broil honey side up 4–5" from heat 3–4 minutes until golden brown. About 155 calories per slice.

Maple Toast: Prepare like honey toast, substituting maple syrup for honey. About 145 calories per slice.

Marmalade Toast: Toast bread on 1 side. Brush untoasted sides with a ½ and ½ mixture of softened butter and orange or other fruit marmalade (1 tablespoon each is enough for 4 slices). Broil spread side up 4–5" from heat 2–3 minutes until lightly browned. About 105 calories per slice.

Orange-Raisin Toast: Mix 1 teaspoon finely grated orange rind with 1 tablespoon each softened butter or margarine and orange juice, 2 tablespoons light brown sugar, and a pinch each cinnamon and nutmeg. Spread on toasted raisin bread and broil spread side up 4–5" from heat 2–3 minutes until bubbly. About 150 calories per slice.

Butterscotch Toast: Blend 2 tablespoons softened butter or margarine with ¼ cup light brown sugar and spread on toast. Sprinkle each slice with about 1 tablespoon minced pecans or walnuts, then broil spread side up 4–5" from heat 3–4 minutes until bubbly and browned. About 210 calories per slice.

Chive Toast: Blend 2 tablespoons softened butter or margarine with 1 teaspoon minced chives, spread on day-old bread (1 side only), then toast about 45 minutes at 300° F. until golden brown and crisp. About 110 calories per slice.

Herb Toast: Prepare like chive toast, substituting 1 teaspoon minced fresh herb (dill, chervil, tarragon, savory, marjoram, or parsley) for the chives. About 110 calories per slice.

Curry Toast: Prepare like chive toast, substituting ½–1 teaspoon curry powder for the chives and adding a pinch each garlic and onion salt. About 110 calories per slice.

Garlic Toast: Blend 2 tablespoons softened butter with ¼ crushed clove garlic, spread on day-old bread, and toast as for chive toast. About 110 calories per slice.

Cheese Toast: Blend 2 tablespoons softened butter or margarine with 1 teaspoon grated Parmesan and, if you like, a pinch garlic or onion powder. Toast as for chive toast. About 112 calories per slice.

How to Make Melba Toast

Slice white or any other bread ⅛" thick, trim off crusts, and halve slices diagonally or cut in small rounds; bake, uncovered, on ungreased baking sheets 10–12 minutes at 300° F. until crisp and lightly browned. Cool and store airtight.

BREADS

How to Make Rusks

Trim crusts from an unsliced loaf of firm-textured white bread, then slice ½" thick; cut in "fingers" 3" long and 1–1½" wide and bake, uncovered, on ungreased baking sheets 30–40 minutes at 300° F. until nicely browned.

How to Make Toast Cups

Trim crusts from thinly sliced, firm-textured white bread and brush 1 side of each slice with melted butter or margarine; press slices, buttered sides down, into muffin cups and brush insides with melted butter. Bake, uncovered, 10–12 minutes at 350° F. until golden brown. Remove from pans and use as patty shells for creamed meats or vegetables.

How to Make Croustades

Trim crusts from an unsliced loaf of firm-textured white bread, then slice 2½" thick; cut each slice into a large cube, rectangle, or round and hollow out centers, leaving walls and bottoms ½" thick (use centers for making bread crumbs). Brush inside and out with melted butter or margarine and bake, uncovered, on ungreased baking sheets 12–15 minutes at 350° F. until golden. Use as patty shells for creamed meats or vegetables.

How to Make Bread Cubes and Crumbs

Bread cubes and crumbs have dozens of uses. Mix into stuffings, toss into salads or casseroles, use as crunchy toppings or coatings.

For Soft Bread Cubes: Stack 2–3 slices bread on a board and cut into strips of desired width, then cut crosswise to form cubes of even size.

For Toasted Bread Cubes: Arrange soft bread cubes on an ungreased baking sheet 1 layer deep and toast in a 300° F. oven, turning occasionally, until evenly golden brown. Or broil 5"–6" from heat, turning often and watching closely.

For Soft Bread Crumbs: Tear fresh slices of bread into small pieces, or buzz bread at high speed in a blender. The job is done zip-quick.

For Dry Bread Crumbs: Put slices of dry bread through fine blade of meat grinder. A neat trick is to tie or rubber band a paper or plastic bag to end of grinder so crumbs drop directly into it. For extra-fine crumbs, sift, then store fine and coarse crumbs separately.

For Buttered Crumbs:

Soft: Toss 1 cup soft bread crumbs with ¼–⅓ cup melted butter or margarine.

Dry: Melt 3–4 tablespoons butter or margarine in a skillet over moderate heat, add 1–1½ cups dry crumbs, and heat, stirring, until golden brown.

For Seasoned Crumbs:

Garlic: Mix ¼ crushed clove garlic with ¼–⅓ cup melted butter or margarine, then toss with 1 cup soft or dry bread crumbs.

Cheese: Toss ¼ cup grated Parmesan cheese with 1 cup dry bread crumbs and 3–4 tablespoons melted butter or margarine.

Herb: Toss 1 cup dry bread crumbs with ¼ cup melted butter, margarine, or olive oil and ¼ teaspoon oregano, marjoram, or thyme.

Yields:

1 standard slice fresh bread
{ about 1 cup soft bread cubes
about ¾ cup toasted bread cubes
about 1 cup soft bread crumbs

1 standard slice dry bread
{ about ⅓ cup dry bread cubes
about ¾ cup dry bread crumbs

CROUTONS

Croutons add flavor and crunch to soups, salads, and casseroles. The ½″ size are best for soups and salads, the ¼″ for casserole toppings. Croutons needn't be cubes, however; cut in triangles, diamonds or discs or into fancy shapes with truffle cutters. Make up a quantity, store airtight, or freeze, then reheat uncovered a few minutes at 425° F. to crispen. Packaged croutons, both plain and seasoned, are also available.
Makes 1 pint

Shortening or cooking oil for deep fat frying
8 slices day-old or stale bread, trimmed of crusts and cut in ¼″ or ½″ cubes

Heat shortening in a deep fat fryer until deep fat thermometer reaches 350° F. Place about ½ cup cubes in fryer basket, lower into fat and fry 10–15 seconds, turning, as needed, until evenly golden brown. Lift out, drain on paper toweling, and fry remaining cubes the same way. (*Note:* Skim crumbs from fat before adding each fresh batch.)

To Skillet Fry: Heat 1″ cooking oil or a ½ and ½ mixture of melted butter or margarine and cooking oil in a large, heavy skillet over moderately high heat until a cube of bread will sizzle. Fry cubes about ½ cup at a time, 15–20 seconds, turning, as needed, until evenly golden brown. Drain on paper toweling.

To Oven "Fry": Preheat oven to 300° F. Butter both sides of bread or brush with melted butter and cut into cubes. Spread out on an ungreased baking sheet and bake, uncovered, 15 minutes; turn croutons and bake about 10 minutes longer until evenly browned.

VARIATIONS:

Garlic Croutons: Shake hot croutons in a bag with 1 teaspoon garlic salt. *Or* spread bread with Garlic Butter, cut in cubes, and oven fry as above.

Italian Croutons: Mix ½ cup each softened butter and grated Parmesan, ½ teaspoon each crushed garlic, basil, and oregano. Spread on bread, cut in cubes, and oven fry.

Herbed Croutons: Mix ⅔ cup softened butter with 2 teaspoons minced chives and ½ teaspoon each minced parsley, basil and chervil. Spread on bread, cut in cubes, and oven fry.

Recipes all too flexible for meaningful calorie counts.

◨ ¢ FRENCH TOAST

If you have stale bread on hand, by all means use it for making French toast.
Makes 4 servings

2 eggs, lightly beaten
⅔ cup milk
¼ teaspoon salt
¼ cup butter, margarine, shortening, or cooking oil
8 slices firm-textured white bread

Beat egg with milk and salt just to blend and place in a piepan. Melt about ¼ the butter in a large, heavy skillet. Quickly dip bread in egg mixture, turning to coat both sides well, then brown on each side in butter (add more butter to skillet as needed). Serve hot with honey, syrup, preserves, or tart jelly and a sprinkling of confectioners' sugar. About 290 calories per serving (without topping).

VARIATION:
Prepare as directed, using raisin or whole wheat bread instead of white. About 330 calories per serving (without topping).

¢ ☒ **MILK TOAST**

Makes 1 serving

1 (¾" thick) slice hot buttered toast or cinnamon toast
1 cup hot milk
Brown sugar (optional)
Nutmeg (optional)

Place toast in a hot shallow soup bowl, pour in milk, sprinkle lightly, if you like, with brown sugar and nutmeg, and serve. About 300 calories per serving if made with buttered toast (without brown sugar topping), about 355 calories per serving if made with cinnamon toast (without brown sugar topping).

YEAST BREADS

Yeast is a delicate living thing that needs food, warmth, moisture, and air if it is to grow and leaven dough. The ingredients mixed with yeast all help provide the proper environment.

Essential Ingredients of Yeast Breads:

Wheat Flour: Flour provides the framework of bread; its skeins of protein (gluten), developed in kneading, stretched as the yeast grows, and set during baking, give bread its characteristic texture. *All-purpose flour* (called for in all the following recipes unless otherwise specified) makes excellent yeast bread; so does *bread flour*, which contains an even higher percentage of protein. But it is not so easily available today. *Cake or pastry flour* is too soft to make good bread. Wheat flour alone may be used in making bread, or it may be mixed with rye flour, oatmeal, corn meal, or other grains.

Sugar: This is the food yeast needs; sugar also helps breads brown.

Salt: Salt isn't just for flavor. It controls the action of the yeast and keeps dough from rising too fast. Too much salt slows rising.

Fat: Lard, shortening, butter, margarine, or cooking oil can be used in making bread. Their functions: to make bread tender, give it fine texture, improve the keeping quality, and aid in browning.

Liquid: Either milk or water can be used to make bread. Milk increases the food value and keeping quality; water gives bread nuttier flavor, chewier texture, and crisper crust.

Yeast: The "life" and leavening of yeast breads. In the old days, women saved bits of yeast sponge from one baking, often mixing in leftover potato cooking water, to use as starters for the next batch. Popular, too, was sour dough—raw dough left to ferment in stone crocks, which could be used in place of yeast.

And when there was no yeast, women made "salt" or "self-rising" bread by using soured corn meal batter as the leavening. Modern yeasts have made the old-fashioned ways unnecessary, though some women still make these rough breads for the joy of it.

Active Dry Yeast: The most widely available form of yeast; it comes in ¼-ounce packets or 4-ounce jars. Kept in a cool, dry spot, it keeps fresh several months. When dissolved in warm water, it does the work of one (⅗-ounce) cake compressed yeast. All of the following recipes call for active dry yeast; if unavailable, substitute one cake compressed yeast for each ¼-ounce package.

Compressed Yeast: Not often seen today, this was the standard before World War II (dry yeast was developed during the war). It must be refrigerated and used within 1–2 weeks, or frozen and used within 6 months. Thaw at room temperature, then use at once. To determine if compressed yeast is still viable, crumble; if it crumbles easily, it's good.

The Care and Handling of Yeast: For most recipes (refrigerator doughs and the new cool-rise method excepted), yeast doughs must be kept warm from start to finish. And that means beginning with a warm bowl (simply rinse a bowl with warm water and dry). As you work with yeast dough, you'll learn what temperature is just right. If you are *aware* that the dough feels cool or warm, then it *is*. At the proper temperature, the dough should be so near your own body temperature that you scarcely feel it.

To Dissolve Yeast: Water (or potato cooking water) is best. It should be warm, between 105° F. and 115° F. Test using a candy thermometer or, if you have none, by the old baby's formula way of letting a drop fall on your forearm. It should feel warm, *not* hot.

About Combining Dissolved Yeast with Other Liquids: A critical step, for a too hot liquid can kill the yeast, a too cold one slows its growth. The perfect temperature is lukewarm, 90–95° F.

Nonessential (but Popular) Ingredients of Yeast Breads: Eggs, fruit, nuts, herbs, and spices are added purely for variety.

Ways to Mix Yeast Breads

Standard Method: Dissolve yeast in warm (105–15° F.) water. Scald milk, mix in sugar, salt, and shortening, and cool to lukewarm; combine with yeast, work in flour, and knead until satiny and elastic. Place in a greased, large warm bowl, turn dough to grease all over, cover with cloth (some people prefer a damp cloth, others a dry one), and set in a warm (80–85° F.) place to rise.

Batter Method: The same as the standard method except that the mixture is much thinner and beaten to blend rather than kneaded.

New Rapid-Mix: A modern refinement in which dry yeast is mixed directly with the dry ingredients (see recipe for Rapid-Mix White Bread).

Sponge Method: The old-fashioned way. Dissolve yeast in water and mix in enough flour to make a soft batter. Set in a warm, dry spot overnight or until mixture becomes "spongy." Next day prepare bread following standard method, mixing sponge into lukewarm milk mixture, then proceeding as directed.

About Kneading

This is the fun part of making bread. The technique isn't difficult, though at first it may seem so. Once you get the rhythm, however, you won't want to stop. Most doughs are kneaded on a lightly floured surface (board or pastry cloth), though extra-soft doughs should be done right in the mixing bowl. (*Note:* If you're lucky enough to have one of the heavy-duty electric mixers with a dough hook, you can knead any dough in the bowl—follow manufacturer's directions.)

To Knead Average Doughs: Shape dough into a large, round ball on a lightly floured bread board and fold over toward you; push down with heels of hands, give dough a quarter turn, and repeat the folding, pushing and turning until dough is satiny, smooth, and elastic, usually 8–10 minutes. Use very little flour on your hands or board, only enough to keep dough from sticking.

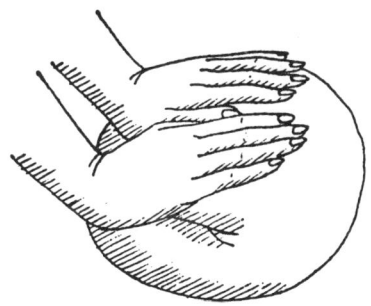

To Knead Very Soft Doughs: Use one hand only; these doughs are supersticky, and if you get both hands involved, you'll be sorry. The technique isn't so much kneading as stretching the dough right in the bowl, pulling it up again and again from the sides of the bowl. Use a large, heavy, shallow bowl, held firmly in place with your free hand. In the beginning, the dough will seem utterly unmanageable, but before long (8–10 minutes) it will begin to blister and to cling to itself, leaving your hand and the bowl relatively clean. It is now ready to rise.

About the Rising Period

This is when the yeast goes to work, leavening the bread. Most breads and rolls get two risings, one before shaping, one after. Some may require three risings, others one only. For the first rising, dough should be allowed to double in bulk; for the second, to double or not as individual recipes direct. Successive risings usually take somewhat less time than the first, so watch carefully. (*Note:* Braids and other intricately shaped breads should be allowed to rise fully after shaping, otherwise they may split during baking. No shaped bread, however, should more than double; if it overrises, it will be coarse and dry and have poor volume.)

Optimum Rising Conditions: A warm (80–85° F.), dry, and draftless spot. Sometimes a turned-off oven can be used (unless pilot light makes oven too hot); sometimes dough can be set over a bowl of warm water. Never, however, use the top of a refrigerator—too much uneven heat.

If Kitchen Is Cool: Use an extra

package of yeast in making the dough; it will not make the bread taste too yeasty.

To Hasten Rising: Use an extra package of yeast in making dough and/or set bowl of dough over a large bowl of warm water, changing water as it cools.

Approximate Rising Times: (first rising):

Soft Doughs: ¾–1 hour to double in bulk

Average Doughs: 1–1½ hours to double in bulk

Heavy Doughs: 1½–2 hours to double in bulk

(*Note:* Times can be approximate at best, since warmth of kitchen and vitality of yeast both affect speed of rising.)

When Is Dough Doubled in Bulk?

Soft Doughs and Batter Breads: Dough or batter should look spongy, puffed, and moist. Press lightly near edge; if imprint remains, dough is doubled in bulk.

Average or Heavy Doughs: Stick two fingers into dough about ½"; if depressions remain, dough is doubled in bulk. If they disappear, give dough another 15–20 minutes to rise, then test again.

About Refrigerator Doughs: The cold of a refrigerator does not kill yeast, merely retards or stops its growth. Once out of the refrigerator, the yeast will begin to work again. Refrigerator doughs usually contain more yeast than standard doughs, also slightly more sugar. Any dough, thus, can be refrigerated if you up the amount of yeast by half or, better still, double it and add an extra tablespoon or so of sugar. How long dough will keep in the refrigerator depends both upon the dough and the temperature inside the refrigerator. Most doughs keep well under refrigeration 3–4 days.

Doughs can be refrigerated as soon as they're mixed or after the first rising; they must be well greased and well covered so that they remain moist and pliable.

When you're ready to bake, take dough from refrigerator. If it has not risen at all, let stand at room temperature 2–3 hours until doubled in bulk; then punch down, shape, and proceed as for unrefrigerated doughs. If the dough has had one rising before going into cold storage, shape as soon as you take it from the refrigerator, let rise until light, about 1 hour, then bake.

About Punching Dough Down

There's a reason for this. Collapsing raised dough evens the texture by breaking up any large bubbles of gas.

Batters: Stir down with a spoon until batter is its original size.

Doughs: Shove a fist deep into the center of the dough so it collapses like a balloon, then fold edges of dough into center.

About Shaping Breads and Rolls

Like sculptor's clay, yeast dough can be fashioned into dozens of shapes, and in European countries it is, especially for holidays and festivals. Some sculpted loaves are museum pieces.

How to Shape Loaves:

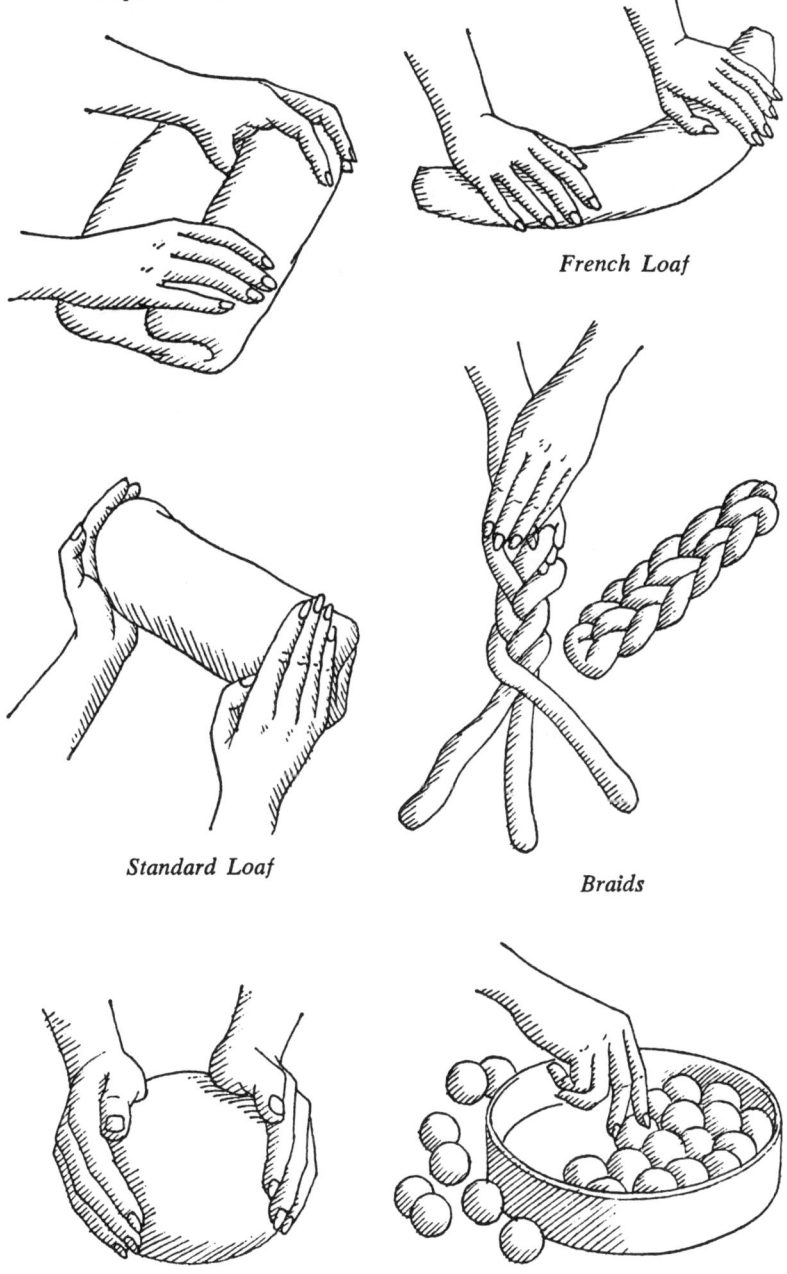

French Loaf

Standard Loaf

Braids

Round Loaf

Pan Rolls

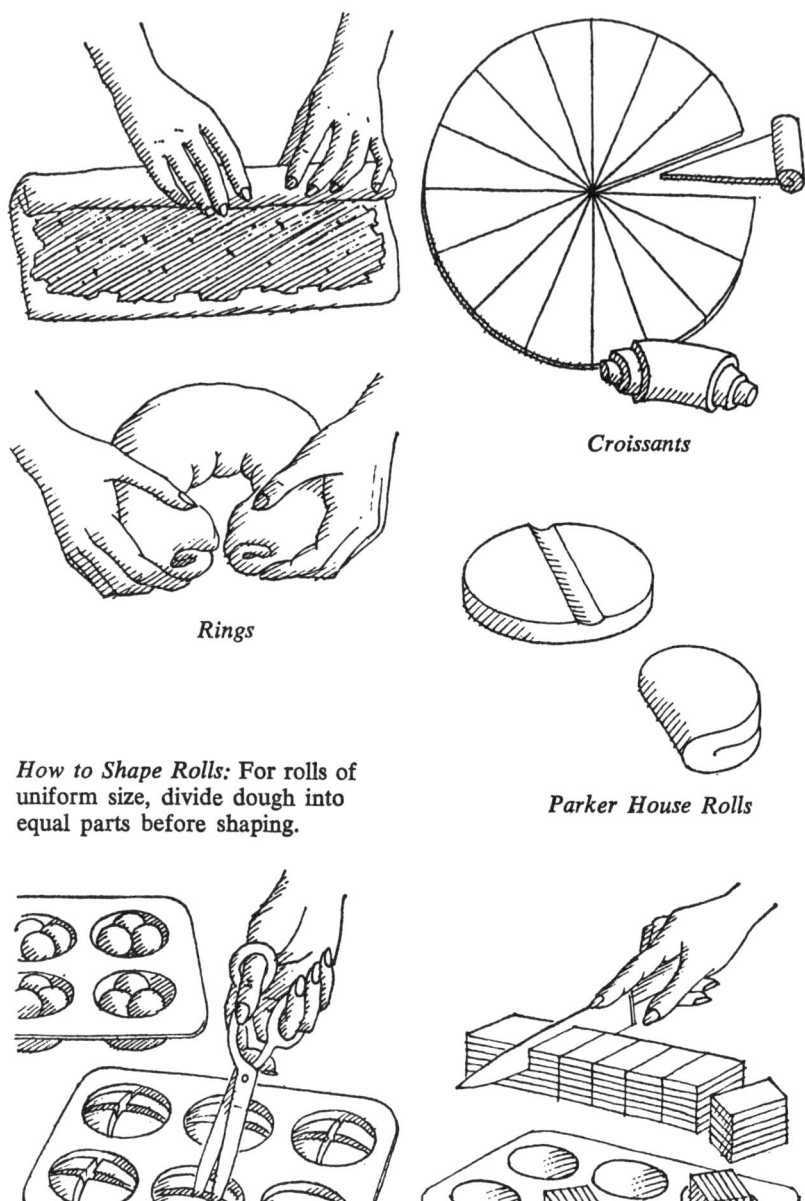

Croissants

Rings

Parker House Rolls

How to Shape Rolls: For rolls of uniform size, divide dough into equal parts before shaping.

Cloverleaf Rolls
Quick Cloverleaf Rolls

Fan Tans

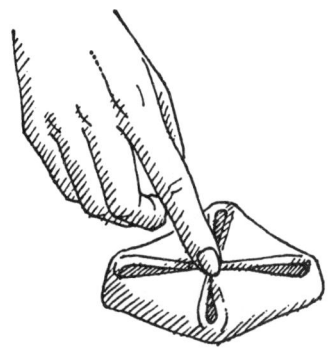
Danish Pastry

About Baking Yeast Breads

Best temperatures are from 350–450° F., the lower heats being better for richer, sweeter breads because there's less danger of overbrowning. The first 10–15 minutes of baking—called "oven spring"—is critical; it is the time when the top of the loaf rises quickly, "breaking" or "shredding" around the edges of the pan, giving bread its characteristic shape and light texture. A perfect loaf has an evenly shredded break. If bread hasn't risen sufficiently before baking, or if the oven temperature is too low, there will be poor volume and little break. If the dough has overrisen, the strands of protein will be stretched to breaking during "oven spring" and the loaf will collapse.

To Give Crusts a Professional Finish

For Soft Brown Crusts: Brush bread or rolls before or after baking with melted butter or margarine, milk, or cream.

For Hard Crusts: Brush bread or rolls before baking with lightly beaten egg white or salty water and bake with a shallow pan of water set on rack underneath.

For Shiny Light Brown Crusts: Brush bread or rolls before baking with 1 egg white lightly beaten with 1 tablespoon cold water; or, if you prefer, brush with mixture during last 10–15 minutes of baking.

For Shiny Dark Brown Crusts: Brush bread or rolls before baking with 1 egg or 1 egg yolk lightly beaten with 1 tablespoon water, milk, or cream (the egg yolk will produce the brownest crust).

For Seed Crusts: Brush bread or rolls before baking with 1 egg or egg white lightly beaten with 1 tablespoon water and sprinkle with poppy, caraway, or sesame seeds.

For Sweet Glazes: See individual recipes for sweet breads that follow.

Why Things Sometimes Go Wrong with Yeast Breads

Small Doughy Loaves: Too much or too little heat during rising *or* too long or too short rising.

Sour or Too Yeasty Bread: Too much heat during rising.

Lopsided Loaves: An unlevel oven or pans touching one another and/or oven walls.

Crumbly Bread: Too long in the rising, especially after shaping.

Coarse or "Holey" Bread: Insufficient kneading; also too long in the rising.

Heavy, Dry Bread: Too much flour.

¢ **BASIC WHITE BREAD**

If you've never made yeast bread, this is a good recipe to begin with. The recipe isn't difficult and the results are delicious.
Makes 2 9″×5″×3″ loaves

½ *cup scalded milk*
3 tablespoons sugar
2 teaspoons salt
3 tablespoons butter, margarine or lard

1½ cups warm water (105–15° F.)
1 package active dry yeast
6 cups sifted flour (about)
1–2 tablespoons melted butter or margarine (optional)

Mix milk, sugar, salt and butter in a small bowl, stirring until sugar dissolves; cool to lukewarm. Pour warm water into a large warm bowl, sprinkle in yeast, and stir until dissolved. Stir in milk mixture, add 3 cups flour, and beat with a wooden spoon until smooth. Mix in enough additional flour, a little at a time, to make a soft dough (you will have to use your hands toward the end). Mixture will be sticky but should leave sides of bowl reasonably clean. Knead on a lightly floured board until satiny and elastic, 8–10 minutes, adding as little extra flour as possible. Shape into a smooth ball, place in a greased large bowl, turning dough to grease all over. Cover with cloth and let rise in a warm draft-free spot until doubled in bulk, about 1 hour. Punch down, turn onto lightly floured board and let rest 5 minutes; knead lightly 2 minutes. Halve piece of dough and shape* each into a loaf about 7″ long and 4″ wide; place in greased 9″×5″×3″ loaf pans, cover, and let rise about 1 hour in a warm spot until doubled in bulk. About 15 minutes before baking, preheat oven to 400° F. When loaves have risen, brush tops with melted butter if you like a soft crust. Bake 35–40 minutes until golden brown and loaves sound hollow when tapped. Turn out immediately and cool on wire racks. About 80 calories per slice.

VARIATIONS:

¢ **Cornell Bread** (a supernutritious bread): Prepare as directed, substituting 6 tablespoons *each* nonfat dry milk powder and soya flour and 2 tablespoons wheat germ for 1 cup of the flour. Mix in at the beginning with the first addition of flour. About 80 calories per slice.

¢ **Raisin Bread:** Prepare as directed, increasing butter and sugar each to ¼ cup and mixing 1¼ cups seedless raisins in after first 3 cups of flour. About 100 calories per slice.

¢ **Bran Bread:** Prepare as directed, substituting ¼ cup molasses for the sugar and 1 cup bran for 1 cup of the flour. About 80 calories per slice.

¢ ☒ **RAPID-MIX WHITE BREAD**

Here is the new streamlined way to make yeast bread.
Makes 2 9″×5″×3″ loaves

5½–6½ cups unsifted flour
3 tablespoons sugar
2 teaspoons salt
1 package active dry yeast
1½ cups water
½ cup milk
3 tablespoons butter, margarine, or shortening at room temperature

Mix 2 cups flour, sugar, salt, and undissolved yeast in large electric mixer bowl. Heat water, milk, and butter over low heat just until warm, not hot. Gradually add to dry ingredients and beat 2 minutes at medium mixer speed. Add about ¾ cup more flour or enough to make a thick batter and beat 2 minutes at high speed, scraping sides of bowl frequently. Stir in enough additional flour to make a soft dough. Knead dough on a lightly floured board until satiny and elastic, 8–10 minutes; place in a greased large bowl, turning to grease all over, cover, and let rise in a warm, draft-free place until doubled in bulk, about 1 hour. Punch dough down, turn onto board, cover, and let rest 15 minutes. Divide in half and shape* into 2 loaves. Place in greased 9"×5" ×3" pans, cover, and let rise until doubled in bulk. Toward end of rising, preheat oven to 400° F. Bake loaves 25–30 minutes until nicely browned and hollow sounding when tapped. Remove from pans and cool on racks. About 75 calories per slice.

VARIATION:

¢ **Cool-Rise Loaves:** Mix dough and knead as directed; leave on board, cover, and let rest 20 minutes. Divide in half, shape* into 2 loaves, and place in greased pans. Brush tops with oil, cover with oiled wax paper, then Saran. Refrigerate 2–24 hours. When ready to bake, preheat oven to 400° F. Uncover loaves and let stand at room temperature 10 minutes; prick any surface bubbles with a greased toothpick. Bake 30–40 minutes until nicely browned and hollow sounding when tapped. Cool as above. About 75 calories per slice.

¢ **POTATO BREAD**

Potato gives the bread extra flavor and softer texture.
Makes 2 9"×5"×3" loaves

½ *cup scalded milk*
¼ *cup shortening, butter, or margarine*
2 *tablespoons sugar*
2 *teaspoons salt*
⅓ *cup warm water (105–15° F.)*
2 *packages active dry yeast*
1½ *cups lukewarm, riced, cooked, unseasoned potatoes*
½ *cup lukewarm potato cooking water*
5¼–5½ *cups sifted flour*

Mix milk, shortening, sugar, and salt; cool to lukewarm. Pour water into a warm large bowl, sprinkle in yeast, and stir to dissolve. Add cooled mixture, potatoes, potato cooking water, and about 2 cups flour; beat until smooth. Mix in enough remaining flour to make a firm dough that leaves the sides of bowl clean. Knead on a lightly floured board until elastic, about 10 minutes. Shape into a ball, place in a greased bowl, turning to grease all over. Cover with cloth and let rise in a warm, draft-free place until double in bulk, about 1 hour. Punch down, cover, and let rise again. Punch down once more and knead lightly 1–2 minutes. Divide dough in half, shape* into 2 loaves, and place in greased 9"×5"×3" loaf pans. Cover and let rise until almost doubled in bulk. Toward end of rising, preheat oven to 400° F. Bake loaves 10 minutes, reduce heat to 350° F., and bake 30–35 minutes longer until well browned and hollow sounding when tapped. Turn out and cool upright on a wire rack before cutting. About 75 calories per slice.

¢ **BATTER BREAD**

This recipe makes smallish loaves with an old-fashioned yeasty flavor and firm, chewy texture.
Makes 2 9"×5"×3" loaves

1 *cup milk, scalded*
3 *tablespoons sugar*
1 *tablespoon salt*
2 *tablespoons butter or margarine, softened to room temperature*
1 *cup warm water (105–15° F.)*
2 *packages active dry yeast*
4¼ *cups unsifted flour*

Mix milk with sugar, salt, and butter, stirring until sugar dissolves; cool to lukewarm. Place warm water in a large warm bowl, sprinkle in yeast, and stir to dissolve; add milk mixture. Stir in flour and beat vigorously until well blended, about 2 minutes.

Batter will be shiny and smooth and leave sides of bowl fairly clean. Use an electric mixer at low speed, if you wish, adding flour a little at a time. When all flour is in, beat at medium speed 2 minutes. Cover dough with cloth and let rise in a warm, draft-free place 40 minutes until slightly more than doubled in bulk. About 15 minutes before batter is fully risen, preheat oven to 375° F. Stir batter down and beat vigorously ½ minute by hand. Divide batter between 2 well-greased 9"×5"×3" loaf pans. Bake 40–50 minutes or until loaves are well browned and sound hollow when tapped. Turn loaves out on wire cake racks to cool. About 55 calories per slice.

SALLY LUNN

A high-rising Southern bread that is almost as rich as sponge cake.
Makes 6–8 servings

2 packages active dry yeast
⅓ cup warm water (105–15° F.)
⅔ cup milk, scalded and cooled to lukewarm
½ cup butter (no substitute), softened to room temperature
⅓ cup sugar
4 eggs
1 teaspoon salt
4 cups sifted flour

Sprinkle yeast over warm water and stir lightly to mix; let stand 5 minutes, then mix in milk and set aside. Cream butter until light, add sugar, and continue creaming until fluffy. Add eggs, one at a time, beating well after each addition; mix in salt. Add flour alternately with yeast mixture, beginning and ending with flour. Beat vigorously with a wooden spoon until smooth and elastic. Place in a well-buttered bowl, cover with cloth, and let rise in a warm, draft-free place until doubled in bulk, about 1 hour. Beat dough hard with a wooden spoon 100 strokes. Transfer to a buttered and floured 3-quart crown mold or bundt pan, cover, and let rise in a warm place 25–30 minutes until doubled in bulk. Meanwhile, preheat oven to 350° F. When dough has risen, bake about ½ hour until well browned and hollow sounding when tapped. Unmold, cut into thick wedges, and serve steaming hot with lots of butter. About 515 calories for each of 6 servings (without butter), 390 calories for each of 8 servings.

¢ SOUR DOUGH BREAD

For those who *truly* want to make bread "from scratch."
Makes 2 round or long, narrow loaves

Sour Dough Starter:
1 cup sifted flour
1 cup cold water
1 tablespoon sugar

Bread:
5 cups sifted flour
1 tablespoon salt
1 tablespoon sugar
1 cup warm water (105–15° F.)
1 package active dry yeast
1 cup sour dough starter

Prepare starter at least 2 days before you plan to use it. Mix flour and water until smooth in a 1-quart bowl or glass jar; add sugar and stir until dissolved. Cover loosely and let stand in a warm (about 80° F.), draft-free place until fermented (mixture will be bubbly and smell sour); stir from time to time during fermentation. For the bread, sift flour with salt and sugar and set aside. Pour warm water into a warm large bowl, sprinkle in yeast, and stir to dissolve. Mix in starter, then flour, a little at a time, working last bit in with your hands. Knead on a lightly floured board until elastic, 8–10 minutes. Shape into a ball, place in a greased bowl, and turn to grease all over. Cover with cloth and let rise in a warm, draft-free place until doubled in bulk, about 1 hour. Punch down, knead lightly 1–2 minutes, and divide in half. Shape* into 2 round or long, tapering loaves and arrange 3" apart on a lightly floured baking sheet. Cover and let rise until nearly doubled in bulk. Toward end of rising, preheat oven to 400° F. Brush tops of loaves with cold water and, if you like, make a diagonal ¼" deep slash the length of loaf with a sharp knife. Bake with a shallow pan half full of hot water on shelf below loaves 35–40 minutes until well browned and hollow sounding when tapped. Cool on wire racks before cutting. About 65 calories per slice.

RICH FRENCH BREAD

A softer, sweeter bread than Pain Ordinaire.
Makes 2 12" loaves

¾ cup scalded milk
2 tablespoons butter or margarine, softened to room temperature
1 tablespoon sugar
2 teaspoons salt
1¼ cups warm water (105–15° F.)
1 package active dry yeast
5¼–5½ cups sifted flour
1 egg yolk lightly beaten with 1 tablespoon cold water (glaze)

Mix milk, butter, sugar, and salt until sugar dissolves; cool to lukewarm. Pour warm water into a warm large bowl, sprinkle in yeast, and stir to dissolve. Add cooled mixture, then mix in 5 cups flour, a little at a time; work in enough extra flour to form a fairly stiff dough. Knead on a lightly floured board until elastic, about 8 minutes. Shape into a ball, place in a greased bowl, turning to grease all over. Cover with cloth and let rise in a warm, draft-free place until doubled in bulk, about 1 hour. Punch down, knead lightly 1–2 minutes, and divide in half. Shape* into 2 loaves about 12" long and 4" wide, tapering ends; arrange 3" apart on a baking sheet sprinkled with corn meal. Cover and let rise until doubled in bulk. Toward end of rising, preheat oven to 425° F. Brush loaves with glaze and make 3 diagonal slashes about ¼" deep across each with a sharp knife. Bake ½ hour, reduce oven to 350° F., and bake 15 minutes longer until golden brown and loaves sound hollow when tapped. Cool on racks before cutting. About 70 calories per slice.

¢ **PAIN ORDINAIRE (CRUSTY FRENCH BREAD)**

Makes 2 12" loaves

1 package active dry yeast
1¾ cups warm water (105–15° F.)
2 teaspoons salt
5¼–5½ cups sifted flour
1 egg white mixed with 1 tablespoon cold water (glaze)

Sprinkle yeast over warm water and stir to dissolve. Mix salt with flour, then add to yeast mixture, a little at a time, working in enough at the end to form a fairly stiff dough. Knead on a lightly floured board until elastic, about 8 minutes. Shape into a ball, place in a greased bowl, turning to grease all over. Cover with cloth and let rise in a warm, draft-free place until doubled in bulk, about 1 hour. Punch dough down, knead lightly 1–2 minutes and divide in half. Shape* into 2 loaves about 12" long and 4" wide, tapering ends; arrange 3" apart on a baking sheet sprinkled with corn meal. Cover and let rise until doubled in bulk. Toward end of rising, preheat oven to 425° F. Brush loaves with glaze and make 3 diagonal slashes about ¼" deep across each with a sharp knife. Bake ½ hour with a shallow baking pan half full of water on rack underneath bread, reduce heat to 350°, and bake 20–25 minutes longer until golden brown and hollow sounding when tapped. Cool on racks before cutting. About 55 calories per slice.

VARIATION:

Hard Rolls (Makes about 2 dozen):

Prepare dough and let rise as directed; punch down, knead 1 minute, and shape into 1½" balls. Place 2" apart on baking sheets sprinkled with corn meal. Cover and let rise until doubled in bulk, about ½ hour. Brush with glaze and slash each roll across the top; bake 15–20 minutes at 425° F. Cool before serving. About 95 calories per roll.

¢ **WHOLE WHEAT BREAD**

This hearty, wholesome bread needs no kneading and toasts beautifully.
Makes 2 9"×5" loaves

1 cup milk
1½ cups cold water
¼ cup molasses
2 tablespoons light brown sugar
1 tablespoon butter or margarine
1 tablespoon salt
½ cup warm water (105–15° F.)
2 packages active dry yeast
4 cups sifted all-purpose flour
5 cups unsifted whole wheat flour
2 tablespoons milk (glaze)

Bring milk and cold water to a boil in a small saucepan. Off heat, mix in molasses, sugar, butter, and salt; cool to lukewarm. Place lukewarm water in a warm large mixing bowl and sprinkle in yeast. Stir cooled mixture into yeast, then beat in all-purpose flour, 1 cup at a time. Finally, mix in whole wheat flour, 1 cup at a time. Place dough in a buttered large bowl, cover with cloth, and let rise about 1 hour in a warm draft-free place until doubled in bulk. Punch dough down and stir briefly (it will be stiff). Divide dough in half and pat firmly into 2 well-greased 9"× 5"×3" loaf pans, rounding tops a little; brush tops with milk to glaze. Cover and let rise 45–50 minutes until almost doubled in bulk. About 15 minutes before you're ready to bake, preheat oven to 400° F. When loaves are risen, bake 20 minutes, reduce oven to 375° F., and bake 45–50 minutes longer or until richly browned and hollow sounding when tapped. Turn loaves out immediately and cool on wire racks. About 105 calories per slice.

¢ **RYE BREAD**

Dark, light, and medium rye flours are all available; use the medium (it's the most widely available) unless you want a particularly dark or light bread.
Makes 2 7" round loaves

2 tablespoons dark brown sugar
2 tablespoons shortening
1 tablespoon salt
1 cup boiling water
½ cup cold water
½ cup warm water (105–15° F.)
1 package active dry yeast
2½ cups unsifted rye flour
3¼–3½ cups sifted all-purpose flour

Mix sugar, shortening, salt, and boiling water in a small bowl, add cold water, and cool to lukewarm. Pour warm water into a warm large bowl, sprinkle in yeast, and stir to dissolve. Add cooled mixture and rye flour and beat well. Mix in 3 cups all-purpose flour, a little at a time, then work in enough additional flour to make a fairly stiff dough that leaves sides of bowl reasonably clean. Knead until fairly smooth and elastic, 8–10 minutes, on a lightly floured board, adding as little extra flour as possible. Shape into a ball, place in a well-greased 3-quart bowl, and turn dough to grease all over. Cover with cloth and let rise in a warm, draft-free place until doubled in bulk, 1½–2 hours. Punch down, knead lightly 1–2 minutes, and divide dough in half. Shape* each into a round loaf about 5½" across and place 3" apart on a baking sheet sprinkled with corn meal. Cover and let rise until doubled in bulk, about 1½ hours. Toward end of rising, preheat oven to 400° F. Bake loaves 30–35 minutes until brown and hollow sounding when tapped. Cool on a wire rack before cutting. About 70 calories per slice.

VARIATIONS:

¢ **Pumpernickel Bread:** Prepare as directed, substituting ⅓ cup dark molasses for the sugar, increasing shortening to ⅓ cup, and omitting cold water. Increase rye flour to 3 cups, reduce white flour to 1⅔ cups, and add 1 cup whole wheat flour. Proceed as directed, allowing extra rising time because the dough is heavier. About 80 calories per slice.

¢ **Swedish Limpa Bread:** Prepare as directed, increasing brown sugar to ⅓ cup and adding ⅓ cup dark molasses, 2 teaspoons each anise seeds, and finely grated lemon or orange rind to shortening, salt, and boiling water; omit cold water. Otherwise, proceed as directed. For a soft crust, brush loaves with milk or melted butter before baking. About 80 calories per slice.

¢ **OATMEAL BREAD**

If you want a lighter, sweeter bread, use a ½ and ½ mixture of molasses and honey or molasses and maple syrup instead of molasses alone. Makes 2 9"×5"×3" loaves

1 cup scalded milk
2 tablespoons shortening or margarine
2 teaspoons salt
1 cup dark molasses or a ½ and ½ mixture of molasses and honey or maple syrup
1 cup cold water
¼ cup warm water (105–15° F.)
1 package active dry yeast
1½ cups uncooked oatmeal
6 cups sifted flour

Mix milk, shortening, salt, and molasses, stir in cold water, and cool to lukewarm. Pour warm water into a warm very large bowl, sprinkle in yeast, and stir to dissolve. Add cooled mixture, oatmeal, and 4 cups flour and mix well. Mix in remaining flour and knead on a lightly floured board until elastic, 5–8 minutes. Shape into a ball, place in a greased bowl, turning to grease all over. Cover with cloth and let rise in a warm, draft-free place until doubled in bulk, about 1½ hours. Punch down and knead lightly 1–2 minutes. Divide dough in half, shape* into 2 loaves, and place in greased 9"× 5"×3" loaf pans. Cover and let rise until almost doubled in bulk. Toward end of rising, preheat oven to 375° F. Bake loaves 40 minutes until browned and hollow sounding when tapped. Turn out and cool upright on a wire rack before cutting. About 110 calories per slice.

¢ **ANADAMA BREAD**

Anadama ("Anna, damn her") was a fisherman's attempt to make something "different" out of his lazy

wife Anna's same old dinner (corn meal and molasses).
Makes a 9"×5"×3" loaf

½ cup corn meal
3 tablespoons shortening
¼ cup dark molasses
2 teaspoons salt
¾ cup boiling water
¼ cup warm water (105–15° F.)
1 package active dry yeast
1 egg, lightly beaten
3 cups sifted flour

Stir corn meal, shortening, molasses, salt, and boiling water in a small bowl until shortening melts; cool to lukewarm. Pour warm water into a warm large bowl, sprinkle in yeast, and stir to dissolve. Add egg, corn meal mixture, and about half the flour. Beat 300 strokes by hand or 2 minutes at medium electric mixer speed. Stir in remaining flour, using hands at the end to mix well. Spoon into a well-greased 9"×5"×3" loaf pan; flour hands and smooth surface. Cover and let rise in a warm, draft-free place until dough is within 1" of top of pan. Toward end of rising, preheat oven to 375° F. If you like, sprinkle top of loaf with a little corn meal; bake 30–35 minutes until well browned and hollow sounding when tapped. Turn loaf out on a wire rack and cool before cutting. About 100 calories per slice.

VARIATION:

¢ **Easy Oatmeal Bread:** Substitute ½ cup uncooked oatmeal for corn meal, reduce flour to 2¾ cups, and proceed as recipe directs. About 100 calories per slice.

CHEESE BREAD

Especially good toasted.
Makes 2 9"×5"×3" loaves

1½ cups milk
2 cups finely grated sharp Cheddar cheese
2 tablespoons shortening
2 tablespoons sugar
2 teaspoons salt
⅓ cup warm water (105–15° F.)
2 packages active dry yeast
1 egg, lightly beaten
6½ cups sifted flour (about)
1 egg yolk, lightly beaten with 1 tablespoon cold water (glaze)
1–2 teaspoons caraway, poppy, or toasted sesame seeds (optional)

Heat milk, cheese, shortening, sugar, and salt over moderate heat, stirring, until cheese is melted; cool to lukewarm. Pour warm water into a warm large bowl, sprinkle in yeast, and stir to dissolve. Add cooled mixture, egg and about 3 cups flour; beat until smooth. Mix in enough remaining flour to make a firm dough. Knead on a lightly floured board until elastic, 5–8 minutes. Shape into a ball, turn in a greased bowl to grease all over, cover with cloth, and let rise in a warm, draft-free place until doubled in bulk, about 1 hour. Punch down and knead 1–2 minutes; divide dough in half, shape* into 2 loaves, and place in greased 9"×5"×3" loaf pans. Cover and let rise until nearly doubled in bulk, about 1 hour. Toward end of rising, preheat oven to 375° F. Brush loaves with glaze and, if you like, sprinkle with seeds. Bake 30–40 minutes until well browned and hollow sounding when tapped. Turn out and cool upright on wire rack before cutting. About 120 calories per slice.

VARIATIONS:

Cheese-Herb Bread: Prepare as directed, adding ¾ teaspoon each marjoram and thyme or 1½ teaspoons oregano to yeast mixture. About 120 calories per slice.

Cheese-Onion Bread: Prepare as directed, adding ¼ cup minced onion to scalded milk. About 120 calories per slice.

Pimiento-Cheese Bread: Prepare as directed but, when shaping loaves, roll into rectangles about 14"×9", sprinkle evenly with ¼–⅓ cup minced pimiento, and roll up from the short side. Bake as directed. About 120 calories per slice.

PIZZA

Makes 2 14" pies

Pizza Dough:
¼ cup warm water (105–15° F.)
1 package active dry yeast
4¼ cups sifted flour
1 teaspoon salt
1 teaspoon sugar
1¼ cups lukewarm water
2 tablespoons olive or other cooking oil

Pizza Sauce:
1 (8-ounce) can tomato sauce
1 (6-ounce) can tomato paste
1 tablespoon olive or other cooking oil
2 tablespoons water
1 clove garlic, peeled and crushed
1 teaspoon oregano
½ teaspoon salt
½ teaspoon sugar
⅛ teaspoon crushed dried hot red chili peppers

Topping:
¾ pound mozzarella cheese, thinly sliced or coarsely grated
⅓–½ cup grated Parmesan cheese
1 teaspoon oregano

Pour warm water into a warm large bowl, sprinkle in yeast, and stir to dissolve. Mix in 2 cups flour, the salt and sugar. Add lukewarm water and oil and beat until smooth. Mix in remaining flour and knead on a lightly floured board until elastic. Shape into a ball, turn in greased bowl to grease all over, cover, and let rise in a warm, draft-free place until doubled in bulk, about 1 hour. Meanwhile, warm all sauce ingredients together in a covered saucepan over lowest heat, stirring now and then, 20 minutes; keep warm until ready to use. Preheat oven to 450° F. Punch dough down, divide in half, refrigerate 1 piece, and roll the other into a circle about 15" across. Place on a greased 14" pizza pan, roll edges under even with rim, and brush with a little oil. Spread half the sauce evenly over dough, sprinkle with half the mozzarella, Parmesan, and oregano. Prepare remaining dough the same way. (Note: Dough may be rolled to fit a 15½"×12" baking sheet if a pizza pan is unavailable.) Bake, uncovered, 20–25 minutes until edges are well browned and cheese bubbly. Cut each pie in 6 wedges and serve hot. Pass extra Parmesan, oregano, and chili peppers if you like. About 300 calories per pie-shaped wedge (6 wedges for each pie).

VARIATIONS:

–The ways to vary pizza topping are as endless as your imagination. Some favorites (to be added between the mozzarella and Parmesan): sliced *fully cooked* sweet or hot Italian sausages; sliced sautéed mushrooms; lightly sautéed strips of green and/or red peppers; lightly sautéed onion rings; drained anchovies; sliced green or ripe olives or any combination of these.

▨ **Quick Pizza** (Makes a 14" pie): Prepare 1 (13¼-ounce) package hot-roll mix by package directions but increase water to 1 cup and omit egg. *Do not let rise.* Roll out to fit a 14" pizza pan and brush with oil. Halve sauce recipe above and mix, substituting ½ teaspoon garlic powder for the garlic; do not heat. Spread on dough and top with half the cheeses and oregano called for. Bake as directed. About 300 calories per pie-shaped wedge (6 wedges per pie).

⊠ **Individual Muffin Pizzas** (Makes 6): Split and toast 3 English muffins; arrange on an ungreased baking sheet. Spread with 1 (8-ounce) can meatless spaghetti sauce. Top with thin slices of mozzarella, sprinkle with Parmesan and oregano. Broil 4″–5″ from the heat about 3 minutes until bubbly. About 165 calories per pizza.

⚖ ¢ **BREAD STICKS**
Makes about 5 dozen

¾ *cup boiling water*
2 tablespoons shortening
2 teaspoons sugar
1 teaspoon salt
¼ *cup warm water (105–15° F.)*
1 package active dry yeast
3½ cups sifted flour
2 egg whites, beaten to soft peaks
1–2 tablespoons milk

Mix boiling water, shortening, sugar, and salt and cool to lukewarm. Pour warm water into a warm mixing bowl, sprinkle in yeast, and stir to dissolve. Add cooled mixture and 1½ cups flour and beat well. Mix in egg whites, then remaining flour. Knead on a lightly floured board until elastic, about 8 minutes. Shape into a ball, place in a greased bowl, turning to grease all over. Cover and let rise in a warm, draft-free place until doubled in bulk, about 1 hour. Punch dough down, knead lightly 1–2 minutes, and divide in half. Roll out 1 portion into a rectangle about 15″ long, 8″ wide, and ⅓″ thick, keeping edges as straight as possible. Cut into strips 8″ long and ½″ wide and roll lightly with floured palms, just enough to round cut edges. Place sticks ½″ apart on greased baking sheets; repeat with remaining dough. Cover and let rise until doubled in bulk, about ½ hour. Meanwhile, preheat oven to 400° F. Brush sticks with milk and bake with a shallow baking pan, half full of water set on rack underneath, 12–15 minutes until lightly browned. Cool on wire racks and store airtight. About 15 calories per bread stick.

VARIATIONS:

⚖ ¢ **Herb Bread Sticks:** Prepare as directed, adding 1 teaspoon each basil and oregano or marjoram to boiling water mixture. About 15 calories per bread stick.

⚖ ¢ **Salt Bread Sticks:** Prepare and shape as directed; after brushing sticks with milk, sprinkle heavily with coarse (kosher-style) salt. Bake as directed. About 15 calories per bread stick.

⚖ ¢ **Poppy or Sesame Seed Bread Sticks:** Prepare and shape as directed; after brushing sticks with milk, sprinkle heavily with poppy or sesame seeds. Brush seeds from baking sheets and bake as directed. About 17 calories per bread stick.

¢ **RICH DINNER ROLLS**
Makes about 2½ dozen

1 cup scalded milk
¼ *cup sugar*
1 teaspoon salt
¼ *cup butter or margarine*
½ *cup warm water (105–15° F.)*
2 packages active dry yeast
2 eggs, lightly beaten
5½ cups sifted flour (about)
1–2 tablespoons melted butter or margarine

BREADS

Mix milk, sugar, salt, and butter in a small bowl, stirring until sugar dissolves; cool to lukewarm. Pour warm water into a warm large bowl, sprinkle in yeast, and stir until dissolved. Stir in milk mixture, eggs, and 2 cups flour, beating with a wooden spoon until smooth. Mix in enough additional flour, a little at a time, to make a soft dough (it will be sticky but should leave sides of bowl clean). Knead on a lightly floured board 8–10 minutes until smooth and elastic; shape into a ball, place in a greased large bowl, turning to grease all over. Cover with cloth and let rise in a warm, draft-free spot until doubled in bulk, 30–40 minutes. Punch dough down. Shape* as desired, place rolls in greased pans, cover, and let rise about ½ hour until doubled in bulk. About 15 minutes before baking, preheat oven to 375° F. Brush tops of rolls with melted butter and bake 15–20 minutes until lightly browned and hollow sounding when tapped. Serve hot. About 110 calories per roll.

¢ **BUTTERMILK ROLLS**

These are unusually light and feathery.
Makes 2 dozen

3 cups sifted flour
1 tablespoon sugar
1 teaspoon salt
¼ teaspoon baking soda
¼ cup chilled lard, butter, or margarine
1 package active dry yeast
¼ cup warm water (*105–15° F.*)
⅔ cup lukewarm buttermilk
1–2 tablespoons melted butter or margarine

Sift dry ingredients into a bowl and cut in lard until the texture of coarse meal. Sprinkle yeast over warm water and stir to dissolve; add buttermilk, pour into a well in flour mixture, and stir until dough comes together. Knead on a lightly floured board until elastic, about 5 minutes. Let rise in a buttered bowl, covered with cloth, in a warm, draft-free spot about ¾ hour until doubled in bulk. Punch dough down, turn onto board, and knead 1 minute. Shape into 1½″ balls, place 2″ apart on greased baking sheets, cover, and let rise until doubled, about ½ hour. Meanwhile, preheat oven to 425° F. Brush rolls with melted butter and bake 15–20 minutes until browned. About 80 calories per roll.

VARIATION:

¢ **Crusty Buttermilk Rolls:** After brushing rolls with butter, sprinkle with corn meal; bake as directed. About 80 calories per roll.

POTATO PUFF ROLLS

People rave about these.
Makes about 3 dozen

¾ cup scalded milk
3 tablespoons shortening
2 tablespoons sugar
2 teaspoons salt
¼ cup warm water (*105–15° F.*)
1 package active dry yeast
1 egg, lightly beaten
1 cup lukewarm, unseasoned mashed potatoes
4 cups sifted flour
2 tablespoons melted butter or margarine

Mix milk, shortening, sugar, and salt and cool to lukewarm. Pour warm water into a warm mixing bowl, sprinkle in yeast and stir to dissolve. Add cooled mixture, egg, potatoes, and 2 cups flour and beat well. Mix in remaining flour and knead on a lightly floured board until satiny and elastic. Shape into a ball, place in a greased bowl, turning to grease all over. Cover and chill in refrigerator at least 3 hours or overnight. Knead dough lightly 1 minute, then divide in half. Roll 1 portion on lightly floured board to a thickness of ½" and cut in rounds with a 2" cutter. Brush tops lightly with butter and fold in half, pressing edges together lightly. Arrange rolls 1" apart on greased baking sheets. Repeat with remaining dough. Cover rolls and let rise in a warm, draft-free place until almost doubled in bulk, about ½ hour. Meanwhile preheat oven to 400° F. Bake rolls 15–17 minutes until golden brown. Serve hot. About 70 calories per roll.

CROISSANTS

Makes about 2–2½ dozen

¾ *cup scalded milk*
2 *teaspoons sugar*
1 *teaspoon salt*
¼ *cup warm water (105–15° F.)*
1 *package active dry yeast*
2¼–2½ *cups sifted flour*
½ *cup butter (no substitute)*
1 *egg yolk lightly beaten with*
   1 *tablespoon cold water (glaze)*

Mix milk, sugar, and salt and cool to lukewarm. Pour warm water into a warm mixing bowl, sprinkle in yeast, and stir to dissolve. Add cooled mixture, then mix in flour, a little at a time, to make a soft dough. Knead on a lightly floured board until satiny and elastic, about 5 minutes. Shape into a ball, place in a greased bowl, turning to grease all over. Cover with cloth and let rise in a warm, draft-free place until doubled in bulk, about 1 hour. Punch down, wrap in wax paper, and chill 20 minutes. Menawhile work butter with your hands until pliable but still cold. Roll dough on a lightly floured board into a rectangle about 12"×16". Dab ½ the butter over ⅔ of dough and fold letter style,

bringing unbuttered ⅓ in first. Pinch all edges to seal. Give dough ¼ turn and roll quickly with short, even strokes into a 12"×16" rectangle. Butter the same way, fold and roll again using remaining butter. Roll and fold twice more (without adding any more butter), then wrap and chill 2–3 hours or overnight. (*Note:* If kitchen is warm, chill dough as needed between rollings.) Halve dough, and keep 1 piece cold while shaping the other: Roll into a 15" circle and cut into 12 or 16 equal-size wedges.

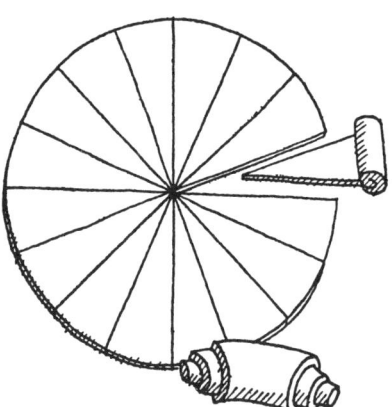

Croissants

Roll up loosely from the wide side and place, triangle points down, 2" apart on ungreased baking sheets. Cover and let rise until almost

BREADS

doubled in size, about 1 hour. Toward end of rising, preheat oven to 375° F. Brush rolls with glaze and bake 15–20 minutes until well browned. Cool slightly before serving or serve at room temperature. About 90 calories for each of 2 dozen croissants, 75 for each of 2½ dozen.

¢ NO-KNEAD REFRIGERATOR ROLLS

Makes about 4 dozen

1 cup boiling water
¼ cup butter or margarine
½ cup sugar
2 teaspoons salt
1 cup warm water (105–15° F.)
2 packages active dry yeast
1 egg, lightly beaten
7 cups sifted flour (about)
1 egg yolk, lightly beaten with
    1 tablespoon cold water (glaze)

Mix boiling water, butter, sugar, and salt in a small bowl, stirring until sugar dissolves; cool to lukewarm. Pour warm water into a large bowl, sprinkle in yeast, and stir until dissolved. Stir in cooled mixture, egg, and about 4 cups flour; beat well with a wooden spoon until smooth. Mix in enough of the remaining flour to make a fairly soft dough, using your hands toward the end. Place dough in a greased large bowl, turn to grease all over, cover with wax paper, then a damp cloth. Refrigerate until doubled in bulk or until 2 hours before needed. (*Note:* Dough will keep 4–5 days in refrigerator and should be punched down occasionally as it rises; keep covering cloth damp.) To use, punch dough down and cut off amount needed. Shape* as desired, place rolls in greased pans, spacing 2" apart, cover with a dry cloth, and let rise in a warm, draft-free spot 1½–2 hours (size of rolls and coldness of dough will determine). About 15 minutes before baking, preheat oven to 400° F. Brush tops of rolls with glaze and bake about 15 minutes until lightly browned and hollow sounding when tapped. Serve warm. About 80 calories per roll.

⊠ QUICK YEAST-RAISED DINNER ROLLS

Makes 16 rolls

¾ cup warm water (105–15° F.)
1 package active dry yeast
2½ cups packaged biscuit mix
1 egg yolk, lightly beaten with
    1 tablespoon cold water (glaze)

Pour warm water into a warm bowl, sprinkle in yeast, and stir until dissolved. Stir in about ⅔ of the biscuit mix and beat vigorously with a wooden spoon. Mix in remaining biscuit mix. Sprinkle a board lightly with biscuit mix, turn out dough, and knead until smooth, 1–2 minutes. Cover with a cloth and let rest 10 minutes. Divide dough into 16 equal pieces, shape into smooth balls, space 2" apart on greased baking sheets, and cover with a cloth. Let rise in a warm, draft-free place ¾–1 hour until doubled in bulk. About 15 minutes before baking, preheat oven to 400° F. Brush tops of rolls with glaze and bake about 15 minutes until lightly browned and hollow sounding when tapped. About 65 calories per roll.

VARIATION:

Sprinkle rolls with sesame or poppy seeds after brushing with glaze; bake as directed. About 65 calories per roll.

¢ BASIC SWEET DOUGH

A good all-round dough to use in making fancy yeast breads.

Makes enough for 2 10" rings or 2 9"×5"×3" loaves or 4 dozen rolls

1 cup scalded milk
¼ cup butter or margarine
½ cup sugar
1 teaspoon salt
¼ cup warm water (105–15° F.)
2 packages active dry yeast
2 eggs, lightly beaten
5 cups sifted flour

Mix milk, butter, sugar, and salt and cool to lukewarm. Pour warm water into a warm large bowl, sprinkle in yeast, and stir to dissolve. Add cooled mixture, eggs, and 3 cups flour and beat well. Mix in remaining flour and knead lightly on a lightly floured board until elastic. Shape into a ball, turn in a greased bowl to grease all over, cover with cloth, and let rise in a warm, draft-free place until doubled in bulk, about 1 hour. Dough is now ready to shape and use as individual recipes direct. About 95 calories per wedge (equal to ⅛ of 1 ring-shaped loaf), 85 calories per 1-inch slice of loaf, and 65 calories per roll.

HOT CROSS BUNS

Makes 4 dozen

1 recipe Basic Sweet Dough
1 cup seedless raisins or dried currants
1 teaspoon allspice
½ cup minced candied citron (optional)
2 egg yolks, lightly beaten with 2 tablespoons cold water (glaze)
2 times the recipe for Easy White Icing

Prepare dough as directed, but add raisins, allspice, and, if you like, citron to yeast along with cooled mixture; proceed as directed and let rise. Divide dough in half and shape into 1½" balls. Arrange 2" apart on greased baking sheets and flatten slightly with palm of hand. Cover and let rise in a warm, draft-free place until doubled in bulk, about ¾ hour. Meanwhile, preheat oven to 400° F. Brush buns with glaze and bake 12–15 minutes until golden brown. Lift to wire racks and, while still warm, draw a cross on top of each with icing. About 110 calories per bun.

BASIC TEA RING

Makes a 10" ring

½ recipe Basic Sweet Dough

Filling:
2 tablespoons melted butter or margarine
¾ cup minced pecans, walnuts, or blanched almonds
½ cup sugar
1½ teaspoons cinnamon

Topping:
1 recipe Easy White Icing

Prepare dough and let rise as directed; punch down and roll on a lightly floured board into a rectangle about 12"×17". Brush with melted butter. Mix nuts, sugar, and cinnamon and sprinkle evenly over dough; roll up from longest side

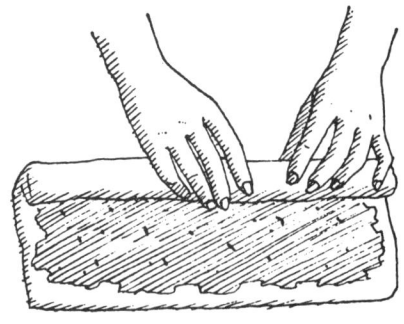

jelly-roll fashion and place seam side down on a greased baking sheet. Bring ends around to form a ring and pinch edges to seal.

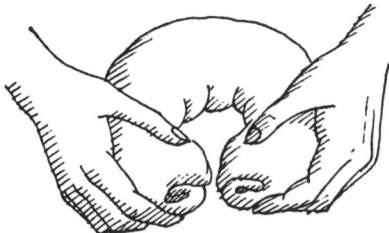

With scissors, snip into ring every 1" and twist slices so cut sides are up. Cover and let rise in a warm, draft-free place until doubled in bulk, about 1 hour. Toward end of rising, preheat oven to 350° F. Bake 35–40 minutes until golden brown. Lift ring to a wire rack set over wax paper and drizzle with icing while still warm. About 160 calories for each of 20 slices.

VARIATIONS:

– Substitute any favorite filling for the one above (see Some Fillings for Coffee Cakes).

Chelsea Buns (Makes 1½ dozen): Prepare and roll dough as directed. For the filling, substitute dried currants for the nuts. Roll up as directed but do not shape into a ring; instead, slice 1" thick and arrange cut sides up 1½" apart on greased baking sheets. Let rise, then bake 15–20 minutes until golden. Lift to racks and drizzle with icing while still warm. About 175 calories per bun.

Caramel Sticky Buns (Makes 1½ dozen): Prepare Basic Tea Ring (above) as directed, but do not shape into a ring; instead, slice 1" thick. Mix 1 cup firmly packed light or dark brown sugar with ½ cup melted butter and 2 tablespoons light corn syrup and spread over the bottom of a greased 13"×9"×2" baking pan. Arrange rolls cut sides up and ½" apart on top, cover, and let rise. Bake 25–30 minutes at 375° F. Let stand in pan 5 minutes, then invert on a wire rack set over wax paper. Serve while still warm. About 275 calories per bun.

¢ **BUBBLE LOAF**

Makes a 9"×5"×3" or 9" tube loaf

½ *recipe Basic Sweet Dough*

Caramel Glaze:
¼ *cup dark corn syrup*
1 tablespoon melted butter or margarine
¼ *teaspoon lemon extract*
¼ *teaspoon vanilla or maple extract*

Prepare dough and let rise as directed. Punch down and let rest 10 minutes. Pinch off bits of dough and roll into 1" balls. Arrange 1 layer deep, ¼" apart, in the bottom of a greased 9"×5"×3" loaf pan or 9" tube pan. Layer in remaining balls, fitting them into spaces in layer below. Cover and let rise in a warm, draft-free place until doubled in bulk, about ¾ hour. Meanwhile, mix glaze ingredients and preheat oven to 350° F. When dough is fully risen, pour glaze evenly over all. Bake 40–45 minutes, cool upright in pan on a wire rack 5 minutes, then invert and cool. There are 2 ways to serve: slicing or pulling off the "individual bubbles." About 90 calories for each of 20 slices.

CHERRY KOLACHE

Makes about 3½ dozen rolls

1 recipe Basic Sweet Dough
2 cups cherry preserves
3 tablespoons melted butter or margarine
Confectioners' or granulated sugar

Prepare dough and let rise as directed. Punch down, roll ½" thick on a lightly floured board, and cut in rounds with a 3" cutter. Arrange 1½" apart on greased baking sheets, cover, and let rise in a warm, draft-free place until doubled in bulk, about ½ hour. With thumb, make a depression in center of each roll and fill with about 2 teaspoons cherry preserves. Let rise 15 minutes; meanwhile, preheat oven to 400° F. Bake 12–15 minutes until golden brown. Transfer to wire racks, brush with melted butter, and dust with sugar. About 135 calories per roll.

Note: Dainty tea-size *kolache* can be made by rolling dough into ¾" balls; let rise as directed, make thumbprints in center, and fill with preserves; bake as directed. Or dough can be rolled into a 12"×15" rectangle, cut in 3" squares and spread with preserves, leaving ¼"–½" margins all round; fold 4 corners in toward center until points touch, then pinch to seal. Let rise and bake as directed. About 35 calories per tea-size roll.

VARIATIONS:

Prune Kolache: Prepare as directed, filling with the following mixture instead of cherry preserves: Mix 2 cups minced pitted cooked prunes (or apricots or figs), ½ cup sugar, 1 tablespoon grated orange or lemon rind, and 1 tablespoon orange or lemon juice. If you like, add ¼–½ teaspoon cinnamon or allspice. About 135 calories per roll.

Poppy Seed-Nut Kolache: Prepare as directed, filling with the following mixture: 1½ cups minced blanched almonds, hazelnuts, or other nuts mixed with ½ cup poppy seeds and ¼ cup warm honey. About 120 calories per roll.

KUGELHUPF

A fruit-filled, sweet yeast bread good with afternoon tea or coffee or as dessert.
Makes a 10" tube loaf

1 recipe Basic Sweet Dough (reduce amount of flour to 4 cups)
2 egg yolks
½ cup seedless raisins
½ cup dried currants
½ cup minced mixed candied fruits (optional)
20 blanched almonds, halved
Confectioners' sugar

Prepare dough as directed, adding extra egg yolks and fruits to yeast along with cooled mixture and 3 cups flour; beat well and add remaining 1 cup flour to make a very soft dough. Do not knead. Grease and flour a 10" tube pan or 3½-quart Turk's-head mold and arrange almonds in bottom. Spoon in dough, cover, and let rise in a warm, draft-free place until doubled in bulk, about 1 hour. Toward end of rising, preheat oven to 400° F. Bake 10 minutes, reduce oven to 350° F., and bake 50–60 minutes longer until lightly browned and springy to the touch. Turn out at once on a wire rack set over wax paper and dust with sifted confectioners' sugar. Slice and serve. About 195 calories for each of 20 slices.

VARIATION:

Instead of using halved almonds, sprinkle prepared mold with ⅓–½ cup minced almonds; spoon in dough and proceed as directed. About 195 calories for each of 20 slices.

DANISH PASTRY

Makes about 3½ dozen

1 recipe Basic Sweet Dough
1 teaspoon cardamom

1 cup butter (*no substitute*)
2 egg yolks, lightly beaten with 2 tablespoons cold water (*glaze*)

Filling:
1 cup (*about*) jelly, jam, almond paste, applesauce, Cheese, Nut, or Prune Filling

Prepare basic dough as directed, mixing cardamom into scalded milk mixture. When dough is fully risen, punch down, cover, and chill 20 minutes. Meanwhile, knead butter until pliable but still cold. Roll dough on a lightly floured board into a rectangle about 12"×10". Dot ½ the butter over ⅔ of dough, leaving ½" margins all round. Fold unbuttered ⅓ in toward center, then far ⅓ on top as though folding a letter; pinch edges to seal.

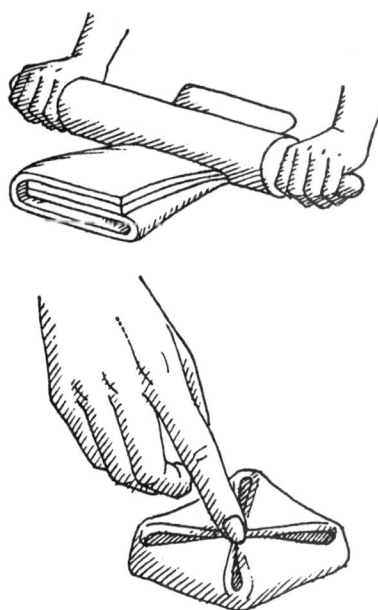

Give package a ¼ turn and roll with short, even strokes into a rectangle about 12"×16". Dot with remaining butter, fold, and roll as before.

Roll and fold twice more, lightly flouring board and pin as needed to keep dough from sticking. Wrap and chill 1 hour. (*Note:* If kitchen is warm, you may need to chill dough between rollings.) Divide dough in half, chill 1 piece while shaping the other. Roll out ⅓" thick and cut in 3" or 4" squares; place 1–2 teaspoons filling in center of each square, moisten edges and fold 2 opposite corners in toward center; press edges to seal. Arrange 2" apart on greased baking sheets, chill 2 hours, or let rise in a warm place until about half doubled in bulk. Preheat oven to 425° F. Brush with glaze, set in oven, and reduce heat at once to 375° F. Bake 15 minutes until browned. Cool on wire racks before serving. About 145 calories per pastry (filled with jelly or jam).

VARIATIONS:

Danish Twists: Prepare dough as directed, let rise, then punch down and roll the butter in as above. Divide in half, chill 1 piece while shaping the other. Roll into a rectangle about 12"×16", brush well with melted butter, and sprinkle with ¼ cup sugar mixed with 1 teaspoon cinnamon. Fold dough in half the long way so you have a strip 6"×16". Cut crosswise into strips ¾" wide. Twist ends of each in opposite directions, arrange on greased baking sheets, let rise, and bake as directed. Shape and bake remaining dough the same way. About 145 calories each.

Danish Ring: Prepare dough as directed, let rise, then punch down and roll butter into dough as above. Divide in half and chill 1 piece while shaping the other. Roll into a rectangle about 12"×16", brush with melted butter, then sprinkle or spread with any of the fillings above. Roll up from the longest side jellyroll fashion, place seam side down on a greased baking sheet, and bring ends around to form a ring, pressing edges to seal. Or, if you prefer, coil snail fashion. Let rise in a warm place until about half doubled in bulk, glaze, and sprinkle with sliced blanched almonds and granulated sugar. Bake 25–30 minutes at 375° F. until golden brown and hollow sounding when tapped. Shape and bake remaining pastry the same way. About 145 calories per 1-inch slice (filled with jelly or jam).

PANETTONE (ITALIAN CHRISTMAS BREAD)

Makes a tall 9" loaf

1 recipe Basic Sweet Dough (reduce amount of scalded milk to ¾ cup)
¼ cup butter or margarine
3 egg yolks, lightly beaten
1 cup sultana raisins
1 cup minced candied citron or mixed candied fruits
½ cup piñon nuts (optional)
2 tablespoons melted butter or margarine
Confectioners' sugar

Prepare basic recipe as directed, adding the ¼ cup butter above to the scalded milk along with the butter, sugar, and salt called for in basic recipe; cool to lukewarm and stir into yeast mixture along with all but last ingredient above. Proceed as basic recipe directs. While dough is rising, prepare pan: Tear off a 30" piece of heavy duty foil and fold over and over again until you have a strip 30" long and 4" wide. Grease 1 side of strip and stand greased side around the inside edge of a greased 9" layer cake pan; secure with a paper clip to form a collar. Punch dough down, knead lightly 1–2 minutes, and shape into a smooth round loaf about 9" across. Place in pan, cover, and let rise in a warm, draft-free place until doubled in bulk, about 1 hour. Toward end of rising, preheat oven to 400° F. Bake 10 minutes, reduce oven to 350° F., and bake 40–50 minutes longer until golden brown and hollow sounding when tapped. Turn out on a wire rack, dust with confectioners' sugar and cool. To serve, cut in thin wedges. About 330 calories for each of 16 wedges.

STOLLEN

Makes 2 large loaves

1 recipe Basic Sweet Dough
1 cup seedless raisins
1 cup minced blanched almonds
¾ cup minced candied fruits or a ½ and ½ mixture of citron and candied cherries
1 tablespoon finely grated lemon rind
3 tablespoons melted butter or margarine
1 recipe Easy White Icing

Prepare dough as directed, adding raisins, almonds, candied fruit, and lemon rind to yeast along with lukewarm mixture. Add remaining flour, knead, and let rise as directed. Divide dough in half and roll or pat out half on a lightly floured board to form an oval about 12"×8". Brush with melted butter, fold in half the long way, and bend ends in slightly to form a crescent; press edges firmly to seal. Transfer to a greased baking sheet and brush with melted butter. Shape remaining dough the same way and place on a baking sheet. Cover loaves and let rise in a warm, draft-free place until doubled in bulk, about ¾ hour. Toward end of rising, preheat oven to 375° F. Bake 35–40 minutes until golden brown. Lift to wire racks set over wax paper and, while still warm, drizzle with icing. For a festive touch, decorate with "flowers" made with blanched almond halves, candied cherries, and slivered angelica. About 140 calories for each of 20 slices.

VARIATION:

Christmas Bread: Prepare dough as directed, using ½ cup each sultana and seedless raisins and adding 1 teaspoon cinnamon and ½ teaspoon nutmeg along with the fruit. Shape into 2 round loaves and place in greased 9" piepans. Or, if you prefer, make 2 braids.* Let rise, bake, and ice as directed. For a shiny crust, brush dough before baking with 1 egg lightly beaten with 1 tablespoon cold water; omit icing. About 140 calories for each of 20 slices.

CINNAMON-RAISIN PINWHEELS

Makes 20 rolls

½ *cup sugar*
3 *tablespoons butter or margarine*
1 *teaspoon salt*
¾ *cup boiling water*
1 *package active dry yeast*
¼ *cup warm water (105–15° F.)*
1 *egg, lightly beaten*
4½ *cups sifted flour*

Filling:
¼ *cup light corn syrup*
¼ *cup melted butter or margarine*
⅓ *cup sugar or firmly packed light brown sugar*
1½ *teaspoons cinnamon*
1½ *cups seedless raisins*

Stir sugar, butter, and salt into boiling water and cool to lukewarm. Dissolve yeast in the warm water in a warm large bowl; add cooled mixture, egg, and 3 cups flour and beat until smooth. Mix in remaining flour, a little at a time. Knead dough on a lightly floured board until elastic, about 5 minutes; place in a greased bowl, and let rise in a warm, draft-free spot 1 hour or until doubled in bulk. Punch dough down, turn onto board, and divide in half. Roll each into a rectangle about 15"×9", brush with corn syrup and melted butter, sprinkle with sugar, cinnamon, and raisins. Roll each jelly-roll style the short way and cut into 10 slices. Lay slices flat, almost touching, in greased layer cake pans, cover, and let rise about ½ hour until doubled in bulk. Meanwhile, preheat oven to 350° F. Brush with melted butter and bake 30–35 minutes until lightly browned. About 210 calories per roll.

SWEDISH CINNAMON RINGS

This is a rich coffee cake, so cut each ring in small wedges. You should be able to get about 20 wedge-shaped slices out of each ring. Makes 3 12" or 4 10" rings

Dough:
2 *packages active dry yeast*
½ *cup warm water (105–15° F.)*
1 *cup butter or margarine*
¾ *cup sugar*
1 *tablespoon crushed cardamom seeds (it's easy to crush them in an electric blender)*
1 *teaspoon salt*
1½ *cups light cream, scalded*
2 *eggs*
8 *cups sifted flour*

Filling:
½ *cup butter or margarine, softened to room temperature*
1 *cup firmly packed light brown sugar*
2 *teaspoons cinnamon*

Decorations (optional):
2 *recipes Lemon Sugar Glaze*
Diced candied red or green cherries

Sprinkle yeast over warm water in a warm large bowl and stir to dissolve. Mix butter, sugar, cardamom and salt with cream and cool to lukewarm. Stir into yeast, then beat in eggs, 1 at a time. Add flour, 1 cup at a time, beating well after each addition. You will probably have to turn dough onto a board and knead in the final cup. Knead dough about 5 minutes until smooth and elastic. Place in a greased large bowl, turn so dough is greased all over, cover with cloth, and let rise in a warm, draft-free place 1½–1¾ hours until doubled in bulk. Punch dough down, turn onto a lightly floured board, and knead 1–2 minutes. Divide dough into 3 or 4 equal parts, depending upon whether you want large- or medium-size rings. Roll each piece of dough into a rectangle (about 14″×18″ for medium-size rings, 18″×22″ for large). Spread lightly with butter; mix brown sugar and cinnamon and sprinkle over butter, then roll up jelly-roll style and shape into a ring. Using sharp scissors, make diagonal snips deep into each ring every 2″ and turn cut-side up. Place rings on lightly greased baking sheets, cover with cloth, and let rise in a warm place until doubled in bulk, 30–40 minutes. Meanwhile, preheat oven to 375° F. When rings have risen, bake 20–30 minutes until nicely browned and hollow sounding when tapped. Transfer to wire racks to cool and, if you like, glaze and decorate. Serve warm or at room temperature. To reheat, wrap in foil and heat 10 minutes at 350° F. If you do not decorate rings, and cut each ring into 20 thin wedge-shaped slices, each slice will be about 140 calories.

PUMPKIN COFFEE CAKE

Makes 8 servings

Dough:
¼ cup milk, scalded
¼ cup sugar
½ teaspoon salt
3 tablespoons butter or margarine
1 package active dry yeast
¼ cup warm water (105–15° F.)
1 egg, lightly beaten
2¼ cups unsifted flour (about)
1 egg yolk, beaten with 1 tablespoon cold water (glaze)

Filling:
¾ cup cooked, mashed pumpkin
½ cup sugar
1 teaspoon cinnamon
½ teaspoon ginger
½ teaspoon salt
1 cup chopped walnuts or pecans
¼ cup seedless raisins

Frosting:
½ cup sifted confectioners' sugar
1 teaspoon milk or light cream
⅛ teaspoon vanilla

Mix milk with sugar, salt, and butter, stirring until sugar dissolves; cool to lukewarm. Sprinkle yeast over warm water and stir until dissolved. Combine milk and yeast mixtures, add egg and half the flour, and beat until smooth. Stir in remaining flour (dough will be fairly soft). Turn onto a lightly floured board and knead 7–8 minutes until smooth and elastic, adding only enough extra flour to keep dough from sticking. Place dough in a greased bowl, turn to grease all sides, cover with cloth, set in a warm, draft-free place, and let rise about 1 hour until doubled in bulk. Punch dough down, turn onto a lightly floured board, and roll into a rectangle about 22″×10″. Mix pumpkin with sugar, spices, and salt and spread evenly over dough, not quite to edges. Sprinkle with ½ cup walnuts and the raisins. Roll up jelly-roll fashion from the wide side, lift to a greased baking sheet, and coil into a ring. Cover and let rise in a warm place about 1 hour until doubled in bulk. Meanwhile, preheat oven to 350° F. Brush ring with egg glaze and bake 30–35 minutes until well browned and hollow sounding when tapped. Mix frosting ingredients together until smooth and frost ring while still warm; sprinkle with remaining nuts. Serve warm or at room temperature. About 400 calories per serving.

Some Fillings for Coffee Cakes and Sweet Breads

Substitute any of the following for fillings called for in Basic Tea Ring, Danish Pastry, Pumpkin Coffee Cake, or other filled yeast bread.

Almond Paste: Cream together until light ⅓ cup each butter and sugar; add 1 egg, ¼ teaspoon almond extract, and ½ cup almond paste and beat until smooth.

Nut: Cream together until light ¼ cup butter and ⅓ cup sugar; mix in 1 tablespoon grated orange or lemon rind. Spread on dough, then sprinkle with 1 cup minced blanched almonds, pecans, or walnuts.

Prune: Heat together over low heat, stirring constantly until thickened, 1 cup coarsely chopped pitted prunes (or dates, dried apricots, or figs), ¼ cup sugar, 2 tablespoons lemon juice, 1 teaspoon grated lemon rind, and 1 tablespoon butter.

Spiced Apple: Mix 2 tablespoons melted butter with ½ cup firmly packed light brown sugar, 1 teaspoon cinnamon, ¼ teaspoon nutmeg, and 1–1½ cups well-drained canned sliced apples. If you like, also mix in ½ cup seedless raisins.

Cottage Cheese: Mix together 1 cup cottage cheese, 1 lightly beaten egg yolk, ⅓ cup superfine sugar, ½ teaspoon vanilla, and 1 teaspoon finely grated lemon or orange rind.

Custard: Mix 1 cup Custard Sauce and ½ cup poppy seeds.

⊠ *Some Quickies:*
– 1 cup any jelly, jam, preserves, or marmalade
– 1 cup mincemeat
– 1 cup canned apple, cherry, or pumpkin pie filling
– 1 cup whipped cream cheese mixed with ¼ cup poppy seeds and 1 teaspoon finely grated lemon or orange rind

BRIOCHE I (TRADITIONAL METHOD)

A difficult recipe, not for beginners. Makes 2 dozen

1 package active dry yeast
2¼ cups warm water (105–15° F.)
4½ cups sifted flour
1 teaspoon salt
3 tablespoons sugar
6 eggs
1½ cups butter (no substitute), softened to room temperature
1 egg yolk, lightly beaten with 1 tablespoon cold water (glaze)

Beat yeast with ¼ cup warm water and ½ cup flour until smooth and sticky. Pour remaining water into a warm bowl; with a rubber spatula, scrape yeast mixture into water, trying to keep in 1 piece, and let sink to the bottom. Let rise in a warm, draft-free spot until yeast mixture floats and is doubled in bulk, 7–10 minutes. Meanwhile, mix remaining flour with salt and sugar on a pastry board and make a large well in the center. Break 3 eggs into a bowl and set aside. Break remaining eggs into well in flour and, using 1 hand, gradually work flour from edges of well into eggs. Add remaining eggs and continue mixing until dough holds together (it will be very sticky). Keeping a metal spatula in 1 hand to help scrape dough from board, scoop up as much dough as possible with other hand and throw or slap hard against board. You won't be able to get all the dough at once and it will stick like glue to your fingers. But keep throwing as much as possible against board, scraping up a little more each time with the spatula.

Continue throwing dough against board until it is smooth, shiny and leaves board and your fingers almost clean, about 100 times. Squeeze ⅓ of butter into dough with your fingers; repeat until all butter is incorporated and dough smooth. Also squeeze in yeast sponge, but not water it was floating in (dough will be soft).

Scoop into a lightly buttered 3-quart bowl, cover with cloth, and let rise in a warm, draft-free place until doubled in bulk, about 2 hours. Stir dough down, cover with foil, and refrigerate 6–8 hours or overnight. Open refrigerator as little as possible during this period.

Dough will rise slightly and become quite firm. Scrape dough onto a lightly floured board, knead lightly with floured hands, and shape quickly into a ball. Cut ball in 4 equal pieces with a floured knife and cut 3 of the quarters into 8 pieces, totaling 24. Roll into smooth balls and place in greased brioche or muffin pans, 1 ball per cup. With dampened index finger, make a deep depression in center of each ball. Roll remaining dough into 24 small balls and place 1 in each depression to form the "topknot." Cover brioches, set in a warm spot and let rise until doubled in bulk, about 1 hour.

About 15 minutes before you're ready to bake, preheat oven to 425° F.; set rack in lower ⅓ of oven. Gently brush brioches with glaze, taking care not to let it run into cracks around topknots (an artist's brush is best). Set pans on baking sheets and bake 12–15 minutes until well browned. (*Note:* You probably won't be able to bake all the brioches at once, so refrigerate 1 batch while baking the other.) Remove from pans at once after baking and serve hot or, if you prefer, cool on wire racks to room temperature. (*Note:* To reheat leftover brioches, bundle loosely in foil and warm 10 minutes at 350° F. These brioches freeze well; thaw before reheating.) About 205 calories per brioche.

BRIOCHE II (EASY METHOD)

So much less complicated than Brioche I and almost as good. Makes 2 dozen

1 package active dry yeast
¼ cup warm water (105–15° F.)
4 cups sifted flour
3 tablespoons sugar
1 teaspoon salt
1½ cups butter or margarine,
softened to room temperature
6 eggs, lightly beaten
1 egg yolk, lightly beaten with 1
tablespoon cold water (glaze)

Mix yeast, warm water, and ¼ cup flour until smooth in a small bowl; set in a pan of lukewarm water (water should come ⅓ of way up bowl) and let stand in a warm spot until bubbles form on yeast mixture, 5–10 minutes. Meanwhile, sift 3 cups flour with the sugar and salt and set aside. Cream butter in a large bowl with an electric mixer until fluffy. Add flour mixture, a little at a time, alternately with eggs. Beat 2 minutes at medium speed. Add yeast mixture, beat ½ minute at low speed, then 2 minutes at medium speed. Add remaining ¾ cup flour by hand. a little at a time, beating with a wooden spoon after each addition. Cover dough with cloth, set in a warm, draft-free spot, and let rise until doubled in bulk, 2½–3 hours. Stir dough down, cover with foil, and refrigerate 6–8 hours or overnight. Now divide dough, shape into 24 brioches, allow to rise, glaze, and bake as directed in Brioche I. About 200 calories per brioche.

BRIOCHE FRUIT LOAVES

Delicious toasted and buttered!
Makes 2 9"×5"×3" loaves

1 recipe Brioche I or II
2 cups mixed dried or candied fruits (seedless raisins, currants, coarsely chopped candied red cherries or citron)
⅓–½ cup slivered or sliced blanched almonds (optional)
1 egg yolk, lightly beaten with 1 tablespoon cold water (glaze)

Prepare brioche up to point of shaping dough; instead of making individual brioches, halve dough. Roll each piece on a lightly floured board into a rectangle 9"×12". Sprinkle with fruit and press in lightly. Roll up the short way, jelly-roll style, and pinch seams together. Place each loaf seam-side down in a greased 9"×5"×3" loaf pan. Slash tops lengthwise down center with a sharp knife and, if you like, sprinkle almonds into slits. Cover with cloth and let rise in a warm, draft-free spot until doubled in bulk, 1–1½ hours. About 15 minutes before you're ready to bake, preheat oven to 350° F. Brush loaves with glaze and bake 35–40 minutes until well browned and hollow sounding when tapped. If tops or almonds brown too fast, cover loosely with foil. Turn loaves out immediately and cool upright on a wire rack. Slice and serve with plenty of butter. (*Note:* These loaves freeze well.) About 155 calories for each of 20 slices (with almonds).

OLD-FASHIONED YEAST-RAISED DOUGHNUTS

Stored airtight, these doughnuts keep fairly well. They're best, of course, eaten straight from the deep fat fryer.
Makes about 3 dozen

¼ cup butter or margarine
⅔ cup scalded milk
⅔ cup warm water (105–15° F.)
2 packages active dry yeast
¾ cup sugar
5 cups sifted flour (about)
2 eggs, lightly beaten
1 teaspoon salt
1 teaspoon cardamom
½ teaspoon cinnamon
½ teaspoon mace
Shortening or cooking oil for deep fat frying

Topping:
½ cup superfine sugar mixed with 1 teaspoon cinnamon

Melt butter in milk and cool to lukewarm. Place water in a warm large mixing bowl, sprinkle in yeast, and stir until dissolved; add milk mixture and sugar. By hand, beat 2½ cups flour in until smooth; mix in eggs, salt, and spices. Mix in remaining flour, adding a little extra, if needed, to form a soft but manageable dough. Knead lightly 1 minute on a floured pastry cloth; shape into a ball, place in a greased large bowl, cover, and let rise in a warm, draft-free spot until doubled in bulk, about 1 hour. Punch dough down, roll ½" thick on pastry cloth, using a floured, stockinette-covered rolling pin. Cut with a floured doughnut cutter and place 1½" apart on ungreased baking sheets. Reroll and cut scraps. Cover with cloth and let rise in a warm spot about 25 minutes until doubled in bulk. Meanwhile, begin heating fat in a deep fat fryer. When doughnuts have risen and fat reaches 375° F., ease 4 doughnuts into fat, 1 at a time. Fry about 2 minutes until golden brown all over, using tongs to turn. Drain on paper toweling. (*Note:* Never fry more than 4 doughnuts at a time and keep fat as near 375° F. as possible; if too hot, doughnuts will brown before they cook inside.) While doughnuts are warm, roll in topping. About 130 calories per doughnut.

VARIATIONS:

Jelly Doughnuts: Prepare as directed, but roll dough ¼" thick instead of ½". Cut in 2½" rounds and put 1 teaspoonful tart jelly in the center of ½ the rounds. Top with remaining rounds, moisten touching edges slightly and pinch to seal. Let rise, then fry as directed. Roll in confectioners' sugar while still warm. About 150 calories per doughnut.

Crullers: Prepare as directed, but instead of cutting into doughnuts, cut in strips 8" long and ½"–¾" wide; let rise, then twist strips several times and pinch ends. Fry at once and roll in topping while still warm. About 130 calories per cruller.

CHAPTER 19

SANDWICHES

Sandwiches are named for the Earl of Sandwich, an eighteenth-century Englishman who was so fond of gambling he had meat or other savory served between slices of bread so that he needn't interrupt his game. Open-face sandwiches are even older, dating to medieval Scandinavia when slices of bread served as plates. Open *or* shut, sandwiches have become universal favorites. And who in those early days could have predicted it?

About Breads

Any bread can be used in making sandwiches, but certain breads and fillings team more happily than others. Here's a quick table of compatibles:

Bread	Suitable Fillings
White bread	Any filling (*Note:* Use day-old bread if filling is soft or runny)
Whole or cracked wheat, oatmeal, rye, or pumpernickel, cheese bread	Cold cuts and cheeses, smoked fish
Fruit or nut breads	Cream cheese, jams, jellies
French or Italian bread	Hero sandwiches, also any meat, egg, or seafood salad
Hard rolls, hamburger, and hot dog buns	Heroes, hamburgers, hot dogs, sloppy Joes, barbecued meat

About Butters and Mayonnaises

These help bind fillings to bread and, at the same time, keep runny fillings from soaking into bread. They can be used straight from the wrapper or jar or flavored any of the following ways (all amounts based on ¼ cup mayonnaise or butter):

	Especially Good with:
Mustard: Blend 1–2 teaspoons mild or spicy prepared mustard with butter or mayonnaise.	Ham, tongue, and other cold cuts
Horseradish: Blend 1 teaspoon prepared horseradish with butter or mayonnaise.	Roast beef
Garlic or Onion: Blend ¼ crushed clove garlic or 1 teaspoon finely grated onion into butter or mayonnaise.	Cold cuts or cheese
Lemon: Blend 1 teaspoon lemon juice and ¼ teaspoon finely grated lemon rind into butter or mayonnaise.	Seafood, chicken, or turkey
Anchovy or Shrimp: Blend 1 teaspoon shrimp or anchovy paste into butter or mayonnaise.	Seafood
Dill: Blend 2–3 teaspoons minced fresh dill or 1 tablespoon minced dill pickle into butter or mayonnaise.	Salami, seafood, egg salad, chicken, or turkey
Parsley or Watercress: Blend 2–3 teaspoons minced parsley or cress into butter or mayonnaise.	Cold cuts, cheese, seafood, chicken, or turkey
Chutney: Blend 1 tablespoon minced chutney into butter or mayonnaise.	Cold sliced chicken, turkey, or lamb
Curry: Blend 1 teaspoon each curry powder, finely minced onion, and chutney into butter or mayonnaise.	Cold sliced chicken, turkey, or lamb; also seafood

Tips for Making Better Sandwiches

Sandwiches in General:

– Leave crusts on all but dainty tea sandwiches; they help keep sandwiches fresh.
– Assemble components, then put sandwiches together just before serving, particularly important if fillings are drippy.
– Soften butter to room temperature so it spreads more easily.
– If filling is creamy, butter 1 slice of bread only.
– Be generous—but not lavish—with butter or mayonnaise; 1 teaspoon per slice is ample.
– Spread butter or mayonnaise *and* filling to edges of bread.
– Use several thin slices of meat or cheese rather than a single thick one.
– Make sure salad-type fillings are creamy, *not soupy.*
– Make toasted sandwiches at the very last minute and do not stack toast—it will become soggy.

Sandwiches to Go:

– Choose sandwich fillings that won't soak into bread.
– Spread bread with butter, then

chill before adding filling so that butter will harden and help keep filling from seeping into bread.
– Pack lettuce leaves, pickles, tomatoes, etc., separately and slip into sandwiches just before serving.
– Keep all salad-type fillings well chilled (especially in transit) and make sandwiches on location.
– Choose less perishable fillings for lunch box sandwiches—cold cuts, sliced cheese, peanut butter, jelly, etc.—instead of quick-to-spoil creamy salad types.
– Keep lunch box sandwiches refrigerated until ready to go and eat within 4 hours.
– Halve sandwiches before wrapping —makes for easier eating.
– Wrap sandwiches individually in wax paper or plastic sandwich bags.

Sandwiches in Quantity:

To Help Compute Quantities:

– 1 (1-pound) loaf averages 20 slices; 1 pullman or sandwich loaf 33–34.
– Allowing a rounded teaspoon per slice, 1 pound butter will spread 50–60 slices or 2½–3 (1-pound) loaves.
– Allowing a rounded teaspoon per slice, 1 pint mayonnaise will spread 50–60 slices or 2½–3 (1-pound) loaves.
– Allowing ¼ cup per sandwich, 1 quart filling will make 16 sandwiches.

To Stretch Butter: Add ½ cup milk to each 1 pound butter and cream until fluffy.

For Quickest Assembly:

– Choose the simplest sandwiches possible.
– Line bread up in rows, pairing slices so they'll match.
– Whip butter or cheese spreads until fluffy so they'll spread zip-quick.
– Place dabs of butter or mayonnaise on alternate rows of slices, then mounds of filling on remaining rows. Spread well to edges, put slices together, and press lightly.
– Use a No. 24 ice cream scoop or ¼ cup measure for apportioning fillings.

Party Sandwiches

– Use a firm, fine-textured bread to avoid ragged edges; if unavailable, use day-old bread and chill well before cutting.
– For attractiveness, slice bread thin and trim off crusts.
– Be sparing about fillings so they don't seep through the bread or ooze out the edges.
– When making sandwiches ahead, cover with wax paper or Saran, never a damp towel. Refrigerate until ready to serve.
– Add garnishes and decorations at the last minute.

How to Cut and Shape Party Sandwiches

(*Note:* Spreads included in the hors d'oeuvre chapter are perfect for party sandwiches.)

Fancy Cutouts: Trim crusts from an unsliced loaf, slice thin lengthwise, spread with filling, then cut, using a sharp bread knife or cookie cutters.

Double Deckers: Make cutouts and mix or match breads and shapes.

Ribbon Loaf: Trim crusts from an unsliced loaf, slice lengthwise about ½" thick, spread, and reassemble. Frost with softened cream cheese, tinted pastel, if you like. Chill well before slicing. For variety, alternate slices of dark and light breads and 2 or more compatible fillings of contrasting color.

Ribbon Sandwiches: Prepare ribbon loaf, chill well, then slice thin. Cut slices into small squares or rectangles.

Round Ribbon Loaf: Trim crusts from unsliced bread, slice and cut slices in circles of the same size. Spread and assemble as for Ribbon Loaf (above). Frost if you like. To serve, cut in thin wedges.

Checkerboards: Prepare 2 ribbon loaves, beginning one with dark bread and the other with light.

Chill well, slice, spread, and restack slices as shown into checkerboards. Chill and slice.

Roll-Ups: Slice extra-fresh bread, spread with a soft filling, roll, and use toothpick to secure. For interest, roll around a sprig of watercress or dill, a carrot or celery stick, cooked asparagus spear, or finger of ham, tongue, or cheese.

Pinwheels: Trim crusts from an unsliced loaf and slice thin lengthwise. Spread each slice with a colorful filling and roll up, jelly-roll style, from the short side. Wrap in dry toweling, chill several hours, then slice thin. (*Note:* If you use extra-fresh, soft bread, it should roll without cracking. Some cooks recommend flattening the bread with a rolling pin, but it shouldn't be necessary if the bread itself is soft. Besides, flattened bread tastes like damp cardboard.)

Decorated Open-Face Sandwiches: Trimmings can be as simple or lavish as time and talent permit: a sprig of dill or a tarragon leaf laid across the filling, an olive slice or fancy truffle cutout, or a showy piped-on design of cream cheese.

About Sandwich Garnishes

Party sandwiches demand garnishes, dainty doll-like ones; Danish sandwiches require something flashier than everyday lunch or supper sandwiches. They don't need trimmings, but how much handsomer they are when garnished. Some trimmings to try (these same garnishes can also be used to decorate meat, fish, and fowl platters):

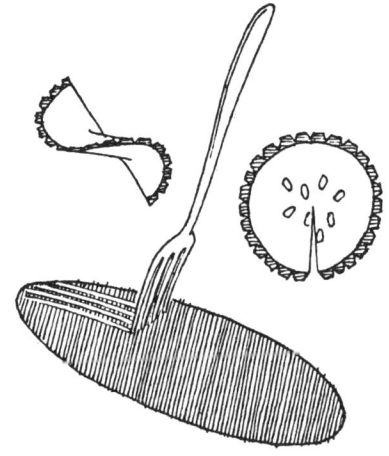

SANDWICHES

Twists or Butterflies
Thin slices of tomato, cucumber, beet, lemon, lime, and orange can all be shaped this way.

Carrot Curls
Bacon curls are rolled the same way. After cutting and rolling carrots, crisp in ice water.

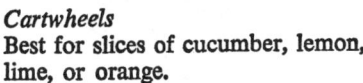

Cartwheels
Best for slices of cucumber, lemon, lime, or orange.

Radish Roses

Celery Frills
Cut as shown above, then crisp in ice water.

Hard-Cooked Egg (Slices, Wedges, and Strips)

Anchovy Rolls and Strips

Onion Rings (Raw and French-Fried)

Herb Sprigs (Chervil, Chives, Dill, Fennel, Cress, Parsley, Tarragon)

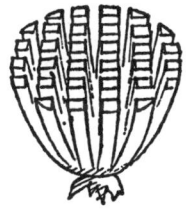

Radish Pompons
Cut, then crisp in ice water.

Pickle Fans

Rind Roses
With knife or vegetable peeler, peel a long, continuous strip of rind, then roll into a rose.

Cutouts (Truffle, Pimiento, Aspic, Cooked Beet or Carrot, Hard-Cooked Egg White work best. Cut out with decorative truffle cutters.)

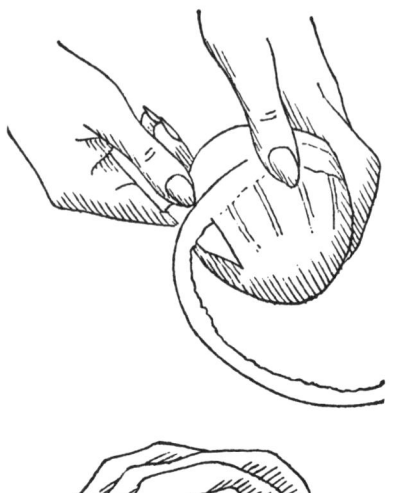

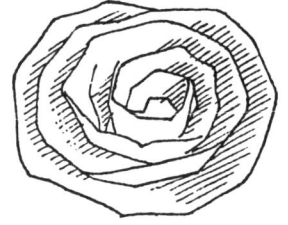

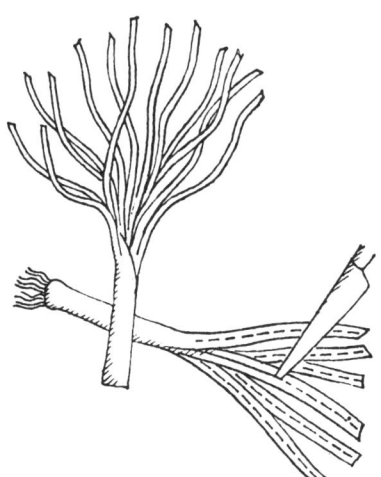

Scallion Ruffles
Cut, then crisp in ice water.

About Toasted Sandwiches

Any filling can be served on toasted bread, but favorites are bacon, lettuce and tomato, cheese, and creamy salad types—tuna salad, egg salad, chicken salad. Toast bread just before making sandwiches and don't stack, lest toast become soggy.

About Grilled Sandwiches

Best sandwiches to grill are those with fairly thick meat or cheese fillings that won't ooze out in the grilling.

How to Grill: Prepare sandwich as directed, then brown lightly 2–3 minutes on a side in 2–3 teaspoons butter or margarine over moderate heat. (*Note:* If you like, sandwich can be dipped in egg—1 egg lightly beaten with ¼ cup milk and a pinch each salt and pepper—then browned as directed. Increase amount of butter slightly if needed.)

About Freezing Sandwiches
(See chapter on freezing.)

Some Sandwiches to Try

What goes into a sandwich can be as exotic or basic as you like because there aren't any hard and fast rules. There are old favorites, of course—and the following list includes them as well as some less familiar combinations. Unless directions specify to the contrary, use any buttered bread or rolls, season fillings to taste with salt and pepper, and serve with a suitable garnish (see About Sandwich Garnishes).

Meat: (*Note:* Sliced hot or cold roast meat sandwiches, Hot Steak Sandwiches, Hamburgers, Sloppy Joes, and Frankfurters are all included elsewhere; see Index for page numbers.)

Basic Meat Salad: Mix any minced cooked meat with enough mayonnaise or salad dressing to make a good spreading consistency. For additional flavor, add any or a combination of the following (tasting as you mix): minced onion, celery, sweet or dill pickles, chives, or parsley; prepared mustard or horseradish; ketchup or chili sauce.

Meat Loaf: Slice any cold meat loaf, not too thin; spread with cold gravy or any of the following: prepared mustard or horseradish, mustard pickle or sweet pickle relish, chili sauce or ketchup.
Optionals: Lettuce and sliced tomato.

Variations: Team meat loaf with any of the following: sautéed sliced onions, pickled red cabbage, fried apple or pineapple rings, applesauce, minced chutney.

Hot Corned Beef or Pastrami: Slice thin and serve on rye bread spread with mustard.

Cold Corned Beef: Slice thin and serve on rye spread with mustard, topped with lettuce, sliced tomato, and mayonnaise. *Variations:* For the lettuce and tomato, substitute any of the following: egg salad, coleslaw, minced Harvard Beets, any sliced cheese or cheese spread.

Ham and Cheese: Sandwich thin slices boiled or baked ham and Swiss, American, or Cheddar cheese between bread spread with mustard and/or mayonnaise. Lettuce optional.

Cold Ham and Egg: Mix equal parts ground cooked ham and minced hard-cooked egg with enough mayonnaise and mustard to bind. Use as a spread. *Or* layer sliced ham and hard-cooked egg between bread spread with mayonnaise and mustard.

Hot Ham and Egg: Sandwich slices of fried ham and a fried egg (cooked until firm) between slices of buttered toast spread with mustard.

B.L.T.: Layer crisp bacon strips, sliced tomato, and lettuce between slices of toast spread with mayonnaise.

Bacon and Beans: Sandwich drained, mashed baked beans between slices of buttered toast with crisp bacon strips and, if you like, thin slices of Bermuda onion.

Poultry: (*Note:* Hot roast chicken or turkey sandwiches are included in the poultry chapter; see Index for page numbers.)

Basic Chicken or Turkey Salad: Follow directions for Basic Meat Salad; also see chapter on salads for specific recipes.

Curried Chicken or Turkey and Nuts: Mix minced or ground cooked chicken or turkey with minced toasted almonds, peanuts, or cashews, curry powder and grated onion to taste, and mayonnaise to bind. Use as a spread.

Chicken or Turkey and Apple: Mix minced or ground cooked chicken or turkey with minced apple, celery, and walnuts and enough mayonnaise to bind; use as a spread.

Chicken or Turkey and Cheese: Mix minced or ground cooked chicken or turkey with grated Swiss or Cheddar cheese, sweet pickle relish to taste, and mayonnaise to bind. Use as a spread.

Chicken or Turkey and Ham: Mix equal parts minced or ground cooked chicken or turkey with minced cooked ham (or tongue, bologna, or other cold cuts), minced scallions or onion to taste, and mayonnaise to bind. Use as a spread.

Sliced Cold Chicken or Turkey: Layer between slices of buttered bread or toast with sliced tomato, lettuce, and mayonnaise. *Optionals:* Any cold cuts or sliced cheese.

Chicken and Avocado: Sandwich slices of cold chicken between slices of bread lavishly spread with Guacamole.

Chopped Chicken Liver: Mince sautéed chicken livers, mix with enough melted butter or mayonnaise to bind, and season, if you like, with a little minced onion. Use as a spread. *Optional:* Mix in a little crisp, crumbled bacon.

Seafood: (*Note:* Hot Crab Burgers, Angels on Horseback, Individual Oyster Loaves, and other specific seafood sandwiches are included in the seafood chapter; see Index for page numbers.)

Basic Seafood Salad: Mix any flaked cooked fish (tuna, salmon, haddock, or other delicate white fish) or minced cooked shellfish (shrimp, lobster, crab, etc.) with enough mayonnaise, Tartar Sauce, or Rémoulade Sauce to bind. *Some Good Additions:* Minced hard-cooked egg; minced onion and celery; minced parsley, tarragon, chervil, or dill; lemon juice; capers; curry powder. (Also see Salads for specific recipes.)

Hot Seafood Sandwiches: Sandwich any fish sticks or cakes, any breaded or batter-fried fish or shellfish between slices of bread or into buns spread with Tartar Sauce or Rémoulade Sauce.

Egg:

Basic Egg Salad: Mix minced hard-cooked eggs with enough mayonnaise or relish-type sandwich spread to bind. *Some Good Additions:* Minced onion and celery; minced dill or sweet pickle; minced parsley, tarragon, chervil, dill, or marjoram; grated Cheddar or Swiss cheese; crisp crumbled bacon; minced ripe or pimiento-stuffed olives; prepared mustard or horseradish. Taste as you mix until flavors seem "just right." (Also see salad chapter for specific recipes.)

Fried Egg: Sandwich a fried egg (cooked until firm) between slices of buttered toast. *Optionals:* Sliced tomato, lettuce, minced scallions, grated Parmesan cheese.

SANDWICHES

Scrambled Egg or Omelet: Sandwich firmly cooked scrambled eggs or any small omelet between buttered toast or buns. *Optionals:* Hollandaise Sauce and/or minced, buttered spinach.

Cheese:

Plain Cheese: Sandwich any thinly sliced cheese between slices of bread spread with butter or mayonnaise and, if you like, mustard. *Optionals:* Lettuce and sliced tomato; any cold cuts.

Grilled Cheese Sandwich: Make a Plain Cheese Sandwich and grill (see How to Grill Sandwiches).

Toasted Cheese Sandwich: (see Cheese Dreams).

Some Spreads to Make with Grated Cheese: Mix coarsely grated Cheddar, American, or Swiss cheese with enough mayonnaise or salad dressing to bind, then add any of the following for flavor: minced pickles, grated onion, crumbled bacon, minced, cooked ham or cold cuts, minced chutney and ground almonds or peanuts. For piquancy, add prepared mustard or horseradish, ketchup or Worcestershire, tasting as you mix.

Cream Cheese and Jelly: Spread any bread with cream cheese, then any jam, jelly, preserves, or marmalade. *Optionals:* Any minced nuts; raisins or minced, pitted dates, prunes, dried figs or apricots.

Cream Cheese and Bacon: Sandwich toast together with cream cheese and crisp crumbled bacon. *Optionals:* Minced ripe or pimiento-stuffed olives; minced, sautéed chicken livers; deviled ham; shrimp or anchovy paste; sliced tomatoes or cucumbers.

Peanut Butter:

Peanut Butter and Jelly: Sandwich buttered bread together with creamy or crunchy peanut butter and any tart jelly, jam, or preserves.

Peanut Butter and Bacon: Sandwich buttered toast together with creamy or crunchy peanut butter and crisp, crumbled bacon. *Optionals:* Lettuce and sliced tomato.

Some Other Things to Team with Peanut Butter: Minced ripe or pimiento-stuffed olives mixed with minced celery and sweet pickle; mashed or sliced ripe bananas; crushed pineapple and flaked coconut; chutney and minced hard-cooked egg or grated Cheddar; seedless raisins and mayonnaise; applesauce and marshmallow cream (children love this one); grated carrot and raisins.

Vegetables:

Lettuce: Sandwich any crisp lettuce leaves between slices of bread spread with mayonnaise or other salad dressing.

Lettuce and Tomato: Layer sliced tomatoes and crisp lettuce leaves between slices of bread spread with mayonnaise or other salad dressing.

Cucumber: Layer thinly sliced cucumbers (sprinkled lightly with vinegar if you like) between buttered slices of bread.

Tomato and Onion: Layer thinly sliced tomatoes and Bermuda onion between slices of bread or toast spread with butter or mayonnaise.

Potato and Pepper: Layer thinly sliced, boiled new potatoes, Bermuda onion, and sweet green or red pepper between slices of bread spread with mayonnaise or relish-type sandwich spread. *Variation:* Substitute Roquefort or Thousand Island Dressing or sour cream for the mayonnaise.

Baked Bean: Spread slices of Boston Brown Bread with cream cheese, mound with cold baked beans, top with a bacon slice, and serve open face.

Mushroom: Sandwich sautéed, sliced mushrooms between slices of bread or toast spread with chive cheese.

Carrot and Raisin: Combine grated carrots and seedless raisins with enough mayonnaise to bind and use as a spread. *Optionals:* A little minced, cooked chicken, turkey, or ham; minced apple.

Club Sandwiches

Whole meals sandwiched between 2 or 3 slices of bread or toast. Junior clubs have similar, though abbreviated, fillings and 2 slices of bread only. Here are some popular combinations with ingredients listed *in order from the bottom up.* Simply build up layers, salting and peppering as you go. When sandwiches are assembled, toothpick layers together at all 4 corners, then halve or quarter diagonally. Cover toothpick ends with olives, cocktail onions, or chunks of pickle.

Simple Club
Buttered slice of white toast
Slice of roast chicken or turkey
Slice of white toast spread with mayonnaise (both sides)
Lettuce leaves
Sliced tomato
Crisp bacon strips
Buttered slice of white toast

Country Club
Slice of cracked wheat toast spread with relish-type sandwich spread
Slice of Swiss cheese
Slice of boiled ham spread with mustard
Buttered slice of white toast (both sides)
Slice of roast chicken or turkey
Thin slice of cranberry jelly
Crisp romaine leaves
Crisp bacon strips
Buttered slice of cracked wheat toast

Pink Lady Club
Slice of white toast spread with tartar sauce
Minced, cooked shrimp or lobster
Buttered (both sides) rye toast trimmed of crusts
Sliced chicken roll or roast chicken
Sliced tomato and watercress sprigs
Slice of white toast spread with mayonnaise

King Club
Slice of buttered rye bread
Sour cream mixed with horseradish
Slice of roast beef
Crumbled French-fried onion rings
Buttered slice of rye bread (both sides)
Slice of Roquefort or blue cheese
Potato salad
Slice of rye bread

Italian Double Decker
Buttered slice of Italian bread
Anchovy fillets
Sliced hard-cooked egg
Sliced pimiento-stuffed olives drizzled with Italian dressing
Buttered slice of Italian bread (both sides)
Slice of mozzarella or provolone cheese
Slice of salami or prosciutto ham
Minced hot red pepper
Slice of Italian bread spread with mayonnaise

SANDWICHES

Deli Double Decker
Slice of pumpernickel spread with pâté, chopped liver, or liverwurst
Slice of Bermuda onion
Sliced dill pickles
Slice of pumpernickel buttered (both sides)
Slice of roast turkey spread with Russian dressing
Slice of pumpernickel

Alligator Triple Decker
Buttered slice of whole wheat toast
Boneless sardines sprinkled with capers
Slice of buttered whole wheat toast (both sides)
Sliced avocado
Sliced tomato spread with Green Goddess Dressing
Slice of whole wheat toast
Tuna salad
Slice of whole wheat toast

Barney's Triple Decker
Buttered slice of rye bread
Slice of corned beef spread with mustard
Drained sauerkraut
Slice of pumpernickel spread with mayonnaise (both sides)
Sliced hard-cooked egg
Minced scallions
Sliced cucumber
Slice of buttered rye bread (both sides)
Slice of pastrami
Shredded lettuce
Slice of pumpernickel spread with mayonnaise

Opera Club
Slice of party rye bread spread with cream cheese
Red caviar
Slice of party rye bread with chive cheese
Slice of smoked salmon or smoked sturgeon
Wilted cucumbers sprinkled with minced fresh dill
Slice of party rye spread with mayonnaise

Heroes or Submarines

Sandwiches Italian-style, whoppers filled to overflowing with sausages, cheeses, peppers—and any of a dozen other things. Begin with split and buttered small Italian loaves or hard rolls, then build up layers, adding anything you fancy. Here are some good combinations, some Italian, some American:

– Slices of prosciutto, provolone cheese, and fried eggplant spread with mustard and chili sauce.
– Slices of Cheddar cheese, dill pickles, Spanish or Italian onion, boiled ham, salami, or liverwurst and tomato, green pepper rings, and shredded lettuce spread with mayonnaise or drizzled with Italian dressing.
– Slices of chicken roll or roast chicken spread with deviled ham; slices of Muenster cheese, cucumbers, and bologna spread with mayonnaise and sprinkled with minced scallions.
– Egg salad, slices of tomato and corned beef.
– Instead of buttering bread or rolls, brush with olive oil and sprinkle with garlic salt; add slices of mozzarella cheese, tomato, and salami, then anchovy fillets and Caponata or hot, sautéed, sliced sweet red peppers. Serve as is or, if you like, wrap in foil and bake 20 minutes at 400° F.

Danish Sandwiches

Lovely to look at and fun to construct. Nearly any combination of bread, meat, filling, and garnish can be used in making these open-face works of art. Here are half a dozen popular combinations, all to be eaten with knife and fork.

– Butter a slice of rye bread and top with a slice of pâté. Mound a few sautéed, sliced mushrooms in the center and lay a crisp bacon strip diagonally across. Place a gherkin fan to one side, tuck a small lettuce leaf underneath, and garnish with a twisted slice of tomato.

– Butter a slice of white bread and top with 2–3 paper thin slices rare roast beef, crumpling slightly instead of laying flat. Add a small lettuce leaf, top with a dollop of Béarnaise, lay a twisted slice of tomato in the center, and add a few shreds of grated horseradish and crumbles of French-fried onions. Garnish with a pickle fan.

– Spread a slice of white or brown bread with unsalted butter or mayonnaise, mound with tiny Danish shrimp, top with cucumber and lemon slices.

– Spread a slice of rye or pumpernickel with butter, mound tissue-thin slices of corned beef on top. Add a twisted slice of tomato, a dill pickle fan, and a few shreds of grated horseradish.

– Spread the bottom half of a soft round bun with butter, top with thin circles of boiled ham, then mound with shrimp or other seafood salad. Garnish with twisted slices of tomato and cucumber, a frill of crinkly lettuce, and slices of hard-cooked egg.

– Spread a slice of pumpernickel with unsalted butter, top with pickled herring, small crisp onion rings, and slices of cherry tomato. Tuck a lettuce leaf to one side and add a sprig of watercress.

PIMIENTO CHEESE SPREAD

Makes about 1¾ cups, enough for 6–8 sandwiches

3 cups coarsely grated sharp Cheddar cheese
2 tablespoons finely grated onion
⅓ cup minced pimiento
½ cup mayonnaise
1 teaspoon prepared spicy brown mustard
1 tablespoon milk or light cream

Mix all ingredients, then beat with a fork until creamy. Cover and let "ripen" in the refrigerator several hours or, better still, overnight. Use as a spread for any bread. About 495 calories for each of 6 sandwiches (2 slices white bread, no butter or mayonnaise), 390 for each of 8 sandwiches.

CREAM CHEESE AND OLIVE SPREAD

Makes about 1 cup, enough for 4 sandwiches

1 (8-ounce) package cream cheese, softened to room temperature
½ cup minced pimiento-stuffed green olives
2 tablespoons milk or light cream
1 teaspoon prepared spicy brown mustard

Beat all ingredients with a fork until creamy, cover, and chill 2–3 hours. Let stand at room temperature 15–20 minutes and use as a spread for any bread. About 355 calories per sandwich (2 slices white bread, no butter or mayonnaise).

☒ CREAM CHEESE AND WATERCRESS SPREAD

Makes about 1½ cups, enough for 4–6 sandwiches

1 (8-ounce) package cream cheese, softened to room temperature

½ cup minced watercress leaves
1 tablespoon grated onion
⅛ teaspoon white pepper

Cream all ingredients together until light and use as a sandwich spread. Especially good for dainty afternoon tea sandwiches. This recipe makes enough filling for 2–2½ dozen tea sandwiches. About 335 calories for each of 4 sandwiches (2 slices bread, no butter or mayonnaise), 265 calories for each of 6 sandwiches, and 35 calories for each tea sandwich.

⊠ EGG AND PARMESAN SANDWICH SPREAD

Makes about 1½ cups, enough for 4–6 sandwiches

4 hard-cooked eggs, peeled and coarsely chopped
¼ cup mayonnaise
¼ cup grated Parmesan cheese
½ teaspoon salt
⅛ teaspoon pepper

Blend all ingredients together and use as a spread for any type of bread. About 370 calories for each of 4 sandwiches (2 slices bread, no butter or mayonnaise), 285 calories for each of 6 sandwiches.

BEEF AND CHEESE SPREAD

Makes about 1 cup, enough for 4 sandwiches

1 (8-ounce) package cream cheese, softened to room temperature
1 (3-ounce) package chipped beef, minced
2 tablespoons minced onion

Mix all ingredients well with a fork and use as a spread for any bread. (*Note:* This spread will be more flavorful if "ripened" in the refrigerator several hours or, better still, overnight.) About 380 calories per sandwich (2 slices bread, no butter or mayonnaise).

⊠ TONGUE AND CHUTNEY SPREAD

Makes about 2 cups, enough for 6–8 sandwiches

1 (1-pound) can tongue, chilled and cut in ¼" cubes
½ cup minced chutney
1 small sweet apple, peeled, cored, and minced

Mix all ingredients and use as a spread for white, whole wheat, or rye bread. About 395 calories for each of 6 sandwiches (2 slices bread, no butter or mayonnaise), 325 calories for each of 8 sandwiches.

⊠ SALMON-CAPER SPREAD

Makes about 1½ cups, enough for 6 sandwiches

1 (1-pound) can salmon, drained
3 tablespoons mayonnaise
2 teaspoons tarragon vinegar
2 teaspoons minced capers
2 tablespoons minced chives

Pick over salmon, discarding any coarse bones and dark skin; mash well. Blend in remaining ingredients and use as a spread for white or brown bread. About 300 calories per sandwich (2 slices bread, no butter or mayonnaise).

WHITSTABLE SANDWICH SPREAD

Whitstable is a little fishing village east of London famous for its tiny shrimp. Women here make lovely tea sandwiches filled with Whitstable shrimp, minced watercress, scallions, and hard-cooked eggs. Makes about 2 cups, enough for 6–8 sandwiches

1 cup cooked, shelled, and deveined shrimp, coarsely chopped
½ cup minced watercress
¼ cup minced scallions (include some tops)
2 hard-cooked eggs, peeled and coarsely chopped
2 tablespoons French dressing

Toss all ingredients together lightly and use as a sandwich spread for white or brown bread. About 205 calories for each of 6 sandwiches (2 slices bread, no butter or mayonnaise), 185 calories for each of 8 sandwiches.

DATE FILLING

Good with moist, sweet breads spread with cream cheese.
Makes 1½ cups, enough for 1½ dozen small sandwiches

1 (8-ounce) package pitted dates, coarsely chopped
½ cup water
¼ cup sugar
2 tablespoons lemon juice
⅓ cup minced pecans, walnuts, or blanched almonds

Simmer dates, water, sugar, and lemon juice, uncovered, about 15 minutes, stirring now and then, until thick. Cool, mix in nuts, and use as a spread for tea sandwiches. About 65 calories per small tea sandwich (2 slices bread, no butter or cream cheese).

VARIATION:

Fig, Apricot, or Prune Filling: Prepare as directed, substituting pitted prunes, dried figs or apricots for the dates. About 65 calories per small tea sandwich (2 slices bread, no butter or cream cheese).

☒ CHEESE DREAMS

Makes 2 servings

4 strips bacon, halved crosswise
4 slices white or whole wheat bread
4 teaspoons butter or margarine
4 sandwich-size slices American cheese
⅛ teaspoon oregano

Preheat broiler. Fry bacon until it begins to curl and turn golden; drain on paper toweling. Toast bread in broiler 4–5″ from heat 3–4 minutes until golden brown; turn and toast 1 minute on second side. Butter lightly toasted sides, top with cheese, a sprinkling of oregano, and bacon. Broil 4–5″ from heat 3–4 minutes until bacon is crisp and cheese melted. Serve piping hot. About 250 calories per serving.

HAWAIIAN CHICKEN SANDWICHES

Makes 6 servings

2 cups minced, cooked chicken meat
⅓ cup minced celery
⅓ cup mayonnaise
½–1 teaspoon salt
¼ teaspoon white pepper
¼ cup finely chopped pecans
6 large round hard rolls
6 pineapple rings, drained well
⅓ cup grated mild Cheddar cheese

Preheat broiler. Mix chicken, celery, mayonnaise, ½ teaspoon salt, pepper, and pecans. Taste for salt and add more if needed. Slice tops off rolls and pull out soft centers—hollows should be large enough to hold about ½ cup chicken mixture. (Save centers for bread crumbs.) Fill rolls with chicken mixture, top with pineapple, and sprinkle with cheese. Broil 3–4″ from heat 2–3 minutes until cheese melts. About 430 calories per serving.

SANDWICHES

DIVAN SANDWICHES

Makes 4 sandwiches

4 slices hot buttered toast
1 (1-pound) can white asparagus
    spears, drained
4 slices cold roast turkey, chicken, or
    ham
½ cup mayonnaise
1 pimiento, minced
1 tablespoon lemon juice
2 egg whites, beaten to soft peaks

Preheat broiler. Lay toast, buttered sides up, on rack in broiler pan; top with asparagus and turkey. Mix mayonnaise, lemon juice, and pimiento; fold in egg whites and spread evenly over turkey, right to edges of toast. Broil 6–7" from heat about 5 minutes until flecked with brown and puffy. Or, if you prefer, bake 3–5 minutes at 450° F. instead of broiling. About 410 calories per sandwich.

WESTERN SANDWICHES

Makes 2 sandwiches

¼ cup minced cooked ham
¼ cup minced yellow onion
¼ cup minced sweet green pepper
1 tablespoon butter or margarine
2 eggs, lightly beaten
2 tablespoons cold water
⅛ teaspoon salt
Pinch pepper
4 slices hot buttered toast, buttered
    bread, or 2 hard rolls, split in half

Stir-fry ham, onion, and green pepper in butter in a heavy 9" skillet over moderate heat 2–3 minutes until onion is limp. Mix eggs, water, salt, and pepper, pour into skillet and fry like a pancake until firm and lightly browned underneath; turn and brown flip side. Halve and sandwich between toast, folding as needed to fit. About 295 calories per sandwich.

POTTED SALMON SANDWICHES

Makes about 1¼ cups filling, enough for 4–6 sandwiches

1 (7¾-ounce) can salmon, drained
1 tablespoon anchovy paste
1 tablespoon lemon juice
Pinch cayenne pepper
⅛ teaspoon cloves
¼ cup butter or margarine, softened
    to room temperature
8–12 slices firm-textured white or
    brown bread
½ medium-size cucumber, peeled
    and sliced paper thin

Pick over salmon, discarding any coarse bones and dark skin; mash with a fork. Add all remaining ingredients except bread and cucumber, mix well to form a smooth paste. Spread *each* slice of bread with salmon, cover half the slices with cucumber, and top with remaining bread. (*Note:* Make these sandwiches shortly before serving—they become soggy on standing.) About 310 calories for each of 4 sandwiches (2 slices bread, no butter or mayonnaise), 245 calories for each of 6 sandwiches.

MONTE CRISTO SANDWICHES

Crisply grilled chicken (or turkey) and cheese sandwiches.
Makes 1 sandwich

4 tablespoons butter or margarine
    (about), softened to room
    temperature
3 slices firm-textured white bread
2 slices cold roast chicken or turkey
2 slices Monterey Jack, Swiss, or
    Cheddar cheese
1 egg, lightly beaten
¼ cup milk
⅛ teaspoon salt

Butter bread, 2 slices on 1 side only,

1 slice on both sides. Lay chicken on a buttered slice, top with doubly buttered slice, cheese, and last slice, buttered side down. Press together lightly; if you like, trim off crusts. Mix egg, milk, and salt, dip in sandwich, coating edges as well as sides. Heat 2 tablespoons butter in a skillet or griddle and brown sandwich over moderately low heat about 2 minutes on each side. About 935 calories per sandwich.

VARIATIONS:

Monte Carlo: Prepare as directed but substitute boiled smoked tongue or ham for the chicken. About 940 calories per sandwich.

Cocktail Monte Cristos: Prepare sandwich as directed, cut in 1" cubes, dip in egg, and fry. Serve with toothpicks as a cocktail snack. About 100 calories each cocktail sandwich.

MOZZARELLA IN CARROZZA (MOZZARELLA IN A CARRIAGE)

Hearty enough for lunch or supper.
Makes 6 servings

Sauce:
½ cup butter or margarine
¼ cup lemon juice
2 tablespoons minced, drained capers
2 tablespoons minced parsley
6 anchovy fillets, finely chopped

Sandwiches:
6 (¼-inch) slices mozzarella cheese
12 slices Italian-style or firm-textured, day-old white bread, trimmed of crusts
⅓ cup milk or evaporated milk
⅓ cup toasted bread crumbs
¾ cup olive or other cooking oil (about)
¼ cup butter or margarine
3 eggs, lightly beaten

Heat all sauce ingredients, uncovered, over low heat 15 minutes. Cover and keep warm at the back of the stove. Sandwich each slice of mozzarella between 2 slices of bread, then trim so edges of bread are even with cheese. Or, using a large round cookie cutter, cut bread and cheese so they are the same size. Dip edges of each sandwich in milk, then in crumbs to coat evenly. Heat oil and butter in a large, heavy skillet over moderately high heat about 1 minute. (*Note:* Oil should be about 1" deep in skillet, so add more if necessary.) Dip sandwiches in beaten eggs to coat well, then fry, a few at a time, in oil about 1 minute on each side until golden brown. Drain on paper toweling. Serve hot, topped with some of the sauce. About 460 calories per serving.

VARIATION:

Prepare as directed, adding a cut-to-fit slice cooked ham to each sandwich. About 530 calories per serving.

☒ HAM AND CHEESE CRESCENTS

A quick, hearty lunch or snack.
Makes 4 servings

1 (8-ounce) package refrigerated dough for crescent rolls
4 teaspoons prepared mild yellow mustard
3 thin sandwich-size slices lean boiled ham, each cut in 3 equal-size pieces
½ cup coarsely grated sharp Cheddar cheese

Preheat oven to 375° F. Spread each triangle of dough with mustard, top with ham, and sprinkle with cheese; roll up jelly-roll fashion and make into crescent shapes following package directions. Arrange on an ungreased baking sheet and bake 15–20

CHEESE TACOS

Makes 6 servings

¼ cup lard or shortening
6 Tortillas (homemade or packaged)
Filling:
6 slices American, Cheddar, or Monterey Jack cheese, coarsely cut up
¼ cup minced yellow onion
1 teaspoon chili powder

Heat lard in a large, heavy skillet over moderate heat and dip in each tortilla 1 or 2 seconds just to soften; spread flat on a baking sheet. Top with cheese and onion and sprinkle with chili powder. Fold in half and fasten with toothpicks. Fry in lard over moderately high heat about 1 minute per side until dappled with brown; drain on paper toweling, and serve. Or, if you prefer, instead of frying, bake uncovered 15 minutes at 400° F. until brown and crisp. About 200 calories per serving.

VARIATIONS:

Chicken Tacos: Omit filling above; fill tortillas with minced, cooked chicken (or pork or beef) moistened with canned enchilada or taco sauce; fold and fry as directed. Serve with sliced radishes, avocado, and shredded lettuce. About 250 calories per serving.

Sausage Tacos: Omit filling above; fill tortillas with minced sautéed chorizo sausage mixed with a little minced onion; fold and fry as directed. About 270 calories per serving.

Bean Tacos: Omit filling above; fill tortillas with Fried or Refried Beans, fold and fry as directed. About 275 calories per serving.

CHAPTER 20

DESSERTS AND DESSERT SAUCES

The category of desserts includes everything from lavish architectural confections to humble bread puddings. There are fruit desserts, puddings hot and cold, ice creams and sherbets, sweet omelets and crepes.

When choosing a dessert, consider the balance of the menu. The richer the main course, the simpler the dessert should be. Cold weather calls for something hot and hearty, summer something cool and light. If the entree contains little protein, add a dessert made with milk, cream, eggs, or cheese. Remember, too, that all desserts don't zoom off the upper limits of the calorie scale. A number included here are well below 100 calories per serving.

Some Ways to Garnish Desserts

Desserts do not demand garnishes, but for a dinner party you may want to glamorize them a bit (opposite).

FRUIT DESSERTS

Once highly seasonal and available primarily where grown, fresh fruits are abundant today around most of the country and much of the calendar. Moreover, such tropical exotics as mangoes, papayas, and passion fruits are beginning to appear in supermarket fruit bins alongside apples and oranges.

Fruits are unusually adaptable; they team well with one another, many can be poached, baked, broiled, or sautéed as well as served *au naturel*. A fruit dessert may be as unpretentious as a pear, crisp and tart, served with a chunk of Cheddar, or as theatrical as Cherries Jubilee, carried flaming into a darkened room. It may be low-calorie (sliced oranges sprinkled with freshly minced mint) or high (strawberry shortcake drifted with whipped cream). Whatever the dessert, the fruit should look

DESSERTS AND DESSERT SAUCES

luscious, fresh, and plump, never fussed over—or left over.

The following directory describes favorite fruits (and a few not so well known), recommends which to cook (and how to cook them), which to serve raw, offers calorie counts and shopping tips.

Some Simple, Basic Ways of Preparing and Serving Fruit

About Peeling, Coring, and Seeding Fruit: Use a stainless-steel knife to prevent fruit from darkening and prepare fruit as you need it, not ahead of time.

Garnish	Appropriate Desserts
Mint, rose geranium, or lemon verbena sprigs	Fruit cups, compotes, ices, sherbets
Lemon or orange wedges, slices or twists, mandarin orange sections	Fruit cups and compotes, lemon or orange puddings, ices, sherbets
Clusters of grapes or berries. (*Note:* for a festive touch, frost by dipping in beaten egg white, then in sugar; let dry thoroughly before using.)	Fruit cups and compotes, steamed fruit puddings
Mini Fruit Kebabs (small pineapple cubes, any firm-ripe grapes, cherries, or berries alternated on toothpicks)	Fruit compotes, steamed fruit puddings, fruit ice cream mousses and bombes
Preserved kumquats	Hot or cold fruit compotes, stewed fruits
Minced crystallized ginger or candied fruits	Vanilla or fruit custards or stirred puddings, fruit sherbets, or ice creams
Flaked or toasted coconut	Fruit cups or compotes, also chocolate, vanilla, or caramel puddings
Minced nuts	Chocolate, vanilla, or caramel puddings
Chocolate curls*	Chocolate, vanilla, caramel, mocha, or coffee puddings or ice creams
Clusters or wreaths of minced or cubed fruit-flavored gelatin	Molded gelatin desserts

Apples, Pears, Figs, and Other Thin, Hard-Skinned Fruits: Use a vegetable peeler or paring knife, paring as thinly as possible. If apples are to be left whole, core with an apple corer, then peel. Otherwise, halve or quarter and cut out core with a paring knife. Pears should be treated the same way; be sure to trim away all gritty flesh surrounding core.

Peaches, Apricots, Nectarines: Plunge fruit in boiling water, let stand about 1 minute, then plunge in cold water and slip off skins. If fruits are to be used whole, do not pit; otherwise, halve and lift pit out.

Citrus Fruits: Cut a thin slice off stem end, then with a paring knife or grapefruit knife cut away rind in an unbroken spiral, taking as much bitter white pith with it as possible.

Grapes: Slit skins lengthwise and "pop" grapes out. To seed, halve and scoop seeds out.

Pineapple: Slice off top and bottom; stand pineapple on counter, and peel straight down from top to bottom. To get the "eyes" out,

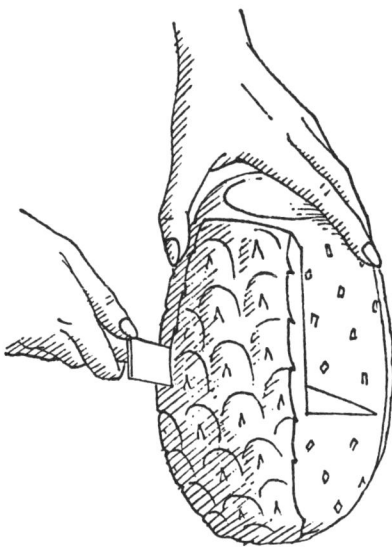

either (1) make spiral, grooved cuts as shown, following line of eyes,

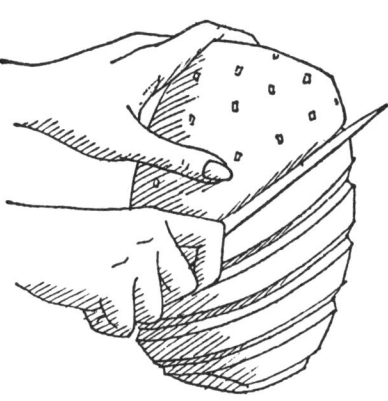

or (2) peel fruit and dig eyes out with the point of a vegetable peeler or knife. *To core:* If pineapple is to be cut in rings, peel and slice, then cut core from each. Otherwise, quarter pineapple lengthwise, then slice off cores—they will be at the point of each quarter.

Avocados: If really ripe, skin can be pulled off with the hands. If firm, halve avocado lengthwise, twist out seed, halve each half lengthwise, and pull or cut skin from each quarter.

Others: Bananas are no problem. Cherries, berries, plums, etc., are usually eaten unpeeled.

About Fruits That Darken: Apples, apricots, avocados, bananas, peaches, nectarines, and some varieties of pear and plum darken after being cut. To keep them bright, dip in lemon or other citrus juice or in an ascorbic acid solution made by mixing ½ teaspoon powdered ascorbic acid (available at drugstores) with ½ cup cold water.

Fruit Cups

These are mixtures of fruit, sometimes fresh, sometimes fresh and frozen or canned, cut in pieces small enough to eat in one bite. For especially pretty fruit cups, team 3–4 fruits of contrasting color, size, shape, and texture: oranges, pineapple, strawberries, and grapes, for example: bananas, tangerines, peaches, and cherries or melon balls; avocado, grapefruit, pears, and plums. For added flavor, mix in a little orange, apple, or pineapple juice, slivered crystallized ginger, grated coconut, minced mint, rose geranium, or lemon verbena. Or, if you prefer, spike with sweet sherry, port or Madeira, or with a fruit liqueur.

Macédoine of Fruit

Named after ancient Macedonia, where fruit desserts were popular, macédoines are mixtures of prettily cut fruits marinated in wine or liqueur. Choose any fresh plump ripe fruits, pare, core, and slice or cube. Layer into a large bowl, sprinkling as you go with superfine sugar, then drizzle with kirsch, Cointreau, Grand Marnier, curaçao, maraschino, other fruit liqueur, or, if you prefer, a fine cognac or brandy. Cover and chill 2–3 hours before serving. Some appealing mixtures:

– Thinly sliced strawberries, pineapple, seedless green grapes with Cointreau.
– Thinly sliced pineapple, pears, and peaches with Grand Marnier or white crème de menthe.
– Sliced oranges with cognac, Grand Marnier, or curaçao.
– Thinly sliced apricots, bananas, and strawberries with kirsch or Cointreau.

Serve macédoines cold, set in a large bowl of crushed ice, or flame.

To Flame: First of all, arrange fruits in a flameproof bowl. After chilling, bring macédoine to room temperature. Warm about ¼ cup brandy, rum, or cognac over low heat about 1 minute, pour over fruit and blaze with a match—stand back, mixture will burst into flames. Serve at once.

Fruit Fools

Wonderfully easy old-fashioned desserts, the kind Grandma served when she had sun-ripened fruits and lots of thick country cream. They are equal parts sweetened fruits and heavy cream, sometimes whipped, sometimes not. Sweet berries make glorious fruit fools; so do soft-ripe peaches and apricots, stewed apples and rhubarb. Fruit purées, if really thick, can be mixed ½ and ½ with whipped cream. A mock but very good fool can be made by combining equal parts fruit and mushy vanilla ice cream. Serve fruit fools unadorned or, for a company touch, scattered with minced pistachios or toasted almonds, slivered preserved ginger, crumbled sugar cookies, gingersnaps, or macaroons.

Fruit Purées

Any soft fruit, raw or stewed, purées well. Force through a fine sieve, a food mill or whirl in an electric blender at high speed (berry purées should be sieved to remove seeds). Serve as is or as a sauce over ice creams or puddings.

Broiled and Sautéed (Fried) Fruits

(See separate recipes that follow.)

Fruit Kebabs

Choose fairly firm but fleshy raw or canned fruits—1″ cubes of apricot, peach, pear, or pineapple, thick banana slices, seedless grapes, sweet cherries—and alternate colorful combinations on short metal skewers. Drizzle with honey or light corn syrup (or Heavy Poaching Syrup) and melted butter. Broil about 4″ from the heat 3–5 minutes, turning and brushing often with additional honey and melted butter. Serve sizzling hot.

FRESH FRUITS — WHEN AND HOW TO USE THEM

Fruit	Description and Season	Buying Tips	Nutritive Value	Best Uses / Preparation Tips
Apples (all-purpose varieties): *The following pie apples: Jonathan, McIntosh, Northern Spy, Stayman, Winesap, Yellow Transparent, York Imperial* (see About Pie Apples, chapter on pies and pastries, for descriptions) *Baldwin:* Round, mottled red; juicy, tart-sweet. SEASON: November-April *Cortland:* Round, red, carmine-striped; tart, snowy flesh that doesn't brown after cutting. SEASON: October-December *Gravenstein:* Round, red-flecked yellow-green; tart, juicy. SEASON: July-September *Grimes Golden:* Round, gold with brown flecks; juicy, sweet, crisp-tender. SEASON: October-February *Wealthy:* Round, bright red; sweet, juicy. SEASON: August-December Apples (cooking varieties): *All pie apples* (see Pies and Pastries) *Rome Beauty:* Plump, round, red, tart; hold shape in cooking. SEASON: November-May Apples (eating varieties): *Delicious (Golden and Red):* Big, long, yellow or red; juicy-sweet. SEASON: September-April	Regardless of type, select firm, fragrant, bruise- and blemish-free apples. Suit variety to use. As a rule, tart crisp apples are best for cooking, sweet, juicy ones are best for eating raw. "Windfalls," often offered as bargains, are perfect for applesauce, apple butter, jams, and jellies.	All apples contain some vitamin A, calcium, and phosphorous, large amounts of potassium. About 70 calories per medium-size apple.	Eating out-of-hand; raw in salads, desserts; general cooking. *Tip:* Unless dipped in lemon or other tart fruit juice, apples will turn brown after being cut open. Baked apples *Tips:* Vegetable peelers speed apple peeling; corers and corer-wedgers handy.

412

Fruit	Selection	Nutrition	Uses
Apricots: Smallish, oval, orange-yellow; flesh smooth, fragrant, sweet. Varietal names unimportant. SEASON: May-September	Choose plump, firm, evenly golden fruit. Allow 1-2 per serving.	High in vitamin A, some C. About 20 calories per apricot.	Eating out-of-hand; raw in desserts, salads; simmered; in pies, puddings. *Tip:* To speed peeling, dip in boiling water.
Avocados: Pear-shaped, smooth green or pebbly black skinned; flesh bland, buttery, nutty. Weigh 1/2-3 pounds each. SEASON: Year round	Choose heavy, medium-size fruit, firm but resilient. Allow 1/4-1/2 avocado per person.	High in B vitamins. Calories vary with maturity, variety; average about 185 per 3½-ounce serving.	Raw in fruit salads, desserts; in ice creams; as container for meat or fish salads. *Tip:* Dip flesh in lemon or other tart juice to prevent darkening. When halving, cut lengthwise.
Bananas: "Seedless," butter-smooth, fragrant tropical fruits. Varietal names unimportant to shopper. SEASON: Year round	Buy firm bananas by the bunch; use as they soften, fleck with brown. Allow 1 banana per person.	Some vitamin A and C; low sodium, low fat; about 85 calories per medium fruit.	Eating out-of-hand; raw in salads, desserts; general cooking. *Tip:* Dip flesh in lemon juice to stop browning.
Berries:			
Blackberries, Dewberries: Plump, glossy, sweet-tart, purple-black; many seeds. *Boysenberries* are large, long Dewberries, *Loganberries* dark red ones. SEASON: Summer	Choose full, lustrous, mold- and bruise-free berries. Allow about 1/4 pound per person.	Some iron, vitamin C. About 60 calories per 1/4 pound portion.	Raw with cream, sugar; in pies, puddings, ice cream, jams, preserves, cordials.
Blueberries: Small, round, dusty blue; tart; tiny seeds. SEASON: Summer	Choose plump, unbroken berries of even size. Allow 1/4 pound per person.	Some iron, vitamin C. About 65 calories per 1/4 pound.	Raw with cream, sugar; in pies, puddings, pancakes, muffins.
Cranberries: Hard, acid, ruby hued. SEASON: September-February	Choose bright, plump berries. Allow 1/4 pound per person.	High in vitamin C. 50 calories per 1/4 pound (unsweetened).	In sauces, relishes, pies, puddings. *Tip:* Be sure to remove wiry stems.
Currants: Small tart red, white or black cousin of gooseberries. SEASON: Summer	Select bright, plump berries with stems attached. Allow 1/4 pound per person.	Some vitamins A, C. About 60 calories per 1/4 pound (unsweetened).	In pies, puddings, jellies, jams, preserves.

FRESH FRUITS – WHEN AND HOW TO USE THEM (continued)

Fruit Description and Season	Buying Tips	Nutritive Value	Best Uses Preparation Tips
Gooseberries: Silver-green berries the size of small grapes; tart. SEASON: Summer	Choose full, evenly sized and colored berries. Allow 1/4 pound per person.	Some vitamins A, C. 45 calories per 1/4 pound (unsweetened).	In pies, puddings, jams. *Tip:* Remove both stem and blossom ends before using.
Lingonberries: Tart red cranberry-like Northern berry. SEASON: Summer	Same as for cranberries. Allow 1/4 pound per person.	Undetermined.	In pancakes, omelets, fruit sauces.
Raspberries: Fragile, cup-shaped, red, black, or golden; juicy-sweet. SEASON: May-December	Choose bright, plump, uncrushed, unmoldy fruit. Allow 1 cup per serving.	Some vitamin C. 70 calories per cup.	Raw with sugar, cream; in pies, puddings, ice cream.
Strawberries: Plump, sweet, juicy, heart-shaped, bright red; gritty external seeds. SEASON: Year round, most plentiful from May-August	Choose clean, solid, well-shaped and colored berries with caps attached; reject leaky boxes. Allow 1 cup per serving.	High in vitamin C. 55 calories per cup.	Raw with sugar, cream; in fruit cups, desserts, pies, puddings, ice cream. *Tip:* Remove stems and caps.
Cherries (sweet): Popular varieties: *Bing* (maroon, heart-shaped), *Chapman* (big, round, purple), *Lambert* (big, round, red-brown), *Royal Ann* (big, heart-shaped, salmon colored), *Tartarian* (heart-shaped, deep purple). SEASON: May-September Cherries (sour): Popular types: *Early Richmond* (dark red, plump, round), *Montmorency* (round, red, juicy), *Morello* (round, black, juicy). SEASON: June-mid-August	Choose plump, bright cherries; firm, if a sweet variety, less so if sour. Allow 1 cup per serving.	Some vitamin A. Calories: about 80 per cup sweet cherries, 60 per cup sour cherries (unsweetened).	In pies, puddings, ice cream, gelatin salads. Sweet cherries also good mixed into fruit desserts. *Tips:* Stem, then scoop out pits using a cherry pitter or point of a vegetable peeler.

Coconuts: Hard-shelled, snowy, nutty-fleshed fruits of a tropical palm. SEASON: Year round	Buy heavy fruit in which milk sloshes. "Eyes" should not be wet or moldy.	Poor. About 400 calories per 1/4 pound.	In pies, cakes, puddings, fruit desserts, candies (see candy chapter for preparation tips).
Crab Apples: Small, hard, wild apples. SEASON: Fall	Choose those as unblemished as possible.	Poor. About 75 calories per 1/4 pound.	For pickling, spicing; in jellies, jams; as garnishes.
Figs: Popular varieties: *Black Mission* (purple, rich, honey-sweet), *Calimyrna* (white, juicy), *Kadota* (green, sweet, fragrant). SEASON: June-October	Choose soft-ripe, plump, unbruised figs; overripe ones smell sour. Allow 3-4 figs per person.	Some vitamin A, minerals. About 30 calories per small fig.	Eating out-of-hand, raw with cream; stewed, in puddings, preserves.
Grapefruit: Type (i.e., pink, seedless, Florida, which has many seeds but is luscious) more important than botanical variety. SEASON: Year round	Choose heavy, firm fruit, not puffy or coarse skinned. Allow 1/2 per person.	High in vitamin C. 55 calories per medium-size 1/2 grapefruit.	Raw as halves, in fruit desserts, salads. *To peel*: Slice off top, cut rind away in spiral. *To section*: Cut down both sides of divider membranes.
Grapes (table varieties): *Red Grapes:* *Cardinal*: Dark red California hybrid of Tokay and Ribier. Few seeds. SEASON: June-August *Catawba*: Oval, maroon, sweet Eastern grape. SEASON: September-November *Delaware*: Small, sweet red Eastern grape. One of the best. SEASON: September-November *Emperor*: Rosy, egg-shaped California grape; bland, some seeds. SEASON: November-May *Red Malaga*: Tender-skinned, firm maroon California grape; delicate. SEASON: July-October	Regardless of type, select plump, clean, unshriveled grapes firmly attached to stems. Bright color, especially with red or black grapes, indicates ripeness. Fully ripe green grapes have an amber cast. Allow 1/4-1/3 pound per person.	All grapes contain some vitamin A and C, calcium and phosphorous. About 75 calories per 1/4 pound, sour grapes somewhat less.	Eating out-of-hand; in table arrangements. Sweet varieties with few seeds (Thompson Seedless) are best for fruit salads, fruit cups, and desserts. Tart strong varieties (Concord) are best for jams and jellies. All grapes make beautiful garnishes.

FRESH FRUITS – WHEN AND HOW TO USE THEM (continued)

Fruit	Description and Season	Buying Tips	Nutritive Value	Best Uses Preparation Tips
	Tokay: Thick-skinned, red California grape; bland; seeds. SEASON: August-October	Regardless of type, select plump, clean, unshriveled grapes firmly attached to stems. Bright color, especially with red or black grapes, indicates ripeness. Fully ripe green grapes have an amber cast. Allow 1/4-1/3 pound per person.	All grapes contain some vitamin A and C, calcium and phosphorous. About 75 calories per 1/4 pound, sour grapes somewhat less.	Eating out-of-hand; in table arrangements. Sweet varieties with few seeds (Thompson Seedless) are best for fruit salads, fruit cups, and desserts. Tart strong varieties (Concord) are best for jams and jellies. All grapes make beautiful garnishes.
Black Grapes:				
	Concord: Tart, blue-black Eastern grape; some seeds. SEASON: September-October			
	Ribier: Large, oblong, jet black, tough-skinned California grape; tart, some seeds. SEASON: July-February			
Green/White Grapes:				
	Almeria: Tough-skinned California grape; not tart, not sweet. SEASON: October-April			
	Muscadine: Large family of Southern grapes, green, russet, or black; includes Scuppernong. Juicy and sweet. SEASON: September-October			
	Niagara: Strong, foxy Eastern grape. SEASON: September-November			
	Thompson Seedless: Luscious, sweet, seedless green California grape. SEASON: June-January			
	White Malaga: Bland California grape being replaced by Thompson Seedless. SEASON: September-November			

Fruit	Selection	Nutrition	Uses
Guavas: Small, oval, thick-fleshed, perfumy tropical fruit. Flesh red or golden; many seeds. SEASON: Year round in Deep South, Florida, California	Choose firm-ripe fruit beginning to soften. Allow 1/4 pound per person.	High in vitamins C, A. About 70 calories per 1/4 pound.	Eating out-of-hand, raw in fruit salads; in jellies and pastes. *Tip:* Peel as thinly as possible.
Kumquats: Tiny, tart, orange citrus fruits eaten skin and all. SEASON: November-February	Buy heavy, unshriveled fruit, 2-3 per person.	High in vitamin A. 70 calories per 1/4 pound.	Eating out-of-hand, raw in desserts; in preserves. *To seed:* Halve lengthwise and scrape out seeds.
Lemons: Sunny, sour citrus fruits. SEASON: Year round	Buy heavy, soft-skinned fruit; green tinges indicate super-sourness.	High in vitamin C, low in calories.	As a flavoring and garnish.
Lichees: Scarlet, cherry-size, leathery shelled Chinese fruits; snowy, juicy, perfumy flesh. Dried lichees, eaten like raisins, are called lichee nuts. SEASON: Summer	Buy unshriveled fruit, 1/3 pound per person.	Some vitamin C. 75 calories per 1/3 pound.	Eating out-of-hand, peeled, raw in fruit desserts. *Tip:* Pit as you would cherries.
Limes: Sour, green citrus fruit. SEASON: Year round	Same as for lemons.	Same as for lemons.	Same as for lemons.
Loquats: Yellow-orange, tart-sweet, downy Chinese plums; many seeds. SEASON: Summer	Buy firm-ripe, bright fruit, 2-3 per person.	Some vitamin A. 25 calories per loquat.	Eating out-of-hand, peeled, raw in fruit salads, dessert. *Tip:* Rub down from skin to remove fuzz before eating.
Mangoes: Large, kidney-shaped, tropical fruits, red-orange and green skinned; flesh orange, peach-like flavor with a hint of pine; one huge seed. SEASON: May-September	Choose fresh, firm fruit. Allow about 1/2 mango per person.	High in vitamins A and C. About 85 calories per 1/2 mango.	Raw in fruit desserts, salads; in pickles, chutney. *To seed:* Halve lengthwise, pry out seed. *Tip:* Peel as thinly as possible.

FRESH FRUITS — WHEN AND HOW TO USE THEM (continued)

Fruit	Description and Season	Buying Tips	Nutritive Value	Best Uses Preparation Tips
Melons:		Regardless of type, select clean, firm, plump melons with clean scars at the stem ends. Ripe cantaloupes will soften slightly at blossom end, and honeydews will yield slightly when pressed. Sniffing the stem or blossom end for fragrance is a test for ripeness. Good ripe watermelons will sound hollow when thumped. Allow 1/2 small melon per person, slices or wedges of larger melons.	Orange-fleshed melons are high in vitamin A, all contain some vitamin C. Calories vary according to type; 1/2 small cantaloupe runs about 60 calories, 1/4 pound watermelon about 40.	All melons can be served more or less the same way — raw, in slices, halves, cubes, or balls; mixed into fruit salads and desserts; puréed into sherbet and ice cream; as garnishes.
Cantaloupe: Plump round melon, buff rind with green netting; sweet, juicy, orange flesh. SEASON: March-December				
Casaba: Large yellow melon, pointed at stem end, ridged rind; sweet, ivory-hued flesh. SEASON: August-November; a Christmas variety available in December				
Crenshaw: Large oval melon with pointed ends, green and yellow rind, sweet salmon flesh. SEASON: July-October				
Honeyball: Round melon, lightly webbed, buff-pink rind; pink, sweet flesh. SEASON: June-November				
Honeydew: Large, round pale green melon with honey-sweet green flesh. SEASON: June-October				
Persian Melon: Like cantaloupe but bigger. SEASON: July-October				
Spanish Melon: Large oblong melon with pointed ends, ridged green skin, pale green, sweet flesh. SEASON: June-October				
Watermelon: Dozens of varieties, some round, some long, some light, some dark green. Newest are midgets with few seeds. SEASON: June-September				

How To Make Melon Baskets

Nectarines: Small, smooth-skinned peaches; richer, sweeter than other types. SEASON: June-September	Buy plump, firm, unblemished, unbruised fruit, 1-2 per person.	High in vitamin A. About 75 calories per nectarine.	Same as for peaches. *Tip:* Dip in citrus juice after cutting to prevent browning.
Oranges (juice types): *Hamlin:* Early Florida-Texas orange, smooth rind; tart, few seeds. SEASON: October-January *Parson Brown:* Heavily seeded Florida orange; coarse flesh; tart. SEASON: October-December *Pineapple:* Midseason Florida orange; tart-sweet, many seeds. SEASON: January-March *Valencia:* Popular variety grown in Florida, Texas, Arizona, and California; deep golden rind, sweet, juicy, few seeds. SEASON: January-November	Regardless of type, oranges should weigh heavy for their size, be plump and firm. Rind color has little to do with quality — many oranges are dyed; those with greenish casts may be fully ripe. Allow 1 orange per person. It takes 2-3 to make 1 cup juice.	High in vitamin C; about 60 calories per medium-size orange, 100-110 calories per cup of juice, depending on sweetness.	Squeezed into juice. Sweeter, less seedy types can be sectioned and mixed into fruit cups, salads, desserts. *To section:* Same as for grapefruit.
Oranges (eating types): *Navel:* Large, thick-skinned, seedless Florida-California orange with navel on blossom end. Sweet, easily peeled and sectioned. SEASON: November-mid-June *Temple:* Popular, large oval Florida orange, thought to be a hybrid of tangerine and orange. Deep orange rind, sweet, rich, and juicy. Many seeds. SEASON: December-April			Eating oranges are best eaten out-of-hand, sectioned or sliced raw into desserts, salads. Temples also juice well.
Oranges (exotic types): *Mandarin:* A variety of tangerine. *Seville or Bigarade:* Sour, bitter Mediterranean oranges, occasionally available in gourmet markets.		How To Make Orange Baskets	In marmalade; for making candied orange rind.

FRESH FRUITS – WHEN AND HOW TO USE THEM (continued)

Fruit	Description and Season	Buying Tips	Nutritive Value	Best Uses / Preparation Tips
Papayas: Tropical melon-like fruit; sweet-musky orange flesh; large cluster of dark seeds in the center; its juice contains an enzyme used in meat tenderizers. SEASON: Year round		Choose yellow fruit, soft but not mushy. Green fruit won't ripen. Sizes: 1-20 pounds. 2-3-pound size best. Allow 1/4 pound per person.	High in vitamins A and C. About 50 calories per 1/4 pound.	Raw in fruit salads, desserts. Also in wedges like melon with lemon or lime. Use seeds as garnishes. *Tip:* Juice can cause skin rash, so wear gloves while peeling and preparing papayas.
Passion fruits (granadillas): Subtropical, purple, egg-shaped, sweet-tart fruits about 3" long; flesh golden. SEASON: Autumn		Select plump, firm-soft, blemish-free fruits, 1-2 per person.	Undetermined. About 50 calories per 1/4 pound.	Eating out-of-hand, peeled; in pies, puddings; also raw in fruit desserts. Juice delicious in punch.
Peaches: Varieties matter less than types: *clingstone* (most are canned commercially) and *freestone* (*Elberta* is a favorite), best for eating, cooking because pits remove easily. Peach flesh may be white, yellow, orange. SEASON: mid-May-October		Choose firm-tender, fragrant, blemish-free fruit showing little green. Allow 1 peach per person.	High in vitamin A, some C. About 35 calories per medium-size peach.	Eating out-of-hand; raw in fruit salads, desserts; in pies, puddings, upside-down cakes, shortcakes. *Tips:* Dip peaches in boiling water and skins will slip off. Dip cut peaches in citrus juice to prevent browning.
Pears (all-purpose varieties): *Anjou:* Big, yellow-russet; crisp, vinous flavor. SEASON: October-May *Bosc:* Large, thin-necked, cinnamon pear; tart. SEASON: October-April		Regardless of type, buy firm-ripe – not hard – pears of good color and shape. Reject unclean, bruised, blemished ones. Allow	Poor for all varieties. About 100 calories per medium-size pear.	Eating out-of-hand; poaching; canning; preserving; in upside-down cakes; sliced raw into fruit salads, cups, and desserts.

Clapp Favorite: Almost round, red-yellow, sweet, smooth, juicy. SEASON: August-November	1 pear per person.	*Tip:* Some types darken after cutting, so dip in citrus juice to be safe. Also trim away any gritty areas surrounding core.
Seckel: Small russet pear; flesh gritty at core; spicy flavor. SEASON: August-December		
Winter Nelis: Large, roundish, russeted dark green pear; buttery, spicy. SEASON: October-May		
Pears (eating varieties):		
Bartlett: Big, bell-shaped, yellow-green pear; smooth, sweet-musky. SEASON: July-mid-October		Eating out-of-hand; raw in fruit cups, desserts, salads. Bartletts also good for canning.
Comice: Large, roundish, chartreuse; fine, juicy-sweet flesh. SEASON: October-March		
Persimmons: Two principal types: *wild American* (small, puckery, good only after first frost) and *Oriental* (plump, vermilion fruits big as apples; flesh soft and sweet). SEASON: October-February	Choose plump, glossy, firm-tender fruit with stems and caps attached. Allow 1 per person.	High in vitamin A, some C. About 80 calories per medium-size Oriental persimmon. Eating out-of-hand (wild varieties only if squishy-ripe); raw in fruit cups, desserts; in puddings, pies. *Tip:* Peel as thinly as possible.
Pineapples: Large prickly tropical fruits, pale to deep yellow; flesh tart and juicy. SEASON: Year round	Buy fresh, clean fruit, heavy for its size with flat "eyes" and strong bouquet. Allow about 1/4 pound per serving.	Some vitamin C; about 60 calories per 1/4 pound serving. Raw in fruit salads, desserts; in pies, puddings, ice creams, upside-down cake. *Tip:* Do not use with gelatin (an enzyme in pineapple keeps it from thickening).

How To Make Pineapple Boats

FRESH FRUITS – WHEN AND HOW TO USE THEM (continued)

Fruit	Description and Season	Buying Tips	Nutritive Value	Best Uses / Preparation Tips
Plums (European types): These are fairly small, tart, blue, green, or black skinned. Popular varieties: *Damson* (small, acid, black), *Green Gage* (green, mild, and sweet), *Prune-Plum* (dark purple, firm, tart). SEASON: Early summer	Regardless of type, buy clean, plump, fresh plums, soft enough to yield when pressed. Reject bruised, sunburned (browned) ones. Allow 1-2 plums per person.	All plums are high in vitamin A and contain some C. Calories vary with sweetness: a medium-size, not too sweet plum averages about 25 calories.	Eating out-of-hand; poaching; in fruit cups, compotes, salads, desserts; in puddings, preserves.
Plums (Japanese types): These are large, lush, scarlet, yellow, or magenta. Popular ones: *Burbank* (vermilion, sweet), *Duarte* (maroon-skinned, scarlet-fleshed, sweet), *Santa Rosa* (red-purple, tart-sweet, juicy). SEASON: August-October				Eating out-of-hand; raw in fruit desserts.
Pomegranates: Curious red Persian fruits, about the size of oranges with fleshy, ruby clusters of kernels, each encasing a dark seed. These are eaten much like grapes, the flesh being sucked from the seeds. SEASON: September-January	Choose medium to large fruits, bright pink or red. Allow about 1/2 fruit per person.	Undetermined. About 40 calories per 1/4 pound.		Eating out-of-hand; pulp good in sherbet, ice cream. *To eat:* Halve lengthwise, remove rind and membrane. Eat ruby kernels, discarding seeds. *To juice:* Halve crosswise and ream as you would an orange. Juice good in punch.

Prickly pears: Fruits of *Opuntia* cactus of the Southwest; flesh may be yellow, red, purple; sweet and watery with little flavor. SEASON: Early autumn	Choose plump, unshriveled fruits about the size of pears with few barbs. Allow 1 per person.	Poor. About 30 calories per medium-size fruit.	Eating out-of-hand; raw in fruit cups and desserts; in jellies. *Tip:* Barbs must be singed off before fruit is peeled.
Pumpkins (see vegetable chapter)			
Quinces: Hard golden fruits; not edible raw. SEASON: October-December	Buy as unblemished fruits as possible.	High in vitamin C. About 50 calories per medium-size fruit.	In jellies, jams, preserves.
Rhubarb: Succulent scarlet stalks; not eaten raw. SEASON: February-August	Choose crisp, straight, bright red stalks. A 1-pound bunch serves 2-4.	Poor. Calories vary according to cooking method.	Stewed; in pies, jams. *Tip:* Roots are poisonous, so trim stalks carefully.
Tangelos: Grapefruit-tangerine hybrids that taste like tart oranges. SEASON: November-March	Buy plump fruit, heavy for its size. Allow 1 per person.	High in vitamin C. About 50 calories per medium-size fruit.	Use as you would oranges or tangerines.
Tangerines: Small, flat, loose-skinned oranges of the mandarin type, easily peeled and sectioned. SEASON: November-May	Choose plump, heavy fruits. Puffiness, flabby skins indicate poor quality. Allow 1 tangerine per person.	High in vitamin C. About 40 calories per medium-size fruit.	Eating out-of-hand; sectioned in fruit desserts and salads.

POACHED (STEWED) FRUITS

Note: For best results, fruits should be firm, not mushy. Quantities are enough for 4 ample servings.

Fruit	Quantity and Preparation	Poaching Syrup	Method	Optional Flavorings (Choose One)
Apples (Rome Beauties are best)	1 quart peeled, cored quarters or eighths OR 4 whole peeled and cored apples	3 cups Thin	Simmer apples, uncovered, in syrup 8-10 minutes until firm-tender. Serve in some syrup.	Cinnamon stick 3-4 cloves Piece crystallized ginger Strip lemon or orange rind Mint, rose geranium sprigs
Apricots, Pears, Oranges	4 peeled whole or halved apricots or pears, 4 peeled whole oranges	2 cups Medium	Simmer, uncovered, in syrup until heated through, about 5 minutes for apricots, 10-15 for pears and oranges. Serve in some syrup.	Cinnamon stick 1 teaspoon curry powder Strip lemon or orange rind Piece crystallized ginger 1" vanilla bean
Cherries	1 quart whole, pitted or unpitted	2 cups Medium	Simmer, uncovered, in syrup 3-5 minutes. Serve in some syrup.	Cinnamon stick 2-3 cloves Strip lemon or orange rind
Berries, Peaches, Plums	1 quart whole berries, 4 whole peeled or halved peaches, 8 whole unpeeled plums	1 cup Heavy	Simmer, uncovered, in syrup until heated through – 2-3 minutes for berries, 5 for plums, peaches about 10. Serve in syrup.	1 cinnamon stick and 1 teaspoon curry powder (for peaches only) 1" vanilla bean 2 lemon or orange slices
Rhubarb	1 quart 1" chunks	1 cup Heavy	Simmer, uncovered, in syrup about 15 minutes until crisp tender. Serve in syrup.	1 teaspoon finely grated orange or lemon rind

VARIATION: Prepare as directed but substitute 1/4-1/3 cup fruit liqueur, rum, brandy, sherry, Porto, or Madeira for 1/4-1/3 cup syrup. (*Note:* Also see separate recipes that follow.)

DESSERTS AND DESSERT SAUCES

POACHING SYRUPS

Type	Sugar	Water	Method	Yield
Thin	1 cup	3 cups	Boil sugar and water uncovered 3-5 minutes until sugar is dissolved.	3 cups
Medium	1 cup	2 cups		2 cups
Heavy	1 cup	1 cup		1 cup

BAKED FRUITS

Fruit	Preparation and Method	Cooking Time and Temperature
Apples (see separate recipes that follow)		
Apricots, pears, peaches	Peel, core, or pit and halve; drizzle with lemon juice, sprinkle with sugar and, if you like, nutmeg and cinnamon. Dot with butter and cover.	15-20 minutes at 425°F. (canned fruit bakes in 10 minutes)
Bananas (see separate recipes that follow)		
Grapefruit, oranges (use Temple or Navel)	Halve grapefruit; peel oranges but leave whole. Sprinkle with sugar or honey and dot with butter. Do not cover.	30-40 minutes at 350°F. Baste occasionally with pan drippings.
Pineapple	Quarter lengthwise, prickly crown and all; do not peel. Cut out core, then score flesh in cubes and loosen. Sprinkle with sugar or honey, dot with butter. Do not cover.	30-40 minutes at 350°F. Baste now and then with pan drippings.
Rhubarb	Cut 2 pounds rhubarb in 1" lengths. Place in a shallow baking dish, sprinkle with 3 tablespoons water and 1½ cups superfine sugar. Also sprinkle lightly with nutmeg and cinnamon, if you like, or drizzle with lemon or orange juice. Cover.	1/2-3/4 hour at 350°F.

About Serving Fruit with Cheese
(See chapter on eggs and cheese.)

About Canned and Frozen Fruits

Nearly all popular fruits—and a number of unusual ones like lichees and papayas—are canned and/or frozen. Some are packed in syrup, others in water for the diet conscious. These are most suitable for compotes and fruit cups, for serving over or under ice creams and puddings. Canned peach, apricot, and pear halves bake and broil well (follow directions for fresh fruits, reducing times slightly).

About Dried Fruits

In the dim days of history, man learned that fruits dried under the sun kept well many months. Today the drying is done mechanically, producing plump, moist, ready-to-use fruits: prunes (dried plums), dates, apricots, raisins (dried grapes). Other commonly dried fruits are apples, currants, peaches, pears, nectarines, and figs.

Dates, raisins, and currants are not cooked except as they are used in breads, cakes, puddings, and pies. Prunes, figs, apricots, and peaches (especially the extra-soft "tenderized" ones) can be used straight from the package or they may be stewed. Dried apples and pears, being a good deal drier, must be cooked.

About Soaking Dried Fruits: Modern techniques have very nearly made soaking a thing of the past. Read and follow label directions carefully. Soaking too long or in too much water makes fruits mushy and flavorless.

About Stewing Dried Fruits:

Apples and Pears: Soak or not as package label directs. Place in a large saucepan, add cold water to cover, set over moderate heat, cover, and simmer about 40 minutes until tender. Sweeten, if you like, adding ¼–⅓ cup sugar per cup of fruit. *For Extra Flavor:* Tuck a couple of lemon slices down into fruit, or a cinnamon stick, or several mint or rose geranium sprigs.

Apricots, Peaches, and Nectarines: Soak or not as directed. Place in a large saucepan, cover with cold water, cover pan, and simmer· 40–45 minutes until tender. Sweeten, if you like, using 3–4 tablespoons sugar per cup of fruit. *For Extra Flavor:* Simmer a few slices lemon, orange, or preserved ginger or a small piece of vanilla bean along with fruit.

Figs: Soak or not as directed. Place in a large saucepan, add cold water to cover, and simmer covered 20–30 minutes until tender. Sweeten, if you like, using about 1 tablespoon sugar or honey per cup of fruit. *For Added Flavor:* Simmer with a few slices lemon or crystallized ginger.

Prunes: Soak or not as label directs. Pit if you like. (*Note:* Pitted prunes are now available.) Place in a large pan, add cold water just to cover, and simmer covered about ¾ hour until tender. (*Note:* "Tenderized" prunes will take only 20 minutes. No need to add sugar.) *For Extra Flavor:* Simmer 2–3 slices lemon studded with cloves along with prunes.

(*Note:* Stewed dried fruits will be plumper, mellower, richer if allowed to stand overnight at room temperature in their cooking liquid before being served.)

To "Plump" Raisins and Dried Currants: If hard and dry, raisins and currants will sink to the bottom of breads and puddings. To prevent this, cover with boiling water and let stand about 5 minutes until they grow plump and soft. Drain well before using. Instead, if you like, soak 5–10 minutes in rum or brandy.

About Cutting and Mincing Dried Fruits: These are sticky and difficult to cut with a knife. Snip with scissors.

⚖ ☒ AMBROSIA

A vitamin-C-rich dessert that everyone likes.
Makes 6 servings

4 large navel oranges, peeled
⅓ cup sifted confectioners' sugar
1 cup finely grated fresh coconut or 1 (3½-ounce) can flaked coconut
¼ cup orange juice

Remove all outer white membrane from oranges and slice thin crosswise. Layer oranges into a serving bowl, sprinkling with sugar, coconut, and orange juice as you go. Cover and chill 2–3 hours. Mix lightly and serve. About 130 calories per serving.

VARIATION:

🔱 Reduce oranges to 2 or 3 and add 2–3 peeled, thinly sliced bananas or 1 small fresh pineapple, peeled, cored, and cut in thin wedges. About 140 calories per serving.

CARIBBEAN COMPOTE

Tropical fruits in port wine.
Makes 8–10 servings

- 1 medium-size pineapple, peeled, cored, and cut in thin wedges
- 3 navel oranges, peeled and sectioned
- 1 small honeydew melon, halved, seeded, peeled, and cut in bite-size chunks
- ⅔ cup superfine sugar
- ⅓ cup tawny port wine
- Juice of 2 limes
- 2 medium-size bananas
- 1 large ripe avocado

Place pineapple, oranges, melon, sugar, and wine in a very large bowl and toss well to mix. Cover and chill 2–3 hours. Place lime juice in a small mixing bowl. Peel bananas and slice about ½" thick, letting slices fall into lime juice; toss lightly. Halve avocado, remove pit, then peel and cut in bite-size cubes, letting these fall into bowl with bananas; toss lightly. Add bananas, avocado, and lime juice to chilled fruits and toss lightly. Re-cover and chill about 30 minutes. Toss lightly and serve in stemmed goblets. About 230 calories for each of 8 servings, 185 calories for each of 10 servings.

HOT FRUIT COMPOTE

A good basic recipe that can be varied a number of ways.
Makes 6–8 servings

- 1 (1-pound) can peach or apricot halves
- 1 (1-pound) can pear halves
- 1 (1-pound) can purple or greengage plums
- 1 cup firmly packed light brown sugar
- ¼ cup lemon juice
- 1 tablespoon finely slivered orange rind
- 2 tablespoons butter or margarine

Preheat oven to 350° F. Drain and measure 1 cup syrup from canned fruits and mix with sugar, lemon juice, and orange rind. Arrange fruits in a large casserole, add sugar mixture, and dot with butter. Bake, uncovered, ½ hour; serve hot with cream or cool and ladle over ice cream or pound cake. About 370 calories for each of 6 servings, 280 calories for each of 8 servings.

VARIATIONS:

Spiced Hot Fruit Compote: Add ½ teaspoon cinnamon and ¼ teaspoon each ginger, nutmeg, and allspice to sugar mixture and proceed as directed. Or omit ginger and substitute ¼ cup ginger marmalade for the lemon juice. About 370 calories for each of 6 servings, 280 calories for each of 8 servings.

Brandied Hot Fruit Compote: Prepare fruit compote as directed, using ½ cup each brandy and syrup drained from fruit; also reduce lemon juice to 2 tablespoons. About 460 calories for each of 6 servings, 350 calories for each of 8 servings.

Curried Hot Fruit Compote: First, heat and stir 1½ teaspoons curry powder in the butter called for in a flameproof casserole 1–2 minutes over moderate heat. Add fruits, substituting 1 (1-pound) can pineapple chunks for the plums, pour in sugar mixture, mix well, and bake as directed. Serve hot with meat or poultry. About 370 calories for each of 6 servings, 280 calories for each of 8 servings.

⚜️ MINTY PINEAPPLE FANS IN COINTREAU

A cooling summer dessert. Low-calorie, too.
Makes 4 servings

1 medium-size ripe pineapple
⅓ cup sugar
8 sprigs mint, washed
⅓ cup Cointreau

Cut off top and stem end of pineapple, then halve, core, and peel. Divide each half lengthwise into 4 wedges, then cut in paper-thin, fan-shaped pieces. Place pineapple fans in a large bowl, add remaining ingredients, and toss well to mix. Cover and marinate in the refrigerator 2–3 hours. Remove mint sprigs and serve. About 160 calories per serving and, if you drain pineapple before serving, about half that.

⚜️ GINGERED HONEYDEW MELON

Makes 4–6 servings

1 medium-size ripe honeydew melon (about 3½–4 pounds)
1½ cups water
½ cup sugar
6 (1-inch) squares crystallized ginger
½ lemon, quartered

Halve melon lengthwise and scoop out seeds; remove rind and cut melon in bite-size cubes; place in a large mixing bowl. Simmer water, uncovered, with sugar and ginger about 30 minutes, stirring occasionally. Off heat, add lemon and cool to lukewarm. Pour syrup and lemon over melon, toss to mix, cover, and chill 3–4 hours. Remove lemon, spoon melon into stemmed goblets, and top with a little of the syrup. About 65 calories for each of 6 servings, 100 for each of 4.

⚜️ ✡ GREEN GRAPES AND SOUR CREAM

One of the easiest elegant desserts.
Makes 4 servings

3 cups seedless green grapes, stemmed, washed, dried, and chilled
½ cup sour cream or unflavored yogurt
¼ cup dark brown sugar

Mix grapes and sour cream, spoon into dessert bowls, sprinkle with sugar, and serve. About 135 calories per serving if made with yogurt.

STRAWBERRIES ROMANOFF

A glamorized version of strawberries and cream.
Makes 4–6 servings

1 quart fresh strawberries, washed, stemmed, and, if large, halved lengthwise
2–3 tablespoons superfine sugar (optional)
⅓ cup orange juice
¼ cup curaçao
¾ cup heavy cream
2 tablespoons confectioners' sugar
¼ teaspoon vanilla

Taste berries and, if tart, sprinkle with sugar. Let stand 10 minutes at room temperature, then toss lightly to mix. Add orange juice and curaçao and toss again; cover and chill several hours, turning berries occasionally. Spoon into a shallow serving dish. Whip cream with sugar and vanilla until soft peaks form, spoon into a pastry bag fitted with a large, fluted tube, and pipe cream over berries, covering completely. About 325 calories for each of 4 servings, 220 calories for each of 6 servings.

⚖ STRAWBERRIES GRAND MARNIER

Dieters won't feel deprived if served this dessert.
Makes 4 servings

1 quart fresh strawberries, washed, stemmed, and halved lengthwise
2–3 tablespoons superfine sugar (optional)
⅓ cup Grand Marnier

Taste berries and, if too tart, sprinkle with sugar. Let stand 10 minutes at room temperature, then toss lightly to mix. Pour Grand Marnier over berries and toss again; cover and chill several hours, turning berries occasionally. Serve topped with some of the Grand Marnier and, if you like, sprigged with mint. About 100 calories per serving (without sugar).

⚖ LICHEES IN PORT WINE

A refreshing and unique summer dessert.
Makes 4–6 servings

2 pounds fresh lichees, peeled, seeded, and halved, or 3 cups halved, drained, canned lichees (both are available in Chinese groceries)
½ cup ruby port wine

Place lichees and port in a small bowl and toss well to mix; cover and chill several hours. Serve in stemmed goblets. About 100 calories for each of 6 servings, 150 for each of 4.

¢ OLD-FASHIONED APPLESAUCE

The kind Grandmother used to make.
Makes 4–6 servings

3 pounds greenings or other tart cooking apples, peeled, cored, and quartered
1 cup sugar
⅔ cup water

Simmer all ingredients uncovered in a large saucepan, stirring frequently, 20–25 minutes until mushy. Serve hot or cold. About 210 calories for each of 4 servings, 140 calories for each of 6 servings.

VARIATION:

¢ **Spicy Applesauce:** Prepare as directed, using light brown sugar instead of granulated, reducing water to ⅔ cup, and adding the juice of ½ lemon, ¼ teaspoon cinnamon, ⅛ teaspoon nutmeg, and 1 tablespoon butter or margarine. About 235 calories for each of 4 servings, 160 calories for each of 6 servings.

GOLDEN SAFFRON APPLES

Makes 4 servings

⅛ teaspoon saffron
½ cup plus 1 tablespoon water
¾ cup sugar
4 large tart cooking apples, peeled, cored, and cut in thick wedges
1 teaspoon lemon juice
1 teaspoon grated orange rind
2 tablespoons toasted, blanched, slivered almonds

Crush saffron and soak in 1 tablespoon water 10 minutes; boil sugar with remaining water, uncovered, stirring occasionally, 4–5 minutes to make a thin syrup. Turn heat to low, strain saffron water into syrup, add apples, lemon juice, and orange rind, cover, and simmer 7–10 minutes until apples are tender but not mushy. Cool apples in their syrup, then chill well. Serve topped with almonds. About 240 calories per serving.

¢ BAKED APPLES

Makes 4 servings

4 large cooking apples (Rome Beauties are best)
⅔ cup sugar
⅔ cup water
1 tablespoon butter or margarine
Pinch cinnamon and/or nutmeg
2–3 drops red food coloring

Preheat oven to 350° F. Core apples, then peel about ⅓ of the way down from the stem end, or, if you prefer, peel entirely. Arrange in an ungreased shallow baking pan. Boil remaining ingredients about 5 minutes to form a clear syrup, pour over apples, and bake uncovered ¾–1 hour, basting often with syrup, until crisp-tender. Serve hot or cold, topped if you like with Custard sauce or whipped cream. About 225 calories per serving (without sauce or whipped cream).

VARIATIONS:

¢ **"Red Hot" Apples:** Core and peel apples as directed; place in pan and in the hollow of each place 2 tablespoons sugar and 1 tablespoon butter or margarine. Prepare syrup as directed but add 1 (1¾-ounce) container red cinnamon candies. Bake as directed, basting often. Fill centers with vanilla ice cream and serve. About 285 calories per serving.

¢ **Brown Sugar Glazed Apples:** Bake apples as directed, remove from oven, baste with syrup, then sprinkle each with 1 tablespoon dark brown sugar mixed with a pinch of cinnamon. Broil 4″ from the heat 1–2 minutes until sugar melts. About 270 calories per serving.

¢ **Baked Stuffed Apples:** Core and peel apples as directed, place in pan and half fill hollows with chopped pitted dates, prunes, or other dried fruit; sprinkle 2 tablespoons sugar into each hollow, finish filling with chopped fruit, and dot with butter or margarine. Omit syrup; instead, pour ½ cup water around apples and bake as directed, but without basting. About 265 calories per serving.

⚔ ¢ ⊠ FRIED APPLE RINGS

Good as dessert or as a garnish for a roast pork platter.
Makes 6 servings

⅓ cup butter or margarine
4 medium-size cooking apples, cored but not peeled and sliced ½″ thick
Unsifted flour

Heat butter in a large, heavy skillet over moderate heat 1 minute. Dredge apples in flour, shake off excess, and sauté, a few at a time, in butter about 10 minutes, turning often until lightly browned. Drain on paper toweling and serve hot. About 155 calories per serving.

VARIATIONS:

⚔ ¢ **Cinnamon Apple Rings:** Fry apple rings as directed, sprinkle with cinnamon sugar, and serve as an accompaniment to meats. Topped with sweetened whipped cream, these make a delicious dessert. About 170 calories per serving (without cream).

⚔ ¢ **Curried Apple Rings:** Prepare as directed but sprinkle with 1–1½ teaspoons curry powder halfway through sautéing. (*Note:* Any of the following sautéed fruits may be curried the same way.) About 155 calories per serving.

Sautéed Pineapple Rings: Pat 6–8 well-drained pineapple rings dry on

DESSERTS AND DESSERT SAUCES

paper toweling, then dredge and sauté as directed about 5–8 minutes. About 175 calories per serving.

⚔ **Sautéed Peaches or Apricots:** Pat 6 fresh or drained canned peach or apricot halves dry on paper toweling, then dredge and sauté 5–6 minutes as directed. About 130 calories per serving.

Sautéed Halved Bananas: Peel 6 underripe bananas and halve lengthwise. Dredge and sauté in butter about 5 minutes. Sprinkle lightly with salt and serve with meat or poultry. About 170 calories per serving.

▨ BAKED BANANAS

Makes 4 servings

4 slightly underripe bananas
¼ cup melted butter or margarine
Sugar, dark brown sugar, or salt

Preheat oven to 350° F. Peel bananas and arrange whole or split lengthwise in a buttered 1-quart *au gratin* dish or shallow casserole; brush well with butter. Bake uncovered 15–20 minutes until soft and pale golden. Sprinkle with sugar and serve as dessert or sprinkle with salt and serve as an accompaniment to roast loin of pork or chicken. About 200 calories per serving.

▨ BANANAS FLAMBÉ

A showy but *easy* dessert you can prepare at the table.
Makes 4 servings

½ cup butter (no substitute)
¾ cup firmly packed light brown sugar
2 tablespoons lemon juice
4 slightly underripe bananas, peeled and halved lengthwise
⅓ cup brandy or light rum

Melt butter in a chafing dish or flameproof casserole (burner-to-table type) over moderately low heat, mix in sugar and lemon juice and heat, stirring until sugar dissolves. Add bananas and simmer, uncovered, about 10 minutes, turning gently with a slotted spatula now and then, to glaze evenly. Warm brandy in a small saucepan, pour over bananas, blaze, and spoon over bananas until flames die. Serve at once. About 440 calories per serving.

VARIATIONS:

Peaches, Pears, or Nectarines Flambé: Substitute 4 large firm peaches, pears, or nectarines for bananas. Peel fruit and leave whole (but core the pears). Proceed as directed. About 420 calories per serving.

Baked Glazed Fruit: Bake any of the above fruits, uncovered, in sugar mixture about ½ hour at 350° F., turning now and then in syrup to glaze. Omit brandy. Recipe too flexible for a meaningful calorie count.

▨ CHERRIES JUBILEE

More culinary pyrotechnics. Bound to impress dinner guests if you bring flaming into a darkened room.
Makes 4–6 servings

1 (1-pound 13-ounce) can pitted Bing cherries
¼ cup sugar
1 tablespoon cornstarch
1 tablespoon lemon juice
1 tablespoon butter (no substitute)
⅓ cup kirsch or brandy

Drain and reserve liquid from cherries. Mix sugar and cornstarch in a saucepan, gradually mix in cherry liquid, and heat, stirring constantly, over moderate heat until boiling. Reduce heat and simmer, uncovered, 3 minutes, stirring now and then. Add lemon juice, butter, and cherries and simmer, uncovered, 2–3 minutes. Meanwhile, warm kirsch in a small saucepan. Transfer cherry mixture to a chafing dish or flameproof serving dish, pour in kirsch, blaze with a match, and carry flaming to the table. Serve as is or spooned over vanilla ice cream. About 255 calories for each of 4 servings (without ice cream), 170 calories for each of 6 servings.

STEWED FRESH FIGS

Makes 6 servings

1 quart firm-ripe figs, peeled
2 cups water
1½ cups sugar
2 tablespoons lemon juice

Place all ingredients in a saucepan and simmer, uncovered, 15–30 minutes until figs are clear and tender; cover and cool in liquid. Serve at room temperature with a little liquid poured over each serving. If you like, pass heavy or light cream. About 225 calories per serving.

VARIATIONS:

Stewed Dried Figs: Substitute 1 pound dried figs for the fresh and simmer as directed until figs are plump and soft. About 355 calories per serving.

Gingered Figs: Simmer 1 (2-inch) piece bruised, peeled gingerroot along with figs; remove before serving. Or use 2 tablespoons minced crystallized ginger and serve along with figs. About 225 calories per serving if made with fresh figs, 355 calories per serving if made with dried figs.

Spiced Figs: Tie 1 stick cinnamon and 4 cloves in cheesecloth and simmer along with figs; remove just before serving. About 225 calories per serving if made with fresh figs, 355 calories per serving if made with dried figs.

Honeyed Figs: Quarter fresh figs and simmer with 1 cup each water and honey and the lemon juice called for. Serve as is or as a sauce over ice cream. About 335 calories per serving (without ice cream).

⊠ ⚖ BROILED GRAPEFRUIT

Good for breakfast or dessert.
Makes 4 servings

2 medium-size grapefruits, halved
4 teaspoons light brown sugar
1 tablespoon melted butter or margarine
4 maraschino cherries

Preheat broiler. Cut around grapefruit sections to loosen, then sprinkle each ½ grapefruit with 1 teaspoon brown sugar and drizzle with ¾ teaspoon melted butter. Broil 5″ from heat 5–7 minutes until golden. Top each ½ grapefruit with a cherry and serve hot. About 100 calories per serving.

VARIATIONS:

⊠ ⚖ **Broiled Sherried Grapefruit:** Just before serving, pour 1 teaspoon sweet sherry over each ½ grapefruit. About 110 calories per serving.

⊠ **Honey-Broiled Grapefruit:** Substitute 1 tablespoon honey or maple syrup for each teaspoon of brown sugar and proceed as directed. About 175 calories per serving.

⊠ ⚖ **Spicy Broiled Grapefruit:** Prepare as directed, adding a pinch cinnamon, nutmeg, or allspice to each ½ grapefruit just before broiling. About 100 calories per serving.

⊠ **Broiled Oranges, Peaches, Apricots, Pears, or Pineapples:** Halved oranges, peaches, and apricots and pineapple rings can all be broiled. Sprinkle cut sides slightly with sugar and butter and broil 3–5 minutes until delicately browned. Recipe too flexible for a meaningful calorie count.

PEARS HÉLÈNE (POIRES HÉLÈNE)

A restaurant classic easily prepared at home.

Makes 4 servings

2 cups water
¾ cup sugar
2 large firm-ripe pears, peeled, halved, and cored
1 teaspoon vanilla
1 pint vanilla ice cream
1 recipe hot Basic Chocolate Sauce

Mix water and sugar in a large skillet (not iron) and heat over moderate heat, stirring until sugar dissolves. Add pears, cover, and simmer 10–12 minutes, turning once in the liquid, until tender but not mushy. Mix in vanilla, then cool pears in liquid. Spoon ice cream into 4 dessert dishes, mounding it slightly. Top each with a pear half, hollow side down. Drizzle some chocolate sauce over pears and pass the rest in a sauceboat. About 605 calories per serving.

BAKED PEARS AU GRATIN

Makes 4 servings

Juice of ½ lemon
3 large firm ripe pears, peeled, cored, and sliced ¼" thick
¼ cup firmly packed light brown sugar
¼ cup light rum
2 tablespoons unsalted butter

Topping:
⅓ cup fine dry bread crumbs
¼ cup sugar
1 tablespoon finely grated Parmesan cheese
3 tablespoons melted unsalted butter

Preheat oven to 400° F. Place lemon juice in a 9" piepan, add pears, and toss lightly to mix; sprinkle with sugar, drizzle with rum, and dot with butter. Mix topping ingredients and sprinkle evenly over pears. Bake, uncovered, 20–25 minutes until lightly browned and bubbly. Serve hot or warm, topped, if you like, with a hearty scoop of vanilla ice cream. About 400 calories per serving (without ice cream).

⊠ PEACH COUPE CHAMPAGNE

Makes 4 servings

2 large ripe peaches
¼ teaspoon lemon juice
1 pint peach, strawberry, or raspberry ice cream
1 pint white or pink champagne, well chilled

Peel peaches, halve, pit, and place in a bowl; sprinkle with lemon juice to prevent darkening. Place a peach half, hollow up, in each of 4 chilled champagne glasses. Mound a generous scoop of ice cream in each peach hollow, fill glasses to the brim with champagne, and serve. About 190 calories per serving.

PEACHES POACHED IN PORT WINE

Makes 4 servings

2 cups dry port wine
1 cup water
½ cup sugar
2 (1-inch × 2-inch) pieces crystallized ginger
1 (2-inch) piece vanilla bean
½ lemon, sliced
4 large ripe peaches, peeled

Boil port, water, sugar, ginger, vanilla bean, and lemon in a large uncovered saucepan 10 minutes; remove lemon. Reduce heat to moderately low, add peaches, and simmer uncovered, turning occasionally, 10–15 minutes. Transfer all to a large bowl, cover, and let stand at room temperature 2–3 hours. Serve peaches topped with some of the cooking liquid. About 270 calories per serving.

PEACH MELBA (PÊCHE MELBA)

Also delicious this way are nectarines and pears.
Makes 6 servings

1 cup water
1 cup sugar
3 large firm-ripe peaches, peeled, halved, and pitted
2 tablespoons lemon juice
1½ pints vanilla ice cream
1 recipe Melba Sauce

Mix water and sugar in a large skillet (not iron) over moderate heat and heat and stir until sugar dissolves; boil, uncovered, 2 minutes. Add peaches and simmer, uncovered, 10–15 minutes, turning once, until tender but not mushy. Mix in lemon juice and cool peaches in syrup. Place scoops of ice cream in individual dessert dishes, top each with a peach half, hollow side down, and add 2–3 tablespoons Melba Sauce. About 360 calories per serving.

PEACH CARDINAL (PÊCHE CARDINAL)

Pears and nectarines are also excellent prepared this way.
Makes 8 servings

1 cup water
1 cup sugar
4 large firm-ripe peaches, peeled, halved, and pitted
1 teaspoon vanilla
2 tablespoons lemon juice
1 quart strawberry ice cream
½ recipe Dessert Cardinal Sauce

Mix water and sugar in a very large skillet (not iron) over moderate heat and stir until sugar dissolves; boil, uncovered, 2 minutes. Add peaches and simmer, uncovered, 10–15 minutes, turning once, until tender but not mushy. Mix in vanilla and lemon juice, and cool peaches in syrup. Place scoops of ice cream in individual dessert dishes, top each with a peach half, hollow side down, and add 2–3 tablespoons Cardinal Sauce. About 245 calories per serving.

BERRY COBBLER

Try this when plump sweet berries are in season.
Makes 6 servings

Filling:
2 quarts fresh berries (any kind), washed and stemmed
6 tablespoons cornstarch
2 cups sugar (about)
2 tablespoons butter or margarine

Topping:
1½ cups sifted flour
2 teaspoons baking powder
¼ cup sugar
½ teaspoon salt
¼ cup butter or margarine
½ cup milk

Preheat oven to 400° F. Place berries in an ungreased 3-quart casserole; mix cornstarch and sugar and stir into berries. Taste and, if too tart, add more sugar. Dot with butter and let stand 20 minutes; stir well. Meanwhile, prepare topping: Sift flour, baking powder, sugar, and salt into a bowl, then cut in butter with a pastry blender until mixture resembles coarse meal. Mix in milk with a fork to form a stiff dough. Drop from a tablespoon on top of berries, spacing evenly. Bake, uncovered, 30 minutes until lightly browned and bubbly. Cool to room temperature before serving. Good topped with whipped cream or vanilla ice cream. About 640 calories per serving (without whipped cream or ice cream).

VARIATION:

Peach Cobbler: Prepare as directed, substituting 6–8 peeled, pitted, thinly sliced ripe peaches for the berries—enough to fill casserole ⅔—and reducing sugar if peaches are very sweet. About 560 calories per serving.

¢ APPLE BROWN BETTY

Always popular. But try the variations, too.

Makes 4–6 servings

1 quart (½-inch) bread cubes or 3 cups soft bread crumbs (made from day-old bread trimmed of crusts)
⅓ cup melted butter or margarine
1 quart thinly sliced, peeled, and cored tart cooking apples
1 cup firmly packed light brown sugar
1 teaspoon cinnamon or ½ teaspoon nutmeg
1 teaspoon finely grated lemon rind
2 tablespoons lemon juice
¼ cup water

Preheat oven to 400° F. Toss bread cubes with butter; set aside. Toss apples with remaining ingredients except water. Beginning and ending with bread cubes, layer bread and apples into a buttered 2-quart casserole. Sprinkle with water, cover, and bake ½ hour. Uncover and bake ½ hour longer until lightly browned. Serve warm with cream, whipped cream, ice cream, or any suitable sauce. About 545 calories for each of 4 servings (without cream or ice cream), 365 calories for each of 6.

VARIATIONS:

Peach or Apricot Brown Betty: Prepare as directed but substitute 2 (1-pound) cans drained sliced peaches or pitted quartered apricots or 3 cups thinly sliced peeled and pitted fresh peaches or apricots for the apples. If you like, substitute ¼ cup syrup drained from canned fruit for the water. About 550 calories for each of 4 servings, 370 calories for each of 6 servings.

Berry-Apple Brown Betty: Prepare as directed, using 2 cups each sliced apples and stemmed blueberries or blackberries. About 545 calories for each of 4 servings, 365 calories for each of 6 servings.

SWISS APPLE CHARLOTTE

Makes 6 servings

6 cups thinly sliced peeled and cored tart cooking apples
1½ cups sugar
1 tablespoon lemon juice
⅛–¼ teaspoon nutmeg
¼ cup butter or margarine
1¾–2 cups fine dry bread crumbs
Heavy cream or sweetened whipped cream (topping)

Preheat oven to 350° F. Mix apples with sugar, lemon juice, and nutmeg to taste and arrange in a buttered 2-quart casserole about 2" deep, scattering small pieces of butter through the apples as you fill the dish. Top with crumbs, cover, and bake 35–45 minutes until apples are tender; uncover and bake 10 minutes longer to brown crumbs lightly. Cool about 5 minutes, then serve with cream. About 380 calories per serving (without cream topping).

▣ QUICK APPLE CRISP

The dessert to serve when time is short.
Makes 4 servings

1 (1-pound 6-ounce) can apple pie filling
1 (5-ounce) stick pastry mix
½ cup firmly packed light brown sugar
¼ teaspoon nutmeg
¼ teaspoon cinnamon

Preheat oven to 375° F. Empty apple pie filling into a greased 8" round layer cake pan. Crumble pastry mix into a bowl, add sugar, nutmeg, and cinnamon, and mix lightly with a fork. Sprinkle pastry mixture evenly over filling and bake, uncovered, 25–30 minutes until golden. Serve hot, topping, if you like, with a dollop of vanilla ice cream or whipped cream. About 460 calories per serving (without ice cream or whipped cream).

VARIATION:

▣ **Quick Peach Crisp:** Prepare as directed, substituting 2 thawed (10-ounce) packages frozen peaches for the apple pie filling and using a 9" pan instead of an 8". About 440 calories per serving (without ice cream or whipped cream).

FRESH PEACH CRISP

The spicy topping makes this Peach Crisp special.
Makes 4–6 servings

4 large peaches, peeled, pitted, and sliced thin
Juice of ½ lemon
¼ cup sugar

Topping:
⅔ cup unsifted flour
1 cup firmly packed light brown sugar
1 teaspoon cinnamon
½ teaspoon ginger
⅛ teaspoon mace
¼ teaspoon salt
½ cup butter or margarine, softened to room temperature

Preheat oven to 350° F. Arrange peaches in an ungreased 9" piepan; sprinkle with lemon juice and sugar. Mix topping ingredients and pat on top of peaches. Bake, uncovered, about 45 minutes until lightly browned and bubbly. (*Note:* It's a good idea to place a piece of aluminum foil under the piepan to catch any drips.) Cool to room temperature and serve as is or topped with whipped cream or vanilla ice cream. About 560 calories for each of 4 servings (without whipped cream or ice cream), 375 calories for each of 6 servings.

VARIATION:

Fresh Apple Crisp: Prepare as directed, substituting 5–6 peeled, cored, and thinly sliced greenings or other tart cooking apples for the peaches. About 630 calories for each of 4 servings, 425 calories for each of 6 servings (without whipped cream or ice cream).

▣ EASY PINEAPPLE CRISP

Couldn't be easier!
Makes 10 servings

1 (1-pound) can crushed pineapple (do not drain)
1 (14-ounce) package butter pecan cake mix
½ cup butter or margarine

Preheat oven to 350° F. Spread pineapple over the bottom of a lightly greased 13"×9"×2" baking pan. Scatter cake mix evenly over pineapple, then dot with butter. Bake, uncovered, about 1 hour until pale golden and slightly crisp. Serve warm with vanilla ice cream or heavy cream. About 425 calories per serving (without ice cream or cream).

SPICY PERSIMMON PUDDING

Makes 12 servings

1⅓ cups sifted flour
1 cup sugar
½ teaspoon baking soda
Pinch salt
½ teaspoon ginger
½ teaspoon cinnamon
½ teaspoon nutmeg
1 cup puréed ripe persimmons
3 eggs, lightly beaten
1 quart milk
½ cup melted butter or margarine

Preheat oven to 300° F. Sift flour with sugar, soda, salt, and spices into a large bowl. Mix persimmons with eggs, milk, and butter and add to dry ingredients, a little at a time, mixing well after each addition. Pour into a greased 13"×9"×2" pan and bake, uncovered, about 1 hour until a silver knife inserted near center comes out clean. Serve warm, topped, if you like, with whipped cream. About 270 calories per serving (without whipped cream).

OLD-FASHIONED STRAW-BERRY SHORTCAKE

Makes 6–8 servings

3 pints strawberries, washed and stemmed
½ cup superfine sugar
1 recipe Extra-Rich Biscuits
Butter
Sweetened whipped cream (optional)

Mash strawberries lightly with a potato masher or fork, mix with sugar, and let stand at room temperature while you make the biscuits. Prepare biscuits as directed and, while still hot, split and butter. Smother with strawberries and, if you like, top with whipped cream. For particularly pretty shortcake, save out 8–10 large perfect berries and use to garnish. About 580 calories for each of 6 servings (without whipped cream), 435 calories for each of 8 servings.

VARIATIONS:

Other Fruit Shortcakes: Prepare as directed but substitute 4–5 cups any prepared sweetened berries or other fruit for the strawberries. Recipe too flexible for a meaningful calorie count.

Southern-Style Shortcake: Serve berries or other fruit on rounds or squares of sponge cake instead of on buttered biscuits. Top with whipped cream. Recipe too flexible for a meaningful calorie count.

PUDDINGS

"Pudding," says Webster, "is a dessert of a soft, spongy or thick creamy consistency." Custard is pudding. So are mousses and Bavarians and creams, dessert soufflés, both hot and cold, gelatin fluffs and sponges. To bring order to the category, puddings are arranged here by type of thickener: Custards and other egg-thickened mixtures, starch puddings, gelatin desserts, etc.

About Custards

When they are good—silky-smooth and tender—they are very, very good, but when they are bad . . . well, the less said the better. What makes custards curdle and weep? Too much heat, invariably, or overcooking (which amounts to the same thing).

Custards cannot be hurried. Like all egg dishes, they must be cooked gently and slowly (read about the techniques of egg cookery in the chapter on eggs and cheese).

Stirred custards should always be cooked in the top of a double boiler *over simmering* water and stirred throughout cooking. Baked custards should bake slowly in moderate or moderately slow ovens and, as an added safeguard against curdling, in a hot water bath.

Should the milk used in custards be scalded? It isn't necessary if the milk is pasteurized; scalding dates to the days of raw milk, which needed heating to destroy microorganisms. Scalding does, however, seem to mellow the flavor of custards, particularly stirred custards, and to shorten cooking time somewhat.

To Test Custards for Doneness:

Stirred Custard: The standard test is to cook until mixture will "coat the back of a metal spoon," not as easy to determine as it sounds because uncooked custard will also leave a film on a spoon. The difference is that cooked custard should leave a thick, translucent, almost jellylike coat about the consistency of gravy. If you suspect that custard is on the verge of curdling, plunge pan into ice water to stop cooking.

Baked Custard: Insert a table knife into custard midway between rim and center (*not* in the middle as cookbooks once instructed). If knife comes out clean, custard is done. Remove at once from water bath and cool. To chill quickly, set custard in ice water—but only if baking dish is one that can take abrupt changes of temperature without breaking.

What to Do About Curdled Custard: If it's baked custard, the best idea is to turn it into a Trifle by mixing with small hunks of cake; if stirred custard, strain out the lumps and serve as a sauce over cake, fruit, or gelatin dessert.

Caution: Keep custards refrigerated; they spoil easily, often without giving a clue.

¢ ⚖ **BAKED CUSTARD**

Makes 10 servings

5 eggs (6 if you plan to bake custard in a single large dish)
⅔ cup sugar
¼ teaspoon salt
1 teaspoon vanilla
1 quart milk, scalded
Nutmeg or mace

Preheat oven to 325° F. Beat eggs lightly with sugar, salt, and vanilla; gradually stir in hot milk. Pour into 10 custard cups or a 2-quart baking dish (buttered if you want to unmold custards). Sprinkle with nutmeg, set in a large shallow pan, and pour in warm water to a depth of 1". Bake, uncovered, about 1 hour until a knife inserted midway between center and rim comes out clean. Remove custards from water bath and cool to room temperature. Chill slightly before serving. About 160 calories per serving. By making custard with skim milk, you can reduce calories to about 125 per serving.

VARIATIONS:

Egg Yolk Custard: Prepare as directed, using 2 egg yolks for each whole egg. About 180 calories per serving.

⚖ **Vanilla Bean Custard:** Prepare as directed, substituting a 2" piece vanilla bean for the extract; heat bean

DESSERTS AND DESSERT SAUCES

in milk as it scalds; remove before mixing milk into eggs. About 160 calories per serving.

¢ **Butterscotch Custard:** Prepare as directed, using light brown sugar and a ½ and ½ mixture of milk and evaporated milk. About 210 calories per serving.

¢ **Chocolate Custard:** Prepare as directed, melting 2 (1-ounce) grated squares unsweetened chocolate in scalding milk. For a richer custard, use a ½ and ½ mixture of milk and evaporated milk. Omit nutmeg. About 190 calories per serving (made with milk, not evaporated milk).

¢ **Crème Caramel:** Mix custard as directed. Spoon about 1 tablespoon caramelized sugar* into each custard cup, add custard, and bake as directed. Chill, then unmold by dipping custards quickly in warm water and inverting. About 210 calories per serving.

STIRRED CUSTARD OR CUSTARD SAUCE

A good basic recipe with nearly a dozen flavor variations.
Makes 4 servings, about 2 cups sauce

2 cups milk, scalded
5 tablespoons sugar
Pinch salt
4 egg yolks, lightly beaten
1 teaspoon vanilla

Heat milk, sugar, and salt in the top of a double boiler over direct, moderate heat, stirring until sugar dissolves. Spoon a little hot mixture into yolks, return to pan, set over *simmering* water, and cook and stir 2–3 minutes until thickened and no raw egg taste remains. Mix in vanilla and serve hot or cool quickly by setting pan in ice water and stirring briskly. Serve as is or over cake, fruit, or pudding. About 200 calories per serving.

VARIATIONS:

¢ ⚖ **Low-Calorie Stirred Custard:** Prepare as directed but use skim milk instead of whole, reduce sugar to ¼ cup, and use 2 lightly beaten eggs instead of all yolks. About 125 calories per ½ cup serving.

¢ **Thin Custard Sauce:** Prepare as directed but increase milk to 2½ cups. About 350 calories per cup. About 22 calories per tablespoon.

¢ **Thick Custard Sauce:** Scald 1½ cups milk; blend remaining ½ cup milk with ¼ cup cornstarch. Mix sugar and salt with hot milk, blend in cornstarch paste and heat and stir over direct, moderate heat until thickened. Mix a little hot sauce into 3 lightly beaten eggs, return to pan, set over simmering water, and heat, stirring constantly, 2–3 minutes until no raw taste of egg remains. Mix in vanilla or, if you prefer, ⅛ teaspoon almond extract. Serve hot, or cool as directed and use in making Trifle or other dessert where a thick custard sauce is called for. About 420 calories per cup, 26 calories per tablespoon.

¢ **Lemon Custard Sauce:** Prepare as directed, substituting ¼ teaspoon lemon extract and 2 teaspoons finely grated lemon rind for vanilla. About 400 calories per cup, 25 calories per tablespoon.

Orange Custard Sauce: Prepare as directed, using 1 cup each orange juice and milk and 1 tablespoon finely grated orange rind instead of vanilla. About 380 calories per cup, 24 calories per tablespoon.

¢ **Chocolate Custard Sauce:** Prepare as directed, blending 1 (1-ounce) coarsely grated square unsweetened chocolate into the scalding milk. About 470 calories per cup, 30 calories per tablespoon.

¢ **Coffee Custard Sauce:** Prepare, using 1 cup each hot strong black coffee and milk; reduce vanilla to ¼ teaspoon. About 320 calories per cup, 20 calories per tablespoon.

¢ **Mocha Custard Sauce:** Prepare Coffee Custard Sauce (above), blending 1 (1-ounce) coarsely grated square unsweetened chocolate into scalding liquid. About 400 calories per cup, 25 calories per tablespoon.

¢ **Maple Custard Sauce:** Prepare as directed, substituting ⅓ cup firmly packed light brown sugar for the granulated and ½ teaspoon maple flavoring for vanilla. About 410 calories per cup, 26 calories per tablespoon.

¢ **Molasses Custard Sauce:** Prepare as directed, using ¼ cup molasses and 2 tablespoons sugar instead of the 5 tablespoons sugar. About 420 calories per cup, 26 calories per tablespoon.

¢ **Caramel Custard Sauce:** Increase sugar to ⅓ cup, caramelize,* then add scalded milk and proceed as directed. About 400 calories per cup, 25 calories per tablespoon.

¢ **Spicy Custard Sauce:** Prepare as directed but reduce vanilla to ¼ teaspoon and add ½ teaspoon cinnamon *or* ¼ teaspoon each cinnamon and nutmeg *or* ¼ teaspoon ginger and a pinch cardamom. About 400 calories per cup, 25 calories per tablespoon.

Coconut Custard Sauce: Prepare as directed but flavor with ¼ teaspoon each vanilla and almond extract; mix in ⅓ cup flaked or toasted coconut. About 460 calories per cup, 29 calories per tablespoon.

Sour Cream Custard Sauce: (Makes about 3 cups): Prepare and cool as directed, then blend in, a little at a time, 1 cup sour cream. About 420 calories per cup, 26 calories per tablespoon.

CRÈME BRÛLÉE

This extra-rich custard with a crackly, broiled-on sugar topping is showy, yet simple to make.
Makes 6 servings

3 cups heavy cream
⅓ cup superfine sugar
½ teaspoon vanilla
6 egg yolks, lightly beaten
¾–1 cup light brown sugar (not firmly packed)

Cook and stir cream, sugar, vanilla, and yolks in the top of a double boiler over simmering water 7–10 minutes until mixture coats a *wooden* spoon. Pour into an ungreased shallow 1½-quart casserole and stir 1–2 minutes. Place wax paper directly on surface of crème, cool to room temperature, then chill 1–2 hours. Preheat broiler. Sprinkle a ¼" layer of brown sugar evenly over crème, set casserole in a shallow bed of crushed ice, and broil 6"–8" from heat about 3 minutes until sugar melts and bubbles (watch so it doesn't burn). Remove from ice, chill 10–15 minutes, then serve, including some of the crackly topping with each portion. About 680 calories per serving.

FLAN

A popular Spanish custard dessert, unusually smooth because it is made with egg yolks only.
Makes 6–8 servings

⅓ cup caramelized sugar*
8 egg yolks
½ cup sugar
¼ teaspoon salt
½ teaspoon vanilla
3 cups milk, scalded

Preheat oven to 325° F. Pour caramelized sugar into a well-buttered 9" layer cake pan. Beat egg yolks lightly with sugar, salt, and vanilla; gradually mix in hot milk. Pour into pan, set in a large, shallow pan, and pour in hot water to a depth of ½". Bake, uncovered, about 1 hour until a knife inserted in the *center* comes out clean. Remove custard from water bath and cool to room temperature. Chill 2–3 hours. Dip pan quickly in very hot water, then invert on serving dish. Cut in wedges and serve. About 270 calories for each of 6 servings, 200 calories for each of 8 servings.

VARIATIONS:

Rum Flan: Prepare as directed, using ½ cup light rum and 2½ cups milk. About 340 calories for each of 6 servings, 255 calories for each of 8 servings.

Pineapple Flan: Prepare as directed, using 2 cups pineapple juice and 1 cup milk; reduce vanilla to ¼ teaspoon and add ¼ teaspoon almond extract. About 270 calories for each 6 servings, 200 calories for each of 8 servings.

FLOATING ISLAND

Makes 4 servings

1 recipe Stirred Custard

Meringue:
2 egg whites
⅛ teaspoon salt
¼ cup sugar

Preheat broiler. Pour custard into 4 custard cups. Beat egg whites with salt until frothy, gradually beat in sugar, a little at a time, and continue to beat until stiff peaks form. Using a serving spoon dipped in cold water, float a large spoonful of meringue on each custard. Set custard cups in a large pan of ice water and broil 4" from heat until tinged with brown. Serve at once. About 255 calories per serving.

VARIATION:

Oeufs à la Neige: Before making custard, prepare meringue as directed. Heat 2 cups milk to simmering in a large skillet (not iron), drop meringue by spoonfuls on milk, and poach 2–3 minutes, turning once with a spoon dipped in hot water. Using a slotted spoon, transfer meringues to a wet plate and cool. Prepare Stirred Custard as directed, using poaching milk. Cool custard. Float poached meringues on custard and chill 2–3 hours before serving. About 255 calories per serving.

TRIFLE OR TIPSY CAKE

Makes 8 servings

1 recipe Easy Sponge Loaf or 1 small sponge or yellow cake
¾ cup strawberry jam
1 (1-pound 14-ounce) can pitted apricots, drained and puréed
1 (11-ounce) can mandarin oranges, drained (optional)
½ cup Marsala or cream sherry
1 recipe Thick Custard Sauce
1 cup heavy cream
¼ cup superfine sugar
¼ teaspoon vanilla
Candied cherries or fruit (garnish)

Split cake into thin layers, spread with jam and about half of the apricot purée, and sandwich back together. Cut in bars about 1"×2" and pack into a 2-quart serving dish; arrange oranges in and around cake if you like. Prick cake well all over and pour Marsala on top; spread with remaining purée and smother with custard sauce. Cover and chill 2 hours. Shortly before serving, whip cream with sugar until stiff; fold in vanilla. Frost on top of Trifle and decorate with candied cherries. About 600 calories per serving.

ZABAGLIONE

Serve this fluffy wine custard hot or cold as a dessert or dessert sauce. Especially good over fresh sliced peaches, strawberries, or homemade Angel Food Cake (a luscious way to use up the yolks). Makes 6 servings

6 egg yolks
⅔ cup superfine sugar
Pinch salt
⅔ cup Marsala wine

Beat egg yolks in top of a double boiler (set on a counter) with a rotary or electric beater until cream colored. Add sugar, a little at a time, beating hard after each addition. Beat in salt and Marsala. Set *over* simmering water (should not touch bottom of pan) and heat and beat constantly with a wire whisk until thick and foamy, about 5–7 minutes. Set double boiler top on counter and continue beating 2–3 minutes. Serve warm or cool further, continuing to beat so mixture does not separate. About 170 calories per serving (without fruit or cake).

¢ ⚖ RENNET CUSTARD

Perfect for those allergic to eggs. Makes 4 servings

2 cups whole or skim milk (fresh milk only)
3 tablespoons sugar
1 teaspoon vanilla
1 rennet tablet (obtainable at most drugstores)
1 tablespoon cold water

Warm milk with sugar until about 110° F. Off heat, mix in vanilla. Crush rennet tablet in the cold water, add to milk and stir 2–3 seconds, no longer. Pour into 4 custard cups and let stand undisturbed 15 minutes. Chill 2 hours and serve. If you like, garnish with preserves, toasted coconut, whipped cream, chopped nuts, or fresh berries. About 115 calories per serving made with whole milk, 80 calories with skim milk (without garnish).

VARIATIONS:

⚖ ¢ **Lemon or Orange Rennet Custard:** Prepare as directed but flavor with ½ teaspoon lemon or orange extract or 1 tablespoon finely grated lemon or orange rind instead of vanilla. Tint yellow or pale orange, if you like, with food coloring. About 115 calories per serving.

Rum-Cream Rennet Custard: Prepare as directed but substitute 1 cup light or heavy cream for 1 cup milk; also substitute 2 tablespoons light rum for the cold water. About 195 calories per serving.

⚖ **Fruit and Rennet Custard:** Arrange 2–3 slices fresh peach, pear, or banana or a few berries in the bottom of each custard cup, then fill with any of the rennet custards. About 130 calories per serving.

VANILLA POTS DE CRÈME

Makes 6–7 servings

6 egg yolks
⅓ cup sugar
1 pint heavy cream
1 (1-inch) piece vanilla bean or 1 teaspoon vanilla

Preheat oven to 325° F. Beat egg yolks with sugar until cream colored. Scald cream with vanilla bean or scald, then add vanilla extract. Remove vanilla bean if used. Gradually stir cream into yolks and strain through a small, fine sieve into 6–7 *pots de crème*. Set pots in a large, shallow pan and pour in warm water to a depth of 1". Bake, uncovered, 25–30 minutes until a knife inserted midway between center and rim comes out clean. Remove pots from water bath, cool, cover, and chill. Serve cold, topped, if you like, with swirls of whipped cream. About 385 calories for each of 6 servings (without whipped cream), 330 calories for each of 7 servings.

VARIATIONS:

Coffee Pots de Crème: Prepare as directed but add 1½ teaspoons instant coffee powder to yolk mixture along with scalded cream and stir until dissolved. If you like, flavor with 1–2 tablespoons coffee liqueur. About 385 calories for each of 6 servings, 330 calories for each of 7 servings.

Brandy (or Rum) Pots de Crème: Prepare as directed but add 3 tablespoons dark rum or brandy to yolk mixture along with scalded cream. About 415 calories for each of 6 servings, 360 calories for each of 7 servings.

CLASSIC POTS DE CRÈME AU CHOCOLAT

A dark chocolate French custard. Very rich!
Makes 4 servings

1 pint heavy cream
1 (1-ounce) square unsweetened chocolate, coarsely grated
6 tablespoons sugar
4 egg yolks, lightly beaten
¼ teaspoon vanilla

Mix cream, chocolate, and sugar in the top of a double boiler, set over simmering water, and heat, beating with a wire whisk, until sugar dissolves and chocolate is blended in. Stir a little hot mixture into egg yolks, then return to pan and cook and stir 2–3 minutes until thickened. Pour mixture into a bowl at once, stir in vanilla, and cool slightly, stirring now and then. Pour into 4 *pots de crème* or custard cups. Cool to room temperature, then chill 2 hours. Serve cold, topped, if you like, with swirls of whipped cream or a few toasted, slivered almonds. About 585 calories per serving (without whipped cream or nuts).

¢ OLD-FASHIONED BREAD AND BUTTER PUDDING

A perfectly delicious way to use up stale bread.
Makes 6–8 servings

4 slices day-old or stale bread
2 tablespoons butter or margarine
½ cup seedless or sultana raisins
¼ teaspoon each cinnamon and nutmeg, mixed together
3 eggs, lightly beaten
⅓ cup sugar
2¼ cups milk

If you like, trim crusts from bread, then butter each slice and quarter. Arrange 2 quartered slices in the bottom of a buttered 1½-quart casserole, sprinkle with half the raisins and half the spice mixture. Top with remaining bread, raisins, and spice mixture. Beat eggs with sugar until cream colored, add milk, and pour over bread. Let stand at room temperature 1 hour. Preheat oven to 350° F. Set casserole in a large, shallow pan and pour in hot water to a depth of 1". Bake, uncovered, about 1 hour until a knife inserted midway between center and rim comes out clean. Cool slightly and serve. If you like, pass cinnamon-sugar to sprinkle on top. About 260 calories for each of 6 servings, 200 calories for each of 8 servings (without cinnamon sugar sprinkled on top).

¢ QUEEN OF PUDDINGS

This lemon-flavored bread pudding is spread with jam, then topped with meringue.
Makes 6 servings

2 cups day-old bread crumbs
1 quart milk, scalded
2 eggs plus 2 egg yolks, lightly beaten
⅓ cup sugar
¼ teaspoon salt
¼ cup melted butter or margarine
Finely grated rind of 1 lemon
½ cup raspberry or strawberry jam or red currant jelly

Meringue:
2 egg whites
¼ cup superfine sugar

Preheat oven to 350° F. Place bread crumbs in a buttered 1½-quart casserole. Slowly mix milk into eggs, then stir in sugar, salt, butter, and lemon rind; pour over bread and let stand ½ hour at room temperature. Mix lightly, set casserole in a shallow pan, pour warm water into pan to a depth of 1", and bake, uncovered, about 1 hour or until a knife inserted midway between center and rim comes out clean. Remove from oven but leave in water bath; spread jam over pudding. Beat egg whites until frothy, slowly beat in sugar, and continue to beat until soft peaks form. Cover jam with meringue; return pudding to oven (same temperature) and bake about 15 minutes until meringue is lightly browned. Cool slightly and serve. About 465 calories per serving.

EXTRA DARK AND RICH CHOCOLATE MOUSSE

Makes 4 servings

4 (1-ounce) squares unsweetened chocolate
⅔ cup sugar
¼ cup heavy cream
⅛ teaspoon salt
2 tablespoons hot water
5 eggs, separated
1 teaspoon vanilla
1 tablespoon cognac or coffee liqueur
Whipped cream (optional topping)

Place chocolate, sugar, cream, and salt in the top of a double boiler, set over simmering water, and heat, stirring occasionally, until chocolate is melted and sugar thoroughly dissolved, about 20 minutes. Add hot water and heat, stirring, until smooth and satiny. Beat in egg yolks, 1 at a time, and remove at once from heat. Beat egg whites to soft peaks; mix about ½ cup whites into chocolate mixture, then lightly fold in the rest, taking care not to break down the volume. Mix in vanilla and cognac, cover, and chill 12 hours before serving. Top, if you like, with fluffs of whipped cream. About 445 calories per serving (without whipped cream).

CHOCOLATE MOUSSE

Not as rich or as difficult to make as Extra Dark and Rich Chocolate Mousse.
Makes 8 servings

6 (1-ounce) squares semisweet chocolate or 1 (6-ounce) package semisweet chocolate bits
2 tablespoons hot water or strong black coffee
5 eggs, separated
1½ teaspoons vanilla
1½ cups heavy cream
Chocolate curls* (optional decoration)

Place chocolate and hot water in the top of a double boiler, set over simmering water, and heat and stir until chocolate is melted. Lightly beat yolks, add a little hot mixture, then stir back into pan and heat and stir over simmering water 1–2 minutes until no raw taste of egg remains. Off heat, mix in vanilla. Beat cream until very thick and glossy (it should almost form soft peaks) and fold into chocolate mixture. Beat egg whites until soft peaks form and fold in, a little at a time, until no flecks of white show. Spoon into a serving dish, cover, and chill at least 12 hours. Scatter with chocolate curls, if you like, just before serving. About 315 calories per serving.

⚖️ **FRUIT WHIP**

Fruit whip will have richer flavor if the dried fruit is stewed the day before and soaked overnight in its stewing liquid. Drain before puréeing.
Makes 6 servings

3 egg whites
¼ teaspoon salt
Pinch cream of tartar
½ cup sugar
1 cup cold puréed stewed prunes, dried apricots, peaches, or figs
⅛ teaspoon cinnamon or nutmeg
1 tablespoon lemon juice

Beat egg whites, salt, and cream of tartar until frothy, gradually beat in sugar, then continue beating until stiff peaks form. Fold remaining ingredients into egg whites, spoon into goblets, and chill well. Serve with Custard Sauce or sweetened whipped cream. About 120 calories per serving (without sauce or whipped cream).

VARIATIONS:

⚖️ **Fruit and Nut Whip:** Prepare as directed, then fold in ¼ cup minced pecans, walnuts, or toasted almonds. About 150 calories per serving.

⚖️ **Baked Fruit Whip:** Prepare as directed but do not chill. Spoon into an ungreased 5-cup soufflé dish or casserole, set in a large, shallow baking pan, pour in hot water to a depth of 1″, and bake uncovered 30–35 minutes at 350° F. until puffy and just firm. Serve warm with cream. About 120 calories per serving (without cream).

About Dessert Soufflés

Dessert soufflés are neither as fragile nor temperamental as reputation would have them. Their biggest shortcoming is that they must be baked at the last minute. They may, however, be partially made ahead of time to avoid last-minute scurrying around. They are prepared exactly like savory soufflés (see About Soufflés in the chapter on eggs and cheese). They can be baked in unbuttered soufflé dishes or straight-sided casseroles or, for glistening brown crusts, in *well-buttered and sugared* ones (butter dish well, spoon in a little granulated sugar, then tilt from one side to the other until evenly coated with sugar; tap out excess).

BASIC HOT DESSERT SOUFFLÉ

From this one basic recipe, you can make seven different soufflés.
Makes 4 servings

2 tablespoons cornstarch
½ cup sugar
1 cup milk
4 egg yolks
2 teaspoons vanilla or the finely grated rind of 1 lemon
4 egg whites
¼ teaspoon cream of tartar

Preheat oven to 350° F. Mix cornstarch and sugar in a heavy saucepan, gradually mix in milk, and heat, stirring constantly over moderate heat, until boiling. Boil and stir 1 minute; mixture will be quite thick. Off heat, beat in egg yolks, 1 at a time; mix in vanilla. Lay a piece of wax paper flat on sauce and cool to room temperature. (*Note:* Soufflé can be made up to this point well ahead of time to avoid last-minute rush.) Beat egg whites with cream of tartar until stiff but not dry, stir about ¼ cup into sauce, then fold in remaining whites. Spoon into a buttered and sugared 6-cup soufflé dish and bake, uncovered, 35–45 minutes until puffy and browned. Serve at once, accompanied, if you like, with Custard Sauce or sweetened whipped cream. About 225 calories per serving (without sauce or whipped cream).

VARIATIONS:

Hot Coffee Soufflé: Prepare as directed, substituting 1 cup cold, very strong black coffee for the milk. About 190 calories for each of 4 servings.

Hot Orange Soufflé: Prepare as directed but use 3 tablespoons cornstarch and substitute 1¼ cups orange juice for the milk; substitute 2 teaspoons finely grated orange rind and 1 teaspoon finely grated lemon rind for the vanilla. About 225 calories per serving.

Hot Chocolate Soufflé: Prepare sauce as directed, increasing sugar to ¾ cup. Before adding yolks, blend in 2 (1-ounce) squares grated unsweetened chocolate or 2 (1-ounce) envelopes no-melt unsweetened chocolate. Proceed as directed, reducing vanilla to 1 teaspoon. About 345 calories per serving.

Hot Nut Soufflé: Prepare sauce as directed but flavor with ½ teaspoon each vanilla and almond extract. Before folding in egg whites, mix in ½ cup minced, toasted, blanched almonds (or minced pecans, walnuts, Brazil nuts, or hazelnuts). Proceed as directed. About 320 calories per serving.

Hot Fruit Soufflé: Prepare sauce as directed but use 3 tablespoons cornstarch, ⅔ cup sugar, ½ cup milk, and 1 cup sieved fruit purée (peach or berry is particularly good). Proceed as directed but bake in a 7-cup soufflé dish. About 300 calories per serving.

Hot Grand Marnier Soufflé: Prepare sauce as directed, using ¾ cup milk and flavoring with the grated rinds of 1 orange and 1 lemon. After adding yolks, beat in ¼–⅓ cup Grand Marnier (or curaçao, Cointreau, or rum). Proceed as directed. About 250 calories per serving.

About Starch-Thickened Puddings

These are really thick sweet sauces, and the techniques of preparing them are the same as for savory starch-thickened sauces (see About Starch Thickeners and Some Tips for Making Better Sauces in the chapter on sauces, gravies, and butters).

The most important points to remember when making starch-thickened pudding are to use a pan heavy enough and a heat low enough to prevent scorching, also to stir constantly as mixture thickens to prevent lumping. Once thickened, starch puddings should mellow several minutes over low heat to remove all

DESSERTS AND DESSERT SAUCES

raw starch flavor. Like custards, they spoil easily and must be kept refrigerated.

¢ BASIC STIRRED VANILLA PUDDING

Makes 4 servings

2 tablespoons cornstarch
½ cup sugar
2 cups milk
1 egg, lightly beaten
1 teaspoon vanilla
1 tablespoon butter or margarine

Mix cornstarch and sugar in a heavy saucepan. Gradually mix in milk and heat, stirring constantly over moderate heat, until mixture boils. Boil and stir 1 minute. Turn heat to very low, mix a little hot sauce into egg, return to pan, and cook and stir 2–3 minutes until no raw taste of egg remains. Do not boil. Off heat, mix in vanilla and butter; cool slightly, pour into serving dishes and serve warm. Or place a circle of wax paper directly on surface of pudding and cool completely; chill and serve cold. If you like decorate with swirls of whipped cream. About 235 calories per serving (without whipped cream).

VARIATIONS:

¢ **Caramel Pudding:** Prepare as directed but substitute ¾ cup firmly packed dark brown sugar for the granulated. If you like, flavor with maple extract instead of vanilla. About 245 calories per serving.

¢ **Chocolate Pudding:** Prepare as directed but increase sugar to ¾ cup and add 1 square coarsely grated unsweetened chocolate along with egg. Reduce vanilla to ½ teaspoon, omit butter, and beat pudding briefly with a rotary beater after removing from heat. About 295 calories per serving.

¢ **Mocha Pudding:** Prepare Chocolate Pudding (above) and add 1 teaspoon instant coffee powder along with chocolate. If you like, serve cold sprinkled with slivered, blanched almonds. About 295 calories per serving (without almonds).

Surprise Fruit Pudding: Slice stale white or yellow cake thin, spread with any jam, cut in small cubes, and place about ¼ cup into each of 6 custard cups. Top with thinly sliced bananas, oranges, or peaches and fill with Vanilla Pudding. Cool and serve. About 340 calories per serving.

¢ ⚖ VANILLA BLANC-MANGE (CORNSTARCH PUDDING)

Slightly thicker than Basic Stirred Vanilla Pudding and not quite so sweet. Try the flavor variations, too.
Makes 8 servings

⅔ cup sugar
6 tablespoons cornstarch
¼ teaspoon salt
1 quart milk
2 teaspoons vanilla

Mix sugar, cornstarch, and salt in the top of a double boiler, then gradually blend in milk. Set over just boiling water and heat, stirring constantly, until thickened. Cook 5–7 minutes, stirring now and then. Remove from heat, add vanilla, and cool 10 minutes, stirring now and then. Pour into a 5-cup mold that has been rinsed in cold water, or into 8 individual molds. Chill until firm, 3–4 hours for large mold, 1–2 hours for small ones. Unmold and serve with any dessert sauce, fresh or stewed fruit. About 165 calories per serving (without sauce or fruit).

VARIATIONS:

Chocolate Blancmange: Prepare as

directed, using 1⅓ cups sugar and 7 tablespoons cornstarch; when thickened, add 3 (1-ounce) squares coarsely grated unsweetened chocolate, stirring until melted, then cook 5 minutes longer. Off heat, beat in 1 teaspoon vanilla. Beat occasionally with a wire whip as mixture cools. Pour into molds and chill as directed. Good with whipped cream. About 290 calories per serving (without whipped cream).

Fruit Blancmange: Prepare as directed, using 2 cups each milk and sieved fruit purée (berries, peaches, pineapple, and banana are good) instead of all milk. Adjust sugar according to sweetness of fruit and tint, if you like, an appropriate color. About 170 calories per serving.

⚖️ **Lemon Blancmange:** Prepare as directed, using 7 tablespoons cornstarch, ½ cup lemon juice, 3½ cups milk, and the finely grated rind of 1 lemon. Tint pale yellow. About 165 calories per serving.

⚖️ **Orange Blancmange:** Prepare as directed, using 7 tablespoons cornstarch, 2 cups each milk and orange juice, and the finely grated rind of 1 orange. Tint orange if you like. About 160 calories per serving.

¢ **TAPIOCA PUDDING**

Tapioca, starch from cassava roots, can be used to thicken soups, sauces, and puddings. It is made into flakes and flour, but more popular are the granules called *quick cooking tapioca* (available plain and in various flavors) and "fisheye" tapioca in medium and large pearl sizes.
Makes 4 servings

⅓ *cup medium or large pearl tapioca*
1 cup cold water
2 cups milk

⅓ *cup sugar*
⅛ *teaspoon salt*
¼ *teaspoon vanilla*

Soak tapioca in cold water at least 3 hours or overnight if you prefer; do not drain. Transfer to a large, heavy saucepan, add remaining ingredients except vanilla, and simmer over lowest heat, stirring now and then, 1 hour. Off heat, mix in vanilla; serve warm or chilled. If you like, top with cream or stewed fruit. About 215 calories per serving (without cream or fruit).

VARIATIONS:

Baked Tapioca Pudding: Prepare pudding as directed, but simmer only ½ hour. Mix in vanilla, pour into a buttered 1-quart casserole, dot with 1 tablespoon butter, and bake, uncovered, 1 hour at 325° F. until lightly browned. About 240 calories per serving.

Chocolate Tapioca Pudding: Prepare as directed but increase sugar to ½ cup and add 1 (1-ounce) square unsweetened chocolate during last half hour of simmering; stir frequently until chocolate melts. About 285 calories per serving.

Butterscotch Tapioca Pudding: Soak tapioca as directed. Warm ¾ cup firmly packed dark brown sugar in 2 tablespoons butter in a large saucepan over moderate heat, stirring frequently, until melted. Mix in tapioca, milk, and salt and proceed as directed. About 235 calories per serving.

¢ **BAKED RICE PUDDING**

Short grain rice, *not* converted, makes the best pudding.
Makes 4–6 servings

⅓ *cup uncooked short grain rice*
1 quart milk

DESSERTS AND DESSERT SAUCES

½ cup sugar
⅛ teaspoon nutmeg or 1 teaspoon vanilla
2–3 tablespoons butter or margarine

Preheat oven to 300° F. Sprinkle rice evenly over the bottom of a buttered 1½-quart casserole. Mix milk and sugar, pour over rice, sprinkle with nutmeg, and dot with butter. Bake, uncovered, 2½ hours, stirring every 15 minutes for the first 1½ hours, until lightly browned. Serve warm, topped, if you like, with cream. About 375 calories for each of 4 servings (without cream), 250 calories for each of 6 servings.

VARIATIONS:

¢ **Raisin Rice Pudding:** Prepare as directed and bake 1½ hours; stir in ⅔–1 cup seedless or sultana raisins and bake 1 hour longer. About 490 calories for each of 4 servings, 325 calories for each of 6 servings.

Creamy Rice Pudding: Prepare pudding as directed and bake 2 hours; mix in ½ cup heavy cream and bake ½ hour longer. About 480 calories for each of 4 servings, 320 calories for each of 6 servings.

¢ **Cold Rice Pudding:** Reduce rice to ¼ cup and proceed as directed. Chill pudding and serve with fresh fruit or whipped cream. About 360 calories for each of 4 servings (without whipped cream or fruit), 240 calories for each of 6 servings.

☒ ¢ **"Quick" Baked Rice Pudding:** Heat milk, sugar, nutmeg, and butter in the top of a double boiler over direct heat until just boiling. Mix in rice, set over boiling water, and cook, stirring now and then, 40 minutes. Transfer to a buttered 1-quart casserole and bake 20 minutes at 350° F. until lightly browned. About 375 calories for each of 4 servings, 250 calories for each of 6 servings.

¢ **Lemon or Orange Rice Pudding:** Prepare as directed but omit nutmeg; mix in 1 tablespoon finely grated lemon rind or 2 tablespoons finely grated orange rind and ½ teaspoon lemon or orange extract. About 375 calories for each of 4 servings, 250 calories for each of 6 servings.

RICE À L'IMPÉRATRICE

An impressive cold rice pudding studded with candied fruit and molded in a decorative mold.
Makes 8 servings

1⅓ cups milk
½ cup uncooked long grain rice
⅓ cup minced mixed candied fruit soaked in 1 tablespoon kirsch
1 cup heavy cream
½ cup sweetened whipped cream (garnish)
Quartered candied cherries and angelica strips (garnish)

Custard:
1 envelope unflavored gelatin
1 cup milk
½ cup sugar
4 egg yolks, lightly beaten
1 teaspoon vanilla

Heat milk to boiling in a small, heavy saucepan, stir in rice, cover, and simmer over lowest heat, stirring now and then, 20–30 minutes until rice is just tender. Fluff rice with a fork and cool. Meanwhile, make the custard: Sprinkle gelatin over milk, let stand 2–3 minutes, mix, and pour into the top of a double boiler. Add sugar, set over simmering water, and heat and stir until steaming. Mix a little milk into egg yolks, return to pan, and cook and stir 2–3 minutes until custard will coat the back of a metal spoon. Remove from heat, mix in vanilla, cool slightly, then stir into rice along with candied fruit; cool to room temperature.

Beat cream until soft peaks form, fold into rice, spoon into an unbuttered 1½-quart decorative mold, cover, and chill several hours or overnight. Unmold and decorate with fluffs of whipped cream, cherries, and angelica. About 320 calories per serving.

VARIATION:

Pears or Peaches à l'Impératrice: Unmold Rice à l'Impératrice in the center of a large, shallow crystal bowl; surround with cold poached or canned pear or peach halves, hollows filled with red currant jelly. Sprig with mint. About 420 calories per serving.

¢ **INDIAN PUDDING**

This New England corn meal pudding is traditionally very soft and may even "weep" (separate) slightly when served. No matter, it's spicy and good.

Makes 6 servings

¼ *cup corn meal*
1 *quart milk*
¾ *cup molasses*
⅓ *cup firmly packed light brown sugar*
¼ *cup butter or margarine*
¼ *teaspoon salt*
½ *teaspoon cinnamon*
½ *teaspoon ginger*
½ *cup seedless raisins (optional)*

Preheat oven to 325° F. Mix corn meal and 1 cup milk. Heat 2 cups milk in the top of a double boiler over simmering water until steaming. Mix in corn meal mixture and cook 15–20 minutes, stirring now and then. Stir in molasses and sugar and cook 2–3 minutes longer. Off heat, mix in butter, salt, spices, and, if you like, raisins. Spoon into a buttered 1-quart casserole and pour remaining milk evenly over top.

Bake, uncovered, about 1½ hours until a table knife inserted midway between center and rim comes out clean. Serve warm with whipped cream or ice cream dusted with nutmeg. About 375 calories per serving (without whipped cream or ice cream).

For a Firmer Pudding: Prepare corn meal mixture as directed; instead of pouring final cup milk over pudding, mix with 2 lightly beaten eggs and blend into pudding. Bake 2 hours at 300° F. just until firm. About 405 calories per serving.

VARIATION:

Apple Indian Pudding: When preparing corn meal mixture, increase meal to ⅓ cup. Toss 1½–2 cups thinly sliced, peeled, and cored tart cooking apples with ⅓ cup sugar, scatter over the bottom of a buttered 2-quart casserole, top with pudding mixture, and bake as directed. About 440 calories per serving.

About Steamed Puddings

These rich, moist puddings aren't often made today. Too troublesome, perhaps. There's no denying they require time and effort. But served on a frosty day, they add such a warm, nostalgic touch, making the bother seem supremely worthwhile.

About Pudding Molds: Unless you make steamed puddings often, you probably won't want to buy proper pudding molds. You can get by using metal cooking bowls, coffee tins, ice-cream bombe molds (if you have them), even custard cups.

About Preparing and Filling Pudding Molds: Butter molds well, then pour in enough pudding batter to fill mold two-thirds—no more;

DESSERTS AND DESSERT SAUCES

steamed puddings must have plenty of room to expand. Cover mold snugly, either with a lid or a well-greased double thickness of aluminum foil tied securely in place.

About Steaming Puddings: Any deep, heavy kettle fitted with a rack can be used for steaming puddings (if the kettle has no rack of its own, use a cake rack). Stand molds upright on rack, pour in enough boiling water to reach halfway up the sides of the molds. Tightly cover kettle and adjust burner so water simmers or boils gently. Check kettle occasionally, adding boiling water as needed to keep molds half submerged throughout steaming. (*Note:* Puddings may be steamed in pressure cookers; follow manufacturer's instructions carefully.)

About Unmolding Steamed Puddings: Remove puddings from steamer and uncover. Let stand a few minutes, then loosen, if necessary with a thin spatula and invert on serving plate. Or, if you prefer, before uncovering mold, dip it quickly in cold water to loosen pudding. Uncover and turn out. If you like a slightly drier pudding, warm 3–5 minutes in a 350° F. oven after unmolding.

To Serve Steamed Puddings: Cut in wedges as you would cake and top with Hard Sauce or other sauce of compatible flavor.

BASIC STEAMED LEMON PUDDING

To avoid a cracked pudding, uncover and let stand 2–3 minutes so that steam can escape, then unmold. There are, by the way, more than a half-dozen different ways to vary the flavor of this basic recipe. Makes 8 servings

1½ cups sifted flour
2 teaspoons baking powder
¼ teaspoon salt
½ cup butter, margarine, or shortening
½ cup sugar
2 eggs
Finely grated rind of 1 lemon
2 tablespoons lemon juice
½ cup milk

Sift flour with baking powder and salt and set aside. Cream butter and sugar until light, add eggs, one at a time, beating well after each addition. Beat in lemon rind and juice. Add flour alternately with milk, beginning and ending with flour; beat well after each addition. Spoon into a well-greased 1½-quart mold or metal bowl, cover with a greased double thickness of foil, and tie around with string. Set on a rack in a large kettle and pour in enough boiling water to come halfway up mold. Cover and steam 1–1½ hours or until metal skewer inserted in center of pudding comes out clean. Keep water simmering throughout, replenishing as needed with boiling water. Uncover mold and let stand 2–3 minutes, then invert on serving dish. Cut in wedges and serve warm with hot Lemon Sauce or Custard Sauce. Leftover pudding may be wrapped in foil and reheated in a 350° F. oven for 20–30 minutes. About 255 calories per serving (without sauce).

VARIATIONS:

Steamed Orange Pudding: Substitute the grated rind of 1 large orange for the lemon; omit lemon juice and use ¼ cup each orange juice and milk instead of all milk. Otherwise, prepare as directed. About 255 calories per serving.

Steamed Chocolate Pudding: Increase sugar to ¾ cup, beat in 3

(1-ounce) envelopes no-melt unsweetened chocolate after eggs and substitute 1 teaspoon vanilla for lemon rind and juice. About 335 calories per serving.

Steamed Ginger Pudding: Substitute ½ cup firmly packed light brown sugar for the granulated; omit lemon rind and juice and add 1½ teaspoons ginger. About 260 calories per serving.

Steamed College Pudding: Prepare batter and mix in ⅓ cup each sultana raisins and dried currants and ¼ cup minced mixed candied fruit and 1 teaspoon allspice. About 300 calories per serving.

Jam or Marmalade Topped Steamed Pudding: Spoon ¼ cup strawberry, raspberry, or black currant jam or orange marmalade into bottom of pudding mold, then add batter and steam as directed. Unmold and top with an additional ⅓ cup hot jam or marmalade. Serve with hot Custard Sauce. About 335 calories per serving (without sauce).

Steamed Date Pudding: Prepare batter as directed and mix in ½ pound finely cut-up pitted dates. About 315 calories per serving.

Individual Steamed Puddings: Prepare any batter as directed and fill greased custard cups two-thirds full, cover with foil, and tie as directed; steam ½ hour.

PLUM PUDDING

The English plum pudding served at Christmas doesn't contain plums; it resembles steamed fruit cake, is made weeks ahead and mellowed in a cool, dry place. If you have no cool spot (about 50° F.), freeze the pudding or make only 1 week ahead and refrigerate. The English hide silver charms or coins in the pudding batter—and lucky the child who finds one.
Makes 12 servings

1½ cups seedless raisins
½ cup dried currants
½ cup finely chopped mixed candied fruit
1 tart apple, peeled, cored, and grated fine
Finely grated rind of 1 lemon
Finely grated rind of 1 orange
¾ cup ale or orange juice or ½ cup ale and ¼ cup brandy or rum
1 cup sifted flour
1 teaspoon baking powder
½ teaspoon salt
1 teaspoon cinnamon
½ teaspoon allspice
¼ teaspoon nutmeg
1 cup fine dry bread crumbs
1 cup firmly packed dark brown sugar
⅓ cup molasses
1 cup finely ground suet
3 eggs, lightly beaten
½ cup minced, toasted, blanched almonds

Mix fruits, rinds, and ale and let stand ½ hour. Sift flour with baking powder, salt and spices, stir in remaining ingredients, add fruit mixture, and mix well. Spoon into 2 well-buttered 1-quart molds or metal bowls, cover with double thicknesses of foil, and tie firmly in place. Set on a rack in a large kettle, add boiling water to come halfway up puddings, cover, and steam 4 hours; keep water simmering slowly and add more boiling water as needed to maintain level. Cool puddings on racks with foil still intact, then store in a cool place, freeze, or refrigerate. To reheat, steam 1 hour exactly the same way you cooked them. Unmold puddings on a hot platter and decorate with holly. If you like, pour ¼ cup warm brandy over each pudding and blaze. Cut in wedges and serve with Hard Sauce. Also good with Brandy or Rum Sauce or Stirred Custard. About 440 calories per serving (without sauce).

ABOUT GELATIN DESSERTS

The beauty of gelatins is that they are both versatile *and* reliable—easy enough for the most inexperienced beginner. A gelatin dessert may be nothing fancier than fruit gelatin, prepared by package directions, chopped or diced, perhaps, then topped with sliced fruit or whipped cream. Or it may be a sparkling mold, jeweled with berries or chunks of fruit, a cool custard-smooth cream, a fluffy sponge, or silky mousse.

Some Basic Ways to Use Gelatins in Dessert

(Also see About Gelatins in the chapter on salads.)

To Whip Gelatin: Dissolve fruit-flavored gelatin as label directs, then cool and chill until just beginning to thicken. Beat hard with a rotary or electric beater until light and fluffy and the consistency of whipped cream. Use in preparing gelatin sponges and mousses. (*Note:* Any gelatin mixture of normal consistency *not* containing solid bits of food may be whipped.)

To Mold Fruits (Makes 4–6 servings): The standard (3-ounce) package of fruit-flavored gelatin will set 2 cups liquid and 2 cups prepared, cut-up, drained fruits. For variety and extra flavor, dissolve gelatin in hot ginger ale or fruit juice instead of water, or a ½ and ½ mixture. Cool, then chill until syrupy before adding fruits so that they won't sink to the bottom or rise to the top. Mix or match fruits and gelatin flavors, putting together any combination that appeals. *Caution: Do not try to congeal fresh or frozen pineapple or pineapple juice. They destroy gelatin's jelling power.*

To Make Your Own Fruit Gelatin (Makes 4 servings): Mix 1 envelope unflavored gelatin and ⅓–½ cup sugar in a heavy saucepan; gradually mix in ½ cup fruit juice and heat and stir over moderately low heat until gelatin and sugar dissolve. Off heat, mix in 1 cup additional fruit juice, cool, chill until syrupy, then fold in 1½ cups prepared berries or cut-up fruit. Spoon into mold and chill until firm.

To Mold Fruit Purée (Makes 4 servings): Mix 1 envelope unflavored gelatin and ⅓ cup cold fruit juice in a small saucepan and heat and stir over moderately low heat until dissolved. Cool slightly, mix in 2 cups fruit purée sweetened to taste and tint an appropriate color if you like. Pour into mold and chill until firm. Good topped with fruit sauce or whipped cream.

To Make Fruit Velvet (Makes 4 servings): Prepare 1 (3-ounce) package fruit-flavored gelatin as label instructs, then cool and chill until syrupy. Beat hard with a rotary or electric beater until foamy, then fold in 1 cup well-drained, prepared, cut-up fruit and 1 cup heavy cream, whipped to soft peaks. Pour into mold and chill until firm.

To Jell Ice Cream (Makes 4–6 servings): Dissolve 1 (3-ounce) package fruit gelatin in boiling water as label directs, cool to room temperature, then beat in 1 pint mushy ice cream of a compatible flavor. Pour into mold and chill until firm. Serve from the bowl—do not unmold.

IMPERIAL PEACH MOLD

Makes 6 servings

1 (3-ounce) package lemon-flavored gelatin
1 (3-ounce) package peach-flavored gelatin
2½ cups peach nectar
1¾ cups ginger ale
4 ripe peaches or 8 canned peach halves, drained
Lemon juice (optional)
2 tablespoons apple or red currant jelly
½ cup heavy cream
6 maraschino cherries

Mix gelatins in a bowl. Heat peach nectar to boiling, pour over gelatins, stirring until they dissolve; add ginger ale and pour into a 1-quart mold. Cool, then chill until firm. Unmold on a large platter. Surround with peeled and pitted peach halves, hollow sides up (dip fresh ones in lemon juice to prevent darkening) and fill hollows with jelly. Whip cream to soft peaks, drop by spoonfuls onto jelly, and top with cherries. About 340 calories per serving.

PORT WINE JELLY

Both simple and sophisticated.
Makes 4–6 servings

1⅓ cups water
2 envelopes unflavored gelatin (3 envelopes if you want to mold the jelly in a decorative mold)
⅔ cup sugar
Juice of 1 lemon, strained through a fine sieve
Juice of 1 orange, strained through a fine sieve
2 cups dark ruby port wine

Place water, gelatin, and sugar in a small saucepan, stir well to mix, then heat, stirring, over moderate heat about 5 minutes until sugar and gelatin are dissolved. Remove from heat and cool slightly. Mix in fruit juices and port. Pour into an ungreased 1-quart bowl or decorative mold, cover, and chill several hours until firm. To serve, spoon jelly into dessert glasses and top, if you like, with sweetened whipped cream. Or, if you have used the decorative mold, unmold on a platter and garnish with fluffs of sweetened whipped cream. About 240 calories for each of 4 servings (without whipped cream), 160 calories for each of 6 servings.

LEMON FLUFF

Tart and lemony, light and billowy.
Makes 5–6 servings

4 eggs, separated
⅔ cup superfine sugar
1½ teaspoons unflavored gelatin
¼ cup cold water
½ teaspoon grated lemon rind
¼ cup lemon juice

Beat egg yolks until very thick and light; add sugar, a little at a time, beating well after each addition, then continue beating until thick and the color of cream. Heat gelatin and water, uncovered, in a small saucepan, stirring occasionally, over low heat until gelatin dissolves; mix in lemon rind and juice and stir into egg mixture. Chill until mixture mounds when dropped from a spoon. Beat egg whites until they form stiff peaks and fold into yolk mixture. Spoon into 5 or 6 parfait glasses or into a 1-quart serving bowl. Cover and chill until serving time. Serve as is or topped with sugared fresh or thawed frozen fruit. (*Note:* Do not spoon from serving bowl into individual dishes until a few minutes before serving or mixture may liquefy.) About 175 calories for each of 5 servings, 145 calories for each of 6 servings.

⚖ LOW-CALORIE GINGERED ORANGE FLUFF

Makes 4 servings

1 cup boiling water
1 envelope low-calorie orange-flavored gelatin (there are 2 envelopes in a ¾-ounce package)
½ cup orange or tangerine juice
½ cup low-calorie ginger ale
Pinch ginger

Mix boiling water and gelatin dessert until dissolved; stir in remaining ingredients. Chill until mixture mounds when dropped from a spoon, then beat with a rotary beater until foamy. Spoon into serving dishes and chill until firm. Serve cold, topped, if you like, with any low-calorie topping. About 25 calories per serving (without topping).

VARIATIONS:

Substitute any other flavor of low-calorie fruit gelatin for the orange, mixing with an appropriate fruit juice: apple and apple juice (26 calories per serving), peach and peach nectar (26 calories per serving), raspberry or strawberry and cranberry juice (30 calories per serving), grape and grape juice (31 calories per serving), pineapple and pineapple juice (28 calories per serving).

MOLDED RASPBERRY MOUSSE

Makes 6–8 servings

2 (10-ounce) packages frozen raspberries, thawed
1 cup water
2 envelopes unflavored gelatin
⅓ cup sugar
⅓ cup rosé wine
¼ cup Cherry Heering
1 pint heavy cream

Topping:
2 (10-ounce) packages frozen raspberries, thawed
2 tablespoons Cherry Heering

Put raspberries through a food mill or purée in an electric blender at high speed; strain and set aside. Heat and stir water, gelatin, and sugar in a small saucepan 4–5 minutes over moderate heat until gelatin and sugar are dissolved. Off heat, mix in purée, wine, and Cherry Heering. Cover and chill until thick and syrupy, about 20–30 minutes, then beat until fluffy; whip cream until soft, glossy peaks form and fold in. Pour into a decorative 2-quart mold, cover, and chill several hours until firm. Meanwhile, purée berries for topping, strain, and mix in Cherry Heering. Chill until ready to use. To serve, loosen mold by dipping quickly in warm water; invert on a large platter. Top with a little of the sauce and pass the rest. About 570 calories for each of 6 servings, 430 calories for each of 8 servings.

VARIATION:

Molded Strawberry Mousse: Prepare as directed, substituting strawberries for raspberries. About 570 calories for each of 6 servings, 430 calories for each of 8 servings.

BASIC COLD SOUFFLÉ (VANILLA)

Makes 4 servings

1 envelope unflavored gelatin
½ cup sugar
1 cup milk
2 eggs, separated
1½ teaspoons vanilla
¾ cup heavy cream

Mix gelatin and sugar in the top of a double boiler, gradually stir in milk, set over simmering water, and heat and stir until sugar dissolves; mix a little hot mixture into lightly beaten egg yolks, return to pan, and cook and stir 2–3 minutes until slightly thickened. Pour into a large bowl and mix in vanilla; cool to room temperature, stirring occasionally, then chill until mixture mounds when dropped from a spoon. Whip cream to soft peaks and fold in. With a separate beater (or the same one well washed), beat egg whites to stiff peaks and fold in. Spoon into a 1-quart soufflé dish and chill until firm. Top, if you like, with whipped cream fluffs, toasted slivered almonds, and/or fresh berries before serving. About 345 calories per serving (without topping).

For a Top Hat Soufflé (Makes 8 servings): Extend height of a 1-quart soufflé dish by wrapping a 4″-wide, double thickness foil strip around outside so it stands 2″ above rim; fasten with cellophane tape. Double any of the cold soufflé recipes, pour into dish, and chill until firm. Remove collar carefully before serving.

VARIATIONS:

Cold Lemon Soufflé: Prepare as directed, substituting ½ cup each lemon juice and water for the milk and ½ teaspoon finely grated lemon rind for the vanilla. About 315 calories per serving.

Cold Orange Soufflé: Prepare as directed, substituting 1 cup orange juice for milk and 1 teaspoon finely grated orange rind for vanilla. About 330 calories per serving.

Cold Fruit Soufflé: Prepare as directed but substitute 1¼ cups any fruit purée for the milk and use 1 egg *yolk* only. Flavor with ¼ teaspoon almond extract instead of vanilla. Otherwise, proceed as directed, folding in whipped cream and beaten egg whites. About 315 calories per serving.

Cold Chocolate Soufflé: Prepare as directed and, while gelatin mixture is still hot, mix in 2½ (1-ounce) coarsely grated squares unsweetened chocolate, stirring until melted. Garnish with chocolate curls* and fluffs of whipped cream. About 435 calories per serving (without chocolate curls and whipped cream).

COLD COFFEE SOUFFLÉ

Makes 10–12 servings

2 envelopes unflavored gelatin
1 cup sugar
¼ teaspoon salt
2½ cups milk
4 eggs, separated
¼ cup plus 1 teaspoon instant coffee powder
1 teaspoon vanilla
1 pint heavy cream
Chocolate curls* and blanched almond halves (optional garnishes)

Heat and stir gelatin, ½ cup sugar, salt, and 2 cups milk in the top of a double boiler directly over moderate heat 5–6 minutes until sugar and gelatin are dissolved. Beat egg yolks lightly with remaining milk, mix in a little of the hot mixture, then return all to pan. Set over simmering water and cook and stir 5–6 minutes until slightly thickened and no raw egg taste remains. Off heat, mix in coffee and vanilla. Place a piece of wax paper flat on sauce and cool to room temperature, then chill, stirring occasionally, until mixture mounds slightly. Meanwhile, wrap a double thickness strip of foil about 4" wide tightly around top of a 1½-quart soufflé dish to form a collar extending 2" above rim; fasten with cellophane tape. Beat egg whites until foamy, add remaining sugar, and beat until stiff; fold into coffee mixture. Beat cream until soft peaks form and fold in. Spoon into soufflé dish, leveling surface. Chill until firm, at least 2 hours. Remove collar and decorate, if you like, with chocolate curls and almond "daisies." About 325 calories for each of 10 servings, 270 calories for each of 12 servings (without garnish).

¢ **SPANISH CREAM**

This silky cool dessert is thickened both with eggs and gelatin.
Makes 6 servings

1 envelope unflavored gelatin
⅔ cup sugar
2½ cups milk
3 eggs, separated
1 teaspoon vanilla

Mix gelatin and ⅓ cup sugar in the top of a double boiler, slowly stir in milk, set over simmering water, and heat and stir until sugar dissolves. Blend a little hot mixture into lightly beaten egg yolks, return to pan, and cook and stir 2–3 minutes until slightly thickened. Pour into a large bowl, mix in vanilla, cool, then chill until mixture mounds slightly when dropped from a spoon. Beat egg whites until frothy, gradually beat in remaining sugar, and continue beating until stiff peaks form. Fold custard mixture into meringue, spoon into a 1-quart mold or 6 goblets and chill until firm. If molded, unmold on a dessert platter. Top, if you like, with fruit, chocolate, or butterscotch sauce. About 200 calories per serving (without fruit or sauce).

VARIATIONS:

¢ **Chocolate Spanish Cream:** Prepare as directed and, while custard is still hot, blend in 1 (1-ounce) coarsely grated square unsweetened chocolate or 1 (1-ounce) square no-melt unsweetened chocolate. About 225 calories per serving.

¢ **Layered Spanish Cream:** Prepare as directed but cool custard mixture only slightly. While still warm, fold into meringue and spoon into a crystal bowl. Chill until firm. Mixture will separate into 2 layers —custard on top, a jellylike mixture underneath. About 200 calories per serving.

BASIC BAVARIAN CREAM (VANILLA)

Bavarian Cream is a cousin of mousses; it has a custard base, which mousses haven't, also whipped cream, which mousses may or may not contain.
Makes 6–8 servings

½ cup sugar
1 envelope unflavored gelatin
1½ cups milk
3 egg yolks, lightly beaten
1½ teaspoons vanilla
¾ cup heavy cream
2 tablespoons confectioners' sugar
3 egg whites (optional)

Mix sugar, gelatin, and milk in the top of a double boiler and heat over simmering water until steaming hot. Mix a little hot mixture into yolks, return to double boiler top, and cook and stir 3–5 minutes until mixture coats the back of a metal spoon. Off heat, mix in vanilla; cool, then chill, stirring occasionally, until mixture mounds when dropped from a spoon. Whip cream with confectioners' sugar until stiff peaks form, then fold into custard mixture. If you like, also beat egg whites to soft peaks and fold in. Spoon into a 1½-quart mold or 6–8 custard cups or parfait glasses and chill 3–4 hours until firm. If molded, unmold on a dessert platter and wreathe, if you like, with crushed sweetened berries, sliced fresh peaches, or any stewed fruit. About 265 calories for each of 6 servings (without fruit), 200 calories for each of 8 servings.

VARIATIONS:

Rum Bavarian Cream: Prepare as directed but use ½ cup light rum and 1 cup milk in the custard mixture instead of all milk and reduce vanilla to ½ teaspoon. (*Note:* Brandy, crème de menthe, or any fruit liqueur may be used in place of rum; tint an appropriate color.) About 340 calories for each of 6 servings, 255 calories for each of 8 servings.

Chocolate Bavarian Cream: Prepare as directed but add 1 (6-ounce) package semisweet chocolate bits to the hot custard mixture, stirring until melted. About 395 calories for each of 6 servings, 300 calories for each of 8 servings.

Mocha Bavarian Cream: Prepare Chocolate Bavarian Cream (above) as directed, using 1 cup milk and ½ cup very strong hot black coffee in the custard mixture. About 395 calories for each of 6 servings, 300 calories for each of 8 servings.

Fruit Bavarian Cream: Prepare as directed, using ½ cup milk and 1 cup puréed berries, peaches, apricots, bananas, or other fruit in the custard mixture; flavor with 1 tablespoon lemon juice instead of vanilla and tint, if you like, an appropriate pastel color. About 395 calories for each of 6 servings, 300 calories for each of 8 servings.

Charlotte Russe (Makes 12–15 servings): Line the bottom and sides of a 9" spring-form pan with split ladyfingers (you'll need about 20), then sprinkle with ¼ cup light rum. Chill while you prepare 2 recipes Basic Bavarian Cream (omit egg whites); spoon into pan and chill 4–6 hours or overnight. Unmold by removing spring form sides and inverting on chilled platter. Garnish with fluffs of whipped cream and maraschino cherries. To serve, cut in wedges as you would a layer cake. About 450 calories for each of 12 servings, 360 calories for each of 15 servings.

SWEDISH CREAM

So rich and smooth it never fails to impress.
Makes 4 servings

1 pint light cream
1 envelope unflavored gelatin
⅔ cup sugar
1 pint sour cream
1 teaspoon vanilla
2 cups sliced fresh or frozen thawed peaches or berries

Heat cream, gelatin, and sugar in a small saucepan over lowest heat, stirring constantly, 15–20 minutes until all sugar and gelatin are dissolved; do not allow to boil. Remove from heat and cool 5 minutes; beat in sour cream with a wire whisk or rotary beater. Stir in vanilla, cover, and chill 2–3 hours until firm. To serve, spoon into individual dessert dishes and top with fruit. About 700 calories per serving.

⚔ LOW-CALORIE POTS DE CRÈME AU CHOCOLAT

Makes 4 servings

1 (½-ounce) envelope low-calorie chocolate pudding mix
1 cup skim milk
1 teaspoon instant coffee powder
1 (1-ounce) square semisweet chocolate, grated
1 teaspoon vanilla

Mix pudding mix and ¼ cup milk in a small saucepan; stir in remaining ingredients. Heat, uncovered, over low heat, stirring constantly, until smooth and thickened; do not boil. Remove from heat, place a piece of wax paper directly on surface of mixture, and cool to lukewarm. Pour into 4 *pots de crème* or ramekins, cover, and chill 2–3 hours until set. Serve cold. About 100 calories per serving.

FROZEN DESSERTS

Ices and ice creams are thought to have originated in ancient China, then traveled the trade routes west to the Mediterranean. Romans served them, but it was sixteenth-century Florentine chefs who glorified them. For the wedding feasts of Catherine de Médicis and Henry II of France, they prepared a new flavor every day. Soon Italian ices and "iced creams" were fashionable throughout Western Europe and their popularity never waned. While abroad, Thomas Jefferson sampled ice cream, copied down a recipe, and on returning to America introduced it at a state dinner at the White House. Today there are many kinds of frozen desserts. Here's a quick lexicon.

The Kinds of Frozen Desserts

Bombe: Ice cream and/or sherbet or ice, frozen in a decorative mold, often in layers of contrasting color and flavor.

Coupe: Ice cream or sherbet served in a broad-bowled goblet topped with fruit and/or whipped cream and *marrons glacés* (glazed chestnuts).

Frappé: Sherbet or ice frozen to the mushy stage.

Granité: A granular Italian ice frozen without stirring. When served, it is scraped into fluffy, snow-like crystals instead of being spooned.

Ice: A watery frozen dessert made of sugar, water, and flavoring (usually fruit juice).

Ice Cream: Originally, frozen sweetened and flavored cream but today almost any creamy frozen dessert. *French ice cream* has an egg custard base.

Mousse: An extra-rich ice cream frozen without being stirred. It often contains whipped cream.

Parfait: Ice cream or whipped cream layered into a tall footed glass with a topping—fruit, chocolate, nut—then frozen.

Sherbet: Fine-textured frozen fruit dessert, originally water-based but today more often made with milk. Gelatin and/or egg white is frequently added to make sherbets smoother.

Sorbet: The French word for *sherbet;* it has come to mean a mushy frozen fruit ice or sherbet, a frappé. It may be served between courses or as dessert.

About Freezing Ice Creams, Sherbets, and Ices

To Freeze in a Crank-Type Freezer (Hand or Electric): Prepare mix according to recipe, cover, and chill 1–2 hours. Meanwhile, wash and scald all freezer parts, then rinse in cold water and dry thoroughly. Set freezer can into freezer, fit dasher into place, and pour in chilled ice cream mix. (*Note:* Mixture will expand as it freezes so never fill freezer can more than two-thirds.) Put lid on can, attach crank top, and lock into place. Add enough crushed ice to fill freezer one-third, distributing evenly around can. Then, using 1 part rock or kosher salt to 8 parts ice (1 to 6 if you want mixture to freeze faster), layer salt and ice into freezer until filled. Let stand 3–5 minutes, then begin turning. If freezer is the hand-crank variety, turn smoothly and slowly, always in the same direction. Stop turning only when mixture is too stiff to crank (electric freezers will shut off or begin to labor heavily). Drain water from freezer and, if necessary, scoop out enough ice to expose top ⅓ of can. Wipe away any salt, paying particular attention to seam around lid. Uncover can, lift out dasher, and scrape all frozen mixture back into can; pack down with a large spoon. Plug hole in can top with a cork (some freezers have an additional solid cover), cover can, then repack freezer, using 1 part salt to 4 parts crushed ice. Cover with heavy paper, cloth, or newspapers and let season ½ hour. Or, if you prefer, pack ice cream into plastic freezer containers and let stand ½ hour in freezer. (*Note:* Don't *store* ice cream in freezer, however. It will become brick hard.)

To Freeze in Refrigerator: Turn temperature setting to coldest point. (*Note:* If you make ice cream often, it's a good idea to have a special set of ice cube trays for just this purpose. Frequently washed ice cube trays lose their finish, causing ice cubes to stick.) Any small excess amounts of ice-cream mix can be frozen in custard cups.

Bombes: Chill a melon or brick bombe mold well in freezer. (*Note:* If you have no mold, use a metal mixing bowl.) Meanwhile soften commercial ice cream or sherbet until workable or, if making your own, freeze only until mushy. Pack into mold, smoothing with a large spoon so that you have an even layer about 1″ thick over bottom and sides; freeze until firm. Add a second layer of contrasting color and flavor, packing tightly against the first layer, and freeze until firm. Fill center with soft ice or ice cream of yet another flavor and freeze until firm. *To Unmold:* Wipe mold with a cloth wrung out in hot water, then invert on a serving platter. (*Note:* Bombes can be frozen by packing them in a mixture of crushed ice and rock or kosher salt—1 part salt to 4 parts ice—but it seems an unnecessary lot of work unless you have no freezer.)

Ice Creams: Prepare base mix as recipe directs and freeze until mushy. Remove from tray and beat at high speed until fluffy. Also whip cream until soft peaks form, fold into base, and freeze until firm. (*Note:* For extra creaminess, beat once again before freezing until firm.)

Mousses: Prepare mix, spoon into shallow trays or mold, cover with foil or wax paper (because of their high cream content, mousses are more apt to pick up refrigerator odors),

DESSERTS AND DESSERT SAUCES

and freeze until firm without beating or stirring.

Parfaits: Layer ice cream or sherbet into parfait glasses with a topping of your choice, then freeze until firm. Some combinations to try:
- Vanilla ice cream with Melba Sauce or Chocolate Sauce or any puréed fruit
- Vanilla ice cream and orange sherbet with Melba Sauce or any puréed berries or peaches
- Chocolate ice cream and whipped cream or Marshmallow Sauce
- Pistachio ice cream, chocolate ice cream, and Chocolate Sauce or Fudge Sauce

Sherbets and Ices: Prepare as recipe directs, spoon into refrigerator trays, and freeze until mushy. Remove from trays, beat until light, then freeze until firm. (*Note:* An extra beating before freezing until firm will make the mixture more velvety.)

◁▷ BASIC FRUIT ICE

An easy recipe you can experiment with. Mix two or more fruit juice flavors, if you like, or use one flavor only.
Makes about 1½ quarts

1 envelope unflavored gelatin
½–1 cup sugar (depending upon sweetness of fruit juice)
1 quart sweet fruit juice (any berry, peach or apricot nectar, pineapple or orange juice) or 1 pint each crushed fruit and water
2 tablespoons lemon juice
Few drops food coloring (optional)
2 egg whites

Mix gelatin and ½ cup sugar in a saucepan, add juice, and heat and stir over low heat until gelatin and sugar dissolve. (*Note:* If using crushed fruit, heat gelatin and sugar with the water and, when dissolved, mix in fruit.) Taste for sugar and adjust as needed. Mix in lemon juice, tint an appropriate color, if you like, pour into 2 refrigerator trays, and freeze until mushy. Spoon into a large bowl and beat hard until fluffy. Beat egg whites to very soft peaks, fold into fruit mixture, spoon into 3 refrigerator trays, cover, and freeze until firm. About 80 calories per ½-cup serving if made with a tart fruit juice and ½ cup sugar.

VARIATIONS:

◁▷ **Lemon or Lime Ice:** Prepare as directed, using 1½ cups sugar, 3 cups water, and 1 cup lemon or lime juice. About 150 calories per ½-cup serving.

◁▷ **Wine Ice:** Mix gelatin with ½ cup sugar and 1 cup each orange juice and water and heat and stir until gelatin and sugar dissolve. Mix in 2 cups dry or sweet white, red, or rosé wine or champagne and proceed as directed. When serving, drizzle a little wine over each portion. About 80 calories per ½-cup serving if made with dry wine.

◁▷ **Spiked Ice:** Prepare Basic Fruit Ice as directed but add ¼–½ cup any compatible fruit liqueur along with the beaten egg whites (orange juice and curaçao, for example, pineapple and crème de menthe, berry juice and crème de cassis, fraise, or framboise). About 100 calories per ½-cup serving.

⊠ ◁▷ LEMON OR LIME GRANITÉ

Granité is a granular ice frozen without being stirred. It can be served at the mush stage or frozen hard, then scraped up in fine, feathery shavings. Particularly good topped with a little fruit liqueur or rum.

Makes about 1½ quarts

1 quart water
2 cups sugar
1 cup lemon or lime juice
1 tablespoon finely grated lemon or lime rind
Few drops yellow and/or green food coloring

Bring water and sugar to a boil in a saucepan, stirring, then reduce heat and simmer, uncovered, 5 minutes. Cool, mix in juice and rind, and tint pale yellow or green. Pour into 3 refrigerator trays, cover, and freeze to a mush without stirring. Spoon into goblets and serve or freeze hard, scrape up with a spoon, and pile into goblets. About 130 calories per ½-cup serving.

VARIATIONS:

⚖ **Orange Granité:** Prepare as directed, substituting 1 quart orange juice for the water, reducing sugar to ¾ cup and lemon juice to 2 tablespoons; also use orange rind instead of lemon. About 85 calories per ½-cup serving.

⚖ **Fruit Granité:** Boil 3 cups water and 1½ cups sugar into syrup as directed. Cool, add 2 tablespoons lemon juice and 2 cups puréed fruit (any berries, peaches, pineapple, sweet cherries); omit rind. Freeze and serve as directed. About 140–50 calories per ½-cup serving depending upon fruit used.

⚖ **Coffee or Tea Granité:** Boil 1 cup each water and sugar into syrup as directed; cool, add 3 cups strong black coffee or tea and to tea mixture, add ¼ cup lemon juice. Freeze and serve as directed. About 65 calories per ½-cup serving.

⚖ **Melon Granité:** Mix 1 quart puréed ripe melon (any kind) with ½–1 cup sugar (depending on sweetness of melon) and 2 tablespoons lemon juice; let stand 1 hour at room temperature, stirring now and then, until sugar is dissolved. Freeze as directed. About 65 calories per ½-cup serving *if* made with ½ cup sugar, 135 calories if made with 1 cup sugar.

⚖ **LEMON OR LIME MILK SHERBET**

Makes about 1½ quarts

1 envelope unflavored gelatin
1⅓ cups sugar
1 quart milk
¾ cup lemon or lime juice
2 teaspoons finely grated lemon or lime rind
Few drops yellow or green food coloring (optional)
2 egg whites

Mix gelatin and sugar in a saucepan, gradually add milk, and heat and stir over low heat until sugar and gelatin dissolve. Cool, add juice and rind, and, if you like, tint pale yellow or green. Pour into 2 refrigerator trays and freeze until mushy. Remove from trays and beat until fluffy. Beat egg whites to very soft peaks and fold into fruit mixture. Spoon into 3 refrigerator trays and freeze until firm. About 150 calories per ½-cup serving.

VARIATIONS:

⚖ **Orange Milk Sherbet:** Heat and stir gelatin with ¾ cup sugar and 2 cups milk until dissolved; cool, add 2 tablespoons lemon juice, 2 cups orange juice, and 1 tablespoon finely grated orange rind. Proceed as directed. About 110 calories per ½-cup serving.

⚖ **Fruit Milk Sherbet:** Heat and stir gelatin with ¾ cup sugar and 2 cups milk until dissolved; cool, add 2 tablespoons lemon juice, ½ cup water, and 1½ cups puréed fruit (berries, sweet cherries, peaches, apricots, pineapple, etc.). Taste for sugar, adding a bit more if needed, then proceed as directed. About 125 calories per ½-cup serving.

☼ **Extra-Low-Calorie Sherbets:** Prepare any of the above sherbets as directed but use skim milk instead of whole, reduce sugar to ½ cup, and use 1 egg white only. About 65 calories per ½-cup serving.

☒ EASY STRAWBERRY OR RASPBERRY LEMON CREAM SHERBET

Makes about 6 servings

2 (10-ounce) packages frozen strawberries or raspberries, thawed
1 (6-ounce) can frozen lemonade concentrate, thawed
1 pint heavy cream

Purée strawberries in an electric blender at low speed, then strain to remove seeds. Add lemonade concentrate and mix well. Beat cream until soft peaks form and fold in. Spoon into 2 refrigerator trays and freeze until firm. About 370 calories per serving.

BASIC REFRIGERATOR ICE CREAM

Turn freezer to coldest setting before beginning this recipe. From this one basic recipe, you can make 14 different flavors of ice cream. Makes 1½ quarts

1 cup sugar
2 teaspoons cornstarch
1 quart milk
3 eggs, separated
2 teaspoons vanilla
1 cup heavy cream, whipped

Mix sugar and cornstarch in top of a double boiler and gradually stir in milk. Add egg yolks and beat until frothy. Set over simmering water and heat 15 minutes, stirring now and then at first, constantly toward the end. Cool and stir in vanilla. Beat egg whites to soft peaks and fold in. Pour into 2 refrigerator trays and freeze until mushy. Spoon into a large bowl, beat hard until fluffy, then beat in cream. Spoon into 3 trays and freeze until firm. (*Note:* For extra smoothness, beat once more before freezing until firm.) About 215 calories per ½-cup serving.

VARIATIONS:

Berry Ice Cream: Prepare as directed but reduce vanilla to 1 teaspoon and add 2 cups any crushed, sweetened-to-taste berries (fresh, frozen, or canned) along with beaten egg whites. About 235 calories per ½-cup serving.

Banana Ice Cream: Prepare as directed but reduce vanilla to 1 teaspoon and add 2 cups puréed ripe bananas (about 6 medium-size bananas) along with egg whites. About 260 calories per ½-cup serving.

Pineapple Ice Cream: Prepare as directed but reduce vanilla to 1 teaspoon and add 1 (1-pound 14-ounce) can crushed pineapple (undrained) along with egg whites. About 280 calories per ½-cup serving.

Peach or Apricot Ice Cream: Prepare as directed but reduce vanilla to ½ teaspoon and add ½ teaspoon almond extract; mix in 2 cups peach or apricot purée along with beaten egg whites. About 250 calories per ½-cup serving.

Orange Ice Cream: Prepare custard mixture as directed, using ¾ cup sugar and 3 cups milk. Add 1 (6-ounce) can thawed frozen orange juice concentrate and 1 cup freshly squeezed orange juice; omit vanilla. Proceed as directed. About 250 calories per ½-cup serving.

Chocolate Ice Cream: Add 2 (1-ounce) squares coarsely grated unsweetened chocolate to hot custard mixture and stir until melted. Reduce vanilla to 1 teaspoon and proceed as directed. About 240 calories per ½-cup serving.

Coffee Ice Cream: Sprinkle ⅓ cup instant coffee powder over hot custard mixture and stir until blended. Reduce vanilla to ½ teaspoon and proceed as directed. About 220 calories per ½-cup serving.

Burnt Almond Ice Cream: Prepare custard mixture as directed, using ½ cup sugar; caramelize* ½ cup sugar and mix in along with vanilla called for. Proceed as directed, mixing 1 cup coarsely chopped toasted, blanched almonds into beaten frozen mixture along with whipped cream. About 285 calories per ½-cup serving.

Butter Pecan Ice Cream: Prepare as directed, mixing 1 cup coarsely chopped, butter-browned pecans into beaten frozen mixture along with whipped cream. About 295 calories per ½-cup serving.

Pistachio Ice Cream: Prepare as directed but reduce vanilla to 1 teaspoon and add ½ teaspoon almond extract. Tint mixture pale green before freezing. Mix ¾ cup coarsely chopped pistachio nuts into beaten frozen mixture along with whipped cream. About 260 calories per ½-cup serving.

Peppermint Ice Cream: Prepare as directed but omit vanilla and add ¼ teaspoon peppermint extract; also mix 1½ cups finely crushed peppermint candy into beaten frozen mixture along with whipped cream. About 270 calories per ½-cup serving.

Rum-Raisin Ice Cream: Soak ⅔ cup minced seedless raisins in ⅓ cup dark rum while preparing recipe; fold into beaten frozen mixture along with whipped cream. About 270 calories per ½-cup serving.

Eggnog Ice Cream: Prepare basic recipe as directed and mix ¼ cup rum or brandy into beaten frozen mixture along with whipped cream. About 240 calories per ½-cup serving.

BASIC FREEZER ICE CREAM (VANILLA)

The principal difference between freezer-cranked and refrigerator ice cream is that, with the former, the cream goes into the freezer mix in the beginning. Avoid using extra-thick or clotted cream—the freezer's churning action may turn it to butter. (*Note:* Any of the refrigerator ice creams can be frozen in a crank freezer. Simply mix in heavy cream —do not whip—at the start.)
Makes about 2 quarts

1 quart light cream
1½ cups superfine sugar
2 tablespoons vanilla or 1 (3-inch) piece vanilla bean, split lengthwise
1 pint heavy cream

Heat and stir light cream and sugar over moderate heat until sugar dissolves thoroughly. If using vanilla bean, heat along with mixture; remove vanilla bean (but not tiny seeds). Cool mixture, mix in vanilla

DESSERTS AND DESSERT SAUCES

extract (if bean wasn't used) and the heavy cream. Chill 1–2 hours, then freeze in a crank-type freezer* (hand or electric) following manufacturer's directions. About 300 calories per ½-cup serving.

VARIATIONS:

Chocolate Freezer Ice Cream: Prepare as directed but heat 3 squares unsweetened chocolate along with the light cream and 2 cups superfine sugar, stirring until melted. About 325 calories per ½-cup serving.

Coffee Freezer Ice Cream: Prepare as directed but heat ⅓ cup instant coffee powder along with light cream and sugar. If you like, stir in ¼ cup coffee liqueur along with vanilla. About 300 calories per ½-cup serving.

Mocha Freezer Ice Cream: Prepare as directed but heat 1 square unsweetened chocolate and ¼ cup instant coffee powder along with light cream and sugar. About 315 calories per ½-cup serving.

Fruit Freezer Ice Cream: Heat 1 pint cream and the sugar as directed. Cool, omit vanilla, but mix in 2 cups any fruit purée (sieved berry, fresh peach, mango, papaya, pineapple, banana, apricot) and the heavy cream. Add ¼ cup lemon or orange juice, and, if flavor is peach, apricot, or pineapple, 1 teaspoon almond extract. Proceed as directed. About 310 calories per ½-cup serving.

Ginger Freezer Ice Cream: Prepare vanilla mix as directed but reduce vanilla to 1 tablespoon. Add 1½ cups minced preserved ginger, 1 cup syrup drained from bottles of ginger, and 2 tablespoons lemon juice. Freeze as directed. About 315 calories per ½-cup serving.

FRENCH VANILLA ICE CREAM

An extra-smooth ice cream made with egg yolks.
Makes 1½ quarts

2 cups milk
1 cup sugar
6 egg yolks, lightly beaten
1 tablespoon vanilla
1 pint heavy cream

Beat milk, sugar, and egg yolks in the top of a double boiler until frothy. Set over simmering water and heat 15 minutes, stirring now and then at first, constantly toward the end. Cool, add vanilla and cream. Freeze in a crank-type freezer* (hand or electric), following manufacturer's directions. About 270 calories per ½-cup serving.

To Freeze in Refrigerator: Prepare custard mixture as directed, cool, and mix in vanilla; pour into 2 refrigerator trays and freeze until mushy. Spoon into a large bowl and beat hard until fluffy. Whip cream until thick and satiny and fold in. Spoon into 3 refrigerator trays, cover, and freeze until firm, stirring twice during the first hour.

VARIATIONS:

French Chocolate Ice Cream: Prepare custard mixture as directed and, while still hot, mix in 3 (1-ounce) coarsely grated squares semisweet chocolate, stirring until well blended. Cool, add 2 teaspoons vanilla, and proceed as directed, freezing either in freezer or refrigerator. About 305 calories per ½-cup serving.

(*Note:* Any of the variations given for Basic Refrigerator Ice Cream can be used for French Vanilla Ice Cream. Simply follow basic recipe above, adding amounts of fruits, flavorings, or nuts called for in the variations.)

☒ DARK CHOCOLATE ICE CREAM

Smooth and dark and super-rich. But so very easy.
Makes 4 servings

1 (6-ounce) package semisweet chocolate bits
1 (7½-ounce) jar marshmallow cream
1 (13-ounce) can evaporated milk
1 teaspoon vanilla
1 cup heavy cream

Melt chocolate bits in the top of a double boiler over simmering water; add marshmallow cream and heat, stirring occasionally, until melted. Pour in milk, a little at a time, mixing well after each addition, then mix in vanilla. Remove from heat and set aside. Whip cream until soft peaks form and fold into chocolate mixture. Pour into a 9"×5"×3" loaf pan and freeze until mushy. Remove from pan and beat until fluffy. (*Note:* With a portable mixer, you can do this *in* the pan. Return to pan and freeze until firm.) When serving, make the portions small. About 700 calories per serving.

☒ BANANA-ORANGE ICE CREAM

Makes 4 servings

3 large ripe bananas, peeled and mashed
1½ cups orange juice (preferably fresh)
Juice of 2 lemons
1 (13-ounce) can evaporated milk
½ cup light corn syrup
½ cup superfine sugar

Mix all ingredients together, pour into 2 refrigerator trays, and freeze until mushy. Remove from trays and beat until fluffy; return to trays and freeze until firm. About 460 calories per serving.

TUTTI-FRUTTI ICE CREAM

Makes 8 servings

1 (1-pound 14-ounce) can crushed pineapple, drained (save juice for drinks)
¼ cup coarsely chopped candied red and green cherries
¼ cup finely chopped citron
⅓ cup coarsely chopped, pitted dates
3–4 tablespoons dark rum (optional)
3 pints vanilla ice cream, softened slightly

Mix together all ingredients, spoon into 3 refrigerator trays or a 9"×5"×3" loaf pan, and freeze until firm. Allow to soften slightly before serving. About 280 calories per serving.

VARIATION:

Tutti-Frutti Party Bombe: Mix as directed, pack in a chilled 2-quart melon mold, and freeze until firm. Unmold and decorate with rum-flavored, sweetened whipped cream put through a pastry bag fitted with a fluted tip. About 280 calories per serving (without whipped cream).

FROZEN COFFEE CREAM

When serving, make the portions small—this is a *very* rich dessert.
Makes 6–8 servings

1 (13-ounce) can evaporated milk
1 cup light cream
1 envelope unflavored gelatin
⅓ cup instant coffee powder
⅔ cup sugar
2 tablespoons coffee liqueur
1 teaspoon vanilla
1 pint heavy cream

Place milk and light cream in a small saucepan and sprinkle gelatin over surface; let stand at room temperature 10 minutes. Mix in coffee powder and sugar, set over lowest heat, and heat, stirring, 20–25 min-

VII. ENTERTAINING

Planked Steak – Rice à l'Impératrice and Crown Roast of Pork – Home candy kitchen

Planked Steak with Vegetables (vol. 1, pp. 265–66 and vol. 2, p. 254)

Rice à la Imperatrice (vol. 2, pp. 449–50); and Crown Roast of Pork (vol. 1, p. 407)

Gifts from the home candy kitchen: fondants and fudges, pralines and brittles, marzipan fruits and mints, hand-dipped chocolates and fruit jellies (vol. 2, pp. 628–44)

utes until gelatin, coffee, and sugar are dissolved; do not boil. Remove from heat and cool to room temperature. Stir in coffee liqueur and vanilla. Pour into a refrigerator tray and freeze until mushy; remove from pan and beat until fluffy. Whip heavy cream until thick and satiny, then beat into coffee mixture. Divide between 2 refrigerator trays and freeze until firm. About 565 calories for each of 6 servings, 425 calories for each of 8 servings.

◧ BISCUIT TORTONI

You can buy the little paper cups used for *tortoni* in Italian delicatessens, also in some gourmet shops. If unavailable, substitute cupcake papers but set in muffin tins to give them extra support. Once tortoni are frozen, lift from tins.
Makes 6 servings

1 cup heavy cream
⅓ cup confectioners' sugar
½ teaspoon vanilla
1 egg white
2 tablespoons light rum
⅓ cup crushed dry macaroons
¼ cup minced, toasted, blanched almonds

Whip cream with sugar and vanilla until soft peaks form. Beat egg white to soft peaks and fold into cream along with rum and macaroons. Spoon into paper cups, sprinkle with almonds, cover with foil circles, and freeze until firm. About 280 calories per serving.

SPUMONI

This Italian ice-cream bombe comes in many flavors, textures, and colors. To vary recipe below, substitute raspberry or chocolate ice cream for the Vanilla-Almond and leave the filling white.
Makes about 1½ quarts

Vanilla-Almond Ice Cream:
2 cups milk
4 egg yolks, lightly beaten
¾ cup sugar
1½ teaspoons vanilla
⅓ cup minced, toasted, blanched almonds

Cream-Fruit Filling:
1 cup heavy cream, tinted pale pink if you like
½ cup sifted confectioners' sugar
1 egg white
¼ cup minced maraschino cherries
2 tablespoons each candied citron, lemon peel, orange peel, and angelica
2 tablespoons light rum or brandy

Set a 2-quart melon mold to chill in freezer. Beat milk, egg yolks, and sugar in the top of a double boiler until frothy. Set over simmering water and heat and stir until mixture will coat a metal spoon and no raw egg taste remains; cool, mix in vanilla and almonds. Pour into a refrigerator tray and freeze until mushy; spoon into a bowl and beat hard until fluffy; return to tray, cover, and freeze until creamy-firm but not hard. Pack firmly into melon mold, smoothing with the back of a spoon to form a thick, even lining. Cover and freeze ½ hour. Meanwhile, prepare filling: Whip cream with sugar until soft peaks form; beat egg white to soft peaks and fold into cream along with remaining ingredients. Spoon into center of melon mold, cover, and freeze overnight. Unmold on a serving platter, loosening, if necessary, by rubbing a cloth wrung out in hot water over bottom of mold. Decorate, if you like, with candied cherries and angelica strips. To serve, cut in wedges. About 250 calories per ½-cup serving.

BAKED ALASKA

A spectacular dessert easy enough for beginners.
Makes 8 servings

1 (9") square firm white or yellow cake, homemade or bought
1 half-gallon brick ice cream (any flavor)

Meringue:
3 egg whites
⅛ teaspoon salt
¼ teaspoon cream of tartar
⅓ cup superfine sugar

Preheat oven to 500° F. Cut cake into a rectangle 5"×7" and place on a foil-lined baking sheet (save scraps for snacks). Halve ice cream lengthwise, place half on cake, and set in freezer while you prepare meringue (also returning remaining ice cream to freezer). Beat egg whites with salt and cream of tartar until foamy, gradually beat in sugar, then continue beating until very stiff peaks form. Remove cake from freezer and quickly frost with meringue, making sure it covers cake and ice cream *entirely* and touches baking sheet all around; swirl meringue into peaks. Bake uncovered on center oven rack about 3 minutes until tan all over. Serve immediately, slicing with a large sharp knife. About 435 calories per serving.

ABOUT DESSERT OMELETS

A favorite with the French, the dessert omelet has never become very popular in this country except among gourmet cooks. Like savory omelets, dessert omelets must be made to order, one at a time. For small dinners, however, they are both practical and impressive *if* the hostess is skilled in the art of omelet making. Before trying the sweet omelet recipe included here, read About Omelets in the chapter on eggs and cheese.

APPLE AND BRANDY OMELET

Makes 2 servings

1 sweet crisp apple, peeled, cored, and sliced thin
2 tablespoons butter
3–4 tablespoons warm Calvados or brandy, warmed slightly
1 Sweet Soufflé Omelet
1 tablespoon sugar

Sauté apple in butter in a small skillet over moderately low heat 8–10 minutes until tender, lightly glazed, and golden. Add 1 tablespoon Calvados and keep warm. Prepare omelet as directed and cover with apples just before folding and turning out. Crease omelet lightly through center, fold, and ease onto a hot platter. Sprinkle with sugar, pour remaining Calvados over surface, and, if you wish, flame before serving. About 465 calories per serving.

SOME SPECIALTY DESSERTS

CREPES SUZETTE

Not as complicated to make as you might think.
Makes 6 servings

1 recipe Simple Dessert Crepes with 1 tablespoon orange juice added to batter

6 sugar lumps
1 orange
1 lemon
½ cup orange juice
½ cup butter (no substitute)
2 tablespoons superfine sugar
¼ cup Cointreau or curaçao
2 tablespoons light rum or Benedictine
¼ cup brandy or Grand Marnier

Mix and cook crepes as recipe directs, then fold each in half and then in half again; keep warm in a 250° F. oven until all are done. Rub sugar lumps on rind of orange and lemon, drop into orange juice, and crush to dissolve. Melt butter in a chafing dish over moderately low heat, add superfine sugar and orange juice, and heat, stirring constantly, until mixture reduces slightly. Doing 1 crepe at a time, lift to chafing dish, unfold in sauce, coating well, then fold as before and push to side of chafing dish. Pour remaining ingredients over crepes—do not stir—and heat, moving pan gently over flame so crepes don't burn. Tilt pan until liqueurs ignite and spoon flaming over crepes. Serve on hot dessert plates topped with some of the sauce. About 435 calories per serving.

⚖ POACHED MERINGUE RING

A beautiful base for sliced fresh berries or any dessert sauce.
Makes 6 servings

6 egg whites
⅛ teaspoon cream of tartar
¼ teaspoon salt
¾ cup superfine sugar
1 teaspoon vanilla
1 teaspoon lemon juice
¼ teaspoon almond extract

Preheat oven to 325° F. Beat egg whites, cream of tartar, and salt with a rotary egg beater until foamy. Add sugar, a little at a time, beating well after each addition. Continue to beat until whites stand in stiff peaks. Fold in vanilla, lemon juice, and almond extract. Pack mixture in an ungreased 6-cup ring mold. Set mold in a shallow pan of cold water and bake, uncovered, 1 hour until meringue is lightly browned and pulls from the sides of mold. Remove meringue from oven and water bath and let cool upright in mold to room temperature. Loosen edges carefully with a spatula and unmold by inverting on a dessert platter. Cut into wedges and serve as is or with a generous ladling of dessert sauce (Algarve Apricot Sauce is especially good) or with sliced fresh berries. About 110 calories per serving (without sauce or fruit).

COEUR À LA CRÈME

For this dessert you will need a heart-shaped basket or perforated metal mold so that the cheese mixture can drain properly. They are stocked by housewares sections of many department stores, also by gourmet food shops.
Makes 8 servings

1 pound cottage cheese
1 pound cream cheese, softened to room temperature
⅛ teaspoon salt
1 pint heavy cream
1 quart fresh strawberries, washed and stemmed, or 2 (10-ounce) packages frozen strawberries, thawed
Sugar (optional)

Press cottage cheese through a fine sieve. Mix with cream cheese and salt and beat until smooth with a rotary beater. Using a wooden spoon, beat in cream, a little at a time. Line a 1½-quart heart-shaped basket or perforated mold with a double thickness of cheesecloth that has been wrung out in cold water; let ends overlap mold, and smooth out as many wrinkles as possible. Spoon cheese mixture into mold, cover with overlapping ends of cloth, and set on a tray deep enough to contain draining whey. Cover loosely with foil and refrigerate overnight; check occasionally to see that whey is not overflowing. To serve: Turn ends of cheesecloth back and invert mold on a large, shallow dish. Garnish with 10–12 large perfect berries; sweeten the rest to taste, crush slightly, and pass as a sauce. About 500 calories per serving.

MONT BLANC AUX MARRONS

An Alp of riced chestnuts snow-capped with sweetened whipped cream. *Not* for calorie counters. Makes 8 servings

1 pound shelled, peeled chestnuts (you'll need about 1½ pounds unshelled chestnuts)
3 cups milk
⅔ cup sugar
2 teaspoons vanilla
1 pint heavy cream
¼ cup sifted confectioners' sugar

Simmer chestnuts, milk, sugar, and 1 teaspoon vanilla in the top of a double boiler over just boiling water 30–40 minutes until very tender. Drain (save milk for pudding or custard). Force chestnuts through a potato ricer or coarse sieve, mounding into a high, fluffy pyramid on a large platter. Chill 2–3 hours. Whip cream with confectioners' sugar and remaining vanilla until very soft peaks form, and gently frost pyramid, letting a bit of the base show.

Serve at once. About 465 calories per serving.

¢ COTTAGE PUDDING

As much cake as pudding and buttery-rich.
Makes 8 servings

2 cups sifted flour
1 tablespoon baking powder
¼ teaspoon salt
½ cup butter or margarine
½ cup sugar
1 egg, lightly beaten
1 teaspoon vanilla or the finely grated rind of 1 lemon
¾ cup milk

Preheat oven to 350° F. Sift flour with baking powder and salt; set aside. Cream butter and sugar until light, add egg, and beat well. Mix vanilla and milk. Add flour and milk alternately to egg mixture, beginning and ending with flour and beating after each addition. Spoon into a buttered 8"×8"×2" baking pan and bake, uncovered, about 50 minutes until top springs back when touched. Cut in squares and serve warm with hot Custard Sauce or whipped cream. About 245 calories per serving (without sauce or whipped cream).

VARIATIONS:

Apple or Cherry Cottage Pudding: Prepare batter as directed and mix in 2 cups very thinly sliced, peeled, and cored tart apples or well-drained, canned pitted red cherries. Bake as directed in a buttered 9"×9"×2" pan. About 260 calories per serving.

Eve's Pudding: Spread 1½ cups applesauce in the bottom of a greased 9"×9"×2" pan, cover with batter, and bake as directed. About 275 calories per serving.

¢ **Raisin Cottage Pudding:** Prepare as directed, using grated lemon rind and adding 2 tablespoons lemon juice and ¾ cup seedless or sultana raisins. About 285 calories per serving.

Castle Pudding: Put 2 tablespoons maple syrup, jam, or jelly into each of 8 buttered custard cups, then fill two-thirds with Cottage Pudding batter. Bake 25 minutes at 350° F., then invert on serving plates. About 300 calories per serving.

CHOCOLATE CHIP PUDDING

Makes 4 servings

2½ cups cubed stale cake (*any flavor*)
2 eggs, lightly beaten
¼ cup sugar
⅛ teaspoon salt
2 cups milk, scalded
¼ cup coarsely chopped pecans or walnuts
½ teaspoon vanilla
¼ teaspoon nutmeg
½ cup semisweet chocolate bits
1 cup light cream (*optional*)

Preheat oven to 350° F. Put cake in a lightly buttered 2-quart casserole; mix together all remaining ingredients except chocolate bits and cream, pour over cake, and mix lightly. Bake, uncovered, 30–35 minutes until barely firm. Sprinkle chocolate bits over surface and bake, uncovered, 10 minutes longer until pudding is firm and chocolate melted. Serve hot, topped, if you like, with cream. About 445 calories per serving (without cream).

EASY DATE AND WALNUT PUDDING

Use scissors dipped in hot water to snip dates quickly.
Makes 20 servings

2 cups boiling water
2 teaspoons baking soda
1 pound pitted dates, coarsely cut up
¼ cup butter or margarine
2 cups sugar
2 cups sifted flour
1 teaspoon vanilla
1 cup coarsely chopped walnuts

Preheat oven to 325° F. Pour water over soda, mix well, and pour over dates. Add butter and stir until melted; cool slightly. Mix sugar and flour in a large bowl, add about ½ date mixture and beat well. Add remaining date mixture and vanilla and beat again. Stir in nuts. Spoon into a well-greased 13"×9"×2" baking pan and bake 50 minutes until springy to the touch. Cut into squares and serve warm or cold with whipped cream or vanilla ice cream. About 240 calories per serving (without whipped cream or ice cream).

DESSERT SAUCES

VANILLA SAUCE

A good basic sauce suited to a variety of desserts.
Makes about 2½ cups

2 tablespoons cornstarch
½ cup sugar
2 cups water or milk
¼ cup butter or margarine
1½ teaspoons vanilla
Pinch nutmeg

Mix cornstarch and sugar in a heavy saucepan, gradually add water, and heat, stirring constantly, until mixture boils. Reduce heat and simmer, uncovered, 2–3 minutes, stirring now and then. Add butter, vanilla, and nutmeg and stir until butter melts and is blended. Serve hot. About 20 calories per tablespoon if made with water, 30 calories per tablespoon if made with milk.

VARIATIONS:

Vanilla Bean Sauce: Scald 2 cups milk, add ½ vanilla bean, split lengthwise, cover, and let steep 20 minutes; discard bean (but not the tiny black seeds). Combine cornstarch and sugar as directed, gradually add milk, and heat and stir until mixture boils. Proceed as directed, omitting vanilla extract and nutmeg. About 20 calories per tablespoon if made with water, 30 calories per tablespoon if made with milk.

French Vanilla Sauce: Prepare Vanilla Bean Sauce (above) as directed, spoon a little hot sauce into 2 lightly beaten egg yolks, return to pan, and heat and stir 1 minute over lowest heat; do not boil. About 35 calories per tablespoon.

Vanilla Sauce Mousseline: Prepare any of the above vanilla sauces as directed; place a circle of wax paper flat on sauce and cool to room temperature. Whip ½ cup heavy cream to soft peaks, fold into sauce, and serve. About 40 to 45 calories per tablespoon, depending upon base sauce used.

✳ EGGNOG SAUCE

Makes about 2 cups

2 egg yolks
½ cup sifted confectioners' sugar
1 teaspoon vanilla
1 cup heavy cream

Beat egg yolks, sugar, and vanilla until thick and creamy. Whip cream to soft peaks, then fold in yolk mixture. Serve with fruit. About 40 calories per tablespoon.

VARIATION:

Orange or Lemon Eggnog Sauce: Just before serving fold in 1 tablespoon finely grated orange or lemon rind and/or 1–2 tablespoons brandy, light rum, or Marsala. About 40 calories per tablespoon (without brandy, rum, or Marsala).

NESSELRODE SAUCE

Serve cold over pudding, fruit, or ice cream.
Makes about 1 quart

1 recipe Stirred Custard
¼ cup Málaga or Marsala wine
¼ cup sultana raisins
¼ cup dried currants
2 tablespoons minced candied red cherries
2 tablespoons minced candied orange peel
2 tablespoons minced candied citron
½ cup shelled, peeled chestnuts, boiled and drained
½ cup heavy cream

Prepare and cool custard as directed. Meanwhile, pour wine over fruits and let stand 1 hour; also purée chestnuts. Mix fruits and chestnuts into custard. Whip cream to soft peaks and fold in. Cover and chill ½ hour before serving. About 30 calories per tablespoon.

✳ BASIC CHOCOLATE SAUCE

Seven sauces from one easy recipe.
Makes about 1 cup

2 (1-ounce) squares unsweetened chocolate
½ cup water
½ cup sugar
½ cup light corn syrup
2 tablespoons butter or margarine
½ teaspoon vanilla

Place chocolate, water, sugar, and syrup in a small, heavy saucepan, set over low heat, and heat, stirring now and then, until chocolate melts. Beat in butter and vanilla. Serve hot or at room temperature. About 85 calories per tablespoon.

VARIATIONS:

Creamy Chocolate Sauce: Substitute ½ cup light cream or evaporated milk for the water. About 100 calories per tablespoon.

Chocolate-Marshmallow Sauce: Omit sugar and add 16 large marshmallows; stir frequently as chocolate and marshmallows melt. About 90 calories per tablespoon.

Chocolate-Peppermint Sauce: Substitute ½ teaspoon peppermint extract for the vanilla. About 85 calories per tablespoon.

Chocolate-Nut Sauce: Prepare sauce as directed and mix in ⅓ cup chopped pecans, walnuts, toasted, blanched almonds, or peanuts. About 110 calories per tablespoon.

Chocolate-Cherry Sauce: Prepare sauce as directed and mix in ¼ cup quartered maraschino cherries before serving. About 90 calories per tablespoon.

Bittersweet Chocolate Sauce: Melt 1 (6-ounce) package semisweet chocolate bits with ½ cup light corn syrup in the top of a double boiler over simmering water. Beat in 1 (5⅓-ounce) can evaporated milk, 2 tablespoons hot water, and ½ teaspoon vanilla; heat and stir until creamy. About 90 calories per tablespoon.

▣ HOT FUDGE SAUCE

Makes 1¼ cups

1½ cups sugar
2 tablespoons flour
¾ cup cold water
3 (1-ounce) squares unsweetened chocolate or 3 (1-ounce) envelopes unsweetened no-melt chocolate
3 tablespoons butter or margarine
1 teaspoon vanilla

Mix sugar and flour in a heavy saucepan, blend in water, and heat, stirring constantly over moderate heat, until boiling and thickened. Reduce heat to low, add chocolate, and heat and stir until chocolate melts. Beat in butter and vanilla. Cool slightly, beating now and then. Serve warm. About 95 calories per tablespoon.

▣ QUICK MOCHA SAUCE

Makes 1¼ cups

2 (6-ounce) packages semisweet chocolate bits
6 tablespoons very hot strong black coffee
1 teaspoon vanilla

Purée chocolate bits, coffee, and vanilla in an electric blender at medium speed until chocolate melts and sauce is smooth. Serve at once over vanilla ice cream or sliced pound cake. This sauce can be stored, covered, in the refrigerator for several days. If too thick, thin with 1–2 tablespoons boiling water. About 82 calories per tablespoon.

▣ MARSHMALLOW CREAM SAUCE

Makes about 1 cup

4–5 tablespoons cold water
1 cup marshmallow cream
¼ teaspoon vanilla

Mix water with marshmallow cream, adding a little at a time, then blend until smooth. Stir in vanilla and serve cold with pudding or fruit. Or heat, stirring constantly, over moderately low heat and serve warm. About 50 calories per tablespoon.

VARIATIONS:

Chocolate Marshmallow Cream: Prepare as directed, set over low heat, and beat in 1 (1-ounce) square coarsely grated unsweetened chocolate or 1 (1-ounce) envelope no-melt unsweetened chocolate. Heat and stir until blended. About 55 calories per tablespoon.

Fruit Marshmallow Cream (About 1½ cups): Prepare as directed and beat in ½ cup strawberry, raspberry, peach, or apricot jam, black or red currant, or grape jelly, and 1 teaspoon lemon juice. Omit vanilla. About 50 calories per tablespoon.

Spicy Marshmallow Cream: Prepare as directed and beat in ¼ teaspoon each cinnamon and nutmeg and 1 teaspoon finely grated lemon rind. Omit vanilla. About 50 calories per tablespoon.

Peppermint Marshmallow Cream: Prepare as directed, substituting ⅛ teaspoon peppermint extract for the vanilla and, if you like, adding a few drops green or red food coloring. About 50 calories per tablespoon.

Liqueur Marshmallow Cream: Prepare as directed, using 2 tablespoons each water and crème de menthe or fruit liqueur instead of all water. Omit vanilla. About 55 calories per tablespoon.

BUTTERSCOTCH SAUCE

Makes about 2 cups

1 cup firmly packed dark brown sugar
1 cup maple syrup
¼ cup butter or margarine
1 teaspoon salt
2 teaspoons vanilla
¾ cup light cream

Heat sugar and syrup in a heavy saucepan over moderately low heat, stirring constantly until sugar dissolves. Raise heat to moderately high and boil uncovered 5 minutes. Off heat, add butter, salt, and vanilla. *Do not stir.* Let stand, uncovered, 5 minutes. Add cream, then beat about 1 minute until creamy, blond, and well blended. Serve warm. About 75 calories per tablespoon.

VARIATION:

Butterscotch Syrup (About 3 cups): Prepare as directed but increase light cream to 1½ cups. Serve over waffles, pancakes, or ice cream. About 60 calories per tablespoon.

✠ CARAMEL SYRUP

Makes 2 cups

1 (1-pound) box dark brown sugar
1½ cups water
2 teaspoons vanilla
¼ teaspoon salt

Heat and stir sugar in a heavy saucepan over low heat until liquid. Off heat, gradually stir in water. Return to low heat and heat and stir until smooth. Cool 5 minutes, mix in vanilla and salt. Pour into a jar, cool, cover, and refrigerate. Use as an ice-cream topping or milk flavoring. About 53 calories per tablespoon.

BASIC NUT SYRUP

Makes about 2 cups

2 cups sugar
1 cup water
¼ cup dark corn syrup
½ teaspoon vanilla
1 cup coarsely chopped walnuts, pecans, toasted almonds, hazelnuts, or blanched, roasted, unsalted peanuts

Mix sugar, water, and syrup in a 1-quart heavy saucepan, set over moderately low heat, and heat and stir until sugar dissolves. Raise heat and boil gently, uncovered, *without stirring* 3 minutes; stir once and, if the consistency of maple syrup, remove from heat; if not, boil 1 minute longer. Cool slightly and add vanilla and nuts. Stir just to mix and serve warm or cool over ice cream. About 80 calories per tablespoon.

VARIATIONS:

Orange-Nut Syrup: Prepare as directed, substituting orange juice for water and the grated rind of 1 orange for vanilla. About 85 calories per tablespoon.

Pistachio Syrup: Prepare as directed, substituting light corn syrup for the dark. Add ⅛ teaspoon almond extract, tint pale green, if you like, and stir in ½ cup shelled and peeled pistachio nuts. About 70 calories per tablespoon.

◨ LEMON OR LIME SAUCE

Spoon over ice cream or yellow cake.

Makes about 2½ cups

2 tablespoons cornstarch
1 cup sugar
1½ cups water
½ cup lemon or lime juice
¼ cup butter or margarine
2 teaspoons finely grated lemon or lime rind

Mix cornstarch and sugar in a heavy saucepan, gradually add water and fruit juice, and heat, stirring constantly, until mixture boils. Reduce heat and simmer, uncovered, 2–3 minutes, stirring now and then. Add butter and rind and stir until butter is melted and well blended. Serve hot. About 30 calories per tablespoon.

VARIATION:

Orange Sauce: Prepare as directed, using 2 cups orange juice instead of water and lemon juice, and grated orange rind instead of lemon. For tartness, add 1–2 tablespoons lemon juice. About 35 calories per tablespoon.

◨ BRANDY OR RUM SAUCE

Delicious over steamed puddings or ice cream.

Makes about 2½ cups

2 tablespoons cornstarch
½ cup sugar
1¾ cups milk
¼–⅓ cup brandy or light rum
¼ cup butter or margarine
½ teaspoon vanilla
Pinch nutmeg

Mix cornstarch and sugar in a heavy saucepan, gradually add milk and brandy, and heat, stirring constantly, until mixture boils. Reduce heat and simmer, uncovered, 2–3 minutes, stirring now and then. Add butter, vanilla, and nutmeg and stir until butter melts and is well blended. Serve hot. About 35 calories per tablespoon.

LEMON-RAISIN SAUCE

Good over gingerbread.

Makes 2⅔ cups

1 cup sugar
2 tablespoons cornstarch
1½ cups cold water
½ cup lemon juice
2 teaspoons finely grated lemon rind
1 egg yolk
2 tablespoons butter or margarine
¼ cup sultana raisins

Mix sugar and cornstarch in a heavy

saucepan, blend in water and lemon juice, and heat, stirring constantly over moderate heat, until mixture boils. Reduce heat and simmer 2–3 minutes, stirring now and then. Mix lemon rind and egg yolk, blend a little hot sauce into egg, return to pan, and beat and stir 1–2 minutes; do not boil. Off heat, add butter and raisins and let stand 2 minutes. Serve warm. About 30 calories per tablespoon.

RED CHERRY SAUCE

Delicious over vanilla ice cream or pound cake.
Makes about 2 cups

1 (1-pound) can pitted sour red cherries (do not drain)
⅔ cup sugar
2 tablespoons cornstarch
¼ teaspoon almond extract
Few drops red food coloring

Drain liquid from cherries and reserve. Mix sugar and cornstarch in a heavy saucepan, blend in cherry liquid, and heat over moderate heat, stirring constantly, until mixture boils. Reduce heat and simmer 2–3 minutes, stirring now and then. Add cherries and almond extract and heat 2 minutes. Off heat, mix in food coloring. Serve hot or cold (thin with a little water if sauce seems thick). About 35 calories per tablespoon.

VARIATION:

Pineapple Sauce: Mix ½ cup sugar with the cornstarch, blend in 1 cup pineapple juice, and proceed as recipe directs, adding 1 (8½-ounce) undrained can crushed pineapple at the end instead of cherries. Omit almond extract and add 1 tablespoon lemon juice. Tint pale yellow if you like. About 35 calories per tablespoon.

☒ JAM OR JELLY SAUCE

Makes about 1½ cups

1 cup jam or jelly (any kind)
2 teaspoons cornstarch
⅔ cup cold water
2 teaspoons lemon juice

Heat jam or jelly in a small, heavy saucepan over moderately low heat. Mix cornstarch and water, blend into jam, and heat and stir until mixture boils. Reduce heat and simmer, stirring now and then, 2–3 minutes. Off heat, mix in lemon juice. Serve warm over pudding. About 30 calories per tablespoon.

VARIATIONS:

Jam and Nut Sauce: Prepare sauce as directed, cool slightly, and mix in ¼–⅓ cup minced pecans, walnuts, or toasted almonds. About 40 calories per tablespoon.

Sultana Jam Sauce: Prepare sauce as directed and mix in ¼ cup sultana raisins; let stand 5 minutes to plump raisins. About 35 calories per tablespoon.

Ginger-Jam Sauce: Prepare sauce as directed, using peach, apricot, or pineapple jam, then mix in ¼ cup minced crystallized ginger. About 35 calories per tablespoon.

Marmalade Sauce: Substitute orange, lemon, or grapefruit marmalade for jam and prepare as directed; omit lemon juice. About 30 calories per tablespoon.

Sherried Peach or Apricot Jam Sauce: Prepare as directed, using ½ cup water and ¼ cup dry sherry (or brandy) instead of the ⅔ cup water; omit lemon juice. About 40 calories per tablespoon.

DESSERTS AND DESSERT SAUCES

⊠ MELBA SAUCE

Serve as a sauce for Peach Melba, ice cream, or fruit or use to flavor milk shakes and sodas.
Makes about 1½ cups

> 1 pint fresh raspberries, washed, or 2 (10-ounce) packages frozen raspberries, thawed
> ⅓ cup red currant jelly
> ⅓–½ cup sugar
> 1 tablespoon cornstarch blended with 2 tablespoons water

Purée raspberries in an electric blender at high speed and strain. Pour into a saucepan, mix in jelly, sugar, and cornstarch paste, and cook and stir over moderate heat until thickened and clear. Cool, taste for sweetness, and add more sugar if needed. About 40 calories per tablespoon if made with fresh berries, 55 calories per tablespoon if made with frozen berries.

VARIATIONS:

Strawberry Sauce: Prepare as directed, substituting 1 pint fresh strawberries or 2 (10-ounce) packages thawed frozen strawberries for the raspberries. About 40 calories per tablespoon if made with fresh berries, 50 if made with frozen berries.

Currant Sauce: Substitute 1 pint very ripe red or black currants for the raspberries and omit the currant jelly. If you like, mix the cornstarch with port wine or blackberry liqueur instead of water. Proceed as directed. About 25 calories per tablespoon.

⚖ DESSERT CARDINAL SAUCE

Use as a dessert sauce for ice cream, sherbet, or fresh fruit.
Makes about 5 cups

> 1 (10-ounce) package frozen raspberries, thawed
> ½ cup superfine sugar
> 1 tablespoon lemon juice
> 2–3 tablespoons kirsch (optional)
> 2 pints fresh strawberries, washed, stemmed, and sliced thin

Purée raspberries in an electric blender at high speed or put through a food mill, then strain. Add ¼ cup sugar, lemon juice, and, if you like, the kirsch; stir well. Mix strawberries with remaining sugar. Gently stir raspberry sauce into strawberries. About 10 calories per tablespoon made without kirsch, 12 calories per tablespoon made with kirsch.

ALGARVE APRICOT SAUCE

In the south of Portugal lies the Algarve, where figs, peaches, and apricots grow. Women make them into a variety of sweets, among them this tart apricot sauce, luscious over a poached meringue.
Makes about 2¼ cups

> 1 (1-pound 14-ounce) can peeled whole apricots (do not drain)
> Juice and grated rind of 1 lemon
> 1 cup firmly packed light brown sugar
> ¼ cup butter

Pit apricots and purée in an electric blender at high speed or put through a food mill. Place in a small saucepan, add lemon juice, rind, and sugar, and simmer uncovered, stirring occasionally, 1 hour until thick and caramel colored. Remove from heat, stir in butter, and cool to room temperature. Serve over Poached Meringue Ring or as a dessert sauce for ice cream, sliced oranges or peaches. About 55 calories per tablespoon.

❧ HONEY SAUCE

Serve warm or cool over pudding, fruit, or ice cream.
Makes 1½ cups

1 cup honey
1 tablespoon cornstarch blended with 1 tablespoon cold water
¼ cup butter or margarine
2 teaspoons lemon juice

Heat honey in a small, heavy saucepan over moderate heat. Stir in cornstarch mixture and heat and stir until boiling; reduce heat and simmer 2–3 minutes. Beat in butter and lemon juice. About 60 calories per tablespoon.

VARIATION:

Honey-Nut Sauce: Prepare sauce as directed, cool, and mix in ½ cup coarsely chopped pecans, walnuts, or toasted almonds. About 80 calories per tablespoon.

❧ EASY PEPPERMINT SAUCE

To save yourself the job of crushing peppermint sticks, buy the small peppermint candies. Best over chocolate ice cream.
Makes 1½ cups

½ pound red-striped peppermint candies or 2 cups coarsely crushed peppermint sticks
1 cup water
½ cup sugar

Heat candy and water in a heavy saucepan over moderate heat, stirring often until candy begins to dissolve, then boil slowly, uncovered, until completely dissolved, stirring now and then. Add sugar and heat and stir 2–3 minutes. Cool and serve over ice cream. About 50 calories per tablespoon.

❧ HARD SAUCE

The perfect sauce for steamed puddings.
Makes about 1 cup

½ cup butter (no substitute), softened to room temperature
2 cups sifted confectioners' sugar
⅛ teaspoon salt
1 tablespoon hot water
1 teaspoon vanilla

Beat butter until creamy; gradually beat in sugar, a little at a time. Beat in remaining ingredients and continue to beat until fluffy. Serve chilled or at room temperature. About 115 calories per tablespoon.

VARIATIONS:

Brandy or Rum Hard Sauce: Omit hot water and vanilla; add 2 tablespoons brandy or rum or 2 teaspoons brandy or rum extract. About 120 calories per tablespoon.

Lemon or Orange Hard Sauce: Omit water and vanilla; instead, beat in 2 tablespoons lemon or orange juice and 1 tablespoon finely grated lemon rind or 2 tablespoons finely grated orange rind. About 115 calories per tablespoon.

Mocha Hard Sauce: Increase hot water to 2 tablespoons and beat in 1 tablespoon instant coffee powder and 2 tablespoons cocoa. About 120 calories per tablespoon.

Cream Fluff Hard Sauce: Prepare sauce as directed but omit water; at the end gradually beat in ¼ cup heavy cream. About 130 calories per tablespoon.

❧ MOCK DEVONSHIRE CREAM

Serve as a topping for fresh fruit, fruit pies, and cobblers.
Makes about 1 pint

DESSERTS AND DESSERT SAUCES

1 cup heavy cream
3 tablespoons sifted confectioners' sugar
1 cup sour cream

Whip cream with the sugar until soft peaks form, then blend in sour cream. About 45 calories per tablespoon.

▣ SWEETENED WHIPPED CREAM

For best results, whip cream by hand just before needed, using a chilled bowl and beater.
Makes about 2 cups

1 cup very cold heavy cream
2 tablespoons sugar or ¼ cup sifted confectioners' sugar
½ teaspoon vanilla or ¼ teaspoon almond, maple, or peppermint extract

Beat cream in a chilled bowl until frothy; slowly beat in sugar and flavoring and continue beating until soft, glossy peaks form, scraping bowl often. (*Note:* If you should slightly overbeat cream, stir in 1–2 tablespoons cold milk.) If you must delay using it, refrigerate, then beat lightly with a wire whisk just before using. About 30 calories per tablespoon.

VARIATIONS:

Plain Whipped Cream: Whip cream as directed but omit sugar and flavoring. About 28 calories per tablespoon.

Decorative Whipped Cream: Whip cream with ⅓ cup sifted confectioners' sugar, flavor, then tint, if you like, a pastel color. Pipe through a pastry tube fitted with a decorative tip. *To Freeze:* Do not color whipped cream; pipe onto wax-paper-lined baking sheets and freeze until hard; wrap frozen fluffs individually, then group in plastic freezer bags. Use within 2 months. Nice on warm pies. About 35 calories per tablespoon.

Chocolate Whipped Cream: Whip as directed, beating in 3 tablespoons sugar blended with 3 tablespoons cocoa; reduce vanilla to ¼ teaspoon. About 40 calories per tablespoon.

Coffee Whipped Cream: Prepare as directed but add 1 teaspoon instant coffee powder. About 30 calories per tablespoon.

Mocha Whipped Cream: Blend 2 tablespoons sugar, 1 tablespoon cocoa, and 1 teaspoon instant coffee powder. Whip into cream as directed. About 35 calories per tablespoon.

Orange or Lemon Whipped Cream: Whip as directed, flavoring with ¼ teaspoon orange or lemon extract and 2 teaspoons finely grated rind instead of vanilla. About 30 calories per tablespoon.

Spiced Whipped Cream: Whip as directed, adding ¼ teaspoon each nutmeg and cinnamon. About 30 calories per tablespoon.

Nutty Whipped Cream: Whip as directed, then fold in ¼–⅓ cup any minced nuts. About 40 calories per tablespoon.

Fruity Whipped Cream: Whip as directed, omitting vanilla, then fold in ⅓ cup any sweetened fruit purée. About 45 calories per tablespoon.

Coconut Whipped Cream: Whip as directed, then fold in ⅓ cup flaked coconut. About 35 calories per tablespoon.

Spiked Whipped Cream: Whip as directed, but flavor with 2–3 tablespoons brandy, rum, bourbon, crème de menthe, or fruit liqueur instead of vanilla. About 35 calories per tablespoon.

Party Whipped Cream (Makes about 2 quarts): Warm 2 teaspoons unflavored gelatin and ¼ cup cold water until gelatin dissolves; cool slightly and gradually mix in 1 quart heavy cream; chill ½ hour. Whip cream, beating in 1 cup sifted confectioners' sugar and 2 teaspoons vanilla. (*Note:* If you use an electric mixer, hold out ⅓ cup cream and stir in after the rest is whipped.) This cream will hold well in the refrigerator about 1 hour. About 30 calories per tablespoon.

⚖ WHIPPED EVAPORATED MILK TOPPING

Makes about 1½ cups

½ cup evaporated milk (do not dilute)
1 tablespoon lemon juice
½ cup sifted confectioners' sugar
½ teaspoon vanilla or ¼ teaspoon almond extract

Chill evaporated milk in an ice cube tray in freezer until ice crystals form around edge, 20–30 minutes. Meanwhile, chill bowl and beater. Whip milk until soft peaks form; add remaining ingredients and beat until stiff peaks form. If not to be used at once, refrigerate and use within 1 hour. About 15 calories per tablespoon.

VARIATIONS:

Any of the Sweetened Whipped Cream flavor variations work well with this topping.

⊠ ⚖ LOW-CALORIE DESSERT TOPPING

Makes 4 servings

3 tablespoons ice water
3 tablespoons nonfat dry milk powder
2 teaspoons lemon juice
Few drops liquid noncaloric sweetener or 2 teaspoons low-calorie granulated sugar substitute
¼ teaspoon vanilla or almond extract

Pour ice water into a chilled bowl, sprinkle powdered milk on surface, and beat with a rotary or electric beater until soft peaks form. Add lemon juice, sweeten to taste, add vanilla, and beat until stiff peaks form. Use at once. About 14 calories per serving.

VARIATIONS:

⊠ ⚖ **Low-Calorie Coffee Dessert Topping:** Substitute 3 tablespoons very strong iced coffee for ice water and omit vanilla. About 14 calories per serving.

⊠ ⚖ **Low-Calorie Orange Dessert Topping:** Substitute 1 tablespoon frozen, slightly thawed orange juice concentrate diluted with 2 tablespoons ice water for the ice water, omit vanilla, and after whipping fold in 1 tablespoon finely grated orange rind. About 20 calories per serving.

HOMEMADE SOUR CREAM

Makes about 1 cup

1 cup heavy cream, at room temperature
¼ cup sour cream or buttermilk

Mix creams in a screw-top jar, cover, and let stand at room temperature about 24 hours until very thick. Chill well before using and keep refrigerated. About 60 calories per tablespoon if made with sour cream, 55 calories per tablespoon if made with buttermilk.

CHAPTER 21

PIES AND PASTRIES

More than any other dessert, pies are typically American. Our speech ("as easy as pie"), our songs ("I'm as normal as blueberry pie . . ."), our literature (to eat "humble pie") are strewn with references. Apple pies, traditionally, usher in autumn, pumpkin pies belong to Thanksgiving, mince pies to Christmas, and cherry pies to George Washington's birthday. Foreign countries have specialties too—if not pies, flaky pastries, honey-drenched or filled with meltingly smooth creams: the éclairs, cream puffs, and Napoleons of France, the tortes of Germany and Austria, the cheese cakes of Italy, the wispy honey-laden pastries of the Middle East. Many can be made at home, some with less effort than seems possible.

The Kinds of Pastry and How to Mix Them

Conventional Pastry: The piecrust pastry, tender and flaky when properly made. The secret is to cut the fat into the flour until it is the texture of coarse meal so that in baking, these flecks of fat melt, leaving the pastry flaky. There are a number of variations on the standard method (see recipes that follow).

Puff Pastry (Pâte Feuilletée): The feathery, many-layered French pastry used for Napoleons, Cream Horns, and dozens of lavish pastries. It is made by rolling and folding chilled butter (or sometimes lard if the pastry is a savory one) into a simple dough so that it separates into tissue-thin "leaves" when baked. A less tedious variation is *Rough Puff Pastry.*

Sweet Short Pastry (also called *Tart* or *Sweet Torte Pastry* and in French, *Pâte Brisée;* the German *Mürbteig* is of this type): Rather like a cookie dough, this egg-rich, sweet pastry is most often used for fruit flans and tarts.

Choux Pastry (Pâte à Choux): A paste containing a high proportion of eggs that is beaten until smooth and elastic enough to "puff" during baking. This is the pastry of cream puffs and éclairs.

Phyllo Pastry (pronounced FEE-lo): The tissue-thin, crisp pastry used for Greek and Middle Eastern pastries. It requires a special hard flour, a special technique, and years of practice. Phyllo leaves, ready to fill and bake, are available in many gourmet markets and Greek groceries.

Strudel Pastry: An elastic dough that is kneaded, rolled, and stretched until big as a table and "thin enough to read a newspaper through." It is filled with fruit, cheese, or poppy seeds, rolled up jelly-roll style, and baked until golden brown and crisp. Strudel dough sheets can be bought at gourmet groceries.

Crumb "Pastries": These aren't pastries but crumbs, crushed dried cereals, nuts, coconut, etc., mixed with sugar or syrup and melted butter and pressed into piepans.

Essential Ingredients of Pastries

Flour: Experts use *pastry flour* for piecrusts because it makes them unusually tender. Available at gourmet groceries (and occasionally through local bakeries), it is softer than all-purpose flour but not so delicate as cake flour. It is not suitable for pastries where elasticity is needed (choux and strudel).

IMPORTANT NOTE: USE ALL-PURPOSE FLOUR FOR PASTRIES IN THIS BOOK UNLESS RECIPES SPECIFY OTHERWISE.

Fat: For most piecrusts, a solid fat is used. It may be vegetable shortening or lard, which many cooks prefer because of its mellow flavor and brittle texture. Mixtures of shortening and butter or margarine may be used, but the proportion of butter (do not use the whipped variety) should be kept low (about 1 to 3) if the pastry is to be flaky. For best results, chill the fat before using. Some pastries are made with cooking oil; it produces a tender (though not very flaky) crust. (*Note:* Use cooking oil only if recipes call for it; do not use interchangeably with shortening or lard.)

Liquid: Water (but occasionally fruit juice, milk, or cream) is used to bind the fat and flour, making pastry workable. For flaky pastry, use cold water; for a denser, mealier texture, warm or hot water.

Salt: Added strictly for flavor; without it, pastries would taste flat.

Extra Ingredients of Pastries

Sugar: Added to tart or torte pastries for sweetness, tenderness, and better browning.

Eggs: Added for richness of flavor and color. Usually egg yolks, rather than whole eggs, are used.

Leavening: Used in cookie dough-type pastries when a certain lightness and sponginess are wanted.

Flavorings: These are merely embellishments—grated cheese or nuts, spices, seeds, grated orange or lemon rind, sometimes vanilla or other extracts—added for variety and interest.

Some Pastry-Making Terms and Techniques

To Brush: To apply a thin coating of liquid, usually glaze or melted butter, with a pastry brush to give pastry a satiny or glistening finish. Bottom crusts are sometimes brushed with beaten egg white to "waterproof" them and keep juices from soaking in.

To Crimp: To pinch or crease edges of pastry in a zigzag or fluted pattern. Crimped edges seal top and bottom crusts together and also act like dams, holding fillings in.

Croûte: The French word for *crust;* en *croûte* refers to something baked in a pastry.

To Cut In: To work fat into flour with a pastry blender, 2 knives, or the fingertips. The motion is literally a cutting one (except when fingers are used), the fat particles being broken up and coated with flour.

To Dot: To dab bits of butter or other solid over the surface of something, usually before baking. In pies, fruit fillings are often dotted with butter.

To Dust: To cover with a thin film of flour.

To Fill: To put filling in a pie shell or other pastry.

To Fit: To press pastry against the contours of a pan.

Flan: The French word for a flat, open-face pie usually filled with fruit or cream filling or a combination of the two; it may be larger than American-style pies or smaller. For baking flan, a *flan ring* (bottomless round metal ring with straight sides) is placed on a baking sheet and the pastry pressed into it.

To Glaze: To coat with glaze. In pastry making, both crusts and fillings may be glazed, crusts with beaten egg or milk and sugar, fillings with syrup, thin gelatin, or clear sweet sauce.

To Line: To cover a pan with a thin layer of pastry, crumb crust, or other material.

Meringue: A stiffly beaten mixture of egg whites and sugar used as a pie topping or dropped from a spoon and baked like cookies.

"Mixture Forms a Ball": The term used to describe pastry when just the right amount of liquid has been added to the flour-shortening mixture. The pastry will just hang together in a ball but be neither sticky (too much liquid) nor crumbly (too little).

Pastry Blender: A gadget indispensable to every pastry cook, 6–8 arched blades or wires, mounted on a wooden handle, that cut fat into flour in record time. If you have none, use 2 table knives instead, cutting back and forth through the fat and flour or, if you prefer, rub fat and flour together with your fingertips. The difficulty of the finger method is that the heat of the hands may melt the shortening and make the pastry tough.

Pastry Cloth: A heavy square of canvas that makes rolling pastry easier because the fabric gives up only a small amount of flour to the pastry yet keeps it from sticking.

Pastry Wheel: A handy cutting wheel with either a plain or zigzag blade mounted on a wooden handle.

To Patch: To fill in cracks, holes, uneven edges of pastry by pressing in small scraps. Sometimes it is necessary to dampen the pastry scraps so they will stick.

Pie Funnel: A heatproof ceramic funnel about 3″ high, often with a decorative top, used in deep-dish pies to help prop up the crust and keep the pie from boiling over. It stands in the center of the pie, its top poking through the pastry.

Pie Shell: Crust fitted into a piepan; it may be baked or unbaked.

To Prick: To pierce pastry, usually a bottom crust, at intervals with a fork so it will lie flat during baking.

To Roll Out: To roll pastry with a rolling pin.

To Roll Up: To roll a pastry over and over, jelly-roll style. The technique is used for making Palmiers and Strudel.

To Seal: To pinch pastry edges together, sealing in filling.

Short: Containing a high proportion of shortening; a short crust is tender and crumbly.

Spring Form Pan: A fairly deep, straight-sided round pan with removable bottom and a side seam that locks and unlocks to facilitate removing pastry. It is most often used for cheese cakes.

Steam Slits or Vents: Decorative slits or holes cut in a top crust to allow steam to escape during baking; these also help keep pies from boiling over.

Stockinette: A knitted cotton "stocking" fitted over a rolling pin to make rolling pastry easier. It works like a pastry cloth, giving up very little flour to the pastry but at the same time keeping it from sticking. Stockinettes are inexpensive and available in nearly every dime store. Wash and dry after each use.

Tart: A small pastry, usually open-face, often with a short sweet crust. It may be bite-size or big enough for one ample dessert portion. Tart shells may be baked in muffin tins or fluted tart tins (see About Making Tarts).

"Texture of Coarse Meal": The term used to describe the consistency of fat when properly cut into flour. In making pastry, the fat should be cut in only until pebbly and coarse. Some cooks prefer the particles even coarser, about the size of small beans, because these solid flecks of fat, scattered throughout the flour, are what make the pastry flaky and crisp.

To Toss: To mix quickly and lightly with a fork, using a tossing motion. This is the technique used in mixing liquid into pastries, the object being to handle as gently as possible so that the fat particles aren't mashed. When the pastry holds together, the mixing's done.

How to Make Better Pies and Pastries

About Pans:

– For richly browned bottom crusts, use heatproof glass, dark metal, or heavy teflon-lined pans. Bright shiny pans deflect the heat, producing pale crusts.
– For best results, use types and sizes of pans recipes call for.
– When making a juicy fruit pie, use a pan with a trough around the rim to catch "boil-ups."
– Do not grease or flour piepan; do, however, make sure it is spotless and dry.

About Mixing Pastries:

– Read recipe before beginning and make sure you have all ingredients and implements on hand.
– For mixing, use a large, heavy, round-bottomed bowl.
– Measure all ingredients before beginning.
– For extra-flaky pastry, chill shortening and water 15–20 minutes before using.
– Use the lightest possible touch in mixing pastries. Cut fat into flour until "the texture of coarse meal" or for a superflaky crust, until "the size of small beans." Scatter liquid over mixture, one tablespoon at a time, tossing with a fork until it just "forms a ball."
– Do not knead pastry unless recipe calls for it (strudel dough, for ex-

ample, must be kneaded). But piecrusts, never.

About Rolling Pastries:

– Lightly gather pastry together with hands and shape loosely into a ball.
– Chill pastry, if you like, about ½ hour before rolling. Some cooks insist that the chilling step is vital if the pastry is to be flaky and tender. But many tests have proved that, if the pastry is properly handled throughout mixing and rolling, the chilling makes little difference.
– Place pastry on a lightly floured pastry cloth or board, flatten lightly into a small circle (or rectangle or square, depending on shape needed), then with lightly floured, stockinette-covered rolling pin, flatten until about ½" thick. Even up any ragged edges.
– Roll pastry from the center outward, using short, firm strokes and changing direction as needed to keep pastry as nearly circular (or rectangular or square) as possible. Always bear in mind the ultimate size and shape you want when rolling and roll toward that end. For most piecrusts, ⅛" is a good thickness. As for diameter, pastry should be about 3" larger in diameter than the pan you plan to use.
– Use as little flour in rolling as possible; it's the extra flour that toughens the pastry.
– If edges crack or pastry is rolled too thin in spots, patch with scraps. Dampen, then press in place and roll. The patchwork should be invisible.
– To transfer pastry easily to pan, place rolling pin across center of pastry, lop half of pastry over rolling pin, and lift gently into pan.

About Fitting Pastries into Pans:

– Center pastry circle in pan so that overhang is equal all around.
– Press gently, fitting against contours of pan.
– *If a single crust pie:* Trim overhang all around with scissors so it is about 1" larger than pan. Roll under, even with rim, and crimp as desired.
– *If a double crust pie:* Do not trim overhang. Brush bottom and sides well with beaten egg white if filling is extra juicy and let air-dry 15–20 minutes. Roll top crust as you did the bottom, making it slightly thinner if you like. Cut decorative steam slits in the center. Add filling to pie shell, mounding it up in the center. Fit top crust over filling, trim both crusts evenly all around so they overhang about ½–1". Roll up and over even with rim, then seal and crimp.

About Baking Pastries:

– Let oven preheat a full 15 minutes before baking.
– Unless recipes direct to the contrary, bake pies as near the center of the oven as possible so they will brown evenly.
– When baking more than one pie at a time, stagger pans on rack or racks, leaving plenty of room between them for heat to circulate. Do not let pans touch oven walls.
– If crust should brown too fast, cover with a piece of foil or dampened piece of cloth. (*Note:* Crimped edges, in particular, brown faster than the rest of the crust.)

To Tell When Pies Are Done:

Double Crust Pies: The crust should be tan and crisp, the filling bubbly.

Single Crust Pies: The crimped edges should be nicely browned and crisp. The filling, if a custard type, should be set (a table knife inserted midway between center and rim should come out clean).

Meringue Pies: Meringue should look "set," be very faint tan with peaks of darker brown.

About Cooling Pies: Follow individual recipes carefully. Most pies should cool a few minutes on a wire rack before being cut; some should be brought to room temperature and others well chilled.

About Storing and Keeping Pies: Pies with custard or cream fillings, also those with whipped cream toppings, should be kept refrigerated (let stand at room temperature about 20 minutes before serving). Other kinds of pie may simply be kept in a cool corner of the kitchen.

About Reheating Pies: Fruit and mince pies are about the only ones that benefit from reheating. They will taste freshly baked if heated about 15 minutes at 325° F. and served hot.

About Freezing Pies: See chapter on freezing.

About Cutting Pies:

In General: Mentally divide pie into the needed number of pieces before making the first cut, then cut, using a pie server to transfer pieces to plates.

Double Crust Pies: Use a very sharp knife with a thin blade.

Single Crust Pies: Cut as you would a double crust pie, but dip knife often in hot water if filling is sticky.

Meringue Pies: Use a sharp knife, dipping into warm water after every cut to keep meringue from sticking.

How to Crimp or Flute a Piecrust

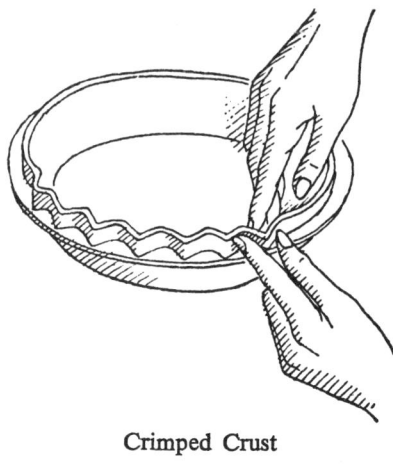

Crimped Crust

Fluted Crust

How to Make Lattice-Top Crusts

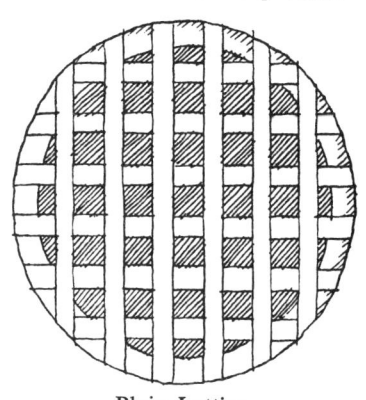

Plain Lattice

PIES AND PASTRIES

Woven Lattice

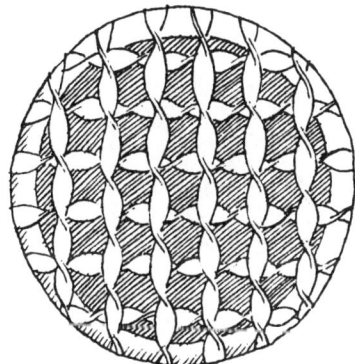

Twisted Lattice

Some Decorative Tricks with Pastry

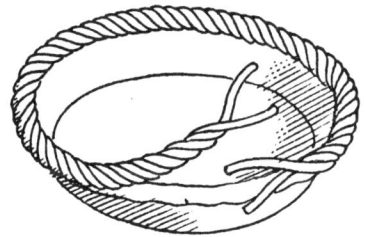

Spiral or Twist

Cut long strips of pastry about ½" wide and twist together, tightly for a spiral, loosely for a twist. Dampen pastry rim and attach by pressing lightly.

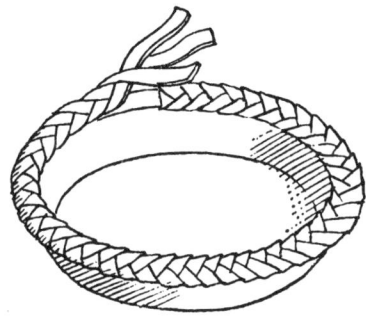

Braid

A variation on the twist made by braiding 3 long thin strips of pastry and attaching to dampened rim.

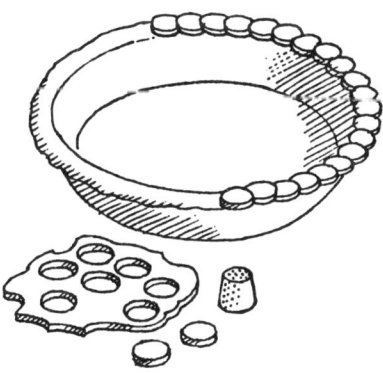

Coin

Cut out tiny pastry circles with a thimble and arrange, overlapping, on dampened rim. To make a button trim, simply perforate centers of circles with a needle so they resemble buttons.

Ruffle

Simply scallop pastry edge using a measuring teaspoon.

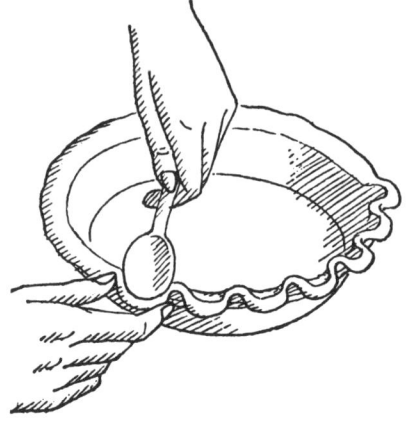

Some Fancy Cutouts for Top Crusts:

           Fruit Cutouts   Wedge Cutouts
Circle in the Square   Christmas Tree Cutouts   Sunburst
        Hatchet Cutouts   Star Burst

¢ FLAKY PASTRY I

For 1 single crust 8", 9", or 10" pie

1¼ cups sifted flour
½ teaspoon salt
⅓ cup chilled vegetable shortening or lard
¼ cup ice water

Place flour in salt in a shallow mixing bowl and cut in shortening with a pastry blender until mixture resembles coarse meal. Sprinkle water over surface, 1 tablespoon at a time, and mix in lightly and quickly with a fork, just until pastry holds together. Shape gently into a ball on a lightly floured pastry cloth, then flatten into a circle about 1" thick, evening up rough edges. Using a lightly floured, stockinette-covered rolling pin and short, firm strokes, roll into a circle about 3" larger than the pan you plan to use. To transfer pastry to pan, lay rolling pin across center of pastry circle, fold half of pastry over pin and ease into pan; press lightly. Seal any cracks or holes by pressing dampened scraps of pastry on top. Trim pastry so it hangs evenly 1" over rim, roll overhang under even with rim and crimp or flute as shown.

To Bake an Unfilled Pie Shell: Preheat oven to 425° F. Prick bottom and sides of pastry well with a fork. To minimize shrinkage, lay a large square of wax paper over crust and fill with uncooked rice or dried beans (experienced cooks keep a jar on hand, using beans or rice over and over). Bake pastry 10–12 minutes, just until tan. Lift out paper of rice. Cool before filling unless recipes direct otherwise.

To Bake a Filled Pie Shell: Follow directions given in individual recipes. About 1090 calories total, 136 for each of 8 wedges and 180 for each of 6 wedges.

VARIATIONS:

Cheese Pastry I: Prepare as directed but toss ½ cup finely grated Cheddar cheese into flour-shortening mixture before adding water. Especially good with apple pie. About 1315 calories total, 165 for each of 8 wedges and 220 for each of 6 wedges.

Orange Pastry I: Prepare as directed but substitute ¼ cup cold orange juice for the water and add 1–2 teaspoons finely grated lemon or orange rind to the flour-shortening mixture. Especially good with fruit or fruit-flavored chiffon pies.

Nut Pastry I: Prepare as directed but toss ¼ cup finely ground nuts (pecans, walnuts, black walnuts, hazelnuts) into flour-shortening mixture before adding water. Especially good with chocolate or other cream or chiffon-type pies. About 1300 calories total, 160 for each of 8 wedges and 215 for each of 6.

¢ **Spicy Pastry I:** Mix ¼ teaspoon each cinnamon, cloves, and allspice and a pinch nutmeg, mace, or ginger with flour; proceed as directed. Good with pumpkin, apple, peach, or other spicy fruit pies.

¢ **Seed Pastry I:** Prepare as directed but toss 1–2 tablespoons poppy, caraway, or toasted sesame seeds with flour-shortening mixture before adding water. The poppy seed crust is good with custard or vanilla cream pies, the caraway with apple, pear, or peach, and the toasted sesame with chocolate or butterscotch cream pies.

The calorie counts for Orange Pastry I, Spicy Pastry I, and Seed Pastry I are all approximately the same as for Flaky Pastry I.

¢ FLAKY PASTRY II

For 1 double crust 8″ or 9″ pie

2 cups sifted flour
1 teaspoon salt
⅔ cup chilled vegetable shortening or lard
4–6 tablespoons ice water

Mix exactly like Flaky Pastry I. Roll half the pastry as directed and fit into pan. Cover loosely and chill while you prepare filling; also wrap and chill unrolled portion. (*Note:* If filling is intricate, make it *before* the pastry.) Just before filling pie shell, roll remaining pastry as you did the first and cut 3 V-shaped slits or decorative holes near center for steam to escape. Fill pie shell and brush rim with cold water. Cover with top crust. For a high fluted edge (best for juicy pies), roll crusts over and even with rim, then crimp. For a flat edge, trim crusts even with rim and press with tines of a fork to seal. Bake according to times given in individual recipes that follow. About 1980 calories total, about 250 calories for each of 8 wedges and 330 calories for each of 6 wedges.

VARIATIONS:

Cheese Pastry II: Prepare as directed but toss 1 cup finely grated Cheddar cheese into flour-shortening mixture before adding water. If necessary, add an extra tablespoon ice water. About 2425 calories total, about 304 calories for each of 8 wedges and about 405 calories for each of 6 wedges.

Orange Pastry II: Prepare as directed but substitute ¼–⅓ cup cold orange juice for the water and add 1 tablespoon finely grated orange or lemon rind. Good with berry or other fruit pies.

¢ **Spicy Pastry II:** Mix ½ teaspoon each cinnamon and allspice and a pinch each ginger, cloves, and nutmeg with flour; then proceed as directed. Good with apple, peach, or other spicy fruit pies.

¢ **Seed Pastry II:** Prepare as directed but toss 2–3 tablespoons poppy, caraway, or toasted sesame seeds with flour-shortening mixture before adding water. The poppy seed crust is good with apple or peach pies, the caraway with apple or pear, and the sesame with apple, peach, or pear.

The calorie counts for Orange Pastry II, Spicy Pastry II, and Seed Pastry II are all approximately the same as for Flaky Pastry II.

¢ HOT WATER PASTRY

A tender crust but not as flaky as Flaky Pastry.

For 1 single crust 8″ or 9″ pie

1¼ cups sifted flour
½ teaspoon salt
¼ teaspoon baking powder
⅓ cup vegetable shortening or lard
3 tablespoons boiling water

Sift flour with salt and baking powder and set aside. With a fork, beat shortening and water until smooth and creamy; chill 20 minutes, then sprinkle in flour, a little at a time, mixing with a fork until pastry begins to hold together. Gather together with fingers and shape into a ball on a lightly floured pastry cloth. Roll and fit into piepan as directed for Flaky Pastry I. To bake an unfilled pie shell, follow directions for Flaky Pastry I; to bake a filled shell, follow instructions given in individual recipes. About 1090 calories total, 136 for each of 8 wedges and 180 for each of 6 wedges.

VARIATION:

Hot Water Pastry for 1 Double Crust 8" or 9" Pie: Use 2 cups sifted flour, double all remaining ingredients, and proceed as directed. Roll pastry into top and bottom crusts as directed for Flaky Pastry II. About 1980 calories total, about 250 calories for each of 8 wedges and 330 calories for each of 6 wedges.

OIL PASTRY

Can be used interchangeably with the more conventional Flaky Pastry II.

For 1 double crust 8" or 9" pie

2 cups sifted flour
1 teaspoon salt
½ cup cooking oil
¼ cup ice water

Sift flour and salt into a bowl; beat oil and water with a fork until slightly thickened and creamy, pour all at once over flour and toss with fork to blend. Gather pastry together (it should just hold together) and, if too dry, add a few additional drops oil and toss again. Shape gently into a ball. Place half of pastry on a 12" square of wax paper and flatten until about 1" thick; even up rough edges. Top with a second square of wax paper and roll from center outward into a circle about 3" larger in diameter than pan you plan to use. (*Note:* If you wipe counter with a damp cloth before rolling, wax paper won't slide around.) Peel off top paper and invert pastry on pan; peel off remaining paper and fit pastry in pan; do not trim overhang. Roll remaining pastry the same way, peel off top paper, and cut 3 V-shaped slits or decorative holes near center for steam to escape. Fill pie shell with desired filling, brush rim with cold water, and invert pastry on filling. Peel off paper and, if pie is juicy, make a high fluted edge. If not, trim crusts even with rim and seal with tines of a fork. Bake according to times given in individual recipes. About 1800 calories total, about 225 calories for each of 8 wedges and 300 calories for each of 6 wedges.

For a Single Crust 8" or 9" Pie: Prepare and roll as directed, using the following quantities: 1¼ cups flour, ½ teaspoon salt, ⅓ cup cooking oil, and 2–3 tablespoons ice water. Fit into pan, crimp, and bake as directed for Flaky Pastry I. About 1170 calories total, about 146 calories for each of 8 wedges and 195 calories for each of 6 wedges.

SOUR CREAM PASTRY

Rich and tender and more flavorful than Flaky Pastry.

For 1 double crust 8" or 9" pie

2 cups sifted flour
½ teaspoon salt
½ teaspoon baking powder
½ cup chilled vegetable shortening
¼ cup sour cream
1 egg, lightly beaten

Sift flour with salt and baking powder, then cut in shortening until mixture resembles coarse meal. Blend sour cream and egg, pour all at once into flour, and mix briskly with a fork until pastry *just* holds together. Wrap in wax paper and chill while you prepare filling. Divide pastry in half, shape into 2 balls, then roll, 1 at a time, on a lightly floured board into a circle 3" larger in diameter than the piepan you're using. Fit 1 circle into pan, pressing gently to smooth out any air bubbles underneath. Fill pie, brush rim of pastry lightly with cold water, top with second pastry circle (it should have steam vents cut in center), and press edges to seal. Roll overhang over until even with rim, and crimp. Bake according to directions given in filling recipe. About 1885 calories total, about 235 calories for each of 8 wedges and 315 calories for each of 6 wedges.

EXTRA-SHORT PASTRY

This short pastry puts the finishing touch on very special pies, whether sweet or savory. It's also perfect for tarts and turnovers, sausage rolls, or tiny meat- or fish-filled appetizers.
For 1 single crust 8" or 9" pie

1½ cups sifted flour
½ teaspoon salt
¼ cup butter or margarine, chilled
¼ cup lard or vegetable shortening, chilled
2 teaspoons lemon juice
3 tablespoons ice water (about)

Mix flour and salt in a shallow bowl and, using a pastry blender, cut in butter and lard until the texture of very coarse meal. Sprinkle lemon juice evenly over surface, then water, 1 tablespoon at a time, mixing lightly with a fork after each addition. Pastry should *just* hold together. Shape into a "brick" on a lightly floured pastry cloth and flatten until about 1" thick; even up rough edges. Place pastry so short side faces you and, using a lightly floured, stockinette-covered rolling pin, roll with short firm strokes to a rectangle 5"×15". Fold near ⅓ of pastry in toward center, then far ⅓. Press edges lightly with rolling pin to seal. Give pastry a ¼ turn and roll again into a rectangle; fold and seal as before. Wrap and chill ½ hour. Roll, fold, and seal 2 more times, flouring board as little as possible, then wrap and chill ½ hour. (*Note:* If kitchen is hot, chill between *each* rolling.) Roll pastry into a circle 3" larger in diameter than the piepan you plan to use if for a pie shell; ½" larger if for a top crust. *For a pie shell,* fit, trim, and bake as directed in Flaky Pastry I. *For a top crust,* follow directions for Rough Puff Pastry. About 1450 calories total, about 180 calories for each of 8 wedges and 240 calories for each of 6 wedges.

TORTE PASTRY

A rich, sweet pastry.
For 1 single crust 8", 9", or 10" pie

½ cup unsalted butter, softened to room temperature
1⅔ cups sifted flour
1½ teaspoons baking powder
1 tablespoon sugar
¾ teaspoon salt
2 egg yolks

Knead all ingredients in a bowl until thoroughly blended. Pat into piepan, pushing dough up sides and crimping edges. About 1600 calories total, about 200 calories for each of 8 wedges and 265 calories for each of 6 wedges.

To Bake an Unfilled Pie Shell: Preheat oven to 375° F. Prick crust well all over with the tines of a fork, and bake 20–25 minutes until lightly browned. Cool before filling.

To Bake a Filled Pie Shell: Follow directions given in individual recipes that follow.

VARIATION:

Sweet Torte Pastry: Increase flour to 1¾ cups and substitute ¼ cup Vanilla Sugar for the sugar; omit salt. Proceed as directed. About 1630 calories total, about 205 calories for each of 8 wedges and 270 calories for each of 6 wedges.

PIES AND PASTRIES

CHOUX PASTRY (PÂTE À CHOUX)

Makes about 1 dozen Cream Puffs or Éclairs; 4½–5 dozen Profiteroles

1 cup water
½ cup butter or margarine
¼ teaspoon salt
1 cup sifted flour
4 eggs at room temperature

Preheat oven to 400° F. Quickly bring water, butter, and salt to boiling. Pull pan almost off burner and turn heat to moderate. Add flour *all at once* and stir quickly with a wooden spoon until mixture forms a ball. Set pan on a damp cloth. Break an egg into a cup and slide into flour mixture. Beat hard with a wooden spoon to blend. Add remaining eggs, 1 at a time, beating well. Each egg *must* be blended in before the next is added; mixture will look odd at first, almost curdled, but as you beat, it will become smooth. Pastry is now ready to use in making Cream Puffs, Éclairs, Profiteroles, Carolines, and Croquembouche. About 130 calories for each Cream Puff or Éclair (unfilled), 25 calories for each of 5 dozen Profiteroles (unfilled).

MÜRBTEIG PASTRY

This German pastry is perfect for fruit flans because it doesn't get soggy. It's delicate and short, so make it on a cool day.
For 1 single crust 8", 9", or 10" pie

2 cups sifted flour
½ cup superfine sugar
Finely grated rind of 1 lemon
¾ cup chilled butter or margarine
3 egg yolks, lightly beaten

Sift flour with sugar and mix in lemon rind. Cut in butter with a pastry blender until mixture resembles fine bread crumbs. Add yolks and mix with a fork until pastry forms a ball. (You may have to use your hands at the end, but handle as lightly as possible.) Wrap pastry and chill 1 hour. Using short, light strokes, roll on a *lightly* floured board into a circle 3" larger than the pan you're using; fit into pan, trimming edges to hang evenly 1" all round. Roll overhang under until even with rim and crimp. Chill pie shell 2 hours. Preheat oven to 450° F. Prick bottom and sides of pastry with a fork, line with wax paper and fill with rice or dried beans to weight down. Bake 5 minutes, lift out paper of rice, reduce oven to 350° F., and bake 12 minutes longer until golden. Cool pie shell before filling.

VARIATION:

Spicy Mürbteig (not authentic but nice with fruit pies): Prepare as directed but sift ¼ teaspoon cinnamon and a pinch nutmeg with flour.

Both versions: About 2585 total calories, about 325 calories for each of 8 wedges and about 430 calories for each of 6 wedges.

ROUGH PUFF PASTRY

Because this pastry is so rich and flaky, it makes a better top than bottom crust. It's usually reserved for pies, casseroles, or cobblers that have no bottom crusts. It can also be used to make Patty Shells, Beef Wellington, Napoleons, and Cream Horns.
For 1 single crust 8" or 9" pie

1½ cups sifted flour
½ teaspoon salt
½ cup chilled butter or margarine
2 teaspoons lemon juice
5–6 tablespoons ice water

Mix flour and salt in a shallow bowl and cut in ¼ cup butter with a pastry blender until the texture of coarse meal. Sprinkle in lemon juice, then water, one tablespoon at a time, mixing lightly and quickly with a fork until pastry *just* holds together. Shape into a "brick" on a lightly floured pastry cloth and flatten until about 1″ thick. Turn so short side faces you, and even up edges. Using a lightly floured, stockinette-covered rolling pin and short, firm strokes, roll into a rectangle 5″×15″. Beginning at far edge, dot ¼ of remaining butter evenly over ⅔ of pastry, leaving ¼″ margins all round. Fold near ⅓ of pastry in toward center, then far ⅓ until even with fold. Press edges lightly with rolling pin to seal. Give pastry a ¼ turn and roll again into a 5″×15″ rectangle. Dot with butter, fold and seal as before; wrap and chill ½ hour. Roll, fold, and seal twice more, using as little flour as possible; wrap and chill ½ hour.

To Use as a Top Crust: Roll into a circle ½″ larger than pan or casserole you plan to use, then trim off excess ½″ in a single long circular strip and reserve. Cut 3 V-shaped slits or decorative holes in center of circle. Lay strip around dampened edge of pan or casserole, center pastry circle over filling, press edges firmly to strip and crimp. Bake according to pie or casserole directions. About 1410 calories total, 175 calories for each of 8 wedges, 235 for each of 6.

To Make Patty Shells: Follow directions for making Small Patty Shells but use Rough Puff Pastry instead of regular Puff Pastry. About 235 calories for each of 6 patty shells.

PUFF PASTRY

Do not attempt this recipe on a hot day—dough will be unmanageable. Make, if possible, with some *pastry* (not cake) flour (obtainable at gourmet groceries), reducing water slightly as needed.
Makes 1 dozen Small Patty Shells or 1 large *Vol-au-vent*

4 cups sifted flour, preferably a ½ and ½ mixture of pastry and all-purpose flour
1½ teaspoons salt
1 cup plus 2 tablespoons ice water
1 tablespoon lemon juice
1 pound unsalted butter, chilled

Mix flour and salt in a bowl. Combine water and lemon juice, sprinkle evenly over flour, about ¼ cup at a time, mixing lightly and quickly with a fork after each addition (pastry should hold together, be firm yet pliable). Add a few drops more ice water if mixture seems dry. Knead on a lightly floured board about 10 minutes until smooth and elastic; cover and let stand at room temperature ½ hour. Meanwhile, knead and squeeze butter until malleable (about consistency of dough), free of lumps, but still cold. Shape into a 5″ square and dust with flour. Shape dough into a "brick" on a lightly floured pastry cloth and, with a lightly floured stockinette-covered rolling pin, flatten to a thickness of 1″; even up ragged edges. Place pastry so short side faces you, and roll with short, firm strokes into a rectangle 6″×18″. Place butter in center, fold near ⅓ of pastry in toward center, then far ⅓. Press edges lightly with rolling pin to seal. Give pastry a ¼ turn and roll again into a rectangle; fold and seal as before. Wrap and chill ¾ hour. Roll, fold, and seal 2 more times, then chill ¾ hour. Roll, fold, and seal twice more and chill 1 hour. Use as little flour as possible when rolling and handle pastry with fingertips. Pastry is now ready to use as recipes direct. To store, wrap and chill overnight or wrap airtight and freeze (thaw in refrigerator before using). About 4850 calories per *Vol-au-vent,* 405 calories per Patty Shell.

VOL-AU-VENT (LARGE PATTY SHELL)

A *Vol-au-vent* filled with creamed poultry or seafood may be oval or round. The oval is traditional, but you may find the round easier to cut. Simply cut 2 (8″) rounds, using a layer cake pan as a guide, then remove a 5″ circle from the center of 1 round.
Makes an 8″ oval

1 recipe Puff Pastry

Glaze:
1 egg, lightly beaten with 1 tablespoon cold water

Make pastry as directed. Also cut an 8″×5½″ oval from cardboard to use as a pattern. Roll half of pastry on a lightly floured pastry cloth into a rectangle 8″×10″ and ½″ thick. Place pattern in center of rectangle and cut out oval. Carefully transfer to a baking sheet brushed with cold water. Roll and cut remaining pastry the same way, then cut a 5″ oval from center, leaving an oval ring about 1½″ wide. Brush ring with cold water and arrange, damp side down, on pastry oval; press seams lightly to seal. Brush ring with cold water and prick bottom of oval to prevent uneven rising. Roll the 5″ oval cutout until it is the size of the bottom oval and lay on pastry shell—sort of like a "lid"; press seams lightly. Make a vertical ridged pattern around sides of pastry shell by pressing at regular intervals with the back of a knife; chill shell ½ hour. Meanwhile, preheat oven to 425° F. Brush top of shell with glaze but do not let run down sides or shell will not rise evenly. Bake on center oven rack 20 minutes, reduce oven to 350° F., and bake 30–40 minutes longer until well browned and crisp. (*Note:* Shell will rise 2–3 times its original height, so make sure second oven rack is out of the way.) Remove "lid" by sliding a knife underneath it and set on a wire rack. With a fork, scoop out soft insides of shell and discard. Return shell to oven and let dry out 5–7 minutes. Using 2 pancake turners, lift to platter. Fill with a hot filling, replace lid, and serve. For cold fillings, cool shell on a wire rack, then fill. (*Note:* Shell can be baked ahead of time and stored airtight several days; reheat 10 minutes at 400° F.) About 4850 calories total.

SMALL PATTY SHELLS (BOUCHÉES)

Small puff pastry shells to be filled with sweet or savory mixtures.
Makes 1 dozen

1 recipe Puff Pastry

Glaze:
1 egg, lightly beaten with 1 tablespoon cold water

Make pastry as directed and roll half to a thickness of ¼″ on a lightly floured board. Cut into rounds with an unfloured 2½″ cookie cutter (wipe cutter with a dry cloth before each cut and, to make shells rise evenly in baking, press cutter straight down through pastry). Arrange ⅓ of the rounds on a baking sheet brushed with cold water, spacing 1″ apart. Cut centers from ⅓ of remaining rounds with a 1¾″ round cutter. Brush tops of rings with cold water and place, tops down, on rounds. Pinch seams lightly to seal and brush rings with cold water. Press the 1¾″ cutter into remaining rounds, just enough to mark with a circle, not to cut clear through. Top each shell with a marked round, marked side up, and pinch seams as before. Brush tops with glaze but do not let glaze run down sides of shells or they will not rise evenly. Roll and cut remaining pastry the same way (also any scraps). Chill shells ½ hour. Meanwhile, preheat oven to 450° F. Bake shells on center oven rack 10 minutes, reduce heat to 350° F., and bake 15–20 minutes longer until golden brown and crisp. With a sharp, pointed knife, lift off marked circle tops from patties and save to use as "lids." With a fork, scoop out and discard soft insides of shells. Return shells to oven for 3–5 minutes to dry out. Patty shells are now ready to be filled with hot creamed mixtures. Cool on wire racks before filling with cold fillings. (*Note:* Stored airtight, these will keep well several days. Reheat, uncovered, 10 minutes at 350° F.) About 405 calories per patty shell.

▣ GRAHAM CRACKER CRUST

Crumb crusts can be substituted for baked pie shells in most recipes. They are especially good with chiffon and cream fillings. If a recipe calls for an unbaked crumb crust, prepare up to point of baking, then chill well, fill, and proceed as individual recipe directs.

For 1 single crust 9″ pie

1½ cups graham cracker crumbs (about 20 cracker squares)
⅓ cup butter or margarine, softened to room temperature
¼ cup sugar

Preheat oven to 350° F. Blend crumbs, butter, and sugar in a bowl. Spoon into a 9″ pie pan and, using the back of a spoon, press firmly against bottom and sides (but not over rim). Bake 8–10 minutes. Cool before filling. About 1440 calories total, about 180 calories for each of 8 wedges, 240 calories for each of 6.

VARIATIONS:

Vanilla Wafer Crust: Substitute vanilla wafer crumbs for the graham cracker, reduce butter to ¼ cup and sugar to 1–2 tablespoons. About 1400 calories total, about 175 calories for each of 8 wedges, 235 calories for each of 6 wedges.

Chocolate Crumb Crust: Substitute crushed chocolate wafers for cracker crumbs, reduce butter to ¼ cup and sugar to 1–2 tablespoons. About 1500 calories total, about 190 calories for each of 8 wedges, 250 calories for each of 6 wedges.

Gingersnap Crumb Crust: Prepare as directed but substitute crushed gingersnaps for the cracker crumbs and omit sugar. About 1400 calories total, about 175 calories for each of 8 wedges, 235 calories for each of 6 wedges.

Cereal Crust: Prepare as directed but substitute 1½ cups crushed cornflakes, rice cereal or wheat cereal for the cracker crumbs. About 855 calories total, about 105 calories for each of 8 wedges, 140 calories for each of 6 wedges.

Nut-Crumb Crust: Reduce crumbs to 1 cup and add ½ cup minced nuts (walnuts, pecans, hazelnuts, toasted blanched almonds, or Brazil nuts). About 1575 calories total, about 195 calories for each of 8 wedges, 265 calories for each of 6.

Marble Crumb Crust: Prepare as directed but toss 2 (1-ounce) squares finely grated semisweet chocolate with the crumbs. About 1720 calories total, 215 calories for each of 8 wedges, 285 calories for each of 6 wedges.

TOASTED COCONUT CRUST

Good with cream or chiffon fillings.
For 1 single crust 9" pie

2 cups flaked coconut
¼ cup melted butter or margarine

Preheat oven to 300° F. Mix coconut and butter. Press firmly against the bottom and sides of a 9" piepan. Bake about 20 minutes until golden. Cool before filling. About 1085 calories total, about 135 calories for each of 8 wedges and 180 calories for each of 6 wedges.

VARIATIONS:

Chocolate-Coconut Crust: Prepare as directed but reduce butter to 2 tablespoons and add 2 (1-ounce) squares melted unsweetened chocolate, 2 tablespoons warm milk, and ⅓ cup sifted confectioners' sugar; mix well. Press into pan and chill 1–2 hours before filling. About 1360 calories total, about 170 calories for each of 8 wedges and 225 calories for each of 6 wedges.

Easy Unbaked Coconut Crust: Substitute 2 cups packaged toasted coconut for the flaked coconut, mix with butter, press into piepan, and chill 1–2 hours before filling. About 1085 calories total, about 135 calories for each of 8 wedges and 180 calories for each of 6 wedges.

▨ TOASTED NUT CRUST

A crunchy, rich, sweet crust, ideal for chiffon fillings.
For 1 single crust 9" pie

1½ cups ground nuts (walnuts, pecans, Brazil nuts, blanched almonds, or hazelnuts)
¼ cup sugar
2 tablespoons butter or margarine, softened to room temperature

Preheat oven to 400° F. Mix nuts, sugar, and butter with your hands, press firmly against bottom and sides of a buttered 9" piepan. Bake 6–8 minutes. Cool before filling. About 1580 calories total, about 195 calories for each of 8 wedges, 265 calories for each of 6 wedges.

VARIATION:

Substitute 1 egg white, beaten to soft peaks, for the butter; mix with a spoon, press into buttered pan, and bake about 10 minutes until tan. Cool before filling. About 1390 calories total, about 175 calories for each of 8 wedges, 230 calories for each of 6 wedges.

▨ COOKIE CRUST

Couldn't be easier!
For 1 single crust 9" pie

1 tablespoon butter or margarine, softened to room temperature
1 tablespoon sugar
1 roll refrigerated slice-and-bake cookie dough (sugar cookie, chocolate, or coconut)

Preheat oven to 375° F. Butter bottom, sides, and rim of a 9" piepan, then coat with sugar. Slice cookie dough ⅛" thick and line sides of pan, overlapping slices slightly and allowing cookies to form a scalloped edge around rim. Line bottom with slices, pressing lightly to fill spaces. Bake 8–10 minutes until tan. Cool before filling. Good with cream fillings. Recipe too flexible for a meaningful calorie count.

⊠ ICE CREAM PIE SHELL

For 1 single crust 9" pie

1 quart vanilla or other flavor ice cream (about), slightly softened

Chill a 9" piepan in the freezer 15–20 minutes. Spoon ice cream into pan, smoothing bottom and sides with the back of a spoon to make a shell. Freeze until firm. Good filled with ice cream of contrasting flavor and color and topped with a cold fruit sauce. Also good filled with fresh fruit and topped with whipped cream. About 1180 calories total (if made with vanilla ice cream), about 150 calories for each of 8 wedges and 195 calories for each of 6 wedges.

Ground Rules for Making Meringues

– Bring egg whites to room temperature before beating.
– Make sure there are no flecks of yolk in the whites; if so, scoop out with a piece of shell.
– Make sure mixing bowl and beater are spotless.
– Follow recipe to the letter.
– Add sugar very slowly, beating well after each addition so it dissolves fully. If it does not, "beads" of syrup or sugar grains will form on baked meringue.
– Be careful not to overbeat egg whites (especially if using electric mixer). Meringue should be *glossy and very stiff but not dry.* If meringue clumps as it's spread, it is overbeaten. To rescue, return to mixing bowl, add 1–2 tablespoons cold water and beat briefly and briskly.
– To keep meringue from shrinking during baking, spread evenly over filling, making sure it touches pie shell all around.

(*Note:* For additional tips, read To Beat Whites in the chapter on eggs and cheese.)

BASIC MERINGUE TOPPING FOR PIES

To Top an 8" Pie, Use:

2 egg whites, at room temperature
⅛ teaspoon cream of tartar
Pinch salt
¼ cup sugar
½ teaspoon vanilla

To Top a 9" Pie, Use:

3 egg whites, at room temperature
¼ teaspoon cream of tartar
⅛ teaspoon salt
6 tablespoons sugar
½ teaspoon vanilla

To Top 10" Pie, Use:

4 egg whites, at room temperature
¼ teaspoon cream of tartar
⅛ teaspoon salt
½ cup sugar
1 teaspoon vanilla

Preheat oven to 350° F. Beat egg whites until frothy, using a rotary beater or electric mixer at moderate speed; add cream of tartar and salt and continue beating, adding sugar, 1 tablespoon at a time. When all sugar is incorporated, add vanilla and beat hard (highest mixer speed) until glossy and peaks stand straight up when beaters are withdrawn. Spoon about half the meringue around edge of *warm* filling, spreading so it touches pastry all around. Pile remaining meringue in center, then spread to cover all filling, pulling into peaks with the back of a spoon or swirling round. If you prefer, pipe meringue over filling, using a pastry bag fitted with a decorative tip. Bake on center oven rack 12–15 minutes until lightly browned. Cool at least 2 hours before serving. To simplify the serving of a meringue pie, dip knife in warm water before cutting each slice.

Meringue for an 8" pie: About 225 calories total, about 35 calories for each of 6 servings.

Meringue for a 9" pie: About 330 calories total, about 40 calories for each of 8 servings.

Meringue for a 10" pie: About 445 calories total, about 55 calories for each of 8 servings.

⚜ MERINGUE PIE SHELL

For 1 single crust 9" pie

3 egg whites at room temperature
⅛ teaspoon cream of tartar
⅛ teaspoon salt
½ cup sugar
1 teaspoon vanilla or ½ teaspoon almond extract

Preheat oven to 250° F. Beat egg whites until foamy; mix in cream of tartar and salt. Add sugar, 1 tablespoon at a time, beating constantly, then continue to beat at highest speed until glossy and stiff enough to stand straight up when beaters are withdrawn. Spoon meringue into lightly greased 9" piepan, then spread with the back of a spoon to cover bottom and sides but not the rim; make sides a little thicker than the bottom and ½"–¾" higher than rim of pan. Bake 1 hour until creamy white and firm, turn oven off and let meringue dry in oven without opening door until oven cools. Shell is now ready to fill as desired. About 430 calories total, about 55 calories for each of 8 wedges, 70 calories for each of 6 wedges.

VARIATION:

Nut Meringue Pie Shell: Prepare meringue as directed, fold in 1 cup ground blanched almonds or hazelnuts, a little at a time, then spoon into pan and bake as directed. About 1280 calories total, about 160 calories for each of 8 wedges, 215 calories for each of 6 wedges.

⚜ MERINGUES

Makes about 2 dozen

6 egg whites, at room temperature
¼ teaspoon cream of tartar
¼ teaspoon salt
¾ cup sugar
¾ cup superfine sugar
1 teaspoon vanilla or ½ teaspoon almond extract
1 or 2 drops any food coloring (optional)

Preheat oven to 250° F. Beat egg whites until foamy; mix in cream of tartar and salt. Mix sugars and add, 1 tablespoon at a time, beating all the while. This will take some time, perhaps 10–12 minutes. Add flavoring and if you like, tint a pastel hue; beat at highest mixer speed until glossy and stiff enough to stand straight up when beaters are withdrawn. Drop by heaping spoonfuls 2" apart on foil-lined baking sheets; smooth into mounds or, if you prefer, pipe meringue onto sheets through a pastry bag fitted with a large plain or star tip. Don't make meringues more than 2½" across or they won't bake properly. Bake 1 hour until creamy white and firm, turn oven off, and let meringues dry several hours or overnight in oven without opening door. Lift off foil and serve as is or with ice cream or fruit. Wrapped airtight, these keep well. About 50 calories each.

VARIATIONS:

⚜ **Meringue Star Shells** (Makes 1 dozen): Beat meringue as directed. Draw 6 (3") circles on 2 foil-lined baking sheets, not too close together, and spread ⅓"–½" deep with meringue. Spoon remaining meringue into a pastry bag fitted with a small star tip. Edge meringue circles with borders of small stars, 1 just touching another, then build up layers to form shells about 1½" deep. Bake and dry out as directed. To serve, fill with any ice cream or fruit. About 100 calories each.

⚜ **Meringues Glacées:** Make and bake meringues as directed, halve, and fill with ice cream. Or sandwich 2 meringues together with ice cream. Top with any dessert sauce or fruit. About 120 calories each if halved and filled with ice cream, about 170 calories each if sandwiched together with ice cream.

Meringues Chantilly: Sandwich baked meringues together with sweetened whipped cream, tinted, if you like, for a party touch. Or if you prefer, tint meringues and leave cream plain. About 200 calories each.

¢ **COUNTRY-STYLE APPLE PIE**

Aromatic of lemon, cinnamon and nutmeg.
Makes 8 servings

1 recipe Flaky Pastry II

Filling:
6 *medium-size tart cooking apples*
¾*–1 cup sugar*
2 *teaspoons lemon juice*
¼ *teaspoon cinnamon*
⅛ *teaspoon nutmeg*
¼ *teaspoon salt*
2 *tablespoons butter or margarine*

Glaze (optional):
1 tablespoon milk
1 tablespoon sugar

Preheat oven to 425° F. Prepare pastry as directed and fit half into a 9" piepan; do not trim edge. Roll top crust, cut steam slits in center, and cover with cloth while you prepare filling. Peel, core, and thinly slice apples, taste, and sweeten as needed with sugar; add lemon juice, spices, and salt and toss gently. Pile apple mixture in pie shell and dot with butter. Brush pastry rim lightly with cold water, fit top crust over apples, trim, seal, and crimp edges. For a shiny crust, brush with milk and sprinkle with sugar. Bake 15–20 minutes with a piece of foil on rack underneath to catch drips, reduce heat to 350° F., and bake 25–30 minutes longer until crust is lightly browned. Cool 5–10 minutes before serving. Serve hot or cold with heavy cream, vanilla ice cream, or chunks of good sharp Cheddar. About 410 calories per serving (without cream, ice cream, or cheese).

DEEP DISH APPLE PIE

Makes 8 servings

1 recipe Flaky Pastry I

Filling:
12 *medium-size tart cooking apples*
1½ cups sugar (about)
½ *teaspoon cinnamon*
¼ *teaspoon nutmeg*
2 *tablespoons flour*
1 tablespoon lemon juice
2 *tablespoons butter or margarine*

Glaze (optional):
1 tablespoon milk
1 tablespoon sugar

Preheat oven to 425° F. Prepare pastry as directed and roll into a 10" square; cut steam slits in center

PIES AND PASTRIES

ABOUT PIE APPLES

There are hundreds of different kinds of apples, most coming into season during the fall and remaining plentiful throughout winter and early spring. All apples, however, do not cook well — the crisp, juicy-sweet apples we love to eat out of hand, for example, lack the tartness and texture needed for successful pies. For best results, use one of these excellent "pie" apples:

Kind of Apple	Description	Season
Jonathan	Small to medium size, deep red with creamy-colored, tart, crisp flesh. Juicy.	October-February
McIntosh	Medium size, bright red with green around stem. White, crisp-tender, juicy flesh.	October-March
Newtown Pippin	Medium size, yellow skin, tart, hard-to-crisp juicy yellowish flesh.	February-June
Northern Spy	Large, bright red with firm, tart, juicy, yellowish flesh.	October-March
Rhode Island Greening	Medium to large, green or yellow-green skin; cream-colored, tart, crisp, juicy flesh.	October-February
Stayman	Striped, dull red apple, medium to large, with tart-crisp, juicy, ivory-hued flesh.	November-April
Winesap	Deep red, small to medium, with some green around stem; firm, crisp, tart, cream-colored flesh.	January-May
Yellow Transparent	Medium, yellow-green with white, juicy, tart flesh.	July-August
York Imperial	Medium-to-large, light or purple-red over yellow; ivory-colored, hard, tart flesh.	October-April

Note: Such all-purpose cooking apples as Gravenstein, Wealthy, Rome Beauty, and Baldwin may also be used in pies, but the nine varieties above give especially fine flavor and texture.

and cover with a cloth while you prepare the filling. Peel, core, and thinly slice apples, taste, and sweeten as needed with sugar; add cinnamon, nutmeg, and flour and toss to mix. Pile apple mixture into an ungreased 9"×9"×2" pan, sprinkle with lemon juice, and dot with butter. Fit pastry over apples, roll overhang under even with rim and crimp edges. For a shiny crust, brush with milk and sprinkle with sugar. Bake 40–50 minutes (with a piece of foil on rack below to catch drips) until crust is browned and apples are tender. (*Note:* If in doubt, poke a skewer through a steam vent to test.) Cool 5–10 minutes before serving. Serve warm or cold in bowls with light cream or ice cream. About 450 calories per serving (without cream).

VARIATIONS:

Deep Dish Berry or Fruit Pie: Double filling recipe of Basic Berry or Fresh Fruit Pie and use to fill the 9" square pan; proceed as recipe directs. About 450 calories per serving (without cream).

Large Family Deep Dish Fruit Pie (Makes 18 servings): Triple the filling recipe of Country-Style Apple, Basic Berry or Fresh Fruit Pie and pile into an ungreased 13"× 9"× 2" pan. Cover with 1 recipe Flaky Pastry II rolled 1" larger than top of pan. Make slits in center, fit over filling, crimp edges, glaze, and bake as directed about 50 minutes. Recipe too flexible for a meaningful calorie count.

¢ APPLE TURNOVERS

Makes 6 servings

1 recipe Flaky Pastry II

Filling:
2 cups peeled and diced tart cooking apples
⅓ cup sugar
¼ teaspoon cinnamon
¼ teaspoon nutmeg
2 tablespoons lemon juice

Glaze:
Milk
Sugar

Preheat oven to 400° F. Make pastry as directed and roll total amount into a rectangle 12"× 18", keeping edges as straight as possible. Cut into 6 (6") squares; brush edges with cold water. Mix filling ingredients and place about ⅓ cup in the center of each square; fold diagonally to form triangles. Press edges together with a floured fork and snip steam slits in tops with kitchen shears. Brush with milk and sprinkle with sugar. Arrange 2" apart on an ungreased baking sheet and bake 25–30 minutes until golden brown. Cool a few minutes on a wire rack. Serve warm or cold with or without cream or ice cream. Or if you like, cool and drizzle with Quick Glacé Icing or Easy White Icing. About 410 calories per serving (without cream, ice cream, or icing).

VARIATIONS:

Fruit Turnovers: Prepare as directed, substituting 2 cups any suitable fresh, frozen, or canned, drained fruit for the apples and adding sugar as needed to sweeten. Recipe too flexible for a meaningful calorie count.

Jam Turnovers (Makes 1 dozen): Roll out pastry and cut into 12 (4") squares. Place 2 tablespoons jam, preserves, marmalade, or mincemeat in the center of each, fold, seal, and glaze. Bake 15 minutes at 425° F. About 305 calories per serving.

Fried Apple Pies (Makes 8 servings): Roll pastry ⅛" thick and cut into 8 (4") circles. Place ¼ cup thick applesauce in the center of each, fold over and seal edges *well*. Do not glaze. Fry in 365° F. deep fat 2–3 minutes, turning as needed, until evenly golden brown. Drain on paper toweling, roll in sugar, and serve warm. About 425 calories per serving.

FRESH FRUIT PIE

This basic recipe can be used for making peach, apricot, plum, pear, cherry, grape, or currant pies.
Makes 8 servings

1 recipe Flaky Pastry II

Filling:
1 quart sliced, pitted, and peeled fresh firm-ripe peaches, apricots, or nectarines; pitted purple or greengage plums; peeled, cored, and sliced pears; stemmed and pitted tart cherries; seeded, halved Tokay or whole seedless green grapes or stemmed currants
¾–1½ cups sugar
¼–⅓ cup sifted flour

⅛ teaspoon salt
1 teaspoon lemon juice (optional)
¼ teaspoon almond extract or nutmeg, cinnamon, or ginger (optional)
2 tablespoons butter or margarine

Glaze (optional):
1 tablespoon milk
1 tablespoon sugar

Preheat oven to 425° F. Make pastry as directed and fit half into a 9" piepan; do not trim edge. Roll out top crust, cut steam slits in center, and cover with a cloth while you prepare the filling. Place fruit in a bowl, add sugar to sweeten, and sprinkle with flour and salt; toss lightly. (*Note:* Cherries will need maximum amount of flour, firmer fruits less.) If you like, sprinkle with lemon juice and almond extract (especially good with peaches, apricots, and cherries). Spoon into pie shell and dot with butter. Brush pastry rim with cold water, fit top crust over fruit, trim, seal, and crimp edges. For a glistening crust, brush with milk and sprinkle with sugar. Bake 35–45 minutes (with a piece of foil on rack below to catch drips) until lightly browned and bubbling. Cool 5–10 minutes before cutting. Serve warm or cold with or without cream or ice cream. About 400 calories per serving (made with ¾ cup sugar and served without cream or ice cream).

VARIATIONS:

Frozen Fruit Pie: Prepare as directed, using 1 quart solidly frozen fruit. About 400 calories per serving (without cream or ice cream).

Canned Fruit Pie: Prepare as directed using 2 (1-pound) cans fruit. Drain fruit well, reserving ½ cup liquid. Mix fruit with enough sugar to sweeten, flour, and seasonings and spoon into pie shell. Pour in reserved liquid (mixed with a few drops red food coloring if it is a cherry pie), dot with butter, and proceed as directed. Recipe too flexible for a meaningful calorie count.

Tapioca Fruit Pie: Substitute 3 tablespoons quick-cooking tapioca for the flour and proceed as recipe directs. About 425 calories per serving.

BASIC BERRY PIE

Makes 8 servings

1 recipe Flaky Pastry II

Filling:
1 quart ripe berries (any kind), hulled, stemmed, and drained
1–1½ cups sugar
¼ cup unsifted flour
⅛ teaspoon salt
1 teaspoon finely grated orange or lemon rind (optional)
2 tablespoons butter or margarine

Glaze (optional):
1 tablespoon milk
1 tablespoon sugar

Preheat oven to 425° F. Make pastry as directed and fit half into a 9" piepan; do not trim edge. Roll top crust, cut steam slits in center, and cover with cloth while you prepare filling. Dry berries on paper toweling, place in a bowl, and sprinkle with 1 cup sugar, the flour, salt, and, if you like, rind; toss *lightly*. Taste berries and if too tart add more sugar. Spoon into pie shell, and dot with butter. Fit pastry rim with cold water. Fit top crust over berries, trim, seal, and crimp edges. For a glistening crust, brush with milk and sprinkle with sugar. Bake 35–45 minutes (with a piece of foil on rack below to catch drips) until lightly browned and bubbling. Cool 5–10 minutes before cutting.

Serve hot or cold with or without cream or ice cream. About 445 calories per serving (made with 1 cup sugar and served without cream or ice cream).

VARIATIONS:

Dutch Berry Pie: Prepare and bake pie as directed. After removing from oven, funnel ⅓ cup heavy cream in through steam slits. Cool and serve. About 475 calories per serving.

Frozen Berry Pie: Prepare as directed, using 1 quart solidly frozen berries for the fresh and increasing flour to ⅓ cup. About 450 calories per serving.

Canned Berry Pie: Substitute 2 (1-pound) cans berries for the fresh; drain well, reserving ½ cup liquid. Mix berries with sugar, flour, and seasonings as directed and spoon into pie shell. Pour in the ½ cup liquid, dot with butter, and proceed as directed. About 445 calories per serving.

FRESH RHUBARB PIE

Makes 8 servings

1 recipe Flaky Pastry II

Filling:
2 pounds rhubarb, trimmed and cut in ½" chunks
1⅓–1¾ cups sugar
⅓ cup unsifted flour
⅛ teaspoon salt
2 or 3 drops red food coloring (optional)
2 tablespoons butter or margarine

Glaze (optional):
1 tablespoon milk
1 tablespoon sugar

Preheat oven to 425° F. Make pastry as directed and fit half into a 9" piepan; do not trim edge. Roll remaining pastry into a 12" circle and cut steam slits in center; cover with cloth while you prepare filling. Toss rhubarb with enough sugar to sweeten, then mix in flour, salt, and food coloring if rhubarb is pale. Pile in pie shell and dot with butter. Brush pastry rim with cold water, fit top crust over rhubarb, trim, seal, and crimp edges. For a glistening crust, brush with milk and sprinkle with sugar. Bake 40–50 minutes (with foil on rack underneath to catch drips) until browned and bubbling. Cool 5–10 minutes before cutting. Good with cream, whipped cream, or vanilla ice cream. About 480 calories per serving (made with 1⅓ cups sugar and served without cream or ice cream).

VARIATION:

Rhubarb-Strawberry Pie: Prepare as directed, using 1 pound rhubarb and 1 pint stemmed, halved strawberries; omit food coloring. For a special occasion, top with a lattice crust.* About 480 calories per serving.

SOUR CREAM PEACH PIE

Peaches and cream baked in a flaky crust and topped with a buttery brown sugar mixture.

Makes 6–8 servings

1 recipe Flaky Pastry I

Filling:
5 ripe peaches
1 cup sour cream
¾ cup sugar
3 tablespoons flour
1 egg
⅛ teaspoon mace
1 tablespoon light rum
¼ teaspoon vanilla

Topping:
¼ cup melted butter or margarine
⅓ cup unsifted flour
½ cup firmly packed light brown sugar

PIES AND PASTRIES

Preheat oven to 400° F. Prepare pastry as directed and fit into a 9" piepan, making a high fluted edge; do not bake. Peel peaches, halve, pit, and slice thin directly into pie shell. Mix remaining filling ingredients and pour over peaches. Bake 25 minutes and remove from oven. Mix topping and crumble evenly over peaches. Return to oven and bake 20 minutes longer. Cool 10–20 minutes before serving. About 550 calories for each of 6 servings, 410 calories for each of 8.

STREUSEL PEACH PIE

Makes 6–8 servings

1 recipe Flaky Pastry I

Filling:
1 quart sliced, pitted, and peeled firm-ripe peaches
½ cup sugar
Finely grated rind and juice of 1 orange

Topping:
½ cup firmly packed light brown sugar
½ cup sifted flour
⅓ cup butter or margarine

Preheat oven to 425° F. Make pastry as directed and fit into a 9" piepan, making a high fluted edge; do not bake. Gently mix peaches, sugar, orange rind and juice and spoon into pie shell. Mix brown sugar and flour, then, using a pastry blender, cut in butter until mixture is crumbly. Sprinkle over peaches, pressing down lightly. Bake (with a piece of foil on rack below to catch drips) about 40 minutes until lightly browned. Serve warm with or without whipped cream or sour cream. About 485 calories for each of 6 servings (without cream), 365 calories for each of 8 servings.

VARIATIONS:

Streusel Pecan-Peach Pie: Make pastry and fill as directed. For the topping: Mix the sugar, ¼ cup flour, and ½ teaspoon cinnamon; cut in butter and toss with ½ cup minced pecans. Spread over peaches and bake as directed. About 535 calories for each of 6 servings, 400 calories for each of 8.

Streusel Apple, Pear, or Plum Pie: Substitute 1 quart peeled, cored, and sliced tart apples or pears or halved pitted plums for the peaches; adjust sugar in filling as needed to sweeten the fruit, then proceed as directed. Recipe too flexible for a meaningful calorie count.

EASY PUMPKIN PIE

Makes 6–8 servings

1 recipe Flaky Pastry I

Filling:
3 eggs, lightly beaten
1 (1-pound) can pumpkin purée
1 (13-ounce) can evaporated milk
1 tablespoon brandy
1 tablespoon molasses
⅔ cup firmly packed light brown sugar
½ teaspoon cinnamon
¼ teaspoon ginger
¼ teaspoon allspice
¼ teaspoon cloves

Preheat oven to 450° F. Make pastry as directed and fit into a 9" piepan, making a high fluted edge; do not bake. Beat all filling ingredients together, using a whisk or rotary egg beater, and pour into pie shell. Bake 10 minutes, reduce temperature to 325° F., and bake 45–50 minutes longer until crust is lightly browned and filling set (a silver knife inserted midway between center and rim should come out clean). Cool to room temperature before serving. About 445 calories for each of 6 servings, 335 calories for each of 8.

OLD-FASHIONED PUMPKIN PIE

Richer and spicier than Easy Pumpkin Pie.

Makes 6–8 servings

1 recipe Flaky Pastry I
1 egg white, lightly beaten

Filling:
1½ cups pumpkin purée
⅔ cup firmly packed dark brown sugar
1¼ teaspoons cinnamon
½ teaspoon ginger
Pinch nutmeg
¼ teaspoon maple flavoring (optional)
¼ teaspoon salt
1 cup milk
1 cup light cream
3 eggs, lightly beaten

Make pastry as directed and fit into a 9" piepan, making a high fluted edge; brush with egg white and chill 1 hour. Preheat oven to 450° F. For the filling, mix pumpkin and sugar until sugar dissolves. Add remaining ingredients, stirring well to blend. Set pie shell on pulled-out center oven shelf, then pour in filling. Bake 10 minutes, reduce heat to 350° F., and bake 30–35 minutes longer until a knife inserted midway between center and rim comes out clean. Serve warm or at room temperature. Good topped with sweetened whipped cream. About 460 calories for each of 6 servings (without whipped cream), about 345 calories for each of 8 servings.

BRANDIED MINCEMEAT IN CHEESE PASTRY

Makes 8 servings

1 recipe Cheese Pastry II

Filling:
1 (1-pound 12-ounce) jar mincemeat
3–4 tablespoons brandy

Preheat oven to 450° F. Empty mincemeat into a strainer set over a bowl and drain 10 minutes; pour off at least 3–4 tablespoons liquid and discard; save the rest. Meanwhile, make pastry as directed and fit half in a 9" or 10" piepan. Roll top crust and make steam slits in center. Mix drained mincemeat with brandy to taste and the reserved liquid and spoon into pie shell. Moisten pastry edges lightly with cold water. Fit top crust over filling, trim edges, seal, and crimp. Bake 10 minutes (with foil on rack underneath to catch drips), reduce heat to 350° F., and bake 20–25 minutes longer until lightly browned. Serve warm or cold with Hard Sauce or wedges of sharp Cheddar. About 590 calories per serving (without Hard Sauce or cheese).

LEMON MERINGUE PIE

Makes 6–8 servings

1 recipe Flaky Pastry I

Filling:
½ cup cornstarch
1½ cups sugar
¼ teaspoon salt
1¾ cups cold water
1 teaspoon finely grated lemon rind
4 egg yolks, lightly beaten
⅓–½ cup lemon juice
2 tablespoons butter or margarine

Meringue:
1 recipe Basic Meringue Topping for a 9" Pie

Make pastry, fit into a 9" piepan, and bake as directed; reduce oven to 350° F. Mix cornstarch, sugar, and salt in a heavy saucepan, slowly blend in water, and heat, stirring constantly, until thickened and smooth. Mix in lemon rind and cook, stirring, 2–3 minutes. Blend a little hot mixture into yolks, return to pan and cook and stir over lowest heat 2–3 minutes; do not boil. Off heat, stir in ⅓ cup lemon juice (½ cup for really tart flavor) and the butter. Spoon filling into pie shell. Prepare meringue as directed, spread over filling, and bake 12–15 minutes until touched with brown. Cool pie at least 2 hours before serving. (*Note:* Pie will cut more easily if knife is dipped in warm water before each cut is made.) About 540 calories for each of 6 servings, 405 calories for each of 8 servings.

VARIATIONS:

Lime Meringue Pie: Prepare as directed, substituting lime juice and rind for the lemon. About 540 calories for each of 6 servings, 405 calories for each of 8 servings.

Orange Meringue Pie: Prepare as directed, using ¼ cup each orange and lemon juice and grated orange rind instead of lemon. About 545 calories for each of 6 servings, 410 calories for each of 8 servings.

KEY LIME PIE

There are dozens of variations of this Florida Keys classic, some made with a graham cracker crust, some topped with meringue. But this particular version is most like the original: a crisp piecrust filled with a creamy, tart lime filling, then crowned with whipped cream. Makes 6–8 servings

1 recipe Flaky Pastry I

Filling:
4 egg yolks, lightly beaten
1 (14-ounce) can sweetened condensed milk
⅔ cup fresh lime juice
Few drops green food coloring

Topping:
1 cup heavy cream, whipped with 3 tablespoons superfine sugar

Make pastry as directed, fit into a 9" piepan, and bake as directed; cool while you make the filling. Beat yolks with condensed milk just to blend, add lime juice, and beat until smooth (the filling will be soft). Tint pale green and pour into baked pie shell. Chill well, then spread whipped cream topping over filling, making sure it touches pastry all around. Return to refrigerator and chill several hours before serving, or better still, overnight, so that filling will firm up somewhat (it will never really be firm). About 680 calories for each of 6 servings, 510 calories for each of 8 servings.

VANILLA CREAM PIE

Makes 6–8 servings

1 recipe Flaky Pastry I

Filling:
¼ cup cornstarch
⅔ cup sugar
¼ teaspoon salt
2½ cups milk
3 egg yolks, lightly beaten
2 teaspoons vanilla
1 tablespoon butter or margarine

Topping (optional):
1½ cups sweetened whipped cream or 1 recipe Basic Meringue Topping for a 9" Pie

Make pastry, fit into a 9" piepan, and bake as directed. Mix cornstarch, sugar, and salt in a saucepan, slowly blend in milk, and heat, stirring, until thickened. Turn heat to lowest point and heat and stir 1–2 minutes. Blend a little hot mixture into egg yolks, return to pan, and cook and stir 1–2 minutes over lowest heat until quite thick; do not boil. Off heat, mix in vanilla and butter. Place a circle of wax paper flat on filling and cool to lukewarm. Fill shell, then chill 2 hours at least. Serve as is or topped with whipped cream. *To top with meringue:* Cool filling slightly, then fill pie shell. Prepare meringue as directed, spread over filling, and bake 12–15 minutes at 350° F. until touched with brown. Cool 2 hours before serving. About 400 calories for each of 6 servings, 300 calories for each of 8 servings (without topping).

VARIATION:

Coconut Cream Pie: Prepare filling as directed, then mix in 1 cup flaked or finely grated coconut. Reduce vanilla to 1 teaspoon and, if desired, serve topped with whipped cream. About 455 calories for each of 6 servings (without whipped cream), about 340 calories for each of 8 servings (without whipped cream).

BUTTERSCOTCH CREAM PIE

Makes 6–8 servings

1 recipe Flaky Pastry I

Filling:
1 cup firmly packed dark brown sugar
¼ cup cornstarch
¼ teaspoon salt
2⅔ cups milk
3 egg yolks, lightly beaten
¼ cup butter or margarine
1 teaspoon vanilla

Topping (optional):
1 cup heavy cream, whipped
or
1 recipe Basic Meringue Topping for a 9" Pie

Make pastry, fit into a 9" piepan, and bake as directed; cool. Mix brown sugar, cornstarch, and salt in a heavy saucepan, slowly add milk, and blend until smooth. Heat, stirring constantly, over moderate heat until almost boiling. Turn heat to low and cook and stir until thickened, about 2 minutes. (*Note:* Mixture scorches easily, so watch.) Blend a little hot mixture into yolks, return to pan, and cook and stir 1–2 minutes over lowest heat until quite thick. Do not boil. Off heat, stir in butter and vanilla. Pour into pie shell, cool to room temperature, then chill 2 hours before serving. If you wish, top with whipped cream. If you prefer to top with meringue, *do not cool and chill filling.* Make meringue, spread on *warm* filling and bake as directed in meringue recipe. About 645 calories for each of 6 servings, 485 calories for each of 8 servings (without topping).

CHOCOLATE CREAM PIE

Makes 6–8 servings

1 recipe Flaky Pastry I

Filling:
2 tablespoons flour
3 tablespoons cornstarch
1 cup sugar
¼ teaspoon salt
2½ cups milk
3 (1-ounce) squares unsweetened chocolate or 3 (1-ounce) envelopes no-melt unsweetened chocolate
3 egg yolks, lightly beaten
1 tablespoon butter or margarine
1 teaspoon vanilla

Topping:
¾ cup heavy cream
3 tablespoons confectioners' sugar (optional)
Chocolate curls* or chopped pistachio nuts (optional garnish)

Make pastry, fit into a 9″ piepan, and bake as directed. Mix flour, cornstarch, sugar, and salt in a heavy saucepan and slowly stir in milk. Heat and stir over moderate heat until thickened and smooth; blend in chocolate. Ladle about ½ cup hot mixture into egg yolks, mix well, and return to pan. Cook and stir 1 minute over lowest heat—do not boil. Off heat, stir in butter and vanilla. Place a circle of wax paper directly on filling and cool to room temperature; stir well and spoon into pie shell. Chill 1–2 hours. Whip cream, adding sugar, if you like, and spread over filling. Decorate with chocolate curls and serve. About 685 calories for each of 6 servings, 515 calories for each of 8 servings.

BLACK BOTTOM PIE

This two-toned pie is chocolate on the bottom, rum chiffon on top. Makes 6–8 servings

1 (9″) crumb crust pie shell (Graham Cracker, Gingersnap, or Chocolate), baked and cooled

Filling:
⅔ cup sugar
2 tablespoons cornstarch
1 envelope unflavored gelatin
2½ cups milk
3 eggs, separated
2 (1-ounce) squares unsweetened chocolate
2 tablespoons light rum
¼ cup superfine sugar
¾ cup heavy cream
Chocolate curls* (garnish)

Mix sugar, cornstarch, and gelatin in the top of a double boiler, gradually mix in milk, and heat, stirring constantly, over simmering water until steaming. Beat egg yolks lightly, stir in a little hot mixture, then return to pan and cook and stir 3–5 minutes until quite thick and smooth. Place a circle of wax paper flat on sauce and cool to lukewarm. Meanwhile, melt chocolate over simmering water and cool. Measure 1½ cups custard sauce into a bowl, blend in chocolate, pour into crust, and chill ½ hour. Cool remaining mixture until it mounds when dropped from a spoon; stir in rum. Beat egg whites until foamy, gradually beat in superfine sugar, and continue to beat until soft peaks form. Fold into rum-custard mixture. Spoon lightly on top of chocolate layer and chill until firm. Whip cream to soft peaks, spread on pie, and decorate with chocolate curls. About 705 calories for each of 6 servings, 530 calories for each of 8 servings.

BANANA CREAM PIE

Makes 6–8 servings

1 recipe Flaky Pastry I

Filling:
2 tablespoons flour
2 tablespoons cornstarch
½ cup sugar
¼ teaspoon salt
1¾ cups milk
3 egg yolks, lightly beaten
1 teaspoon vanilla
1 tablespoon butter or margarine
3 ripe bananas

Topping:
¾ cup heavy cream, whipped

Make pastry, fit into a 9″ piepan, and bake as directed. Mix flour, cornstarch, sugar, and salt in a saucepan. Slowly blend in milk and heat and stir until thickened and smooth; turn heat to lowest point and heat and stir 1–2 minutes. Blend a little hot mixture into egg yolks, return to pan, and cook and stir 1–2 minutes over lowest heat until quite thick; do not boil or mixture will curdle. Off heat, mix in vanilla and butter. Place a circle of wax paper directly on mixture and cool to room temperature. Stir filling and spoon half into pie shell. Peel bananas, slice ¼" thick, and arrange evenly over filling. Top with remaining filling. "Frost" with whipped cream, chill 20–30 minutes and serve. (*Note:* If you know you won't eat all the pie at one sitting, top individual servings with whipped cream instead of frosting the whole pie—whipped cream breaks down in the refrigerator.) About 640 calories for each of 6 servings, 480 calories for each of 8 servings.

SOUR CREAM RAISIN PIE

Makes 6–8 servings

1 recipe Flaky Pastry I

Filling:
3 eggs
1 cup sugar
¼ teaspoon salt
1½ teaspoons cinnamon
½ teaspoon nutmeg
1 cup sour cream
1¼ cups seedless raisins

Preheat oven to 450° F. Make pastry as directed and fit into a 9" piepan, making a high fluted edge; do not bake. Beat eggs until thick and cream colored, add sugar gradually, beating well after each addition. Continue beating until thick and light. Blend in remaining ingredients and spoon into pie shell. Bake 10 minutes. Reduce heat to 350° F., and bake 30 minutes longer or until a knife inserted midway between center and rim comes out clean. Cool 15 minutes before cutting. Serve warm or at room temperature. About 535 calories for each of 6 servings, 400 calories for each of 8 servings.

¢ SHOOFLY PIE

In Pennsylvania Dutch country you may find this pie served for breakfast. Its original function was to distract flies from other foods.

Makes 6–8 servings

1 recipe Flaky Pastry I

Filling:
⅔ cup boiling water
½ teaspoon baking soda
½ cup molasses

Crumb Topping:
1½ cups sifted flour
¼ teaspoon salt
¾ cup firmly packed light brown sugar
⅓ cup butter, margarine, or shortening

Preheat oven to 350° F. Prepare pastry as directed and fit into a 9" piepan, making a high fluted edge; do not bake. Mix filling. Also mix flour, salt, and sugar and cut in butter with a pastry blender until the texture of coarse meal. Sprinkle about ⅓ cup topping into pie shell, pour in filling, and sprinkle evenly with remaining topping. Bake on center oven rack 35–40 minutes until well browned. Cool on a wire rack and serve slightly warm or cold. Good with whipped cream or vanilla ice cream. About 540 calories for each of 6 servings (without whipped cream or ice cream), 405 calories for each of 8 servings.

CUSTARD PIE

For a crisp bottom crust, use the Slipped Custard Pie recipe (see Variations below).

Makes 6–8 servings

1 recipe Flaky Pastry I

Filling:
4 eggs
⅔ cup sugar
½ teaspoon salt
2½ cups milk
1 teaspoon vanilla
¼ teaspoon nutmeg

Make pastry as directed and fit into a 9" piepan, making a high fluted edge; do not bake. Preheat oven to 425° F. With a rotary beater, beat eggs lightly, add sugar and salt, and beat until thick and cream colored. Gradually beat in milk and vanilla, then strain through a fine sieve and pour into pastry shell. Sprinkle with nutmeg and bake 15 minutes; reduce temperature to 350° F. and bake 12–15 minutes longer or until a silver knife inserted midway between center and rim comes out clean. (*Note:* Center will still be soft but will set on standing.) Do not overbake or custard will curdle. Cool on a wire rack to room temperature before serving, or serve well chilled. About 400 calories for each of 6 servings, 300 calories for each of 8 servings.

VARIATIONS:

Rich Custard Pie: Prepare as directed, substituting 1 cup heavy cream for 1 cup of the milk. About 515 calories for each of 6 servings, 385 calories for each of 8 servings.

Coconut Custard Pie: Prepare as directed but, just before pouring custard into pie shell, fold in ¾ cup flaked coconut. Pour into shell, sprinkle with ¼ cup flaked coconut (omit nutmeg), and bake as directed. About 455 calories for each of 6 servings, 340 calories for each of 8 servings.

Egg Yolk Custard Pie: Prepare as directed, using 8 egg yolks for custard instead of 4 whole eggs. About 425 calories for each of 6 servings, 320 calories for each of 8 servings.

Slipped Custard Pie: Make and bake a 9" pie shell as directed in Flaky Pastry I. Prepare and strain custard mixture, pour into a well-buttered 9" piepan, and sprinkle with nutmeg. Set piepan in a larger pan, add enough hot water to come halfway up piepan. Bake at 350° F. 30–35 minutes or until custard tests done; cool on a wire rack to room temperature. Gently loosen custard from sides of piepan with a spatula, hold level, and shake to loosen bottom. Now tilt and carefully slide into pie shell; hold pans close together and coax custard along. Let custard settle a few minutes before serving. About 400 calories for each of 6 servings, 300 calories for each of 8 servings.

RICH COCONUT PIE

For a truly exquisite pie, use freshly grated coconut.
Makes 6–8 servings

1 recipe Flaky Pastry I

Filling:
¼ cup butter or margarine, softened to room temperature
1 cup superfine sugar
2 eggs
2 tablespoons flour
½ cup milk
¼ teaspoon almond extract
2 cups finely grated coconut

Preheat oven to 350° F. Make pastry as directed and fit into a 9" piepan, making a high fluted edge; do not bake. Cream butter and sugar until light, beat in eggs, 1 at a time. Sprinkle in flour and blend until smooth. Mix in remaining ingredients and spoon into pastry shell. Bake 45 minutes until browned and springy to the touch. Cool on a wire rack and serve at room temperature. About 540 calories for each of 6 servings, 405 calories for each of 8 servings.

VANILLA CHIFFON PIE

Plenty of flavor variations here to try.
Makes 6–8 servings

1 (9") pie shell, baked and cooled (Flaky Pastry I or a crumb crust)
Filling:
¾ cup sugar
1 envelope unflavored gelatin
1 cup milk
4 eggs, separated
2 teaspoons vanilla
⅓ cup heavy cream (*optional*)
¼ teaspoon nutmeg

Mix ½ cup sugar and the gelatin in the top of a double boiler, gradually mix in milk, and heat and stir over simmering water until steaming hot. Beat egg yolks lightly, blend in a little hot milk mixture, and return to pan. Cook and stir 3–5 minutes until thickened and no raw taste of egg remains. Mix in vanilla, set pan over cold water, and place a circle of wax paper flat on sauce. Cool, stirring now and then, until mixture mounds slightly on a spoon. Whip cream, if you like, and fold into sauce. Beat egg whites until foamy, gradually beat in remaining sugar, and beat to soft peaks; fold into sauce. Spoon into pie shell and chill until firm, at least 3–4 hours. Sprinkle with nutmeg and serve. (*Note:* If you prefer, use cream to garnish pie instead of mixing into filling.) About 405 calories for each of 6 servings, 305 calories for each of 8 servings (with pastry crust and without optional heavy cream).

VARIATIONS:

Chocolate Chiffon Pie: Prepare as directed but use only 3 egg yolks and add 2 (1-ounce) squares unsweetened chocolate. Beat ½ cup sugar with 3 egg whites and fold into sauce; reduce vanilla to 1 teaspoon and omit nutmeg. Decorate with chocolate curls.* About 525 calories for each of 6 servings, 395 calories for each of 8 servings.

Coffee Chiffon Pie: Prepare as directed but add 2 tablespoons instant coffee powder or freeze-dried coffee along with egg yolks; reduce vanilla to 1 teaspoon. About 405 calories for each of 6 servings, 305 calories for each of 8 servings.

Coconut Chiffon Pie: Prepare as directed but reduce vanilla to ½ teaspoon and add ½ teaspoon almond extract. Fold in ¾ cup finely grated coconut along with beaten egg whites. Chill, then serve topped with toasted, flaked coconut. About 460 calories for each of 6 servings, 345 calories for each of 8 servings.

Lemon, Lime, or Orange Chiffon Pie: Prepare as directed but use ⅓ cup lemon or lime juice or ⅓ cup thawed frozen orange juice concentrate and ⅔ cup water instead of milk; also use 2 tablespoons finely grated lemon, lime, or orange rind instead of vanilla. Tint filling an appropriate color, if you like, before spooning into pie shell. Omit nutmeg. About 415 calories for each of 6 servings, 310 calories for each of 8 servings.

Berry Chiffon Pie: Prepare as directed but substitute 1 cup crushed, sieved ripe berries for the milk, omit egg yolks, and flavor with 1 tablespoon finely grated lemon rind instead of vanilla. (*Note:* If you use frozen berries, reduce sugar to ½ cup —¼ cup in the sauce, ¼ cup in the beaten egg whites.) Fold in the whipped cream, then the beaten egg whites. Cover pie shell, if you like, with ½ cup sliced berries before pouring in filling. Chill until firm; omit nutmeg. About 435 calories for each of 6 servings, 325 calories for each of 8 servings.

Peach or Apricot Chiffon Pie: Prepare like Berry Chiffon Pie (above) but use 1 cup peach or apricot purée instead of berries. If you like, cover bottom of pie shell with a layer of sliced peaches or apricots before pouring in filling. About 435 calories for each of 6 servings, 325 calories for each of 8 servings.

Pumpkin Chiffon Pie: Mix 1¼ cups pumpkin purée with ¾ cup firmly packed light brown sugar and the gelatin called for; proceed as recipe directs but use only 2 egg yolks. Omit vanilla and add ½ teaspoon each cinnamon and nutmeg. Cool, fold in 2 egg whites beaten with ¼ cup sugar, fill pie shell, chill well, then serve topped with fluffs of whipped cream. About 420 calories for each of 6 servings (without whipped cream), 315 calories for each of 8 servings.

STRAWBERRY BAVARIAN PIE

Strictly speaking, a Bavarian does *not* contain egg whites. If you hate having leftover whites, however, beat to soft peaks and fold into filling at the end.
Makes 6–8 servings

1 (9") pie shell (*Flaky Pastry I, Sweet Torte, or Graham Cracker Crust*), baked and cooled

Filling:
½ cup sugar
1 envelope unflavored gelatin
½ cup milk
3 egg yolks, lightly beaten
1 tablespoon lemon juice
1 cup puréed strawberries
Few drops red food coloring
¾ cup heavy cream
2 tablespoons confectioners' sugar
3 egg whites (*optional*)

Mix sugar, gelatin, and milk in the top of a double boiler and heat over simmering water until steaming hot. Mix a little hot milk mixture into yolks, return to pan, and cook and stir 3–5 minutes until thickened and no raw taste of egg remains. Off heat, mix in lemon juice, berries, and food coloring; cool, stirring occasionally, until mixture mounds when dropped from a spoon. Whip cream with confectioners' sugar until firm peaks form, then fold into strawberry mixture. If you like, also beat egg whites to soft peaks and fold in. Spoon into pie shell and chill at least 4 hours before serving. About 435 calories for each of 6 servings (made with pastry crust and optional egg whites), 325 calories for each of 8 servings.

VARIATIONS:

Rum Bavarian Pie: Prepare filling as directed, using 1 cup milk and omitting lemon juice, berries, and food coloring; flavor with ½ cup light rum. About 520 calories for each of 6 servings, 390 calories for each of 8 servings.

Chocolate Bavarian Pie: Prepare filling as directed but use 1½ cups milk and 1 (6-ounce) package semisweet chocolate bits; omit lemon juice, berries, and coloring and flavor with 1 teaspoon vanilla. About 655 calories for each of 6 servings, 490 calories for each of 8 servings.

Mocha Bavarian Pie: Prepare Chocolate Bavarian Pie (above) as directed, using 1 cup milk and ½ cup very strong hot black coffee. About 640 calories for each of 6 servings, 480 calories for each of 8 servings.

Almond Bavarian Pie: Prepare filling as directed, using 1¼ cups milk; omit lemon juice, berries, and coloring and mix in ¾ cup finely ground blanched almonds and ½ teaspoon almond extract. About 540 calories for each of 6 servings, 405 calories for each of 8 servings.

Nesselrode Pie: Prepare filling as directed, using 1¼ cups milk; omit lemon juice, berries, and coloring and add 2 tablespoons light rum. Just before adding whipped cream, fold in ¼ cup finely chopped mixed candied fruits and 3 egg whites, beaten to soft peaks. Proceed as directed, and just before serving decorate with candied fruits. About 515 calories for each of 6 servings, 385 calories for each of 8 servings.

GRASSHOPPER PIE

This tastes very much like the Grasshopper cocktail—a mixture of crème de menthe and crème de cacao.
Makes 6–8 servings

1 (9") pie shell (Graham Cracker Crust, Flaky Pastry I, or Mürbteig), baked and cooled

Filling:
¾ cup sugar
1 envelope unflavored gelatin
½ cup cold water
3 eggs, separated
⅓ cup green crème de menthe
¼ cup crème de cacao
½ cup heavy cream
Few drops green food coloring (optional)

Topping:
½ cup heavy cream, whipped to soft peaks
Chocolate curls*

Heat and stir ½ cup sugar, gelatin, and water in the top of a double boiler over simmering water until gelatin dissolves. Lightly beat egg yolks, blend in a little hot mixture, then return to pan. Cook and stir 3–5 minutes until thickened and no raw taste of egg remains. Off heat, mix in liqueurs; place a circle of wax paper flat on sauce and cool until mixture mounds when dropped from a spoon. Whip cream to soft peaks, fold into sauce, and, if you like, tint pale green. Beat egg whites until foamy, gradually beat in remaining sugar, and continue to beat until soft peaks form; fold into sauce. Spoon into pie shell and chill until firm, at least 3–4 hours. Top with swirls of whipped cream and sprinkle with chocolate curls. About 675 calories for each of 6 servings, 505 calories for each of 8 servings.

VARIATION:

Brandy Alexander Pie: Prepare as directed but substitute ⅓ cup brandy for the crème de menthe. About 675 calories for each of 6 servings, 505 calories for each of 8 servings.

OLD-FASHIONED SOUTHERN PECAN PIE

Almost too good to be true.
Makes 6–8 servings

1 recipe Flaky Pastry I

Filling:
1 cup pecan halves
1 (1-pound) box light brown sugar
¼ cup unsifted flour
½ teaspoon salt
½ cup milk
1½ teaspoons vanilla
3 eggs
½ cup melted butter or margarine

Preheat oven to 325° F. Make pastry as directed and fit into a 9" pie-pan; do not bake. Arrange pecans in concentric rings over bottom of pastry. Blend sugar, flour, and salt, then mix in milk and vanilla. Beat in eggs, 1 at a time, using a wire whisk or rotary beater; mix in butter, a little at a time. Pour filling over pecans. Bake pie 1 hour and 15 minutes or until filling is puffy and crust golden. Serve at room temperature. And cut the pieces small—the pie is *rich*. About 695 calories for each of 6 servings, 520 calories for each of 8 servings.

LEMON CHESS PIE

The South's favorite pie is "chess" (probably a corruption of "cheese" from the English "lemon cheese"). Lemon is a popular chess flavor, but there are others—so many no one knows which is the original. Here are three especially good ones.
Makes 6–8 servings

1 recipe Flaky Pastry I

Filling:
*1½ cups sugar
2 tablespoons flour
Finely grated rind of 2 lemons
5 eggs
Juice of 2 lemons
⅓ cup melted butter or margarine*

Preheat oven to 325° F. Make pastry as directed and fit into a 9" piepan; do not bake. Mix sugar, flour, and rind, then, beat in eggs, 1 at a time. Stir in lemon juice and finally the melted butter, adding a bit at a time and beating well after each addition. Pour filling into pie shell and bake about 1 hour until puffy and golden (filling will seem unset). Cool pie to room temperature (filling will settle and thicken). Serve at room temperature. About 545 calories for each of 6 servings, 410 calories for each of 8 servings.

BROWN SUGAR CHESS PIE

Rich, rich, *rich!*
Makes 6–8 servings

1 recipe Flaky Pastry I

Filling:
*1 (1-pound) box light brown sugar
4 eggs
¼ cup milk
1½ teaspoons vanilla
½ teaspoon salt
½ cup melted butter or margarine*

Preheat oven to 325° F. Make pastry as directed and fit into a 9" piepan; do not bake. Blend together all filling ingredients except butter, then mix in butter, a little at a time; pour into pie shell and bake about 1 hour until puffy and golden. Cool pie to room temperature before serving (filling will settle and thicken). Cut the pieces small. About 560 calories for each of 6 servings, 420 calories for each of 8 servings.

COLONIAL CHESS PIE

This chess pie, unlike the others, contains raisins and walnuts. And is it RICH!
Makes 6–8 servings

1 recipe Flaky Pastry I

Filling:
*½ cup unsalted butter
1⅔ cups sugar
1 cup light cream
1⅓ cups seedless raisins
6 egg yolks, lightly beaten
1½ cups coarsely chopped walnuts
½ teaspoon vanilla
½ teaspoon salt*

Preheat oven to 425° F. Make pastry as directed and fit into a 9" piepan; do not bake. Heat and stir butter, sugar, cream, and raisins over moderate heat just until boiling; remove from heat. Blend a little hot mixture into yolks, return to pan, and stir in remaining ingredients. Pour into pie shell and bake 15 minutes, reduce oven to 375° F. and bake 45–50 minutes longer until puffy and golden. Cool to room temperature before serving. About 970 calories for each of 6 servings, 730 calories for each of 8 servings.

THE VERY BEST CHEESE PIE

Unbelievably smooth.
Makes 10 servings

Crust:
18 graham crackers rolled to crumbs (there should be 1½ cups)
¼ cup sugar
5 tablespoons melted butter or margarine

Filling:
2 (8-ounce) packages cream cheese, softened to room temperature
2 eggs
½ cup sugar
1 teaspoon vanilla

Topping:
1 cup sour cream
¼ cup sugar
1 teaspoon vanilla

Preheat oven to 375° F. Mix crust ingredients and pat firmly into the bottom and ⅓ of the way up the sides of a 9″ spring form pan. Beat filling ingredients with a rotary beater or electric mixer until satiny and pour into crust. Bake 20 minutes, remove from oven, and cool 15 minutes. Meanwhile, raise oven to 475° F. Blend topping ingredients and spread gently over cheese filling. Return pie to oven and bake 10 minutes longer. Cool in pan to room temperature, then cover with foil and chill 10–12 hours before serving. Cut in *slim* wedges. About 430 calories per serving.

CHERRY TOPPING FOR CHEESE CAKE

The following toppings can be spread over Cottage Cheese Cake or the Very Best Cheese Pie after they have been baked and thoroughly cooled.

Makes enough to top a 9″ cheese cake

½ cup sugar
2 tablespoons cornstarch
1 (1-pound) can sour red cherries, drained (reserve liquid)
Cherry liquid plus enough water to total ¾ cup
1 teaspoon lemon juice
Few drops red food coloring

Mix sugar and cornstarch in a saucepan, gradually blend in cherry liquid, and heat, stirring, until boiling. Reduce heat and simmer 5 minutes, stirring occasionally. Off heat, mix in lemon juice, cherries, and food coloring. Cool 5 minutes, spread on top of cooled cheese cake, and chill several hours. About 850 calories total, about 85 calories for each of 10 servings and 70 calories for each of 12.

VARIATIONS:

Blueberry Topping: Prepare as directed but substitute 1 (1-pound) can blueberries for cherries and reduce sugar to ¼ cup; omit food coloring. About 660 calories total, about 66 calories for each of 10 servings and 55 calories for each of 12.

Cranberry Topping: Substitute 1 (1-pound) can whole cranberry sauce (do not drain) for cherries. Mix sauce with ⅓ cup sugar, 1 tablespoon cornstarch blended with ¼ cup orange juice and proceed as directed. About 1100 calories total, about 110 calories for each of 10 servings and 90 calories for each of 12.

Pineapple Topping: Drain liquid from 1 (8-ounce) can crushed pineapple and add enough canned pineapple juice to total ½ cup. Blend ¼ cup sugar and 1 tablespoon cornstarch, mix into pineapple juice, and heat and stir as above until thickened and clear. Mix in lemon juice and pineapple (but not food coloring), cool, and spread over cheese cake as directed. About 450 calories total, about 45 calories for each of 10 servings and 40 calories for each of 12.

COTTAGE CHEESE CAKE

Makes 12 servings

Crust:
2½ cups graham cracker crumbs
⅓ cup sugar
⅓ cup melted butter or margarine

Filling:
2 pounds cottage cheese
4 eggs, separated
½ cup sugar
¼ cup sifted flour
2 tablespoons lemon juice
1 teaspoon finely grated lemon rind

Preheat oven to 325° F. Mix crust ingredients and pat firmly over the bottom and up the sides of a 9" spring form pan. Purée cottage cheese in an electric blender 1–2 minutes at high speed until smooth or press through a fine sieve; set aside. Beat egg yolks until thick, slowly add sugar, and beat until the color of cream. Beat in flour, lemon juice and rind, and cottage cheese. In a separate bowl, beat egg whites to soft peaks; with a wire whisk mix into cheese mixture until completely blended. Spoon into crust and bake 1 hour on center oven rack until lightly browned. Turn off oven, open door, and let cake cool in oven ½ hour. Lift to a wire rack and cool in pan to room temperature, remove spring form, cover cake with foil, and chill well before serving. About 340 calories per serving.

STRAWBERRY TOPPING FOR CHEESE CAKE

Makes enough to top a 9" cheese cake

1 quart strawberries, washed and stemmed
⅓ cup sugar
1 tablespoon cornstarch
¼ cup water
Few drops red food coloring

Crush enough small berries to make 1 cup and press through a fine sieve. Mix sugar and cornstarch in a saucepan, blend in sieved berries and water, and heat and stir over moderate heat until boiling; lower heat and simmer 2–3 minutes, stirring until thickened and clear. Add coloring and cool slightly. Arrange whole berries, points up, on a baked, cooled cheese cake, spoon sauce over all, and chill 2 hours. About 500 calories total, about 50 calories for each of 10 servings and 40 calories for each of 12.

LEMON ANGEL PIE

A shattery meringue crust billowing with a creamy lemon filling.
Makes 6–8 servings

1 (9") Meringue Pie Shell, baked and cooled

Filling:
4 egg yolks
½ cup sugar
¼ cup lemon juice
2 tablespoons finely grated lemon rind
1 cup heavy cream

Beat egg yolks in the top of a double boiler until thick and cream colored. Gradually beat in sugar, then lemon juice and rind. Set over simmering water and cook, stirring constantly, about 5–8 minutes until thick. Remove from heat, place a circle of wax paper flat on mixture, and cool to room temperature. Whip cream until soft peaks form, and spread half in bottom of pie shell. Cover with filling and top with remaining whipped cream. Or fold lemon mixture into whipped cream, then fill pie shell. Chill overnight. About 320 calories for each of 6 servings, 230 calories for each of 8 servings.

VARIATIONS:

Lime Angel Pie: Prepare as directed but substitute ¼ cup lime juice and 1 tablespoon grated lime rind for the lemon juice and rind. About 320 calories for each of 6 servings, 240 calories for each of 8 servings.

Orange Angel Pie: Prepare as directed but substitute ¼ cup thawed, frozen orange juice concentrate and 2 tablespoons finely grated orange rind for the lemon juice and rind. About 340 calories for each of 6 servings, 255 calories for each of 8 servings.

CHOCOLATE ANGEL PIE

If chocolate is your choice, you'll prefer this angel pie to the lemon. Makes 6–8 servings

1 (9") Meringue Pie Shell, baked and cooled

Filling:
¼ cup hot water
1 (12-ounce) package semisweet chocolate bits, melted
1 cup heavy cream
½ cup sifted confectioners' sugar
1 teaspoon vanilla

Blend water and chocolate bits until smooth and cool to room temperature. Beat cream and sugar to stiff peaks, fold into chocolate mixture, flavor with vanilla, and spoon into meringue shell. Chill well before serving. About 535 calories for each of 6 servings, 400 calories for each of 8 servings.

VARIATION:

Mocha Angel Pie: Prepare as directed but use ¼ cup strong hot black coffee instead of water. About 535 calories for each of 6 servings, 400 calories for each of 8 servings.

PEACH SUNDAE PIE

Makes 8 servings

1 (9") pie shell (Graham Cracker, Nut-Crumb, Toasted Coconut, Flaky Pastry I, or Sweet Torte Pastry), baked and cooled

Filling:
1 quart peach or vanilla ice cream
3 ripe peaches, peeled, pitted, and sliced thin
¼ cup Melba Sauce
¾ cup heavy cream, whipped to soft peaks (optional)
¼ cup minced nuts (walnuts, pecans, pistachios, toasted almonds)

Soften ice cream slightly, spread in pie shell, making edges a little higher than center, and freeze until firm. Top with peaches, drizzle with sauce, "frost," if you like with whipped cream, and sprinkle with nuts. Serve at once. About 400 calories per serving (made with graham cracker crust and with whipped cream).

VARIATIONS:

Other Flavors: Prepare as directed, using any favorite combinations of ice cream and fruit—strawberry and raspberry, lemon and strawberry, orange and blueberry, etc. Or, if you prefer, omit the fruit and whipped cream and spread ice cream with any favorite sundae topping. Recipe too flexible for a meaningful calorie count.

Alaska Pie: Fill pie shell with ice cream (not sherbet or ice milk, which will melt too fast) and freeze until hard. Omit peaches, sauce, and whipped cream. Cover ice cream *completely* with 1 recipe Basic Meringue Topping for a 9" Pie and bake 3–5 minutes at 500° F. until touched with brown. Serve at once. About 350 calories per serving.

STRAWBERRY ICE CREAM PARFAIT PIE

Makes 8 servings

1 (9") pie shell (any kind), baked and cooled

Filling:
1 (3-ounce) package strawberry-flavored gelatin
1¼ cups boiling water
1 pint strawberry ice cream
1½ cups sliced strawberries
¾ cup heavy cream, whipped to soft peaks

Mix gelatin and water in a large bowl. Add ice cream by spoonfuls and stir until melted and well blended. Chill until mixture mounds when dropped from a spoon, then fold in berries. Spoon into pie shell and chill until firm. Garnish with whipped cream. About 340 calories per serving (made with standard piecrust).

VARIATIONS:
Prepare as directed but use any of the following combinations of gelatin, ice cream, and fruit instead of that given above: raspberry-flavored gelatin, raspberry ice cream, and raspberries; orange-flavored gelatin, vanilla ice cream, and orange sections; lemon-flavored gelatin, peach ice cream, and sliced peaches; mixed fruit-flavored gelatin, pistachio ice cream, and sliced bananas. Recipe too flexible for a meaningful calorie count.

ABOUT MAKING TARTS

Tarts, in classical cuisine, are short cookie-like pastry shells filled with raw or cooked fruit, often accompanied with custard or cream filling. They are usually open face (at least they are never sealed under a top crust) and may be small, medium, or large. The most beautiful are arrangements of fruit jeweled under a clear sweet glaze.

In America, tarts are simply little pies, single or double crusted, sometimes enough for one serving, sometimes no more than a mouthful. Almost any pie recipe can be used for tarts. (*Note:* You will probably need 1½–2 times the amount of pastry because it takes more to line several little pans than a single large one.)

Some Ways to Shape Tart Shells: Prepare pastry, roll out ⅛" thick, then cut in circles about 1" larger all around than tin you plan to use. Fluted tart tins, available in many housewares departments, make especially dainty tarts, but tarts can also be fitted into muffin pans or over upside-down custard cups or gelatin molds.

About Baking Tarts: Follow individual pie recipes, making the following adjustments in baking times and temperatures:

Unfilled Tart Shells: Preheat oven to 450° F. Roll and fit pastry into tins, prick well all over, and bake 10–15 minutes until crisp and tan. Cool in pans on wire racks a few minutes, then ease out, using a metal skewer to free stubborn spots. Cool thoroughly before filling. (*Note:* Preserves or jams may be used to fill small tarts instead of pie fillings.)

Filled Tarts: Preheat oven to 425° F. Roll and fit pastry into tins; do not prick. Add filling, enough to fill each tart ½–⅔, no more. Add top crust, if any, crimp edges, and seal. Bake 15–20 minutes until pastry is crisp and tan and filling bubbly. Cool or not as individual recipes direct.
(*Note:* To minimize breakage, keep tarts in tins until just before serving.)

Some Ways to Decorate Tarts: Keep decorations simple, in proportion to the tart and appropriate to the occasion. Here are a few suggestions:

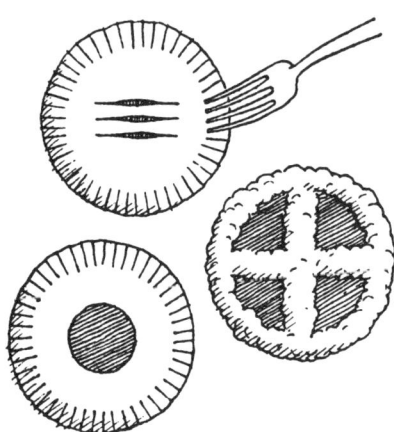

SWISS STRAWBERRY TART

Makes 6–8 servings

1 recipe Flaky Pastry I

Filling:
3 tablespoons flour
¼ cup sugar
⅛ teaspoon salt
1 cup milk
½ teaspoon vanilla
2 egg yolks, lightly beaten
⅓ cup heavy cream
3 cups ripe strawberries, washed, stemmed, and dried

Glaze:
¾ cup red currant jelly

Make pastry, fit into a 9″ piepan, and bake as directed; cool. Mix flour, sugar, and salt in the top of a double boiler, add milk slowly, stirring until smooth, then cook and stir over direct moderate heat until thickened and smooth; stir in vanilla. Blend a little hot mixture into yolks, return to top of double boiler, set over simmering water, and cook and stir 3–4 minutes until thick and no taste of raw egg remains. Remove from heat, place a circle of wax paper flat on sauce and cool to room temperature. Whip cream and fold into sauce. Spread over bottom of pie shell and arrange strawberries, points up, on top. To glaze, melt jelly over low heat, cool to barely lukewarm, then spoon evenly over berries. Cover and chill until serving time (but no longer than 1–2 hours or pastry will become soggy). About 485 calories for each of 6 servings, 365 calories for each of 8 servings.

VIENNESE FRUIT FLAN

Cut the pieces small—this one's rich!
Makes 8–10 servings

1 (9″) Sweet Torte or Mürbteig pie shell, baked and cooled

Filling:
1 cup heavy cream
¼ cup superfine sugar

1 teaspoon vanilla
1 quart stemmed strawberries or a mixture of sliced peaches, seedless green or seeded black grapes, and any stemmed berries

Glaze:
1 cup water
2 tablespoons sugar
4 teaspoons arrowroot or cornstarch blended with 2 tablespoons cold water
1 teaspoon lemon juice
Few drops red food coloring

Beat cream with sugar and vanilla until soft peaks form; spread over bottom of pie shell and arrange fruit artistically on top. Mix glaze (omitting coloring) and heat, stirring, over low heat until thickened and *clear*. Tint pale pink, cool to lukewarm, then spoon evenly over fruit. Keep in a cool place (not the refrigerator) and serve within 2–3 hours. About 380 calories for each of 8 servings, 305 calories for each of 10 servings.

TRUDY'S VIENNESE LINZERTORTE

Makes an 8" torte

Pastry:
1½ cups sifted flour
¼ cup sugar
½ teaspoon baking powder
½ teaspoon salt
1 teaspoon cinnamon
½ cup firmly packed dark brown sugar
½ cup butter, chilled (*no substitute*)
1 egg, lightly beaten
½ cup finely ground unblanched almonds

Cream Filling:
1 egg
⅓ cup sugar
¼ cup sifted flour
¼ teaspoon salt
1½ cups scalding hot milk
1 teaspoon vanilla

Raspberry Topping:
1 (10-ounce) package thawed frozen raspberries (*do not drain*)
2 tablespoons sugar
2 tablespoons cornstarch
1 tablespoon lemon juice

Sift flour with sugar, baking powder, salt, and cinnamon, then, using a pastry blender, cut in brown sugar and butter until mixture resembles coarse meal. Add egg and almonds and blend with a fork until mixture forms a ball. Wrap half the pastry and chill. Press remaining pastry into the bottom and up the sides of an 8" piepan, cover, and chill. To prepare filling, beat egg until frothy, add sugar gradually, and beat 2–3 minutes until thick. Add flour and salt slowly and blend until smooth. Gradually add milk, stirring constantly. Transfer to the top of a double boiler, set over simmering water, and cook, stirring, 2–3 minutes until thickened and smooth. Reduce heat, cover, and cook 5 minutes, stirring frequently. Off heat, mix in vanilla; place a piece of wax paper directly on surface and cool to room temperature. Meanwhile, prepare topping: Mix all ingredients in a saucepan and bring to a boil, stirring; reduce heat and simmer, uncovered, 5–7 minutes, stirring occasionally, until thick; cool to room temperature. Preheat oven to 375° F. Spoon filling into pastry shell and carefully spread with topping. Roll remaining pastry into an 8" circle and cut in strips ½" wide; arrange lattice-fashion over filling. Lay 1–2 long strips around rim to cover lattice ends and press gently to seal. Bake 30–35 minutes until lightly browned. Cool several minutes before serving. About 300 calories for each of 12 servings.

APPLE STRUDEL

You can make strudel with all-purpose flour, but bread flour will produce a thinner, flakier pastry. Remove your rings before pulling and stretching strudel pastry; also make sure fingernails are clipped so you don't tear it. (*Note:* You can buy ready-to-fill strudel pastry at some gourmet groceries if you don't feel up to making it from scratch.) Makes 12 servings

Pastry:
1 ½ cups sifted flour (preferably bread flour)
¼ teaspoon salt
1 egg, lightly beaten
1 tablespoon cooking oil
⅓ cup lukewarm water
Cooking oil (for brushing pastry)

Filling:
¾ cup (about) melted butter (no substitute)
1 cup toasted fine bread crumbs
5 medium-size tart cooking apples, peeled, cored, and minced
⅔ cup sugar, mixed with 1 teaspoon cinnamon
¾ cup seedless raisins
½ cup minced, blanched almonds
2 teaspoons finely grated lemon rind

Topping:
Sifted confectioners' sugar

Mix flour and salt and make a well in the center. Combine egg, oil, and water, pour into well, and, using a fork, pull dry ingredients into liquid; mix to form a soft dough. Knead on a lightly floured board 3–4 minutes until smooth and elastic. Place dough in an oiled bowl, turn to grease all over, cover, and let stand in a warm place ½ hour. Meanwhile, cover a table about 3 feet square with an old tablecloth or sheet, smooth out, pull taut and fasten underneath with tape. Sprinkle all over with flour, adding a little extra in the center. With a lightly floured rolling pin, roll dough into an 18″ circle. Brush all over with oil. Slip floured hands, backs up, underneath pastry, then gently and evenly stretch dough, working from the center toward edges and moving hands around circle to stretch all areas as evenly and thinly as possible. The fully stretched dough should be semitransparent and cover the table. Work carefully to avoid tearing holes, but if small ones appear, ignore or pinch together (don't try to patch). Let pastry hang over edge of table and let stand, uncovered, 10 minutes (no longer or it may become brittle). Preheat oven to 400° F. Brush pastry generously with butter and with kitchen shears cut off thick edges and square up sides. Sprinkle crumbs over top half of pastry, leaving 2″ margins at the top and both sides. Cover crumbs with apples, sprinkle with sugar, raisins, almonds, and lemon rind; drizzle with 2–3 tablespoons melted butter. Fold top margin down and side margins in over filling. Grasping cloth at the top, tilting and holding taut with both hands, let strudel roll itself up, jelly-roll fashion. Ease strudel onto a buttered baking sheet and curve into a horseshoe. Brush with butter and bake on center rack 20 minutes; reduce oven to 350° F., brush again with butter, and bake 20–25 minutes longer, brushing once more with butter after 10 minutes or so. When strudel is richly browned, transfer to a wire rack and cool. Dust with confectioners' sugar and slice 2″ thick. Serve slightly warm or cool, with or without whipped cream. About 365 calories per serving (without cream).

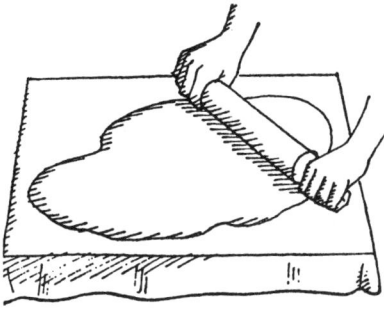

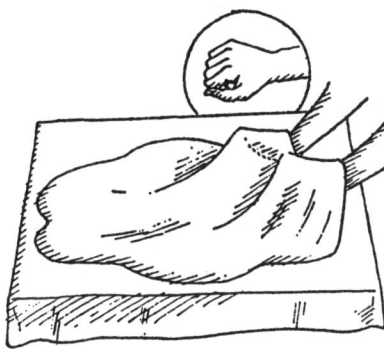

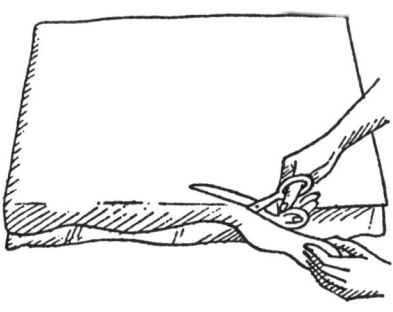

How to Roll and Stretch Strudel

VARIATIONS:

Cherry Strudel: Prepare as directed, using Cherry Strudel Filling instead of apple. About 390 calories per serving.

Cheese Strudel: Use Cheese Strudel Filling instead of apple and place on stretched pastry in a row at the top, leaving 2" margins at top and sides. Fold the margins in over filling, roll, and bake strudel as directed. About 420 calories per serving.

Poppy Seed Strudel: Prepare and stretch pastry as directed; brush with melted butter and ½ cup warm honey, then sprinkle top half with crumbs. Across the top end in a single row place 2 cups ground poppy seeds, ½ cup sugar, 1 cup seedless raisins, the finely grated rind of 1 lemon, leaving a 2" margin at the top and each side. Drizzle with ½ cup heavy cream. Fold margins in over filling, roll, and bake strudel as directed. About 380 calories per serving.

Jam Strudel: Prepare and stretch pastry as directed; brush with melted butter, scatter crumbs over top half of pastry, leaving 2" margins as above. Spread 1½–2 cups warmed strawberry, raspberry, or apricot jam over crumbs, top with ¾ cup sultana raisins and ½ cup minced blanched almonds. Fold margins in over filling, roll, and bake as directed. About 435 calories per serving.

CHERRY STRUDEL FILLING

Enough to fill 1 strudel

2 (1-pound) *cans pitted tart red or sweet dark cherries, drained*
½–1 *cup sugar*
¼ *teaspoon almond extract*
1 *cup minced, blanched almonds*

Quarter the cherries, toss with the minimum amount of sugar, and let stand 10 minutes; taste for sweetness and add more sugar if needed. Mix in extract and almonds and use as strudel filling. About 1925 calories total (with 1 cup sugar).

VARIATION:

Fresh Cherry Strudel Filling: Simmer 1 quart stemmed, pitted, ripe tart red or dark sweet cherries with ½–1 cup sugar and ¼ cup water 5 minutes until softened. Cool in liquid and drain; taste for sugar and adjust, then mix with extract and almonds. About 1555 calories total (with 1 cup sugar).

CHEESE STRUDEL FILLING

Enough to fill 1 strudel

1 pound cottage cheese
⅓ cup sugar
1 egg plus 1 egg white, lightly beaten
¼ cup heavy cream
1 cup seedless raisins
1 cup minced walnuts
Finely grated rind and juice of 1 lemon

Purée cottage cheese in an electric blender 1–2 minutes at high speed until smooth or press through a fine sieve. Mix with remaining ingredients and use as strudel filling. About 2290 calories total.

PALMIERS

Makes about 5 dozen

1 recipe Puff Pastry
½ cup sugar (about)

Make pastry as directed, divide in 3 equal parts, and roll, one at a time, into a 12½" square about ⅛" thick. With a sharp knife, cut ¼" off all margins, making edges ruler straight. Brush square with cold water, sprinkle evenly with about 2 tablespoons sugar. Make a light mark down center of square and fold each side in toward center as shown so folds meet exactly; fold again through center of each half, then fold 1 roll over on top of the other. Wrap and chill 1 hour. Preheat oven to 450° F. With a very sharp knife, slice rolls cross-

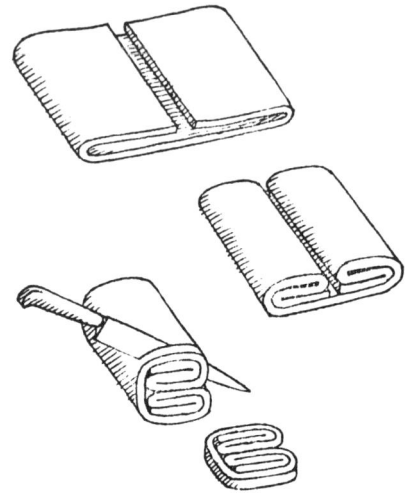

How to Fold and Cut Palmiers

wise every ½", dip both cut sides of slices in sugar, arrange 1½" apart on ungreased baking sheets, and bake 5–7 minutes until browned on the bottom; turn, using a pancake turner, reduce heat to 375° F. and bake 5 minutes longer until browned underneath. Cool on wire racks. Serve as is or, if you like, sandwiched together with sweetened stiffly whipped cream. About 90 calories each (unfilled, unsandwiched).

NAPOLEONS

Napoleons are best eaten the day they're made. If you must prepare them ahead of time, spread pastry thinly with hot sieved apricot preserves before filling to keep Napoleons crisp. Also refrigerate until about 20 minutes before serving. Makes about 1 dozen

1 recipe Puff Pastry
2 recipes Pastry Cream or 1 quart sweetened stiffly whipped cream
Sifted confectioners' sugar

Prepare pastry as directed, divide in

3 equal parts, and roll out 1 piece on a lightly floured board into a rectangle 12½"×14½" and ⅛" thick, keeping edges as straight as possible. With a sharp knife, trim ⅛" off all margins. Roll pastry over a lightly floured rolling pin and unroll on a baking sheet brushed with cold water; prick well all over, cover, and chill ½ hour. Meanwhile, preheat oven to 450° F. Roll remaining 2 pieces the same way, transfer to baking sheets and chill. (*Note:* If you do not have 3 baking sheets, keep pastry chilled and roll when a sheet is free—make sure it is cool.) Bake pastry, 1 sheet at a time, on center oven rack 10 minutes until golden brown and crisp. Ease onto an extra-large wire rack (or 2 racks tied together) and cool thoroughly. Place pastry sheets on a large, flat surface and even up margins (all 3 pieces should be about the same size). Cut each the long way into strips 4" wide and, as though making triple decker sandwiches, sandwich strips together, 3 deep, with filling (do not spread filling on top layer). Chill 1 hour. Using a sharp knife held vertically and a sawing motion, cut strips crosswise at 2" intervals. Dust with confectioners' sugar and serve as soon as possible. About 400 calories each.

VARIATION:

Prepare and bake 3 pastry sheets as directed. Cut 2 into strips as above; spread the third uncut sheet with 2 recipes Quick Glacé Icing. Melt 4 (1-ounce) squares semisweet chocolate and drizzle in parallel lines over icing; before it hardens, draw a toothpick across lines every ½" or so to make a crisscross design; when icing hardens, cut sheet into strips as you did the other two. Assemble Napoleons as above, using glazed strips as the top ones. About 550 calories each.

CREAM HORNS

For this recipe, you will need cream horn tubes, obtainable at gourmet shops or confectionery supply houses.

Makes about 2½ dozen

1 recipe Puff Pastry

Glaze:
1 egg, lightly beaten with 1 tablespoon cold water
Sugar

Make pastry as directed and roll out half at a time on a lightly floured pastry cloth to a thickness of ⅛", keeping sides as straight as possible. You will need long strips, so roll for length rather than width (it will take a 30" strip to wrap a cream horn tube 5" long). Cut pastry in strips ½" wide. Brush cream horn tubes with cold water and, starting at the point, wind with pastry strips, overlapping edges slightly but taking care not to stretch pastry. If it is necessary to piece pastry (when one strip is not long enough for the tube), make seams as smooth as possible. Cover pastry horns and chill ½ hour. Meanwhile, preheat oven to 450° F. Arrange horns 1" apart on baking sheets brushed with cold water. Brush horns with glaze, then sprinkle with sugar. Brush any spilled sugar from baking sheets and bake horns 10 minutes; reduce oven to 350° F. and bake 3–5 minutes longer or until golden brown and crisp. Remove tubes from horns by twisting free. Cool pastry horns on wire racks and serve filled with sweetened whipped cream or Pastry Cream.

About 240 calories each (filled with sweetened whipped cream).

CREAM PUFFS

Makes 1 dozen

1 recipe Choux Pastry
1 egg yolk, mixed with 1 tablespoon cold water (glaze)
2 recipes Pastry Cream or 1 quart ice cream or any suitable cream filling
¼ cup sifted confectioners' sugar

Preheat oven to 400° F. Make pastry as directed and drop by rounded tablespoonfuls 3″ apart on an ungreased baking sheet to form 12 puffs, or put through a pastry bag fitted with a large, plain tip. Brush tops with glaze and bake 45–50 minutes until puffed, golden brown, and hollow sounding when tapped. (*Note:* Do not open oven door during first quarter hour.) Cool puffs on wire racks away from drafts. To fill, cut a ¾″ slice off the top of each puff and pull out any soft dough inside. Fill, replace tops, cover, and chill until serving time. Dust with confectioners' sugar and serve. About 240 calories each (filled with pastry cream).

VARIATIONS:

– Frost tops of filled puffs with any favorite icing.
– Top with hot or cold chocolate or butterscotch sauce.
– Fill with fresh, canned, or frozen fruit mixed with whipped cream instead of pastry cream.
– Fill with softened ice cream (any flavor); wrap airtight and freeze. Thaw 5–10 minutes before serving. These will keep about 1 month in the freezer.

All variations too flexible for meaningful calorie counts.

CHOCOLATE ÉCLAIRS

Makes 1 dozen

1 recipe Choux Pastry
1 egg yolk, mixed with 1 tablespoon cold water (glaze)
2 recipes Pastry Cream
1 recipe Chocolate Glacé Icing

Preheat oven to 400° F. Make pastry as directed and drop by rounded tablespoonfuls 2″ apart in rows that are 6″ apart on an ungreased baking sheet to form 12 equal-sized mounds. Using a spoon and a spatula, shape each mound into an oval about 4″ long, 1½″ wide, and 1″ high. Or put mixture through a pastry bag fitted with a large, plain tip. Brush tops with glaze and bake 40–45 minutes until puffed, golden brown, and hollow sounding when tapped. Cool away from drafts on wire racks. Halve éclairs lengthwise and gently pull out any soft dough inside. Fill with pastry cream and replace tops. Arrange on a wire rack with a piece of wax paper underneath. Spoon icing evenly over each and allow to harden. Serve within 1–2 hours. Do not refrigerate. About 280 calories each.

PROFITEROLES

Bite-size Cream Puffs. Perfect for a tea if served plain without sauce.

Makes about 4½ dozen

1 recipe Choux Pastry
1 egg yolk, mixed with 1 tablespoon cold water (glaze)
3 recipes Pastry Cream or 7 cups sweetened whipped cream (about)
⅓ cup sifted confectioners' sugar

Preheat oven to 400° F. Prepare pastry as directed and drop by rounded teaspoonfuls 2″ apart on ungreased baking sheets or put through a pastry bag fitted with a medium-size plain

PIES AND PASTRIES

tip. Smooth into little round "pillows" about 1" high and brush tops lightly with glaze. Bake 20–25 minutes until puffed, golden brown, and crisp. Cool on wire racks away from drafts. Just before serving make a small slit in the side of each Profiterole and squirt in filling with a pastry bag filled with a small, plain tip. Dust with confectioners' sugar and serve. Good with chocolate sauce. About 100 calories each (without chocolate sauce).

VARIATIONS:

Profiteroles au Chocolat: Fill with Chocolate Cream Filling, arrange in a large bowl, or pile in a small pyramid and pour Dark Chocolate Sauce over all. (*Note:* Pyramid will be easier to shape if you use chocolate sauce as a "glue" to stick profiteroles together.) About 150 calories each.

Ice Cream Profiteroles: Fill with any softened ice cream; wrap airtight and freeze. Thaw 10 minutes before serving. Top with Butterscotch or Fudge Sauce. These keep about 1 month in the freezer. About 160 calories each (without sauce).

Carolines: Make profiteroles as directed but fill with a cold savory mixture instead of a sweet one (creamed meat, seafood, or eggs are all suitable). To serve Carolines hot, reheat pastries *before filling*—5–7 minutes at 325° F. Split, fill with hot savory mixture, and serve. Hot or cold, these make good cocktail or buffet food. Recipe too flexible for a meaningful calorie count.

CROQUEMBOUCHE

This pastry pyramid must be made on a dry day so that the glaze will harden properly. It can be made with Meringue Kisses as well as Profiteroles and, for a really showy dessert, wreathed in spun sugar.*
Makes 15–18 servings

1 recipe Profiteroles

Glaze:
1 cup water
1½ cups sugar

Base:
1 (9") *cardboard circle covered with foil*

Topping:
¼ cup sifted confectioners' sugar

Prepare *profiteroles* as directed. Heat and stir glaze ingredients until sugar dissolves, then boil uncovered, stirring occasionally, 10–15 minutes until the color of amber; keep warm over lowest heat. Place base on a large round platter and set near range. Using glaze as a "glue," stick a ring of profiteroles, browned sides up, around edge of base. Form a second, slightly smaller ring on top by sticking profiteroles in spaces of first row and slanting slightly toward center. Fill middle with unglazed Profiteroles to support "walls." Continue building pyramid and top with

a single Profiterole. (*Note:* If syrup should harden, add 1–2 tablespoons boiling water and heat until again syrupy.) Dust confectioners' sugar over Croquembouche. To serve, start at the top and pull off Profiteroles with 2 forks; allow 3–4 per person. About 190 calories for each of 15 servings, 160 calories for each of 18 servings.

BAKLAVA

A terrific (and calorific) Greek-Middle Eastern pastry, dripping with honey syrup. Packages of phyllo pastry leaves (sheets) are available in Middle Eastern groceries and bakeries.
Makes 30 servings

1 (1-pound) package phyllo pastry leaves at room temperature
1½ cups (about) melted unsalted butter (no substitute)
Filling:
1 pound walnuts or toasted, blanched almonds, chopped fine
½ cup sugar
1 teaspoon cinnamon
Syrup:
1 cup honey
1 cup sugar
1 cup water
2 tablespoons lemon juice
2 (1") strips lemon rind

Preheat oven to 350° F. Unroll pastry leaves and separate into 3 stacks of equal height; place 1 stack in a buttered 17"×12"×2" baking pan and brush every second sheet with melted butter. Mix filling and scatter ⅓ of it over pastry stack in pan; top with half of the leaves from the second stack, brushing every other one with butter. Sprinkle with another ⅓ filling, top with remaining leaves from second stack, again brushing with butter. Sprinkle with remaining filling and top with third stack of pastry leaves, again brushing every second leaf with butter. With a sharp knife, cut Baklava into 30 squares. Measure remaining butter and add a little extra, if needed, to total ½ cup; brown lightly over low heat, then pour evenly over pastry. Bake on center rack ½ hour, reduce oven to 300° F., and bake ½ hour longer. Meanwhile, prepare syrup: Heat and stir all ingredients in a heavy saucepan over moderate heat until sugar dissolves, then boil slowly 20 minutes. Strain syrup and pour over Baklava as soon as it comes from the oven. Serve warm or cold. About 310 calories per serving.

CHAPTER 22

CAKES, FILLINGS, AND FROSTINGS

The old-fashioned art of cake making is being threatened by the dozens of excellent mixes on the market, also by a growing calorie consciousness. Consequently, this chapter is somewhat slimmer than cake chapters of other basic cookbooks. Still, there are plenty of recipes—some easy, some involved—for those who love to make cakes from "scratch" and those who want to learn how.

The Kinds of Cakes and How to Mix Them

There are dozens of different kinds of cakes, descended from three basic types: *the butter or creamed cakes* (those containing butter or some fat, also baking powder or soda to leaven), *the sponge cakes* (air-leavened cakes made with a great many eggs or egg whites) and *the chiffon* (a combination of the butter and sponge, containing some fat—usually cooking oil—and a high proportion of eggs). The type of cake determines the method of mixing:

Butter Cakes:

Conventional Method of Mixing (this can be done either by hand or electric mixer): Have butter, margarine, or shortening at room temperature (except in sultry summer weather, when butter or margarine is best used straight from the refrigerator); cream (moderate mixer speed) until light, gradually add sugar, and cream until fluffy. Add eggs (or egg yolks), one at a time, beating well after each addition. Add sifted dry ingredients (lowest mixer speed) alternately with the liquid, beginning and ending with the dry and adding ¼ to ⅓ at a time. Finally, if eggs have been separated, beat whites to soft peaks and fold in by hand. (*Note:* If cake contains minced fruits and/or nuts, gently fold in at the end. To keep them from sinking to the bottom of the cake during baking, hold out a bit [about ¼–⅓] of the dry ingredients, toss with the minced fruits or nuts and fold in along with them.)

Quick or One-Bowl Method: This streamlined way of mixing cakes more or less arrived with electric mixers and should not be used for old-fashioned butter cakes. It is closer to the muffin method of mixing than the conventional cake method in that the sifted dry ingredients go into the bowl first, the combined liquids are added all at once, and the two beaten just enough to blend (use low, then moderate mixer speed and scrape down beaters and sides of bowl as needed). Sometimes the eggs are separated, the yolks being added along with the other liquid ingredients and the whites folded in at the last.

Sponge Cakes (these include Angel Food as well as the different types of sponge):

True Sponge: Have egg yolks at room temperature and beat until frothy; add sugar gradually and beat until very thick and the color of cream (use moderate to high mixer speed or lots of elbow grease if beating by hand). Add sifted dry ingredients a little at a time and mix well after each addition (low mixer speed). Beat egg whites (also at room temperature) to soft peaks and fold in by hand.

Angel Food: These cakes can be made by electric mixer, but you'll get better volume if you do the beating by hand, preferably with a balloon whip in an unlined copper bowl. The trouble with mixers is that they overbeat and break down the egg whites. Even with hand beating there is great temptation to whip the whites into tall stiff peaks. Properly beaten, however, the peaks should be soft and the whites flow, not run, when the bowl is tipped. For greatest stability, they should be beaten with a little of the sugar; the remainder is sifted and added with the flour, a little at a time.

Chiffon Cakes: These are best made with an electric mixer. Flour, sugar, and other dry ingredients go into the bowl first; oil, egg yolks, liquids, and flavorings are added to a well in the dry ingredients and the mixture beaten at slow, then moderate speed, until batter is smooth and satiny. Egg whites, beaten to very stiff peaks, are then folded in just enough to blend.

About Essential Ingredients for Cakes

A cake will be no better than what goes into it. Choose ingredients of top quality; do not improvise, substituting one ingredient for another, but use the types of sugars, flours, shortenings, and leavenings recipes specify.

Fat: Essential to butter cakes for texture, tenderness, and flavor. Butter adds the best flavor, but vegetable shortening, some cooks believe, produces a higher, more tender cake. By combining the two, you can produce a cake of exceptionally fine flavor and volume. Do not use margarine interchangeably for butter unless recipe gives it as an alternate; margarine has somewhat greater shortening power than butter, and in a cake of delicate balance it may make the cake fall or split. Do not use hard fats like lard for making cakes and do not use cooking oil unless recipes call for it.

Sugar: This, of course, means granulated sugar unless recipe specifies light or dark brown sugar. When using brown sugar, make sure it is fresh and soft and moist (it is virtually impossible to remove or beat out hard lumps from old, dried sugar). And when measuring brown sugar, *pack* the sugar into the measuring cup.

Eggs: Egg sizes vary enormously

CAKES, FILLINGS, AND FROSTINGS

(see chapter on eggs and cheese); those used in developing these recipes were large. For greater cake volume, have eggs at room temperature.

Flour: Cake and all-purpose flour can both be used in making cakes but should not be used interchangeably for one another, at least, not measure for measure. To use one in place of the other, make the following adjustments:

1 cup sifted cake flour = ⅞ cup sifted all-purpose flour

1 cup sifted all-purpose flour = 1 cup plus 2 tablespoons sifted cake flour

Cake flour produces an exceptionally fine-textured, tender cake, and experts prefer it, especially for butter cakes. All-purpose flour, with slightly more body, is more reliable and a better choice for beginners. Self-rising flour, which contains both baking powder and salt, can be used in recipes calling for both baking powder and salt. To use, simply sift and measure the amount of flour called for and omit baking powder and salt. A word of caution: Self-rising flour should be absolutely fresh, otherwise it may not do a proper job of leavening. No matter what kind of flour you're using, always sift before measuring, spoon into the measure lightly, and level off top with the edge, not the flat side, of a knife or spatula. *A note about the presifted flours:* Though excellent for sauces and gravies, they do not produce as fine-grained cakes as the old-fashioned sift-yourself flours.

IMPORTANT NOTE: *All cake recipes in this book should be made with all-purpose flour unless recipe specifies cake flour.*

Leavenings: Air can leaven a cake and so can steam, but when we speak of leavenings, we usually mean baking soda (if cake contains sour milk or other acid ingredient) or baking powder. There are three basic kinds of baking powders: *double-acting,* which releases leavening gases on contact with moisture and again during baking; *tartrate,* a single-acting powder that releases a volume of gas the instant it's dampened, and *phosphate,* a slightly slower-to-react single-acting powder. Read can labels carefully to determine which type of baking powder you're dealing with. Do not substitute one type for another unless you bear in mind that 1 teaspoon double-acting powder has the leavening power of 1½ teaspoons phosphate powder and 2 teaspoons tartrate powder. Tartrate powder is particularly tricky and should not be used unless the cake is mixed zip-quick and popped straight into the oven; it does, however, produce cakes of unusually fine grain. All baking powders lose potency on standing, so it's best to buy in small quantities and store tightly covered. *To test a baking powder's effectiveness:* Mix 1 teaspoon baking powder with ⅓ cup warm water; if it fizzes, the baking powder's good; if it doesn't, better buy a new supply. If you're in the middle of a cake and discover that your can of baking powder is inactive or empty, you can get by using this *emergency homemade baking powder:*

2 teaspoons cream of tartar
1 teaspoon baking soda
½ teaspoon salt

} to leaven each 1 cup flour

IMPORTANT NOTE: *Baking powder in the cake recipes that follow is double-acting baking powder.*

Milk: Milk, in a cake recipe, means sweet whole milk.

Flavorings: Always use finest quality true extracts or flavorings, not perfumy imitations that can spoil an otherwise fine cake. Also make sure nuts are strictly fresh.

Some Cake-Making Terms and Techniques

To Beat: This refers to vigorous mixing with a spoon (use a comfortable, long-handled wooden spoon for best results) in a round and round motion, also to beating with a rotary or electric mixer.

To Blend: To combine one ingredient with another until absolutely homogeneous, as in blending chocolate into a batter.

To Cream: To work one or more ingredients, usually fat or fat and sugar, by beating with an electric mixer or by pressing over and over against the side of a bowl with the back of a spoon until soft and creamy. Properly creamed for a cake, butter (or butter and sugar) will be very pale yellow, fluffy, and neither greasy nor sugary. This will take 3–4 minutes in an electric mixer, sometimes, when eggs are added, mixture will seem to curdle; this will not affect the cake.

To Dredge: To toss chopped nuts, dried or candied fruits with flour, sugar, or other dry ingredients to prevent their sinking to the bottom of a cake during baking.

Dry Ingredients: Flour, baking powder or other leavening, salt (and sometimes cocoa or other dry ingredients) sifted together.

To Fill: To put layers of a cake together with filling (usually a softer mixture than frosting).

To Fold In: To incorporate one mixture into another, usually a light one such as beaten egg whites, into a batter using a very gentle over and over motion with minimum loss of

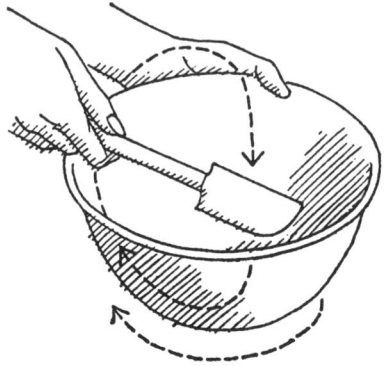

lightness and air. A rubber spatula is the best implement to use, though spoons, even portable electric mixers set at lowest speed and drawn through the mixture with a folding motion, work well.

To Frost: To spread with frosting.

To Glaze: To cover thinly with hard icing, fruit purée, or other shiny mixture.

To Ice: To frost.

To Mix: To blend a number of ingredients together by stirring or beating.

To Sift: To separate fine from coarse particles or to blend dry ingredients by passing them through a fine sieve or flour sifter.

To Stir: To mix in a circular motion, gently without beating.

To Whip: To beat rapidly with a whisk, rotary or electric beater to incorporate as much air as possible as in whipping cream or beating egg whites to stiff peaks.

To Work: To soften or blend by kneading or creaming.

CAKES, FILLINGS, AND FROSTINGS

How to Make Better Cakes

About Pans and Preparing Pans:

– For lightly, evenly browned cakes, use shiny baking pans rather than dark or discolored ones, which will overbrown—even burn—the cake. Do not use glass baking dishes unless you compensate for their slow heat conduction by raising oven temperature 25° F. They bake cakes too slowly, may dry them out, or form a thick hard crust all round. When using the new nonstick pans, follow manufacturer's directions closely, also watch baking cakes carefully until you learn how fast or slow pans conduct heat.

– Grease or grease and flour pans or not as recipes direct. As a general rule, any batter containing butter or other fat must be baked in a greased pan and, if extra rich, in a greased and floured pan. Grease bottoms of pans only unless recipes direct to the contrary. Cakes will rise more evenly all round if they can cling to ungreased pan sides.

– For greasing, use melted clarified butter* (unsalted) if you aren't on a budget, and shortening or cooking oil if you are. Apply thinly and evenly with a pastry brush or wad of paper toweling.

(*Note:* If batter is extra rich or contains sticky fruit, you may even need to grease the new nonstick pans.) To grease and flour, simply shake a small amount of flour into a greased pan, tilt back and forth until there is a thin, even layer of flour over bottom, then tap out excess.

– To simplify dishwashing, line pan bottoms with wax paper cut to fit or with packaged cake pan liners, available in most large department stores, then grease or not, as directed.

– *For best results, always use pan sizes recipes specify.* There are occasions, however, when a different shape is needed, and there are a number of batters that will bake successfully in pan shapes or sizes other than those recommended: all of the simple butter cakes, Real

Recommended Pan Size	Alternate Pan Size
2 (8″) layers 3 (8″) layers	1½–2 dozen cupcakes 2 (9″×9″×2″) pans
1 (9″) layer	1 (8″×8″×2″) pan
2 (9″) layers	1 (13″×9″×2″) pan 1 (15½″×10½″×1″) jelly-roll pan 2 (8″×8″×2″) pans 1 (9″) tube pan 2½ dozen cupcakes
1 (13″×9″×2″) pan	2 (8″×8″×2″) pans 1 (10″) tube pan 2 (9″) layers 2 (15½″×10½″×1″) jelly-roll pans 2 (9″×5″×3″) loaves
1 (9″×5″×3″) pan	1 (9″×9″×2″) pan 2 dozen cupcakes

Sponge Cake, Devil's Food Cake, Nut Cake, Spice Cake, White Wedding Cake, Burnt Sugar Cake, Basic White Cake. Avoid changing pans for Pound Cake, any of the chiffons, other sponges and loaf cakes. Use the table above as a guide and, unless recipe specifies to the contrary, fill pans no more than half full. Bake any leftover batter as cupcakes.

About Mixing Cakes:

– Read recipe through before beginning it and make sure you have all ingredients on hand.
– Have all utensils out, pans prepared, and ingredients measured and sifted before beginning.
– Have all ingredients at room temperature (except in very hot weather) before beginning. In summer, simply take straight from refrigerator.
– When using an electric mixer, use a medium speed for the creaming but a low speed for working in dry and liquid ingredients unless recipes direct to the contrary.
– When mixing by hand, use a comfortable, long-handled wooden spoon.
– Always cream fat and sugar thoroughly—it's virtually impossible to overbeat at this point. *But* mix in dry ingredients with a light touch, just enough to blend. Overbeating at this point will make the cake tough.
– Fold in beaten egg whites last, *very gently,* so you don't break down the volume.

About Placing Batter in Pans:

– Always put batter in cool pans and never fill more than ½–⅔ full.
– Spread batter well to edges of pan.
– When making a layer cake, apportion batter evenly between pans so layers will be of equal size. Using an ice cream ball scoop and filling pans by adding a scoopful of batter first to one pan and then the other is a trick experts use.
– Once pans are filled, tap gently to break any large air bubbles.

About Baking:

– Have oven checked and regulated often by a local serviceman so it is as accurate as possible. Also make sure it stands level on the floor, otherwise cakes may be lopsided.
– Let oven preheat a full 15 minutes before baking.
– Unless recipes direct otherwise, bake cakes as near the center of the oven as possible. Those placed too low may burn on the bottom, those placed too high on top.
– When baking several cakes or layers at once, stagger on shelves, leaving plenty of room around them so heat can circulate evenly. Never let pans touch each other or oven walls.
– Cake baking time breaks down into 4 quarters, the first 2 being the most critical (don't open oven door during this time or jar oven in any way).

First Quarter of Baking . . . cake begins to rise
Second Quarter of Baking . . . cake continues to rise and browns slightly
Third Quarter of Baking . . . cake continues browning
Fourth Quarter of Baking . . . cake finishes browning and shrinks from sides of pan

To tell when cakes are done, use the following tests:

– Insert cake tester or toothpick in center of cake; if it comes out clean with no crumbs adhering, cake is done.

—Gently press top of cake; if it is springy to the touch and finger leaves no imprint, cake is done.
—Examine edges of pan; if cake has pulled away from pan, it is done.

About Cooling Cakes and Removing from Pans:

Butter Cakes:
—Cool upright in pans on a wire rack about 10 minutes before turning out.
—Loosen edges of cake with a spatula, invert cake on rack, then turn right side up and cool thoroughly before frosting.

Sponge and Chiffon Cakes:
—Cool cake thoroughly upside down in pan. If pan does not have "feet" so that it will stand upside down, simply "hang" on a 1-quart soft drink bottle by inserting bottle neck into pan tube.
—Loosen cake edges (and around center tube) and invert on cake plate. Do not turn right side up.

About Storing and Keeping Cakes: Any cake with a custard or whipped cream filling or frosting should be kept refrigerated. Others last longest kept in a cake keeper in a cool spot. Fruit cakes should be wrapped in rum- or fruit-juice-soaked cheesecloth, then in foil and stored airtight in a cool, dark place.

About Freezing Cakes: Nearly all cakes freeze well; for details, see the chapter on freezing.

About Cutting Cakes (solid lines indicate cuts that should be made first, dotted lines successive cuts). Use a thin, sharp-pointed knife for butter cakes, a serrated knife or fine thread and a seesaw motion for sponge, angel, and chiffon cakes.

Layer Cakes:

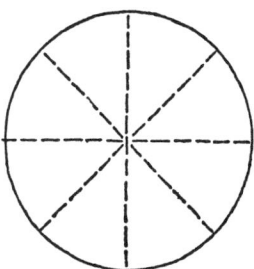

Conventional Way

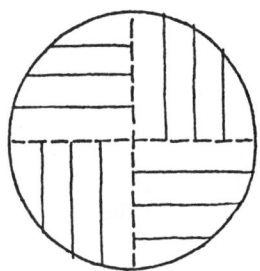

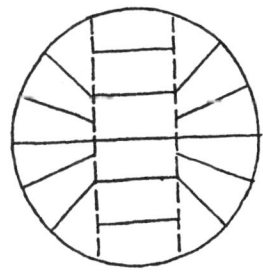

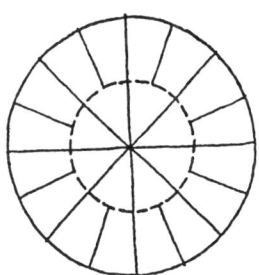

For More Servings

Tiered Wedding Cakes:

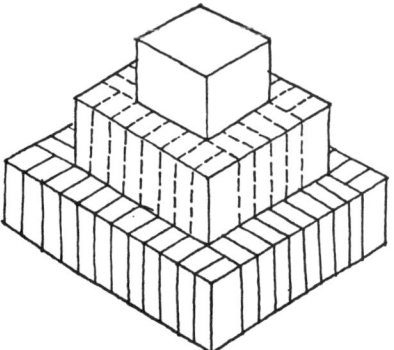

The cutting procedure for tiered cakes, whether round or square, is essentially the same. Cut bottom tier all around, then cut middle tier, again cut bottom tier, lift off top tier and present to bride, finally, cut remaining middle tier.

Loaf Cakes:

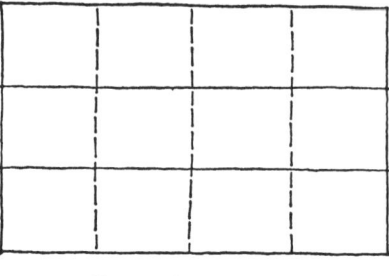

Conventional Way

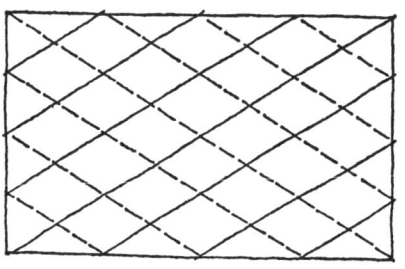

For More Servings

Why Things Sometimes Go Wrong With Cakes

Occasionally, despite all care and precaution, a cake will fail. Here are some common causes of cake failures, how to recognize and remedy them.

Description	Cause
Collapsed Center	Too much sugar or shortening; too little baking powder; underbaking
Fallen Cake	Same as collapsed center; also too little flour
Lopsided Cake	Unlevel oven shelves; also, sometimes, cake pans touching one another or oven walls
Cake Overflowing Pan	Using too small a pan
Heavy Cake	Too much sugar or too little baking powder
Dry Cake	Too much flour or too little shortening; also overbaking
Coarse Texture	Too much shortening or baking powder; undermixing; too low an oven heat
Uneven Texture	Undermixing

CAKES, FILLINGS, AND FROSTINGS

Cracked or Uneven Top	Too much flour or too hot an oven
Sticky Top or Crust	Too much sugar
Uneven Browning	Crowding oven rack; using dark pans; baking at too high a temperature

Note: For tips on baking cakes at high altitudes, see section High Altitude Cooking.

¢ BASIC TWO-EGG BUTTER CAKE

An economical all-purpose cake. Makes 2 8" layers

1¾ cups sifted cake flour
2 teaspoons baking powder
¼ teaspoon salt
½ cup milk
1 teaspoon vanilla
½ cup butter or margarine, softened to room temperature
1 cup sugar
2 eggs

Preheat oven to 375° F. Sift flour with baking powder and salt and set aside; combine milk and vanilla. Cream butter until light, add sugar gradually, continuing to cream until fluffy. Add eggs, one at a time, beating well after each addition. Add dry ingredients alternately with milk, beginning and ending with the dry and adding about ⅓ of total at a time. Beat *just* until smooth. Spoon into 2 greased and floured 8" layer cake pans and bake 25–30 minutes until cakes shrink slightly from sides of pans and are springy to the touch; cool upright in pans on wire racks 5–7 minutes, then invert on racks. Turn layers right side up and cool completely. Fill and frost as desired. About 175 calories for each of 12 servings (unfrosted).

BASIC THREE-EGG BUTTER CAKE

Slightly richer than the Two-Egg Butter Cake (above). Makes 2 9" layers

2 cups sifted cake flour
2 teaspoons baking powder
¼ teaspoon salt
½ cup milk
1 teaspoon vanilla
½ cup butter or margarine, softened to room temperature
1 cup sugar
3 eggs, separated

Preheat oven to 375° F. Sift flour with baking powder and salt and set aside; combine milk and vanilla. Cream butter until light, add sugar gradually, continuing to cream until fluffy. Add egg yolks, one at a time, beating well after each addition. Add dry ingredients alternately with milk, beginning and ending with the dry and adding about ⅓ of total at a time; beat *just* until smooth. Beat egg whites until soft peaks form, and gently fold into batter. Spoon into 2 greased and floured 9" layer cake pans and bake 25–30 minutes until cakes shrink slightly from sides of pans and are springy to the touch; cool upright in pans on wire racks 5–7 minutes; then invert on racks. Turn right side up and cool completely. Fill and frost as desired. About 165 calories for each of 16 servings (unfrosted).

VARIATION:

Poppy Seed Cake: Pour milk called for over ⅓ cup poppy seeds and let stand at room temperature 3–4 hours, then proceed as recipe directs. Fill with Poppy Seed Cream Filling and frost with a butter cream frosting. About 165 calories for each of 16 servings (unfrosted).

SWEET LEMON LOAF

This cake is very tender, so slice it thick.

Makes a 9"×5"×3" loaf

1½ cups sifted flour
1½ teaspoons baking powder
¼ teaspoon salt
½ cup butter or margarine, softened to room temperature
1 cup sugar
2 eggs
½ cup milk
Finely grated rind and juice of 1 lemon
½ cup coarsely chopped pecans or walnuts (optional)

Glaze:
Juice of 1 lemon
¼ cup sugar

Preheat oven to 350° F. Sift flour with baking powder and salt and set aside. Cream butter until light, slowly add sugar and beat until fluffy. Add eggs, one at a time, beating well after each addition. Add dry ingredients alternately with milk, beginning and ending with the dry and adding about ⅓ of the total at a time. Add lemon rind and juice and beat *just* until smooth. Stir in nuts, if you like, and spoon into a greased and floured 9"×5"×3" loaf pan. Bake about 1 hour until cake pulls from sides of pan and is springy to the touch. Let cool upright in pan on a wire rack while you make the glaze. Heat lemon juice and sugar over low heat, stirring until sugar dissolves. Pour evenly over top of cake and let cake cool thoroughly in pan before turning out. Wrap tightly and store overnight before cutting. About 450 calories for each of 8 servings (without optional nuts).

BASIC WHITE OR SILVER CAKE

For a really silvery cake, use vegetable shortening.

Makes 2 9" layers

2½ cups sifted cake flour
1 tablespoon baking powder
½ teaspoon salt
⅔ cup butter, margarine, or vegetable shortening
1½ cups sugar
1 teaspoon vanilla
½ teaspoon almond extract
¾ cup milk
4 egg whites, at room temperature

Preheat oven to 375° F. Sift flour with baking powder and salt and set aside. Cream butter until light, gradually add 1¼ cups sugar, continuing to cream until fluffy. Add vanilla and almond extract and at low speed, mix in dry ingredients alternately with the milk, beginning and ending with the dry and adding about ⅓ of the total at a time. In a separate bowl beat egg whites until frothy, slowly add remaining sugar, and beat to very soft peaks. Fold into batter just until blended. Spoon into 2 greased and floured 9" layer cake pans and bake 20–25 minutes until cakes shrink slightly from sides of pans and are springy to the touch. Cool upright in pans on wire racks 5 minutes, then invert on racks, turn right side up, and cool completely. Fill and frost as desired. About 200 calories for each of 16 servings (unfrosted).

VARIATIONS:

Marble Cake: Prepare batter as directed and divide in half. Blend 3 tablespoons cocoa with 3 tablespoons hot water and mix into half the batter. Drop alternate spoonfuls of white and chocolate batter into pans, dividing amounts equally; zigzag a knife through batter to marbleize and bake as directed. About 210 calories for each of 16 servings (unfrosted).

Rainbow Cake: Prepare batter as directed and divide in 3 equal parts. Tint one pink, one yellow, and one green (or, if you prefer, leave one plain). Layer equal amounts of each color in each pan and bake as directed. When cool, put layers together with any white or pastel frosting (7-Minute is particularly good). Divide remaining frosting in 3 parts and tint as you did cake batter. Put alternate spoonfuls of each color on top and sides of cake, then swirl with a broad spatula to marbleize. If you like, scatter crushed peppermint candy on top. About 200 calories for each of 16 servings (unfrosted).

Lady Baltimore Cake: Prepare cake as directed; also prepare 1 recipe 7-Minute Frosting. To about ⅓ of the frosting, add ¾ cup coarsely chopped pecans or walnuts, ½ cup seedless raisins, ⅓ cup diced dried figs, and ¼ teaspoon almond extract; put cake layers together with the fruit frosting, then ice with remaining 7-Minute Frosting. About 270 calories for each of 16 servings (frosted and filled).

Coconut Cream Cake: Prepare cake as directed; also prepare a double recipe of Basic Vanilla Cream Filling; divide in half and mix ½ cup flaked coconut into one part. Put cake layers together with coconut filling. Spread remaining filling over top and sides of cake, then coat thickly with flaked coconut (about 1½ cups). About 250 calories for each of 16 servings (frosted and filled).

BOSTON CREAM PIE

Makes a 9" 2-layer cake

2 9" layers Basic Three-Egg Butter Cake, Real Sponge Cake, or layers made from a yellow cake mix
1 recipe Basic Vanilla Cream Filling, Double Cream Filling, or 1½ cups sweetened whipped cream
1 recipe Chocolate Glaze

Sandwich cake layers together with filling, spread glaze on top, and let stand until glaze hardens. Store in refrigerator. About 250 calories for each of 16 servings (made with Basic Three-Egg Butter Cake and Basic Vanilla Cream Filling).

WHITE WEDDING CAKE

Begin recipe about 3–4 days before the wedding. For a 3-tier cake, each 2 cake layers thick, you will need to triple the batter recipe given below. Make 3 separate lots rather than a giant unmanageable one. You will need: 1 (13") round cake pan about 2½" deep, 2 (10"), and 2 (7") round cake pans of similar depth (these special wedding cake pans can be bought at specialty shops and confectionery supply houses); a heavy 16" circle of plywood neatly covered with heavy foil; 1 (10") and 1 (7") white cardboard cake divider; a large lazy Susan to simplify decorating and a pastry bag and decorative star tip.

Makes a 3-tier cake, about 100 servings

Batter (Make Up 3 Separate Batches):

6 cups sifted flour
2 tablespoons baking powder
2 teaspoons salt
2 cups milk, at room temperature
2 teaspoons vanilla

1 pound butter or margarine or 1⅓
 cups margarine and ⅔ cup
 vegetable shortening
4 cups sugar
8 eggs, at room temperature
2 teaspoons lemon extract
2 tablespoons finely grated lemon
 rind

Filling:
1 recipe Pineapple-Coconut Filling

Frosting:
4 times the recipe Basic Lemon or
 Orange Butter Cream Frosting,
 tinted pale pink or yellow if you
 like

Decorations:
About 4 yards narrow white satin
 ribbon
Small sprays of artificial or real
 flowers matching bride's bouquet

Preheat oven to 325° F. Sift flour with baking powder and salt and set aside. Combine milk and vanilla. Cream butter until light, add sugar gradually, continue to cream until fluffy. Add eggs, one at a time, beating well after each addition. Mix in lemon extract and rind. Add dry ingredients alternately with milk, beginning and ending with the dry and adding about ⅛ of the total at a time. Beat just until smooth. Spoon into one ungreased 13" and one ungreased 7" round cake pan lined on the bottom with wax paper, *filling no more than half full* (this is a high-rising batter). Cover small pan with wax paper and refrigerate; bake large layer 60–65 minutes until it pulls from sides of pan and is springy to the touch. Cool upright in pan on wire rack 10 minutes, then loosen and invert on rack; peel off paper, turn right side up, and cool thoroughly.

Meanwhile, mix a second batch of batter, cover bowl, and refrigerate until needed. Wash, dry, and reline 13" pan with wax paper, half fill with batter; also half fill second 7" pan, cover, and refrigerate. Bake 13" layer as before, turn out and cool. Mix a third batch of batter, spoon into the 2 (10") pans, ungreased but lined on the bottom with wax paper, filling no more than half full; cover with wax paper and refrigerate. When both large layers are baked, raise oven to 350° F. and bake the 2 small- and 2 medium-size layers, staggering on oven shelves and allowing plenty of space between pans. Small layers will bake in 40–45 minutes, the medium in about 50. Cool and turn out as you did the large layers. When all cakes are thoroughly cool, wrap airtight in foil and store in a cool place, not refrigerator. (*Note:* Any leftover batter can be baked as cupcakes—do not more than half fill muffin cups.)

To Assemble and Frost Cake: Center foil-covered plywood circle on lazy Susan and cover outer rim with wax paper triangles, letting points hang over (these are to catch frosting drips). Center 1 (13") layer on board, spread with filling and top with second (13") layer, bottom side up. Spread lightly with frosting, just to seal in crumbs. Place a 10" layer on a 10" divider, spread with filling, and center on 13" tier; top with second (10") layer, bottom side up, and frost top lightly. Set 7" layer on 7" divider, spread with filling, and center on 10" tier; top with final 7" layer. Beginning at the top, lightly frost sides of each tier to seal in crumbs and let dry at room temperature 1–2 hours. Starting again at the top, frost entire cake.

(*Note:* If you plan to decorate with frosting, make surface as smooth as possible.) For a simple finish, swirl frosting into waves with a wide

CAKES, FILLINGS, AND FROSTINGS

metal spatula. Let dry 2 hours before decorating further.

To Decorate: Beginning at the top, pipe decorative borders around base of top and middle tiers, then add rosettes, scrolls, any designs you fancy (see Tips on Decorating Cakes). Pull out wax paper triangles around base of cake and pipe a decorative border around base of cake. Keep in a cool, dust-free place or invert a very large cardboard carton over cake, making sure top and sides do not touch.

Final Trimmings: On the day of the wedding, make rosettes from the ribbon and arrange with tiny flower sprays between the tiers, "gluing" to cake with a little frosting. Decorate top with small posies wreathed in ribbon or any suitable commercial decorations. Keep cool until serving time.

To Serve: See About Cutting Cakes. About 140 calories for each of 100 servings.

POUND CAKE

Here is a truly old-fashioned pound cake made without baking powder so the texture will be firm, fine, and moist.
Makes a 9"×5"×3" loaf

2¼ cups sifted cake flour
¼ teaspoon salt
⅛ teaspoon nutmeg or mace
1 cup butter (*no substitute*), softened to room temperature
1 cup sugar
5 eggs, separated
1 teaspoon vanilla or orange extract or 1 tablespoon finely grated lemon rind

Preheat oven to 350° F. Line a 9"×5"×3" loaf pan with greased wax paper (let paper lop over rim about ½" to make removing cake easier). Sift flour, salt, and nutmeg together and set aside. Cream butter until light, then add sugar slowly, creaming until fluffy. Beat egg yolks until thick and light, add to butter mixture, a little at a time, beating well after each addition. Blend flour in gradually, then mix in vanilla and beat *just* until smooth. Beat egg whites until soft peaks form and fold gently into batter. Spoon into pan and bake 65–70 minutes until cake pulls slightly from sides of pan. Cool upright in pan on a wire cake rack 30 minutes before slicing. About 360 calories for each of 10 servings.

THELMA'S 1, 2, 3, 4 CAKE

This cake keeps well if wrapped airtight; it also freezes well.
Makes a 9" tube cake

3 cups sifted flour
2 teaspoons baking powder
¼ teaspoon salt
1 cup milk
1 teaspoon vanilla or almond, lemon or orange extract
1 cup butter or margarine, softened to room temperature, or vegetable shortening
2 cups sugar
4 eggs, separated

Preheat oven to 350° F. Sift flour with baking powder and salt and set aside; combine milk and vanilla. Cream butter until light; add sugar gradually, continuing to cream until fluffy. Beat egg yolks until thick and pale yellow; mix into creamed mixture. Add dry ingredients alternately with milk, beginning and ending with the dry and adding about ⅓ of the total at a time. Beat *just* until smooth. Beat egg whites until soft peaks form and gently fold into batter. Spoon into a greased and floured 9" tube pan and bake about 1 hour until cake shrinks slightly from sides of pan and is springy to the touch. Cool cake upright in its pan on a wire rack 25–30 minutes; loosen edges, invert on rack, and cool thoroughly. Serve plain or frost with a butter cream frosting. About 305 calories for each of 16 servings (unfrosted).

BASIC CHOCOLATE BUTTER CAKE

Makes 2 9" layers

2 cups sifted cake flour
¾ teaspoon baking soda
½ teaspoon salt
¾ cup buttermilk or sour milk
1 teaspoon vanilla
½ cup butter or margarine, softened to room temperature
1⅓ cups sugar
3 eggs
3 (1-ounce) squares unsweetened chocolate, melted or 3 (1-ounce) envelopes no-melt unsweetened chocolate

Preheat oven to 350° F. Sift flour with baking soda and salt and set aside. Combine buttermilk and vanilla. Cream butter until light, add sugar gradually, beating until fluffy. Add eggs, one at a time, beating well after each addition; mix in chocolate. Add dry ingredients alternately with milk, beginning and ending with the dry and adding about ⅓ of the total at a time. Beat *just* until smooth. Spoon into 2 greased and floured 9" layer cake pans and bake 30–35 minutes until cakes shrink slightly from sides of pans and are springy to the touch. Cool upright in pans on wire racks 5–7 minutes, then invert on racks. Turn cakes right side up and cool thoroughly. Fill and frost as desired. About 220 calories for each of 16 servings (unfrosted).

VARIATION:

Mocha Butter Cake: Prepare as directed but blend 1 tablespoon instant coffee powder with buttermilk and vanilla. Fill and frost with Mocha Butter Cream Frosting. About 220 calories for each of 16 servings (unfrosted).

☒ CRAZY CHOCOLATE CAKE

"Crazy" in that the method of mixing is wholly unconventional. The cake, however, is unusually fine-grained.

Makes 2 9" layers

Group I:
2 cups sugar
1 cup sour milk
1 cup butter, softened to room temperature (no substitute)
1½ teaspoons vanilla
3 cups sifted cake flour

Group II:
2 eggs
¾ cup unsifted cocoa
2 teaspoons baking soda
¼ teaspoon salt
1 cup boiling strong coffee

Preheat oven to 325°F. Add ingredients to a large mixing bowl by alternating between Groups I and II. For example, first into bowl would be sugar, second eggs, third sour milk, fourth cocoa, and so on. Do not mix. When all ingredients are in the bowl, beat 1 minute with an electric mixer at moderate speed or 3 minutes by hand. Pour into 2 well-greased 9" layer cake pans and bake 45–50 minutes until cakes shrink slightly from sides of pans and are springy to the touch. Cool upright in pans on wire racks 5–7 minutes, then invert to remove. Turn cakes right side up and cool thoroughly. Fill and frost as desired (good with 7-Minute Frosting). About 300

CAKES, FILLINGS, AND FROSTINGS

calories for each of 16 servings (unfrosted).

¢ DEVIL'S FOOD CAKE

Dark and rich.
Makes 2 9" layers

2 cups sifted cake flour
2 cups sugar
½ cup cocoa
1 teaspoon baking soda
½ teaspoon salt
½ cup vegetable shortening
1¼ cups milk
1 teaspoon vanilla
3 eggs
1 teaspoon baking powder

Preheat oven to 350° F. Sift flour, sugar, cocoa, baking soda, and salt into large electric mixer bowl. Drop in shortening and add ¾ cup milk and the vanilla. Mix at lowest speed 15 seconds just to blend. (*Note:* Hold a towel over bowl to catch splatters.) Beat 2 minutes at medium speed, scraping bowl and beaters once or twice. Add remaining ingredients and beat 2 minutes longer. Spoon into 2 ungreased (9") layer cake pans lined with wax paper and bake 40–45 minutes until cakes shrink slightly from sides of pan and are springy to the touch. Cool upright in pans on wire racks 5 minutes, then invert on racks, peel off paper, turn right side up, and cool completely. Fill and frost as desired. About 250 calories for each of 16 servings (unfrosted).

VARIATIONS:

¢ **Devil's Food Loaf:** Prepare as directed and bake in an ungreased 13"×9"×2" pan lined with wax paper. Same time, same temperature. About 165 calories for each of 24 servings (unfrosted).

Mocha Fudge Cake: Prepare as directed but substitute 3 melted (1-ounce) squares unsweetened chocolate or 3 (1-ounce) envelopes no-melt unsweetened chocolate for the cocoa, add 1 tablespoon instant coffee powder and mix in with the shortening. About 260 calories for each of 16 servings (unfrosted).

SACHERTORTE

Sachertorte, Vienna's famous chocolate cake, is densely dark and rich. It was invented 150 years or so ago by Franz Sacher for Prince Metternich when calories meant nothing.
Makes a 9" cake

1 cup sifted cake flour
¼ teaspoon salt
6 (1-ounce) squares unsweetened or semisweet chocolate
¾ cup butter, softened to room temperature (no substitute)
1 cup sugar
6 egg yolks
8 egg whites
1 cup apricot preserves
1 recipe Chocolate Glaze
1 cup heavy cream, whipped to soft peaks (optional topping)

Preheat oven to 350° F. Sift flour with salt and set aside. Melt chocolate over simmering water, then cool. Cream butter until light, gradually add ¾ cup sugar and cream until fluffy. Add egg yolks, one at a time, beating well after each addition. Beat in chocolate, scraping bowl often until thoroughly blended. In a separate bowl, beat egg whites until frothy; gradually add remaining sugar and beat until soft peaks form. Stir about ½ cup egg whites into creamed mixture. Sift and fold in flour alternately with remaining egg whites, beginning and ending with flour and adding about ¼ at a time. Spoon into a 9" spring form pan lined on the bottom with wax paper, then greased and floured on bottom and sides. Tap pan lightly on counter to break any large bubbles. Bake on center oven rack 45–55 minutes, until top is springy to the touch. Cool upright in pan on a wire rack 10 minutes, loosen cake, and remove spring form; invert cake on rack, remove pan bottom, and carefully peel off paper. Turn right side up and cool completely on rack. Halve cake horizontally, spread with preserves, put layers together and spread top thinly with preserves. Spoon chocolate glaze on top and let stand until set. Cut in small pieces and serve topped with whipped cream. About 365 calories for each of 16 servings (without cream).

BÛCHE DE NOËL (CHRISTMAS LOG)

A rich chocolate log traditionally served on Christmas Eve in France. Makes 1 roll

½ *cup sifted cake flour*
¾ *teaspoon baking powder*
¼ *teaspoon salt*
4 *eggs, at room temperature*
¾ *cup sugar*
1 *teaspoon vanilla*
3 *(1-ounce) squares unsweetened chocolate, melted, or 3 (1-ounce) envelopes no-melt unsweetened chocolate*
2 *tablespoons very strong warm black coffee*
Sifted cocoa
2 *recipes Mocha or Chocolate Butter Cream Frosting*

Preheat oven to 400° F. Line the bottom of a 15½" × 10½" × 1" jelly-roll pan with wax paper. Sift flour with baking powder and salt and set aside. With electric or rotary beater, beat eggs at high speed until foamy; slowly add sugar, a little at a time, and beat until very thick and cream colored. Mix in vanilla, blend chocolate with coffee and mix into batter. Fold in dry ingredients just until blended. Spoon into pan, spreading batter evenly. Bake 12–14 minutes until springy to the touch. Loosen edges of cake and invert on a clean dish towel heavily sprinkled with sifted cocoa. Peel off paper and cut off crisp edges with a sharp knife. Beginning at the short side, roll cake and towel up; cool completely on a wire rack. Unroll, remove towel, spread about 1 cup mocha frosting to within ½" of edges and carefully reroll. Wrap loosely in foil and chill 1 hour. With a sharp knife, cut a small piece from each end on the diagonal and reserve to make "branches." Place roll seam side down on serving plate and tuck a strip of wax paper under each side. Spread with remaining frosting, then draw fork tines in a wavy pattern the length of log to resemble bark or use a serrated ribbon tip and a pastry bag to force frosting out in a ridged bark effect. Lay trimmed-off ends on roll cut side down at an angle, off center. Press into frosting lightly, then frost edges. If you wish, sprinkle log with minced pistachio nuts and write "Noel" in white decorative icing. About 680 calories for each of 12 servings.

BURNT SUGAR CAKE

Makes 2 9" layers

Burnt Sugar Syrup:
¾ *cup sugar*
¾ *cup boiling water*

Cake:
3 *cups sifted cake flour*
1 *tablespoon baking powder*
½ *teaspoon salt*
½ *cup milk*
1 *teaspoon vanilla*
1 *teaspoon maple flavoring (optional)*
½ *cup burnt sugar syrup*

¾ cup butter or margarine
1⅓ cups sugar
3 eggs

Frosting:
⅓ cup butter or margarine
1 (1-pound) box confectioners' sugar, sifted
¼ cup burnt sugar syrup
1 teaspoon vanilla
¼ teaspoon salt

For syrup: Melt sugar in a heavy skillet or saucepan over low heat, stirring now and then. Heat, stirring constantly, until amber colored. Off heat, gradually stir in boiling water (it will foam up), return to low heat, and stir until sugar dissolves. Cool to room temperature. Preheat oven to 350° F. Sift flour with baking powder and salt and set aside. Mix milk with flavorings and ½ cup burnt sugar syrup. Cream butter until light, add sugar gradually, creaming until fluffy. Add eggs, one at a time, beating well after each addition. Add dry ingredients alternately with milk mixture, beginning and ending with the dry and adding about ⅓ of the total at a time. Beat just until smooth. Spoon into 2 ungreased 9" layer pans lined with wax paper. Bake about ½ hour until cakes pull from sides of pan and are springy to the touch. Cool upright in pans on wire racks 5 minutes, loosen, and invert on racks; peel off paper, turn right side up, and cool. For the frosting: Cream butter until fluffy, beat in sugar, a little at a time, adding alternately with the syrup. Mix in vanilla and salt and beat until satiny and of good spreading consistency. If mixture seems stiff, thin with a little additional syrup. Put cake layers together with some frosting, then frost with the remainder. About 445 calories for each of 16 servings.

NUT CAKE

Use the nuts you like best for making this cake.
Makes a 13"×9"×2" cake

2 cups sifted cake flour
1½ teaspoons baking powder
½ teaspoon salt
⅓ cup milk, at room temperature
1 teaspoon vanilla
½ teaspoon almond extract
1 cup butter or margarine
1 cup sugar
3 eggs
1¼ cups finely chopped toasted nuts (pecans, walnuts or black walnuts, filberts, or almonds)
Few untoasted nut halves (garnish)

Preheat oven to 350° F. Sift flour with baking powder and salt and set aside. Mix milk, vanilla and almond extract. Cream butter until light, add sugar gradually, continuing to cream until fluffy. Add eggs, one at a time, beating well after each addition. Add flour alternately with milk, beginning and ending with flour. Stir in chopped nuts. Spoon into an ungreased 13"×9"×2" pan lined on the bottom with wax paper and scatter nut halves on top. Bake about ½ hour until cake pulls from sides of pan and is springy to the touch. Cool upright in pan on a wire rack 10 minutes, loosen edges of cake, invert on rack, peel off paper, turn right side up, and cool thoroughly. (*Note:* If you prefer, omit garnish and, when cake is cool, frost as desired.) About 140 calories for each of 24 servings (unfrosted).

VARIATIONS:

Nut Layer Cake: Prepare batter as directed, spoon into 2 ungreased (9") layer cake pans lined on the bottom with wax paper and bake 25–30 minutes at 350° F. until cakes test done. Cool as directed; fill and frost as desired. About 210 calories for each of 16 servings (unfrosted).

Nut-Seed Cake: Add 2 tablespoons caraway or poppy seeds to cake batter along with flour. About 140 calories for each of 24 servings (unfrosted).

Nut-Candied Fruit Cake: Add ½ cup minced mixed candied fruit to cake batter along with flour. About 160 calories for each of 24 servings (unfrosted).

Orange-Nut Cake: Prepare as directed but add the finely grated rind of 2 oranges to creamed mixture before adding eggs. About 140 calories for each of 24 servings (unfrosted).

Chocolate-Nut Cake: Prepare as directed but add 4 melted (1-ounce) squares semisweet chocolate to creamed mixture before adding eggs. About 175 calories for each of 24 servings (unfrosted).

ORANGE, DATE, AND NUT LOAF

Makes a 13"×9"×2" cake

- *4 cups sifted flour*
- *1 teaspoon salt*
- *1 teaspoon baking soda*
- *1 cup butter or margarine, softened to room temperature*
- *2 cups sugar*
- *4 eggs*
- *1 teaspoon vanilla*
- *2 tablespoons finely grated orange rind*
- *1½ cups buttermilk*
- *1½ cups coarsely chopped pecans or walnuts*
- *1 cup minced, pitted dates or ½ cup each minced dates and sultana raisins*

Preheat oven to 350° F. Sift flour with salt and baking soda and set aside. Cream butter until light, add sugar gradually and cream until fluffy. Add eggs, one at a time, beating well after each addition. Blend in vanilla and orange rind. Add dry ingredients, about ⅓ at a time, alternately with buttermilk, beginning and ending with the dry. Stir in nuts and dates and spoon into a greased and floured 13"×9"×2" pan. Bake about 1 hour and 10 minutes or until cake shrinks slightly from sides of pan and top is springy to the touch. Cool cake upright in its pan on a wire rack. Cut in squares and serve. About 285 calories for each of 24 servings.

WALNUT TORTE

No flour needed in this *torte;* the nuts and bread crumbs give it body. Makes a 9" 2-layer cake

- *1 cup lightly packed, finely ground walnuts or black walnuts*
- *½ cup fine dry bread crumbs*
- *6 eggs, separated*
- *1 cup sugar*
- *¼ teaspoon almond extract*
- *2 teaspoons finely grated orange or lemon rind*

Preheat oven to 350° F. Mix nuts and crumbs and set aside. Beat egg yolks until thick and pale yellow, slowly add ¾ cup sugar, and beat until very thick and the color of cream. In a separate bowl, beat egg whites until frothy, gradually add remaining sugar, and beat until soft peaks form. Fold egg whites into yolk mixture alternately with nut mixture, beginning and ending with whites. Stir in almond extract and grated orange or lemon rind. Spoon into 2 ungreased (9") round pans lined on the bottom with wax paper. Bake about 20 minutes or until a faint imprint remains when top is touched. Cool upright in pans on wire racks

CAKES, FILLINGS, AND FROSTINGS

5–7 minutes, carefully loosen cakes with a spatula, invert on racks, peel off paper, turn right side up, and cool thoroughly. Fill and frost as desired —especially good with Mocha or Nut Butter Cream Frosting. About 140 calories for each of 16 servings (unfrosted).

VARIATION:

Hazelnut Torte: Prepare as directed, using finely ground, blanched hazelnuts or filberts instead of walnuts. About 140 calories for each of 16 servings (unfrosted).

APPLESAUCE CAKE

A moist old-fashioned cake. It contains no eggs, so it is suitable for those allergic to them.
Makes a 9" cake

2 cups sifted flour
½ teaspoon baking soda
1 teaspoon baking powder
½ teaspoon salt
¾ teaspoon cinnamon
½ teaspoon nutmeg
¼ teaspoon cloves
2 tablespoons milk
1 teaspoon vanilla
1 cup applesauce
½ cup butter or margarine
1 cup firmly packed light brown sugar
¾ cup seedless raisins
¾ cup minced pecans or walnuts

Preheat oven to 350° F. Sift flour with baking soda, baking powder, salt and spices and set aside. Mix milk, vanilla, and applesauce. Cream butter until light, add sugar gradually, continuing to cream until fluffy. Add dry ingredients alternately with applesauce mixture, beginning and ending with the dry and adding about ⅓ of the total at a time. Beat just until smooth. Mix in raisins and nuts. Spoon into an ungreased 9" pan lined with wax paper and bake 35 minutes until cake shrinks slightly from sides of pan and is springy to the touch. Cool upright in pan on a wire rack 5 minutes, then invert on rack, peel off paper, turn right side up, and cool completely. Frost or not as desired or serve slightly warm with Lemon-Raisin Sauce. About 225 calories for each of 16 servings (unfrosted).

¢ SPICE CAKE

Makes an 8"×8"×2" cake

1½ cups sifted flour
1½ teaspoons baking powder
¼ teaspoon salt
1 teaspoon cinnamon
¾ teaspoon nutmeg
¼ teaspoon allspice
¼ teaspoon cloves
¼ teaspoon ginger
½ cup plus 2 tablespoons milk
1 teaspoon vanilla
½ cup butter or margarine
1 cup sugar
1 egg

Preheat oven to 350° F. Sift flour with baking powder, salt, and spices and set aside. Mix milk and vanilla. Cream butter until light, add sugar gradually, continuing to cream until fluffy. Add egg and beat well. Add dry ingredients alternately with milk, beginning and ending with the dry and adding about ⅓ of the total at a time. Spoon into an ungreased 8"×8"×2" pan lined on the bottom with wax paper. Bake about 45 minutes until cake pulls from sides of pan and is springy to the touch. Cool upright in pan on a wire rack 10 minutes, loosen edges, and invert on a rack. Peel off paper, turn right side up and cool. Frost or not as desired. About 200 calories for each of 12 servings (unfrosted).

VARIATIONS:

¢ **Spice Layer Cakes:** Double the ingredients, prepare batter as directed, and bake in 2 ungreased 9" layer cake pans lined on the bottom with wax paper about 45 minutes at 350° F. About 240 calories for each of 20 servings (unfrosted).

¢ **Lemon-Spice Cake:** Prepare as directed but add 1 teaspoon lemon extract and the finely grated rind of 1 lemon along with the egg. About 200 calories for each of 12 servings (unfrosted).

¢ **Raisin-Spice Cake:** Add ¼ cup seedless raisins to batter with final addition of flour. About 210 calories for each of 12 servings (unfrosted).

¢ **GINGERBREAD**

Makes a 9"×9"×2" cake

2½ cups sifted flour
1½ teaspoons baking soda
½ teaspoon salt
1¼ teaspoons ginger
1 teaspoon cinnamon
½ teaspoon cloves
½ teaspoon allspice
½ cup vegetable shortening
½ cup sugar
1 egg
1 cup molasses
1 cup boiling water

Preheat oven to 350° F. Sift flour with soda, salt, and spices and set aside. Cream shortening until fluffy, then add sugar, a little at a time, beating well after each addition. Beat in egg. Combine molasses and boiling water and add alternately with the sifted dry ingredients, beginning and ending with the dry and beating after each addition just enough to mix. Pour into a greased, wax-paper-lined 9"×9"×2" pan and bake 50–60 minutes until gingerbread pulls from sides of pan and is springy to the touch. Cool gingerbread upright in its pan on a wire rack. Cut in large squares and serve. About 200 calories for each of 16 servings.

¢ **GRANDMOTHER'S SOFT GINGER CAKE**

This thin batter bakes into an unusually soft-crumbed cake.

Makes a 9"×9"×2" cake

2½ cups sifted cake flour
1½ teaspoons baking soda
¼ teaspoon salt
1 teaspoon cinnamon
1 teaspoon cloves
1 teaspoon ginger
¼ teaspoon nutmeg
½ cup vegetable shortening
⅔ cup sugar
1 egg
⅔ cup molasses
1¼ cups boiling water

Preheat oven to 375° F. Sift flour with soda, salt, and spices and set aside. Cream shortening until fluffy, add sugar, a little at a time, creaming well after each addition. Beat in egg. Combine molasses and boiling water and add alternately with sifted dry ingredients, beginning and ending with the dry. Beat after each addition to mix. Pour into a lightly greased 9"×9"×2" pan and bake 40–45 minutes until cake pulls from sides of pan and is springy to the touch. Cool cake upright in its pan on a wire rack. To serve, cut in large squares and top, if you like, with whipped cream or vanilla ice cream. About 165 calories for each of 16 servings (without whipped cream or ice cream).

PINEAPPLE UPSIDE-DOWN CAKE

Makes a 10" round or 9" square cake

⅓ cup butter or margarine
½ cup firmly packed light or dark brown sugar
1 (1-pound 4-ounce) can sliced pineapple, drained

CAKES, FILLINGS, AND FROSTINGS

8 maraschino cherry halves, well drained
14–16 pecan halves

Cake:
1⅓ cups sifted flour
1 cup sugar
2 teaspoons baking powder
½ teaspoon salt
⅓ cup vegetable shortening
⅔ cup milk
1 teaspoon vanilla
½ teaspoon lemon extract
1 teaspoon finely grated lemon rind
1 egg

Preheat oven to 350° F. Melt butter in a heavy 10″ skillet (with ovenproof handle) or in a 9″×9″×2″ pan over low heat. Off heat, sprinkle brown sugar evenly over butter. Arrange pineapple in a pattern on sugar and fill spaces with cherries and pecans. Set aside while mixing cake. Sift flour, sugar, baking powder, and salt into large mixer bowl, drop in shortening and milk and beat at lowest speed just to blend. (*Note:* It's a good idea to hold a towel over bowl to prevent spills at first.) Beat 2 minutes at medium speed, scraping bowl and beaters once or twice. Add remaining ingredients and beat 2 minutes longer, scraping bowl now and then. Pour batter evenly over fruit. Bake 40–50 minutes until cake is golden brown and pulls from sides of pan. Cool upright in pan on wire rack 3–4 minutes, loosen edges of cake, invert on heatproof serving plate, and leave pan over cake 1–2 minutes. Remove pan and serve warm or cold with sweetened whipped cream. About 250 calories for each of 16 servings (without whipped cream).

VARIATIONS:

Apricot or Peach Upside-Down Cake: Substitute 1 (1-pound 4-ounce) can drained apricot or cling peach halves for pineapple rings; arrange hollow side up on sugar. Or use well-drained sliced cling peaches. Proceed as directed. About 250 calories for each of 16 servings.

Apple Upside-Down Cake: Peel, core, and thinly slice 2 large tart apples and arrange in an attractive pattern on top of sugar. If you like, dot here and there with pitted cooked prunes, seedless or sultana raisins. Proceed as directed. About 230 calories for each of 16 servings (without prunes or raisins).

Gingerbread Upside-Down Cake: Prepare fruit layer as directed. Prepare cake batter substituting ⅓ cup each dark molasses and boiling water for the milk; mix and cool before adding. Also add 1 teaspoon each ginger and nutmeg along with egg and other flavorings. Bake as directed. About 265 calories for each of 16 servings.

⚜ REAL SPONGE CAKE

Note all the variations you can make from this one basic recipe.
Makes 2 9″ layers

6 eggs, separated, at room temperature
1 cup sifted sugar
½ teaspoon salt
2 teaspoons vanilla
1 cup sifted cake flour

Preheat oven to 350° F. Beat egg yolks until thick, slowly add sugar, salt, and vanilla, beating constantly; continue beating until very thick and the color of cream. Slowly mix in flour (lowest mixer speed). Beat egg whites to soft peaks (they should *just* flow when bowl is tipped) and fold lightly into batter, about ¼ at a time. Spoon into 2 wax-paper-lined 9″ layer cake pans and bake 25 minutes until golden and springy. Cool upright in pans on a wire rack 5 minutes, then loosen carefully with a spatula and turn out. Peel off paper, turn right side up, and cool completely. Fill and frost as desired. About 100 calories for each of 16 servings (unfrosted).

To Bake in Other Pans:

⚖️ **Tube Pan:** Spoon batter into an ungreased 10" tube pan and bake 45 minutes at 350° F. Invert at once and cool completely in pan. (*Note:* If cut in 12 wedges and served unfrosted, each slice will total about 125 calories.)

⚖️ **Loaf Pan:** Spoon batter into a wax-paper-lined 13"×9"×2" loaf pan and bake ½ hour at 350° F. Cool upright in pan 5 minutes, invert, peel off paper, turn right side up, and cool. 63 calories per unfrosted 2" square.

⚖️ **Muffin Pans** (Makes 2 Dozen Cupcakes): Spoon batter into muffin tins lined with cupcake papers, filling each ¾ full; bake 12–15 minutes at 350° F. Remove from pans and cool upright on wire racks. 63 calories per unfrosted cupcake.

VARIATIONS:

⚖️ **Lemon Sponge Cake** (Approximately the same calorie counts as above): Prepare as directed but flavor with 1 teaspoon lemon extract and 1 tablespoon each lemon juice and finely grated rind instead of vanilla.

⚖️ **Orange Sponge Cake** (Approximately the same calorie counts as above): Prepare as directed but flavor with 1 teaspoon orange extract, 1 tablespoon lemon juice, and 2 tablespoons finely grated orange rind instead of vanilla.

Nut Sponge Cake: Prepare as directed but just before folding in whites mix in ¾–1 cup minced pecans, walnuts, or toasted, blanched almonds. About 150 calories for each of 16 servings (unfrosted).

⚖️ **Chocolate Sponge Cake:** Sift ¼ cup cocoa with flour and add to egg-sugar mixture alternately with vanilla and 2 tablespoons cold water, beginning and ending with flour. Proceed as directed. About 115 calories for each of 16 servings (unfrosted).

⚖️ **Coffee Sponge Cake:** Beat egg yolks, sugar, salt, and vanilla as directed; add flour alternately with 1 tablespoon instant coffee powder dissolved in 2 tablespoons cold water; proceed as directed. About 100 calories for each of 16 servings (unfrosted).

⚖️ **Mocha Sponge Cake:** Prepare Chocolate Sponge Cake (above) as directed but dissolve 1 tablespoon instant coffee powder in the 2 tablespoons cold water. Mix in alternately with flour as directed. About 115 calories for each of 16 servings (unfrosted).

Coconut Cream Sponge Cake: Prepare Real Sponge Cake as directed and put layers together with sweetened whipped cream mixed with ½ cup flaked coconut. Frost with sweetened whipped cream and sprinkle with flaked coconut (about 1 cup). About 185 calories for each of 16 servings (frosted).

¢ ⚖️ **Economy Sponge Cake:** Sift the flour with 1½ teaspoons baking powder. Beat 3 egg yolks with the sugar as directed, then add flour alternately with ¼ cup cold water mixed with 2 teaspoons vanilla, beginning and ending with dry ingredients. Beat 3 egg whites with ¼ teaspoon cream of tartar and proceed as directed. Bake 20–25 minutes at 350° F. in the 9" layer cake pans. Do not put layers together but serve unfrosted, each layer cut in 12 wedges. About 55 calories for each of 12 servings. (*Note:* This recipe is a good choice for persons on low-cholesterol diets.)

¢ ⚜ **Economy Chocolate Sponge Cake:** Prepare Economy Sponge Cake as directed but sift ¼ cup cocoa along with the flour. About 60 calories for each of 12 servings.

☒ ⚜ **EASY SPONGE LOAF**

Makes an 8"×8"×2" cake

3 eggs
¾ cup sugar
⅛ teaspoon salt
1 teaspoon vanilla
¾ cup sifted flour

Preheat oven to 350° F. Beat eggs until frothy, slowly add sugar and salt, beating constantly; continue beating until thick and the color of cream. Mix in vanilla, then flour, a little at a time. Spoon into an 8"×8"×2" pan lined with greased wax paper and bake 35 minutes until golden and springy to the touch. Cool cake upright in its pan on a wire rack 5 minutes, then loosen carefully with a spatula and turn out. Peel off wax paper and cool before cutting or using in Trifle or other recipes. About 70 calories per 2" square (unfrosted).

⚜ **GÉNOISE**

Génoise, the classic European sponge cake, is the foundation of showy *Gâteaux* and *Petits Fours*. It can be made entirely by mixer instead of the more traditional way given here. But eggs should be slightly warmed before beating, then beaten until very thick and creamy in a warm bowl about 15 minutes (beware of overheating mixer). Makes a 9" cake

4 eggs, at room temperature
¾ cup superfine sugar
1 teaspoon vanilla
1 teaspoon finely grated lemon or orange rind
¾ cup sifted cake flour
3 tablespoons melted clarified butter,* cooled to lukewarm (no substitute)

Preheat oven to 350° F. Butter a 9" spring form pan, line bottom with wax paper, butter paper, and dust bottom and sides of pan with flour. Place eggs, sugar, vanilla, and rind in a large stainless-steel or copper mixing bowl and set *over*, not in, a large pan ⅓ filled with barely simmering water. With a large wire whisk, beat until mixture foams and is almost doubled in volume, about 5–6 minutes. Transfer to large mixer bowl and beat at moderately high speed until very thick (when beaters are raised, mixture should drop in a slowly dissolving ribbon). Set bowl on damp cloth, sift in ¼ cup flour, fold in gently, then fold in 1 tablespoon butter. Continue adding flour and butter the same way, the same amounts each time, until all are incorporated. Pour batter into pan, tap lightly on counter to break any large bubbles, and bake on center oven rack 30–35 minutes until cake shrinks slightly from sides of pan and is springy to the touch. Cool upright in pan on a wire rack 10 minutes (cake will sink a little in the middle), then loosen edges carefully with a spatula and remove spring form sides. Invert on rack, lift off pan bottom, peel off paper, turn cake right side up, and cool thoroughly. Slice into 2 or 3 layers and fill and frost as desired. About 125 calories for each of 12 servings (unfrosted).

VARIATIONS:

Favorite Génoise: Sprinkle cut surfaces of Génoise with 2–3 tablespoons kirsch or other fruit liqueur and sandwich layers together with apricot purée and sweetened whipped cream. Frost with Basic or Coffee Butter Cream Frosting and scatter thickly with minced filberts or pistachio nuts. Recipe too flexible for a meaningful calorie count.

⚔️ **Génoise for Petits Fours:** Prepare batter as directed and pour into an ungreased 13"×9"×2" pan lined on the bottom with wax paper. Bake 25 minutes at 350° F. Cool as directed. Cake is now ready to cut and make into Petits Fours. About 30 calories for each of 48 petits fours (unfrosted).

⚔️ **Génoise for a Four-Layer Cake:** Use 6 eggs, 1 cup superfine sugar, 1½ teaspoons each vanilla and grated rind, 1 cup sifted cake flour, and ¼ cup clarified butter. Prepare batter as directed and divide between 4 wax-paper-lined, greased, and floured 9" layer cake pans. Bake 15 minutes at 350° F., then cool as directed. About 125 calories for each of 16 servings (unfrosted).

PETITS FOURS

The tricky part of petits fours is frosting them evenly. A base coat of Apricot Glaze seals in loose crumbs, makes the icing go on more smoothly, and keeps the little cakes moist. A help, too, is frosting with Quick Glacé Icing instead of dipping —the more traditional and tedious way—in melted fondant.
Makes about 4 dozen

1 *(1–2-day-old) Génoise for Petits Fours or any firm-textured white or yellow cake baked in a 13"×9"×2" pan*
1 *recipe Apricot Glaze*
3 *recipes Quick Glacé or Chocolate Glacé Icing (or some of each)*
1 *recipe Decorative Butter Cream Frosting or Royal Icing*
Silver dragées, candied violets, chocolate shot (optional)

Cut all hard edges from cake, then even up loaf by trimming off browned top so it is uniformly 1½" thick. Cut in 1½" squares or rounds, small rectangles or triangles and brush off loose crumbs. Spear cakes, 1 at a time, on a fork and dip in apricot glaze to coat top and sides. Place uncoated side down about 2" apart on wire racks set over baking sheets. Let stand uncovered 1 hour. Prepare icing as directed, then, using a large spoon, ladle over cakes, one at a time, so top and sides are evenly coated. (*Note:* Enough must be poured over all at once to create a smooth finish.) Scrape up run-over on baking sheets and remelt. Let cakes dry thoroughly before decorating. Tint decorative icing as desired and pipe on tiny flowers, leaves, stars, scrolls, any design you like. Or decorate with silver *dragées*, candied violets, chocolate shot (see Tips on Decorating Cakes). Store in a cool, dry place until serving time. (*Note:* Petits fours can be frozen but their frosting won't be quite so glossy.) About 240 calories each.

VARIATION:

⚔️ **Simple Petits Fours:** Frost top of a trimmed sheet of cake with Basic Butter Cream Frosting or any flavored butter cream frosting, then cut in desired shapes with a sharp knife, wiping blade after each cut. Decorate with bits of candied cherries, slivered almonds, strips of angelica, colored sugar, or toasted coconut. About 100 calories each.

JELLY ROLL

The filling *needn't* be jelly, as these variations prove.
Makes 1 roll

CAKES, FILLINGS, AND FROSTINGS

¾ cup sifted cake flour
¾ teaspoon baking powder
¼ teaspoon salt
4 eggs, at room temperature
¾ cup sugar
1 teaspoon vanilla
Confectioners' sugar
1 cup any fruit jelly or jam or 1½ cups sweetened whipped cream

Preheat oven to 400° F. Line the bottom of a 15½"×10½"×1" jelly-roll pan with wax paper. Sift flour with baking powder and salt and set aside. With electric or rotary beater, beat eggs at high speed until foamy; slowly add sugar, a little at a time, and continue beating until very thick and the color of mayonnaise. Mix in vanilla. Fold in flour mixture just until blended. Spoon into pan, spreading batter evenly. Bake 12–14 minutes until golden and springy to the touch. Loosen edges of cake, invert on a clean dish towel lightly dusted with sifted confectioners' sugar. Peel off paper carefully and trim off crisp edges with a very sharp knife. Starting from short side, roll cake and towel up together and cool on a wire rack. Unroll, remove towel, spread jelly to within ½" of edges and reroll. Place seam side down and sift confectioners' sugar on top. (*Note:* If jelly or jam is stiff, warm slightly before spreading.) When serving, make slices about 1" thick. About 190 calories for each of 12 servings (made with jelly or jam).

VARIATIONS:

Lemon Jelly Roll: Prepare cake as directed but omit vanilla; add ½ teaspoon lemon extract and 1 tablespoon each lemon juice and finely grated lemon rind. Fill with Lemon Cheese or Lemon Filling instead of jelly. About 190 calories for each of 12 servings.

Orange Jelly Roll: Prepare as directed but omit vanilla and flavor with ½ teaspoon orange extract and 1 tablespoon finely grated orange rind. Fill with Orange Filling. About 190 calories for each of 12 servings.

Strawberry Jelly Roll: Prepare batter as directed and mix in 2 or 3 drops red food coloring; bake as directed. Spread with 1 cup heavy cream, sweetened and whipped to soft peaks, and 1½–2 cups thinly sliced strawberries and roll; or fill with Strawberry Filling. Wrap in foil and chill 1 hour. Sprinkle with confectioners' sugar before serving. About 180 calories for each of 12 servings (made with whipped cream and sliced strawberries).

Chocolate Jelly Roll: When making cake, reduce flour to ⅔ cup, add ¼ cup cocoa and sift with flour, baking powder, and salt. Add 1 tablespoon cold water along with vanilla; bake as directed. Fill with Chocolate Cream Filling or Chocolate, Mocha, or Coffee Butter Cream Frosting. Dust with confectioners' sugar before serving. About 380 calories for each of 12 servings (made with Chocolate, Mocha, or Coffee Butter Cream Frosting).

ANGEL FOOD CAKE

If you follow the directions exactly, you'll bake a tall and tender cake.
Makes a 10" tube cake

1½ cups sifted sugar
1 cup sifted cake flour
1 teaspoon cream of tartar
¼ teaspoon salt
12 egg whites, at room temperature
1 teaspoon vanilla
½ teaspoon almond extract
1 teaspoon lemon juice

Preheat oven to 325° F. Sift ¾ cup sugar with the flour and set aside.

Sprinkle cream of tartar and salt over egg whites; beat with a wire whisk or rotary beater until *very soft* peaks form (whites should *flow, not run*, when bowl is tipped). Sift a little of the remaining sugar over whites and gently fold in, using a whisk; repeat until all sugar is mixed in. Now sift a little sugar-flour mixture over whites, and fold in with the whisk; repeat until all is incorporated (it may take as many as 10 additions). Fold in vanilla, almond extract, and lemon juice. Pour batter into an *ungreased* 10″ tube pan and bake 1–1¼ hours until cake is lightly browned and has pulled from the sides of pan. Invert pan and cool cake thoroughly in pan; then loosen edges with a spatula and turn out. Leave plain or frost as desired. About 120 calories for a piece equal to $\frac{1}{12}$ of the cake (unfrosted).

BASIC CHIFFON CAKE

For maximum volume use 1–2 more egg whites than yolks.
Makes a 10″ tube cake

2¼ cups sifted cake flour
1½ cups sugar
1 teaspoon salt
1 tablespoon baking powder
½ cup cooking oil
6 egg yolks, at room temperature
¾ cup cold water
2 teaspoons vanilla
1 teaspoon lemon juice
7–8 egg whites, at room temperature
½ teaspoon cream of tartar

Preheat oven to 325° F. Sift flour, sugar, salt, and baking powder into a bowl. Make a well in the center and add, in the order listed, the oil, egg yolks, water, vanilla, and lemon juice. Beat until smooth. Using largest bowl and electric mixer or rotary beater, beat egg whites and cream of tartar until they will form *very stiff peaks* (whites should be stiffer than for Angel Food Cake or Meringue). With a rubber spatula, gently fold into batter, ¼ at a time, just until blended. Pour into an *ungreased* 10″ tube pan and bake 55 minutes; raise oven to 350° F. and bake 10 minutes longer until cake is lightly browned and has pulled from sides of pan. Invert and cool cake thoroughly in pan; loosen edges with a spatula and turn out. Leave plain or frost as desired. About 290 calories for each of 12 servings (unfrosted).

VARIATIONS:

Lemon Chiffon Cake: Prepare as directed but reduce vanilla to 1 teaspoon and add ½ teaspoon lemon extract and 2 tablespoons finely grated lemon rind. About 290 calories for each of 12 servings (unfrosted).

Orange Chiffon Cake: Prepare as directed but reduce vanilla to 1 teaspoon, substitute ¾ cup orange juice for the cold water, and add 2 tablespoons finely grated orange rind. About 290 calories for each of 12 servings (unfrosted).

Spiced Chiffon Cake: Prepare as directed but reduce vanilla to 1 teaspoon and add 1 teaspoon cinnamon and ½ teaspoon each nutmeg, cloves, and allspice. About 290 calories for each of 12 servings (unfrosted).

Butterscotch-Maple Chiffon Cake: Prepare as directed but substitute 2 cups firmly packed light brown sugar for the granulated, reduce vanilla to 1 teaspoon, omit lemon juice, and add 1–2 teaspoons maple flavoring. If you like, fold in ¾ cup finely chopped pecans or walnuts just before folding in egg whites. About 300 calories for each of 12 servings (without nuts and unfrosted).

Chocolate Chiffon Cake: Blend ⅓ cup cocoa with ¾ cup boiling water, then cool to room temperature. Reduce flour to 1¾ cups, sift with dry ingredients as directed, then add oil, egg yolks, cocoa mixture, and 1 teaspoon vanilla (omit lemon juice) and beat until smooth. Proceed as recipe directs. About 320 calories for each of 12 servings (unfrosted).

Mocha Chiffon Cake: Prepare Chocolate Chiffon Cake (above) as directed but blend cocoa with ¾ cup very strong hot black coffee instead of boiling water. About 320 calories for each of 12 servings (unfrosted).

LIGHT FRUIT CAKE

Makes a 9″×5″×3″ loaf

1¼ cups sifted flour
½ teaspoon baking powder
½ teaspoon salt
½ teaspoon nutmeg
¼ teaspoon ginger
½ cup butter or margarine
½ cup sugar
3 eggs
1 teaspoon vanilla
½ teaspoon almond extract
1 cup sultana raisins
1 pound mixed candied fruits (pineapple, orange, and lemon peel, citron), chopped fine
¼ pound candied red cherries, coarsely chopped
1 cup toasted, slivered almonds or coarsely chopped pecans or walnuts
Blanched almond halves (garnish)
Candied cherry halves (garnish)

Preheat oven to 300° F. Grease, then line the bottom and sides of a 9″×5″×3″ loaf pan with foil; grease foil lightly. Sift flour with baking powder, salt, and spices and set aside. Cream butter until light, gradually add sugar, continuing to cream until fluffy. Add eggs, 1 at a time, beating well after each addition. Mix in vanilla and almond extract. Add dry ingredients, about ⅓ cup at a time, beating just to blend. Toss raisins with candied fruits, cherries, and nuts, and stir into batter. Spoon into pan and decorate with almond and cherry halves. Bake 1½–1¾ hours until cake shrinks slightly from sides of pan, is lightly browned, and a metal skewer inserted in center comes out clean. Cool cake upright in pan on a wire rack ½ hour. Invert on rack, peel off foil, turn right side up and cool thoroughly. Wrap in brandy-, rum-, or fruit-juice-soaked cheesecloth, then in foil and store airtight 2–3 weeks before serving. About 260 calories for each of 20 servings.

JAMAICAN RUM CAKE

A superrich dark fruit cake that takes 2 days to make and 3 weeks to ripen.
Makes 2 9″×5″×3″ loaves

1 cup dried currants
1½ cups seedless raisins
1 cup seeded raisins
¾ cup coarsely chopped dried black figs
¾ cup coarsely chopped pitted dates
½ cup coarsely chopped candied cherries
1½ cups minced mixed candied fruits
1½ cups dark Jamaican rum
2 cups sifted flour
2 teaspoons baking powder
1 teaspoon cinnamon
1 teaspoon nutmeg
½ teaspoon salt
1 cup butter or margarine, softened to room temperature
2 cups firmly packed dark brown sugar

5 eggs
¾ cup blanched, toasted, sliced almonds

The day before you bake the cake, place all fruits in a large bowl, add rum, mix well, cover, and let stand overnight at room temperature. Next day grease and line the bottom and sides of 2 (9"×5"×3") loaf pans with brown paper or foil; grease linings well. Preheat oven to 275° F. Sift flour, baking powder, cinnamon, nutmeg, and salt together into a bowl. Cream butter until light; add sugar gradually and cream until fluffy. Beat in eggs, one at a time. Add dry ingredients, about ½ cup at a time, alternately with fruits (including any liquid in bottom of bowl), beginning and ending with dry ingredients. Fold in almonds. Spoon batter into pans and, if you wish, decorate tops with candied cherries and/or blanched almond halves. Place on center oven rack; half fill a roasting pan with water and place on rack below. Bake 4 hours until cakes shrink slightly from sides of pan. Cool upright in pans on wire racks 1 hour. Carefully turn out and peel off paper. Turn cakes right side up and cool thoroughly. Wrap in rum-soaked cheesecloth, then in foil and store in an airtight container about 3 weeks to ripen. About 235 calories for each of 20 servings (from 1 loaf).

ROYAL FRUIT WEDDING CAKE

The rich dark fruit cake served alongside the bride's white cake used to be called the groom's cake. Today, either may be served as the wedding cake. There are advantages to the fruit cake: It can be made well ahead and, in fact, improves on standing (it's the best choice if the top tier is to be saved for the first anniversary). Disadvantages? Its hard Royal Icing, though more durable, is difficult to cut and in humid weather may "weep." This next recipe is a hundred years old. It makes an outstanding Christmas cake (⅓ of the recipe will make a 10" tube cake).
Makes a 3-tier cake, about 150 servings

Fruit Mixture:
1½ pounds citron, chopped fine
¾ pound candied orange peel, chopped fine
¾ pound candied lemon peel, chopped fine
6 ounces candied ginger, chopped fine
3 pounds seedless raisins
1½ pounds sultana raisins
1½ pounds dried currants
¾ pound candied cherries, coarsely chopped
¾ pound shelled pecans or walnuts, minced
Finely grated rind of 6 lemons
1½ cups orange marmalade
¾ cup lemon juice
¾ cup orange juice
1½ teaspoons vanilla
1 teaspoon almond extract

Cake Mixture:
6 cups sifted flour
1 tablespoon cinnamon
1½ teaspoons nutmeg
¾ teaspoon mace
¾ teaspoon cloves
¾ teaspoon allspice
1½ teaspoons baking powder
1½ teaspoons salt
1½ pounds butter or margarine
3 cups sugar
18 eggs

Decorations:
6 times the recipe Marzipan (make in 2 or 3 batches)
Lightly beaten whites of 2 eggs

3–4 times the recipe *Royal Icing* (make one batch at a time, as needed)
1 recipe *Sugar Bells*

Make cakes at least 2 weeks before the wedding; if properly stored, they can be made 2 months ahead. Place fruit mixture in a large bowl, toss well, cover, and let stand overnight at room temperature. Grease, then line bottom and sides of a 13", a 10", and a 7" round cake pan with a double thickness of brown paper; grease paper well. Preheat oven to 250° F. Sift together twice the flour, spices, baking powder, and salt and set aside. Cream butter until light, add sugar gradually, and cream until fluffy. Add eggs, 1 at a time, beating well after each addition. Add dry ingredients, about 1 cup at a time, beating just to blend. (*Note:* Unless you have an extra-large mixing bowl, you will have to transfer batter to a large kettle before all dry ingredients are incorporated.) Stir in fruit mixture. Spoon batter into pans, filling to within ½" of tops. Cover 13" pan with foil and refrigerate. Bake smaller 2 cakes on center oven rack with a pan of water on rack underneath 4½–5 hours until cakes pull slightly from sides of pan and a metal skewer inserted in centers comes out clean. If cakes brown too fast, cover loosely with foil. Cool upright in pans on wire racks ½ hour, invert on racks, peel off paper, turn right side up, and cool thoroughly. Bake 13" cake the same way 5½–6 hours. When all cakes are cool, wrap in brandy-, rum-, or fruit-juice-soaked cheesecloth, then in foil and store airtight.

To Decorate: A few days before the wedding, unwrap cakes and prepare *marzipan*. Turn cakes upside-down and fill small holes with marzipan. Cut a wax paper circle the size of each cake, sprinkle lightly with confectioners' sugar, then with a stockinette-covered rolling pin, roll marzipan out on wax paper circles ⅛" thick. Trim away ragged edges so you have perfect circles; brush tops of cakes with lightly beaten egg white and invert circles on cakes of matching size. Peel off paper. Roll remaining marzipan ⅛" thick and, using a ruler, cut in strips exactly the depth of each cake. Brush sides of cakes with egg white, then wrap a marzipan strip around each, *not* overlapping edges but trimming so they just meet; press lightly until as smooth as possible. (*Note:* Side strips may be put on in 2 or 3 pieces if easier, but surface *must be absolutely smooth.*) Let dry 3–4 hours at room temperature. At this point, each cake should be placed on a heavy cardboard circle cut to fit or metal divider disc (obtainable from confectioners' supply houses). If tiers are to be separated by pillars, the supporting posts should be inserted and interlocking ornamental pillars attached (cakes are frosted and decorated individually on their respective divider discs). Make up Royal Icing, a batch at a time as needed, and frost top and sides of each cake *thinly* (if too thick, icing will crack), making surface as smooth as possible (it will help to dip spreading spatula in hot water occasionally, also to work with tier set on a lazy Susan). Let cakes dry overnight in a cool, dry, dust-free spot. Next day, make up additional icing as needed and pipe on decorations (see Tips on Decorating Cakes).

To Assemble: If cake is a simple tiered one, center largest tier on a serving tray (or plywood circle covered with heavy foil). Top with middle tier, then small one, and pipe a fluted border of icing around base of each tier. Add Sugar Bells and any other final decorative touches you like. Keep cake cool until serving time. If cake is a towering pillared one, decorate individual tiers and put together on location shortly before the reception.

To Cut and Serve: See About Cutting Cakes.

About 340 calories for each of 150 servings.

About Cupcakes

Cupcakes can be made from almost any cake batter if you use the following guide for filling pans: fill each muffin pan cup ⅔ full for conventional butter cake batters, fill ½ full for quick-method batters like that used for Easy Yellow Cupcakes, fill ¾ full for true sponge batters, and fill ⅞ full for chiffon cake batters. Use cupcake papers to save greasing and washing pans and to give cupcakes better shape. Or, if you prefer, grease and flour unlined muffin pan cups. Bake cupcakes at 375° F., 12–25 minutes, depending on batter, until springy to the touch.

⚖ ¢ ▨ EASY YELLOW CUPCAKES

Makes 1½ dozen

1⅓ cups sifted flour
¾ cup sugar
2 teaspoons baking powder
¼ teaspoon salt
¼ cup vegetable shortening
⅔ cup milk
1 egg
1 teaspoon vanilla

Preheat oven to 375° F. Sift flour, sugar, baking powder, and salt together into a large mixing bowl. Add shortening and milk, stir to blend, then beat slowly about 1½ minutes with an electric mixer. Add egg and vanilla and beat slowly 1½ minutes. Spoon batter into muffin tins lined with cupcake papers, filling each half full. Bake 20–25 minutes until cakes are golden brown and springy to the touch. Remove cakes from pans and cool upright on wire racks. Frost as desired. About 105 calories each (unfrosted).

VARIATIONS:

⚖ ¢ ▨ **Easy Chocolate Cupcakes:** Prepare as directed but add 2 (1-ounce) melted squares unsweetened chocolate or 2 (1-ounce) envelopes no-melt unsweetened chocolate along with egg and vanilla. About 125 calories each (unfrosted).

⚖ ¢ ▨ **Easy Butterscotch-Spice Cupcakes:** Substitute ¾ cup firmly packed dark brown sugar for the granulated and 1 teaspoon maple flavoring for vanilla. Also sift ½ teaspoon each cinnamon and nutmeg along with dry ingredients, then proceed as directed. About 110 calories each (unfrosted).

▨ **Easy Raisin-Nut Cupcakes:** Prepare as directed and mix in ½ cup each seedless raisins (or dried currants, minced pitted prunes, or dates) and minced walnuts or pecans. About 155 calories each (unfrosted).

¢ ⚖ ▨ **Easy Orange Cupcakes:** Prepare as directed but use ⅓ cup each orange juice and milk instead of all milk; omit vanilla and add 2 teaspoons finely grated orange rind. About 105 calories each (unfrosted).

¢ ⚖ ▨ **Easy Lemon Cupcakes:** Prepare as directed but substitute ¼ teaspoon lemon extract for vanilla and add the finely grated rind of 1 lemon. About 105 calories each (unfrosted).

CAKES, FILLINGS, AND FROSTINGS

▣ **Chocolate Chip Cupcakes:** Prepare as directed and fold in 1 (6-ounce) package semisweet chocolate bits. About 170 calories each (unfrosted).

⚖ **SOUR CREAM PATTY CAKES**

You can quickly sour fresh cream by adding a little vinegar and letting stand in a warm place about ½ hour. For the amount of cream called for below, use 5 tablespoons heavy cream and 1 tablespoon vinegar. Makes 1 dozen

1 cup sifted flour
1 teaspoon baking powder
6 tablespoons sugar
¼ teaspoon salt
¼ cup butter or margarine, chilled
1 egg, lightly beaten
6 tablespoons soured or unsoured fresh light cream
1 teaspoon grated orange or lemon rind
½ teaspoon orange or lemon extract

Preheat oven to 425° F. Sift flour with baking powder, sugar, and salt. Cut in butter with a pastry blender until mixture resembles coarse meal. Add egg and cream and mix well. (*Note:* If you use soured cream, mix curds with whey before measuring.) Stir in rind and extract. Spoon into greased and floured muffin tins, filling each cup ⅔ full. Bake 12 minutes or until tops spring back when touched. Remove cakes from pans and cool upright on a wire rack. About 125 calories each.

VARIATION:

Fruit or Nut Patty Cakes: Prepare as directed, adding 2–3 tablespoons chopped candied cherries or nuts or ¼ cup dried currants or seedless raisins along with the rind and extract. About 140 calories each.

EASY INDIVIDUAL FRUIT CAKES

Makes about 2 dozen

1 (1-pound 1-ounce) package pound cake mix
¾ cup brandy or sweet white wine
⅛ teaspoon cloves
¼ teaspoon ginger
¼ teaspoon nutmeg
¼ teaspoon cinnamon
¼ teaspoon orange extract
⅛ teaspoon almond extract
1 cup minced mixed candied fruit
½ cup seedless raisins
½ cup dried currants
1 tablespoon flour
1 cup finely chopped walnuts
Candied cherries or blanched almond halves (garnish)

Preheat oven to 325° F. Prepare cake mix by package directions, using the eggs but substituting brandy or wine for the liquid called for. Beat in spices and extracts. Dredge fruit in flour, then mix into batter along with nuts. Spoon into muffin tins lined with cupcake papers, filling each ⅔ full. Decorate tops with candied cherries or "daisies" made of almond halves. Bake 35–45 minutes until golden and springy to the touch. Cool cakes in papers (but not in pans) on wire racks. Peel off papers, wrap cakes in brandy- or wine-soaked cheesecloth, then in foil and "season" about 1 week in an airtight container. About 205 calories each.

FILLINGS AND FROSTINGS

"The icing on the cake" . . . the finishing touch. Not every cake needs an icing; some, in fact—pound cake, angel cake, fruit cake—are better without it. But most cakes are bare without frosting of some sort. Generally speaking, superrich cakes call for less-than-superrich icings, plain cakes for something a little showy. The same holds true for layer cakes that are filled (between the layers) as well as frosted.

Some Tips on Frosting Cakes

Preparing the Cake:
– Cool cake thoroughly before frosting unless recipe directs otherwise.
– Trim cake so that it is symmetrical.
– Brush or rub off loose crumbs and trim away ragged edges with scissors; also trim or, using a fine grater, remove any overbrown top or bottom crust.
– Choose a flat plate 2″ larger in diameter than the cake and cover plate rim, petal-fashion, with triangles of wax paper, letting points hang over edge (these are to catch drips and keep plate clean). When cake is frosted, simply pull out wax paper.
– Center cake on plate, bottom side up if a tube cake, right side up if a layer or loaf cake.
– To make the frosting easier, set cake plate on a lazy Susan or turned-upside-down bowl so that you can rotate it as you spread on frosting.

Filling the Cake:
– Place one layer bottom side up on plate as directed above.
– Prepare and cool filling before using unless recipe calls for a warm filling (warm fillings usually seep into cakes too much, making them soggy).
– Spread filling, not too thick, to within ¼″ of edge and, if extra soft, to within 1″ of edge. Add next layer, bottom side up (*unless* it is the top layer) and press lightly into filling.
– Repeat until all layers are in place, remembering that the final layer should be placed right side up.
– Wipe off any filling that has squished out from between layers onto sides of cake.

Frosting the Cake:

If Frosting Is Thick:
– Using a metal spatula, spread a thin layer over top and sides of cake to seal in crumbs. Let dry at room temperature 10 minutes.
– Refrost sides of cake, working from bottom up, to form a slight "rim" around top of cake; this helps keep sides straight and top level.
– Pile remaining frosting on top and spread out to meet edges.
– If frosting is soft, swirl into waves with spatula or draw fork tines lightly over surface.

If Frosting Is Thin:
– Avoid using glazes or hard-drying thin frostings like Royal Icing in humid weather; they may never harden.
– Spoon frosting or glaze over top of cake and let run down sides. This is a good way to ice chiffon, angel, or sponge cakes.
– To give Royal Icing a glass-smooth finish, frost top and sides as quickly as possible, dipping spatula often in hot water and shaking off excess (don't worry at this point about smoothing surface). Then hold edge of spatula blade against sides of cake, slightly at an angle, and rotate cake slowly, scraping off roughened places.
– Dip spatula in hot water and repeat process, smoothing out all rough spots.
– Smooth off top, dipping spatula in hot water as needed.

Frosting Cupcakes:
— Cool cupcakes thoroughly; meanwhile, prepare frosting.
— Holding cupcakes by the bottom, dip one at a time into frosting, then lift out with a slight twirling motion so there is a curlicue on top.
— Set on wire racks and let dry thoroughly. Or, if you like, while frosting is still soft, stud with walnut or pecan halves, chocolate bits, candied cherries, raisins, or chunks of dried fruit. Or scatter lightly with flaked coconut or minced nuts, fine cookie crumbs, or grated semisweet chocolate.

What to Do with Leftover Frosting:
— Cover and refrigerate until needed.
— Bring to room temperature and use to frost cupcakes or cookies.
— Use as a dessert topping (particularly good with steamed puddings).

Tips on Decorating Cakes

The Simplest Decorations: These require no icing and are usually nothing more than confectioners' sugar, sifted through a lace doily onto a cake; a poured-on glaze of melted semisweet chocolate or warmed preserves; a dusting of colored sugar, cocoa, or cinnamon sugar. Quick, easy, and inviting.

Easy Ways to Dress Up Frosted Cakes: Ready-made colored frostings in squirt-on cans or tubes make decorating a snap. They need no refrigeration, are quick and easy to use. Also available in some supermarkets and most gourmet shops: decorating jellies in assorted colors; colored sugars and decorettes; silver dragées; chocolate and butterscotch bits; hard candies and gumdrops; birthday candles and holders. Take whatever is available, add imagination, and create an original special occasion cake.

Flower Cakes: Dot frosted cakes with real flowers (daisies, chrysanthemums, rosebuds, violets), crystalized violets or roses (available in gourmet shops), or fashion flowers out of blanched almonds, slivers of candied fruits, or well-drained mandarin orange sections.

Marble Cakes: Frost top of cake with Snow Glaze (double recipe but add only 3 tablespoons milk to make frosting stiffer). Prepare ½ recipe Chocolate Glaze and drizzle in parallel lines over snow glaze. Before chocolate hardens, draw a toothpick across lines, creating a zigzag effect.

Simple Anytime Decorations:
— Frost a chocolate or mocha cake with Basic or Coffee Butter Cream Frosting and sprinkle top with chocolate curls.*
— Frost any yellow or white butter cake with Whipped Cream Frosting, arrange a ring of miniature meringues on top, and fill center with fresh strawberries.
— Frost sides of a chocolate cake with Basic Butter Cream Frosting, cover top with Chocolate Glaze, and coat sides with chocolate shot or minced nuts.

More Intricate Decorations:

About Cake-Decorating Equipment:

Cake-Decorating Sets: These are widely available in metal or plastic and include a slim selection of decorating tips. Good for beginners.

Pastry (or Decorating) Bags: The best are plastic-lined cotton bags and come in a variety of sizes; they are waterproof, washable, and if properly cared for will last almost indefinitely. Also available: transparent plastic bags, also washable and reusable.

To Make Your Own Decorating Bag:
- Cut an 8" square of parchment, wax paper, or heavy typewriter bond, then halve diagonally into 2 triangles.
- Roll into a sharp-pointed cone and fold points down.

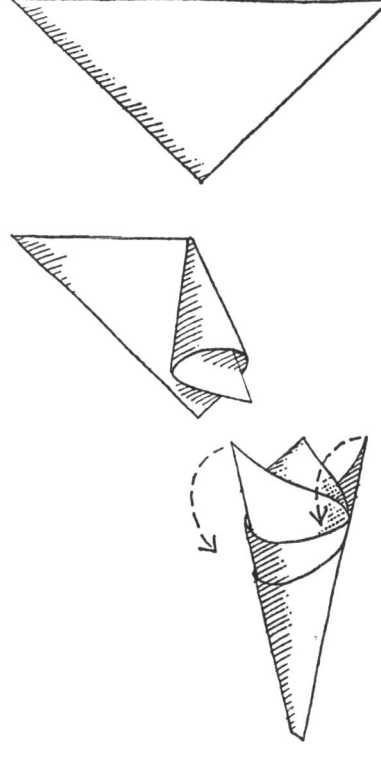

- To make fine lines (flower stems, dots, writing), snip point off to make a tiny hole.
- For broader lines, snip a little more off point.
- For making stars, scrolls, and leaves, snip still more off point and cut with a single or double notch.

- To use with decorative tips, cut ½" -¾" off point and drop in desired tip.
- To fill: Spoon enough frosting into cone to half fill, then fold corners in and top down. (*Note:* If bag should go limp before decorating is done, cut off directly above decorating tip, drop tip into a fresh cone, and squeeze frosting from old bag into the new.)

Decorating Tips (*also called Decorating Tubes*): These may be bought singly or in partial or complete sets (more than a hundred tips) from gourmet shops and confectionery supply houses. Decorating guides come with the sets.

A beginner's set might include:
Tips #2 and 5 (for writing, making flower buds, scrolls)
Tips #14, 18, 22 (for stars, swags, large scrolls)
Tip #30 (for large stars and shells)
Tip #6 (for fancy borders)
Tips #66 and 90 (for small and large leaves)

To Use Pastry Bags and Decorative Tips:
- Never more than half fill bag.
- Roll or fold top down and push frosting out, using steady, gentle pressure so decorations will have crisp outlines. Practice, if you like, on a piece of wax paper or turned-upside-down cake pan until you get the hang of it.
- If you set bag aside for a while, push out a bit of frosting before resuming decoration; some of it may have hardened.
- For really intricate designs, sketch out patterns on paper and use as a guide.

Flower Nails: These look like oversized thumbtacks, are made of metal

CAKES, FILLINGS, AND FROSTINGS

or plastic, and are useful for shaping flowers. Top nail head with a tiny square of wax paper, form flower, then lift off paper and let flower dry. Peel off paper and place flower on cake. For a make-shift flower nail, use a small jar with a lid.

Decorating Stencils: Cardboard and plastic stencils in a variety of patterns and letters are available in gourmet shops and confectionery supply houses. You can also make your own (manila folders work especially well). To use, hold stencil over frosting and fill cut-out spaces with colored sugar, decorettes, thin colored frosting or melted semisweet chocolate.

Decorating Combs: Available in plastic and aluminum. To use, simply draw comb through soft frosting in straight or wavy lines.

About Decorative Frostings: Use Royal Icing for intricate designs and Decorative Butter Cream Frosting for softer, simpler ones.

To Color Frostings: Use liquid or paste food colors (available in a wide range of colors at gourmet shops). Always add colors *gradually*, drop by drop for liquid colors, and dabbed on the end of a toothpick for the paste. Mix in thoroughly before adding more color. It's far better to undercolor than overcolor (many colored frostings will darken on drying). Prepare more of each color than you think you will need so that you will not have to mix up another batch (it will be virtually impossible to match the colors exactly). (*Note:* Always keep frostings covered with damp cloth or paper toweling as you work to prevent their drying out.)

How to Mix Colors

Orange=red+yellow (more yellow than red)
Strawberry=red+yellow (more red than yellow)
Lime Green=yellow+green (more green than yellow)
Chartreuse=yellow+green (more yellow than green)
Violet=blue+red (more blue than red)
Maroon=blue+red (more red than blue)
Brown=yellow+red and a smidgen of green

About Decorating with Chocolate: Always use type of chocolate called for in a recipe and do not substitute cocoa for chocolate.

To Grate Chocolate: Chill chocolate well, then grate into a deep bowl (it tends to fly all over).

To Melt Chocolate: Break into small pieces and melt over hot, not boiling water (chocolate scorches easily, so melt very slowly). Or place chocolate in a custard cup and set in a pan of hot water. Cool melted chocolate slightly before adding to any frosting. *To Smooth Out Lumps:* If a drop of water falls into melted chocolate, the chocolate will lump. To make it smooth again, stir in ½–1 teaspoon vegetable shortening for each ounce of chocolate. It won't affect the flavor.

To Make Chocolate Curls: Warm chocolate (semisweet or German sweet) in wrapper in your hands, just enough to soften outside slightly. Unwrap and shave into thin curls over a piece of wax paper, using a vegetable peeler. Scatter onto cakes as decoration.

To Make Chocolate Cutouts: Melt

6 (1-ounce) packages semisweet chocolate over hot water and blend in 1 teaspoon vegetable shortening. Spread evenly and thinly on a baking sheet lined with wax paper and quick-chill in freezer or refrigerator until chocolate begins to harden. Cut out in desired shapes with cookie cutters (or, for very small decorations, with truffle cutters). Return to refrigerator or freezer and let harden thoroughly. Lift off decorations and use to decorate cakes. To store: Layer into a cakebox, separating layers with wax paper, cover, and keep in refrigerator or freezer.

To Write with Chocolate: Melt semisweet chocolate and blend with a few drops light corn syrup; cool until slightly thickened, then drizzle off the end of a spoon in a thin even stream or, if thick enough, push through a pastry bag fitted with a fine, plain tip.

To Glaze with Chocolate: Melt unsweetened or semisweet chocolate, cool slightly, then spoon or drizzle over a frosted cake. (*Note:* Let frosting harden several hours before adding chocolate. This works especially well with 7-Minute Frosting.)

Some General Decorating Hints:
— Choose a firm-textured cake that will support weight of decorations rather than a delicate sponge or angel food.
— Allow plenty of time for decorating; it is often necessary to let part of the decorations harden before adding more.
— Choose a cool, dry day for the decorating, not a hot, humid one, when icings will not harden.
— If your hands are warm, put only a small amount of frosting in pastry bag at a time, lest body heat soften it too much to be workable.
— Keep designs simple, in proportion to size of cake.
— Suit the designs to the occasion.

☒ BASIC BUTTER CREAM FROSTING

Try the flavor variations that follow or experiment with ideas of your own. This frosting is superbly adaptable.

Makes enough to fill and frost an 8" or 9" 2-layer cake or 24 cupcakes

⅓ *cup butter or margarine, softened to room temperature*
1 (1-pound) box confectioners' sugar, sifted
5–6 tablespoons light cream
2 teaspoons vanilla
¼ *teaspoon salt*

Cream butter until fluffy; beat in sugar, a little at a time, adding alternately with cream. Mix in vanilla and salt and beat until satiny and of good spreading consistency. If mixture seems too stiff, thin with a little additional cream. Add 250 calories to each serving if cake is cut in 12 pieces, 190 to each serving if cake is cut in 16 pieces, and 125 calories to each of 24 cupcakes.

VARIATIONS:

Browned Butter Cream Frosting: Brown butter lightly instead of creaming, then beat in sugar and proceed as directed. Calorie counts the same as for Basic Butter Cream Frosting.

Coffee Butter Cream Frosting: Prepare by basic method above, beating 2 teaspoons instant coffee powder into butter along with sugar. Calorie counts the same as for Basic Butter Cream Frosting.

Mocha Butter Cream Frosting: Prepare by basic method above, beating 2 teaspoons instant coffee powder and 2 (1-ounce) squares melted unsweetened chocolate into creamed butter before adding sugar. Add 275 calories to each serving if cake is cut in 12 pieces, 210 calories if cut in 16 pieces, and 140 calories to each of 24 cupcakes.

Chocolate Butter Cream Frosting: Prepare by basic method but blend 3 (1-ounce) squares melted unsweetened chocolate or ½ cup sifted cocoa into creamed butter before adding sugar. Proceed as directed. Add 290 calories to each serving if cake is cut in 12 pieces, 220 calories to each serving if cake is cut in 16 pieces, and 145 calories to each of 24 cupcakes.

Maple Butter Cream Frosting: Prepare by basic method, substituting ½ cup maple syrup for the light cream and reducing vanilla to ½ teaspoon. Calorie counts approximately the same as for Mocha Butter Cream Frosting.

Nut Butter Cream Frosting: Prepare as directed and, when of good spreading consistency, mix in ⅓–½ cup minced walnuts, pecans, blanched filberts, or almonds. Calorie counts approximately the same as for Chocolate Butter Cream Frosting.

Orange or Lemon Butter Cream Frosting: Prepare by basic method, substituting 4–5 tablespoons orange or lemon juice for the cream; omit vanilla and add 3–4 teaspoons finely grated orange or lemon rind and ¼ teaspoon almond extract. Add 230 calories to each serving if cake is cut in 12 pieces, 175 to each serving if cake is cut in 16 pieces, and 115 calories to each of 24 cupcakes.

Cherry Butter Cream Frosting: Prepare by basic method, substituting 5–6 tablespoons maraschino cherry juice for the light cream; omit vanilla. When frosting is of good spreading consistency, fold in ¼ cup minced, well-drained maraschino cherries. About 10 calories more per serving than Basic Butter Cream Frosting.

Pineapple Butter Cream Frosting: Prepare by basic method, substituting ⅓ cup drained, canned crushed pineapple for the cream; reduce vanilla to ½ teaspoon and add ¼ teaspoon almond extract. Calorie counts the same as for Basic Butter Cream Frosting.

Berry Butter Cream Frosting: Prepare by basic method, substituting ⅓ cup sieved, puréed fresh or thawed frozen strawberries, raspberries, or blackberries for the cream. Omit vanilla and add 1 teaspoon lemon juice. Calorie counts the same as Basic Butter Cream Frosting.

Decorative Butter Cream Frosting: Prepare Basic Butter Cream Frosting as directed but reduce cream to 1–2 tablespoons; if you want a really snowy frosting, substitute vegetable shortening for butter and add a drop of blue food coloring. (*Note:* Use only on firm frostings or decorations may sink in. On warm or humid days, add a little extra confectioners' sugar so decorations will hold their shape.) About 10 calories less per serving than Basic Butter Cream Frosting.

❊ CREAM CHEESE FROSTING

Slightly firmer than butter frosting, this one also invites improvisation. Makes enough to fill and frost an 8″ or 9″ 2-layer cake

2 (3-ounce) packages cream cheese, softened to room temperature
1 (1-pound) box confectioners' sugar, sifted

1 teaspoon vanilla
1–2 tablespoons milk, light cream, or evaporated milk

Beat cream cheese until very soft, then gradually beat in confectioners' sugar. Mix in vanilla and enough milk to make a good spreading consistency. Add approximately 185 calories to each of 16 servings of cake.

VARIATIONS:

Sour Cream–Cream Cheese Frosting: Prepare as directed but substitute ¼ cup sour cream for the milk. Add approximately 190 calories to each of 16 servings of cake.

Chocolate Cream Cheese Frosting: Beat cream cheese until soft, mix in 2 (1-ounce) squares melted unsweetened chocolate and proceed as directed, increasing milk to 3 tablespoons. Add about 205 calories to each of 16 servings of cake.

Coffee Cream Cheese Frosting: Prepare as directed, adding 1 tablespoon instant coffee powder along with sugar. Add about 185 calories to each of 16 servings of cake.

Orange or Lemon Cream Cheese Frosting: Prepare as directed but omit vanilla and use orange or lemon juice instead of milk. Flavor with the finely grated rind of 1 lemon or orange. Add about 185 calories to each of 16 servings of cake.

⊠ WHIPPED CREAM FROSTING

Spread on cakes shortly before they're cut and eaten.
Makes enough to fill and frost a 9″ tube or 2-layer cake

1 pint heavy cream, well chilled
1 cup sifted confectioners' sugar
1 teaspoon vanilla

In a chilled bowl with chilled beaters, beat cream until frothy. Gradually add confectioners' sugar, then vanilla. Continue beating until thick enough to spread. Use at once. Add about 140 calories to each of 16 servings of cake.

VARIATIONS:

Chocolate Whipped Cream Frosting: Sift ½ cup cocoa with confectioners' sugar and beat into cream as directed. Add about 150 calories to each of 16 servings of cake.

Coffee Whipped Cream Frosting: Mix 1 tablespoon instant coffee powder with the cream and proceed as directed. Add about 140 calories to each of 16 servings of cake.

Fruit Whipped Cream Frosting: Prepare as directed but flavor with ½ teaspoon orange or lemon extract, instead of vanilla, and the finely grated rind of 1 lemon or orange. Add about 140 calories for each of 16 servings of cake.

Nut Whipped Cream Frosting: Prepare as directed but flavor with maple flavoring or almond extract instead of vanilla and fold in ¾ cup minced pecans, filberts, boiled chestnuts, or toasted almonds. Add about 170 calories to each of 16 servings of cake.

Tipsy Whipped Cream Frosting: Prepare as directed but flavor with brandy or rum extract instead of vanilla or 1–2 tablespoons brandy, rum, or bourbon. (*Note:* For a really Tipsy Cake, pierce unfrosted cake layers all over with a metal skewer and drizzle with a little liquor; cover loosely and let stand 1 hour before filling and frosting.) Add about 145 calories to each of 16 servings of cake.

CAKES, FILLINGS, AND FROSTINGS

Coconut Whipped Cream Frosting: Prepare as directed and fold in 1 cup flaked or toasted flaked coconut. Add about 160 calories to each of 16 servings of cake.

Neapolitan Fruit Cream Filling: Use this only as a filling, it's too soft for frosting. Make half the recipe and fold in ½ cup minced, well-drained peaches, pears, apricots, pineapple, or fruit salad or ½ cup thinly sliced bananas or berries. Add about 145 calories to each of 16 servings of cake.

Warm Weather Whipped Cream Frosting: Blend 1 teaspoon unflavored gelatin and 2 tablespoons cold water in a custard cup. Set in a small pan of simmering water and stir until gelatin dissolves; cool. Gradually beat into cream, then proceed as recipe directs. Add about 140 calories to each of 16 servings of cake.

7-MINUTE FROSTING

Some electric mixers will whip up 7-Minute Frosting in *less* than 7 minutes. Makes enough to fill and frost an 8" or 9" 2-layer cake or 24 cupcakes

2 egg whites
1½ cups sugar
¼ teaspoon cream of tartar or 1 tablespoon light corn syrup
⅓ cup cold water
1 teaspoon vanilla

Mix all ingredients except vanilla in the top of a double boiler and set over just boiling water. Beat constantly with rotary or electric beater until stiff peaks form, 4–7 minutes. Off heat, add vanilla and beat until of good spreading consistency. Add about 75 calories to each of 16 servings of cake, 50 calories to each of 24 cupcakes.

VARIATIONS:

Orange or Lemon 7-Minute Frosting: Prepare as directed but use orange or lemon juice instead of water and ½ teaspoon orange or lemon extract instead of vanilla. If you like, fold in the finely grated rind of 1 orange or lemon just before using and tint pale orange or yellow. Calorie counts approximately the same as for 7-Minute Frosting.

Peppermint 7-Minute Frosting: Prepare as directed but flavor with ½ teaspoon peppermint extract or ¼ teaspoon oil of peppermint instead of vanilla. Tint pale pink and fold in ⅓ cup crushed peppermint candy. Add about 105 calories to each of 16 servings of cake, 70 calories to each of 24 cupcakes.

Coffee 7-Minute Frosting: Prepare as directed but use ½ cup firmly packed dark brown sugar and 1 cup granulated; also dissolve 1 tablespoon instant coffee powder in the water before adding. Calorie counts approximately the same as for 7-Minute Frosting.

Caramel 7-Minute Frosting: Prepare as directed but use 1 cup firmly packed dark brown sugar and ½ cup granulated; flavor with maple flavoring instead of vanilla. Calorie counts approximately the same as for 7-Minute Frosting.

Fruit or Nut 7-Minute Frosting: Prepare as directed, then fold in ½–¾ cup prunes, or raisins or ½–¾ cup coarsely chopped nuts. Add about 100 calories to each of 16 servings of cake, 65 calories to each of 24 cupcakes.

Chocolate 7-Minute Frosting: Prepare as directed, then fold in 2 melted and cooled (1-ounce) squares unsweetened chocolate. Do not beat, just stir to mix. Add about 95

calories to each of 16 servings of cake, 65 calories to each of 24 cupcakes.

Marshmallow 7-Minute Frosting: Prepare as directed, then fold in 1 cup snipped marshmallows. Add about 90 calories to each of 16 servings of cake, 60 calories to each of 24 cupcakes.

Coconut 7-Minute Frosting: Prepare as directed, tint pastel, if you like, then fold in ½ cup flaked coconut. After frosting cake, sprinkle with additional flaked coconut. Add about 85 calories to each of 16 servings of cake, 55 calories to each of 24 cupcakes.

WHITE MOUNTAIN FROSTING

A fluffy white frosting that you don't have to beat *on* the stove.
Makes enough to fill and frost an 8" or 9" 2-layer cake

¾ *cup sugar*
¼ *cup light corn syrup*
¼ *cup water*
3 *egg whites, at room temperature*
1 *teaspoon vanilla or* ½ *teaspoon almond extract*

Mix sugar, corn syrup, and water in a small, heavy saucepan, insert candy thermometer, partially cover pan, and bring to a boil over moderate heat. Remove cover and boil *without stirring* until thermometer registers 240–42° F. or until a drop on the tip of a spoon will spin a 6"–8" thread. Just before syrup reaches proper temperature, begin beating egg whites with an electric mixer until soft peaks form. When syrup reaches correct temperature, set mixer at high speed and pour syrup into whites in a slow thin stream. Continue beating until glossy and firm enough to hold a shape. Beat in vanilla. Add about 55 calories to each of 16 servings of cake.

VARIATIONS:

Pink Mountain Frosting: Prepare as directed but substitute ¼ cup maraschino cherry liquid for water and use almond extract. Calorie count the same as for White Mountain Frosting.

Lemon or Orange Mountain Frosting: Prepare as directed but substitute lemon or orange juice for water and flavor with ½ teaspoon lemon or orange extract and the finely grated rind of 1 lemon or orange. Calorie count the same as for White Mountain Frosting.

Marble Mountain Frosting: Prepare as directed and just before spreading swirl in 1 (1-ounce) square coarsely grated unsweetened chocolate or 1 (1-ounce) envelope no-melt unsweetened chocolate to create a marbleized effect. Add about 65 calories to each of 16 servings of cake.

Maple Mountain Frosting: Use ¾ cup firmly packed light brown sugar instead of granulated and substitute 1 teaspoon maple flavoring for vanilla. Calorie count the same as for White Mountain Frosting.

Rock Candy Mountain Frosting: Prepare as directed but flavor with ½ teaspoon peppermint extract instead of vanilla and, just before serving, fold in ½ cup crushed peppermint sticks. Add about 85 calories to each of 16 servings of cake.

Marshmallow Mountain Frosting: Prepare as directed up to point of adding vanilla. With scissors, snip 8 marshmallows into small bits and fold into frosting along with vanilla. Add about 70 calories to each of 16 servings of cake.

CAKES, FILLINGS, AND FROSTINGS

SEAFOAM FROSTING

Almost as good as seafoam candy. Delicious on chocolate or burnt sugar cakes.

Makes enough to fill and frost an 8" or 9" 2-layer cake

⅔ cup firmly packed light brown sugar
¼ cup light corn syrup
1 egg white
⅛ teaspoon cream of tartar
⅛ teaspoon salt
2 tablespoons water
1 teaspoon vanilla

Combine all ingredients except vanilla in the top of a double boiler, set over boiling water, and beat with a rotary beater or portable electric mixer until mixture stands in peaks. Off heat, add vanilla and continue beating until mixture will hold deep swirls. Use at once. Add about 50 calories to each of 16 servings of cake.

FUDGE FROSTING

Really fudgy.
Makes enough to frost an 8" or 9" round or square cake

1½ cups sugar
½ cup water or milk
1 tablespoon light corn syrup
1 tablespoon butter or margarine
2 (1-ounce) squares unsweetened chocolate, coarsely grated, or 2 (1-ounce) envelopes no-melt unsweetened chocolate
1 teaspoon vanilla

Place all ingredients except vanilla in a heavy saucepan with a candy thermometer, set over moderate heat, and stir once or twice as chocolate melts. Boil *without stirring* until thermometer reaches 234° F. or until a little mixture dropped into cold water forms a very soft ball. Remove from heat at once and cool without stirring to 120° F. (lukewarm); mix in vanilla and beat until thick and of good spreading consistency. (*Note:* If frosting seems thick, add a little milk or light cream; if too thin, beat in a little sifted confectioners' sugar.) Add about 100 calories to each of 16 servings of cake (if frosting is made with water), 105 calories (if frosting is made with milk).

VARIATIONS:

Vanilla Fudge Frosting: Prepare as directed but use milk, light or sour cream instead of water and omit chocolate. Add about 90 calories to each of 16 servings (if frosting is made with milk), about 100 calories (if made with light or sour cream).

Caramel Fudge Frosting: Prepare as directed, using 1 cup firmly packed light or dark brown sugar and ½ cup granulated sugar; also use milk, dark corn syrup and, if you like, add 1 teaspoon maple flavoring in addition to vanilla. Omit chocolate. Add about 95 calories to each of 16 servings of cake.

✖ EASY FUDGE FROSTING

Makes enough to fill and frost an 8" or 9" 2-layer cake

2 cups sugar
¼ cup light corn syrup
½ cup butter or margarine
½ cup milk
2 (1-ounce) squares unsweetened chocolate, coarsely grated, or 2 (1-ounce) envelopes no-melt unsweetened chocolate
1 teaspoon vanilla

Stir all ingredients except vanilla in a heavy saucepan over low heat until chocolate melts. Bring to a full rolling boil, stirring constantly, then boil 1 minute. Off heat, beat until lukewarm; stir in vanilla and continue stirring until a good spreading consistency. Add about 185 calories to each of 16 servings of cake.

VARIATION:

Easy Caramel Fudge Frosting: Prepare as directed but use 2 cups firmly packed light or dark brown sugar instead of granulated sugar; omit corn syrup and chocolate. Add about 160 calories to each of 16 servings of cake.

❈ BROILED PENUCHE ICING

A fast frosting for simple cakes.
Makes enough to top a 9″ square cake

⅔ cup firmly packed light or dark brown sugar
¼ cup butter or margarine, softened to room temperature
¼ cup heavy cream
½ cup finely chopped nuts

Preheat broiler. Mix all ingredients and spread evenly on warm cake. Set on wire cake rack over baking pan and broil 5″ from the heat 3–4 minutes until mixture bubbles and browns lightly. Cool slightly before cutting. Add about 100 calories to each of 16 servings of cake.

For a 13″ × 9″ × 2″ Cake: Use 1 cup sugar, ⅓ cup each butter and cream and ¾ cup nuts. Add about 90 calories to each of 24 servings of cake.

VARIATIONS:

Broiled Coconut Icing: Prepare as directed but substitute ½ cup flaked coconut for nuts. Add about 100 calories to each of 16 servings of cake.

Broiled Peanut Butter Icing: Prepare as directed but substitute ¼ cup peanut butter for butter and use ½ cup minced *unsalted* toasted, blanched peanuts. Add about 125 calories to each of 16 servings of cake.

❈ ROYAL ICING (ORNAMENTAL FROSTING)

This frosting holds its shape well, dries hard, and is ideal for making durable decorations. It also helps keep cakes moist.
Makes enough to decorate an 8″, 9″, or 10″ cake

3 egg whites, at room temperature
¼ teaspoon cream of tartar
1 (1-pound) box confectioners' sugar, sifted

Beat egg whites and cream of tartar until foamy. Gradually beat in sugar, then beat at high speed until very thick and glossy (beaters when withdrawn should leave sharp, firm peaks). Use to frost and decorate cakes. Keep bowl of frosting covered with damp cloth as you work to prevent "crusting." If frosting should lose stiffness, beat at high speed until firm again, or if necessary (sometimes true in humid weather) beat in a little additional confectioners' sugar. About 2310 calories total (amount per serving of cake depends entirely upon how lavishly the cake is decorated).

❈ QUICK GLACÉ ICING

This icing dries hard with a lovely glossy finish.
Makes enough to glaze about 1⅓ dozen Petits Fours

3 cups sifted confectioners' sugar
3 tablespoons light corn syrup
3 tablespoons water
Few drops any food coloring (optional)

Place all ingredients except food coloring in the top of a double

CAKES, FILLINGS, AND FROSTINGS

boiler over *simmering* water and heat, stirring, until sugar dissolves and mixture is smooth. Do not allow water underneath to boil or icing will not be glossy. Tint with food coloring as desired. Spoon over Petits Fours or any small cakes set on wire racks over baking sheets. Scrape up run-over from baking sheet, return to double boiler, and warm again until of pouring consistency. If thick, add a few drops warm water. Add about 105 calories to each of the petits fours.

VARIATION:

Chocolate Glacé Icing: Prepare as directed and, when sugar is dissolved, add 1½ ounces semisweet chocolate broken into bits and heat, stirring until blended. Add 1–2 tablespoons warm water to thin to pouring consistency; do not overheat or icing will not be glossy. Add about 155 calories to each of the petits fours.

▨ SNOW GLAZE

A quick and easy topping for any simple cake.
Makes enough to glaze a large loaf or tube cake or 24 cupcakes

1 cup sifted confectioners' sugar
2 tablespoons warm milk
¼ teaspoon almond extract

Sprinkle confectioners' sugar slowly into milk and blend smooth. Mix in almond extract, spread on cake, and let stand until glaze hardens. Add about 30 calories to each of 16 servings of cake, 20 calories to each of 24 cupcakes.

VARIATIONS:

Sugar Glaze: Prepare as directed but substitute warm water for milk. Calorie counts the same as for Snow Glaze.

Lemon or Orange Sugar Glaze: Prepare as directed but substitute warm lemon or orange juice for milk and flavor with 1 teaspoon finely grated lemon or orange rind. Calorie counts the same as for Snow Glaze.

Tutti-Frutti Glaze: Prepare as directed but substitute 1 lightly beaten egg white for milk. Spread glaze on cake and decorate with slivered mixed candied fruit peel, candied red cherries, angelica, and thinly sliced blanched almonds. Recipe too flexible for a meaningful calorie count.

Easy White Icing (perfect for icing hot sweet breads): Prepare as directed but use cold milk and reduce quantity to about 1 tablespoon. Flavor with ¼ teaspoon vanilla instead of almond extract. Calorie counts approximately the same as for Snow Glaze.

▨ CHOCOLATE GLAZE

Makes enough to glaze an 8″ or 9″ cake or 6–8 Éclairs

2 (1-ounce) squares unsweetened chocolate
1 teaspoon butter or margarine
1 cup sifted confectioners' sugar
3 tablespoons warm water

Melt chocolate and butter in the top of a double boiler over simmering water; stir to blend well. Set top of double boiler on a damp cloth, add ½ cup confectioners' sugar and 1 tablespoon water; beat until smooth. Add remaining sugar and water and beat until glossy. Use to glaze éclairs, other pastries, or the tops of cakes. Add about 40 calories to each of 16 servings of cake, 100 calories to each of 6 éclairs and 75 calories to each of 8 éclairs.

APRICOT GLAZE

An excellent base coat for Petits Fours and other small cakes to be covered with thin, hard, smooth icings.

Makes enough to glaze 4 dozen Petits Fours

2 cups apricot preserves
½ cup water

Heat preserves and water in a saucepan over low heat, stirring constantly, until mixture bubbles; heat and stir 2–3 minutes longer, press through a fine sieve, and cool slightly before using. Add about 50 calories to each of the petits fours.

BASIC VANILLA CREAM FILLING

Makes about 1 cup, enough to fill an 8″ or 9″ 2-layer cake

2 tablespoons cornstarch
⅓ cup sugar
¾ cup milk
1 egg yolk, lightly beaten with ¼ cup milk
1 teaspoon vanilla

Blend cornstarch, sugar, and milk in a small saucepan and heat, stirring constantly, over moderate heat until mixture boils and is thick; boil and stir ½ minute longer. Off heat, beat a little hot mixture into egg yolk, return all to pan *gradually*, beating constantly. Mix in vanilla and cool to room temperature, beating now and then. Add about 30 calories to each of 16 servings of cake.

VARIATIONS:

Poppy Seed Cream Filling: Prepare as directed and mix in 2 tablespoons poppy seeds. Add about 30 calories to each of 16 servings of cake.

Double Cream Filling: Prepare as directed and fold in ⅓ cup heavy cream whipped to soft peaks. (*Note:* Also good with any of the flavor variations.) Add about 50 calories to each of 16 servings of cake.

Chocolate Cream Filling: Prepare as directed but increase sugar to ½ cup and add 2 (1-ounce) squares melted semisweet chocolate or 2 (1-ounce) envelopes no-melt unsweetened chocolate along with vanilla; blend well. If mixture seems thick, thin with a little milk. Add about 60 calories to each of 16 servings of cake.

Butterscotch Cream Filling: Substitute ½ cup firmly packed dark brown sugar for the granulated and, if you like, use maple flavoring instead of vanilla. Add about 30 calories to each of 16 servings of cake.

Coffee Cream Filling: Add 1½ teaspoons instant coffee powder along with the sugar. Add about 30 calories to each of 16 servings of cake.

Fruit Cream Filling: Prepare as directed but omit vanilla and add ¼ teaspoon lemon or orange extract and 2 teaspoons finely grated lemon or orange rind. Add about 30 calories to each of 16 servings of cake.

Coconut Cream Filling: Prepare as directed and mix in ½–⅔ cup flaked coconut. Add about 40 calories to each of 16 servings of cake.

PASTRY CREAM

What to put inside feathery French pastries.

Makes enough to fill a 3-layer cake or 1 dozen Cream Puffs or Éclairs

½ cup sifted flour
½ cup sugar

⅛ teaspoon salt
2 cups milk
2 eggs plus 2 egg yolks, lightly beaten
1 teaspoon vanilla

Mix flour, sugar, and salt in the top of a double boiler. Add milk slowly, blending until smooth. Heat and stir over direct moderate heat until thickened and smooth. Mix about ½ cup hot mixture into eggs, then return to pan. Set over simmering water and cook and stir 2–3 minutes until thick. Off heat, stir in vanilla. Place a piece of wax paper flat on sauce to prevent a skin from forming and cool. Stir well, cover, and chill until ready to use as a pastry filling. Add about 75 calories to each of 16 servings of cake, about 100 calories to each of 12 cream puffs or éclairs.

LEMON FILLING

Makes enough to fill an 8″ or 9″ 2-layer cake

3 tablespoons cornstarch
1 cup sugar
½ cup lemon juice
1 cup hot water
2 tablespoons butter or margarine
2 tablespoons finely grated lemon rind
Few drops yellow food coloring

Mix cornstarch and sugar in a saucepan, stir in lemon juice, and water and bring to a full boil, stirring constantly. Reduce heat slightly and heat and stir until thickened and clear. Off heat, beat in butter and lemon rind, then tint pale yellow. Place wax paper flat on sauce and cool to room temperature. Beat with a whisk or rotary beater before using. Add about 70 calories to each of 16 servings of cake.

VARIATIONS:

Lime Filling: Prepare as directed but substitute lime juice and rind for the lemon. Tint pale green. Add about 70 calories to each of 16 servings of cake.

Orange Filling: Prepare as directed, using 1 cup orange juice and ½ cup hot water; substitute orange rind for the lemon. Tint pale orange with a red and yellow food coloring. Add about 70 calories to each of 16 servings of cake.

Pineapple Filling: Mix cornstarch with sugar, add 1 cup pineapple juice, ¼ cup hot water, and ½ cup well-drained crushed pineapple. Heat and stir until thickened; off heat, beat in the butter and ¼ teaspoon lemon rind. Do not tint. Add about 85 calories to each of 16 servings of cake.

Rich Fruit Filling: Prepare any of the preceding recipes in the top of a double boiler over direct heat. When cornstarch mixture is thickened and clear, mix a little into 2 lightly beaten egg yolks, return to pan, set over simmering water, and heat and stir 1–2 minutes. Proceed as directed but do not tint. Recipe too flexible for a meaningful calorie count.

Fruit Cream Filling: Prepare Lemon, Lime, Orange, or Pineapple Filling as directed and, just before using, mix in 1 cup softly whipped cream. For the Lemon, Lime or Orange Fillings add about 95 calories for each of 16 servings of cake. For the Pineapple Filling, add about 110 calories for each of 16 servings of cake.

STRAWBERRY FILLING

Soft and fluffy. Use to fill angel, white, or yellow cakes or jelly rolls. Makes enough to fill a 9″ or 10″ 3-layer cake

1 (6-ounce) package strawberry-flavored gelatin
1 cup very hot water
1 (10-ounce) package thawed frozen, sliced strawberries or 1 pint fresh strawberries, hulled and sliced thin
1 teaspoon almond extract
½ cup heavy cream

Mix gelatin and water, stirring until gelatin dissolves. Add strawberries and almond extract and mix well. Cover and chill until thick and syrupy, but not firm. Whip cream to soft peaks, then fold into strawberry mixture. Chill 20–30 minutes until thick but not set. Use to fill Angel Food Cake, cut in 3 layers, any 3-layer white or yellow cake, or roll up inside jelly roll. Add about 55 calories to each of 16 servings of cake.

PINEAPPLE-COCONUT FILLING

Makes enough to fill a 3-tier wedding cake

2 (1-pound 4-ounce) cans crushed pineapple (do not drain)
1½ cups sugar
¼ cup lemon juice
¼ cup cornstarch blended with ½ cup cold water or pineapple juice
2 (3½-ounce) cans flaked coconut

Mix all but last ingredient in a saucepan, set over moderate heat and heat and stir until thickened and clear and no taste of cornstarch remains. Cool 10 minutes, stir in coconut, and cool to room temperature, stirring now and then. Add about 25 calories to each of 100 pieces of wedding cake.

SUGAR BELLS

For wedding cakes. You will need 1 (3¼″), 1 (2″), and 1 (1¼″) plastic bell molds (obtainable from confectioners' supply houses and sometimes local bakeries). Makes 3 large, 10 medium, and 16 small bells

2½ pounds superfine sugar
1 egg white
Cornstarch
1 recipe Royal Icing (optional)

Place sugar and egg white in a bowl and rub between your palms until evenly moist and mixed. Dust each mold inside with cornstarch, tapping out excess. Pack sugar firmly into molds, level off bottoms, and invert on wax paper; carefully lift off molds. Repeat until all sugar is molded. Let bells dry 1–2 hours until hard about ¼″ in from the outside. With a small spoon or spoon handle, scoop out soft insides, leaving shells ⅛″–¼″ thick. Cover scooped-out sugar with damp cloth and use for molding more bells. Let bells dry overnight at room temperature. Pipe icing around edges, if you like, to give a more finished look. Use to decorate any wedding or anniversary cake. Calorie counts will vary considerably according to how much each sugar bell is hollowed out and how lavishly it is decorated with royal icing. As a very rough estimate, figure about 130 calories per medium-size bell.

CHAPTER 23

COOKIES

Take a wintry afternoon, add an oven full of cookies scenting the air with their warm, sugary promise and you have one of the memories dear to most of us. Cookies are where most of us begin our cooking lessons because they're fast, fun, and practically disaster-proof—a little too much liquid or flour won't destroy them *or* the cook's enthusiasm.

Basically, there are six different types of cookies: *Drop, Rolled, Molded or Pressed, Refrigerator, Bar,* and *No-Bake.* We'll discuss them one by one, but first, some tips that apply to them all.

How to Make Better Cookies

About Pans and Preparing Pans:

— For delicately browned cookies, choose shiny baking sheets rather than dark ones. Dark surfaces absorb heat more quickly and cookies tend to overbrown on the bottom. When using the new nonstick pans, keep a close eye out until you learn how fast they bake.
— For uniform baking, make sure baking sheets are 1″–2″ smaller all round than the oven (heat must circulate freely). Also make certain pans do not touch oven walls at any point.
— Grease pans only when recipes specify doing so.
— For greasing, use melted clarified butter* (unsalted) if you can afford it and shortening or cooking oil if you can't. Apply evenly and thinly with a pastry brush or small crumple of paper toweling, coating *bottoms of pans only*. To simplify dishwashing, grease only those areas cookies will actually touch.
(*Note:* Even the new nonstick pans need greasing if the cookies contain much sugar or fruit.)
— When baking cookies in quantity, line baking sheets with foil or, better still, with baking pan liner paper, a silicone-coated parchment that eliminates greasing altogether. It is available in kitchen departments of large department stores. Have several sheets of foil or paper cut to size, then as each batch of cookies comes from the oven, lift them off, paper and all, and slide a fresh sheet into place.
— If you have no baking sheets, use a turned-upside-down roasting pan—turned upside down because cookies bake poorly in high-sided pans.

About Mixing Cookies:

— Read recipe through carefully before beginning it.
— Have all utensils out, pans prepared,

and ingredients measured before beginning.

– When using an electric mixer, use a medium speed for creaming shortening, sugar, and eggs and low speed for working in dry ingredients unless recipes specify otherwise.

– When mixing by hand, use a spoon with a long, comfortable handle—wooden spoons are especially good.

– Always mix in dry ingredients with a light hand and only enough to blend. Overbeating at this point tends to make the cookies tough.

About Placing Cookies on Pans:

– Always put cookies on *cool* baking sheets; if sheets are warm, cookies will spread unnecessarily. When baking in quantity, use 2 or 3 sheets so that there is time to cool each before adding a fresh batch of cookies.

– Allow plenty of spreading room when spacing cookies on sheets (recipes specify just how much). As a rule, the thinner the dough or the higher the butter or shortening content, the more cookies will spread.

– Whenever you have less than a full sheet of cookies to bake, use a turned-upside-down pie tin or small baking pan. An unfilled sheet of cookies will bake unevenly.

– Avoid placing cookies too near edges of baking sheets; they will brown much more quickly than those in the center.

– Always scrape crumbs from a used sheet and wipe it thoroughly with paper toweling before reusing.

About Baking:

– Let oven preheat a full 15 minutes before baking cookies.

– Unless recipe states otherwise, bake cookies as near the center of oven as possible. Those placed too low tend to burn on the bottom, those placed too high will be brown on top but raw in the middle.

– Unless your oven is very large, do not attempt to bake more than one sheet, certainly no more than 2 sheets of cookies at a time. Whenever you bake 2 sheets at once, stagger them, one slightly above the other, so heat can circulate freely and reverse positions of pans halfway through baking.

– Because there is some heat buildup in even the best of ovens, you can expect second, third, and fourth sheets of cookies to bake slightly faster than the first.

– Turn baking sheets as needed during baking so that cookies will brown as evenly as possible.

– Always use a timer when baking cookies.

– Check cookies after minimum baking time and, if not done, bake maximum time.

– If, despite all precautions, some cookies are done ahead of others, simply remove from baking sheet.

– *To tell when cookies are done, use the following tests:*

Crisp, Thin Cookies: Check color; cookies should be firm to the touch, delicately browned or lightly ringed with brown.

Fairly Thick Dropped or Shaped Cookies: Press lightly in the center; if no imprint remains, cookies are done.

Meringue Kisses: Tap lightly; if kisses sound hollow, they are done.

Bars: Press lightly in center; mixture should feel firm yet springy. Bars should also have pulled from sides of pan.

– To rescue cookies that have burned on the bottom, grate off blackened parts with a fine lemon rind grater.

About Removing Cookies from Baking Sheets:

– Use wide spatulas or pancake turners.
– Unless recipe states otherwise, lift cookies at once to wire racks to cool. Exceptions are very soft cookies, which must be firm before a spatula can be slipped underneath them.

About Cooling Cookies:

– Never overlap cookies on racks and never arrange more than one layer deep; cookies will stick to one another.
– Remove to canisters as soon as cool.

About Storing Cookies:

Soft Cookies: Store in canisters with tight-fitting covers and, if necessary, with a chunk of apple or bread to keep them moist (replace apple or bread often). Brownies and other bars can be stored in their baking pans, tightly wrapped in foil or plastic food wrap.

Crisp Cookies: Blanket statements can't be made because much depends on weather. Crisp cookies, for example, will soon go limp if stored in a loosely covered container in a muggy climate; in such areas they *must* be stored airtight. But in dry areas, the treatment is just the opposite: Store in loosely covered containers. If cookies should soften, crispen by heating three to five minutes at 350° F.

About Freezing Cookies: (See the chapter on freezing and canning).

About Packing and Shipping Cookies:

– Choose soft, sturdy, undecorated cookies that won't crumble in transit (a list is given in the Cookie Chart).
– For shipping, pick a sturdy cardboard box and line with wax paper. Cushion bottom with a thick layer of crumpled wax paper, cellophane "excelsior" or unseasoned popcorn. For long-distance shipping, pack cookies in a metal canister and cushion it in the box.
– Wrap cookies individually in plastic food wrap or, if flat, in pairs back to back. Tape each packet shut.
– Layer cookies in rows, always putting heaviest cookies on the bottom. Before adding a second layer, fill all holes and crevices with unseasoned popcorn. Add a cushioning layer of paper toweling (several thicknesses), then another layer of cookies. You'll have better luck if you don't try to send more than two or three layers of cookies.
– Cover top layer with crushed wax paper or paper toweling.
– Tape box shut, wrap in heavy paper and tie securely in several places.
– Print address clearly and mark package "fragile."
– If cookies are to be shipped great distances, use air parcel post.

About Decorating Cookies

Cookies can be decorated either before or after baking. Simple, sprinkled, or pressed-on designs can be applied before cookies go into the oven, but intricate designs, whether painted or piped on, are best done after baking.

To Decorate Before Baking:

Most Suitable Cookies: Simple, relatively flat cookies: dropped or rolled cookies, molded or cookie press cookies, refrigerator or commercial slice-and-bake cookies.

Sprinkle-On Decorations: Brush unbaked cookies with milk, cream, or lightly beaten egg white and sprinkle with colored sugar or coconut, silver *dragées*, chocolate jimmies, decorettes, finely chopped nuts or candied fruit, cinnamon sugar (supermarket shelves are loaded with jiffy decorator items). Brush any spilled sugar or decoration from baking sheet, then bake as directed. For an extra-special touch, cut paper stencils out of heavy paper—bells, stars, initials—and color cut-out areas only.

Press-On Decorations: Brush unbaked cookies with milk or cream and press on raisins, dried currants, candied cherries, nuts, chocolate or butterscotch bits, mini-marshmallows, gumdrops, cinnamon "red hots" in desired designs.

Paint-On Decorations: These are best for light-colored rolled cookies. Make an egg paint by mixing 1 egg yolk with ¼ teaspoon cold water and 2 or 3 drops food coloring (this amount will be enough for 1 or 2 colors). Using fresh new paintbrushes, paint simple designs on unbaked cookies, then bake as directed until firm but not brown. If paint thickens on standing, thin with a few drops cold water.

To Decorate After Baking:

Most Suitable Cookies: Large, simple, flat cookies, especially rolled cookies.

Paint-On Decorations: Cool cookies and frost with a smooth, thin layer of Royal Icing. Keep bowl of icing covered with a damp cloth or paper toweling to keep it from hardening while you work. For an absolutely smooth surface, keep dipping knife or spatula in hot water and use long sweeping strokes. Let icing harden thoroughly. Paint on designs, using clean, fresh paintbrushes and paste food colors (liquid colors will soften icing too much).

Pipe-On Decorations: Cool cookies and, if you like, frost with Royal Icing as directed for Paint-On Decorations. Tint small amounts of icing desired colors and put through pastry tubes fitted with plain or decorative tips, tracing outlines of cookies or adding any decorative touches you like. Be sure to keep each container of icing covered with a damp cloth so it won't dry out.

To Make Hanging Cookies (wonderful as Christmas tree decorations):

Most Suitable Cookies: Large decorated rolled cookies, particularly fancy cutouts.

To Attach Hangers to Unbaked Cookies: "Stick" large loops of thin ribbon or thread to backs of unbaked cookies with tiny dabs of dough. Bake as directed, then decorate.

To Attach Hangers to Baked Cookies (good only for those that are not shattery-crisp): While cookies are still warm and pliable, quickly draw lengths of coarse thread through top, using a sturdy needle. Don't insert too close to edge or cookies may break. Allow 6"–8" thread for each cookie so it can easily be hung. Decorate as desired.

How to Dress Up Commercial Slice-and-Bake Cookies

The rolls of refrigerator cookie dough in supermarket coolers needn't just be sliced and baked. You can mix the flavors (as in Bullseyes and Checkerboards), roll the dough into balls or bake into chewy bars. You can crown the cookies with frosting or sandwich them together with cream fillings. Here are some quickies to try. (All, incidentally, are easy enough for children to make.)

Bullseyes: Take 1 light and 1 dark roll refrigerated slice-and-bake cookie dough and slice each ¼" thick (some good combinations: sugar cookie and chocolate or butterscotch, butterscotch and chocolate). Cut center from each slice with a 1½" round cutter, then remove small circles from the "centers" with a 1" round cutter. Reassemble cookies, mixing dark and light to form bullseyes. Lift to ungreased baking sheets with a pancake turner and bake 6–8 minutes at 375° F. until just firm. Cool 1 minute on sheets before transferring to wire racks to cool.

Checkerboards: Take 1 light and 1 dark roll refrigerated slice-and-bake cookie dough and quarter each lengthwise. Roll slightly with hands to round edges of each quarter. Reassemble rolls, checkerboard style as shown, and press lightly together.

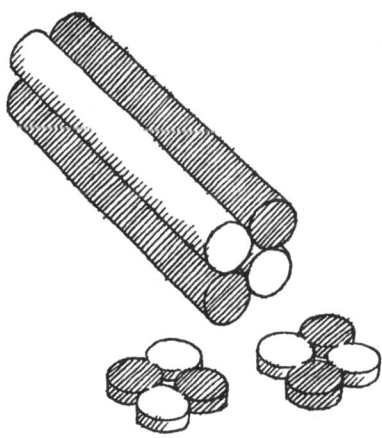

Slice ¼" thick, bake and cool by package directions.

Cutouts: Slice 1 roll sugar or coconut cookie dough ¼" thick. With tiny decorative cutters (truffle cutters are perfect), cut out centers of half the slices (save scraps, pinch together, and use for Nut Balls). Bake all and cool by package directions. Sandwich plain and cut-out rounds together with any frosting, jelly or preserves, marshmallow cream or bottled ice-cream sundae topping.

Nut Balls: Slice 1 roll any flavor slice-and-bake cookie dough ¼" thick and shape each slice into a small ball; roll in finely chopped nuts. Arrange 1" apart on ungreased baking sheets and flatten slightly; top each with a nut half. Bake about 8 minutes at 375° F. until pale tan. Cool 1 minute on sheets, then transfer to wire racks.

Coconut Balls: Prepare like Nut Balls, substituting flaked coconut for nuts.

Snow-Capped Fudgies: Slice 1 roll chocolate slice-and-bake cookie dough ¼" thick and bake as package directs—but only for 5 minutes. Top each cookie with 5–6 miniature marshmallows, grouping them close together. Bake 2–3 minutes longer until marshmallows are lightly browned and slightly melted. Cool on wire racks.

Quick Marguerites: Slice and bake 1 roll sugar cookie dough as directed; cool cookies and spread with peach, apricot, or berry preserves; top with marshmallow cream and serve. Or, if you prefer, top cookies with preserves, then miniature marshmallows and return to oven 2–3 minutes to brown lightly.

Butterscotch or Chocolate Dot Cookies: Slice 1 roll sugar cookie, butterscotch, or chocolate cookie dough ¼" thick, arrange on baking sheets and lightly press 10–12 butterscotch, semisweet, or milk chocolate bits onto each cookie. Bake and cool as directed.

Coconut or Raisin Cookies: Slice 1 roll sugar cookie, coconut, or butterscotch cookie dough ¼" thick and bake 5 minutes. Sprinkle each cookie with 1–2 teaspoons flaked coconut or dot with seedless raisins and press in lightly. Bake 2–3 minutes longer until cookies are pale tan. Cool as package directs.

Cherry Twinks: Slice 1 roll sugar or coconut cookie dough ¼" thick and shape around well-drained maraschino cherries (you'll need 2 slices for each cherry). Bake on ungreased sheets about 8 minutes at 375° F. until light tan. Cool cookies on wire racks, then dip tops in vanilla frosting mix, prepared by package directions.

VARIATION:

Prepare as directed, substituting ½ dried fig, pitted date, or prune for each cherry.

Chocolate-Nut Thins (delightful thin bars): Halve 1 roll sugar or coconut cookie dough crosswise, then slice each piece *lengthwise* ¼" thick. Arrange 2 rows of 8 slices on an ungreased baking sheet, allowing ¼" between slices (this will be only half the slices). Bake 8 minutes at 375° F. Remove from oven, and while still on baking sheet, spread with 2 (1½-ounce) bars melted milk chocolate or ½ (5¾-ounce) package melted milk chocolate bits and sprinkle with ⅓ cup minced pecans, walnuts, or blanched almonds. Cool on sheet 15 minutes, then halve each slice crosswise. Bake and frost remaining slices the same way.

Coconut-Chip Chews: Slice 1 roll chocolate chip slice-and-bake cookie dough 1" thick and quarter each piece; space evenly over bottom of an ungreased 9"×9"×2" baking pan. Bake 5 minutes at 375° F., remove from oven, and spread partially baked pieces lightly to make an even layer. Cover with 2 cups flaked coconut mixed with 1 lightly beaten egg. Bake 25 minutes longer until coconut is delicately browned. Cool upright in pan on a rack about 15 minutes and cut into bars.

Chewy Slice-and-Bake Bars: Slice 1 roll any flavor slice-and-bake cookie dough 1" thick and quarter each piece; space evenly over the bottom of an ungreased 9"×9"×2" baking pan and bake 5 minutes at 375° F. Remove from oven and spread partially baked pieces, making an even layer. Bake 15–20 minutes longer until top is just firm and mixture pulls slightly from edges of pan. Cool upright in pan on a wire rack 15 minutes, then cut into bars.

Streusel-Topped Bars: Prepare Chewy Slice-and-Bake Bars (above) through point of spreading partially baked dough into a single layer. For *streusel* topping: Mix ⅓ cup each sifted flour and firmly packed light brown sugar, then cut in 3 tablespoons butter with a pastry blender until the size of small peas. Scatter mixture evenly over bars and proceed as directed.

Praline Bars: Using nut or butterscotch cookie dough, prepare Chewy Slice-and-Bake Bars (above) through point of spreading partially baked dough into a single layer. Quickly cream ¼ cup softened butter and ½ cup firmly packed light or dark brown sugar, dot evenly over all, and sprinkle with 1 cup finely chopped pecans. Proceed as directed.

✠ ¢ BASIC COOKIE MIX

A good mix to have on hand because there are ten different quick cookies you can make from it.
Makes about 9 cups

4 cups sifted flour
4 cups sugar
1½ cups nonfat dry milk powder
1½ tablespoons baking powder
1½ teaspoons salt

Place all ingredients in a large bowl and mix well with a spoon; sift mixture twice. Store in a tightly covered container. Keeps several weeks at room temperature.

10 Quick Cookies to Make from the Basic Mix

Sugar Cookies (Makes 3 dozen): With a spoon, mix 2 cups Basic Cookie Mix, ½ cup melted butter or margarine, 1 lightly beaten egg, and 1 teaspoon vanilla. Lightly flour hands and shape in 1″ balls; arrange 2″ apart on well-greased baking sheets. Bake 12–15 minutes at 350° F. until golden. Cool 1–2 minutes on sheets, then transfer to wire racks to cool. About 60 calories per cookie.

Raisin Cookies (Makes 3 dozen): Prepare Sugar Cookie dough as directed, mix in ½ cup seedless raisins or sultanas, shape and bake as directed. About 70 calories per cookie.

Coconut Cookies (Makes 3 dozen): Prepare Sugar Cookie dough as directed, mix in ½ cup flaked coconut, shape and bake as directed. About 65 calories per cookie.

Chocolate Chip Cookies (Makes 3 dozen): Prepare Sugar Cookie dough as directed, mix in ½ cup semisweet chocolate bits, shape and bake as directed. About 70 calories per cookie.

Nut Cookies (Makes 3 dozen): Prepare Sugar Cookie dough as directed, mix in ½ cup chopped walnuts, pecans, or blanched almonds, shape and bake as directed. About 70 calories per cookie.

Spice Drops (Makes 3 dozen): Mix 2 cups Basic Cookie Mix with 1 teaspoon cinnamon, ¼ teaspoon each ginger and allspice, and ⅛ teaspoon nutmeg. Stir in 1 lightly beaten egg, ½ cup melted butter or margarine, and 1–2 tablespoons water, just enough to make mixture a good consistency for dropping from a spoon. Drop from a teaspoon onto well-greased baking sheets, spacing cookies 2″ apart, and bake 12–15 minutes at 350° F. until golden. Cool 1–2 minutes on sheets, then transfer to wire racks to cool. About 60 calories per cookie.

Chocolate Drops (Makes 3 dozen): Mix 2 cups Basic Cookie Mix with ¼ cup sifted cocoa. Stir in 1 lightly beaten egg, ½ cup melted butter, ¼ cup water, and 1 teaspoon vanilla. Drop from a teaspoon onto well-greased baking sheets, spacing cookies 2″ apart, and bake 12–15 minutes at 350° F. until lightly browned around edges. Let cool 1–2 minutes on sheets, then lift to wire racks to cool. About 70 calories per cookie.

Peanut Butter Balls (Makes 3 dozen): Mix 2 cups Basic Cookie Mix with 1 lightly beaten egg, ¼ cup melted butter or margarine, ½ cup crunchy or creamy peanut butter, and 1 teaspoon vanilla. With lightly floured hands, shape into 1″ balls and space 2″ apart on lightly greased baking sheets. Bake 12 minutes at 350° F. or until the color of sand. Transfer to wire racks to cool. About 70 calories per cookie.

Brownies (Makes 16): With a spoon mix 2 cups Basic Cookie Mix, 1 lightly beaten egg, ⅓ cup each cold water and melted butter or margarine, 1 teaspoon vanilla, and 2

(1-ounce) envelopes no-melt unsweetened chocolate or ¼ cup sifted cocoa. Fold in ½–¾ cup chopped pecans or walnuts. Beat by hand 1 minute, spoon into a greased 9"×9"×2" baking pan, and bake 25 minutes at 375° F. or until top springs back when touched. Cool upright in pan on rack, then cut into large squares. About 150 calories per brownie.

Oatmeal Bars (Makes 32): With a spoon mix 2 cups Basic Cookie Mix, 1½ cups uncooked quick-cooking oatmeal, 1 lightly beaten egg, ¾ cup melted butter or margarine, ¼ cup cold water, 1 teaspoon vanilla, and ½ teaspoon almond extract. Spoon into a greased 13"×9"×2" baking pan and bake 30–35 minutes at 350° F. until top is golden and sides shrink slightly from sides of pan. Cool upright in pan 10 minutes, then cut into small bars. About 120 calories per bar.

DROP COOKIES

These are old favorites because they're so quick to mix and bake. They can be plain or studded with nuts, chocolate, or fruit; they can be crisp or chewy, thick or thin, rich or slimming (well, at least fairly low in calories). Best of all, they do not have to be rolled or shaped or pushed through a cookie press—simply dropped from a spoon and popped in the oven.

Some Tips:
– To minimize spreading during baking, chill dough slightly, then mound in center when dropping onto cookie sheets.
– Space cookies on sheets carefully, remembering that the thinner the dough, the more the cookies will spread (recipes specify just how much room to leave between cookies).
– For more interesting or uniform size cookies, put dough through a pastry bag fitted with a large, plain round tube, piping directly onto baking sheets. Cookies without nuts, fruit, or other obstructive bits can be pressed through a large open star tip. (*Note:* Don't fill pastry bag more than ⅔ full because the heat of your hands will soften the dough and make cookies spread more than usual.)

✷ CREAM CHEESE FLAKES

Being egg-free, these cookies are good for those with an allergy to eggs.
Makes 5 dozen

1 cup butter or margarine
1 (3-ounce) package cream cheese, softened to room temperature
1 cup sugar
½ teaspoon salt
1 tablespoon light cream or milk
1 tablespoon finely grated lemon or orange rind
2½ cups sifted flour

Preheat oven to 350° F. Cream butter and cheese, add sugar and salt, and continue creaming until light and fluffy. Add cream and lemon rind; slowly blend in flour. Drop from a teaspoon onto ungreased baking sheets, spacing cookies 2" apart; flatten cookies slightly and bake 15 minutes until lightly ringed with brown. Transfer at once to wire racks to cool. About 60 calories per cookie.

⊠ LEMON WAFERS

Nice and tart.
Makes about 4½ dozen

½ cup butter or margarine, softened to room temperature
1⅓ cups sugar
3 eggs
3 tablespoons lemon juice
Grated rind of 1 lemon
2 cups unsifted flour
¼ teaspoon mace
¼ teaspoon salt

Preheat oven to 375° F. Cream butter until light and fluffy, then beat in sugar. Mix in eggs, one at a time, beating well after each addition. Stir in lemon juice and rind; mix in flour, mace, and salt. Drop from a teaspoon onto lightly greased baking sheets, spacing cookies 2" apart. Bake about 15 minutes until cookies are lightly ringed with brown. While still warm, transfer to wire racks to cool. About 55 calories per cookie.

⊠ ¢ BROWN SUGAR DROPS

Try the variations as well as the basic recipe.
Makes 6 dozen

3½ cups sifted flour
1 teaspoon baking soda
1 teaspoon salt
1 cup butter or margarine or ½ cup each vegetable shortening and butter, softened to room temperature
2 cups firmly packed light or dark brown sugar
2 eggs
½ cup sour milk or buttermilk
2 teaspoons maple flavoring (optional)

Preheat oven to 400° F. Sift flour with soda and salt and set aside. With a rotary beater or electric mixer cream butter, sugar, and eggs until well blended. Mix in sour milk and maple flavoring. Slowly mix in dry ingredients. Drop by rounded teaspoonfuls 2" apart on greased baking sheets and bake 8–10 minutes until nearly firm (cookie should barely retain fingerprint when lightly touched). Transfer cookies to wire racks to cool. About 70 calories per cookie.

VARIATIONS:

Coconut Drops: Prepare as directed, mixing 1½ cups flaked coconut into dough at the end. Bake as above. About 80 calories per cookie.

Filled Brown Sugar Drops: Prepare as directed and drop by level teaspoonfuls; make a thumbprint or small well in center of each cookie and fill with dabs of jam, marmalade, peanut butter, or Fig Filling. Cover with a dab of cookie dough and bake 10–12 minutes. About 100 calories per cookie.

Hermits (Makes about 8 dozen): Prepare as directed but substitute ½ cup cold coffee for the sour milk. Mix 1½ teaspoons cinnamon and ½ teaspoon nutmeg into dough, then 1½ cups minced walnuts or pecans and 2 cups chopped seedless raisins. Bake as directed. About 80 calories per cookie.

Rocks (Makes 8 dozen): Prepare as directed, then stir in 2 cups seedless or sultana raisins, 1½ teaspoons nutmeg, and ½ cup finely chopped candied citron. Bake as directed. About 80 calories per cookie.

Fruit Drops (Makes 8 dozen): Prepare as directed, then stir in 2 cups of any of the following: dried currants, minced dates, prunes, dried apricots or figs, candied cherries, or mixed candied fruits. Bake as directed. About 80 calories per cookie.

COOKIE CHART*
OR WHICH COOKIE RECIPES TO

	Halve	Double	Let Children Try	Pack and Ship
Drop Cookies:				
Applesauce Cookies		X	X	
Benne Wafers	X			
Brandy Snaps		X		
Brown Sugar Drops	X		X	X
Carrot Cookies		X		X
Chocolate Drops			X	X
Chocolate Macaroons	X			X
Chocolate Pecan Wafers				X
Coconut Discs		X	X	X
Coconut Drops	X		X	X
Cream Cheese Flakes	X			
Dropped Oatmeal Chippies	X	X	X	X
Filled Brown Sugar Drops	X		X	
Florentines		X		
Fruit Drops	X		X	X
Hermits	X		X	X
Maude's Cookies		X	X	X
Mincemeat Discs		X	X	X
Mincemeat Hermits	X		X	X
Old-Fashioned Ginger Biscuits		X	X	X
Orange-Almond Lace Cookies	X			
Pecan Crisps	X	X	X	X
Rocks	X		X	X
Spice Drops			X	X
Sugarless Oatmeal Drops	X	X		
Sugar Pillows	X		X	X
Toll House Cookies		X	X	X
Rolled Cookies:				
Butterscotch Sugar Cookies	X			
Chocolate Sugar Cookies	X			
Coconut Sugar Cookies	X			
Decorative Cookies	X		X	
Fig Newtons	X			X
Gingerbread Boys	X	X	X	
Golden Cheddar Rings	X			
Moravian Christmas Cookies	X			
Nut Sugar Cookies	X			
Pepparkakor	X		X	

*Those cookies not listed are not very well suited to any category.

COOKIE CHART
OR WHICH COOKIE RECIPES TO (continued)

	Halve	Double	Let Children Try	Pack and Ship
Rolled Cookies (continued)				
Soft Sugar Cookies	X			
Spitzbuben	X			
Springerle	X			
Sugar Cookies	X			
Molded or Pressed Cookies:				
Almond Butterballs	X	X		X
Butterballs	X	X		X
Chocolate Chip Cookies			X	X
Chocolate Spritz	X		X	X
Coconut Butterballs	X			
Coconut Cookies			X	X
Nut Cookies			X	X
Old-Fashioned Butter "S" Cookies	X			
Orange-Almond Balls			X	X
Peanut Butter Balls			X	X
Peanut Butter Cookies	X		X	X
Pressed Molasses Spice Cookies			X	X
Raisin Cookies			X	X
Snickerdoodles	X		X	X
Spritz	X		X	X
Sugar Marbles			X	X
Thumbprint Cookies	X	X		X
Refrigerator Cookies:				
Almond-Orange Icebox Cookies		X		X
Basic Refrigerator Cookies		X		X
Chocolate Checkerboards		X		X
Chocolate Refrigerator Cookies		X		X
Fig and Almond Pinwheels				X
Filled Refrigerator Cookies		X		
Nut Refrigerator Cookies		X		X
Oatmeal Icebox Cookies		X		X
Orange-Chocolate Jewels				X
Bars:				
Apple-Oatmeal Bars				X
Basic Brownies		X	X	X
Black Walnut and Coconut Bars				X
Brownies			X	X
Brown Sugar Brownies		X	X	X
Butterscotch Brownies		X	X	X
Chewy Pecan-Cinnamon Bars				X
Coconut Brownies		X	X	X

COOKIE CHART
OR WHICH COOKIE RECIPES TO (continued)

	Halve	Double	Let Children Try	Pack and Ship
Bars (continued)				
Coconut Topped Brownies		X		X
Congo Squares			X	X
Currant and Raisin Bars				X
Date-Oatmeal Bars				X
Fig-Oatmeal Bars				X
Fruit Bars				X
Fruit and Nut Bars				X
Fudgey Saucepan Brownies			X	X
German Date Squares				X
Layered Apricot Bars				X
Marble Brownies				X
Minted Double Chocolate Tea Brownies		X		X
Mocha Brownies		X		X
Oatmeal Bars			X	X
Scottish Shortbread	X			X
Snowy Coconut Chews		X	X	X
Toll House Brownies		X	X	X
Two-Tone Brownies				X
Wheat and Milk-Free Brownies			X	X
No-Bake Cookies:				
Butterscotch Haystacks		X	X	X
Chocolate Haystacks		X	X	X
Fruit Balls	X	X	X	X
Fudge Nuggets			X	X
No-Bake Chocolate Bon-Bons	X	X	X	X
No-Bake Rum Balls	X	X		X
Peanut Butter Bars			X	X
Porcupines	X		X	X

Note: All of the suggestions given in How to Dress Up Commercial Slice-and-Bake Cookies are easy enough for children to do.

⊠ TOLL HOUSE COOKIES

Makes about 4 dozen

1 cup plus 2 tablespoons sifted flour
½ teaspoon baking soda
½ teaspoon salt
½ cup butter or vegetable shortening, softened to room temperature
⅓ cup plus 1 tablespoon sugar
⅓ cup plus 1 tablespoon firmly packed light brown sugar
1 teaspoon vanilla
1 egg
1 (6-ounce) package semisweet chocolate bits
½ cup coarsely chopped pecans

Preheat oven to 375° F. Sift flour with baking soda and salt and set aside. Cream butter, sugars, and vanilla until light and fluffy. Beat in egg. Mix in dry ingredients; stir in chocolate bits and pecans. Drop by well-rounded ½ teaspoonfuls on lightly greased baking sheets, spacing cookies 2″ apart. Bake 10–12 minutes until lightly edged with brown. Transfer immediately to wire racks to cool. About 65 calories per cookie.

⊠ PECAN CRISPS

Rather like a praline cookie.
Makes about 5 dozen

1 cup butter (no substitute)
1 (1-pound) box light brown sugar
2 eggs
2½ cups unsifted flour
½ teaspoon baking soda
½ teaspoon salt
1 teaspoon vanilla
1½ cups coarsely chopped pecans

Preheat oven to 350° F. Cream butter until light, add sugar, and continue creaming until fluffy. Beat in eggs, one at a time. Mix in flour, soda, and salt, then remaining ingredients. Drop from a teaspoon onto lightly greased baking sheets, spacing cookies about 2″ apart, and bake 12–15 minutes until lightly browned. Remove at once to wire racks to cool. About 100 calories per cookie.

⚖ ⊠ MAUDE'S COOKIES

A centuries-old Quaker recipe. The cookies are buttery and bland but the crystallized ginger decoration adds bite. Moreover, they are fairly low-calorie.

Makes 3½–4 dozen small cookies

½ cup butter (no substitute), softened to room temperature
⅓ cup sugar
1 egg, well beaten
¾ cup sifted flour
½ teaspoon vanilla
3½–4 dozen pieces crystallized ginger about the size of raisins

Preheat oven to 350° F. Cream butter until fluffy, add sugar, and continue creaming until light. Beat in egg, then mix in flour and vanilla. Drop from a half teaspoon onto *lightly* greased baking sheets, spacing cookies 2″ apart—they spread quite a bit. Press a piece of candied ginger into the center of each cookie and bake 8–10 minutes until ringed with tan. Transfer at once to wire racks to cool. About 35 calories per cookie.

FROSTED ORANGE DROPS

Makes about 4 dozen

½ cup vegetable shortening
1 cup sugar
½ teaspoon salt
4 egg yolks
1 tablespoon finely grated orange rind
½ cup orange juice
2½ cups sifted flour
1½ teaspoons baking powder
½ cup coarsely chopped black walnuts

Frosting:
1 tablespoon butter or margarine
1 tablespoon orange juice
1 teaspoon finely grated orange rind
1 cup sifted confectioners' sugar
¼ teaspoon salt

Preheat oven to 375° F. Cream shortening with sugar, salt, and egg yolks until light; mix in orange rind and juice. Sift flour with baking powder, and stir into creamed mixture; mix in nuts. Drop from a teaspoon onto greased baking sheets, spacing 2" apart. Bake 12–15 minutes until touched with brown. Meanwhile, prepare frosting: Cream butter, orange juice, and rind until light, stir in confectioners' sugar and salt, and beat until smooth. Cool cookies slightly on wire racks, then frost. About 80 calories per cookie.

CHOCOLATE PECAN WAFERS

Dark and chewy.
Makes 4 dozen

½ cup butter or margarine
1 cup sugar
¼ teaspoon salt
1 teaspoon vanilla
2 eggs
¾ cup sifted flour
4 (1-ounce) squares semisweet chocolate, melted
¾ cup finely chopped pecans

Cream butter, sugar and salt until light and fluffy, add vanilla and eggs, and beat well. Slowly mix in flour and remaining ingredients. Chill mixture in bowl ½ hour. Meanwhile, preheat oven to 350° F. Drop by rounded teaspoonfuls 2" apart on greased baking sheets and flatten with bottom of a glass dipped in sugar (resugar glass for each cookie). Bake 15 minutes until tops retain almost no impression when touched. Transfer immediately to wire racks to cool. About 65 calories per cookie.

BENNE WAFERS

In the South, sesame seeds are called "benne." This recipe is a Charleston favorite.
Makes about 4 dozen

1 cup sifted flour
¼ teaspoon salt
½ teaspoon baking powder
2 cups firmly packed dark brown sugar
½ cup butter or margarine
2 eggs, lightly beaten
1 teaspoon vanilla
⅔ cup toasted sesame seeds

Preheat oven to 325° F. Sift flour with salt and baking powder and set aside. Cream sugar and butter until thoroughly mixed; beat in eggs and vanilla. Slowly mix in flour, then sesame seeds, mixing just to blend. Drop mixture by level teaspoonfuls 5" apart on well-greased baking sheets. Bake 10 minutes until lightly browned; cool on sheets about ½ minute, then lift to wire racks with a pancake turner. Store airtight when cool. About 80 calories per cookie.

⚖ ¢ CARROT COOKIES

A cookie somewhat more nutritious than most.
Makes about 5 dozen

½ cup butter or margarine
1 cup sugar
1 cup cooled, mashed, cooked carrots (unseasoned)
1 egg
½ teaspoon vanilla
½ teaspoon cinnamon
¼ teaspoon ginger
¼ teaspoon allspice
1 tablespoon finely grated orange rind
2 cups sifted flour

2 teaspoons baking powder
¼ teaspoon salt

Preheat oven to 350° F. Cream butter until fluffy; add sugar gradually, beating well after each addition. Mix in carrots, egg, vanilla, spices, and orange rind. Sift flour with baking powder and salt and beat in gradually. Drop from a teaspoon 1½" apart onto lightly greased baking sheets and bake 12–15 minutes until firm but not brown. Let cool about 1 minute on baking sheets, then transfer to wire racks to cool. About 40 calories per cookie.

PUMPKIN COOKIES

Because the cookies are made with pumpkin, raisins, and nuts, they provide a little more than just "empty calories."
Makes 4 dozen

2 cups sifted flour
1 teaspoon baking soda
¼ teaspoon salt
1 teaspoon cinnamon
¼ teaspoon nutmeg
½ cup butter or margarine
1 cup sugar
1 teaspoon vanilla
1 cup canned pumpkin
1 cup seedless raisins
1 cup chopped pecans or walnuts

Preheat oven to 375° F. Sift flour with soda, salt, and spices and set aside. Cream butter with sugar until light, add vanilla and pumpkin, and mix well. Slowly add dry ingredients, then stir in raisins and nuts. Drop by rounded teaspoonfuls 2" apart on greased baking sheets and bake 15 minutes until lightly browned. Transfer to wire racks to cool. About 95 calories per cookie.

◨ COCONUT DISCS

Try making these cookies with freshly grated coconut instead of canned flaked coconut. They will taste nuttier and not quite so sweet.
Makes 2 dozen

2 tablespoons butter or margarine, softened to room temperature
½ cup sugar
1 egg, lightly beaten
¼ teaspoon almond extract
1 cup packaged biscuit mix
2 tablespoons milk
⅔ cup flaked coconut

Preheat oven to 375° F. Mix butter with sugar, egg, and almond extract. Add biscuit mix and milk and blend until smooth. Stir in coconut. Drop by rounded teaspoonfuls 2" apart on greased baking sheets and bake 10 minutes until lightly browned. Transfer to wire racks to cool. About 70 calories per cookie.

VARIATION:

Mincemeat Discs (Makes 2 dozen): Substitute firmly packed light brown sugar for the granulated, omit almond extract, milk, and coconut. Prepare as directed, blending in ⅔ cup mincemeat at the end. Drop and bake as directed. About 85 calories per cookie.

◨ APPLESAUCE COOKIES

If you like caraway seeds, by all means stir them into the cookie dough. They give the cookies quite a different flavor.
Makes 2½ dozen

2 tablespoons butter or margarine, softened to room temperature
½ cup sugar
1 egg, lightly beaten
1 cup packaged biscuit mix
½ cup applesauce
1 teaspoon finely grated lemon rind
1½ teaspoons caraway seeds (optional)

Preheat oven to 375° F. Cream butter well with sugar and egg; mix in remaining ingredients until smooth. Drop from a teaspoon 2″ apart on well-greased baking sheets and bake 8 minutes until golden around the edges. Transfer at once to wire racks to cool. (*Note:* Since these cookies brown nicely on the underside but not on top, they're more attractive served bottom side up.) About 50 calories per cookie.

OLD-FASHIONED GINGER BISCUITS

For crisp cookies, store airtight; for softer ones, store loosely covered. To crispen again in humid weather, heat 3–5 minutes at 350° F., then cool.
Makes 4½ dozen

2 cups sifted flour
½ teaspoon salt
2 teaspoons ginger
½ teaspoon cloves
2 teaspoons baking soda
¾ cup butter or margarine
1¼ cups sugar
1 egg, lightly beaten
¼ cup molasses

Preheat oven to 350° F. Sift flour with salt, spices, and baking soda and set aside. Cream butter and sugar until light and fluffy. Add egg and molasses, beating well after each addition. Mix in dry ingredients just until blended. Drop by rounded teaspoonfuls 3″ apart on greased baking sheets and bake 15 minutes until golden brown. (*Note:* Keep unused dough chilled until ready to bake.) Cool cookies on sheets 1–2 minutes, then transfer to wire racks to cool. About 60 calories per cookie.

▣ DROPPED OATMEAL CHIPPIES

Makes 3½ dozen

1 cup sifted flour
2 teaspoons baking powder
½ teaspoon salt
½ cup butter or margarine, softened to room temperature
1 cup firmly packed light brown sugar
1½ cups uncooked quick-cooking oatmeal
2 eggs, lightly beaten
1 teaspoon vanilla
1 cup chopped pitted dates or seedless raisins

Preheat oven to 350° F. Sift flour with baking powder and salt. Stir butter and sugar together until just mixed; blend in flour, oatmeal, eggs, and vanilla. Stir in dates. Drop by rounded teaspoonfuls 2″ apart on greased baking sheets and bake 15–18 minutes until lightly browned and tops spring back when touched. Transfer at once to wire racks to cool. About 75 calories per cookie.

⚖ ▣ SUGARLESS OATMEAL DROPS

Makes 2½ dozen

1 cup sifted flour
2 teaspoons baking powder
¼ teaspoon salt
½ cup butter or margarine, softened to room temperature
1 cup low-calorie granulated sugar substitute
2 eggs, lightly beaten
1½ teaspoons vanilla
1⅓ cups uncooked oatmeal
½ teaspoon cinnamon (optional)

Preheat oven to 350° F. Sift flour with baking powder and salt. Cream butter until light and blend in sugar substitute. Mix in remaining ingredients. Drop by level teaspoonfuls 1″ apart on greased baking sheets and bake 15 minutes or until edges are lightly browned and cookies just firm to the touch. Transfer to wire racks to cool. About 50 calories per cookie.

⚔ ⊠ MONTROSE DROP CAKES

These little rose-flavored Scottish cakes are usually baked in tiny tart tins, but they can be dropped from a spoon directly onto baking sheets. Because the cakes are so small, they are fairly low-calorie. Rose water, used to flavor these cookies, is available at specialty food shops.

Makes about 5 dozen

½ cup butter (no substitute)
⅔ cup sugar
3 eggs
1 tablespoon brandy
1 teaspoon rose water
¼ teaspoon nutmeg
1 cup sifted flour
½ teaspoon baking powder
¼ teaspoon salt
⅔ cup dried currants

Preheat oven to 375° F. Cream butter until fluffy, add sugar gradually, beating well after each addition. Beat in eggs, one at a time, then brandy, rose water, and nutmeg. Sift flour with baking powder and salt and mix in a little bit at a time. Stir in currants. Drop from a teaspoon onto greased baking sheets, spacing cookies 3″ apart. Bake 8–10 minutes until ringed with tan. Let cool on baking sheets about 1 minute, then transfer to wire racks to cool. About 40 calories per cookie.

⚔ MACAROONS

These cookies are milk- and wheat-free, good for anyone with those specific allergies.

Makes about 4½ dozen

1 (½-pound) can almond paste
3 egg whites
1 cup sugar
½ cup sifted confectioners' sugar

Preheat oven to 300° F. Using a sharp knife, slice almond paste ¼″ thick, then chop until the consistency of coarse meal. Place in a large mixing bowl, add egg whites, and mix using your hands. Knead in the sugar, a little bit at a time, then work in the confectioners' sugar until smooth. Line 2 baking sheets with heavy brown paper, then drop macaroons onto paper from a teaspoon, making each about 1″ in diameter and spacing about 2″ apart. Bake on lowest oven shelf 25–30 minutes until crazed and faintly tan. Remove from oven and let cool on paper to room temperature. Dampen paper by setting on top of moist towels, then peel off macaroons. Let cookies dry on wire racks at room temperature 1 hour, then store airtight. About 45 calories per cookie.

⚔ CHOCOLATE "MACAROONS"

Makes 4 dozen

4 egg whites
2 cups sifted confectioners' sugar
2 cups fine vanilla wafer crumbs
2 (1-ounce) squares semisweet chocolate, grated
1½ teaspoons cinnamon

Preheat oven to 325° F. Beat egg whites until foamy, slowly add confectioners' sugar, and continue beating until firm peaks form. Stir in crumbs, chocolate, and cinnamon. Drop by level teaspoonfuls 2″ apart on well-greased baking sheets and bake 20 minutes. Transfer at once to wire racks to cool. About 40 calories per cookie.

COCONUT MACAROONS

Makes about 3 dozen

4 egg whites
¼ teaspoon salt
¾ teaspoon vanilla
¼ teaspoon almond extract
1⅓ cups sugar
2 (3½-ounce) cans flaked coconut

Preheat oven to 325° F. Beat egg whites with salt, vanilla, and almond extract until soft peaks form. Add sugar gradually, about 2 tablespoons at a time, and continue beating until stiff peaks form. Fold in coconut. Drop by rounded teaspoonfuls onto greased baking sheets, spacing cookies about 2" apart. Bake 18–20 minutes until very delicately browned and firm to the touch. Cool briefly on sheets (just until macaroons can be lifted without losing their shape), then transfer to wire racks to cool. About 60 calories per cookie.

⚔ MERINGUE KISSES

It's said that Marie Antoinette loved meringue kisses so she often made them herself. If you've never made them, see Ground Rules for Making Meringue in the chapter on pies and pastries before beginning this recipe.

Makes about 3½ dozen

4 egg whites, at room temperature
¼ teaspoon salt
¼ teaspoon cream of tartar
1 cup sugar
¾ teaspoon vanilla or ¼ teaspoon almond extract
1 or 2 drops red or green food coloring (optional)

Preheat oven to 250° F. Line baking sheets with foil. Beat egg whites with a rotary beater or electric mixer at moderate speed until foamy; stir in salt and cream of tartar. Add sugar, 1 tablespoon at a time, beating well after each addition. Add vanilla and food coloring, if you wish, to tint meringue a pastel color. Beat hard at highest mixer speed until meringue is glossy and forms peaks that stand straight up when beater is withdrawn. Drop by rounded teaspoonfuls 2" apart on prepared baking sheets; leave surface peaked or smooth into rounded caps. If you prefer, pipe meringue through a pastry bag fitted with a medium-size plain or star tip making each kiss about 1½" in diameter. Bake 35–45 minutes until creamy-white and firm. For crisp kisses: Turn off oven and let kisses cool in oven 2–3 hours without opening door. For chewier kisses, lift foil and kisses to wire rack and cool. Peel kisses from foil, using a spatula to help loosen them if necessary. Store airtight. About 20 calories per cookie.

VARIATIONS: (With the exception of Filled Kisses and Rainbow Kisses, all are low-calorie.)
Frosted Kisses: Dip tops of baked, cooled kisses in Chocolate or Fudge Frosting; let dry on wire racks. About 30 calories per cookie.
Filled Kisses: Sandwich 2 kisses together with a favorite filling or frosting. Recipe too flexible for a meaningful calorie count.
Rainbow Kisses: Before baking, divide meringue into 3 equal parts and tint pastel yellow, green, and pink. Bake as directed and cool. Sandwich different colors together with plain or tinted sweetened whipped cream. About 65 calories per cookie.
Meringue Chews: Preheat oven to 325° F. Prepare kisses as directed, then bake 10–12 minutes until tops are just firm to the touch. Cool on

foil on wire racks. About 20 calories per cookie.

Candied Kisses: Prepare meringue mixture as directed, then fold in ⅔ cup very finely chopped candied fruits or mixed candied red and green cherries; shape and bake as directed. About 30 calories per cookie.

Nut Kisses: Prepare meringue mixture as directed, then fold in 1 cup finely chopped nuts: pecans, walnuts, blanched almonds, filberts, pistachios. Shape, sprinkle tops with a few additional nuts, and bake as directed. About 45 calories per cookie.

Chocolate Kisses: Prepare meringue mixture as directed, then fold in 2 melted and cooled (1-ounce) squares unsweetened or semisweet chocolate, leaving a marbled effect if you like. About 30 calories per cookie.

Coconut Kisses: Prepare meringue mixture as directed, fold in 1½ cups flaked coconut, shape and bake as directed. About 30 calories per cookie.

Brown Sugar Kisses: When making meringue, substitute 1 cup light brown sugar for the granulated and proceed as recipe directs. (*Note:* For especially good flavor, use 1 teaspoon maple flavoring instead of vanilla, or ½ teaspoon each vanilla and maple flavoring.) About 20 calories per cookie.

Coffee Kisses: Prepare meringue mixture as directed, then beat in 1 teaspoon vanilla and 4 teaspoons instant coffee powder dissolved in 1 tablespoon boiling water. Shape and bake as directed, then let stand in turned-off oven at least 4 hours or until crisp and dry. About 25 calories per cookie.

Fruit Kisses: Prepare meringue mixture as directed, then beat in ⅓ cup sieved, *thick* berry preserves (strawberry, raspberry, black raspberry, etc.), adding 1 rounded teaspoonful at a time and beating well after each addition. Omit vanilla and almond extract. Shape and bake 3½ hours at 200° F., then let stand at least 4 hours in turned-off oven. About 30 calories per cookie.

⚖ **HAZELNUT KISSES**

Makes about 5 dozen

2 egg whites
⅛ teaspoon salt
1 cup sifted confectioners' sugar
1 cup finely ground unblanched hazelnuts or filberts
1 (1-ounce) square unsweetened chocolate, grated fine
½ teaspoon cinnamon
¼ teaspoon finely grated lemon rind (optional)
Candied red cherry slices (optional garnish)

Preheat oven to 300° F. Beat egg whites with salt until stiff peaks form; mix in remaining ingredients except cherries and drop from a half teaspoon onto ungreased, foil-lined baking sheets, spacing cookies about 1½" apart. Decorate each, if you like, with a slice of candied cherry. Bake 20 minutes until faintly browned, remove from oven, and cool about 2 minutes before removing from foil. Cool on wire racks. About 25 calories per cookie.

BRANDY SNAPS

Don't attempt these on a wet or humid day; they won't be crisp.
Makes 1½ dozen

¼ cup molasses
¼ cup butter or margarine, softened to room temperature

⅓ cup sugar
½ cup sifted flour
½ teaspoon ginger
1–2 teaspoons brandy

Brandy Cream (optional filling):
½ cup heavy cream
¼ cup sifted confectioners' sugar
1–2 tablespoons brandy

Preheat oven to 325° F. Bring molasses just to a boil over moderate heat, add butter and sugar, and stir until melted. Off heat mix in flour, ginger, and brandy. Stand pan in a bowl of very hot water to keep mixture soft as you work, replenishing hot water as needed. Drop mixture from level teaspoons onto greased baking sheet, spacing 3″ apart. Bake one sheet at a time, 5 minutes in top ⅓ of oven, then 2–3 minutes on middle rack. Cool cookies on sheet about 1 minute or until they can be lifted with a pancake turner; while still warm and pliable, bend into a tube around the handle of a wooden spoon. Cool on wire racks. If cookies harden too soon, return quickly to oven to soften. If you like, fill just before serving with Brandy Cream. To make, whip cream and confectioners' sugar until soft peaks form; fold in brandy. (*Note:* the easiest way to fill cookies is with a pastry bag fitted with a plain or rosette tip.) About 100 calories per cookie if unfilled, about 140 per cookie if filled.

To Serve as Flat Wafers: Let cookies stand a little longer on baking sheets so they won't curl between rack rungs as they cool.

⚖ ORANGE-ALMOND LACE COOKIES

Makes 4 dozen

½ cup butter (*no substitute*)
½ cup sugar
½ teaspoon finely grated orange rind
½ cup ground blanched almonds
2 tablespoons flour
2 tablespoons milk

Preheat oven to 350° F. Mix all ingredients in a saucepan and heat and stir over moderate heat just until mixture bubbles; remove from heat at once. Drop by half teaspoonfuls 4″ apart on ungreased baking sheets (you will only get 4 or 5 cookies on each sheet). Bake 6–7 minutes until golden brown and bubbly. Let stand 1 minute, just until cookies are firm enough to lift off sheet with a pancake turner. Cool on wire racks, then store airtight. About 30 calories per cookie.

To Curl Cookies: As you lift each cookie from baking sheet, curl around handle of wooden spoon to form a cornucopia or "cigarette"; cool seam side down. If cookies cool too quickly to curl, return to oven briefly to soften.

FLORENTINES

Makes 2 dozen

¼ cup butter or margarine
⅓ cup firmly packed light brown sugar
¼ cup sifted flour
¼ cup plus 1 tablespoon heavy cream
¾ cup finely chopped or slivered blanched almonds
⅓ cup minced candied orange peel or mixed candied peel and candied cherries
4 (*1-ounce*) squares semisweet chocolate
3 tablespoons butter or margarine

Preheat oven to 350° F. Cream butter and sugar until light and fluffy. Stir in flour alternately with cream; then stir in almonds and peel. Drop mixture by level teaspoonfuls 3″

apart on greased and floured baking sheets; with a knife dipped in cold water, spread into 2" rounds. Bake about 12 minutes until lacy and golden brown, watching carefully toward the end. Cool 1–2 minutes on sheets, then, using a pancake turner, carefully transfer to wire racks to cool. If cookies cool too much to remove easily, return to oven 1–2 minutes to soften. Melt chocolate and butter together in a double boiler over simmering water, stirring frequently; cool slightly. Arrange cookies flat side up on wax paper and spread with chocolate. When chocolate hardens, store cookies airtight. About 120 calories per cookie.

⚜ LADYFINGERS

If you've never tasted homemade ladyfingers, you don't know what you're missing.
Makes 1½ dozen

3 eggs, separated
⅔ cup sifted confectioners' sugar
½ teaspoon vanilla
Pinch salt
½ cup sifted cake flour

Preheat oven to 325° F. Beat egg yolks until pale lemon colored, slowly add ⅓ cup confectioners' sugar and continue beating until thick and the color of mayonnaise. Beat in vanilla. Beat egg whites until soft peaks form, add salt and 2 tablespoons confectioners' sugar, and continue beating until stiff. Mix flour with remaining confectioners' sugar. Fold egg whites into yolk mixture, about ¼ at a time and alternately with flour, beginning and ending with whites. (*Note:* Sift flour onto yolk mixture for more even distribution and don't try to fold in every speck of egg white each time before adding more.) Spoon mixture into a pastry bag (no tube necessary because the bag opening is the perfect size) and press out evenly but lightly into strips 4" long, spacing them 2" apart on buttered and floured baking sheets. (*Note:* You can shape ladyfingers with 2 tablespoons or simply drop mixture by rounded teaspoonfuls without shaping.) Bake in center or upper ⅓ of oven 12–15 minutes until pale golden. Cool on sheets 1 minute, then, using a wide spatula, transfer to wire racks to cool. Serve as is, sprinkled with confectioners' sugar or sandwiched together with jam, chocolate frosting, or sweetened whipped cream. About 50 calories per cookie.

For a Crisper Crust (nice for Charlotte Russe): Sprinkle ladyfingers with confectioners' sugar just before baking.

¢ ⚜ MADELEINES

Madeleines are spongy little cakes baked in small individual molds. The molds come in sets of a dozen and are available in kitchen departments of large department stores, also at gourmet shops. You'll need two dozen molds for this recipe because the batter is unusually light and must be baked the minute it's mixed.
Makes 2 dozen

2 tablespoons clarified butter*
½ cup sifted cake flour
⅛ teaspoon salt
2 eggs
⅓ cup sugar
½ teaspoon finely grated lemon rind
¼ cup butter (no substitute), melted
Confectioners' sugar

Preheat oven to 350° F. Brush madeleine molds with clarified butter and refrigerate until needed. Sift together flour and salt. Beat eggs until frothy, add sugar, 2 tablespoons at a time, beating well after each addition, then continue beating at high mixer speed until very thick and lemon colored. Fold in flour, ⅓ at a time. Mix lemon rind and butter; fold into batter, 1 tablespoon at a time, working quickly with a rubber spatula. (*Note:* Make very sure spatula reaches bottom of bowl when folding in butter.) Fill molds ⅔ full, place on baking sheets, and bake 15–17 minutes until golden and tops spring back when touched. Cool in molds 1–2 minutes, then lift out with a spatula. Cool fluted side up on wire rack. Dust generously with confectioners' sugar before serving. About 40 calories per cookie.

ROLLED COOKIES

Children adore these cookies—as much to make as to eat. They love the feel of the dough, they love rolling it out, cutting it into plain and fancy shapes. But most of all, they delight in decorating the cookies— strewing them with colored sugar, frosting them, and "squirting" or painting on designs (the aerosol cans of decorator frostings are perfect for children, as are the spillproof paste colors available in gourmet shops; they're as easy to use as poster paints).

All rolled cookie doughs, of course, aren't suitable for children. Many are so tender and rich even skillful cooks find them a challenge (for a list of rolled cookies children *can* make with relative ease, see the Cookie Chart).

Temperature is all-important when it comes to rolling dough—temperature of the day, of the kitchen, of the dough, and of your hands. All should be cool if you're to succeed.

Some Tips:

– Chill dough until firm but not hard; if dough is too cold and hard, especially a butter-rich dough, it will crack and split and be difficult to roll. The perfect temperature for rolling is when dough yields slightly when pressed but does not stick to your fingers.

– If dough is unusually soft or sticky, chill board and rolling pin as well as the dough.

– If your hands are warm, keep a bowl of ice water handy and cool them from time to time by dipping into the water. Rolling dough is especially difficult for women with warm hands because the heat of their hands oversoftens the dough, making it stick to everything.

– Roll only a small amount of dough at a time (about 1 cup) and keep the rest in the refrigerator until needed.

– Before rolling, shape dough roughly into the form you want— circle, rectangle, or square—and when rolling, shift position of dough on board and direct rolling pin strokes as needed to achieve that shape.

– When rolling, bear down on pin *lightly,* only enough to stretch and move dough in the direction you want.

– Resist the temptation of adding flour whenever the dough threatens to stick. Flour does make the dough easier to work, but it also makes the cookies tough and dry. The secret of crisp-tender rolled cookies is using little or no flour in the rolling. Here are two ways:

(1) Use a pastry cloth and stockinette-covered rolling pin. Both need

only the lightest flouring because the porousness of the cloth holds the flour and releases very little into the dough.

(2) Roll dough between 2 sheets of wax paper. This method is particularly good for soft, butter-rich doughs and for cookies that must be rolled tissue-thin. The process is a bit tricky, but it does work. Place a small amount of dough between 2 sheets of wax paper (no flour needed) and roll quickly and lightly until dough is ¼"–½" thick; peel off top sheet of paper and invert it on board so used side is down. Flop dough over onto sheet, peel off top sheet, and reverse it also so that fresh side touches dough. Continue rolling to desired thickness, reversing or replenishing wax paper as needed. If dough threatens to stick despite frequent changes of paper, simply pop into refrigerator in its semirolled state, paper and all. A few minutes' chilling will firm up the dough and make the paper peel off like magic. When dough is desired thickness, remove top sheet and cut cookies (bottom sheet should still be in place). Chill cookies briefly on wax paper so they can be lifted with ease to baking sheets. With this method, you should be able to roll dough without using any additional flour. But if at the end dough tends to stick despite all precautions, dust *very* lightly with flour (with an exceedingly soft dough, this may be necessary to keep top sheet of wax paper from sticking after final rolling).

– Flour cutters *only* if dough is soft and sticky and then only *lightly*. A quick way to do it is to sift a little flour into a shallow bowl, then simply dip cutter into it, shaking off any excess.

– When cutting cookies, cut as close together as possible so there will be few scraps to reroll. Unless you've used very little flour in rolling, the rerolls will be tough.
– If dough is unusually soft, cut into the simplest shapes—circles, diamonds, squares—to reduce breakage.
– Use a wide spatula or pancake turner for transferring cookies to baking sheets. The spatula need not be floured unless dough is supersoft.
– Space cookies ¾"–1" apart on baking sheets unless recipes specify otherwise; most rolled cookies spread very little during baking.

About Cookie Cutters

Lucky the woman who owns a set of old-fashioned tin cookie cutters. They do really cut (unlike the plastic and aluminum cutters made today) and their designs are enchanting. It is still possible to find these old cutters, but it requires a bit of sleuthing in antique shops both at home and abroad. The best of the contemporary cutters are European, best in design, best in cutting ability. They're available at most gourmet shops as single cutters, cutter blocks, and cutter wheels.

You can, of course, design your own cutters. All you have to do is make a pattern, take it to a tinsmith and let him worry about the rest. Failing a handy tinsmith, you can still make cookies from your own designs. Simply sketch your designs on heavy paper (Manila file folders are the perfect weight and grease resistant to boot), cut them out, lay on rolled-out dough, and "trace" around them with a very sharp knife.

¢ SUGAR COOKIES

A good basic cookie with plenty of flavor variations to try.
Makes about 7 dozen

3¾ cups sifted flour
1½ teaspoons baking powder
1 teaspoon salt
1 cup butter or margarine
1½ cups sugar
2 teaspoons vanilla
2 eggs

Preheat oven to 375° F. Sift flour with baking powder and salt and set aside. Cream butter, sugar, and vanilla until light and fluffy. Add eggs, 1 at a time, beating well after each addition. Slowly mix in dry ingredients until just blended (lowest speed if you use mixer). If your kitchen is very hot, wrap dough in wax paper and chill about 1 hour so it will roll more easily. Roll ¼ of dough at a time on a lightly floured board to 1/16″–⅛″ thickness and cut with plain or fluted cutters (a 2″ or 3″ size is good). Transfer to lightly greased baking sheets with a pancake turner, spacing cookies 2″ apart. If you like, brush with milk and sprinkle lightly with sugar. Bake in top ⅓ of oven 8–9 minutes until pale tan. Transfer to wire racks to cool. Reroll and cut trimmings.

For Softer Cookies: Roll dough ⅛″–¼″ thick and cut with a 3″ cutter; bake as directed 10–12 minutes until edges are just golden.

For Slice-and-Bake Cookies: Shape dough into a log about 2″ in diameter, then chill several hours until firm or freeze. Slice ¼″ thick and bake about 10 minutes until firm but not brown. About 55 calories per cookie.

VARIATIONS:

Sugar Pillows: Reduce flour to 3 cups and prepare dough as directed. Drop by rounded teaspoonfuls on lightly greased baking sheets, spacing cookies 2″ apart. Lightly butter the bottom of a water glass, dip in sugar, then flatten cookies until ¼″ thick (you'll have to resugar the glass about every other cookie). Bake 10–12 minutes until firm but not browned. Cool on wire racks. About 55 calories per cookie.

Chocolate Sugar Cookies: Add 4 (1-ounce) squares melted and cooled semisweet chocolate or 4 (1-ounce) envelopes no-melt semisweet chocolate to creamed mixture after adding eggs. Proceed as recipe directs. About 70 calories per cookie.

Pinwheels: Prepare dough as directed; mix half of it with 2 (1-ounce) envelopes no-melt semisweet chocolate. Roll ⅓ of the plain dough into a rectangle 6″×8″ and ¼″ thick. Roll ⅓ of chocolate dough into a rectangle the same size, and, using a pancake turner, carefully place on top of plain dough. Roll the 2 together to a thickness of ⅛″, keeping shape as nearly rectangular as possible, then roll up jelly-roll style, from the short side. Repeat with remaining dough. Wrap and chill rolls ½ hour, then slice ¼″ thick and bake 10–12 minutes until cookies barely show a print when lightly pressed. Cool as directed. About 65 calories per cookie.

Sugar Marbles: Reduce amount of flour to 3 cups and prepare dough as directed. Into half mix 2 (1-ounce) envelopes no-melt semisweet chocolate. Pinch off about ½ teaspoon each plain and chocolate dough, then roll the 2 together into a small ball, squeezing slightly, to achieve a marbled effect. Repeat until dough is used up. Space marbles 2″ apart on greased cookie sheets and bake about

10 minutes. About 55 calories per cookie.

Butterscotch Sugar Cookies: Substitute 2 cups firmly packed light or dark brown sugar for the 1½ cups sugar and proceed as directed. About 65 calories per cookie.

Nut Sugar Cookies: Work 1 cup finely chopped pecans, walnuts, filberts, pistachios, Brazil nuts, or toasted, blanched almonds into dough after dry ingredients. Roll and bake as directed. About 75 calories per cookie.

Coconut Sugar Cookies: Chop 1½ cups flaked coconut fairly fine and mix into dough after dry ingredients. Substitute 1½ teaspoons almond extract for the vanilla. Roll and bake as directed. About 75 calories per cookie.

Lemon or Orange Sugar Cookies: Substitute 1 teaspoon lemon or orange extract for vanilla and add 2-3 tablespoons finely grated lemon or orange rind along with eggs. Roll and bake as directed. About 55 calories per cookie.

Decorative Cookies: If fancy cutouts are to be made, increase amount of flour in basic recipe by about ½ cup (there'll be less breakage while you decorate cookies). Roll and cut cookies. For ideas on decorating, see About Decorating Cookies. About 60 calories per cookie.

SAND TARTS

This dough lends itself to all kinds of quick variations that will delight children.
Makes 4 dozen

⅔ *cup butter or margarine*
1 *cup sugar*
¼ *teaspoon salt*
1 *egg*
1 *teaspoon vanilla*
2¾ *cups sifted flour*

Glaze:
1 *egg white, lightly beaten*
¼ *cup sugar*
Blanched, halved almonds (optional decoration)

Cream butter, sugar, and salt until light and fluffy; beat in egg, then vanilla. Mix in flour, ⅓ at a time, beating just to blend. Wrap dough and chill 1 hour. Preheat oven to 375° F. Roll, a small amount of dough at a time, ⅛" thick and cut with a 2" round cutter. Arrange 1" apart on greased baking sheets, brush with egg white and sprinkle with sugar. If you like, top each with an almond half. Bake 8-10 minutes until pale golden. Cool on wire racks. About 80 calories per cookie.

VARIATIONS:

Slice-and-Bake Sandies: Prepare dough as directed and chill 1 hour; shape into a 2" roll, wrap in foil, and chill overnight. Slice ⅛" thick, glaze and bake as directed. About 80 calories per cookie.

Jumbles: Prepare and roll cookies as directed; cut with a 2½" fluted round cutter, and in the center of half the cookies put ½ teaspoon tart jam or jelly, marmalade or mincemeat, semisweet chocolate bits or chopped mixed candied fruits. Top with remaining cookies, press edges together and snip tiny steam vents in centers with scissors. Do not glaze. Bake about 12 minutes until pale golden and cool on wire racks. About 155 calories per cookie.

Jelly Cutouts: Prepare, roll, and cut cookies as directed in basic recipe, then cut out centers of half the cookies, using a 1" round cutter or decorative truffle cutters. Glaze cutout cookies only. Bake all as directed, then sandwich together with jelly, using cutout cookies as the top layer. (*Note:* Centers can be rerolled and cut, or baked—2–3 minutes will do it.) About 150 calories per cookie.

Turnovers: Prepare and roll cookies as directed but cut with a 3" round cutter. Drop ½ teaspoon any jam or preserves on half of each cookie, fold over, and seal edges. Glaze and bake 12 minutes. Cool on wire racks. About 90 calories per cookie.

ROSE TREE COOKIES

A buttery-crisp old Quaker cookie that's tricky to make (don't attempt it in warm weather or in a warm kitchen). The secret is to cream the butter and sugar until fluffy and white and to roll the dough paper thin, using as little flour as possible.
Makes about 5 dozen

1 cup butter (no substitute)
1½ cups sugar
1 egg
1¼ teaspoons baking soda, dissolved in 2 teaspoons hot water
2 teaspoons vanilla
2½ cups sifted flour

Cream butter and sugar until fluffy and white (about 10 minutes with an electric mixer at low speed). Beat in egg, then soda mixture and vanilla. Work in flour slowly. Divide dough in half and spoon each onto a large sheet of wax paper; flatten into large circles or rectangles about 1" thick, wrap, and chill 1–2 hours until firm enough to roll but not brittle. When you're ready to roll dough, preheat oven to 375° F. Roll about ¼ of each package at a time between 2 sheets of wax paper. (*Note:* You should be able to roll the dough paper thin with very little additional flour if you change sheets of paper when dough begins to stick—the wax paper will peel off zip-quick if you chill all briefly.) Cut with a 2½"–3" round cutter, chill 5–10 minutes more so circles can be lifted off paper easily, then space 1½" apart on an ungreased baking sheet. Bake cookies 5–7 minutes until pale tan, cool on sheet about 1 minute, then lift to wire rack to cool. Store airtight. About 60 calories per cookie.

GINGERBREAD BOYS

Let the children help make and decorate these.
Makes 2 dozen

2½ cups sifted flour
½ teaspoon salt
2 teaspoons ginger
½ cup butter or margarine
½ cup sugar
½ cup molasses
½ teaspoon baking soda
¼ cup hot water

Decorations:
Cinnamon candies ("red-hots")
Seedless raisins

Easy Icing:
1 cup sifted confectioners' sugar
¼ teaspoon salt
½ teaspoon vanilla
1 tablespoon heavy cream (about)

Sift flour with salt and ginger and set aside. Melt butter in a large saucepan over low heat, remove from heat and mix in sugar, then molasses. Dissolve soda in hot water. Add dry ingredients to molasses mixture alternately with soda-water, beginning and ending with dry ingredients. Chill dough 2–3 hours. Preheat oven to 350° F. Roll out dough, a small portion at a time, ⅛" thick. Cut with gingerbread boy cutter, handling dough carefully, and transfer cookies to ungreased baking sheets (they should be spaced about 2" apart). Press on cinnamon candies for buttons and raisins for eyes and bake 10–12 minutes until lightly browned. Cool 2–3 minutes on sheets, then lift to wire racks. While cookies cool, prepare icing: Mix sugar, salt, and vanilla; add cream, a few drops at a time, mixing well after each addition until icing is smooth and will hold a shape. Using a decorating tube, pipe outlines for collars, boots, cuffs, and belts. If you like, make a little extra icing, tint yellow, and use to pipe in hair. When frosting has hardened, store airtight. (*Note:* Gingerbread boys can be made several days ahead and piped with icing shortly before serving. If they soften in storage, warm 3–5 minutes at 350° F. to crispen, then cool on racks.) About 130 calories each.

⚛ GOLDEN CHEDDAR RINGS

Serve as a cookie or as an appetizer with cocktails.
Makes about 7½ dozen

¾ cup butter (no substitute), softened to room temperature
2 cups sifted flour
1 teaspoon paprika
½ teaspoon salt
¼ teaspoon cayenne pepper
1 pound sharp Cheddar cheese, coarsely grated
2 tablespoons superfine sugar

Preheat oven to 400° F. Rub butter, flour, paprika, salt, and cayenne together, using your hands, until smooth and creamy. Add cheese and knead on a piece of foil 3–4 minutes until smooth and thoroughly blended. Roll dough thin, half at a time, on a lightly floured pastry cloth (it should be about as thin as piecrust). Cut into rings with doughnut cutter and bake on ungreased baking sheets 4–6 minutes until *faintly* browned. Remove at once to wire racks to cool and, while still hot, sprinkle lightly with sugar. Scraps and "holes" can be rerolled and cut. About 45 calories each.

¢ MORAVIAN CHRISTMAS COOKIES

These dark ginger-molasses cookies store beautifully, so you can make them well ahead of the Christmas rush. The Moravian women of Old Salem, North Carolina, roll them paper thin and cut in fancy shapes.
Makes 4½ dozen

4 cups sifted flour
1 teaspoon ginger
1 teaspoon cinnamon
1 teaspoon mace
½ teaspoon cloves
¼ cup butter or margarine
¼ cup lard
½ cup firmly packed dark brown sugar
1 cup molasses
1½ teaspoons baking soda
1 tablespoon very hot water

Sift flour with spices. Cream butter, lard, and sugar until light and fluffy; add molasses and beat well. Dissolve soda in water. Mix ¼ of dry ingredients into creamed mixture, then stir in soda-water. Work in remaining dry ingredients, ⅓ at a time. Wrap dough and chill 4–6 hours. Preheat oven to 350° F. Roll dough, a little at a time, as thin as possible (⅛″ is maximum thickness, ⅟₁₆″ far better). Cut with Christmas cutters, space cookies 1½″ apart on lightly greased baking sheets, and bake about 8 minutes until lightly browned. Cool 1–2 minutes on sheets, then transfer to wire racks. When completely cool, store airtight. About 70 calories per cookie.

To Decorate: Make an icing by mixing 1 cup sifted confectioners' sugar with 2–3 teaspoons heavy cream. Trace outlines of cookies with icing by putting through a pastry tube fitted with a fine tip. About 80 calories per cookie.

MARGUERITES

The rose water flavoring is what makes these cookies distinctive. It is available at many drugstores, also at specialty food shops.
Makes 4 dozen

3¼ cups sifted flour
½ teaspoon salt
½ teaspoon cinnamon
½ teaspoon nutmeg
¼ teaspoon mace
1 cup butter or margarine
1 cup sugar
3 egg yolks
¼ cup rose water

Topping:
3 egg whites
4 cups sifted confectioners' sugar
2 tablespoons lemon juice
½ (1-pound) jar peach or apricot preserves or marmalade

Sift flour with salt and spices. Cream butter and sugar until light and fluffy; beat in yolks, 1 at a time. Mix in dry ingredients alternately with rose water, beginning and ending with dry ingredients and beating only enough to blend. Chill dough 1–2 hours. Preheat oven to 350° F. Roll dough, a small amount at a time, ¼″ thick and cut in rounds with a 2½″ cutter. Space cookies 2″ apart on greased baking sheets and bake 10–12 minutes until light tan. Cool cookies on sheets 2–3 minutes, then transfer to wire racks. When all cookies are done, reduce oven temperature to 325° F. and prepare topping: Beat egg whites until frothy, add confectioners' sugar, ¼ cup at a time, beating well after each addition. Add lemon juice and beat until stiff peaks form. Spread each cookie, not quite to edge, with 1 teaspoon preserves, top with a rounded teaspoon meringue and spread to cover. Arrange 1″ apart on ungreased baking sheets and bake 15 minutes until topping is creamy white and firm. Cool on wire racks. About 140 calories each.

VARIATION:

⚖ ☒ **Jiffy Marguerites:** Instead of making cookies, spread soda crackers with preserves and meringue and bake as directed. For 1½ dozen crackers, use the following meringue proportions: 1 egg white, 1⅓ cups sifted confectioners' sugar, and 2 teaspoons lemon juice. About 50 calories each.

CHOCOLATE-FILLED PECAN DREAMS

Makes about 4 dozen

¾ cup butter or margarine
⅔ cup sifted confectioners' sugar
1 egg yolk
¾ cup very finely chopped pecans
1⅔ cups sifted flour

Filling:
¼ cup butter or margarine
1 cup sifted confectioners' sugar
1 egg white
¼ teaspoon vanilla
2 (1-ounce) envelopes no-melt semisweet chocolate

Cream butter and sugar until light and fluffy; add egg yolk and mix well. Mix in nuts and flour just until blended. Chill dough 1–2 hours. Preheat oven to 350° F. Roll out dough, a small amount at a time, ¼″ thick and cut with a 2″ round cookie cutter. Space 2″ apart on ungreased baking sheets and bake 10–12 minutes until pale tan. Transfer to wire racks to cool. For the filling: Cream butter and sugar until light and fluffy, add egg white and vanilla and beat well; blend in chocolate. When cookies are cold, sandwich together with filling. (*Note:* If cookies are not to be served the same day, do not fill; store airtight, then assemble shortly before serving.) About 85 calories per cookie.

CREAM-FILLED MOLASSES COOKIES

Makes about 5 dozen

¾ cup vegetable shortening
1 teaspoon salt
1 cup molasses
¾ cup sugar
1 egg
4½ cups sifted flour
2 teaspoons ginger
1 teaspoon soda

Cream Filling:
1 tablespoon butter
1 cup sifted confectioners' sugar
⅛ teaspoon salt
¼ teaspoon ginger
⅛ teaspoon cinnamon
1 tablespoon boiling water

Preheat oven to 350° F. Cream shortening with salt, molasses, sugar, and egg until light; sift flour with ginger and soda and add, 1 cup at a time, to creamed mixture, beating smooth after each addition. If dough seems very soft, chill until firm enough to roll. Roll, about ¼ of dough at a time, on a lightly floured board to a thickness of ⅛"–¼". Cut half of dough with a doughnut cutter, other half with round cookie cutter of the same diameter. Repeat until all dough is rolled and cut. Bake on greased baking sheets 10–12 minutes, remove to wire racks to cool. Meanwhile, prepare filling: Cream butter, sugar, salt, ginger and cinnamon until light, then beat in boiling water. To assemble cookies, spread rounds with filling, top with doughnut-shaped cookies, and press lightly into place. About 105 calories per cookie.

FIG NEWTONS

Not as difficult to make as you might think and so much better than the store-bought.
Makes 3 dozen

3 cups sifted flour
½ teaspoon salt
½ teaspoon cinnamon (optional)
⅔ cup butter or margarine
½ cup firmly packed dark brown sugar
½ cup firmly packed light brown sugar
2 egg whites
1 teaspoon vanilla

Fig Filling:
2 cups finely chopped dried golden figs
1 cup water
2 tablespoons sugar
2 tablespoons lemon juice

Sift flour with salt and, if you like, cinnamon. Cream butter and sugars until very fluffy; beat in egg whites and vanilla. Slowly work in flour; wrap dough and chill 2–3 hours. Meanwhile, prepare filling: Simmer all ingredients together, stirring frequently, 5–7 minutes until thick. Cool but do not chill. When dough has chilled long enough, preheat oven to 350° F. Roll out dough, a small portion at a time, ¼" thick and cut in pieces about 2½" wide and 3" long. Place a level teaspoon fig mixture in center of each, fold dough around filling as though folding a business letter. Flatten cookies slightly and place seam side down

1″ apart on ungreased baking sheets; bake about 12 minutes until lightly browned and just firm. Cool on racks. About 100 calories each.

SPITZBUBEN

Delicate almond cookies sandwiched together with jelly or jam (vary their flavors if you like).
Makes 2½ dozen

2 cups sifted flour
½ teaspoon salt
1 cup sugar
½ cup finely chopped blanched almonds
⅔ cup butter (no substitute), softened to room temperature
1 teaspoon vanilla
2 tablespoons heavy cream
1 (1-pound) jar red currant jelly or raspberry jam
Vanilla Sugar or sifted confectioners' sugar

Preheat oven to 350° F. Sift flour with salt and sugar; mix in nuts. Using your hands, work in butter until thoroughly blended. Mix vanilla and cream and add, a few drops at a time, mixing with a fork until mixture holds together. (*Note:* If kitchen is warm, chill dough about 1 hour or until a good consistency for rolling.) Roll out, a small amount at a time, ⅛″ thick and cut with a 2″ scalloped round cookie cutter. Space cookies 2″ apart on ungreased baking sheets and bake about 12 minutes until golden brown. Cool on sheets 3–4 minutes, then transfer to wire racks. When cool, sandwich cookies together with jelly and dust with vanilla sugar or confectioners' sugar. (*Note:* Being egg-free, these cookies are good for those with egg allergies.) About 170 calories per cookie.

PFEFFERNÜSSE (GERMAN PEPPERNUTS)

The secret of good "peppernuts" is to ripen the dough 2–3 days before baking and to store the cookies 1–2 weeks with a piece of apple before eating.
Makes 3½ dozen

3 cups sifted flour
1 teaspoon cinnamon
⅛ teaspoon cloves
¼ teaspoon white pepper
3 eggs
1 cup sugar
⅓ cup very finely chopped blanched almonds
⅓ cup very finely chopped mixed candied orange peel and citron
Vanilla Sugar or confectioners' sugar (optional)

Sift flour with spices and set aside. Beat eggs until frothy, slowly add sugar, and continue beating until thick and lemon colored. Slowly mix in flour, then almonds and fruit peel. Wrap in foil and refrigerate 2–3 days. When ready to bake, preheat oven to 350° F. Roll, about ⅓ of dough at a time, ¼″–½″ thick and cut with a 1¾″ round cutter. Space cookies 1″ apart on greased baking sheets and bake 15–18 minutes until light brown. Cool on wire racks and store with ½ an apple in a covered container 1–2 weeks before eating. If you like, dredge in vanilla sugar or dust with confectioners' sugar before serving. About 70 calories per cookie if not dredged in sugar, 80 calories if dredged in sugar.

PEPPARKAKOR (CHRISTMAS GINGER SNAPS)

These gingery brown cookies are Sweden's favorite at Christmas time. They are rolled very thin, cut into stars, bells, angels, and Santa

Clauses, and hung upon either the Christmas tree or the small wooden *pepparkakor* tree.
Makes about 5 dozen

3½ cups sifted flour
1 teaspoon baking soda
½ teaspoon salt
1½ teaspoons ginger
1½ teaspoons cinnamon
1½ teaspoons cloves
1 cup butter or margarine
1 cup firmly packed dark brown sugar
2 egg whites

Icing:
4 cups sifted confectioners' sugar
2 egg whites

Sift flour with soda, salt, and spices. Cream butter and sugar until very fluffy; beat in egg whites. Slowly work in dry ingredients. Wrap and chill 12 hours. Preheat oven to 350° F. Roll out dough, a small portion at a time, ⅛" thick on a lightly floured board and cut in decorative shapes; space cookies about 1" apart on ungreased baking sheets and bake 10–12 minutes until lightly browned around the edges. Transfer to wire racks to cool. While cookies cool, prepare icing: Slowly blend confectioners' sugar into egg whites and beat until smooth. Fit pastry bag with a fine, plain tip and pipe icing onto cookies, tracing outlines, filling in details, or adding any decorative touches you wish. (*Note:* To make hanging cookies, see directions given in About Decorating Cookies.) About 100 calories per cookie.

LEBKUCHEN

A spicy German cookie studded with candied fruits.
Makes about 4½ dozen

3 cups sifted flour
½ teaspoon baking soda
1 teaspoon cinnamon
½ teaspoon nutmeg
½ teaspoon cloves
1 cup firmly packed dark brown sugar
1 cup honey, at room temperature
1 egg
1 teaspoon finely grated lemon rind
1 tablespoon lemon juice
½ cup finely chopped blanched almonds
½ cup finely chopped mixed candied orange peel and citron

Frosting:
1 cup sifted confectioners' sugar
4–5 teaspoons milk

Decoration:
Blanched halved almonds
Slivered or halved candied cherries

Sift flour with baking soda and spices. Beat sugar, honey and egg until well blended; add lemon rind and juice. Slowly mix in dry ingredients just until blended; stir in almonds and fruit peel. Wrap and chill 12 hours. Preheat oven to 400° F. Roll out ⅓ of dough at a time ¼" thick and cut with a 2" round cookie cutter *or* cut in rectangles 2½" × 1½". Arrange 2" apart on lightly greased baking sheets and bake 8 minutes until edges are lightly browned and tops spring back when touched. Cool on wire racks. For the frosting: Mix sugar and milk until smooth; spread a little on top of each cookie or dip cookie tops in frosting. Decorate with almonds and cherries. Let frosting harden before storing cookies. About 80 calories per cookie.

For Drop Cookies: Reduce flour to 2½ cups; drop by rounded teaspoonfuls and bake as directed. About 75 calories per cookie.

SPRINGERLE

The original 3-D cookies, *Springerle* date to pagan Germany when the poor, having no animals to sacrifice at the Winter Festival, made effigies of them out of cookie dough. Today, springerle are square or rectangular cookies with pressed-in designs, made either by rolling dough on a springerle board or with a springerle rolling pin (available in gourmet shops). Sometimes used, too, are individual wooden cookie blocks called *Spekulatius* blocks. Makes about 5 dozen

4 cups sifted flour
1 teaspoon baking powder
½ teaspoon salt
4 eggs
2 cups sugar
2 teaspoons finely grated lemon rind (optional)
Anise seeds

Sift flour with baking powder and salt. Beat eggs until lemon colored, slowly add sugar, ½ cup at a time, beating well after each addition; continue beating until very thick and pale, about 10 minutes with a mixer. Slowly mix in lemon rind and dry ingredients, beating just to blend. Wrap and chill dough 3–4 hours. Roll, ⅓ at a time, slightly less than ½″ thick, keeping shape as nearly rectangular as possible and about the width of the rolling pin. Roll a lightly floured springerle rolling pin over dough 1 time, pressing firmly so dough is about ¼″ thick and evenly so imprint is clear. If using springerle board, roll dough ¼″ thick on lightly floured board, using regular rolling pin, then invert on lightly floured surface. If using spekulatius block, roll dough ¼″ thick, then press firmly and evenly, using block like a stamp. (*Note:* In warm weather, chill springerle pin or board along with dough to make rolling easier.) Cut on imprint lines to separate individual cookies, transfer to a lightly floured surface, and let stand uncovered overnight. Preheat oven to 325° F. Sprinkle greased baking sheets generously with anise seeds, lift cookies to sheets, and bake 15 minutes until golden but not brown. Cool 1 minute on sheets before transferring to racks to cool. (*Note:* Some people like to mellow springerle about a week in an airtight canister before serving.) About 110 calories per cookie.

MOLDED OR PRESSED COOKIES

These three-dimensional cookies are great favorites everywhere, but especially in Europe, where women are artists at shaping dough (Scandinavian museums exhibit cookie masterpieces alongside other folk art). Almost as soon as a little girl can toddle into the kitchen, she is given a dab of dough to shape. By the time she reaches her teens, she knows how to fashion wreaths and rings, rosettes and ribbons, pinwheels and pretzels and checkerboards. She has learned to use the cookie press with speed and skill and has built up a delectable cookie repertoire (the better to catch a husband).

The dough for molded and pressed cookies is quite short (rich in butter or shortening) and has the look and feel of shortbread. There are three basic ways to handle it:
(1) Roll into chunky logs (à la refrigerator cookies), chill until firm, slice thin, and bake.
(2) Hand-shape into little balls, pillows, crescents, or logs.
(3) Push through a pastry bag or cookie press. (*Note:* Only the softer doughs are suitable for pressing.) There are a number of kinds of cookie presses. Before buying, shop around, talk with friends, and if possible borrow a press to try.

Some Tips:
— Choose a cool day for making molded or pressed cookies. Heat makes the dough too soft to hold a shape.
— When using cookie press, always follow manufacturer's instructions.
— Never fill cookie press or pastry bag more than ½ to ⅔ full; the heat of your hands will soften dough faster than you can press it. Invariably the last of the dough must be removed from the press, chilled, and then *re*-pressed.
— Never try to press a dough containing bits of fruit or nuts that may clog the works.
— Always press cookies onto cool or cold baking sheets.
— If dough seems too soft to press or mold, chill slightly.
— When shaping cookies, flour hands only when absolutely necessary and then *very* lightly. Most doughs can be shaped with unfloured hands.

BUTTERBALLS

They will melt in your mouth.
Makes 4 dozen

2 cups sifted flour
½ teaspoon salt
1 cup butter (no substitute)
½ cup superfine sugar
2 teaspoons vanilla or 1½ teaspoons vanilla and ½ teaspoon almond extract
½ cup sifted confectioners' sugar or Vanilla Sugar (optional)

Sift together flour and salt and set aside. Cream butter and sugar until light and fluffy; add flavoring. Slowly mix in flour, ½ cup at a time, until just blended. Chill dough 1–2 hours. Preheat oven to 325° F. Shape dough into 1" balls, handling quickly and lightly, space 2" apart on ungreased baking sheets, and bake about 15 minutes until the color of pale sand. Transfer to wire racks to cool. If you like, roll in confectioners' sugar before serving. About 65 calories per cookie.

VARIATIONS:

Coconut Butterballs: Stir 1 cup flaked coconut into prepared dough, then proceed as directed. If you like, brush cooled, baked cookies with beaten egg white and roll in plain or colored flaked coconut before serving. About 70 calories per cookie.

Almond Butterballs: Prepare as directed, using vanilla-almond extract combination and mixing in ½ cup finely chopped toasted blanched almonds after flour. Chill, shape into balls, roll in finely chopped toasted blanched almonds (you'll need about ¾ cup altogether), then bake as directed. (*Note:* Other nuts may be used instead of almonds; particularly good are pecans, walnuts, hazelnuts, piñons, pistachio nuts, or unsalted peanuts.) About 85 calories per cookie.

Thumbprint Cookies: Mix, chill, and shape cookies as directed. Make a deep thumbprint in center of each, fill with tart jam or jelly, and bake as directed. About 80 calories per cookie.

OLD-FASHIONED BUTTER "S" COOKIES

Makes 4 dozen

1 cup butter (*no substitute*)
1 cup sugar
6 egg yolks, lightly beaten
2 tablespoons finely grated lemon rind (*optional*)
3 cups sifted flour

Preheat oven to 325° F. Cream butter and sugar until light and fluffy, add egg yolks 1 at a time, beating well after each addition; if desired, add lemon rind. With a spoon, mix in flour. Refrigerate half the dough while shaping the rest. Pinch off a piece of dough and roll between lightly floured hands into a rope ½" in diameter; cut in 4" lengths and shape into *s*'s on ungreased baking sheets. Cookies should be spaced 2" apart. Bake 18–20 minutes or until lightly browned at the edges. Cool a few minutes on sheets, then carefully transfer to wire racks. When cool, store airtight. About 80 calories per cookie.

VARIATIONS:

Other flavorings may be substituted for the lemon rind: 2 teaspoons vanilla, 1 teaspoon almond extract, or 2 tablespoons finely grated orange rind. About 80 calories per cookie.

ALMOND CRUNCHIES

Makes about 8 dozen

4 cups sifted flour
1¼ cups sugar
1½ teaspoons baking powder
¼ teaspoon nutmeg
1½ cups butter (*no substitute*), softened to room temperature
1 egg
1 teaspoon vanilla
¼ teaspoon almond extract

Topping:
1 egg, lightly beaten
⅓ cup finely chopped blanched almonds
½ cup coarsely crushed sugar cubes

Preheat oven to 350° F. Sift flour, sugar, baking powder, and nutmeg together into a large bowl. Blend in butter, egg, vanilla, and almond extract. Shape into 1" balls and place, 2" apart, on lightly greased baking sheets. To apply the topping, press each ball down to a thickness of about ¼", using a fork dipped in the beaten egg. Sprinkle with almonds and crushed sugar and bake 10–12 minutes until delicately browned. Cool on wire racks. About 60 calories per cookie.

PEANUT BUTTER COOKIES

Makes 6 dozen

2½ cups sifted flour
1 teaspoon baking powder
½ teaspoon salt
1 cup butter or margarine or ½ cup each vegetable shortening and butter
1 cup sugar
1 cup firmly packed light brown sugar
2 eggs
1 cup crunchy peanut butter

Sift flour with baking powder and salt and set aside. Cream butter and sugars until light and fluffy; add eggs, 1 at a time, beating well after each addition. Beat in peanut butter. Slowly mix in dry ingredients, about ⅓ at a time, until just blended.

Chill dough 2 hours. Preheat oven to 375° F. Shape dough into 1" balls, arrange 3" apart on greased baking sheets, and flatten by pressing lightly with a floured fork in a crisscross fashion. Bake 10–12 minutes until golden. Transfer to wire rack to cool. (*Note:* Dough freezes well.) About 80 calories per cookie.

☒ SNICKERDOODLES

Children will have fun making these. Makes about 6 dozen

2¾ cups sifted flour
¼ teaspoon salt
1 teaspoon baking soda
2 teaspoons cream of tartar
1 cup butter or margarine, softened to room temperature
1½ cups sugar

Topping:
2 tablespoons sugar, mixed with 2 tablespoons cinnamon

Preheat oven to 350° F. Sift flour with salt, baking soda, and cream of tartar. Cream butter until light, add sugar gradually, continuing to cream until fluffy. Work in dry ingredients slowly and beat *just* until smooth. Shape into 1" balls and roll in topping. Arrange 2" apart on ungreased baking sheets and bake 18–20 minutes or until light tan. Transfer at once to wire racks to cool. Store airtight. About 55 calories per cookie.

MEXICAN WEDDING CAKES

Meltingly tender filbert cookies. Makes about 5 dozen

1 cup butter or margarine, softened to room temperature
⅔ cup plus 3 tablespoons unsifted confectioners' sugar
1 tablespoon vanilla
¼ teaspoon salt
2⅓ cups sifted flour
1½ cups finely ground, toasted, unblanched filberts

Cream butter until light and fluffy. Add ⅔ cup confectioners' sugar and continue creaming until smooth; beat in vanilla and salt. Mix in flour, then the filberts. Wrap dough in foil and chill several hours until firm. Preheat oven to 350° F. Pinch off bits of dough and roll into 1" balls. Place 2" apart on ungreased baking sheets and flatten each ball with the palm of your hand until ¼" thick; even up any ragged edges. Bake 12–15 minutes until edged with brown. Transfer to wire racks to cool, then sift remaining 3 tablespoons confectioners' sugar over cookies to dust lightly. About 65 calories per cookie.

KOURABIEDES

These butter-rich Greek cookies are traditionally served on saints' days and at Christmas. Makes about 3½ dozen

1 cup unsalted butter (no substitute)
⅓ cup sifted confectioners' sugar
1 egg yolk
2¼ cups sifted flour
2 tablespoons brandy
½ cup very finely chopped walnuts or blanched almonds (optional)
Confectioners' sugar

Cream butter until light, slowly add confectioners' sugar, and continue creaming until light and fluffy; beat in egg yolk. Slowly mix in flour, adding alternately with brandy. If you like, mix in nuts. Wrap dough in wax paper and chill 1 hour. Preheat oven to 350° F. Using a rounded teaspoon as a measure, scoop up bits of dough and with lightly floured hands roll into strips 3" long. Bend into crescents and arrange 2" apart on ungreased baking sheets. Bake 15 minutes or until the color of sand. Cool 2–3 minutes on sheets, then carefully transfer to wire racks. Cool and roll in confectioners' sugar. About 80 calories per cookie (with nuts).

VARIATION:

Instead of shaping into crescents, roll dough into 1¼" balls and, if you like, stud each with a clove. Bake 17–18 minutes. About 80 calories per cookie.

ALMOND TARTS (SWEDISH SANDBAKELSEN)

Makes 2½ dozen

½ cup butter (no substitute), softened to room temperature
⅓ cup sugar
1 egg yolk, lightly beaten
½ teaspoon almond extract
1 cup plus 2 tablespoons sifted flour
½ cup finely ground blanched almonds

With a wooden spoon, mix butter, sugar, egg yolk, and almond extract until well blended. Mix in flour and almonds; wrap and chill 1 hour. Preheat oven to 325° F. Press ¼" layers of dough into buttered and floured 1½"–2" tartlet tins. Stand tins on a baking sheet and bake 18–20 minutes until tarts are pale golden (watch closely toward the end). Transfer tins to a wire rack and cool until easy to handle. To remove tarts from tins, tap bottoms of tins lightly and ease tarts out. You may need to squeeze tins lightly to loosen tarts or use a large, sturdy needle to help pry them out. Cool tarts thoroughly, then store airtight. Just before serving, fill with sweetened whipped cream or invert and dot with crystallized fruit or dabs of red currant jelly. About 70 calories per cookie.

SPRITZ

From the German word meaning "to squirt," *Spritz* are cookies "squirted" through a cookie press into delicate designs.

Makes about 5 dozen

1 cup butter or margarine, softened to room temperature
⅔ cup sugar
2 egg yolks, lightly beaten
1 teaspoon vanilla
2½ cups sifted flour

Optional Decorative Frostings:
Plain: *Blend 1 cup sifted confectioners' sugar until smooth with 2 tablespoons each softened butter and heavy cream.*
Chocolate: *In a double boiler over hot, not boiling, water, heat and stir 1 cup semisweet chocolate bits with 2 tablespoons each light corn syrup and hot water until smooth. Keep over hot water but remove from stove, while frosting cookies.*

Preheat oven to 375° F. With a wooden spoon, beat butter, sugar, egg yolks and vanilla until well mixed. Add flour, ½ cup at a time, mixing well after each addition. Press dough in desired designs through a cookie press onto ungreased baking sheets, spacing cookies 1" apart. Bake 7–9 minutes or until cookies are almost firm but not brown. Cool on sheets 2–3 minutes, then carefully transfer to wire racks. Store airtight. About 55 calories per cookie.

To Decorate: Dip baked, cooled cookies in either of the frostings above, then sprinkle with colored sugar or decorettes, silver dragées, chocolate sprinkles, flaked coconut, shaved Brazil nuts, chopped, toasted almonds, pistachio nuts, walnuts or pecans, minced candied cherries or crystallized fruit. About 70 calories per cookie.

VARIATION:

Chocolate Spritz: Follow basic recipe above but before adding flour mix 2 (1-ounce) envelopes no-melt semisweet or unsweetened chocolate into batter. Proceed as directed. Frost and decorate if you wish. About 60 calories per cookie if unfrosted and undecorated, 75 calories per cookie if frosted and decorated.

BUTTER STARS

Makes 4½ dozen

⅔ cup butter (no substitute)
1 cup sugar
1 egg
1 teaspoon vanilla or ½ teaspoon almond extract
2¼ cups sifted flour
Colored sugar

Preheat oven to 350° F. Cream butter and sugar until light and fluffy; add egg and vanilla and beat well. Mix in flour just until blended. Put through cookie press fitted with a star design onto ungreased baking sheets, spacing cookies 1½" apart. Sprinkle lightly with colored sugar. Bake 10–12 minutes until firm and golden at the edges, not brown. Transfer immediately to wire racks to cool. About 70 calories per cookie.

VARIATIONS:

Butter Planks: Prepare dough as directed above and put through cookie press fitted with serrated ribbon tip, making each plank about 3" long. Bake 8 minutes at 350° F. Sandwich baked cookies together with Chocolate or Mocha Butter Cream Frosting. About 155 calories per cookie.

Almond Pretzels: Prepare dough as directed but use almond extract for flavor instead of vanilla and blend in ½ cup very finely chopped, toasted, blanched almonds after the flour. Use fluted tube attachment for cookie press and form into pretzels about 3" in diameter. Bake as directed. About 80 calories per cookie.

Peanut Butter Stars: Prepare dough as directed, but reduce amount of butter to ½ cup and blend well with ½ cup creamy peanut butter. Omit vanilla from recipe and reduce flour to 2 cups. Press and bake as directed. About 70 calories per cookie.

Scotch Orange Crisps: When making dough, substitute ½ cup firmly packed dark brown sugar for ½ cup of the granulated; omit vanilla and add 1 tablespoon finely grated orange rind. Put through cookie press fitted with desired design and bake as directed. About 70 calories per cookie.

SUGAR PRETZELS

Christmas favorites in Germany and Scandinavia.
Makes 2½ dozen

1 cup butter (no substitute)
⅔ cup sugar
2 egg yolks, lightly beaten
1 teaspoon vanilla
2 cups plus 2 tablespoons sifted flour

Decoration:
1 egg white, lightly beaten
¼ cup green, red, or plain sugar

Preheat oven to 375° F. Cream butter until white, slowly add sugar, and continue beating until light and fluffy. Add egg yolks and vanilla and beat well. By hand mix in flour just until blended. Spoon mixture into a pastry bag fitted with a rosette tube and pipe pretzel-shaped cookies on greased and floured baking sheets. Make the cookies about 2½" in diameter and space them 2" apart. Brush lightly with egg white and sprinkle with colored or plain sugar. Bake 10–12 minutes until just firm but not brown. Cool 1–2 minutes, then lift to racks with a spatula. When cool, store airtight. About 110 calories per cookie.

VARIATIONS:

Berliner Kränze (Wreaths): Pipe dough into 1½"–2" wreaths, brush with egg white, and decorate with green sugar and slivers of candied red cherries. Bake as directed. About 110 calories per cookie.

Nut Rings: Pipe dough into 1"–1½" rings, brush with egg white, and sprinkle with ground pecans, walnuts, filberts, or flaked coconut instead of colored sugar. Bake as directed. About 110 calories per cookie.

⚖ ¢ **PRESSED MOLASSES SPICE COOKIES**

Makes 4 dozen

2 cups sifted flour
½ teaspoon cinnamon
½ teaspoon nutmeg
¼ teaspoon ginger
¼ teaspoon salt
¼ teaspoon baking soda
½ cup butter or margarine
½ cup sugar
¼ cup molasses
1 egg

Preheat oven to 375° F. Sift flour with spices, salt, and soda. Cream butter and sugar until light and fluffy; beat in molasses and egg. Slowly add dry ingredients, mixing just to blend. (*Note:* If weather is cool, you may need to soften dough with 2–3 teaspoons milk to make it a good consistency for the cookie press.) Press dough through cookie press in desired designs onto ungreased baking sheets, spacing cookies 1" apart. Bake 10 minutes until firm. Cool 2 minutes on baking sheets, then transfer to wire racks. About 50 calories per cookie.

REFRIGERATOR COOKIES

In this day of extra-large freezers and refrigerators, refrigerator cookies are a hostess's best friend; a roll of cookie dough "on ice" is excellent insurance against drop-in guests. It's there whenever you need it, ready to slice and bake.

Most refrigerator cookie doughs are soft and butter-rich, much like molded or pressed cookie doughs (*these*, too, can be shaped into rolls, chilled, sliced, and baked). Extra-soft refrigerator cookie doughs need not be chilled if you're in a rush; simply drop from a spoon and bake as you would drop cookies.

Some Tips:
– If dough is extra soft, chill briefly in bowl until firm enough to shape.
– For "square" cookies, line an empty carton in which wax paper or plastic food wrap came with foil and pack dough in firmly. Chill until firm.
– For cookies with colored or flavored borders, roll chilled dough in colored or cinnamon sugar, ground nuts, or flaked coconut before slicing and baking.
– Always use your sharpest knife for slicing refrigerator cookies.
– When slicing dough, give roll a quarter turn every now and then so that it doesn't lose its round shape.
– Remember that refrigerator cookie dough freezes especially well and can be sliced and baked while still solidly frozen.

COOKIES

⚜ ¢ BASIC REFRIGERATOR COOKIES

Makes about 6 dozen

2 cups sifted flour
½ teaspoon salt
½ teaspoon baking soda
½ cup butter or margarine
1 cup granulated, light or dark brown sugar
1 egg
2 teaspoons vanilla

Sift flour with salt and baking soda and set aside. With rotary beater or electric mixer cream butter, sugar, egg, and vanilla until light and fluffy. Slowly mix in dry ingredients; shape dough into a roll about 2″ in diameter; wrap in foil or plastic food wrap and chill several hours or overnight. Preheat oven to 400° F. Slice roll ⅛″ thick and arrange slices ½″ apart on ungreased baking sheets. Bake 8–10 minutes until pale tan. Cool cookies on wire racks. About 35 calories per cookie.

VARIATIONS:

⚜ **Nut Refrigerator Cookies:** Prepare as directed, mixing in 1½ cups minced nuts (pecans, walnuts, filberts, Brazil, pistachio, or blanched, toasted almonds) along with dry ingredients. Proceed as directed. About 50 calories per cookie.

⚜ ¢ **Chocolate Refrigerator Cookies:** Add 2 (1-ounce) envelopes no-melt semisweet chocolate to creamed mixture, add dry ingredients, and proceed as directed. About 40 calories per cookie.

Filled Refrigerator Cookies: Prepare and slice cookies as directed. Make "sandwiches" by putting 2 slices together with 1 teaspoon jam, jelly, or preserves; snip a cross in center of each top cookie to expose filling. Bake about 10 minutes. About 90 calories per cookie.

⚜ ¢ **Chocolate Checkerboards:** Prepare dough as directed; into half mix 1 (1-ounce) envelope no-melt

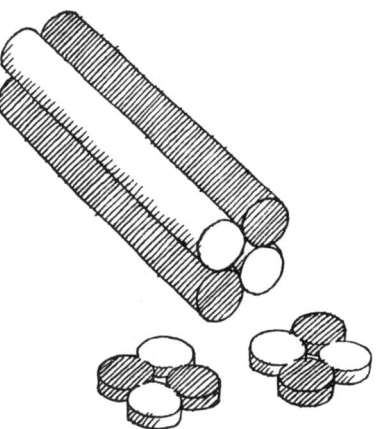

semisweet chocolate. Divide plain and chocolate doughs in half and roll each into a rope about ½″–¾″ in diameter. Lay 1 chocolate and 1 plain rope side by side and touching each other on counter and top with remaining 2 ropes, reversing colors as shown to form checkerboard. Press together lightly, then wrap and chill overnight. Slice and bake as directed. About 40 calories per cookie.

⚜ ¢ **Chocolate Pinwheels:** Prepare dough as directed; into half mix 1 (1-ounce) envelope no-melt semisweet chocolate. Flatten chocolate dough on a large piece of wax paper into a rectangle roughly 12″×9″×¼″. On another piece of wax paper, flatten vanilla dough into a rectangle the same size. Carefully invert vanilla dough on the chocolate, aligning edges as well as possible; peel off wax paper, roll up like a jelly roll, wrap, and chill overnight. Slice and bake as directed. (*Note:* To reverse colors in pinwheels, simply invert chocolate dough on vanilla instead of vice-versa.) About 40 calories per cookie.

⚜ BUTTERSCOTCH ICEBOX COOKIES

Makes 8 dozen

3½ cups sifted flour
2 teaspoons baking powder
½ teaspoon salt
1 cup butter, margarine, or vegetable shortening
2 cups firmly packed light brown sugar
1 egg
1½ teaspoons vanilla
3 tablespoons heavy cream

Sift flour with baking powder and salt and set aside. Cream butter and sugar until light; add egg and vanilla and beat well. Slowly add dry ingredients and cream. Shape dough into rolls about 2" in diameter; wrap and chill several hours until firm. Preheat oven to 400° F. Slice rolls ⅛"–¼" thick and arrange 1" apart on ungreased baking sheets. Bake 6–10 minutes until lightly browned. Transfer to wire racks to cool. About 50 calories per cookie.

MOLASSES ICEBOX COOKIES

Makes about 6 dozen

3¼ cups sifted flour
½ teaspoon baking soda
¼ teaspoon salt
1 tablespoon ginger
½ teaspoon cinnamon
¼ teaspoon allspice
1 cup butter, margarine, or shortening
1 cup firmly packed light brown sugar
½ cup molasses

Sift flour with soda, salt, and spices and set aside. Cream butter and sugar until very light and fluffy.

Work dry ingredients in alternately with molasses, beginning and ending with dry ingredients. Divide dough in half and shape into 2 rolls about 2" in diameter. Wrap and chill several hours until firm. Preheat oven to 350° F. Slice rolls ⅛" thick, space cookies about 1½" apart on ungreased baking sheets and bake 8–10 minutes until just firm to the touch. Let cool about 1 minute on baking sheets before transferring to wire racks to cool. About 60 calories per cookie.

⚜ ALMOND-ORANGE ICEBOX COOKIES

Makes 8 dozen

2¾ cups sifted flour
¼ teaspoon salt
¼ teaspoon baking soda
1 cup butter or shortening
½ cup sugar
½ cup firmly packed light brown sugar
2 tablespoons orange juice
1 tablespoon finely grated orange rind
1 egg
½ cup blanched, slivered almonds

Sift flour, salt, and soda together and set aside. Cream butter until fluffy and beat in sugars. Mix in orange juice, rind and egg and beat well. Gradually stir in dry ingredients, then almonds. Shape into rolls about 1½" in diameter, wrap and chill several hours until firm. Preheat oven to 375° F. Using a very sharp knife (because of almonds in dough), slice ⅛" thick and place 1½" apart on greased baking sheets. Bake 10–12 minutes until lightly ringed with brown. Transfer to wire racks to cool. About 40 calories per cookie.

VARIATION:

⚜ **Orange-Chocolate Jewels:** Prepare as directed but omit almonds; instead, stir in 2 (1-ounce) squares finely grated semisweet chocolate. Shape, chill, slice, and bake as directed. About 40 calories per cookie.

OATMEAL ICEBOX COOKIES

Makes 6 dozen

¾ cup sifted flour
½ teaspoon salt
½ teaspoon baking soda
½ cup butter or margarine
½ cup firmly packed light brown sugar
½ cup sugar
1 egg, lightly beaten
1 teaspoon vanilla
1½ cups uncooked quick-cooking oatmeal
½ cup finely chopped pecans, walnuts, or blanched, toasted almonds

Sift together flour, salt, and baking soda and set aside. Cream butter and sugars until light and fluffy. Beat in egg and vanilla; mix in dry ingredients, oatmeal, and nuts. Divide dough in half, turn out on lightly floured board, and shape into 2 rolls about 10″ long and 1½″ in diameter. Wrap in foil or plastic food wrap and chill well or freeze. About 10 minutes before cookies are to be baked, preheat oven to 375° F. Slice rolls ¼″ thick and arrange cookies 2″ apart on lightly greased baking sheets. Bake about 10 minutes until tan. Cool 5 minutes on baking sheet, then transfer to wire rack and cool completely. About 55 calories per cookie.

PEANUT BUTTER REFRIGERATOR COOKIES

Children especially like these.
Makes about 5 dozen

2 cups sifted flour
¾ teaspoon baking powder
½ teaspoon cinnamon
⅓ cup butter, margarine, or vegetable shortening
¼ cup creamy or crunchy peanut butter
¾ cup sugar
1 egg
½ cup finely chopped, roasted, blanched peanuts

Sift flour with baking powder and cinnamon and set aside. Cream butter, peanut butter, and sugar until light; add egg and beat well. Slowly add dry ingredients; stir in nuts. Shape dough into a roll 2″–2½″ in diameter; wrap and chill several hours until firm. Preheat oven to 400° F. Slice roll ⅛″ thick, arrange 1″ apart on ungreased baking sheets, and bake 6–8 minutes until pale tan. Cool 1 minute on sheets before transferring to wire racks. About 55 calories per cookie.

FIG AND ALMOND PINWHEELS

Wrapped in foil, rolls of dough can be kept in the freezer several months. Simply slice and bake as needed.
Makes about 6 dozen

2 cups sifted flour
½ teaspoon baking powder
⅛ teaspoon baking soda
½ teaspoon salt
½ cup butter or margarine
2 tablespoons vegetable shortening
½ cup sugar
⅓ cup firmly packed light brown sugar
1 egg, lightly beaten
¾ teaspoon vanilla

Fig and Almond Filling:
1¼ cups finely chopped dried figs (about ½ pound)
¼ cup sugar

¾ cup water
2 teaspoons lemon juice
½ cup very finely chopped, blanched almonds

Sift flour with baking powder, soda, and salt and set aside. Cream butter, shortening, sugar, and brown sugar until light and fluffy. Add egg and vanilla and beat well. Slowly mix in dry ingredients just to blend. Chill dough 6–8 hours. Meanwhile, make the filling: Mix figs, sugar, and water in a saucepan and simmer 8–10 minutes, stirring constantly, until thickened. Off heat, add lemon juice; cool and stir in nuts. Divide dough in half; roll out 1 portion to measure 9"×11" (it should be about ¼" thick). Spread with half the filling, leaving ½" margins all around. Roll up from longest side jelly-roll fashion; pinch seam together, wrap in foil or wax paper, and freeze until firm. Repeat with remaining dough and filling. To bake: Preheat oven to 400° F. Slice rolls ⅛" thick, arrange cookies 2" apart on ungreased baking sheets, and bake about 8 minutes until lightly browned. Cool 2–3 minutes on sheets before transferring to wire racks to cool. About 70 calories per cookie.

BAR COOKIES

Here's the fastest way to fill the cookie jar. Simply stir up a batter, bake in one pan, then cool and cut in bars or squares. Most bars are as much cake as cookie, though some, the superrich, are half cookie, half candy. The advantages of bar cookies, in addition to how fast they can be made, are that they store well and are adored by nearly everyone.

Some Tips:
– If batter is very rich or contains much fruit, grease *and* flour pan.
– Always use the pan sizes given in recipes; an incorrect size can give bars an altogether different (and often unpleasant) texture.
– When placing batter in pan, spread well to corners.
– Always let bars cool upright in their pan on a wire rack several minutes before cutting (recipes specify how long).
– Use a very sharp knife for cutting bars, and if mixture is hard or sticky, dip knife in hot water.
– If your hand is unsteady, use a metal-edged ruler to guide you when cutting bars.

BASIC BROWNIES

Chewy chocolate brownies. But try the variations, too.
Makes 16 brownies

⅓ cup butter or margarine
2 (1-ounce) squares unsweetened chocolate
¾ cup sifted flour
½ teaspoon baking powder
¼ teaspoon salt
1 cup sugar
2 eggs
1 teaspoon vanilla
¾ cup coarsely chopped pecans or walnuts

Preheat oven to 350° F. Melt butter and chocolate in a small, heavy saucepan over lowest heat; cool to room temperature. Sift flour with baking powder and salt and set aside. Beat sugar, eggs, and vanilla until light and fluffy; slowly mix in chocolate mixture, then dry ingredients. Stir in nuts. Spoon into a greased 8"×8"×2" pan and bake 30–35 minutes until brownies just begin to pull from sides of pan. Cool to room temperature upright in pan on a wire rack. Cut into 16 squares and serve. About 165 calories per brownie.

To Make with Cocoa: Increase amount of butter to ½ cup and, instead of melting, cream with sugar until fluffy. Beat in eggs and vanilla. Sift ⅓ cup sifted cocoa with flour, baking powder, and salt and work into creamed mixture. Stir in nuts and bake as directed. About 170 calories per brownie.

To Make with No-Melt Chocolate: Instead of melting butter, soften to room temperature and mix with 2 (1-ounce) envelopes no-melt unsweetened chocolate. Beat into creamed mixture and proceed as directed. About 170 calories per brownie.

VARIATIONS:

Mocha Brownies: Stir 2 tablespoons instant coffee powder into melted butter and chocolate and proceed as directed. About 165 calories per brownie.

Brown Sugar Brownies: Prepare as directed, substituting 1 cup firmly packed light brown sugar for the sugar. About 165 calories per brownie.

Minted Double Chocolate Tea Brownies: Prepare recipe as directed, but chop nuts fine. Stir ½ cup mint-flavored semisweet chocolate bits into batter along with nuts and spread in a greased 13"×9"×2" pan. Bake 20–25 minutes, cool as directed, and cut into 40 bars. About 70 calories per brownie.

Frosted Brownies: Prepare, bake, and cool brownies as directed; before cutting, spread with Chocolate Butter Cream Frosting (you'll need half the recipe). About 275 calories per brownie.

Filled and Frosted Tea Brownies: Prepare recipe as directed and bake in a greased 13"×9"×2" pan 20–25 minutes; cool and spread half of surface with Chocolate Butter Cream Frosting and other half with Coffee, Maple, or Orange Butter Cream Frosting (you'll need about ½ recipe of each). Cut each half into 24 equal-size bars and sandwich together in pairs with chocolate frosting on top. About 245 calories per brownie.

Two-Tone Brownies: Prepare recipe as directed but omit chocolate. Spoon half the batter into a greased 8"×8"×2" pan; mix 1 (1-ounce) envelope no-melt unsweetened chocolate into remaining batter and carefully spread on top. Bake as directed. About 155 calories per brownie.

Coconut Brownies: Prepare as directed, substituting ⅔ cup flaked coconut for nuts. About 145 calories per brownie.

Coconut Topped Brownies: Prepare Coconut Brownies; before baking spread with ⅔ cup flaked coconut mixed with 1 tablespoon each sugar and melted butter. Bake as directed. About 175 calories per brownie.

Snowy Coconut Chews: Omit chocolate and stir 1 cup flaked coconut into batter along with nuts. Spread in a greased 13"×9"×2" pan, bake 20–25 minutes, cool, and cut in 2" squares. About 100 calories each.

⊠ FUDGY SAUCEPAN BROWNIES

Truly dark and chewy. "The best," brownie lovers say.
Makes 16 large brownies

¾ cup butter or margarine
4 (1-ounce) squares unsweetened chocolate

2 cups sugar
4 eggs
1½ cups unsifted flour
½ teaspoon salt
1½ teaspoons vanilla
1¾ cups coarsely chopped pecans

Preheat oven to 375° F. Melt butter and chocolate in a large, heavy saucepan over lowest heat. Off heat, mix in remaining ingredients in order listed, beating well after each addition. Pour batter into a greased 9"×9"×2" pan and bake 40 minutes until brownies just begin to pull from sides of pan. Cool pan of brownies upright on a wire rack to room temperature, then cut in 16 squares. About 350 calories per brownie.

⊠ WHEAT- AND MILK-FREE BROWNIES

Most children adore brownies. For those with wheat and/or milk allergies, here's a special recipe.
Makes 2 dozen

⅓ cup margarine, softened to room temperature
1 cup firmly packed light brown sugar
2 eggs, lightly beaten
2 (1-ounce) envelopes no-melt semisweet chocolate or 2 (1-ounce) squares semisweet chocolate, melted
1 teaspoon vanilla
⅔ cup unsifted rice flour
½ teaspoon baking powder
¼ teaspoon salt
½ cup coarsely chopped pecans or walnuts

Preheat oven to 350° F. With a spoon, mix margarine and sugar well; add all remaining ingredients except nuts and blend until smooth. Stir in nuts and pour into a greased 8"×8"×2" or 9"×9"×2" pan. Bake 30 minutes or until sides shrink slightly from pan and top springs back when touched. Cool upright in pan on a wire rack, then cut into squares. About 105 calories per brownie.

MARBLE BROWNIES

Makes 16 brownies

Chocolate Layer:
1 (4-ounce) package sweet chocolate
3 tablespoons butter or margarine
2 eggs
¾ cup sugar
½ cup unsifted flour
½ teaspoon baking powder
Pinch salt
1 teaspoon vanilla
⅔ cup chopped pecans or walnuts

Vanilla Layer:
1 (3-ounce) package cream cheese
2 tablespoons butter or margarine
¼ cup sugar
1 egg
1 tablespoon flour
¾ teaspoon vanilla

Preheat oven to 350° F. Begin chocolate layer: Melt chocolate with butter over lowest heat, stirring to mix; cool to room temperature. Meanwhile, prepare vanilla layer: Beat cheese and butter until fluffy, gradually add sugar, creaming until fluffy. Beat in egg, flour, and vanilla; set aside while you finish chocolate layer. Beat 2 eggs until pale in color, add sugar slowly, and beat until mixture is quite thick. Stir in flour, baking powder, and salt, then cooled chocolate mixture, vanilla, and nuts. Spread half the chocolate layer in a greased 9"×9"×2" baking pan, top with vanilla layer, then remaining chocolate layer. Zigzag a knife through batter to create marbled effect. Bake 35–40 minutes until brownies pull from sides of pan. Cool upright in pan on a wire rack,

BUTTERSCOTCH BROWNIES

Makes 16 brownies

⅔ cup sifted flour
1 teaspoon baking powder
¼ teaspoon salt
¼ cup butter or margarine
1 cup firmly packed light or dark brown sugar
1 egg
1 teaspoon vanilla
¾ cup coarsely chopped walnuts or pecans

Preheat oven to 350° F. Sift flour with baking powder and salt and set aside. Melt butter in a saucepan over low heat, add sugar, and stir until dissolved; cool 5 minutes. Beat in egg and vanilla, mix in dry ingredients and nuts. Spoon into a greased 8"×8"×2" baking pan and bake 30–35 minutes until brownies just begin to pull from sides of pan. Cool upright in pan on a wire rack to room temperature, then cut in 16 squares. About 135 calories per brownie.

VARIATION:

Toll House Brownies: Prepare as directed but reduce amount of nuts to ½ cup; stir ½ cup semisweet chocolate bits into batter along with nuts and bake as directed. About 155 calories per brownie.

SCOTTISH SHORTBREAD

The secret of good shortbread lies in the kneading. The dough *must* feel satin-smooth, and getting it that way may take as long as 15 minutes. Makes 2 dozen slim, pie-shaped pieces

3¼ cups sifted flour
¼ cup sifted rice flour
¼ teaspoon salt
1 cup butter (*no substitute*), softened to room temperature
½ cup sugar

Preheat oven to 350° F. Sift flour with rice flour and salt. Using your hand or a wooden spoon, work butter and sugar together until light in color; blend in dry ingredients. Keeping dough in bowl, knead vigorously until satin-smooth and no sugar grains remain. Divide dough in half, place each on an ungreased baking sheet or 9" pie tin, and press flat into 9" circles, using palms of hands. Crimp edges as you would piecrust and cut each circle into 12 wedges (but don't separate). Bake 25 minutes until pale golden, not brown. Cool in pans on wire rack 10 minutes, then carefully recut to separate wedges; cool thoroughly. If you like, sprinkle shortbread lightly with sugar as soon as it comes from oven. About 145 calories per piece.

VARIATION:

Shortbread for Those with Milk Allergies: Make as directed, substituting ¾ cup margarine or vegetable shortening for the butter. About 125 calories per piece.

LEMON SPONGE SQUARES

Makes about 2½ dozen

Cake:
1½ cups sifted flour
½ teaspoon salt
¼ teaspoon baking powder
½ cup butter or margarine
1 cup sugar
3 eggs, separated
⅓ cup lemon juice
1 tablespoon finely grated lemon rind
1 cup sifted confectioners' sugar

Frosting:
1 cup sifted confectioners' sugar
1 tablespoon heavy cream or evaporated milk
2 tablespoons butter or margarine, softened to room temperature

Preheat oven to 350° F. Sift flour with salt and baking powder and set aside. Cream butter and sugar until light and fluffy; add egg yolks, one at a time, beating well after each addition. Mix in dry ingredients alternately with lemon juice, beginning and ending with dry ingredients. Mix in lemon rind. In a spearate bowl beat egg whites until soft peaks form. Add confectioners' sugar, ¼ cup at a time, beating well after each addition, then continue to beat until stiff peaks will form. Fold egg white mixture into batter and pour into a well-greased and floured 13″×9″×2″ baking pan. Bake 35–40 minutes on center oven rack until top springs back when lightly touched. Cool upright in pan on a rack 3–5 minutes. Meanwhile, mix frosting ingredients together until smooth. While cake is still warm, spread top evenly with frosting. Cool in pan, then cut into squares. About 130 calories per piece.

CHINESE CHEWS

The easiest way to "chop" dates is to snip them into small pieces with kitchen shears. To simplify the job, chill dates slightly before cutting. Makes about 3 dozen

¾ cup sifted flour
1 cup sugar
1 teaspoon baking powder
Pinch salt
1 cup coarsely chopped dates
1 cup coarsely chopped walnuts
3 eggs, beaten until fluffy
½ teaspoon vanilla (optional)
⅔ cup sifted confectioners' sugar

Preheat oven to 350° F. Sift dry ingredients together and mix in dates and walnuts. Fold in eggs and, if you like, add vanilla. Spread evenly in a greased and floured 15½″×10½″×1″ jelly-roll pan (it will seem at first as though there isn't enough batter, but keep spreading it toward the corners; layer will be *very* thin). Bake 20 minutes until lightly browned and top springs back when touched. Cool upright in pan on a wire rack 10–12 minutes, then cut in 1¼″–1½″ squares. Roll in confectioners' sugar while still warm, then cool before serving. About 80 calories each.

MERINGUE NUT BARS

These cookies are wheat- and milk-free, good for those with either or both of these allergies.
Makes 4 dozen

2 egg whites
1⅓ cups sugar
1 tablespoon lemon juice
4 cups very finely chopped nuts (pecans, walnuts, or filberts)
1 teaspoon vanilla

Preheat oven to 325° F. Beat egg whites until frothy. Add sugar, 1 tablespoon at a time, beating well after each addition. Add lemon juice, then beat hard (highest mixer speed) 2–3 minutes. (*Note:* All sugar won't dissolve as it does in regular meringues, but mixture should be stiff and glossy.) Measure out 1 cup of the meringue mixture and set aside. Mix nuts and vanilla into remaining mixture; roll half of it out on a well-floured board into a rectangle about 6″ wide and ¼″ thick (the length doesn't matter, but the width should be 6″ so that bars of uniform size can be cut easily). Spread ½ cup reserved plain meringue on top. With a floured knife, cut into bars 3″ long and 1½″ wide and arrange 2" apart on a greased and floured baking sheet. Roll, spread, and cut remaining nut meringue mixture the same way. Bake 25 minutes or until topping is creamy white and firm. Cool on wire racks. About 80 calories each.

CHEWY PECAN-CINNAMON BARS

Makes about 5 dozen

1 cup sifted flour
½ teaspoon baking powder
1 tablespoon cinnamon
¼ teaspoon salt
1 cup butter or margarine
1 cup plus 1 tablespoon sugar
2 eggs, separated
1 cup finely chopped pecans

Preheat oven to 300° F. Sift flour with baking powder, cinnamon, and salt. Cream butter with 1 cup sugar until light and fluffy; add egg yolks one at a time, beating well after each addition. Mix in dry ingredients. Spread mixture in an ungreased 14"×17" baking sheet with a slightly raised edge. Beat egg whites until frothy, add remaining sugar and continue beating until stiff; spread evenly over mixture on sheet; sprinkle with nuts. Bake 40–45 minutes until golden. Cool upright in pan on a rack 10 minutes, cut in bars, and cool. About 65 calories each.

▣ CONGO SQUARES

Filled with nuts and chocolate bits. And so quick to make.
Makes 4 dozen

½ cup butter or margarine, softened to room temperature
1 (1-pound) box dark brown sugar
3 eggs, lightly beaten
2½ cups sifted flour
½ teaspoon salt
1 teaspoon vanilla
1 (6-ounce) package semisweet or 1 (5¾-ounce) package milk chocolate bits
1 cup coarsely chopped walnuts or pecans

Preheat oven to 350° F. Cream butter with sugar and eggs until well blended; mix in remaining ingredients in the order listed. Spread in a greased 15½"×10½"×1" jelly-roll pan and bake 30–35 minutes until top springs back when touched. Cool upright in pan on a wire rack, then cut into squares. About 110 calories each.

GREEK WHEAT AND WALNUT BARS (KARYDATA)

Makes 16

¾ cup butter or margarine
¾ cup sugar
3 eggs, separated
1 cup uncooked farina or wheatina
1 teaspoon cinnamon
1½ cups finely chopped walnuts
¼ teaspoon salt

Syrup:
¼ cup sugar
2 tablespoons warm water

Topping:
Sifted confectioners' sugar

Preheat oven to 375° F. Cream butter until fluffy and add sugar, a little at a time, beating well after each addition. Beat egg yolks in, one at a time. Stir in farina, cinnamon, and nuts. Beat egg whites with salt until soft peaks form and fold into batter. Spread in a greased and floured 9"× 9"×2" baking pan and bake 20–25 minutes until just firm to the touch. Meanwhile, prepare syrup: Boil sugar and water in a very small, heavy saucepan until clear and slightly thickened, about 3–5 minutes. Remove pan from oven, spoon syrup over top, distributing it as evenly as possible; return to oven and bake 5–10 minutes longer until mixture pulls from sides of pan. Cool upright in pan 5 minutes on a wire rack, then loosen and turn out. When cold, dust *lightly* with confectioners' sugar and cut into 16 bars. About 230 calories each.

BISHOP'S BARS

Like dates, candied cherries are more easily snipped into small pieces than chopped.
Makes 20

2 eggs
⅔ cup sugar
⅔ cup sifted flour
½ teaspoon baking powder
¼ teaspoon salt
1 (6-ounce) package semisweet chocolate bits
1 cup coarsely chopped pecans or walnuts
¾ cup coarsely chopped dates
⅔ cup coarsely chopped candied red cherries
½ teaspoon vanilla

Preheat oven to 375° F. Beat eggs until fluffy and pale; gradually beat in sugar and continue beating until about the color and consistency of mayonnaise. Sift flour with baking powder and salt, add chocolate bits, nuts, dates, and candied cherries, and toss well to dredge; stir into egg mixture, then mix in vanilla. Spread in a greased and floured 9"×9"×2" baking pan and bake 30–35 minutes until lightly browned and mixture begins to pull from sides of pan. Cool upright in pan 10–15 minutes on a wire rack, then cut into large bars (make 5 cuts one way and 4 the other). About 165 calories each.

GERMAN DATE SQUARES

Makes about 3 dozen

½ cup butter
1 cup sugar
3 eggs
½ cup sifted flour
2 teaspoons baking powder
¼ teaspoon salt
1 cup finely chopped walnuts
1 cup finely chopped, pitted dates
1 teaspoon vanilla

Preheat oven to 250° F. Cream butter until light, add sugar and continue creaming until fluffy. Add eggs, one at a time, beating well after each addition. Sift flour with baking powder and salt and mix into batter. Stir in walnuts, dates, and vanilla. Spoon into a lightly greased 9"×9"×2" baking pan and bake, uncovered, 3 hours (mixture should be quite firm and tan and crackly on top). Cool upright in pan on a wire rack several hours, then cut into 1½" squares (no larger because these cookies are rich). About 90 calories each.

LAYERED APRICOT BARS

Makes 2 dozen

⅔ cup dried apricots
1 cup water
½ cup butter or margarine, softened to room temperature
¼ cup sugar
1⅓ cups sifted flour
½ teaspoon baking powder
¼ teaspoon salt
1 cup firmly packed light brown sugar
2 eggs, lightly beaten
1½ teaspoons brandy flavoring or 1 teaspoon vanilla
½ cup finely chopped walnuts

Preheat oven to 350° F. Place apricots and water in a small saucepan,

COOKIES

cover, and simmer 10 minutes; drain, cool, and chop fine; set aside. Stir butter and sugar together until well mixed; blend in 1 cup flour. Spread mixture in a greased 9"× 9"×2" pan and bake 25 minutes. Meanwhile, sift remaining flour with baking powder and salt. Beat brown sugar and eggs until thick; add flavoring. Slowly mix in dry ingredients, apricots, and walnuts. Spread lightly and evenly over baked layer and bake ½ hour longer. Cool upright in pan on a wire rack, then cut into bars, using a knife dipped in warm water. About 130 calories each.

¢ APPLE-OATMEAL BARS

Makes 2 dozen

1 cup sifted flour
½ teaspoon salt
½ cup firmly packed light brown sugar
⅓ cup plus 2 tablespoons butter or margarine
1 cup uncooked quick-cooking oatmeal

Filling:
2½ cups finely chopped or thinly sliced, peeled apples
¼ cup sugar
¼ teaspoon nutmeg

Preheat oven to 400° F. Sift flour with salt and add brown sugar. Using a pastry blender, cut in ⅓ cup butter until the size of small peas; mix in oatmeal. Pack half the mixture into a well-greased 9"×9"× 2" pan; top with apples and sprinkle with sugar and nutmeg. Dot with remaining butter and cover with remaining oatmeal mixture, pressing down lightly. Bake 45–50 minutes until tan on top. Cool upright in pan on a wire rack and cut into bars. About 100 calories each.

VARIATIONS:

Date-Oatmeal Bars: Prepare oatmeal mixture as directed but, instead of preparing filling, simmer 2 cups chopped, pitted dates, uncovered, with 1 cup water and 2 tablespoons sugar 7–10 minutes until thick; cool to room temperature. Spread evenly over bottom oatmeal layer; do not dot with butter as above. Top with remaining oatmeal mixture and bake as directed. About 140 calories each.

Fig-Oatmeal Bars: Prepare like Date-Oatmeal Bars, substituting 1 cup chopped dried figs for 1 cup of the dates. About 140 calories each.

Prune-Oatmeal Bars: Prepare like Date-Oatmeal Bars, substituting 1 cup chopped, pitted prunes for 1 cup of the dates. About 140 calories each.

CURRANT AND RAISIN BARS

Makes 32 bars

1 cup sifted flour
1 teaspoon baking powder
½ teaspoon salt
2 eggs
1 teaspoon lemon extract
1 cup sugar
¾ cup seedless raisins
¾ cup dried currants

Optional Topping:
Confectioners' sugar or Lemon Sugar Glaze

Preheat oven to 350° F. Sift flour with baking powder and salt and set aside. Beat eggs until thick and lemon colored, add lemon extract, then gradually add sugar, ¼ cup at a time, beating well after each addition. Slowly mix in dry ingredients until just blended. Stir in raisins and currants. Spread mixture in a well-greased 13"×9"×2" baking pan and bake 30 minutes until top springs back when lightly touched. Cool upright in pan on wire rack 10 minutes, cut into 32 bars, and cool completely in pan. If you like, sift confectioners' sugar over bars before serving or frost with Lemon Sugar Glaze. About 70 calories each if unglazed, 85 calories if glazed.

VARIATIONS:

Fruit Bars: Prepare as directed, substituting 1½ cups finely diced, pitted dates, prunes, dried apricots, or figs for currants and raisins. About 70 calories each.

Fruit and Nut Bars: Stir ¾–1 cup coarsely chopped walnuts, pecans, almonds, or hazelnuts into batter after adding fruit; bake as directed. *Or* scatter nuts evenly on top of batter after spreading in pan and bake as directed. About 90 calories each.

Black Walnut and Coconut Bars: Omit raisins and currants; stir 1½ cups flaked coconut and 1 cup coarsely chopped black walnuts into batter; bake as directed. About 95 calories each.

NO-BAKE COOKIES

These are an American invention and a good one, too. They require very little time, effort, or expertise to make and, when properly stored, will keep longer than any other type of cookie. Many, especially those rich in fruit or flavored with liquor, will actually improve on standing.

◨ NO-BAKE RUM BALLS

Makes about 2½ dozen

1 ¾ cups fine vanilla wafer crumbs
1 cup finely ground pecans
1 cup unsifted confectioners' sugar
¼ cup cocoa
3 tablespoons light corn syrup
¼ cup light rum or bourbon
⅓ cup sifted confectioners' sugar (for dredging)

Place all but last ingredient in a bowl and mix well, using your hands. Roll into 1″ balls and dredge in confectioners' sugar. (*Note:* These cookies keep well up to 10 days when stored in airtight canisters.) About 100 calories each.

FOUR-FRUIT BALLS

These cookies are milk-, egg-, and wheat-free, good for those with any or all of these allergies.
Makes 5 dozen

½ pound pitted dates
1 (12-ounce) package dried figs
1½ cups seedless raisins
12 pitted prunes
2 ounces crystallized ginger
1½ cups walnuts or pecans
Juice of ½ lemon
2 tablespoons pineapple or other fruit juice or rum or brandy
½ teaspoon cinnamon
Confectioners' sugar

Put dates, figs, raisins, prunes, ginger, and nuts through fine blade of meat grinder. Mix well, using your hands, sprinkle in fruit juices and cinnamon and mix again. Shape into 1″ balls and roll in confectioners' sugar to coat. Let stand at room temperature 3–4 hours, then store airtight. About 100 calories each.

ORANGE-ALMOND BALLS

Makes 5 dozen

½ cup butter or margarine
1 (6-ounce) can frozen orange juice concentrate, thawed

1 (1-pound) box confectioners'
    sugar, sifted
1 (12-ounce) box vanilla wafers
1 cup sliced, blanched almonds
1 cup toasted, blanched almonds,
    chopped fine, or 1 cup toasted or
    colored* flaked coconut, chocolate
    jimmies, colored sugar, or
    decorettes

Heat butter and orange concentrate in a large saucepan over low heat, stirring until butter melts. Off heat, mix in confectioners' sugar. Crush vanilla wafers in an electric blender at high speed or with a rolling pin; add to mixture along with sliced almonds and mix well. Shape into 1″ balls and roll in toasted almonds. Arrange on a tray or baking sheet and chill 2–3 hours before serving. Store airtight and, if weather is warm, in refrigerator. About 100 calories each.

▣ PORCUPINES

Makes 3 dozen

2 eggs, lightly beaten
1 cup finely chopped, pitted dates
¾ cup sugar
1 cup finely chopped pecans or
    walnuts
2 cups toasted rice cereal
2 cups flaked coconut (about)

In a saucepan over moderate heat, heat eggs, dates, and sugar, stirring constantly about 10 minutes until mixture thickens. Cool 5 minutes and stir in nuts and cereal. Cool 10 minutes longer, then drop by rounded teaspoonfuls into flaked coconut; roll in coconut and shape into balls. About 85 calories each.

NO-BAKE CHOCOLATE BONBONS

Makes 2 dozen

¼ pound sweet chocolate
1 cup sifted confectioners' sugar
1 cup finely crushed vanilla wafer
    crumbs
¼ cup light corn syrup
2 tablespoons honey
½ cup finely chopped walnuts or
    pecans
Sifted confectioners' sugar (for
    dredging)

Melt chocolate in top of double boiler over simmering water. Off heat stir in remaining ingredients except dredging sugar in order listed; as mixture stiffens, use hands to blend well. Shape into 1″ balls and roll in confectioners' sugar. Let ripen 1–2 days before serving. About 95 calories each.

▣ CHOCOLATE HAYSTACKS

Makes 2 dozen

1 (6-ounce) package semisweet
    chocolate bits
1 (6-ounce) package butterscotch
    bits
½ cup coarsely chopped pecans,
    walnuts, or almonds
1 (3-ounce) can chow mein noodles

Melt chocolate and butterscotch bits in a double boiler over simmering water. Off heat mix in nuts and noodles. Drop by tablespoonfuls on wax paper and cool to room temperature. About 85 calories each.

VARIATION:

Butterscotch Haystacks: Prepare as directed, using 2 (6-ounce) packages butterscotch bits instead of 1 chocolate and 1 butterscotch. About 85 calories each.

FUDGE NUGGETS

Not as high-calorie as you might think.
Makes 3 dozen

2 cups sugar
1 cup milk
2 (1-ounce) squares semisweet chocolate
½ teaspoon instant coffee powder
2 tablespoons butter or margarine
1 teaspoon vanilla
1¾ cups graham cracker crumbs

Mix sugar and milk in a large, heavy saucepan; insert candy thermometer. Boil over moderate heat without stirring until thermometer registers 230° F.; mixture will foam up, so adjust heat as needed to prevent its boiling over. Off heat, stir in chocolate, coffee, butter and vanilla; mix until chocolate melts. Stir in crumbs and, working quickly, drop by rounded teaspoonfuls on wax paper. Cool thoroughly and serve. About 80 calories each.

MRS. BOULDIN'S DATE-NUT FINGERS

Makes about 4 dozen

½ cup margarine
1 cup sugar
1 egg, lightly beaten
1 (8-ounce) package pitted dates, chopped fine
1¼ cups toasted rice cereal
1 cup finely chopped pecans or walnuts
1 cup finely shredded coconut (about)

Melt margarine in the top of a double boiler over simmering water. Stir in sugar and egg. Heat, stirring every 5 minutes, for 20–30 minutes over simmering—not boiling—water until mixture is thick and will coat the back of a wooden spoon. Pour over dates, add cereal and nuts, and mix well. Cool to room temperature, then shape into "fingers" about 2" long and 1" wide and roll in coconut to coat evenly. Store airtight. About 125 calories each.

⊠ PEANUT BUTTER BARS

Crunchy and sweet.
Makes 4 dozen

1 cup sugar
1 cup light corn syrup
1 (12-ounce) jar crunchy peanut butter
4 cups toasted rice cereal
1 cup coarsely chopped unsalted peanuts (optional)

Heat and stir sugar, syrup, and peanut butter in a very large saucepan over moderate heat until mixture boils. Off heat mix in remaining ingredients. Pack into a well-greased 9"×13"×2" baking pan and cool. Cut into bars. About 90 calories each (without peanuts), 110 calories (with peanuts).

SPECIAL COOKIES

The two following recipes don't fit any of the basic cookie categories. Both are deep-fat-fried, both are Continental classics. And neither, surprisingly, is very high in calories.

SWEDISH ROSETTES (STRUVOR)

For these you will need a special rosette iron, available in housewares sections of many large department stores. Read instructions accom-

VIII. EATING ALFRESCO

Charcoal Broiled Shish Kebabs – "All-American" picnic – Spiced Blue Crabs – French Chocolate Ice Cream

Charcoal Broiled Shish Kebabs (vol. 1, p. 370); and Spit-Roasted Leg of Lamb (vol. 1, pp. 361–63)

Crisp-Fried Chicken (vol. 1, p. 557); Jiffy Deviled Eggs (vol. 2, p. 19); Herbed Potato Salad (vol. 2, p. 299); and Creamy Sweet-Sour Coleslaw (vol. 2, pp. 294–95)

Spiced Blue Crabs (vol. 1, p. 686)

French Chocolate Ice Cream (vol. 2, p. 465)

panying iron carefully before beginning this recipe.
Makes 4 dozen

Shortening or cooking oil for deep fat frying
2 eggs plus 1 egg yolk
¾ cup light cream
⅓ cup sugar
1 cup sifted flour
¼ teaspoon salt
Sifted confectioners' sugar

Begin heating fat in a deep fryer over moderate heat; insert deep fat thermometer. Beat eggs, cream, and sugar just to blend; sprinkle in flour and salt, a little at a time, and beat until smooth. When fat reaches 355–65° F., heat rosette iron by submerging in the hot fat about 10 seconds. Lift out, shake off excess fat, and dip iron carefully into batter so that its top is *exactly level* with that of the batter—any deeper and you won't be able to get the rosette off the iron. Plunge batter-coated iron into fat and, as soon as batter starts to "puff," gradually lift out iron so that rosette will slip back into fat. When lightly brown on one side, flip gently with a fork to brown other side. (*Note:* The whole procedure takes only a few seconds so you'll have to work fast.) Lift rosette out with a fork or slotted spoon and drain on paper toweling. Repeat with remaining batter, reheating iron for each rosette and never frying more than 2 rosettes at a time and keeping fat as near to 355–65° F. as possible. Spread rosettes out in a single layer on several thicknesses of paper toweling to cool. Dust with confectioners' sugar and serve.

These are best eaten the day they're made, but if stored airtight, they will keep fairly well about a week. About 60 calories each.

¢ ⚖ **PORTUGUESE FILHOS**

These crisp, wine-flavored, fried cookies are best served the day they are made and are especially good with a glass of port or Madeira.
Makes 3½ dozen

Shortening or cooking oil for deep fat frying
1 egg, lightly beaten
1 tablespoon port wine
3 tablespoons cold water
¼ teaspoon vanilla
2 teaspoons melted butter
2 tablespoons sugar
¼ teaspoon salt
1½ cups plus 2 tablespoons sifted flour
Confectioners' sugar

Begin heating shortening in a deep fat fryer over low heat; insert deep fat thermometer. Mix egg, port, water, vanilla, butter, sugar, and salt; sprinkle in flour and mix well. Turn out on lightly floured board and knead 1 minute just until smooth. Divide dough in half and roll, one piece at a time, *paper thin.* Cut in 2½" squares; make a slit in one corner and pull opposite corner through. When fat reaches 375° F., drop in *filhos,* 4 or 5 at a time, and fry about 2 minutes until golden; turn them over to brown evenly if they don't flip on their own. Lift out with a slotted spoon and drain on paper toweling. Cool, then dredge with confectioners' sugar. About 50 calories per cookie.

CHAPTER 24

CANDIES AND NUTS

How many good cooks' love of food began with a batch of fudge? Dozens, probably, because nothing draws children to the kitchen faster than candy making. And nothing *involves* them more quickly in cooking. It's fun to beat divinity, pull taffy or mints, shape marzipan. Fun, too, to lick the spoon. As long as everyone's had a good time, it doesn't matter if the candy isn't perfect. The next batch will be better and the next batch better still.

Tips for Making Better Candies

– First, the weather. It does make a difference, with cooked candies especially. So choose a dry, cool, clear day. If you must make candy on a damp day, cook 2° higher on the candy thermometer than recipe specifies so that candy will harden.
– Measure ingredients precisely.
– Do not double or halve recipes for cooked candies and do not make substitutions in ingredients.
– Follow recipes to the letter; candies are critical (apt to fail) and do not take to improvisation.
– Use a heavy, deep, straight-sided pan about four times the volume of combined recipe ingredients so that candy has plenty of room to boil up without boiling over. Also choose pan with an insulated handle so you won't burn yourself.
– Use a wooden spoon for stirring—less chance of the candy's turning to sugar and less chance of burning yourself. And make sure spoon is clean and dry each time it is put into the candy.
– *Use a candy thermometer.* Clip to side of pan, making sure bulb is immersed but does not touch bottom. Some cooks recommend inserting thermometer after candy boils (to reduce risk of crystallization), but the wait isn't necessary except for fondant. Moreover, a cold thermometer may break if shoved into boiling syrup. Keep an eye on the mercury; it will climb to 220° F. at a snail's pace, but race on thereafter and, unless watched, overshoot its mark. Read thermometer at eye level and, if in doubt about its accuracy, also use one of the tests described below. *To test accuracy of thermometer:* Insert in a pan of cold water and bring gradually to a boil; boil 10 minutes. Temperature should be 212° F. If not, note difference and adjust recipe temperatures accordingly. For example, if thermometer reads 210° F. at the boiling point,

CANDIES AND NUTS

cook candy 2° lower than recipes suggest; if it registers 214° F., cook 2° higher.
- Use a marble slab for working candy or, failing that, a large ironstone platter or heavy metal tray.
- To simplify beating at the end, use a portable electric mixer.

- *To help keep creamy candies from turning to sugar:* There's no guarantee, but the following precautions should all help:
- If candy contains butter, cook in a buttered pan; also butter end of thermometer.
- Brush down crystals that collect on

CANDY-MAKING TEMPERATURES AND TESTS

Thermometer Reading	Candy Stage	Test (use fresh water for each test)
230–34° F.	Thread	Syrup dropped from a spoon will form a 2″ thread.
234–40° F.	Soft Ball	A drop of syrup forms a soft ball in cold water that flattens on removal.
244–48° F.	Firm Ball	A drop of syrup forms a firm, pliable ball in cold water that holds its shape on removal.
250–65° F.	Hard Ball	A drop of syrup forms a hard but still pliable ball in cold water.
270–90° F.	Soft Crack	Syrup dropped in cold water forms pliable strands.
300–10° F.	Hard Crack	Syrup dropped in cold water forms brittle strands.

Note: These thermometer readings are slightly higher than those marked on standard candy thermometers, but they have proved more reliable.

sides of pan and thermometer with a damp pastry brush (just one crystal can turn a whole batch of candy gritty).
- When making fondant or other simple water-sugar candies, cover and boil about three minutes after sugar is dissolved; steam will wash away crystals that have gathered on sides of pan.
- Do not stir candy after sugar has dissolved.
- Do not hurry the cooking or the cooling; let syrup cool to 110° F. before beating. If speed is important, cool in a larger pan of cold water.
- Do not scrape pan when turning candy out.
- Knead cooled, cooked candy to reduce size of sugar crystals and work in any nuts afterward.
- Do not overcook candy; use a clean, dry spoon each time you make a test.
- Do not overbeat candy before turning out; it should be about the consistency of a butter frosting and just losing its gloss. Once candies begin turning, they turn fast, so you must work quickly. If candy becomes too hard, pick up and knead until soft again, then pat into a pan with your hands or shape into a roll and slice.

Some Special Candy-Making Techniques

To Color Sugar: Put about ½ cup sugar (granulated) in a small bowl and add food color, 1 drop at a time; rub sugar quickly between fingers after each addition to distribute color evenly. Be careful not to overcolor.

To Make Vanilla Sugar: Place 1 pound sugar in a canister with an airtight lid and push 2 vanilla beans deep down in. Cover and let stand at least one week before using. If you want a supply of vanilla sugar on hand, replenish sugar as needed and add a fresh vanilla bean every 6 months. Use vanilla sugar wherever vanilla extract is called for—in making candies, cookies, custards, dessert soufflés, and sauces. Allow 1 tablespoon vanilla sugar for each ¼ teaspoon vanilla and decrease recipe's total quantity of sugar accordingly. Thus, in a recipe calling for 2 cups sugar and 1 teaspoon vanilla, you would use 4 tablespoons vanilla sugar and 1¾ cups sugar.

To Spin Sugar: Pastry cooks love to frame their masterpieces with clouds of spun sugar, and frankly, the spinning's a sticky business best left to the pros. Attempted at home without the proper technique or utensils, it can quickly wreck both cook and kitchen. However, for those who want to try their luck, here is a method that has worked fairly well at home. Pick a dry, crisp day. Place 1 cup sugar, ½ cup hot water, and ⅛ teaspoon cream of tartar in a small, heavy pan; insert candy thermometer. Heat, stirring until sugar dissolves, then boil slowly, uncovered, without stirring until thermometer reaches 310° F. While syrup cooks, cover counter near stove (and floor beneath it) with newspapers. Stand 2 clean quart-size soda bottles on counter about 2 feet apart. When syrup reaches 310° F., turn heat off; let cool a few minutes, then dip in a wooden spoon and pull out. If syrup spins a long, fine hair, temperature is right for spinning. Dip in a wire whisk, then spin by drawing threads from one bottle to the other, using a quick whipping motion. Continue dipping and spinning until you have an inch-wide skein of threads, then carefully lift off and set on wax paper. Continue spinning, reheating syrup if it should harden too much. *How to Use Spun Sugar:* Use as soon as possible—to wreathe a compote of fruits, a showy pastry or cake or shape into a nest on a circle of cardboard, fill with delicate candies, and use as a *bonbonnière*-centerpiece.

To Toast Grated Coconut: Spread coconut out in an ungreased shallow baking pan and toast uncovered, stirring often, 30–40 minutes at 300° F. until golden.

To Color Grated Coconut: Dip a toothpick in food color, stir through coconut, then rub with your fingers to distribute. Repeat until color is the intensity you want.

To Dip Candies in Fondant: (see Fondant).

To Dip Candies in Chocolate: This isn't just a matter of melting chocolate and sloshing candy through it. It's a tricky technique requiring years to master, so don't be discouraged if your chocolates are streaked or ragged around the edges.

For best results:
– Choose a cool, crisp day and have kitchen cool.
– Choose dippable candies—fondant balls, firm caramels, candied cherries.
– Have both chocolate and candies

CANDIES AND NUTS

to be dipped at room temperature.
– Use semisweet chocolate (once called dot or dipping chocolate) and work with no more than 2 pounds at a time and no less than 1.
– Holding chocolate by wrapper, grate fine into the top of a double boiler, handling as little as possible; insert a candy thermometer.
– Melt very slowly over hot—*not boiling*—water, stirring until chocolate reaches 130° F. Do not add any water to chocolate. Set chocolate over—not in—cold water and cool to 85° F. Also cool water in double boiler bottom to 85° F. Replace chocolate over warm water and keep there throughout dipping.
– Using a dipping fork or 2-pronged kitchen fork, dip candies one at a time into chocolate to coat evenly; set on wax-paper-covered wire racks, twirling tail end of chocolate into curlicues on top of candies.
– Let chocolates harden 5–10 minutes before removing from paper. Trim off any ragged edges and store airtight (not in the refrigerator, which will cause chocolate to whiten and streak). (*Note:* You must work quickly with chocolate. If it hardens before candies are dipped, remelt and cool as before. Semisweet chocolate bits can be used for dipping but are stiffer and lack the finish of semisweet chocolate.)

About Special Candy Flavorings

Essences and oils are used to flavor candies as well as the familiar extracts available at supermarkets. Gourmet shops usually carry a full line of essences (butterscotch, peppermint, spearmint, etc.), also such exotics as rose, violet, and orange flower water. Drugstores are the best places to buy oils—peppermint, wintergreen, clove, etc.—because all are used in pharmacy. These are potent and must be added drop by drop.

About Decorating Candies

Candies need little decoration and, in fact, are extremely difficult to decorate because of their small size. Bar candies are best left alone, but won't be overdecorated if topped by nut halves or candied cherries. Fondant and uncooked fruit balls can be rolled in finely ground nuts, grated coconut (plain, colored, or toasted), in sugar (plain or colored), in chocolate shot or decorettes. Fondant-dipped candies can be adorned with piped-on icing designs (the same decorative icings used for cakes). But keep designs simple—a tiny star or flower or leaf. When tinting icings, use a light touch, remembering that colors often darken as icing dries. Liquid food colors work well, but the number of colors is limited. For a broader palette, investigate paste colors sold in specialty shops.

About Wrapping and Keeping Candies

When it comes to wrapping and storing, candies fall into two groups: those that dry on standing and those that absorb moisture from the air. Fudges, fondants, and other creamy candies are the drying kind; caramels and hard candies just the opposite. Always store the two kinds separately so that one doesn't give up moisture to the other. Caramels and hard candies should be individually wrapped as soon as they've cooled in wax paper, cellophane, plastic food wrap, or foil, then placed in airtight canisters. The drying kind needn't be wrapped unless you hope to keep it some time, but it *should* be stored airtight.

About Packing and Shipping Candies

Sturdy, undecorated candies are the best travelers—fudge, fondant, caramels, nougats, fruit balls, etc. Wrap each piece separately, then pack and ship as you would cookies (see About Packing and Shipping Cookies).

COOKED CANDIES

¢ ⚖ **FONDANT**

Fondant is more a base for other confections than a candy to be eaten by itself.
Makes about 1 pound

2 cups sugar
1½ cups hot water
⅛ teaspoon cream of tartar or ¼ teaspoon lemon juice

Heat and stir all ingredients in a large, heavy saucepan over moderate heat until sugar dissolves; cover and boil 3 minutes. Uncover, insert candy thermometer that has been heated under hot tap, and cook *without stirring* to 238° F. or until a drop of fondant forms a soft ball in cold water. (*Note:* Wipe crystals from sides of pan with a damp pastry brush as they collect —fondant will be less apt to turn grainy.) Remove fondant from heat and let stand 1–2 minutes until bubbles subside; pour—*without scraping pan*—onto a marble slab or large, heavy platter rubbed lightly with a damp cloth; cool undisturbed until barely warm. (*Note:* If you have an extra candy thermometer, insert as soon as fondant is poured.) When fondant has cooled to 110° F., scrape from edges with a broad spatula in toward center again and again until it thickens and whitens; pick up and knead until velvety. Wrap fondant in cloth wrung out in cold water and "season" ½ hour before using. (*Note:* Covered with damp cloth and stored in an airtight jar, fondant will keep 3–4 days.) About 25 calories per 1″ ball.

To Flavor Fondant: Knead in about ½ teaspoon extract (vanilla, almond, rum, spearmint, rose or orange water) or a few drops oil of peppermint or wintergreen. Add these *by the drop,* tasting as you go so you don't *overflavor.*

To Color Fondant: Dip a toothpick in desired food color, then pierce fondant in several places. Knead to distribute color; if too pale, repeat—but keep colors pastel.

To Use Fondant for Dipping: Melt fondant (either plain or flavored) in the top of a double boiler over simmering water, stirring until smooth. Drop in candy center, nut or fruit to be dipped, turn with a long-handled, two-tined fork to coat evenly, lift to wax paper, and for a professional touch twirl tag end of fondant into a curlicue on top of each piece when removing fork. Let harden, then lift from paper.

VARIATIONS:

⚜ **Coffee Fondant:** Prepare as directed, substituting 1½ cups strong black coffee for the water and 2 tablespoons light corn syrup for the cream of tartar. About 25 calories per 1″ ball.

⚜ **Honey Fondant:** Prepare as directed but add 2 tablespoons honey and omit the cream of tartar. About 25 calories per 1″ ball.

⚜ **Butter Fondant:** Prepare as directed, using the following ingredients: 2 cups sugar, 1 cup milk, 1 tablespoon light corn syrup, and 1 tablespoon butter. About 30 calories per 1″ ball.

⚜ **Opera Creams:** Prepare as directed, using the following ingredients: 2 cups sugar, 1 cup heavy cream, and ⅛ teaspoon cream of tartar. Do not boil covered; instead, after sugar dissolves, cook without stirring to 238° F. (*Note:* This fondant takes longer to cream up on the marble slab than regular fondant.) About 35 calories per 1″ ball.

Confections to Make with Fondant

Stuffed Fruits: Shape fondant into small balls and stuff into pitted dates, prunes, or dried apricots. Roll in granulated sugar. About 50 calories each.

Nut Bonbons: Sandwich large walnut or pecan halves together with small fondant balls. About 50 calories each.

Frosted Nuts or Fruits: Dip large walnut or pecan halves, whole blanched almonds, candied cherries, pitted dates, or dried apricots into melted fondant. About 50 calories each.

Snow-Capped Fudge Balls: Prepare Best Chocolate Fudge as directed but omit nuts; instead of pouring into pan, pour onto a damp marble slab or heavy platter and, when cool enough to handle, knead until soft and velvety. Shape into small balls and dip in melted fondant. About 100 calories each.

Pinwheels: Take equal parts fondant and fudge (without nuts) or two flavors and colors of fondant and knead separately until smooth. Flatten one piece into a rectangle about 6″×8″ and ⅛″ thick. Pat remaining candy on top to fit, then roll jelly-roll fashion and slice ¼″ thick. About 60 calories each.

⚜ **Thin Mints:** Flavor fondant with peppermint, tint pale green and flavor with spearmint, or tint pale pink and flavor with wintergreen. Melt in the top of a double boiler over simmering water, stirring until smooth; drop from a teaspoon onto wax paper and let harden. About 25 calories each.

Sugarplums: Roll fondant around small pieces of fruit—candied cherries, small pitted dates, cubes of preserved ginger, pieces of dried apricots. About 60 calories each.

⚜ **Snowballs:** Shape fondant into small balls and roll in flaked coconut. About 35 calories each.

Nut Balls: Shape fondant into small balls and roll in ground nuts—pecans, walnuts, almonds, pistachios, Brazil nuts, hazelnuts. About 40 calories each.

Christmas Balls: Shape fondant into small balls and roll in chocolate or silver shot, colored sugar, or decorettes. About 40 calories each.

⚜ **Coffee Drops:** Shape fondant into small balls and roll in instant coffee powder. About 25 calories each.

DIVINITY

Makes about 1½ pounds

2½ *cups sugar*
½ *cup light corn syrup*
½ *cup water*
2 *egg whites*
1 *teaspoon vanilla*
1½ *cups coarsely chopped walnuts or pecans*

Place sugar, syrup, and water in a large, heavy saucepan; insert candy thermometer. Heat and stir over moderate heat until sugar dissolves; lower heat slightly and cook uncovered *without stirring* to 260° F. Toward end of cooking, beat egg whites until soft peaks form. When syrup reaches 260° F., add to egg whites in a very slow, fine stream, beating hard all the while. Continue adding, more quickly toward the end, until all syrup is in. Add vanilla and beat until stiff peaks form; fold in nuts. Drop from rounded teaspoons onto wax-paper-lined baking sheets and cool thoroughly. About 40 calories per piece.

VARIATIONS:

Seafoam: Prepare as directed but use firmly packed light brown sugar instead of granulated. About 40 calories per piece.

⚜ **Confetti Divinity:** Prepare as directed but omit nuts; instead, stir in 1 cup minced mixed candied fruit. About 35 calories per piece.

⚜ **Fruit Divinity:** Prepare as directed but omit nuts; instead, stir in 1 cup minced pitted dates, prunes, or dried apricots. About 30 calories per piece.

Christmas Divinity: Prepare as directed but reduce nuts to ¾ cup; also stir in ¾ cup minced mixed red and green candied cherries. About 40 calories per piece.

⚜ **Pistachio Divinity:** Prepare as directed but reduce vanilla to ½ teaspoon and add ¼ teaspoon almond extract. Tint pale green if you like, beat until stiff, and fold in 1½ cups minced pistachio nuts. About 40 calories per piece.

BEST CHOCOLATE FUDGE

Makes about 2 pounds

4 *cups sugar*
1 *cup milk*
3 *(1-ounce) squares unsweetened chocolate*
¼ *teaspoon salt*
¼ *cup light corn syrup*
¼ *cup butter or margarine*
1 *teaspoon vanilla*
1–1½ *cups coarsely chopped pecans or walnuts (optional)*

Heat sugar, milk, chocolate, salt, and corn syrup, uncovered, in a large, heavy saucepan with a candy thermometer over moderate heat, stirring constantly, until sugar dissolves. Continue cooking, uncovered, *without stirring* but occasionally moving a wooden spoon back and forth over bottom of pan until thermometer reaches 236–38° F. or mixture forms a soft ball in cold water. Remove from heat, drop in butter, and cool, without stirring, to 110° F. Add vanilla and beat until fudge is quite thick and begins to lose its gloss. Quickly mix in nuts, if you like, and spread in a well-buttered 8″×8″×2″ baking pan. Cool until firm and cut into 1″ squares. For better flavor, store airtight and ripen 24 hours. About 80 calories per piece (with 1 cup nuts).

BLOND FUDGE

A good choice for those allergic to chocolate.

Makes about 1 pound

2 cups sugar
¼ cup light corn syrup
1⅓ cups milk
⅓ cup light cream
1 teaspoon vanilla
1 tablespoon butter
1¼ cups coarsely chopped pecans or walnuts (optional)

Place sugar, syrup, milk, and cream in a large, heavy saucepan (mixture tends to boil up, so pan should be at least 4 times combined volume of ingredients); insert candy thermometer. Heat and stir over moderate heat until sugar dissolves, reduce heat slightly and cook, uncovered, stirring only if mixture threatens to boil over, until thermometer reaches 238° F. or a drop of candy forms a soft ball in cold water. Toward end of cooking, mixture will be very thick, so watch closely and move spoon gently across bottom of pan occasionally to keep it from scorching. Remove from heat, add vanilla and butter *without stirring*, and cool to 110° F. Beat until thick and no longer glossy, quickly mix in nuts, if you like, and turn into a buttered 8″×8″×2″ pan, spreading to edges. Cool until firm and cut in 1″ squares. About 50 calories per piece (with nuts).

VARIATIONS:

Coconut Fudge: Prepare as directed but omit nuts; instead, stir in 1¼ cups flaked coconut. Turn out, cool, and cut as directed. About 45 calories per piece.

Toll House Fudge: Prepare as directed but reduce nuts to ¾ cup; at the same time, mix in 1 cup semisweet chocolate bits. Turn out, cool, and cut as directed. About 65 calories per piece.

PENUCHE

Makes about 1 pound

1 (1-pound) box light brown sugar
¾ cup milk
2 tablespoons butter or margarine
1 teaspoon vanilla

Heat sugar, milk, and butter in a large, heavy saucepan with a candy thermometer over moderate heat, stirring until sugar dissolves. Lower heat slightly and cook, uncovered, *without stirring* to 240° F. or until mixture forms a soft ball in cold water. Off heat, add vanilla—do not stir—and cool to 110° F. Beat until thick and no longer shiny, pour into a buttered 8″×8″×2″ pan, spreading to edges. Score in 1″ squares and cool to room temperature. Cut into 1″ squares and serve. About 40 calories per piece.

VARIATIONS:

Nut Penuche: Prepare as directed but mix in ⅔ cup coarsely chopped pecans or walnuts just before pouring into pan. About 50 calories per piece.

Coconut Penuche: Prepare as directed but mix in ⅔ cup flaked coconut just before pouring into pan. About 45 calories per piece.

Maple Penuche: Prepare as directed but use maple flavoring instead of vanilla. For a more delicate flavor, use 1 cup granulated sugar and 1¼ cups firmly packed light brown sugar instead of all brown sugar. About 40 calories per piece.

Coffee Penuche: Prepare as directed but use ¼ cup heavy cream and ½ cup very strong black coffee instead of milk. About 45 calories per piece.

PRALINES

A friend said of these, "Best I ever ate!"
Makes about 2 dozen

2 cups sugar
½ cup firmly packed light brown sugar
1 teaspoon baking soda
¼ teaspoon salt
⅛ teaspoon cinnamon
1 cup buttermilk
¼ cup butter or margarine
2 cups pecan halves

Mix sugars, soda, salt, cinnamon, and buttermilk in a large, heavy saucepan; drop in butter. Insert candy thermometer. Heat, uncovered, and without stirring over moderately high heat until candy thermometer registers 238° F. or mixture forms a soft ball in cold water. Remove from heat at once and stir in pecans. Beat briskly with a wooden spoon about 1 minute, then drop onto wax-paper-lined baking sheets, making each praline 2″–2½″ in diameter. Let harden thoroughly before serving. About 165 calories each.

CARAMELS

Cook very slowly in your heaviest saucepan. This mixture is sweet and thick—apt to scorch.
Makes about 1 pound

1 cup sugar
⅔ cup light corn syrup
1½ cups light cream
⅛ teaspoon salt
1 teaspoon vanilla

Place sugar, syrup, and ½ cup cream in a large, heavy saucepan; insert candy thermometer. Heat and stir over moderate heat until sugar dissolves. Turn heat to low and cook, uncovered, stirring occasionally, to 238° F. Mix in ½ cup cream and cook, stirring as needed to keep from sticking, to about 236° F. or until mixture forms a soft ball in cold water. Mix in remaining ½ cup cream and heat, stirring constantly, until very thick and a drop firms up quickly in cold water. Thermometer may register only 230° F., but if mixture firms up, take from heat. Mix in salt and vanilla and pour into a buttered 8″×8″×2″ pan. Cool until just warm and score in 1″ squares. Cool thoroughly, cut in squares, and wrap individually in wax paper or cellophane. About 40 calories per piece.

VARIATIONS:

Nut Caramels: Prepare as directed but just before pouring into pan stir in ⅔ cup minced walnuts or pecans. About 45 calories per piece.

Chocolate Caramels: Prepare as directed but add 1½ (1-ounce) squares melted unsweetened chocolate along with final ½ cup cream. Watch closely to see that mixture doesn't scorch during final cooking. About 45 calories per piece.

ALMOND NOUGAT

For best results, use 2 candy thermometers, one in each syrup.
Makes 1 pound

First Syrup:
½ cup sugar
½ cup light corn syrup
2 tablespoons water

Second Syrup:
1½ cups sugar
½ cup light corn syrup
¼ cup water

2 egg whites

¼ cup butter or margarine, softened to room temperature
¼ teaspoon almond extract
1 cup minced blanched almonds or ½ cup each minced almonds and minced candied red cherries

Mix first syrup in a small, heavy saucepan, insert candy thermometer, and heat over moderately high heat until sugar dissolves; cook, uncovered, *without stirring* to 246° F. Combine second syrup ingredients in a larger, heavy saucepan meanwhile, insert candy thermometer, and heat and stir over moderate heat until sugar dissolves; pull pan to side of burner. Beat egg whites to stiff peaks in large mixer bowl; add first syrup in a slow, *thin* stream, beating at moderate speed. At the same time, heat second syrup, uncovered, *without stirring* to 285° F. or until a drop forms pliable strands in cold water. Continue to beat whites at slow speed. Add second syrup in a fine, slow stream, beating at moderate speed. Add almond extract and beat until very thick; stir in nuts and, using buttered hands, press into a well-buttered 8" × 8" × 2" pan. Cover loosely with wax paper and let stand in a cool place (not refrigerator) overnight. Cut in 1" squares and let ripen 2–3 days before eating. Wrap pieces individually and store airtight. About 60 calories per piece.

OLD ENGLISH TOFFEE

Makes 1 pound

1 cup butter (*no substitute*)
¼ cup light cream or evaporated milk
2 cups firmly packed light brown sugar
1 teaspoon vanilla

Melt butter in a large, heavy saucepan over moderate heat; mix in cream and sugar, insert candy thermometer, and heat uncovered, stirring occasionally, until sugar dissolves. Continue cooking uncovered, moving a wooden spoon across bottom of pan *occasionally* (but not actually stirring) until thermometer reaches 280° F. or a little mixture dropped in ice water separates into firm but not brittle strands. Remove from heat, let bubbling subside, add vanilla, and stir only to blend. Pour into a well-buttered 8" × 8" × 2" pan and cool 10 minutes—candy should be hardening but still plastic. Turn onto a foil-lined board and score in 1" squares. Cool to room temperature, break into squares, and wrap each in foil, cellophane, or wax paper. Store airtight. About 55 calories per piece.

PEANUT BRITTLE

Makes about 1¾ pounds

2 cups roasted, blanched peanuts
2 cups sugar
½ cup water
½ cup light corn syrup
¼ cup butter or margarine
¼ teaspoon baking soda
½ teaspoon vanilla

Warm peanuts in a large, heavy skillet over low heat 5–7 minutes, shaking skillet occasionally; keep warm while making brittle. Mix sugar, water, and corn syrup in a large, heavy saucepan; insert candy thermometer. Set over high heat and heat, stirring, until sugar dissolves, then heat, uncovered, *without stirring* but moving a wooden spoon back and forth across bottom of pan occasionally to prevent scorching. When thermometer reaches 310° F. or a little hot syrup dropped in ice water turns brittle, remove from heat, add butter, peanuts, soda, and vanilla, and mix just to blend. Let bubbles subside, pour out as thin as possible on buttered baking sheets, spreading mixture with a buttered spatula. *For extra-thin brittle:* Cool until easy to handle, then pull out and stretch with buttered fingers. When brittle is cold, crack into bite-size pieces. (*Note:* Flavor will be best if brittle ripens 24 hours in an airtight canister.) About 80 calories per piece.

VARIATIONS:

Lacy Brittle: Prepare as directed, heating ¼ teaspoon cream of tartar with sugar mixture and increasing soda to ½ teaspoon. About 80 calories per piece.

Pecan Brittle: Prepare as directed, substituting roasted pecan halves for peanuts. About 80 calories per piece.

Walnut Brittle: Prepare as directed, substituting walnut halves for peanuts. About 80 calories per piece.

Almond Brittle: Prepare as directed, substituting toasted, blanched whole almonds for peanuts. About 80 calories per piece.

BLACK WALNUT-MOLASSES CANDY

Makes about 1 pound

1½ cups molasses
1 cup sugar
1 cup light cream or evaporated milk
2 tablespoons butter or margarine
½ teaspoon baking soda
½–¾ cup finely chopped black walnuts

Mix molasses, sugar, and cream in a large, heavy saucepan, drop in butter, and insert candy thermometer; heat, stirring constantly, over moderately low heat until sugar dissolves. Cook uncovered, moving a wooden spoon across bottom of pan *occasionally* (but not actually stirring) to 250° F. or until a drop of candy forms a hard ball in cold water. Off heat, add soda, then nuts and stir *just to blend.* Pour into a well-buttered 9"×9"×2" pan; do not scrape pan. Cool 15 minutes, score in 1" squares and, when hardening but still pliable, turn out on a baking sheet. Cool to room temperature and cut in 1" squares. Wrap each piece and store airtight. About 40 calories per piece.

Some Pointers on Pulled Candies

– Don't attempt to make pulled candies in a cool kitchen; candies will harden too fast.
– Rally the troops; pulling candy calls for teamwork and young strong arms.
– Remove rings—candy can pull the settings out.
– Make sure counter underneath platter or tray of hot candy is heat resistant; if not, it may get scorched.
– While candy is still too hot to handle, begin the pulling with a buttered spatula by lifting and stretching.
– Use buttered bare hands for the pulling (gloves are hopeless) and keep rebuttering them as needed to keep candy from sticking.

¢ **VANILLA TAFFY**

Makes 1 pound

2 cups sugar
⅔ cup light corn syrup
⅓ cup water
3 tablespoons butter or margarine
½ teaspoon vanilla

Mix sugar, syrup, and water in a heavy saucepan, drop in butter, and insert candy thermometer. Heat, stirring constantly, over moderately high heat until sugar dissolves, then cook, uncovered, *without stirring* to 270° F. or until a drop of candy forms firm, pliable strands in cold water. Pour at once onto a buttered marble slab, large ironstone platter, or heavy metal tray; do not scrape pan. Cool 1–2 minutes, then sprinkle with vanilla and, using a buttered spatula, fold edges in toward center to distribute heat evenly. When candy is cool enough to handle, pull and stretch with buttered hands until light and no longer shiny. When too stiff to pull further, stretch into a rope about ½" in diameter, and with buttered kitchen shears cut across the grain every 1". Separate pieces, dry thoroughly, then wrap and store airtight. About 40 calories per piece.

VARIATION:

¢ **Peppermint Taffy:** Prepare as directed but omit vanilla; sprinkle taffy instead with 8 drops oil of peppermint and, if you like, a few drops green coloring. Proceed as above. About 40 calories per piece.

¢ **MOLASSES TAFFY**

Makes 1¼ pounds

2 cups sugar
1 cup dark molasses
1 cup water
¼ cup butter or margarine

Mix sugar, molasses, and water in a heavy saucepan, drop in butter, and insert candy thermometer. Heat, stirring constantly, over moderately high heat until sugar dissolves, then cook, uncovered, *without stirring* to 270° F. or until a drop of the mixture forms firm, pliable strands in cold water. Pour onto a buttered marble slab at once, or large ironstone platter or heavy metal tray.

Cool 1–2 minutes, then fold edges toward center to distribute heat. When cool enough to handle, pull and stretch with buttered hands until light and no longer shiny. When too stiff to pull further, stretch into a rope about ½" in diameter and with buttered kitchen shears cut across the grain every 1". Separate pieces as you cut, cool thoroughly, then wrap individually and store airtight. About 40 calories per piece.

MRS. B's PULLED MINTS

A difficult recipe, not for beginners. At first these mints are chewy and taffy-like, but after several days of "ripening," they soften magically and will melt in your mouth.
Makes 1½ pounds

4 cups sugar
2 cups boiling water
½ cup unsalted butter (no substitute)
6–8 drops oil of peppermint
4–5 drops green food coloring (optional)

Mix sugar and water in a heavy saucepan, drop in butter, and insert candy thermometer. Heat, stirring constantly, over moderately high heat until sugar dissolves, then cook, uncovered, *without stirring* to 258° F. or until a drop of mixture forms a hard ball in cold water. Immediately pour onto a buttered marble slab, large ironstone platter, or heavy metal tray; do not scrape out pan. Sprinkle with oil of peppermint and, if you like, coloring. Cool slightly but as soon as possible begin pulling and stretching with buttered hands. When candy pales and begins to lose its gloss, pull and twist into a rope ¾"–1" in diameter and cut across the grain with buttered kitchen shears every ½"–¾". Spread pieces out on wax paper and, when thoroughly cool, store airtight. Let "ripen" 2–3 days—mints will cream up. About 50 calories per piece.

⚖ ¢ FRUIT JELLIES

This mixture froths up, so use an extra-large pan.
Makes about 1 pound

2 envelopes unflavored gelatin
1½ cups sugar
1½ cups cold water
1 cup light corn syrup
½ teaspoon lemon juice
¼ teaspoon lemon, orange, mint, or strawberry flavoring
Few drops food coloring
Sugar or cornstarch for dredging

Mix gelatin and sugar in a large, heavy saucepan, slowly mix in water, then syrup; insert candy thermometer. Heat over moderate heat, stirring constantly, until sugar dissolves, then cook *without stirring* to 222° F. Gently set pan in a larger pan half full of cold water and cool jelly to 160° F. Mix in lemon juice, flavoring, and appropriate color. Pour into an oiled 9"×9"×2" pan and cool to room temperature. Refrigerate overnight, turn out on wax paper sprinkled with sugar or cornstarch, ease jelly out and sprinkle top with sugar or cornstarch. Cut in 1" squares with a knife dipped in hot water. Let dry 2–3 hours and store airtight. About 35 calories per 1" square if dredged in cornstarch.

APRICOT-ALMOND BALLS

An old-fashioned sweetmeat.
Makes 4 dozen

1 pound dried apricots
1½ cups sugar
¼ cup orange juice
Finely grated rind of 1 orange
1 cup minced, blanched almonds
Sifted confectioners' sugar for dredging

Put apricots through fine blade of meat grinder. Place in the top of a double boiler, set over just boiling water, and mix in sugar, orange juice, and rind. Cook, stirring now and then, ½ hour; mix in nuts and cook 5 minutes longer. Cool in pan until just slightly warm, then drop from a teaspoon into confectioners' sugar and shape into 1" balls. When all balls have been shaped, roll again in confectioners' sugar. Store airtight. About 65 calories per piece.

CANDIED APPLES

Prepare a batch for Halloween.
Makes 6

6 wooden skewers or lollipop sticks
6 medium-size red apples, washed, dried, and stemmed
2 cups sugar
2 cups light corn syrup
1 cup water
¼ cup red cinnamon candies
½ teaspoon red food coloring

Insert skewers in stem ends of apples. Place all remaining ingredients except food coloring in a heavy saucepan; insert candy thermometer and heat over moderate heat, stirring constantly, until sugar and candies dissolve; do not boil. Mix in coloring, then boil *without stirring* until thermometer reaches 300° F. or a drop of syrup turns brittle in cold water. Remove from heat. Working quickly, dip apples, one at a time, in syrup to coat evenly, twirling so excess drains off. Cool on wax-paper-lined baking sheet. About 360 calories each.

VARIATION:

Caramel Apples: Instead of preparing syrup above, melt 1½ pounds vanilla caramels with 3 tablespoons water in the top of a double boiler, stirring until smooth. Dip apples as directed, scraping excess caramel off on rim of pan. Cool until caramel hardens. About 500 calories each.

¢ CANDIED CITRUS PEEL

Some grapefruits have excessively bitter peel. To overcome it, soak peel overnight in heavily salted water (weight peel so it stays submerged).
Makes about 1 pound

Peel from 2 grapefruits, 3 large thick-skinned oranges (navel are good), or 4 large lemons or limes
5 quarts cold water
3 cups sugar
½ cup hot water
1 teaspoon gelatin mixed with 1 tablespoon cold water

Cover peel with 1 quart cold water, bring to a boil, then drain. Repeat process 4 times until peel is tender. If peel has thick pith, scoop out excess. Cut peel in thin strips or petal shapes. Heat 2 cups sugar and hot water in a heavy saucepan over moderately low heat, stirring constantly until sugar dissolves. Add peel and boil slowly until clear and candy-like, about 25 minutes, moving a wooden spoon occasionally over bottom of pan to keep peel from sticking. Add gelatin, cook and stir 5 minutes longer. Remove from heat and let stand 3-5 minutes; remove peel, a few pieces at a time, allowing excess syrup to drain off, then roll in remaining sugar to coat thickly. (*Note:* Toothpicks are handy for doing this messy job. Dry peel on wire racks and store airtight.) About 70 calories per piece.

For Brightly Colored Peel: Tint syrup color of fruit used or roll candied peel in colored sugar.

¢ LOLLIPOPS

Makes 1½ dozen

2 cups sugar
½ cup light corn syrup
½ cup water
⅛–¼ teaspoon oil of orange, lime, peppermint, or spearmint (obtainable at drugstores)
Few drops food coloring
1½ dozen lollipop sticks or wooden skewers

Mix sugar, corn syrup, and water in a heavy saucepan, insert candy thermometer, and heat, stirring constantly, over moderately high heat until sugar dissolves; cook, uncovered, *without stirring* to 300° F. or until a drop of syrup turns brittle in cold water. Cool 2-3 minutes. Meanwhile, lay lollipop sticks 3″ apart on buttered baking sheets. Add flavoring and coloring to syrup, mix gently, creating as few bubbles as possible, then drop from a teaspoon onto sticks forming lollipops about 2½″ in diameter. Cool, lift off sheets —not by sticks, but by loosening with the point of a knife. About 60 calories each.

VARIATIONS:

Licorice Lollipops: Flavor syrup with ¼ teaspoon oil of anise and color black with 1 teaspoon paste food coloring. About 60 calories each.

Butterscotch Lollipops: Prepare as directed but heat ½ cup firmly packed light brown sugar and 2 tablespoons butter along with other ingredients. Flavor with ¼ teaspoon vanilla or butterscotch extract; do not color. About 90 calories each.

UNCOOKED CANDIES

✠ UNCOOKED FONDANT

Makes about 1 pound

¼ cup butter (*no substitute*), softened to room temperature
2 tablespoons light corn syrup
3 tablespoons heavy cream
1 (*1-pound*) box confectioners' sugar, sifted
½ teaspoon vanilla

Cream butter with corn syrup and heavy cream until smooth; slowly add sugar, a little at a time, beating well after each addition and kneading in the last bit if necessary. Work in vanilla. Roll into 1″ balls or use to stuff pitted dates, prunes, or dried apricots or to sandwich together large pecan or walnut halves. About 40 calories per piece, 90 if used to sandwich together nut halves.

VARIATION:

Citrus-Rum Fondant: Prepare as directed, substituting 3 tablespoons dark rum for the cream and 1 teaspoon grated fresh orange or tangerine rind and ⅛ teaspoon orange extract for the vanilla. About 40 calories per piece.

✠ QUICK RAISIN-PECAN FONDANT

Makes about 2 pounds

⅔ cup sweetened condensed milk
1 teaspoon vanilla or maple flavoring
4 cups sifted confectioners' sugar
½ cup seedless raisins
1 cup coarsely chopped pecans

Mix milk and vanilla, add confectioners' sugar about ½ cup at a time, stirring constantly; before adding final ½ cup, work in raisins and pecans with your hands. Knead in remaining sugar, press mixture into an ungreased 8″×8″×2″ baking pan, cover loosely with foil, and chill 2–3 hours until firm. Cut in 1″ squares and let ripen 24 hours in an airtight canister before serving. About 60 calories per piece.

VARIATION:

Chocolate-Covered Fondant Squares: Dip* fondant squares in melted semisweet chocolate to coat evenly. Arrange on wax paper, decorate tops with pecan halves or candied cherries, and let stand in a cool place until chocolate hardens. Wrap airtight. About 110 calories per piece.

KENTUCKY COLONELS

Bourbon-filled, chocolate-covered, butter-cream balls.
Makes 3½ dozen

½ cup butter (*no substitute*)
1 (*1-pound*) box confectioners' sugar, sifted
1 tablespoon evaporated milk or heavy cream
2 tablespoons bourbon (*about*)
1 (*6-ounce*) package semisweet chocolate bits
¼ cup hot water
42 pecan halves

Cream butter until light and fluffy, slowly blend in sugar and evaporated milk, and beat until smooth. Scoop up by rounded measuring teaspoonfuls, shape into balls and arrange 1½″ apart on ungreased baking sheets. With little finger, make deep dents in tops of balls and, using an eyedropper, add a few drops bourbon; pinch tops to seal. Chill ½ hour. Melt chocolate bits in the top of a double boiler over simmering water, add water a little at a time and beat until smooth. Keeping chocolate warm over hot water so it doesn't harden, spoon over balls, coating evenly. Top each ball with a pecan. Chill 2–3 hours before serving. Store airtight in refrigerator or other cool place. About 115 calories per piece.

☒ UNCOOKED FUDGE

As velvety and chocolaty as old-fashioned cooked fudge.
Makes about 1½ pounds

2 (3-ounce) packages cream cheese, softened to room temperature
4 cups sifted confectioners' sugar
2 tablespoons evaporated milk
1 (6-ounce) package semisweet chocolate bits
½ teaspoon vanilla
⅛ teaspoon salt
1 cup coarsely chopped pecans

Beat cream cheese until smooth, slowly blend in sugar and evaporated milk, and beat until creamy. Melt chocolate bits in the top of a double boiler over simmering water, add to cheese mixture along with vanilla and salt, and beat until smooth. Stir in pecans, press into a well-buttered 9″×9″×2″ pan, cover, and chill overnight. Cut in 1″ squares and store in refrigerator or other cool place. About 45 calories per piece.

VARIATIONS:

Uncooked Almond Fudge: Prepare as directed but substitute ½ teaspoon almond extract for vanilla and 1 cup coarsely chopped blanched almonds for pecans. About 45 calories per piece.

Uncooked Cocoa Fudge: Prepare as directed but use ½ cup cocoa instead of chocolate bits and add 2 extra teaspoons milk. About 40 calories per piece.

Uncooked Coconut Fudge: Prepare as directed but stir in 1 cup shredded or flaked coconut instead of pecans. About 45 calories per piece.

Uncooked Peanut Butter Fudge: Prepare as directed but omit chocolate; mix in 1 cup creamy peanut butter and 1 cup coarsely chopped unsalted roasted peanuts instead of pecans. About 55 calories per piece.

Uncooked Maple Fudge: Prepare as directed but omit chocolate and use maple flavoring instead of vanilla. After turning candy into pan, sprinkle with 1 cup finely grated maple sugar and press in lightly. About 42 calories per piece.

☒ MARZIPAN

Delicately shaped and tinted marzipan fruits, flowers, vegetables, and animals are ancient Christmas confections. Special molds, used for the shaping, are sold in housewares departments of many large stores, also by candy supply houses. Pure almond paste can be bought at gourmet shops.
Makes about ½ pound

½ pound pure almond paste
1 egg white, lightly beaten
1½ cups sifted confectioners' sugar

Break up almond paste in a bowl, add egg white and about ½ cup confectioners' sugar, and mix well. Knead in remaining sugar until mixture is smooth and malleable. Marzipan is now ready to color and shape or use in other recipes. About 80 calories per 1″ ball.

To Make Fruits and Vegetables: Knead in appropriate food color, drop by drop, until marzipan is the right color. Pinch off small pieces and shape as desired. To tint or shade, dilute coloring with water and paint on with an artist's brush. Pipe on stems and leaves of green Basic Butter Cream Frosting. To give texture to citrus fruits and strawberries, dust a thimble with confectioners' sugar, then press over surface of candy. (*Note:* Beginners may find it helpful to work from real life fruit.) Stored airtight in refrigerator, candy keeps well several weeks.

VARIATIONS:

Cocoa Marzipan: Prepare marzipan, then knead in 2 tablespoons cocoa. Use to make "mushrooms" or "potatoes" (roll in cocoa after shaping and make "eyes" with a toothpick or skewer). If you prefer, roll into small (about 1") balls and dip* in melted semisweet chocolate. About 85 calories per piece (undipped).

Chocolate-Dipped Marzipan: Prepare marzipan, then knead in ½ teaspoon vanilla, rum or brandy flavoring, and 1 tablespoon instant coffee powder. Sprinkle hands and board with confectioners' sugar, then roll marzipan, a little at a time, into ropes 1" in diameter. Cut in ½" lengths, flatten into ovals, and dip* in melted semisweet chocolate. Before chocolate hardens, top with almond halves. Store airtight. About 125 calories per piece.

SPICY UNCOOKED FRUIT-NUT BARS

Makes about 1½ pounds

1 cup pitted prunes
½ cup dried figs
1 cup seedless raisins
1 cup pitted dates
½ cup coarsely chopped pecans, walnuts, or blanched almonds
¼ teaspoon cloves
¼ teaspoon cinnamon
¼ teaspoon salt
Few drops orange juice (just to moisten)
Sifted confectioners' sugar (for dredging)

Put fruits and nuts through fine blade of meat grinder, mix in seasonings and just enough orange juice to make mixture hold together. Roll or pat out ¼" thick, cut in squares or small circles, and dredge in confectioners' sugar. If you prefer, roll into small balls and dredge. About 40 calories per piece.

⊠ DOUBLE PEANUT CLUSTERS

Makes about 3½ dozen

½ cup sugar
½ cup light corn syrup
¾ cup creamy peanut butter
1 cup roasted, blanched peanuts
1 cup ready-to-eat, concentrated protein cereal

Bring sugar and corn syrup to a boil in a saucepan over moderately low heat, stirring constantly; remove from heat, add peanut butter, and blend until smooth. Quickly mix in remaining ingredients, then drop from a teaspoon onto wax paper, or cool until easy to handle and shape into 1" balls. Let stand in a cool place (not the refrigerator) until firm. Store airtight. About 80 calories per piece.

NUTS

Any nuts can be used in making candies, most can be toasted and eaten out of hand, but the favorites are almonds, walnuts, pecans, peanuts, and pistachios. For variety, try some of the less familiar: Brazil

CANDIES AND NUTS

nuts, cashews, chestnuts, hazelnuts and their European cousin, filberts, macadamias, piñons (pine nuts), or if you're lucky enough to live where you can gather your own, hickory, beech, and butternuts. Nuts *do* run to calories, but fortunately not "empty calories" because they are a high protein food with impressive vitamin and mineral content.

About Buying Nuts

Supermarkets carry all the popular nuts in a variety of forms. Which you buy depends on your budget and time schedule. You'll save money by buying nuts in the shell or unblanched, but you'll spend considerable time preparing them. Obviously, the more nearly ready to use nuts are (toasted, chopped, ground, etc.), the more expensive they will be.

Nuts in the Shell (1 pound unshelled nuts = ½ pound shelled nuts): This is the way to buy nuts if they must be kept some time (some unshelled nuts will keep as long as a year). Choose nuts without splits, scars, holes, or mold. Nuts commonly available in the shell: almonds, Brazil nuts, chestnuts, filberts or hazelnuts, pecans, peanuts, pistachios, and walnuts.

Shelled, Unblanched Nuts: Recipes sometimes call for unblanched nuts (skins add color, flavor, and texture). Those often available this way: almonds, filberts and hazelnuts, peanuts, pistachios. (*Note:* Pecans and walnuts are never blanched.)

Shelled, Blanched Nuts: Almonds, Brazil nuts, filberts, hazelnuts, peanuts, piñons, and pistachio nuts are frequently sold this way.

Shelled, Blanched, Roasted, or Toasted Nuts: Almonds, pecans, peanuts, cashews, hazelnuts, filberts, and macadamias are all available; also mixed roasted nuts. The newest entries are the dry-roasted nuts—lower in calories than the regular roasted nuts. For candies, it's best to use unsalted nuts unless recipes specify to the contrary.

Nut Halves and Meats: A handy form of almonds, pecans, and walnuts. If packaged in plastic bags, sniff for signs of rancidity (these nuts don't stay fresh long). If you are particular about your cooking, you'd do well to prepare your own nuts.

About Preparing Nuts

To Crack:

Thin- or Soft-Shelled Nuts (peanuts and almonds): Crack with your hands and pull out kernels. (*Note:* Chestnuts are soft-shelled but need special techniques—see Vegetables.)

Thick- or Hard-Shelled Nuts: Crack with a nutcracker, pull off shells, and with a nut pick extract kernels. (*Note:* Pecans have a bitter red-brown inner partition that must also be removed.)

To Blanch:

Almonds, Peanuts, Pistachios: Shell, cover with boiling water, and let stand 2 minutes; drain, cool slightly and slip off skins.

Chestnuts: (see vegetable chapter).

Filberts, Hazelnuts: These nuts are so tedious to blanch you'll probably want to pay a little more and buy them already blanched. But if you're counting pennies: Shell nuts, cover with boiling water, and boil 6 minutes; drain and cover with hot tap water. Lift nuts from water, one at a time, and slip and scrape off skins, using a paring knife. The skins are stubborn, will cling to the nuts and your fingers. An easier although not a 100-per-cent-successful method is to drain the blanched nuts, bundle in a turkish towel and rub together briskly.

To Chop Nuts: Do only about ½ cup at a time, using a chopping board and heavy chopping knife. Or, if a quantity must be done, use a chopping bowl and curved chopper.

To Shave Nuts (almonds and Brazil nuts, either blanched or unblanched, are the most suitable): Peel off thin slivers using a vegetable peeler.

To Grate Nuts: The quickest way is to use a rotary grater.

To Grind Nuts: Buzz a few nuts at a time in an electric blender at high speed, stopping and stirring as needed to keep nuts from clumping. Do not use a meat grinder.

To Toast or Roast Nuts: Blanch or not, as you like. Spread out in an ungreased shallow baking pan and roast uncovered, stirring often, ½–1½ hours at 300° F. until lightly browned (size and kind of nut will determine, so watch closely). If you like (and if nuts are blanched), drizzle with melted butter and sprinkle with salt. Toss well to mix and store airtight.

To Deep Fry (best for almonds and peanuts): Blanch nuts. Pour about 2″ corn or peanut oil in a large, heavy skillet and heat to 360° F. Fry nuts, about 1 cup at a time, stirring often, until pale golden. Lift to paper-towel-lined baking sheets with a slotted spoon and cool. (*Note:*

Nuts will continue cooking slightly as they cool, so don't fry more than *pale* golden.) Sprinkle with salt and toss to mix. Store airtight.

About Fresh Coconut

Coconuts have double, hard shells, but most sold today wear the inner monkey-faced shell only. Choose those that are heavy for their size and full of liquid (you can tell by shaking them).

To Open: Pierce "eyes" with a screwdriver and drain liquid into a bowl (it can be used in recipes). Break coconut open with a hammer and chisel *or* place coconut on a baking sheet and heat 20 minutes at 400° F. Tap all over to loosen meat, then crack with a hammer or mallet. Pry chunks of white meat from shell and peel off brown skin with a knife or vegetable peeler.

To Grate: Grate coarse or fine with a flat or rotary grater, or cut in small cubes and buzz, a few at a time, in an electric blender at high speed. From 1 medium-size coconut, you'll get 3–4 cups grated coconut and 1 cup liquid. (*Note:* When measuring grated coconut, do not pack the measure.)

How to Color or Toast Coconut: (see Some Special Candy-Making Techniques).

COCONUT MILK OR CREAM

Makes about 1 quart

1 medium-size coconut
Liquid from coconut plus enough water, milk, or light cream to total 1 quart

Open coconut,* reserving liquid; grate meat moderately fine and place in a large, heavy saucepan with liquid mixture. Heat slowly, stirring constantly, just until mixture boils. Remove from heat, cover, and cool to room temperature. Press through a double thickness of cheesecloth or a fine sieve, forcing out as much liquid as possible. Discard coconut pulp. Use milk in making curries, confections, desserts, and beverages. Store in refrigerator.

To Make with Canned Coconut: Prepare as directed, substituting 3 (4-ounce) cans flaked or shredded coconut for the fresh and using 1 quart milk or light cream. (*Note:* If your Scottish nature rebels at discarding the coconut, spread out in a large, shallow baking pan, drizzle lightly with melted butter, and toast, stirring often, ¾–1 hour until crisp and golden. Flavor will be bland, but coconut can be used to garnish candies and fruit desserts or as a condiment for curry.)

About 10 calories per cup (fresh or canned coconut) if made with water, 110 calories per cup if made with milk, and 315 calories per cup if made with light cream.

CHINESE COCONUT CANDY

Sugared strips of fresh coconut.
Makes about 1 pound

1 medium-size coconut
Coconut liquid plus enough cold water to total 1 cup
2 cups sugar

Open coconut,* reserving liquid. Remove coconut meat in as large pieces as possible and trim off brown skin with a vegetable peeler. Cut in strips about 2" long and ⅜" wide. Mix sugar and coconut liquid in a large, heavy saucepan, insert candy thermometer, and heat, stirring constantly, over moderate heat until sugar dissolves. Add coconut and boil, uncovered, to 240° F. or until a drop of candy forms a soft ball in cold water; stir once or twice just to keep coconut from sticking. Remove from heat and stir gently until mixture sugars and coats coconut. Using 2 forks, lift strips to wax-paper-lined baking sheets, separate into individual pieces, and cool. Store airtight. About 50 calories per piece.

SUGARED NUTS

Such a dainty sweetmeat. Easy to make, too.
Makes about 1 pound

1¼ cups sugar
⅔ cup water
2 tablespoons light corn syrup
Pinch salt
2 cups pecan or walnut halves, whole blanched pistachio nuts, or toasted, blanched almonds or filberts

Place sugar, water, syrup, and salt in a heavy saucepan; insert candy thermometer. Heat and stir over moderate heat until sugar dissolves, reduce heat slightly, and cook uncovered *without stirring* to 240° F. Remove from heat, stir in nuts, and pour onto a wax-paper-lined baking sheet. Spread out as thin as possible and let cool until hard. Break apart, separating into individual nuts. About 40 calories per nut.

VARIATIONS:

Sugared and Spiced Nuts: Prepare as directed but mix 1 teaspoon vanilla, ½ teaspoon cinnamon, and a pinch nutmeg into syrup just before adding nuts. Pour out, cool, and separate as directed. About 40 calories per nut.

Orange-Sugared Nuts: Prepare as

directed but substitute strained orange juice for the water and add the finely grated rind of 1 orange. Proceed as above. About 40 calories per nut.

GLAZED NUTS

These must be made on a cool, dry day if they're to harden properly. Makes about 1 pound

- 2 cups sugar
- 1 cup hot water
- ⅛ teaspoon cream of tartar
- 1 pound whole blanched almonds or filberts, pecan or walnut halves

Mix sugar, water, and cream of tartar in a heavy saucepan; insert candy thermometer. Heat and stir over moderate heat until sugar dissolves, reduce heat slightly, and cook, uncovered, *without stirring* until syrup is 310° F. and the color of straw. Remove from heat and set very gently in a large pan of boiling water (be careful because water will sputter). Using tongs, dip nuts into syrup, one at a time; dry on wax-paper-lined baking sheets. When thoroughly cool, store airtight. (*Note:* These candies quickly pick up moisture from the air and become sticky, so serve as soon after making as possible. If syrup should harden before all nuts are dipped reheat slowly to soften.) About 35 calories per nut.

VARIATION:

⚖ **Glazed Fruits:** Prepare syrup as directed and use for dipping dried apricot halves, pitted dates, firm, fresh, well-dried strawberries or grapes, well-dried orange or tangerine sections, candied cherries. Handle fruit carefully so you don't puncture it. From 20 to 35 calories per fruit, depending upon whether fresh or dried fruits are used. The dried fruits are higher in calories.

GARLICKY COCKTAIL ALMONDS

Makes 1 pound

- 1 pound whole blanched almonds
- 2 tablespoons melted butter or margarine
- 1 clove garlic, peeled and crushed
- ¾ teaspoon salt

Preheat oven to 275° F. Spread almonds out in a large, shallow roasting pan. Mix butter with garlic and drizzle over nuts; stir well. Roast uncovered, stirring occasionally, about 2 hours until golden brown. Drain on paper toweling. When cool, sprinkle with salt and toss to mix. About 235 calories per ¼ cup.

TOASTED CURRIED ALMONDS

Makes 1 pound

- 1 pound whole blanched almonds
- 3 tablespoons melted butter or margarine
- 1 tablespoon curry powder
- ½ teaspoon Worcestershire sauce
- ¼ teaspoon liquid hot red pepper seasoning
- 1 teaspoon salt mixed with 1 teaspoon curry powder

Preheat oven to 275° F. Spread almonds out in a large, shallow roasting pan. Mix butter with curry powder, Worcestershire sauce, and liquid hot red pepper seasoning, drizzle over nuts and stir well. Roast uncovered, stirring every 20 minutes, about 2 hours until golden brown. Drain on paper toweling. When cool, sprinkle with salt-curry powder mixture and toss well to mix. Drain on fresh paper toweling before serving. About 250 calories per ¼ cup.

HOT BUTTERED POPCORN

Makes about 4 servings

⅓ cup cooking oil
⅔ cup unpopped popcorn
3 tablespoons butter or margarine
½ teaspoon salt

Heat oil in a large, heavy saucepan over high heat about 1 minute until a kernel of corn will sizzle. Add corn, cover saucepan, and once corn begins to pop, shake pan vigorously just above burner until all corn is popped—it will take only 2–3 minutes. Pour corn into a very large bowl. Drop butter into pan and heat until it melts and bubbles up, drizzle over popcorn, and toss lightly to mix. Sprinkle with salt and toss again. About 160 calories per serving.

POPCORN BALLS

Makes 9 3″ balls or 1½ dozen 1½″ balls

1 cup sugar
1 cup light corn syrup
1 teaspoon cider vinegar
3 tablespoons butter or margarine
1 teaspoon vanilla
2 quarts popped, unseasoned popcorn

Place sugar, corn syrup, and vinegar in a heavy saucepan; insert candy thermometer and heat and stir over moderately high heat until sugar dissolves. Cook uncovered *without stirring* to 260° F. or until a drop of syrup forms a hard ball in cold water. Off heat, mix in butter and vanilla. Pour over popcorn in a large bowl and stir quickly so all pieces are coated. With buttered hands, scoop up and shape into large or small balls. Cool on wax paper. Wrap individually in wax paper or plastic food wrap. About 255 calories per large popcorn ball, 130 per small popcorn ball.

VARIATIONS:

Molasses Popcorn Balls: Prepare as directed but substitute 1 cup dark molasses for the sugar. Same calorie counts as for popcorn balls.

Colored Popcorn Balls: Prepare as directed but tint syrup desired color after sugar dissolves. Same calorie counts as for popcorn balls.

Cereal and Popcorn Balls: Prepare as directed but use a ½ and ½ mixture of popcorn and puffed rice or wheat cereal. Same calorie counts as for popcorn balls.

Popcorn and Peanut Balls: Prepare as directed, but substitute ¼ cup creamy peanut butter for the butter and add 1 cup roasted peanuts to the popcorn. About 360 calories per large ball, 180 per small ball.

Caramel Popcorn Balls: Instead of making syrup above, melt ¾ pound vanilla or chocolate caramels with 3 tablespoons water in the top of a double boiler, stirring until smooth. Pour over popcorn and shape into balls. About 200 calories per large ball, 100 calories per small ball.

CHAPTER 25

PICKLES, PRESERVES, JAMS, AND JELLIES

Pickling and preserving are two of the oldest forms of food conservation because man learned early that overly acid, sweet, or salty foods did not spoil readily. Cleopatra adored pickles, gave them credit for her beauty, and Ceasar, something of a health faddist, insisted that his legions eat pickles to stave off scurvy. In the more recent past, women pickled and preserved foods so that their families would eat well throughout the winter. Today, with the winter's food supply at the supermarket, pickling and preserving have become labors of love. Odd as it may seem, a number of sophisticated New York City women look forward each summer to the "preserving season." They enjoy the homeliness of putting up a dozen or so jars of pickles and another of fruit preserves. Needless to add, family and friends welcome the fruits of their labor—reason enough for getting down the big kettles and cartons of jars.

Note: Because there is not space here to do more than cover the basics, we recommend the excellent and detailed booklets prepared by the U. S. Department of Agriculture, state agricultural extension services, manufacturers of preserving jars, and processors of liquid and powdered pectins.

The Ways of Pickling and Preserving

Brining: This is the old-fashioned slow cure in which vegetables are submerged for weeks in heavy brine ("heavy enough to float an egg," recipes used to read). Not often used today, except for making Sauerkraut (see recipe), because there are shorter, surer methods.

Fresh-Pack or Quick Process: This is the modern way of pickling—easy, efficient, and reliable. Foods—usually vegetables or fruits—are heated in vinegar, brine, or a mixture of vinegar and salt, often with sugar and spices, then packed hot into hot sterilized jars and sealed; or they may be packed cold into jars, covered with boiling hot pickling liquid and processed in a hot water bath to prevent spoilage. (*Note:* For pickles, the water bath should be hot 180–85° F.), not boiling. Hot pack pickles and relishes, if sufficiently acid or salty, usually need no processing.

Open Kettle Preserving: The method recommended for preserves, jams, jellies, fruit butters, chutneys, ketchups, and conserves, which involves nothing more complicated than cooking all ingredients in a large, open kettle until of desired consistency. Very tart or sweet mixtures, ladled boiling hot into hot sterilized jars, do not need to be processed in a hot water bath; cooler or less concentrated mixtures may (as for pickles, the water bath should be 180–85° F., not boiling).

The Equipment of Pickling and Preserving

All of the paraphernalia of canning (which see) is needed for pickling and preserving. Kettles, however, should be extra large (1½–2 gallons or more), providing plenty of boil-up room. They should be made of enameled metal, stainless steel, or other inert material, never copper, tin, zinc, or galvanized metals that can react with the acid of pickles or preserves to produce poisonous salts. Aluminum kettles are safe but sometimes darken pickles and preserves, giving them a metallic taste. Additional equipment you'll find useful: wide-mouth stone crocks for brining, large sieves, a food mill and meat grinder and for making jellies, cheesecloth or, better still, a jelly bag (French-seamed flannel bag for straining fruit juices) and a jelmeter (calibrated glass tube used to determine jelling power of fruit juices); both of these items are stocked by good housewares departments or can be ordered by them. A candy thermometer is handy to have, also a potato masher. Jelly glasses, lids, and paraffin are also essential.

PICKLES AND RELISHES

Any food almost can be pickled—preserved in brine or vinegar. But certain vegetables and fruits pickle better than other foods—cucumbers, sweet peppers, green tomatoes, cauliflower, corn, and green beans, to name a few. The difference between a pickle and a relish? It's merely a matter of size. When foods are left whole or in large chunks or slices, they are pickles. When minced or chopped, they become relishes. (*Dieters Note:* Most tart pickles and relishes are low-calorie.)

Essential Ingredients of Pickling

Salt: Pickling salt (fine-grained pure salt) is best, dairy or kosher salts (coarse, flaked pure salts) next best; table salt contains adulterants that will cloud the brine. (*Note:* Because of their coarseness, dairy and kosher salts, measure for measure, are not equal to pickling salt. When substituting either one for pickling salt, use 1½ times the amount of pickling salt called for.) The recipes that follow specify which salt to use.

Vinegar: Vinegars should be plain, unflavored, of top grade and 4–6 per cent acid strength (this information is included on the label). They may be cider (brown) or distilled (white) but must be clear and free of sediment. White vinegars are best for white or delicately colored vegetables; brown vinegars will darken them. Never use a vinegar of unknown acid strength; a too weak vinegar can cause pickles to soften and spoil.

Sugar: Granulated sugar is the standard, though occasionally, when a mellower, darker product is wanted, light or dark brown sugar will be called for.

Spices: Whole dried spices, freshly bought, are preferable because they can be neatly tied in cheesecloth, simmered along with the pickles, then quickly fished out of the kettle. Powdered spices darken pickles and so will whole spices if left in too long.

Water: It should be soft—either naturally or artificially so. Hard water can produce ugly white scum on pickles or, if high in iron, turn them black. To soften water: Boil hard 15 minutes, let stand 24 hours, then skim scum from top. Carefully ladle water into a clean container, leaving any sediment behind.

Fruit and Vegetables: These should be garden fresh (never picked more than a day ahead of time), a shade underripe, free of blemishes, soft or decayed spots, and for especially pretty pickles, of small-to-medium, uniform size.

Slaked Lime (Calcium Hydroxide) and Alum: These aren't essential to pickling except when supercrisp pickles are wanted. They're used with unfermented pickles only, most often watermelon rind or green tomato. Both can be bought in drugstores and hardwares specializing in canning equipment.

Tips for Making Better Pickles and Relishes

– Read recipe through carefully before beginning and follow directions to the letter.
– Have all ingredients and equipment assembled before beginning. Make sure preserving jars are the proper type (those made specifically for preserving) and in perfect condition (no cracks or chips), spotless and sterilized (directions for sterilizing jars and closures are included in the chapter on canning). Lids should be perfect too—not warped, dented, or bent. If using closures requiring rubber rings, buy new ones of the proper size.
– Do not attempt to pickle vast quantities at a time; work instead with amounts you can handle comfortably in your kitchen.
– Use highest quality fruits and vegetables, picked, if possible, just before pickling.
– Use freshly bought vinegars, spices, salts, and sugars, never those that have been sitting around on the shelf.
– Never add chemicals to pickles or relishes to heighten their color—copper sulfate, for example, or vitriol. And do not, as Grandmother did, pickle green vegetables in copper kettles to brighten the green—vinegar, coming in contact with copper, produces a poison.
– Measure or weigh ingredients carefully.
– Pack jars, one at a time, as recipes direct, allowing amount of head space (room at the top of the jar) recommended. Jars to be processed in a hot water bath should have

PICKLES, PRESERVES, JAMS, AND JELLIES

about ¼″ of head space so that there is room for expansion of food as it sterilizes; jars requiring no processing should be filled to within ⅛″ of tops. Jars processed in a pressure cooker need the most head space of all—usually 1″, but follow recipe and manufacturer's directions.
— As you pack jars, run a small spatula around inside of jar to remove air bubbles.
— Make sure pickling liquid covers solids; if there is not enough, pour in a little additional vinegar or brine (same strength as that in the recipe).
— Before sealing jars, wipe tops and threading with a clean, damp cloth.
— When packing hot pickles, make sure that they *and* the pickling liquid are *boiling hot.*
— If pickles have been packed cold, do not remove metal screw bands after sealing and processing. Leave intact until jars are opened.
— When cooling sealed jars, stand several inches apart and away from drafts so that air will circulate evenly.
— Test seals after jars have cooled 12 hours. If a jar has not sealed, refrigerate and serve within the week. *Or* empty contents into a saucepan, bring slowly to a boil, and pack into a hot sterilized jar. Reseal and cool.
— Store pickles and relishes in a dark, cool, dry place and let stand some weeks before serving so that flavors will mellow and mingle.
— To keep pickles from fading, wrap jars in newspaper before storing.

Why Things Sometimes Go Wrong with Pickles

Soft or Slippery Pickles: Vinegar too weak or pickles not kept submerged in brine or pickling liquid.

Hollow Pickles ("Floaters"): Cucumbers picked too long before pickling.

Dark Pickles: Iron in the water used.

Shriveled Pickles: Pickling solution too acid, too salty, or too sweet.

Faded Pickles: Pickles kept too long on the shelf or stored in too bright a spot.

¢ ⚖ DILL PICKLES

Because cucumbers brined in barrels need controlled conditions not always attainable at home, these recipes use the newer, easier fresh-pack method.
Makes about 8 pints

3–3½ dozen small- to medium-size cucumbers (about 4″ long), washed and left whole or halved lengthwise (do not peel)
1 gallon cold water mixed with ¾ cup pickling salt (brine)
16 sprigs fresh dill or pickling dill or 8 tablespoons dill seeds
8 teaspoons mustard seeds
1 quart white vinegar
1 quart water
½ cup pickling salt
½ cup sugar
3 tablespoons mixed pickling spices, tied in cheesecloth

Let cucumbers stand in brine overnight. Wash and sterilize 8 (1-pint) jars and closures. Drain cucumbers and pack into hot jars, leaving ¼″ head space. To each jar add 2 sprigs dill (or 1 tablespoon dill seeds) and 1 teaspoon mustard seeds, poking halfway down in jar. Set uncovered jars on a baking sheet and keep hot in a 250° F. oven. Simmer vinegar, water, salt, sugar, and pickling spices, uncovered, 15 minutes in an enamel or stainless-steel saucepan, stirring now and then. Pour boiling hot into jars, filling to within ⅛" of tops. Wipe rims and seal. Or, if you prefer, fill jars to within ¼" of top, seal, and process in a hot water bath* 10 minutes. Take from water bath and secure seals if necessary. Cool, check seals, label, and store in a cool, dark, dry place. Let unprocessed pickles stand 4–6 weeks before using, processed ones 3 weeks. About 20–30 calories per pickle, depending on size.

VARIATIONS:

⚖ **"Kosher" Dill Pickles:** When packing cucumbers, add to each jar 1 peeled and bruised clove garlic, 1 bay leaf, and 1 (3"×½") strip hot red chili pepper in addition to seasonings above. Proceed as directed. Same calorie counts as for dill pickles.

¢ **Sweet Dill Pickles:** Prepare as directed but, instead of vinegar mixture called for, simmer 5 cups vinegar and 5 cups sugar with the 3 tablespoons spices. Pour into jars as directed, leaving ¼" head space at the top, and process in a hot water bath* 10 minutes. About 50–60 calories per pickle, depending on size.

AUNT FLORRIE'S BREAD AND BUTTER PICKLES

Makes about 6 quarts

4 quarts paper-thin unpeeled cucumber slices
8 medium-size white onions, peeled and sliced paper thin
2 medium-size sweet green peppers (or 1 green and 1 red), washed, cored, seeded, and coarsely chopped
½ cup pickling salt
1 quart cracked ice
5 cups sugar
1½ teaspoons turmeric
½ teaspoon cloves
2 tablespoons mustard seeds
1 teaspoon celery seeds
5 cups cider or white vinegar

Mix all vegetables, salt, and ice in a very large colander, weight down, pressing out liquid, set over a large kettle, and let stand 3 hours (in refrigerator if possible). (*Note:* If kitchen is warm and you haven't refrigerator space, add more cracked ice after 1½ hours.) Meanwhile, wash and sterilize 6 (1-quart) jars and closures, stand on a baking sheet, and keep hot in a 250° F. oven until needed. Mix sugar, spices, and vinegar in a very large enamel or stainless-steel kettle. Drain vegetables well and add to kettle. Heat, uncovered, over moderate heat *just* to the boiling point, moving a wooden spoon through mixture occasionally but not actually stirring. Ladle boiling hot into jars, filling to within ⅛" of tops, wipe rims, and seal. Cool, check seals, label, and store in a cool, dark, dry place. Let stand 4–6 weeks before serving. About 100 calories per ¼ cup.

MUSTARD PICKLES

Makes 4 pints

1 medium-size cauliflower, washed, trimmed, and divided into small flowerets
2 medium-size cucumbers, peeled, seeded, and cut in ¼" cubes
3 medium-size sweet green peppers, washed, cored, seeded, and coarsely chopped
1 medium-size sweet red pepper, washed, cored, seeded, and coarsely chopped
1 pint tiny white onions or shallots, peeled
1 quart cold water mixed with ⅓ cup pickling salt
½ cup sifted flour
1 cup sugar

3 tablespoons powdered mustard
1½ teaspoons turmeric
1 quart white vinegar

Place all vegetables and salt water in a large bowl, cover, and refrigerate overnight. Wash and sterilize 4 (1-pint) jars and their closures; stand on a baking sheet and keep hot in a 250° F. oven until needed. Transfer vegetables and brine to a large enamel or stainless-steel kettle, cover, bring to a boil over high heat, then boil 1 minute; drain in a colander and set aside. In the same kettle, mix flour, sugar, and spices; slowly blend in vinegar and heat, stirring constantly, over moderate heat until thickened. Add vegetables, cover, and heat, stirring occasionally, 8–10 minutes, just until boiling. Ladle into jars, filling to within ¼" of tops, wipe rims, and seal. Process 10 minutes in a hot water bath.* Cool, check seals, label, and store in a cool, dark, dry place. Let stand 4–6 weeks before serving. About 45 calories per ¼ cup.

¢ ⚖ **EASY ICE WATER CUCUMBER PICKLES**

Gherkins may be substituted for cucumbers in this next recipe.
Makes 6 quarts

6–6½ dozen small cucumbers (do not peel)
Ice water
6 tablespoons pickling salt
6 tablespoons mixed pickling spices
12 tablespoons sugar
2–3 white onions, peeled and sliced thin
3 quarts boiling white vinegar

Cover cucumbers with ice water and let stand 3–4 hours, replenishing ice as needed. Wash and sterilize 6 (1-quart) jars and closures, stand on a baking sheet, and keep warm in a 250° F. oven until needed. Drain cucumbers and pack into hot jars, filling to within ¼" of the top. Add 1 tablespoon salt, 1 tablespoon pickling spice, and 2 tablespoons sugar to each jar, top with 1–2 slices onion, and fill to within ¼" of the top with vinegar. Wipe rims and seal. Process in a hot water bath* 10 minutes. Remove jars and secure seals if needed. Cool, check seals, label, and store in a cool, dark, dry place 4–6 weeks before serving. About 2 calories per pickle.

⚖ **GREEN TOMATO PICKLES**

Makes about 5 pints

2 quarts sliced, unpeeled green tomatoes (slices should be about ½" thick)
2 tablespoons pickling salt
1 cup granulated sugar
1 cup dark brown sugar
1 pint cider vinegar
2 tablespoons mustard seeds
1 teaspoon celery seeds
2 bay leaves, crumbled
2 large yellow onions, peeled and sliced thin
2 large sweet green peppers, cored, seeded, and minced
1 large sweet red pepper or 1 small hot chili pepper, cored, seeded, and minced

Mix tomatoes and salt, cover, and refrigerate overnight; drain well. Wash and sterilize 5 (1-pint) jars and closures, stand on a baking sheet, and keep hot in a 250° F. oven until needed. Mix sugars, vinegar, spices, and onions in a very large enamel or stainless-steel kettle, cover, and boil slowly 10 minutes. Add tomatoes and peppers and simmer, uncovered, stirring now and then, 5 minutes. Ladle boiling hot into jars filling to within ⅛" of tops and making sure liquid covers vegetables. Wipe rims and seal; cool, check seals, label, and store in a cool, dark, dry place 4–6 weeks before using. About 25 calories per pickle.

⚔ DILLED GREEN TOMATOES

Makes 4 pints

3 pounds small, firm green tomatoes, washed and stemmed
4 sweet green peppers, washed, cored, and seeded
8 cloves garlic, peeled
1 teaspoon celery seeds
1 quart water
1 pint cider or white vinegar
½ cup pickling or kosher salt
2 tablespoons pickling dill

Wash and sterilize 4 wide-mouth (1-pint) preserving jars and closures. Blanch tomatoes and peppers but do not skin; cut peppers in strips ½″ wide. Place 2 garlic cloves and ¼ teaspoon celery seeds in each jar, then fill to within ½″ of top with tomatoes and pepper strips, distributing as evenly as possible. Boil water, vinegar, salt, and dill, uncovered, 5 minutes and pour over tomatoes, filling jars to within ⅛″ of tops. Seal jars, cool, label, and store in a cool, dark, dry place. Let stand 4–6 weeks before serving. About 25 calories per ¼ cup.

⚔ DILLED GREEN BEANS

Choose the straightest beans for this recipe—makes packing jars easier.
Makes 6 pints

3 pounds green beans
6 cloves garlic, peeled and halved
3 teaspoons mustard seeds
1½ teaspoons peppercorns
12 large sprigs fresh dill or 3 teaspoons dill seeds
3 cups cider vinegar
3 cups water
¼ cup pickling salt

Wash and sterilize 6 (1-pint) jars and closures. Snap ends off beans, cut in 4½″ lengths, and pack vertically in jars, filling centers with odd lengths. Add 2 halves garlic, ½ teaspoon mustard seeds, ¼ teaspoon peppercorns, and 2 sprigs fresh dill (or ½ teaspoon dill seeds) to each jar. Heat vinegar, water, and salt to boiling, then pour in jars, filling to within ¼″ of the top. Wipe rims and seal. Process in a hot water bath* 5 minutes. Tighten seals if necessary, cool, check seals, label, and store in a cool, dark, dry place 4–6 weeks before serving. About 10 calories per ¼ cup.

VARIATIONS:

⚔ Dilled Carrots:
Prepare as directed but substitute 3 quarts parboiled (4″) carrot sticks for beans. About 15 calories per ¼ cup.

⚔ Dilled Zucchini:
Prepare as directed but substitute 3 quarts unpeeled (4″) zucchini strips for beans. (*Note:* Baby zucchini are best.) About 10 calories per ¼ cup.

⚔ ¢ SAUERKRAUT

Makes about 7 quarts

7–8 medium-size firm green cabbages, quartered, cored, and shredded fine
1 cup pickling salt

Wash and scald a 4-gallon crock. Mix 5 pounds of the shredded cabbage thoroughly with ¼ cup salt and pack firmly into crock, pressing down with a potato masher. Continue filling crock, adding 5 pounds shredded cabbage mixed with ¼ cup salt each time and pressing down well to extract enough liquid to cover cabbage. Cover with 4 thicknesses of cheesecloth, tucking ends down in jar. Weight down with a sterilized heavy plate topped with a sterilized

PICKLES, PRESERVES, JAMS, AND JELLIES

large jar full of water (plate should be submerged in cabbage liquid). Set crock on a tray (it may bubble over during fermentation), drape more cheesecloth on top, and let stand at room temperature (70° F.) until fermentation stops, 2–3 weeks in warm weather, 4 weeks in cool. Fermentation will begin the day after packing; for best results, keep temperature as near 70° F. as possible. Skim scum from crock each day, covering with fresh cheesecloth if necessary. When bubbling stops, tap jar gently; if no bubbles rise, fermentation is completed (sauerkraut should be cream colored with no white spots). Wash and sterilize 7 (1-quart) jars and closures and keep hot in a 250° F. oven. Pack, one at a time, with sauerkraut, filling to within ½" of tops and making sure kraut is covered with liquid. (*Note:* If there is insufficient liquid, fill with brine made by dissolving 2 tablespoons pickling salt in 1 quart boiling water.) Wipe rims and seal. Process in a boiling water bath* ½ hour. Tighten lids if needed, cool, check seals, label, and store in a cool, dark, dry place. (*Note:* If you have a cool cellar—55° F. or less—kraut can be stored there in the crock through the winter. Just be sure kraut is weighted down in its juices and crock loosely covered.) About 15 calories per ½ cup.

¢ PICKLED RED CABBAGE

Because this cabbage is packed cold, store with screw bands tightly screwed down.
Makes about 3 pints

- 2 *quarts moderately finely shredded red cabbage (about 1 large head)*
- 1 *quart cold water mixed with ¼ cup pickling salt (brine)*
- 1 *quart cider vinegar*
- 1 *cup sugar*
- 2 *tablespoons mixed pickling spices, tied in cheesecloth*

Mix cabbage and brine, cover, and let stand overnight; drain well. Wash and sterilize 3 (1-pint) jars and closures. Pack cabbage into jars, filling to within ½" of tops. Boil vinegar, sugar and spices in an enamel or stainless-steel saucepan 10 minutes, then fill jars to within ⅛" of tops. Wipe rims and seal. Cool, label, and store in a cool, dark, dry place 4–6 weeks before serving. About 45 calories per ¼ cup.

⚖ PICKLED WHOLE BEETS

Makes 4 pints

- 4 *pounds small beets, boiled and peeled (they should be hot)*
- 2 *teaspoons pickling salt*
- 1 *pint white vinegar*
- 2 *cups sugar*
- 1 *tablespoon mixed pickling spices (optional)*

Wash and sterilize 4 (1-pint) jars and closures. Pack beets in hot jars, filling to within ½" of the top, halving some to fill gaps; add ½ teaspoon salt to each jar. Meanwhile, bring remaining ingredients to a boil, pour over beets, filling jars to within ¼" of the top. Wipe rims and seal. Process in a hot water bath* ½ hour. Remove jars from bath and secure seals if necessary. Cool, check seals, label, and store in a cool, dark place. Let stand 2–3 weeks before serving. About 20 calories per beet.

VARIATION:

⚖ **Pickled Sliced Beets** (Makes 3 pints): Prepare as directed but slice cooked beets ¼" thick. (*Note:* You can use larger beets for this recipe.) About 35 calories per ¼ cup.

⚖ PICKLED ONIONS

Makes 8 pints

7 pounds small white onions, peeled and parboiled 2 minutes
1 cup pickling salt
2 quarts cider or white vinegar
½ cup sugar
4 teaspoons mustard seeds, lightly crushed
8 bay leaves

Place onions in a large bowl, cover with cold water, add salt and stir to dissolve; cover and let stand at room temperature 24 hours. Next day, wash and sterilize 8 (1-pint) jars and closures; stand on a baking sheet and keep hot in a 250° F. oven until needed. Rinse onions under cold running water and drain well. Bring vinegar, sugar, and spices to a boil in an enamel or stainless-steel saucepan, stirring occasionally. Meanwhile, pack onions into jars; pour in boiling vinegar, filling jars to within ⅛" of tops and distributing mustard seeds and bay leaves evenly. Wipe rims and seal. Cool, check seals, label jars, and store in a cool, dark, dry place. Let stand 1 week before using. About 15 calories per onion.

⚖ PICKLED MUSHROOMS

Makes 4 pints

3 pounds mushrooms (button to medium size), wiped clean
1 quart water mixed with 3 tablespoons pickling salt (brine)
4 cloves garlic, peeled and bruised
4 bay leaves
1 teaspoon whole cloves
1 teaspoon peppercorns
4 chili pequins (tiny hot dried red peppers)
1 quart white vinegar
¼ cup olive oil

Wash and sterilize 4 (1-pint) jars and closures, stand on a baking sheet, and keep hot in a 250° F. oven until needed. Simmer mushrooms in brine, covered, 5 minutes, then drain. Into each hot jar place 1 clove garlic, 1 bay leaf, ¼ teaspoon each cloves and peppercorns, and 1 chili pequin. Heat vinegar and oil to boiling in an enamel or stainless-steel saucepan, add mushrooms and simmer, uncovered, 5 minutes. Remove mushrooms with a slotted spoon and pack into jars, then pour in boiling vinegar mixture, filling to within ⅛" of tops. Wipe rims and seal. Cool, check seals, label, and store in a cool, dark, dry place 2–3 weeks before serving. About 30 calories per ¼ cup.

¢ WATERMELON RIND PICKLES

Makes 4 pints

1 (15–16-pound) slightly underripe watermelon with thick, firm rind
2 quarts cold water mixed with ½ cup pickling salt (brine)

Syrup:
4 pounds sugar
1 quart cider vinegar
1 quart water
2 lemons, sliced thin
2 teaspoons whole cloves
2 teaspoons whole allspice
4 cinnamon sticks, broken up

Quarter melon, remove green skin and pink flesh, and cut rind in 1" cubes; measure 4 quarts cubed rind, cover with brine, and soak overnight. Drain rind, rinse with cold water, place in a very large kettle, cover with water, and simmer covered about ½ hour until barely tender and translucent. Meanwhile, prepare syrup: Mix sugar, vinegar, and water in a very large enamel or stainless-steel kettle, add lemon and spices, tied in cheesecloth, and slowly boil uncovered 20 minutes. Also wash and sterilize 4 (1-pint) jars and closures, stand on a baking sheet in a 250° F. oven until needed. Drain rind, add to syrup, and simmer uncovered until rind is clear, about ½ hour. Remove spice bag. Using a slotted spoon, pack rind into jars, then pour in boiling syrup, filling to within ⅛" of tops. Wipe rims and seal. Cool, check seals, label, and store in a cool, dark, dry place several weeks before serving. About 40 calories per ¼ cup.

SPICED CANTALOUPE

Makes 3 pints

- *1 (3½–4-pound) underripe cantaloupe*
- *2 quarts cold water mixed with ½ cup pickling salt (brine)*

Syrup:
- *6 cups sugar*
- *2 quarts water*
- *2 cinnamon sticks, broken up*
- *1 tablespoon whole cloves*
- *1 tablespoon whole allspice*
- *1 (2") piece gingerroot, peeled and bruised*
- *1 pint cider vinegar*

Quarter melon, remove seeds, peeling, and rind, then cut flesh in ½" cubes; measure out 3 quarts, cover with brine, and soak 3 hours. Meanwhile, prepare syrup: Slowly boil 4 cups sugar and the water, uncovered, in a very large enamel or stainless-steel kettle 5 minutes. Drain and rinse cantaloupe, add to syrup, and boil, uncovered, ½ hour. Remove from heat, set lid on kettle askew, and let stand overnight. Next day, tie spices in cheesecloth and add to kettle along with vinegar and remaining sugar. Slowly boil, uncovered, until cantaloupe is clear, about ½ hour. Meanwhile, wash and sterilize 3 (1-pint) jars and closures and keep hot on a baking sheet in a 250° F. oven until needed. Using a slotted spoon, pack cantaloupe into jars, then pour in boiling syrup, filling to within ⅛" of tops; wipe rims and seal. Cool, check seals, label, and store in a cool, dark, dry place several weeks before serving. About 40 calories per ¼ cup.

PICKLED PEACHES

Dipping peaches and apricots in boiling water makes skins slip right off. Try not only the peaches but some of the other fruits included among the variations.

Makes about 10 pints

- *8 pounds small, firm-ripe peaches (clingstone varieties are best)*
- *1 gallon cold water mixed with 2 tablespoons each pickling salt and white vinegar*
- *2 tablespoons whole cloves (about)*

Basic Pickling Syrup:
- *1 quart white vinegar*
- *1 quart water*
- *3 pounds sugar*
- *4 cinnamon sticks, broken and tied in cheesecloth*

Peel peaches, then drop in water-salt-vinegar mixture to prevent discoloration; leave whole or halve but do not remove pits. Stud each peach with 2 cloves. Place syrup ingredients in a large enamel or stainless-steel kettle and bring to a boil. Add peaches, a few at a time, and simmer uncovered 5–7 minutes until barely tender. Remove peaches with a slotted spoon and set aside while cooking the rest. When all are cooked, bring syrup to a boil and pour over peaches; cover and let stand overnight (this plumps peaches and gives them better flavor). Next day, wash and sterilize 10 (1-pint) jars and their closures. At the same time, drain syrup from peaches and bring to a boil; discard spice bag. Pack peaches into hot jars, then pour in boiling syrup, filling to within ¼" of the top. Wipe rims and seal. Process in a hot water bath* 10 minutes. Remove jars from bath and secure seals if necessary. Cool, check seals, label, and store in a cool, dark, dry place 4–6 weeks before serving. About 50 calories per peach.

VARIATIONS:

Pickled Apricots: Substitute 8 pounds apricots for peaches; peel, leave whole, or halve and pit. Proceed as directed. About 50 calories per apricot.

Pickled Pears: Substitute 8 pounds small, firm-ripe pears for peaches. Leave stems on but remove blossom ends. Proceed as directed. About 80 calories per pear.

Pickled Apples: Substitute 10 pounds peeled, quartered, and cored small tart apples for peaches. Add cloves to pickling syrup instead of studding fruit, then proceed as directed. About 65 calories per apple.

Pickled Crab Apples: Substitute 8 pounds unpeeled crab apples for peaches. Remove blossom ends but not stems, then prick in several places to prevent bursting. Add cloves to pickling syrup and simmer crab apples 7–10 minutes, depending on size. Proceed as recipe directs. About 45 calories per crab apple.

Pickled Quinces: Substitute 8 pounds firm-ripe quinces for peaches. Peel, quarter, core, and slice thin. For pickling syrup use 1 pint each vinegar and water and 4 pounds sugar; add cloves and cinnamon. Simmer quinces 30–40 minutes in syrup until translucent. Proceed as directed. About 45 calories per ¼ cup.

Spiced Fruits: Prepare any of the preceding pickled fruits as directed, but tie cinnamon and cloves in cheesecloth along with 2 tablespoons whole allspice and 2 (2") pieces bruised, peeled gingerroot. If you like, add 1 or 2 slices lemon to each jar. Same calorie counts as the individual pickled fruits.

California Fruit Pickles: Prepare any of the preceding pickled fruits as directed but use a ½ and ½ mixture of granulated and light or dark brown sugar in the pickling syrup. Same calorie counts as the individual pickled fruits.

BRANDIED PEACHES

Makes 4 pints

4 pounds small firm-ripe peaches (clingstone varieties are best)
2 quarts cold water mixed with 1 tablespoon each pickling salt and lemon juice
1 quart water
4 cups sugar
1 pint brandy (about)

Wash and sterilize 4 (1-pint) jars and closures, stand them on a baking sheet, and keep hot in a 250° F. oven until needed. Peel peaches, then drop in water-salt-lemon juice mixture to prevent darkening. Bring water and sugar to a boil in an enamel or stainless-steel saucepan; reduce heat, add peaches, a few at a time, and simmer 5–7 minutes until barely tender. Remove peaches with a slotted spoon and pack in hot jars, filling to within ½" of tops. When all peaches are cooked, return filled but uncovered jars to 250° F. oven. Insert candy thermometer in syrup and boil, uncovered, until thermometer registers 222° F. Cool syrup 5 minutes, measure out 1 pint,

PICKLES, PRESERVES, JAMS, AND JELLIES

and stir in 1 pint brandy; pour into jars, filling to within ¼" of the top. (*Note:* If you need more liquid, mix equal quantities of syrup and brandy.) Wipe jar rims and seal. Process in a hot water bath* 10 minutes. Remove jars and secure seals, if necessary. Cool, check seals, label, and store in a cool, dark, dry place. Let stand 4–6 weeks before serving. About 55 calories per peach.

VARIATION:

Brandied Pears: Substitute 4 pounds small firm-ripe pears for peaches. Peel and remove blossom ends but leave stems on if you wish. Proceed as recipe directs. About 120 calories per pear.

⚖ PRESERVED CINNAMON APPLE RINGS

Delicious with ham or roast pork.
Makes 2 pints

1 pint boiling water
1 cup red cinnamon candies
8 medium-size tart apples, peeled, cored, and sliced ½" thick
4 cups sugar

Wash and sterilize 2 (1-pint) jars and their closures, set on a baking sheet in a 250° F. oven, and keep hot until needed. Mix water and candies in a large, heavy saucepan, stirring until candies dissolve; add apples, cover, and simmer 10 minutes until transparent. Pack apples into jars and set, uncovered, in oven. Add sugar to saucepan and boil, uncovered, 3 minutes. Pour syrup over apples, filling jars to within ¼" of tops. Wipe rims, seal, and process in a hot water bath* 20 minutes. Remove jars and secure seals if necessary. Cool, check seals, label, and store in a cool, dark, dry place. About 20 calories per apple ring.

GINGERED PEARS

Serve with any meat.
Makes 4 pints

5 pounds firm-ripe pears, peeled, quartered, and cored
½ cup lemon juice
5 cups sugar
1 tablespoon finely grated lemon rind
⅓ cup minced gingerroot or ½ cup minced preserved ginger

Wash and sterilize 4 (1-pint) jars and closures, stand them on baking sheet, and keep warm in a 250° F. oven until needed. Simmer all ingredients, uncovered, in a heavy enamel or stainless-steel kettle until pears are tender and translucent, about 30–40 minutes. Ladle into hot jars, filling to within ⅛" of tops. Wipe rims and seal. Cool, check seals, label, and store in a cool, dark, dry place 2–3 weeks before using. About 50 calories per pear quarter.

TOMATO KETCHUP

Ketchup can be made from mushrooms, grapes, cranberries, green tomatoes, in fact from many fruits and vegetables. But the favorite is bright red tomato ketchup.
Makes 2 pints

8 pounds unpeeled ripe tomatoes, coarsely chopped
1 cup minced yellow onions
1 teaspoon celery seeds
1 teaspoon mustard seeds
1 teaspoon whole allspice
1 cinnamon stick
½ teaspoon peppercorns
2 bay leaves
1 tablespoon salt
1 cup white vinegar
1 cup sugar

Mix tomatoes and onions in a large (at least 1 gallon) enamel or stainless-steel kettle, cover, and simmer 20–30 minutes, stirring now and then, until mushy. Purée, a little at a time, at low speed in an electric blender or put through a food mill, then press through a fine sieve. Place in a clean large kettle and cook, uncovered, at a slow boil until volume reduces by half. (*Note:* It's important that kettle be large to keep ketchup from spattering kitchen.) Meanwhile, wash and sterilize 2 (1-pint) jars and their closures, stand them on a baking sheet, and keep warm in a 250° F. oven until needed. Tie all spices and bay leaves in cheesecloth and add to kettle along with salt, set lid on askew, and simmer ½ hour. Remove spice bag, add vinegar and sugar, and cook, uncovered, at a slow boil, stirring frequently, until very thick. (*Note:* Toward the end, you will have to stir constantly to prevent scorching.) Ladle ketchup into jars, filling to within ⅛″ of tops, wipe rims, and seal. Cool, check seals, and store in a cool, dark, dry place. Let stand 2 weeks before using. (*Note:* To keep ketchup bright red over a long period of time, wrap jars in foil.) About 25 calories per tablespoon.

VARIATIONS:

Easy Ketchup: Substitute 2 (1-pound 12-ounce) cans tomato purée for fresh tomatoes, omit onion, and cook down as recipe directs to about ⅓ of original volume. Add spices called for but only 1½ teaspoons salt; proceed as directed. About 25 calories per tablespoon.

Cranberry Ketchup: Substitute 2 pounds cranberries for tomatoes and simmer with 1 cup water until mushy. Proceed as recipe directs but increase sugar to 2 cups. About 50 calories per tablespoon.

Hot Chili Sauce: Peel and core tomatoes before chopping; simmer as directed with 2 cups each minced onions and minced, cored, and seeded sweet red peppers and 1–2 minced, cored, and seeded hot red peppers (or ¼–½ teaspoon crushed dried hot red chili peppers). Purée mixture but do not strain. Proceed as for Tomato Ketchup (above), adding 1 tablespoon mixed pickling spices to the spices called for and increasing vinegar to 1½ cups. About 30 calories per tablespoon.

GREEN TOMATO CHUTNEY

Makes 6–7 pints

10 pounds green tomatoes, washed, stemmed, and coarsely chopped
3 tart apples, peeled, cored, and minced
1 pint cider vinegar
3 cups sugar
2 cups firmly packed dark brown sugar
2 teaspoons salt
1½ teaspoons curry powder
1 teaspoon powdered mustard
½ teaspoon cayenne pepper
½ teaspoon turmeric
½ teaspoon ginger
½ pound sultana raisins

Wash and sterilize 7 (1-pint) preserving jars and closures. Mix all ingredients in a very large enamel or stainless-steel kettle, cover, and bring slowly to a boil. Uncover and *simmer*, stirring occasionally, 1½–2 hours until thick. Ladle into jars, filling to within ⅛″ of tops. Wipe rims and seal. When cool, check seal and label. Store in a cool, dark, dry place. Let stand at least 2 weeks before serving. About 25 calories per tablespoon.

APPLE CHUTNEY

When doubling this recipe, speed up the preparation by putting fruit and vegetables through the coarse blade of a meat grinder.
Makes about 4 pints

2 quarts coarsely chopped, peeled tart apples
1 cup minced, seeded sweet red peppers
1 cup minced yellow onions
1 clove garlic, peeled and minced
1 pound seedless raisins
1 (1-pound) box dark brown sugar
1 pint cider vinegar
1 tablespoon ginger
1 tablespoon cinnamon
2 teaspoons powdered mustard
2 teaspoons salt
¼ teaspoon crushed dried hot red chili peppers

Wash and sterilize 4 (1-pint) jars and their closures and stand them on a baking sheet in a 250° F. oven until needed. Mix all ingredients in a very large enamel or stainless-steel kettle, cover, and bring slowly to a boil. Uncover and simmer, stirring occasionally, 1–1½ hours until thick. (*Note:* Stir more frequently toward the end to prevent scorching.) Ladle boiling hot into jars, filling to within ⅛″ of tops. Wipe rims and seal. When cool, check seals and label. Store in a cool, dark, dry place. Let stand 1 month before serving. About 35 calories per tablespoon.

VARIATIONS:

Pear or Peach Chutney: Prepare as directed but substitute 2 quarts coarsely chopped, peeled firm-ripe pears or peaches for apples and omit red peppers. About 35 calories per tablespoon.

Mango Chutney: Substitute 4 pounds peeled, pitted, and thinly sliced green mangoes for apples, increase sugar to 2 pounds and vinegar to 1 quart. Add 1 pound dried currants and 3 tablespoons minced fresh gingerroot. Mix all ingredients in kettle, cover, and let stand overnight. Next day, proceed as directed. About 65 calories per tablespoon.

MINCEMEAT

True mincemeat should contain ground beef; if you include it, the mincemeat must be pressure processed to prevent spoilage. Mincemeat made without meat or suet need not be processed.
Makes about 6 quarts

2 pounds ground lean beef (optional)
1 cup water (optional)
5 pounds tart apples, peeled, cored, and chopped fine
1 pound seedless raisins
1 pound sultana raisins
1 pound dried currants
½ pound citron or mixed candied fruits, minced
½ pound finely ground suet (optional)
2 (1-pound) boxes dark brown sugar
1 quart apple cider, or 3 cups cider and 1 cup brandy or rum
1 tablespoon cinnamon
1 tablespoon allspice
1 tablespoon nutmeg
¼ teaspoon ginger
2 oranges or 3 large tangerines
1 lemon

Wash and sterilize 6 (1-quart) jars and closures and keep hot on a baking sheet in a 250° F. oven until needed. If using meat, simmer in water 10 minutes, breaking up with a spoon. Mix remaining ingredients except oranges and lemon in a large enamel or stainless-steel kettle. Finely grate orange and lemon rinds; also discard white pith and seeds and finely chop oranges and lemon. Add rind and fruit to kettle, also meat and liquid if you like, and simmer uncovered 1 hour, stirring occasionally at first, more often as mixture thickens. *If mixture contains meat and/or suet:* Ladle into jars, filling to within 1" of tops, wipe rims and seal. Process in a pressure cooker* 20 minutes at 10 pounds pressure. Remove from pressure cooker, secure seals if needed, cool, and label. *If mixture contains no meat or suet:* Ladle into jars, filling to within ⅛" of tops. Seal, cool, and label. Store mincemeat in a cool, dark, dry place several weeks before using. About 635 calories per cup (with meat and suet), 250 calories per cup (without).

⚜ PICCALILLI

Makes about 6 pints

- *4 pounds green tomatoes, quartered but not peeled or cored*
- *2 medium-size sweet green peppers, cored and seeded*
- *2 medium-size sweet red peppers, cored and seeded*
- *4 medium-size unpeeled cucumbers, halved and seeded*
- *2 medium-size yellow onions, peeled and quartered*
- *3 cups cider vinegar*
- *2 cups firmly packed light brown sugar*
- *2 teaspoons mustard seeds*
- *2 teaspoons celery seeds*
- *1 teaspoon allspice*
- *1 tablespoon prepared horseradish*

Wash and sterilize 6 (1-pint) jars and closures, stand them on baking sheet, and keep hot in a 250° F. oven until needed. Put all vegetables through the medium blade of a meat grinder, then drain well. Place in a very large enamel or stainless-steel kettle, add remaining ingredients, set lid on askew, and boil slowly ½ hour, stirring now and then. Ladle into jars, filling to within ⅛" of tops, wipe rims, and seal. Cool, check seals, label, and store in a cool, dark, dry place 4–6 weeks before using. About 12 calories per tablespoon.

⚜ CHOW CHOW RELISH

A great way to use up garden tag ends.

Makes about 4 pints

- *4 medium-size green tomatoes, cored and minced but not peeled*
- *4 medium-size sweet green peppers, cored, seeded, and minced*
- *2 medium-size sweet red peppers, cored, seeded, and minced*
- *2 large yellow onions, peeled and minced*
- *1 small cabbage, shredded fine*
- *1 medium-size cauliflower, separated into flowerets, or 3 cups cut green beans*
- *2 quarts cold water mixed with ½ cup pickling salt (brine)*
- *3 cups white vinegar*
- *2 cups sugar*
- *1 tablespoon celery seeds*
- *1 tablespoon mustard seeds*
- *1 teaspoon powdered mustard*
- *1 teaspoon turmeric*
- *1 teaspoon allspice*

Mix all vegetables with brine, cover, and let stand 1 hour. Meanwhile, wash and sterilize 4 (1-pint) jars and closures, stand them on a baking sheet, and keep hot in a 250° F. oven until needed. Drain vegetables well and set aside. Mix vinegar with remaining ingredients in a very large enamel or stainless-steel kettle and simmer, uncovered, 15 minutes. Add vegetables and simmer, uncovered, 10 minutes. Ladle boiling hot

PICKLES, PRESERVES, JAMS, AND JELLIES

into jars, filling to within ⅛" of tops. Wipe rims and seal. Cool, check seals, label, and store in a cool, dark, dry place 1 month before serving. About 10 calories per tablespoon.

⚖ PEPPER RELISH

To save time, peppers can be put through the medium blade of a meat grinder instead of being minced. Makes about 6 pints

- 1 dozen sweet green peppers, cored, seeded, and minced
- 1 dozen sweet red peppers, cored, seeded, and minced
- 2 cups minced yellow onions
- 1 cup minced celery
- 3 cups white vinegar
- 1½ cups sugar
- 1 tablespoon pickling salt
- 1 tablespoon mustard seeds
- 1 teaspoon celery seeds

Sterilize 6 (1-pint) jars and closures, stand them on a baking sheet, and keep warm in a 250° F. oven until needed. Mix all ingredients in a large, heavy enamel or stainless-steel kettle, cover, and simmer 15 minutes. Ladle into jars, filling to within ⅛" of tops and making sure liquid covers vegetables. Wipe rims and seal. *Or*, if you prefer, leave ½" head space, seal jars, and process in a hot water bath* 15 minutes. Remove jars, secure seals if necessary. Cool, check seals, label, and store in a cool, dark, dry place 3-4 weeks before using. About 10 calories per tablespoon.

VARIATIONS:

⚖ **Hot Pepper Relish:** Prepare as directed but substitute 1 dozen hot red chili peppers for the sweet red peppers. About 10 calories per tablespoon.

⚖ **Pepper Slaw** (Makes about 14 pints): Finely shred 2 large heads green cabbage, mix with ¼ cup pickling salt, cover, and refrigerate overnight. Next day, drain thoroughly, mix with Pepper Relish ingredients, increasing sugar and vinegar each to 6 cups and mustard and celery seeds each to 2 tablespoons. Simmer 20-30 minutes, then ladle into jars and seal as directed. About 15 calories per tablespoon.

⚖ CORN RELISH

To simplify cutting corn from cobs, boil corn 3 minutes and plunge into cold water.
Makes about 6 pints

- 2 quarts whole kernel corn (corn cut from about 1½ dozen ears)
- 1 cup minced yellow onions
- 1 cup minced sweet green pepper
- 1 cup minced sweet red pepper
- 1 cup minced celery
- 3 cups cider vinegar
- 1½ cups sugar
- 1 tablespoon pickling salt
- 1 tablespoon mustard seeds
- 2 teaspoons turmeric
- 1 teaspoon celery seeds

Sterilize 6 (1-pint) jars and closures, stand them on a baking sheet, and keep warm in a 250° F. oven until needed. Mix all ingredients in a large, heavy enamel or stainless-steel kettle, cover, and simmer 20 minutes. Ladle into jars, filling to within ⅛" of tops and making sure liquid covers vegetables. Wipe rims and seal. *Or* leave ½" head space, seal, and process in a hot water bath* 15 minutes. Remove jars and secure seals if needed. Cool, check seals, label, and store in a cool, dark, dry place 3-4 weeks before using. About 15 calories per tablespoon.

VARIATION:

⚖️ **Corn-Cranberry Relish** (Makes 7½ pints): Prepare as directed but add 1 pound washed and stemmed cranberries put through the medium blade of a meat grinder and increase sugar to 3 cups. About 15 calories per tablespoon.

⚖️ JERUSALEM ARTICHOKE PICKLE RELISH

Note how very low in calories this relish is.

Makes 6 pints

- 5 *pounds Jerusalem artichokes*
- 2 *medium-size yellow onions, peeled and coarsely chopped*
- 1 *cup sugar*
- 3 *cups cider vinegar*
- 1 *tablespoon turmeric*
- 1 *tablespoon mustard seeds*
- 1 *tablespoon celery seeds*
- 2 *tablespoons pickling salt*
- 1 *cinnamon stick*
- ½ *teaspoon crushed dried hot red chili peppers*

Wash and sterilize 6 (1-pint) jars and closures, stand them on a baking sheet, and keep hot in a 250° F. oven until needed. Using a stiff vegetable brush, scrub artichokes carefully under cold running water; scrape away any blemishes but do not peel, then put through the coarsest blade of a meat grinder. Place artichokes and remaining ingredients in a large, heavy enamel or stainless-steel kettle and simmer, uncovered, ½ hour, stirring occasionally; remove cinnamon. Ladle into jars, filling to within ¼" of tops; wipe rims and seal. Process 10 minutes in a hot water bath.* Cool, check seals, label, and store in a cool, dark, dry place. Let stand 4–6 weeks before serving. About 3 calories per tablespoon.

HAMBURGER RELISH

Makes about 8 pints

- 4 *pounds ripe tomatoes, peeled, cored, and coarsely chopped*
- 4 *pounds unpeeled green tomatoes, cored and coarsely chopped*
- 3 *medium-size sweet green peppers, cored, seeded, and minced*
- 3 *medium-size sweet red peppers, cored, seeded, and minced*
- 2 *large yellow onions, peeled and minced*
- 1 *quart minced celery*
- ½ *cup pickling salt*
- 1 *quart cider vinegar*
- 2 *(1-pound) boxes light brown sugar*
- 1 *cup granulated sugar*
- 1 *teaspoon powdered mustard*
- ½ *teaspoon pepper*

Mix all vegetables, sprinkle with salt, cover, and let stand overnight in a cool place. Drain well and mix with remaining ingredients in a very large enamel or stainless-steel kettle. Simmer, uncovered, stirring now and then, about 1½ hours until thick. Meanwhile, wash and sterilize 8 (1-pint) jars and closures, stand them on a baking sheet, and keep hot in a 250° F. oven until needed. Ladle relish boiling hot into jars, filling to within ⅛" of tops. Wipe rims and seal. Cool, check seals, label, and store in a cool, dark, dry place 3–4 weeks before using. About 25 calories per tablespoon.

PEACH RELISH

Makes 6 half pints

- 4 *pounds firm-ripe peaches (clingstone types are best), peeled, pitted, and sliced thin*
- 1 *cup sultana raisins*
- 1½ *cups firmly packed light brown sugar*
- ¾ *cup cider vinegar*
- 1 *teaspoon cinnamon*

½ teaspoon cloves
¼ teaspoon ginger
½ cup slivered almonds (optional)

Place all ingredients except nuts in an enamel or stainless-steel kettle, cover, and heat very slowly to simmering; uncover and simmer ¾ hour, stirring frequently. Meanwhile wash and sterilize 6 half-pint jars and closures, stand them on a baking sheet, and keep hot in a 250° F. oven until needed. If you like, add nuts to relish. Ladle boiling hot into jars, filling to within ⅛″ of tops. Wipe rims and seal. Cool, check seals, label, and store in a cool, dark, and dry place several weeks before serving. About 30 calories per tablespoon (without almonds).

BERRY RELISH

Tart-sweet berry relishes go well with most meats and poultry.
Makes 6 half pints

- 2 quarts firm-ripe berries (blueberries, huckleberries, cranberries, red or black currants, elderberries, or gooseberries), washed and stemmed
- 4 cups sugar
- ¾–1 cup cider vinegar
- 1½ teaspoons cinnamon
- ½ teaspoon allspice
- ¼ teaspoon ginger

Wash and sterilize 6 half-pint jars and closures, stand them on a baking sheet, and keep hot in a 250° F. oven until needed. Place berries in a large enamel or stainless-steel saucepan and crush a few with a potato masher. Cover and simmer, stirring now and then, until berries are soft. Mix in remaining ingredients, insert a candy thermometer, and boil slowly, stirring now and then, until thermometer registers 218° F. Ladle into jars, filling to within ⅛″ of tops. Wipe rims and seal. Cool, check seals, label, and store in a cool, dark, dry place 3–4 weeks before serving. About 40 calories per tablespoon.

RANCH RELISH

Makes 3 cups

- 3 medium-size ripe tomatoes, peeled, seeded, and cut in ¼″ cubes
- 1 medium-size yellow onion, peeled and minced
- 1 large sweet green pepper, washed, cored, seeded, and minced
- 2 teaspoons salt
- ½ cup chili sauce

Mix all ingredients, cover, and chill at least 2 hours to blend flavors (overnight is better). Serve with barbecued beef, broiled steaks and chops. About 6 calories per tablespoon.

CRANBERRY-ORANGE RELISH

Makes 1 pint

- 1 pound cranberries, stemmed, washed, and drained
- 2 large oranges
- 1¾ cups sugar
- ⅛ teaspoon salt

Pick cranberries over, discarding any underripe ones. Finely grate orange rinds; remove white pith and seeds from oranges, then coarsely chop. Put cranberries and oranges through the medium blade of a meat grinder. Mix with sugar and salt, cover, and let stand at room temperature 1 hour; mix again. Serve as is or slightly chilled. Stored airtight in the refrigerator, relish will keep several weeks. About 50 calories per tablespoon.

VARIATIONS:

Cranberry-Pear Relish: Prepare as

directed but substitute 4 peeled and cored pears (firm) for oranges and add ¼ cup minced crystallized ginger. About 60 calories per tablespoon.

Preserved Cranberry-Orange Relish (Makes 4 half pints): Leave cranberries whole, add grated rind and coarsely chopped oranges, then simmer, uncovered, with the sugar, salt, and 1 cup orange juice about ¾ hour, stirring now and then. Ladle boiling hot into 4 sterilized half-pint jars, filling to within ⅛" of tops, wipe rims, and seal; cool, check seals, label, and store. About 50 calories per tablespoon.

Fruit-Nut Conserve (Makes 5 half pints): Prepare Preserved Cranberry-Orange Relish (above) as directed but add ¾ cup seedless raisins along with sugar and juice. After simmering, add ¾ cup toasted, slivered almonds or coarsely chopped, blanched filberts; pack into jars as directed. About 65 calories per tablespoon.

SOME QUICK AND EASY RELISHES

These are jiffy relishes to mix up and serve, not ones to can. Store in the refrigerator.

Cran-Apple Relish (Makes about 1 pint): Mix 1 (1-pound) can undrained whole cranberry sauce with 1 unpeeled, cored, and diced tart cooking apple and 1 teaspoon lemon juice. Or mix cranberry sauce with ½ cup applesauce. About 25 calories per tablespoon.

Cranberry-Chutney Relish (Makes about 2½ cups): Mix 1 (1-pound) can undrained whole cranberry sauce with ½ cup minced chutney. About 40 calories per tablespoon.

Cranberry-Pineapple Relish (Makes about 3 cups): Mix 1 (1-pound) can undrained whole cranberry sauce with 1 (8-ounce) can drained crushed pineapple and 1 teaspoon minced mint. About 30 calories per tablespoon.

Cranberry-Walnut Relish (Makes about 3 cups): Mix 1 (1-pound) can undrained whole cranberry sauce with ⅓ cup each minced walnuts and celery. About 30 calories per tablespoon.

⚖ *Onion Relish* (Makes about 1 cup): Mix 1 large peeled and minced yellow, Bermuda, or Spanish onion with 2 tablespoons each cider vinegar and sugar and ¼ teaspoon salt. If you like add 1 minced pimiento. Let stand at room temperature ½ hour before serving. About 10 calories per tablespoon.

⚖ *Pineapple Relish* (Makes about 3 cups): Mix 1 (1-pound 4-ounce) can drained crushed pineapple with ½ cup each minced sweet green or red pepper and celery, 3 tablespoons each firmly packed light brown sugar and cider vinegar. Let stand at room temperature ½ hour before serving. About 15 calories per tablespoon.

⚖ *Quick Corn Relish* (Makes about 3 cups): Mix 2 cups drained canned whole kernel corn with ⅓ cup each minced yellow onion and sweet green or red pepper, ¼ cup each minced celery and sweet pickle relish, ½ teaspoon salt, and 2 tablespoons each sugar and cider vinegar. Let stand at room temperature ½ hour before serving. About 15 calories per tablespoon.

⚖ *Quick Pickled Beets* (Makes 1 pint): Sprinkle 1 (1-pound) can sliced beets with ¼ teaspoon garlic salt. Add ⅓ cup hot cider vinegar

PICKLES, PRESERVES, JAMS, AND JELLIES

mixed with 2 tablespoons sugar and ⅛ teaspoon cloves. Chill before serving. About 10 calories per tablespoon.

Quick Pickled Peaches (Apricots, Pears, Prunes, or Figs) (Makes 6 servings): Drain syrup from 1 (1-pound) can peach halves (apricot or pear halves, whole prunes or figs) into a saucepan, add ⅓ cup each cider vinegar and sugar, ¼ teaspoon each whole allspice and mustard seeds, and 1 stick cinnamon. Simmer, uncovered, 3–4 minutes, pour over fruit, which has been studded with cloves (3–4 for each piece). (*Note:* Omit cloves if using prunes or figs.) Cool and chill. From 40–100 calories per fruit (prunes, pears, and figs are the highest, peaches and apricots the lowest).

⚔ *Radish, Zucchini, and Lettuce Relish* (Makes about 1½ cups): Mix ½ cup each minced, unpeeled radishes and zucchini, 1 cup finely shredded iceberg lettuce, 2 tablespoons each cider vinegar and sugar, ¼ teaspoon salt, and ⅛ teaspoon caraway seeds. Let stand 15 minutes at room temperature, mix well again, and serve. About 5 calories per tablespoon.

▨ HOT MUSTARD FRUITS

Delicious with baked ham or boiled tongue.
Makes 6 servings

2 tablespoons butter or margarine
⅓ cup firmly packed light brown sugar
3 tablespoons prepared spicy brown mustard
1 cup drained canned sliced peaches
1 cup drained canned apricot halves
1 cup drained canned pineapple slices, cut in half

Preheat oven to 325° F. Melt butter in a small saucepan over low heat, add sugar and mustard, and heat and stir about 5 minutes until sugar dissolves. Place fruits in an ungreased shallow 1-quart casserole and pour in mustard mixture. Bake, uncovered, ½ hour, stirring and basting fruits once or twice. Serve as a vegetable substitute. About 200 calories per serving.

VARIATION:

Hot Curried Fruits: Prepare as directed but add 2–3 teaspoons curry powder to melted butter along with sugar and mustard. About 200 calories per serving.

⚔ ▨ HOMEMADE "PREPARED" MUSTARD

Refrigerated, this mustard keeps almost indefinitely.
Makes ½ cup

1 (1½-ounce) can powdered mustard
2 tablespoons sugar
1 teaspoon salt
3 tablespoons cider vinegar
2 tablespoons olive or other cooking oil
1 tablespoon cold water
½ teaspoon Worcestershire sauce

Mix mustard, sugar, and salt, add remaining ingredients gradually, and beat until smooth. Spoon into a sterilized jar, cover tightly, and refrigerate. About 10 calories per tablespoon.

VARIATIONS:

⚔ **Spicy Hot Mustard Spread:** Prepare as directed but add ¼ teaspoon each ginger and turmeric and ⅛ teaspoon cayenne pepper. About 10 calories per tablespoon.

⚔ **Horseradish Mustard:** Prepare as directed but add 2 tablespoons prepared horseradish. About 10 calories per tablespoon.

⚔ **Mild Mustard Spread:** Substitute 1 tablespoon white wine vinegar for cider vinegar and increase water to ¼ cup. About 10 calories per tablespoon.

⚔ **White Wine Mustard:** Mix yellow or brown powdered mustard (the brown is available in oriental groceries) with the sugar and salt called for. Blend in 2 tablespoons white wine vinegar, ¼ cup dry white wine, 1 tablespoon olive oil, ¼ teaspoon turmeric, and ⅛ teaspoon cayenne pepper. About 10 calories per tablespoon.

⚔ **FRESH HORSERADISH**

Stored in the refrigerator, this will keep almost indefinitely.
Makes 1 pint

½ *pound horseradish root, scrubbed and peeled*
½ *cup white vinegar*
2 *teaspoons salt*

Remove any discolored parts from root with a vegetable peeler, then coarsely chop root. (*Note:* If you are doing more than this amount at one time, drop horseradish into cold water to prevent browning.) Chop very fine, a little at a time, in an electric blender or put twice through the fine blade of a meat grinder. Mix with vinegar and salt. Pack into sterilized jars, cover tightly, and let ripen in refrigerator 1 week before using. About 5 calories per tablespoon.

JELLIES

Few cooking achievements seem more magical than the transformation of plump, freshly picked fruits into sparkling, quivery jellies. Yet there is nothing mysterious about the process. Or difficult. Three essentials are needed to make jelly: *pectin* (the jelling agent found naturally in certain fruits), *acid* (also found naturally in fruits, which strengthens the pectin), and *sugar* (which stretches and tenderizes the pectin; either beet or cane sugar may be used). With a delicate balance of the three comes perfect jelly: one that quivers but does not run, is firm enough to stand alone when unmolded yet tender enough to cut easily with a spoon.

How to Make Jelly

Suitable Fruits for Natural Jellies (those requiring no commercial liquid or powdered pectins): Tart apples, crab apples, Concord grapes, currants, quinces, blackberries, cranberries, gooseberries, and raspberries. For best results, fruits should be firm-ripe, when pectin content is at its peak. Neither green nor overripe fruits have sufficient pectin for making jelly.

Preparing the Fruit:

Apples, Crab Apples, Quinces: Wash, cutting away any blemishes; remove stems and blossom ends, then slice thin, quarter, or coarsely chop. *Do not peel, core, or seed* (these all contain pectin).

Grapes, Currants, and Berries: Stem, wash, and sort, discarding any soft or blemished fruits, then crush with a potato masher (leave skins and seeds in).

Extracting the Juice: Place prepared fruit in a large kettle, add amount of water called for in the following chart, and boil uncovered, stirring

PICKLES, PRESERVES, JAMS, AND JELLIES

JUICE EXTRACTION TABLE

Kind of Fruit	Quantity of Prepared Fruit	Amount of Water Needed per Quart of Fruit	Recommended Boiling Time
Apples and crab apples	1 quart	1 cup	20 minutes
Quinces	1 quart	2 cups	25 minutes
Raspberries	1 quart	None	10 minutes
Blackberries, gooseberries, and currants	1 quart	¼ cup	10 minutes
Concord grapes	1 quart	¼ cup	15 minutes
Cranberries	1 quart	1 cup	10 minutes

Note: The extracted juice (jelly stock) can be bottled and the jelly made at a later date in small quantities as needed (makes for clearer jelly). Simply heat juice to 190° F., ladle into hot sterilized jars, filling to within ¼" of tops, seal, and process 10 minutes in a hot water bath.* Cool, check seals, and store in a cool, dark, dry place until ready to make jelly.

occasionally, the recommended amount of time. Pour into a damp jelly bag suspended over a large bowl (most jelly bags come equipped with their own stands) or into a cheesecloth-lined colander set in a large bowl. Let juices drip through undisturbed; squeezing the bag to force out juices will cloud the jelly. You can, however, massage the bag *very gently* once or twice. Extracting juice is a painstaking process so don't be alarmed if it takes an hour or more. (*Note:* If extracted juice seems cloudy, strain through several thicknesses of cheesecloth.)

Testing for Pectin: Knowing how much pectin fruit juice contains is vital to making good jelly because the pectin content determines the amount of sugar needed. There are 2 tests:

With a Jelmeter (the most reliable test): These, available in housewares departments, come with full instructions; follow them. Jelmeters are calibrated glass tubes through which the extracted juice is drained, the speed of drainage indicating the pectin content and thus the quantity of sugar needed.

With Alcohol: In a small glass mix 1 teaspoon grain (*ethyl*) alcohol (available at drugstores) with 1 teaspoon room-temperature extracted juice; let stand one minute, then pour into a second glass. If a firm precipitate forms, juice is high in pectin and should be mixed, measure for measure, with sugar. If precipitate is curdy, use ¾ as much sugar as fruit juice and, if soft, half as much sugar as juice.

The sugar-to-juice ratios given in the table below are averages and should be used as a guide only when it is not possible to make one of the more accurate pectin tests.

Cooking the Jelly: Place juice and required amount of sugar in a very large, heavy kettle (at least 4 times the volume of fruit put into it—jellies bubble higher and higher as they thicken and, unless kettle is big enough, will boil over). Set over low

BASIC PROPORTIONS FOR JELLIES

Kind of Fruit Juice	Average Amount of Sugar Needed per Cup Extracted Juice
Apple, crab apple, cranberry, and currant	1 cup
Blackberry, gooseberry, raspberry, Concord grape, and quince	¾ cup

heat, insert a candy thermometer, and heat and stir, using a long-handled wooden spoon, until sugar is dissolved. Raise burner heat and boil rapidly, uncovered and without stirring, until thermometer registers 8° F. higher than the boiling point of water in your area. At sea level, the jelling temperature is about 220° F. Begin testing for sheeting, however, shortly after mixture boils (when thermometer reads about 215° F.).

Testing for Sheeting: This is the standard jelly test, fortunately a quick and reliable one. Take up a small amount of the hot mixture on a cold metal spoon, cool slightly, then tilt. When drops cling together, forming a jelly-like sheet, jelly is done.

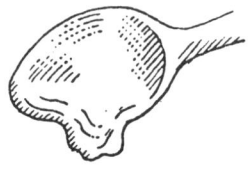

Sheeting
(done)

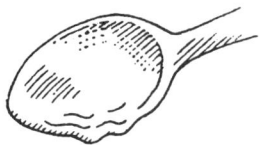

Syrupy
(not done)

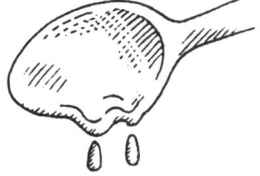

Thick Drops
(not done)

Preparing Jelly Glasses and Lids: These can be washed and sterilized while jelly cooks (follow directions in canning chapter). Invert sterilized glasses on paper toweling, stand lids right side up, and keep away from drafts.

Melting Paraffin: Because hot paraffin is flammable, the melting should never be done over direct heat but in the top of a double boiler. Or, better still, in a small deep coffeepot (one used exclusively for melting paraffin) set in a saucepan of boiling water (with the coffeepot, pouring's a snap). Paraffin melted slowly and kept just at the point of liquefaction will do a far better job of sealing jellies than smoking-hot paraffin which, on hardening, will shrink from the sides of the glass, split, or crack.

Filling Jelly Glasses: Place glasses on a level counter near kettle of jelly, turn right side up, one by one, as you're ready to fill them. Have jelly boiling hot, then ladle into glass, holding ladle as close to glass as possible to prevent air bubbles from forming in jelly. Fill glass to within

PICKLES, PRESERVES, JAMS, AND JELLIES

¼" of the top and seal with ⅛" melted paraffin, making sure it touches glass all round. Prick any bubbles in paraffin before it hardens so all air will be sealed out. (*Note:* A single thin layer of paraffin works better than a thick one because it remains malleable, fitting itself to the contours of the cooling jelly. Thick paraffin layers are apt to become brittle on hardening and pull from the sides of the glasses.) Cool jelly, cap glasses, label, and store in a cool, dark, dry place. (*Note:* Jelly can, if you like, be poured into small preserving jars—the half-pint size is good.) Simply pour *boiling hot* into jars, filling to within ⅛" of tops, wipe rims with a clean damp cloth, and seal. Invert jars for about 10 seconds so hot mixture will destroy any microorganisms in the head space, then stand right side up and cool. Check seals, label, and store.

How to Rescue Runny Jelly

Sometimes jelly made with the greatest care refuses to jell, hardly a disaster because there are several ways to salvage it:

Without Adding Commercial Pectin: Empty jelly into a saucepan, bring to a boil, and continue cooking until mixture will sheet (see Testing for Sheeting). Ladle into clean sterilized glasses and reseal with paraffin.

With Commercial Powdered Pectin: Measure jelly and for each 1 quart measure ¼ cup sugar, ¼ cup water, and 4 teaspoons powdered pectin. Mix pectin and water in a large saucepan, bring to a boil, stirring constantly to prevent scorching, then mix in jelly and sugar. Boil hard for exactly ½ minute. Remove from heat, ladle into clean sterilized glasses, and reseal with paraffin.

With Commercial Liquid Pectin: Measure jelly and for each 1 quart measure ¾ cup sugar, 2 tablespoons strained lemon juice, and 2 tablespoons liquid pectin. Bring jelly to a full boil over high heat, quickly mix in sugar, lemon juice, and pectin, and heat, stirring constantly, until mixture comes to a full rolling boil. Boil hard one minute, remove from heat, ladle jelly into clean sterilized glasses, and reseal with paraffin.

About Jellies Made with Commercial Pectins

Liquid and powdered pectins, in making it possible to jell any fruit juice, have revolutionized jelly making. They must, however, be used carefully—amounts required vary considerably from juice to juice, depending on sweetness, tartness, and pectin content. No master recipe, alas, can be drawn up for the commercial pectins, so the best plan is to follow the manufacturer's recipes explicitly.

Tips for Making Better Jellies

Because so many of these tips are the same as for jams and preserves, they are included at the end of that section.

Why Things Sometimes Go Wrong with Jellies

Soft, Runny Jelly: Too little pectin or sugar or both; also undercooking.

Stiff Jelly: Too much pectin or acid or both.

Dull, Cloudy Jelly: Fruit juice not carefully extracted.

Grainy or Crystalline Jelly: Too much sugar, too little cooking.

Gummy Jelly: Overcooking.

Weepy Jelly: Fruit too acid or paraffin layer too thick.

Darkened or Off-Color Jelly: Stored at too high a temperature.

Faded Jelly: Stored in too bright a room.

JAMS, MARMALADES, FRUIT BUTTERS, PRESERVES, AND CONSERVES

These preserved fruits and fruit spreads are easy to make and foolproof enough to invite improvisation. What distinguishes one from another? Here's a fast run-down:

Jams: Crushed berries or cut-up fruits cooked with a little water and a lot of sugar until thick, slightly jelled, and of good spreading consistency.

Marmalades: Clear, tender, jelly-like spreads usually made of citrus fruits and containing shreds of rind and bits of cooked fruit.

Fruit Butters: Melba-smooth, honey-sweet spreads made by cooking strained fruit pulp with sugar and spices long and slow in an open kettle.

Preserves: Whole or cut-up fruits cooked in a sugar syrup until clear; syrup may be very thick or fairly thin.

Conserves: Jam-like spreads made of a mixture of fruits and nuts.

How to Make Jam

Suitable Fruits: Apricots, blackberries, blueberries, cherries, gooseberries, grapes, peaches, pears, plums, raspberries, rhubarb, and strawberries. Also combinations of these.

Preparing the Fruit:

Berries and Other Soft Fruits: Wash and sort fruit, removing caps, stems, and any bruised or blemished spots, then crush.

Firm Fruits: Peel, core, and pit, then quarter, dice, or coarsely chop. (*Note:* Grapes and plums will have better texture if cooked until tender with a little water—about ¼ cup for each quart prepared fruit—before being mixed with sugar.)

Cooking the Jam: Measure prepared fruit and for each quart add 3 cups sugar. Place in a very large, heavy kettle (at least 4 times volume of fruit put into it) and heat and stir over low heat until sugar dissolves. Insert a candy thermometer, then boil rapidly uncovered, stirring often, until very thick, about 218–22° F. on thermometer. Test for sheeting (see Jelly); when mixture sheets, jam is done.

Preparing Jelly Glasses, Melting Paraffin: Follow directions given for jelly.

Filling Glasses: Remove jam from heat and let stand 1–2 minutes to settle foam; skim froth from surface, then ladle into jelly glasses or preserving jars as directed for jelly. Cool, label, and store in a cool, dark, dry place.

PICKLES, PRESERVES, JAMS, AND JELLIES

How to Make Marmalade
(see separate recipes that follow)

How to Make Fruit Butters

Suitable Fruits: Apples and crab apples, apricots, peaches, pears and plums, grapes and quinces.

Preparing the Fruit: Prepare as directed for jam.

Making the Fruit Pulp: Measure prepared fruit and for each 1 quart add ½ cup water. Cook in a large kettle, stirring now and then, until mushy; press through a sieve or purée in a food mill.

Cooking the Fruit Butter: Measure fruit pulp and for each quart add 3 cups sugar; if you like, tie a few whole cloves, allspice, and a broken cinnamon stick in cheesecloth. Heat and stir over low heat in a large kettle until sugar dissolves, then slowly boil, uncovered, until quite thick, 1–1½ hours, stirring often to prevent scorching, especially toward the end.

Preparing Glasses, Melting Paraffin: Prepare as directed for jelly.

Filling Glasses: Remove fruit butter from heat, let stand 2 minutes, and skim off froth. Fill glasses or jars as directed for jelly. (*Note:* Many fruit butter recipes call for less sugar than this basic method; if the proportion of sugar to fruit pulp is less than 3 to 4—3 cups sugar to 4 cups pulp—there will be less chance of spoilage if the fruit butter is poured into hot sterilized preserving jars to within ¼" of tops.) Seal and process in a hot water bath* about 10 minutes. Check seals after processing, then label jars and store in a cool, dark, dry place.

How to Make Preserves

Suitable Fruits: Cherries, figs, peaches, pears, pineapple, raspberries, and strawberries.

Preparing the Fruit:

Cherries and Berries: Wash, stem, and sort, discarding any that are bruised or blemished. Leave sweet cherries whole but halve and pit the sour.

Figs: Wash and stem, then peel carefully, trying not to cut too close to the seeds. Leave whole.

Peaches and Pears: Peel, pit or core, and slice. (*Note:* Pears are also good cut into small chips or thin pieces.)

Pineapple: Peel, core, and cube or slice thin.

Cooking the Preserves:

Soft Fruits (Berries and Peaches): Measure prepared fruit and for each 1 quart add 3 cups sugar; mix and let stand at room temperature 10 minutes to draw some of the juices from the fruit. Set over low heat and cook and stir until sugar dissolves; cover, remove from heat, and let stand overnight so fruits will plump up. Next day, bring to a boil, add a few whole cloves and a broken cinnamon stick tied in cheesecloth, if you like, and cook slowly, stirring occasionally, until fruit is clear and syrup thick. Remove spices.

Firm Fruits: Measure prepared fruit and for each 1 quart measure ½ cup water and 3 cups sugar. Mix water and sugar, bring to a boil in a large kettle, stirring until sugar dissolves. Add fruit and boil, uncovered, stirring occasionally, until fruit is clear and syrup thick. If you like, tie a few whole spices in cheesecloth—cloves, allspice, a cinnamon stick—and cook along with fruits; remove when preserves are done—the fruit clear and syrup thick.

Preparing Glasses, Melting Paraffin: Prepare as directed for jelly.

Filling Glasses: Rich jam-like preserves made of small berries or fairly finely cut fruit can be ladled into jelly glasses and sealed under paraffin. But fruits preserved whole in syrup should be packed hot in hot sterilized jars. In either case, before filling jars, let preserves stand off heat 2 minutes to settle foam; skim off froth, then pack in glasses or jars as directed for jelly. (*Note:* Preserves packed in jars should be processed 10 minutes in a hot water bath.*) Cool preserves, label, then store in a cool, dark, dry place.

How to Make Conserves

These are really simple variations on jams—mixtures of two or more fruits (use any suitable for jam) cooked with minced nuts and/or raisins. Prepare conserves like jam, teaming any combination of fruits you fancy, and using 3 cups sugar and ½ cup seedless raisins and/or chopped pecans, walnuts, or blanched almonds to each 1 quart prepared raw fruit. For better texture and flavor, add nuts during last 5 minutes of cooking.

TIPS FOR MAKING BETTER JELLIES, JAMS, PRESERVES, AND CONSERVES

In General:
— Read recipe through carefully before beginning and follow directions.
— Pick a clear, dry day for making jellies, jams, or preserves.
— Assemble equipment and ingredients before starting. Make sure jars or glasses are spotless, free of cracks and nicks.
— Make jellies, jams, and preserves in small quantities; do not double recipes.
— Measure or weigh ingredients carefully.
— Use extra-large, flat-bottomed kettles, heavy enough to reduce risk of scorching and made of an inert material, like enameled metal or stainless steel, that will not alter color or flavor of fruit.
— Use a candy thermometer to help determine doneness and check it for accuracy before using (for directions, see Candies and Nuts).
— For soft jams and preserves, slightly undercook; for stiff ones, slightly overcook.
— If you live in a hot climate or have no cool space for storing preserves, pack in preserving jars and process 10–15 minutes in a hot water bath* instead of ladling into jelly glasses and sealing with paraffin.
— When sealing with paraffin, make layer no more than ⅛" thick, see that it touches glass all around and has no air bubbles.
— Wipe cooled, sealed glasses and

jars with a clean damp cloth before storing.
— When cooling jars, allow plenty of space between them so air can circulate. Also, cool away from drafts.
— Test seals about 12 hours after cooling. If a jar has failed to seal, empty contents into a saucepan, bring to a boil, ladle into a clean, hot, sterile jar, reseal, and cool. Or, store in refrigerator and serve within 2 weeks.
— Store jams, jellies, and preserves in a dark, cool, dry place and let mellow several weeks before serving. Also, try to serve within a year, sooner if possible.

Jellies:
— Use firm-ripe fruit instead of fully ripe or, if you wish, ¼ slightly underripe fruit and ¾ ripe (but not overripe).
— Do not rush juice extraction but let it drip through jelly bag at its own snail's pace.
— If extracted juice lacks tartness (essential to making jelly jell), add 1 tablespoon strained lemon juice to each cup fruit juice.
— Do not overcook fruit when preparing for juice extraction—destroys pectin.

Jams, Marmalades, Fruit Butters, Preserves, and Conserves:
— To save money, use less-than-perfect fruits, *but* prepare carefully, trimming away all blemishes and moldy spots that might cause spoilage.
— When making preserves, have fruits of as uniform size and shape as possible.
— To keep fruit from floating to the top of jams and preserves, use fully ripe fruits and plump overnight in the sugar syrup.
— Watch all thick fruit mixtures closely during cooking and stir as needed to prevent scorching.
— Remove any whole spices immediately after cooking to prevent fruit from darkening.
— To reduce risks of spoilage (and make jams and preserves prettier) skim off as much froth or foam as possible before ladling into jars.

¢ **OLD-FASHIONED APPLE JELLY**

Apples that make particularly good jelly are Rhode Island Greenings. Do not double this recipe.
Makes enough to fill 5 8-ounce jelly glasses

5 pounds Rhode Island Greenings, washed, stemmed, and sliced thin but not peeled or cored
5 cups water
½ cup plus 2 tablespoons lemon juice
3¾ cups sugar (about)

Place apples (include seeds and cores), water, and lemon juice in a very large enamel or stainless-steel kettle, cover, and boil 15–20 minutes until apples are mushy. Meanwhile, suspend 2 damp jelly bags over large, heatproof bowls or line 2 large colanders with 4 thicknesses of cheesecloth, letting ends hang over rims, and set colanders in bowls. Pour half of the apples and their juice into each bag or colander and let juice drip through. (Note: Cheesecloth can be tied into bags and suspended over bowls.) For sparkling, clear jelly, don't force pulp through bags. You may, however, massage bags gently, encouraging juice to trickle through. Have patience—this takes a long time. Meanwhile, sterilize 5 (8-ounce) jelly glasses and stand upside down on several thicknesses paper toweling. When juice has been extracted (you should have about 5 cups), place in a clean, large enamel or stainless-steel kettle and stir in ¾ cup sugar for each 1 cup juice; insert a candy thermometer. Boil mixture uncovered, without stirring, 20–25 minutes until thermometer registers 218–20° F.; begin testing for "sheeting" after mixture has boiled 10 minutes. Take up a little juice in a large metal spoon, cool slightly, then tilt; if drops slide together forming a jelly-like sheet, jelly is done. Remove from heat and skim off froth. Fill glasses to within ¼″ of tops and seal with ⅛″ melted paraffin. Cool, cover, label, and store in a cool, dark, dry place. About 45 calories per tablespoon.

VARIATIONS:

¢ **Old-Fashioned Rose Geranium Jelly:** Place a small rose geranium leaf in the bottom of each jelly glass, pour in apple jelly, press a second leaf into jelly, then seal with paraffin. About 45 calories per tablespoon.

¢ **Crab Apple Jelly:** Prepare as directed, substituting 5 pounds crab apples for Greenings (¼ should be slightly underripe, the rest ripe) and omitting lemon juice. Test extracted juice for pectin* (crab apples contain considerable pectin) and add the quantity of sugar indicated (usually 1 cup sugar for each 1 cup extracted crab apple juice is about right). Proceed as directed. About 45 calories per tablespoon.

¢ **Spiced Apple or Crab Apple Jelly:** Prepare as directed but, when cooking apples and water for juice, add 6–8 whole cloves, 1 broken cinnamon stick, and 2–3 whole allspice, tied in cheesecloth. Remove spice bag before pouring apples into jelly bags. About 45 calories per tablespoon.

¢ **Minted Apple or Crab Apple Jelly:** Prepare as directed but when cooking apples and water for juice add 1 cup bruised mint leaves tied in cheesecloth; remove mint bag before pouring apples into jelly bags. About 45 calories per tablespoon.

Quince Jelly: Prepare as directed, substituting 5 pounds coarsely chopped, unpeeled firm-ripe quinces for Greenings and omitting lemon juice; cook quinces and water (2 cups water to each quart prepared fruit) 25–30 minutes until mushy. Extract juice, test for pectin,* and add quantity of sugar indicated (usually ¾ cup sugar for each 1 cup extracted juice). Proceed as directed. About 45 calories per tablespoon.

OLD-FASHIONED CONCORD GRAPE JELLY

Makes enough to fill 4 8-ounce jelly glasses

3 pounds Concord grapes, washed and stemmed but not peeled
¾ cup cold water
2¼ cups sugar (about)

Place grapes and water in a large enamel or stainless-steel kettle and mash well with a potato masher. Cover and bring to a boil over high heat; reduce heat slightly and boil gently 15 minutes.

Meanwhile, suspend 2 damp jelly bags over large heatproof bowls or line 2 large colanders with 4 thicknesses of cheesecloth, letting ends hang over rims; stand colanders in large bowls.

Pour half of grape mixture into each bag or colander and let juice drip through undisturbed. (*Note:* Cheesecloth can be tied into bags and suspended over bowls.) While juice is being extracted, sterilize 4 (8-ounce) jelly glasses and stand upside down on several thicknesses of paper toweling.

When most of the juice has dripped through, measure carefully—you should have about 3 cups. Place juice in a clean large enamel or stainless-steel kettle and add ¾ cup sugar for each 1 cup juice; insert a candy thermometer.

Bring mixture to a boil over high heat, reduce heat slightly, and boil uncovered, without stirring, 10–15 minutes until thermometer reaches 218–20° F. Begin testing for sheeting, however, after 5 minutes of cooking. Take up a little juice in a large metal spoon, cool slightly, then tilt; if drops run together in a jelly-like sheet, jelly is done. Remove from heat and skim off froth. Fill glasses to within ¼" of tops and seal with ⅛" melted paraffin. Cool, cover, label, and store in a cool, dark, dry place. About 40 calories per tablespoon.

☒ WINE JELLY

Serve as a condiment with poultry, game, or game birds.
Makes 2½ cups

1½ cups medium-dry port, red or white wine, or 1 cup wine and ½ cup water
1 cup currant or grape jelly
3 whole cloves
½ stick cinnamon
1 tablespoon lemon juice
1 envelope unflavored gelatin softened in ¼ cup cold water

Simmer wine, jelly, spices, and lemon juice, uncovered, 10 minutes; add gelatin and heat and stir until dissolved. Strain through a cheesecloth-lined sieve, cool, then chill until firm. Break up slightly with a fork and serve cool—not straight out of the refrigerator. About 30 calories per tablespoon.

☒ UNCOOKED BERRY JAM

This recipe can be made with a variety of berries.
Makes enough to fill 5 8-ounce jelly glasses

1 quart berries, stemmed, washed, and drained well
2 pounds sugar
2 tablespoons lemon juice
½ (6-ounce) bottle liquid pectin

Sterilize 5 (8-ounce) jelly glasses or, if you plan to store jam in freezer, freezer jars. Mash berries with a potato masher, then measure. You will need 1 pint mashed fruit. Strain out some of the seeds, if you like, but add extra mashed berries as needed to fill out the 1-pint measure. Mix berries and sugar well; combine lemon juice and pectin and add to berries; stir 3 minutes. (*Note:* A little undissolved sugar may remain.) Fill glasses to within ¼" of tops, cover with lids or rounds of foil, and let jam "set up" at room temperature; this may take 24 hours. Refrigerate and use within 3 weeks or freeze and use within 1 year. About 45 calories per tablespoon.

ORANGE MARMALADE

Make only small amounts of marmalade at a time so it doesn't scorch.
Makes 4 half pints

2 large thick-skinned oranges (navel or Valencia are best)
1 small lemon
2 cups water
4 cups sugar (about)

Peel oranges and lemon, trim away inner white part so rind is about ⅜" thick; cut in fine slivers about ½" long. Discard pith and seeds in fruit, then chop fruit fine, saving juice. Mix rind, fruit, and juice in a very large, heavy enamel, stainless-steel, or flameproof glass saucepan, add water, and simmer uncovered 10 minutes. Cover and let stand in a cool place overnight. Next day, wash and sterilize 4 half-pint jars and closures, stand them on a baking sheet, and keep hot in a 250° F. oven until needed. Measure fruit mixture and for each cup add 1 cup sugar. Return to pan, insert candy thermometer, slowly heat uncovered to boiling, stirring until sugar dissolves; boil slowly uncovered, stirring now and then, 30–40 minutes until thermometer reaches 218–20° F. Take up a little of the juice in a large metal spoon, cool slightly, then tilt; if drops slide together in a sheet, marmalade is done. Remove from heat, stir 1 minute, skim off froth, and ladle into jars, filling to within ⅛" of tops. Wipe rims and seal. Cool, check seals, label, and store in a cool, dark, dry place. About 50 calories per tablespoon.

VARIATIONS:

Bitter Orange Marmalade: Prepare as directed, using the slivered rind and chopped fruit of 4–5 Seville oranges; omit lemon. Tie seeds in cheesecloth and simmer along with rind, chopped fruit and juice, and water called for for 30–40 minutes until rind is almost tender; remove seeds and let stand overnight. Measure mixture, add enough water to total 1 quart, then proceed as directed, using 1–1½ cups sugar per cup of mixture, depending on how sweet a marmalade is wanted. About 50 calories per tablespoon.

Grapefruit Marmalade: Prepare as directed, using the rind of 2 large grapefruits instead of oranges; after trimming and slivering rind, measure 1½ cups to use in the marmalade; combine with lemon rind. Bring rinds and 1 quart water to a boil in a small saucepan, then drain; repeat twice. Mix rind and chopped, seeded grapefruit sections, add the 2 cups water called for, and proceed as directed. About 50 calories per tablespoon.

Lemon Marmalade: Prepare as directed for Orange Marmalade (above) but use the rind and chopped, seeded fruit of 4 large lemons; also use 1½ cups sugar for each 1 cup fruit and rind mixture. About 75 calories per tablespoon.

Ginger-Lime Marmalade: Prepare as directed, using the slivered rind and chopped fruit of 4–5 limes (you'll need 3 cups fruit and rind mixture) and the slivered rind and chopped fruit of 1 lemon. Use 1½ cups sugar for each cup fruit mixture and add ⅓ cup slivered crystallized ginger. Cook and bottle as directed. About 80 calories per tablespoon.

Kumquat Marmalade: Prepare as directed, using 1 quart slivered kumquat rind and chopped fruit (you'll need about 1¾ pounds ripe kumquats). (*Note:* The easiest way to prepare these small fruits is to halve lengthwise, scrape out seeds and core, then to sliver fruit and rind together.) Use 1½ cups water and ½ cup lemon juice when cooking, otherwise proceed as for Orange Marmalade. About 52 calories per tablespoon.

Calamondin Marmalade (Makes 5 half pints): These supertart, tiny citrus fruits, available in Florida and California, make excellent marmalade. Prepare like Kumquat Marmalade (above), substituting calamondins for kumquats, using 2 cups water instead of water *and* lemon juice and increasing amount of sugar for each cup fruit mixture to 2–2½ cups. About 83 calories per tablespoon.

GINGERED PEAR AND PINEAPPLE PRESERVES

Makes 15 half pints

Grated rind of 2 lemons
Juice of 2 lemons
10 pounds underripe pears
1 medium-size firm pineapple
1 pound crystallized ginger, coarsely chopped
5 pounds sugar

Place lemon rind and juice in a very large enamel or stainless-steel kettle. Peel, quarter, and core pears, one at a time; divide each quarter lengthwise into 3 wedges, then slice thin, letting pear fall into lemon juice in kettle and tossing occasionally to mix. Peel pineapple, quarter lengthwise, and remove hard core; cut quarters into long, slim wedges, then slice thin; add to kettle along with ginger and sugar. Set, uncovered, over moderately high heat and bring to a boil, stirring occasionally. Adjust heat so mixture boils *very gently* and boil uncovered, stirring occasionally, 1–1¼ hours until the consistency of marmalade. Meanwhile, wash and sterilize 15 half-pint jars and closures; stand them on a baking sheet and keep hot in a 250° F. oven until needed. Ladle preserves into jars, filling to within ⅛" of the tops; wipe rims and seal. Cool, check seals, label, and store in a cool, dark, dry place. Let stand 2–3 weeks before using. About 45 calories per tablespoon.

BLUE RIDGE APPLE BUTTER

Makes 4 half pints

4 pounds tart cooking apples, washed, cored, and sliced but not peeled
3 cups apple cider or water
2 cups sugar (about)
1 teaspoon cinnamon
¼ teaspoon allspice
¼ teaspoon cloves
¼ teaspoon salt

Boil apples and cider, uncovered, in a large enamel or stainless-steel kettle, stirring frequently, about 20 minutes until mushy; put through a fine sieve, pressing out as much liquid as possible. Measure apple pulp and for each 1 cup add ½–¾ cup sugar, depending on how sweet you like things. Put pulp, sugar, spices, and salt in a clean enamel or stainless-steel kettle and cook, uncovered, very slowly about 1½ hours, stirring often, until very thick (spoon a little mixture on a cold saucer, if it cools into a smooth firm mass, butter is done). Meanwhile, wash and sterilize 4 half-pint jars and closures and keep hot on a baking sheet in a 250° F. oven until needed. Spoon apple butter into jars, filling to within ¼" of tops, wipe rims, seal, and process in a hot water bath* 10 minutes. Cool, check seals, label, and store in a cool, dark, dry place several weeks before serving. About 35 calories per tablespoon.

⊠ LEMON CHEESE (LEMON CURD)

Use as a filling for cakes, pies, sweet rolls, or as a spread for hot breads.
Makes about 1 quart

1 cup butter
2 cups sugar
3 tablespoons finely grated lemon rind
⅔ cup lemon juice
⅛ teaspoon salt
4 eggs

Melt butter in the top of a double boiler over simmering water. Add sugar, lemon rind, juice, and salt and stir until sugar dissolves, 2–3 minutes. Beat eggs until frothy, mix in about 1 cup lemon mixture, return to double boiler and cook and stir 7–9 minutes until thick. Ladle into small jars, cover and cool to room temperature. Store in refrigerator. About 55 calories per tablespoon.

CHAPTER 26

CANNING AND FREEZING

CANNING

Canning dates to the Napoleonic Wars, when the French Government offered twelve thousand francs to the man who could discover a way of preserving rations. The man who did was François Appert, his method being to seal food in bottles and boil them in water. Appert did not know why the process worked; Louis Pasteur would determine that half a century later.

Canned food revolutionized world eating habits by making seasonal and regional foods widely available year round. Groceries and home pantries alike towered with tins of meat, fish, fruit, and vegetables. But their popularity declined abruptly after World War II with the mass availability of commercial frozen foods, which, everyone marveled, "tasted every bit as good as the fresh."

Freezing also proved to be an easier, more economical and reliable method of conserving food at home and has since made home canning of meats, poultry, fish, and game almost obsolete. The section on freezing covers these foods fully. Because space is limited, there is room here only to cover the rudiments of canning and to concentrate upon those foods still commonly canned at home—fruits and vegetables. Those seeking fuller coverage should obtain U. S. Department of Agriculture bulletins on the canning of meat, poultry, fruits, and vegetables (available through county agricultural extension offices or by writing the Office of Information, U.S.D.A., Washington, D.C. 20250). Invaluable, too, are the excellent booklets published by manufacturers of preserving jars.

The Equipment of Canning

1½–2-Gallon Kettles, preferably stainless-steel or enamel, for sterilizing jars, blanching and precooking foods.

Water Bath Canner: Any big kettle fitted with a wire or wooden rack and tight lid will work.

Pressure Cooker for canning low-acid vegetables, meats, poultry, fish, and game.

Preserving Jars and Closures: There are a number of types, each available in half-pint, pint, quart, and half-gallon sizes, but those most suitable for home use are the half pint, pint, and quart. Most popular today are the *Standard* and *Wide-Mouth Jars with Screw Bands and Dome Caps* (use dome caps one time only but reuse screw bands if in good condition). Also available are *Jars with Porcelain-Lined Zinc Caps and Rubber Sealing Rings* (the jars and caps are reusable, but the rubber rings should be used one time only if you are to be assured of a tight vacuum seal); and finally, *Old-Fashioned Jars with Glass Lids, Clamp-Down Springs, and Rubber Sealing Rings* (again the jars and lids are reusable if in perfect condition—no chips or cracks—but the rubber rings should be used only once).

Other Useful Implements:
Wide-Mouth Funnel for easier jar filling

Colanders and Large Strainers for washing and preparing foods to be canned

Scales

Clock or Timer

Blanching or Deep-Fat-Frying Basket

Cup, Pint, and Quart Measuring Cups; Measuring Spoons

Large and Small Knives; Long-Handled Forks, Ladles, Spoons, and Slotted Spoons

Tongs or Bottle Holder

About Pressure Cookers

The most expensive single piece of equipment needed for canning, a pressure cooker should be chosen carefully. It should be sturdy, of heavy metal construction with a tightly fitting lid equipped with a *pressure gauge* (to indicate steam pressure inside cooker), a *petcock* (valve to allow air and steam to escape when opened and pressure to build up when closed), and a *safety valve* (emergency steam release that "blows" when pressure overbuilds).

Caring for a Pressure Cooker:
– Sponge (but do not scour) kettle in hot soapy water after each use and dry thoroughly. The lid should never be immersed in water; sponge off and wipe dry, paying special attention to edges, crevices, and valves. Take care not to bang or roughen rims of kettle or cover.
– Keep petcock, pressure gauge, and safety valve clean and unclogged by drawing a string through the openings. If safety valve is the ball-and-socket variety, wash well after each use.
– Have pressure gauge checked at the beginning of each canning season (county agricultural extension agents and some manufacturer's dealers can assist you). If the gauge is 5 pounds off or more, invest in a new pressure cooker. Otherwise, mark prominently on kettle or tag the lid with the test results, i.e., "pressure 1 pound high" or "pres-

sure 2 pounds low" so that you will automatically compensate when using kettle.
– If cooker has a rubber gasket, keep clean and grease-free. Also check before using to make sure it shows no signs of age (cracking or softening). If so, replace with a new gasket.
– Never use metal brighteners in a pressure cooker; they may wear off the finish.
– Never subject a pressure cooker to abrupt temperature changes by pouring cold water into a hot cooker or plunging it in cold water. Doing so may warp or crack the cooker.
– Store cooker uncovered, stuffed with paper toweling to absorb any odors and moisture. Wrap lid separately and set on kettle askew *and* upside down.

Using a Pressure Cooker: Keep manufacturer's instructions handy and reread carefully at the beginning of each new canning season or whenever you have not used pressure cooker for some months.

TO PROCESS AT 10 POUNDS PRESSURE

If Gauge Reads Low by:	*If Gauge Reads High by:*
1 pound, process at 11 pounds	1 pound, process at 9 pounds
2 pounds, process at 12 pounds	2 pounds, process at 8 pounds
3 pounds, process at 13 pounds	3 pounds, process at 7 pounds
4 pounds, process at 14 pounds	4 pounds, process at 6 pounds

The Care of Preserving Jars and Closures

– Carefully examine jars before using, rejecting any with nicks or cracks. Also discard warped, dented, or rusty lids or screw bands or caps with loose linings.
– Do not reuse rubber rings or dome caps; they may not seal properly.
– Wash jars and closures in hot soapy water after each use and then again *before* using. Rinse well in hot water.
– *To Sterilize Jars and Closures* (essential for foods *not processed* in a boiling water bath or pressure cooker). Stand jars on a rack in a large kettle, add water to cover, bring to a full rolling boil, cover kettle, and boil 10 minutes. Closures usually need only to be scalded, but treatment varies according to type, so follow manufacturer's instructions.
– Whether sterilized or not, jars and closures should be immersed in hot water until they are needed; for pickles, preserves, jams, and jellies, they may be kept hot in a 250° F. oven.

The Terms and Techniques of Canning

Acid and Low-Acid Foods: Any food with a high acid content—either natural, as in fruit, or artificial, as in pickles—is an acid food. Vegetables (except tomatoes), all meats and fish are low-acid foods. Acid foods are processed in a water bath, low-acid foods must be pressure processed.

To Blanch: To dip raw food in boiling water or to steam briefly to set juices, reduce bulk, intensify color, or facilitate peeling.

Botulism: A serious, often-fatal form of food poisoning that develops in low-acid foods. Sadly, it usually gives no clues. The best preventive is to can foods with the utmost care, using equipment in perfect working order. Whenever in doubt about a can of food, *boil, covered, a full 15 minutes before tasting* (corn should be boiled 20 minutes). If food should foam during heating or develop an off odor, discard immediately (where neither children nor animals will find it). Also wash and sterilize any implements that touched the food before using again.

Closure: A cap, lid, or its component parts used to seal preserving jars airtight.

Enzymes: Natural chemical agents in food which, if not destroyed in canning, will alter color, texture, and flavor of food.

Flat-Sour: A common form of spoilage among canned foods, easily detected by its sour smell. Careful canning procedures prevent it.

Head Space: The distance between the food level and the top of a jar. Pickles, jams, and jellies should have ⅛" head space only; they are not processed and food needs no expansion room. With few exceptions, foods processed in a water bath should have ¼"–½" head space and those in a pressure cooker 1".

Microorganisms: The microscopic yeasts, molds, and bacteria that can cause food to spoil. The purpose of processing is to destroy them.

To Pack: To fill jars with food to be preserved. There are two methods:

Hot Pack: Packing food at or near the boiling point into hot jars. Sometimes the food is cooked or partially so, sometimes merely brought to boiling.

Cold (or Raw) Pack: Packing cold, raw food into hot jars. Food is then covered with boiling liquid (syrup, juice, or water), sealed, and processed.

To Precook: To partially or fully cook food prior to canning. The purpose is to drive out air, making food more compact.

To Process: To destroy microorganisms in canned food by heating in a pressure cooker or water bath prescribed lengths of time. Pickles and preserves should be processed in a *hot water bath* (water temperature 180–85° F., not boiling) but fruits and tomatoes in a *boiling water bath* (212° F.).

To Sterilize: To kill microorganisms on preserving jars and lids by scalding or boiling in water.

To Seal: To make jar closures airtight.

To Vent or Exhaust: To force air or steam from a pressure cooker.

Steps to Successful Canning

Initial Preparations:

— At the beginning of the canning season, assemble all equipment and make sure it is in good working order. Have pressure cooker gauge checked for accuracy.

— Examine jars and closures, rejecting any imperfect ones. Buy whatever additional jars and fittings you need early, including spares to replace midseason casualties. At the height of the season, it may be impossible to buy the particular sizes or types you need.

— Buy fresh supplies of dome caps or rubber rings. Wash rubber rings before using and check for resilience, *not* by stretching, which may pull rings out of shape, but by folding in half or pleating. Examine folds closely and reject any rings showing cracks or softness. Also reject any

that do not spring back when released.
- If in doubt about a jar or closure, test for leakage. Half fill with water, screw on cap, and stand jar upside down. If water oozes out, try lid on a jar you know to be good, also a good lid on the questionable jar. Discard all faulty jars and lids.
- Reread all instruction booklets for equipment you plan to use.
- Do not attempt to do a season's canning in one day; 1–2 canner loads are sufficient.
- Wash and sterilize jars and closures and keep covered with boiling water until needed.
- Have ready whatever canning syrups you will need.
- Never short-cut safe methods by using canning powders or aspirin.
- Never shorten processing times.
- Follow canning procedures carefully.

Selecting Fruits and Vegetables:
- Choose firm, ripe, garden fresh fruits and vegetables of highest quality. If possible gather your own (some orchards and farms encourage the practice).
- Sort food according to size and color. They will be prettier and process more evenly.
- Can food as soon after gathering as possible. If delayed, store in a cool, well-ventilated spot.

Preparing Fruits and Vegetables:
- Wash carefully, whether or not food is to be peeled. Do small amounts at a time, sloshing up and down in several changes of cool water and handling gently to avoid bruising. Lift from—rather than drain off—the final rinse water, leaving dirt and grit behind. Rinse sink or basin well between washings.
- Do not soak food in water; it will lose flavor and food value.
- Peel and cut fruits and vegetables as the Canning Guide recommends.
Tip: Peaches, apricots, plums, tomatoes, and other thin-skinned fruits peel quickly, cleanly if plunged in boiling water, then in ice water.

Packing Jars:

In General:
- Lift jars from hot water, one at a time, as you are ready to fill them.
- If using closures requiring rubber rings, lift rings from hot water, fit on jar ledge just below rim, and press flat. Reject and use a fresh ring if first one bulges or buckles.

Cold Pack:
- Fill hot jar quickly with raw food, arranging as attractively as possible and packing all but limas, peas, and corn snugly (being starchy, these will expand during processing; other foods will shrink). Peaches and other large fruit halves will be prettiest layered into wide-mouth jars, slightly overlapping, with hollows down. To pack berries without crushing, spoon into jar, shaking down occasionally.
- Leave ample head space (follow directions in Canning Guide).
- Pour in enough boiling syrup, water, or juice to cover food, at the same time leaving required head space. To cover food in a 1-quart jar, you will need ½–1½ cups liquid.

Hot Pack:
- Fill hot jars rapidly, one at a time, packing loosely.
- Leave recommended head space (see Canning Guide).
- If food has insufficient juices of its own to cover, add boiling syrup, water, or juice, leaving necessary head space.

Sealing Jars:

In General:
- Work air bubbles out of jar by running a knife around inside walls

where bubbles congregate.
— Seal each jar as you fill it.

Jars with Screw Bands and Dome Caps:
— Wipe jar rim with a hot, damp cloth.
— Fit dome cap on with sealing ring against rim.
— Screw metal band on tight—by hand only.

Jars with Porcelain-Lined Zinc Caps:
— Wipe jar rim *and* rubber ring carefully with a hot, damp cloth (a tiny seed or bit of food can prevent a proper seal).
— Screw cap down tight, then turn back ¼″. As soon as jar is processed, cap will be screwed down tight, completing seal.

Jars with Clamp-Type (Lightning) Closures:
— Wipe jar rim *and* rubber ring well with a hot, damp cloth.
— Put glass lid on so it rests squarely on rubber ring.
— Push long wire clamp up into notch on lid; leave short wire up until after processing. Then snap down against jar shoulder to complete the seal.

Processing Jars of Food: (*Caution:* Never process in an oven; food will not heat through sufficiently and jars may explode.)

In a Boiling Water Bath (212° F.): *For Fruits and Tomatoes.*
— If food is *Cold Pack,* have water hot but not boiling lest abrupt temperature change crack jars. If food is *Hot Pack,* have water boiling.
— Using tongs or jar holder, lower jars, one at a time, into water bath, adjusting so each stands steady on rack, does not touch its neighbor or canner sides, and is not apt to tilt or tumble during processing.
— When all jars are in the water bath, make sure water level is 1″–2″ above jar tops. Add boiling water, if needed, taking care not to pour directly on jars.
— Cover water bath and, when water comes to a full rolling boil, begin timing the processing (use timetables in Canning Guide).
— Keep water boiling steadily and add boiling water to kettle as needed to keep level well above jars.

Note: Times given in Canning Guide are for altitudes near sea level. If you live at 1,000 feet above sea level or higher, adjust times as below.

— Remove jars from water bath to a wire rack as soon as processing time is up.

In a Pressure Cooker: For Vegetables except Tomatoes.
— Familiarize yourself with pressure cooker and its operation before beginning.
— Place rack in cooker and pour in boiling water to a depth of 2″–3″.
— Stand jars on rack, allowing plenty of space around them. If cooker is deep enough to accommodate 2 layers, place a rack on first layer and stagger jars so they do not stand directly above one another.
— Fasten canner cover as manufacturer directs so steam can escape only through petcock or weighted gauge opening.
— Adjust heat under cooker so that steam streams steadily out of petcock or weighted gauge opening a full 10 minutes, driving air from cooker.
— Close petcock or attach weighted gauge and begin building up pressure.
— When pressure reaches 10 pounds (internal temperature will be 240° F. at altitudes near sea level), begin counting processing time.

CANNING AND FREEZING

WATER BATH PROCESSING TIME ADJUSTMENTS FOR HIGH ALTITUDES

Feet above Sea Level	IF TOTAL PROCESSING TIME Is 20 Minutes or Less, Increase by:	IF TOTAL PROCESSING TIME Is More than 20 Minutes, Increase by:
1,000	1 minute	2 minutes
2,000	2 minutes	4
3,000	3	6
4,000	4	8
5,000	5	10
6,000	6	12
7,000	7	14
8,000	8	16
9,000	9	18
10,000	10	20

Note: For more detailed instructions, contact local agricultural extension office or home economics departments of local universities or utility companies.

PRESSURE ADJUSTMENTS FOR HIGH ALTITUDES

Feet above Sea Level	Pressure Needed (Equivalent to 10 Pounds at Sea Level)
2,000	11 pounds
4,000	12
6,000	13
8,000	14
10,000	15

Processing times remain constant.

— Keep pressure constant by adjusting burner heat and protecting cooker from drafts, *never by opening petcock.*

Note: At altitudes 2,000 feet or more above sea level, pressure greater than 10 pounds will be needed to achieve the necessary 240° F. inside cooker. Follow manufacturer's directions, or make adjustments as above.

— When processing time is up, remove cooker from heat and let stand undisturbed until *2 minutes after pressure has dropped to zero.*

— Open petcock slowly or remove weighted gauge.
— Unlock cover and open cooker, tilting cover away to deflect sudden bursts of steam.
— Lift jars to wire racks, allowing plenty of space around them.

Cooling Processed Jars:
— Complete seals on jars, if necessary, as you lift them to wire rack:

Jars with Screw Bands and Dome Caps: No adjustment needed.

Porcelain-Lined Zinc Caps: Screw down tightly.

Lightning-Type Closures: Snap short wire loop down against jar shoulder.
— Let jars cool at least 12 hours on wire racks, allowing plenty of space between them for air to circulate. Protect from drafts but do not cover with dish towels. (*Caution:* Never set hot jars directly on a cold counter—they may break.)
— If liquid in a jar has boiled down in processing, do not open jar and add more. Leave jar sealed; food may darken but it is unlikely to spoil.

Checking Seals (the day after canning):

Screw Band Closures:
— Remove screw bands, wiping if necessary with a hot damp cloth to loosen.
— Press center of dome cap; if it moves, jar has not sealed. Also tap center of cap; if it makes a clear ringing sound, seal is tight. If it sounds thudding, jar may not have sealed. To test further, slowly turn jar upside down. If there is no leakage, jar is probably properly sealed. *But,* mark jar as questionable and inspect carefully for spoilage before using.

Porcelain-Lined Zinc Caps and Lightning-Type Closures:
— Turn jar halfway over. If there is no leakage, jar is sealed.

If a Jar Has Not Sealed:
— Refrigerate and use contents within 3–4 days.
— *Or* start all over again, packing into a clean, hot jar, reprocessing, and cooling.
— Check questionable jar and closure for defects before reusing.

Labeling and Storing Home-Canned Food:
— Label each jar clearly, including description of contents, canning date, and, if more than one canner load was done that day, load number.
— Include on label any remark to indicate whether seal may be faulty.
— Store jars in a cool, dark, dry place. Dampness can corrode or rust caps, inviting spoilage; warmth and light reduce quality and storage life; freezing may break jars or seals.

Using Home-Canned Foods:
— Use, if possible, within a year after canning. Though safe to eat for several years, home-canned foods lose color, texture, flavor, and food value after a year on the shelf.
— Once a jar is opened, store any unused portion in refrigerator.
— Be alert to symptoms of spoilage (see Why Things Sometimes Go Wrong with Canned Foods). Reject jars with bulging or leaky lids, off colors or odors, mold. Also discard those that fizz or spurt when opened. With low-acid vegetables there is also the danger of botulism (see Terms and Techniques of Canning for a discussion of this serious form of food poisoning).

Boil sugar and water, stirring occasionally, until sugar dissolves. Use boiling hot for canning fruits, ice cold for freezing. (*Note:* To cover 1 pint fruit packed for freezing, you will need ½–¾ cup syrup; to cover 1 quart fruit packed for canning, 1–1½ cups.)

To Add Ascorbic Acid (to prevent fruits from darkening): Prepare any of the above syrups as directed, then add to the full amount, just before using, ½ teaspoon ascorbic acid powder or crystals mixed with 1 tablespoon cold water. (*Note:* If using the commercial solutions, add as labels direct.)

CANNING AND FREEZING

SUGAR SYRUP FOR CANNING AND FREEZING

Type of Syrup	Amount of Sugar or Sugar and Corn Syrup	Amount of Water	Yield
Thin	2 cups sugar OR ⅔ cup light corn syrup and 1⅓ cups sugar	1 quart	5 cups
Medium	3 cups sugar OR 1 cup light corn syrup and 2 cups sugar	1 quart	5½ cups
Heavy	4¾ cups sugar OR 1½ cups light corn syrup and 3¼ cups sugar	1 quart	6½ cups
Extra heavy	7 cups sugar OR 2⅓ cups light corn syrup and 4⅔ cups sugar	1 quart	7¾ cups

WHY THINGS SOMETIMES GO WRONG WITH CANNED FOODS

Condition	Causes	Safe to Eat?
Bulging lids or can ends	Spoilage	No
Darkened food at top of jar of fruit or pickles	Exposure to air, insufficient liquid to cover, not processed long enough to destroy enzymes.	Yes, IF there is no off odor or other sign of spoilage.
Rose or purple cast in apples, pears, peaches	Chemical reaction during processing.	Yes
Darkened or grayed vegetables	Water used in canning hard OR a reaction of vegetable acids, tanins, or sulfur with metal of cooker or canner.	Probably safe if there is no off odor or other sign of spoilage. If in doubt, discard *without* tasting.
White sediment or cloudy liquid in jar	POSSIBLE SPOILAGE. May also be caused by vegetable starches, minerals in water, or fillers in salt.	No. DO NOT TASTE. Discard.
Floating fruit	Canning syrup too heavy.	Yes
Jar unseals during storage	Spoilage	No
Jar fails to seal	Faulty jar or lid, bit of food on jar rim, failure to follow canning procedures.	Yes — IF discovered immediately after canning and *used* immediately.

NOTE: Beware of and discard — *never taste* — any food that is moldy, mushy, cloudy, soft or slimy, any that bubbles, fizzes, or spurts, any that has an off odor or color.

CANNING GUIDE FOR FRUITS AND ACID VEGETABLES

— *To Prevent Darkening*, dip apples, apricots, peaches, and pears after cutting in 1 gallon cold water mixed with 2 tablespoons each vinegar and salt. Do not let fruit stand in mixture longer than 20 minutes; drain well before proceeding.

— *Syrup Quantity Needed*: Depending on fruit's juiciness, use 1-1½ cups syrup per quart prepared fruit.

— *Simmering Temperature*: 185-210° F. *Boiling Temperature*: Varies with mixture; it is reached whenever mixture bubbles actively.

— *About Filling Jars*: For *Hot Pack*, hot food goes into *hot jars*; for *Cold Pack*, raw food goes into *hot jars*. Always leave 1/4"-1/2" head space and make sure food is submerged in juices. Wipe jar rims and screw on caps before processing. *Note*: For best results, follow Steps to Successful Canning, outlined earlier.

Food	Amt. Needed per Quart Canned Food	Preparation	Method	Time in Boiling Water (212° F.) Bath	
				Pints	Quarts
Apples	2½-3 lbs.	Peel, core, cut in wedges; dip to prevent darkening.*	*Hot Pack*: Boil, uncovered, 5 minutes in Thin Syrup; fill jars, cover apples with boiling syrup, leaving 1/2" head space.	20 min.	20 min.
Applesauce	3-4 lbs.	Prepare as recipe directs; heat to simmering.	*Hot Pack*: Fill jars to within 1/2" of tops.	20 min.	20 min.
Berries (except strawberries), currants	1½-3 lbs.	Stem, sort, wash, and drain.	*Hot Pack* (for firm berries): Add 1/2 cup sugar to each quart prepared fruit; let stand, covered, 2 hours. Heat to boiling, fill jars to within 1/2" of tops; if not enough syrup to cover, pour in boiling water to within 1/2" of tops.	10 min.	15 min.
			Cold Pack (for soft berries): Pour 1/2 cup boiling Thin or Medium Syrup into each jar, add raw berries, shaking to pack without crushing, filling to 1/2" of tops. Pour in boiling syrup to cover; leave 1/2" head space.	15 min.	20 min.

Cherries	2-2½ lbs.	Stem, sort, wash, and drain. Pit or not, as you like; if not, prick cherries with sterilized pin to prevent bursting.	*Hot Pack:* Add 1/2-3/4 cup sugar per quart prepared cherries; if unpitted, also add a little water to prevent scorching; heat to simmering. Fill jars with cherries to within 1/2" of tops, cover with boiling Thin Syrup, leaving 1/2" head space.	10 min.	15 min.
			Cold Pack: Pour 1/2 cup boiling Medium or Heavy Syrup into each jar, fill to within 1/2" of tops with cherries, shaking down to pack without crushing. Cover with boiling syrup, leaving 1/2" head space.	20 min.	25 min.
Figs	1½-2½ lbs.	Use firm figs only; wash and drain but do not peel or stem.	*Hot Pack:* Cover figs with water, bring to a boil, let stand off heat 5 minutes; drain. Fill jars with figs to within 1/2" of tops, add 1 tablespoon lemon juice to each quart, cover figs with boiling Thin Syrup; leave 1/2" head space.	1 hr. and 25 min.	1½ hrs.
Fruit juices	—	Extract juice from fruit as in making jelly.* Sweeten to taste.	*Hot Pack:* Pour simmering hot into jars, leaving 1/2" head space.	5 min.	5 min.
Fruit purées	—	Use fleshy, ripe fruit. Wash, stem, and pit; do not peel. Add a little water to prevent sticking; simmer until soft. Purée in a food mill or sieve, sweeten to taste.	*Hot Pack:* Pack simmering hot in jars, leaving 1/2" head space.	10 min.	10 min.
Grapes	2-2½ lbs.	Stem, wash, and drain but do not pee or seed.	*Cold Pack:* Pour 1/2 cup boiling Medium Syrup into each jar; fill with grapes to within 1/2" of tops, add more boiling syrup; leave 1/2" head space.	15 min.	20 min.

CANNING GUIDE FOR FRUITS AND ACID VEGETABLES (continued)

Food	Amt. Needed per Quart Canned Food	Preparation	Method	Time in Boiling Water (212° F.) Bath Pints	Time in Boiling Water (212° F.) Bath Quarts
Peaches, pears, nectarines, apricots	2-3 lbs.	Peel peaches, pears; apricots, nectarines may or may not be; halve, pit, or core, removing gritty, stringy flesh; dip to prevent darkening,* drain and rinse.	*Hot Pack:* Heat fruit to simmering in Medium Syrup; pack, hollows down, to within 1/2" of jar tops. Cover with boiling syrup, leaving 1/2" head space. *Cold Pack* (for all except pears): Pack *raw* fruit, hollows down, to within 1/2" of jar tops. Cover with boiling Medium Syrup; leave 1/2" head space.	20 min. 25 min.	25 min. 30 min.
Persimmons (wild)	—	Prepare as for Fruit Purée.	*Hot Pack:* Pack boiling hot in jars, leaving 1/2" head space.	15 min.	20 min.
Plums	1½-2½ lbs.	Choose firm plums; wash and peel or not; if unpeeled, prick with sterilized pin to prevent bursting.	*Hot Pack:* Cover plums with Heavy or Medium Syrup and heat to boiling. Cover and let stand *off* heat 1/2 hour. Pack plums in jars and cover with boiling syrup, leaving 1/2" head space.	20 min.	25 min.
Rhubarb	1-2 lbs.	Wash and trim stalks but do not peel; cut in 1" chunks.	*Hot Pack:* Mix each quart prepared rhubarb with 3/4-1 cup sugar, cover, let stand 3-4 hours. Bring slowly to boiling; boil 1/2 minute. Pack in jars, leaving 1/2" head space.	10 min.	10 min.

Tomatoes*	2½-3½ lbs.	*Cold Pack:* Pack whole tomatoes in jars to within 1/2" of tops; press gently to fill space. Add no liquid. Add 1/2 teaspoon salt to each pint, 1 teaspoon to each quart.	35 min. 45 min.
	Same as above except quarter tomatoes instead of leaving whole.	*Hot Pack:* Heat and stir tomatoes until boiling. Pack into jars, leaving 1/2" head space; add 1/2 teaspoon salt to each pint jar, 1 teaspoon salt to each quart.	10 min. 15 min.
Tomato juice*	3-3½ lbs.	Wash, core, and dice soft-ripe tomatoes; heat and stir until mushy; strain. Add 1 teaspoon salt to each 1 quart juice.	
		Hot Pack: Pour boiling hot into jars, filling to within 1/4" of tops.	10 min. 15 min.

*Note: For canning, use only *vine-ripened* tomatoes that are red, juicily plump, and filled with a rich tomato bouquet. Tomatoes picked green may lack the natural acids needed in order for them to can safely by the Boiling Water Bath method.

CANNING GUIDE FOR LOW-ACID VEGETABLES

Note: Only those vegetables particularly suited to canning are included here, those that remain firm, colorful, flavorful.

Not Recommended for Canning: Broccoli, Brussels sprouts, cabbage, cauliflower, eggplant, leafy greens, okra, onions, rutabaga, turnips.

— Before beginning, read About Pressure Cookers and Steps to Successful Canning.
— *About Filling Jars:* The *Cold Pack* method, once thought risky for low-acid vegetables, has recently been proved safe for asparagus, carrots, green and black-eyed peas, lima, green, and wax beans, corn. It is included along with the *Hot Pack* method.

Food	Amt. Needed per Quart Canned Food	Preparation	Method	Processing Time at 10 lbs. Pressure	
				Pints	Quarts
Asparagus	2½–4½ lbs.	Use tender, tight-tipped stalks; wash, remove woody ends, scales. Rinse, leave whole or cut in 1" lengths.	*Hot Pack:* Boil 3 minutes in water to cover; if whole, pack close together, stems down to within 1" of jar tops. Add 1 teaspoon salt to each quart, cover with boiling cooking water, leaving 1" head space.	25 min.	30 min.
			Cold Pack: Pack *raw* asparagus as for Hot Pack, adding salt, covering with fresh boiling water and leaving 1" head space.	25 min.	30 min.
Beans (green and wax)	1½–2½ lbs.	Use young, tender beans. Wash, drain, string, trim off ends, and cut in 2" lengths.	*Hot Pack:* Boil 3 minutes in water to cover; pack in jars to within 1" of tops; add 1 teaspoon salt per quart, cover with boiling cooking water, leaving 1" head space.	20 min.	25 min.
			Cold Pack: Pack *raw* beans as directed for Hot Pack, add salt, cover with fresh boiling water, filling to within 1" of jar tops.	20 min.	25 min.

Beans (lima)	3-5 lbs. (unshelled)	Select young tender beans; wash, drain, and shell. Wash once more.	*Hot Pack:* Boil 3 minutes in water to cover; spoon beans in jars to within 1" of tops; add 1 teaspoon salt to each quart, cover with boiling water, leaving 1" head space. *Cold Pack:* Loosely spoon *raw* beans into jars, add salt as directed for Hot Pack and pour in fresh boiling water, leaving 1" head space.	40 min. 50 min. *Note:* If beans are large, process an extra 10 minutes.
Beets	2-3½ lbs. (minus tops)	Sort beets by size; cut off tops, leaving 1" stems on, also leave roots on. Wash well and boil in water to cover 15-25 minutes until skins slip off. Skin, trim, If small, leave whole; if not, halve, quarter, slice, or dice.	*Hot Pack:* Fill jars with hot beets to within 1" of tops, add 1 teaspoon salt to each quart; cover with fresh boiling water, leaving 1" head space.	30 min. 35 min.
Carrots	2-3 lbs. (minus tops)	Wash carrots, peel, and wash again. Leave whole, slice, or cube.	*Hot Pack:* Boil 3 minutes in water to cover; fill jars with carrots, to within 1" of tops, add 1 teaspoon salt per quart; pour in boiling cooking water, leaving 1" head space. *Cold Pack:* Pack raw carrots in jars as directed for Hot Pack, add salt, and cover with fresh boiling water, leaving 1" head space.	25 min. 30 min. 25 min. 30 min.
Celery	1½-2 lbs. (minus tops)	Discard tops; scrub well, rinse; trim stalks of coarse parts and cut in 2" lengths.	*Hot Pack:* Boil 3 minutes in water to cover; pack celery in jars to within 1" of tops, add 1 teaspoon salt to each quart, cover with boiling cooking water, leaving 1" head space.	30 min. 35 min.

CANNING GUIDE FOR LOW-ACID VEGETABLES (continued)

Food	Amt. Needed per Quart Canned Food	Preparation	Method	Processing Time at 10 lbs. Pressure	
				Pints	Quarts
Corn (cream-style)	10-16 ears	Husk corn, remove silks; following directions in vegetable chapter, cut corn from cobs as for cream-style corn.*	*Hot Pack:* Measure corn pulp; to each quart add 2½ cups boiling water and 1 teaspoon salt; boil together 3 minutes, ladle into pint jars, filling to within 1" of tops.	1 hr. and 25 min.	Not Recommended
			Cold Pack: Fill *pint* jars to within 1" of tops with *raw* corn pulp; add 1/2 teaspoon salt to each jar, add boiling water; leave 1" head space.	1 hr. and 35 min.	Not Recommended
Corn (whole kernel)	8-16 ears	Husk corn, remove silks; following directions in vegetable chapter, cut corn from cobs as for whole kernel corn.*	*Hot Pack:* Measure kernels; to each quart add 1 pint boiling water and 1 teaspoon salt; boil 3 minutes, then fill jars to within 1" of tops.	55 min.	1 hr. and 25 min.
			Cold Pack: Loosely fill jars with *raw* kernels to within 1" of tops; add 1 teaspoon salt to each quart, cover with boiling water, leaving 1" head space.	55 min.	1 hr. and 25 min.
Parsnips	2-3 lbs.	Scrub well, peel, and wash. Slice or leave whole.	*Hot Pack:* Boil 3 minutes in water to cover; pack in jars to within 1" of tops; add 1 teaspoon salt to each quart, cover with boiling cooking water, leaving 1" head space.	30 min.	35 min.
Peas (black-eyed)	3-6 lbs. (unshelled)	Shell peas, wash, and drain.	*Hot Pack:* Boil 3 minutes in water just to cover; pour into jars, leaving 1" head space. Add 1 teaspoon salt to each quart, also, if needed, boiling water to cover peas.	35 min.	40 min.
			Cold Pack: Pack raw peas loosely in jars to within 1" of tops; add salt as for Hot Pack, also boiling water to cover, leaving 1" head space.	35 min.	40 min.

Peas (green)	3-6 lbs. (unshelled)	Shell peas and wash; drain well.	*Hot Pack:* Boil small peas 3 minutes in water just to cover, large peas 5 minutes; pour into jars, leaving 1" head space; add 1 teaspoon salt to each quart and, if needed, boiling water to cover peas.	40 min.	40 min.
			Cold Pack: Loosely pack *raw* peas in jars, leaving 1" head space; add 1 teaspoon salt to each quart. Pour in boiling water to within 1" of jar tops.	40 min.	40 min.
Potatoes (Irish)	5-6 lbs.	Use freshly dug new potatoes of uniform size; scrub, peel, and wash. Leave whole.	*Hot Pack:* Boil 10 minutes, drain well. Pack potatoes in jars to within 1" of tops; add 1 teaspoon salt per quart, add boiling water to cover potatoes, leaving 1" head space.	30 min.	40 min.
Potatoes (sweet)	2-3 lbs.	Use freshly dug, small-to-medium sweet potatoes. Scrub well, parboil 20 minutes to loosen skins. Do not prick. Skin, leave whole, halve, or quarter.	*Hot Pack (Dry):* Pack hot potatoes in jars, filling to within 1" of tops; press gently to fill spaces; add no salt or liquid.	65 min.	1 hr. and 35 min.
			Hot Pack (Wet): Fill jars to within 1" of tops with hot potatoes; add 1 teaspoon salt to each quart; cover with boiling water or Medium Syrup (see Canning Syrups), leaving 1" head space.	55 min.	1½ hrs.
Pumpkin and winter squash	1½-3 lbs.	Halve pumpkin or squash, remove seeds, cut in 2" chunks, and peel. Steam until tender, 20-25 minutes; purée in a food mill.	*Hot Pack:* Heat and stir purée to simmering; ladle into jars, filling to within 1" of tops. Add no liquid or salt.	65 min.	1 hr. and 20 min.
Summer squash	2-4 lbs.	Select, tender-skinned young squash. Wash well but do not peel. Slice 1/2" thick.	*Hot Pack:* Steam 3 minutes, pack hot in jars, leaving 1" head space. Add 1 teaspoon salt to each quart, pour in boiling water to cover squash; leave 1" head space.	30 min.	40 min.
Tomatoes	(see Canning Guide for Fruits and Acid Vegetables)				

FREEZING

Frozen food is as old as the Eskimos. Throughout history, men have sought scientific ways of freezing food, and no less a person than Sir Francis Bacon caught his death trying to freeze chickens by packing them with snow. Early in the twentieth century an American scientist named Clarence Birdseye sampled frozen venison and fish while on expedition to Labrador and found both remarkably like the fresh. He also watched fish, pulled live from the sea, freeze solid in minutes. Quick-freezing, Birdseye suspected, was the key to quality, and he set to work devising mechanical means of quick-freezing fish, meat, fruits, and vegetables. His frozen foods went on sale in the 1930's, but unfortunately few people could afford them. It was not until after World War II that the Age of Frozen Foods arrived.

Today the home freezer ranks in importance with the range and refrigerator. Nearly a third of America's families own home freezers—"minimarkets" stocked with out-of-season fruits and vegetables, meats bought "on special," the catch of fishing and hunting expeditions, brown-and-serve breads, instant dinners and party snacks. Freezing is not only the fastest, easiest, and most economical way of preserving foods at home, it is also the one that alters flavor, color, and food value the least. The intense heat of canning required to kill microorganisms and stop enzymatic action changes the character of food. Not so freezing, which does not destroy microorganisms or enzymatic action, merely stops them cold.

About Home Freezers

To freeze food successfully, a freezer must maintain a temperature of 0° F. or lower. Most refrigerator frozen food compartments average 20–32° F. and, though suitable for storing frozen foods short periods of time, are not adequate for freezing food. A home freezer is essential; which size and model you choose depends upon your individual needs and preferences.

The Equipment of Home Freezing

Most of the paraphernalia of canning is useful: large kettles (stainless-steel, enameled metal, or other material that will not react with acid foods), sieves, colanders, blanching baskets, long-handled spoons and forks, funnels, cup measures, measuring spoons, knives, etc. (see The Equipment of Canning). In addition, the following will be useful:

Hand or Electric Vegetable Shredder-Chopper-Slicer for shredding, chopping, or slicing foods to be frozen.

Food Mill or Electric Blender for puréeing foods.

Meat Grinder for grinding foods.

Potato Masher for mashing foods.

Pancake Turner for handling foods to be frozen.

Shallow Baking Pans for freezing rolls or cookies. Once foods are frozen, they can be removed from pans and bundled in plastic bags, freeing pans for use.

CANNING AND FREEZING

Freezer Thermometer for checking freezer temperature.

Freezer Packaging Materials (Note: To be effective, freezer wraps must be both moisture- and vaporproof).

—*Aluminum Foil:* Multipurpose but especially suited to wrapping meats, fish, poultry, and bulky, irregular-shaped foods and covering to-be-frozen casseroles. (*Tip:* Pad sharp bones with "wads" of foil—keeps them from piercing outer wrapper.)

—*Plastic Food Wraps:* Unusually soft and pliable; best for wrapping irregular shapes and soft foods.

—*Plastic Bags, Pouches:* Good for all but sharp or extra-large foods. *Tip:* To fill quickly, spoon food into a wide-mouth jar, invert bag over top, then turn upside down.

—*Laminated Papers:* Double-ply papers (cellophane, plastic, or foil bonded to heavy paper). Best for wrapping large, heavy roasts, poultry, or fish. These are reusable but must be sterilized by soaking 15 minutes in 1 quart warm water mixed with 1 teaspoon liquid chlorine bleach.

—*Outer Wraps:* Cloth stockinettes (available in most housewares departments) and butcher paper can both be used. They're needed to reinforce extra-large or heavy packages against freezer wear and tear.

—*Freezer Tapes:* A special, pliable tape that holds fast in subzero temperatures.

—*Pasteboard and Plastic Containers:* Sturdy and available in assorted sizes (the 1-pint size holds 3–4 vegetable or soup servings, 2–3 meat servings). Ideal for juicy or fragile foods. Reusable but, like laminated papers, these must be sterilized (use the same method).

—*Freezer Jars:* Wide-mouth glass jars available in half-pint, pint, and 3-cup sizes. Best for liquids, juicy or highly seasoned foods. Sterilize jars and closures before using (follow directions for sterilizing jars in canning section).

About Additives and Antibrowning Agents Used in Freezing

Sugar: Most fruits are packed in sugar or sugar syrup; use granulated sugar, not brown, which will darken fruits.

Salt: Vegetables to be frozen are sometimes washed or rinsed in salt water; use the uniodized to prevent discoloration.

Water: If hard or brackish, the water used for blanching foods may cause darkening. Soften water, if necessary, following method described in chapter on pickles, preserves, jams, and jellies.

Antibrowning Agents: Unless specially treated, apples, avocados, peaches, apricots, most varieties of pears and plums will darken during freezing. The most common preventives are:

Ascorbic Acid (Vitamin C): Available in tablet, powder, and crystalline form, also commercial solutions (usually sweetened mixtures of ascorbic and citric acid; use as labels instruct).

Citric Acid: The acid of citrus fruits and a less effective antibrowning agent than ascorbic acid; follow label directions.

Lemon Juice: Recommended only when ascorbic or citric acid is unavailable. To use, mix ¼ cup lemon juice with 1 gallon cold water and dip cut fruits; drain before packing.

Sodium Sulfite or Bisulfite: For apples only. Buy pharmaceutical grades at drugstores and use as labels direct.

Steps to Successful Freezing

Initial Preparations:
- Before starting out, assemble all ingredients and equipment.
- Make sure you have plenty of suitable packaging materials and freezer containers (sterilize if necessary).
- Check freezer space and freeze only what food it can accommodate. Most manufacturers recommend adding no more than 2-3 pounds food per cubic foot freezer space.
- Have ready whatever freezing syrups and antibrowning agents you will need.
- Reread freezer and freezer container manufacturer's instruction booklets and freezing procedures before beginning.

Food Selection and Handling:
- Choose top quality fruits, vegetables, meats, poultry, and seafood.

- *Avoid foods that freeze poorly:*
Avocados (except puréed)
Bananas
Cabbage, Sauerkraut
Celery
Cheese (except hard types)
Cream (except whipped)
Cucumbers
Custard or Cream Pies (or cream-filled pastries, cakes, cookies)
Eggs (in the shell, hard-cooked whites)
Egg or Cream-Thickened Sauces, Mayonnaise, Salad Dressings
Gelatins
Lettuce or Other Salad Greens
Long-Grain Rice
Irish Potatoes (except fried)
Tomatoes (except puréed and cooked)
- Wrap and quick-freeze all foods as soon as possible after obtaining. If necessary to postpone freezing, keep refrigerated.
- Handle foods to be frozen as little as possible.
- Freeze in practical meal-size portions.
- Follow freezing directions carefully; don't take short cuts.

Packing and Wrapping:
- Pack liquid or fragile foods in sturdy, leakproof containers.
- Use drugstore or butcher wrap for wrapping meats, poultry, seafood, other large, firm pieces.
- Double-wrap large, bulky, or angular pieces as an extra precaution against freezer wear and tear.
- Always wrap snugly, pressing out all air pockets. Sloppy wrapping invites "freezer burn" (streaked, faded, shriveled spots) and spoilage.
- Use freezer tape only for sealing packages; cellophane tape will come unstuck.
- Wipe container rims before sealing; a wide-mouth funnel reduces spillage.
- Wipe spills from packages before freezing.
- Leave ½"-¾" head space in freezer jars, containers or bags (unless otherwise directed) to allow for expansion of food during freezing.
- Label packages clearly with wax pencil, noting kind of food, weight or number of servings, date, and any cooking or serving tips.

Freezing and Storing:
- If freezer has a temperature control, turn to coldest setting 24 hours before adding food. The quicker food is frozen, the smaller the ice crystals and the better the food's texture.
- Place packages directly on freezing

CANNING AND FREEZING

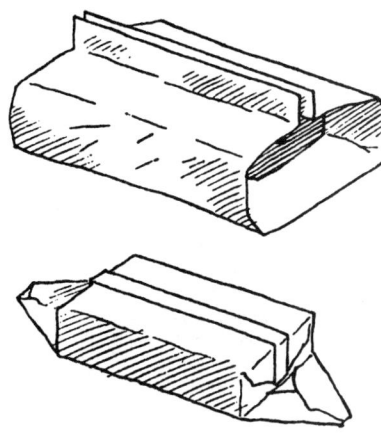

Drugstore Wrap

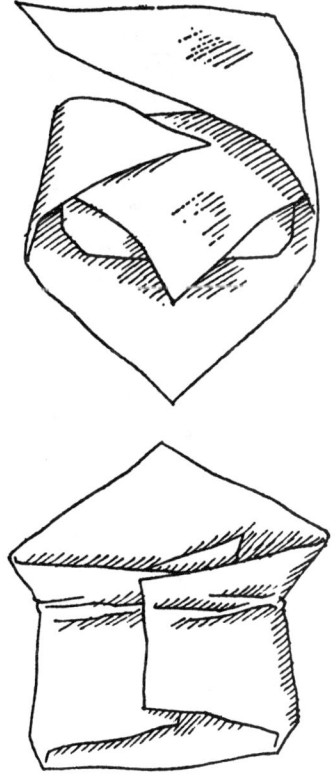

Butcher Wrap

surfaces, leaving 1" space around each.
— Allow 12 hours for food to freeze; if not solid in that length of time, check freezer temperature. If above 0° F., transfer unfrozen food to refrigerator and use as soon as possible.
— If you overestimate freezer capacity, refrigerate overflow packages and use within 24 hours.
— For most efficient freezer use, keep fully loaded.
— Stack frozen foods compactly in freezer and check occasionally for torn wrappers. Overwrap ripped packages or use within 1–2 weeks.
— Rotate food in freezer so that older packages are used first. Also group food by type so it will be easier to find.
— Maintain freezer temperature at 0° F. and open freezer only when necessary.
— Keep freezer inventory up to date.

— *If power should fail:* Leave freezer closed. In a fully loaded freezer, food will stay frozen up to 2 days, even in hot weather; in a half-full freezer, about 24 hours. If power will be off longer than 2 days, transfer food to a locker plant or pack in dry ice; 25 pounds dry ice will hold a fully loaded 10-cubic-foot freezer 3–4 days, a half-full freezer 2–3 days. (*Note:* Ventilate room while using dry ice.)

Thawing and Using Frozen Foods:
— Defrost foods before cooking or using only if necessary. Fruits are best thawed only enough to separate; so are minced onions or peppers and sliced mushrooms. Most vegetables should be cooked from the solidly frozen state in a minimum of water (corn on the cob is the exception; unwrap and thaw 20 minutes, then boil 5–8 minutes in plenty of un-

FREEZING GUIDE FOR FRUITS

Fruit	Amt. Needed To Fill 1 Pint	Preparation	Method, Recommended Packs
Apples (use crisp varieties)	1½ lbs.	Peel, core, slice medium thick, letting drop in 1 gal. cold water mixed with 2 T. salt; drain, rinse. If to be packed in sugar or unsweetened, soak 5 minutes in 1 gal. cold water mixed with 1 t. sodium sulfite (obtainable in drugstores). Drain.	*Syrup Pack:* Follow basic method, using Medium Syrup *with* ascorbic acid. *Sugar Pack:* Pack by basic method, using 1/2 t. ascorbic acid and 1/2 cup sugar per quart prepared fruit. *Unsweetened:* Mix 1/2 t. ascorbic acid with each quart prepared fruit; fill containers, leaving required head space.
Applesauce	1 pint	Prepare any recipe, adding 1/2 t. ascorbic acid per cup sugar used. Chill well.	Fill containers, leaving recommended head space.
Avocados	3 medium size	Peel, pit, and mash or purée.	*Sugar Pack:* Follow basic method, mixing 1/2 t. ascorbic acid and 1 cup sugar into each quart purée. Use for desserts. *Unsweetened:* Mix 1/4 t. ascorbic acid or 2 t. lemon juice with each quart purée. Pack in containers, leaving required head space, or in avocado shells (wrap in foil).
Berries (except strawberries),	1-1⅓ pints	Sort, wash, drain; stem or hull; leave berries and currants whole; pit cherries but leave whole.	*Syrup Pack:* Pack as directed, using Medium or Heavy Syrup. *Sugar Pack:* Follow basic method, using 3/4 cup sugar per quart prepared fruit. *Unsweetened:* Pack dry, covering if you like, with berry juice, OR freeze spread on trays and package. (*Note:* Not recommended for cherries.)
Cherries, Currants	1-1½ lbs.		

FREEZING GUIDE FOR FRUITS (continued)

Fruit	Amt. Needed To Fill 1 Pint	Preparation	Method, Recommended Packs
Fruit purées	—	Purée fruit as directed in Canning Guide for Fruits. When sweetening, use 2/3-1½ cups sugar per quart purée, depending on tartness of fruit.	*Sugar Pack:* If fruit is type that darkens, mix 1/2 t. ascorbic acid with each quart sweetened purée. Pack as directed. *Unsweetened:* Do not sweeten purée but add ascorbic acid as for Sugar Pack. Fill containers, leaving recommended head space.
Oranges, Grapefruit	2-4 medium size	Peel, section or slice, and seed.	*Syrup Pack:* Follow basic method, using Medium Syrup with ascorbic acid. *Unsweetened:* Pack in containers, leaving required head space. Add no liquid.
Grapes	1¼ lbs.	Sort, stem, wash. If seedless, leave whole; if not, halve, seed.	*Syrup Pack:* Pack as directed, using Medium Syrup.
Melons	1½ lbs.	Halve, seed, slice, cube, or cut into balls.	*Syrup Pack:* Follow basic method, using Medium Syrup.
Peaches, Apricots, Nectarines	1-1½ lbs.	Peel, halve, and pit. Leave as halves or slice.	*Syrup Pack:* Follow basic method, using Medium Syrup *with* ascorbic acid. *Sugar Pack:* Mix 1/2-2/3 cup sugar and 1/2 t. ascorbic acid with each quart prepared fruit. Pack as directed. *Unsweetened:* Mix 1/2 t. ascorbic acid in 1 quart cold water. Pack fruit in containers, leaving required head space, cover with water mixture.
Pears	1½ lbs.	Peel, halve, and core. Leave as halves, quarter, or slice.	*Syrup Pack:* Follow basic method, using Medium Syrup *with* ascorbic acid.

FREEZING GUIDE FOR FRUITS (continued)

Fruit	Amt. Needed To Fill 1 Pint	Preparation	Method, Recommended Packs
Persimmons (wild or cultivated)	—	Prepare like Fruit Purées, sweetening each quart purée with 1 cup sugar.	*Sugar Pack:* Mix 1/8 t. ascorbic acid with each quart sweetened purée. Pack as directed. *Unsweetened:* Do not sweeten purée. Add ascorbic acid as for Sugar Pack, fill containers, leaving recommended head space.
Pineapple	1 small	Peel, core, and remove eyes. Slice, dice, cube, or cut in wedges or sticks.	*Syrup Pack:* Pack as directed, using Medium Syrup. *Unsweetened:* Fill containers, leaving required head space; add water to cover if you like.
Plums	1 lb.	Sort and wash; do not peel. Leave whole or halve and pit.	*Syrup Pack:* Pack as directed, using Medium or Heavy Syrup *with* ascorbic acid. *Unsweetened:* Sprinkle each quart prepared fruit with 1/4 t. ascorbic acid mixed with 2 T. water. Pack in containers, leaving recommended head space.
Rhubarb	1 lb.	Wash and trim stalks; cut in 1"-2" lengths.	*Syrup Pack:* Pack as directed in Heavy Syrup. *Sugar Pack:* Mix 1 cup sugar with each quart prepared fruit. Pack as directed. *Unsweetened:* Fill containers, leaving head space; add no liquid, *OR* freeze spread on trays, then pack.
Strawberries	1½ pints	Wash, sort, and hull. Leave berries whole unless large, then halve or quarter.	*Syrup Pack:* Pack as directed in Medium or Heavy Syrup. *Sugar Pack:* Mix 3/4 cup sugar with each 1 quart prepared fruit; pack as directed. *Unsweetened:* Fill containers, leaving required head space, covering, if you like, with juice from some of the berries. Or spread on trays, freeze, then package.

FREEZING GUIDE FOR VEGETABLES

- Use mature, top quality produce; avoid vegetables that do not freeze well (charts include "good freezers" only).
- Wash in cool water (unless chart notes otherwise) and trim (for detailed preparation steps, see vegetable chapter).
- Blanch as charts recommend, about 1 quart vegetables at a time, in plenty of boiling water, using a fine mesh basket. *Tip:* For small vegetables or those cut fine, line basket with cheesecloth. (*Note:* At altitudes of more than 5,000 feet, add an extra minute to total blanching time.)
- Quick-chill blanched vegetables under cold running water or in ice water. Drain well; do not allow to soak. Pat small vegetables dry on paper toweling.
- Pack in containers (sturdy ones for fragile vegetables), leaving 1/2" head space for pints, 3/4" for larger containers *unless* chart directs otherwise.
- Seal, label, and quick-freeze.

Vegetable	Amount Needed to Fill 1 Pint	Preparation for Freezing	Recommended Blanching Time in Minutes
Asparagus	1-1½ lbs.	Use tender, tightly budded stalks; wash in tepid water, snap off woody ends, remove scales. Sort by size, cut in jar or 2" lengths, blanch, chill, pack snugly, alternating stems and tips for compactness. Leave no head space.	Slim stalks: 2 Medium stalks: 3 Thick stalks: 4
Beans (green and wax)	1 lb.	Use tender young beans; wash, drain, string if needed, trim off ends. Cut in 2" lengths, French or leave whole. Blanch, chill, and pack.	3
Beans (lima)	2-2½ lbs. (unshelled)	Wash, drain, shell, sort by size. Blanch, chill, and pack.	Small beans: 2 Medium beans: 3 Large beans: 4
Beets	1-1½ lbs.	Sort by size, cut off tops, but leave 1" stems on, also roots. Scrub, boil 35-45 minutes until tender; peel, trim, leave whole, slice, or dice. Chill, pack.	None
Broccoli	1 lb.	Remove coarse stems, leaves; peel stalks, wash, separate into stalks of equal size, halving if need be. Make X-cuts in stem ends. Blanch, chill, and pack. Leave no head space.	3
Brussels sprouts	1 lb.	Remove stem ends, coarse outer leaves, make X-cuts in stem ends. Wash in cold salted water, sort by size. Blanch, chill, and pack. Leave no head space.	Small sprouts: 3 Medium sprouts: 4 Large sprouts: 5

FREEZING GUIDE FOR VEGETABLES (continued)

Vegetable	Amount Needed to Fill 1 Pint	Preparation for Freezing	Recommended Blanching Time in Minutes
Carrots	1¼ lbs.	Wash, peel, and trim; wash again. Leave whole if small, otherwise slice, dice, or cut in julienne strips. Blanch, chill, and pack.	Whole carrots: 5 Cut carrots: 2
Cauliflower	1 small	Divide in flowerets, trim, wash, blanch, chill, pack. Leave no head space.	3
Corn on the cob		For All Styles: Choose tender young ears; husk and remove silks. Blanch, chill, wrap ears individually in double thickness foil.	Small ears: 3 Medium ears: 5 Large ears: 7
Whole kernel	2-2½ lbs.	Blanch and quick-chill ears, then, following directions in vegetable chapter, cut corn from cobs as for whole kernel corn.* Pack.	All ears: 4
Cream-style		Blanch and quick-chill ears, then cut from cobs as for cream-style corn* in vegetable chapter. Pack.	All ears: 4
Eggplant	1 small	*Do not freeze raw.* Prepare Fried Eggplant recipe, undercooking slightly. Drain on paper toweling; spread 1 layer deep on foil-lined trays and freeze hard. Layer in container, return to freezer. *To serve:* Heat (thawed or unthawed) uncovered in a 350°F. oven 5-10 minutes until of good serving temperature.	None
Greens (beet, chard, collards, kale, mustard, spinach, turnip greens)	1-1½ lbs.	Use young, tender greens; wash, trim off coarse stems, wash again. Blanch, chill, and pack.	Collards: 3 Other greens: 1½-2
Kohlrabi	1¼ lbs.	Trim off leaves, stems; wash, peel, cut in 1/2" cubes. Blanch, chill, pack.	1
Mushrooms	1 lb.	Cut off woody stems; wipe clean, sort by size. Leave whole if small (1" or less across); slice if large. Blanch, adding 1/4 cup lemon juice per gallon water. Chill and pack.	Sliced or button mushrooms: 2 Whole: 3

Vegetable	Amount	Preparation	Blanching time (minutes)
Okra	1 lb.	Choose tenderest young pods. Remove stems but not caps. Wash well, leave whole or slice 1" thick. Blanch, chill, pack.	Whole pods: 4 Sliced pods: 3
Onions	1 lb.	*Do not freeze whole.* Peel, mince, blanch, chill and pack.	1
Parsnips	1¼ lbs.	Trim, scrub, peel and cut in 1/2" cubes. Blanch, chill and pack.	2
Peas (green, black-eyed)	2-2½ lbs. (unshelled)	Shell, sort by size, blanch, chill and pack.	Baby peas: 1 Medium size: 2
Peppers (sweet green and red)	3-4 medium size	Wash, core and seed. Leave whole, halve crosswise, slice in rings or mince. Blanch, chill and pack.	Whole, halved: 3 Sliced: 2 Minced: 1
Potatoes (Irish)	3 medium	*Do not freeze raw.* Prepare Twice-Fried French Fries recipe *but fry and drain once.* Spread 1-layer deep on foil-lined trays and freeze hard. Pack in containers, return to freezer. *To serve:* Fry second time (solidly frozen) as recipe directs, allowing 1-2 minutes longer.	None
Potatoes (sweet)	3 medium	*Do not freeze raw.* Prepare Mashed Sweet Potatoes recipe, cook, pack, and freeze. Or prepare Orange-Candied Sweet Potatoes, omitting sectioned orange; cool, pack, and freeze. *To use:* Thaw and Thaw slightly and reheat slowly.	None
Pumpkin	3-4 lbs.	Prepare Pumpkin Purée recipe; cool, pack, and freeze. Thaw before using.	None
Rutabaga, turnips	1½ lbs.	Trim, peel, wash, cut in 1/2" cubes. Blanch, chill, and pack.	2
Summer squash	1 lb.	Trim, scrub; do not peel if tender; slice 1/2" thick, blanch, chill, and pack.	2
Tomatoes	2 lbs.	*Do not freeze raw.* Wash, peel, core, coarsely chop. Simmer, covered, 15-20 minutes; purée. Simmer, uncovered, until cooked down to 1 pint. Cool, pack, and freeze. *To use:* Thaw and use as you would tomato purée, seasoning to taste.	None
Winter squash	3-4 lbs.	*Do not freeze raw.* Halve, seed, cube, and peel. Steam or boil until tender, 20-25 minutes; drain and mash or purée. Cool, pack, and freeze. *To serve:* Thaw slightly and reheat slowly.	None

salted water). Directions for cooking frozen meat, poultry, and seafood are included in each of those chapters.
– Unless directed to the contrary, thaw frozen foods in their wrappers. Set in a pan to catch drips (savory juices can be used in gravies, sauces, and stews).
– Thaw at room temperature or in the refrigerator (refrigerator thawing takes twice as long. A 1-pint package will thaw in 2–3 hours at room temperature, in 4–6 in the refrigerator).
– Never thaw frozen food in warm water unless directions recommend it.
– Check thawing packages frequently, also turn often, and use while still well chilled. Never allow to come to room temperature.

About Refreezing Thawed Food:
– Never refreeze any food that has reached 40° F. internal temperature (check with a freezer thermometer). That registering less than 40° F. or still showing ice crystals may be safely refrozen, though flavor, color, and texture will suffer.
– Inspect partially thawed food carefully and do not refreeze any that has an off color or aroma. Be particularly careful about seafood and poultry; they spoil more quickly than red meats.
– Never risk eating any food you suspect may be spoiled; and don't feed to pets (they get food poisoning too).

FREEZING GUIDE FOR FRUITS

– Freeze fruit varieties that freeze well; county home agents can recommend best local "freezers."
– Freeze fruits in sturdy, leakproof containers. (*Tip:* 1 quart size fills a 9″ pie.)
– Use one of the following methods of packing and treat apples, apricots, pears, peaches, plums, and other fruits that darken on exposure to air with ascorbic acid or other antibrowning agent (read About Additives and Antibrowning Agents Used in Freezing).
– Pack, seal, and freeze as fast as possible. Note type of pack on label as well as date, kind of fruit, number of servings, etc.

Basic Packing Methods

Syrup Pack: Prepare Sugar Syrup for Canning and Freezing (recipe in canning section) in strengths the preceding charts specify, adding ascorbic acid if fruit is type that darkens; chill syrup. *To Pack:* Pour ⅓ cup syrup in container, half fill with fruit, shaking down to pack snugly without crushing, add fruit to fill, cover with syrup, leaving required head space. If fruit floats, push under syrup with a wad of plastic food wrap or foil and put lid on container.

Sugar Pack: Measure fruit, spread on trays (not tin), sprinkle with amount of sugar charts recommend (granulated, not brown), mix gently, and let stand until juices appear and sugar dissolves. If fruit is type to darken, mix ½ teaspoon ascorbic acid with each 1 cup sugar *before* adding to fruit. Fill containers, shaking fruit down and leaving necessary head space.

Unsweetened Pack: Do not use artificial sweeteners. If fruit is darkening type, sprinkle each quart fruit with ¼ teaspoon ascorbic acid dissolved in 2 tablespoons cold water, *or* if fruit will be packed in water or juice, add ½ teaspoon ascorbic acid to each quart liquid. Pack fruit dry in containers *or* pack dry, then cover with cold water or juice made by crushing some of the fruit, in each case leaving required head space. *Or* spread fruit one layer deep on foil-lined trays and freeze solid, then fill containers to tops.

Head Space Recommended for All Packs: ½" for pints, ¾"–1" for larger containers. (*Note:* Exception is fruit that is frozen spread out, then packed; in such instances, fill containers to the brim.)

Notes:
– Ascorbic acid called for is powder or crystalline form; if using commercial solutions, add as labels instruct.
– In preceding charts, T=tablespoon, t=teaspoon.

ABOUT FREEZING MEAT, GAME, POULTRY, AND GAME BIRDS

Nearly all uncooked, uncured meat, variety meats, poultry, and game birds freeze well. Use top qualities only (meat and poultry should be federally inspected, game and poultry fully dressed). No meat or poultry will improve during freezing, though ice crystals and enzymes both work to tenderize them (a not-so-tender steak, for example, will be tender enough to broil after 1–2 months in the freezer).

General Tips for Freezing Meat, Game, Poultry, and Game Birds:
  Wrap and quick-freeze as soon after obtaining as possible.
– Trim off excess fat (pull loose fat from poultry body cavities) and, whenever possible, remove bones to conserve freezer space.
– Shape hamburgers, sausage patties, meat balls and loaves before freezing.
– Package in meal-size portions or amounts suitable for family use. Separate chops, steaks, meat patties, pieces of chicken with 2 layers of freezer paper so they can be easily separated while solidly frozen.
– Wrap snugly, fitting wrapping to contours of food and pressing out as much air as possible. Pad sharp bones with wads of wrapping so they will not pierce wrapper. Double-wrap delicate or fragile meats (skinned game birds, variety meats, etc.).
– Freeze liver, heart, kidneys, tongue, pork and beef sausages uncooked; blanch sweetbreads and brains (see sections on sweetbreads and brains); fully cook tripe.
– Label packages carefully, indicating date, cut, and kind of meat or poultry, weight, and pertinent remarks (whether chicken is a stewing fowl or broiler-fryer).

Special Tips for Freezing Poultry and Game Birds:
– Remove any pinfeathers and hairs, also traces of lung or windpipe in body cavity.
– Wash giblets, pack and freeze separately.
– Never stuff poultry prior to freezing.

About Thawing and Cooking Frozen Meat, Game, Poultry, and Game Birds: Roasts, steaks, chops, hamburgers, meat loaves do not need to be thawed before cooking. Most poultry and variety meats do. See chapters on meat, poultry, game and game birds for specific instructions.

GUIDE TO FREEZING PARTIALLY PREPARED OR FULLY COOKED FOODS

Food	Preparation for Freezing	Serving Tips
Meat, Poultry, Seafood		
Stews, casseroles	Cook until barely tender; underseason; omit potatoes, pasta, or other starchy ingredient. Cool, pack in containers or oven-to-table casseroles, and freeze.	Thaw slightly, reheat slowly as recipe directs. Add potatoes or pasta in time to cook fully.
Pies	Bake fully and freeze or cook filling only, fill pan, add top crust, and freeze without baking. (*Note:* Use an aluminum or other nonrusting piepan.)	*Large Pies:* Thaw, then reheat or bake. *Small Pies:* Bake or reheat without thawing.
Meat loaves, meat balls	Cook fully and freeze or freeze raw.	*Uncooked Loaves:* Bake without thawing, increasing time 1½ times. *Cooked Loaves:* Thaw and reheat. *Uncooked Meat Balls:* Thaw before cooking. *Cooked Meat Balls:* Reheat without thawing.
Leftovers	Freeze leftover roasts in as large pieces as possible or sliced and covered with gravy; remove all bone, fat, skin, etc. Also, remove stuffing from body cavities of poultry, bones, and shells from seafood and scrape off any sauce or gravy.	Thaw and serve cold or use in recipes calling for cooked meat, poultry, or seafood.
Breads	Bake, cool, wrap, and freeze. (*Note:* Rolls can be baked until just beginning to brown, then cooled and frozen; they will finish baking during reheating.)	Thaw in wrapper or loosened wrapper, then heat to serving temperature. (*Note:* Toast sliced bread unthawed.)

Sandwiches	Butter both slices of bread; use meat spreads, savory butters as fillings, not mayonnaise mixtures, which freeze poorly. To prevent ice crystal formation, avoid contact with freezer shelves.	Thaw in wrappers.
Pies and pastries	*Pie Shells:* Freeze baked or unbaked. *Pies:* Do not freeze custard or cream pies. Double-crust fruit pies can be frozen raw or baked (increase cornstarch or other thickener in filling by 1 tablespoon.) If to be frozen raw, do not cut steam vents in top crust. Use aluminum or other nonrusting piepans.	*Pie Shells:* If raw, bake unthawed 5 minutes at 450°F., prick and bake 15 minutes longer. If baked, thaw and fill. *Pies:* If raw, cut steam vents in top crust, bake without thawing 3/4-1 hour at 425°F. If baked, heat without thawing 3/4 hour at 350°F.
Cakes	Use pure flavorings — synthetics may turn bitter. Bake cake but do not fill or frost; wrap and freeze. *(Note:* If necessary to freeze a frosted cake, freeze and then wrap.)	Thaw unfrosted, unfilled cakes in wrappers, then fill and frost. If frosted, loosen wrapper and thaw in refrigerator.
Cookies	Freeze baked or unbaked.	Refrigerator-type cookie dough can be sliced and baked while frozen; others should be thawed.
Gravies, sauces	Do not freeze egg- or cream-thickened sauces; increase starch slightly in starch-thickened sauces; when cooling, beat briskly to lessen chance of separation in freezing.	Reheat slowly without thawing, in top of a double boiler if thick, stirring or beating often.
Stocks, broths	Boil uncovered to reduce volume and save freezer space.	Reheat without thawing, diluting as needed with water.

ABOUT FREEZING SEAFOOD

Not all seafood freezes well; watery fish turns mushy and flavorless; oily or gamy fish becomes overly strong. Because of "flash freezing," commercial packers can freeze fish far more successfully than can the person with a home freezer. Still, freezing is a better way of preserving a fisherman's catch than canning.

Fish: Prepare fish for freezing exactly as for cooking; clean and scale, leave whole, fillet, or cut in steaks. Drugstore-wrap airtight in foil or other pliable freezer wrapping, separating steaks or fillets with 2 layers of wrapping material so they can be pulled apart while solidly frozen. Label, then store in freezer in plastic bags to seal in fishy odors.

Shrimp: Pack shelled or unshelled, raw or boiled; if boiled, quick-chill before freezing.

Hard-shell Crabs, Lobsters: Boil or steam, remove meat from shell, cool, and pack. (*Note:* If shells are needed, scrub, wrap, and freeze separately.)

Soft-shell Crabs: Prepare as for cooking, wrap individually, and freeze.

Oysters, Clams: Shuck, saving liquor. Pack in containers, cover with liquor (if insufficient, make up with brine made by mixing 1 tablespoon salt to 1 cup water).

Scallops: Wash, drain, pack in containers, and cover with brine (1 tablespoon salt to 1 cup water).

About Thawing and Cooking Frozen Seafood: Detailed instructions are included in the sections on fish, and shellfish.

About Freezing Herbs

Pick fresh herbs just before they bloom, preferably on a dry day, choosing tenderest young shoots. Wash only if dirty, rinse in cool water, and gently shake off excess moisture. Freeze by one of the following methods. (*Note:* Frozen herbs have approximately the same flavor power as fresh herbs, about ½–⅓ as much as dried herbs.)

Blanching Method: Tie herb stalks in groups of 2 or 3, blanch one minute in boiling water, then quick-chill in ice water. Remove leaves from stalks and wrap in plastic food wrap—about 5 large or 1 tablespoon small leaves to a package. Wrap each plastic packet in foil to seal in fragrance, label, and quick-freeze. Once frozen, bundle packets into a plastic bag so they won't get lost in freezer. *To Use:* Mince solidly frozen leaves and add to recipe.

Ice Cube Method: Mince herb, spoon 1 tablespoon into each compartment of an ice cube tray, add water to fill and freeze. Once frozen, empty all herb cubes of a flavor into a plastic bag (all tarragon, for example, or all dill or chives) and label bag. Bundle, if you like, in a larger plastic bag and store in freezer.

To Use: Add herb cube to soup, sauce, or stew or, if a "dry" herb is needed for a salad or other dish, thaw cube in a small strainer set over a small bowl. Add thawed herb to recipe (and liquid to soups, sauces, or stews—it will have some herb aroma).

CANNING AND FREEZING

ABOUT FREEZING DAIRY PRODUCTS

Do not try to freeze milk, and cream only if whipped (see To Freeze Decorative Whipped Cream in the dessert chapter). Butter, margarine, and lard can be frozen in their original cartons and kept about a month; to store longer, remove from cartons and wrap tightly in foil or other freezer wrap. As for cheese, only hard varieties, like Parmesan, freeze with any success; wrap snugly in foil or plastic food wrap.

ABOUT FREEZING EGGS

Note: Freeze only absolutely fresh eggs.

To Freeze Whole Eggs: Break eggs into a bowl, stir just to mix, trying not to make any bubbles. Measure eggs and for each 1 cup, mix in 1 tablespoon sugar or light corn syrup (such eggs can be used in desserts) or 1 teaspoon salt (use for savory recipes). Pack in 1-cup leakproof cartons, label, and quick-freeze. Be sure to note on label how many eggs there are in the carton and whether they have had sugar or salt added. Thaw before using.

To Freeze Yolks: Stir yolks just enough to break, measure, and for each 1 cup yolks add 1 tablespoon sugar or light corn syrup or 1 teaspoon salt. Proceed as for whole eggs.

To Freeze Whites: Do not stir whites or add sugar or salt. Break directly into ice cube trays, allowing one white per compartment. Freeze solid, then empty into plastic bags and store in freezer. Thaw before using.

ABOUT FREEZING PARTIALLY PREPARED OR FULLY COOKED FOODS

A number of recipes in this book indicate at which point preparations may be interrupted and the dish frozen. Many more can be doubled, tripled, or quadrupled and frozen for future use.

Some General Tips

– Slightly undercook foods to be frozen, particularly pasta dishes like lasagne and ravioli.
– Whenever possible, omit potatoes, pasta, rice, or other starchy foods from stews and juicy casseroles; they turn mushy and occupy unnecessary freezer space. Add to recipe when reheating.
– Underseason recipes slightly; some seasonings fade in the freezer, others gain strength. Adjust seasonings when reheating.
– Quick-chill any hot food before packing and freezing.
– Whenever practical, freeze casseroles or stews in freezer-to-oven-to-table dishes. Or freeze in foil-lined pans or casseroles and, when brick hard, lift out and wrap airtight. To reheat, unwrap and refit in pan.

– Freeze small amounts of stock, broth, and vegetable cooking water in ice cube trays; when solid, bundle cubes in plastic bags. Use in soups, sauces, stews.

– Apportion meat and vegetable leftovers in TV dinner trays, cover, label, and freeze.

– Whenever possible, reheat frozen cooked foods without thawing.

APPENDIX

EAT WELL, KEEP WELL

Astonishing as it may seem in this age of abundance, a great many Americans (about 20 per cent, according to a recent Department of Agriculture survey) are malnourished. Not for lack of money. But for lack of understanding about how foods function in the body. We tend to eat what we like, often without restraint, and in America preferences run to carbohydrates (starches and sweets).

What we eat affects how we look, feel, and to some extent behave. The killing and crippling diseases of yesterday—scurvy, pellagra, beriberi, rickets—were all eventually traced to specific nutritional deficiencies, a vitamin C deficiency for scurvy, niacin for pellagra, thiamine for beriberi, and vitamin D for rickets. Such desperate vitamin inadequacies, fortunately, are rarely seen in America today, but poor nutrition manifests itself in bad complexions and other skin problems, in obesity, in irritability and listlessness.

Nutritionists maintain that, with rare exceptions, a person who eats moderately and wisely, selecting a variety of foods each day from The 4 Basic Food Groups, will be properly nourished.

The 4 Basic Food Groups

GROUP I—THE MILK GROUP: Milk (all kinds), cream, cheese needed to supply calcium, high-quality protein, vitamin A, and riboflavin (a B vitamin). The *Recommended Daily Amount* varies according to age and sex:

	8-ounce glasses needed per day
Children under 9	2–3
Children 9–12	3 or more
Teen-agers	4 or more
Adults	2 or more
Pregnant Women	3 or more
Nursing Mothers	4 or more

Note: Some "milk" may be taken as cheese or ice cream:

½ cup ice cream=¼ cup milk
½ cup cottage cheese=⅓ cup milk
1 (1″) cube Cheddar cheese=½ cup milk

GROUP II—THE MEAT GROUP: All meats and organ meats, poultry and eggs, fish and shellfish, and, as occasional meat substitutes, dry beans and peas, lentils, nuts, and peanut butter. This group supplies the body with top quality protein, iron, and three important B vitamins —thiamine, riboflavin, and niacin. *Recommended Daily Amounts:* 2 or more servings from the group. Any of the following count as 1 serving: 3 ounces cooked lean meat, poultry or seafood; 2 eggs; 1 cup cooked dried beans, peas or lentils; ¼ cup peanut butter.

GROUP III—THE FRUIT AND VEGETABLE GROUP: The source of vitamin-A-rich foods (dark green and yellow vegetables such as broccoli and winter squash and such fruits as apricots, cantaloupe, mangoes, persimmons, and pumpkin); also the source of vitamin-C-rich foods (citrus fruits, cantaloupe, strawberries, sweet green and red peppers). *Recommended Amounts:* 1 serving daily of a vitamin-C-rich food, 1 serving every other day of a vitamin A food, and 2–3 additional servings daily of any other foods in the group.

GROUP IV—THE BREAD-CEREAL GROUP: All whole grains, enriched or restored breads and cereals (see chapter on cereals, rice, and pasta), necessary for B vitamins, protein, iron, and energy. *Recommended Daily Amounts:* 4 or more servings, 5 or more if breads only are eaten.

OTHER FOODS: Fats, oils, sweets, refined cereals are all important to the body as energy foods. But they are so rarely lacking in the diet it's not necessary to remind people to eat them.

About Individual Nutrients

What are proteins exactly? Carbohydrates? Vitamins? Minerals? What do they do in the body? Why are they important?

Protein: The substance of life, the body's building material. It is essential to the maintenance and repair of all bodily tissues, to the production of enzymes, hormones, and infection-fighting antibodies. Protein also provides energy to fuel the body. In truth, protein is not a single compound but many, composed of simpler compounds called *amino acids.* To date, 22 amino acids have been isolated, eight of them *essential,* meaning the body cannot manufacture them and that they must be taken in as food. The highest quality proteins are those providing the best supply of essential amino acids—animal foods, invariably, such as meat, seafood, poultry, milk, cheese, and eggs.

Carbohydrates: The energy foods—sugars and starches. The danger here is not eating too few but too many.

Fats and Oils: Complex chemical substances, controversial today because they have been implicated in circulatory and heart diseases. Their chief role in the body is to provide energy, and this they do, about twice as well as carbohydrates and proteins. But the specter of *cholesterol* looms and television commercials, hammering away at us to use this mono- or polyunsaturated fat, won't let us forget it. Cholesterol is not a fat but a related fatty substance used by the body to form vitamin D and certain hormones. Its presence in the body (particularly its accumulation in and clogging of blood vessels) is being investigated in relation to the saturation of a fat. Saturation refers, simply, to the hydrogen content of a fat and, in a far more practical sense, to the consistency. Generally speaking, the more hydrogen a fat contains, the more saturated it is and the harder or stiffer. Hydrogenated shortenings, to illustrate, are vegetable oils pumped full of hydrogen so that they become creamy and thick. The subject is far too complicated to discuss further here, not to mention unresolved. But for those who would explore it more thoroughly, we recommend an excellent free pamphlet, "Nutritional Facts About Fats," written for lay persons and available from Cornell University. Write for: Home Economics Extension Leaflet 32, New York State College of Human Ecology, Cornell University, Ithaca, New York.

Vitamins: These chemical compounds, found in minute quantities in foods, are essential to good health. The most important of them are:

Vitamin A: Helps eyes adjust to changing light intensities, helps prevent night blindness, necessary for healthy mucous membranes. *Good Sources:* Dark yellow or orange fruits, dark green and yellow vegetables, cream, butter, whole milk, fortified margarine, liver. (*Note:* Vitamin A can be stored by the body, so avoid overdoses of vitamin pills.)

The B Group: There are about a dozen B vitamins, the most important of which are *thiamine* (B_1), *riboflavin* (B_2), and *niacin*. If the body receives enough of these three, it is unlikely to be deficient in any others of the B group.

Thiamine helps keep muscles, heart, and nerves functioning properly, promotes appetite and aids carbohydrate metabolism. *Good Sources:* Meat (particularly pork), fish, poultry, enriched breads and cereals, milk, dried peas, and beans.

Riboflavin is essential for the utilization of oxygen within the body and enzyme function. *Good Sources:* The same as for thiamine.

Niacin, like riboflavin, is necessary for proper tissue use of oxygen, also for healthy skin, tongue, and digestive system. *Good Sources:* Lean meats, poultry, whole and enriched cereals, peanuts, dried peas, and beans.

Vitamin C (Ascorbic Acid) has literally to do with holding the body together—tissues, bones, teeth, blood vessels. It speeds healing of wounds, helps stave off infection. *Good Sources:* Citrus fruits, cantaloupe, strawberries, tomatoes, sweet green peppers, raw cabbage, collards and kale, broccoli, freshly dug Irish potatoes.

THE EFFECT OF COOKING ON VITAMINS

Vitamin	Destroyed by Heat	Leached Out in Cooking Water	Destroyed by Sunlight	Destroyed by Exposure to Air
A	not apt to be affected by cooking			
Thiamine	X	X		
Riboflavin		X	X	
Niacin		X		
C	X	X		X
D	not apt to be affected by cooking			
E	not apt to be affected by cooking			

Vitamin D: Essential to calcium metabolism and the formation of sound bones and teeth. *Good Sources:* Eggs, fish liver oils, sardines, salmon, tuna, sunshine (it converts a substance on the skin to vitamin D which can then be used by the body. *Caution:* Bathing or showering after a sunbath destroys the vitamin D). Like vitamin A, vitamin D can be stored by the body and indiscriminate use of vitamin pills may cause overdoses and illness.

Vitamin E: Despite faddists' cure-all claims for vitamin E, scientists have yet to substantiate any of them. Physicians have used vitamin E successfully to treat a certain anemia in children. Its primary role, however, seems to be as a biological antioxidant (preventing unwanted oxidation of certain fatty acids) in both the body and in foods. It is important that the diet contain adequate amounts of vitamin E, but because it is so widely found in foods we eat (vegetable oils, eggs, butter and margarine, legumes and nuts, green leafy vegetables, wheat germ), deficiencies are unlikely.

Minerals:

Calcium and Phosphorous: Necessary for strong bones and teeth, good muscle tone, sound nervous system. *Good Sources:* Milk and milk products, dark leafy greens such as kale, collards, mustard and turnip greens.

Iodine: Needed for normal thyroid function. *Good Sources:* Seafood, iodized salt.

Iron: Essential for rich, red blood. *Good Sources:* Organ meats (particularly liver), red meats, oysters, dark green leafy vegetables, eggs, dried fruits, whole or enriched cereals.

Note: There are a number of other minerals and vitamins but they have not been included here either because they are unlikely to be missing in the diet or because their function and requirement are still undetermined.

About Water

Though not a nutrient, water is nonetheless vital. The human body, about ⅔ water, must have water in order to survive—to regulate body temperature, to aid digestion, to carry off wastes. Most foods contain water, it's true, but they may not provide the body as much water as it needs. The old rule of "6–8 glasses of liquid a day" still holds.

About Calories

Calories do count, alas, and the only way to lose weight safely and successfully is to reduce the daily calorie intake—forever if necessary. There simply is no magic pill or potion to melt away unwanted pounds. Crash diets do produce immediate results— sometimes drastic ones—but in the long run they fail because the dieter not only regains all lost weight but usually an extra few pounds as well. This sort of seesaw dieting is dangerous. So, too, are starvation diets limiting calories to less than 1,000 a day. If you have more than 5 or 10 pounds to lose, see your doctor and have him advise the reducing diet that is best for you. Most doctors discourage losing more than 2–3 pounds a week, and most agree that the only sane way to diet is to eat foods from each of the Basic 4

Food Groups, merely less of each. (A week's balanced 1,200-Calorie-a-Day Menus are included in the chapter on menu planning).

What is a calorie? Technically, a unit of heat used to measure the fuel potential of food in the body. To maintain body weight, the calorie intake (via food) must equal the outgo (via energy expended in the day's activities). When the intake exceeds the outgo, the balance is converted to fat. When the reverse is true, as in reducing diets, the body's fat reserves are tapped to provide energy.

"Middle age spread" is simply a failure to adjust eating habits to a slower life-style. We continue to stuff ourselves as we did in our teens and yet are far less active. To compound the problem, our basal metabolism is slowing down. It will continue to decline throughout life, and the woman who would keep her figure (or the man his physique) will cut daily calorie intake by about 150–200 every 10 years after the age of 25. At 35, for example, all factors remaining equal (height, weight, activity), the body will need about 150 calories less per day than it did at 25, and at 45, about 150 less than it did at 35. And so it goes throughout life.

How many calories are enough? It varies, obviously, according to age, sex, size, activity, and a number of other factors, but you can make a rough estimate. Take your *desirable body weight* (see accompanying height-weight charts), then multiply this figure by:

16 calories if you are sedentary
20 calories if you are active
24 calories if you are a woman and very active
28 calories if you are a man and very active

This is the number of calories you need each day to maintain *desirable body weight*. Desirable body weight is considered to be mid-20's weight. In other words, what you weighed at the age of 25 (assuming you were neither over- nor underweight). Maintaining this weight throughout life is extremely difficult for most people because excess weight comes so slowly, perhaps only 1–2 pounds a year (1 pound body fat=3,500 stored calories). The temptation is to watch the scale creep upward, reaching new plateaus, until we realize one day with a start that we are 10 or 20 pounds too heavy. Then come the remorse and the resolutions to diet.

The **Recommended Daily Dietary Allowances** chart shows several nutrients essential for maintenance of good nutrition in healthy, normally active persons in this country. They can be attained with a variety of common foods which will also provide nutrients of less defined requirements.

More detailed information may be obtained for "Recommended Dietary Allowances," publication 1146 mentioned in the Source note in the chart, page 723.

RECOMMENDED DAILY DIETARY ALLOWANCES[1][2]
Designed for the maintenance of good nutrition of practically all healthy persons in the U.S.A.
(Allowances are intended for persons normally active in a temperate climate)

Persons	Age in years[5] From	Age in years[5] up to	Weight in pounds	Height in inches	Food Energy[3] Calories	Protein Grams	Calcium Grams	Iron Milligrams	Vitamin A International units	Thiamine Milligrams	Riboflavin Milligrams	Niacin Equivalent[4] Milligrams	Ascorbic Acid Milligrams	Vitamin D International units
Men	18	35	154	69	2,900	70	0.8	10	5,000	1.2	1.7	19	70	
	35	55	154	69	2,600	70	.8	10	5,000	1.0	1.6	17	70	
	55	75	154	69	2,200	70	.8	10	5,000	.9	1.3	15	70	
Women	18	35	128	64	2,100	58	.8	15	5,000	.8	1.3	14	70	
	35	55	128	64	1,900	58	.8	15	5,000	.8	1.2	13	70	
	55	75	128	64	1,600	58	.8	10	5,000	.8	1.2	13	70	
Pregnant (second and third trimester)					+200	+20	+.5	+5	+1,000	+.2	+.3	+3	+30	400
Lactating					+1,000	+40	+.5	+5	+3,000	+.4	+.6	+7	+30	400
Infants[6]	0	1	18	—	lb. × 52 ± 7	lb. × 1.1 ± 0.2	.7	lb. × 0.45	1,500	.4	.6	6	30	400
Children	1	3	29	34	1,300	32	.8	8	2,000	.5	.8	9	40	400
	3	6	40	42	1,600	40	.8	10	2,500	.6	1.0	11	50	400
	6	9	53	49	2,100	52	.8	12	3,500	.8	1.3	14	60	400
Boys	9	12	72	55	2,400	60	1.1	15	4,500	1.0	1.4	16	70	400
	12	15	98	61	3,000	75	1.4	15	5,000	1.2	1.8	20	80	400
	15	18	134	68	3,400	85	1.4	15	5,000	1.4	2.0	22	80	400
Girls	9	12	72	55	2,200	55	1.1	15	4,500	.9	1.3	15	80	400
	12	15	103	62	2,500	62	1.3	15	5,000	1.0	1.5	17	80	400
	15	18	117	64	2,300	58	1.3	15	5,000	.9	1.3	15	70	400

[1] Source: Adapted from Recommended Dietary Allowances, Publication 1146, 59 pp., revised 1964. Published by National Academy of Sciences — National Research Council, Washington, D.C., 20418. Price $1.00. Also available in libraries.

[2] The allowance levels are intended to cover individual variations among most normal persons as they live in the United States under usual environmental stresses.

[3] Tables 1 and 2 and figures 1 and 2 in Publication 1146 (see footnote 1) show calorie adjustments for weight and age.

[4] Niacin equivalents include dietary sources of the preformed vitamin and the precursor, tryptophan. 60 milligrams tryptophan represents 1 milligram niacin.

[5] Entries on lines for age range 18 to 35 years represent the 25-year age. All other entries represent allowances for the midpoint of the specified age periods, i.e., line for children 1 to 3 is for age 2 years (24 months); 3 to 6 is for age 4½ years (54 months), etc.

[6] The calorie and protein allowances per pound for infants are considered to decrease progressively from birth. Allowances for calcium, thiamine, riboflavin, and niacin increase proportionately with calories to the maximum values shown.

Note: The Recommended Daily Dietary Allowances should not be confused with Minimum Daily Requirements. The Recommended Dietary Allowances are amounts of nutrients recommended by the Food and Nutrition Board of National Research Council, and are considered adequate for maintenance of good nutrition in healthy persons in the United States. The allowances are revised from time to time in accordance with newer knowledge of nutritional needs.

The minimum Daily Requirements are the amounts of various nutrients that have been established by the Food and Drug Administration as standards for labeling purposes of foods and pharmaceutical preparations for special dietary uses. These are the amounts regarded as necessary in the diet for the prevention of deficiency diseases and generally are less than the Recommended Dietary Allowances. The Minimum Daily Requirements are set forth in the Federal Register, vol. 6, No. 227 (Nov. 22, 1941), beginning on p. 5921, and amended as stated in the Federal Register (June 1, 1957), vol. 22, No. 106, p. 3841.

DESIRABLE WEIGHTS FOR WOMEN, AGE 25 AND OVER*

Note: for girls between 18 and 25, subtract 1 pound for each year under 25.

Height (in shoes, 2″ heels)		Weight in Pounds (in indoor clothing)		
		Small Frame	Medium Frame	Large Frame
Feet	Inches			
4	10	92–98	96–107	104–119
4	11	94–101	98–110	106–122
5	0	96–104	101–113	109–125
5	1	99–107	104–116	112–128
5	2	102–110	107–119	115–131
5	3	105–113	110–122	118–134
5	4	108–116	113–126	121–138
5	5	111–119	116–130	125–142
5	6	114–123	120–135	129–146
5	7	118–127	124–139	133–150
5	8	122–131	128–143	137–154
5	9	126–135	132–147	141–158
5	10	130–140	136–151	145–163
5	11	134–144	140–155	149–168
6	0	138–148	144–159	153–173

* Prepared by the Metropolitan Life Insurance Company.

DESIRABLE WEIGHTS FOR MEN, AGE 25 AND OVER*

Height (in shoes, 1″ heels)		Weight in Pounds (in indoor clothing)		
		Small Frame	Medium Frame	Large Frame
Feet	Inches			
5	2	112–120	118–129	126–141
5	3	115–123	121–133	129–144
5	4	118–126	124–136	132–148
5	5	121–129	127–139	135–152
5	6	124–133	130–143	138–156
5	7	128–137	134–147	142–161
5	8	132–141	138–152	147–166
5	9	136–145	142–156	151–170
5	10	140–150	146–160	155–174
5	11	144–154	150–165	159–179
6	0	148–158	154–170	164–184
6	1	152–162	158–175	168–189
6	2	156–167	162–180	173–194
6	3	160–171	167–185	178–199
6	4	164–175	172–190	182–204

* Prepared by the Metropolitan Life Insurance Company.

ADDRESS BOOK

The following companies will fill mail order requests for specialty foods and equipment. Most have catalogues; others will answer specific inquiries.

Special Cooking Equipment

Bazaar de la Cuisine (catalogue)
1003 Second Avenue
New York, New York 10022

Bazar Français (catalogue)
666–68 Sixth Avenue
New York, New York 10010

The Bridge Company
212 East Fifty-second Street
New York, New York 10022

Dione Lucas Gourmet Center
226 East Fifty-first Street
New York, New York 10022

Hammacher Schlemmer (catalogue)
147 East Fifty-seventh Street
New York, New York 10022

Maid of Scandinavia (catalogue)
3245 Raleigh Avenue
Minneapolis, Minnesota 55416

Foreign and Specialty Foods

Byrd Mill
RFD 5
Louisa, Virginia
(Whole grain, stone-ground, flours and meals)

Casa Moneo
210 West Fourteenth Street
New York, New York 10011
(Spanish and Latin American foods, utensils; list available; catalogue)

Charles and Company
340 Madison Avenue
New York, New York 10017
(Assorted delicacies; catalogue)

Cheese-of-All-Nations
153 Chambers Street
New York, New York 10007
(Imported Cheeses)

GNL Shallot Distributors
51 De Shibe Terrace
Vineland, New Jersey 08360
(Shallots)

H. Roth and Son
Lekvar-by-the-Barrel
1577 First Avenue
New York, New York 10028
(Hungarian and Middle European foods, herbs, and spices, cooking utensils; catalogue)

Kassos Brothers
570 Ninth Avenue
New York, New York 10036
(Greek foods)

Katagiri
224 East Fifty-ninth Street
New York, New York 10022
(Japanese foods)

Maison Glass
52 East Fifty-eighth Street
New York, New York 10022
(Assorted delicacies; catalogue)

Manganaro Foods
488 Ninth Avenue
New York, New York 10018
(Italian foods and cooking utensils; catalogue)

Maryland Gourmet Mart
1072 First Avenue
New York, New York 10022
(Game, assorted delicacies; catalogue)

Paprikás Weiss Importer
1546 Second Avenue
New York, New York 10028
(Paprika, Hungarian and Middle European foods, spices, herbs, gourmet utensils; catalogue)

Schapira Coffee Company
117 West Tenth Street
New York, New York 10011
(Coffees, teas; catalogue)

Trinacria Importing Company
415 Third Avenue
New York, New York 10016
(Near and Middle Eastern foods, utensils)

Information on Foods and Cooking, Marketing, Food Conservation, and Gardening:

Superintendent of Documents
Government Printing Office
Washington, D.C. 20402
(Publication lists available)

INDEX

A

Address book
  for foreign foods, 725–26
  for special cooking equipment, 725
  for specialty foods, 725–26
Aioli sauce, 94
Alaska pie, 519
Albuféra sauce, 82
Algarve-style apricot sauce, 477
Allemande sauce, 79–80
Almond(s)
  broccoli with, 170
  bulgur kasha with apples and, 50–51
  butterballs, 607
  candy
    -apricot balls, 640
    brittle, 638
    fudge, 643
    nougat, 636–37
  celery with, 193
    scalloped, 194
  cocktail, with garlic, 648
  cookies
    crunchies, 608
    fig pinwheels with, 615–16
    -orange, 614
    -orange balls, 624–25
    pretzels, 611–12
    tarts, 610
  green beans with, 153
  ice cream, 464
  noodles with, 60
  -oyster stuffing, 121
  pie, Bavarian-style, 514
  rice with, 39
  sherried rice stuffing with raisins and, 116
  -sour cream sauce, 98
  stuffing for fish, 124
  tarts, 610
  toasted curried, 648
  wax beans with, 153
  wild rice with, 49
Ambrosia, 426–27
Ambrosia salad, 311
American-style Russian dressing, 331
Amish-style bread and potato stuffing, 116
Anadama bread, 373–74
Anchovy(ies)
  artichokes stuffed with, Roman-style, 144
  broccoli with, Roman-style, 170–71
  butter, 100
  deviled eggs with, 18
  egg salad with, 307
  mayonnaise, 94
  for sandwiches, 392
  sauce, 78
    marinara, 104–5
    -olive, 107
    -sour cream, 98
  tomatoes broiled with cheese and, 277
  tuna salad with, 308
Andalusian-style mayonnaise, 94
Angel food cake, 530–32
Appetizers
  grits and Gruyère, 55
  Monte Cristo sandwiches, 405–6
Apples
  baked, 430
    stuffed, 430
  -bread and raisin stuffing, 115
  brown Betty, 435
  brown sugar glazed, 430
  bulgur kasha with almonds and, 50–51
  butter, 675
    Blue Ridge, 681
  candied, 640
  canning, 692
  caramel, 640–41
  chicken sandwiches with, 398
  chutney, 663
  cinnamon rings, 430, 661
  cottage pudding, 470
  -cranberry relish, 668
  crisp, 436
  curried rings, 430
  dessert omelet with brandy and, 468
  freezing, 704
  fried rings, 430
  gold saffron, 429–30
  Indian pudding, 450
  jelly, 670–74, 677–78
    with mint, 678
    spiced, 678
  pancakes, 351
  -pecan stuffing, 120
  pickled, 660
    cinnamon rings, 661
  pie, 500–2
    country-style, 500
    deep dish, 500–2
    fried, 502
    general data on, 501
    streusel, 505
  -prune-cranberry stuffing, 121

red cabbage with, Flemish-style, 179–80
red hot, 430
rutabaga scalloped with, 263
with saffron, 429–30
strudel, 522–23
Swiss-style Charlotte, 435
turkey sandwiches with, 398
turnovers, 502
upside-down cake, 549
yam casserole with raisins and, 259
Applesauce
  cake, 547
  canning, 692
  cookies, 589–90
  freezing, 704
  mayonnaise, 94
  old-fashioned, 429
  spicy, 429
Apricot(s)
  Algarve-style sauce, 477
  -almond balls, 640
  bars, 622–23
  -bread stuffing, 116
  broiled, 432
  brown Betty, 435
  butter, 675
  canning, 694
  freezing, 705
  frosting glaze, 572
  ice cream, 463
  jam, 674
  -pecan bread, 347
  pickled, 660
  pie, chiffon, 513
  and pineapple salad, 318
  relish, 669
  rice, 38
  sandwiches, 404
  sautéed, 431
  upside-down cake, 549
Argenteuil-style artichoke bottoms, 143
Armenian-style
  rice, 41
  zucchini custard, 273
Arroz amarillo, 38
Artichoke(s), 141–47
  bottoms
    Argenteuil-style, 143
    Brittany-style, 143
    cold, 143
    Florentine-style, 143
    Lyonnaise-style, 143
    à la Parisienne, 144
    Piedmontese-style, 143
    princesse, 143
    soubise, 143
    stuffed with vegetables, 143
  frittata, 15
  general data on, 141–42
  globe, 141–45
    basic steamed, 142–43
  hearts
    DuBarry, 143

    marinated, Italian-style, 145
  Jerusalem
    baked, 146
    boiled, 145–46
    creamed, 146–47
    hash brown, 146
    low-calorie, 146
    purée, 146
    relish, 666
  low-calorie, 143, 146
  Provençal-style, braised, 144–45
  Roman-style, stuffed with anchovies, 144
  tomatoes marinated with, 291
Asparagus, 147–50
  buttered tips, 148
  canning, 696
  with capers, 148
  casserole with cheese, 148–49
  Chinese-style, 149
  cold, 148
  creamed tips, 148
  crepes au gratin, 173
  with dill, 148
  Divan, 149
  freezing, 707
  general data on, 147
  low-calorie, 148
  Polonaise-style, 148
  salad, 301
  Spanish-style, 149–50
  steamed, 147–48
  vinaigrette, 300–1
Aspic
  eggs in, 20–21
  ham, 317
  salad, 313–14
  seafood, 314
  tomato, 313–14
  vegetable, 313–14
Aunt Florrie's bread and butter pickles, 654
Aurore sauce, 80
Austrian-style cabbage, 176
Avgolemono sauce, 93
Avocado(s)
  chicken sandwiches with, 398
  freezing, 704
  -lemon aspic, 314–15
  mayonnaise, 94
  mousse, 315–16
  -rice stuffing, 117
  salad
    with Belgian endive, 310
    with grapefruit, 310
    -lemon mold, 315
    -lime mousse, 315
    mousse, 315–16
    with orange, 310
    with papaya, 310
    shellfish with eggs and, 309
    with tomatoes, 310
    with tomatoes and Roquefort, 291
  salad dressing, 327

INDEX

with tomatoes
  ribbon aspic, 320
  rice, 39

B

Baccalà, fettuccine con, 66
Bacon
  biscuits, 340
  and corn pie, 204
  and eggs
    with onions, creamed, 18
    pie, 16–17
    scrambled with hominy, 55
  green beans with dill and, 153
  hot salad dressing, 293
  lima beans with
    and carrots, 156
    in sour cream, 156
  muffins, 337
  rutabaga with sour cream and, 263
  sandwiches
    with beans, 397
    with cream cheese, 399
    with lettuce and tomato, 397
    with peanut butter, 399
  -sour cream sauce, 98
  spinach with, 266
  wax beans with dill and, 153
  wild rice with mushrooms and, 48
Baked Alaska, 468
Baking powder, general data on, 531
Baklava, 528
Banana(s)
  baked, 431
  flambé, 431
  glaze, 431
  ice cream, 463
    -orange, 466
  pie, cream, 509–10
  sautéed, 431
  tea bread, 348
  Waldorf salad with, 311
Bannocks, 341
Barbecue
  beef
    gravy for, 107
    sauce for, 107
  dried beans, 162–63
  sauces, 107–8
Barley, 34
  baked casserole with mushrooms, 51–52
  stewed with vegetables, 51
Basil
  -mint salad dressing, 324
  sauce, Genoese-style spaghetti with, 63
Basque-style
  eggplant with peppers and tomatoes, 209
Batarde sauce, 93
Batter
  bread, 369–70
  for fried foods, 356–57
  tempura, 357

vegetable fritter, 357
Bavarian cream, 457–58
Bavarian-style pie, 513–14
Bean(s), 150–66
  general data on, 150–52
  varieties, 150
  See also Dried beans; names of beans
Bean powders, 152
Bean sprouts
  sweet-sour salad, 301–2
Bearnaise sauce, 92
  blender, 93
Béchamel sauce, 78–79
Beef
  gravy for barbecue, 107
  ground
    cannelloni filled with, 69–70
    ravioli filled with, 67–68
  marinade for, 109
  meat balls
    spaghetti and, in tomato sauce, 63
    pisto with, 211
    rigatoni stuffed with sausage and, 66–67
  sauce, 105–6
    barbecue, 107
  steak
    Japanese-style sauce for, 111
  tufoli stuffed with sausage and, 66–67
  See also Corned beef
Beer
  marinade, 109
Beet(s), 166–68
  baked, 167
    with sour cream and caraway seeds, 168
  boiled, 166–67
  in burgundy, 168
  canning, 697
  cold, 167
  dried bean salad with, 302
  freezing, 707
  general data on, 166
  with grapes, 168
  Harvard, 167
  with horseradish, 167
  hot spicy, shredded, 167–68
  orange-glazed, 167
  in orange-lemon sauce, 168
  pickled, 657
  pickled eggs and, 21
  relish, 668–69
  with sour cream and dill, 167
  Tokay, 168
Beet greens
  freezing, 708
  steamed, 168
Belgian endive, 213–15
  general data on, 213–14
  au gratin, 214
  ham with, 214
  low-calorie, 214
  salad with avocado, 310
  Swiss-style, 214–15
Belgian-style tomato salad, 291

INDEX

Benne wafers, 588
Bercy butter, 100
Bercy sauce, 80
Berliner kränze, 612
Berry(ies)
 -apple brown Betty, 435
 biscuits, 340
 butter cream frosting with, 565
 canning, 692
 cobbler, 434–35
 freezing, 704
 ice cream, 463
 jam, 679
 pancakes, 351
 pie, 503–4
  basic, 503–4
  canned berries, 504
  chiffon, 512–13
  deep dish, 501
  Dutch-style, 504
  frozen, 504
 relish, 667
 shortcake, 437
Beurre manié, 78
Beurre noir, 100
Bigarade sauce, 86
Biscuit tortoni, 467
Biscuits, 338–41
 bacon, 340
 baking powder, 338–39
 berry, 340
 buttermilk, 339
 cheese, 340
 -corn meal, 340–41
 drop, 339
 dumplings, 355–56
 extra-quick, 339
 extra-rich, 339
 herb, 340
 lemon, 340
 make-ahead, 340
 onion, 340
 orange, 340
 party, 340
 savory pinwheel, 340
 stir-and-roll, 339
 sweet pinwheel, 339–40
 topping for casseroles, 339
Bishop's bars, 622
Black bean(s)
 boiled, 158
 Brazilian-style, 166
 Florida-style, with peppers, 165–66
 general data on, 151
Black bottom pie, 509
Blackberry(ies)
 jam, 674
 jelly, 670–74
Black-eyed peas
 boiled, 157
 canning, 698
 Carolina-style, 157
 freezing, 709
 fresh, boiled, 157
 general data on, 150, 151
 hopping John, 164
 rice salad, with, 303
 Southern-style, 164
Blancmange, 448
Blini, 353
Blintzes, cheese, 33
Blood as a thickener, 75
Blue cheese
 celery casserole with, 194
 -sour cream sauce, 98
Blue Ridge Apple Butter, 681
Blueberry
 jam, 674
 muffins, 337
 topping for cheese cake, 516
 waffles, 354
Bolognese-style tomato sauce, 104
Bontemps sauce, 80
Bordelaise sauce, 87
Boston-style baked beans, 159
 brown bread, 349
Bouchées, 495–96
Bourbonnaise-style quiche, 31
Bourguignonne-style beef, sauce, 87
Bran, 34
 bread, 368
 -nut muffins, 338
 -raisin muffins, 338
Brandy(brandied)
 Alexander pie, 514
 baked beans, 159
 dessert omelet with apple and, 468
 hard sauce, 478
 hot fruit compote with, 427
 mincemeat pie, 506
 peaches, 660–61
 pears, 661
 pots de crème, 443
 sauce, 475
 snaps, 592–93
 wild rice with, 49
 stuffing with corn bread and chestnuts, 117–18
Brazilian-style black beans, 166
Bread(s), 334–90
 anadama, 373–74
 apricot-pecan, 347
 banana tea, 348
 bannocks, 341
 as a basic food group, 718
 batter, 369–70
 Boston brown, 349
 bran, 368
 bubble loaf, 381
 and butter pudding, 443–44
 cheese, 374–75
 Christmas, 384
  Italian-style, 384
 cool-rise loaves, 369
 corn
  basic, 343

INDEX

muffins, 344
sticks, 343–44
stuffing, 118
stuffing, -wild rice with brandy and chestnuts, 117–18
corn meal mush, 345–46
fried, 346
Cornell, 368
crackling, 344
cranberry-nut, 348
croustades, 359
croutons, 360
crumbs, 359–60
cubes, 359
currant-nut, 347–48
date-nut, 347
dumplings, 356
freezing, 712
French-style
crusty, 371–72
garlic, 357
rich, 371
garlic, 357–58
Hilda's Yorkshire scones, 342
hushpuppies, 346
Irish soda, 341–42
Johnnycake, 344–45
kugelhupf, 382
oatmeal, 373
orange-nut, 348
panettone, 384
popovers, 342
potato, 369
prune and walnut, 347
pumpernickel, 373
quick, 336–61
  mixing methods, 334
  tips on making, 334–36
raisin, 368
  -nut, 347–48
Rhode Island-style jonnycakes, 344–45
rye, 372–73
Sally Lunn, 370
for sandwiches, 391
sour dough, 370–71
spoon, 345
sticks, 376
stuffing, 114–17
  Amish-style, with potatoes, 116
  for fish, 122–23
  with ham and green peppers, 115
  herbed, 120, 121
Swedish-style limpa, 373
sweet dough, 379–80
tea ring, 380–81
tortillas, 346–47
  chili, 347
white
  basic, 367–68
  rapid-mix, 368–69
whole wheat, 372
yeast, 361–90
  baking, 367
  crusts, 367
  essential ingredients, 361–62
  kneading, 363
  mixing methods, 362–63
  problems, 367
  punching dough down, 364
  rising period, 363–64
  shaping, 365–66
Yorkshire pudding, 342–43
Bread sauce, 110
Breadfruit, 168–69
Brioche, 387–88
  fruit loaves, 389
Broccoli, 169–73
  amandine, 170
  with anchovies, Roman-style, 170–71
  baked in mustard sauce, 172
  casserole with eggs and sour cream, 172
  Castilian-style, sautéed with ripe olives, 171
  cold, 170
  crepes au gratin with, 172–73
  eggs au gratin with, 16
  freezing, 707
  general data on, 169
  low-calorie, 170
  Osaka-style skillet, 171–72
  with Parmesan cheese, 170, 171
  with peanut butter sauce, 171
  steamed, 169
  in white wine sauce, 171
Broth
  cucumbers braised in white wine and chicken broth, 206
  freezing, 713
  See also Stock
Brown sauce, 84–91
Brown sugar
  chess pie, 515
  cookie drops, 583
  glaze for apples, 430
Brownies, 616–19
Brussels sprouts, 173–75
  boiled, 173
  with chestnuts, 174
  creamed with celery, 175
  dilled, in sour cream, 174
  freezing, 707
  general data on, 173
  au gratin, 174
  low-calorie, 173
  in onion sauce, 174–75
  parmigiana, 174
  veronique, 174
Bûche de Noël, 544
Buckwheat, 34–35
  kasha, 50
  pancakes, 352
Bulgur, 36
  croquettes, 47
  kasha, 50
  with apples and almonds, 50–51
  with mushrooms, 51

INDEX

-pecan stuffing, 119
pilaf, 41
Buns
  caramel sticky, 381
  Chelsea, 381
  hot cross, 380
Burgundy
  beets with, 168
Butter, 100–3
  anchovy, 100
  apple, 675
    Blue Ridge, 681
  apricot, 675
  Bercy, 100
  black, 100
  browned, 100
  caper, 100
  chili, 101
  chive, 101
  crab apple, 675
  curry, 101
  dill, 101
  drawn, 100
  freezing, 715
  fruit, 675
  garlic, 101
  grape, 675
  green, 101
  herb, 101
  horseradish, 101
  lemon, 101
  lobster, 101
  maître d'hôtel, 101
  marchands de vin, 102
  mushroom, 102
  mustard, 102
  noisette, 102
  orange, 102
  paprika, 102
  parsley, 101
  peach, 675
  pear, 675
  pimiento, 102
  plum, 675
  quince, 675
  for sandwiches, 391
  seasoned, 102
  shallot, 102
  shrimp, 102
  tarragon, 102
  tomato, 102–3
  tuna, 103
  for vegetables, 130–35
  watercress, 103
Buttermilk
  biscuits, 339
  marinade, 109
  mayonnaise, 94
  pancakes, 351
  rolls, 377
  salad dressing, 325
    chive, 332–33
  waffles, 354

Butterscotch
  chiffon cake with maple and, 554–55
  cookies
    brownies, 619
    dot, 579
    haystacks, 625
    icebox, 614
  cream cake filling, 572
  custard, 439
  lollipops, 641
  pie, cream, 508
  pudding, tapioca, 448
  sauce, 474
  spice cupcakes with, 558
  sugar cookies with, 599
  syrup, 474
  toast, 358

C

Cabbage, 175–81
  Austrian-style, 176
  baked, 178
  and bean hot pot, 160–61
  Chinese
    low-calorie, 180
    sautéed with sesame seeds, 180
    steamed, 180
  colcannon, 177–78
  creamy, 176
  Creole-style, 176–77
  general data on, 175–76
  kale and, 219
  low-calorie, 176
  Pennsylvania Dutch-style, 177
  red
    with chestnuts, 179
    Flemish-style, with apples, 179–80
    pickled, 657
    sweet-sour, 179
  with saffron, 177
  Savoy, with chestnuts, 179
  scalloped, 178
  shredded ruby, 179
  spicy East Indian-style, 178
  steamed, 176
  See also sauerkraut
Cacik, 297–98
Caesar salad, 292
Cajun-style rice, 44
Cakes, 529–74
  angel food, 530–31
  apple upside-down, 549
  applesauce, 547
  apricot upside-down, 549
  Boston cream, 539
  bûche de Noël, 544
  burnt sugar, 544–45
  butter, 529–30
    basic three-egg, 537
    basic two-egg, 537
  cheese, 516–17
    blueberry topping for, 516

INDEX

cherry topping for, 516
cranberry topping for, 516–17
pineapple topping for, 517
strawberry topping for, 517
chiffon, 530, 554
  butterscotch-maple, 554–55
  chocolate, 555
  lemon, 554
  mocha, 555
  orange, 554
  spiced, 554
chocolate
  basic, 542
  chiffon, 555
  crazy, 542–43
Christmas log, 544
coconut cream, 539
coffee
  cinnamon, 349
  fillings for, 387
  pumpkin, 386–87
  Swedish-style cinnamon rings, 385–86
cottage cheese, 517
decorating, 561–64
devil's food, 543
  loaf, 543
fillings, 572–74
  butterscotch cream, 572
  chocolate cream, 572
  coconut cream, 572
  coffee cream, 572
  double cream, 572
  fruit, 573
  fruit cream, 572, 573
  lemon, 573
  lime, 573
  Neapolitan-style fruit cream, 567
  orange, 573
  pastry cream, 572–73
  pineapple, 573
  pineapple-coconut, 574
  poppy seed cream, 572
  strawberry, 573–74
  vanilla cream, 572
freezing, 713
frostings, 559–72
  broiled, 570
  butter cream, 564–65
  cream cheese, 565–66
  fudge, 569–70
  glacé, 570–71
  glaze, 571–72
  ornamental, 570
  royal, 570
  seafoam, 569
  7-minute, 567–68
  tips on, 560–61
  whipped cream, 566–67
  white, 571
  white mountain, 568
fruit
  individual, 559
  light, 555

  royal wedding, 556–58
Génoise, 551
gingerbread, 548
  upside-down, 549
Grandmother's soft ginger, 548
hazelnut torte, 547
ingredients for, 530–32
Jamaican rum, 555–56
jelly roll, 552–53
kinds of, 529
Lady Baltimore, 539
lemon, sweet loaf, 538
marble, 538–39
mixing, 529–30, 534
mocha, 542
  chiffon, 555
  fudge, 543
nut, 545
orange with dates and nuts, 546
peach upside-down, 549
petits fours, 552
pineapple upside-down, 548–49
poppy seed, 537
pound, 541
problems, 536–37
rainbow, 539
Sachertorte, 543–44
silver, 538
sour cream, 559
  -fruit, 559
  -nut, 559
spice, 547–48
sponge, 530, 549–50
sugar bells for, 574
terms and techniques, 532
Thelma's 1, 2, 3, 4, 541–42
tips on making, 533–36
tipsy, 441–42
trifle, 441–42
walnut torte, 546–47
white
  basic, 538
  wedding, 539–41
Calamondin marmalade, 680
Calcium, 720
Calves liver
  risotto with, 42–43
California style
  fruit pickles, 660
  orange-ginger barbecue sauce, 108
  sour cream salad dressing, 326
Calories
  general data on, 720–21
  See also end of each recipe
Camembert cheese, cream salad dressing, 327
Candied fruit, nut cake with, 546
Candy, 628–44
  almond
    -apricot balls, 640
  brittle, 638
  fudge, 643
  nougat, 636–37

734 INDEX

apple
  candied, 640
  caramel, 640–41
caramels, 636
  chocolate, 636
  nuts, 636
chocolate
  caramels, 636
  -covered fondant squares, 642
  -dipped marzipan, 644
  Christmas balls, 633
  citrus peel, 641
coconut
  Chinese-style, 647
  fudge, 635–43
  penuche, 635
coffee
  drops, 634
  fondant, 633
  penuche, 635–36
cooked, 632–41
decorating, 631
divinity, 634
fondant, 632
  butter, 633
  chocolate-covered squares, 642
  citrus-rum, 642
  coffee, 633
  honey, 633
  opera creams, 633
  raisin pecan, 642
  uncooked, 642
fruit
  divinity, 634
  frosted, 633
  jellies, 640
  -nut bars, 644
  stuffed, 633
fudge
  -almond, 643
  best chocolate, 634
  blond, 635
  cocoa, 643
  -coconut, 635, 643
  maple, 643
  -peanut butter, 643
  snow-capped balls, 633
  Toll House, 635
  uncooked, 643
keeping, 631–32
Kentucky Colonels, 642–43
lollipops, 641
marzipan, 643–44
mints
  Mrs. B's pulled, 639–40
  thin, 633
nut
  balls, 633
  bonbons, 633
  caramels, 636
  frosted, 633
  -fruit bars, 644
  penuche, 635

Old English toffee, 637
packing and shipping, 632
peanut brittle, 637–38
peanut butter fudge, 643
peanut clusters, 644
pecan
  brittle, 638
  -raisin fondant, 642
  penuche, 635
  pinwheels, 633
  pralines, 636
  pulled, 638
  snowballs, 633
  special flavorings, 631
  special techniques, 629–31
  sugarplums, 633
  taffy, 638–39
  thermometer, 628–29
tips for making, 628–29
uncooked, 642–44
walnut, 638
wrapping, 631–32
Cannellini
  boiled, 158
  general data on, 151
Cannelloni, 69–71
  Garibaldi, 70
  homemade pasta dough, 58
  with meat filling, 69
  alla Nerone, 70
  squares, 69
Canning, 683–99
  closures for, 685
  equipment, 684
  general data on, 683
  guide for
    fruits, 692–95
    vegetables, 692–99
  jars for, 685
  problems, 691
  steps to follow, 686–90
  sugar syrup for, 691
  terms and techniques, 685–86
Cantaloupe, pickled, 659
Cantonese-style
  carrots with green pepper and celery, 185–86
Caper(s)
  asparagus with, 148
  butter, 100
  chicken salad with eggs and, 305
  lettuce with onions and, 223
  salmon sandwiches with, 403
  sauce, 78
    -horseradish, 78
    lemon, 95
    -sour cream, 98
    -yogurt, 99
Caramel
  apples, 640–41
  candy, 636
    chocolate, 636
    nut, 636

INDEX

custard, 440
crème, 439
fudge frosting with, 570
glaze
  parsnips in, 236
popcorn balls, 649
pudding, 447
  7-minute frosting with, 567
sticky buns, 381
syrup, 474
Caraway seed(s)
  beets baked with sour cream and, 168
  coleslaw with, 295
  dumplings, 356
  nut cake with, 546
  pastry, 489, 490
  rice, 39
  sauerkraut, with, 181
Carbohydrates, 718
Cardoons, 181–82
Caribbean-style compote, 427
Carolina-style
  black-eyed peas, 157
  coleslaw with celery seed, 295
  wilted lettuce, 293
Carrots, 182–86
  baked, with rice, 186
  boiled, 183
  canning, 697
  and celery
    curry, 193–94
    with green peppers Cantonese-style, 185–86
  cold, 183
  cookies, 588–89
  with dill, 656
  Flemish style, 185
  freezing, 708
  general data on, 182
  lemon glazed, 183
  lima beans with bacon and, 156
  low-calorie, 183
  macédoine of vegetables
    cold, 184
    hot, 184
  mashed, 183–84
  and onion pie, 186
  Provençal-style, 185
  rosemary, 183
  sandwiches with raisins, 400
  with squash, 270
  Turkish-style fried beans and, 161
  Venetian-style, in cream, 184–85
  Vichy, 184
Casseroles
  asparagus and cheese, 148–49
  barley, baked with mushrooms, 51–52
  biscuit topping for, 339
  broccoli with eggs and sour cream, 172
  celery-blue cheese, 194
  freezing, 712
  hominy, 54

  potato, 248
  cottage, 253–54
  pumpkin and onion, 262
  three bean, 160
  toasted rice and vegetables, 40
  wild rice, chicken livers, and sausage, 49–50
  yam, with apples and raisins, 259
Castilian-style broccoli, sautéed with ripe olives, 171
Cauliflower, 186–90
  baked in wine and cream sauce, 190
  boiled, 187
  Caruso, 188–89
  in cider and cream, 188
  deviled, 188
  freezing, 708
  general data on, 186
  au gratin, 190
  Polonaise, 187–88
  pudding, 189–90
  puréed, à la DuBarry, 189
  salad, raw, 297
  soufflé, 189
Caviar
  egg salad with, 307
  mayonnaise, 94
  omelets with, 13
  salad dressing, 332
Celeriac, 191–92
  boiled, 191
  cold, 191
  creamed, 191
  general data on, 191
  au gratin, 192
  low calorie, 191
  puréed, 191
Celery, 192–95
  with almonds, 193
  scalloped, 194
  boiled, 192–93
  Brussels sprouts creamed with, 175
  canning, 697
  and carrots
    curry, 193–94
    with green peppers Cantonese-style, 185–86
  casserole with blue cheese, 194
  cold, 193
  general data on, 192
  au gratin, 193
  hearts, 192
  macédoine of vegetables
    cold, 184
    hot, 184
  salad, Victor, 300
  stir-fried, 194–95
Celery seed, Carolina-style
  coleslaw with, 295
Cereals, 34–56
  as a basic food group, 718
  dressing up, 36–37
  forms of, 34 36

INDEX

general data on, 34
kinds of, 34–36
pie crust, 496
See also names of cereals
Champ, 234
Champagne, peaches with, 433
Chantilly sauce, 92
Charcutière sauce, 88
Chard, 195–96
  boiled, 195
  cold, 196
  freezing, 708
  general data on, 195
  low calorie, 196
  puréed, 196
Charlotte russe, 458
Chasseur sauce, 88
Chateaubriand sauce, 88
Chaud-froid sauce, 83
Chayotes, 196
Cheddar cheese
  bake, 29
  -beer fondue, 27–28
  cookie rings, 601
  macaroni loaf with, 61–62
  -onion tart, 32
  sauce, onions in, 233
Cheese, 21–33
  asparagus with
    casserole, 148–49
    crepes, 173
  bake, 29
  Belgian endives with, 214
    and ham, 214
  blintzes, 33
  bread, 374–75
  bread crumbs, 359
  breaded, fried, 32–33
  broccoli crepes with, 172
  Brussels sprouts with, 174
  cake, 516–17
    blueberry topping for, 516
    cherry topping for, 516
    cranberry topping for, 516–17
    pineapple topping for, 517
    strawberry topping for, 517
  cauliflower with, 190
  celeriac with, 192
  celery with, 193
  cooking tips, 25
  -corn fritters, 204
  -corn meal biscuits, 340–41
  crackers, 343
  croque-Madame, 32
  croque-Monsieur, 32
  cucumbers with, 205
  curds and sour cream, 28–29
  dried bean purée with, 158
  dumplings, 356
  eggs with
    and broccoli, 16
    croquettes, 20
    deviled, 18
  fondue, 27–28
  freezing, 715
  fried beans with, 162
  garlic bread, 357
  general data on, 21–22
  gnocchi, 52
  green beans with, 154
  grouped by type, 22–25
    blues, 24
    firm, 23
    hard (grating), 25
    semisoft, 23
    soft, ripened, 22
    soft, unripened, 22
  ham with cheese salad, 307
  hominy casserole with, 54
  kohlrabi with, 220
  leeks with, 221
  lemon, 681
  lima beans with, 154, 156
  macaroni and, 61–62
    -mushroom sauce, 77
  noodles with, 60
    ring, 59
  omelets filled with, 11
  -onion tart, 32
  pancakes, 352
  pastry, 489, 490
  pears baked with, 433
  pie, 516
  potatoes with, 249
  puff, 29
  pumpkin with, 261
  quiche, 31
    bourbonnaise, 31
    clam, 31–32
    corn, 204
    Lorraine, 31
    niçoise, 31
    onion, 31
  ravioli, 67–68
  rice with, 40
    croquettes, 47
    Spanish-style, 43
  rutabaga with, 263
  sandwiches
    with chicken, 398
    with chipped beef, 403
    dreams, 404
    grilled, 399
    with ham, 399
    with ham, crescents, 406–7
    -pimiento, 402
    plain, 399
    spread, 399
    tacos, 407
    toasted, 399
    with turkey, 398
  sauce, 77
    eggs in, 17
    eggs in, stuffed, 16
    Italian-style, 82
    -sour cream, 98

INDEX

scalloped potatoes with, 252
serving, 25–26
soufflés, 29–31
spinach with, 266
squash with, 271–72
strudel, 524
toast, 358
tomatoes and
  aspic, 314
  broiled with anchovies, 277
  pie with corn, 279–80
  ribbon loaf, 320
tuna salad with, 308
turnips with, 282
turnovers, Ukrainian-style, 33
vegetable purée with, 158
waffles, 354
wax beans with, 154
Welsh rabbit, 26
  -tomato, 26–27
See also Cottage cheese; Cream cheese; names of cheeses
Chef's salad, 304
Chelou, 46
Chelsea buns, 381
Cherry(ies)
  butter cream frosting with, 565
  canning, 693
  chocolate sauce with, 473
  cookie twinks, 580
  cottage pudding, 470
  freezing, 704
  jam, 674
  jubilee, 431–32
  kolache, 381–82
  -pecan salad, 318–19
  preserves, 675–76
  sauce, 476
  strudel, 523–24
  topping for cheese cake, 516
Chestnut(s), 196–98
  boiled, 197
  braised, 198
  -bread stuffing, 115
  Brussels sprouts with, 174
  creamed, 197
  Mont Blanc aux marrons, 470
  -mushroom stuffing, 119
  peeling, 197
  puréed, 198
  red cabbage and, 179
  riced pyramid, 197–98
  roasted, 198
    hearth-, 198
  sautéed, 197
  shelling, 197
  wild rice stuffing with brandy and corn bread, 417–18
Chevreuil sauce, 86
Chicken
  aspic, 314
  cucumbers braised in white wine and chicken broth, 206

gravy, 84
livers
  chopped, sandwiches, 398
  -mushroom stuffing, 121
  -rice stuffing, 116
  risotto with, 42
  wild rice casserole with sausage and, 49–50
macaroni salad with, 303
manicotti stuffed with mushrooms and, 71
marinades for, 108–9
ravioli stuffed with prosciutto and, 68
salad, 305
  chow chow, 306
  curried, 309
  with eggs and capers, 305
  with ham, 305
  jellied, 317
  with olives and walnuts, 305
  sandwiches, 398
  with seafood, 305
  with vegetables, 305
  Waldorf, 306
sandwiches
  with apple, 398
  with avocado, 398
  with cheese, 398
  chopped liver, 398
  curried with nuts, 398
  with ham, 398
  Hawaiian-style, 404
  salad, 398
  sliced, 398
  tacos, 407
and tomato ribbon loaf, 320
Chick-peas
  baked pilaf, 164–65
  boiled, 157–58
  eggplant stuffed with mushrooms and, 213
  general data on, 151
  Greek-style, with tomatoes, 165
  and kasha, 165
  and tomato salad, 302
Chiffon sauce, 77–78
Chili
  butter, 101
  -garlic bread, 357–58
  hot ketchup, 662
  rice, 39
  sauce, 109
  tostado, 347
Chinese cabbage
  low-calorie, 180
  sautéed, with sesame seeds, 180
  steamed, 180
Chinese-style
  asparagus, 149
  barbecue sauce, 108
  celery, stir-fried, 194–95
  coconut candy, 647
  cookie chews, 620
  cucumbers in soy sauce, 206
  hot mustard sauce, 111

rice
  fried, 45
  fried eggs and, 45
  snow peas, 241
  sweet-sour sauce, 111
Chives, 230
  butter, 101
  -buttermilk salad dressing, 332–33
  dumplings, 355
  -sour cream sauce, 98
  toast, 358
  wild rice with sour cream and, 48
  -yogurt sauce, 99
Chivry sauce, 80
Chocolate
  Bavarian cream, 458
  blancmange, 447–48
  butter cream frosting with, 565
  cake
    basic, 542
    chiffon, 555
    crazy, 542–43
  candy
    caramels, 636
    -covered fondant squares, 642
    -dipped marzipan, 644
  -coconut piecrust, 497
  cookies, 613
    bonbons, 625
    checkerboard, 613
    dot, 579
    -filled pecan dreams, 602–3
    haystacks, 625
    macaroons, 591
    -nut thins, 580
    pecan wafers, 588
    pinwheels, 613–14
    quick, 581
  cream cake filling, 572
  cream cheese frosting with, 566
  crumb piecrust, 496
  cupcakes, 558
  custard, 439, 440
  dessert soufflé, 446, 456
  doughnuts, 350
  éclairs, 526
  frosting glaze, 571
  glacé, 571
  ice cream, 464
    dark, 466
    French-style, 465
  jelly roll, 553
  marshmallow cream sauce with, 474
  meringue kisses, 593
  mousse, 444–45
  nut cake with, 546
  pie
    angel, 518
    Bavarian-style, 513
    chiffon, 512
    cream, 508–9
  pots de crème, 443
    low-calorie, 459

profiteroles, 527
pudding, 447
  steamed, 451–52
  tapioca, 448
  sauce, 472–73
  7-minute frosting with, 567–68
Spanish cream, 457
sponge cake, 550–51
spritz, 611
whipped cream with, 479
whipped cream frosting with, 566
Chocolate chip
  cookies, 581
  cupcakes, 559
  pudding, 471
Choron sauce, 92
Choux pastry, 493
Chow chow relish, 664–65
Christmas bread, 385
  Italian-style, 384
Christmas log, 544
Chutney
  apple, 663
  -cranberry relish, 668
  cream cheese salad dressing with, 327
  green tomato, 662
  mango, 663
  mayonnaise, 94
  peach, 663
  pear, 663
  for sandwiches, 392
  -sour cream sauce, 98
  tongue sandwiches with, 403
  -yogurt sauce, 99
Cider
  cauliflower in cream and, 188
  vinegar, 322
Cinnamon
  apple rings with, 430, 661
  coffee cake, 349
  -pecan bars, 621
  -raisin pinwheels, 385
  Swedish-style rings, 385–86
  toast, 358
Citrus peel
  candied, 641
  -rum fondant, 642
Clam(s)
  freezing, 714
  quiche, 31–32
  sauce
    red, 104
    white, 64, 106
  spaghetti with white clam sauce, 64, 106
  stuffing for fish, 124
Cobblers, 434–35
Cocktail appetizers
  mayonnaise for shellfish, 95
Cocktail sauce, 109–10
Cocoa
  fudge, 643
  marzipan, 644

INDEX

Coconut
  broiled frosting with, 570
  butterballs, 607
  cake filling with pineapple, 574
  candy
    Chinese-style, 647
    fudge, 635, 643
    penuche, 635
  coloring, 630
  cookies, 580
    balls, 579
    and black walnut bars, 624
    brownies, 617
    -chip chews, 580
    discs, 589
    drops, 583
    macaroons, 592
    quick, 581
  cream cake, 539
  cream cake filling, 572
  custard, 440
  fresh, 646
  meringue kisses, 593
  milk, 646–47
  pie, 511–12
    chiffon, 512
    cream, 508
    custard, 511
  piecrust, 497
  7-minute frosting with, 568
  sponge cake, 550
  sugar cookies with, 599
  toasting, 630
  whipped cream with, 479
  whipped cream frosting with, 567
Cod, salt
  fettuccine with, 66
Coeur à la crème, 469–70
Coffee
  butter cream frosting with, 564
  candy
    drops, 634
    fondant, 633
    penuche, 635–36
  chiffon pie, 512
  cream cake filling, 572
  cream cheese frosting with, 566
  custard, 440
  dessert soufflé, 446, 456–57
  granité, 462
  ice cream, 464, 465, 466–67
  low-calorie dessert topping, 480
  meringue kisses, 593
  pots de crème, 443
  7-minute frosting with, 567
  sponge cake, 550
  whipped cream with, 479
  whipped cream frosting with, 566
Coffee cake
  cinnamon, 349
  fillings for, 387
  pumpkin, 386–87
  Swedish-style cinnamon rings, 385–86

Cointreau, pineapple fans with mint in, 428
Colbert sauce, 90
Colcannon, 177–78
Coleslaw
  with caraway seeds, 295
  Carolina-style, with celery seed, 295
  red and green, 295
  sweet-sour, 294–95
Collards, 198
  boiled, 199
  freezing, 708
  low-calorie, 199
Colonial chess pie, 315–16
Cookies, 575–627
  almond
    crunchies, 608
    fig pinwheels with, 615–16
    -orange, 614
    -orange balls, 624–25
    pretzels, 611
    tarts, 610
  applesauce, 589–90
  apricot bars, 622–23
  bar, 616–24
    chart, 585–86
    general data on, 616
  basic mix, 581–82
  benne, 588
  Bishop's bars, 622
  brandy snaps, 593–94
  brown sugar drops, 583
  brownies, 616–19
  butter
    old-fashioned "S," 608
    planks, 611
    stars, 611
  butterballs, 607
    almond, 607
    coconut, 607
    thumbprint, 608
  butterscotch
    brownies, 619
    dot, 579
    haystacks, 625
    icebox, 614
  carrot, 588–89
  Cheddar rings, 601
  cherry twinks, 580
  chewy slice-and-bake bars, 580
  Chinese-style chews, 620
  Christmas
    ginger snaps, 604–5
    Moravian-style, 601–2
  chocolate, 613
    bonbons, 625
    checkerboards, 613
    dot, 579
    -filled pecan dreams, 602–3
    haystacks, 625
    macaroons, 591
    -nut thins, 580
    pecan wafers, 588
    pinwheels, 613–14

quick, 581
chocolate chip, 581
coconut, 580
  balls, 579
  and black walnut bars, 624
  brownies, 617
  -chip chews, 580
  discs, 589
  drops, 583
  macaroons, 592
  quick, 581
commercial, dressing up, 578-80
Congo squares, 621
cream cheese flakes, 582
cutters, 597
date
  German-style squares, 622
  -nut fingers, 626
  -oatmeal bars, 623
decorating, 577-78
drop, 582-96
  chart, 584
  general data on, 582
fig
  and almond pinwheels, 615-16
  Newtons, 603-4
  -oatmeal bars, 623
Florentines, 594-95
freezing, 713
fruit
  bars, 624
  drops, 583
  four-fruit balls, 624
  and nut bars, 624
fudge nuggets, 626
German-style peppernuts, 604
ginger, old-fashioned biscuits, 590
gingerbread boys, 600
Greek-style wheat and walnut, 621-22
hermits, 583
kourabiedes, 609-10
ladyfingers, 595
lebkuchen, 605
lemon
  sponge squares, 619-20
  wafers, 583
macaroons, 591-92
Madeleines, 595-96
Marguerites, 602
  quick, 579
Maude's, 587
meringue kisses, 592
Mexican-style wedding cakes, 609
mincemeat discs, 589
molasses
  creamed-filled, 603
  icebox, 614
  pressed spice, 612
molded, 606-12
  chart, 585
  general data on, 606-7
Montrose drop, 591
Mrs. Bouldin's date-nut fingers, 626

no-bake, 624-26
  chart, 586
  general data on, 624
nut, 613
  balls, 579
  -chocolate thins, 580
  -date fingers, 626
  and fruit bars, 624
  meringue bars, 620-21
  quick, 581
oatmeal
  -apple bars, 623
  -date bars, 623
  dropped chippies, 590
  -fig bars, 623
  icebox, 615
  -prune bars, 623
  quick, 582
  sugarless drops, 590-91
orange
  -almond, 614
  -almond balls, 624-25
  -almond lace, 594
  -chocolate jewels, 615
  drops, 587-88
  Scotch-style crisps, 611
packing and shipping, 577
peanut butter, 608, 615
  bars, 626
  quick, 581
  stars, 611
pecan
  chocolate-filled dreams, 602-3
  chocolate wafers, 588
  -cinnamon bars, 621
  crisps, 587
pepparkakor, 604-5
pfeffernüsse, 604
piecrust, 497
porcupines, 625
Portuguese-style filhos, 627
praline bars, 580
pressed, 606-12
  chart, 585
  general data on, 606-7
pumpkin, 589
raisin, 580
  and currants, 623-24
  quick, 581
refrigerator, 612-16
  basic, 613
  chart, 585
  general data on, 612
rocks, 583
rolled, 596-606
  chart, 584-85
  general data on, 596-97
rose tree, 600
rum balls, 624
sand tarts, 599
shortbread, Scottish-style, 619
snickerdoodles, 609
snow-capped fudgies, 579

spice
  pressed molasses, 612
  quick, 581
spitzbuben, 604
springerle, 606
spritz, 610–11
storing, 577
streusel-topped bars, 580
sugar, 598–99
  butterscotch, 599
  chocolate, 598
  coconut, 599
  decorative, 599
  lemon, 599
  marbles, 598–99
  nut, 599
  nut rings, 612
  orange, 599
  pillows, 598
  pinwheels, 598
  pretzels, 611
  quick, 581
  wreaths, 612
Swedish-style rosettes, 626–27
tips on making, 575–77
Toll House, 587
  brownies, 619
types of, 575
Corn, 199–204
  boiled
    on the cob, 200
    creamy, 201
    fresh whole kernel, 201
    with vegetables, 201
  canning, 698
  confetti, 202
  freezing, 708
  fritters, 204
    -cheese, 204
  general data on, 199–200
  gumbo, 203
  herbed, in cream, 201–2
  oysters, 204
  and pepper pancakes, 352
  -pepper stuffing, 121
  pie, 203–4
    with bacon, 204
    tomato-cheese, 279–80
  pudding, 203
  quiche, 204
  relish, 665–66, 668
  roasted, 200–1
  scalloped, 202–3
  succotash, old-fashioned, 202
Corn bread
  basic, 343
  muffins, 344
  sticks, 343–44
  stuffing, 118
    wild rice, with brandy and chestnuts, 117–18
Corn meal, 35
  -cheese biscuits, 340–41

  mush, 345–46
    fried, 346
Corned beef sandwiches, 397
Cornell bread, 368
Cottage cheese
  cake, 517
  homemade, 28
  salad
    and cream cheese mold, 315
    with spinach, 298–99
Cottage pudding, 470–71
Couscous, 35
  boiled, 53
Cowpeas
  boiled, 157–58
  general data on, 151
Crab(s)
  freezing, 714
  ravigote, 309–10
  stuffing for fish, 124
Crab apple(s)
  butter, 675
  jelly, 670–73
    with mint, 678
    spiced, 678
  pickled, 660
Crackling bread, 344
Cranberry(ies)
  -corn bread stuffing, 118
  jelly, 670–73
  ketchup, 662
  mayonnaise, 94
  nut bread, 348
  -prune-apple stuffing, 121
  relish, 666, 667–68
  salad
    frozen ribbon, 321
    mold, 319
    -pecan mold, 319
  sauce
    -orange, 112
    spicy, 112
    whole, 112
  topping for cheese cake, 517
  -wild rice stuffing, 117
Cranberry beans
  boiled, 157
  general data on, 150, 151
Cream
  freezing, 715
  sauce
    -horseradish, 96
    -wine, cauliflower baked in, 190
  Spanish-style, 457
  Swedish-style, 458
Cream cheese
  cookie flakes, 582
  and cottage cheese salad mold, 315
  frosting, 565–66
  salad dressing, 327
  sandwiches
    with bacon, 399
    with jelly, 399

with olives, 402
with watercress, 402-3
sauce, hearts of palm in, 217-18
tomato aspic with olives and, 313
Cream horns, 525-26
Cream puffs, 526
Crème brûlée, 440
Creole-style
  cabbage, 176-77
  tomato sauce, 103
Crepes
  asparagus, au gratin, 173
  broccoli, au gratin, 172-73
  dessert, 354-55
  savory filled, 354
  Suzette, 468-69
Croissants, 378-79
Croque-Madame, 32
Croquembouche, 527-28
Croque-Monsieur, 32
Croquettes
  bulgur, 47
  egg, 20
  kasha, 47
  potato, 249
  rice, 46-47
Crostini alla mozzarella, 32-33
Croustades, 359
Croutons, 360
Crullers, 390
Cucumber(s), 204-7
  aspic, 314
  baked stuffed, 206-7
  boiled, 205
  braised in white wine and chicken broth, 206
  Chinese-style, in soy sauce, 206
  general data on, 204-5
  au gratin, 205
  low-calorie, 205
  Provençal-style, 206
  salad, 297-98
  sandwiches, 399
  sautéed, 205-6
  -sour cream sauce, 98
  vegetable stuffed, 206
  -yogurt sauce, 99
Cumberland sauce, 110
Cupcakes, 558-59
Currant(s)
  freezing, 704
  -glazed parsnips, 236
  jelly, 670-73
  muffins, 337
  -nut bread, 347-48
  and raisin bars, 623-24
  red
    -sour cream sauce, 99
  rice, 38
  sauce, 477
Curry(ied)
  apple rings, 430
  asparagus salad, 301

butter, 101
celery and carrot, 193-94
chicken
  sandwiches with nuts, 398
  eggs, 17-18
  deviled, 19
  salad, 307
  garlic bread, 357-58
  hot fruit compote, 427-28
  hot fruit relish, 669
  mayonnaise, 329
  rice, 39
  for sandwiches, 392
  sauce, 82-83
  shrimp
    salad, 309
    -sour cream sauce, 98
  spinach, 267
  toast, 358
  turkey
    sandwiches with nuts, 398
    -yogurt sauce, 99
Custard, 437-40
  baked, 438-39
  brandy pots de crème, 443
  butterscotch, 439
  caramel, 440
  crème, 439
  chocolate, 439, 440
  chocolate pots de crème, 443
    low-calorie, 459
  coconut, 440
  coffee, 440
    pots de crème, 442-43
  crème brûlée, 440
  egg yolk, 438
  flan, 440-41
    fruit, Viennese-style, 520-21
    pineapple, 441
    rum, 441
  floating island, 441
  general data on, 437-38
  lemon, 439
  low-calorie, 439
  maple, 440
  mocha, 440
  molasses, 440
  oeufs à la neige, 441
  orange, 439
  pie, 510-11
  rennet, 442
  sauce, 439-40
  sour cream, 440
  spicy, 440
  spinach, 268
  stirred, 439
  thick, 439
  thin, 439
  vanilla bean, 438
  vanilla pots de crème, 442-43
  zabaglione, 442
zucchini, Armenian-style, 273

INDEX

D

Dandelions, 207
  general data on, 207
  wilted, 207
Danish style
  new potatoes, 257
  pastry, 382–84
  sandwiches, 401–2
Dasheens, 207–8
Date(s)
  cookies
    German-style squares, 622
    -nut fingers, 626
    -oatmeal bars, 623
  muffins, 337
  -nut bread, 347
  orange cake with nuts and, 546
  pudding, steamed, 452
  rice, 38
  sandwiches, 404
  Waldorf salad with marshmallows and, 310
  walnut pudding, 471
Dessert(s), 408–71
  frozen, 459–68
  fruit, 408–37
  garnishes for, 409
  gelatin, 453–59
  puddings, 437–53
  speciality, 468–71
  See also names of desserts; types of desserts
Dessert sauces, 471–80
  apricot, Algarve-style, 477
  brandy, 475
  butterscotch, 474
  caramel syrup, 474
  cardinal, 477
  cherry, 476
  chocolate, 472–73
  currant, 477
  custard, 439–40
  eggnog, 472
  hard, 478
  honey, 478
  hot fudge, 473
  jam, 476
  jelly, 476
  lemon, 475
    -raisin, 475
  lime, 475
  low-calorie topping, 480
  marshmallow cream, 473–74
  Melba, 477
  mocha, 473
  mock Devonshire cream, 478
  Nesselrode, 472
  nut syrup, 474–75
  orange, 475
    -nut syrup, 475
  peppermint, 478
  pineapple, 476
  pistachio syrup, 475
  rum, 475
  sour cream, homemade, 480
  strawberry, 477
  vanilla, 471–72
  vanilla bean, 472
  whipped cream, 479–80
Devil's food cake, 543
  loaf, 543
Devonshire cream, mock, 478–79
Dhal, 222
Diable sauce, 86
Dietary allowances, recommended daily, 721–24
Dijonnaise-style sauce, 96–97
  vegetables, 141
Dill
  asparagus with, 148
  beets with sour cream and, 167
  Brussels sprouts with sour cream and, 174
  butter, 101
  egg salad with, 307
  green beans with bacon and, 153
  lima beans with, 156
  mayonnaise, 94
  pickles, 653–56
    carrots, 656
    green beans, 656
    green tomato, 656
    kosher, 654
    sweet, 654
    zucchini, 656
  salsify with sour cream and, 264
  for sandwiches, 392
  sauce
    new potatoes in, 256–57
    -sour cream, 98
    -yogurt, 99
  wax beans with bacon and, 153
Diplomate sauce, 81
Divinity, 634
Doughnuts, 349–50
  chocolate, 350
  jelly, 390
  lemon, 350
  old-fashioned yeast-raised, 389–90
  orange, 350
  spicy baking powder, 349–50
  sugar puffs, 350
Dressing. *See* Salad dressing
Dried beans
  alphabet of, 151
  baked
    Boston-style, 159
    rummy, 159
    sandwiches, 400
    sandwiches with bacon and, 397
    Swedish-style, 163–64
  barbecued, 162–63
  boiled, 157–58
  brandied, 159
  and cabbage hot pot, 160–61
  cold, 158

creamed purée of, 158
fried, 162
hominy with salt pork and, 55
Mexican-style, 162
Neapolitan-style with Parmesan, 161
in onion sauce, 161
salad, 302
savory, 158
south-of-the-border bean pot, 163
Spanish-style bean pot, 164
three bean casserole, 160
Turkish-style
  fried with carrots, 161
white bean stew, 160
See also names of beans
Duck
  eggs, 2
  marinades for, 108–9
Dumplings, 355–56
  basic, 355
  biscuit, 356
  bread, 356
  caraway seed, 356
  cheese, 356
  chive, 355
  Nockerln, 61
  with parsley, 355
  peas and, 239
  quick, 356
  saffron, 356
  sage, thyme and onion, 355
Dutch-style berry pie, 504
Duxelles sauce, 88

E

East Indian-style cabbage, 178
  rice and lentils, 45–46
Éclairs, 526
Eggs, 1–21
  Americano-style, 9
  asparagus Divan with, 149
  in aspic, 20–21
  bacon and
    with onions, creamed, 18
    pie, 16–17
    scrambled with hominy, 55
  baked, 7
    in toast caps, 15–16
    in tomatoes, 15
    in tomatoes, low-calorie, 15
  Benedict, 8
  blood specks in, 2
  and broccoli
    casserole with sour cream, 172
    au gratin, 16
    parmigiana, 170
  chicken salad with capers and, 305
  Chinese-style fried rice and, 45
  color of, 1
  cooked in the shell, 4–5
  creamed, 17–18
  croquettes, 20
  deviled, 18–19
    in aspic, 20–21
  dried, 2
  duck, 2
  fertile, 2
  Florentine-style, 9
  Foo Young, 9–10
  freezing, 2, 715
  freshness of, 1–2
  fried, 6
    French-style, 6
  garnishes for, 7
  general data on, 1–2
  goose, 2
  huevos rancheros, 9
  leftover yolks and whites, 4
  in a nest, 8
  noodles, 58–59
  pickled, 21
  poached, 5
  quality of, 1
  ranch-style potato pie, 17
  rosemary, 19–20
  salad, 306–7
  sandwiches, 398–99, 403
  sauce, 80
  Scotch woodcock, 7–8
  scrambled, 6
    with hominy and bacon, 55
  shellfish salad with avocado and, 309
  shirred, 7
  size of, 1
  skillet potato breakfast and, 7
  special terms and techniques, 2–4
  stuffed
    in aspic, 20
    basic, 19
    in cheese sauce, 16
    French-style, 16
    in mushroom sauce, 16
    rosy, 16
  as thickeners, 74
  tomato aspic with, 313
  yolk
    custard, 438
    custard pie, 511
  See also Omelets
Eggnog
  ice cream, 464
  sauce, 472
Eggplant, 208–13
  Basque-style, with peppers and tomatoes, 209
  broiled, 209
  freezing, 708
  fried, 208–9
  general data on, 208
  Italian-style tomato sauce
    with mushrooms and, 104
  Izmir-style, 209–10
  low-calorie, 209
  parmigiana, 212
  pisto, 211

ratatouille, 210
ravioli, 68
stuffed
  with mushrooms and chick-peas, 213
  with pilaf and raisins, 212
  Turkish-style, 213
  Sultan's, 211
Endive. *See* Belgian endive
English muffins, individual pizzas, 376
English-style
  crumpets, 353
Espagnole sauce, 85–87
Estouffat, 160
Eve's pudding, 470

F

Farina, 35
  gnocchi parmigiana, 53
Fats, 718–19
Fava beans, 151
Fennel, 215–16
  boiled, 215–16
  butter-braised, 216
  cold, 216
  general data on, 215
  low-calorie, 216
  parmigiana, 216
Ferns, 216–17
  buttered, 216–17
  general data on, 216
Fettuccine
  con baccalà, 66
  and fish, 66
Fig(s)
  canning, 693
  cookies
    and almond pinwheels, 615–16
    Newtons, 603–4
    -oatmeal bars, 623
  with ginger, 432
  with honey, 432
  preserves, 675–76
  relish, 669
  rice, 38
  sandwiches, 404
  spiced, 432
  stewed, 432
Figaro sauce, 92
Financière sauce, 89
Finnish-style
  onions in sour cream, 235
  tomato salad, 291
Fish
  fettuccine and, 66
  stuffing for, 122–23
  See also names of fish
Fisherman's baked shells, 62
Flageolets
  boiled, 158
  general data on, 151

Flan, 440–41
  fruit, Viennese-style, 520–21
  pineapple, 441
  rum, 441
Flemish-style
  carrots, 185
  red cabbage and apples, 179–80
Floating island, 441
Florentines, 594–95
Florentine-style
  artichoke bottoms, 143
  eggs, 9
  noodles, 60
Florida-style black beans with peppers, 165–66
Fondant
  butter, 633
  chocolate-covered squares, 642
  citrus-rum, 642
  coffee, 633
  honey, 633
  opera creams, 633
  raisin-pecan, 642
  uncooked, 642
Fondue
  cheese, 27–28
Food groups, 4 basic, 717–18
Forcemeat, 121–22
  amount needed, 114
  as a garnish, 122
  general data on, 113–14
  leftovers, 114
  tips on, 113–14
  veal, 121–22
Franconia potatoes, 248
Frankfurters
  hominy casserole with, 54–55
Freezing, 700–16
  additives for, 701–2
  antibrowning agents for, 701–2
  dairy products, 715
  eggs, 715
  equipment, 700–1
  fruits, 704–6, 710–11
  fully cooked food, 712–13, 715–16
  game, 711
  game birds, 711
  general data on, 700
  general tips on, 715–16
  herbs, 714
  home freezers, 700
  meat, 711, 712
  partially prepared food, 712–13, 715
  poultry, 711, 712
  seafood, 714
  steps to follow, 702–3, 710
  sugar syrup for, 691
  vegetables, 707–9
French-fried
  onion rings, 232
  parsnips, 237
  potatoes, 251

INDEX

shoestring, 251
  twice-fried, 251
French-style
  bread
    crusty, 371-72
    garlic, 357-58
    rich, 371
  ice cream, 465
  mayonnaise, 94
  omelets, 12-13
  peas, 240
  salad dressing, 323-24
  stuffed eggs, 16
  toast, 360-61
  tomato salad, 291
  vanilla sauce, 472
Frijoles fritos, 162
Frijoles mexicanos, 162
Frijoles refritos, 162
Fritters
  corn, 204
  -cheese, 204
  grits and Gruyère, 55
  vegetable, 140
  vegetable batter, 357
Frostings. *See* Cakes, frostings
Fruit(s)
  as basic food group, 718
  Bavarian cream, 458
  blancmange, 448
  brioche loaves, 389
  butter, 675
  cake
    individual, 559
    light, 555
    royal wedding, 556-58
    cake filling, 573
    candied nut cake with, 546
  candy
    divinity, 634
    frosted, 633
    jellies, 640
    -nut bars, 644
    stuffed, 633
  canned, 425
  canning guide for, 692-95
  chart, 412-25
  compote, 427-28
  cookies
    bars, 624
    drops, 583
    four-fruit balls, 624
    and nut bars, 624
  coring, 409-10
  cream cake filling, 572
  cup, 410-11
  dessert soufflé, 446, 456
  desserts, 408-37
  dried, 425-26
  fools, 411
  freezing guide for, 704-6, 710-11
  frozen, 426
  glazed, 648

granité, 461-62
  -herbed bread stuffing, 121
  ice, 461
  ice cream, 465
  juice, canning, 693
  kebabs, 411
  lettuce stuffed with, 294
  macédoine of, 411
  marshmallow cream sauce with, 474
  mayonnaise, 329
  meringue kisses, 593
  Neapolitan-style cream cake filling, 567
  -nut conserve, 668
  omelets filled with, 12
  peeling, 409-10
  pickled, 660
  pie, 502-3
    deep dish, 501
    tapioca, 503
  poached, 424
  pudding, 442, 447
  purée, 411
    canning, 693
    freezing, 705
  relish, 668, 669
  and rennet custard, 442
  salad
    combinations, 290
    five fruit, 311
    frozen, 320-21
  salad dressing
    cooked, 330
    with cream cheese, 327
    low-calorie, 327-28
    with sour cream, 326
  seeding, 409-10
  7-minute frosting with, 567
  sherbet, 462-63
  sour cream cake with, 559
  squash glazed with, 275
  stuffing for fish, 124
  turnovers, 502
  Viennese-style flan, 520-21
  whip, 445
  whipped cream with, 479
  whipped cream frosting with, 566
Fudge
  -almond, 643
  best chocolate, 634
  blond, 635
  -cocoa, 643
  coconut, 635, 643
  frosting, 569-70
    caramel, 569, 570
    vanilla, 569
  maple, 643
  mocha cake, 543
  nuggets, 626
  peanut butter, 643
  snow-capped balls, 633
  Toll House, 635
  uncooked, 643

INDEX

G

Game
  blood as a thickener, 75
  freezing, 711
  marinade for, 109
  wild rice for, 48
Game birds
  freezing, 711
  marinade for, 108-9
Garbanzos, boiled, 158
Garlic
  bread, 357-58
  bread crumbs, 359
  butter, 101
  cocktail almonds with, 648
  croutons, 360
  French dressing, 323
  general data on, 230
  -herb salad dressing, 324-25
  noodles with, 60
  rice, 39
  -Roquefort salad dressing, 326-27
  for sandwiches, 392
  sauce, 91
  toast, 358
  vinegar, 322-23
Gelatin, 311-13
  desserts, 453-58
Genoese-style spaghetti with basil sauce, 63
Génoise, 551-52
German-style
  date squares, 622
  peppernuts, 604
  potato salad, 299-300
Giblets
  gravy, 84
  stuffing, 121
Ginger
  figs with, 432
  Grandmother's soft cake with, 548
  honeydew melon with, 428
  ice cream, 465
  jam sauce with, 476
  Japanese-style rice with toasted seaweed and, 45
  lime marmalade with, 680
  old-fashioned cookie biscuits, 590
  -orange California-style barbecue sauce, 108
  orange fluff with, 455
  parsnips with, 236
  pear and pineapple preserves with, 681
  pickled pears with, 661
  pudding, steamed, 452
Ginger snaps
  Christmas, 604-5
  crumb piecrust, 496
Gingerbread, 548
  boys, 600-1
  upside-down cake, 549
Glacé, 570-71
Glace de viande, 90

Glaze(glazed)
  banana, 431
  brown sugar, for apples, 430
  caramel, parsnips in, 236
  currant, parsnips in, 236
  fruit, 648
    for squash, 275
  lemon
    for carrots, 183
    frosting, 571
    for new potatoes, 256
  nectarines, 431
  nuts, 648
  onions, 231
  orange
    for beets, 167
    frosting, 571
    for parsnips, 236
  peaches, 431
  pears, 431
  for turnips, 282
Gnocchi
  cheese, 52
  farina parmigiana, 53
  potato, 52
Goose
  eggs, 2
  marinades for, 108-9
Gooseberry
  jam, 674
  jelly, 670-74
Graham cracker piecrust, 496
Grand Marnier
  dessert soufflé, 446
  strawberries with, 429
Grand Veneur sauce, 86-87
Granité, 461-62
Grape(s)
  beets with, 168
  butter, 675
  canning, 693
  freezing, 705
  green, and sour cream, 428
  jam, 674
  jelly, 670-74, 678-79
  Waldorf salad with, 310-11
  -wild rice stuffing, 117
Grapefruit
  broiled, 432
  freezing, 705
  marmalade, 680
  and pineapple mold, 318
  salad with avocado, 310
Grasshopper pie, 514
Gravy, 84-85
  for barbecue beef, 107
  chicken, 84
  freezing, 713
  giblet, 84
  glace de viande, 90
  herb, 84-85
  au jus, 84
  jus lié, 85

milk, 85
mushroom, 85
quick, 85
onion, 85
pan, 84
sour cream, 85
turkey, 84
wine, 85
Great Northern beans
  boiled, 157-58
  general data on, 151
Greek-style
  chick-peas and tomatoes, 165
  marinade for salads, 323
  omelet, shepherd's, 14
  vegetables, 140-41
  wheat and walnut bars, 621-22
Green bean(s)
  amandine, 153
  with bacon and dill, 153
  boiled, 152
  canning, 696
  cold, 153
  with dill, 656
  freezing, 707
  general data on, 150
  au gratin, 154
  low-calorie, 153
  lyonnaise, 154
  macédoine of vegetables
    cold, 184
    hot, 184
  with mushrooms, 153
  in mustard sauce, 153
  with oil and vinegar, 153
  with onions in sour cream, 153
  Oriental-style, with water chestnuts, 155
  Pompeii-style, 154-55
  Provençal-style, 154
  salad, 301
  succotash, 202
  sweet-sour, 153
Green Goddess dressing, 331-32
Green onions, 230
Green pepper(s), 242-45
  and bread stuffing, with ham, 115
  carrots with celery and,
    Cantonese-style, 185-86
  celery stir-fried with scallions and, 195
  and corn pancakes, 352
  -corn stuffing, 121
  eggplant with tomatoes and,
    Basque-style, 209
  Florida-style black beans with, 165-66
  freezing, 709
  general data on, 242-43
  Italian-style, with onions, 244
  marinated roasted, 244
  mushrooms with onions and, 226
  relish, 665
  sandwiches with potatoes, 399-400
  sautéed, 243-44
  stuffed, 243
  with macaroni marinara, 243
  with Spanish-style rice, 243
  with Spanish-style rice and meat, 243
  sweet-sour
    sauce, with pineapple, 110-11
  in Swiss cheese sauce, 244-45
  -tomato stuffing for fish, 123
Green sauce, 97
Grenache mayonnaise, 94
Gribiche sauce, 97
Grits, 35
  with Gruyère cheese
    appetizers, 55
    fritters, 55
  with Smithfield ham patties, 55-56
Groats, 35
Gruyère cheese
  grits with
    appetizers, 55
    fritters, 55
Gumbo
  corn, 203
  vegetable, 228-29

H

Ham
  asparagus and, Divan, 149
  aspic, 314
  Belgian endive with
    and cheese, 214
  -bread and pepper stuffing, 115
  -corn bread and olive stuffing, 118
  lentils and, 222
  omelets
    with mushrooms and tomatoes, 13
    and tomato frittata, 14-15
  patties, with grits, 55-56
  pisto with, 211
  salad, 307
    with cheese, 307
    with chicken, 305
    jellied, 317
  sandwiches
    and cheese, 397
    and cheese crescents, 406-7
    and chicken, 398
    and egg, 397
  scalloped potatoes with, 252
  with turkey
    sandwiches, 398
  and veal
    forcemeat, 122
  waffles, 354
  wild rice with, 48
Hamburger relish, 666
Hard sauce, 478
Hawaiian-style
  chicken sandwiches, 404
Hazelnut(s)
  kisses, 593
  mushroom caps baked with, 226
  torte, 547

INDEX

Hearts of palm, 217
  braised in white wine, 217
  in cream cheese sauce, 217–18
  general data on, 217
  marinated, 295–96
  sautéed, 218
Herbs (herbed)
  biscuits, 340
  bread
    cheese, 374
    crumbs, 359–60
    garlic, 357
    sticks, 376
    stuffing, 120–21
  butter, 101
  cheese
    soufflé, 30
  corn in cream with, 201–2
  croutons, 360
  egg salad with, 307
  fines sauce, 88
  freezing, 714
  gravy, 84–85
  mayonnaise, 95
  noodles with, 60
  omelets with, 13
  potatoes with
    new, 256
    salad, 299
  rice, 39
  salad dressing, 324
    -garlic, 324–25
    for salads, 287–88
  salsify with, 264
  sauce, 91
    -sour cream, 98
    -yogurt, 99
  spaghetti with, 65
  toast, 358
  tuna salad with, 308
  for vegetables, 130–35
  vinegar, 323
  wild rice with, 48
Hermits, 583
Heroes, 401
Herring
  Scandinavian-style salad, 308
Hilda's Yorkshire scones, 342
Hollandaise sauce, 91–92
  blender, 93
  mock, 95
  with mustard, 92
  -sour cream, 98–99
Hominy, 35
  with beans and salt pork, 55
  casserole, 54–55
  -green bean succotash, 202
  scrambled with bacon and eggs, 55
Honey
  figs with, 432
  fondant, 633
  grapefruit broiled with, 432

  sauce, 478
  toast, 358
Honeydew melon with ginger, 428
Hopping John, 164
Hors d'oeuvre. *See* Appetizers; names of hors d'oeuvre
Horseradish
  beets with, 167
  butter, 101
  fresh, 670
  mustard, 669
  for sandwiches, 392
  sauce
    -caper, 78
    -cream, 96
    hot, 78–79
    -sour cream, 99
    whipped, 96
    -yogurt, 99
Huevos rancheros, 9
Hungarian-style noodles, 60
Hushpuppies, 346

I

Ice cream, 463–67
  almond, 464
  apricot, 463
  baked Alaska, 468
  banana, 463
    -orange, 466
  berry, 463
  biscuit tortoni, 467
  chocolate, 464
    dark, 466
  coffee, 464, 465, 466–67
  eggnog, 464
  freezer, 464–67
  freezing, 460–61
  French-style, 465
  fruit, 465
  ginger, 465
  mocha, 465
  orange, 463–64
    -banana, 466
  peach, 463
  pecan, 464
  peppermint, 464
  pie shell, 498
  pineapple, 463
  pistachio, 464
  profiteroles, 527
  refrigerator, 463–64
  rum-raisin, 464
  spumoni, 467
  strawberry parfait pie, 519
  tutti-frutti, 466
  vanilla, 464–65
Ices
  freezing, 460–61
  fruit, 461
  wine, 461
Imam Bayildi, 213

INDEX

Indian pudding, 450
Indian-style
  rice pilaf, 41
  sauce, 80–81
Iodine, 720
Iranian-style rice, baked, 46
Irish-style
  soda bread, 341–42
Iron, 720
Italian-style
  artichoke hearts, marinated, 145
  Christmas bread, 384
  croutons, 360
  macaroni, pimiento, and cheese loaf, 62
  peppers and onions, 244
  sauce, 88
    cheese, 82
    tomato, 104
    tomato, with mushrooms and eggplant, 104
  sausage
    polenta baked with, 54
  spinach, 266
  tomato salad, 291
  zucchini, 270
Izmir-style eggplant, 209–10

J

Jam
  apricot, 674
  berry, 679
  blackberry, 674
  blueberry, 674
  cherry, 674
  general data on, 674
  ginger sauce with, 476
  gooseberry, 674
  grape, 674
  omelets filled with, 12
  peach, 674
  pear, 674
  plum, 674
  pudding, steamed, 452
  raspberry, 674
  rhubarb, 674
  sauce, 476
  strawberry, 674
  strudel, 523
  tips for making, 676–77
  turnovers, 502
Jamaican-style
  rice, 44–45
  rum cake, 555–56
Jambalaya, 43–44
Japanese-style
  ginger rice with toasted seaweed, 45
  steak sauce, 111
  vegetable salad with sesame seeds, 294
Jellied
  meat salad, 317
  shellfish salad, 317–18
  tongue salad, 317
  turkey salad, 317
  vegetable salad, 316
Jelly, 670–74
  apple, 670–74, 677–78
    with mint, 678
    spiced, 678
  blackberry, 670–74
  with commercial pectins, 673
  crab apple, 670–74
    with mint, 678
    spiced, 678
  cranberry, 670–74
  cream cheese sandwiches with, 399
  currant, 670–74
  doughnuts, 390
  gooseberry, 670–74
  grape, 670–74, 678–79
  juice extraction table, 671
  omelets filled with, 12
  peanut butter sandwiches with, 399
  port wine, 454
  problems, 673–74
  quince, 670–74, 678
  raspberry, 670–74
  rose geranium, 678
  runny, rescuing, 673
  sand tart cutouts, 599–600
  sauce, 476
  tips for making, 676–77
  wine, 679
Jelly rolls, 552–53
Johnnycake, 344
Joinville sauce, 81
Jonnycakes, Rhode Island-style, 344–45
Juniper berry(ies)
  sauerkraut braised with, 181
Jus lié, 85

K

Kale, 218–19
  boiled, 218–19
  with cabbage, 219
  freezing, 708
  general data on, 218
  low-calorie, 219
Karydata, 621–22
Kasha, 35
  buckwheat, 50
  bulgur, 50
    with apples and almonds, 50–51
    with mushrooms, 51
  chick-peas and, 165
  croquettes, 47
  with walnuts, 51
Kentucky Colonels, 642–43
Ketchup, 661–62
  cranberry, 662
Key lime pie, 507
Khichiri, 45–46
Kidneys
  lamb
    -rice stuffing, 116

INDEX

Kohlrabi, 219-20
Kolache, 381-82
Kosher dill pickles, 654
Kourabiedes, 609-10
Kugelhupf, 382
Kumquat marmalade, 680

L

Lady Baltimore cake, 539
Ladyfingers, 595
Lamb-kidney rice stuffing, 116
Lasagne, 68
  homemade pasta dough, 58-59
  meat ball, 69
Lebkuchen, 606
Leek(s), 220-21
  pie, 221
  zucchini pudding-soufflé with, 272-73
Leftovers
  egg yolks and whites, 4
  freezing, 712
  pasta, 58
  potatoes, 248-49
    casserole, 248
    creamed, 249
    croquettes, 249
    cups, 248-49
    au gratin, 249
    -onion pie, 249
    patties, 249
  rice, 38
  stuffing, 114
  truffles, 280
Lemon
  -avocado aspic, 314-15
  -avocado mold, 315
  biscuits, 340
  blancmange, 447-48
  -bread stuffing for fish, 123
  butter, 101
  butter cream frosting with, 565
  cake
    chiffon, 554
    spice, 548
    sponge, 550
    sweet loaf, 538
  cake filling, 573
  cheese, 681-82
  cookies
    sponge squares, 619-20
    sugar, 599
    wafers, 583
  cream cheese frosting with, 566
  cupcakes, 558
  curd, 681-82
  custard, 439
    rennet, 442
  dessert soufflé, 456
  doughnuts, 350
  fluff, 454-55
  glaze
    for carrots, 183

  frosting, 571
  for new potatoes, 256
  granité, 461-62
  ice, 461
  jelly rolls, 553
  -lime salad dressing, 325
  marmalade, 680
  pie
    angel, 517-18
    chess, 515
    chiffon, 512
    meringue, 506-7
  rice pudding, 449
  for sandwiches, 392
  sauce, 83, 475
    -caper, quick, 95
    -eggnog, 472
    hard, 478
    -orange, beets in, 168
    -raisin, 475-76
    -7-minute frosting with, 567
  sherbet, 462
  whipped cream with, 479
  white mountain frosting with, 568
Lentil(s), 221-23
  boiled, 222
  dhal, 222
  East Indian-style rice with, 45-46
  general data on, 221
  with ham, 222
  red, with rice, 222-23
  savory, 222
Lettuce, 223
  butter-braised, 223-24
  general data on, 223, 285-86
  with onions and capers, 223
  relish with radishes and zucchini, 669
  salad, 293-94
  sandwiches, 397, 399
  types of, 285-86
Lichees in port wine, 429
Licorice lollipops, 641
Lima beans
  with bacon and sour cream, 156
  boiled, 155, 158
  canning, 697
  with carrots and bacon, 156
  with cheese, 154, 156
  cold, 156
  with dill, 156
  dried, savory with wine, 161-62
  general data on, 150, 151
  with parsley and paprika, 156
  with pecans, 156
  succotash, 156-57
Lime
  -avocado mousse, 315
  cake filling, 573
  granité, 461-62
  ice, 461
  -lemon
    salad dressing, 325
    marmalade with ginger, 680

INDEX

pie
  angel, 518
  chiffon, 512
  Key, 507
  meringue, 507
  sauce, 475
  sherbet, 462
Linguine alla romana, 66
Linzertorte, Trudy's Viennese-style, 521–22
Liqueurs
  marshmallow cream sauce with, 474
  omelets filled with, 12
Liquor
  omelets filled with, 12
Liver
  calf's
    risotto with, 42–43
  chicken
    chopped, sandwiches, 398
    -mushroom stuffing, 121
    -rice stuffing, 116
    risotto with, 42
    wild rice casserole with sausage and, 49–50
Lobster
  butter, 101
  freezing, 714
  sauce, 81
Lollipops, 641
Lorette potatoes, 255
Louisiana-style
  rice and red kidney beans, 44
  shellfish salad, 309
Lyonnaise-style
  artichoke bottoms, 143
  fried tomatoes, 277
  green beans, 154
  noodles, 60
  omelets, 13
  potatoes, 250
  sauce, 88–89
  wax beans, 154

M

Macaroni, 61–62
  and cheese, 61–62
  fisherman's bake shells, 62
  peppers stuffed with, marinara, 243
  salad, 303
Macaroons, 591–92
Madeira wine
  sauce, 89
    with mushrooms, 85, 226
Madeleines, 595–96
Maître d'hôtel butter, 101
Maize. See Corn
Malt vinegar, 322
Maltese sauce, 92
Mango
  chutney, 663
Manicotti, 69
  baked meatless, 70–71
  chicken and mushroom stuffed, 71
  homemade pasta dough, 59
Maple
  -butter cream frosting, 565
  chiffon cake with butterscotch, 554–55
  custard, 440
  fudge, 643
  mashed sweet potatoes, 258
  penuche, 635
  toast, 358
  white mountain frosting, 568
Marchands de vin butter, 102
Marchands de vin sauce, 88
Marguerites, 602
  quick, 579
Marinara sauce, 104
  -anchovy, 104–5
  -mushroom, 104
  peppers stuffed with macaroni in, 243
Marinière sauce, 80
Marmalade
  calamondin, 680
  general data on, 674
  grapefruit, 680
  kumquat, 680
  lemon, 680
  lime, with ginger, 680
  orange, 679–80
    bitter, 680
  pudding, steamed, 452
  sauce, 476
  toast, 358
Marrons. See Chestnuts
Marrowfat beans
  boiled, 158
  general data on, 151
Marshmallow(s)
  chocolate sauce with, 473
  -cream sauce, 473–74
  frozen pineapple salad with, 321
  7-minute frosting with, 568
  sweet potato puff with, 259
  Waldorf salad with dates and, 310
  white mountain frosting with, 568
Marzipan, 643–44
Masa harina, 35
Maude's cookies, 587
Mayonnaise, 328–29
  anchovy, 94
  Andalusian-style, 94
  applesauce, 94
  avocado, 94
  blender, 328
  buttermilk, 94
  caviar, 94
  Chantilly, 329
  chutney, 94
  cranberry, 94
  curry, 329
  dill, 94
  French-style, 94
  fruit, 329
  green, 332

INDEX

grenache, 94–95
herb, 95
homemade, 328
mint, 95
mustard, 95
Niçoise, 329
perfection, 95
pimiento and olive, 95
rémoulade, 329
Russian-style, 329
for sandwiches, 392
sauce, 94–96
verte, 328
shellfish cocktail, 95
thin, 329
tuna, 95
watercress, 95
Meat
as a basic food group, 717–18
freezing, 711, 712
See also Beef; Lamb; Pork; Veal
Meat balls
beef
spaghetti and, in tomato sauce, 63
lasagne, 69
Meat loaf
sandwiches, 397
Melba sauce, 477
Melba toast, 358
Melon(s)
freezing, 705
granité, 462
Meringue, 498–500
basic, 498–99
Chantilly, 500
glacées, 500
kisses, 592–93
nut bars, 620–21
pie shell, 499
poached ring, 469
rules for making, 498
star shells, 500
Mexican-style
deviled eggs, 18
dried beans, 162
fried beans, 162
wedding cakes, 609
Middle East-style rice pilaf, 41
Milk
coconut, 646–47
freezing, 715
gravy, 85
toast, 361
Milkweed, 283
Millet, 35
Mincemeat, 663–64
pie, brandied, 506
stuffing, 121
Mint
apple jelly with, 678
-basil salad dressing, 324
crab apple jelly with, 678
mayonnaise, 95

peas with, 238
pineapple fans in Cointreau with, 428
rice with, 39
sauce, 77, 111–12
Mints
Mrs. B's pulled, 639–40
thin, 633
Mocha
Bavarian cream, 458
brownies, 617
butter cream frosting with, 564–65
cake, 542
chiffon, 555
fudge, 543
sponge, 550
custard, 440
hard sauce, 478
ice cream, 465
pie
angel, 518
Bavarian-style, 513
pudding, 447
sauce, 473
whipped cream with, 479
Molasses
cookies
cream-filled, 603
icebox, 614
pressed spice, 612
custard, 440
popcorn balls, 649
taffy, 639
walnut candy with, 638
Mole sauce, 105
Mont Blanc aux marrons, 470
Monte Carlo sandwiches, 406
Monte Cristo sandwiches, 405–6
cocktail, 406
Montrose drop cakes, 591
Moravian-style Christmas cookies, 601–2
Mornay sauce, 79
Mousse
avocado, 315–16
chocolate, 444–45
lime-avocado, 315
raspberry, molded, 455
strawberry, molded, 455
Mousseline sauce, 92
Mozzarella cheese
breaded, fried, 32–33
in carrozza, 406
Mrs. Bouldin's date-nut fingers, 626
Mrs. B's pulled mints, 639–40
Muffins, 336–38, 344
Mung beans, 152
Mürbteig pastry, 493
Mushroom(s), 224–26
barley casserole with, 51
-bread and sage stuffing, 115
broiled, 225
buckwheat kasha with, 50
bulgur kasha with, 51
butter, 102

754   INDEX

caps baked with hazelnuts, 226
celery stir-fried with, 195
-chestnut stuffing, 119
chicken with
  -liver stuffing, 121
  creamed, 225-26
eggplant stuffed with chick-peas and, 213
general data on, 224
gravy, 85
  quick, 85
green beans with, 153
Italian-style tomato sauce with eggplant and, 104
low-calorie, 225
in Madeira sauce, 226
manicotti stuffed with chicken and, 71
omelets with ham and tomatoes, 13
  with onions and green peppers, 226
pickled, 658
ravioli, 68
rice, 39
  stuffing, 117
risotto with, 42
turnips stuffed with, 283
salad, raw, 296
sandwiches, 400
sauce, 77
  with beef and sausage, 105-6
  -cheese, 77
  -Madeira, 85, 226
  -marinara, 104
  quick, 77
  stuffed eggs in, 16
  -sausage stuffing, 121
sautéed, 224
skillet, 225
spaghetti with butter, cream and Parmesan cheese, 65
spinach baked with, 267
stuffing for fish, 124
wild rice with bacon and, 48
-wild rice stuffing, 117
Mustard
  butter, 102
  egg salad with, 307
  homemade, 669-70
  hot fruit relish, 669
  mayonnaise, 95, 329
  pickles, 654-55
  salad dressing, 330-31
  for sandwiches, 392
  sauce, 77
    broccoli baked in, 172
    -hollandaise, 92
    green beans in, 153
    hot, 77
    hot, Chinese-style, 111
    -mayonnaise, 95
    -sour cream, 99
    -yogurt, 99
    wine, 670
Mustard greens, 226-27
  boiled, 199

freezing, 708
general data on, 226-27
low-calorie, 199

N

Nantua sauce, 79
Napoleons, 524-25
Nasturtium salad, 293
Navy beans
  boiled, 157-58
  general data on, 151
Neapolitan-style
  dried beans with Parmesan, 161
  fruit cream cake filling, 567
Nectarines
  baked, glazed, 431
  canning, 694
  flambé, 431
  freezing, 705
Nesselrode pie, 514
Nesselrode sauce, 472
Nettles, 283
New England-style
  baked pumpkin, 261
Niçoise-style
  mayonnaise, 329
  onion tart, 235
  quiche, 31
  salade, 298
Nockerln, 61
Noisette butter, 102
Noodles, 59-60
  Alfredo, 65
  amandine, 60
  with cheese, 60
  creamed, 60
  egg, 58-59
  Florentine-style, 60
  fried, 60
  with garlic, 60
  with herbs, 60
  homemade, 58-59
  Hungarian-style, 60
  Lyonnaise-style, 60
  noisette, 60
  with onions, 60
  Oriental-style, 58
  Polonaise-style, 60
  with poppy seeds, 60
  ring, 59
  sauce for, 60
  savory, 59
  Smetana-style, 60
  spätzle, 60-61
Normandy-style
  sauce, 81
Nut(s), 644-48
  -bran muffins, 338
  butter cream frosting with, 565
  cake, 545-46
  candy
    balls, 633

INDEX 755

bonbons, 633
caramels, 636
  frosted, 633
  -fruit bars, 644
  penuche, 635
chicken sandwiches with curry and, 398
chocolate sauce with, 473
cookies, 613
  balls, 579
  -chocolate thins, 580
  -date fingers, 626
  and fruit bars, 624
  meringue bars, 620–21
  quick, 581
-cranberry bread, 348
cream cheese salad dressing with, 327
-crumb piecrust, 496
cupcakes with raisins and, 558
-currant bread, 347–48
-date bread, 347
dessert soufflé, 446
frozen fruit salad with, 321
fruit conserve, 668
fruit whip with, 445
general data on, 644–45
glazed, 648
honey sauce with, 478
jam sauce with, 476
meringue kisses with, 593
meringue pie shells with, 499
muffins, 337
omelets filled with, 12
-orange
  bread, 348
  cake with dates, 546
  syrup, 475
pancakes, 351
pastry, 489
-poppy seed kolache, 382
-raisin bread, 347
rice, 39
7-minute frosting with, 567
sponge cake, 550
sugar cookies with, 599
sugared, 647–48
toasted, piecrust, 497
turkey sandwiches with curry and, 398
waffles, 354
whipped cream with, 479
whipped cream frosting with, 566
See also names of nuts

O

Oatmeal
  bread, 373
  cookies
    -apple bars, 623
    -date bars, 623
    dropped chippies, 590
    -fig bars, 623
    icebox, 615
    -prune bars, 623
  quick, 582
  sugarless drops, 590–91
Oats, 35
O'Brien potatoes, 250
Oeufs à la neige, 441
Oeufs en cocottes, 7
Oil(s)
  general data on, 321–22, 718–19
  and vinegar, 96–97
Okra, 227–29
  boiled, 227
  freezing, 709
  fried, 227–28
  general data on, 227
  low-calorie, 227
  salad, 296
  vegetable gumbo, 228–29
Olive(s)
  -anchovy sauce, 107
  -bread and onion stuffing, 116
  broccoli sautéed with, Castilian-style, 171
  chicken salad with walnuts and, 305
  -corn bread and ham stuffing, 118
  cream cheese sandwiches with, 402
  egg salad with, 307
  -pimiento mayonnaise, 95
  rice, 39
  Spanish-style rice with saffron and, 43
  tomato aspic with cream cheese and, 313
  tuna salad with, 308
Olive oil
  green beans with vinegar and, 153
  spinach with vinegar and, 267
  wax beans with vinegar and, 153
Omelets, 10–15
  artichoke frittata, 15
  caviar, 13
  dessert, 468
    fillings, 468
  fines herbes, 13
  French-style, 12–13
  general data on, 10
  Greek-style shepherd's, 14
  ham
    with mushrooms and tomatoes, 13
    and tomato frittata, 14–15
  Lorraine, 13
  Lyonnaise-style, 13
  onion frittata, 14
  piperade, 15
  plain, 12–13
  puffed, 13–14
  sandwiches, 399
  savory fillings, 11
  soufflé, 13–14
  Spanish-style, 13
  tips on making, 10–11
Onion(s), 229–35
  baked, 232
  biscuits, 340
  boiled, 231
  -bread and olive stuffing, 116
  and carrot pie, 186

in Cheddar sauce, 233
-cheese bread, 374–75
cheese soufflé with, 30
cheese tart with, 32
creamed, 231
dumplings with sage and, 355
eggs and bacon creamed with, 18
Finnish-style, in sour cream, 235
freezing, 709
French-fried rings, 232
frittata, 14
general data on, 229–30
glazed, 231
gravy, 85
green beans with, in sour cream, 153
lettuce with capers and, 223
low-calorie, 231
mushrooms with green peppers and, 226
noodles with, 60
pan-braised, 231
pancakes, 352
peppers and, Italian-style, 244
pickled, 658
pissaladière, 235
potato pie, 249
and pumpkin casserole, 262
quiche, 31
relish, 668
rice, 38–39
roasted, 232–33
sage dressing, 118–19
for sandwiches, 392
sauce
 Brussels sprouts in, 174–75
 dried beans in, 161
sautéed, 231–32
skillet squash and, 270
skillet turnips and, 282
spinach and sour cream baked with, 267–68
stew, 233
stuffed, 234
tart à la niçoise, 235
tomato sandwiches with, 399
See also Scallions
Opera creams, 633
Orange(s)
 avocado salad with, 310
 biscuits, 340
 blancmange, 448
 broiled, 432–33
 butter, 102
 butter cream frosting with, 565
 cake
  chiffon, 554
  with dates and nuts, 546
  filling for, 573
 candied sweet potatoes with, 258
 cookies
  -almond, 614–15
  -almond balls, 624–25
  -almond lace, 594
  -chocolate jewels, 615

 drops, 587–88
 Scotch-style crisps, 611
 -cranberry relish, 667–68
 cream cheese frosting with, 566
 cupcakes, 558
 cups, spicy mashed squash in, 274
 custard, 439
  rennet, 442
 dessert soufflé, 446, 456
 doughnuts, 350
 eggnog sauce with, 472
 fluff, with ginger, 455
 freezing, 705
 glaze
  for beets, 167
  frosting, 571
  for parsnips, 236
 granité, 462
 ice cream, 463–64
  -banana, 466
 jelly rolls, 553
 low-calorie dessert topping, 480
 marmalade, 679–80
  bitter, 680
 mashed sweet potatoes with, 257–58
 muffins, 337
 -nut
  bread, 348
  cake with dates, 546
  syrup, 475
 pastry, 489, 490
 peas with mint and, 239
 pie
  angel, 518
  chiffon, 512
  meringue, 507
 pudding, steamed, 451
 -raisin toast, 358
 rice, 38
 rice pudding, 449
 sauce, 86, 475
  -cranberry, 112
  -ginger, California-style barbecue, 108
  hard, 478
  -lemon, beets in, 168
  -nut syrup, 475
 7-minute frosting with, 567
 sherbet, 462
 sponge cake, 550
 sugar cookies with, 599
 -sugared nuts, 647–48
 -sweet potato stuffing, 119–20
 whipped cream with, 479
 white mountain frosting with, 568
Oriental-style
 cucumber salad, 298
 green beans with water chestnuts, 155
 noodles, 58
Osaka-style skillet broccoli, 171–72
Ouillade, 160–61
Oyster(s)
 -almond stuffing, 121
 -bread stuffing, 115

INDEX

corn, 204
-corn bread stuffing, 118
freezing, 714
sauce, 81
oyster plant. *See* Salsify

P

Pain ordinaire, 371–72
Palm. *See* Hearts of palm
Palmiers, 524
Paloise sauce, 92
Pancakes, 351–53
  potato, 255
  rice, 47–48, 351
  toppings for, 355
Panettone, 384
Papaya salad, with avocado, 310
Paprika
  butter, 102
  lima beans with parsley and, 156
Parfait, strawberry ice cream pie, 519
Parisienne-style
  artichoke bottoms, 144
  potatoes, 248
Parmesan cheese
  broccoli with, 170, 171
  Brussels sprouts with, 174
  dried bean salad with, 302
  egg sandwiches with, 403
  eggplant with, 212
  farina gnocchi with, 53
  fennel with, 216
  Neapolitan-style dried beans with, 161
  polenta with, 54
  -sour cream salad dressing, 297
  spaghetti with butter and cream, 64–65
  squash with, 275
  stuffed, 271
Parsley (parsleyed)
  butter, 101
  dumplings, 355
  lima beans with paprika and, 156
  potatoes with, 247
  new, 256
  for sandwiches, 392
  sauce, 77
  turnips with, 281
Parsnip(s), 236–37
  boiled, 236
  cakes, 237
  canning, 698
  carrots mashed with, 184
  freezing, 709
  fried, 237
  general data on, 235–36
  gingery, 236
  glazed, 236
  mashed, 236
  roasted, 237
Pasta, 56–71
  amount needed, 57
  general data on, 56
  homemade dough, 58–59
  how to eat, 58
  kinds of, 56–57
  leftovers, 58
  sauces for, 103–7
  verde, 59
  See also names of pasta
Pastrami sandwiches, 397
Pastry, 481–96
  caraway seed, 489, 490
  cheese, 489, 490
  choux, 493
  cream filling for, 572–73
  Danish-style, 382–84
  extra-short, 492
  flaky, 490
  freezing, 713
  hot water, 490–91
  ingredients for, 482
  kinds of, 481–82
  mixing, 481–82
  Mürbteig, 493
  nut, 489
  oil, 491
  orange, 489, 490
  patty shells, 495–96
  poppy seed, 489, 490
  puff, 493–95
  sesame seed, 489, 490
  sour cream, 491–92
  spicy, 489, 490
  terms and techniques, 482–84
  tips on, 484–88
  torte, 492
Pâté
  -wild rice stuffing, 117
Patty shells, 495–96
  Swedish-style, 350–51
Pea beans
  boiled, 157–58
  general data on, 151
Peach(es)
  baked, glazed, 431
  broiled, 432
  brown Betty, 435
  butter, 675
  canning, 694
  cardinal, 434
  chutney, 663
  cobbler, 435
  coupe champagne, 433
  crisp, 436
  flambé, 431
  freezing, 705
  ice cream, 463
  à l'Impératrice, 450
  imperial mold, 454
  jam, 674
  Melba, 434
  pickled, 659–60
  with brandy, 660–61
  pie, 504–5
    chiffon, 513

-pecan, 505
sour cream, 504–5
streusel, 505
sundae, 518
poached in port wine, 433–34
preserves, 675–76
relish, 666–67, 669
sautéed, 431
upside-down cake, 549
Peanut(s)
brittle, 637–38
candy clusters, 644
popcorn balls, 649
Peanut butter
broiled frosting with, 570
cookies, 608–9, 615
bars, 626
quick, 581
stars, 611
fudge, 643
sandwiches, 399
sauce, broccoli with, 171
Pear(s)
baked
glazed, 431
au gratin, 433
broiled, 432–33
butter, 675
canning, 694
chutney, 663
-cranberry relish, 667–68
flambé, 431
freezing, 705
Hélène, 433
à l'Impératrice, 450
jam, 674
pickled, 660
with brandy, 661
with ginger, 661
pie, streusel, 505
preserves, 675–76
and pineapple, with ginger, 681
relish, 669
vinegar, 322
Waldorf salad with, 311
Peas, 237–42
boiled, 238, 241
à la bonne femme, 240
canning, 699
cold, 238
in cream, 238
and dumplings, 239
farm-style, 240–41
freezing, 709
French-style, 240
general data on, 237–38
macédoine of vegetables
cold, 184
hot, 184
with mint, 238, 239
puréed, 239
with rosemary, 238
with soy sauce, 239–40

See also Black-eyed peas; Snow peas; Split peas
Pecan(s)
-apple stuffing, 120
-apricot bread, 347
-bread stuffing, 115
-bulgur stuffing, 119
candy
brittle, 638
-raisin fondant, 642
-cherry salad, 318–19
cookies
chocolate-filled dreams, 602–3
chocolate wafers, 588
-cinnamon bars, 621
crisps, 587
-cranberry mold, 319
ice cream, 464
lima beans with, 156
pie
-peach, 505
Southern-style, 514–15
-yam soufflé, 259–60
Pennsylvania Dutch-style
cabbage, 177
fried tomatoes, 277
Penuche, 635–36
Pepparkakor, 604–5
Pepper sauce, 86
Peppermint
chocolate sauce with, 473
ice cream, 464
marshmallow cream sauce with, 474
sauce, 478
7-minute frosting with, 567
taffy, 639
Peppers. See Green peppers; Red peppers
Périgourdine sauce, 89
Périgueux sauce, 89
Persimmon(s)
canning, 694
freezing, 706
pudding, 437
Petits fours, 552
Pfeffernüsse, 604
Phosphorous, 720
Piccalilli, 664
Pickles (pickled), 651–64
apples, 660
cinnamon rings, 661
apricots, 660
Aunt Florrie's bread and butter, 654
beets, 657
cantaloupe, 659
crab apples, 660
dill, 653–54, 656
carrots, 656
green beans, 656
green tomato, 656
kosher, 654
sweet, 654
zucchini, 656
egg salad with, 306–7

eggs, 21
equipment, 651
fruits, 659–60
general data on, 650–51
green tomato, 655–56
ice water cucumber, 655
ingredients for, 651–52
mushrooms, 658
mustard, 654–55
onions, 658
peaches, 659–60
  with brandy, 660–61
pears, 660
  with brandy, 661
  with ginger, 661
piccalilli, 664
problems, 653
quince, 660
red cabbage, 657
sauerkraut, 656–57
tips for making, 652–53
watermelon rind, 658–59
Piedmontese-style artichoke bottoms, 143
Pies, 481–519
Alaska, 519
almond, 514
apple, 500–2
  country-style, 500
  deep dish, 500–2
  fried, 502
  general data on, 501
  streusel, 505
apricot, chiffon, 513
bacon and egg, 16–17
banana cream, 509–10
Bavarian-style, 513–14
berry, 503–4
  basic, 503–4
  canned berries, 504
  chiffon, 512–13
  deep dish, 501–2
  Dutch-style, 504
  frozen, 504
Black Bottom, 509
Boston cream, 539
brandy Alexander, 514
brown sugar chess, 515
butterscotch cream, 508
carrot and onion, 186
cheese, 516
chocolate
  angel, 518
  Bavarian-style, 513
  chiffon, 512
  cream, 508–9
cobblers, 434–35
coconut, 511–12
  chiffon, 512
  cream, 508
  custard, 511
coffee chiffon, 512
colonial chess, 515–16
corn, 203–4
  with bacon, 204
  tomato cheese, 279–80
custard, 510–11
freezing, 712, 713
fruit, 502–3
  deep dish, 500–2
  tapioca, 503
grasshopper, 514
leek, 221
lemon
  angel, 517–18
  chess, 515
  chiffon, 512
  meringue, 506–7
lime
  angel, 518
  chiffon, 512
  Key, 507
  meringue, 507
mincemeat, brandied, 506
mocha
  angel, 518
  Bavarian-style, 513
Nesselrode, 514
orange
  angel, 518
  chiffon, 507
  meringue, 507
peach, 504–5
  chiffon, 513
  -pecan, 505
  sour cream, 504–5
  streusel, 505
  sundae, 518
pear streusel, 505
pecan
  -peach, 505
  Southern-style, 514–15
plum streusel, 505
potato
  with onions, 249
  ranch-style, with eggs, 17
pumpkin, 505–6
  chiffon, 513
rhubarb, 504
  -strawberry, 504
rum Bavarian, 513
shoofly, 510
sour cream-raisin, 510
strawberry
  Bavarian-style, 513
  ice cream parfait, 519
  -rhubarb, 504
tips on, 484–88
vanilla
  chiffon, 512
  cream, 507–8
Pilaf
  baked chick-pea, 164–65
  bulgur, 41
  eggplant stuffed with raisins and, 212
  rice, 40–41

Pimiento(es)
butter, 102
-cheese bread, 375
-cheese sandwiches, 402
Italian-style macaroni and cheese loaf with, 62
-olive mayonnaise, 95
Pineapple(s)
broiled, 432–33
butter cream frosting with, 565
cake filling, 573
crisp, 436–37
fans in Cointreau, with mint, 428
flan, 440–41
freezing, 706
ice cream, 463
preserves, 675–76
and pears, with ginger, 681
relish, 668
rice, 38
salad
and apricots, 318
frozen marshmallow and, 321
and grapefruit mold, 318
sauce, 476
sautéed rings, 430–31
sweet-sour sauce, 110–11
topping for cheese cake, 517
upside-down cake, 548–49
Pink beans, 151
Piñon nuts
spaghetti with butter, cream, Parmesan cheese and, 65
Pinto beans
boiled, 157–58
general data on, 151
Piperade sauce, 15
Piquante sauce, 86
Pissaladière, 235
Pistachio nut
divinity, 634
ice cream, 464
syrup, 475
Pisto, 211
Pizza, 375–76
individual English muffin, 376
Plantains, 245
Plum(s)
butter, 675
canning, 694
freezing, 706
jam, 674
pie, streusel, 505
pudding, steamed, 452–53
sauce, 112
Poires Hélène, 433
Poivrade sauce, 86
Pokeweed, 283
Polenta, 53–54
Pompeii-style
green beans, 154–55
wax beans, 154–55

Popcorn
balls, 649
hot buttered, 649
Popovers, 342
Poppy seed
bread sticks, 376
cake, 537
cream cake filling, 572
noodles with, 60
nut cake with, 546
-nut kolache, 382
pastry, 489, 490
rice, 39
strudel, 523
Porcupines, 625
Pork
hominy with beans and, 55
and veal forcemeat, 121–22
See also Bacon; Ham; Sausages
Port wine
jelly, 454
lichees in, 429
peaches poached in, 433–34
sauce, 89
Portuguese-style
filhos, 627
tomato sauce, 103
Potato(es), 245–57
Amish-style stuffing with bread and, 116
Anna, 255–56
baked, 247–50
balls, 247
boiled, 246–47, 249
bread, 369
-bread stuffing Amish-style, 116
canning, 699
carrots mashed with, 183
cottage casserole, 253–54
Dauphine, 254
duchess, 254
farmhouse topping, 253
freezing, 709
French-fried, 251
shoestring, 251
twice-fried, 251
general data on, 245–47
gnocchi, 52
hashed brown, 250
leftovers, 248–49
casserole, 248
creamed, 249
croquettes, 249
cups, 248–49
au gratin, 249
-onion pie, 249
patties, 249
Lorette, 255
Lyonnaise-style, 250
mashed, 247, 249–50
new, 256–57
O'Brien, 250
pancakes, 255
with parsley, 247

INDEX

pie
  with onions, 249
  ranch-style, with eggs, 17
  planked, 254
  puffs
    rolls, 377–78
  pumpkin and, 261
  riced, 247
  roasted, 248
  rösti, 255
  salads, 299–300
  sandwiches with peppers, 399–400
  scalloped, 252–53
  skillet egg breakfast with, 7
  soufflé, 251–52
  -pudding, 253
  See also Sweet potatoes
Poulette sauce, 80
Poultry
  freezing, 711, 712
  marinades for, 108–9
  wild rice for, 48
  See also Chicken; Duck; Goose; Rock Cornish game hens; Turkey
Pound cake, 541
Pralines, 636
  cookie bars, 580
Preserves
  cherry, 675–76
  equipment, 651
  fig, 675–76
  general data on, 650–51, 674
  omelets filled with, 12
  peach, 675–76
  pear, 675–76
    and pineapple, with ginger, 681
  pineapple, 675–76
    and pears, with ginger, 681
  raspberry, 675–76
  strawberry, 675–76
  tips for making, 676–77
Pressure cookers, 684–85, 688–89
Pressure cooking
  vegetables, 127–29
Profiteroles, 526–27
Prosciutto
  ravioli stuffed with chicken and, 68
Proteins, 718
Provençal-style
  braised artichokes, 144–45
  carrots, 185
  cucumbers, 206
  fried tomatoes, 277
  green beans, 154
  ratatouille, 210
  tomato salad, 291–92
  tomato sauce, 103–4
Prune(s)
  -apple-cranberry stuffing, 121
  kolache, 382
  -oatmeal bars, 623

relish, 669
sandwiches, 404
  and walnut bread, 347
Pudding(s)
  blancmange, 447
  bread and butter, 443–44
  caramel, 447
  cauliflower, 189–90
  chocolate, 447
    blancmange, 447–48
    steamed, 451–52
    tapioca, 448
  chocolate chip, 471
  corn, 203
  cottage, 470–71
  date and walnut, 471
  dessert, 437–53
  fruit, 442, 447
  Indian, 450
  mocha, 447
  persimmon, 437
  plum, steamed, 452–53
  potato soufflé, 253
  queen of, 444
  rice, 448–50
  rum-cream rennet, 442
  squash, 271
  starch-thickened, 446–47
  steamed, 450–53
  tapioca, 448
  vanilla, 447
  Yorkshire, 342–43
  zucchini and leek soufflé, 272–73
  See also Custard
Puff pastry, 493–95
Pumpernickel, 373
Pumpkin, 260–62
  baked, 261
  boiled, 260
  canning, 699
  casserole with onions, 262
  coffee cake, 386–87
  cookies, 589
  freezing, 709
  general data on, 260
  au gratin, 261
  mashed, 260–61
  pie, 505–6
    chiffon, 513
  potatoes and, 261
  purée, 261–62
Purslane, 283–84

Q

Quiche, 31–32
  bourbonnaise-style, 31
  clam, 31–32
  corn, 204
  Lorraine, 31
  niçoise, 31
  onion, 31

INDEX

Quince(s)
  butter, 675
  jelly, 670–74, 678
  pickled, 660

R

Radish
  relish with zucchini and lettuce, 669
  salad, 296
Raisin(s)
  -bran muffins, 338
  bread, 368
  -apple stuffing, 115
  -nut, 347–48
  -cinnamon pinwheels, 385
  cookies, 580
    and currants, 623–24
    quick, 581
  cottage pudding, 471
  cupcakes with nuts and, 558
  eggplant stuffed with pilaf and, 212
  jam sauce with, 476
  -lemon sauce, 475
  muffins, 337
  -orange toast, 358
  -pecan fondant, 642
  rice, 38
  rice pudding, 449
  -rum ice cream, 464
  sandwiches with carrots, 400
  sauce, 89, 112
  sherried rice stuffing with almonds and, 116–17
  sour cream pie, 510
  spice cake with, 548
  yam casserole with apples and, 259
Raspberry
  jam, 674
  jelly, 670–74
  -lemon cream sherbet, 463
  mousse, molded, 455
  preserves, 675–76
  sherbet, 463
Ratatouille, 210
Ravigote sauce, 81, 97
Ravioli, 67–68
  homemade pasta dough, 58–59
Red cabbage
  with chestnuts, 179
  Flemish-style, with apples, 179–80
  pickled, 657
  sweet-sour, 179
Red kidney beans
  boiled, 157–58
  general data on, 151
  Louisiana-style rice with, 44
Red peppers, 242–43
  -bread and ham stuffing, 115
  freezing, 709
  general data on, 242–43
  Italian-style, with onions, 244
  relish, 665

  sautéed, 243–44
  stuffed, 243
  with macaroni marinara, 243
  with Spanish-style rice, 243
Réforme sauce, 87
Regency-style sauce, 89
Relish, 664–69
  apricot, 669
  beet, 668–69
  berry, 667
  chow chow, 664–65
  corn, 665–66, 668
  cranberry, 666, 667–68
  fig, 669
  fruit, 667–68, 669
  general data on, 631
  hamburger, 666
  Jerusalem artichoke, 666
  onion, 668
  peach, 666–67, 669
  pear, 669
  pepper, 665
  pineapple, 668
  prune, 669
  radish, zucchini, and lettuce, 669
  ranch, 667
  tips for making, 652–53
Rémoulade dressing, 329
Rennet custard, 442
Rhode Island-style jonnycakes, 344–45
Rhubarb
  canning, 694
  freezing, 706
  jam, 674
  pie, 504
  -strawberry, 504
Rice, 35–50
  amandine, 39
  apricot, 38
  Armenian-style, 41
  Arroz amarillo, 38
  avocado-tomato, 39
  Cajun-style, 44
  caraway seed, 39
  carrots baked with, 186
  with cheese, 40
  chelou, 46
  chili, 39
  Chinese-style
    fried, 45
    fried eggs and, 45
  confetti, 39
  croquettes, 46–47
  currant, 38
  curried, 39
  date, 38
  dressing up, 38–40
  East Indian-style, with lentils, 45–46
  fig, 38
  garlic, 39
  general data on, 35
  green, 39
  herbed, 39

INDEX

Iranian-style, baked, 46
Jamaican-style, 44–45
Jambalaya, 43–44
Japanese-style, with ginger and toasted seaweed, 45
khichiri, 45–46
leftovers, 38
Louisiana-style, with red kidney beans, 44
with mint, 39
mushroom, 39
stuffing, 116–17
nut, 39
olive, 39
onion, 38–39
orange, 38
pancakes, 47–48, 351
pilaf, 40–41
pineapple, 38
poppy seed, 39
pudding, 448–50
raisin, 38
red lentils and, 222–23
ring, 40
risotto, 42–43
turnips stuffed with, 283
saffron, 38
shellfish salad with, 309
salad, 303–4
savory, 39
sour cream, 40
soy, 40
Spanish-style, 43
baked with cheese, 43
with olives and saffron, 43
peppers stuffed with, 243
stuffing, 116–17
toasted, 40
vinegar, 322
See also Wild rice
Ricotta cheese, ravioli stuffed with spinach and, 68
Rigatoni, beef and sausage stuffed, 66–67
Risi e bisi, 42
Risotto, 42–43
turnips stuffed with, 283
Robert sauce, 89
Rock candy, white mountain frosting with, 568
Rock Cornish game hens, marinades for, 108–9
Roebuck sauce, 86
Rolls
buttermilk, 377
hard, 372
kolache, 381–82
no-knead refrigerator, 379
potato puff, 377–78
quick yeast-raised, 379
rich, 376–77
Romaine sauce, 89–90
Roman-style
artichokes stuffed with anchovies, 144
broccoli with anchovies, 170–71
linguine, 66
Roquefort cheese
French dressing, 324
quiche, 31
salad dressing, 326–27
tomato and avocado salad with, 291
Rose geranium jelly, 678
Rose tree cookies, 600
Rosemary
carrots with, 183
eggs with, 19–20
zucchini with, 272–73
Rosettes, 350–51
Rösti, 255
Rouennaise sauce, 87
Rum
baked beans with, 159
balls, 624
Bavarian cream, 458
-citrus peel fondant, 642
-cream rennet custard, 442
flan, 441
hard sauce, 478
Jamaican cake, 555–56
pie, Bavarian-style, 513
pots de crème, 443
-raisin ice cream, 464
sauce, 475
Russian-style
mayonnaise, 329
salad, 298
salad dressing, 331
Rutabaga, 262–63
with bacon and sour cream, 263
boiled, 262
carrots mashed with, 184
cottage-style, 263
freezing, 709
general data on, 262
au gratin, 263
hashed brown, 263
low-calorie, 262
mashed, 262–63
scalloped, with apples, 263
Rye, 35
bread, 372–73
muffins, 338

S

Sachertorte, 543–44
Saffron
apples with, 429–30
cabbage with, 177
dumplings, 356
rice, 38
shellfish salad with, 309
Spanish-style, with olives, 43
Sage
-bread and mushroom stuffing, 115
dumplings with thyme and onion, 355
-onion dressing, 118–19
Ste. Michele scalloped potatoes, 252–53

INDEX

Salad, 285–321
  ambrosia, 311
  asparagus, 300–1
  aspic, 313–15
  avocado
    with Belgian endive, 310
    with grapefruit, 310
    -lemon mold, 315
    -lime mousse, 315
    mousse, 315–16
    with orange, 310
    with papaya, 310
    shellfish with eggs and, 309
    with tomatoes, 310
    with tomatoes, ribbon loaf, 320
    with tomatoes, and Roquefort, 291
  Caesar, 292
  cauliflower, raw, 297
  celery, Victor, 300
  chef's, 304–5
  cherry-pecan mold, 318–19
  chicken, 305
    chow chow, 306
    curried, 309
    with eggs and capers, 305
    with ham, 305
    jellied, 317
    with olives and walnuts, 305
    sandwiches, 398
    with seafood, 305
    with vegetables, 305
    Waldorf, 306
  chick-pea and tomato, 302
  coleslaw
    with caraway seeds, 295
    Carolina-style, with celery seed, 295
    red and green, 295
    sweet-sour, 294–95
  cottage cheese
    and cream cheese mold, 315
    and spinach, 298–99
  crab ravigote, 309–10
  cranberry
    frozen ribbon, 321
    mold, 319
    -pecan mold, 319
  cucumber, 297–98
  dried bean, 302
  egg, 306–7
    sandwiches, 398
  fruit
    combinations, 290
    five fruit, 311
    frozen, 320–21
    garnishes for, 290–91
  gelatin, 311–13
  general data on, 285
  grapefruit
    with avocado, 310
    and pineapple mold, 318
  green bean, 301
  greens, 285–89
    crisping, 286–87
    making tossed salads, 287–89
    washing, 286–87
  ham, 307
    with cheese, 307
    with chicken, 305
    jellied, 317
  hearts of palm, marinated, 295–96
  herbs for, 287–88
  herring, Scandinavian-style, 308
  jellied meat, 317
  lemon-avocado mold, 315
  lettuce, 293–94
  lime-avocado mousse, 315
  macaroni, 303
  molded, 311–13
  mushroom, raw, 296
  nasturtium, 293
  niçoise, 298
  okra, 296
  perfection, 316–17
  pineapple
    and apricots, 318
    frozen marshmallow and, 321
    and grapefruit mold, 318
  potato, 299–300
  radish, 296
  rice, 303, 304
  Russian-style, 298
  seafood
    with chicken, 305–6
    sandwiches, 398
  shellfish, 308–9
    jellied, 318
  shrimp, curried, 309
  soufflé, 317
  spinach, 293, 298–90
  sweet-sour bean sprout, 301–2
  tabbouleh, 304
  three bean, 301
  tomato
    artichokes marinated with, 291
    with avocado, 310
    with avocado, ribbon loaf, 320
    with avocado and Roquefort, 291
    Belgian-style, 291
    and cheese ribbon loaf, 320
    and chicken ribbon loaf, 320
    with chick-peas, 302
    Finlandia, 291
    French-style, 291
    frosted, 291
    Italian-style, 291
    Mediterranean-style, 291
    Provençal-style, 291–92
    stuffed, al pesto, 303–4
  tongue, 307
    jellied, 317
  tuna, 307, 308
  turkey, 305
    chow chow, 306
    curried, 309
    jellied, 317
    sandwiches, 398

vegetable
  with chicken, 305
  combinations, 290
  Japanese-style, with sesame seeds, 294
  jellied, 316
  ribbon, 316
  vinaigrette, 300-1
  Waldorf, 310-11
    with chicken, 306
  winter health, 292
  zucchini, raw, 296
Salad dressings, 321-33
  avocado, 327
  basil-mint, 324
  buttermilk, 325
  -chive, 332-33
  Camembert cream, 327
  caviar, 332
  cooked, 329-30
  cream cheese, 327
  French, 323-24
  fruit
    cooked, 330
    with cream cheese, 327
    low-calorie, 327-28
    with sour cream, 326
  garlic-herb, 324-25
  garlic-Roquefort, 326-27
  Greek-style marinade, 323
  Green Goddess, 332-33
  herb, 324
    -garlic, 324-25
  hot bacon, 293
  lemon-lime, 325
  low-calorie, 326, 331
  mustard, 330-31
  oil, 321-22, 718-19
    and vinegar, 96-97
  rémoulade, 329
  Roquefort, 326-27
  Russian, 331
  shallot, 325
  sour cream, 326
    with Parmesan cheese, 297
  Spanish-style, 324
  sweet-sour, 325
  Thousand Island, 331
  tips on making, 322
  vinaigrette, 323
  vinegar, 322-23
    oil and, 97-98
  watercress, 332
  wine, 325-26
  yogurt, 326
  See also Mayonnaise
Sally Lunn, 370
Salmon
  sandwiches
    with capers, 403
    potted, 405
Salsa fría, 105
Salsify, 263-64
  boiled, 264

creamed, 264
  with dill and sour cream, 264
  general data on, 263-64
  herbed, 264
Salt cod
  fettuccine with, 66
Salt pork
  hominy with beans and, 55
Sand tarts, 599-600
Sandbakelsen, 610
Sandwiches, 391-407
  anchovy for, 392
  apricot, 404
  bacon
    with beans, 397
    with cream cheese, 399
    with lettuce and tomato, 397
    with peanut butter, 399
  baked bean, 400
  bean tacos, 407
  bread for, 391
  butters for, 391-92
  carrot and raisin, 400
  cheese
    with chicken, 398
    with chipped beef, 403
    dreams, 404
    grilled, 399
    with ham, 399
    and ham crescents, 406-7
    -pimiento, 402
    plain, 399
    spread, 399
    tacos, 407
    toasted, 399
    with turkey, 398
  chicken
    with apple, 398
    with avocado, 398
    with cheese, 398
    chopped liver, 398
    curried, with nuts, 398
    with ham, 398
    Hawaiian-style, 404
    salad, 398
    slice, 398
    tacos, 407
  chipped beef with cheese, 403
  chutney for, 392
  club, 400-1
  corned beef, 397
  cream cheese
    with bacon, 399
    with jelly, 399
    with olives, 402
    with watercress, 402-3
  cucumber, 399
  curry for, 392
  cutting, 393-94
  Danish-style, 401-2
  date, 404
  dill for, 392
  Divan, 405

egg, 398–99, 403
fig, 404
freezing, 713
garlic for, 392
garnishes for, 394–96
grilled, 396–97
ham
  and cheese, 397
  and cheese crescents, 406–7
  with chicken, 398
  and egg, 397
heroes, 401
horseradish for, 392
lemon for, 392
lettuce, 397, 399
mayonnaise for, 391–92
meat loaf, 397
Monte Carlo, 406
Monte Cristo, 405–6
  cocktail, 406
mozzarella in carrozza, 406
mushroom, 400
mustard for, 392
omelet, 399
onion for, 392
parsley for, 392
pastrami, 397
peanut butter, 399
pimiento cheese, 402
potato and pepper, 399–400
prune, 404
salmon
  with capers, 403
  potted, 405
sausage
  tacos, 407
seafood, 398
shaping, 393–94
shrimp, 392
submarines, 401
tips for making, 392–93
toasted, 396
tomato
  with bacon and lettuce, 397
  with lettuce, 399
  with onions, 399
tongue with chutney, 403
turkey, 398
watercress for, 392
Western-style, 405
Whitstable spread, 403–4
Sauce, 72–112
aioli, 94
Albuféra, 82
Allemande, 79–80
anchovy, 78
  marinara, 104–5
  olive, 107
  sour cream, 98
aurore, 80
avgolemono, 93
barbecue, 107–8
basil, Genoese-style spaghetti with, 63
batarde, 93
béarnaise, 92
blender, 93
Béchamel, 78–79
beef, 105–6
Bercy, 80
beurre manié, 78
bigarade, 86
bontemps, 80
bordelaise, 87
bourguignonne-style, 87–88
bread, 110
brown, 84–90
butter
  drawn, 100
caper, 78
  -horseradish, 78
  -lemon, 95
  sour cream, 98
  yogurt, 99
Chantilly, 92
charcutière, 88
chasseur, 88
Chateaubriand, 88
chaud-froid, 83–84
Cheddar cheese
  onions in, 233
cheese, 77
  eggs in, 17
  eggs in, stuffed, 16
  Italian-style, 82
  -sour cream, 97–98
chevreuil, 86
chiffon, 77–78
chili, 109
chivry, 80
Choron, 92
clam
  red, 104
  white, 64, 106
cocktail, 109–10
Colbert, 90
cranberry
  orange, 112
  spicy, 112
  whole, 112
cream
  -horseradish, 96
  -wine, cauliflower baked in, 190
cream cheese, hearts of palm in, 217–18
Cumberland, 110
curry, 82–83
demi-glace, 87–90
diable, 86
dijonnaise, 96–97
dill
  for new potatoes, 256–57
  -sour cream, 98
  -yogurt, 99
diplomate, 81
duxelles, 88
egg, 80
eggnog, 472

INDEX

espagnole, 85–87
Figaro, 92
financière, 89
fines herbes, 88
freezing, 76, 713
garlic, 91
general data on, 72
glace de viande, 90
Grand Veneur, 86–87
green, 97
gribiche, 97
half glaze, 87–90
hard, 478
herb, 91
  -sour cream, 98
  -yogurt, 99
hollandaise, 91–92
  blender, 93
  mock, 95
  with mustard, 92
  -sour cream, 98–99
honey, 478
horseradish
  -caper, 78
  -cream, 96
  hot, 78–79
  -sour cream, 99
  whipped, 96
  -yogurt, 99
Indian, 80–81
Italian-style, 88
Japanese-style steak, 111
Joinville, 81
keeping, 75–76
lemon, 83
  -caper, quick, 95
  -orange, beets in, 168
lobster, 81
low-calorie, 99
Lyonnaise-style, 88–89
Madeira, 89
  with mushrooms, 85, 226
Maltese, 92
marchands de vin, 89
marinara, 104
  -anchovy, 104–5
  -mushroom, 104
  peppers stuffed with macaroni in, 243
marinière, 80
mayonnaise, 93–96
  for shellfish, 95
  verte, 328–29
mint, 77, 111–12
mocha, 473
molé, 105
Mornay, 79
mousseline, 92
mushroom, 77
  with beef and sausage, 105–6
  -cheese, 77
  -Madeira, 85, 226
  -marinara, 104
  quick, 77
  stuffed eggs in, 18
mustard, 77
  broccoli baked in, 172
  green beans in, 153
  -hollandaise, 92
  hot, 77
  hot, Chinese-style, 111
  -mayonnaise, 95
  -sour cream, 99
  -yogurt, 99
Nantua, 79
for noodles, 60
Normandy-style, 81
oil and vinegar, 96–97
olive-anchovy, 107
onion
  Brussels sprouts in, 174–75
  dried beans in, 161
orange, 86
  -cranberry, 112
  -ginger, California-style barbecue, 108
  -hard, 478
  -lemon, beets in, 168
  -nut syrup, 475
oyster, 81
paloise, 92
parsley, 77
for pasta, 103–7
peanut butter, broccoli with, 171
pepper, 86
peppermint, 478
périgourdine, 89
périgueux, 89
piquante, 86
plum, 112
poivrade, 86
port wine, 89
poulette, 80
raisin, 89, 112
ravigote, 81, 97
réforme, 87
Regency-style, 89
Robert, 89
roebuck, 86
romaine, 89–90
rouennaise, 87
salsa fría, 105
shallot, 90–91
shrimp, 83
Smitane, 100
soubise, 79
sour cream, 97–99
  -sherry, 99
soy
  Chinese-style celery, stir-fried with sesame seeds, 194–95
  Chinese-style cucumbers in, 206
  peas with, 239–40
  rice with, 40
suprême, 81–82
sweet-sour, 110
Swiss cheese, peppers in, 244–45
Talleyrand, 82

INDEX

tarragon, 90
tartar, 95–96
tempura, 111
teriyaki, 108
terms and techniques, 72–75
  tips on, 75
tomato
  bolognese-style, 104
  Creole-style, 103
  Italian-style, 104
  Italian-style, with mushrooms and eggplant, 104
  Portuguese-style, 103
  Provençal-style, 103–4
  savory beef, 106
  sour cream, 99
  spaghetti and meat balls in, 63
  tortue, 90
  tuna, 106–7
  for vegetables, 130–35
  velouté, 79–82
  Victoria, 87
  Vincent, 95
  white, 76–84
  wine
    broccoli in, 171
    -cream, cauliflower baked in, 190
  yogurt, 99
  Yorkshire, 87
  zingara, 90
  See also dessert sauces
Sauerkraut, 180–81
  braised, with juniper berries, 181
  with caraway seeds, 181
  general data on, 180–81
  pickled, 656–57
  stuffing, 120
Sausages
  -bread stuffing, 116
  -corn bread stuffing, 118
  hominy casserole with, 54–55
  Italian-style
    polenta baked with, 54
  with mushrooms
    stuffing, 121
  pancakes, 352
  ravioli with, 68
  rigatoni stuffed with beef and, 66–67
  sauce with beef, mushrooms and, 105–6
  tacos, 407
  tufoli stuffed with beef and, 66–67
  See also frankfurters
Scallions, 230
  celery stir-fried with green peppers and, 195
  champ, 234
  creamed, 233
  snow peas with, 241
  squash with, 270
Scallops
  freezing, 714
  Scandinavian-style herring salad, 308
Scones, Hilda's Yorkshire, 342

Scotch-style
  orange crisps, 611
  shortbread, 619
  woodcock, 7–8
Seafoam
  divinity, 634
  frosting, 569
Seafood
  aspic, 314
  freezing, 712, 714
  omelets filled with, 11
  salad, with chicken, 305–6
  sandwiches, 398
  See also Fish, shellfish; names of fish and shellfish
Seasonings
  for vegetables, 130–35
Semolina, 35
  boiled, 53
Sesame seed(s)
  bread sticks, 376
  Chinese cabbage sautéed with, 180
  Chinese-style celery, stir-fried with soy sauce, 195
  Japanese-style vegetable salad with, 294
  pastry, 489, 490
  -sour cream sauce, 99
Shallot(s)
  butter, 102
  general data on, 230
  salad dressing, 325
  sauce, 90–91
Shellfish
  cocktail, mayonnaise for, 95
  macaroni salad with, 303
  salad, 308–9
  jellied, 318
  See also names of shellfish
Sherbet
  freezing, 460–61
  fruit, 462–63
  lemon, 462
  lime, 462
  low-calorie, 463
  orange, 463
  raspberry, 463
  strawberry, 463
Sherry (sherried)
  apricot jam sauce with, 476
  grapefruit broiled with, 432
  peach jam sauce with, 476
  -rice stuffing with raisins and almonds, 116–17
  -sour cream sauce, 99
Shoofly pie, 510
Shortbread, Scottish-style, 619
Shortcake
  strawberry, 437
Shrimp
  butter, 102
  salad, 309
  freezing, 714
  marinated, 109

INDEX

salad, curried, 309
sandwiches, 392
sauce, 83
stuffing for fish, 124
Sildesalat, 308
Smitane sauce, 100
Smithfield ham
  patties, grits with, 55–56
Snickerdoodles, 609
Snow peas
  boiled, 241
  Chinese-style, 241
  with scallions, 241
  with water chestnuts, 241
Snowballs, 633
Soda bread, Irish-style, 341–42
Sofrito wax beans, 155
Sorrel, 264
Soubise sauce, 79
Soufflés
  cauliflower, 189
  cheese, 29–30
  dessert, 260, 445–46
    cold, 456–57
    hot, 445–46
  omelets, 13–14
  pancakes, 352
  potato, 251–52
  -pudding, 253
  salad, 317
  vegetable
    basic, 139–40
    chart, 136–37
  yam-pecan, 259–60
  zucchini and leek pudding, 272–73
Soup
  glace de viande, 90
  -sour cream sauce, 99
Sour cream
  beets with
    baked with caraway seeds, 168
    and dill, 167
  braised lettuce with, 223
  broccoli casserole with eggs and, 172
  Brussels sprouts with dill and, 174
  cake, 559
    -fruit, 559
    -nut, 559
  cream cheese frosting with, 566
  cucumbers in, 297
  curds and, 28–29
  custard, 440
  fried tomatoes with, 276
  gravy, 85
  green beans and onions with, 153
  green grapes with, 428
  homemade, 480
  lima beans with bacon and, 156
  onions in, Finnish-style, 235
  pastry, 491–92
  peach pie with, 504–5
    raisin pie, 510
  rice with, 40

rutabaga with bacon and, 263
salad dressing, 326
  with Parmesan cheese, 297
salsify with dill and, 264
sauce, 97–100
  -sherry, 99
spinach and onions baked with, 267–68
Waldorf salad with, 311
wild rice with chives and, 48
sour dough bread, 370–71
South American-style hot barbecue sauce, 108
Southern-style
  black-eyed peas, 164
  fried okra, 227–28
  strawberry shortcake, 437
South-of-the-border bean pot, 163
Soy sauce
  Chinese-style celery, stir-fried with sesame seeds, 195
  Chinese-style cucumbers in, 206
  peas with, 239–40
  rice with, 40
Soybeans, 152
Spaghetti, 63–65
  all'amatriciana, 64
  with butter, cream, and Parmesan cheese, 64–65
  carbonara, 65
  Genoese-style, with basil sauce, 63
  with herbs, 65
  and meat balls, in tomato sauce, 63
  al pesto, 63
  with white clam sauce, 64, 106
Spanish-style
  asparagus, 149–50
  bean pot, 164
  cream, 457
  omelet, 13
  potato salad, 300
  rice, 43
    baked with cheese, 43
    with olives and saffron, 43
    peppers stuffed with, 243
  salad dressing, 324
  shellfish salad, 309
  vegetable stew, 211
Spätzle, 60–61
Spice cake, 547–48
Spice cookies
  pressed molasses, 612
  quick, 581
Spinach, 265–68
  with bacon, 266
  baked, 267
  chopped, 266
  cold, 266
  creamed, 266
  curried, 267
  custard, 268
  freezing, 708
  general data on, 265
  au gratin, 266

Italian-style, 266
low-calorie, 266
with oil and vinegar, 267
puréed, 266
ravioli stuffed with ricotta and, 68
ring, 266–67
salad, 293, 298–99
steamed, 266
Spitzbuben, 604
Split peas
purée, 242
Sponge cake, 530, 549–51
Spoon bread, 345
Spring onions, 230
Springerle, 606
Spritz, 610–11
Spumoni, 467
Squash, 268–75
baked, 274
boiled, 270, 273–74
candied, 274
canning, 699
and carrots, 270
cold, 270
freezing, 709
fruit-glazed, 275
general data on, 268–69
au gratin, 271–72
low-calorie, 270
mashed, 273, 274
with Parmesan cheese, 275
stuffed, 271
pudding, 271
and scallions, 270
scalloped, 270–71
skillet, with onions, 270
summer, 268–69
winter, 269
See also Zucchini
Stew
freezing, 712
onion, 233
ratatouille, 210
vegetable, Spanish-style, 211
white bean, 160
Stock
freezing, 713
See also Broth
Stollen, 384–85
Strawberry(ies)
cake filling, 573–74
freezing, 706
Grand Marnier, 429
jam, 674
jelly roll, 553
lemon cream sherbet, 463
mousse, molded, 455
pie
Bavarian-style, 513
ice cream parfait, 519
-rhubarb, 504
preserves, 675–76
Romanoff, 428–29

sauce, 477
sherbet, 463
shortcake, 437
tart, Swiss-style, 520
topping for cheese cake, 517
Strudel
apple, 522–23
cheese, 523
cherry, 523
jam, 523
poppy seed, 523
Struvor, 626–27
Stuffings, 113–24
apple-pecan, 120
bread, 114–16
for fish, 122–23
with ham and green peppers, 115
herbed, 120, 121
chestnut-mushroom, 119
chicken liver-mushroom, 121
corn bread, 118
-wild rice, with brandy and chestnuts, 117–18
corn-pepper, 121
for fish, 122–24
general data on, 113–14
giblet, 121
leftovers, 114
mincemeat, 121
orange-sweet potato, 119–20
oyster-almond, 121
pecan-bulgur, 119
prune-apple-cranberry, 121
rice, 116–17
sage and onion, 118–19
sauerkraut, 120
sausage-mushroom, 121
tangerine-cracker, 120
wild rice, 117–18
Submarine sandwiches, 401
Succotash
green bean, 202
New England-style, 157
old-fashioned, 202
quick, 156–57
Sugar
-vanilla, 630
Sugar bells, 574
Sugar cookies, 598–99
butterscotch, 599
chocolate, 598
coconut, 599
decorative, 599
lemon, 599
marbles, 598–99
nut, 599
nut rings, 612
orange, 599
pillows, 598
pinwheels, 598
pretzels, 611–12
quick, 581
wreaths, 612

INDEX

Sugarplums, 633
Sultan's eggplant, 211
Suprême sauce, 81–82
Swedish-style
  baked beans, 163–64
  cinnamon rings, 385–86
  cream, 458
  limpa, 373
  patty shells, 350–51
  rosettes, 626–27
  sandbakelsen, 610–11
Sweet potato(es), 257–58
  baked, 258
  boiled, 257
  cakes, 258–59
  canning, 699
  freezing, 709
  general data on, 257–58
  mashed, 257
  -orange stuffing, 119–20
  orange-candied, 258
  puff, 259
  See also Yams
Sweet-sour
  bean sprout salad, 301–2
  coleslaw, 294–95
  green beans, 153
  red cabbage, 179
  salad dressing, 325
  sauce, 110–11
  wax beans, 153
Swiss chard. *See* Chard
Swiss cheese puff, 29
Swiss-style
  apple Charlotte, 435
  Belgian endive, 214–15
  strawberry tarts, 520
Syrup, 474–75

T

Tabbouleh, 304
Tacos, 407
Taffy, 638–39
Talleyrand sauce, 82
Tangerine-cracker stuffing, 120
Tapenade, 96
Tapioca
  fruit pie, 503
  pudding, 448
Tarragon
  butter, 102
  eggs in aspic, 20
  French dressing, 324
  sauce, 90
Tartar sauce, 95, 96
Tarts, 519–20
  almond, 610
  Cheddar cheese and onions, 32
  onion, à la niçoise, 235
  sand, 599–600
  strawberry, Swiss-style, 520
  tips on making, 519–20

Tea, granité, 462
Tempura
  batter, 357
  sauce, 111
Teriyaki
  sauce, 108
Thelma's 1, 2, 3, 4 cake, 541–42
Thermometers
  for candy, 628, 629
Thickeners, 75
Thousand Island dressing, 331
Thyme, dumplings with sage and onion, 355
Tipsy cake, 441–42
Toast, 358
  cups, eggs baked in, 15–16
  French-style, 360–61
  milk, 361
Toffee, old English, 637
Toll House cookies, 587
  brownies, 619
Tomato(es), 275–80
  aspic, 313–14
  -avocado rice, 39
  baked, 277–78
  broiled, 277
  butter, 102–3
  canning, 695
  eggplant and, 209–10
  eggs baked in, 15–16
  freezing, 709
  fried, 276–77
  fried beans with, 162
  general data on, 275–76
  Greek-style chick-peas and, 165
  green
    chutney, 662
    pickles, 655–56
  -green pepper stuffing for fish, 123
  juice, canning, 695
  ketchup, 661–62
  omelets with ham and mushroom, 13
  pie with cheese and corn, 279–80
  rice-stuffed, al pesto, 303–4
  salad
    artichokes marinated with, 291
    with avocado, 310
    with avocado, ribbon loaf, 320
    with avocado, and Roquefort, 291
    Belgian-style, 291
    and cheese ribbon loaf, 320
    and chicken ribbon loaf, 320
    with chick-peas, 302
    Finlandia, 291
    French-style, 291
    frosted, 291
    Italian-style, 291
    Mediterranean-style, 291
    Provençal-style, 291–92
    stuffed, al pesto, 303–4
  sandwiches
    with bacon and lettuce, 397
    with lettuce, 399
    with onion, 399

sauce, 103–5
  bolognese-style, 104
  Creole-style, 103
  Italian-style, 104
  Italian-style, with mushrooms and eggplant, 104
  Portuguese-style, 103
  Provençal-style, 103–4
  red clam, 104
  savory beef, 106
  -sour cream, 99
  spaghetti and meat balls in, 63
  scalloped, 279
  stewed, 279
  Welsh rabbit with, 26–27
Tongue
  aspic, 314
  salad, 307
  jellied, 317
  sandwiches with chutney, 403
Torte
  hazelnut, 547
  pastry, 492
  walnut, 546–47
Tortillas, 346–47
  chili, 347
Tortue sauce, 90
Tostados, 347
Trifle cake, 441–42
Trudy's Viennese-style linzertorte, 521–22
Truffles (truffled), 280
  canned, 280
  general data on, 280
  leftover, 280
  spaghetti with butter, cream, and Parmesan cheese, 65
Tufoli, beef and sausage stuffed, 66
Tuna
  butter, 103
  mayonnaise, 95
  salad, 307, 308
  sauce, 106–7
Turkey
  aspic, 314
  curry sandwiches with nuts, 398
  gravy, 84
  marinade for, 108–9
  salad, 305
    chow chow, 306
    curried, 309
    jellied, 317
  sandwiches, 398
Turkish-style
  cucumber salad, 297–98
  fried beans and carrots, 161
  stuffed eggplant, 213
Turnip(s), 280–83
  boiled, 281–82
  carrots mashed with, 184
  freezing, 709
  general data on, 280–81
  glazed, 282
  au gratin, 282
  low-calorie, 281
  macédoine of vegetables
    cold, 184
    hot, 184
  mashed, 281–82
    with parsley, 281
  roasted, 282
  skillet, with onions, 282
  stuffed with mushroom risotto, 283
Turnip greens, 708
  boiled, 199
  general data on, 280–81
  low-calorie, 199
Turnovers
  apple, 502
  cheese, Ukrainian-style, 33
  fruit, 502
  jam, 502
Tutti-frutti
  frosting glaze, 571
  ice cream, 466

U

Ukrainian-style
  cheese turnovers, 33

V

Vanilla
  Bavarian cream, 457–58
  blancmange, 447–48
  cream cake filling, 572
  dessert soufflé, 456
  fudge frosting with, 569
  ice cream, 464–65
  pie
    chiffon, 512
    cream, 507–8
  pots de crème, 442–43
  pudding, 447
  sauce, 471–72
  sugar, 630
  taffy, 638–39
Vanilla bean
  custard, 438–39
  sauce, 472
Vanilla wafer piecrust, 496
Variety meats. See Liver; Tongue
Veal
  forcemeat, 121–22
  forcemeat balls, 122
Vegetable(s), 125–284
  artichoke bottoms stuffed with, 143
  aspic, 313
  as a basic food group, 718
  canning, 126
    guide, 692–99
  chicken with
    salad, 305

INDEX

corn boiled with, 201
cucumbers stuffed with, 206
à la dijonnaise, 141
freezing, 707–9
fritters, 140
  batter, 357
frozen, 126
general data on, 125
à la grecque, 141
gumbo, 228–29
leftovers, 126
macédoine of
  cold, 184
  hot, 184
omelets filled with, 11
pressure cooking, 127–29
purée of, au gratin, 158
salad
  with chicken, 305
  combinations, 290
  Japanese-style, with sesame seeds, 294
  jelled, 316
  ribbon, 316
  vinaigrette, 300–1
sauces for, 130–35
seasonings for, 130–35
soufflé
  basic, 139–40
  chart, 136–37
stew, Spanish-style, 211
stewed barley with, 51
storing, 126
stuffing for fish, 123
tips on, 125–26
toasted rice casserole and, 40
tomatoes stewed with, 279
See also names of vegetables
Velouté sauce, 79–82
Venetian-style carrots in cream, 184–85
Victoria sauce, 87
Viennese-style
  fruit flan, 520–21
  Trudy's linzertorte, 521–22
Vinaigrette, 323
  vegetables, 300–1
Vincent sauce, 95
Vinegar, 322–23
  green beans with olive oil and, 153
  oil and, 96–97
  spinach with olive oil and, 267
  wax beans with olive oil and, 153
Vitamins, 719–20
Vol-au-vent, 495

W

Waffles, 353–54
Waldorf salad, 310–11
  with chicken, 306
Walnut(s)
  candy, 638
  chicken salad with olives and, 305
  -coconut bars, 624

-cranberry relish, 668
-date pudding, 471
kasha with, 51
-prune bread, 347
-torte, 546–47
-wheat bars, 621–22
Water, 720
Water chestnut(s)
  -bread stuffing, 115
  Oriental-style green beans with, 155
Watercress
  butter, 103
  buttered, 224
  cream cheese sandwiches with, 402–3
  mayonnaise, 95
  salad dressing, 332
  for sandwiches, 392
Watermelon rind pickles, 658–59
Wax beans
  amandine, 153
  with bacon and dill, 153
  boiled, 152
  canning, 696
  cold, 153
  freezing, 707
  general data on, 150–51
  au gratin, 154
  low-calorie, 153
  Lyonnaise-style, 154
  macédoine of vegetables
    cold, 184
    hot, 184
  with mushrooms, 153
  with oil and vinegar, 153
  Pompeii-style, 154–55
  sofrito, 155
  sweet-sour, 153
Weight charts, 724
Welsh rabbit, 26
  tomato, 26–27
Western-style sandwiches, 405
Wheat, 35–36
  -walnut bars, 621–22
Whipped cream, 479–80
  frosting, 566–67
White sauce, 76–84
Whitstable sandwich spread, 403–4
Whole wheat
  bread, 372
  muffins, 337
  pancakes, 351–52
Wild rice, 48–50
  amandine, 49
  basic boiled, 48
  brandied, 49
  cakes, 49
  casserole with chicken livers and sausage, 49–50
  for game, 48
  general data on, 35
  with ham, 48
  with herbs, 48
  with mushroms and bacon, 48

for poultry, 48
with sour cream and chives, 48
stuffing, 117–18
Wine(s)
cheese soufflé with, 30
cucumbers braised in chicken broth and, 206
gravy, 85
hearts of palm braised in, 217
ice, 461
jelly, 679
mustard, 670
salad dressing, 325–26
sauce
  broccoli in, 171
  -cream, cauliflower baked in, 190
  savory dried lima beans with, 161–62
vinegar, 322
Woodcock, Scotch, 7–8

Y

Yams, 257–60
baked, 258
boiled, 257–58
carrots mashed with, 183
casserole with apples and raisins, 259
general data on, 257–58
mashed, 257–58
orange-candied, 258
-pecan soufflé, 259–60
See also Sweet potatoes
Yogurt
salad dressing, 326
sauces, 99
Yorkshire pudding, 342–43
Yorkshire sauce, 87

Z

Zabaglione, 442
Zingara sauce, 90
Zucchini
Armenian-style custard, 273
with dill, 656
general data on, 269
Italian-style, 270
and leek pudding-soufflé, 272–73
ratatouille, 210
relish with radishes and lettuce, 669
with rosemary, 272
salad, raw, 296

How to Use This Book

Whenever the name of a recipe is capitalized (Medium White Sauce, for example), the recipe is included elsewhere in the book. Consult Index for page numbers.

How-to information is described in full detail elsewhere in the book; see Index for page numbers. For example, a method or technique ("braise, sauté*") is marked with an asterisk.

Three symbols are used throughout the book to key recipes:

⚖	= Low-Calorie
¢	= Budget
⌛	= Quick and Easy

Whenever specific sizes of pans, casseroles, or molds are given, they are essential to the success of a recipe.

Do not make substitutions unless a recipe specifies alternate ingredients (margarine for butter, for example; oil for shortening; syrup for sugar).

Preheat oven or broiler a full 15 minutes before using.

Use middle oven rack for general baking and roasting; whenever a higher or lower rack position is essential, recipe will so direct.

"Cool" as used in recipes means to bring a hot food to room temperature; "chill" means to refrigerate or place in an ice bath until chilled throughout.

Read each recipe through carefully before beginning it, making sure that all necessary ingredients and utensils are on hand and that instructions are clear.

Recipe yields are given in average-size servings or portions.

Calorie counts for average-size servings are set down in round numbers (130 calories per serving instead of 128.5).

About Ingredients

Unless recipes specify otherwise:
Flour called for is all-purpose flour, sifted before measuring.
Baking powder is double-acting baking powder.
Butter is salted butter.
Sour cream is the commercial type.
Eggs are large eggs.
Brown sugar is measured firmly packed.
Garlic cloves are of medium size.
Herbs and spices are dried.
All measures are standard, all measurements level.

OVEN TEMPERATURES

Below 300° F. = very slow
300° F. = slow
325° F. = moderately slow
350° F. = moderate
375° F. = moderately hot
400-25° F. = hot
450-75° F. = very hot
500° F. or more = extremely hot

FAHRENHEIT/CELSIUS (CENTIGRADE) SCALE

	Boiling Point F.		Boiling Point C.	
(of Water)	212°	–	100°	(of Water)
	200°	–	93.3°	
	190°	–	87.8°	
	180°	–	82.2°	
	170°	–	76.7°	
	160°	–	71.1°	
	150°	–	65.6°	
	140°	–	60°	
	130°	–	54.4°	
	120°	–	48.9°	
	110°	–	43.3°	
	100°	–	37.8°	
	90°	–	32.2°	
	80°	–	26.7°	
	70°	–	21.1°	
	60°	–	15.6°	
Freezing Point (of Water)	50°	–	10°	Freezing Point (of Water)
	40°	–	4.4°	
	32°	–	0°	

Conversion Formula:
Fahrenheit to Celsius (Centigrade):
Subtract 32 from Fahrenheit reading, divide by 1.8.

What It Will Mean to Cook with Metric Measures

The metric system is a way of measuring based on the decimal system with larger measures being subdivided into units of ten. Food researchers and European cooks have always used the metric system because it is more precise than American weights and measures.

In recipes, the principal difference between our present way of measuring and the metric is that dry ingredients like flour and sugar are weighed rather than measured in a cup.

Meats, fruits, and vegetables will be sold by the kilogram instead of the pound and, in recipes, will be called for by weight rather than by cup (whether sliced, diced, or whole).

Small measures — tablespoons, teaspoons, and fractions thereof — are not likely to change.

Liquids are measured in measuring cups, but the calibrations are marked in liters, ½ liters, ¼ liters, and milliliters instead of in cups. (See opposite.) There will be no more such cumbersome measurements as ½ cup plus 1 tablespoon or 1 cup minus 3 teaspoons.

TABLE OF EQUIVALENTS OF U.S. WEIGHTS AND MEASURES

Note: All measures are level.

Pinch or dash = less than 1/8 teaspoon
3 teaspoons = 1 tablespoon
2 tablespoons = 1 fluid ounce
1 jigger = 1½ fluid ounces
4 tablespoons = ¼ cup
5 tablespoons + 1 teaspoon = 1/3 cup
8 tablespoons = ½ cup
10 tablespoons + 2 teaspoons = 2/3 cup
12 tablespoons = ¾ cup
16 tablespoons = 1 cup
1 cup = 8 fluid ounces
2 cups = 1 pint
2 pints = 1 quart
4/5 quart = 25.6 fluid ounces

1 quart = 32 fluid ounces
4 quarts = 1 gallon
2 gallons (dry measure) = 1 peck
4 pecks = 1 bushel

SOME FRACTIONAL MEASURES

½ of ¼ cup = 2 tablespoons
½ of 1/3 cup = 2 tablespoons + 2 teaspoons
½ of ½ cup = ¼ cup
½ of 2/3 cup = 1/3 cup
½ of 3/4 cup = ¼ cup + 2 tablespoons
1/3 of ¼ cup = 1 tablespoon + 1 teaspoon
1/3 of 1/3 cup = 1 tablespoon + 2 1/3 teaspoons
1/3 of ½ cup = 2 tablespoons + 2 teaspoons
1/3 of 2/3 cup = 3 tablespoons + 1 2/3 teaspoons
1/3 of 3/4 cup = ¼ cup

SOME DRY WEIGHTS (Avoirdupois)

4 ounces = ¼ pound
8 ounces = ½ pound
16 ounces = 1 pound

METRIC WEIGHTS AND MEASURES

FLUID MEASURES

10 milliliters = 1 centiliter
10 centiliters = 1 deciliter
10 deciliters = 1 liter
10 liters = 1 decaliter
10 decaliters = 1 hectoliter
10 hectoliters = 1 kiloliter

CUBIC MEASURES

1000 cubic millimeters = 1 cubic centimeter
1000 cubic centimeters = 1 cubic decimeter
1000 cubic decimeters = 1 cubic meter

WEIGHTS

10 milligrams = 1 centigram
10 centigrams = 1 decigram
10 decigrams = 1 gram
10 grams = 1 decagram
10 decagrams = 1 hectogram
10 hectograms = 1 kilogram

LINEAR MEASURES

10 millimeters = 1 centimeter
10 centimeters = 1 decimeter
10 decimeters = 1 meter
10 meters = 1 decameter
10 decameters = 1 hectometer
10 hectometers = 1 kilometer

METRIC EQUIVALENTS OF U.S. WEIGHTS AND MEASURES

WEIGHTS (Avoirdupois)

5 grams = 1 teaspoon (approx.)
28.35 grams = 1 ounce
50 grams = 1¾ ounces
100 grams = 3½ ounces
227 grams = 8 ounces
1000 grams (1 kilogram) = 2 lbs. 3¼ oz.

FLUID MEASURES

1 deciliter = 6 tablespoons + 2 teaspoons
¼ liter = 1 cup + 2¼ teaspoons
½ liter = 1 pint + 4½ teaspoons
1 liter = 1 quart + 3 tablespoons
4 liters = 1 gallon + ¾ cup
10 liters = 2½ gallons + 1 pint

LINEAR MEASURES

2½ centimeters = 1 inch
1 meter (100 centimeters) = 39 1/3 inches

Some Abbreviations Used in European Cookbooks: g. = gram; kg. = kilogram; cm. = centimeter; c. = cuiller (spoon), usually qualified by type (coffee spoon, soupspoon, or tablespoon); dl. = deciliter.